3

As God Shall Ordain

as
GOD
shall
ORDAIN

A HISTORY OF THE

FRANCISCAN SISTERS OF CHICAGO

1894 - 1987

Sister Anne Marie Knawa, OSF

As God Shall Ordain

If this plan . . . is of men, it will fail; but if it is of God, you will not be able to overthrow it.

Acts 5:38–39

Toward the end of May, Father [Barzynski] announced that we would have to accept orphans. I became alarmed at this because I thought that we were not as yet too well instructed in the religious life, nor were we aware of how a religious should conduct herself. I told Father that if it had to be done, we would need more spiritual instruction and guidance in the matter of rearing the orphans. Father [Barzynski] answered simply: "As God shall ordain." It was left at that.

The "Chronicle" of Mother Mary
Theresa Dudzik

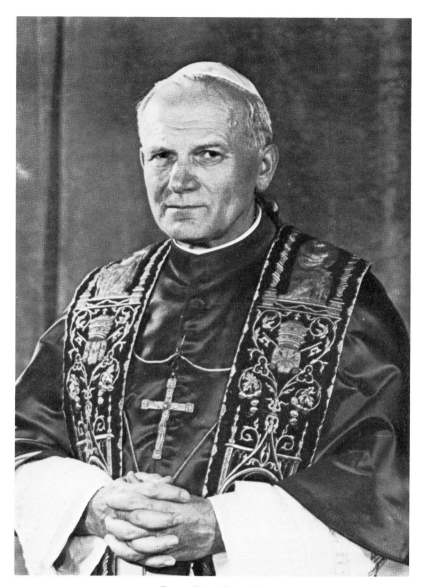

Pope John Paul II
Bishop of Rome, Vicar of Jesus Christ,
Successor of the Prince of the Apostles,
Supreme Pontiff of the Universal Church

Joseph Cardinal Bernardin
Fifth Cardinal, Seventh Archbishop
and Twelfth Bishop
of Chicago

**The Servant of God
Mother Mary Theresa, OSF
(Josephine Dudzik)
Foundress of the Congregation
of the
Franciscan Sisters of Chicago**

To Mary,
the Immaculate Conception,
patroness of
the Franciscan Sisters of Chicago,
and to my beloved parents,
John and Mary Knawa,
who first taught me to love
the Holy Mother of God

TABLE OF CONTENTS

ILLUSTRATIONS   xviii

FOREWORD   xxi

PREFACE   xxii

ACKNOWLEDGMENTS   xxvi

PART ONE:
IT WAS NOT YOU WHO CHOSE ME   1860–1909

1	The Dudzik Family	3
2	Land of Birth	13
3	St. Stanislaus Kostka Parish	21
4	Chicago: "City of the Big Shoulders"	43
5	Arrival in America	52
6	New Beginnings	64
7	Foundation Days	76
8	New Crises	83
9	Triumph of Spirit	94
10	A Dream Fulfilled	106
11	Amid Sadness and Joy	120
12	St. Vincent's Orphan Asylum	131
13	The Apostolate of Education	149
14	Growth and Expansion	162
15	Progress in Early Ventures	171
16	St. Elizabeth's Day Nursery	178
17	Undertakings in Missouri	186
18	New Ways and New Works	196
19	Death and Life	216
20	Moving Toward the Future	223

PART TWO:

IT WAS I WHO CHOSE YOU TO GO FORTH AND BEAR FRUIT   1910–1946

21	The First General Chapter: Mother M. Anna Wysinski	247
22	From Illinois to Texas	266
23	School Apostolate Extension	289
24	A Term Concluded	314
25	The Second General Chapter: Mother M. Aloysia Holysz	324
26	Expanding the School Apostolate	333
27	Guardian Angel Day Care Center	350
28	Victory in Death	364
29	The Spirituality of Sister M. Theresa Dudzik	374
30	A Milestone Reached	389
31	The Third General Chapter: Mother M. Vincent Czyzewski	401
32	Woodland Park: Our Lady of Victory Convent	414
33	Final Events	428
34	The Fourth General Chapter: Mother M. Aloysia Holysz	435
35	Added Blessings	441
36	The Fifth General Chapter: Mother M. Antonina Osinski	458
37	Areas of Domestic Service	472
38	Our Lady of Victory Convent for the Aged and Infirm Sisters	488
39	Mount Alvernia Convent	505
40	St. Anthony's Home	514
41	The Franciscan Sisters in North Dakota	526
42	The Sixth General Chapter: Mother M. Mechtilde Zynda	537
43	Boys Town, Nebraska	548
44	The Franciscan Sisters in the Southland	568
45	Towards New Horizons	581
46	Meeting Apostolic Needs	588

PART THREE:

AND YOUR FRUIT MUST ENDURE   1947–1987

47	The Seventh General Chapter: Mother M. Jerome Dadej	603
48	Developing Missions	617
49	St. John Hospital and School of Nursing	629
50	The Growing Hospital Apostolate	667
51	Madonna High School	678

52 The Eighth General Chapter: Mother M. Jerome Dadej 720

53 Expansion in Health Care Services 727

54 The Challenge of the Fifties 756

55 Era of Growth and Transition 762

56 The Ninth General Chapter: Mother M. Beatrice Rybacki 773

57 In the Midst of Change 780

58 Our Lady of Victory Convent: The New General Motherhouse 788

59 The Tenth General Chapter: Mother M. Beatrice Rybacki 804

60 The Winds of Change: The First Extraordinary Chapter of Affairs 818

61 The Eleventh and Twelfth General Chapters: Sister M. Hugoline
Czaplinski 841

62 St. Anthony Medical Center 862

63 The Thirteenth General Chapter: Sister Martha Joan Sempolski 878

64 Challenge and Response 887

65 Further Ministerial Witness 895

66 The Fourteenth General Chapter: Sister Joseph Marie Zenda 902

APPENDICES

Appendix A: The Constitutions of the Congregation of the
Franciscan Sisters of Chicago 921

Appendix B: The Beatification and Canonization Process of the
Servant of God, Mother Mary Theresa Dudzik,
Foundress of the Congregation of the Franciscan
Sisters of Chicago 934

Appendix C: The Emblem of the Congregation of the Franciscan
Sisters of Chicago 946

Appendix D: Major Superiors of the Congregation of the Franciscan
Sisters of Chicago 948

Appendix E: Superiors General and Members of the General Council
of the Congregation of the Franciscan Sisters of Chicago 949

Appendix F: Houses and Institutions Staffed by the Congregation of the
Franciscan Sisters of Chicago 951

Appendix G: Present Membership of the Congregation of the
Franciscan Sisters of Chicago 956

Appendix H: Deceased Members of the Congregation of the
Franciscan Sisters of Chicago 958

Appendix I: Key Personnel of the Congregation of the Franciscan
Sisters of Chicago 963

Appendix J: Directresses of Formation and Field Supervisors of
               Instruction in the Congregation of the Franciscan
               Sisters of Chicago   984

Appendix K: Delegates to the General Chapters and Special Chapters
               of Affairs of the Congregation of the Franciscan Sisters
               of Chicago   991

Appendix L: A Prayer for Our Daily Needs Written by Mother Mary
               Theresa Dudzik, Foundress of the Congregation of the
               Franciscan Sisters of Chicago   992

Appendix M: Prayer for the Beatification of the Servant of God, Mother
               Mary Theresa Dudzik, Foundress of the Congregation
               of the Franciscan Sisters of Chicago   992

NOTES AND REFERENCES   Found after each chapter

BIBLIOGRAPHY   993

INDEX   1010

ILLUSTRATIONS

Pope John Paul II		Frontis.
Joseph Cardinal Bernardin		Frontis.
Mother M. Theresa Dudzik		Frontis.
Parish Church	Kamien Krajeński, Poland	4
Dudzik Family Cottage	Płocicz, Poland	4
The Dudzik Family		6
Vocational School	Kamien Krajeński, Poland	7
Josephine and Her Brother Joseph		9
Partitions of Poland		15
Reverend Vincent Michael Barzynski, CR		26
St. Stanislaus Kostka Parish Complex	Chicago, Illinois	31
First Home of Community	Chicago, Illinois	57
Opening Page of Dudzik Manuscript		64
Blessed Kunegunda		69
Second Home of Community	Chicago, Illinois	95
Original Motherhouse Complex	Chicago, Illinois	107
Women Residents of St. Joseph Home for the Aged and Crippled	Chicago, Illinois	108
Reverend Andrew Spetz, CR		124
Most Reverend Patrick A. Feehan		134
Original St. Vincent's Orphan Asylum	Chicago, Illinois	136
Orphans at St. Vincent's Orphan Asylum	Chicago, Illinois	136
Sierota [The Orphan] Magazine		136
Foundation Group		139
SS. Peter and Paul School and Convent	Spring Valley, Illinois	151
St. Stanislaus Bishop and Martyr Convent	Chicago, Illinois	156
St. Stanislaus Bishop and Martyr School	Chicago, Illinois	156
Original Frame Houses for Aged	Chicago, Illinois	163
St. Casimir Convent	Cleveland, Ohio	165
St. Casimir School	Cleveland, Ohio	166
St. Michael School and Convent	Berlin, Wisconsin	172
St. Josaphat School	Oshkosh, Wisconsin	174
St. Elizabeth's Day Nursery	Chicago, Illinois	179
St. Casimir Church and School	St. Louis, Missouri	187
St. Stanislaus Convent	St. Louis, Missouri	190
St. Stanislaus Church and School	St. Louis, Missouri	190
St. Adalbert School	Whiting, Indiana	200
St. John Cantius Convent	Indiana Harbor, Indiana	203
St. John Cantius / Catholic Elementary School	Indiana Harbor, Indiana	204
St. Adalbert Convent	East St. Louis, Illinois	208
St. Adalbert School	East St. Louis, Illinois	208
St. Florian Convent	Chicago, Illinois	219
St. Florian School	Chicago, Illinois	219
St. Hedwig Convent	Gary, Indiana	225
St. Hedwig School	Gary, Indiana	226
St. Stanislaus Kostka Convent	Youngstown, Ohio	229
St. Stanislaus Kostka Church and School	Youngstown, Ohio	230
Church Vestment Workshop	Chicago, Illinois	234
Early Spiritual Directors		242–243
Mother M. Anna Wysinski		250

St. Stanislaus Bishop and Martyr Church, School, and Convent	Posen, Illinois	267
St. Roch	La Salle, Illinois	269
Holy Trinity Church, Convent, and School	Falls City, Texas	272
Five Holy Martyrs Convent	Chicago, Illinois	291
Five Holy Martyrs School	Chicago, Illinois	291
St. Casimir Convent	Johnstown, Pennsylvania	298
St. Casimir / West End Catholic Consolidation School	Johnstown, Pennsylvania	298
Assumption of the Blessed Virgin Mary Convent	Conemaugh, Pennsylvania	304
Assumption of the Blessed Virgin Mary / Conemaugh Catholic Consolidation School	Conemaugh, Pennsylvania	306
St. Mary of Częstochowa Convent	Hammond, Indiana	315
St. Mary of Częstochowa School	Hammond, Indiana	316
Sacred Heart of Jesus Convent	Gary (Tolleston), Indiana	318
Sacred Heart of Jesus Church and School	Gary (Tolleston), Indiana	319
Sacred Heart of Jesus Convent	La Porte, Indiana	334
Sacred Heart of Jesus Church and School	La Porte, Indiana	334
St. Adalbert School	Farrell, Pennsylvania	336
St. Michael Church and School	Glen Campbell, Pennsylvania	337
SS. Peter and Paul Church and School	Arcadia, Pennsylvania	339
St. Casimir School	Streator, Illinois	341
St. Mary of Częstochowa Church and School	Madison, Illinois	342
St. Joseph Convent	East Chicago, Indiana	345
St. Joseph School	East Chicago, Indiana	345
Guardian Angel Day Care Center	Chicago, Illinois	351
Free Clinic	Chicago, Illinois	353
Mother M. Theresa Dudzik		379
Assumption of the Blessed Virgin Mary School and Hall	New Chicago, Indiana	390
Assumption of the Blessed Virgin Mary Convent	New Chicago, Indiana	391
Sacred Heart of Jesus School	Cleveland, Ohio	394
Sacred Heart of Jesus Convent	Cleveland, Ohio	397
Walker Mansion	Lemont, Illinois	417
Our Lady of Victory Statue		419
Original Our Lady of Victory Convent; Novitiate House; Present Mother Theresa Museum	Lemont, Illinois	419
Procession	Lemont, Illinois	422
St. Pancratius Convent	Chicago, Illinois	429
St. Pancratius School	Chicago, Illinois	430
Earlier St. Joseph Home	Chicago, Illinois	442
St. Joseph Home of Chicago	Chicago, Illinois	446
Chapel: St. Joseph Home of Chicago	Chicago, Illinois	447
Our Lady of Spring Bank Manor	Okauchee, Wisconsin	473
Anthony Brady Memorial Hall	Washington, DC	477
Our Lady of Victory Convent for the Aged and Infirm Sisters; Present Mother Theresa Home	Lemont, Illinois	489
Shrine: St. Francis of Assisi	Lemont, Illinois	492
Shrine: Our Lady of Lourdes	Lemont, Illinois	495
Altar: Our Lady of Częstochowa	Lemont, Illinois	497
Farm	Lemont, Illinois	498
Mount Alvernia Convent	East Cleveland, Ohio	506

Garden: Mount Alvernia Convent	East Cleveland, Ohio	507
Original St. Anthony's Home	Crown Point, Indiana	516
South Heart Public School	South Heart, North Dakota	528
Convent: South Heart Public School	South Heart, North Dakota	529
St. Joseph Home for the Aged	Cleveland, Ohio	543
Father Flanagan and Sisters	Boys Town, Nebraska	553
Immaculate Conception Convent	Boys Town, Nebraska	554
St. Peter Claver Church and School	Mobile, Alabama	569
St. Peter Claver Convent	Mobile, Alabama	571
St. Joseph the Provider School	Campbell, Ohio	590
St. Joseph the Provider Convent	Campbell, Ohio	591
Former Superiors General of the Franciscan Sisters of Chicago		598–599
Sister M. Gonzaga Raniszewski		606
Sister M. Doloretta Radzienda		609
Madonna Hall	Cleveland, Ohio	618
St. Philip of Jesus Community Center	Chicago, Illinois	620
St. John Regional Medical Center	Huron, South Dakota	637
Nurses' Home	Huron, South Dakota	648
St. John Hospital School of Nursing	Huron, South Dakota	651
Mother of Grace Hospital (Gregory Community Hospital)	Gregory, South Dakota	672
Original Madonna High School	Chicago, Illinois	683
Madonna High School	Chicago, Illinois	695
Madonna High School Convent	Chicago, Illinois	701
SS. Philip and James Church and School	Cleveland, Ohio	723
SS. Philip and James Convent	Cleveland, Ohio	725
Our Lady of the Sandhills (Atkinson Memorial Hospital)	Atkinson, Nebraska	731
St. Anthony's Hospital	Martin, South Dakota	740
Mount Alverna Home	Parma, Ohio	748
Mount Alverna Home and Convent	Parma, Ohio	749
St. Leo the Great School	Cleveland, Ohio	764
St. Leo the Great Convent	Cleveland, Ohio	765
St. Louise de Marillac School	La Grange Park, Illinois	768
St. Louise de Marillac Convent	La Grange Park, Illinois	769
Reverend Henry M. Malak		778
Blessed Sacrament School	Gary, Indiana	783
General Motherhouse: Our Lady of Victory Convent	Lemont, Illinois	790
Sacred Heart Chapel: Our Lady of Victory Convent	Lemont, Illinois	792
Community Cemetery	Lemont, Illinois	795
St. Anthony Home	Crown Point, Indiana	809
St. Anthony Medical Center Convent	Crown Point, Indiana	864
St. Anthony Medical Center	Crown Point, Indiana	866
St. Anthony Medical Center Complex	Crown Point, Indiana	867
St. Francis House of Prayer	Lemont, Illinois	889
Holy Family Child Care Center	Crown Point, Indiana	897
St. Anthony of Padua School	Parma, Ohio	898
St. Anthony of Padua Convent	Parma, Ohio	900
Sister Joseph Marie Zenda, Superior General		903
Ordinaries and Bishops		916–917
Religious Habit: Past and Present		918–919

FOREWARD

Who can explain the promptings of the human heart? Who can explain a person's unquenchable thirst for knowledge, truth, and love? Who can explain why, throughout human history, men and women drawn from all walks of life and from all parts of this known world mysteriously follow some divine calling or quest and, forgetful of their own needs, achieve heroic virtue, fame, or fortune?

As God Shall Ordain is a response to that which no one can explain—of how a single, simple, and unassuming woman founded a religious institute whose members still follow the way of the Lord unreservedly. It is a scholarly record of living history which recaptures the original inspiration of the foundress and attests to God's action and providential care in her life, in the lives of the Sisters, and in the growth and ministries of the congregation.

Because the author has closely interwoven the early history of the congregation with the cultural, economic, social, and political milieu, the reader can better understand the conditions and needs of the immigrant Church of Chicago as well as the spirit and devotion which characterized the Sisters in their apostolic endeavors. There are descriptive accounts of human events, incidents of faith and courage, and records of human frailty. There are delightful stories of women and men, clergy and lay, whose lives were interwoven with the lives of our early members and whose decisions often influenced a young and striving community. As you read this account of our history, you will find yourself drawing from your memories and experiencing a powerful sense of gratitude.

It is my fondest hope that this work of love written by Sister Anne Marie Knawa may find its way into thousands of homes and that the strength of its message may influence the minds and hearts of other young and valiant women. May it also enshrine the noble example of our pioneers as models worthy of imitation by all present and future members. This recording of our past is an attempt to share our religious life and its beginnings with our families and friends who have helped and loved us through the years.

The Sisters express their profound gratitude to Sister Anne Marie Knawa, author of this historical work, and to Sister Mary Jude Kruszewski, assistant and editor, for their perseverance and dedication to this formidable project. Our wholehearted appreciation is extended also to the Sisters and laity who contributed in any way to this publication.

History not only records the accomplishments of the past but also provides the foundation and inspiration for our future. With faith in God's providence, the Franciscan Sisters of Chicago shall preserve that future "as God shall ordain."

Sister Joseph Marie Zenda, OSF
Superior General
January 28, 1989

PREFACE

In 1894, God ordained that a new religious congregation be established in the city of Chicago. An exceptional woman, Josephine Dudzik, an immigrant Pole, filled with steadfast faith, ardent hope, and immense charity, was moved to shelter, in her own home, the aged, poor, disabled, and abandoned whom she encountered in her neighborhood. As a consequence of her desire to bring comfort and relief to those who suffered human misery, Josephine Dudzik, destined to become Mother M. Theresa, founded the Franciscan Sisters of Chicago, the first religious Sisterhood established in the city of Chicago, and the first Polish-American Sisterhood founded in the United States.

Most people have a tendency to look upon founders and foundresses of religious congregations as saints. And rightly so. The author is inclined to agree with the noted psychologist Eugene Kennedy who in his book of reflections, *The Joy of Being Human*, so vividly capsulates the essence of sanctity:

> The contemporary saint is not the person who is famous for long
> fasts and longer prayers as much as the man or woman, whether engaging
> in these activities or not, *is there* when people need his response. The
> saint is not recognized by his heavenly glow, but, by his earthly *presence*
> at a time *when we desperately need what only another human being can
> provide for us in terms of understanding, encouragement, or support.*

Josephine Dudzik was present at a time when the Church, her parish, and her neighborhood needed her. Filled with the characteristic Franciscan reverence for life, she was imbued with a charism which reflected Christ's presence in the world and which contributed to the building up of the Body of Christ, his Church. The gift of the Spirit granted to Josephine Dudzik—Mother M. Theresa—enabled her to come to the aid of the neglected, deprived, and suffering aged and orphaned of her time. Eventually, her followers would enter the fields of education, health care, and social services with the same vision, hope, and dedication which had first inspired their beloved foundress.

It should be noted by the reader that the congregation at its foundation was called the Franciscan Sisters of Blessed Kunegunda, presumably upon the advice of its spiritual director, the Reverend Vincent Barzynski, CR. At the First Extraordinary Chapter of Affairs held in 1968, a decree was passed to change the name of the congregation to the Franciscan Sisters of Chicago. The Sisters chose to be recognized as followers of St. Francis of Assisi, and like him, to be identified with their place of foundation. For the sake of clarity, therefore, throughout this history, the congregation will always be referred to as the Franciscan Sisters of Chicago.

No complete history of the Congregation of the Franciscan Sisters of Chicago has appeared to the present time. The first and most accurate source of the congregation's beginnings is to be found in "The Chronicle of the Franciscan Sisters Under the Patronage of St. Kunegunda in Chicago" written in 1910 by Mother M. Theresa Dudzik at the request of the Reverend Andrew Spetz, CR, her spiritual director at that time. Sister M. Gonzaga Raniszewski, who served as the secretary general of the Franciscan Sisters of Chicago for twenty-four years, wrote a brief two-part history of the congregation in the Polish language. The first part dates from the birth of Mother M. Theresa Dudzik to 1910, and the second part from 1910 to 1940. Only the first part was published in 1947. When the author made application to the Franciscan Sisters of Chicago, it was Sister M. Gonzaga who welcomed her to the Motherhouse. The author has always considered it an honor to continue the work originally begun by Sister M. Gonzaga.

The Second Vatican Council emphasized the importance and the obligation of religious to be faithful to the spirit and the aim of their founder or foundress and to study their congregation's past. The decision of the Sister-delegates to the Eleventh General Chapter of Elections held in 1970 reflected the recommendation of the Second Vatican Council by decreeing that a history be written so that Mother M. Theresa Dudzik might be known and that the Sisters themselves might learn of the congregation's foundation, development, traditions, and ministries. The author took up the task at the specific request of Sister M. Hugoline Czaplinski who had been elected the superior general of the congregation in 1970. As the exacting task of writing the history and drawing the composite of the person and the spirit that was Mother M. Theresa Dudzik began, an incident in the Gospel of St. Luke became clear to the author. The evangelist Luke relates that on one occasion, Jesus crossed the Sea of Galilee to the shores of Tiberias where he fed five thousand hungry people. When they had all eaten, Jesus instructed his disciples to "gather up the fragments" so that nothing be lost. Thus, the author has attempted to "gather up the fragments" which have survived through the years and which constitute the congregation's history—that nothing be lost.

In the Preface to her brief account of the congregation, Sister M. Gonzaga listed several reasons for writing her history. It was undertaken primarily to acquaint others with Mother M. Theresa Dudzik and the congregation which she founded. Sister M. Gonzaga hoped to imbue the members of the congregation with the spirit of Mother M. Theresa and that of the pioneer Sisters. The book also had as one of its objectives to show the Sisters' gratitude to the Congregation of the Resurrection, who, from the very beginning, provided spiritual guidance and loving support to Mother M. Theresa and the foundation group. Finally, Sister M. Gonzaga hoped that her history would serve to manifest the glory of God and reveal his Divine Providence in the lives of his creation.

It would appear that the reasons for the publication of the congregation's first brief history were entirely commendable and, as such, could not be improved upon by the present author. In truth, however, there are a few more reasons besides those expressed by Sister M. Gonzaga which justify the presentation of a new and larger history. This account attempts to highlight the lives of the Franciscan Sisters of Chicago who have contributed significantly to the shaping of the Church and of America. This history aims at introducing the reader to or contributing to a fuller understanding of Mother M. Theresa whose cause for sainthood is currently undergoing inquiry in Rome. It is meant to present the inspiration, sacrifice, and dedication of those Sisters who have gone before and have left to the members of the congregation, present and future, a humble but proud heritage. It is also an attempt to share the religious spirit of the Franciscan Sisters of Chicago with their families, friends, benefactors, and co-workers who have loved and supported them throughout the congregation's long history. The author's final sentiment regarding the significance of the history is to be found in the Nobel Prize Acceptance Speech of the American writer, William Faulkner, who accepted his award " . . . not for glory or least of all for profit, *but to create out of the materials of the human spirit something which did not exist before."*

For the reader, certain vital facts should be clarified from the very beginning. While Mother M. Theresa Dudzik never served as the superior general of the congregation which she founded, the title of "Mother" was accorded her as a gesture of recognition and respect at the Sixth General Chapter of Elections. Since Mother M. Theresa died in 1917 and the title was not conferred until 1940, she is always referred to as Sister M. Theresa in the text.

It should be noted also that throughout the history, the names of the Sisters used in the text are those used by the Sisters at the present time. If a Sister returned to her baptismal name, Appendix G will give her former name.

Because the reader may not be acquainted with terms regularly used in religious life or in the Church before the advent of the Second Vatican Council, an attempt has been made to define them, generally in the Notes and References section.

In many instances, actual letters or excerpts from them are used because the correspondent's letter expresses a state of mind or a given situation much better than could have been stated by the author. Likewise, the history contains many photographs which represent a reality and immediacy which supersede any description evoked by the written word.

Lastly, although this book is called a history, the author prefers to look upon it rather as a chronicle, for it is indeed a register of persons, places, and events in the order of time. Perhaps in some instances, the related episodes might seem to be of little value or effect. The final aim was always to recount persons, places, or events that in some way colored the history of the congregation. There are some occurrences which might appear to be of a controversial or rather sensitive nature. The accounts of these episodes are meant to maintain their historical accuracy or their bearing on a particular event.

Certain obstacles presented themselves to the author as the work, admittedly challenging in itself, was begun. There were many futile attempts to secure some of the needed material. Very often there were too few primary sources of information to draw upon. Many useful sources of information might have been lost, destroyed unintentionally, or perhaps had never existed at all. Because of the lack of historical records or sources of information, the material in some portions of the historical narrative is rather meager. Parish histories, in particular, too often were vague or at times somewhat inaccurate. While the histories of some parishes or institutions as presented herein have been more faithfully depicted, in all probability, some discrepancies will still be present. It is important to emphasize at this point that the author found it necessary to translate much of the material contained in this history from the Polish.

Because of the research conducted, the archives and the library of the congregation have been vastly enriched with valuable books, excellent souvenir books of parishes, schools, and institutions; pamphlets, brochures, and histories of numerous congregations; precious photographs; and valuable correspondence.

The ministerial service and the spiritual life-witness of Mother M. Theresa and the Franciscan Sisters of Chicago as presented in this account is a long and honorable history in terms of loving aid to the sick, the poor, the aged, the orphaned, the children in elementary schools and the young women in high schools, and all the People of God anxious to hear the Good News of the Gospel. As the Franciscan Sisters of Chicago continue their ministries into the 21st century while striving to live out their ecclesial commitment, they abandon themselves to the wisdom of St. Augustine: "Trust the PAST to the mercy of God, the PRESENT to his love, and the FUTURE to his Providence." The Franciscan Sisters of Chicago simply add—"As God shall ordain."

Sister Anne Marie Knawa, OSF

ACKNOWLEDGMENTS

A famous French writer, Massieu, once wrote: *La reconnaissance est la memoire du coeur,* "Gratitude is the memory of the heart." My heart remembers, then, God, our Father, who called the Congregation of the Franciscan Sisters of Chicago into existence. It recalls fondly our beloved patroness, Mary, the Immaculate Conception, who has interceded for the congregation during these past ninety-four years. My heart preserves the memory of our beloved foundress, Mother Mary Theresa Dudzik, who has left us a legacy of deep love for and abiding trust in Divine Providence. Fondly, I call to remembrance all the Franciscan Sisters of Chicago, both living and deceased, whose zealous endeavors and dedicated lives I have had the privilege of recording on these pages.

In my gratitude, I want to thank especially the superiors general, Sister M. Hugoline Czaplinski, Sister Martha Joan Sempolski, and Sister Joseph Marie Zenda for initiating this project, for encouraging its completion, and for providing the time and the means which made it possible. I would also like to acknowledge the kind support and encouragement of the general councils of each administration, and, in particular, I wish to thank Sister M. Alvernia Groszek and Sister M. Francine Labus for access to historical sources in the archives of the congregation. I also wish to thank Clara Rolowicz, the administrative secretary, for her kind assistance.

I extend my heartfelt thanks to diocesan chancellors, pastors of parishes, members of religious congregations of men and women, principals of schools, administrators of institutions, and lay persons who responded to my requests for information and, in many cases, offered their genuine hospitality during my visitations. I would like to thank them for their kindness and cooperation.

Many historians, librarians, and archivists in various parts of the United States gave generously of their time and talent to help. Accordingly, I am indebted to the late Reverend Menceslaus J. Madaj, archivist for the Archdiocese of Chicago; Sister Gertrude Cook, MMSA, archivist for the Archdiocese of San Antonio, Texas; the Reverend Donald Bilinski, OFM, former curator of the Polish Museum of America; Francis P. Clark, University of Notre Dame Memorial Library; Sister M. Chrysantha Rudnik, CSSF, and Sister M. Julianne Chudy, CSSF, of Montay College Library, Chicago; Sister M. Jane Coogan, BVM; Sister M. De Chantal, CSFN; Sister M. Frances Romana, SSND; Sister Margaret Mary Curry, CCVI; Sister Rita Prendergast, CCVI; Sister M. Bernadette Anderwald, CCVI; Sister M. Margaret Bright, CCVI; the Reverend John Iwicki, CR; the Reverend Edward Janas, CR; the late Reverend Edwin Zygmunt, CR; the Reverend Dennis Sanders, CR; Sister M. Loyola Dymanowski, OSF; and the Most Reverend Alfred L. Abramowicz, auxiliary bishop of Chicago, for material from his private collection. I also owe special thanks to the library staffs of Newberry Library, Chicago; the Gilpin Library of the Chicago Historical Association, Chicago; *The Chicago Catholic* (formerly *The New World*) newspaper office; Loyola and De Paul Universities, Chicago; Rosary College, River Forest, Illinois; the Municipal Reference Library, Chicago; the Chicago Public Libraries; St. Louis University, St. Louis, Missouri; The Catholic University of America, Washington, DC; Columbia University of New York City; Harvard University; the University of Chicago; and St. John College of Cleveland.

A special word of thanks is due to the following for the photographs contained in this history many of which are reproduced for the first time: Sister M. Jude Kruszewski for photos of places too numerous to mention; Sister M. Josetta Kuczmarski for photos of St. Anthony of Padua School, Parma, Ohio; Sister M. Aloysilla Kedzior for photos of Mount Alverna Home, Parma, Ohio; Sister M. Gabriel Lazarski for photos of St. Anthony Hospital, St. Anthony Home, and Holy Family Child Care Center, Crown Point, Indiana; Sister M. Joella Bielinski and Mr. Richard Buckley for photos of Madonna Hall, SS. Philip and James School, St. Leo the Great School, Sacred Heart School, and St. Casimir School, all in Cleveland, Ohio; Sister Gail Stackpole, IHM, for photos of St. Peter Claver School, Mobile, Alabama: the Most Reverend Alfred L. Abramowicz, auxiliary bishop of Chicago, for photos of the home, school, and parish church of Josephine Dudzik; the Reverend Henry M. Malak, for assorted photos; Root Photographers of Chicago for photos of the Motherhouse, St. Joseph Home of Chicago, Mother Theresa Home, the former Our Lady of Victory Convent, and the Madonna High School residency; Jim Kilcoyne of the *Chicago Catholic;* and Ed Ziganto of Brookfield Photo Service in Brookfield, Illinois, for developing and enlarging scores of photos.

I offer my sincerest thanks to Janis Boehm of Janis Boehm Design for the beautiful cover and layout. Her wholehearted and generous cooperation in preparing this history for publication deserves more thanks than I could ever adequately express. Deep gratitude for helping to shape this book is due also to Carla Babrick, proofreader; to Tim Basaldua of Automated Graphics for the electronic page composition; to Robert Garvey Jr., for production editing; and to John Stec, who prepared the index. My thanks also extend to Armin Von der Heydt of Worzalla Publishing Company for his invaluable assistance.

I wish to extend my appreciation to my dearest family, kind friends, and all well-wishers for their prayers and support. I am grateful, also, to the many, many others who are not named but who have helped me in any way.

My warmest thanks, however, are reserved for my loyal friend and collaborator, Sister M. Jude Kruszewski, who from research to print rendered me invaluable assistance. I am grateful to her for editing the manuscript and for preparing the footnotes and bibliography. Her proofreading ability was excellent. When driving me to and from appointments and visitations, her patience was most commendable. She gave me acute criticism, sound advice, and much-needed confidence. It was she who sustained me in times of doubt and tribulation. I can say in truth that if it were not for her expert assistance and sincere encouragement, I would never have been able to complete this project. Sister M. Jude has left a permanent imprint on this book.

Finally, if indeed "Gratitude is the memory of the heart," then for all the memories I have neglected to mention, or was not aware of, or did not do justice to, I truly apologize.

I treasure the memory of this experience, and for everyone connected with this history, I pray:

> The Lord bless you and keep you;
>
> May He show His face to you and
>   have mercy on you.
>
> May He turn His countenance to you
>   and give you peace.
>
> The Lord bless you.

Sister Anne Marie Knawa, OSF

PART ONE

IT WAS NOT YOU WHO CHOSE ME
1860–1909

CHAPTER 1

The Dudzik Family

Not far from the industrial city of Poznań, approximately 175 miles west of Warsaw, near Chojnice in the Pomeranian Region of Western Poland when the former Republic of Poland was under the rule of Prussia, lay the tiny and obscure village of Płocicz. There, on August 30, 1860, John and Agnes [née Polaszczyk] Dudzik, a religious and industrious couple, welcomed the third of their six children.[1] On September 2, 1860, in the parish church of the Immaculate Conception in Kamień Krajeński, which belonged to the Archdiocese of Gniezno near Poznań,[2] the child was baptized. She was given the name of a saint beloved by the Polish nation. In honor of St. Joseph, the child was baptized Josephine. Written in German, the language of Poland's Prussian oppressors,[3] her baptismal record which also established her date of birth is recorded in this manner:

The English translation reads:

Baptismal Certificate
Josephine Dudzik, Catholic, Daughter of John D. and his spouse Agnes, née Polaszczyk, was born on August 30, 1860 at Ploetrig, County Flatów and was baptized on September 2 of the same year. In certification thereof —Kamień, August 8, 1908.

(Signed) Lessel, Pastor[4]

The parish church in Kamień Krajeński where Josephine Dudzik was baptized and made her First Holy Communion

The small cottage in the village of Płocicz where Josephine Dudzik was born on August 30, 1860

This concise, seemingly uniform and insignificant account contains the heart of a life, which as it unfolded and grew, would lead Josephine Dudzik to dedicate herself as a gift to God and the Catholic Church in the service of her neighbor. Her desire to bring comfort and relief to those who suffered human misery resulted in her becoming the foundress of the Franciscan Sisters of Chicago, a new religious congregation in the Church. The social service and life-witness of Josephine Dudzik—later Sister Mary Theresa—found roots in the Gospel message of Jesus: "You have not chosen Me; but I have chosen you and have appointed you, that you should go and bear fruit, and that your fruit should remain."[5] Herein was the beginning of a life marked with great faith, ardent hope, magnanimous charity, and extraordinary faithfulness to the inspiration of the Holy Spirit.

John Dudzik, Josephine's father, was born in Poland on August 20, 1822, the son of John and Anna (née Mulzów) Dudzik who were peasant farmers.[6] He married Agnes Polaszczyk who was born in Poland in 1828. Unfortunately, there is no other information available concerning the Dudziks' early life. It is known that John Dudzik had a younger brother Joseph, who in 1866, emigrated to America with his wife, Frances. Upon their arrival in the New World, Joseph and Frances Dudzik made their home on the Northwest Side of Chicago in the vicinity of St. Stanislaus Kostka Church where Frances Dudzik was employed as a housekeeper at the large rectory.

Before Josephine's birth, her parents had owned a small house and a parcel of land in the little village of Komirowo. It was here that their first child, Rosalie, was born in 1856.[7] In 1873, Rosalie Dudzik, a young woman of seventeen, left Poland for America and made her home in Chicago with her now widowed Aunt Frances.[8] On June 15, 1873, Rosalie married Adam Frank[9] who is listed in the parish annals as one of the pioneer settlers of Chicago having lived in St. Stanislaus Kostka Parish since 1868.[10] The Reverend John Wołłowski, CR, a member of the Congregation of the Resurrection who staffed the parish, officiated at the wedding.[11] In time, Rosalie and Adam Frank were to become the parents of thirteen children.[12]

Marianne, the second child of John and Agnes Dudzik, was also born in Komirowo in 1858. Encouraged by her older sister Rosalie, Marianne left Poland for America in 1873, and upon her arrival in Chicago, was welcomed at the home of Rosalie and Adam Frank. In 1877, Marianne married August Budnik at St. Stanislaus Kostka Church.[13] A daughter, Anne, was born to the young couple on April 8, 1878. Five months later, on September 24, 1878, Marianne Budnik died and was laid to rest in St. Adalbert's Cemetery in Chicago's early northwest suburb of Niles.[14] After Marianne's untimely death, the Franks adopted Anne, the godchild of Rosalie Frank.

By the time of Josephine's birth, John and Agnes Dudzik had moved south of the village of Komirowo to another tiny hamlet called Płocicz. In its resemblance to most European villages at that time, it was a mere cluster of simple homes surrounded by farmland.[15] In 1862, two years after Josephine's birth, a son was born to the Dudziks whom they named Joseph. A fifth child, Frances, was born in 1864. At the age of sixteen,

The Dudzik Family:
Sitting, left to right: John Dudzik, Katherine Dudzik, Agnes Dudzik
Standing, left to right: Rosalie Dudzik Frank, Joseph Dudzik, Frances Dudzik, Josephine Dudzik

Frances left the village of Płocicz and made her home in Chicago with her sister and brother-in-law, Rosalie and Adam Frank. Three years later, in 1867, the youngest member of the Dudzik family, Katherine, was born.

Together with her sisters and brothers, Josephine Dudzik was raised in an atmosphere of affection and piety. The children learned their lessons in the love of God and faithfulness to the Catholic Church from the good example of their parents. Of Josephine's childhood and youth, very little is known. During World War II, all records of the parish church were destroyed; therefore, the date of her First Communion is not recorded in the *Spis Sióstr* [Register of Sisters] of the congregation and is not known. According to the same *Register,* however, Josephine Dudzik was confirmed by Archbishop John Marwicz of the Archdiocese of Gniezno, although the date of the Confirmation is not recorded.[16]

Josephine attended one of the small village schools and received a basic elementary education in a curriculum and by methods of instruction fashioned by her country's Prussian dictators.[17] While the Prussians had maintained eight-year compulsory schooling for the Poles, all education was conducted solely in the German language. The history of Prussia was emphasized and Polish studies were excluded.[18] We can assume that

Josephine attended religion classes at her parish church of the Immaculate Conception in Kamień Krajeński and that she learned the basic tenets of the Catholic faith from her devout parents.

Having completed her elementary studies, Josephine was unable to pursue a higher education because the Prussian government had declared that there were "too many" secondary schools and thus proceeded to close many of them.[19] Denied an opportunity to study at the secondary level, Josephine was determined to enter one of the various types of vocational schools for girls where nursing, housekeeping, horticulture, house management, and other skills were taught.[20] Josephine chose to enter a vocational school conducted by the Congregation of the Sisters of St. Elizabeth in Kamień Krajeński where she learned sewing and needlework.[21] In the course of time, Josephine was able to establish herself as a competent seamstress in her home town of Płocicz.[22] This skill was to be her chief source of income when she emigrated to the United States with her family and settled in Chicago.

To all appearances, Josephine Dudzik was a normal child with tender affection for her family. If we embrace the universal truth as proposed by the English poet, William Wordsworth, that "the child is father to the man," or as the great English poet and satirist, Alexander Pope, has stated: "Just as the twig is bent, so the tree is inclined," then we might assume further that Josephine was a generous, idealistic, determined, and unassuming child and adolescent whose natural goodness was heightened by a vigorous

The vocational school conducted by the Congregation of the Sisters of St. Elizabeth in Kamień Krajeński where Josephine learned sewing and needlework

prayer life engendered by a deep Christian faith. In maturity, the outward manifestation of her faith, sobriety, and spirit of self-sacrifice found expression in her intense love for the old, the sick, the abandoned, and the crippled. It was said of her that if it were humanly possible, "she would have walked the streets and picked up all the needy, old, crippled, and forsaken in order to clothe, feed, and love them."[23] Years later, in a manuscript called "Kronika Sióstr Franciszkanek pod opieką Św. Kunegundy w Chicago, Illinois" [The Chronicle of the Franciscan Sisters under the patronage of St. Kunegunda in Chicago, Illinois] which she wrote in obedience to her spiritual director, she gives an account of the circumstances which eventually gave rise to the formation of the Congregation of the Franciscan Sisters of Chicago. Josephine's own words offer valuable insight into the motives which prompted her dedication to others:

> Very often, I felt drawn to greater sacrifice for others. Consequently, I was constantly occupied with the thought of how I could be of service to the needy and the poor.[24]

Her spirituality, we might assume also, had been developing from early childhood. As her interior life grew in intensity, it urged her to a permanent commitment of herself to God and to the needy, abandoned, and suffering, all of whom she looked upon as her brothers and sisters who were less fortunate than she.

In 1947, a brief history of the congregation was written by Sister M. Gonzaga Raniszewski called *Rys historyczny Zgromadzenia Sióstr Franciszkanek Błogosławionej Kunegundy. Część pierwsza, 1860–1910* [A historical survey of the Franciscan Sisters of Blessed Kunegunda. Part one, 1860–1910]. In it, Sister M. Gonzaga states:

> When commissioned to write the *Rys,* it was necessary to give some facts concerning the childhood and youth of the foundress [Sister M. Theresa Dudzik]. Sister M. Ladislaus Wroblewski personally knew Josephine's sister, Rosalie Frank. Sister M. Ladislaus and I went to Mrs. Frank for some information. She accepted us pleasantly, and she answered promptly and eagerly any questions about Sister M. Theresa's childhood, youth, emigration, and the foundation of the congregation. It was she who supplied the family photographs of Josephine and her family. I wrote down the things Mrs. Frank told me and for the rest [of the information] I depended on the "Chronicle."[25]

Josephine's physical appearance is known through her photographs, and her sister, Rosalie Frank, aided in the description:

> Josephine was of average height with brown hair and blue eyes. Her pleasant features were heightened by her dignified and courteous manner. She seemed always to possess a happy and pleasant disposition which rendered her sensitive to the needs of others. She possessed a simple, unassuming manner bordering on shyness. [26]

Josephine Dudzik and her brother Joseph

A further profile of Josephine Dudzik by her sister is supplied by Sister M. Gonzaga in the *Rys:*

> From her early childhood, Josephine was characterized by piety and love. As many times as there were opportunities to come to the aid of a neighbor, she willingly did so. She always shared what she had with others. Josephine could not bear to see people in need without coming to their aid—she would share her supper with a poor girl; she took food to a sick neighbor; she aided another by sitting with her children so that the neighbor could attend Mass; with money she saved, she bought medicine for others; she aided those in sorrow; there was not a week when she did not perform some good deed. In all honesty, these were small offerings,

but God does not look at the size of a good deed but at the heart. The small, oftentimes unseen deeds one performs are more meritorious than large ones in which one's glory is often sought. Josephine succeeded in hiding her good deeds so that very few people were able to uncover in this lively girl such a delicate and sensitive nature and such a good heart.[27]

Josephine's profile continues:

She truly loved the hidden life—simple, given to prayer and work. Like the Blessed Virgin Mary, she intended to keep the purity of her body and soul for God. There were many instances when she wanted to spend time at the feet of Our Lord in the Eucharist, but because of the distance to the church from her house she could not do so. She was able to attend church on Sundays and holydays only, and then she remained longer at prayer so that near to Jesus, she could gain the strength and determination she needed to live a truly virtuous life.[28]

At home with her family in Płocicz, Josephine shared their joys and hardships though always impelled by a spirit and vision she herself did not understand:

At this time in her life, Josephine was not yet dreaming of the future. During the winter she was occupied with sewing, and in the summer, she helped on the farm. She always seemed satisfied, amiable, with a song on her lips. Deeds of kindness gave her great happiness and she would have given herself over to the performance of more of them except that she sometimes received censure from her family for devoting so much time to others. Desirous of being obedient in everything to her parents, Josephine attempted to restrain her visits of mercy to the poor. She yearned for a more spiritual life, but she had no spiritual director to depend upon. She begged God that she might know herself better, and, therefore, know in what manner to strive for perfection. Josephine prayed for direction and inspiration for the road she was so eager to travel.[29]

Josephine had often read and surely understood what the Evangelist Matthew had recorded in the sixteenth chapter of his Gospel concerning Christ:

If anyone wants to be a follower of Mine, let him renounce himself and take up his cross and follow Me. For anyone who wants to save his life will lose it, but anyone who loses his life for My sake will find it.[30]

Josephine Dudzik had prayed for spiritual guidance, and it would be granted to her. Eventually she was to renounce herself, take up her cross, and lose her life for the sake of Christ. But the time, the place, and the manner in which this would occur would be of God's own choosing.

THE DUDZIK FAMILY

[1]Writing in her short history, Sister M. Gonzaga states: "Josephine was the fourth in a line of the children of John Dudzik and Agnes Polaszczyk." This would indicate that another child was born before Josephine since she is generally regarded as the third child. The proof of the birth of a child who did not survive before Josephine could not be substantiated by the author. Sister M. Gonzaga Raniszewski, OSFK, *Rys historyczny Zgromadzenia Sióstr Franciszkanek Błogosławionej Kunegundy. Część pierwsza, 1860–1910* [A historical survey of the Franciscan Sisters of Blessed Kunegunda. Part one, 1860–1910] (Chicago: By the Author, 1947), p. 10.

[2]Poznań is located on a broad fertile plain on the Warta River in west-central Poland. It is one of Poland's oldest cities, having been established about A.D. 800, and was the residence of Polish kings until 1296. In 1815, it became the capital of Prussian Poland.

[3]Josephine Dudzik needed the baptismal record before taking her perpetual vows in 1909. She, therefore, obtained it herself in 1908 as the baptismal record indicates. Baptismal Record (AFSCL).

[4]Because Prussia was determined to suppress Catholicism and outlaw the Polish language, legal and administrative affairs were conducted in German. As a result of these repressive measures, family names and names of villages were changed to look German. Sometimes they were replaced by entirely new German names. For example, Płocicz, the village where Josephine Dudzik was born, was changed to Ploetrig; Gdańsk was changed to Danzig; Poznań to Posen, Chojnice to Konitz, etc. Sister M. Assumpta Pogorzelska, "A Historical Study of Religion and Education as Underlying Influences in the Localization of the Poles of Cleveland up to 1915" (M.A. thesis, St. John's College of Cleveland, 1951), p. 21.

[5]John 15:16.

[6]*St. Stanislaus Kostka Church: Burial Register, 1882–1890*, vol. 3 (Chicago, Illinois), p. 212.

[7]*Album Pamiątkowy Złotego Jubileuszu Parafii Świętego Stanisława Kostki, 1867–1917* [A Commemorative Album of the Golden Jubilee of St. Stanislaus Kostka Parish, 1867–1917] (Chicago: 1917), p. 264.

[8]Ibid., p. 264; and Secretaries General, *Community Chronicle, 1904* (AFSCL).

[9]Adam Frank was born in Poland on May 11, 1851. He died on April 21, 1906 and was buried on April 24 in St. Adalbert's Cemetery. The Reverend Andrew Spetz officiated at his funeral. Rosalie Frank outlived her husband by many years. She died on November 8, 1940, and was also buried in St. Adalbert's Cemetery. *Album SSK*, p. 264; and *St. Stanislaus Kostka Church: Burial Register, 1904–1907*, vol. 14 (Chicago, Illinois), p. 218.

[10]*Album SSK*, p. 264.

[11]*St. Stanislaus Kostka Church: Registram Matrimoniorum, 1869–1882*, vol. 1 (Chicago, Illinois).

[12]Two of the thirteen children entered the Congregation of the School Sisters of Notre Dame. Helen Frank (Sister M. Romania) and Clara Frank (Sister M. Salesia) left the congregation in 1942. *Book of Correspondence:* Letter from Sister M. Frances Romano, SSND, to author, 8 September 1975 (AFSCL).

[13]A search of the *Registram Matrimoniorum* at St. Stanislaus Kostka Church does not contain the entry for the 1877 marriage date. The same book, however, contains the following entry on page 85 for July 29, 1879 and reveals what happened to her husband: "August Budnik (widower), age 23, and Julianna Januszewski (age 18). The Reverend Vincent Barzynski officiated at the wedding." *St. Stanislaus Kostka Church: Registram Matrimoniorum, 1869–1882*, vol. 1 (Chicago, Illinois), p. 85.

[14]*St. Stanislaus Kostka Church: Burial Register, 1877–1882*, vol. 2 (Chicago, Illinois), p. 27.

[15]Raniszewski, p. 10.

[16]*Spis Sióstr* (AFSCL).

[17]Wojciech Świętosławski, "Education," in *Poland,* ed. Bernadotte E. Schmitt (Berkeley and Los Angeles: University of California Press, 1964), p. 257.

[18]Świętosławski, p. 257; and Sister M. Valentia, "Some Aspects of Polish Immigration to the United States with Special Reference to the Period 1870–1905" (M.A. thesis, Marquette University, 1942), p. 10.

[19]Frank J. Drobka, "Education in Poland Past and Present" (Ph.D. dissertation, Catholic University of America, 1927), p. 46.

[20]Świętosławski, p. 257.

[21]Raniszewski, p. 10.

[22]Ibid.

[23]Ibid., p. 24.

[24]Matka Maria Teresa Dudzik, "Kronika Sióstr Franciszkanek pod opieką Św. Kunegundy w Chicago, Illinois" [The Chronicle of the Franciscan Sisters under the patronage of St. Kunegunda in Chicago, Illinois] Chicago, 1910. (Unpublished manuscript, AFSCL.), p. 1.

[25]Raniszewski, p. 12.

[26]Ibid.

[27]Ibid.

[28]Ibid.

[29]Ibid., pp. 12–14.

[30]Matt. 16:24–25.

CHAPTER 2

Land of Birth

Poland has been called "the Land of Graves and Crosses."[1] It is easy to understand why after reading its turbulent history. Poland, once the largest country in Europe and the "pillar of Western Civilization,"[2] has had a tragic history of bloody defense against numerous adversaries and has suffered partition by its unscrupulous and greedy neighbors. The Poles' passion for freedom, however, has never allowed them to succumb totally to their unprincipled conquerors. The Poles have constantly defended their intense religious faith and their ideals of patriotism by deeds of heroic proportion. Because of their indomitable will to survive as a nation in spite of almost insurmountable obstacles, history has always seen the triumph of the Polish spirit.[3] It was in this land and of these people that Josephine Dudzik was born. A brief sketch of her native land and its tragic history will help to explain why Josephine and her family left the tenuous security of their homeland for the sanctuary of America.

Perhaps the most significant date in Polish history is the year A.D. 966 which marks Poland's formal acceptance of Christianity. That year, King Mieszko I (966–992), the first of the Piast rulers, introduced Roman Catholicism to his kingdom thereby giving Poland the Western orientation it has had ever since.[4] With the marriage of Jadwiga (Hedwig), Queen of Poland, to Lithuania's Grand Duke Władysław Jagiełło in 1386, the resulting union of the two nations created a period of great prosperity for Poland—its "Golden Age"—which continued for the next 150 years. By the sixteenth century, Poland had reached its zenith of glory. With over a thousand years of culture and historical tradition, Poland emerged as the most powerful state in Europe[5] and the "harbor and asylum of all peoples."[6]

Located as it was, however, on the wide, windswept plains[7] in the very center of Eastern Europe, Poland had no natural borders, and, as a consequence, no natural defenses except the Carpathian and Sudeten Mountains on the south. Bounded by the Baltic Sea on the north, Poland was further situated between the two powerful empires of Germany in the west and Russia on the east. Thus, its boundaries and open plains made Poland tragically vulnerable to its envious neighbors. Poland's perilous location has subsequently affected the history of its people, its society, and its culture.[8] By the end of the eighteenth century, the grandeur of medieval Poland had declined due to the political and economic distress engendered within its own societal and governmental structure. T. Lindsay Baker summarizes the causes of this decline:

> An increasing distinction arose between the middle and lower classes on one hand and the land-holding nobles on the other. The greed of these nobles for individual wealth and power weakened the central government. The king of Poland had become little more than a life-president with very restricted powers. The parliament of Poland, which might have unified the country, served further to disable it. An individual member could veto any measure before the body or even could dissolve the entire assembly with a single vote to that effect. In such a situation, Poland was becoming a weak centralized state while its neighbors, Prussia, Russia, and Austria were becoming strong centralized empires.[9]

Besides its internal strife, Poland had also undergone a series of defensive wars against marauding Swedes, Turks, Cossacks, Tartars, and Russians which further weakened it as a nation.[10] In the last quarter of the eighteenth century, therefore, Poland's neighbors, Prussia, Russia, and Austria took advantage of the political disorder and disintegration which prevailed in Poland and joined forces to overpower the already weakened country. Thus, the First Partition of Poland took place in 1772, when approximately one-third of its territory and one-half of its population were appropriated by Prussia, Russia, and Austria.

In 1791, the Polish Parliament decreed the famous "Constitutions of the Third of May," using as its foundation the American and French ideas of democracy.[11] Frightened by the possible emergence of a stronger and more unified Poland, both Prussia and Russia subjected Poland to a Second and even larger Partition in 1793.[12] Valiant Poles, under Kościuszko, attempted a revolt—against their Russian oppressors in particular—but were severely defeated.

A Third and Final Partition in 1795 wiped Poland from the map of Europe as an independent political state. Prussia appropriated the northwest section of Poland, the east was claimed by the Russians, and Austria took the south. For the next 123 years,[13] Poland ceased to exist as a sovereign state, and her dismembered parts lived as three separate social, constitutional, and economic regions. Poland, however, proved to be quite "indigestible"—it survived the Partitions as a nation if not as a country as Karl Marx wisely observed.[14]

During the years of oppression which followed Poland's actual dismemberment, the countries of Prussia, Russia, and Austria were united in one last ruthless and desperate effort. They aimed specifically to exterminate Poland's very soul—its religion, its culture, and its nationalism. An intense program of Russification and Germanization followed. The

The Partitions of Poland. Reproduced courtesy of Northern Illinois University Press from Polish Catholics in Chicago, 1850–1920: A Religious History, by Joseph John Parot, 1981.

use of the Polish language in schools and in the conduct of legal and administrative affairs was forbidden. Education was severely restricted. Catholic clergy were imprisoned for resisting state control of seminaries, institutions, and parishes. Determined efforts were made to force the Polish peasant from the land. All three of the dominating powers demanded compulsory military service.[15] In Russian-dominated Poland, there was widespread confiscation of property, countless executions, expulsions to Siberia, and a fierce persecution of the Catholic Church.[16] When Bismarck, the Iron Chancellor of Germany, took control of the German empire, his ruthless attack against Polish nationalism was intensified by the *Kulturkampf,* his bitter struggle against the Roman Catholic Church, which lasted from 1872 to 1887. Although Austria proved the most tolerant and least vindictive of Poland's three oppressors, Galicia, the unprogressive and underdeveloped southeast section under her control, abounded in poverty.[17] In spite of the despised Partitions, however, Poland continued to exist as a cultural entity. The Poles steadfastly maintained their Catholic faith, their native language, and worked their land awaiting what they hoped would be Poland's eventual resurrection.[18] Thousands of Poles, however, weary of the persistently repressive measures of Prussia, Russia, and Austria sought refuge in exile.[19]

The Poles had long been settlers in other sections of the world including America, the "New World," the *Nowy Świat.*[20] Wytrwal divides the emigration of Poles to America into three major periods. The first period, generally marked from 1608 to 1776, saw the departure from Poland of noblemen, military leaders, refugees, and adventurers. In the second period, lasting from 1776 to 1870, political émigrés and skilled workmen chiefly left the country. But during the third period, from 1870 to the twenties of the present century, a new phase of Polish emigration began consisting mainly of peasants and unskilled workers. This turned into a mass movement.[21]

While there is no doubt that Polish emigration to the United States had been motivated by religious and political reasons, the great wave of emigration which began in the latter half of the nineteenth century was motivated chiefly by pressing social and economic needs.[22] Dissatisfaction at home and the promise of a better life in America spurred the massive Polish emigration. Henry Sienkiewicz, the brilliant Polish novelist, tersely declared the reason for the mass exodus of Poles to the New World: "To search for bread and freedom that were lacking at home."[23] Anthony Kuzniewski, SJ, is emphatic in his conclusion concerning the reasons for emigration:

> To Poland, as elsewhere in Europe, the land ultimately proved insufficient to sustain the lives of the rapidly growing population. The number of people in the Russian Partition tripled in the course of the nineteenth century; in Galicia, where the subdivided parcels of land were too small to be recorded on official charts, 55,000 people were starving to death each year in the late 1880s. The necessity to stay alive and the lack of urban industries to employ the landless peasants led to the emigration.[24]

The Poles of the Prussian Partition were the first to start their mass emigration to America in the late 1870s. They came mostly from Silesia (Śląsk), the province of Posen (Poznań), and Pomerania (Pomorze).[25] The next group of Polish immigrants came from Austrian Poland from the area known as Galicia and from the Górale region in the Carpathian Mountains. They began their mass emigration about the turn of the century when the agrarian crises deepened.[26] About 1890, the mass emigration of Poles in the territory under Russian domination began, i.e., Lithuania, Livonia, and the Ukraine.[27] According to Kuzniewski, more than 2.2 million Poles entered the United States by 1914. Other writers who have described this period have generally reached the same conclusion in regard to the number of Poles who emigrated.[28]

Although most of the immigrants came from farming areas in Poland, less than one-fifth of them settled in rural areas.[29] Very few of them went into business for themselves. Thousands of Poles worked in factories, mills, mines, auto industries, railroads, and packinghouses.[30] The majority of the Polish immigrants settled in the large industrial cities of Buffalo, Cleveland, Chicago, Detroit, Milwaukee, and Pittsburgh.[31] Chicago, in particular, emerged as the acknowledged metropolis of immigrant Poles because of its excellent lines of communication with the seaboard and its vast opportunities for employment.[32] By the 1890s, approximately 77.9 percent of Chicago's population were foreign-born and the Poles constituted 5.4 percent.[33] By the time of the First World War, Chicago had Polish settlers in every corner of the city. There were thirty-four parishes by 1916, and nearly a quarter-million Polish residents in a city of two million people.[34]

As in Poland, the parish church became the center of family and community life for the Poles in America since they sought companionship and consolation with others like themselves.[35] The Roman Catholic Church helped the Polish immigrant adjust to the New World. When the first immigrant Poles came to Chicago, they generally settled in one of five distinct settlements. The first to be established was that located on the Northwest Side centering on the intersection of Milwaukee, Ashland, and Division Streets about a mile and a half from Downtown Chicago in the parish of St. Stanislaus Kostka.[36] While the beginning and development of Polish parishes in the city followed basically the same pattern, the history of Chicago's oldest Polish settlement, St. Stanislaus Kostka Parish, where Josephine Dudzik and her family took root, was anything but typical.

LAND OF BIRTH

[1]Father John B. Terbovich, "Poland's Culture and Its People," *The Immaculate* 17 (1966): 50.

[2]Ibid.

[3]Even as these words are being written, the Polish people are once again undergoing a crisis of great magnitude. From this crisis has evolved "one of history's most improbable heroes," Lech Wałęsa, according to *Time* 116 (December 1980): 26. This courageous shipyard worker became organizer and leader of the Communist world's only independent Polish labor union called *Solidarność* [Solidarity]. He single-handedly rallied his fellow workers to stand up against the might of the Soviet Union and challenge its corrupt and ineffective regime. As a consequence, he was imprisoned by the Polish government as it imposed martial law on Poland on December 13, 1981, in an effort to crush Solidarity. *Time* magazine voted Wałęsa "Man of the Year" for 1981. Wałęsa was *Time's* first imprisoned "Man of the Year" since India's Mahatma Gandhi appeared on the magazine's cover. Wałęsa was also the recipient of the Nobel Peace Prize in 1981. Another hero of our times is the Reverend Jerzy Popieluszko, an outspoken pro-Solidarity priest, who was slain in 1984 by four secret-service police officers in Poland.

Poland's history is studded with lengthy periods of oppression, invasion, occupation, and poverty. But the Polish national anthem boldly states: "Poland has not perished as long as we are alive," and the ideals that Wałęsa and Popieluszko represent today have their roots in more than one thousand years of Polish history.

[4]Lindsay T. Baker, "The Early History of Panna Maria, Texas" (Ph.D. dissertation, Texas Tech University, 1975), p. 5.

[5]Casimir Stec, "The National Orientation of the Poles in the United States 1608–1935" (M.A. thesis, Marquette University, 1946), p. 47.

[6]Mary Assumpta Pogorzelska, "A Historical Study of Religion and Education as Underlying Influences in the Localization of the Poles of Cleveland up to 1915" (M.A. thesis, St. John's College of Cleveland, 1951), p. 77.

[7]Poland is a vast plain or field, which is literally the very meaning of *pole* from which the country derives its name.

[8]The following sources are suggested for excellent reading on the history of Poland: Clifford Barnett, *et al. Poland: Its People; Its Society; Its Culture* (New York: Grove Press, Inc., 1958); Francis Dvornik, *The Slavs in European History and Civilization* (New Brunswick, New Jersey: Rutgers University Press, 1962); Roman Dyboski, *Outlines of Polish History,* 2nd ed. (London: George Allen and Unwin, 1941); Aleksander Giejsztor, Stefan Kieniewicz, Emanuel Rostworowski, Janusz Tazbir, and Henryk Wereszycki, *History of Poland* (Warsaw: PWN: Polish Scientific Publishers, 1968); Oscar Halecki, *A History of Poland,* rev. ed. (London: J. M. Dent and Sons, 1955); Stefan Kaniewicz, *The Emancipation of the Polish Peasantry* (Chicago: University of Chicago Press, 1969); Herbert H. Kaplan, *The First Partition of Poland* (New York: Columbia University Press, 1962); Robert Leslie, *Reform and Insurrection in Russian Poland, 1856–1865* (London: Athlone Press, 1963); Robert Howard Lord, *The Second Partition of Poland* (Cambridge: Howard University Press, 1915); Bernadotte Schmitt, editor, *Poland* (California: University of California Press, 1947); W. F. Reddaway, *et al. From Augustus II to Pilsudski* (1697–1935), vol. 2, *The Cambridge History of Poland* (Cambridge: Cambridge University Press, 1941); W. F. Reddaway, *et al. From the Origins to Sobieski* (to 1696), vol. 1, *The Cambridge History of Poland* (Cambridge: Cambridge University Press, 1950). Piotr Wandycz, *The Lands of Partitioned Poland, 1795–1918* (Seattle: Seattle University of Washington Press, 1974).

[9]Baker, "The Early History of Panna Maria, Texas," p. 5.

[10]Joseph A. Wytrwal, *America's Polish Heritage: A Social History of the Poles in America* (Detroit: Endurance Press, 1961), p. 107.

[11]Ibid., p. 11.

[12]Ibid., p. 15.

[13]At the end of World War I, Poland took its place once more in the commonwealth of Europe as an independent state but now with the full extent of its historical boundaries. This newly found freedom, was, unfortunately, short-lived. Twenty-one years later, Poland was again shamefully attacked and occupied by Nazi Germany and Soviet Russia. As a result of the Yalta Conference in 1945, Poland was placed under Communist domination and remains so to this day.

[14]"Focus," *Chicago Tribune,* 7 May 1982.

[15]M. Golawski, M.A., *Poland Through the Ages.* (London: Orbis Limited, 1971), p. 145.

[16]Ibid., p. 44.

[17]Ibid., p. 146.

[18]Wytrwal, p. 13.

[19]Sister M. Francis Borgia, OSF, in *He Sent Two* (Milwaukee: Bruce Publishing Co., 1965), p. 36, remarks: "There occurred in Europe a phenomenon the like of which the human race had never witnessed before and has not witnessed since. The pull was to the New World. Between 1830 and 1920, more than 33,800,000 emigrated to America." From all available statistics, it is very obvious that the Poles were a part of this huge migration.

[20]Joseph J. Parot, *Polish Catholics in Chicago, 1850–1920* (De Kalb, Illinois: Northern Illinois University Press, 1981), p. 3.

[21]Wytrwal, p. 108.

[22]Ibid., p. 148.

[23]Theresita Polzin, *The Polish American: Whence and Whither* (Pulaski, Wisconsin: Franciscan Publishers, 1973), p. 46.

[24]Anthony J. Kuzniewski, SJ, "The Catholic Church in the Life of the Polish-Americans," in *Poles in America,* ed. Frank Mocha (Stevens Point, Wisconsin: Worzalla Publishing Co., 1978), pp. 399–422.

[25]Stefan Włoszczewski, *History of Polish American Culture.* (Trenton, New Jersey: White Eagle Publishing Co., 1946), p. 60.

[26]Pogorzelska, p. 24.

[27]Parot, p. 5.

[28]It is generally understood that the exact statistics on Polish emigration are difficult to determine and are sometimes unreliable. According to Helen Znaniecka Lopata, "The Function of Voluntary Associations in an Ethnic Community: Polonia," (Ph.D. dissertation, University of Chicago, 1954), p. 15, often the immigrant Poles were not classified as Poles, but as Germans, Austrians, or Russians, depending on what partitioned section they came from. There is, however, the ardent research on Polish-American growth in the United States done by the eminent Polish-American historian, Miecislaus Haiman, and upon which we can rely. Haiman has studied all the available records in each state and in the Federal Bureau of Statistics in Washington, DC. He also consulted contemporary newspapers, both American and foreign. Haiman's conclusions are listed in *Polish Past in America, 1608–1865* (Chicago, Polish Museum of America, 1975, pp. 68–70. They are as follows: in 1860 some 10,000 Poles with ten settlements; 50,000 Poles in 1870 with twenty settlements; in 1875, approximately 200,000 Poles in three hundred settlements; in 1890, at least 1,000,000 Poles in 150 parishes with 125 parochial schools; an increase of 1,000,000 Poles in 1900, with about four hundred parishes. By the first years of the twentieth century, there were 3,000,000 Poles with 530 parishes and three hundred schools. There were Poles in every state of the United States. These figures are substantiated by Joseph A. Wytrwal, *America's Polish Heritage* (Detroit: Endurance Press, 1961), p. 78; Bessie Louise Pierce, *A History of Chicago,* vol. 3: *The Rise of a Modern City* (New York: Alfred A. Knopf, 1957), p. 15; M. J. Madaj, "Chicago: The Polish Capital of the United States," *The New World,* 9 April 1971, p. 26; Mary Inviolata Ficht, "Noble Street in Chicago: Socio-cultural Study of Polish Residents Within Ten Blocks" (M.A. thesis, De Paul University, 1952), p. 68; Mieczysław Szawlewski, *Wychodztwo Polskie w Stanach Zjednoczonych Ameryki* (Lwów: Narodowego Imienia Ossolinckich, 1924), p. 17; Theresita Polzin, *The Polish*

American (Pulaski, Wis.: Franciscan Publishers, 1973), p. 58; and Jay P. Dolan, *The American Catholic Experience: A History from Colonial Times to the Present* (Garden City: Doubleday and Company, Inc., 1985), p. 133.

[29]Włoszczewski, p. 62.

[30]Mary Valentia Karolczak, "Some Aspects of Polish Immigration to the United States with Special Reference to the Period 1870–1905" (M.A. thesis, Marquette University, 1942), p. 39.

[31]Wytrwal, p. 42.

[32]During the 1840s and 1860s, immigrants flocked to Chicago. These immigrants were mainly Yankees and Southerners who came from states on the Atlantic coast. The Germans, Swedes, and Irish arrived next. By the 1880s and 1890s, hundreds of thousands of Czechs, Slovaks, Italians, Greeks, Russians, and Poles had settled in Chicago. Martha Bennett King, *The Key to Chicago* (New York: J. B. Lippincott Co., 1961), p. 39.

[33]M. J. Madaj, "Chicago: The Polish Capital of the United States," *The New World*, 9 April 1971, pp. 1–29.

[34]Edward R. Kantowicz, *Polish American Politics in Chicago, 1888–1940* (Chicago: The University of Chicago Press, 1975), p. 26.

[35]Harold M. Mayer and Richard E. Wade, *Chicago: Growth of a Metropolis* (Chicago: The University of Chicago Press, 1969), p. 152.

[36]Generally, whenever a group of Poles settled in a particular area, they formed a society under the patronage of a saint. The next step was to petition the bishop of the diocese for a Polish priest who was eventually named the pastor. The pastor and the society, or committee, would then organize the new parish and build a church which was oftentimes combined with a school. It usually followed that the church was named after the particular saint under whose patronage the society was initially formed. Karol Wachtel, *Polonia w Ameryce* [The Poles in America] (Philadelphia: Polish Star Co., 1944), p. 85.

CHAPTER 3

St. Stanislaus Kostka Parish

Miecislaus Haiman, the illustrious pioneer historian of Polish America, traced the history of the Poles in Chicago to a group of exiles who had come to the city in the autumn of 1834 with plans of founding a "New Poland" in Illinois on land granted to them by the Congress of the United States. The exiles were delegates of 235 Polish officers and soldiers who had fled Poland after the failure of the November Insurrection of 1830–1831 against the Russians. Although their plans for establishing a purely Polish colony in Illinois[1] never materialized due to many legal and technical difficulties, Polish emigration to Chicago gained momentum after 1834.[2]

Among the earliest permanent settlers was Anthony Smarzewski-Schermann[3] who came to Chicago in 1851 with his wife and three children with the hope of establishing a Polish colony and trading center. They settled in the area of Noble[4] and Bradley[5] Streets where Schermann[6] eventually opened a grocery store in what was then a suburb of Chicago.[7] At that time, the city had already assumed great importance due to its excellent location on the southern shores of Lake Michigan which connected it with strategic waterways. With many railroad lines also serving the city, Chicago was fast becoming a giant in the industrial and commercial world. The city's vast natural resources made its growth rapid and prosperous. In the immediate vicinity of Schermann's settlement west of the Chicago River, however, the area was basically farmland where Chicagoans hunted wild ducks and rabbits and held occasional picnics. The vast prairies were dotted with a few frame houses, and cattle and chickens fed freely on the open grasslands. The swampy and sometimes virtually muddy plains stretched out at great length offering only Plank Road,[8] later called Milwaukee Avenue, running southeast, as the main outlet to the steadily growing city of Chicago.[9] By what stretch of the imagination could Schermann have envisioned that, after his initial modest settlement, Chicago would someday rank second only to Warsaw as the city containing the largest number of Poles in the world.

When the second uprising of Poland against her Czarist oppressors failed in 1863, large numbers of Poles set out for America and found their way to Chicago. Newly arrived immigrants came also from the sections of Silesia (Śląsk), Pomerania (Pomorze), and

Greater Poland (Wielkapolska).[10] At the close of America's Civil War, Chicago's energetic and prosperous industry and commerce also beckoned many immigrants. Poles gravitated to the new metropolis of the Midwest attracted by the city's strong and expanding labor market. Each year the city grew in size, wealth, and importance. It is no surprise that Chicago's population increased from 200,000 in 1866 to 334,270 by 1870.[11]

In 1864, there were approximately thirty families rooted in the area of Noble Street and Milwaukee Avenue.[12] That same year, a Union army officer named Peter Kiołbassa[13] arrived in Chicago on furlough and visited the tiny Schermann settlement. Learning of the Poles' desperate need for the services of a Polish priest, Kiołbassa succeeded in contacting the Reverend Leopold Moczygemba,[14] a missionary priest whom he had met in Texas, and convinced him to come to Chicago. When Father Moczygemba arrived in February 1864, the Poles viewed his visit among them as a sign of the permanency of what was to become the "village of St. Stanislaus Kostka," *Stanisławowo*,[15] the *Polonia*[16] of Chicago. At a historic meeting held in Schermann's house, a society for mutual benefit and cooperation was formed called the Society of St. Stanislaus Kostka.[17] Its official organizers were listed as Anthony Smarzewski-Schermann, president; Peter Kiołbassa, vice-president; John Niemczewski, secretary; John Arkuszewski and Paul Kurr, committee members.[18] While the group seriously discussed plans for the formation of a parish and the erection of a church, they lacked the necessary funds to put their plans into action. As a consequence, the Society of St. Stanislaus Kostka was inactive for the next two years. In the meantime, the Poles attended services at the German churches of St. Joseph's[19] near Chicago Avenue and La Salle Street and St. Michael's[20] at North Avenue and Cleveland Street.[21] Upon Kiołbassa's return to Chicago after the Civil War, he zealously reactivated the Society of St. Stanislaus Kostka. He provided it with a written constitution which was designed to reflect its religious spirit by means of the practice of the corporal and spiritual works of mercy.[22] It was structured to form a parish which held loyalty to the Catholic Church as one of its principal aims and the maintenance of "peace" between emerging factions in *Stanisławowo*.[23]

By 1867, with 150 families in the prairie area, plans were underway to purchase land near Wesson and Oak Streets for the proposed church.[24] Instead, four lots were purchased at the corner of Noble and Bradley Streets for $1,700. After a lengthy delay, the construction of a modest two-story structure with a cross and steeple rising eighty-five feet in the air was begun in 1869. On June 18, 1871, the Most Reverend Thomas Foley,[25] bishop of Chicago, dedicated the church which the parishioners had proudly named St. Stanislaus Kostka. The first floor of the twelve-foot-high building was designed for classroom use and meeting halls; the second floor, twenty-two feet high, served as the church.[26]

In the meantime, the parish was faced with the problem of securing a permanent pastor. Until this time, the Poles had been ministered to by a Jesuit, the Reverend F. X. Szulak, SJ, and the Reverend Joseph Molitor, the Czech pastor of nearby St. Wenceslaus Church on De Koven Street.[27] In February of 1869, the Reverend Simon Wieczorek, CR,[28] while on a missionary visit to Polish and German Catholics in Iowa, learned of the great number of Poles in Chicago who had no Polish priest to minister to them. He informed his regional superior, the Reverend Eugene Funcken, CR, of the matter, and as a result, the Reverend John Wołłowski, CR,[29] from Parisville, Michigan, was sent to preach a mission to the Chicago Poles in April. Upon his arrival, he found a city of over 300,000 people with about four hundred Polish families whose spiritual life had been sorely neglected.[30] Because of the persistent efforts of Peter Kiołbassa, who had carried on correspondence with the Congregation of the Resurrection in Rome with the hope of receiving a Resurrectionist priest for the Chicago mission, Father Wołłowski returned to Chicago to assume his role as the permanent pastor of St. Stanislaus Kostka Church.[31] When he arrived in November 1869, however, he learned that other plans had been made during the summer. The administrator of the Diocese of Chicago, the Reverend John Halligan,[32] had appointed the Reverend Joseph Juszkiewicz, a diocesan priest, as pastor of St. Stanislaus Kostka Church on the personal recommendation of Father Szulak. Disheartened, Father Wołłowski returned to the Resurrectionist headquarters in Canada.[33]

In 1870, the Reverend Adolph Bakanowski, CR,[34] who had been laboring for four years as a missionary in the Polish colonies of Texas, arrived in Chicago.[35] He had been recalled to Europe by his superiors, but the outbreak of the Franco-Prussian War in 1870 now prevented him from continuing his journey. With the approval of the superior general of the Resurrectionists, the Reverend Jerome Kajsiewicz, CR,[36] Father Bakanowski obtained the necessary consent of Bishop Foley to remain in Chicago temporarily to serve the Poles of St. Stanislaus Kostka Parish who now numbered over five hundred families.[37] The membership begged him to remain permanently at the parish, but he reminded them of his obligation to return to Rome. Father Bakanowski had indeed arrived in the parish at a critical and unfortunate time, for violent controversies raged between Father Juszkiewicz, the pastor, and his parishioners. Dissatisfied with what they termed his negligence of parish affairs and his tyrannical policies, the people now stood in strong opposition to Father Juszkiewicz.[38] The constant disputes and wranglings mounted until they became exceedingly crucial and ended almost fatally for Father Juszkiewicz.[39] He left the parish after one year, and Father Bakanowski obtained permission to remain in Chicago until the Franco-Prussian hostilities in Europe had ceased. In September of 1870, Bishop Foley appointed him temporary pastor. When Father Jerome Kajsiewicz, as superior general, formally accepted the parish as a Resurrectionist mission, Father Bakanowski became the first member of the Congregation of the Resurrection to become pastor of St. Stanislaus Kostka Church.[40] Consequently, the Congregation of the Resurrection began its long and memorable association with the parish. This event is noted by the Reverend Leonard Long, CR, in *The Resurrectionists:* "Under the Resurrectionists, the parish reached its zenith of glory, achieved renown as the model Catholic parish, and under every aspect, became the foremost parish not only in the Archdiocese of Chicago, but in the entire country." [41]

The Resurrectionists were ideally suited for this endeavor. Known officially as the Congregation of the Resurrection, it had its beginning in Paris on February 17, 1836. After the abortive November Insurrection of 1830–1831 by the Poles against their Russian oppressors, several thousand Poles sought refuge in Paris. The Polish émigrés, influenced by France's own internal turmoil, were soon engulfed in a wave of anticlericalism and materialistic socialism. Among the exiles who fought the rising surge of irreligion was the great Polish poet, Adam Mickiewicz (1798–1855), who exerted a profound influence upon his compatriots in the early years of the Paris emigration. He perceived the salvation of the Polish exiles to lie in the formation of a distinctly Polish religious order. He suggested an associate, Bogdan Jański (1808–1840), a convert from the socialism of Saint-Simon, as the person to bring about the religious revival among the Poles.[42] Inspired by the French Catholic lay apostolate movement headed by Count Charles Montalembert, Pere Jean Lacordaire, OP, and Frederick Ozanam, Jański attempted a similar work among the Poles in Paris. Influenced by Jański's profound example, Peter Semenenko (1814–1886), and Jerome Kajsiewicz (1812–1873), two scholars who had returned to the practice of the Catholic faith only a few years earlier, joined Jański in living a common life in a rented house on the rue Notre Dame des Champs on February 17, 1836. Jański died in 1840, unable to see the full realization of his initial undertakings. Two years later, on the Easter morning of March 27, 1842, Semenenko and Kajsiewicz, along with five other clerics, professed their first vows under Pope Gregory XVI in the chapel of SS. Peter and Paul in the catacombs of San Sebastian in Rome. They called themselves the Congregation of the Resurrection. Father Semenenko, who composed the first Rule for the Resurrectionists, was elected the first superior general.

The Resurrectionists came to the United States with the initiation of missionary activity in Parisville, Michigan, in 1865. The next year, their work spread to Texas with the appointment of the Reverend Adolph Bakanowski, CR, the Reverend Vincent Barzynski, CR, and a cleric, Felix Zwiardowski. In Chicago, as has already been noted, Resurrectionist history began with the appointment of the Reverend Adolph Bakanowski to the permanent pastorate of St. Stanislaus Kostka Church.[43]

Father Bakanowski's pastorate, however, was not without its share of unpleasantness. One of the most vexing problems which erupted during his administration was the infiltration of Masonic and Socialist influences which were beginning to make themselves felt in the parish.[44] Dissident groups attempted to create ill will toward the bishop of Chicago over the question of church property. Bishop Foley maintained that all Church properties should be held in the name of the bishop of the diocese to preserve order and to secure a high degree of centralization within each diocese.[45] The dissidents argued that the church and the land on which it stood belonged to the people of the parish. They were totally opposed to handing over their property to an "Irish" bishop. Father Bakanowski, having won their trust, was able to convince them of the necessity and the legality of transferring ownership of the parish to the bishop of Chicago according to the statutes of the Councils of Baltimore which stated that the deed to all the Church properties should be in the name of the bishop of the diocese.[46]

Unfortunately, the amicable settlement of the matter was short-lived, for in the space of a year, a similar conflict further divided the Polish community of *Stanisławowo* into two irreconcilable factions. The strained situation was further intensified by another event which occurred in October 1871. On a trip to Chicago, Father Kajsiewicz had an audience with Bishop Foley in which they formally concluded an agreement by which the Resurrectionists were placed in charge of all the Polish churches in the Diocese of Chicago for the next ninety-nine years. Besides continuing to staff St. Stanislaus Kostka Church, the Resurrectionists were to provide Polish priests for all future Polish parishes.[47] These significant actions would prove to have unfortunate results for the future "peace" of *Stanisławowo.*

During this period of agitation, nevertheless, Father Bakanowski proceeded in the matter of completing the construction of St. Stanislaus Kostka Church which was blessed and dedicated by Bishop Foley on June 18, 1871. Approximately twenty-two thousand jubilant parishioners as well as numerous fraternities and associations from neighboring parishes joined in a large and colorful parade through the streets of the city in conclusion of the day's celebration. The parish population at this time was rapidly approaching fifteen thousand families.[48]

A few months after the spirited dedication of St. Stanislaus Kostka Church, an event occurred which altered the history of Chicago, and to no small degree, that of *Stanisławowo.* On the evening of October 8, 1871, the Great Chicago Fire erupted bringing death, ruin, and devastation.[49] While the loss in life and property for Chicagoans was staggering, the Polish community of St. Stanislaus Kostka suffered relatively small losses. Out of the Great Fire, however, came a new and greater city. To aid in Chicago's feverish restoration and growth, thousands of people, a great number of them Poles, came to Chicago seeking employment.[50] Another event, the emergence of the *Kulturkampf*[51] in Bismarck's Germany, sent a new wave of Polish immigrants to Chicago, and most particularly, to *Stanisławowo.*[52] As a consequence, the parish continued to grow at such a phenomenal rate that by 1872, the Church was severely and dangerously overcrowded. By 1873, the number of Poles in the *Stanisławowo* area was estimated at twenty thousand.[53]

In an effort to alleviate the situation, Father Bakanowski called a parish meeting to decide whether St. Stanislaus Kostka Church should be enlarged or whether another church should be erected to accommodate all worshippers. The matter was left in the hands of the two main but antagonistic associations at the parish, namely, the older Society of St. Stanislaus Kostka and the younger Society of St. Joseph which had been organized in 1871. Both societies were at odds with each other, but the Society of St. Joseph was given permission by Father Bakanowski to construct a new church at Division and Noble Streets. Completed in 1873, it was named Holy Trinity.[54] The history of Holy Trinity Church, popularly called *Trójcowo,* is dimmed somewhat by the controversy which surrounded its organization, and which profoundly affected the Polish community in Chicago and throughout the United States. It was in this fashion that Holy Trinity Church,[55] the eldest daughter of St. Stanislaus Kostka Church, also became its principal rival.

Father Bakanowski remained as pastor at St. Stanislaus Kostka Church until May

1874, when he was summoned to Rome as a delegate to the general chapter of the Congregation of the Resurrection. He never returned to the United States. His position as administrator of St. Stanislaus Kostka Church was shared by three priests, respectively, for the next four months. They were the Reverend John Wołłowski, CR, the Reverend Felix Zwiardowski, CR,[56] and the Reverend Simon Wieczorek, CR.

Reverend Vincent Michael Barzynski, CR, Founder of the Resurrectionist Missions in Chicago 1874–1899, Spiritual Director of Mother M. Theresa Dudzik and the pioneer Franciscan Sisters of Chicago

On September 18, 1874, however, "a man of Providence, given not only to the people of St. Stanislaus Kostka Parish, but also to the entire population of America," assumed his duties as pastor.[57] This was the Reverend Vincent Michael Barzynski, CR, the "Founder of the Resurrectionists in the United States,"[58] who for the next twenty-five years was the acknowledged spiritual and social leader of the Polish colony in America. He may well have been nominated "the most outstanding parish priest in the history of the Chicago diocese" for that he proved to be.[59] Under his guidance, St. Stanislaus Kostka Church emerged as the largest parish in the United States and, eventually, in the world. In *The First One Hundred Years*, the Reverend John Iwicki, CR, gives a capsule view of this eminent priest's effect on *Stanisławowo:*

When Father Barzynski assumed the pastorate in 1874, there were about 400 families in the parish, a wooden church, a school and a rectory, valued at $20,000. In 1897, two years before his death, St. Stanislaus numbered 40,000 souls, a little over 8,000 families. The parish buildings were valued at half a million dollars. There were 3,000 pupils in the parish school staffed by 40 School Sisters of Notre Dame, 7 lay teachers, and 5 priest teachers. The parish counted 51 societies with an aggregate membership of 12,000. The parish choir had 300 members. In the years following, these numbers increased and remained constant for several decades.[60]

Father Barzynski was truly an extraordinary man. He was born on September 20, 1838, in the village of Sulisławice, near Sandomierz in the Congress Kingdom, that part of Poland dominated by the Russians. His parents were Joseph and Marianne (née Sroczyński) Bara. Three days after his birth he was baptized Vincent Michael in St. Mary's Church.[61] At the time of the baptism, the entire family used the surname *Bara,* a name still common today in the village. It appears that at some later date, the family added the suffix *-ski* to its name, resulting in the modified surname Barzynski, which tended to identify it with the gentry and nobility.[62] Vincent finished the local elementary school in the town of Tomaszów Lubelski, but instead of attending the county gymnasium,[63] he was privately tutored. In 1856, he went to Lublin to study philosophy and theology at the diocesan seminary and was ordained a priest on October 28, 1861. While returning to his home town of Tomaszów after the celebration of his First Mass, he caught a cold that forced him to remain at his father's house for six months. The cold was the beginning of a lung problem which afflicted him for the rest of his life and which, eventually, was to contribute to his death.[64]

In 1862, while still recovering from his illness, he was assigned to the village of Horodło on the Bug River. Subsequently, he served as parish priest at Zamość, and then returned to Tomaszów, the town of his childhood, at a most difficult time. In January 1863, the Polish Insurrection had taken place, and the Russians had attacked Tomaszów killing twenty-two people and ransacking numerous houses.[65] The Polish provisional government appointed Father Barzynski a "regional organizer" thereby commissioning him with the task of supplying arms to the Polish insurgents. After six months, in order to avoid Russian arrest, Father Barzynski escaped to Cracow in Austrian Poland. The Austrians jailed him for ten months for entering the country without permission and the necessary documents.[66] After his release from prison, Father Barzynski fled to Paris where a large Polish community was already in exile. Here he became acquainted with members of the Congregation of the Resurrection operating among the Polish émigrés. He joined the congregation, and after completing his novitiate in Rome, made his profession of vows on September 18, 1866.[67] On September 28, 1866, the Reverend Jerome Kajsiewicz, the father general of the Resurrectionists; the Reverend Alexander Jełowicki, the superior of the Resurrectionists in Paris; and the Most Reverend Claude-Marie Dubuis, bishop of Galveston, signed an agreement for the Resurrectionists to supply Polish priests for the Polish parishes in Texas. Even before the agreement was signed, three priests had already been selected. The Reverend Adolph Bakanowski, CR, and a seminarian, Felix Zwiardowski, were ordered to Panna Maria, Texas. Father Barzynski was ordered to San Antonio where he arrived on November 8, 1866. The Poles had no parish organization or place of worship. By 1868, Father Barzynski had built a church combined with a parish school and rectory which he named St. Michael's. He took an active role in establishing numerous lay organizations and ministering to isolated groups in other Polish colonies in Texas. He labored incessantly. Father Barzynski himself described his dedication in a letter to his father general in these words: "I work . . . like a mother at the wedding of her only daughter."[68]

In November of 1872, Father Barzynski left St. Michael's Parish in San Antonio. He moved to the Polish settlement of St. Hedwig's, approximately twenty miles away, laboring in the Annunciation of the Blessed Virgin Mary Parish. Early in 1873, he was transferred to Panna Maria, Texas,[69] where he remained for ten months. On September 6, 1874, Father Barzynski arrived in Chicago for a "visit" and resided at St. Stanislaus Kostka Parish. On September 19, 1874, Bishop Foley appointed him pastor, and for the next twenty-five years, Father Barzynski served as confessor, educator, and protector of the thousands of immigrant Poles flooding the city.[70] Throughout his twenty-five years in Chicago, he was the major advisor to Bishop Foley and Archbishop Feehan on Church affairs in the Polish community.[71] This ingenious priest, organizer, patriot, and social worker exerted his influence in every direction and was associated with major events during his pastorate. Besides being administrator of the largest Polish parish and grade school in America, Father Barzynski is credited with many other contributions. Among the most important, according to the Reverend John J. Iwicki, CR, in *The First One Hundred Years*, are the following:

> He was co-founder of the Polish Roman Catholic Union of America, a fraternal insurance organization for the immigrant Poles (1873); he invited the Sisters of the Holy Family of Nazareth to the United States and established them at their first mission of St. Josaphat's school (1885); he founded the Polish Publishing Company for the dissemination of Catholic books and periodicals (1887); he founded the Society of Priests Under the Protection of the Sacred Heart, an auxiliary unit of the Polish Roman Catholic Union, to foster mutual peace and unity and to aid the bishops (1887); he built and organized the Holy Family Orphanage on Division and Holt Streets in Chicago and placed the orphans under the care of the School Sisters of Notre Dame (1890); he founded the *Polish Daily News* [Dziennik Chicagoski], a Catholic daily in the Polish language (1890); he was the founder and initiator of St. Stanislaus Kostka College, presently Weber High School (1890); he was instrumental in

organizing St. Mary of Nazareth Hospital in Chicago in conjunction with the Sisters of the Holy Family of Nazareth (1894); he was negotiating to bring the Sisters of the Resurrection to the United States (1898–1899); he was the first Provincial Superior of the Resurrectionist missions in the United States (1898–1899); and he inspired the Reverend Francis Gordon, CR, to organize the *Polish Alma Mater* [Macierz Polska] for youth (1897).[72]

In addition, Father Barzynski organized six Polish Resurrectionist parishes in Chicago and helped organize many more. Among those he directly or indirectly established or inspired were: St. Adalbert (1874); Immaculate Conception, South Chicago (1882); SS. Cyril and Methodius, Lemont (1883); St. Josaphat (1884); St. Mary of Perpetual Help (1884); St. Joseph (1886); St. Hedwig (1888); St. John Cantius (1893); St. Stanislaus Bishop and Martyr (1893); St. Hyacinth (1894); Sacred Heart, Melrose Park (1895); St. Michael, South Chicago (1897); and St. Mary of the Angels (1899).

In "Polish Churches Along the Kennedy Expressway," the authors Lilien and Pyrek-Ejsmont state:

> As visitors to Chicago head north on the Kennedy, they often express amazement at the sudden sight of these magnificent edifices, imposed serenely and towering majestically against the western skyline. They are part of what Chicago's notable visitor, Pope John Paul II, lauded as the contributions made by his compatriots, "the sons and daughters of our first homeland."[73]

For this invaluable legacy, gratitude is due to the Reverend Vincent Barzynski, CR.[74]

As did his predecessor, Father Bakanowski, Father Barzynski strove to unite the parish into a harmonious and closely knit unit, and thus St. Stanislaus Kostka Parish emerged as a model for all the other Polish parishes of Chicago. To accomplish this end, Father Barzynski was forced to battle the insidious influences of the period, namely, Socialism, Masonry, and the Polish Independent Church Movement among others.[75] In the process, he was often attacked by his adversaries and could not escape becoming, at times, a rather controversial figure.[76] One fact remains constant. Father Barzynski influenced the history, development, and progress of the Catholic Poles in Chicago, and his name is inseparable from the history of the Polish immigrants in America. Although Father Barzynski was the recipient of numerous honors and accolades during his lifetime, the *Dziennik Chicagoski* [Polish Daily News] after his death, paid him the supreme compliment by calling Father Barzynski simply, "a good priest."[77]

Prior to the arrival of Father Barzynski in 1874, the School Sisters of Notre Dame from Milwaukee had been invited to staff the elementary school of St. Stanislaus Kostka Parish.[78] Mother M. Caroline, commissary general, had responded to the invitation by sending Sister M. Rogeria, SSND,[79] Sister M. Melaria, SSND, and a postulant who arrived on February 2, 1874. While Mother M. Caroline did her utmost to provide Sisters for the Catholic schools and for the children of all immigrant nationalities, she seemed to have a special fondness for the Poles. In *Mother Caroline and the School Sisters of Notre Dame in North America,* the author states: "For the Polish people, she [Mother Caroline] seemed to have a particular affection because of their noble traits of character, their deep piety, and the sufferings they had endured to preserve the faith."[80]

On opening day of school in February of 1874, eighty-nine pupils were registered. By September, 350 pupils were registered to begin the new school year.[81]

In spite of the erection of Holy Trinity Church, which had initially been built to alleviate the overcrowded conditions at St. Stanislaus Kostka, a larger church was now an urgent necessity. In 1875, therefore, Father Barzynski initiated construction of a new St. Stanislaus Kostka Church on the southwest corner of Noble Street and Ingraham Street, now called Evergreen, at the cost of $11,500. The result was one of the largest and most beautiful churches in Chicago.[82] Built in the form of a Roman basilica, the church stood two hundred feet long and eighty feet wide with a seating capacity of fifteen thousand people. Both the upper and the lower church were used for liturgical services.[83] The cornerstone was laid on July 1, 1877, and the first mass was offered on December 24, 1877, in the lower church. The construction of the church went on for another three years, and on July 10, 1881, it was finally blessed. The need for a larger school was also obvious. In 1889, a huge, four-story, 212-foot-long school was erected facing Bradley Avenue. It contained sixteen classrooms, four large meeting halls, and an immense auditorium with accommodations for approximately four thousand people. It was equipped with a stage and was used exclusively for dramatic presentations and other public gatherings.[84] At the time, the auditorium was considered to be the second largest in the city.[85] In 1892, two church towers and the statue of St. Stanislaus Kostka were erected in the facade of the church building.[86] In 1893, the year of the Columbian Exposition[87] in Jackson Park on Chicago's South Side, visitors from all over the world came to Chicago. St. Stanislaus Kostka Church appeared as one of the scheduled stops for tourists. They flocked to see the impressive parish complex billed as the largest in the world, and the statistics for the year proved it. There were 2,277 baptisms, 382 marriages, and 883 funerals.[88] By 1898, there were forty thousand people in the parish, a little over eight thousand families, and three thousand children in the school.[89] At the time of Father Barzynski's death in 1899, the parish census had risen to fifty thousand.[90] The Reverend Joseph Wiśniewski, CR, relates an interesting anecdote recorded in the archives of the Congregation of the Resurrection in Rome:

> When the Very Reverend John Kasprzycki, CR, was rendering his report on the Resurrectionists to Pope St. Pius X and remarked that St. Stanislaus Kostka parish in Chicago which his Congregation administered had close to 4,000 children in its parochial school, the Holy Father retorted: "Why that is more like a diocese than a parish!"[91]

Indeed, anyone reading a more detailed history of the parish would never doubt that statement. It was a rare historic time and occurrence which shall not repeat itself.

On May 21, 1899, the Reverend John Kasprzycki, CR, was appointed the pastor of St. Stanislaus Kostka Church after the death of Father Barzynski which had occurred on May 2. By 1902, because of the lack of accommodations for the 3,675 pupils at the school, the parish auditorium was converted into twenty-four additional classrooms. In 1905, Father Kasprzycki was elected superior general of the Resurrectionists and was replaced by the Reverend Francis Gordon, CR, who proceeded to erect an immense school, a convent to house sixty-five Sisters, and a beautiful auditorium.[92] Unfortunately, on the night of December 22, 1906, a tragic fire destroyed the entire complex under construction since spring of that year.[93] Undaunted, Father Gordon began the work of rebuilding the school. The new school stood five stories high and contained fifty-four classrooms plus three meeting halls making it the largest elementary school in the United States. Eventually the church, the auditorium, the Sisters' residence, the school, the rectory, and the gymnasium covered the entire city block at Noble, Ingraham, and Bradley Streets.[94] The complex was solemnly blessed by the Most Reverend James Quigley, archbishop of Chicago, on May 10, 1908, with tens of thousands in attendance.[95] There were thirty-five

The St. Stanislaus Kostka Parish Complex: the church, auditorium, Sisters' residence, school, rectory, and gymnasium which occupied the entire city block at Noble, Ingraham, and Bradley Streets, opposite Pulaski Park, c. 1908

thousand people on the parish roster in 1908. By 1910, there were 3,829 pupils under the care of sixty-five School Sisters of Notre Dame.[96]

In 1925, St. Stanislaus Kostka parish, with 2,700 children still enrolled, had the second largest grammar school in the archdiocese but slowly began to show signs of diminishing numbers as Polish families moved to newer parishes. St. Stanislaus Kostka Parish remained relatively stable until the 1950s when plans to build the Northwest Expressway, now the Kennedy Expressway, were announced.[97]

Poland observed its Millennium of Christianity in 1966.[98] Because of Chicago's huge Polish community, its observance was one of the largest in the world. The Most Reverend Stanislaus Rubin, representing Stefan Cardinal Wyszynski, the Primate of Poland, opened his Chicago visit with a mass at St. Stanislaus Kostka Church, the "Mother Church."[99] In 1978, the grammar school was razed. Today, only the church and high school, now serving as the elementary school, remain. Although Poles now live in all parts of the city and suburbs, St. Stanislaus Kostka Church will always remain the "Cradle of the Polish Colony in Chicago."[100]

In 1881, Josephine Dudzik, her parents, her brother Joseph, and youngest sister, Katherine, left their cruelly partitioned homeland for America and settled in St. Stanislaus Kostka Parish. In *Neighborhood*, noted author and priest-sociologist, Andrew Greeley, quotes a colleague, Gerald Suttles: "Neighborhood is where one lives with one's family and friends. The boundaries of the neighborhood are the boundaries of an important segment of one's life."[101] For Josephine Dudzik, this important segment consisted of approximately sixteen years spent in the neighborhood of St. Stanislaus Kostka Parish where she and her family resided upon their arrival in America—in a city and in an area which sometimes promised more than it was capable of rendering its newly arrived immigrants.

ST. STANISLAUS KOSTKA PARISH

[1]Congress made a grant to the Poles of selected land located on the banks of the Rock River near the present city of Rockford. Lucille Wargin, "The Polish Immigrant in the American Community" (Ph.D. dissertation, De Paul University, 1948), p. 6.

[2]Miecislaus Haiman, "The Poles in Chicago," in *Poles of Chicago: A History of One Century of Contribution to the City of Chicago, Illinois, 1837–1937*, ed. Polish Pageant, Inc. (Chicago: By the Author, 1937), p. 1.

[3]He was born in Kcynia, near Posen in 1818. Initially, he was an agent for an association which maintained a fleet of ships and was thus responsible for securing passage to America for more than 100,000 people, mostly Poles. Smarzewski-Schermann died in 1900 at eighty-two. *Album Pamiątkowy Złotego Jubileuszu Parafii Świętego Stanisława* [A Commemorative Album of the Golden Jubilee of St. Stanislaus Kostka Parish] (Chicago: 1917), p. 234.

[4]By 1873, Noble Street was the principal trading center of the Polish community, the traditional "main street" of the district. Noble Street was known as the "Polish Corridor," and for Poles today, Noble Street stands "as their monument and a still vital memory." Sister M. Inviolata Ficht, "Noble Street in Chicago: Socio-cultural Study of Polish Residents Within Ten Blocks" (M.A. thesis, De Paul University, 1952); and Andrew Greeley, *Neighborhood* (New York: The Seabury Press, 1977), p. 53.

[5]The name of Bradley Street was later changed to Potomac Avenue.

[6]Smarzewski-Schermann legally changed his name to Schermann in America. Joseph J. Parot, *Polish Catholics in Chicago, 1850–1920* (De Kalb, Illinois: Northern Illinois University Press, 1981), p. 34.

[7]Rev. M. J. Madaj, "Chicago: The Polish Capital of the United States," *The New World*, 9 April 1969, pp. 1–29.

[8]Plank Road consisted of twenty-three miles of long three-inch flat pieces of timber laid over a dirt road. It was, unfortunately, planked on one side of the street only.

[9]*Diamond Jubilee, 1867–1942: St. Stanislaus Kostka Church* (Chicago: 1942), p. 58.

[10]*Diamond Jubilee, 1867–1942: St. Stanislaus Kostka Church*, p. 58; Ficht, p. 45; and Parot, p. 16.

[11]John J. Iwicki, *The First One Hundred Years: A Study of the Apostolate of the Congregation of the Resurrection in the United States, 1866–1966* (Rome: Gregorian University Press, 1966), p. 47.

[12]*Diamond Jubilee, 1867–1942: St. Stanislaus Kostka Church*, p. 58.

[13]Among the leading figures at St. Stanislaus Kostka Parish was Peter Kiołbassa. Born in Swib, Upper Silesia, Poland, in 1837, he came to the United States in 1855 with his parents and settled in Panna Maria, Texas. The Kiołbassas soon moved from Panna Maria to Castroville, and finally to San Antonio, arriving in 1858.

When the Civil War broke out, Peter Kiołbassa joined the Texas Cavalry. He was captured by the Union forces and sent to Illinois. There he enlisted with the Union Army becoming a corporal in the Sixteenth Illinois Cavalry and served until 1866. It was during one of his furloughs in Chicago in 1864 that he became intensely involved in establishing the Society of St. Stanislaus Kostka among the Poles.

Settling in Chicago after the War, Kiołbassa became a recognized leader in the Polish community. He joined the Chicago police force in which he served until 1869. From 1870–1871, he worked as a teacher and organist in the Resurrectionist mission of Panna Maria. Returning to Chicago in 1872, he was named City Tax Collector, a post he held for fourteen years. He also served as a member of the Illinois State Legislature for two years, making him the first Polish-born state legislator in the United States. From 1891 to 1893, he served as Chicago's City Treasurer. By his practice of returning all interest accrued on city funds to the treasury instead of keeping it for private use while in office as had been the custom of his predecessors, he earned a reputation for integrity and the nickname, "Honest Pete." In 1898, he was elected an alderman; in 1900, a city supervisor. In 1904, he served as Public Works Inspector, a position he held until his death on June 23, 1905. Helen Busyn, "Peter Kiołbassa—Maker of Polish America," *Polish American Studies* 8 (1951): 77; and *The Polish Texans* (San Antonio: University of Texas, 1972), no pagination.

[14]The Reverend Leopold Moczygemba had a most interesting and colorful life. Called the "Patriarch of American Polonia," Father Moczygemba was born in Upper Silesia in 1824. He was ordained a priest in the Order of Friars Minor Conventuals in 1847. Emigrating as a missionary priest to America in 1852, he founded the first Polish settlement at Panna Maria, Texas, in 1854. His later life is equally important in both ethnic and Catholic American history. In 1858, Father Moczygemba left Texas and went on to build the core of Franciscan Minor Conventual churches and friaries in the eastern United States; to establish a number of Catholic parishes; to help found the Polish Roman Catholic Union, the largest Polish organization in the country; and to co-found a seminary in Detroit with the Reverend Joseph Dombrowski.

In 1879, he asked for and received permission from the Holy See to transfer to the Congregation of the Resurrection. Six years later, he received a dispensation from the Resurrectionist community and eventually died as a priest of the Detroit Archdiocese on February 23, 1891, at the age of sixty-five.

It is interesting to note that Father Moczygemba's missionary activities took him to Lemont, Illinois, in 1882, where he served as pastor of St. Alphonsus Church. He was also responsible for establishing SS. Cyril and Methodius Church in Lemont in 1883. T. Lindsay Baker, "The Reverend Leopold Moczygemba, Patriarch of Polonia," *Polish American Studies* 41 (Spring 1984): 66–109.

For further biographical details of Father Moczygemba's novel life, see T. Lindsay Baker, "The Early History of Panna Maria, Texas," *Texas Tech University Graduate Studies* No. 9 (Lubbock, Texas: Texas Tech Press, 1975), pp. 14–29, 52–55; Edward J. Dworaczyk, *The First Polish Colonies of America in Texas* (San Antonio: The Naylor Company, 1936), pp. 1–19, 90–156; Dworaczyk, *The Millennium History of Panna Maria, Texas, the Oldest Polish Settlement in America, 1854–1966*, a revised version of "The Centennial History of Panna Maria, Texas," 1954; Jacek Przygoda, *Texas Pioneers from Poland: A Study in the Ethnic History* (Waco, Texas: privately printed, 1971), pp. 13–60; Reverend Joseph Swastek, *Priest and Pioneer: Reverend Leopold Moczygemba*, Reprint from *The Seraphic Chronicle*, The Conventual Press, 1951, Detroit, Michigan, Polish Builders of America Series, pp. 41–69.

[15]The usual way of naming Polish-American communities was to call the community surrounding the church by the church name with the addition of the suffix *owo*. *Stanisławowo*, therefore, was the name given to the St. Stanislaus Kostka Church district. The neighborhood around Holy Trinity Church was called *Trójcowo*, St. Hedwig, *Jadwigowo*, St. Pancratius, *Pankracowo*, etc. Edward R. Kantowicz, *Polish-American Politics in Chicago, 1888–1940* (Chicago: The University of Chicago Press, 1975), p. 15; and Joseph Parot, "The American Faith and the Persistence of Chicago Polonia, 1870–1920" (Ph.D. dissertation, Northern Illinois University, 1971), p. 3.

[16]*Polonia* is a term frequently applied to entire numbers of Poles in America, or, on a lesser scale, to the local community of Poles. *Polonia* was a complex entity composed of Polish Catholic institutions, traditions, and values, coupled with American urban, industrial conditions and democratic ideals. The definition still serves today. Joseph Swastek, *The Polish American Story* (Buffalo: Felician Sisters, 1953), p. 7.

[17]Generally, whenever a group of Poles settled in a given community, they formed a society under the patronage of a saint whose name was later transferred to the church. Casimir Stec, "The National Orientation of the Poles in the United States 1608–1935" (M.A. thesis, Marquette University, 1946), p. 43.

The early settlers of the area under discussion chose the name of a saint who had long been considered one of the principal protectors of Poland. Born in 1550, St. Stanislaus Kostka was the son of a senator of the Kingdom of Poland. He was sent to the Jesuit college at Vienna at fourteen.

Despite his father's bitter opposition, Stanislaus was determined to become a member of the Society of Jesus. He undertook a journey to Rome to seek admittance, and upon his arrival there in 1567, was admitted to the Society by its general, St. Francis Borgia. Stanislaus died less than a year later on August 15, but not before he had edified everyone with his humility, innocence, and obedience. He was canonized in 1726, but already before this date, Zygmunt III of Poland had obtained leave from Rome for the feast of St. Stanislaus Kostka to be kept throughout the country. Hundreds of Polish churches in America have been named after this holy youth. Christopher St. John, *A Little Book of Polish Saints* (London: Burns and Oates, 1918), pp. 66–71.

[18]*Diamond Jubilee 1867–1942: St. Stanislaus Kostka Church* (Chicago: 1942), p. 58.

[19]St. Joseph's Church was two miles away from the area with a river dividing its boundary. Most of the people had to walk the river's bank and then take the ferry across the stream. This often proved most inconvenient since it demanded scrupulous punctuality on the part of those attending the church services. Unfortunately, the Great Fire of 1871 destroyed the beautiful buildings of St. Joseph's Parish and the homes of more than five hundred of its parishioners. *The Annals of St. Boniface Parish, 1862–1926* (Chicago: 1926), pp. 12–13.

[20]St. Michael's Church, organized in 1852, was one of the few buildings on the North Side of the city to escape total destruction in the Great Chicago Fire. Only the shell of the church was left intact, but by 1873, St. Michael's Church had been restored and rededicated. Rev. Msgr. Harry Koenig, STD, ed., *A History of the Parishes of the Archdiocese of Chicago*, 2 vols. (Chicago: Catholic Bishop of Chicago, 1980), p. 634.

[21]Madaj, p. 11.

[22]Parot, "The American Faith and the Persistence of Chicago Polonia," p. 13.

[23]It is presumed that the emerging factions represented various geographical areas of Poland that were culturally as well as socially alien to the Poles already settled in the area. The chief faction, the *Gmina Polska* [Polish Commune] was led by Ladislaus Dyniewicz and his group who later became the mainstays of the rival Society of St. Joseph which was established in 1871. Dyniewicz published the first Polish paper in Chicago in 1867 called the *Gazeta Polska* [Polish Gazette] and later opened a Polish publishing house. Parot, p. 12.

While both groups were "intensely loyal Americans and passionately patriotic Poles," the "nationals" led by Dyniewicz stood for more secular ideals such as greater lay ownership in the Church and support for an independent Polish homeland as opposed to the "clericals" of *Stanisławowo*. These were simply two basic divisions in the early movement to organize the Polish-American community of *Stanisławowo*, but the consequences of their division altered the history of the area. Greeley, p. 53; and Frank Renkiewicz, *The Poles in America, 1608–1972: A Chronology and Fact Book* (Dobbs Ferry, New York: Oceana, 1973), p. 6.

[24]This is the site of the Montgomery Ward and Company offices and warehouse at the present time.

[25]The Most Reverend Thomas P. Foley was born in Baltimore and ordained there in 1846. He served as chancellor of the Diocese of Baltimore, and in 1870, was named coadjutor and administrator of the Diocese of Chicago during the illness of the Most Reverend James Duggan, then bishop of Chicago.

During Bishop Foley's tenure of office, the Holy Name Church was rebuilt after the Great Fire of 1871 and designated the Cathedral of the diocese. Bishop Foley died in Chicago on February 18, 1879. Rev. Joseph Thompson, ed., *Diamond Jubilee of the Archdiocese of Chicago, 1920* (Des Plaines, Illinois: St. Mary's Training School Press, 1920), pp. 45–49.

[26]Iwicki, p. 51.

[27]*Diamond Jubilee, 1867–1942: St. Stanislaus Kostka Church*, p. 60.

[28]The Reverend Simon Wieczorek, CR, labored in the Congregation of the Resurrection in Michigan and Iowa from 1868 to 1874. In Chicago, he was the administrator of St. Stanislaus Kostka Church from July to September 1874, while also serving at Holy Trinity Church. He left the congregation in December 1874, to labor in the Diocese of Green Bay, Wisconsin. Edward T. Janas,

CR, *Dictionary of American Resurrectionists, 1865–1965* (Rome: Gregorian University Press, 1967), pp. 118–119.

[29]The Reverend John Wołłowski, CR, was born in Lithuania and made his profession in the Congregation of the Resurrection in 1868. He served as pastor of St. Mary's Church, Parisville, Michigan, from 1868 to 1869. He acted as administrator of St. Stanislaus Kostka Church from May to September 1873, thus earning the distinction of being the first member of the Congregation of the Resurrection to come to Chicago. After further apostolic ministry in Rome and Bulgaria, he left the congregation in 1875. Janas, p. 119.

Father Wołłowski officiated at the wedding of Josephine Dudzik's eldest sister Rosalie to Adam Frank on June 15, 1873. *Registram Matrimoniorum,* vol. 1: 1869–1882 (St. Stanislaus Kostka Church, Chicago, Illinois).

[30]Busyn, p. 74; and Iwicki, p. 49.

[31]Iwicki, p. 50.

[32]The Reverend John Halligan served as the interim administrator between the terms of Bishop Duggan and Bishop Foley. Bishop Duggan had suffered a nervous breakdown in 1869, from which he never recovered, and was sent to a sanitarium in St. Louis. The Diocese of Chicago, therefore, was at this time very unsettled. Thompson, p. 43.

[33]By now Kiołbassa had become devoted to the Congregation of the Resurrection and was elated over its acceptance of the Chicago mission. This unforeseen turn of events, however, so disturbed Kiołbassa that he left Chicago to accept a position as a schoolteacher and organist at the Resurrectionist mission of Panna Maria, Texas, in 1870. Iwicki, p. 52.

[34]The Reverend Adolph Bakanowski was born in Russian Poland in 1840 of the landed gentry. He was ordained as a secular priest in 1863. That same year he joined the ill-fated insurrection against the Russians. Forced to flee to Austria, he received a false passport and fled to Rome where he entered the Congregation of the Resurrection in 1864.

In 1866, he was sent to Panna Maria, Texas, where he established the first foundation in the United States for the Congregation of the Resurrection. He also founded St. Joseph School, the first Polish Catholic School in the United States. In 1870, he came to Chicago and became the first Resurrectionist pastor of St. Stanislaus Kostka Church. He left for Rome as a delegate to the general chapter of the congregation held in 1873. Father Bakanowski continued to serve the congregation in London, Vienna, and Cracow, Poland, where he died on May 22, 1916. T. Lindsay Baker, "The Early Years of Reverend Wincenty Barzynski," *Polish American Studies* 32 (1975): 37; and Janas, pp. 4–6.

[35]According to the Reverend Wacław Kruszka, the noted priest-historian, Kiołbassa was instrumental in directing Father Bakanowski to Chicago. Kiołbassa was in Texas from 1869 to 1870 as we have already seen. See Chapters 15 and 18 for further reference to Father Kruszka.

[36]The Reverend Jerome Kajsiewicz, CR, was one of the founding priests of the Resurrectionists.

[37]*Diamond Jubilee, 1867–1942: St. Stanislaus Kostka Church,* p. 60.

[38]Ficht, p. 74; and Long, p. 79.

[39]One night six masked gunmen gained entrance to the rectory under the pretext of a "sick call" and physically assaulted Father Juszkiewicz. They further threatened him with death if he did not leave the parish. Ficht, p. 74; and Andrew M. Greeley, "Catholicism in America: 200 Years and Counting, " *The Critic,* Summer 1976, p. 29.

[40]Iwicki, p. 55.

[41]Leonard Long, CR, *The Resurrectionists* (Chicago: By the Author, 1971), p. 14.

[42]Robert Kurtz, CR, the present superior general of the Congregation of the Resurrection, states in *Resurrection Studies,* July 1980:

It is no accident that one of the major influences in the life of Jański (and one might add the names of Semenenko and Kajsiewicz as well) was the Romantic poet, Adam Mickiewicz, who is the founder of the Romantic Movement in Polish letters and its most notable exponent. Mickiewicz stands on a par with Byron, Shelley, and Keats in English literature and Goethe in German literature. It was the professed Catholicism of Mickiewicz that attracted Bogdan Jański and eventually Peter Semenenko and Jerome Kajsiewicz to the Church. Adam Mickiewicz is also credited with suggesting the foundation of a religious community to Bogdan Jański. The poet was a man of Utopian vision. He was the major spokesman for the ideas of Slavic messianism, sometimes known as Pan-Slavism, the theory in which Poland was seen as God's instrument for the re-unification of Eastern and Western Christendom. Jański's community with a universal apostolate parallels Mickiewicz's Romantic vision.

[43]Over one hundred years later, the Congregation of the Resurrection is represented in Italy, Poland, Bulgaria, Austria, Canada, Australia, Bermuda, Brazil, and Bolivia. In the United States, Resurrectionists labor in Florida, Alabama, Missouri, California, and Illinois. They also engage in parish ministry, education, chaplaincies, counseling, retreat work, and missionary service. The Chicago Province of the Congregation, which continues to staff St. Stanislaus Kostka Church to this day, is engaged in the administration of eight parishes, two mission churches, and Resurrection Center, a retreat house in Woodstock, Illinois. The congregation also conducts the well-known and well-reputed Weber High School and Gordon Technical High School which have a combined enrollment of approximately 3,700 young men.

For further information on the congregation and its celebrated founders, see James Antosz, CR, "A Short History of the Congregation of the Resurrection," Chicago, 1942. (Mimeographed.); John J. Iwicki, CR, *The First One Hundred Years: A Study of the Apostolate of the Congregation of the Resurrection in the United States, 1866–1966* (Rome: Gregorian University Press, 1966); Edward T. Janas, CR, "Father Peter Semenenko, CR, and His Message," *Polish American Studies* 13 (January–June 1956): 1–18; Leonard Long, CR, *The Resurrectionists* (Chicago: By the Author, 1971), p. 93.

[44]Iwicki, pp. 55–56; and Edward T. Janas, CR, *Dziennik Chicagoski*, 27–28 October 1967, p. 8.

[45]Lawrence Orzell, "A Minority Within a Minority: The Polish National Catholic Church, 1896–1907," *Polish American Studies* 36 (1979): 8.

[46]Ibid.

[47]Iwicki, p. 58.

[48]*Diamond Jubilee 1867–1942: St. Stanislaus Kostka Church,* p. 60.

[49]The Great Fire of 1871 is discussed at greater length in Chapter 4.

[50]Mary Dulcissima Małolepszy, "A Historical Survey of the St. Hedwig's Home, An Institution for the Care of Dependent Children, Archdiocese of Chicago" (M.A. thesis, Loyola University, 1945), p. 9.

[51]The *Kulturkampf* and its effects were previously mentioned in Chapter 2.

[52]Joseph A. Wytrwal, *America's Polish Heritage: A Social History of the Poles in America* (Detroit: Endurance Press, 1961), pp. 125–130.

[53]Marya Lilien and Małgorzata Pyrek-Ejsmont, "Polish Churches along the Kennedy Expressway" (Chicago: Chicago Historical Society, 1980), pp. 19–29.

[54]The Society of St. Joseph wanted to call their church St. Joseph's, but with another St. Joseph's Church serving the German community only a short distance away, Bishop Foley asked them to call their church Holy Trinity. Roger J. Coughlin and Cathryn A. Riplinger, "The Story of Charitable Care in the Archdiocese of Chicago, 1844–1959" (Chicago: The Catholic Charities, 1959), p. 157.

[55]Holy Trinity is located on the west side of Noble Street between Division Street and Milwaukee Avenue several blocks south of St. Stanislaus Kostka Church. Founded in 1873 by the

Society of St. Joseph, under the guidance of the Reverend Adolph Bakanowski, CR, the church was originally built to accommodate the overflow of parishioners from St. Stanislaus Kostka Church. It was meant to remain a part of St. Stanislaus Kostka Parish under the control of the Congregation of the Resurrection.

In 1874, when Father Barzynski was appointed pastor of St. Stanislaus Kostka Church, he announced his decision to build a new and large parish church, and to use Holy Trinity Church as a school or parish hall. This decision was vehemently opposed by the Society of St. Joseph, long a rival of St. Stanislaus Kostka Church and the Congregation of the Resurrection. The Society of St. Joseph demanded a separate parish since they now had their own church, maintained their own treasury, and did not want the Resurrectionists in control. Although 1873 is considered to be the founding date of Holy Trinity Church, the parish was not established canonically until 1893 due to a twenty-year struggle during which the church was closed several times.

The situation became more acute when the Society of St. Joseph allied itself with the Polish National Alliance (Alliancists), while the Society of St. Stanislaus was associated strictly with the Polish Roman Catholic Union (Unionists). The enmity between the two groups is summed up by Joseph Wytrwal in *America's Polish Heritage:*

> The Polish Roman Catholic Union was organized in 1873 by the clergy as an effort to keep the Polish immigrant close to the clergy and the church; the Polish National Alliance was organized in the 1880s by exiles of the unsuccessful 1863 insurrection in an effort to rally the Polish immigrants to work for the eventual liberation and restoration of Poland. The PNA was a lay organization and controlled by the people of all creeds and faiths of Polish ancestry.

During this period of bitter factionalism between the Alliancists and the Unionists, Holy Trinity was closed three times by the archbishop of Chicago. It was obvious that the Alliancists would never accept Father Barzynski as their pastor since he was a Unionist. The Resurrectionists, however, were committed to staffing all Polish parishes by an exclusive contract with the archbishop of Chicago. The long-standing controversy was resolved in 1893 when Francis Cardinal Satolli, the first Apostolic Delegate to the United States, placed Holy Trinity Church under the administration of the priests of the Congregation of the Holy Cross from South Bend, Indiana. The parish owed its rapid and successful development to its first pastor, the Reverend Casimir Stuczko, CSC. Under his leadership, a magnificent Romanesque church, a parochial school, and a high school were built. Holy Trinity Parish became a vibrant center of Polish life and nationalism as well as a center of cultural attractions.

The admirable Father Stuczko was born in Mirosław, Poland, in 1867. At fifteen, he came to the United States and received his education at the University of Notre Dame. At the completion of his studies, he entered the Congregation of the Priests of the Holy Cross. In 1891, he was ordained. He was appointed pastor of Holy Trinity Church on June 27, 1893, and served with great distinction in that capacity for fifty-six years. To him is due much of the credit for the mutual support and esteem which characterize the Polish Roman Catholic Union of America, as it is known today, and the Polish National Alliance.

In an ironic turn of events, the administration of Holy Trinity Church returned to the Resurrectionist Fathers in 1975 when the priests of the Congregation of the Holy Cross withdrew from the parish. Iwicki, pp. 68–72; Koenig, vol. 1, pp. 403–411; and Wytrwal, p. 227.

[56]The Reverend Felix Zwiardowski, CR, was born in Poland in 1840. Ordained in 1867, he was sent to the Texas mission while still a cleric. He was, thus, the first member of the Congregation of the Resurrection to be ordained in the United States. He served mainly as a missionary among Poles, Mexicans, and Indians in Texas.

In Chicago, he served as pastor of St. Stanislaus Kostka Church from September 1873 to July 1874, at which time he returned to Texas. The next year, he founded the first Polish Sisterhood of American origin, the Sisters of the Immaculate Conception or the "Blue Sisters," as they were popularly known in Panna Maria, Texas. The group disbanded in 1880.

Father Zwiardowski made several return trips to Chicago after 1880 and assisted at various Resurrectionist parishes including St. Stanislaus Kostka Church. It was here that he became acquainted with the Dudzik family who were newly arrived from Poland.

In 1884, Father Barzynski appointed him the pastor of the newly founded St. Josaphat Church in the Lakeview section of Chicago. While administering St. Josaphat Church, Father Zwiardowski became well acquainted with Josephine Dudzik's youngest sister, Katherine, who was often referred to by Father Zwiardowski as "my spiritual child." Iwicki, pp. 28–36; and Janas, pp. 77–78.

[57] *Diamond Jubilee, 1867–1942: St. Stanislaus Kostka Church,* p. 61; Thompson, p. 379.

[58] Iwicki, p. 61.

[59] Coughlin and Replinger, p. 151.

[60] Iwicki, p. 63.

[61] T. Lindsay Baker lays to rest the long-held belief, propagated by the Reverend Wacław Kruszka that Wincenty (Vincent) was originally baptized Michael. Kruszka held that when Wincenty was critically ill, his mother offered him to the service of God before a miraculous picture of St. Vincent Ferrer. Sister M. Gonzaga Raniszewski also recounts this anecdote which Baker calls a "charming but probably inaccurate story." Baker, pp. 29–52; Wacław X. Kruszka, *Historja Polska w Ameryce* [The history of the Poles in America] (Milwaukee: Kuryer Publishing Co., 1937); and Siostra M. Gonzaga Raniszewski, OSFK, *Rys historyczny Zgromadzenia Sióstr Franciszkanek Błogosławionej Kunegundy. Część pierwsza, 1860–1910* [A historical survey of the Franciscan Sisters of Blessed Kunegunda. Part one, 1860–1910] (Chicago: By the Author, 1947), p. 18.

[62] Baker, pp. 29–30.

[63] A *gymnasium,* in most European countries, was a secondary school for students preparing to enter a university. It is commonly called "high school" in America.

[64] Baker, p. 32.

[65] Ibid., p. 34.

[66] Janas, p. 7.

[67] Baker, p. 35.

[68] Ibid., p. 43.

[69] Several references have already been made to the town of Panna Maria, Texas. The background of this oldest Polish colony in Texas is most interesting and edifying.

Panna Maria, Texas, fifty miles southeast of San Antonio, was the site of the first permanent Polish settlement in the United States. The beginnings of the town and parish are attributed to the Reverend Leopold Moczygemba, who was at that time a Conventual Franciscan. As a result of his efforts, one hundred families from his native village in the Opole District of Upper Silesia in Prussia, left their homeland in the fall of 1854, seeking economic, political, and religious freedom. According to tradition, they landed in Galveston and *walked* until they reached Indianola two weeks later. Eventually they arrived at the site chosen for them by Father Moczygemba, two miles north of the junction of the San Antonio and Cibolo Rivers, on Christmas Eve, 1854. At midnight, under a large oak tree, mass was offered for the first time in thanksgiving. In fulfillment of a vow, the immigrants named the site *Panna Maria,* the Virgin Mary.

These early settlers passed through untold hardships in the open prairies of Texas. They suffered from the hot summers, prolonged dry weather, snakes, and insects. They were also victims of discrimination because of their "strange" language, customs, and culture. But the Poles survived. They built their first church in 1856 and dedicated it to the Immaculate Conception. It was destroyed by lightning in 1877. A new church, built in 1878, is still standing. In 1868, the first Polish private school in America called St. Joseph's was established in Panna Maria. Today the building houses the Museum of the Panna Maria Historical Association.

Eventually a number of the Polish pioneers left the foundation group and settled in places like Cestohowa, Kosciuszko, St. Hedwig, Pawelekville, and Bandera thus earning Panna Maria the title of "Mother Colony" of the numerous Silesian settlements in Texas. Another group of Silesian Poles settled in Falls City, Texas, the only site of the ministry of the Franciscan Sisters of Chicago in that state.

In 1974, the Centennial Year of the Archdiocese of San Antonio, the Poles succeeded in bringing back to Texas the remains of Father Moczygemba. His remains were transferred from Mount Elliott Cemetery in Detroit and liturgically reinterred in Panna Maria on October 13, 1974. About one hundred feet north of the church, the large oak tree under which mass was offered for the first time in 1854 still stands, a living but mute witness to the faith and sufferings of the first Polish settlers in Texas. T. Lindsay Baker, 14–29; Rev. Edward Dworaczyk, *The First Polish Colonies in Texas* (San Antonio: The Naylor Co., 1936), no pagination; Jacek Przygoda, *Texas Pioneers from Poland: A Study in Ethnic History* (Waco, Texas: No Imprint, 1971), no pagination. See fn. 14 above.

[70]Iwicki, p. 61.

[71]Coughlin and Riplinger, p. 151.

[72]Iwicki, p. 62.

[73]Lilien and Pyrek-Ejsmont, p. 29.

[74]Baker, "The Early Years of Reverend Wincenty Barzynski," pp. 29–52; Iwicki, 61–110; Janas, pp. 7–10; and Long, pp. 82–87.

[75]Iwicki, pp. 62–63.

[76]While Father Barzynski has been called the "magnanimous leader of the Poles and the greatest Pole that American Polonia has possessed," there are writers who do not entirely share this view. The reader is directed to Coughlin and Riplinger; *Diamond Jubilee, 1867–1942: St. Stanislaus Kostka Church*; Kantowicz; Parot, *The American Faith and the Persistence of Chicago Polonia, 1870–1920; Polish Catholics in Chicago, 1850–1920*; and Sister M. De Chantal, *Out of Nazareth* (New York: Exposition Press, 1974).

[77]*Dziennik Chicagoski,* 3 May 1899.

[78]The actual invitation to staff the school was extended by the Reverend Felix Zwiardowski during his brief tenure as pastor. Iwicki, p. 63, fn. 49.

[79]Sister M. Rogeria, SSND, served as principal at the school for over forty-four years. She finally resigned in 1918 because of ill health. Thompson, p. 381.

[80]A School Sister of Notre Dame, *Mother Caroline and the School Sisters of Notre Dame in America,* vol. 2 (St. Louis: Woodward and Tiernan Co., 1928), p. 203.

[81]Among the prominent laymen who were added to the staff from approximately 1882 to 1909 and assigned to teach the older boys were Szczęsny Zahajkiewicz, a poet and author of numerous dramatic works; Stanislaus Szwajkart, the editor-in-chief of the *Dziennik Chicagoski* [Polish Daily News]; and Dr. Boleslaus Klarkowski, a noted physician, teacher, and historian. *Diamond Jubilee, 1867–1942: St. Stanislaus Kostka Church,* p. 64.

[82]The accomplished architect was the well-known Patrick C. Keeley who also designed the Holy Name Cathedral in Chicago. In "Polish Churches along the Kennedy Expressway," the authors state: "Of all the churches built by the Polish immigrants, St. Stanislaus Kostka is perhaps the most unusual architecturally . . . it makes a striking impression. But the exterior of this landmark is not nearly as effective as its beautiful Romanesque sanctuary whose paintings were executed by the distinguished Tadeusz Zukotynski in 1895–1899." Lilien and Pyrek-Ejsmont, pp. 19–29.

[83]From 1900 to 1915 as many as twelve masses were celebrated each Sunday using both the upper and the lower church. Iwicki, p. 67.

[84]The spacious auditorium, complete with stage, played an important role in the cultural lives of the parishioners. The Dramatic Circle was begun in 1891 when the parishioners united all the societies in a three-day observance of the centenary of the historic adoption of the Polish Constitution of the Third of May. Sister M. Andrea, SSND, "The Societies of St. Stanislaus Kostka

Parish," *Polish American Studies* 9 (1952): 34–36. Father Barzynski commissioned the gifted teacher, lecturer, poet, and playwright, Szczęsny Zahajkiewicz to produce a special play for the occasion. The result was *Jasna Góra* [Bright Mountain], adapted from *Potop* by Henry Sienkiewicz. The play was so successful that amateur productions began to be staged regularly. In 1892, Helena Modjeska [Modrzejewska], the noted Polish dramatic actress often compared to Bernhardt or Duse, graced the stage of St. Stanislaus Kostka in a play called *Chłopi Arystokraci* [The Peasant Aristocrats]. She also appeared in the title role of *Królowo Jadwiga* [Queen Hedwig] written especially for her by Zahajkiewicz. As the Dramatic Circle's tireless director for many years, Zahajkiewicz wrote over sixty plays and also translated plays from the English, French, and other languages into Polish, Born in Galicia, Poland, in 1861, Zahajkiewicz came to Chicago in 1889 at the request of the Resurrectionist priests to teach at St. Stanislaus Kostka Parish where he remained for the rest of his life. He also was editor of the *Dziennik Chicagoski* [Polish Daily News] until 1912. He died in Chicago in 1917.

The Dramatic Circle attracted many gifted writers and dramatic talent. Dr. Karol Wachtel was another successful poet, writer, director, and producer. Shakespearean plays staged in Polish were especially popular as directed by Dr. Wachtel. He was the founder of three Polish-American companies which presented plays in downtown theaters of Chicago. Born in Jarosław, Poland, in 1876, he came to America in 1903 and in that same year, received his Ph.D. from De Paul University in Chicago. In 1907, he was named editor of the *Dziennik Chicagoski* and in 1918, he became its editor-in-chief. He went to Poland after World War I but returned to the United States in 1926. He was the editor of a weekly published in Philadelphia until his death.

Critical reviews praised the efforts of St. Stanislaus Kostka's performing arts. When the steady rise in school enrollment made it necessary to convert the parish theater into classrooms, however, the Dramatic Circle ceased activities until 1908 when it was revived in the new auditorium. Anthony C. Tomczak, "The Poles in Chicago," *Poland* 12 (1931): 28, 68–70; and Joseph A. Wiśniewski, St. Stanislaus Kostka Parish in "Chicago: Its Spiritual, Educational, and Cultural Legacy to the 600,000 Americans of Polish Extraction, 1869–1908" (M.A. thesis, De Paul University, 1964), p. 82.

[85]*Diamond Jubilee 1867–1942: St. Stanislaus Kostka Church*, p. 19.

[86]Lightning struck the church's south tower on June 19, 1964, and completely destroyed it. Rather than rebuild the tower at great expense, it was simply leveled off.

[87]The Columbian Exposition was a national and international celebration in commemoration of the 400th anniversary of the discovery of America by Columbus. It is discussed at greater length in Chapter 4.

[88]*Diamond Jubilee 1867–1942: St. Stanislaus Kostka Church*, p. 20.

[89]Iwicki, p. 63.

[90]Haiman, p. 4 and Madaj, p. 7.

[91]Wiśniewski, p. 88.

[92]St. Stanislaus Kostka Convent could appropriately have been called a mini-Motherhouse. With the number of aspirants, postulants, and senior novices teaching there, it could also have been termed a novitiate. "Teaching Pioneers at St. Stanislaus Kostka Grade and High School," *Bulletin of St. Stanislaus Kostka Church* (Chicago: 1974), no pagination.

[93]*St. Stanislaus Kostka Centennial Book 1867–1967* (Chicago: 1967), p. 38.

[94]This complex included one of the first high schools on the Northwest Side of Chicago under the direction of two priests of the Congregation of the Resurrection. Called St. Stanislaus College, it opened in 1890 in the old frame church which had been converted into classrooms. Relocated and renamed Weber High School, it continues to thrive as a modern educational institution. In 1914, the St. Stanislaus Kostka High School for Ladies (later shortened to St. Stanislaus Kostka High School) came into existence under the supervision of the School Sisters of Notre Dame. The school, unfortunately, closed in 1977 due to a decline in enrollment.

[95]The Honorable Charles Warren Fairbanks, the vice-president of the United States, was

among the speakers at the banquet held that night.

[96]"Teaching Pioneers," *Bulletin,* no pagination.

[97]As planned by the city, the Kennedy Expressway was slated to cut through the parish property and would necessitate the demolition of St. Stanislaus Kostka Church as well as several other parish buildings. Opposition to the plan came from the largest Polish Catholic community in the entire city. While the church itself was spared, the cutting and constructing of the Kennedy Expressway in 1958 along a diagonal artery from Downtown Chicago to O'Hare International Airport forced the residents to leave. Thousands of homes were demolished including the first home of the Congregation of the Franciscan Sisters of Chicago—the Dudzik home on Chapin Street.

In the ensuing years, the area has become home to one of the strongest concentrations of Puerto Ricans, blacks, and Mexicans in the city although many Poles still remain in the area. Greeley, *Neighborhood,* p. 40.

[98]It was a celebration of Poland's one thousand years of Christianity. See Chapter 59 for further mention of this very significant event.

[99]The vitality of the "Mother Church" is well indicated by the number of vocations it has provided to the priesthood and religious life. The figure indicated in the *Bulletin* issued in February 1974, by the School Sisters of Notre Dame on the occasion of the 100th Anniversary of their coming to St. Stanislaus Kostka School indicated the following: the Congregation of the Resurrection, 24; Other, 40 for a total of 64; the School Sisters of Notre Dame, 197; Other, 157, for a total of 354. The figures include Mother M. Theresa Dudzik and Mother M. Anna Wysinski, the foundress and co-foundress of the Franciscan Sisters of Chicago; also, Mother M. Hilaria Matz and her sister, Mother M. Ernestine Matz, the foundresses of the Congregation of the Sisters of Our Lady of Perpetual Help of St. Louis, Missouri. The author has made no attempt to update the 1974 figures. "Teaching Pioneers," *Bulletin,* no pagination.

[100]Haiman, p. 4.

[101]Greeley, *Neighborhood,* p. 24.

CHAPTER 4

Chicago: "City of the Big Shoulders"

Carl Sandburg, the "poet laureate of industrial America," describes the city of Chicago in a poem which has since become characteristically identified with him. Published in 1912, the poem, entitled appropriately enough, "Chicago," is a tribute to the city's strength and vitality. Sandburg's vigorous lyrical epithets summarize Chicago's proletarian character when he extols the city as:

> Hog Butcher for the World,
> Tool Maker, Stacker of Wheat,
> Player with Railroads and the Nation's Freight Handler:
> Stormy, husky, brawling,
> City of the Big Shoulders.

This booming giant of a Chicago was not always the truly wonder city which Sandburg extols so proudly. At one time, Chicago was just acres and acres of weeds when the great cities of the East were already established.[1] Founded on a swamp, this parcel of land on the southwest shores of Lake Michigan eventually grew to be the nation's second largest city and the nation's leading industrial and transportation center. Its historical good fortune, excellent geographic location, and most assuredly—the indefatigable spirit and indomitable strength of its inhabitants—contributed to this growth.

In 1673, Father Jacques Marquette and Louis Joliet, the former a French Jesuit missionary and the latter a French-Canadian mapmaker, visited the site of Chicago. Robert Cavelier sieur de La Salle and other French explorers followed, but the location did not seem to attract settlers. It was not until 1779 that a prosperous fur trapper named Jean Baptiste Point du Sable established a trading port on the north bank of the Chicago River which became the center of a permanent settlement.

Early in 1803, the army built Fort Dearborn, but it was destroyed when unfriendly Indians massacred the settlers and once again, Chicago was a wilderness. Finally, in 1833, Chicago was incorporated as a village with a population listed at more than 150 settlers. In 1837, Chicago was incorporated as a city with approximately 4,170 inhabitants, and it began its climb to progress and prosperity.[2] By 1861, the English journalist and war correspondent William Howard Russell, who was generally critical of things American, wrote of Chicago:

> There has sprung up in thirty years a wonderful city of fine streets, luxurious hotels, handsome shops, magnificent stores, great warehouses, extensive quays, capacious docks; and as long as corn holds its own, and the mouths of Europe are open, and her hands full, Chicago will acquire greater importance, size, and wealth with every year.[3]

From 1861 to 1865, the Civil War years, Chicago grew with vigor. After the War, immigrants mainly from Germany, Ireland, and Sweden poured into Chicago. Crowded neighborhoods of factory workers living in small wooden cottages sprang up around the city. The population rose to 300,000,[4] but a great tragedy awaited the prospering city. This tragedy, the Great Chicago Fire of 1871, began on the West Side of the city on the corner of Jefferson and De Koven Streets, south of the business district. Legend attributes the start of the devastating fire to Patrick and Catherine O'Leary's cow that upset a lantern causing the hay in their barn to ignite.[5] The fire erupted at approximately eight-forty-five o'clock on the evening of Sunday, October 8, 1871, and raged incessantly until October 10, twenty-seven hours after the first flames appeared. Although the exact cause of the tragedy is unknown, its remote cause can be attributed to the city and the vigorous winds which helped to spread the fire among the "tinderboxes," those flimsy, wooden cottages, stores, and factories in which two-thirds of the city's population lived and worked. Contributing to the inferno were the wooden sidewalks and the streets' paving blocks as well as the wooden bridges.[6] Compounding the calamity was the firefighters' equipment which broke down causing much delay and confusion.[7] It is estimated that the disaster left over 250 people dead and at least 100,000 people homeless.[8] Approximately three and a half square miles and 17,450 buildings valued at $220 million were destroyed.[9] After the fire was extinguished, thousands at home were seriously hurt, and many died as a result of the cold. A smallpox epidemic also claimed many lives.[10] Some 104,000 Chicagoans were homeless, one-third of the entire population.[11]

Many people predicted the demise of Chicago after the Great Fire of 1871, but the undaunted Chicagoans epitomizing the vigor and urgency of the spirit that made the city's slogan, "I WILL," began anew to build. Many residents left the city, but many more realized Chicago's potential for growth and prosperity, and the city census rose to half-a-million by 1880 with Chicago as the nation's fourth largest city.[12] Chicago began to construct replacement buildings, and a building boom followed. Enterprising men renewed or began their businesses, and Chicago returned to its former economic strength. The city was emerging from the ashes of the Great Fire as a giant railroad center, meatpacker, labor dealer, and trader of grain. Like a phoenix, Chicago rose from the ashes of the Great Fire of 1871. Chicago was even being called the "Rome of the Midwest" with all roads leading to this young and self-confident city.[13]

After the Great Fire of 1871, most of Chicago's business community began to build with higher standards and better planning. Unfortunately, however, the areas in which Chicago's working class lived were a reflection of the crudities of life as they existed in the city. Caring little for safety, durability, or comfort, greedy builders hurriedly constructed and soon created a squalid area of wooden tenements which became home for growing immigrant nationalities in all sections of the city. There were three ethnic areas in Chicago in particular which suffered from bad housing and living conditions. One was the Italian and Jewish section in the Hull House area;[14] the Bohemian neighborhood in the tenth ward was the second; the third was the Polish settlement directly across from St. Stanislaus Kostka Church.[15] Fearing the stresses which poverty, isolation, and loneliness create, the Poles, like most immigrants in America, had settled in separate neighborhoods, and the parish church had become the center of their religious, social, and cultural lives.[16] As early as 1873, as we have seen, most of Chicago's estimated twenty thousand Poles were concentrated on the Near Northwest Side close to Noble and Division Streets in the vicinity of St. Stanislaus Kostka Church.

Dr. Joseph Parot in *The American Faith and the Persistence of Chicago Polonia, 1870–1920,* writes of that era and the neighborhood of St. Stanislaus Kostka whose housing and living conditions were by far the worst in the city of Chicago:

> The City Homes Association's Report clearly showed the extent of the wretched housing conditions facing Stanislawians. The total population of the area was 13,825, an average of 339.8 inhabitants per acre. This final tally showed that the density of that Polish quarter was three times that of the most crowded portions of Tokyo, Calcutta, and many other Asiatic cities. What was even more appalling was the fact that the Polish settlement contained 7,306 children. Of this difficult-to-believe number of children, it was shown that one single block—bounded by Division, Dickson, Blackhawk, and Holt—contained 1,349 children! The block bounded by Bradley, Holt, Blackhawk, and Cleaver was the densest of all, with a total of 1,601 people, of which 832 were children;[17] 315 families occupied this small bit of space. The average density per acre was 457. In one final brutal statistic, it was shown that the 10 block Stanislawian area contained 2,716 families.[18]

Parot continues the description:

> The swollen numbers might not have been so shattering if there had been housing adequate enough to shelter this congested multitude. One of the worst features of *Stanisławowo's* housing was the high number of rear dwellings built helter-skelter behind the facades of the front dwellings. Behind the 529 front dwellings in the 10 block area stood 242 rear buildings, an average of 31.4 percent of all the buildings standing. With

almost every available square foot of the land covered with some form of dwelling, *Stanisławowo* appeared to the contemporary observer to be nothing more than wall-to-wall concrete. Another horrible feature of the 771 buildings standing was that they were divided up and subdivided again as the population increased, a tendency which made the "apartments" smaller and smaller as time went by.[19]

Because of the "wall-to-wall concrete" of the area, very little sunlight was available, and half the rooms had inadequate lighting. Because of the congestion, even fresh air became a luxury. With the large number of bathrooms on the basement levels and the poor drainage they offered, rainstorms became a dreaded crisis since the basements would contain floating raw sewage. With so many houses and basement apartments, the sanitary conditions were hazardous. Garbage disposal was a constant problem; usually it was dumped in the narrow passageways between buildings. In this situation, vermin were uncontrollable. In addition, with the presence of 202 horse stables and manure boxes in *Stanisławowo*, it is no wonder that the death rate was as high as 37.17 per thousand.[20] By 1888, the St. Stanislaus Kostka area had a death rate higher than that of the city as a whole.[21]

An interesting correlation appears in Di Donato's book, *Immigrant Saint: The Life of Mother Cabrini*. In 1899, Mother Cabrini was summoned to a mission in a new territory which the author claims was every bit as awful as New York had been, if not worse— Chicago! Di Donato writes:

> She [Mother Cabrini] explored in detail the ugly anatomy of social evils which existed. She learned the grim, dark truths of the immigrants' life. Home, for the immigrant, was a small flat in a dilapidated multiple dwelling. Usually there were three buildings, a front, middle, and rear, cramped on a shoestring lot, and narrow alleys separated row on row of deteriorated wooden tenements. The plumbing usually consisted of a single water tap in the hallway for a dozen large families. The alleyways were choked with garbage, decomposing animal and vegetable matter, dead cats and dogs, and toilet overflow. With the sweltering heat in the congested tenements, typhoid and impetigo were summer's gifts. During winter, rheumatism and tuberculosis blossomed in the freezing rooms, while pneumonia visited at random. Asphyxiation from faulty coal stoves and kerosene heaters in the airless rooms took a heavy toll as well. In the factories where the immigrants worked, the loss of limbs or of life itself was an everyday occurrence.[22]

Chicago, citywide, could not hide some of its grim underlying problems. The shambles of some of the older parts of the city bred tuberculosis, malaria, smallpox, cholera, and diphtheria.[23] Housing continued to be a major problem. Many families continued to live in crowded, unsanitary conditions in cheap wooden houses built without basements, sewer connections, or running water. The condition of the streets was bad, and air and water were increasingly polluted.[24]

Besides the obvious fact of low wages, working conditions in general in the city were also miserable. As early as 1873, a financial panic erupted which lasted for at least six years and precipitated considerable social unrest. By 1874, unemployment had brought with it the consequences of fury since Chicago had become a center of strife and violence between labor and capital. Among the more devastating and historically memorable occurrences in Chicago was the Haymarket Riot of 1886 when a bomb had been thrown into a meeting where 180 policemen had been called to subdue an unruly crowd of laborers and anarchists. A strike at McCormick's International Harvester Plant also added to the unrest. The Pullman Strike brought out the federal troops when the workers at Pullman went on strike as did the American Railway Union.[25] Between 1887 and 1894, there were 582 strikes in Chicago involving 282,611 employees.[26]

Despite its numerous problems and setbacks, by 1890, Chicago became the second largest city in the United States with more than a million people. Strikingly, nearly 80 percent of them were Czech, Slovak, Italian, Greek, Russian, or Polish immigrants or the children of immigrants.[27] Although the immigrants were mostly unskilled laborers who did not know the English language, they found employment in the Union Stock Yards on Chicago's South Side and in the steel mills of South Chicago. They labored in the quarries and breweries near 17th Street and Ashland Avenue as well as the tanneries near Milwaukee Avenue and Division Street.[28] Chicago continued to grow into a major trade and manufacturing center. It gained in importance as a grain mart, lumber market, heavy-manufacturing center, and the leader of the meat-packing industry in the world.[29] Bismarck, the famous German statesman, was said to have remarked: "I wish I could go to America if only to see that Chicago!"[30]

In the summer of 1893, Chicago was host for the celebration of the 400th anniversary of the discovery of America by Christopher Columbus. The World's Columbian Exposition, also called the Chicago World's Fair, opened formally on May 1, 1893, with great magnificence in Chicago's Jackson Park on the city's South Side. The 666 acres of converted swampland extending about two miles along the shores of Lake Michigan held approximately 150 buildings of beautiful architecture which were finished in plaster and fiber and shone like white marble. It was aptly titled "White City." Gustav Kobbé, writing of the World's Columbian Exposition says:

> I have seen many descriptions of the World's Fair, but none has quite expressed what seems to me its most beautiful characteristic. That is neither its size nor its magnificence, but its gracious beauty and engaging loveliness, which linger in the memory like the remembrance of a pleasant dream . . . we have something that is simply beautiful.[31]

This national and international fair drew more than twenty-seven million visitors from the United States and abroad who came to see everything that was new in architecture, engineering, and transportation.[32] Chicagoans are said to have bragged so much about the Columbian Exposition that Charles A. Dana, a New York newspaper editor, nicknamed Chicago the "Windy City."[33]

As a reflection of the "actual" Chicago, however, the World's Columbian Exposition was a colorful and lovely facade. Beautiful with its lacy-white buildings, "White City" masked a city of congestion, squalor, and poverty. Indeed, the wonders on display seemed to have little to do with the economic friction outside "White City."[34] While Jackson Park was all glittery and cheerful inside, outside in "Gray City," men roamed the streets, slept in parks, and pondered a bleak and uncompromising future.[35]

After the World's Columbian Exposition closed on October 20, 1893, what had begun with such excitement and pride ended in misery.[36] The "hard times" which had already begun in the winter of 1891–1892, burst into a severe economic crisis which gripped the city and the nation. The World's Columbian Exposition ended in the worst Depression of the nineteenth century. Twenty-four banks failed during the first eight months of the year, and business failures increased by 50 percent. Throughout the state, scores of factories, mills, and mines closed down. Bands of unemployed men roamed the streets of Chicago begging for food and jobs while laborers from the mines and farms fled in desperation to the city where thousands were already out of work.[37] As if to add to the misery of the situation, the winter of 1893 was a bitter one, and the rough winds of Lake Michigan blew upon the dingy tenements which now lacked fuel.[38] Many of the younger members of the neighborhoods fled to what were advertised as more "prosperous" cities or farmlands often leaving behind their children or aged and dependent parents. Every day saw the poor begging on the steps of churches.[39] One could see the unemployed sleeping by thousands on the floors and stairways of City Hall and in parks and police stations. Abandoned children filled the orphanages beyond capacity. This state of affairs continued into the first two decades of the new century.[40] Priests, ministers, philanthropists, concerned neighbors, and a few kind hearted employers generally came to the aid of the distressed poor.[41] But the city of Chicago, itself caught up in welfare agencies that were not very effective, and caught up in a corrupt municipal government, seemed immune to the hopeless existence of a large segment of its population.[42] The lack of organization among the charitable forces of the city was painfully revealed in the terrible days after the World's Columbian Exposition when the great financial depression throughout the country was so intensified in Chicago.

At this time in history, social workers did not exist and there was no known woman's role in the social services. But when Jane Addams, "the civic saviour of Chicago,"[43] became aware of the social ills plaguing the West Side of the city, she founded Hull House, a social settlement destined to become world-famous, and was eventually awarded the Nobel Peace Prize. In like fashion, Josephine Dudzik, who had emigrated to

Chicago in 1881, and who was destined to spend more than sixteen years in the vicinity of St. Stanislaus Kostka Parish also became painfully aware of the social problems existing in the city and especially in her Northwest Side neighborhood. Her conscience and her compassion aroused by the plight of her poor, aged, and distressed neighbors, Josephine would eventually make a decision which would change the course of her life and the lives of hundreds of women, who, through the years, would be inspired by her vision, courage, and love for humanity.

CHICAGO: "CITY OF THE BIG SHOULDERS"

[1]Robert Howard, *Illinois: A History of the Prairie State* (Grand Rapids, Michigan: William B. Eerdmans Publishing Co., 1972), p. 391.

[2] Lois Wille, "Chicago" in *The World Book Encyclopedia,* vol. 3 (Chicago: World Book–Childcraft International, Inc., 1982), p. 345.

[3]*Illinois Guide and Gazetteer* (Chicago: Rand McNally and Co., 1969), p. 121.

[4]Dominic A. Pacyga and Ellen Skerrett, *Chicago: City of Neighborhoods* (Chicago: Loyola University Press, 1986), p. 3.

[5]"The precise cause of the fire is now a mystery and must ever remain so," A. T. Andreas wrote in his *History of Chicago* published in 1886. Today, one hundred years later, it is still a mystery.

[6]Commissioner Lewis W. Hill, *Historic City: the Settlement of Chicago* (Chicago Department of Development and Planning, 1976), p. 37; Howard, p. 175; and Herman Kogan and Lloyd Wendt, *Chicago: A Pictorial History* (New York: Bonanza Books, 1958), pp. 115–125.

[7]Kogan and Wendt, p. 115.

[8]One of the few surviving buildings is the Gothic water tower, now a civic landmark, on the Near North Side of the city. The Chicago Fire Academy, built in 1959, now stands on the site where the fire began.

[9]Stephen Longstreet, *Chicago, 1860–1919* (New York: David McKay Co., Inc., 1973), p. 134; and Kogan and Wendt, p. 124.

[10]*Diamond Jubilee, 1867–1942: St. Stanislaus Kostka Church,* p. 64.

[11]Hill, p. 47.

[12]Robert Cross, "The Heartland in World History," *Chicago Tribune Magazine,* 23 May 1976, sec. 9, p. 39; and Howard, p. 352.

[13]Kenan Heise and Michael Edgerton, *Chicago Center for Enterprise,* vol. 2: *The Twentieth Century* (Woodland Hills, California: Windsor Publications, Inc., 1937), p. 315; and Howard, p. 391.

[14]The Poles living in the Hull House area were living in the same wretched conditions as the Poles in *Stanisławowo.* See *Residents of Hull House, Hull House Maps and Papers: A Presentation of Nationalities and Wages in a Congested Area of Chicago* (Boston, 1895); Joseph J. Parot, "The American Faith and the Persistence of Chicago Polonia 1870–1920" (Ph.D. dissertation, Northern Illinois University, 1971), p. 249, fn. 2.

[15]Parot, p. 169.

[16]Joseph A. Wytrwal, *America's Polish Heritage: A Social History of the Poles in America* (Detroit: Endurance Press, 1961), p. 159.

[17]This block was cleared in 1911 and the 3.8 acres became the site of the present Pulaski Park. Sister M. Inviolata Ficht, "Noble Street in Chicago: Socio-cultural Study of Polish Residents Within Ten Blocks" (M.A. thesis, De Paul University, 1952), p. 127.

[18]Parot, pp. 169–170.

[19]Ibid., pp. 170–171.

[20]Ibid., pp. 171–174.

[21]Edward R. Kantowicz, "Polish Chicago: Survival Through Solidarity," in *The Ethnic Frontier,* ed. Melvin G. Holli and Peter d' A. James (Grand Rapids, Micigan: William B. Eerdmans Publishing Co., 1977), p. 15.

[22]Pietro Di Donato, *Immigrant Saint: The Life of Mother Cabrini* (New York: McGraw-Hill Book Co., Inc., 1960), pp. 139–142.

[23]Glenn A. Bishop and Paul T. Gilbert, *Chicago's Accomplishments and Leaders* (Chicago: Bishop Publishing Co., 1932), pp. 82–83; and Finis Farr, *Chicago: A Personal History of America's Most American City* (New Rochelle, New York: Arlington House, 1973), p. 175.

[24]Hill, p. 43.

[25]Cornelia Meigs, *Jane Addams, Pioneer for Social Justice* (Boston: Little, Brown, and Co., 1970), p. 97; and Kogan and Wendt, p. 151.

[26]Hill, p. 44.

[27]Martha Bennett King, *The Key to Chicago* (New York: J. B. Lippincott Co., 1961), p. 39.

[28]Rev. M. J. Madaj, "Chicago: The Polish Capital of the United States," *The New World* 9 April 1971, pp. 1–29.

[29]Di Donato, p. 140.

[30]Longstreet, p. 137.

[31]Gustave Kobbé in *Prairie Street: Impressions of Illinois, 1673–1967, by Travelers and Others,* ed. Paul M. Angle (Chicago: The University of Chicago Press, 1968), p. 20.

[32]Allan Carpenter, *Illinois, Land of Lincoln* (Chicago: Childrens Press, 1968), p. 76; and *Illinois Guide and Gazetteer,* p. 121.

[33]Wille, p. 345.

[34]Cross, p. 41.

[35]Harold M. Mayer and Richard E. Wade, *Chicago: Growth of a Metropolis* (Chicago: The University of Chicago Press, 1969), p. 193.

[36]Meigs, p. 117.

[37]Federal Writers' Project of the Work Projects Administration for the State of Illinois, *Illinois: A Descriptive and Historical Guide* (Chicago: A. C. McClurg and Co., 1939), no pagination.

[38]Edward Wegenknecht, *Chicago* (Oklahoma: University of Oklahoma Press, 1964), p. 18.

[39]Sister M. Martha Bywalec, "The Chronicle of St. Joseph Home," 26 July 1975. (Unpublished manuscript sent to author.)

[40]Farr, pp. 193, 199; Federal Writers' Project, p. 41; Mayer and Wade, p. 193; and Meigs, p. 79.

[41]Cross, p. 42.

[42]Farr, p. 200.

[43]Bessie Louise Pierce, *A History of Chicago,* vol. 3: *The Rise of a Modern City, 1871–1893* (New York: Alfred A. Knopf, 1957), p. 465.

CHAPTER 5

Arrival in America

When the Dudzik family made the painful decision to leave Poland, they, like thousands of Poles before them, were impelled to emigrate for a number of reasons. Among them were Poland's religious persecution, its political oppression, and the grave economic hardships caused by the Partitions. There was the need also to escape the dire and unrelenting effects of Bismarck's *Kulturkampf,* particularly this hated attempt at abolishing Catholicism and Polish nationalism. It is assumed that another important reason for their leaving Poland at this time might have been the justifiable fear that Joseph Dudzik, now nineteen years old, would be forced to undergo compulsory military training in the Prussian army. In truth, very few details concerning the motives which finally prompted the Dudziks to emigrate are known. But one thing is quite certain. Rosalie and Adam Frank, who, together with another Dudzik daughter, Frances, were already happily settled in America, wrote letters to their loved ones in Poland, and begged the rest of the Dudzik family to share the security and the opportunity which the New World offered.[1] Migration regulations at this time were not restrictive either in Poland or in the United States.[2] Although emigrating posed many hazards and hardships, the cost of transportation was generally affordable. Since there is no available information, it is presumed that the Dudziks arrived in America by steamship after having traveled steerage class. It does not appear that the journey posed any particular problems for the Dudziks. According to the National Archives in Washington, DC, most immigrants during the nineteenth century came through the Port of New York at Ellis Island. There is no evidence to prove that the same was not true of the Dudzik family.[3] While emigrating to a strange and distant country undoubtedly required a large amount of faith, hope, and courage, the Dudzik family's experience of living under foreign and ruthless domination in their native Poland had given them ample opportunity to cultivate those virtues.

Once in Chicago, the Dudzik family was welcomed into the flat prepared for them in the home of Rosalie and Adam Frank at 34 N. Crittenden Street.[4] Josephine, now a young woman of twenty one,[5] helped support her family as a seamstress working out of her home.[6] Her brother Joseph, it is generally believed, was hired by the Resurrectionist

52

Fathers at St. Stanislaus Kostka rectory as a drayman while her sister Frances worked at the same rectory as a housekeeper assisting her aunt. Josephine's youngest sister Katherine was a student at St. Stanislaus Kostka elementary school.

When Frances Dudzik, who had already been in America for three years, reached her nineteenth birthday, she expressed a desire to dedicate herself to God in the religious life. Influenced by the example of the School Sisters of Notre Dame,[7] who staffed St. Stanislaus Kostka School, and encouraged in her resolve by her pastor and confessor, Father Vincent Barzynski, Frances Dudzik entered the Congregation of the School Sisters of Notre Dame as a candidate on December 8, 1883.[8] She was received into the novitiate on May 24, 1887, at which time she received the name Sister M. Leovina. Eleven years later, she professed perpetual vows in the congregation in which she was to die in 1931.[9]

In little less than a year, Katherine Dudzik, now seventeen, made known her wish to follow her sister Frances into a convent. Katherine, however, had become acquainted with the Congregation of the Sisters of Charity of the Incarnate Word of San Antonio, Texas,[10] who staffed St. Josaphat's School which was in close proximity to St. Stanislaus Kostka Parish.[11] The fact that the Motherhouse of the congregation was located in Texas did not deter Katherine from presenting herself as a candidate on December 6, 1884.[12] She was invested with the habit on August 2, 1885, and received the name Sister St. Barbara of the Blessed Sacrament.[13] The young congregation, in existence for approximately twenty years, was destined to suffer much sorrow when in 1886, many of the Sisters died from dengue or typhoid fever. Sister Helen Finck, CCVI, writing in *The Congregation of the Sisters of Charity of the Incarnate Word of San Antonio, Texas,* states: "The Angel of Death visited the Community frequently during the foundation days to take from it Sisters, who in the freshness of their youth and in the height of their usefulness, were overcome by disease."[14]

At first, when Sister M. Barbara became ill, it was believed that she was among those victims of typhoid or dengue fever.[15] Sister M. Barbara, however, died on November 23, 1886, of consumption, the disease which had agonized her for over six months.[16] She had pronounced her first vows from the Santa Rosa Infirmary on August 14, 1886, and her perpetual vows on November 21, 1886, two days before she died at the age of nineteen.[17] On the morning of November 24, 1886, the Most Reverend John C. Neraz, bishop of San Antonio, offered a Requiem Mass in the Motherhouse chapel for the repose of her soul. The burial itself took place at two o'clock in the afternoon. All the Sisters from the Santa Rosa Infirmary who could be spared attended, and little orphan children walked in procession to the San Fernando Parish Cemetery, Number One.[18] A telegram had been sent to Father Barzynski in Chicago informing him of Sister M. Barbara's death. The task of making known the heart-breaking news to the Dudzik family was his responsibility. Thus, in the brief span of eight years, the Dudziks had lost two young daughters, and Josephine had lost two beloved sisters to death. The remaining Dudziks, armed with ardent faith in God and affectionate love for each other, sustained themselves in their mutual sorrow.

It is difficult to determine whether Josephine Dudzik, in the years that ensued, wished to follow her sisters into the religious life. As a loving and conscientious young woman, however, she realized that, for the time being at least, she was largely responsible for the welfare of her aging parents. Nonetheless, this obligation did not prohibit her from membership and active involvement in the numerous parish organizations at St. Stanislaus Kostka Church which provided her with ample opportunities to enrich her spiritual life and to perform frequent exercises of charity.

Because the faith of the Poles was so closely united to their culture, it was inevitable that many of their activities centered around the church and their priests. Transplanted as they were from villages in Poland into new surroundings, the Poles of St. Stanislaus Kostka Church made the parish the chief center of their religious, educational, social, and cultural lives. Organized as the parish was, according to the directives of Father Peter Semenenko's[19] well-known *Instrument of Conducting a Parish*, the liturgy, parish school, confraternities, and societies were all means of uniting the Poles in their faith and love of neighbor.[20] Father Barzynski strove to apply the principle of a "multitude of believers who have but one heart and one soul," in his labors at St. Stanislaus Kostka Church and was very successful in forming a large Christian family.[21] As a consequence, numerous parochial organizations sprang into existence.[22] According to a study made by Sister M. Andrea, SSND, the organizations at St. Stanislaus Kostka Parish fell into six categories. The first included those societies which were responsible for the foundation and development of the parish. The second included organizations which emphasized the practice of the spiritual and corporal works of mercy. These included such groups as the Ladies' Rosary Society, the Young Ladies' Rosary Society, three branches of the Third Order of St. Francis, and the Archconfraternity of the Immaculate Heart of Mary. The third group consisted of societies whose purpose was to assist the pastor in various projects of a humanitarian, educational, and charitable nature. The fourth group concerned itself with organizations which helped to provide recreation. To foster love and appreciation for the Polish language, culture, and traditions was the aim of the fifth group. The sixth group had as its function to participate in parades, rallies, pageants, and other Polish and American celebrations. Collectively, these splendidly functioning societies were largely responsible for the "keen sense of loyalty, generosity, and cooperation" which existed at St. Stanislaus Kostka Parish.[23]

It was certain that Josephine Dudzik would find her way into several of the benevolent societies and even be instrumental in their erection and administration. In 1874, one of the largest groups in the parish, the First Branch of the Young Ladies' Rosary Society, was organized by Father Felix Zwiardowski, CR. It had as its chief aim to instill in its members a deep devotion to the Blessed Virgin Mary, especially through the Holy Rosary and the performance of charitable works.[24] Because it had so many members, a Second Branch was organized in 1883 by Father Barzynski. Josephine Dudzik, elected its second prefect, served in the group for thirteen years.

In 1885, with the aid of Father Barzynski, Josephine Dudzik co-founded the Archconfraternity of the Immaculate Heart of Mary with two friends, Rosalie Wysinski and Josephine Kopciak.[25] It had as its chief function to imbue its members with Marian idealism as well as to promote devotion to the Immaculate Heart of Mary. On the more immediate level, Josephine Dudzik's services included decorating the altars, sewing altar linens, and leading the church congregation in singing the devotion of the *Godzinki,* the "Little Hours of the Blessed Virgin Mary." Both she and Rosalie Wysinski visited private homes and led families in the recitation of the rosary.[26] Eventually, Josephine Dudzik succeeded succeed Josephine Kopciak as the prefect of the Archconfraternity.[27] From this Archconfraternity over forty young women entered religious life.[28]

Perhaps the fraternal association which made the deepest impression on Josephine was the Third Order of St. Francis. Third Orders, which had their beginnings in the thirteenth century, were aimed at lay men and women who sought to deepen their lives in union with and according to the spirit of a religious order. The Third Order of St. Francis was founded in 1209 to enable its members to share in the Franciscan movement by living according to the Christ-like example of St. Francis of Assisi.[29] While the members were not bound by any vows, it was a true religious order with a novitiate, Rule, profession, daily Office, and a habit.[30] The tertiary[31] strove for love of neighbor, goodness in action, the exercise of modesty, chastity, simplicity in living, and fidelity to the duties of one's state of life.[32] According to Hanley and Fink in *The Franciscans: Love at Work:* "With the Rule as a guide, the tertiary becomes a good Christian, and if progress is made in this, apostolic activity comes as naturally as breathing."[33]

In 1886, the Third Order of St. Francis for young women was canonically founded at St. Stanislaus Kostka Parish by a Franciscan priest whose services Father Barzynski had secured for that purpose.[34] Among the first members accepted were Josephine Dudzik, Rosalie Wysinski, and Josephine Kopciak. Father Barzynski was successful in obtaining the aid of Mother M. Raphael Lubowidzka, CSFN, the first provincial superior of the Congregation of the Sisters of the Holy Family of Nazareth in the United States, to train and prepare the tertiaries for their religious commitment.[35] In a letter to Rome dated September 14, 1887, from Mother M. Raphael to the foundress of the congregation, Mother Mary of Jesus the Good Shepherd (Frances Siedliska), Mother M. Raphael wrote:

> . . . Father Vincent [Barzynski] very earnestly asked me to prepare the Third Order members to the novitiate and to profession. Because they work all day, they can only come in the morning for meditation and at night for a conference. Father Barzynski wants to make me the spiritual guide of these young women.[36]

Another letter followed in December which stated in part:

> . . . a retreat was held with the tertiaries who are preparing for their novitiate; there are eight, and at the head are the *poczciwa,* ["good-natured"] Josephine Dudzik and Rosalie Wysinski.[37]

After their profession in the Third Order, Rosalie, who as a tertiary was called

Sister Anna, was elected the first superior; Josephine Dudzik, who as a tertiary had chosen the name Sister Theresa in honor of the great St. Teresa of Avila,[38] was elected the mistress of novices, an office she held for almost thirteen years. By this time, both Josephine and Rosalie were being referred to as *świętobliwy panny,* the "pious women" of St. Stanislaus Kostka Parish.[39]

Besides serving her family unselfishly, Josephine Dudzik found in the societies of St. Stanislaus Kostka Church an outlet for her "natural as breathing" charitable activities. In addition to increasing the depth of Josephine's spiritual life, the societies provided concrete opportunities to help the less fortunate in the huge and overcrowded parish as far as the duties of her state of life allowed.

A function of the third type of society existing at St. Stanislaus Kostka parish, it will be remembered, was to assist the pastor in various projects of a humanitarian and charitable nature. Since it was true that most of the Polish immigrants' activities centered around their parish church, it was equally true that the parish priest played a most important role in the life of the Polish people. He was their friend, helper, guide, and guardian in the New World as he had been in the Old.[40] This was emphatically true of the Reverend Vincent Barzynski. As pastor of St. Stanislaus Kostka Church, he felt it was his duty to find solutions to the problems of the needy within his parish community. Although there were mutual aid insurance societies, these societies had limitations. It was up to the pastor and the Resurrectionist priests to find solutions to the problems of unemployment, alcoholism, juvenile delinquency, child welfare, and the homeless aged.[41] For a long time, Father Barzynski had been searching for a solution to the special problem of providing for the neglected aged poor of his parish. As Josephine Dudzik's pastor, confessor, spiritual guide, and family friend, he soon came to feel that perhaps Josephine might be the answer to his prayers. Father Barzynski had early recognized in the young Josephine Dudzik a woman of sincere piety, fervent dedication, and genuine compassion. He now began to refer some of the needy and unfortunate aged and homeless women of the parish to Josephine for consolation, inspiration, and material aid.[42]

Josephine Dudzik was thirty years old when, in January of 1890, Chicago was engulfed by an epidemic of influenza which was then encircling the world. The dread disease had crossed the Atlantic and invaded the eastern seaboard cities. At first only isolated cases were reported in all sections of Chicago, but in a few days, a full-blown epidemic developed.[43] Unfortunately, the Dudziks had earlier been made aware of the presence of the deadly disease, for on May 12, 1889, John Dudzik had died at the age of sixty-seven. The *Burial Register* of St. Stanislaus Kostka Church indicates that he was buried in St. Adalbert's Cemetery on the same day.[44] The *Burial Register* reveals that many parishioners were often buried on the same day or a day later. According to the Department of Health Report of the City of Chicago, public funerals of persons dying of influenza and from pneumonia-complicated influenza were prohibited as soon as it became evident that the local outbreak of influenza would assume epidemic proportions. Even church funerals were forbidden, and priests performed the funeral rites at the homes of the deceased who were taken directly from the place of death to the cemetery. There is every reason to believe that John Dudzik was a possible victim of this outbreak of influenza and pneumonia.

After the death of her father, Josephine and her mother and brother left the flat at Crittenden Street and moved to a small house also owned by Rosalie and Adam Frank. Although the Dudziks remained parishioners of St. Stanislaus Kostka Church, their new home at 11 Chapin Street was located approximately one-half block from Holy Trinity Church. They had lived in the vicinity less than two years when Joseph Dudzik announced his intention to marry Josephine Kopciak, Josephine Dudzik's faithful tertiary companion. Joseph Dudzik and Josephine Kopciak were wed on January 22, 1891, in a ceremony performed by Father Barzynski.[45] So it happened that less than ten years after the joyous arrival and reunion of the Dudziks in America, Josephine and her mother were now alone in their house on Chapin Street. Josephine Dudzik had learned early the profound lesson of *Ecclesiastes:* "For everything there is a season, and a time for every affair under the heavens; . . . a time for giving birth, a time for dying; . . . a time for tears, a time for laughter; . . . a time for searching, and a time for losing."[46]

The first house of the newly founded community at 11 Chapin Street (changed later to 1341 Haddon Avenue). Built in 1885, the house was demolished on January 22, 1965, as part of the Chicago Department of Urban Renewal's Project Noble-Division.

ARRIVAL IN AMERICA

[1]There is no doubt that the letters of immigrants to their families were often the cause for the families' joining their loved ones in America. According to the U.S. Department of Labor, nearly all European immigrants admitted at entrance that they were joining their family or friends. *The Report of the Commissioner General of Immigration,* vol. 12 (Washington, DC: 1901).

[2]Victor E. Greene, "Pre-World War I Polish Emigration to the United States: Motives and Statistics," *The Polish Review* 6 (Summer 1961): 68.

[3]According to the *Chicago Sun-Times,* 24 October 1976, records of immigrants are available, but the passenger lists for the years 1847–1896 are not indexed and each page would have to be searched. The National Archives in Washington, DC, do not perform research but do make the records available for people to search through. The newspaper also stated that immigrants probably arrived at Ellis Island almost faster than records could be kept.

[4]The address of the Dudziks' first home in America was obtained from the Congregation of the Sisters of Charity of the Incarnate Word, "Addresses to the Parents of Our Postulants," no. 55 (Texas: 28 October 1883), p. 26—"Miss Catharina Dudzik, Mr. Johann Dudzik, Critenden [*sic*] Street, No. 34, North—Chicago, Ill." Crittenden (the correct spelling) Street is now called Thomas Street.

[5]Sister M. Gonzaga Raniszewski, OSFK, in *Rys historyczny Zgromadzenie Sióstr Franciszkanek Błogosławionej Kunegundy, Część pierwsza, 1860–1910* [A historical survey of the Franciscan Sisters of Blessed Kunegunda. Part one, 1860–1910] (Chicago: By the Author, 1947), p. 13, writes that Josephine Dudzik left Poland in 1878 thus making her eighteen years old at the time of departure. According to the *Book of Admittances,* St. Joseph Home for the Aged and Crippled in Chicago, pp. 194–195, however, Agnes Dudzik, Josephine's mother, was admitted to the Home on December 22, 1894. An entry in the *Book of Admittances* indicates that Agnes Dudzik arrived in America in 1881. Since Josephine Dudzik came to America with her parents, this entry also established the date of her arrival and her age. Additional proof for the year 1881 as the year of the Dudziks' arrival is found in the *Obituaries, 1931,* of the School Sisters of Notre Dame concerning Frances Dudzik: "In 1881 her parents emigrated to America and settled in Chicago in St. Stanislaus Parish."

[6]Raniszewski, *Rys,* p. 14.

[7]Frances Dudzik chose to enter one of the largest and most renowned congregations of religious women in the Church. Originally, the Congregation of the School Sisters of Notre Dame was founded in the French Province of Lorraine in 1597 by St. Peter Fourier, an Augustinian Canon. His hopes for a religious congregation dedicated exclusively to teaching were realized in the consecration of Blessed Alice Le Clerc and her companions who gave themselves to God as Canonesses of St. Augustine or the Congregation of Notre Dame. The congregation grew rapidly and spread throughout France and Germany. By 1809, because of the secularization brought about by Napoleon, all the houses of the congregation were suppressed, and all the Sisters were forced to disperse. In 1833, Caroline Gerhardinger, a former pupil of the suppressed Notre Dame Sisters, together with Anna Hotz and Anna Braun, re-established the congregation, now called the School Sisters of Notre Dame, in Bavaria. In this endeavor, they were aided and encouraged by the Most Reverend Michael Wittman, the saintly bishop of Ratisbon, and his pious friend, the Reverend Francis Sebastian Job.

In 1847, Caroline Gerhardinger, who was called Mother Teresa of Jesus, brought the first band of Sisters to America to care for the children of German immigrants. After working for three years in the East, the Sisters moved to Milwaukee, Wisconsin, where they founded their Motherhouse. Mother Teresa of Jesus appointed Sister Caroline Friess the first mother superior, a title she bore until 1880, when with the approval of Pope Leo XIII, a commissariat was established in America. The following year, Mother Caroline Friess, rightfully called the foundress of the Sisterhood in America, was elected the first commissary general.

Today, the School Sisters of Notre Dame are an international congregation numbering nearly ten thousand women who are engaged in the ministry of education in its broadest sense. They serve the Church as teachers, nurses, missionaries, lawyers, secretaries, journalists, social workers, and religious educators on all levels. Their aim, the formation of genuine Christian community arrived at through prayer and service, is a reaffirmation of the ideal of Mother Teresa of Jesus, their foundress. *Book of Correspondence:* "Brief Historical Sketch of the Community of the School Sisters of Notre Dame," from Sister M. Frances Romano, SSND, Mequon, Wisconsin, to author, 26 October 1973 (AFSCL); and Sister M. Nobilis, SSND, "The First Polish School in the United States," *Polish American Studies* 4 (January–June 1947): 1–5.

[8]School Sisters of Notre Dame, "Candidature Records, 1871–1880 and 1881–1890" (Motherhouse Archives, Mequon, Wisconsin).

[9]In a letter to the author, September 15, 1975, Sister Esther Smith wrote the following, which was taken from *Home Chronicles,* St. Casimir's Mission, Milwaukee:

> Sister M. Leovina was stationed for a number of years at St. Hyacinth's mission in Milwaukee. In 1895, she was transferred to St. Casimir's Parish in the same city where she worked efficiently for fifteen years as superior and teacher. A model superior, she was loyal to the Order and conscientious and faithful in the observance of the Holy Rule. She was a true mother to the Sisters, a good and conscientious religious, and a zealous laborer who worked for the good of the pupils, teachers, and the parish. Forty-two girls from the parish entered the School Sisters of Notre Dame during Sister M. Leovina's time.

Sister M. Leovina also served the congregation in Radom, Illinois, as superior and teacher from 1910 to 1922. After her active teaching career, she spent her last years as sacristan at St. Hedwig's and St. Stanislaus missions in Milwaukee where she was a model of diligence, humility, and respectful submission to authority.

Her death was as quiet as her life had been. She suffered a brain hemorrhage, and the last rites of the Church were administered to her on April 8, 1931. She died on April 10. At her deathbed was the pastor of St. Stanislaus Church, the Reverend Louis Jurasinski, one of her former pupils. Her remains are buried in the congregation's cemetery in Elm Grove, Wisconsin, section F, grave 13. *Book of Correspondence:* Letter from Sister M. Frances Romano, SSND, to author, 21 July 1975 (AFSCL); School Sisters of Notre Dame, "Candidature Records, 1871–1880 and 1881–1890," p. 37; and School Sisters of Notre Dame, "Obituaries 1931." (Original copies in Motherhouse archives, Mequon, Wisconsin).

[10]In 1866, Bishop Claude M. Dubuis of Galveston saw the need for Catholic hospitals to care for the victims of yellow fever which was raging along the Texas coast. Since there was no hospital conducted by Sisters in his diocese, which then comprised the whole state of Texas, he went to France to secure religious women to found a hospital in Galveston. He was unable to obtain any, but at least he found three young women who were willing to devote their lives to missionary work in Texas. In Lyons, France, at the cloistered convent of the Order of the Incarnate Word and Blessed Sacrament, Mother M. Angelique, the superioress, admitted the three volunteers and trained them in the practice of religious life. After their brief preparation, they left for Galveston in the fall of 1866. Later, two groups of four and six members were received at Lyons and followed the three pioneer Sisters to Galveston. Bishop Dubuis sent three Sisters from Galveston to establish a hospital in San Antonio in 1869. With the establishment of the Santa Rosa Infirmary in San Antonio, an independent foundation of the Sisters of Charity of the Incarnate Word was created. The religious chosen to make this first foundation and nurse the sick in the second Catholic hospital in all of Texas were Mother M. Madeleine, Mother St. Pierre, and Sister Agnes. Because of the difficulties of travel between San Antonio and Galveston, Bishop Dubuis declared the new house independent of the Galveston Community in 1872.

The congregation increased rapidly, and by 1892, the Sisters of Charity of the Incarnate

Word were engaged in the three areas of apostolic activity for which they were established: care of the sick, the orphans, and education.

In 1922, provinces of the congregation were established in San Antonio, St. Louis, and Mexico. A juniorate in Ireland was opened that same year. Today the congregation numbers approximately nine hundred and fifty professed Sisters. *Archdiocese of San Antonio: Diamond Jubilee, 1874–1949* (San Antonio: 1949), pp. 120–122.

[11]Katherine Dudzik met the Sisters of Charity of the Incarnate Word when St. Josaphat's Church was founded in 1883 by Father Barzynski in the section of Chicago called Lakeview. Father Barzynski appointed the Reverend Felix Zwiardowski, CR, the first pastor, but because of ill health, he was succeeded by the Reverend Francis Breitkopf, CR, in May 1884. Father Barzynski was instrumental in securing the services of the Congregation of the Sisters of Charity of the Incarnate Word to staff the school. With the consent of Bishop Neraz of San Antonio, the Sisters were sent to St. Josaphat's School in Chicago, and to the Immaculate Conception School in South Chicago whose founding the Resurrectionist Fathers had also promoted. Although both schools were extremely promising, Mother St. Pierre felt obliged to withdraw the Sisters because she was unwilling to establish in Chicago a novitiate exclusively for Polish postulants which the Resurrectionist Fathers advocated. In 1884, the Sisters of Charity of the Incarnate Word withdrew from both schools and returned to the South. When the Sisters withdrew from St. Josaphat's School, Mother Mary of Jesus, the Good Shepherd (Frances Siedliska), foundress of the Congregation of the Sisters of the Holy Family of Nazareth, sent her Sisters to staff the school thereby opening the first mission of her congregation in the United States.

In 1885, Sister M. Barbara wrote to her family that Father Felix Zwiardowski, stationed at Annunciation, BVM Church, approximately four miles from the Motherhouse of the Sisters of Charity of the Incarnate Word in San Antonio, had visited her at least four times. He often referred to her as his "spiritual child." Father Zwiardowski had been an assistant at St. Stanislaus Kostka Church in Chicago during the early 1880s, and had obviously become acquainted with the Dudzik family when they had settled in the parish in 1881. *Book of Correspondence:* Letter from Sister M. Barbara Dudzik to the Dudzik family, 17 April 1885 (AFSCL); *Book of Correspondence:* Letter from Sister Margaret Mary Curry, CCVI, secretary general to author, 11 December 1973 (AFSCL); *Immaculate Conception BVM Diamond Jubilee, 1882–1957* (Chicago: 1957), p. 85; John J. Iwicki, *The First One Hundred Years: A Study of the Congregation of the Resurrection in the United States, 1866–1966* (Rome: Gregorian University Press, 1966), pp. 75–76; and Sister M. Helena Finck, *The Congregation of the Sisters of Charity of the Incarnate Word of San Antonio, Texas* (Washington, DC: The Catholic University of America, 1925), p. 82.

[12]There should be little or no surprise that Katherine was not hesitant about traveling to San Antonio. For a young woman who had already crossed the Atlantic Ocean at fourteen, the journey to far-off Texas would hardly have filled her with alarm. There does appear, however, to be a slight discrepancy as to whether Katherine entered the congregation in June or December of 1884. The record reads: "Number 146, p. 42, Le 6 Juin (*Juin* is crossed and *Dec.* written above it) 1884. Mlle. Kate Dudzik Polonaise agée de 17 a fait son entrée comme postulante daus notre CTE Sister St. Pierre Sup., Sr. St. Gabriel, Sec." *Livre des postulantes de la Communaute des Soeurs de Charitē du Verbe Incarnē dans la ville de San-Antonio, Diocêse de San-Antonio, Texas, Etats-Unis d'Amē rique. Entrēe des Postulantes dans la Communautē des Religieuses du Verbe Incarne de San-Antonio Hopital de Santa Rosa.* Sons la direction de la regnante Reverende Mere Ste. Madeleine l[ère] [Superērieure de l'establissement].

[13]On August 2, 1885, the following entry is made in the "Motherhouse Diary, 1883–1889" of the Sisters of Charity of the Incarnate Word kept daily by Sister M. Gabriel: "Four Postulants took the habit: Miss Katie Dudzik—in religion Sister Barbara of the Blessed Sacrament. The ceremony was performed by the Right Reverend Bishop (J. C. Neraz) assisted by Reverend Father Parisot of Brownsville, Texas, at 5:30 p.m." Also, the Act of Vesture of Sr. M. St. Barbara of the Blessed Sacrament is found in *Livre, No. 1 Actēs de prises d'habits des Soeurs de Charitē du Verbe-Incarnē,*

dans la ville de San-Antonio, diocêse de San-Antonio, Texas, Etats-Unis d'Amērique, p. 55 number 102).

[14]Finck, p. 92.

[15]Sisters of Charity of the Incarnate Word, "The Motherhouse Diary, 1883–1889."

[16]*The Bureau of Vital Statistics, Texas* Department of Health, County of Bexar, Standard Certificate of Death, p. 41, #49, 1886, lists Sister M. Barbara's death from consumption. Two other entries in convent records substantiate this. In *Livre, No. 1, Actēs de prises d'habits des Soeurs de Charitē du Verbe-Incarnē, dans la ville de San-Antonio, diocêse de San-Antonio, Texas, Etats-Unis d'Amērique*, p. 55, #102, a notation next to Sister M. Barbara's Act of Vesture says: "Died, November 23, 1886, of consumption." *The Annual Profession Book II*, #93, has a marginal note written next to the name of Sister M. Barbara of the Blessed Sacrament: "Died on the 23rd of November, 1887 [*sic*] of consumption."

[17]*The Motherhouse Diary, 1883–1889 of the Sisters of the Incarnate Word* reads that from October 22, 1886, Sister M. Barbara took a turn for the worse. On November 21, 1886, on the feast of the Presentation of the Blessed Virgin Mary, she pronounced her perpetual vows. The notation in the *Diary* for November 23, 1886, the day Sister M. Barbara died, is especially moving:

> Again the Incarnate Word has visited this little community and this evening at 9:30 plucked another flower from our novitiate, Sister M. Barbara. Our beloved Sister was confined to her bed for the past three months, and although suffering intensely, edified all by her unalterable patience and resignation. Our cherished Sister was well-prepared to meet her heavenly Spouse, having made her perpetual vows recently, received Extreme Unction, and more than once the final absolution. She had full possession of her mental faculties, and recognized all around her to the end. She did not seem to have any agony, but expired as calmly as an infant. Though our hearts bled to lose our beloved Sister, yet we cheerfully submitted to the Holy Will of Him Who knows what is best for us, and breathed once more 'Fiat.' The absence of our Reverend Mother was keenly felt by all. Our beloved Bishop was there to soothe her in her last moments.

[18]In 1930, the remains of Sister M. Barbara were reinterred in the congregation's cemetery adjacent to the Incarnate Word Generalate in San Antonio. Author's visit to the congregation's cemetery in San Antonio, Texas.

[19]The reader will recall that Father Peter Semenenko was one of the three founders of the Congregation of the Resurrection.

[20]Iwicki, p. 60.

[21]Ibid.

[22]Father Barzynski was so successful that by 1900 and until the late 1930s, St. Stanislaus Kostka Church had sixty-one societies, seven confraternities, and eleven fraternal organizations. In addition, there were five groups within the parish choir and two dramatic and theatrical associations. Iwicki, p. 67.

[23]Sister M. Andrea, SSND, "The Societies of St. Stanislaus Kostka Parish." *Polish American Studies* 9 (January–June 1952): 27–37.

[24]*Album Pamiątkowy Złotego Jubileuszu Parafii Świętego Stanisława Kostki, 1867–1917* [A Commemorative Album of the Golden Jubilee of St. Stanislaus Kostka Parish, 1867–1917] (Chicago: 1917), p. 100.

[25]These two women will discussed in later chapters.

[26]*Book of Depositions:* Sister M. Paul Kirschbaum (AFSCL).

[27]*Album, SSK*, p. 112.

[28]Ibid.

[29]Boniface Hanley, OFM, and Salvator Fink, OFM, *The Franciscans: Love at Work*

(Paterson, New Jersey: St. Anthony's, 1962), p. 213.

[30]It consisted of a scapular and a cord. The scapular, two small squares of cloth, usually wool, joined by cords, was worn around the neck with one square hanging in front and one in back. A thin cord was worn around the waist under ordinary clothing.

[31]*Tertiary* is the name given to a member of the Third Order Secular of St. Francis. The Third Order Secular was called "third" because its foundation followed the establishment of the "first" (for men) and the "second" (for women) religious orders with which they are associated. Today, the Third Order Secular of St. Francis is called Secular Franciscans.

[32]Albert Paul Schimberg, *The Larks of Umbria* (Milwaukee: The Bruce Publishing Co., 1942), p. 159.

[33]Hanley and Fink, p. 214.

[34]*Album, SSK,* p. 126.

[35]This congregation, to which the Franciscan Sisters of Chicago are indebted for providing Josephine Dudzik and Rosalie Wysinski with valuable spiritual training as tertiaries, was founded by a noble Polish woman, Mother Mary of Jesus the Good Shepherd (Frances Siedliska) in 1875 in Rome to relieve needy persons through social and charitable activities, as well as the Christian education of youth. The Most Reverend Patrick A. Feehan summoned the Sisters to Chicago to give assistance to the poor Polish immigrants who formed such a large part of his flock. When they arrived in Chicago, Father Barzynski provided transportation to their first mission, St. Josaphat's parish, where they cared for orphans and school children.

The Sisters today staff elementary schools, high schools, colleges, hospitals, retirement homes, child-care centers, nursing homes, and retreat centers. The daughters of Mother Siedliska, whose cause for beatification was formally introduced in 1940, serve in Italy, Poland, France, the United States, England, Ireland, Puerto Rico, Peru, and Australia. *St. Adalbert: A Tribute to 100 Years of Service, 1874–1974* (Chicago: 1974), p. 23; and Antonio Ricciardi, *His Will Alone,* trans. Regis N. Barwig (Rome: Edizioni Agiografiche, 1970), p. 180.

[36]Letter from Mother M. Raphael Lubowidzka, first provincial superior of the Congregation of the Sisters of the Holy Family of Nazareth, Holy Family Academy, 130 W. Division St. (now 1444 W. Division St.), Chicago, Illinois, to Mother Mary of Jesus the Good Shepherd (Frances Siedliska), foundress of the Congregation of the Sisters of the Holy Family of Nazareth, in Rome, Italy, 14 September 1887 (Original copy in the archives at the Motherhouse of the Congregation of the Sisters of the Holy Family of Nazareth, in Rome, Italy).

[37]Ibid., 4 December 1887.

[38]Josephine's chosen patron saint, St. Teresa, is one of the glories of Spain and the Church. Born in the ancient fortress-city of Avila on March 28, 1515, as the first rumblings of revolt and heresy were threatening the unity of the Catholic Church, the attractive and spirited Teresa entered the Carmelite monastery of the Incarnation at eighteen against the wishes of her widowed father. As in all monasteries of that time, the Ancient Rule of Carmel had been replaced by a less austere Rule with little or no emphasis on strict enclosure, complete poverty, silence, solitude, and perpetual abstinence which were so necessary for a life of prayer and sacrifice. According to her account, St. Teresa's own spiritual life was lukewarm until she underwent a conversion in 1556.

Alarmed at the devastating effects of the heresy in Germany, England, and France, and wishing to pray for the welfare of the Church, St. Teresa obtained permission to return to the Primitive Rule of Carmel, and founded the first Monastery of the "Reform" on August 24, 1562. In spite of bitter opposition, she zealously set up fifteen convents, including one for men, and left the task to St. John of the Cross to establish other men's monasteries. Her autobiographical and mystical works make her equally renowned as a writer. Death came to her at Alba de Tormes on October 15, 1582.

Biographers speak of St. Teresa of Avila as a practical, level-headed woman possessed of great idealism yet maintaining a gentle sense of humor. She had superhuman perseverance in the midst of the trials of life, and monumental patience and trust in God's goodness. These qualities helped her never to compromise when a matter of principle was involved. In choosing St. Teresa as her patron, Josephine Dudzik chose a saint whose character proved to be very much like her own as this history reveals. *Dictionary of Catholic Biography,* p. 1104; and John Coulson, ed., *The Saints* (New York: Guild Press, 1957), p. 96.

[39]*Interview* with Sister M. Ernest Blazonczyk, 12 May 1974 (AFSCL).

[40]Joseph A. Wisniewski, CR, "St. Stanislaus Kostka Parish in Chicago: Its Spiritual, Educational, and Cultural Legacy to the 600,000 Americans of Polish Extraction, 1869–1908" (M.A. thesis, De Paul University, 1964), p. 45.

[41]Roger J. Couglin and Cathryn A. Riplinger, *The Story of Charitable Care in the Archdiocese of Chicago, 1844–1959* (Chicago: The Catholic Charities, 1959), p. 153.

[42]Siostra M. Gonzaga Raniszewski, OSFK, *Zarys Połwiecza Zgromadzenia Sióstr Franciszkanek Bł. Kunegundy* [Sketch of the fifty-year history of the Congregation of the Franciscan Sisters of Bł. Kunegunda] (Chicago: By the Author, 1944), p. 13.

[43]Swayne Wickersham, Commissioner of Health, in the annual report of the Department of Health in Chicago, 1890, describes the outbreak:

> It reached its height in our city the last week of January, at which time it is my belief that over 100,000 of our citizens were sufferers from that cause alone. The deaths directly attributed to it by the attending physicians, as shown by the certificates, were 112. But in a very large number of death certificates presented to this department for burial permits, it was prominently mentioned as a complicating cause. It undoubtedly hastened the death of a large number who were suffering from consumption, also those who contracted pneumonia and other diseases of the respiratory organs. The largest monthly mortality for the year was in January which was 2,501. The total mortality for the year was 21,856.

John Dill Robertson, MD, commissioner of health, *A Report on an Epidemic of Influenza in the City of Chicago in the Fall of 1918,* Reprinted from the *Octennial Report 1911–1918,* Educational Series, #15, Department of Health (Chicago: 1918). Contains a report of the 1890 epidemic by Swayne Wickersham, commissioner of health, 1890, under "Previous Influenza Epidemics in Chicago."

[44]*St. Stanislaus Kostka Church: Burial Register, 1882–1890,* vol. 3 (Chicago: 1890), p. 212.

[45]The wedding, at which Josephine served as bridesmaid, is recorded in *Zapowiedzie, 1890,* vol. 13, p. 157, *St. Stanislaus Kostka Church.* Eventually they were the parents of three children: one, a son, is presumed to have died in infancy. Joseph Dudzik died on July 4, 1919, in Kentucky, where he had been in the employ of the Resurrectionist Fathers in much the same capacity as he had worked for them at St. Stanislaus Kostka rectory in Chicago. He was buried in the family plot at St. Adalbert's Cemetery.

[46]Eccles. 3:1–8.

CHAPTER 6

New Beginnings

The illustrious American essayist and poet, Henry David Thoreau, wrote: "There is no remedy for love, but to love more." Alone now with her mother in their home on Chapin Street, Josephine Dudzik's continued growth in piety was accompanied by a growth in her spirit of self-denial which caused her to turn with greater attention to the needs of the aged, destitute, and crippled. It is obvious from the entries in her "Chronicle,"[1] that her solicitude for the needy and unfortunate whom she encountered in the parish, or who were directed to her by Father Barzynski, did not diminish with the passage of time. Instead, her love for God in the person of her neighbor grew to such an extent that she now began to shelter homeless and needy women in her small, inadequate home much to the growing displeasure and discomfort of her mother. Later, on the first page of her "Chronicle," Josephine, in all simplicity, would reveal her concern:

Opening page of Mother M. Theresa Dudzik's manuscript, a short history of the community. The account begins in 1893 and ends in 1910. The original manuscript in Polish is preserved in the archives of Our Lady of Victory Convent, General Motherhouse, Lemont, Illinois.

For a number of years, I had already been contemplating in what way better comfort and lodging might be given to poor girls, widows, and to the sick who were unable to do hard work. I had frequently sheltered too many of them in the limited quarters of my home. As a result, my mother often hindered me in my work of mercy because she was exposed to various inconveniences for which I was reproached. She also remarked that not only I suffered, but this action of mine compelled her to suffer, too.[2]

Josephine tried to pacify her mother and surround her with greater care and concern. She even made extravagant promises to be more disciplined in the performance of her works of charity. Nevertheless, when another aged, homeless, ill, or widowed woman sought shelter, Josephine forgot her promises to her mother in the hope of bringing solace and practical aid to someone who needed help.[3] More and more frequently now, when Father Barzynski encountered a woman in the parish in dire need, he would refer her to Josephine. She, in turn, would extend to the woman the genuine hospitality of her heart and home. Josephine's own words offer valuable insight into the motives which prompted this genuine solicitude for others:

I felt the misery and sufferings of others, and it seemed to me that I could not love Jesus, or even expect heaven if I were concerned only about myself . . . not suffering any inconvenience, but simply living in comfort. Very often, I felt drawn to greater sacrifice for others. Consequently, I was preoccupied with the thought of how I could be of service to the needy and the poor. In my mind, I was already arranging the beds and preparing all things necessary for this purpose. The thought haunted me day and night even though I was unaware of the means by which this could be accomplished.[4]

Trusting in Divine Providence, Josephine prayed and waited for enlightenment. It was not long in coming. Once again, her own words express her sentiments:

Once while at prayer, a thought suddenly occurred to me to rent or purchase a home in the vicinity of St. Stanislaus Kostka Church and assemble all the tertiaries from this parish who would desire to join me in a common life of prayer, labor, and service.[5]

Josephine, elated by her inspiration,[6] confided her plan in greater detail to her trusted friend and sister tertiary, Rosalie Wysinski, who not only praised Josephine's noble goal but also expressed a desire to join her in making this inspiration a reality. Rosalie agreed that Josephine's proposal should be discussed at the next meeting of the members of the Third Order of St. Francis.

On Sunday, October 1, 1893, after the conclusion of the business portion of the meeting, Josephine presented her plan to the assembled tertiaries. A woman of insight,

Josephine informed them of the obvious need to minister to the many ill, widowed, and needy women of the parish. She told them of her plan to gather a group of zealous co-workers who would desire to live the common life and lend mutual aid and encouragement to one another in this work of mercy. The tertiaries, inspired by Josephine Dudzik's vision, responded with great enthusiasm and some, like Josephine herself, pressed for immediate action. Rosalie Wysinski, however, urged the group to refrain from proceeding with any plan for at least a year, so that through prayerful reflection, they might more easily discern the Will of God. Josephine had some misgivings at the thought of waiting a year for a matter which she perceived needed immediate attention. Nevertheless, she readily conceded to Rosalie's spirit of faith and good judgment in the matter.[7]

On October 7, 1894, the feast of Our Lady of the Most Holy Rosary, the tertiaries gathered for their regular monthly meeting. Josephine Dudzik restated the plan she had proposed a year earlier—to form a lay apostolate with women such as herself, who would live a common life of prayer, labor, and service to neighborhood women in need. Her enthusiasm quickly gave way to dismay and disappointment when it became obvious that while many of the tertiaries had given some thought to her proposed plan, others had dismissed it entirely from their minds. Some had even altered their original intention to join her. Nonetheless, Josephine was jubilant when seven tertiaries submitted their names. They were Rosalie Wysinski, Marianne Bezler,[8] Susanna Chelewski, Katherine Marzanek, Victoria Milewski, Marianne Steltman, and Clara Szrambek with Josephine herself as the eighth volunteer.[9]

Reserved and shy by nature, Josephine waited a month before approaching Father Barzynski with her plan and the names of the tertiaries who had volunteered to join her. Father Barzynski received her plan most favorably and urged Josephine and the tertiaries to pursue their benevolent cause without further delay. For years, Father Barzynski had been aware of the plight of the aged, orphaned, crippled, and abandoned members of his parish. Perhaps he did not dare to dream that a young woman like Josephine Dudzik would present him with a solution to a plan he had long been harboring secretly—the institution of a religious congregation committed to the corporal and spiritual works of mercy in his parish.[10] For his part, he promised Josephine and the tertiaries his spiritual counsel as well as his practical advice and protection.[11] Father Barzynski stipulated one condition, however, which caused Josephine Dudzik some apprehension. Unless the group adopted the structure of a religious community, lived together in religious obedience, and wore a distinctive religious habit,[12] Father Barzynski would not grant his approval and support. His insistence on the necessity for the women to form a religious community, he explained, was to ensure the stability of the group should the initial zealous dedication of the members diminish with the passage of time.[13] Awed at first with the prospect of founding a new Franciscan community in the Church, Josephine was determined to overcome her fears: "I resolved to obey him [Father Barzynski] in everything that he might command in this respect."[14] She was convinced that this was God's work since it had met with Father Barzynski's approval.

Josephine Dudzik and the tertiaries met as a group with Father Barzynski for the first time on November 10, 1894. While initially Josephine's plan had been "to provide comfort and lodging for poor girls, widows, and the sick [women] who were unable to do hard work,"[15] Father Barzynski now urged Josephine Dudzik and the tertiaries to alter their original aim. He proposed that the Franciscan tertiaries care for both aged and disabled men and women "not in a home on Noble Street near St. Stanislaus Kostka Church, but on the outskirts of the city in either Avondale or Cragin."[16] Father Barzynski advised them to begin their charitable work in either of these areas in order to avoid the noisy and overcrowded St. Stanislaus Kostka vicinity. In the Avondale and Cragin districts,[17] he reasoned, the land was less expensive, and there was more room to build and expand should the eager Franciscan tertiaries succeed in their plan to erect a home for the aged in the future.[18] Josephine and the women accepted Father Barzynski's altered plan with all sincerity and docility and listened attentively as he explained the nature and purpose of religious life. Their savings and belongings were to be placed into a common treasury. They would be bound to obedience, to common prayer, and other spiritual exercises. They would practice lifelong celibacy. Father Barzynski then spoke to each tertiary personally in order to discern her reason for joining the group. At that meeting also, each prospective candidate's personal possessions were duly recorded so that later, if a candidate chose to leave, all her material goods would be returned to her.[19] During this interview, Susanna Chelewski withdrew her intention to join the group. The thought of leaving Chicago for the outskirts of the city did not appeal to her, nor did she wish to place her savings of $1,000 into the common treasury. The seven other candidates remained staunch in their commitments with one modification.[20] Rosalie Wysinski, who approved most heartily of the plan and wished to cooperate in its formation, expressed the fear that she could not begin the life in common with the other volunteers since she was the sole support of her parents and her sister Matilda, a deaf mute,[21] and was thus forced to remain with them. Nonetheless, she was committed to joining the group in living the common life at the earliest opportunity.

At a subsequent meeting held on November 24, 1894, Josephine's home at 11 Chapin Street[22] was chosen as the residence in which the women would begin their life in common. That day, to their great joy and surprise, another tertiary, Constance Topolinski, asked to be accepted. Father Barzynski proposed that after a six-month probation period, the tertiaries should receive a religious habit. This unnerved Josephine for she could not imagine wearing the garb of a religious without having had a suitable spiritual preparation. Moreover, she could not envision living a structured religious life without a permanent residence. She would write in her "Chronicle":

> I wondered how we could live as a community since we had no permanent home. No doubt, in this instance, we would be following the example of our Holy Father Francis, who also had no permanent home. This thought consoled me and brought me peace of mind.[23]

At the conclusion of the meeting, Father Barzynski urged Josephine and her tertiary companions to begin a novena with the greatest devotion to the Immaculate Conception. It would begin on November 27 and conclude on December 8, the day of the feast. He further proposed asking the parishioners of St. Stanislaus Kostka Church to join the tertiaries in begging the Mother of God for help in the difficult undertaking upon which they had so willingly embarked.[24]

In the meantime, Father Barzynski sought permission[25] for the erection of the new community in the Church from the Most Reverend Patrick A. Feehan, archbishop of Chicago.[26] Archbishop Feehan was enthusiastically receptive to Father Barzynski's concept of a congregation of religious women solely dedicated to the care of aged and crippled men and women. Fully aware of the success of Father Barzynski's numerous charitable activities in the Archdiocese of Chicago and of his tremendous influence among the Poles of Chicago, Archbishop Feehan believed that the project would be blessed by God.[27] Since the women were Franciscan tertiaries, they planned to adopt the Rule of the Third Order Regular of St. Francis and be known as the Sisters of the Third Order of St. Francis under the patronage of Blessed Kunegunda.[28]

One wonders why the community was placed under the patronage of Blessed Kunegunda. The explanation for the name choice is supplied by Sister M. Gonzaga Raniszewski, in *Rys historyczny Zgromadzenia Sióstr Franciszkanek Błogosławionej Kunegundy. Część pierwsza, 1860–1910* [A historical survey of the Franciscan Sisters of Blessed Kunegunda. Part one, 1860–1910]:

> When Father Barzynski presented a plan to Archbishop Feehan about founding a Polish community of Sisters in Chicago with the goal of aiding the aged and crippled, Archbishop Feehan was impressed and supportive. When Father Barzynski informed the Archbishop that the new community would be named the Sisters of the Third Order of St. Francis under the patronage of Blessed Kunegunda to whom Father Barzynski had a special devotion, Archbishop Feehan approved and praised the name choice. He reasoned that since the Sisters would be working among the Poles, it would be wise to have a Polish patroness.[29]

Historically, then, the choice of the name can be directly attributed to Father Barzynski and the influence of the Resurrectionist Fathers. The year 1893 marked the 600th anniversary of the death of Blessed Kunegunda. Every parish conducted by the Resurrectionist Fathers became involved in the commemoration of the anniversary. In that same year, as part of the festivities, there was a renewal of interest in the canonization process of Kunegunda who had been beatified and called "Blessed" in 1690 by Pope Alexander VIII. There was now a determined effort to have her declared a "Saint." Because the renewal of interest in the canonization process of Blessed Kunegunda took on such a joyous and triumphant tone, it seemed that she would have little difficulty being proclaimed a saint. She was already being addressed prematurely as "Saint" on many

Blessed Kunegunda, Daughter of Bela IV, King of Hungary
Wife of Boleslaus V, King of Poland
Patroness of the Congregation

occasions. Seemingly, then, at Josephine's own conviction and at the urging of Father Barzynski, the young women adopted Blessed Kunegunda, a model of Christian charity and patroness of Poland, as the patroness of their new community.[30]

Father Barzynski and Josephine Dudzik continued to have numerous private meetings during which he explained the importance of the decision she had made and the spirit with which she might hope to accomplish her goal. In her "Chronicle," Josephine admits that Father Barzynski subjected her to various trials to determine whether or not she possessed the qualities to guide the tertiaries. Josephine assured Father Barzynski that with the grace of God, she would be equal to any task with which she was confronted.[31] One of these meetings, Josephine relates, was of extreme significance:

He [Father Barzynski] demanded a promise from me to care for this community in times of difficulty as well as in times of prosperity. When I made the promise, I did not foresee any problems. Later, when difficulties and adversities did arise, I remembered my promise. Consequently, I was able to bear hardships more easily.[32]

Josephine Dudzik had no way of foreseeing the pain, contradiction, and excruciating periods of doubt which awaited her when she made this generous offering of herself to God in the service of the needy, but she looked upon Father Barzynski as a saintly and prudent man. He had explained the gravity and the responsibility of her obligation, and she had willingly accepted it out of love for God and humanity. She would later have occasion to recall her promise to Father Barzynski when many times pain and contradictions made themselves felt:

I recalled my promise. Consequently, I was able to bear sorrow more easily. The thought that I had freely agreed upon this undertaking for Jesus Christ sustained me.[33]

At the last group meeting, which took place on December 12, 1894, all the women except Clara Szrambek expressed their eagerness to begin life in common.[34] Father Barzynski extended his blessing to the group and urged them to assemble at Josephine Dudzik's home on Chapin Street to begin their religious life in common before Christmas Day. He also announced that the new community would be placed under the special patronage of the Immaculate Conception and would, thereafter, date its beginning to December 8, 1894.[35] Now Josephine could truly pray with the Psalmist: "Thou hast held me by my right hand and by Thy Holy Will Thou hast sustained me."[11]

NEW BEGINNINGS

[1]In 1910, Sister M. Theresa Dudzik wrote "Kronika Sióstr Franciszkanek, pod opieką Św. Kunegundy w Chicago, Illinois" [The Chronicle of the Franciscan Sisters under the patronage of St. Kunegunda in Chicago, Illinois], at the command of the Reverend Andrew Spetz, CR, who was, at that time, the spiritual director of the newly established congregation. The "Chronicle" covers the years from 1893 to 1910 and contains, in the words of Sister M. Theresa, "only the more important occurrences insofar as I remember them." This "Chronicle," then, is invaluable since it represents the only written word of Sister M. Theresa Dudzik.

[2]Matka Maria Teresa Dudzik, "Kronika Sióstr Franciszkanek pod opieką Św. Kunegundy w Chicago, Illinois" [The Chronicle of the Franciscan Sisters under the patronage of St. Kunegunda in Chicago, Illinois] Unpublished manuscript, 1910 (Lemont, Illinois, AFSCL), p. 1.

[3]Ibid.

[4]Ibid.

[5]Ibid., p. 2.

[6]In *The Rise of a Modern City,* Bessie Louise Pierce writes of Jane Addams whom she calls "the civic saviour of Chicago." Jane Addams, a native of Illinois, opened Hull House, a social settlement destined to become world-famous for the devotion of its leader and her programs to social reform. A look at the lives of Jane Addams and Josephine Dudzik makes their backgrounds appear disparate enough to preclude any resemblance or comparison therein, but in the circumstances which called their work into existence, in the motives which impelled them to dedication to the less fortunate, and in the ideals which governed and influenced the growth of their foundations, they are remarkably similar. In terms of time and circumstances, Chicago produced these two noble women, truly great heralds of vision, resourcefulness, courage, and profound dedication in the area of humanitarian service. Jane Addams, a self-appointed social reformer, came to the rescue of Chicago's West Side colony of immigrant Bohemians, Russians, Germans, and Italians impelled by the motives she outlined in her book, *Twenty Years at Hull-House:*

> It is hard to tell just when the very simple plan which afterwards developed into the Settlement House began to form itself in my mind . . . but I gradually became convinced that it would be a good thing to rent a house in a part of the city where many primitive and actual needs are found, in which young women, who had been given over too exclusively to study, might learn from life itself.

In a most remarkable parallel, Josephine Dudzik, confronted by the existing social problems on Chicago's Northwest Side, likewise began her pioneer humanitarian work with words that appear to be a re-echoing of the words of her contemporary, Jane Addams. The author pursued the parallelism to such an extent that it resulted in a paper presented at the annual meeting of the Polish American Historical Association on December 28, 1977, in Dallas, Texas. A revised version of the paper appeared in *Polish American Studies* 35 (Spring–Autumn) 1978 under the title, "Jane Addams and Josephine Dudzik: Social Service Pioneers." Bessie Louise Pierce, *A History of Chicago,* vol. 3: *The Rise of a Modern City, 1871–1893* (New York: Alfred A. Knopf, 1957); and Jane Addams, *Twenty Years at Hull-House* (New York: The MacMillan Co., 1910), p. 85.

[7]Dudzik, p. 3.

[8]Marianne Bezler had joined the pioneer band of the Sisters of St. Felix of Cantalice (Felicians) as a postulant in December 1876. Her name in religion was Sister M. Hyacinth, the name by which she was known in the new community of Franciscan tertiaries. Sister M. Theophane Kalinowski, CSSF, "The First Decade of the Sisters of St. Felix in America, 1874–1884" (M.A. thesis, Loyola University, Chicago, 1956), p. 53.

[9]Dudzik, p. 3.

[10]Father Barzynski's specific plan to have Josephine Dudzik found an entirely new

congregation in the Church has sometimes led to his being credited as the actual founder. The original inspiration to live a common life of prayer and to labor for the sake of the unfortunate and needy was, without a doubt, Josephine Dudzik's. The Franciscan Sisters of Chicago had their origin in a manner similar to many other congregations in the Church. It has often been the case that the establishment of a community of women was guided by a priest who acted as the spiritual director from its conception. For example, the Reverend Sebastian Schwarz of Austria directed a group of pious young women to the needs of preschool children who were exposed to the dangers of the street, and the Congregation of the School Sisters of the Third Order of St. Francis in Savannah, Missouri, was formed. The Congregation of the Franciscan Sisters of Christian Charity of Manitowoc, Wisconsin, came about as the result of the Reverend Joseph Fessler's plan to begin a parish school for the many immigrants settling around St. Nazianz, Wisconsin. One of the local girls offered her aid and was soon joined by others. The Congregation of the Sisters of St. Felix of Cantalice (Felicians) was organized in Warsaw, Poland, in 1885 by Sophia Truszkowski as a charitable institute to serve orphaned and neglected children. She placed herself under the guidance of the Reverend Honorat Koźminski.

It is equally true that certain pious societies, such as the Third Order of St. Francis to which Josephine and the foundation group belonged, were the nuclei of religious orders. The Sisters of the Third Order of St. Francis of Assisi in Milwaukee, Wisconsin, trace their origin to 1849 when six young tertiaries of the Third Order of St. Francis in Augsburg, Germany, came to Milwaukee and established one of the first Motherhouses in that state. Likewise, the Congregation of the Daughters of Mary of the Immaculate Conception in New Britain, Connecticut, founded in 1904 by the Reverend Lucian Bojnowski, had its beginning with a group of devout Marian sodalists in the parish who were concerned over the sad fortune of orphaned children. The reader is directed to the splendid book written by John M. Lozano, CMF, called *Foundresses, Founders and Their Religious Families* written in 1983 and published by the Claret Center for Resources in Spirituality.

[11]Siostra M. Gonzaga Raniszewski, *Zarys Półwiecza Zgromadzenia Sióstr Franciszkanek Bł. Kunegundy* [Sketch of the fifty-year history of the Congregation of the Franciscan Sisters of Bl. Kunegunda] (Chicago: By the Author, 1944), p. 13.

[12]A religious habit is the special dress or attire proper to many members of religious congregations in the Catholic Church. Many foundresses never initiated or proposed a religious habit for their members. Indeed, such was the case with the Congregation of the Sisters of Charity of the Blessed Virgin Mary, whose foundress, Mother M. Frances Clarke, and her early followers dressed in a conservative and becoming dress worn by women of the day. Mother M. Clarke felt that there was no reason for the adoption of a distinctive religious habit, nor is it at all certain that she planned for her Sisters to wear one. Although the congregation was established in 1831, the Sisters did not formally wear a religious habit until 1853. For another, the Society of the Daughters of the Heart of Mary have never worn a religious garb. Today, many congregations no longer wear a distinctive garb identifying them as members of a particular Sisterhood. M. Jane Coogan, BVM, *The Price of Our Heritage*, 2 vols. (Dubuque, Iowa: Mount Carmel Press, 1975) 1:274.

[13]Dudzik, p. 4.

[14]Ibid.

[15]Ibid., p. 1.

[16]Ibid., p. 4.

[17]Avondale, about six miles from Chicago's Loop and near Milwaukee Avenue, was, in 1894, a highly undeveloped district. Cragin was also a rural area on the outskirts of Chicago about five and a half miles from St. Stanislaus Kostka Church. Approximately seven families were settled in the area at this time amid large stretches of farm land and wide prairies. Both Avondale and Cragin will be discussed in greater detail in later chapters.

[18]Raniszewski, p. 33.

[19]Dudzik, p. 4.

[20]Ibid.

[21]Raniszewski, p. 30.

[22]In later years, the name of the street and the house number were changed from 11 Chapin Street to 1341 Haddon Avenue. On January 22, 1965, this "first" home of the congregation was razed. It was demolished as part of the Chicago Department of Urban Renewal's Project Noble–Division on the Near Northwest Side, a redevelopment program designed to provide space for new housing. When the house was in the process of being demolished, the weather-beaten date-stone bearing the year of erection—1864—was removed from beneath the roof of the deteriorated two-story brick building by workmen. It was presented to Mother M. Beatrice Rybacki by John Duba, Commissioner of the Department of Urban Renewal. The general council of the congregation, the pastor of Holy Trinity Church, and a number of city officials also were present. The historical date-stone is now on the grounds of the Mother Theresa Museum in Lemont. Some attempts were made to preserve the historically significant building, but its poor condition indicated that any efforts at renovation would prove far too costly to the congregation.

[23]Dudzik, p. 5.

[24]Ibid.

[25]There is no record in the archives of the congregation nor in the archives of the Archdiocese of Chicago of any written permission obtained by Father Barzynski. The permission must have been given to him verbally.

[26]The first archbishop appointed to the See of Chicago was Patrick Augustine Feehan. Born in Killenaule, Tipperary, Ireland, in 1829, he studied at seminaries in Ireland. He came to America at the invitation of Archbishop Kenrick of St. Louis, and studied at Carondolet Seminary in St. Louis where he later taught and became president. He served as pastor at two parishes in St. Louis. During this period, he also spent a great deal of time in prison work and as a volunteer chaplain to the wounded soldiers of the Civil War. In 1865, he was consecrated bishop of Nashville. He succeeded in rebuilding his war-ravaged diocese and won the affection of Nashville's citizens during the cholera epidemic of 1878.

On September 11, 1880, the Diocese of Chicago was raised to an archdiocese and the Right Reverend Patrick A. Feehan was appointed its first archbishop. He was installed on November 28, 1880. Chicago was rebuilding after the Great Fire of 1871, and Archbishop Feehan devoted his energy to solving many of the city's problems. His years in Chicago were a time of rapid growth. His administration was faced with the problem of integrating the Irish, German, Polish, Italian, and other immigrants who daily arrived in the archdiocese. Through his efforts, many religious orders were founded to serve the various nationalities in Chicago parishes.

Archbishop Feehan was a patient, gentle, thoughtful man and an indefatigable worker. His legacy to his successor, Archbishop Quigley, was 566 priests, 100 seminarians, 55 missions, 7 orphan asylums, 15 hospitals, 4 industrial schools, and 10 charitable institutions. He established 119 parishes in Cook and Lake Counties between 1880 and 1902. Sixty-three of these parishes were national, designed to meet the special needs of the foreign-born. His zeal for Catholic education earned him the title, "The Apostle of the Schools." The first official Catholic newspaper in Chicago, *The New World* (now *The Chicago Catholic*), was established by Archbishop Feehan in 1892.

Archbishop Feehan died at his archiepiscopal residency on July 11, 1902, at the age of seventy-three. His remains are buried in the Bishops' Crypt in Mount Carmel in Hillside. The Congregation of the Franciscan Sisters of Chicago is particularly indebted to Archbishop Feehan for the following: permission to found their congregation; confirmation of the erection of St. Joseph Home for the Aged and Crippled and St. Vincent's Orphan Asylum; permission to open the novitiate of the congregation; and confirmation of the First Constitutions of the Franciscan Sisters of Chicago. *Dictionary of Catholic Biography,* pp. 4–6; Rev. M. J. Madaj, *The New World,* 16 August 1974, sec. 2, pp. 7–8; Rev. Joseph Thompson, ed., *Diamond Jubilee of the Archdiocese of Chicago, 1920* (Des Plaines, Illinois: St. Mary's Training School Press, 1920), pp. 51–67.

[27]Raniszewski, p. 94.

[28]It comes as a bit of a surprise to learn that Blessed Kunegunda, venerated as queen and mother of the Polish people during her lifetime, and accepted as the patroness of the congregation after its foundation, was not herself a Pole. Blessed Kunegunda, or Kinga, as she is often called, was born in 1224, the daughter of Bela IV, King of Hungary. She was descended from sainted ancestors—the sister of Blessed Jolanta, the niece of St. Salomea, and also the niece of the beloved St. Elizabeth of Hungary. At the age of sixteen, Kunegunda was given in marriage to Boleslaus V of Poland in dowry and to ally the Poles with the Hungarians in the event of an attack by their common enemy, the Tartars. For forty years, Kunegunda and Boleslaus lived in voluntary chastity. Many pious legends surround Blessed Kunegunda, and it is sometimes difficult to extricate the fact from the fantasy. What we do know indicates that in foregoing natural motherhood, Kunegunda became a mother according to Christ's love. She spent her days visiting the poor, the sick, and the deprived. She distributed medicine and food to the unfortunate. With her wealth, she endowed churches and hospitals and ransomed Christians. To her Polish subjects, she was both queen and mother, and therefore, some of the legends which persist fall heavily in the area of her participation in Poland's political and social life. For example, the salt mines in Southern Poland are inexorably linked with her. It is said that in the salt mines in Hungary, she threw in her ring as a sign of her ownership of the mine. Later, the same ring was found in a lump of salt in Bochnia. Since that time, salt is mined in Bochnia and its vicinity, and salt commerce grew to such large proportions that Poland accumulated great wealth, and the peasant had the opportunity to purchase salt at a nominal price. Another legend tells us that in a neighborhood devoid of water, a clear and abundant stream appeared after Kunegunda prayed. When Tartar hordes plundered Poland and Kunegunda learned of their approach, she prayed to SS. Gervase and Protase for help and actually foretold the victory of the Poles over the barbarous Jadzwingów. In general, these legends abound and merely accentuate the love of the Polish people for their queen.

When the first Franciscans came to Cracow, Kunegunda, her aunt Salomea, and sister Jolanta received the habit of the Third Order of St. Francis from Father Bartholomew Morawczyk. At Kunegunda's request, Boleslaus also received the habit in 1274. Kunegunda was an especial benefactor to the Order of Friars Minor and the Poor Clares. She founded the monastery of Poor Clares at Stary Sącz in 1257, and at her husband's death in 1279, she joined the monastery and eventually became its abbess. She died on July 24, 1292. When she was beatified in 1690 by Pope Alexander VIII, she was named the patroness of Poland.

Her cult has not entirely disappeared. The monastery which she founded still exists after seven centuries during which time its existence has been threatened by wars waged by aggressors. As late as 1935, there was still a movement to canonize her. As a consequence, the terms "Blessed" and "Saint" were used arbitrarily. There is a good deal of correspondence between the abbess of Stary Sącz and Mother M. Antonina Osinski in the archives having to do with the impending canonization. Unfortunately, World War II intervened. In 1966, Mother M. Beatrice Rybacki still kept contact with the Poor Clares in Stary Sącz. The abbess, Mother Bonaventure, acknowledged each gift with sincere gratitude. "Bł. Kunegunda, 1224–1292," *Posłaniec* (Pulaski, Wisconsin, Franciscan Fathers, Assumption of Blessed Virgin Mary Province, 1937), p. 207; *Franciscan Echo* (Lemont, Illinois: 1966); "O Kanonizacje Błog. Kingi, Królowej Polski i Klaryski," *Kronika Seraficka* (Hartland, Wisconsin), p. 287; *Minutes of General Council Proceedings*, 9 December 1935 (AFSCL); and Sister M. Gonzaga Raniszewski, *Zarys Półwiecza Zgromadzenia Sióstr Franciszkanek Bł. Kunegundy* [Sketch of the fifty-year history of the Congregation of the Franciscan Sisters of Bl. Kunegunda] (Chicago: By the Author, 1944), p. 51.

[29]Siostra M. Gonzaga Raniszewski, OSFK, *Rys historyczny Zgromadzenia Sióstr Franciszkanek Błogosławionej Kunegundy. Część pierwsza*, 1860–1910 [A historical survey of the Franciscan Sisters of Blessed Kunegunda. Part one, 1860–1910] (Chicago: By the Author, 1947), p. 34.

[30]Rev. Henry Malak, *The Forgotten Heart of Kinga* (London: Veritas Publishing Co., 1959), pp. 181–87.

[31]Dudzik, p. 6.

[32]Ibid.

[33]Ibid.

[34]At this meeting, Clara Szrambek asked that her name be withdrawn. She expressed a desire to join a congregation already firmly established.

[35]Dudzik, p. 7.

[36]Ps. 73:23–24.

CHAPTER 7

Foundation Days

The zealous Franciscan tertiaries who comprised the foundation group of aspiring religious were settled in Josephine's home by December 20, 1894. The last one to be welcomed was Constance Topolinski who arrived that day. Upon the advice of Father Barzynski, the group prepared for the election of its first religious superior on Sunday, December 23. Before casting their votes, the women prayed to the Holy Spirit and to the Mother of God.[1] The tertiaries had recognized in Josephine Dudzik a sensitivity to the needs of others as well as the ardent determination of a natural leader. Her unfailing gentleness and kind disposition had won the women's trust and loyalty, and Josephine was unanimously elected the superior. Since all the women were members of the Third Order of St. Francis, they resolved to call themselves by the names they had received as tertiaries. Josephine Dudzik was now called Sister Theresa, and the other tertiaries were known as Sister Anna (Rosalie Wysinski); Sister Hyacinth (Marianne Bezler); Sister Frances (Katherine Marzanek); Sister Felixa (Marianne Steltman); Sister Joachim (Victoria Milewski); and Sister Angeline (Constance Topolinski). Although Rosalie Wysinski was present that day to participate in the elections, she was still unable to join the tertiaries permanently because of her obligations to her family.[2] Living with the Sisters at this time were Mrs. Dudzik, the mother of Sister Theresa, and Mrs. Steltman, the widowed mother of Sister Felixa.[3]

On Monday, the Eve of Christmas, the Sisters prepared the traditional Christmas Eve supper and invited Father Barzynski to share the Christmas wafer with them.[4] He arrived, blessed their home, and expressed his delight and approval of the selection of Sister Theresa as the superior. Since the tertiaries did not as yet have a Rule or any Constitutions, Father Barzynski promised to draw up a "horarium" or daily program for them to follow. For the rest of the Christmas holidays, the atmosphere in the home on Chapin Street among the seven Franciscan tertiaries who now called each other "Sister" was one of peace and contentment. The Sisters were happy and no one happier, perhaps, than Sister Theresa who felt that she had at last succeeded in attaining her goal, and that only days of joy, tranquility, and fulfillment could follow.

Father Barzynski presented Sister Theresa with the long-awaited horarium on January 15, 1895. The Sisters attempted to follow faithfully this order of the day based on the Tertiary Rule of the Third Order of St. Francis. Daily rising was set for four-thirty o'clock in the morning. Morning prayers, in common, consisted of the Litany of the Holy Name of Jesus, the "Little Hours,"[5] and the prescribed Third Order prayers, namely, the Our Father, Hail Mary, and Glory Be recited twelve times. This was followed by Holy Mass at St. Stanislaus Kostka Church. The morning meditation, spiritual reading, the rosary, the daily examen, and evening prayers comprised the rest of the spiritual exercises which they performed in common. Silence, meant to attain communion with God and foster a spirit of tranquility, was maintained as much as possible. An alloted time for common recreation was also provided. The Reverend Simon Kobrzynski, CR,[6] the local superior of the Resurrectionist Fathers at St. Stanislaus Kostka Church, presented the Sisters with a book of meditations called *The Year of Christ*[7] which they used daily. During the evening meal, they listened to readings from *Spiritual Life*,[8] a gift from Father Barzynski.[9] As elected superior of the group, Sister Theresa was in charge of the household and assigned the Sisters to their daily duties. In keeping with their life in common, there was the immediate need to support themselves. Sister Theresa and Sister Angeline, both proficient seamstresses, sewed custom-made dresses in their convent home. At Father Barzynski's suggestion, Sister Felixa, Sister Frances, Sister Hyacinth, and Sister Joachim were assigned to domestic work at the large St. Stanislaus Kostka Rectory. Their household duties also included washing and ironing for eight priests and brothers in residence. Sometimes the rectory housed as many as twelve resident Resurrectionists, and scores of priests, newly arrived from Europe, often sought temporary lodging at the rectory. The many liturgical services and popular devotions at the church drew a large number of priests, and the Sisters were expected to handle all of their laundry needs.[10] For this labor, they received $40 a month; Sister Anna, who mended the church linens, was paid an additional $15 a month. After attending to their immediate necessities, the Sisters placed the remainder of their meagre earnings into a common fund set aside to build a home for the aged in the near future.[11]

After a short while, however, the initial spirit of sacrifice and self-denial of the group began to fade. They seemed to have forgotten the words of Lamartine: "To love for the sake of being loved is human, but to love for the sake of loving is angelic." When the women had resolved to live in common, they had agreed that all of their material possessions were to be placed into the general treasury. Sister Joachim, in particular, found it difficult to comply with this voluntary obligation. As a result, she kept all her possessions in a locked trunk which was contrary to the group's proposed spirit of trust and the sharing of all goods in common. It also indicated a visible lack of dependence on Divine Providence for all their present and future needs. In an effort to enforce the regulation relating to the possession of all goods in common, Sister Theresa sent a Sister, in her stead, to advise Sister Joachim either to surrender her possessions or to leave the small community if she found it difficult to conform to the regulations which she had willingly taken upon herself to obey. Sister Joachim's attitude and subsequent action fostered discontent and conflict within the group which eventually brought matters to a sad conclusion. Severely displeased by the rebuke which she had received only indirectly from Sister Theresa, Sister Joachim chose to leave the group on January 28.[12] Upon learning of Sister Joachim's departure, Father Barzynski reprimanded Sister Theresa for what he believed was imprudence and haste in dealing with a matter so directly related to her duty as superior. He denounced her inability to assert herself and warned that if her timidity proved to be a problem in the future, it would be better for the group to disband rather than cause him any further distress. Sister Theresa, who had promised Father Barzynski to keep the group together under any circumstances, was alarmed and saddened at this suggestion. She apologized to him for her lack of tact in dealing with Sister Joachim. Father Barzynski was pacified, and in turn, urged Sister Theresa to maintain the group with confidence, love, and fortitude even amid the most trying times.[13]

Sister Theresa's fervent hope for stability and harmony within the group was short-lived. Disruptive differences and antipathies continued to make themselves felt. In the early part of February, another source of discontent made itself visible. The three Sisters engaged in the arduous tasks at St. Stanislaus Kostka Rectory rebelled at what they felt was an unequal distribution of duties. They accused Sister Theresa and Sister Angeline of assuming the less demanding task of sewing within the comforts of the convent home, while they were assigned the more demanding physical labor at St. Stanislaus Kostka Rectory.[14] Sister Theresa, anxious to restore the household to peace, decided that the matter would best be settled by taking upon herself the laundry duties in order to set an example for the other Sisters. Her mother was distressed at Sister Theresa's decision and envisioned a premature death for her daughter since excessive physical labor had been expressly forbidden by Sister Theresa's physician.[15] However, fortified by her faith in Divine Providence and anxious to create harmony and love among the Sisters, Sister Theresa devoted herself to this difficult task for the next nine years. She readily admits in her "Chronicle":

> I often chose the hardest tasks. I say this not to praise myself, but to admit God's ready assistance . . . when it was necessary to sacrifice myself to bring about peace, I did not hesitate; I trusted in God and he came to my aid.[16]

After Sister Joachim's departure, Sister Hyacinth assumed the role of agitator in the small community. Now displeased with her newly assigned duties in the home, she complained incessantly. As a result, she, too, left the small community in April of 1895. Unable to secure peace of mind at home, however, Sister Hyacinth begged Sister Theresa for readmittance. While Sister Theresa hesitated to grant her this request, Father Barzynski gave permission for her return. Only two days after her return, however, Sister Hyacinth again showed signs of displeasure and resentment when she was given the lowest rank in the group. Formerly, she had ranked second only after Sister Theresa. Still, there was some cause for rejoicing when on April 4, 1895, Katherine Gill, called Sister Josepha as a tertiary, asked to join the community and was eagerly accepted.[17]

The joyous feast of Easter arrived. The small community shared the traditional Easter egg[18] with one another, but much of the delightful and hope-filled spirit which had surrounded the celebration of their first Christmas together seemed to be missing. Possessed of a cheerful disposition, Sister Theresa found it difficult to accustom herself to the sullen and moody temperaments of some of the Sisters. At this point, she wrote in her "Chronicle:"

> Although I hummed "Haec Dies" or "Regina Coeli"[19] from time to time since I loved to sing very much, there was no joy in my singing, at least not such a sense of jubilation as I had experienced while I was living alone with my mother. When something occurred to make me unhappy, I offered it to Jesus and simply hoped for the best.[20]

In the days ahead, Sister Theresa often had cause to recall her promise to Father Barzynski to care for the community in time of difficulty as well as in time of prosperity. She realized that in renouncing her own will for the love of God, she had opened herself to pain and adversity as well as to the animosity of others. She did not waver. Relentlessly, she sustained herself with the words of St. Paul: "Let us not be weary in well doing; for in due season we shall reap, if we faint not."[21]

FOUNDATION DAYS

[1]Matka Maria Teresa Dudzik, "Kronika Sióstr Franciszkanek pod opieką Św. Kunegundy w Chicago, Illinois" [The Chronicle of the Franciscan Sisters under the patronage of St. Kunegunda in Chicago, Illinois] Unpublished manuscript, 1910 (AFSCL), p. 7.

[2]Dudzik, p. 8.

[3]According to the "Chronicle," Mrs. Dudzik and Mrs. Steltman prepared breakfast which enabled the Sisters to worship at mass and fulfill their morning spiritual exercises. When Mrs. Dudzik was in good health, she also prepared some other meals. Dudzik, p. 11.

[4]The Christmas Eve supper, known as *wigilia,* the vigil, is a beautiful tradition among Poles. It begins with the appearance of the first star that night. Traditionally, the meatless menu contains an uneven number of courses usually including herring, a beet or mushroom soup, fish, cooked wheat, dumplings or noodles, sauerkraut, compote from dried fruit, and Christmas cakes. At the beginning of the meal, the head of the family breaks the blessed wafer and shares it with everyone present wishing each the joys of Christmas. The thin unleavened wafers, embossed with religious scenes from the Nativity are called *opłatki.* Those present then break the wafer with each other in a mutual exchange of love, joy, and forgiveness. In some households, the dinner is set for more people than are present as a reminder of those who are absent. Usually a layer of straw is spread on the table at which the meal is eaten in memory of the Christ Child's humble birth. A Polish proverb attaches still another meaning to the charming custom: "Hay in the hut and misery out of it"—an obvious reference to the belief that God's blessing will reign in the household that year. Ann Chrypinski, ed., *Polish Customs* (Detroit: Friends of Polish Art, 1972), p. 106.

[5]The "Little Hours," commonly referred to in Polish as *Godzinki,* is a devotion to the Blessed Virgin Mary arranged in imitation of the prayers in the Divine Office. The custom of saying the "Little Hours" of Our Lady's Office arose in the fourteenth or fifteenth century. They were translated into Polish by a Jesuit scripture scholar in the sixteenth century.

[6]The Reverend Simon Kobrzynski, CR, was born in the Lublin District of Poland in 1834. Ordained in Lublin in 1860, he entered the Congregation of the Resurrection in 1864, in Paris, where he fled after taking part in the Polish Insurrection of 1863 against the Russians. In the United States, he was stationed at St. Stanislaus Kostka Church from 1888 to 1896. He also served from March to September 1889 at Holy Trinity Church before the Congregation of the Resurrection was forced to relinquish it to the Congregation of the Holy Cross. He served as a general councilor in Rome for five years and was appointed novice master from 1896 to 1899. He died in Rome in 1905. While at the Lublin seminary, he was one year ahead of the illustrious Vincent Barzynski, the priest destined to play such an important role in the life of Josephine Dudzik. Edward T. Janas, CR, *Dictionary of American Resurrectionists, 1865–1965* (Rome: Gregorian University Press, 1967), p. 32.

[7]This book provided the group with their main source of daily meditation for the next thirteen years. Its title in Polish is *Rok Chrystusowy czyli Rozmyślania na każdy dzień roku o życie i nauce Pana Naszego Jezusa Chrystusa.* Published in 1867 in Berlin, it has no author given except *Xiądz* [Priest]. Father Edward T. Janas, CR, believes that it might have been authored by a member of his congregation, the Reverend Alexander Jełowicki, the appointed Missionary Apostolic for the Poles living in France. A sample of its spiritual content follows; it is a reflection for the Friday after the Fourth Sunday of Advent:

> I. Mary carried her son without pain and without difficulty. Love makes everything easier and sweeter. It appears difficult and hard to you to carry Christ's word and perform His teachings because you do not love enough.

> II. Take heed of the graces with which the Lord enriched Mary during the time He spent in her womb, when He, from the first moment of her existence, showered her with so many graces. O with what light He enlightened her soul!

With what fire He lit her soul! From where does your coldness and blindness come even though you so often receive Christ in your heart? From this, that you do not heed Him, you abandon Him, and you are soon dissipated and return to worldly ways.

III. The dignity of a mother flows to her children, but here the dignity of the Son elevates the Mother. Mary is the Queen of all because she is the Mother of the King of all. And your dignity results from your labors, not from veneration from people, but from your acts performed in the following of Christ.

[8]*Spiritual Life* [*Życie Duchowne*], the spiritual classic authored by Reverend Joseph Sebastian Pelczar, can be found in the archives of the congregation. Father Barzynski presented it as a gift to Josephine Dudzik, and she strove to adopt the spiritual guidelines contained therein. The book, containing 455 pages, embraces varied topics suitable to the religious life: the three roads to perfection, interior recollection, false pleasures of the world, the virtue of perseverance, the daily examination of conscience, etc. The Appendix contains instructions in regard to the vows for all persons who have dedicated their lives to God in the religious state.

The author, Joseph Sebastian Pelczar, was born on January 17, 1842, in Korczyna, Poland. He completed his theological training in the seminary of Przemyśl and was ordained to the priesthood in 1864. From 1870 to 1877, he taught pastoral theology and canon law in the seminary of Przemyśl. From 1877 to 1899, he was a canon of the Chapter in Cracow and professor at the Jagiellonian University. In 1894, he founded the Congregation of the Servants of the Sacred Heart. In 1899, he was named auxiliary bishop of Przemyśl and became bishop of the same diocese in 1900.

He died on March 28, 1924. A harmonious blending of prayer and apostolic works acquired through his interior life made him an ideal priest and bishop. He was a prolific author and an outstanding preacher. The reputation for holiness accorded him caused the Diocese of Przemyśl and the Congregation of the Servants of the Sacred Heart to introduce his cause for beatification in 1954. Sisters of the Sacred Heart, "Beatification Leaflet" (2311 Arch Street, Cresson, Pennsylvania).

Sister M. Sylvestra Pelczar, a member of the Franciscan Sisters of Chicago from 1905 until her death in 1956, was the niece of Bishop Pelczar. She was also the aunt of Sister M. Agnes Zywiec, presently a member of the congregation.

Another spiritual book preserved in the archives is *Progress in Perfection and Virtues* [*O Postępowaniu w Doskonałości i Cnotach*] *Book I* and *Book II,* written by the Reverend Alphonse Rodriguez, SJ. The book was translated from the original Spanish into Polish. A brief note by Mother M. Antonina Osinski written on the flyleaf of *Book II* states that the book was read aloud in the chapel to foster the Sisters' spiritual growth. Alphonse Rodriguez, SJ, *Progress in Perfection and Virtues,* 3 vols.; trans. Casimir Riedl, TJ (Kraków: X. Michael Mycielski, TJ, 1894).

[9]Dudzik, p. 9.

[10]*St. Stanislaus Kostka Centennial Book, 1867–1967* (Chicago: 1967), p. 36.

[11]Siostra M. Gonzaga Raniszewski, OSFK, *Rys historyczny Zgromadzenia Sióstr Franciszkanek Błogosławionej Kunegundy. Część pierwsza, 1860-1910* [A historical survey of the Franciscan Sisters of Blessed Kunegunda. Part one, 1860–1910] (Chicago: By the Author), p. 41.

[12]Raniszewski, p. 41.

[13]Ibid.

[14]Ibid., p. 11.

[15]Ibid., p. 12.

[16]Ibid.

[17]Sister Theresa speaks of Sister Josepha Gill in her "Chronicle" as a fine and industrious young woman, but one for whom life under religious obedience was not suitable. A reliable and responsible person, Sister Josepha was sorely missed by Sister Theresa when the former left the small community on August 14, 1898, after having spent three years and five months with the group. Dudzik, p. 11.

[18]For Poles, eggs are a major item among the foods blessed on Holy Saturday. After the long Lenten fast, the joyful Easter Sunday meal begins with a blessed egg, the symbol of life. The head of the family shares small pieces of the Easter egg with each member of the family wishing them a holy and happy feast and blessings for happiness and a long life.

[19]These are traditional and much-loved Latin Easter hymns.

[20]Dudzik, p. 13.

[21]Gal. 6:9.

CHAPTER 8

New Crises

While Sister Theresa was somewhat dismayed over the lack of harmony within the small community, she became extremely aware of the anxiety and concern which now engulfed Father Barzynski. A major controversy had developed among the parishioners at nearby St. Hedwig's Church which he had established in 1888.[1] The controversy had erupted into a factional dispute, and in February 1895, many of St. Hedwig's parishioners left the Roman Catholic Church and became members of the Independent Church of All Saints under the leadership of the rebellious priest, the Reverend Anthony Kozłowski.[2] The situation sapped Father Barzynski of his strength and necessitated his leaving Chicago for an undetermined period of time. He returned in April, not fully recuperated, and as a consequence, devoted less time and attention to the Sisters who truly felt the loss of his direction. To compound the existing problems, one of the tertiaries, Sister Frances, whose sister had joined the Independent Church, begged Sister Theresa to allow her to visit her sister more often in an effort to bring her back into the Roman Catholic Church.[3] Upon returning from the visits to her sister, however, Sister Frances, more often than not, praised the merits of the dissident Father Kozłowski. Consequently, heated disagreements arose among the Sisters forcing Sister Theresa to intervene. In an effort to discourage Sister Frances' disobedient and offensive behavior, Sister Theresa suggested that she seek the counsel of Father Barzynski.[4] In anger and retaliation, Sister Frances withdrew from the group at the end of June 1895, and urged the other Sisters to follow her lead. In her intense devotion to the Independent Church, Sister Frances was instrumental in assembling the nucleus of a Sisterhood there.[5]

Poles belonging to the Independent All Saints Church were often ignorant of the fact that the Independent Church was in conflict with the Roman Catholic Church, or else they did not understand the significance of the conflict being waged by their spiritual leaders. Two women, Anna Schreiber and Martha Barczewski,[6] had been members of the Independent Church before their entrance into the small band of Franciscan tertiaries. The story of Sister M. Magdalen (the former Anna Schreiber) is especially interesting. She was born in Chicago in 1882. When she was thirteen years old, her mother died, and she was sheltered by a family who belonged to the Independent Church. At sixteen, she entered the community of Sisters founded at Independent All Saints Church by Katherine Marzanek (the former Sister Frances) and remained with it for three years. Due to the efforts of the Reverend Andrew Spetz, CR, and Sister Theresa, Anna Schreiber left the Independent Church and entered the community of Franciscan tertiaries on July 7, 1901, where she was received warmly by Sister Theresa. After a trial period of four months, she asked to be accepted as a member. Sister M. Magdalen's entire life in the congregation was spent at the Motherhouse. She died on October 7, 1968, a faithful member of the congregation.[7]

Back in the little community, Sister Felixa, goaded by her mother's open displeasure with the small band of tertiaries, also left them in June 1895.[8] Before her departure, however, she succeeded in inducing Sister Hyacinth to leave with her. Both women claimed that the community was doomed to fail, and that they were exercising good judgment in leaving. Father Barzynski's frequent illnesses, they reasoned, would soon lead to his death, and the Sisters, lacking a competent spiritual leader and guide, would abandon the whole idea of a new community.[9]

By July of that year, only Sister Theresa, Sister Angeline, Sister Josepha, and Sister Anna remained of the group, although Sister Anna continued to live at home with her parents. While Sister Theresa was visibly distressed at the departure of the four women, still she realized that "our outlooks on religious life differed greatly."[10] In addition, she was painfully aware that the new form of life they were attempting to lead offered little or no attraction. To join the tertiaries in living a common life of prayer and service to the poor and unfortunate meant to rise very early and to work late into the night; it meant to conform to a horarium in which every waking hour was dictated by regulation or by need; it meant to submit to a religious superior and be guided by her commands; it meant to experience painful frugality and the lack of even the necessities of life; it meant mortification and constant denial of self. The tertiaries were, for the most part, not readily adaptable, since it must be remembered that they were older women who had exercised some degree of freedom, choice, and financial independence before joining Sister Theresa in her project. It is well to recall at this point that Sister Theresa herself was thirty-five years old. Sister Anna was forty-five years old and Sister Angeline was thirty-nine. It is a fair assumption that these were the proximate ages of the other tertiaries. Perhaps some members of the group were not prepared for life in a convent and felt the common life and work a burden. Sister Theresa, aware of the spirit of sacrifice, fortitude, and good will the tertiaries who left had originally shown, sincerely regretted their leave-taking. Aware of St. Paul's admonition to the faithful Ephesians: "Do not give in to discouragement . . . surpassing power comes from God," Sister Theresa resolved, now more than ever, to make the little community succeed.[11] She urged the remaining Sisters to rededicate themselves to the service of God in the person of his sick, aged, and poor.

The Sisters started along practical lines. Because of the loss of the tertiaries, a decision was made to have Sister Theresa, Sister Angeline, Sister Josepha, and Mrs. Dudzik move to a smaller apartment on the second floor of the Chapin Street house. To spare the Sisters the backbreaking toil of doing the laundry at St. Stanislaus Kostka Rectory by hand, Father Barzynski succeeded in making arrangements for the Sisters to use the washing machines at the Holy Family Orphanage conducted by the School Sisters of Notre Dame on Division Street.[12] Because Sister Theresa and Sister Josepha could not have access to the washing machines until Thursday of the week, they were forced to work most hurriedly that day since Friday and Saturday had to be spent in ironing and distributing the laundry. In the meantime, Sister Theresa and Sister Josepha also continued their housekeeping chores at St. Stanislaus Kostka Rectory. Before long, Sister Josepha's health was affected and she was hospitalized in the early part of October.[13] While Sister Josepha recuperated, Sister Theresa was forced to assume all the duties they had previously shared until she hired a lay woman to assist her. In the meantime, Sister Angeline continued to sew custom-made dresses at the convent home while Sister Theresa's mother helped by preparing their meals. Sister Theresa summed up this painful period of adjustment after the departure of the tertiaries by stating in her "Chronicle" with characteristic simplicity: "We continued to attain the goals for which we had banded together."[14]

An additional disadvantage the women suffered at this time was Father Barzynski's prolonged bouts with lung problems which often compelled him to leave Chicago for warmer climates for long periods of time. His presence and advice were sorely missed by the Sisters, especially by Sister Theresa, who felt deprived of the human consolation and encouragement she would have received from him. Once again, her "Chronicle" reveals her feelings and her resolution:

> In spite of any adversity, I maintained my happy disposition since I saw
> the Will of God in all life's events. I remembered the promise I had made
> freely to Father Barzynski to preserve the community. I resolved not to
> lose heart in adversity, but to labor all the more energetically for the
> survival of the community.[15]

A year later, Sister Theresa felt that the appropriate time had come to do what had been uppermost in her mind for the last few years. It was necessary to purchase some lots and build a permanent home for the aged and crippled. Father Barzynski had suggested that Sister Theresa and Sister Anna search for suitable land in the district of Avondale near the site of St. Hyacinth's Church which he was in the process of constructing.[16] Although transportation was poor and the streets were muddy and unpaved, Father Barzynski was aware that lots in Avondale were readily available at low costs. There was good reason to be optimistic about Avondale's future.

After a long and fruitless search for an appropriate site, Sister Theresa and Sister Anna sought the advice of a good and trustworthy friend, Ignatius Palubicki, a professional bricklayer who had emigrated from Sister Anna's village of Bruss in Poland.[17] He helped them determine the type of building they required, and he was also instrumental in securing an architect, Mr. Wilkowski, to whom the Sisters paid $229 for his services.[18]

On October 15, 1895, Sister Theresa and Sister Anna purchased a tract of land consisting of twelve lots at Hamlin and Schubert Avenues for $5,000. They made a down payment of $1,000 from savings which Sister Theresa had accumulated and kept in the house treasury. After Peter Kiołbassa examined the agreement-of-sale papers and acknowledged them sound, the land was recorded as sold to Josephine Dudzik and Rosalie Wysinski on November 1, 1895. At that time, an additional payment of $900 was made leaving the remaining $4,000 as a debt to be paid at the earliest possible opportunity.[19] The purchase of the land seemed to revitalize both Sister Theresa and Sister Anna since now they had to redouble their efforts to meet the demands of the payments. The burden of the transaction lay chiefly upon the shoulders of Sister Theresa since Sister Anna was still obligated to provide for her father, her mother who was bedridden, as well as for her handicapped sister Matilda.[20]

Sister Theresa was beset with other difficulties as well. Both her brother Joseph Dudzik and her sister Rosalie Frank had earlier requested loans from her in order to purchase some property. They had both assured Sister Theresa that the money would be repaid when she would be in need of it. Unfortunately, neither her brother nor her sister was in a position to repay the money when Sister Theresa requested its return in order to pay for the purchased land. When she sought the advice of Father Barzynski in regard to the purchase of the land and the matter of handling the unpaid debt, she discovered that he had left for Texas because of his recurring ill health. Once again it appeared that the Sisters were "left as orphans without a father."[21] During Father Barzynski's absence, Sister Theresa sought the advice and encouragement of Father Simon Kobrzynski, the local superior of the Resurrectionist Fathers at St. Stanislaus Kostka Church. Father Kobrzynski was also ill at this time and, unfortunately, his condition ushered in still another problem. When Sister Theresa visited the rectory to obtain the customary $40 payment for laundry services, the priest in charge during Father Kobrzynski's illness met her with some degree of unpleasantness.[22] Speaking bluntly to Sister Theresa, he claimed that the Sisters were overpaid for this manual labor, and, thereafter, the payments would be reduced to $25 a month. Sister Theresa was hurt and dismayed by the priest's attitude and decision since the laundry payment was one of the chief means of livelihood for the small community. The money was also needed to help pay for Sister Josepha's hospitalization. Even the $15 which Sister Anna had been receiving for mending church linens was to be withheld from now on. Finally, the unrelenting priest declared his intention to secure lay women in the parish to attend to the laundry chores. Sister Theresa wrote in her "Chronicle" concerning these unhappy events:

> When I was notified that my services were no longer needed, I cried in
> secret, unnoticed by anyone except the Lord Jesus. I could not refrain
> from shedding tears, thinking that I took upon myself the responsibility
> of caring for the new community and maintaining it by the labor of my
> own hands. And here, even the source of our income had been taken

away. Even though Father knew the purpose of our organization and the cause for which we had been saving our earnings, that is, for a home for the aged and crippled, he ignored us in permitting the other women to take the work from us. I considered his act unchristian and felt angry toward him.[23]

When Father Kobrzynski returned to good health, Sister Theresa informed him of the unfortunate incident which had occurred. Father Kobrzynski insisted on keeping the services of the Sisters, but stated that their salary would be lowered to $35 dollars a month.[24] After reflecting upon the entire matter, Sister Theresa inserted this optimistic line into her "Chronicle" shortly after that unsettling incident: "Life, however, has a way of going on amid the sorrows and the joys that befall us."[25] In spite of the problems which had produced so much pain and uneasiness concerning the Sisters' salary, the news of Father Barzynski's return from Texas caused her much joy.

At their first meeting upon his return, Father Barzynski advised Sister Theresa to organize a Home Planning Committee to assist the Sisters in their proposal to build a permanent home for the aged and the crippled. One of the first persons to accept the invitation to join the committee was Klemens J. Beliński,[26] the president of the Polish Roman Catholic Union. Other members included the Reverend John Radziejewski,[27] the pastor of St. Adalbert's Church on the Southwest Side of Chicago,[28] and Mr. Polenz, a member of St. Adalbert's Church. He was later intrumental in organizing a society in the parish under the patronage of St. Joseph to provide financial assistance to the new Sisterhood. Among the committee members from St. Stanislaus Kostka Church were Father Barzynski, Peter Kiołbassa, John Maca, W. Jendrzejek, and John Gniot, who was chosen the treasurer of the Home Planning Committee. While the Reverend John Piechowski, pastor of St. Hedwig's Church, and Mr. Kielczynski of St. John Cantius Church[29] had also joined, they never became active members of the group.[30]

Prior to the first meeting of the Home Planning Committee, Father Barzynski had instructed Sister Theresa and the Sisters to begin a collection in all the Polish parishes at the end of July to help meet their financial obligations. Sister Theresa was personally repulsed at the suggestion of "begging" since she looked upon it as a disagreeable and humiliating practice. It had never occurred to her that this mode of action might be necessary when she began her charitable venture since she had firmly resolved to maintain the community by the labor of her hands.[31] Sister Theresa resolutely determined to overcome her repugnance for the task since the custom of begging alms for the love of God was never alien to the spirit of Franciscans.[32] Fortunately for Sister Theresa, another Franciscan tertiary, Pauline Dzik, called Sister Agnes, had requested permission to join the community in July.[33] She offered much encouragement to Sister Theresa by showing no disdain at the prospect of begging. Father Barzynski made an initial contribution of $15 and offered words of encouragement to the Sisters together with his blessing. With the exception of the pastors of St. John Cantius and St. Adalbert Parishes, the pastors of many of the other Polish churches in Chicago frowned upon the Sisters' request to collect alms in their churches.[34] Although the Sisters wore no distinctive religious garb as yet, their plain attire was totally in keeping with the nature of their mission.[35] Sister Theresa was surprised and hurt, however, at the reception she received in her home parish of St. Stanislaus Kostka. While some parishioners responded generously, others were darkly suspicious of her motives for collecting alms. She records this in her "Chronicle":

> Although many parishioners knew me through sixteen years of active participation in parish activities, they were now inclined to think that I did not care to work and was, therefore, innovating some new and mysterious project as an excuse to beg for my own welfare.[36]

If Sister Theresa was shocked and confused by the display of hostility on the part of many parishioners of St. Stanislaus Kostka Parish, it would not be long before she would be forced to endure hostility and humiliation almost beyond endurance.

NEW CRISES

[1]St. Hedwig's Church at the corner of Webster and Hoyne was founded in 1888 to aid the steady stream of Polish immigrants who settled in the vicinity of St. Stanislaus Kostka Church. The Reverend Joseph Barzynski, a diocesan priest and brother of the Reverend Vincent Barzynski, CR, was the first pastor of St. Hedwig's. He labored with great zeal for the good of the parish, and as it grew, he found the need for an assistant priest. In May 1894, Father Vincent Barzynski obtained for his brother the services of a young, personable, and energetic secular priest, the Reverend Anthony Kozłowski, who had recently emigrated from Europe. Within a few months, Father Kozłowski's desire to secure Father Barzynski's position as pastor became obvious. Various parish leaders began to level criticism at Father Joseph Barzynski's management of the parish and allied themselves with the rebellious Father Kozłowski. The dissidents welcomed Father Kozłowski's stand on favoring the trustee system of church ownership in regard to parochial administration. Another reason for the power struggle occurring at St. Hedwig's Parish was Father Kozłowski's hope, as well as that of the dissidents, that St. Hedwig's would follow the example of Holy Trinity Parish and remove the Resurrectionist Fathers from administration of the parish. Father Kozłowski was dismissed from St. Hedwig's Church for his rebellious stand, and a wave of separation from the parish by his faithful followers took place. Great havoc was created among the good, simple people of the parish, who, through either ignorance or misguided loyalty to Father Kozłowski broke away from St. Hedwig's Parish and formed the Independent Church of All Saints in a rented store at Lubeck and Hoyne Avenues. The disruptive spirit and ecclesiastical insubordination fostered by the dissenters exploded into violence and near bloodshed forcing Archbishop Feehan to close St. Hedwig's Church a number of times and forcing Father Joseph Barzynski to resign his pastorate. Father Kozłowski was eventually excommunicated from the Roman Catholic Church by Archbishop Feehan and formed an Independent Church with his followers. The Reverend John Piechowski, CR, succeeded Father Barzynski as pastor of St. Hedwig's and with zealous perseverance, prevailed in restoring peace to the divided parish. He was eager not only to promote the spiritual welfare of his parishioners, but also to build a badly needed church which remains to this day one of the more beautiful churches in Chicago. St. Hedwig's Parish is still a thriving, vibrant parish, but it has felt the pangs of urban progress with the erection of the Kennedy Expressway which cut through the parish resulting in a substantial decrease in enrollment.

In all justice to Father Kozłowski and his followers, however, part of the blame for the volatile situation which developed at the parish can be attributed to the unrest among the immigrant Poles due to the serious economic problems which gripped the city of Chicago and the country as a whole at that time in history. John I. Iwicki, CR, *The First One Hundred Years: A Study of the Apostolates of the Congregation of the Resurrection in the United States, 1866–1966* (Rome: Gregorian University Press, 1966), pp. 79–95; and *St. Hedwig Church: Diamond Jubilee, 1888–1963* (Chicago: 1963), p. 23.

[2]The Reverend Anthony Kozłowski was ordained in 1885 in Taranto, Italy. In 1894, he came to the United States and served as assistant pastor at St. Hedwig's Church for one year at the invitation of Father Vincent Barzynski. The violent conflict at the parish which his presence created led to his dismissal and his subsequent organization of the Polish "Independent" Church of All Saints at Lubeck and Hoyne Avenues (now at 2019 W. Charleston). In 1895, Father Kozłowski was excommunicated by Archbishop Feehan, and all those who remained with him were in schism.

On November 13, 1897, Father Kozłowski was consecrated bishop of the Old Catholic Church in Berne, Switzerland, by Bishop E. Herzog. Before his death in 1907, Father Kozłowski had succeeded in organizing twenty-three parishes in the United States and south central Canada which were known as the Polish Old Catholic Church. In 1907, All Saints Cathedral Polish Old Catholic Church voted to join the Polish National Catholic Church, thus becoming the first of Chicago's Polish National Catholic parishes. The Polish National Church had its origin in 1897 when the Reverend Francis Hodur formed it as a single independent congregation in Scranton, Pennsylvania. According to John Tracy Ellis in *American Catholicism* (Chicago: University of Chicago Press,

1956), p. 127, the Polish National Church is the only significant American schism of the Roman Catholic Church. Iwicki, pp. 80–95; and Reverend Joseph Swastek, *The Polish American Story* (Buffalo: Felician Sisters, 1953), pp. 1–19.

[3]Matka Maria Teresa Dudzik, "Kronika Sióstr Franciszkanek pod opieką Św. Kunegundy w Chicago, Illinois" [The Chronicle of the Franciscan Sisters under the patronage of St. Kunegunda in Chicago, Illinois] Unpublished manuscript, 1910 (AFSCL), p. 14.

[4]According to Sister Theresa, Sister Frances' belligerent attitude was accompanied by her claims of having been favored with "visions" and "revelations" of a divine nature. Dudzik, p. 15.

[5]Theodore L. Zawistowski writes: "There had even been active nuns in the Polish National Catholic Church, converts from the Roman Catholic Church, but they were not allowed to recruit novices and eventually died out." An attempt by the author to secure more information on the subject from All Saints Cathedral, the headquarters of the Polish National Church in Chicago, proved futile. Dudzik p. 15; and Theodore L. Zawistowski, "The Polish National Catholic Church: An Acceptable Alternative," in *Poles in America,* ed. Frank Mocha (Stevens Point, Wisconsin: Worzalla Publishing Co., 1978), pp. 423–434.

[6]Sister M. Hyacinth, the former Martha Barczewski, was born in 1885 in Chicago. She entered the community on October 3, 1902. In the community, Sister M. Hyacinth was a teacher, but she served also as a principal and superior at various schools for a period of ten years. She also rendered service at Our Lady of Spring Bank Abbey in Oconomowoc, Wisconsin. In 1942, she was assigned to Boys Town where she performed various duties and remained for eighteen years. Sister M. Hyacinth retired to the Motherhouse in Lemont in 1965 and died there on November 5, 1972. She was eighty-seven years old and had been in the congregation for seventy years. *Spis Sióstr* (AFSCL).

[7]*Book of Correspondence:* Letter from Sister M. Martha Bywalec to author, 6 November 1975 (AFSCL); *Book of Depositions:* Sister M. Magdalen Schreiber (AFSCL); and *Spis Sióstr* (AFSCL).

[8]Dudzik, p. 15.

[9]Ibid.

[10]Ibid., p. 16.

[11]Eph. 3:12–19.

[12]This orphanage was to play an important role in the lives of the Franciscan tertiaries and is discussed more fully in Chapter 12.

[13]In her "Chronicle," Sister Theresa Dudzik states that Sister Josepha was placed in a "Polish" hospital. The *Official Catholic Directory* for 1899 lists St. Mary of Nazareth as the city's first Polish hospital. Operated by the Congregation of the Sisters of the Holy Family of Nazareth since 1894, the hospital, directed by Sister M. Sophie, CSFN, was a three-story, twenty-four–bed facility at 258 W. Division Street. Today, an ultramodern St. Mary of Nazareth Hospital ministers to the needs of Chicago's inner-city residents in a new location at 2233 W. Division Street.

[14]Dudzik, p. 17.

[15]Ibid., p. 18.

[16]The first and oldest parish in the area called Avondale was that of St. Hyacinth. Originally a district that was unfavorably located, Avondale was soon settled by immigrant Poles who could no longer be accommodated at St. Stanislaus Kostka Parish. By 1894, there were about forty families who had settled in the area and urged Father Barzynski to establish a parish. Because of the economic depression which engulfed Chicago at the time, Father Barzynski urged the parishioners to wait until it would be economically feasible to build a church and a school. In the meantime, however, the threat of the establishment of the Polish Old Catholic Church in Avondale prompted him to acquire property on Wolfram Street, the site on which the "Independent" Church planned to build.

At first, a two-story wooden combination church and school was built on Central Park and Milwaukee Avenues. The Reverend John Piechowski, CR, was appointed its first pastor. When he was reassigned to St. Hedwig's Church to stem the growing separation of the "Independent" faction, he was succeeded by the Reverend John Gieburowski, CR.

In 1899, St. Hyacinth's Parish was relocated on Wolfram Street since the Milwaukee Avenue area had proven unsuitable because of the noisy and constant traffic. With the continued growth of the parish, a permanent church and school combination was constructed in 1906. It was a most adequate structure with large classrooms and an ample church. From this church, Mother M. Anna Wysinski, the first superior general of the Franciscan Sisters of Chicago, was buried on February 1, 1917, amid a large group of mourners.

In 1917, with approximately 2,100 families residing in the parish, the present large Renaissance-style church on George Street was constructed. It was blessed in 1921 by the Most Reverend George Mundelein, archbishop of Chicago, after years of considerable labor and financial reversals. Today, St. Hyacinth's is the largest Polish parish in the Archdiocese of Chicago. For the last several years, Madonna High School, owned and operated by the Franciscan Sisters of Chicago, has held its annual commencement exercises at St. Hyacinth's historic church. *St. Hyacinth Church: Golden Jubilee, 1894–1944* (Chicago: 1944), pp. 16–48.

[17]According to the records of St. Joseph Home for the Aged, Ignatius Palubicki was born in 1862 in Bruss, Poland. In Chicago, he was a member of St. Stanislaus Kostka Church. Admitted to St. Joseph Home for the Aged on February 21, 1937, he died there on May 24 of the same year. He was buried from St. Stanislaus Kostka Church and laid to rest in St. Adalbert's Cemetery. His son, the Reverend John Palubicki, was the first altar boy at St. Joseph Home for the Aged and Crippled, and served at the blessing of its cornerstone. Born in Bruss, Poland, in 1886, he attended St. Stanislaus Kostka School upon his arrival in America. In 1909, he was ordained for the Archdiocese of Omaha by Archbishop John Ireland. After a varied and colorful apostolate, which included serving as resident missionary on the Santee and Ponca Indian Reservations, he was appointed pastor of Blessed Sacrament Church in Omaha in 1936. He served there until his death in 1956. *Book of Correspondence:* Letter from James R. Cain, chancellor, Archdiocese of Omaha, 3 September 1975; Raniszewski, *Rys,* Part two, p. 51.

[18]Dudzik, p. 19; and "Rachunki: Domu Św. Józefa dla Polskich Starców i Kalek w Avondale, Illinois, 1894—" (AFSCL).

[19]Dudzik, p. 19.

[20]Ibid.

[21]Ibid., p. 20.

[22]Sister Theresa does not mention the name of the priest involved in the incident in her "Chronicle." Any attempt to identify him at this point would be mere conjecture.

[23]Dudzik, p. 21.

[24]Ibid.

[25]Ibid., p. 22.

[26]Klemens J. Beliński, a noted civic leader, was president of the Polish Roman Catholic Union of America from 1886 to 1887, and again from 1895 to 1897. He was elected from Chicago to the state legislature in 1939. In her "Chronicle," Sister Theresa states: "We owe him [Beliński] a debt of gratitude because he was the one, who, after Father Barzynski, did the most towards having our new home built." Francis Bolek, ed., *Who's Who in America: A Biographical Directory of Polish American Leaders and Distinguished Poles Resident in the Americas,* 3rd. ed. (New York: Harbinger House, 1943; Arno Publishers, 1970), p. 34; *Book of Correspondence:* Report from Edward G. Dykla, secretary general, PRCUA, to author (AFSCL); and Dudzik, p. 22.

[27]The Reverend John Radziejewski was a diocesan priest associated with the apostolate of the Congregation of the Resurrection. Born in Poland in 1844, he was ordained in Rome in 1869 and served as a pastor in a parish in Poznań for four years. As a consequence of the repressive "May Laws" enacted by Bismarck, he fled to Paris and was an assistant at a parish when the Reverend

Vincent Barzynski informed him of the need for Polish-speaking priests in America. He came to Chicago in 1881 and served as an assistant at St. Stanislaus Kostka Church. On the recommendation of Father Barzynski, he was made the pastor of Immaculate Conception Church in South Chicago in 1882. In 1884, he was appointed pastor of St. Adalbert's Church in Chicago in which capacity he remained until his death in 1904. *Immaculate Conception BVM Diamond Jubilee, 1882–1957* (Chicago: 1957), p. 80; and Iwicki, p. 73.

[28]In 1864, the Congregation of the Resurrection assisted in founding St. Adalbert's Church on the Southwest Side of Chicago at 17th Street and Paulina Avenue. The Reverend H. Klimecki, an assistant at St. Stanislaus Kostka Church, was appointed St. Adalbert's first pastor on the recommendation of the Reverend Simon Wieczorek, CR, pastor of St. Stanislaus Kostka Church. The third and most outstanding pastor of this progressive parish was the Reverend John Radziejewski, a diocesan priest, who was appointed with the support of Father Barzynski.

St. Adalbert's Church has played a distinguished role in the history of the Archdiocese of Chicago. Since its foundation, it has been the center of cultural and civic activity on Chicago's Southwest Side. The first American of Polish descent to become a bishop in the United States, the Most Reverend Paul Peter Rhode, and the Right Reverend Monsignor James J. Strzycki, pastor of Five Holy Martyrs for thirty-five years, were members of St. Adalbert's parish.

By 1920, there were over three thousand families with 2,614 children in school under the direction of the Congregation of the Sisters of the Holy Family of Nazareth and fifty-seven societies attending to the social, benevolent, and cultural needs of the Polish community. The difficulties the parish is facing in the present day are a reflection of the emerging demographic and social changes being experienced by many ethnic parishes in the city. *St. Adalbert: A Tribute to 100 Years of Service, 1874–1974* (Chicago: 1974), no pagination; Iwicki, pp. 72–73; and Reverend Joseph Thompson, ed., *Diamond Jubilee of the Archdiocese of Chicago, 1920* (Des Plaines, Illinois: St. Mary's Training School Press, 1920), pp. 433–435.

[29]With the continued influx of Polish immigrants, there arose the need for yet another division of St. Stanislaus Kostka Parish. The Reverend Vincent Barzynski established St. John Cantius Church in an area that soon acquired the name, "Polish Patch," located about one and one-eighth miles from Chicago's Main Post Office. Father Barzynski entrusted the organization and building of the church and parish to the Reverend John Kasprzycki, CR, the first pastor. Although the initial construction of the church began in 1893, severe economic depression delayed its completion until 1898. When it was completed, there emerged an inspiring Renaissance-Baroque structure with a capacity for holding two thousand people.

The booming parish school was staffed by the School Sisters of Notre Dame. In 1918, the school numbered 2,300 pupils; in 1943, it had 376.

By the early 1950s, however, time and change had visited this vibrant and enthusiastic parish. The construction of the Kennedy Expressway, which demolished thousands of homes and forced the people to move from the area, as well as the changing ethnic population saw the decline of the once solid Polish region. Today, the parish of St. John Cantius consists of several hundred families, and the former parish schoolhouses the headquarters for the Montessori Midwest Teacher Training Center. The former convent is now the official headquarters of the Archdiocesan Confraternity of Christian Doctrine. *St. John Cantius Church 1893–1968* (Chicago: 1968), pp. 40–49.

St. John Cantius Parish has had fifty-eight young women enter the Congregation of the Franciscan Sisters of Chicago including Mother M. Antonina Osinski, the fourth superior general of the congregation, and Mother M. Jerome Dadej, the sixth superior general.

[30]Dudzik, p. 25.

[31]Ibid., p. 21.

[32]A feature which is characteristic of the Franciscan Order is the custom called mendicancy, that is, the begging of alms for the love of God. The Franciscan Order was called a mendicant order which means that the members were essentially supported by free will offerings and

the income they received for rendering spiritual services. In the First Rule of St. Francis, chapter seven, he writes: "When there is need for it, let them go out for alms." The Second Rule, chapter six, says: "Nor should they be ashamed of it, for our Lord made himself poor in this world for our sake."

There are many religious orders which are not mendicant. Among them is the Congregation of the School Sisters of Notre Dame. The fact that they could not solicit alms had a great influence on the small band of Franciscan tertiaries. See Chapter 12.

[33]Apolonia (Pauline) Dzik was born on June 2, 1866, in Straszewo, Poland. She joined the small community of Franciscan tertiaries on July 9, 1896, from St. Stanislaus Kostka Parish. Previously, she had been a postulant in the Congregation of the Sisters of the Holy Family of Nazareth. The *Sisters' Registry, 1909–1919* reveals that she joined the Franciscan Sisters of Joliet, Illinois, after leaving the Sisters of the Holy Family of Nazareth. She is not, however, recorded in the annals of the Franciscan Sisters of Joliet. Later, Pauline Dzik would prove wholly unsuited to religious life with the Franciscan tertiaries and be dismissed. *Book of Correspondence:* Letter from Sister Rose Marie Machalski, CSSN, quoting from the *Sisters Registry, 1909–1919,* p. 4 to author (AFSCL); Letter from Sister Marian Voelker, OSF, archivist, Sisters of St. Francis, Joliet to author, 9 March 1977 (AFSCL); and Dudzik, p. 23.

[34]Siostra M. Gonzaga Raniszewski, OSFK, *Rys historyczny Zgromadzenia Sióstr Franciszkanek Błogosławionej Kunegundy. Część pierwsza, 1860–1910* [A historical survey of the Franciscan Sisters of Blessed Kunegunda. Part one, 1860–1910] (Chicago: By the Author, 1947), p. 52.

[35]In her deposition, Sister M. Cyprian Lewandowski states that her mother informed her that the Sisters wore lay clothes which were basically alike. In the winter, when they went outdoors, the Sisters wore black hats and long black shawls crossed over their shoulders. Sister M. Hyacinth Barczewski substantiates this. *Book of Depositions:* Sister M. Cyprian Lewandowski and Sister M. Hyacinth Barczewski (AFSCL).

[36]Dudzik, p. 23.

CHAPTER 9

Triumph of Spirit

At the end of September 1895, the Home Planning Committee met at St. Stanislaus Kostka Rectory. Both Sister Theresa and Sister Anna were able to attend the meeting. The initial topic covered was the use of the money which the Sisters had collected. They had received $450 in parish donations, and Matilda Wysinski, Sister Anna's sister, had loaned the Sisters $400. A woman whom the Sisters had sheltered, Mrs. Elizabeth Karnowski, brought her savings of $150 and thus a total of $1,000 was realized. Sister Theresa suggested that this money be used to lower the debt on the recently acquired lots, and the Home Planning Committee approved.[1] The next topic centered on building a permanent home for the aged and crippled. Sister Theresa had accepted three new dependents[2] into their home on Chapin Street, and the Sisters, therefore, desperately needed larger quarters.[3] The Home Planning Committee suggested that instead of building a new structure, an old house could be purchased and moved to the newly acquired lots. Sister Theresa opposed such a purchase as being too costly and only a temporary solution to a persistent need. If the Sisters were not allowed to build a new home for the aged and crippled at this time, Sister Theresa suggested that they be allowed to seek larger accommodations for their dependents. When Sister Anna supported Sister Theresa's opinion, Father Barzynski became impatient and chided both Sisters saying that they "dream of building a mansion or a palace when they should, instead, be occupied with the lowly tasks required of them when ministering to the sick and the aged."[4] Rebuked, the Sisters refrained from expressing any further opinions. The Home Planning Committee, however, agreed with Sister Theresa and Sister Anna on the more prudent plan of seeking larger temporary quarters to enable the Sisters to accept more of the aged and crippled who continually sought shelter.[5]

On the very next day after the meeting, Sister Theresa and Sister Anna began their search for larger quarters to house the four tertiaries, Sister Theresa's mother, and the three women they sheltered. The Sisters were fortunate in being directed to the owners of an apartment house still under construction. The large, brick, three-story, multifamily building at 1368 Ingraham Street seemed perfect for their needs.[6] Sister Theresa arranged to rent three apartments at $22.50 a month. At the beginning of November 1896, the Sisters and their dependents moved in. Sister Theresa, her mother, and three aged women had sleeping quarters in the rear of the first floor where the kitchen was also located. Sister Angeline, Sister Josepha, and Sister Agnes occupied sleeping quarters on the second floor in the rear where the oratory and a workroom were arranged. The other apartments were occupied by the owners of the building as well as by a private renter.[7]

The second house (extreme right) of the newly founded community at 1368 Ingraham Street (presently Evergreen Street) opposite St. Stanislaus Kostka Church. The Sisters and aged residents occupied apartments on the first and second floors. Built in 1896, the house is still standing. The first house is the residence of Congressman Daniel Rostenkowski.

The Sisters continued to observe the horarium which had served them well in the house on Chapin Street. Now, however, they could attend mass at St. Stanislaus Kostka Church daily, and it was very convenient for them to be closer to the rectory where they continued to work. On Sundays, the Sisters attended High Mass.[8] Because of the large number of worshippers, the Sisters had a special pew reserved in what was called the "lower" church.[9] After mass, they read the *Advanced Catechism,*[10] and on Sunday afternoons, they were able to attend Vespers at the church.[11]

Hardships and sufferings were not strangers in the convent home on Ingraham Street. There were now eight virtually penniless women and a young boy without legs whom Sister Theresa had accepted early in January of 1897.[12] The members of the Home Planning Committee who had encouraged Sister Theresa and Sister Anna to seek larger quarters to accommodate the growing number of aged and crippled, and who so frequently sent the unfortunate to the Sisters to be sheltered, now failed to render any assistance.[13] Sister Angeline continued to sew at the convent home while Sister Theresa did the laundry and domestic work at the rectory. Any income the women received was used as partial payment on the lots and also for the purchase of beds, linens, and other essential items for their home and dependents. In addition, the Sisters needed money for the immediate needs of food and clothing as well as for rent and fuel. Since all the dependents were without any means of support, the costs of maintenance mounted rapidly. Prompted by Sister Theresa, the Sisters turned with ever-increasing confidence to the mercy of God and begged for help. They also sought the intercession of St. Joseph, whom Sister Theresa had selected as the patron of their house ministry as, indeed, had her patroness, the great St. Teresa of Avila.[14] Sister Theresa confidently called St. Joseph the *gospodarz*,[15] the real "master" of their home and of their material goods. She had resolved also to name the proposed new institution St. Joseph Home for the Aged and Crippled. Her faith in St. Joseph was unfailing as the following incident reveals:

> One day I had only a penny in the treasury when a Sister approached me and asked me for a new dress. The one she was wearing was completely threadbare. Undeniably, she needed a new dress. I explained the situation to her and promised to buy some material for dresses for all of us as soon as I would be able to do so. Not only was she dissatisfied with my explanation, but she was annoyed by it to such a degree that she poured out all the grievances she held against me in words full of anger. I was afraid that the good God might be offended by these words. When the Sister left me, tears welled up in my eyes, and it seemed as though I could do nothing to hold them back. But I just had to do something for the poor Sister so that there would be peace again. I asked myself: "Doesn't St. Joseph care for us anymore?" I then presented my problem to him, and with confidence in his assistance, I did not worry any more. Help actually came. I do not say that it was the result of my inadequate prayer, because I firmly believe that St. Joseph would grant help to anyone in need—just as he did to me that day.
>
> In the afternoon, a lady came to visit me. A few years ago, I had sewn some dresses for her daughters, as well as for others, before I had to give that up and tend to the laundry duties. These women for whom I had sewn were disappointed when I could no longer sew for them, and they took their orders elsewhere. I had some unhappy moments about this situation. This woman, however, had forgotten to pay what she owed me for the sewing I had done for her years ago. Now she not only paid the $6.40 which she owed me, but she added a fifty cent donation since I had waited so long for the payment. I was very grateful and sincerely thanked St. Joseph to whom I attributed this unexpected help. I had completely

forgotten that this money was due me until I actually saw the woman that day, and then it all came back to me.[16]

The days in the house on Ingraham Street did not all pass in peace and harmony. When more aged and abandoned women were sheltered, they frequently resorted to loud quarreling among themselves because of the cramped quarters they shared. Even the neighbors complained about the noise erupting from the house.[17] Oftentimes, when Sister Theresa returned from the Holy Family Orphanage where she spent the major part of the day in strenuous laundry chores, she was forced to act as peacemaker in the home. Her "Chronicle" contains an example of the joy and sadness which she often encountered:

> Despite all the difficulties and trouble I endured, I never felt completely exhausted. My greatest joy was to kneel down to say the evening prayers and rosary with the residents, and I saw how fervently and willingly they participated in the religious exercises. The situation was quite the reverse when they first came to us. Many had the deplorable habit of cursing, and I insisted strenuously that they get rid of that fault. When a few admonitions did not help, I threatened to expel anyone who did not cease cursing. This threat proved effective in each case. It seemed to me that God was pleased even with the little good that I could do for His glory. Prior to the admission of these aged women, most of them had not attended church for many years. It was a great encouragement to me to witness their improvements.[18]

In the spring of 1897, Sister Theresa reminded Father Barzynski about the plans for the construction of a permanent home for the aged and crippled. He suggested that the Home Planning Committee meet to discuss the issue. Of all the members, only Father Piechowski, the pastor of St. Hedwig's Church, refused to attend. This saddened her.[19] When the day of the meeting approached, Sister Anna fell ill and Sister Theresa was forced to appear alone before the committee which was something she disliked doing.[20] In an attempt at light humor during the meeting, Peter Kiołbassa remarked: "Let's proceed differently in this matter. Our treasurer, Mr. Gniot, is a widower; it would be much easier to make wedding arrangements."[21] Sister Theresa was visibly embarrassed by Mr. Kiołbassa's remark and the turn the conversation had taken. Father Barzynski came to her rescue by redirecting the conversation to the business at hand, namely, the proposed structure and the architect to be hired.

Soon Sister Theresa was destined for a very painful experience. A woman in the parish of St. Stanislaus Kostka began to circulate malicious rumors about Sister Theresa when the news concerning the purchase of the lots was made public. It was an established fact, well known in the parish, that Adam Frank, Sister Theresa's brother-in-law, dealt in the buying and selling of houses. With the unfortunate economic crisis of the late 1890s and its attendant depression, it was very possible that Adam Frank lost both money and houses because of financial reversals. It was also well known in the parish that his wife, Rosalie Frank, the sister of Sister Theresa, often borrowed money for her husband from the neighbors. With this money he bought property. Now gossip was being circulated by the unknown woman that Rosalie Frank had given the money she had borrowed from her neighbors to Sister Theresa. It was rumored that Sister Theresa intended to abandon the elderly and to build a fine new house for herself on the newly acquired lots. Other hearsay suggested that the Frank family was to move in with Sister Theresa and share her good fortune.[22] To Sister Theresa's great dismay, many parishioners believed the contemptible rumors. She wrote in her "Chronicle" at this time of stress: "The storm in all its fury hit me. The persons with whom I had lived in friendship for many years turned against me."[23] Sister Theresa continued to be met with disparaging and defamatory remarks.[24] To compound this most unfortunate situation, the malicious gossip began to reflect upon the person of Father Barzynski.[25] He was now a victim of the same detractions, and even the members of the Home Planning Committee were loud in their criticism of him. Sister Anna, Sister Theresa's main support during this traumatic time, verbalized her fears concerning the future. Her faith shaken by the gossip, Sister Anna began to doubt the permanency of the little Franciscan sisterhood and the actualization of the plans for building a home for the aged and crippled.[26]

In the midst of all the adversity which surrounded her, however, Sister Theresa maintained her confidence as she reveals in her "Chronicle":

> I did not believe this for a second. I could not believe that all our plans [for the Home] would be dropped. I recalled Father Barzynski's prediction made at the start of our community. He had foretold all these numerous sufferings and hardships, although I never thought that it would ever reach such proportions. The facts spoke for themselves. Sometimes, however, I felt guilty because I caused people to offend God by my actions. Father Vincent told me to put such thoughts completely out of my mind, and encouraged me to continue working for the glory of God.[27]

With the $1,500 debt on the lots still remaining, Father Barzynski found it very difficult to secure a loan for the new building project. All his attempts met with failure. In spite of the situation still existing at St. Stanislaus Kostka Parish concerning the vicious rumors, Sister Theresa, after conferring with Sister Anna, decided to approach the Women's Rosary Society and the Young Ladies' Rosary Society for a donation. The former group donated $1,000 while the latter gave $500.[28] The problem of the debt on the lots was now resolved, but there was no money left for the building fund. A short time later, Father Barzynski summoned Sister Theresa and Sister Anna to the rectory where he informed them that a loan for $10,000 at 4 percent interest with which to start the building of the home could be secured, but it would be necessary to transfer the ownership of the lots to him.[29] In this manner, he would be able to secure a loan on his recognizance since no one wished to make a loan to the Sisters. When Sister Theresa and Sister Anna agreed to Father Barzynski's proposal, he promptly engaged an attorney, Nikodem L. Piotrowski,[30] to transact the entire matter.[31]

As soon as Father Barzynski obtained the loan and made arrangements to pay the architect, the construction of the home for the aged and the crippled began in earnest in the early part of September of 1897. On the day of the groundbreaking ceremony, Father Barzynski requested Sister Theresa and the Sisters to pray earnestly for the success of the project. Thereupon, Sister Theresa was led to much reflection. She was acutely aware that with the actual building of the institution for the aged and the crippled, she would have to assume leadership not only in regard to its operation on a day-to-day basis, but also as religious superior to the women who had trustingly come together at her invitation to live according to the norms of an established religious community. She was filled with a feeling of inadequacy and wrote:

> I was overcome with a kind of misgiving. I knew that it would not be easy
> to learn how to be a good religious. How could I impart such knowledge
> when I myself was simple and uneducated both in spiritual and secular
> matters? . . . Nevertheless, I only wished that God's Will be done; I
> placed all my trust in him and allowed him to do with me what he
> wanted.[32]

Perhaps in her humility, Sister Theresa had forgotten the words of St. Paul which, in reality, characterized her entire life:

> For consider your call, brethren: not many of you are learned in a worldly
> sense, not many in high station, not many well-born. On the contrary,
> God chose the simple things of the world to confound the learned; and
> God chose the weak things of the world to confound the powerful.[33]

Sister Theresa and Sister Anna now made plans to move into the new building. First, however, they rented an apartment near the location of the new structure where Sister Anna could live with her parents until St. Joseph Home for the Aged and Crippled was completed, and they could be admitted.[34] The Sisters found an apartment on Ridgeway Avenue and moved into it on November 11, 1897. Although Sister Anna had not as yet lived with the Sisters in community, that date marks her arrival in the Avondale area.[35]

Meanwhile, Sister Theresa waited impatiently for St. Joseph Home for the Aged and Crippled to be completed so that the Sisters could leave the vicinity of St. Stanislaus Kostka Parish where she continued to be so misjudged and maligned. Now the young community was being harassed with predictions of the failure of their charitable venture and by various other unflattering remarks. One day, utterly exhausted and disheartened, Sister Theresa went to the building site of St. Joseph Home in Avondale to note the progress being made. She reveals her sentiments when she was finally able to view the development of St. Joseph Home for the Aged and Crippled:

As soon as I was able to see the skeleton of the building, I was overcome with fear and happiness. My heart was filled with gratitude to God, the sentiments which He alone could understand. I then ascended the ladder to the top of the building in order to see the progress made so far and to pray. No one saw me but God to whom I felt so close at that moment. When I realized that here, on this site which seemed to have been chosen by God Himself, so far from any church or people, the Holy Sacrifice of the Mass would be offered and glory given to God, I cried from joy.[36]

The structure was to have been completed by Christmas, but the digging and laying of the foundation had progressed so slowly that by the middle of October, only the cornerstone had been blessed. The laying of the cornerstone had been conducted in a private ceremony performed by Father Barzynski in the presence of a few loyal Home Planning Committee members. Neither Sister Theresa nor Sister Anna were present, and the "Chronicle" provides no reason for their absence, or worse, for their lack of an invitation to be present.

In December, Sister Theresa paid a visit to Sister Anna and her parents. She found them worried and dismayed over difficulties with their Swedish neighbors. Sister Theresa suggested that Sister Anna and her parents move to a small, roughly built shelter intended as a storage place which had been constructed near St. Joseph Home. The building was habitable with plastered walls and a chimney so that a stove could be attached. As might be expected, when Sister Anna and her parents moved into the building, all imaginable inconveniences were theirs; sometimes even the necessities of life were lacking.[37] While Sister Anna and her parents lived in the vicinity, however, they were able to supervise the malingering construction workers and prod them to complete their work. In the meantime, Sister Theresa continued to take upon herself the laundry duty in the rectory at St. Stanislaus Kostka at which she worked late into the night since she was occupied most of the day with ministering to the aged residents in the convent home.[38]

When news of the completion of the home for the aged and the crippled spread, a woman resident, Theodosia Troeder,[39] whom Sister Theresa had accepted into the house on Chapin Street the year before and whose crippled hand had been successfully mended by surgery, asked to be admitted as a member of the community. She joined the group of tertiaries on November 21, 1897, and was called Sister Frances. That same day, another young woman asked to be accepted. She was Marianne Ogurek, who, because she was not a tertiary, retained her baptismal name.[40] Born on May 6, 1875, in Makowarsk, Poland, Marianne Ogurek came to the United States in 1884 and settled in St. Stanislaus Kostka Parish. A member of the Young Ladies' Rosary Society, she came to the small community to be sheltered as a convalescent. Impressed with the simplicity and prayerfulness of the Sisters' lives, she determined to join them. Upon entering the novitiate, Marianne Ogurek was given the name Sister M. Clara. A fervent religious, Sister M. Clara exhibited great love for the congregation and a conscientious devotion to duty all the days of her religious life. According to the Sisters who shared their lives with her, she excelled in religious obedience and respect for the Holy Rule and the Constitutions. She was especially loved by the novices and postulants[41]

On December 7, 1897, another tertiary, Caroline Baut, joined the group.[42] Known in religion as Sister M. Elizabeth, Caroline Baut was born in Moszczenice, Poland, on August 9, 1871. She came to America in 1893 after the death of her parents and lived in St. Stanislaus Kostka Parish. Upon meeting Sister Theresa in the Young Ladies' Rosary Society, Caroline Baut joined the group determined to help Sister Theresa in her dedicated work for the aged and the crippled. Sister Elizabeth was extremely mild-mannered and humble by nature. Very small in stature, she was a powerhouse of piety, simplicity, and kindness.[43]

Sister Theresa rejoiced with the generous women who came to join the small group in service to the aged and the crippled. Thus, on the third anniversary of the foundation of the community, there were eight Sisters just as there had been at its beginning. Sister Theresa assigned Sister Frances Troeder to domestic duties in the house, Sister Marianne Ogurek to sewing duties, and Sister Elizabeth Baut to helping with the laundry chores. Sister Theresa could now turn her full attention to the care of their aged dependents, who with the coming of winter, frequently became ill. There were now eight Sisters, twelve women and three men in the group.[44] The time was slowly approaching when they would leave the familiar area of St. Stanislaus Kostka Church and bid farewell to Chicago to settle in the new home for the aged and crippled built in Avondale. The heart of Sister Theresa was full as she wrote this entry in her "Chronicle":

> Slowly the time drew near when it was necessary to bid farewell to Chicago, such a pleasant place [miłe miejsce], and especially to the church of St. Stanislaus Kostka where the Lord Jesus had bestowed so many graces on me. Nevertheless, I did not feel too unhappy, knowing that this was the Will of God. I knew that He would continue to enrich me with His grace if I would only continue to cooperate with Him.[45]

Sister Theresa maintained her spiritual equanimity even in the most severe trials and misunderstandings, and deserved to be rewarded, for she lived the words of St. Paul: "Do not forget kindness and charity, for by such sacrifices God's favor is obtained."[46] Now three more young women had entered the small community. Two of them were destined to remain in the community until their deaths, firmly rooted in the affection of Sister Theresa Dudzik and the traditions and the aspirations of the community which she had founded.

TRIUMPH OF SPIRIT

[1]Matka Maria Teresa Dudzik, "Kronika Sióstr Franciszkanek pod opieką Św. Kunegundy w Chicago, Illinois" [The Chronicle of the Franciscan Sisters under the patronage of St. Kunegunda in Chicago, Illinois] Unpublished manuscript, 1910 (AFSCL), p. 24.

[2]According to the *Book of Admittances, St. Joseph Home for the Aged and Crippled, Chicago, Illinois, 1898–1920* (AFSCL), p. 112, Mrs. Frances Konkowski was sent to the Sisters on September 2, 1896, by Mr. Kielczynski of St. John Cantius Parish. She died on January 24, 1902, at the home.

The young blind girl mentioned in the "Chronicle" on p. 25 is Josephine Gagala. Theodosia Troeder, of whom more will be written later, was the woman with the crippled hand. The fourth woman was, of course, Mrs. Elizabeth Karnowski.

[3]Dudzik, p. 24.

[4]Ibid., p. 25.

[5]Ibid.

[6]The home at 1368 Ingraham Street, which is now called Evergreen Street, was presumably owned by Matthew Lewandowski, the grandfather of two members of the Franciscan Sisters of Chicago. Sister M. Cyprian, the former Mary Lewandowski, entered in 1915 and died in 1964 in the congregation. Her sister, Sister M. Remigia, the former Alice Lewandowski, entered in 1930.

In her deposition for the cause of beatification of Mother M. Theresa, Sister M. Cyprian testified that she was "fortunate to have been born in the home where Sister M. Theresa Dudzik had lived." She stated that her grandparents lived in the front apartment on the second floor, while her parents lived in the front apartment on the first floor. Sister M. Cyprian also stated that her mother told her many things concerning Sister M. Theresa and the small community. She also said her mother often left her in the care of the Sisters when she was busy doing the laundry or had to leave the house for some reason.

The house, located across the street from St. Stanislaus Kostka Church, is still standing. The interiors of many of the apartments are being renovated and modernized providing quaint apartments. Two houses to the right of the Lewandowski house is the renovated residence of Congressman Daniel Rostenkowski who still represents this district in Congress. *Book of Depositions:* Sister M. Cyprian Lewandowski (AFSCL).

[7]Dudzik, p. 26.

[8]High Mass or Solemn High Mass, as it was called, was one with a celebrant who was assisted by a deacon or subdeacon plus other servers. In the complete ritual of the former Liturgy of the Mass, parts of it were sung, the ministers, people, and altar were incensed, and the kiss of peace was given.

[9]Between the years 1900 and 1915, St. Stanislaus Kostka Parish with its "upper" and "lower" churches had as many as twelve masses each Sunday to accommodate its parishioners. John J. Iwicki CR, *The First One Hundred Years: A Study of the Apostolate of the Congregation of the Resurrection in the United States, 1866–1966* (Rome: Gregorian University Press, 1966), p. 67.

[10]The *Advanced Catechism,* as the name implied, was an advanced version of the standard catechism which, as a manual for moral and religious instruction, summarized Catholic doctrine. The basic or standard catechism in the United States was the so-called *Baltimore Catechism* which takes its name from the Third Baltimore Council which authorized it.

Because of the controversy which had occurred at St. Hedwig's Church and the establishment of the "Independent" Polish National Church of All Saints, perhaps it was necessary to instruct the Sisters in the basic beliefs of the Roman Catholic Church. In Chapter 8, mention was made of two Sisters who belonged to the Independent All Saints Church and were ignorant of the fact.

In pioneer days, it was safe to assume that some of the young women who presented themselves as postulants lacked knowledge of the fundamental truths of their faith.

[11]Dudzik, p. 27.

[12]According to the deposition of Sister M. Elizabeth Baut, a young boy named Joseph, who had no legs, was sheltered by the Sisters. His relatives paid the Sisters $5 a month for his support. In her "Chronicle," Sister Theresa makes reference to him when she says she "taught the boy the *Catechism* and general prayers since he knew nothing concerning the Catholic faith." Later, Sister Elizabeth contends, Joseph worked in a railroad yard at the guard box and thus supported himself.

In her deposition, Sister M. Hyacinth Barczewski, who entered the infant community in 1902, and was also a parishioner of St. Stanislaus Kostka Church, states that she often saw the boy Joseph accompany Josephine Dudzik as they made their way to church and presumed that the boy was her son. Upon her entrance into the community, Sister M. Hyacinth was, of course, made aware of the truth of the matter. *Book of Depositions:* Sister M. Hyacinth Barczewski; Sister M. Elizabeth Baut (AFSCL); and Dudzik, p. 27.

[13]Dudzik, p. 28.

[14]St. Teresa of Avila's devotion to St. Joseph is well known. As patron saint of her convent, St. Joseph was implored for help by St. Teresa more often than any other saint. One of her favorite mottoes was: "Go to Joseph." She said of him: "I cannot call to mind that I have ever asked him at any time for anything which he has not granted. I only ask, for the love of God, that any who doubts what I say make a test of it and see from actual experience the great benefits that come from this glorious Patriarch."

[15]The word literally means "landowner." It is a title of respectful address.

[16]Dudzik, p. 29.

[17]Ibid., p. 30.

[18]Ibid., p. 27.

[19]Although Sister Theresa was very hurt by Father Piechowski's refusal to attend the meeting, it is easy to see why he did not do so. The "controversy" at St. Hedwig's Church was taking place. Since much of it concerned Father Joseph Barzynski, the brother of Father Vincent Barzynski, it would have been, perhaps, "uncomfortable" for Father Piechowski, who had taken Father Joseph Barzynski's place, to be present. At any rate, he did wish the Sisters success in their building plans. In later years, Father Piechowski would prove to be a kind and loyal patron of the young community. Dudzik, p. 30.

[20]Ibid.

[21]John Gniot was first mentioned in Chapter 8 when he was named treasurer of the Home Planning Committee. According to the *Registram Matrimoniorum*, vol. 1, 1869–1882, p. 22 and *Spis Slubów*, 1898, vol. 23, p. 81, Father Barzynski had officiated at the marriage of John Gniot to Julianna Lamkoska on January 9, 1876, at St. Stanislaus Kostka Church. Gniot's wife died in 1896. At the time of this incident at the Home Planning Committee meeting, Gniot was forty-five years old; Sister Theresa was thirty-seven. Gniot did marry again, however, on April 19, 1898. His second wife was Anna Obert, a widow of forty-two.

Gniot, who was of great assistance to Sister Theresa when the Sisters left the St. Stanislaus Kostka district for Avondale, was familiar in the parish. He was the president of the Society of the Sacred Heart which he helped organize with Father Barzynski and Michael Relewicz on December 29, 1889. He also served as vice president of the Polish Roman Catholic Union of America from 1886 to 1887 and as treasurer from 1887 to 1892. *Album Pamiątkowy Złotego Jubileuszu Parafii Świętego Stanisława Kostki, 1867–1917* [A Commemorative Album of the Golden Jubilee of St. Stanislaus Kostka Parish, 1867–1917] (Chicago, Illinois, 1917), p. 160; *Book of Correspondence:* Letter from Edward G. Dykla, secretary general of the PRCUA, to author, 3 September 1975 (AFSCL); and Mieszysław Haiman, *Zjednoczenie Polskie Rzymsko-Katolickie w Ameryce, 1873–1948* [The History of the Polish Roman Catholic Union of America, 1873–1948] (Chicago, Illinois, 1948), p. 76.

[22]*Book of Depositions:* Sister M. Gonzaga Raniszewski (AFSCL); and Dudzik, p. 32.

[23]Among them was Mr. Jendrzejek, a member of the Home Planning Committee to whom the woman first made the accusation. As a result, he withdrew his name from the Home Planning Committee and refrained from rendering any further help. Dudzik, p. 32.

[24]Siostra M. Gonzaga Raniszewski, OSFK, *Rys historyczny Zgromadzenia Sióstr Franciszkanek Błogosłowionej Kunegundy. Część pierwsza, 1860–1910* [A historical survey of the Franciscan Sisters of Blessed Kunegunda. Part one, 1860–1910] (Chicago: By the Author, 1947), p. 62.

[25]Dudzik, p. 32.

[26]Ibid., pp. 32–33.

[27]Ibid.

[28]In spite of the controversy surrounding Sister Theresa, Sister M. Gonzaga Raniszewski in *Rys,* p. 64, suggests that the societies probably responded so generously because of their affection for Sister Anna.

[29]Legal documents (AFSCL).

[30]A prominent professor and lawyer, Nikodem L. Piotrowski, was born in Poland and studied there and in Germany. He arrived in the United States in 1882, studied at the University of Notre Dame, and graduated from the University of Indiana at Valparaiso. He was elected president of the Polish Roman Catholic Union of America in 1918. He taught law at Loyola University in Chicago, and during World War I, served as war correspondent for the *Chicago Tribune*. Francis Bolek, ed., *Who's Who In Polish America: A Biographical Directory of Polish American Leaders and Distinguished Poles Resident in the Americas,* 3rd ed. (New York: Harbinger House, 1943; Arno Publishers, 1970), p. 350.

[31]Dudzik, p. 34.

[32]Ibid.

[33]I Cor. 1:26–27.

[34]Matilda Wysinski remained with another sister in Chicago temporarily.

[35]*Spis Sióstr* (AFSCL).

[36]Dudzik, p. 35.

[37]Ibid., p. 36.

[38]Raniszewski, p. 67.

[39]Theodosia Troeder was born on May 28, 1873, in Neunberg, West Prussia. She belonged to St. Stanislaus Kostka Parish. Her postulancy began on May 21, 1899, and her novitiate on June 4, 1900. After making her first profession of vows on June 6, 1902, Sister Frances left the community on July 29 of that same year. *Spis Sióstr* (AFSCL).

[40]In the small community of Franciscan tertiaries which, in time, became the Congregation of the Franciscan Sisters of Chicago, Sister M. Clara had an active and varied life. From 1916 to 1922, she held the office of assistant general and first councilor to Mother M. Aloysia Holysz. For fourteen years, she worked in the Church Vestment Workshop at the Motherhouse, and served in numerous schools and institutions as teacher and superior. Her later years were spent in retirement at Our Lady of Victory Convent in Lemont where she died on December 18, 1971, at the age of ninety-six. *Spis Sióstr* (AFSCL).

[41]Dudzik, p. 37; *Interview* with Sister M. Loyola Dymanowski and other Sisters; and *Spis Sióstr* (AFSCL).

[42]At the beginning of her religious life, Sister M. Elizabeth did household duties, sought alms, and served as sacristan at St. Joseph Home for the Aged and Crippled. In 1922, she was sent to St. Casimir's School in Streator, Illinois, to attend to household duties. After one year, she returned to the Motherhouse where she was engaged in various duties until she was assigned to Our Lady of Victory Convent in Lemont, Illinois, in 1937. She was never seriously ill, however, until months before her death on June 18, 1960, at the age of eighty-nine. *Spis Sióstr* (AFSCL).

[43]*Interview* with Sister M. Loyola Dymanowski and other Sisters; and *Spis Sióstr* (AFSCL).

[44]John Lewandowski, completely deaf, was the first adult male resident accepted. He was a widower from St. Stanislaus Kostka Parish. Accepted on January 9, 1898, he remained there until his death on October 15, 1912, at the age of eighty-five. *Book of Admittances, St. Joseph Home for the Aged and Crippled, Chicago, Illinois, 1898–1920* (AFSCL) pp. 2–3; Dudzik, p. 38; and *St. Stanislaus Kostka Church: Book of Records.*

[45]Dudzik, p. 38.

[46]Heb. 13:16.

CHAPTER 10

A Dream Fulfilled

On the feast of St. Joseph, in 1898 celebrated on March 23, Sister Theresa and the seven Sisters together with ten women and three men left St. Stanislaus Kostka Parish. That morning, they had all received Holy Communion at mass with the intention of asking God's blessing upon their new undertaking. After breakfast, the move began to Avondale and to the new structure which now stood completed. The new residence for which they were destined was called St. Joseph Home for the Aged and Crippled in honor of the selected patron and master of their home.[1]

Avondale in the 1890s remained a desolate section of land without gas, water, sewers, or paved roads. It was a wide area of land on the Northwest Side of Chicago about six miles from Chicago's Loop and near Milwaukee Avenue, one of Chicago's main streets. Avondale was settled principally by Poles who, keenly aware of the overpopulation in St. Stanislaus Kostka Parish, purchased land in the area for eventual settlement. After 1893, however, the period of Chicago's economic decline prohibited many of them from building in large numbers. Consequently, by 1894 only forty families were settled in Avondale. The section was largely undeveloped, overgrown with large trees and high grass where goats grazed and flocks of geese abounded. Because of its location, there was little communication with the rest of the city. The lack of paved streets, sidewalks, transportation, and stores was a major inconvenience that the pioneer residents of Avondale were forced to endure. There was, unfortunately, an added unplesantness in the fact that the Scandinavians living in the near vicinity of Logan Square found it rather difficult to welcome their new Polish neighbors. As a consequence, frequent animosity and misunderstanding arose between the groups.[2]

Moving to their new home in Avondale involved many difficulties. Father Barzynski had suggested that the Sisters rent a large wagon by which to transport all their goods, but the Sisters were refused rental of any wagon because of the excessive mud in the vicinity of Avondale. Except for Milwaukee Avenue,[3] the mud roads made by the thawing snow were difficult to travel on. The Sisters did succeed, however, in obtaining the services of a grocer, John Thiel, and of John Gniot, who offered the use of their horses and wagons and helped to haul much of the furniture from the old quarters to the new home. A third wagon, belonging to the Sisters, was driven by Sister Theresa's brother, Joseph Dudzik.[4] At twilight, the last wagonload arrived in Avondale bringing an exhausted Sister Angeline and Sister Marianne who had remained in Chicago until they had completed the last of their sewing orders.

The St. Joseph Home for the Aged and Crippled was a brick, three-story, medium-sized structure. It was not a very large building, yet it served as both an institution for the aged and as a Motherhouse for the young community. Now, filled with eight Sisters, ten aged women, three aged men, and the parents of Sister Anna, the home was already overcrowded. Dining rooms for the Sisters and their elderly residents plus a kitchen were located on the first floor. A small chapel had been arranged on the second floor as well as sleeping quarters for the men. Sister Anna's parents also slept in this area. The third floor contained a workshop as well as sleeping quarters for the Sisters and the women residents.

There was more than enough work for the eight Sisters in caring for the aged as well as in maintaining the institution. Sister Theresa divided the work among the Sisters who all endured the exhausting labor and dire poverty which seemed to dictate their lives. The expenses for the maintenance of St. Joseph Home for the Aged and Crippled were heavy, and the Sisters had no funds readily available from which to draw. Besides the expenses connected with the home, there was the added burden of the interest which still remained to be paid on the loan which the Sisters had taken. None of the aged residents provided financial support and were thus totally dependent on the Sisters for survival. Requests continued to pour in from all sides asking and sometimes begging the Sisters to accept the aged into the home. Sister Theresa was forced to refuse many requests because

The original Motherhouse Complex on Hamlin and Schubert Avenues. Left: St. Vincent's Orphan Asylum. Center: St. Joseph Home for the Aged and Crippled. Right: the Novitiate House.

Sister M. Theresa Dudzik and residents of St. Joseph Home for the Aged and Crippled, c. 1900.

of the overcrowded conditions. She suffered a great deal of unpleasantness from disgruntled people because of these refusals. She denied requests to shelter the elderly when she knew that they had children who could support them although she realized that the elderly were often better cared for at St. Joseph Home than by unkind and unsympathetic relatives.[5]

One of the chief problems which faced Sister Theresa and her Sister companions was the constant shortage of food, especially bread, which could not be obtained in large quantities in order to meet the demands of so many people. The bakers did not deliver goods to the home, and the grocery stores in the neighborhood were quite unprepared to supply their buyer's needs in such large quantities. The winter was unduly severe and the coal companies in Chicago did not want to make deliveries to Avondale because of the bad roads. Sometimes Joseph Dudzik, Sister Theresa's brother, helped with the deliveries. To secure the coal and all needed supplies, Sister Theresa used the wagon belonging to the Sisters and a horse donated by the Resurrectionist Fathers at St. Stanislaus Kostka Church. Although Sister Josepha was physically weak because of her illness, she drove the horse and wagon always accompanied by Sister Theresa. At times, when it was necessary, Sister Theresa took the reins herself. It was just one more burden which she assumed. She had already given much time and energy to the necessary tasks at St. Joseph Home and had even attempted the needed carpentry work at which, on many occasions, she bruised her hands. Sister Theresa and Sister Anna also walked, back and forth, more than twenty miles to the Union Stock Yards[6] on Chicago's far South Side in order to buy a much-needed cow and two pigs with money that had been returned to them as a debt. By far the biggest problem which still weighed heavily upon the mind of Sister Theresa was the fact that the

Sisters had no guaranteed income from any source. By leaving Chicago, they lost their chief source of support from dressmaking and domestic work at the St. Stanislaus Kostka Rectory. In the largely uninhabited area of Avondale, there was little call for dressmaking orders and certainly not enough to support twenty-three people.[7] This was a time of dire need and anxiety.

In the midst of this tribulation, plans were being made for the blessing of St. Joseph Home for the Aged and Crippled. On May 1, 1898, the feast of the Solemnity of St. Joseph, Father Barzynski offered Holy Mass in the small convent chapel assisted by the Reverend Eugene Sedlaczek, CR, the pastor of St. Hyacinth's Church and the Sisters' temporary confessor.[8] Father Barzynski delivered a sermon which inspired the large gathering of friends and benefactors. He spoke sincerely and eloquently of the Sisters' dedication to the aged, crippled, and needy. He took the occasion to foretell the growth of the small community of women, and of the eventual expansion of St. Joseph Home.

Shortly after the dedication, a young crippled girl, Angela Osinski, was admitted to the home. Her admission in May was followed by that of Mrs. Theophila Łagodzinski, a widow from Holy Trinity Parish. Fortunately, she brought with her an offering of $250 which was desperately needed.[9] At the beginning of June, a new candidate, Antoinette Graff, asked to be admitted to the small community and was accepted.[10]

With the absolute need to feed, clothe, and house the many people entrusted to their care, Sister Theresa, in desperation, decided to send the Sisters to collect alms and to gather donations of food. Until this time, the Sisters had worn secular clothes; but now they were outfitted with black dresses and short, black veils. Having received the approval of Father Barzynski, the appointed Sisters went out on their first begging assignment in August using their horse and wagon. Much to their surprise, the Sisters were well received by the public and brought back enough food for several days and $16 in cash. Happy with these results, the Sisters continued to maintain themselves and the aged by begging.[11] The Sisters and some of the more hardy elderly at the home tilled the soil in the convent garden and planted various vegetables which also helped meet their needs. For the time being, Sister Theresa ceased worrying about hunger.[12]

Of necessity, most of the physical work attached to the care of the animals fell to Sister Theresa and Sister Josepha. Before long, the heavy labor affected Sister Josepha to such a degree that she fell seriously ill again and this time seemed unable to recuperate fully. As a consequence, she resolved to leave the band of Sisters of which she was so vital a part. Sadly, she returned to her relatives on August 14, 1898. She was followed on the next day by the candidate Antoinette Graff.[13] The loss of the two women was balanced, however, by the acceptance on August 15 of Anna Welter, who, as Sister Mary, was destined to remain in the congregation until death.[14]

In the latter part of 1898, it became apparent that because of ill health, Father Barzynski was not as actively involved in the guidance of the young Franciscan community as he had formerly been. Now he was assigning more and more responsibility for the spiritual leadership of the Sisters to his young assistant at St. Stanislaus Kostka

Parish, the zealous and solicitous Reverend Andrew Spetz, CR. As a consequence, Father Spetz became aware of the fact that the Sisters, as an emerging community in the Church, were in need of a definable and adaptable set of Constitutions based on the Rule of the Third Order of St. Francis rather than the prescriptions of the Tertiary Rule of St. Francis which they had been following thus far. The Sisters yearned to have their own Constitutions to better govern their daily lives. To this end, Father Spetz contacted the Congregation of the Sisters of the Third Order of St. Francis in Milwaukee, Wisconsin, requesting them to provide him with a set of their Constitutions. The Sisters very obligingly sent a copy to Father Spetz, who in turn, used it as a guide for the Constitutions which he wrote for the small community in Avondale since the Sisters' objectives were similar.[15] After formulating the Constitutions, Father Spetz gave a copy of them to Sister Theresa and Sister Anna for approval. The Sisters returned the Constitutions to Father Spetz several times asking for greater clarification concerning particular articles, and when these were defined, the Constitutions were accepted by both Sisters as being adequate and able to be observed.

Since almost all the Sisters were Franciscan tertiaries, they looked forward to the celebration of the feast of St. Francis of Assisi on October 4, 1898. Sister Theresa, especially, anticipated the arrival of Father Barzynski who had promised to celebrate mass at St. Joseph Home. Instead, the Reverend Vincent Rapacz, CR,[16] came to offer mass in the chapel for the intention of the Sisters on this festive occasion. Later in the afternoon, however, Father Barzynski made an unexpected visit to the Sisters and requested that they all assemble in the chapel. There, to everyone's surprise, Father Barzynski announced the removal of Sister Theresa as superior of the community. Offering no apology or explanation, Father Barzynski deposed Sister Theresa and appointed Sister Anna Wysinski, Sister Theresa's good friend and confidante, to succeed her as the new superior.

Although the announcement stunned her, Sister Theresa gracefully accepted her removal with peace and resignation, obedient to her spiritual director.[17] She had always submitted to his direction with simplicity and humility and in a spirit of deep faith. This circumstance was no different. If God had seen fit to establish the community of Franciscan tertiaries using Sister Theresa as his human instrument, the price exacted was not to be paid without deep pain.

The Sisters, who were admittedly fond of Sister Anna, accepted the change without question although they wondered how Sister Anna, who was so frequently ill, could discharge the duties of the superior. While the reason for such an abrupt removal was never made known, and the docile and humble Sister Theresa and the Sisters never requested to know, it appears that the removal of Sister Theresa as superior was deemed necessary by Father Barzynski. In spite of the fact that the Sisters were deeply involved in establishing and maintaining St. Joseph Home, there were people in St. Stanislaus Kostka Parish, it will be remembered, who persisted in spreading offensive and derogatory stories about Sister Theresa. Many parishioners of St. Stanislaus Kostka Parish initially mistook Sister Theresa's aim to build a home for the aged as being an excuse simply to collect money to purchase a dwelling for her own comfort, thereby deceiving all those who had donated alms toward the establishment of St. Joseph Home.[18] These false accusations did not stop once the small community left the district of St. Stanislaus Kostka Parish. It appears that more and more of the offensive rumors were beginning to affect the reputation of Father Barzynski and the fledgling group of Sisters he helped establish.[19] Sister M. Gonzaga, writing in the *Rys* states:

> The people [of St. Stanislaus Kostka Parish] judged rashly that if Sister Theresa were the superior of the Sisters, then the whole of St. Joseph Home belonged to her. To put an end to these rumors and to attempt to change the malicious criticism of the parishioners, Father Barzynski took a stringent course of action. He removed Sister Theresa as superior and appointed Sister Anna in her place. He believed that the people of St. Stanislaus Kostka Parish would thus be persuaded to stop spreading offensive stories.[20]

With all due respect to Father Barzynski, he believed that the removal of Sister Theresa would restore peace and harmony to his agitated parish. In all actuality, matters did settle down at St. Stanislaus Kostka Parish after Sister Anna became the superior.[21] While this does not justify Father Barzynski's removal of Sister Theresa as the superior, it does indicate the spirit of self-surrender God sometimes demands of a chosen soul and the fulfillment of the words of Jesus:

> Amen, amen, I tell you: if the grain of wheat does not fall into the earth it remains alone; but if it dies, it yields much fruit. The man who loves his life will lose it, but the man who disregards his life in this world will keep it into life eternal. If somebody wants to serve me, he will have to follow me, and wherever I am, my servant will be there also. If somebody serves me, the Father will crown him with honor.[22]

Because of her removal from office, Sister Theresa could now devote more time to her spiritual life and the care of her beloved aged. Thoroughly free of any bitterness, Sister Theresa felt, as she herself states in her "Chronicle," "as if a heavy stone had fallen from around my neck, and I perceived unusual happiness."[23] What was of more importance to her at this time, was the fact that the Blessed Sacrament was not as yet reserved in the chapel, and she felt "like a fish out of water without the Blessed Sacrament."[24] The nearest church, St. Hyacinth's, was about a half-mile away. Although some of the Sisters could not attend mass daily because of their pressing duties with the aged, many of them were able to do so especially in the summertime. During the winter, because of the distance and the inclement weather, the Sisters were forced to forego attendance at mass. On Sundays and holydays, however, Father Barzynski came to celebrate mass in the chapel, or else he sent Father Spetz.[25] The need to worship at mass was most important to the Sisters, especially to Sister Theresa, who revealed her feelings in her "Chronicle": "At times I felt such a great yearning for Jesus in the Blessed Sacrament that I was ready to run to church at any time, even late in the evening."[26]

Unfortunately, Father Barzynski did not quite share her sentiments as the next entry reveals:

> I believed this yearning [for Jesus in the Blessed Sacrament] was just a
> temptation. Father Barzynski suggested, instead, that I think about my
> residents and not dream. As much as I tried to follow his advice, the
> longing for Jesus in the Blessed Sacrament returned again and again.[27]

The feast of the Immaculate Conception was once again approaching and marked the fourth anniversary of the community's founding. Father Barzynski suggested that the Sisters make the customary novena to the Blessed Virgin Mary prior to the community's special feast. In addition, he instructed Sister Theresa, Sister Angeline, Sister Anna, and Sister Agnes to observe a week of retreat in preparation for their admittance to the postulancy[28] on December 8, 1898. He promised that they would receive their religious habits and be admitted to the novitiate[29] in early spring of the next year.[30]

Until this time, the Sisters had had no experience in making a formal retreat and their circumstances at this time did not permit them to do so. They resolved, then, to perform their daily spiritual exercises with greater attention and devotion, and to maintain recollection by means of silence as much as was possible in their circumstances. To the already crowded horarium, they added another meditation in the afternoon, and while at work, they attempted recollection by placing themselves in the presence of God often, begging him for the graces needed to live the life of a good religious. Father Barzynski promised to deliver several conferences throughout the retreat. The Sisters were overjoyed at the prospect of beginning their postulancy, and Sister Theresa was especially happy:

> I was so overwhelmed [by the prospect of beginning our postulancy on
> December 8] that I began to plan in what way I could most solemnly
> honor the feast of the Immaculate Conception since this was the feast I
> loved best in the whole year.[31]

On the vigil of the feast of the Immaculate Conception, each Sister made a confession of her entire life in preparation for entering the postulancy.[32] Somewhere during the course of the retreat, it occurred to Sister Theresa to secure an organ for the celebration of Midnight Mass on Christmas Eve:

> I wished that the organ would be played and that we could sing together
> at Midnight Mass in honor of the Child Jesus . . . we could thank him for
> all the graces he had showered upon us, especially because he had led us
> to this peaceful environment, a desert as it were, a retreat from the
> Babylon[33] of Chicago.[34]

Sister Anna shared Sister Theresa's opinion and confirmed her petition to Father

Barzynski regarding the organ for the chapel. The Young Ladies' Rosary Society at St. Stanislaus Kostka Parish had already agreed to supply the organ, but while granting the society the necessary permission to purchase it, Father Barzynski said: "I will give them an organ! They are to make a good retreat and here they are longing for music!"[35] Nevertheless, Father Barzynski suggested that they secure the eminent Professor Emil Wiedemann,[36] the distinguished Andrew Kwasigroch,[37] or his gifted daughter-in-law, Rose Kwasigroch[38] to provide organ lessons. It was almost a year later, however, that Sister Theresa was able to secure the popular and talented Brother Adalbert Góralski, CR,[39] the organist and choir director of St. Hyacinth's Church to instruct the Sisters.[40]

On the morning of December 8, Father Barzynski celebrated mass for the Sisters in the chapel and they all received Holy Communion. They were very happy and no one was happier than Sister Theresa who was thoroughly prepared to undergo any further sacrifices this new life might entail.[41] Father Barzynski delivered a brief sermon in which he extolled the dignity of their religious consecration and the spirit of dedication it required. He wished them the grace of holy perseverance and the continued growth of the community in the midst of any hardships and disillusionment. From that day on, the four Sister-postulants wore the same kind of brown dress with a white collar.[42] Although they attempted to live the religious life well, the peace and harmony of their Sisterhood was shaken. The enormity of their tasks with the aged, with each other, and with their own struggling human nature in the faithful observance of the Rule and the Constitutions was extremely exacting at times. Sister Theresa herself noted in her "Chronicle":

> It was difficult. We were to train ourselves to live according to the Rule
> and at the same time we still engaged in criticism, gossiping, suspicion,
> and the like. The shortcomings in our conduct were even more evident in
> the new home.[43]

Learning of the spirit of dissension that sometimes prevailed, Father Barzynski reproved Sister Theresa coldly. He urged her to reduce what the Sisters perceived to be her "rigidity" and to allow a more relaxed atmosphere to prevail by means of less adherence to the Rule and the Constitutions and the practice of silence in particular. As postulant mistress, a position Sister Theresa acquired from the day the Sisters entered the postulancy, she felt that the practice of silence was absolutely necessary to encourage peace and to promote union with God:

> Even though the order of the day was somewhat modified, I tried to
> observe it [silence] because I considered that advancement in spiritual
> life would result by adhering to this practice. It was not too difficult since
> there was a small number of us at that time, and whoever entered tried to
> conduct herself according to the Rule. As soon as the Rule was relaxed, it
> became more difficult. Consequently, it was always worse for me since I
> recalled the promises that I had made [to maintain the community in spite

of all adversity]. I was not able to look peacefully on such a life and for my part, I tried to encourage the observance of the Rule in keeping silence as formerly. Because of this good example, I brought upon myself great displeasure from almost every Sister . . . they reminded me that I was not the superior; therefore, I should have little to say about maintaining silence.[44]

If trials and difficulties were to come, the pain and disappointment were all the greater since they came from the very community she had worked so steadfastly to establish. While it was true that she was no longer the legitimate superior of the group, she did have the role of postulant mistress. As such, she felt responsible for the interpretation and the preservation of the Rule and Constitutions. Imbued as she was by her vision of what religious life should be, she sought to promote a community where a genuine religious spirit might prevail and the Rule and Constitutions might be strictly observed. It was obvious to her that she would have to exert her greatest energies in training the first members of the community. Sister Theresa bore the harsh recriminations directed against her with patience and love. She often had unpleasant confrontations with the Sisters.[45] These episodes were often related to Father Barzynski, and as a consequence, he frequently admonished Sister Theresa in the presence of all the Sisters. She bore these humiliations with equanimity and resignation. The result of these actions was Sister Theresa's determination to refrain further from reprimanding any Sister in regard to her observance of the Rule and the Constitutions. Nevertheless, she continued to be appalled by the laxity of religious observance by some of the Sisters and dismayed by their hostile attitudes. Saddened by their lack of religious fervor, Sister Theresa was soon tempted to return to the former simple life she had led with her mother in the house on Chapin Street. She even admonished herself for having founded the community of tertiaries and secretly regretted the sacrifices she had endured in order to bring the community about:

> I wondered whether it were possible for life to be like this in a convent. Finally, a violent temptation came upon me, and I was disturbed with these thoughts—how foolish you are! Could you not have remained quietly with your mother, served God better and accomplished more good than now? In this way of life, you can condemn yourself because you cannot live here as the Rule prescribes nor can you observe the commandments of God. Here you will condemn yourself . . . these thoughts spun through my mind and it appeared as if everything were falling apart. When these thoughts would materialize, I assured myself that I could manage anywhere.[46]

Anguish seemed to overtake her and the thought of actually leaving passed through her mind:

> Although I had submitted my money toward the payment of the lot, I

came to the conclusion that I would not take anything from here [when I left]. I would earn as much anywhere for my mother's and my own meagre support; I never dreamed of conveniences. As much as I was able to, I reassured myself with the thought that whatever I did, I would do for the greater glory of God. And if God did not demand further work from me [concerning the founding of the community], I would even agree to His wishes.

This blissful peace, however, did not last long. The promises which I made to God and to Father Barzynski in the early stages of the foundation resounded in my heart. I recalled when Father Barzynski said that perhaps I would be solicitous about this community as long as everything went well . . . but as soon as obstacles would arise, I would become discouraged and forsake everything. Father remarked that in this way I would bring him and myself to ridicule as well as the Church which permits such foundations. Most of all, I would deceive those persons whom I accepted into the community. After much reflection, I promised God, and him [Father Barzynski] that as long as I lived, I would try, as much as my strength allowed, to sustain this community and persevere in it.[47]

Because the Sisters did not have a regular confessor at this time, Sister Theresa was further disheartened since she had no particular spiritual director, outside of Father Barzynski, in whom she could confide. What remained for her to do was to pray that God would change the circumstances in which she found herself. These interior sufferings disheartened her but did not diminish her courage nor weaken her confidence in the days that lay ahead. Rather than yield to frustration and defeat, she gained encouragement from knowing that she could take her problems to Jesus, the font of all human trust. In her "Chronicle," therefore, she wrote: "I began to present our difficulties to Jesus more frequently and to seek help from him alone."[48] With St. Paul, Sister Theresa could now pray: "There is nothing love cannot face, there is no limit to its faith, its hope, and its endurance."[49] Calling upon her profound courage, ardent spirit of sacrifice and boundless confidence in the Providence of God, Sister Theresa was determined, now more than ever, to renew her commitment to God and to reaffirm her promise to Father Barzynski to pray, sacrifice, and labor perseveringly for the survival of the community which she had founded and loved.

A DREAM FULFILLED

[1]Josephine Dudzik received her baptismal name in honor of St. Joseph. This "just man" of whom the Gospel tells us so little has traditionally been one of the Church's most popular saints. He is especially loved by the Polish people who have dedicated numerous Sisterhoods, churches, and schools to him. They especially honor him as the protector of youth, model of all fathers, and patron of a happy death. So warmly have the Polish adopted St. Joseph as their own that even today, one of the Sisters, laughingly but lovingly, recalls that she cried when she learned St. Joseph was Jewish and not Polish as she had believed and taken pride in all through her elementary school days! It was this godly, holy man that Josephine loved and to whom she had prayerful devotion throughout her lifetime. It was to him that she and the founding Sisters dedicated the first visible fruits of their labor—the St. Joseph Home for the Aged and Crippled. From its very foundation, the congregation was entrusted to the protection of St. Joseph for all its spiritual and material needs. As a consequence, the Franciscan Sisters of Chicago have special affection for St. Joseph and celebrate his feastday with particular joy.

[2]Chicago Plan Commission, *Forty-Four Cities in the City of Chicago* (Chicago: City of Chicago, 1942), p. 83; and *St. Hyacinth Church: Golden Jubilee, 1894–1944* (Chicago, 1944), pp. 16–18.

[3]With the laying of Plank Road, now Milwaukee Avenue in 1848, and the arrival of the Chicago and Northwestern, and the Chicago, Milwaukee, and St. Paul Railroads in the middle 1850s, rapid growth occurred in all the communities in the Northwest section. In 1889, Avondale and nearby Logan Square merged with Chicago.

Milwaukee Avenue tells a great deal about the growth of Chicago. Milwaukee Avenue began as a pioneer trail leading into a prairie and later became a magnet for ethnic groups such as Scandinavians, Jews, and Germans before the Columbian Exposition of 1893. After that time, the area was settled by Central Europeans, especially Poles, who began to build churches and organizations that bound them tightly to the area and to each other. After 1900, to most Chicagoans, Milwaukee Avenue meant "Polish," since the area claimed thousands of Poles, making it the second largest concentration of Poles in the world. Avondale today is a large and thickly populated section embracing the largest Polish parish in the city, St. Hyacinth's, and also that of St. Wenceslaus. While Milwaukee Avenue has a special meaning for Chicago Poles and they still predominate, the area today has the feel of the inner city after having undergone ethnic and racial change and movement. James David Besser, "A Street Called Home: Why Milwaukee Avenue is Really Chicago's Main Street," *Chicago Sun-Times Midwest Magazine,* 3 November 1974; Chicago Plan Commission, *Forty-Four Cities,* p. 83; and *St. Hyacinth's Golden Jubilee,* pp. 16–18.

[4]Matka Maria Teresa Dudzik, "Kronika Sióstr Franciszkanek pod opieką Św. Kunegundy w Chicago, Illinois" [The Chronicle of the Franciscan Sisters under the patronage of St. Kunegunda in Chicago, Illinois] Unpublished manuscript, 1910 (AFSCL), p. 39.

[5]Siostra M. Gonzaga Raniszewski, OSFK, *Rys historyczny Zgromadzenia Sióstr Franciszkanek Błogosławionej Kunegundy. Część pierwsza, 1860–1910* [A historical survey of the Franciscan Sisters of Blessed Kunegunda. Part one, 1860–1910] (Chicago: By the Author, 1947), p. 72.

[6]The enormous Union Stock Yards complex, which was constructed in 1865 at 41st and Halsted Streets, was once the greatest livestock market in the world. The surrounding area, known as the "Back of the Yards," became one of the most vibrant business entities in the city of Chicago. In the year 1894, for example, more than one million head of cattle went through the stockyards. Chicago was once the leader in livestock trading and meatpacking making it deserving of poet Carl Sandburg's descriptive term, "Hog Butcher for the World." The meatpacking industry eventually abandoned Chicago for new plants in the West, and the stockyards closed officially on August 1, 1971. *Book of Correspondence:* Letter from Larry P. Caine, vice president and general manager, International Amphitheatre, Chicago, Illinois, to author, 9 February 1976; and *Chicago Sun-Times,* 27 August 1981.

[7]Dudzik, p. 40.

[8]The Reverend Eugene Sedlaczek, CR, was born in Poznań, Poland. He studied philosophy and theology in Rome where he was ordained in 1892. An assistant at St. Stanislaus Kostka Church for several years, he served as pastor of St. Hedwig's Church for two weeks during the factional disturbances there. He then became rector of St. Stanislaus Kostka Parochial School, and for some time, was president of St. Stanislaus College. He served as pastor of St. Hyacinth's Church from 1897 to 1899, and that year, was appointed pastor of St. John Cantius Church.

Father Sedlaczek was very active in promoting the interests of the Polish Roman Catholic Union. In conjunction with Casimir Neumann, he was editor and publisher of the first Catholic youth magazine written in Polish in the United States from 1894 to 1896 called *Nadzieja* [Hope]. He left the Congregation of the Resurrection in 1902 and labored in New York as a secular priest. Edward T. Janas, CR, *Dictionary of American Resurrectionists, 1865–1965* (Rome: Gregorian University Press, 1957), pp. 109–111.

[9]Dudzik, p. 44.

[10]She was the first candidate who applied for admission to the community at St. Joseph Home for the Aged and Crippled. She was admitted with reluctance by Sister Theresa who considered her an unsuitable candidate. Nevertheless, upon the recommendation of Father Barzynski, Sister Theresa welcomed her in June. *Spis Sióstr* (AFSCL).

[11]Dudzik, p. 44.

[12]Raniszewski, p. 74.

[13]Dudzik, p. 44.

[14]Anna Welter was born on November 29, 1881, in Sempolno, Poland. She came to the United States in 1893, and settled with her parents in St. Stanislaus Kostka Parish. As a professed religious, Sister Mary Welter served principally as a teacher in the congregation's schools for over twenty years. She was stationed at the Motherhouse for twelve years and was sent to Our Lady of Victory Convent, Lemont, in 1939. She died there on October 17, 1955, at the age of seventy-four. *Spis Sióstr* (AFSCL); and *Congregation Membership Records* (AFSCL).

[15]*Book of Correspondence:* Sister Diana Tergerson, OSF, to author, 27 August 1975 (AFSCL).

[16]The Reverend Vincent Rapacz, CR, was born in 1865 in the Galicia region of Poland. In 1889, he entered the Congregation of the Resurrection and was ordained in 1895. In Chicago, he was assigned to St. Stanislaus Kostka Church from 1895 to 1899. Appointed to St. John Cantius Church in 1899, he served there for thirty-two years until his death in 1931. Because of his exemplary religious life and total dedication to the people of St. John Cantius Church, he was revered by the parishioners as another St. John Vianney. Father Rapacz also served as master of novices at St. Stanislaus College from 1903 to 1905. John J. Iwicki, CR, *The First One Hundred Years: A Study of the Apostolate of the Congregation of the Resurrection in the United States, 1866–1966* (Rome: Gregorian University Press, 1966), p. 97; and Janas, p. 51.

[17]The histories of religious communities are replete with the names of founders and foundresses who were unjustifiably removed as leaders of the congregations they themselves founded. The names of St. Benedict who began the great Benedictine Order and St. John of the Cross who headed the men's congregation of Carmelites easily come to mind. St. Therese Couderc, foundress of the Congregation of the Sisters of the Cenacle, for example, was deposed as superior and foundress because of a supposed lack of administrative ability. In later years, Mother Therese Couderc was again acknowledged as the foundress and was eventually canonized in 1970. Mother Theodore Guerin, foundress of the Congregation of the Sisters of Providence, was deposed from her office by Bishop de la Hailandiere who proceeded to appoint a new superior to replace her. The history of the Congregation of the Resurrection, so closely allied to the foundation of the Franciscan Sisters of Chicago, reveals the same injustice done to its main founder, the Reverend Peter Semenenko.

[18]See Chapter 9.

[19]Roger J. Coughlin and Cathryn A. Riplinger, *The Story of Charitable Care in the Archdiocese of Chicago, 1844–1959* (Chicago: The Catholic Charities, 1959), p. 154; and Edward R. Kantowicz, *Polish-American Politics in Chicago, 1888–1940* (Chicago: The University of Chicago Press, 1975), p. 39.

[20]Raniszewski, p. 77.

[21]Ibid., p. 89.

[22]John 12:24–26.

[23]All was not hardship and strife in spite of the circumstances. In her deposition, Sister M. Clara Ogurek recalls that on November 19, the feast of St. Elizabeth of Hungary, Sister Theresa, who loved laughter and gaiety, helped dress Sister Elizabeth Baut in colored robes to represent the Hungarian saint. The Sisters danced in homage to the "queen" and Sister Theresa's hair, ordinarily plaited in braids, became undone in the spirited dance. *Book of Depositions:* Sister M. Clara Ogurek (AFSCL); and Dudzik, p. 45.

[24]Dudzik, p. 45.

[25]Ibid., p. 54.

[26]Ibid., p. 45.

[27]Ibid.

[28]The postulancy is the first period of training in a religious house by means of a preliminary experience of the life. Before the renewal of religious life ushered in by the Second Vatican Council, the usual community exercises and manner of life were followed under the guidance of a postulant mistress. Traditionally, candidates for admission to a religious order usually spend a year or less in this stage before entering the next stage which is the novitiate. It is obvious that a strict interpretation of the postulancy is not entirely workable here since the postulants were actually the foundation group of the community.

[29]The novitiate is the period following the postulancy in which the novice undergoes a term of probation in preparation for temporary vows in a religious community. Again, the term "novitiate" like that of the "postulancy" is used loosely in applying it to the years that the foundation group spent as both postulants and novices. It can readily be seen that this was their only time of probation and their only preparation for the religious life. No one would deny that it was indeed a most difficult period to undergo in a budding community.

[30]Dudzik, p. 46.

[31]Ibid.

[32]Ibid.

[33]One has only to read Sister Theresa's own "Prayer over the City of Chicago" (see Appendix L) to know that she loved this great metropolis. In her "Chronicle" she speaks of Chicago as a "pleasant place in which to live." Here, however, Sister Theresa is alluding to the ancient city of Babylon on the Euphrates River famous for its riches, luxury, and vice. While loving Chicago, Sister Theresa was not blind to its faults. In this instance, she figuratively compares the tumult of the city to the relative peace and seclusion of Avondale.

[34]Dudzik, p. 47.

[35]Ibid.

[36]Professor Emil Wiedemann was born in Skurcz, Poland, in 1862. At twenty, he emigrated to the United States and settled in Chicago where he devoted his entire career to music. He was an organist at Immaculate Conception Church and St. Michael's Church, both in South Chicago, as well as at St. Adalbert's Church in Buffalo, New York, before becoming choirmaster at St. Hedwig's Church in Chicago in 1896. He remained there for over fifty years. An organist, composer, instructor, and choir director, Professor Wiedemann deservedly is one of the most respected and distinguished Polish-American musicians. Karol Wachtel, *Polonja w Ameryce* [The Poles in

America] (Philadelphia: Polish Star Co., 1944), p. 131.

[37]Andrew Kwasigroch emigrated to America from Poland in 1872. He was the organist at St. Stanislaus Kostka Church for more than forty-six years. Under his direction, the St. Stanislaus Choir was the first to present theatrical performances in the Polish language in Chicago. During the World Exposition held in Chicago in 1893, he was the general director of the three Polish choirs of St. Stanislaus Kostka Church which sang on "Polish Day," October 7, in Festival Hall. Francis Bolek, ed., *Who's Who in Polish America: A Biographical Directory of Polish American Leaders and Distinguished Poles Resident in the Americas,* 3rd ed. (New York: Harbinger House, 1943; Arno Publishers, 1970), p. 251; and Joseph A. Wiśniewski, CR, "St. Stanislaus Kostka Parish in Chicago: Its Spiritual, Educational, and Cultural Legacy to the 600,000 Americans of Polish Extraction, 1869–1908" (M.A. thesis, De Paul University, 1964), p. 94.

[38]Rose Kwasigroch, who sang at St. Stanislaus Kostka Church from 1890 to 1900, was an outstanding name in the musical circles of the Chicago Poles. The daughter of the noted Peter Kiołbassa, she was the wife of Francis Kwasigroch, a public official and one of the most influential Poles in Chicago. A student of world-famous opera stars, she appeared in operatic arias under Theodore Thomas, founder and first conductor of the Chicago Symphony Orchestra. She was also a soloist at Holy Name Cathedral in Chicago for many years. Bolek, p. 251.

[39]Brother Adalbert Góralski, CR, was the first organist and director of choir at St. Hyacinth's Church in Chicago. Born in 1852 in Polish Pomerania, Lubawa Province, Poland, he made his profession in the Congregation of the Resurrection in 1888 in Cracow. He arrived in Chicago in 1893, and was stationed at St. Hyacinth's Church from 1896 to 1912. In 1896, he organized the first choir at the parish giving it the name of his patron saint. The St. Adalbert Choir made frequent public appearances and for many years was the most active organization in the parish. After 1915, the choir was known as the St. Hyacinth's parish choir. Brother Adalbert served at St. Hedwig's Church from 1915 to 1917, and then returned to St. Hyacinth's Church. He died in Chicago on April 2, 1917.

Brother Adalbert compiled and edited approximately twelve Polish sacred song books in Chicago from 1909 to 1915. He also wrote many original compositions which his choir sang. Janas, p. 85; Iwicki, p. 101; and *St. Hyacinth: Golden Jubilee,* p. 43.

[40]Dudzik, p. 48.

[41]Ibid., p. 49.

[42]Raniszewski, p. 79.

[43]Dudzik, p. 49.

[44]Ibid., p. 50.

[45]An entry in the "Chronicle" says simply: "The one Sister who spread false rumors left the community." It is obvious that she is referring to Antoinette Graff who left the group after two months. Ibid.

[46]Ibid.

[47]Ibid., p. 51.

[48]Ibid., p. 52.

[49]I Cor. 13:7.

CHAPTER 11

Amid Sadness and Joy

After the feast of Christmas in 1898, Father Barzynski appeared to be in worse health than ever before. He continued to delegate Father Spetz to attend to much of the young community's spiritual and material matters. On the feast of the Espousals of the Blessed Virgin Mary, celebrated then on January 23, Father Barzynski felt well enough to celebrate Holy Mass for the Sisters and to hear their confessions. He appeared unusually happy, and during breakfast with the Sisters, he chatted amiably. He also gave the Sisters some religious admonitions and expressed his joy and satisfaction at their dedication to the aged and the crippled. Before leaving St. Joseph Home, he presented the Sisters with a chalice to be used during Holy Mass in the convent chapel.[1]

Upon his departure from St. Joseph Home, Father Barzynski met with a near-fatal accident. As he alighted from the streetcar on Division Street, he stumbled and fell to the ground, and only by hanging onto the exit pole was he able to save himself from the wheels of an oncoming streetcar. He was taken to the rectory of St. Stanislaus Kostka Church in an unconscious state, and his life hung precariously in the balance. Upon learning of the accident, the Sisters were thoroughly unnerved at the possibility of losing their beloved spiritual director. The thought of his dying, especially when his friendship and guidance were so badly needed, was most upsetting. Unfortunately, the near-tragic accident gave rise to another round of malicious gossip. The parishioners of St. Stanislaus Kostka Church now accused the Sisters of having burdened Father Barzynski with worry to such an extent that he was stricken ill while at St. Joseph Home for the Aged and Crippled.[2] The Sisters ardently prayed for Father Barzynski's return to good health. Their prayers were answered, for on March 19, the feast of St. Joseph, Father Spetz hired a horse and wagon and drove Father Barzynski to St. Joseph Home for an unexpected call on the Sisters. At the home, Father Barzynski delivered a brief conference to the Sisters and also informed them that they would be admitted into the novitiate as soon as he had received the necessary permission from Archbishop Feehan.[3]

Approximately three weeks later, Father Barzynski told the Sisters that they would be accepted into a formal novitiate on April 23, the feast of the patronage of St.

Joseph. In anticipation of this event, Sister Theresa and Sister Anna had been engaged in designing a religious garb to be worn as an external sign of the Sisters' consecration. They wished to conform to what they believed was the traditional Franciscan habit.[4] The result was a long, brown, one-piece habit with four deep pleats at the front yoke and four in the back folded in such a way that the top pleat, eleven inches wide, formed a scapular. The sleeves were wide, deep, and long with large cuffs. A cord made of white wool with tasseled fringes encircled the waist and was held in place by a single knot. It hung down the right side with three knots in the larger part. The three knots were to symbolize the three vows; every knot had five sections to symbolize the five wounds of Christ. On the left side was worn the Rosary of the Seven Joys of the Blessed Virgin Mary.[5] The headdress consisted of a coif, guimpe, brow band, and a stiff white cornet to which a white veil was sewed and pinned in three folds. The veil was lined with a white starched material and formed a circular headpiece.[6] A large collar in three suggested folds at the neck, and a crucifix made of wood and suspended from the neck completed the religious garb. The candidates who were to be received into the postulancy on the same day were to be dressed in long black dresses with wide sleeves, and a circular white collar. On their heads, they were to wear a black bonnet to which a veil could be added when they left the house.

The joyful preparation for the Sisters' reception into the novitiate and the postulancy was interrupted by the news that Father Barzynski had taken a turn for the worse and was now confined at the Alexian Brothers Hospital then located at Belden and Lakewood Avenues. Sister Theresa and Sister Anna received permission from Father Spetz to visit Father Barzynski on April 5. In his illness, Father Barzynski received the Sisters most cordially and voiced the hope that he would be able to receive them into the novitiate on the proposed date of April 23. The Sisters had no way of knowing that this visit to Father Barzynski in the hospital would be their last meeting with him on earth.

When April 23 finally arrived, Father Barzynski, now recovered, eagerly waited to be driven by Father Spetz to St. Joseph Home. In the meantime, however, Sister Anna, fearing for Father Barzynski's health, had postponed the date of the reception of the Sisters into the novitiate and postulancy to May 21, the feast of the Ascension. She had failed, however, to notify him of this change. As a result, Father Barzynski never had the joy of investing the Sisters with the habit which he had so long desired to do. He died on May 2, 1899. Only the day before, he had been taken for a carriage ride in Lincoln Park by an old and prominent parishioner, and Father Barzynski, still weakened from his long illness, caught a cold which developed into pneumonia.[7] Early on the morning of May 2, the Sisters learned that he had been hospitalized. During the day they prayed for his return to good health, but at evening prayer, they heard the tolling of the church bells for the deceased. Their worst fears were confirmed when on their way to mass on the morning of May 3, they were informed of Father Barzynski's death. The Sisters cried aloud upon reaching the church. Sister Theresa wrote of that moment:

To me, this was the greatest sorrow which I had experienced in my life. My present grief was greater than when my parents died whom I dearly loved. We needed Father Vincent more than ever since we still did not have the habit. We were busily preparing to receive it and had hoped to receive it from his hands. There were other reasons for our feeling of abandonment. I felt the loss of a good spiritual father, who, for almost sixteen years, had been my confessor. After God and the Mother of God, I owed the greatest gratitude to him. My success, while still in the world, was due to his directing me on the road of self-denial. His exemplary life of mortification, great love of neighbor, and other virtues which shone so during his lifetime, and which I had observed for so many years, now disappeared with him forever. My only consolation was in knowing that I did not place all my hopes in him as almost everyone believed. I tried to conform to his advice which he so often gave. But he also reminded me not to place my confidence in him but in God. If I had placed my confidence solely in him, it would have been the end of the community as so many people believed. However, we did not waver, but fastened our hopes on God. Since God had begun this work through him [Father Barzynski], He would continue it for His glory.[8]

The funeral took place on May 5, 1899, and all eight Sisters attended. Leaving St. Joseph Home for the Aged and Crippled in the care of Divine Providence, the Sisters traveled by streetcar to St. Stanislaus Kostka Church.

Hundreds of clergymen from throughout the United States were present as well as scores of Sisters. Thousands from every parish, society, and fraternity in Chicago attended. In spite of the immense crowd, the Sisters were able to be seated in the church having been recognized by the members of the Home Planning Committee. Sister Theresa used the barest of words to sum up the fullness of heart each Sister experienced as she sat in the church waiting for the Solemn Requiem Mass to begin. "There," she wrote in her "Chronicle," "we wept and prayed."[9]

The death of Father Barzynski engulfed Chicago, as well as the entire Polonia in America, in deep sorrow. The city had never before witnessed a funeral marked with such universal and genuine grief.[10] The first page of the *Dziennik Chicagoski* of May 3, 1899, boldly stated that with the death of Father Barzynski, the Polish people everywhere had lost a person "whose name was interwoven with the history of Polish immigrants in America forever."[11] In a letter from Father Spetz to the Reverend Wacław Kruszka, Father Barzynski was referred to as "a great patriot and one of the most worthy Polish priests in America . . . a man of largess of heart and the true spirit of God . . . a zealous priest who worked beyond his strength."[12] When the remains of Father Barzynski were carried out of St. Stanislaus Kostka Church, the Sisters walked slowly alongside his coffin. When the funeral cortege passed the nearby Holy Family Orphanage on Division Street, almost every orphan was outdoors, tearfully bidding farewell to this most beloved guardian.[13] Sadness gripped Sister Theresa at the thought of what would now happen to the children. She was aware of the difficulties the Holy Family Orphanage was experiencing and how much Father Barzynski had suffered on that account.[14] For the time being, however, she put those thoughts aside.

Gigantic crowds lined the way to St. Adalbert's Cemetery.[15] When the Sisters reached Milwaukee Avenue, they took the streetcar to Jefferson Park which was as far as the streetcar line extended.[16] From there the Sisters proceeded on foot to the cemetery, approximately twenty blocks or two and one-half miles away. They walked briskly in order to arrive before the funeral cortege. When they reached the designated burial place, they stood a short distance from the graveside, in tears, unable to get closer because of the huge crowd. Sister Theresa wrote sadly of this event in her "Chronicle":

> During the ceremonies, many eyes were turned in our direction and many
> pointed us out to their friends. Some expressed their sympathy for us, and
> wondered what would happen to us now. Others smiled at us with pity,
> asking: "What will become of these old maidens now?"[17]

At the graveside, Archbishop Feehan gave the final absolution of the Church, and the Reverend Francis Gordon, CR, the editor of the *Dziennik Chicagoski* and a close friend of Father Barzynski, gave the final invocation.[18] Thus ended the funeral of this "intensely loyal American, fiercely devout Catholic, and passionately patriotic Pole."[19]

When the ceremonies at the cemetery were concluded, the Sisters headed toward home on foot and offered this mortification for the repose of the soul of Father Barzynski. By this time, night had fallen, and when the Sisters arrived at St. Joseph Home, they found the aged men and women in great panic. With the Sisters absent for such a length of time, the residents feared that they had been deserted. Even worse, they believed that perhaps upon their return, the Sisters would ask them to leave the shelter of St. Joseph Home.[20] In all the excitement of the day, even the cows had wandered away, but luckily, were found again. Soon the Sisters were so busy easing the fears of the elderly that they had little time left to grieve for Father Barzynski. The elderly, so happy that they would not be asked to leave St. Joseph Home, kissed the hands of the Sisters out of gratitude and showered verbal blessings upon them.[21]

Although Father Barzynski's death was a terrible blow to the small group of religious women, and they grieved at the loss of their spiritual mentor, their sorrow was alleviated by the presence of Father Barzynski's young assistant, the Reverend Andrew Spetz, CR. In her "Chronicle," Sister Theresa wrote: "After the loss of Father Barzynski, God did not forsake us because He sent us the Reverend Andrew Spetz."[22] In the pious and enthusiastic Father Spetz, the Sisters had gained another faithful and gentle counselor. Sister M. Theresa, in particular, found in him a good friend and prudent director.

The noble character of Father Spetz was apparent from the beginning of his ministry to the young community. Called "another St. Vincent de Paul" among the poor of

Reverend Andrew Spetz, CR, Second Spiritual Director of the
Franciscan Sisters of Chicago

St. Stanislaus Kostka Parish, Father Spetz possessed not only deep faith and piety, but was
also a man with "keen insight into public affairs, and ever active where the honor of God,
the good of the Church, the welfare of the people, or Christian education were
concerned."[23]

    The Reverend Andrew Spetz was born on December 16, 1858, in Berlin (now
Kitchener), a town in the province of Ontario, Canada. In 1876, he graduated from St.
Jerome's College located in the town of his birth. In 1878, he went to Rome where he
entered the Congregation of the Resurrection. Desiring to labor among the Slavs because
of the scarcity of priests in their mission lands, Father Spetz set out in 1881, with the
consent of his superiors, to Adrianople in Bulgaria, to labor there and bring the Bulgarians
back to the Church of Rome. On May 4, 1884, he was ordained a priest in Adrianople. For
three years he acted as procurator for the mission, and in 1889, was summoned to Rome to

become the vice-rector of the Polish Papal College. In 1893, he was transferred to St. Mary's College in St. Mary, Kentucky, where he was professor of classic and modern languages.[24] Father Spetz spoke English, German, Greek, Italian, Bulgarian, and Turkish with great ease[25] and learned to speak Polish quite fluently which was an added advantage when dealing with the Sisters.[26] This modest, conscientious, and exemplary priest seemed ideally suited to assume the spiritual direction of the struggling community, which in its formative period still mourned the passing of Father Barzynski.

To assure the Sisters of his support, loyalty, and valuable direction, Father Spetz designated Pentecost Sunday, May 21, 1899, the date originally set, as the day on which they would receive the habit and begin their formal novitiate. He arranged, therefore, for the Sisters to begin a four-day retreat under the direction of the Reverend Florian Matuszewski, CR.[27] Father Matuszewski encouraged the Sisters to hold fast to the life to which they had dedicated themselves, and through his conferences, the Sisters obtained a greater knowledge of the religious life. They now felt that they were better prepared to assume the obligations of the novitiate than they had of the postulancy. Although the Sisters still performed their full share of daily duties, they tried in every way to devote more time to their spiritual exercises and to prepare interiorly for the moment after which they had so long aspired. On the vigil of Pentecost, Father Spetz brought the ciborium containing the Blessed Sacrament to the chapel of St. Joseph Home where the Eucharist would now be permanently reserved and become truly the center of the community. Sister Theresa could scarcely withhold her joy:

> I could not contain my happiness at the thought that from this day forward, we would have the Blessed Sacrament in our small chapel. Now that Our Lord would be dwelling so near to us, it would be possible to speak with Him more frequently and to present our various cares and concerns to Him.[28]

The chapel itself had been furnished in a simple and dignified manner for the occasion. When the Sisters first moved into St. Joseph Home, the Archconfraternity of the Immaculate Heart of Mary at St. Stanislaus Kostka parish had donated a statue of Our Lady of Victory[29] as well as one of St. Joseph and of St. Francis of Assisi. The altar was obtained from the oratory of St. Stanislaus Kostka Church, and the pews were donated by the Women's Rosary Society of St. Stanislaus Kostka Church on the occasion of the fiftieth wedding anniversary of Sister Anna's parents.

On the feast of Pentecost, May 21, 1899, at seven-thirty o'clock in the morning, Father Spetz presented the religious habit to the Sisters in a very simple but impressive ceremony. Each Sister to be received into the novitiate had her religious garb laid out in the pew before her. When Father Spetz intoned the "Veni, Creator,"[30] the Sisters joined in the singing of the hymn. He blessed their habits, delivered a brief sermon in which he exhorted the Sisters to be worthy religious, and then placed in their hands the religious habit and a candle.[31] The Sister-novices went to an adjoining room, dressed themselves in their religious garb, and returned with lighted candles to the chapel to continue the ceremony. Father Spetz then announced that to their tertiary names would now be added the lovely name of *Mary* in honor of the Immaculate Conception.[32] Thus the Sister-novices were now called Sister Mary Theresa Dudzik, Sister Mary Anna Wysinski, Sister Mary Angeline Topolinski, and Sister Mary Agnes Dzik. The Sister-candidates received into the postulancy were Marianne Ogurek (Sister Mary Clara); Caroline Baut (Sister Mary Elizabeth); Theodosia Troeder (Sister Mary Frances); and Anna Welter (Sister Mary). Since they already wore the postulant's dress, they now received a black bonnet from Father Spetz to complete their outfits.[33] The aged men and women witnessing the reception were moved to tears as were the Sisters themselves.[34] Father Spetz then celebrated a Low Mass[35] during which the Sisters received Holy Communion. After mass, the Sisters sang the "Magnificat"[36] in gratitude to God for all the graces with which they had been blessed. Although the Sisters had had no time to prepare properly for the rendering of the "Magnificat," they sang with all their hearts and with the greatest devotion.[37]

Although it was a memorable day and one to be shared with loved ones, no relatives or guests had been invited to the ceremonies. Since the Sisters attended to all the duties associated with St. Joseph Home themselves, they would have had no one to take care of their guests. Instead, the Sisters rejoiced on this momentous occasion with the jubilant aged and crippled residents. In the afternoon, however, the Sisters welcomed some visitors who came for the most part out of curiosity to see the religious habit with which the Sisters had been invested.[38]

On the following day, the Reverend John Piechowski, CR,[39] the pastor of St. Hedwig's Church, arrived with four Sisters of the Congregation of the Holy Family of Nazareth who staffed St. Hedwig's School. After celebrating Holy Mass for all the Sisters, he joined them at breakfast. He congratulated the new Sister-novices and the Sister-postulants and wished them God's blessings together with the sincere hope for continued growth of the community. He told the Sisters of several young women who had expressed a desire to enter religious life and promised to direct them to the new community.[40] That same day, the Reverend Joseph Gieburowski, CR,[41] an assistant at St. Hedwig's Church, also visited the Sisters. In the days which followed, Father Gieburowski proved to be a God-send. As confessor to the Sisters, he instructed them in the nature of the vows and the obligations which they entailed. With Father Spetz, he composed morning and evening prayers for the Sisters, and on many occasions, arrived at the chapel early in the morning to pray with them. He also directed the Sisters in the methods of meditation, oftentimes making the meditation aloud for their instruction. He made the Sisters conscious of their calling, so beautifully expressed by St. Paul: "If you and I belong to Christ, guaranteed as his anointed, it is all God's doing; it is God also who has set his seal upon us, and as a pledge of what is to come has given the Spirit to dwell in our hearts."[42]

When Father Gieburowski left America in 1901, the Reverend Vincent Rapacz, CR, the Reverend Stephen Kowalczyk, CR,[43] and the Reverend Francis Dembiński, CR,[44] served as the Sisters' spiritual guides and confessors.

AMID SADNESS AND JOY

[1]Matka Maria Teresa Dudzik, "Kronika Sióstr Franciszkanek pod opieką Św. Kunegundy w Chicago, Illinois" [The Chronicle of the Franciscan Sisters under the patronage of St. Kunegunda in Chicago, Illinois] Unpublished manuscript, 1910 (AFSCL), p. 52.

[2]Ibid., p. 53.

[3]Ibid.

[4]It is traditionally believed that St. Francis' habit was a coarse gray tunic. Actually, St. Francis did not strictly regulate the habit of his first followers. The shape and the color were of small importance in his eyes. In 1260, however, St. Bonaventure sought to restrict the garb of the Friars Minor to a single type notably by seeking to prohibit exaggerated length and width of sleeves, cowls, and colors. Alexandre Masseron and Marion A. Habig, OFM, *The Franciscans* (Chicago: Franciscan Herald Press, 1959), pp. 86–87; and Arnoldo Mondadori, *The Life and Times of St. Francis* (Philadelphia and New York: The Curtis Publishing Co., 1967), p. 51.

[5]The Rosary of the Seven Joys is also known as the Franciscan Crown and consists of reciting the Our Father once and the Hail Mary ten times in each of the seven decades in honor of the seven joys of the Blessed Virgin Mary. At the end, Hail Mary is added twice more to complete the seventy-two years Mary is presumed to have lived. It is the tradition of the Franciscans that in the year 1422, a young novice was about to leave because he no longer had the opportunity to crown Our Lady's statue as had been his custom before his entrance into the order. As a consequence, Mary appeared to him and taught him how to weave a spiritual crown of prayers in honor of her joys.

[6]There seems to be little doubt, as early photos reveal, that the headdress and collar of the Congregation of the School Sisters of Notre Dame were the basic pattern for those of the Franciscan tertiaries. It would not be presumptuous to believe that Sister Theresa and Sister Anna were guided in their choice of a style so similar to that of the School Sisters of Notre Dame because these Sisters staffed St. Stanislaus Kostka School. It must also be remembered that both Sister Theresa and Sister Anna had sisters in the Congregation of the School Sisters of Notre Dame, and this fact, no doubt, also influenced their design of a headdress and collar for their new Franciscan community.

[7]Shortly after his ordination, Father Barzynski had developed a lung problem which afflicted him for the rest of his life. See Chapter 3.

[8]Dudzik, pp. 56–57.

[9]Ibid.

[10]Miecislaus Haiman, "The Poles in Chicago," in *Poles of Chicago: A History of One Century of Contribution to the City of Chicago, Illinois,* ed. Polish Pageant, Inc. (Chicago: By the Author, 1937), p. 177.

[11]*Dziennik Chicagoski,* 3 May 1899.

[12]Wacław Kruszka, *Historya Polska w Ameryce* [The History of Poles in America], 12 vols. (Milwaukee: Kuryer Press, 1905), 9:243.

[13]Dudzik, p. 57.

[14]The particular problems which faced Father Barzynski at this time are made clearer in Chapter 12 which deals with the Holy Family Orphanage and the various issues connected with it.

[15]Mention has already been made of St. Adalbert's Cemetery as the final resting place of many members of the Dudzik family. This historically relevant cemetery was organized by the Resurrectionist Fathers for the Polish, Bohemian, and Czech Catholics in the Archdiocese of Chicago. In October 1872, the Reverend Adolph Bakanowski, CR, pastor of St. Stanislaus Kostka Church, and the Reverend Joseph Molitor, pastor of St. Wenceslaus (Bohemian) Church, purchased twenty-one acres of land in Niles, Illinois, to serve as a common cemetery. Father Barzynski was buried in St. Adalbert's Cemetery, but in 1901, was reinterred in an imposing mausoleum with his monument above it. It was erected by his many friends and sympathizers in grateful recognition of

his enormous contributions to the development of the Polish-American people. Enlarged in 1925, the mausoleum is the final resting place for all members of the Congregation of the Resurrection in the Chicago Province. John J. Iwicki, CR, *The First One Hundred Years: A Study of the Apostolate of the Congregation of the Resurrection in the United States, 1866-1966* (Rome: Gregorian University Press, 1966), p. 119.

[16]Jefferson Park, an early suburb of Chicago, was a settlement on the old Plank Road, now Milwaukee Avenue. It is said to have been a trading post several years before Chicago was incorporated. It is an area lying west of the Chicago, Milwaukee, and St. Paul Railroad tracks and north of Gunnison Avenue. It is bounded on the west by Narragansett Avenue, goes north to Bryn Mawr and then Austin Avenue from that point to the Forest Preserve. Chicago Plan Commission, *Forty-Four Cities in the City of Chicago* (Chicago: City of Chicago, 1942), p. 92.

[17]Dudzik, p. 58.

[18]*Centennial: St. Stanislaus Kostka Church, 1867–1967* (Chicago: 1967), p. 39.

[19]Andrew M. Greeley, "Catholicism in America: 200 Years and Counting," *The Critic,* Summer 1976, p. 31.

[20]Dudzik, p. 58.

[21]Ibid., p. 59.

[22]Ibid., p. 54.

[23]Reverend Joseph Thompson, ed., *Diamond Jubilee of the Archdiocese of Chicago, 1920* (Des Plaines, Illinois: St. Mary's Training School Press, 1920), p. 385.

[24]St. Mary's College, *Memorare, 1821–1871* (St. Mary, Kentucky, 1871), p. 34.

[25]Siostra M. Gonzaga Raniszewski, OSFK, *Rys historyczny Zgromadzenia Sióstr Franciszkanek Błogosławionej Kunegundy. Część pierwsza, 1860–1910* [A historical survey of the Franciscan Sisters of Blessed Kunegunda. Part one, 1860–1910] (Chicago: By the Author, 1947), p. 85.

[26]Andrew Spetz, CR, *Epistolae, 1893–1912* (Archives of the Congregation of the Resurrection: Rome, Italy).

[27]The Reverend Florian Matuszewski, CR, was an assistant at several parishes assigned to the Congregation of the Resurrection, notably St. Stanislaus Kostka. He served there in 1893 and again from 1898 to 1901. He left the Congregation in 1901 and labored as a secular priest in Minnesota. Edward T. Janas, CR, *Dictionary of American Resurrectionists, 1865–1967* (Rome: Gregorian University Press, 1967), pp. 106–107.

[28]Dudzik, p. 60.

[29]The statue of Our Lady of Victory became a cherished item in the history of the Franciscan Sisters of Chicago. The statue, brought over from France by Father Barzynski, has not been duplicated in the United States. For many years, the statue remained in the chapel of St. Joseph Home until it was transferred to the Mother Theresa Museum in Lemont. A replica of this revered statue, made of Carrara marble, was placed in the foyer of the new Our Lady of Victory Convent Motherhouse on June 7, 1968.

Mary's title of "Our Lady of Victory" and "Help of Christians" came about as a consequence of the famous victory which the Christians gained over the Turks near Lepanto in the Ionian Sea. For more than a hundred years before the Battle of Lepanto, the Turks had gained numerous victories and had threatened the Christian faith of all of Europe. Alarmed at the threat to Christendom, Pope St. Pius V assured the Christian world of victory if Mary, the Mother of God, were invoked in prayer. A great battle took place on October 7, 1571, at Lepanto, and the Christians emerged victorious. To leave a perpetual memorial of this blessing, Pope St. Pius V added, "Help of Christians, pray for us," to Mary's litany and a special feast on the Church calendar. Pope Gregory XIII ordered it celebrated on the first Sunday of October. It has from then on been called "Rosary Sunday" The day designated as the feast of Our Lady of Victory was May 24. In 1683, the Turks were again repelled in battle by the invocation of Mary. Historically, these victories preserved Christendom for Europe. Today, the Church calendar lists October 7 as the feast of Mary under her titles, "Our Lady of the Rosary," and "Our Lady of Victory." *Book of Correspondence:* Unpublished instruction given by the founder, the Reverend J. J. Sigstein, Victory Noll, Indiana, 1935; received by author from Sister Margaret Campbell, Victory Noll Sisters, Huntington, Indiana, 13 November 1975 (AFSCL).

[30]"Veni, Creator," [Come, Creator Spirit], the oldest hymn in the Catholic Church to the Holy Spirit, was usually sung at the ceremonies connected with the reception of the religious habit and the profession of vows in the older established congregations.

[31]Candles, used in many rites and ceremonies of the Church, are a mark of joy and show honor to God. They also symbolize Christ as the "Light of the World."

[32]Since this first investiture, it has been the custom of the congregation to add the name of "Mary" or "Marie" to the new name each novice receives at her reception to the novitiate. The custom is still carried on except, of course, in instances where the Sister chooses to retain her baptismal name.

[33]Dudzik, p. 61.

[34]Ibid.

[35]"Low Mass" was a simplified form of the Liturgy of the Mass as said by one priest in contrast to "High Mass" which was sung and had three priests.

[36]The "Magnificat," often sung on solemn occasions, is the canticle of the Blessed Virgin Mary, spoken on the occasion of her visit to her cousin, Elizabeth, and derives its name from the first words of the Latin version, "Magnificat anima mea Dominum," that is, "My soul doth magnify the Lord."

It was the congregation's customary hymn of thanksgiving since that time for every reception to the novitiate and to the postulancy. It was also sung after the *Little Office of the Blessed Virgin Mary* every Sunday in gratitude for the graces received that week in every house of the congregation. The practice was generally discontinued after the First Extraordinary Chapter of Affairs of 1968 and its singing was optional. With the introduction of *Christian Prayer: The Liturgy of the Hours* in 1972, however, every Evening Prayer concludes with the recitation of the "Magnificat." It is sung on Sundays and holydays and at the funeral of a Sister of the congregation. Dudzik, p. 62.

[37]Dudzik, p. 62.

[38]Ibid.

[39]The Reverend John Piechowski, CR, referred to in earlier chapters, was born in Poland on December 27, 1863. After his ordination in 1891, he was assigned to the College of the Resurrection Fathers in Lwów, Poland. He was then transferred to the United States where he became an instructor in the newly founded St. Stanislaus College. In 1892, Father Barzynski appointed him principal of the school, a position he occupied until 1895. His faith and trust in God regarding the aim of the school convinced many reluctant immigrant parents of the necessity of a higher education for their children.

From January to June 1895, he served as the first pastor of St. Hyacinth's Church. From June 1895, to January 1909, he was the pastor of St. Hedwig's Church where he was called to halt the Polish Independent Church Movement. His personality together with his patience, understanding, and diligence enabled him to deal with the situation effectively and to cause the virtual rebirth of the parish. During his fourteen-year pastorate, many dissenters returned to the Church, and within ten years, that is, by 1905, the parish had 1,500 families, over 1,300 school children, and thirty-four societies. He was a most zealous administrator, and the erection of the magnificent St. Hedwig's Church is credited to him. His last assignment was at St. Stanislaus Kostka Church where he served from 1917 until his death in 1921.

He founded a monthly publication in 1907 at St. Hedwig's called *Wiara i Ojczyzna* [Faith and Fatherland]. The magazine was edited by Szczęsny Zahajkiewicz, an illustrious writer, who also taught at St. Hedwig's School. The magazine was short-lived; it lasted from January to April. Prior to that, he had founded a Polish Catholic juvenile magazine called *Przyjaciel Młodzieży* [Friend of Youth] which lasted from 1895 to 1897. Casimir Neuman, the editor of the *Dziennik Chicagoski* was also the editor of this magazine. Iwicki, pp. 91–93, 212; and Janas, pp. 48–49.

[40]Many parish priests acted as spiritual directors to the young women who came to them in confession. Consequently, they had the opportunity to guide many of the young women to religous congregations suited to them or to their particular abilities.

[41]An outstanding missionary and preacher, the Reverend Joseph Gieburowski, CR, served as a spiritual moderator of the Franciscan Sisters of Chicago from 1899 to 1901.

Born and educated in Poland, he received his philosophy and theology training in Rome where he was ordained in 1892. He served as an assistant at St. Stanislaus Kostka Church from 1892 to 1895 during which time he observed the charitable works of Josephine Dudzik.

Father Gieburowski was a vigorous opponent of the Polish "Independent" Church Movement which had its origin at St. Hedwig's Church. His appointment as temporary pastor in 1895 brought about a momentary peace among the opposing factions in the parish. He returned to serve the parish again in 1897 and remained until 1901. He returned to apostolic labor in Austria and Poland and died in Lwów on November 25, 1932. Iwicki, p. 135; and Janas, pp. 21–22.

[42]II Cor. 1:21–22.

[43]The Reverend Stephen Kowalczyk, CR, was an assistant at St. John Cantius Church from 1909 to 1915, and pastor from 1921 to 1930. He was chosen to succeed Father Andrew Spetz as superior and rector of St. John Cantius Seminary in St. Louis in 1918 when the former died. His kindness and generosity inspired many young men at Weber High School in Chicago to enter the novitiate of the congregation. His contributions to the spiritual and material welfare of the St. Joseph Novitiate in Chicago make him memorable in the annals of the Congregation of the Resurrection. Iwicki, pp. 178, 185; and Janas, p. 35.

[44]The Reverend Francis Dembiński, CR, the "Fatherly Priest," was an assistant at several Resurrectionist parishes in Chicago. He served as the assistant at St. Stanislaus Kostka Church from 1909 to 1915, and was appointed the pastor from 1915 to 1920. Janas, p. 15.

CHAPTER 12

St. Vincent's Orphan Asylum

Historically, the Great Fire of 1871 left in its aftermath a legacy of disaster for Chicago. The "Black Death Pox" raged and the number of deaths it caused almost equaled the number of people who had perished in the Great Fire itself.[1] Along with the ruination of homes and property there was the destruction of factories which deprived countless families of wage earners. Conditions worsened when the devastating economic crisis which gripped Chicago in the 1890s left many families without a father's wages, and the effect on the family was bleak. The wave of influenza which raged during the 1890s, as well as waterborne diseases such as typhoid fever caused further devastation to families. Added to these facts was the high incidence of mortality among child-bearing mothers due to the unsanitary conditions of the rapidly growing city. Thus, many children were orphaned or sometimes simply abandoned by bereaved fathers or troubled families. As with all other ethnic groups in Chicago, the growth of the Polish population meant a proportional growth in social and welfare problems for the Poles. The need arose now to address the problems of the orphaned, abandoned, and delinquent children. Care had to be provided for those children requiring shelter if the family were in temporary need of assistance. Care also had to be provided for illegitimate children as well as for those whose parents were desirous of relinquishing them.

Father Barzynski had founded the first institution for the children of Polish immigrants at St. Josaphat's Parish in the Lakeview area in 1885. Under the guidance of the Congregation of the Sisters of the Holy Family of Nazareth, ten orphans were housed in the parish school and convent. The expense of their care was met by the financial contributions of the parishes of both St. Stanislaus Kostka and St. Josaphat Churches.[2] When the number of orphans sharply increased, Father Barzynski received permission from Archbishop Feehan to build a large, four-story dwelling on Division and Holt Streets in the vicinity of St. Stanislaus Kostka Church to harbor the orphans of all Polish and Bohemian parishes. The Sisters of the Congregation of the Holy Family of Nazareth staffed the orphanage which they aptly named the Holy Family Orphanage. All Polish and Bohemian pastors supplied the necessary finances to maintain the institution, and a board of directors was formed consisting of ten Polish and Bohemian pastors with Father Barzynski as chairman. Because the Sisters of the Holy Family of Nazareth and Father Barzynski failed to agree on vital issues concerning the future of the orphanage,[3] it was transferred to the care of the Congregation of the School Sisters of Notre Dame on September 4, 1890.[4] By 1892, the number of orphans had risen to 123 and was growing steadily.

In 1898, the Bohemian pastors withdrew their financial support of the orphanage to establish an independent Bohemian orphanage in Lisle, Illinois.[5] The Holy Family Orphanage continued to be supported with donations of food and money provided chiefly by the Polish parishes of St. Stanislaus Kostka, St. Hedwig, Holy Trinity, St. Adalbert, and St. Michael in South Chicago.[6] The sole responsibility for maintaining the orphanage now fell primarily to Father Barzynski and the Congregation of the Resurrection. Because of the protracted lack of funds so vitally needed to continue day-to-day operation of the institution, Father Barzynski requested the School Sisters of Notre Dame to take up a collection in St. Stanislaus Kostka Parish. Because the Constitutions and Customs of their congregation did not allow them to solicit alms, the Sisters suggested placing the orphans in the care of a congregation which had no restrictions in regard to begging. After consulting with Archbishop Feehan, Father Barzynski made the decision to transfer the orphans to the young Franciscan community in Avondale. Father Barzynski had already discussed the matter with Sister M. Theresa early in 1898, indicating to her that someday the Sisters might be obliged to assume this responsibility. Sister M. Theresa was alarmed at the suggestion when Father Barzynski had presented it to her. She realized that she and the Sisters were not, as yet, sufficiently grounded in the essentials of the spiritual life, nor were they fully aware of the complete and binding responsibilities that living an authentic religious life demanded. At the time of Father Barzynski's suggestion, Sister M. Theresa had voiced these legitimate fears to him. She steadfastly maintained that the Sisters would have to have more spiritual guidance and instruction as well as some practical training in child care in order to rear and educate the orphans properly. Father Barzynski had simply answered: "As God shall ordain." The entire matter was left at that.[7] Sister M. Theresa knew that Father Barzynski's reply implied total and implicit surrender to the care of Divine Providence and utter trust in His Divine Will. Before Father Barzynski could finalize any plans for the complete transfer of the orphans to St. Joseph Home for the Aged and Crippled in Avondale, however, he died. To Father Spetz was left the matter of providing support for the orphans. At the end of May 1899, he proposed to Sister M. Theresa that the Sisters make plans for sheltering them. As for the Holy Family Orphanage, the Congregation of the Resurrection was formulating plans to convert it into St. Stanislaus College for young men.[8]

Sister M. Anna, the mother superior, and Sister M. Theresa prepared to accept the orphans in July. They realized, of course, that the conditions at St. Joseph Home were far from ideal for the kind of care the orphans required. The overcrowded St. Joseph Home already housed nine Sisters and twenty aged men and women. The Sisters had no alternative but to remodel the attic of St. Joseph Home in order to provide sleeping quarters for the orphans. The laundry, the area used for doing the washing and ironing in the winter, was converted into a kitchen. The Sisters gave up their refectory for use as the orphans' dining room.

On July 18, 1899, twenty-seven older orphan girls moved into St. Joseph Home. The younger boys and girls remained at the Holy Family Orphanage in the care of the Reverend John Kruszynski, CR,[9] the superior of St. Stanislaus College, and one Resurrectionist brother. The School Sisters of Notre Dame left the Holy Family Orphanage on August 16, 1899.[10] Before their departure, however, they brought over twelve more young girls and infants. Twenty-seven boys still remained at the orphanage. Two weeks later, Father Spetz asked Mother M. Anna to send at least two Sisters "to the rescue of the Resurrectionist brother!"[11] The two Sister-postulants, Sister M. Clara Ogurek and Sister Mary Welter were sent. A short while later, Sister M. Clara was joined by a new candidate, Rosalie Kubera,[12] when Sister Mary Welter was recalled to St. Joseph Home.[13]

With the addition of the young girls and infants, St. Joseph Home was now seriously overcrowded. The workload of the Sisters was oppressive. Besides having charge of all the infants and children, the Sisters maintained the dormitories and laundry. They conducted a school for the orphans with lessons geared to their particular ages.[14] The children were also instructed in the fundamentals of the Catholic faith and prepared for the reception of their First Holy Communion or, in the case of the older children, for the sacrament of Confirmation.[15] The Sisters' main source of income at this time was voluntary offerings received from people who were acquainted with their plight or the offerings of money and food gathered by begging. Whatever the circumstances, however, the aged and the orphans had a substantial amount of nourishing food and no one ever went hungry, except on occasion, the Sisters themselves.[16]

After a few months, the Sisters came to the conclusion that only a new structure would suffice to house the orphans properly. Without funds but with unbounding confidence in Divine Providence, the Sisters determined to construct a separate home for the orphans. Relying on Father Spetz's ability to negotiate a loan for $12,000, construction of a three-story brick structure began at the end of September. The work progressed so well that the building was ready for occupancy by December 21, 1899. On that day, the twenty-seven remaining boys were transferred from the Holy Family Orphanage, and now sixty-six children lived in the new St. Vincent's Orphan Asylum, so-named in honor of the patron saint of the orphans' beloved Father Vincent Barzynski.[17] The boys occupied the first floor; the girls lived on the second floor, while the third floor was reserved as a much-needed chapel.

Shortly after the work had commenced on St. Vincent's Orphan Asylum, the Sisters received the first official "Document of Erection" from the Most Reverend Patrick Feehan, archbishop of Chicago, approving the St. Joseph Home for the Aged and Crippled and St. Vincent's Orphan Asylum.[18] It read:

Most Reverend Patrick A. Feehan
First Archbishop of Chicago 1880–1902

I hereby approve of St. Joseph's Home for the Aged and Crippled, and St. Vincent's Orphan Asylum on Schubert and Hamlin Avenues established and conducted by the Ladies of the Third Order of St. Francis under the direction of the R. R. Fathers of the Congregation of the Resurrection.

At the same time I recommend these benevolent institutions to the faithful of the archdiocese and to the well-known charity of the Chicago public.

P. A. Feehan
Archbishop of Chicago[19]

18th Oct.
1899

On Christmas Eve, 1899, St. Vincent's Orphan Asylum and the chapel were blessed by the Reverend John Kasprzycki, CR,[20] the pastor of St. Stanislaus Kostka Church. It was a private dedication with only Father Spetz and several parishioners attending.[21] After the guests had departed, Father Spetz transferred the Blessed Sacrament from the former small chapel in St. Joseph Home to the new chapel in St. Vincent's Orphan Asylum. Father Spetz had secured an organ for the new chapel, and at the Christmas Midnight Mass, August Kochanski, the organist at St. Hyacinth's Church, played and the St. Cecilia Choir of that parish sang. During the second mass celebrated that day, Brother Adalbert Góralski accompanied the Junior Choir of St. Hyacinth's Church at the organ. For the first time, the Sisters had Benediction of the Most Blessed Sacrament in the chapel during which they joyfully sang the "Te Deum," a hymn of praise and thanksgiving. Thus, at the end of the nineteenth century, the former band of Franciscan tertiaries consisted of four novices, four postulants, and ten candidates in charge of seventeen aged women, seven aged men, and sixty-six orphans.[22]

Unlike Holy Family Orphanage, St. Vincent's Orphan Asylum did not receive financial assistance from many of the parishes but was supported mainly by the donations of friends and the solicitation of alms through a door-to-door collection by the Sisters. Even the $12,000 loan obtained by Father Spetz to build the orphanage remained for the Sisters to defray.[23] Sometimes, parents, who could afford to, paid according to their means. This letter, found in the archives of the congregation, is typical of the spirit and tone of the letters received by the Sisters:

> Sister Angels!
>
> You will excuse me for not writing to you before. I have been waiting to get a little money to send you. I will send you some in a few days. I hope is _____ well and happy. I feel satisfied that he has every care better than I could give him in my trouble. [*sic*] In regards to adopting _____, I will be perfectly willing to in case anything should happening [*sic*] to me, but I wish you keep him as your own child, and not to give him to any one, but I hope I can live to see him grow to be a man, and in regards to his age and birthplace, he was born in Goshen, Indiana, on July 7, 1896. I do not wish to give him up as long as I live. I think he is getting along fine in school as he has been sick so much last winter. Did ever [sic] his Uncle come to see him since I left Chicago [*sic*] please let me know in your next letter. Tell _____ to write me again as I so much enjoy his letters. I hope he is now entirely well and is able to go out in this nice spring weather. Please tell me how he is and how he is enjoying himself. I will close for this time wishing prompt reply and I will send you some money in my next letter. I am feeling a little better at prassent [sic] and doing some little work.
>
> With love and kisses to _____ from his Mother and many kind regards to yourself. [*sic*]
>
> I remain yours very respectfully
>
> Mrs. _____
>
> Marion, Ohio[24]

The original St. Vincent's Orphan Asylum erected in 1899. Later, the Church Vestment Workshop was located on the second floor. In 1949, Madonna High School opened on the first floor.

Orphans at St. Vincent's Orphan Asylum, Chicago, Illinois, c. 1906

Sierota [The Orphan], a monthly magazine founded in 1900 by the Resurrectionist Fathers to give financial aid to the orphans of St. Vincent's Orphan Asylum

136

Subsidies from many Polish parishes which referred the children to St. Vincent's Orphan Asylum and which had previously supported the Holy Family Orphanage were no longer forthcoming.[25] Occasionally, groups like the Young Ladies' Rosary Sodality of St. Stanislaus Kostka Parish sponsored a picnic or bazaar for the benefit of the orphans. The burden for the maintenance of the orphanage, therefore, rested mainly on the Sisters and the Congregation of the Resurrection. To help support the Sisters and the orphans, the Reverend Stanislaus Siatka, CR,[26] founded a modest monthly literary magazine called *Sierota* [The Orphan], consisting of thirty-two pages selling for $1 a year. It succeeded in deftly combining religious and factual articles concerning the orphans and the aged. It listed the names of benefactors to whom the Sisters accorded public thanks.[27] The publication, which made its appearance on March 15, 1900, was well received because of its simple, clear, and informative style and content. In 1903, the publication became a semimonthly with sixteen pages. Later, it was published weekly and sold for five cents a copy. The Reverend Felix Ładon, CR,[28] succeeded Father Siatka as editor of the magazine until a lack of subscribers caused it to be discontinued.[29]

As the number of elderly who were admitted to St. Joseph Home for the Aged and Crippled and the number of children accepted at St. Vincent's Orphan Asylum were increasing, the young Franciscan community was solidly growing in membership. Sister M. Theresa was thankful to God for the generous and compassionate spirit of the many women who asked for admittance to the community. In her "Chronicle," Sister M. Theresa states: "God, seeing our difficult circumstances, sent more candidates to the community."[30] Nothing pleased Sister M. Theresa and the Sisters more than when new applicants arrived to carry on their charitable work. These young women appeared eager to share the poverty and simplicity of the Sisters' lives, and seemed to be led by a spirit of genuine dedication since they knew that the community was supported chiefly by the collection of alms, a duty to which the Sisters were frequently assigned. After returning to St. Joseph Home for the Aged and Crippled and St. Vincent's Orphan Asylum at the end of a day spent begging for alms, the candidates had to wash and iron the laundry of the aged and the orphans, serve the sick and the aged, and oftentimes perform the lowliest tasks for the incapacitated residents. Many of the candidates had already passed through a struggle with either their parents or families who would have preferred that their daughters enter an established community rather than resort to begging for their livelihood as well as for that of their dependents.[31]

Among the candidates who were accepted during the summer months of 1899 were Monica Zawadzka (Sister M. Andrea) from Holy Trinity Parish; Marianne Pinkowski (Sister M. Kunegunda); Estelle Holysz (Sister M. Aloysia); and Marianne Gorski (Sister M. Rose), all from St. Hedwig's Parish. The last to enter, in the latter part of August, was Louise Maka (Sister M. Veronica) from St. Stanislaus Kostka Parish. On November 1, 1899, four more candidates entered from St. Hedwig's Church: Marianne

Czyzewski (Sister M. Vincent); Martha Grabowski (Sister M. Salomea); Barbara Reich (Sister M. Stanislaus); and Philomena Suchomski (Sister M. Josepha). All of these women were destined to play important roles in the history of the congregation.

The candidates wore a black secular dress, of any style, for a month after entrance, after which they received the postulant's garb from Sister M. Theresa and a black bonnet from the presiding priest in a simple ceremony in the chapel.[32] Sister M. Theresa was assigned the care of the candidates, although, of course, she was only a novice herself.[33] In addition, Sister M. Theresa was also in charge of her Sister-novices, the postulants, and still exclusively in charge of the aged and the crippled. She also supervised the laundry chores which were now considerably increased since the Sisters had begun once more to wash, mend, and distribute the laundry from St. Stanislaus Kostka Rectory. Through this labor, an added source of income was available. Since Sister M. Anna exercised the duties of mother superior, Sister M. Angeline served as the treasurer and secretary. She was also in charge of all the sewing, mending, and the teaching of sewing to the postulants and orphans. Sister M. Agnes took charge of the orphan girls while Sister M. Frances Troeder had the boys under her care.[34]

While intensely occupied with her duties, Sister M. Theresa realized that the brief time of novitiate was drawing to a close. Although she sincerely longed to seal her commitment to God by professing the vows of poverty, chastity, and obedience, she was not anxious to see the time of novitiate end for herself or for the other Sisters. In her humility, she felt unworthy and ill prepared for the act of professing her vows. There was still the continuing attitude of religious laxity among the Sisters which she sincerely felt was not in keeping with the religious spirit and was not conducive to the common good. While these feelings disturbed Sister M. Theresa, she resolved her uneasiness as she states in the "Chronicle": "Many of my doubts [concerning my unpreparedness for first profession] disappeared after I submitted myself to the Will of God and the designs of Divine Providence."[35]

As the small community entered the twentieth century, the future looked promising. There were four novices and fourteen postulants in charge of seventeen aged women, three aged men, and sixty-three orphans. Two more candidates joined the ranks of the community, namely, Estelle Karwata (Sister M. Felixa) and Cecilia Lama (Sister M. Philipine). During the holy season of Lent, Father Spetz purchased the Stations of the Cross for the chapel thus initiating this unique Franciscan spiritual exercise into the community. He invited the Franciscan Fathers from old St. Peter's Church, then located on Polk Street, to bless the stations on the First Friday of Lent.[36]

Father Spetz designated June 3, 1900, the feast of Pentecost, as the day on which the novices would make their first profession of vows in the community. In preparation, the Sisters began a five-day retreat under the direction of the Reverend Stephen Dąbkowski, CR.[37] Since eight postulants were also to participate in the retreat, the eight new candidates took over the retreatants' duties so that the novices and postulants were freer to attend to their spiritual preparation.

The pioneer Sisters on the day of their First Profession of Vows, June 3, 1900. Left to right: Sister M. Anna Wysinski, Sister M. Angeline Topolinski, Sister M. Agnes Dzik, Sister M. Theresa Dudzik

On the day of the first profession of vows, during a mass celebrated by Father Spetz, Sister M. Theresa, Sister M. Anna, Sister M. Angeline, and Sister M. Agnes pronounced their vows for one year. An account of this memorable event appeared in the *Sierota* magazine under the title, "From the Orphanage":

> On Pentecost Sunday, June 3, 1900, a beautiful ceremony took place in the chapel of St. Vincent's Orphan Asylum. Four Sisters from the newly erected Community of Sisters of the Third Order of St. Francis, approved by the Right Reverend Patrick Feehan, bishop of Chicago, for the Archdiocese of Chicago only, made their religious vows for one year in the hands of the Reverend Andrew Spetz, CR. At the ceremony, the Sisters received a small silver cross to wear around the neck as a symbol of their profession. The names of these Sisters are Sister M. Anna Wysinski, Sister M. Theresa Dudzik, Sister M. Angeline Topolinski, and Sister M. Agnes Dzik.[38]

In her "Chronicle," Sister M. Theresa writes of this occasion also, but not without a tinge of humor:

> The ceremony [for the first profession of vows] was more solemn than our reception to the novitiate, but, for me, the lack of a competent organist proved a terrible source of distraction. We asked Professor Wiedemann from St. Hedwig's parish to play. Instead of coming himself, he sent a man who had not rehearsed with the Sisters. Consequently, they did not harmonize and the result was unnerving. I would never wish to hear another rendition like that one![39]

Fortunately for everyone concerned, in the afternoon for the Benediction Service and on the following day for mass, the Sisters had the assistance of an organist from St. Stanislaus College.[40]

In another ceremony which took place on the next day, June 4, eight postulants received the habit from the Reverend John Kasprzycki, CR, who was assisted by Father Spetz. Unlike the first reception to the novitiate held the year before, on this occasion the parents and the relatives of the novices and postulants were invited to witness the ceremony. The following is an account of the event as recorded in the magazine, *Sierota*:

> On Monday, June 4, 1900, the second feast took place when eight postulants entered the novitiate and received the habit from the hands of Father John Kasprzycki, CR, provincial of the Congregation. Their names are Theodosia Troeder (Sister M. Frances); Marianne Ogurek (Sister M. Clara); Caroline Baut (Sister M. Elizabeth); Anna Welter (Sister Mary); Rosalie Kubera (Sister M. Hedwig); Monica Zawadzki (Sister M. Andrea); Marianne Pinkowski (Sister M. Kunegunda); and Louise Maka (Sister M. Veronica).
>
> The ceremony was very lovely. The chapel overflowed with parents, relatives, friends, and acquaintances of the Sisters. This community has supervision over the orphans and the aged in the home at Avondale. May God grant them perseverance on the road to perfection.[41]

From the day of her first profession of vows, Sister M. Theresa was officially appointed and called the mistress of novices and postulants.[42] She performed this duty with great dedication, fidelity, and zeal and attempted to instill the love of God and neighbor, the love of community life, and the spirit of poverty into her novices.[43]

Unfortunately, it appears that personal difficulties seemed to increase after the Sisters pronounced their vows.[44] The Sisters who disturbed the equanimity and peace of the convent household were often those Sisters for whom the observance of the Rule and Constitutions was too heavy for them to bear. Sister M. Theresa felt that not all members had been called to live in community and to share the common life. Some women, she believed, had a selfish motive in entering the community, and, as a result, proved to be a source of trial and disedification to others. They were disturbers of peace and silence, and even worse, incited other Sisters to discontent. Instead of developing interior calm and union with God, some of the Sisters proved vexatious and quarrelsome. Regrettably, many of the adverse feelings were directed personally at Sister M. Theresa. Those Sisters who were unfavorably disposed to her and even showed their dislike openly created difficulties and misunderstandings as she struggled to consolidate the community. A few Sisters testify to this in their depositions:

> Some Sisters did not like Sister M. Theresa when she reminded them of

their failings, and her observance of the Rule irritated them because they wished to live "loosely." They were unkind to her but she bore all this with patience.[45]

It certainly appeared as though the trials and obstacles which had tested the purpose, faith, and perseverance of many religious founders also awaited Sister M. Theresa. It might be well to remember, at this point, that the community was still in its formative stage and perhaps the Sisters, either through their own inadequacies or the circumstances at the time, were unable to measure up to the standards that Sister M. Theresa had set for herself.

There are several factors which might have influenced the conduct of these early Sisters. It must be noted that the days of these first Sisters were devoted chiefly to working arduously. Great personal sacrifices, never-ending struggles with poverty, burdensome and thankless duties, and, perhaps, very little time for recreation marked the pioneer days. While Sister M. Theresa acted as mistress of novices, postulants, and candidates, and was thus responsible for their spiritual formation, the time and the opportunity for ideal spiritual formation simply did not exist. Perhaps the depositions of some Sisters state the matter in truth:

> Sister M. Theresa had us under her care in the postulancy and novitiate; we saw her only in the refectory because she had so much work with the old folks. We were like sheep without a shepherd. We had brief meetings during the year to learn about religious life.[46]

It should also be made quite clear at this time that other circumstances existed which provided numerous opportunities to test the Sisters' virtue. Since every Sister had a distinct character, it was inevitable that personalities should contend. Most religious communities, in the beginning, were distinguished according to their ethnic origins. Thus, it is important to remember that because many of the early Sisters came from Poland or were American-born Poles, they represented regional areas of Poland made by the Partitions headed by Austria, Prussia, and Russia.[47] During the years of Poland's "captivity" by the three oppressive nations mentioned above, the distinguishing marks of the occupying countries remained clearly recognizable in the portion they ruled. For example, the Sisters who entered from St. Hedwig and St. Stanislaus Kostka Parishes were mainly from the section of Poland under Prussian domination while the Sisters who entered from St. John Cantius were mainly from Galicia which was under Austrian domination. Many of the Sisters still referred to themselves by their regional areas and strongly identified with them. These regional identifications were strong enough at the beginning to cause conflict and ill will at times.

Other factors appeared which made it extremely difficult for the Sisters to be ideally "of one mind and one heart." Many of the early Sisters were not educated, and some, in fact, had never gone to school. Most of the early Sisters had entered the community at an older age; not a few of them had had responsible employment and a sense of independence before entering and thus were of a less pliable nature. No doubt, they often found obedience a strain. There were also indications that some women had relied on their confessors for guidance; these, in turn, directed the women to the young community while not having adequately discerned their qualifications for religious life.[48]

Devoid of a strong faith, firm hope, and deep love, some Sisters operated on a natural level only. It is certainly most probable that Sister M. Theresa understood the frailty of human nature and recognized that some of the early Sisters were not truly suited for religious life. Sister M. Theresa, however, had become accustomed to their murmuring and criticizing since she had already borne these vexations for six years as she states in her "Chronicle." While the situation caused her much anguish, her attitude was in keeping with her faith and fortitude:

> Criticism of my conduct served as an advantage in overcoming my pride. I desired to bear more so long as God would not be offended. I would consider it even great happiness to be able to suffer for the greater glory of God and the good of this Community.[49]

In spite of those who showed her their ill will, Sister M. Theresa was, in fact, much loved as is evident from the article appearing in *Sierota* entitled, "The Feastday of Sister Theresa in the Orphanage":

> Already on the vigil of Sister Theresa's feastday [St. Teresa of Avila], there was an unusual spirit in the home for Polish orphans in Avondale. They were getting ready for the solemn observance of the feastday of the mistress of novices and postulants, as well as the sensitive and thoughtful guardian of the orphans and the aged. In each face could be read the longing with which they awaited this day when they were to express their sentiments of love and gratitude to their superior and guardian.
>
> For several weeks, the orphans were getting ready to deliver their wishes. All preparations were being made in secret so as to create a bigger surprise. For lack of space, the refectory was to be used.
>
> Sunday afternoon, several girls and boys went to nearby woods for leaves and branches to make floral arrangements. They did this with such enthusiasm! The girls made wreathes, the boys were putting up tables, while others were rehearsing their verses and songs.
>
> Mass was offered for the intention of Sister M. Theresa the next day. The chapel was beautifully decorated. After Mass, everyone went to the social hall. Here poems were recited and songs and comical skits were enacted. It was obvious that the children understood and meant what they said.
>
> After the children's recital, another surprise awaited Sister M. Theresa. The elderly, with whom she deals exclusively, got together to

show their gratitude. It was a very moving scene when a woman, over one hundred years old, thanked her and wished her well. Sister M. Theresa truly appreciated these sentiments which were a reward for her work and hardships.

Another ceremony followed that. A four-year-old black child, in the orphanage for a few weeks, received the sacrament of Baptism and responded to the priest's queries in Polish. Father Spetz baptized him.[50]

On December 8, 1900, the sixth anniversary of the foundation of the community, six postulants were received into the novitiate. They were Estelle Holysz (Sister M. Aloysia); Marianne Gorski (Sister M. Rose); Marianne Czyzewski (Sister M. Vincent); Martha Grabowski (Sister M. Salomea); Barbara Reich (Sister M. Stanislaus); and Philomina Suchomski (Sister M. Josepha). The retreat preceding the reception of the young women into the novitiate was conducted by the Reverend Joseph Gieburowski who also presented the Sisters with the religious habit and celebrated mass.[51] *Sierota* magazine had the following account of the event:

Last Saturday, December 8, a moving ceremony of the reception of six candidates to the novitiate of the Franciscan Sisters was held in the Avondale orphanage. Friends and relatives filled the chapel.

This Community is growing beyond expectations and although young, is rendering valuable service to God and men. St. Hedwig's parish has provided most of the Sisters so far, but there are others from St. Stanislaus Kostka, Holy Trinity, St. Adalbert, and even one from Baltimore, Maryland.[52] Together there are twenty-five Sisters. Their spiritual advisor is Father Joseph Gieburowski of St. Hedwig's parish, who for two years has performed this duty with zeal. It must be admitted that the growth of the Community of Franciscan Sisters as well as the orphanage under their care, is forging ahead.

The guidance of Father Gieburowski was a real blessing especially for the newly-founded Community which so badly needed an enlightened director in spiritual matters. Such an extraordinary guide was Father Gieburowski. It is too bad that he could not fulfill his obligation longer since during Lent of 1901, he was assigned to Europe and never returned to America.[53]

In June of 1901, the professed Sisters were preparing to renew their vows for another year, and the novices were getting ready to make their first profession of vows.[54] The Sisters began their retreat on June 1 under the direction of the Reverend Stanislaus Siatka, CR. Because there were more Sisters to help with the manual labor, more time could be devoted to spiritual exercises and spiritual formation.[55] Sister M. Theresa, Sister M. Anna, and Sister M. Angeline renewed their vows for one year on June 6, 1901, the feast of Corpus Christi that year. Unfortunately, Sister M. Agnes Dzik was not among the Sisters renewing their vows. She had been dismissed from the community for her inability to live socially and religiously in a group.[56]

The next postulants were received into the novitiate on July 27, 1901. A five-day retreat conducted by the Reverend Stanislaus Rogalski, CR, preceded the reception of the five postulants: Estelle Karwata (Sister M. Felixa); Cecelia Lama (Sister M. Philipine); Martha Zamrowski (Sister M. Seraphine); Frances Zimna (Sister M. Gertrude)[57] and Josephine Roszak (Sister M. Agnes).[58]

Before the close of the year, another profession of first vows took place. On December 8, 1901, six novices were to have professed their first vows.[59] The ceremony was postponed, however, until December 15, due to the fact that Father Spetz had gone to the dedication of the new school of SS. Peter and Paul in Spring Valley, Illinois. When he returned, he arranged for the retreat under the direction of another Resurrectionist priest.

ST. VINCENT'S ORPHAN ASYLUM

[1]Sister M. Dulcissima Małolepszy, "A Historical Study of St. Hedwig's Home, An Institution for the Care of Dependent Children, Archdiocese of Chicago," (M.A. thesis, Loyola University, 1945), p. 3.

[2]John J. Iwicki, CR, *The First One Hundred Years: A Study of the Apostolate of the Congregation of the Resurrection in the United States, 1866–1966* (Rome: Gregorian University Press, 1966), p. 120.

[3]This matter in all its entirety and ramifications will not be discussed here. The reader is referred to Iwicki, p. 120; Małolepszy, p. 4; and Sister M. De Chantal, CSFN, *Out of Nazareth, A Centenary of the Sisters of the Holy Family of Nazareth in the Service of the Church* (New York: Exposition Press, Inc., 1974), pp. 64–69, 76–77, 81–85.

[4]In *Mother Caroline and the School Sisters of Notre Dame in North America*, 2 vols. (St. Louis: Woodward and Tiernan Co., 1928) 2:53, the orphanage is called the Holy Family Home for Polish Orphans.

[5]*Interview* with the Right Reverend Abbot Thomas J. Havlik, St. Procopius Abbey, Lisle, Illinois, with author, 17 March 1977 (AFSCL).

[6]Iwicki, p. 121.

[7]Matka Maria Teresa Dudzik, "Kronika Sióstr Franciszkanek pod opieką Św. Kunegundy w Chicago, Illinois" [The Chronicle of the Franciscan Sisters under the patronage of St. Kunegunda in Chicago, Illinois] Unpublished manuscript, 1910 (Chicago, Illinois, AFSCL), p. 63.

[8]St. Stanislaus Kostka Parish was the "cradle" of St. Stanislaus College founded in 1890 by Father Barzynski for the sons of Polish immigrants. The frame building which served as the first St. Stanislaus Kostka Church opened in 1890 as one of the first high schools for boys on the Northwest Side of Chicago. From 1899, St. Stanislaus College used the building which had formerly served as the Holy Family Orphanage. The word "college" at this time meant an institution for secondary education more on the order of a high school.

Father Barzynski appointed the Reverend Joseph Halter, CR, an experienced and devoted teacher, and his very capable assistant, the Reverend John Piechowski, CR, to staff the school. These pioneer educators were instrumental in overcoming the negative attitude of many immigrant parents in regard to higher education for their sons and were responsible for the schools' eventual successful development. In 1930, the old St. Stanislaus College was renamed Weber High School.

Through the years, increasing enrollment and an expanding curriculum eventually required a new location for Weber. The site chosen was Palmer and Latrobe Avenues in the vicinity of St. Stanislaus Bishop and Martyr Church called Cragin. Classes in the new Weber High School began in September of 1950, and by 1962, an expansion program saw the construction of a million-dollar addition making Weber High School capable of accommodating almost 1,250 young men. *Album Pamiątkowy Złotego Jubileuszu Parafii Świętego Stanisławawa Kostki, 1867–1917* [A Commemorative Album of the Golden Jubilee of St. Stanislaus Kostka Parish, 1867–1917] (Chicago: Illinois, 1917), p. 325; and *Weber's New Frontier: Souvenir Book of Dedication* (Chicago, 27 May 1962), no pagination.

[9]The Reverend John Kruszynski, CR, was born in Poland in 1863. Before his entry into the Congregation of the Resurrection, he was a teacher in Prussian-dominated Poland for more than five years. In Chicago, he was the rector of St. Stanislaus Kostka School from 1885 to 1902. Father Kruszynski was appointed the first master of novices at the North American novitiate established in 1901 at St. Stanislaus College. He served an an assistant at several Resurrectionist parishes and was appointed chaplain of St. Joseph Home for the Aged from 1912 to 1914. He died while on sick leave in Tucson, Arizona in 1917. Edward T. Janas, CR, *Dictionary of American Resurrectionists, 1865–1965* (Rome: Gregorian University Press, 1967), pp. 34–35.

[10]*School Sisters of Notre Dame,* pp. 52–53.

[11]Dudzik, p. 64.

[12]Rosalie Kubera, who entered in June, was destined to play a vital role in the congregation's history as Sister M. Hedwig. For a biography of Sister M. Hedwig, see Chapter 18.

[13]Dudzik, p. 63.

[14]Andrew Spetz, CR, "Annual Report to the Board of State Commissioners of Public Charities at Springfield, Illinois," (Chicago, 30 January 1908) (AFSCL).

[15]Siostra M. Gonzaga Raniszewski, OSFK, *Rys historyczny Zgromadzenie Sióstr Franciszkanek Błogosławionej Kunegundy. Część pierwsza, 1860–1910* [A historical survey of the Franciscan Sisters of Blessed Kunegunda. Part one, 1860–1910] (Chicago: By the Author, 1947), p. 132.

[16]*Book of Depositions:* Sister M. Ludwina Prokuszka and Sister M. Mercy Witczak (AFSCL).

[17]Dudzik, p. 64.

[18]*The Official Catholic Directory of 1901,* p. 47 contains the following information: Under "Communities of Women," is written: Ladies of the Third Order of St. Francis—St. Vincent Orphan Asylum (Polish) and St. Joseph's Home for the Aged and Crippled, Chicago. On p. 46, under "Orders of Women" is written: "St. Vincent's Orphan Asylum and St. Joseph's Home for the Aged and Crippled, Hamlin and Schubert Avenues, Ladies of the Third Order of St. Francis (Polish), Sister Rosalie, Superior, 75 orphans, 30 old people and cripples."

[19]"Document of Erection" from the Most Reverend Patrick A. Feehan, 18 October 1899 (AFSCL).

[20]The Reverend John Kasprzycki, CR, was a recognized sacred orator, leader, and organizer. He was born in 1858 in Poland, then under Prussian government, where he received his primary and secondary education. In 1879, he went to Rome where he entered the Congregation of the Resurrection and was ordained in 1886. In 1887, he was appointed assistant novice master in Rome. His superiors sent him to America in 1890 to work among the Polish immigrants at St. Stanislaus Kostka Parish in Chicago. From 1893 to 1899, he organized and was pastor of St. John Cantius Parish. He succeeded Father Barzynski as pastor of St. Stanislaus Kostka Church, and was also elected provincial superior of the Resurrectionists. He guided the parish until 1905 when he was elected superior general of the entire congregation. He served in Rome until 1920. Upon his return to Chicago, he was master of novices from 1923 to 1925, and remained at the St. Joseph Novitiate as superior until his death in 1933. Janas, pp. 29–30.

The site of the St. Joseph Novitiate for the Congregation of the Resurrection until 1950 was in the area called Cragin in the vicinity of St. Stanislaus Bishop and Martyr Church. The novitiate, established in 1917, was not without its difficulties, and the *St. Joseph Novitiate Chronicle* reveals that the Franciscan Sisters of Chicago came to the aid of the newly established novitiate by donating twelve roosters and thirteen hens for their farm. Since the Sisters were very adept in needlework, they contributed numerous corporals, purificators, altar linens, palls, and ciborium veils for the St. Joseph Novitiate chapel. Iwicki, p. 175.

[21]Dudzik, p. 65.

[22]Ibid., p. 67.

[23]St. Vincent's Orphan Asylum, "Financial Report" (AFSCL).

[24]*Book of Correspondence:* Letter from Mrs. J. C. to the Franciscan Sisters at St. Vincent's Orphan Asylum, 10 April 1903 (AFSCL).

[25]Children were admitted from various parishes throughout the years. A listing of the parishes revealed the following: St. Stanislaus Kostka, 190; St. John Cantius, 109; St. Hedwig, 55; Holy Trinity, 36; St. Mary of Perpetual Help, 32; St. Casimir, 25; St. Hyacinth, 20; St. Mary of the Angels, 13; Immaculate Conception, South Chicago, 14; St. Josaphat, 9; SS. Peter and Paul, 9; St. Florian, 7; Holy Innocents, 7; St. George, 6; St. Joseph, 6; St. Andrew, Hammond, Indiana, 6; St.

Anne, 1. Some numbers of children admitted were listed only by location: South Bend, Indiana, 2; Kenosha, Wisconsin, 2; Briggsville, Wisconsin, 2; Pullman Area of Chicago, 1. Reference is also made to nine children of unspecified nationalities or parishes. As a matter of record, the Sisters had found a black boy on Sunday and called him "Joey Sunday." Sister M. Gonzaga states that two black boys were converted to Catholicism and even learned to speak Polish. *Book of Depositions:* Sister M. Ludwina Prokuszka; and Raniszewski, p. 101.

[26]The Reverend Stanislaus Siatka, CR, a dedicated priest, author, and publicist, was born and educated in Poland. In preparation for the priesthood, he studied philosophy and theology in Rome in 1896. After ordination, he was appointed vice-rector of the Polish College in Rome. He came to Chicago in 1897, and for fifteen years was an assistant at several parishes conducted by the Resurrectionists. To Father Siatka is given the credit for initiating the commercial courses for girls at St. Stanislaus Kostka School in 1914. He served as president of the Polish Publishing Company from 1914 to 1933, and as a staff member on the *Dziennik Chicagoski* [The Polish Daily News], and in 1931, was named the manager. Father Siatka compiled and edited *Wiązek Nabożenstw* [A Manual of Devotions]. From 1923 to 1926, he was professor of Polish language and literature at St. Mary of the Lake Seminary in Mundelein, Illinois. He died in 1933. Iwicki, p. 67; and Janas, pp. 55–56.

[27]Raniszewski, p. 102.

[28]The Reverend Felix Ładon, CR, was a renowned catechist, writer, publisher, and ardent promoter of Polish Catholic culture in the United States. Born in Poland in 1870, he entered the Congregation of the Resurrection in 1895. He taught mathematics and biology in Adrianople, Turkey, from 1895 to 1910. He wrote the first manual of mathematics in the Bulgarian language and was professor of mathematics and sciences at St. Stanislaus College in 1900. Father Ładon served as an assistant at several Resurrectionist parishes, notably St. Stanislaus Kostka from 1900 to 1909. He organized a two thousand volume parish library at St. Stanislaus Kostka School, only to see it totally destroyed in 1906 when the school suffered a fire. He was the editor of many religious books, textbooks, and novelettes. He accompanied the first four pioneer Sisters of the Congregation of the Resurrection when they left Rome in 1900 to begin their apostolate in America at St. Mary of the Angels School in Chicago. He died in Chicago in 1920. Iwicki, p. 105; and Janas, pp. 40–42.

[29]In December of 1906, the magazine was assimilated by the Catholic monthly youth magazine called *Macierz Polska* [The Polish Alma Mater] Iwicki, p. 211.

[30]Dudzik, p. 64.

[31]Raniszewski, p. 132.

[32]Ibid.

[33]Dudzik, p. 64.

[34]Raniszewski, p. 93.

[35]Dudzik, p. 68.

[36]The Way of the Cross, a devotion instituted by the Church to help the faithful meditate on Christ's passion and death, was begun by the Franciscans who had charge of the holy places in the Holy Land. Pope Innocent XI granted an indulgence to all Franciscans and to those connected with the Franciscan Order for making the Stations. In 1726, Pope Benedict XIII extended these indulgences to all the faithful.

[37]The Reverend Stephen Dąbkowski, CR, was an assistant at St. Stanislaus Kostka Parish in 1897 and again in 1903. He also served as assistant at St. Hyacinth's Church and St. Hedwig's Church and performed the duties of pastor at St. John Cantius Church for one year. On sick leave, he died in 1917 in St. Louis. Janas, p. 14.

[38]Reverend Stanislaus Siatka, CR, ed., "From the Orphanage," *Sierota* [The Orphan] 1 (June 1900), no pagination (AFSCL).

[39]Dudzik, p. 69.

[40]Ibid.

[41]Siatka, *Sierota* [The Orphan].

[42]Dudzik, p. 69.

[43]Siostra M. Gonzaga Raniszewski, OSFK, *Zarys Połwiecza Zgromadzenia Sióstr Franciszkanek Bł. Kunegundy* [Sketch of the fifty year history of the Congregation of the Franciscan Sisters of Bł. Kunegunda] (Chicago: By the Author, 1944), p. 21.

[44]Dudzik, p. 70.

[45]*Book of Depositions:* Sister M. Martha Bywalec, Sister M. Bridget Czuj, Sister M. Gerard Gorzkowski, Sister M. Barbara Grochola, Sister M. Pius Wojcicki, Sister M. Eustace Borowski, Sister M. Hilary Dadej, Sister M. Brunona Szwagiel, and Mother M. Antonina Osinski (AFSCL),

[46]*Book of Depositions:* Sister M. Sophie Ciurkot and Mother M. Jerome Dadej (AFSCL).

[47]See Chapter 2.

[48]*Book of Depositions:* Early members of Franciscan Sisters of Chicago (AFSCL).

[49]Dudzik, p. 70.

[50]Siatka, "The Feastday of Sister Theresa in the Orphanage," *Sierota* [The Orphan] 1 (October 1900), no pagination (AFSCL).

[51]The only disturbing element at the ceremony seems to have been Sister M. Clara's organ playing, but Sister M. Theresa hastens to add that Father Gieburowski knew that the Sisters were not, as yet, proficient in music. Dudzik, p. 72.

[52]The *Sisters' Registry* [*Spis Sióstr*, 1909–1919] does not verify this fact. The only Sister to come from a parish other than one in Chicago was Sister M. Colette Nowak who is listed as entering from St. John the Evangelist Church in New York City on May 18, 1901.

[53]Siatka, *Sierota* [The Orphan] I (January 1901) no pagination (AFSCL).

[54]The novices who made their first profession of vows were Sister M. Andrea Zawadzki, Sister M. Clara Ogurek, Sister M. Elizabeth Baut, Sister M. Frances Troeder, Sister M. Hedwig Kubera, Sister M. Kunegunda Pinkowski, Sister Mary Welter, and Sister M. Veronica Maka. *Spis Sióstr* (AFSCL).

[55]Dudzik, p. 72.

[56]Ibid.

[57]Frances Zimna (Sister M. Gertrude) was not destined to remain in the congregation. She had entered from St. Hedwig's Parish on July 2, 1900. She was admitted to the novitiate on July 27, 1901, and made her first profession of vows on August 2, 1902. On May 29, 1911, she professed perpetual vows. Sister M. Gertrude was assigned to household duties at St. Stanislaus Bishop and Martyr Convent, St. Elizabeth's Day Nursery, and St. Joseph Home for the Aged and Crippled until her departure from the congregation on July 17, 1915. *Spis Sióstr* (AFSCL).

[58]Sister M. Agnes Roszak was thirty-six years old when she entered the postulancy from St. Joseph Church in the Town of Lake area on Chicago's Southwest Side. This is the first recorded admission of a widow to the congregation. After her first profession, she was sent to St. Casimir School in Cleveland to attend to household duties. In 1906, she returned to the Motherhouse where she remained in charge of the laundry until her death of a heart attack on April 7, 1931. She was sixty-seven years old and had been in the congregation for thirty-one years. *Spis Sióstr* (AFSCL).

[59]The novices were Sister M. Aloysia Holysz, Sister M. Josepha Suchomski, Sister M. Rose Gorski, Sister M. Salomea Grabowski, Sister M. Stanislaus Reich, and Sister M. Vincent Czyzewski. *Spis Sióstr* (AFSCL).

CHAPTER 13

The Apostolate of Education

As the community grew in membership, its basic concentration had been centered on the initiation of the Sisters into the life of the community and their training in the spirit and ideal of the religious life. The community's main apostolate continued to be the care of the aged and crippled at St. Joseph Home and the care of the orphans at St. Vincent's Orphan Asylum. As Father Spetz continued to guide the women, it soon became obvious to him that many pastors, chiefly from areas where rapidly growing Polish settlements were being established and parishes were being organized, were conscious of the new Franciscan community in the Church, its works of mercy, and its potential for growth. In 1866, the Second Plenary Council of Baltimore had directed priests to open schools in their parishes. The American bishops, afraid that attendance at public schools constituted a great danger to the faith and the morals of Catholic children, believed that the parochial schools would remedy this situation. Numerous requests were then sent for Sisters to staff them. In the same fashion, Polish clergy began turning to Polish Sisterhoods to staff the schools attached to their churches following the example of other national groups such as the Irish and the German.[1]

In 1901, the Reverend Andrew Drewnicki, the pastor of SS. Peter and Paul Parish in Spring Valley, Illinois, wrote to Sister M. Anna Wysinski, the mother superior of the community, with a plea for three Sisters to teach in his school. Upon receiving the request, Sister M. Anna and Sister M. Theresa discussed the matter with Father Spetz. Although the education of children in elementary schools was not in their original plans, the Sisters realized that a vocation in the field of education was truly apostolic and rendered authentic service to the Church and to society. They were also aware that the Poles looked to the parish schools to preserve their culture and their faith, their special liturgy, their language and their customs, and were willing to make sacrifices to finance their new churches and parochial schools.[2] So imbued were Sister M. Anna and Sister M. Theresa with the desire to be of service to the Church and its people that they determined to respond to the appeals of the clergy and undertake as many schools as they were able to staff. Father Spetz asked the Most Reverend Patrick Feehan, archbishop of Chicago, for permission to send the

Sisters to teach in Polish parochial schools. Archbishop Feehan not only gave his permission willingly, but he also strongly encouraged the Sisters to enter into this important apostolate since the Church in America was deeply concerned for the welfare and faith of the immigrant Catholics.[3]

As soon as Sister M. Anna undertook the staffing of elementary schools, it became necessary to prepare the Sisters for their teaching apostolate. Sister M. Anna and Sister M. Theresa arranged, therefore, for the academic preparation of the Sisters under the tutorship of public school teachers Miss Grace W. Elsworth, Miss Ann Boldmen, and Miss Anna Mortimer.[4] Because of the inability of many of the Sisters to speak English, these teachers taught English to the Sisters and instructed them in academic subjects so that the Sisters would be prepared to teach religion, reading, writing, history, arithmetic, and geography.[5] Because the pastors made ample provision for the Polish language and culture in the program of the parochial schools, the Sisters were also instructed in Polish history, literature, and language as taught by several distinguished scholars, namely, Dr. Karol Wachtel,[6] Szczęsny Zahajkiewicz, and N. Gołaszewski. Bible history was taught by the Reverend Felix Ładon, CR. Dr. Wachtel, in particular, was engaged for over twenty years as a teacher of Polish literature at St. Stanislaus College and the Motherhouse of the Franciscan Sisters of Chicago.[7]

The efforts of the young band of Franciscan Sisters were met with difficulties encountered by almost all other religious congregations at this time in history. Most of the Sisters had a rather limited education themselves since many of them had completed no more than elementary school. In some instances, the Sisters were scarcely older than the pupils they were sent out to teach. So pressed were mothers general by overanxious pastors to supply Sisters for their schools that as soon as Sisters, novices, and even postulants were available, they were sent to classrooms. Because of this urgent demand for teachers in the American Catholic parochial schools, religious training was often limited to one year of canonical novitiate and very little postulant direction.[8] The Franciscan Sisters of Chicago, like most congregations at the time, attempted to correct these weaknesses through practices such as individual instruction, lectures, and most often, some training from the older, more experienced Sister-teachers. Eventually, provisions would be made for the Sisters to attend summer schools in order to equip them with the proper academic and professional training.

In spite of these obstacles, most of the Sisters handled themselves with maturity and genuine common sense beyond their years. Nurtured in homes that provided solid character training and examples of virtuous living, the Sisters were, in many ways, solidly equipped to meet the challenges of their teaching vocations born of prayer, faith, and love for the Church. It must also be remembered that the Sisters were encouraged in their endeavors by the generosity, love, and confidence of devoted parishioners.

In 1901, Spring Valley was a thriving coal mining and industrial region spilling out of steep bluffs on the floodplain on the north bank of the Illinois River. The parish of SS. Peter and Paul had been officially organized on September 30, 1891, for the Poles and

Left: SS. Peter and Paul School and Convent
Spring Valley, Illinois (1901–1903) (1910–1918)

the Lithuanians of the region who had been among the first of the ethnic groups to settle there.[9] Father Spetz eagerly accepted the invitation to send the Franciscan Sisters to their first teaching mission as is indicated by the following letter:

> Dear Brother Stanislaus:
>
> This week, Father Kosinski[10] and myself [sic] to Spring Valley next Sunday when the Bishop will bless a new school and confirm. To Spring Valley, I have sent three Sisters from the Orphan Asylum[11] to teach and now I go to visit them to see how they are getting along. (They are the Sisters of the Third Order established by Father Barzynski and now under my direction) . . . you see we are busy people here. Study well so that you may return for we have plenty of work.
>
> Yours in Christ devoted,
Andrew Spetz, CR[12]

On August 27, 1901, the three Sisters selected for the first teaching mission of the community left for Spring Valley. They were Sister M. Kunegunda Pinkowski, who was appointed superior and principal, Sister M. Clara Ogurek, and Sister Mary Welter, who was assigned to household duties.[13] All three Sisters had just made their first profession of vows that June, and, quite understandably, the assignment was a challenge to them. From the moment of their arrival, the Sisters endured many hardships and inconveniences, for neither their promised residence nor the school was finished, and several months elapsed before they were satisfactorily completed.[14] In time, however, a small, two-story frame structure was built consisting of three classrooms, a chapel, and rooms to house the Sisters.[15] There were 130 children enrolled in the school.[16]

The following year, Sister M. Kunegunda and Sister M. Clara returned to Spring Valley with Sister M. Seraphine Zamrowski who was assigned to household duties. In February 1903 an epidemic of smallpox erupted which affected the whole town. As a consequence, all the schools were closed. The three Sisters left Spring Valley and returned to Chicago without anyone's knowledge. Upon their arrival, they were forbidden to reside at the Motherhouse by strict orders of the doctor who insisted firmly that they be isolated. The Sisters were given shelter in St. Joachim Home, one of the frame houses that the community had purchased on Ridgeway Avenue.[17] The winter was an unusually severe one, and the Sisters were forced to endure the extreme cold; the stove in St. Joachim Home was small and did not adequately warm the house. Three beds had been quickly set up, but, unfortunately, there was a shortage of blankets. Many times, even their frugal meals which had to be carried over from the Motherhouse to St. Joachim Home were cold upon arrival. When the danger of communicating the disease to others no longer existed, the three Sisters were warmly greeted at the Motherhouse.[18]

It was not until early April that Sister M. Kunegunda and Sister M. Clara learned that it was safe to return to Spring Valley. Sister M. Seraphine did not accompany them, however, and Sister M. Salomea Grabowski was sent in her place. Shortly after the Sisters' return to SS. Peter and Paul School, the pastor, the Reverend Casimir Ambrosaitis, left Spring Valley for "an unspecified time" without arranging for a substitute. The Sisters were forced to conduct the school and settle all school matters during his absence. To fulfill their spiritual obligations, the Sisters attended St. Ann's (Lithuanian) Church about a mile away. This proved to be an added hardship since the early spring thaws sometimes forced them to walk ankle-deep in mud.[19] When the Sisters returned to Chicago at the end of the school year in June, Sister M. Anna and her advisory council voted to withdraw the Sisters from SS. Peter and Paul School because of the unsettled state of affairs which existed. Sister M. Aloysia in her brief "Chronicle of the Franciscan Sisters of St. Kunegunda" tersely states: "In 1903, the mission in Spring Valley was closed because of a riot which occurred in the parish."[20] The Community Chronicle for that period states that the Sisters withdrew "among much commotion and disorder in the parish."[21] Whether the unfortunate circumstances which existed were the result of conditions at the parish level or in the city of Spring Valley itself is difficult to determine due to the scarcity of information concerning this mission. Some problems might have arisen because of the strike by the coal miners which resulted in massive unemployment and grave food shortages.[22] On the other hand, friction had existed between the pastors and parishioners of SS. Peter and Paul and the neighboring parish of St. Ann's for a number of years.[23]

In the latter part of 1903, the Reverend Martin Piechota was appointed the new pastor of SS. Peter and Paul Church. He was successful in securing another congregation, the Franciscan Sisters of Our Lady of Perpetual Help of St. Louis, Missouri, to staff the school. They remained until 1910 when the extreme tension between the Sisters and the Reverend Joseph Cieśla, who had assumed the pastorate in 1909, forced the Sisters to withdraw from the school.[24]

As early as April 1910, Father Cieśla had petitioned Sister M. Theresa Dudzik, who had been appointed the mother superior in 1909, to once again accept SS. Peter and Paul School when the Franciscan Sisters of Our Lady of Perpetual Help left in June. Sister M. Theresa and her advisory council voted unanimously to accept the school for the second time.[25] The Sisters who reopened the school in September of 1910 were Sister M. Colette Nowak, the superior and principal; Sister M. Francis Drufke, Sister M. Wenceslaus Gorski, and Sister M. Barbara Grochola who was assigned to household duties. Father Cieśla was very pleased with the Sisters and asked Sister M. Theresa that they all be reassigned to the school the following September.[26]

In 1911, the Reverend Anton Deksnis, pastor of the nearby St. Ann's (Lithuanian) Church, earnestly begged the newly elected superior general, Mother M. Anna Wysinski, for three Sisters to staff his new school. He had appealed to Mother M. Anna because he had been informed that the congregation had several members of Lithuanian extraction, and he hoped that these Sisters could be sent to his school.[27] More than five years later, in July 1917, the request to staff St. Ann's School was finally accepted. There are no records which contain the names of the Sisters who were assigned to the school, but when the appointed Sisters, who were not Lithuanian, did arrive in August to take charge, they were met by hostile parishioners who demanded Sisters of their own nationality to teach their children.[28] The pastor who had succeeded Father Deksnis in 1917 urgently appealed to Father Cieśla to straighten out the matter which resulted in the Franciscan Sisters' prompt return to the Motherhouse.[29]

The Sisters remained at SS. Peter and Paul School for eight years. Throughout those years, however, the relationship between Father Cieśla and the Sisters slowly deteriorated. The *Sisters' Registry* indicates that six superior-principals had been appointed in those eight years. In 1918, therefore, Sister M. Clara Ogurek, the assistant general of the community, paid a visit to Spring Valley to discuss the matter with Father Cieśla. When it became apparent that the differences between Father Cieśla and the Franciscan Sisters of Chicago could not be resolved, he agreed to the permanent withdrawal of the Sisters at the close of the school year in 1918.[30] By 1924, SS. Peter and Paul School no longer existed, and the school building was converted into a parish hall. The building was literally cut down to a one-story building in 1936 and became the American Legion Hall which it remains today. The present rectory bears the distinction of being the oldest house in Spring Valley.[31] In spite of the turbulent history of SS. Peter and Paul School, the Franciscan Sisters are beneficiaries of three vocations from Spring Valley which have endured, namely, Sister M. Grace Kujawa,[32] Sister M. Eusebius Kolupka, and her sister, Sister M. Clarissa Kolupka.

Encouraged by their success in the Spring Valley parish school, the small band of Franciscan Sisters of Chicago accepted a second school, their first in the Archdiocese of Chicago, in a rural area called Cragin on the city's far Northwest Side.[33] As early as 1893, the area had attracted Polish-speaking settlers who petitioned the Most Reverend Patrick A. Feehan, archbishop of Chicago, to establish a Catholic church. The archbishop assigned the Reverend Vincent Barzynski to organize the parish which was placed under the patronage of St. Stanislaus Bishop and Martyr.[34]

Amid the wide stretches of prairie and open farmland, spirited Polish immigrants had erected a two-story frame structure, the upper floor of which was the church. The lower floor contained a small hall with a stage at one end and a classroom at the other. The building, located on Long Avenue, was dedicated by Father Barzynski on June 30, 1893. From 1893 to 1901, St. Stanislaus Bishop and Martyr Church was a "mission parish" served by the priests of the Congregation of the Resurrection who traveled by horse and buggy from St. Stanislaus Kostka Church to the Cragin settlement.[35] In 1897, the school opened with Miss Cecilia Klinger as the sole teacher of three grades in the first floor classroom of the church-school combination.[36]

On October 21, 1901, the Reverend John Obyrtacz, CR,[37] was appointed the first resident pastor of St. Stanislaus Bishop and Martyr Church. He invited the Franciscan Sisters of Chicago to take charge of the school which now had an enrollment of eighty-five students. The first Sisters sent to staff the school arrived on August 26, 1902. They were Sister M. Aloysia Holysz, superior and principal; Sister M. Philipine Lama, and Sister M. Gertrude Zimna, who was assigned to household duties.[38] The Sisters made their home in a frame house on Long Avenue next door to the rectory.[39] The parish was a long distance from the city, and because of poor transportation, the Cragin area made little progress for several years. Conditions at the St. Stanislaus Bishop and Martyr mission remained relatively stable until January 1905, when Sister M. Aloysia became ill and was forced to return to the Motherhouse. Sister Mary Welter and Sister M. Susanna Kielpinski were then sent to teach, and Sister M. Cajetan Tabasz and a postulant were sent to help Sister M. Gertrude with household duties.[40] The new superior and principal who replaced Sister M. Aloysia was Sister M. Philipine whose name will always be linked with the history of St. Stanislaus Bishop and Martyr Church.[41]

The morning of Tuesday of Holy Week, March 26, 1907, began as a typically beautiful spring day. In the early part of the afternoon, however, a severe storm threatened the area, and by three o' clock, when the children were about to be dismissed, a violent storm swept in from the northwest. The storm, accompanied by lightning, struck the church tower and set the church-school combination on fire. Within seconds, Sister M. Philipine ordered the immediate evacuation of the building, and the children were quickly sent home.[42] Sister M. Philipine dispatched a student to inform the fire department of the disaster and another to inform the pastor, who, unfortunately, was in the city on a business call. Taking a few older students with her, Sister M. Philipine headed for the sacristy in an attempt to rescue the church goods. Seeing the courageous nun, several men hurried after her and were successful in salvaging as much of the church goods as was possible. Sister M. Philipine waited impatiently for the pastor, hoping he would arrive in time to rescue the Blessed Sacrament from the main altar. When the roof caved in over the church choir, however, she ran to the burning church and removed the Blessed Sacrament to the safety of the convent chapel. She had barely left the church when the entire roof collapsed. The local two-hose fire engine, drawn by four horses, had arrived too late, the muddy roads preventing them from arriving in time to save the frame structure. To compound the problem, the hoses, rusted from lack of use, were unserviceable. The firemen made several futile attempts to clean them at the site of the burning structure which was in utter ruins within two hours.[43]

The Reverend Andrew Spetz was notified of the fire and hurried to the scene. Using the trolley car to get there, he was informed, incorrectly by the conductor, that four Sisters and several children had perished in the fire. When he arrived at the convent, he began to count each Sister as she made her appearance on the convent porch. After being assured of their safety and that of the children, both he and the Reverend Daniel Luttrell, the pastor of the neighboring parish of St. Genevieve, salvaged the church documents from the rectory.[44] Father Luttrell offered both his church and his school for the use of the parishioners of St. Stanislaus Bishop and Martyr Parish until such time as their church and school could be rebuilt. Instead, the Most Reverend Peter Muldoon, auxiliary bishop of Chicago, granted the pastor, Father Obyrtacz, permission to use a large hall belonging to a parishioner for use as a temporary church and school.[45] Bishop Muldoon, on the same occasion, praised the prudence and courage of Sister M. Philipine.[46] The hall, one block south of the destroyed church, was attended to by the Sisters who prepared it for the first service held there, the Adoration of the Cross on Good Friday. In this hall, services were held on weekdays, Sundays, and holydays. After the daily mass the hall served as the school. The school, which had been destroyed, had contained only four classrooms, but six grades were taught with an enrollment of 150 pupils.[47] Now all the children were taught in the hall. It was necessary for everyone to adjust to what must have been an intolerable situation since the respective grades were obviously all contained in the same area. In addition, there was a serious lack of desks and chairs, chalkboards, and other vital school supplies. Sharing this particular hardship with Sister M. Philipine, the principal, were Sister Mary Welter, Sister M. Stanislaus Reich, and Sister M. Gerard Gorzkowski.[48] These unfavorable conditions prevailed for several months until a new brick building in Gothic style, designed to serve as a combination church and school, was completed on Long Avenue. It was consecrated by the Most Reverend James Quigley, archbishop of Chicago, on December 8, 1907. At this time the parish had only eighty-five families, but within two years, the number of families increased to more than two hundred.

In January 1909, Father Obyrtacz was succeeded by the Reverend Stanislaus Świerczek, CR,[49] during whose eighteen-year tenure the parish thrived.[50] When in November 1919, the Most Reverend George Mundelein, archbishop of Chicago, visited the parish and saw with what difficulty the pupils, as well as the Sisters, were being accommodated, he ordered Father Świerczek to build an additional school building and a house for the Sisters.[51] In 1920, a new school, a brick structure on Lorel Avenue, was built to serve the more than seven hundred children who were enrolled. Part of the school building was used as living quarters for the pastor and the assistants. In the meantime, the old rectory was remodeled and converted into a convent for the Sisters.[52]

St. Stanislaus Bishop and Martyr School
Chicago, Illinois, (1901–)

St. Stanislaus Bishop and Martyr Convent
Chicago, Illinois

In 1926, a new, magnificent brick church, in Renaissance style, was erected. This enabled the old church-school combination on Long Avenue to be completely utilized as a school. School records reveal that by 1930, there were 1,365 children enrolled.[53] The growing school population demanded a corresponding increase in Sister personnel, and in 1928, the pastor, the Reverend Francis Kubiaczyk, CR,[54] authorized the construction of a spacious, modern convent on Lorel Avenue.[55] At the present time, when the decline in vocations has necessitated the closing of many schools, it is interesting to note an entry in the 1936–1937 convent journal which states not only the names of the teaching Sisters, but also the convent personnel which included a laundress, two cooks, a church sacristan, an assistant church sacristan, a convent chapel sacristan, a portress and seamstress, and a music teacher. By 1940, there were twenty-two Sisters on the teaching staff alone.[56]

Apart from the general school curriculum which the Sisters managed most effectively throughout the years, the Sisters arranged dramatic, musical, and patriotic programs of outstanding value and quality. The school band, organized in 1936, and consisting of approximately sixty students, achieved well-deserved prominence.[57] In 1940, the band performed at the request of the visiting Polish consul, and that year, the band won the coveted first prize in the Archdiocesan School Band Contest.[58]

The oldest school staffed by the Franciscan Sisters of Chicago is today very much alive and well. St. Stanislaus Bishop and Martyr Church has grown from a small, rural parish to the vibrant, stable parish it is today. There are presently six dedicated Sisters and fifteen lay teachers on the staff with an enrollment of approximately five hundred children. It is estimated that from 40 to 50 percent of the parishioners are recent immigrants from Poland, a historical repetition of the period in 1893 when this splendid and flourishing parish was born.

THE APOSTOLATE OF EDUCATION

[1]Frank Mocha, ed., *Poles in America* (Stevens Point, Wisconsin: Worzalla Publishing Co., 1978), p. 429.

[2]Albert Q. Maisel, *They All Chose America* (New York: Thomas Nelson and Sons, 1957), p. 214; and Casimir Stec, "The National Orientation of the Poles in the United States 1608–1935" (M.A. thesis, Marquette University, 1946), p. 48.

[3]Siostra M. Gonzaga Raniszewski, OSFK, *Rys historyczny Zgromadzenia Sióstr Franciszkanek Błogosławionej Kunegundy. Część pierwsza, 1860–1910* [A historical survey of the Franciscan Sisters of Blessed Kunegunda. Part one, 1860–1910] (Chicago: By the Author, 1947), pp. 107–109.

[4]Any attempts to secure more information concerning these teachers at the Board of Education in Chicago met with defeat. Raniszewski, pp. 107–108.

[5]Ibid.

[6]Dr. Wachtel was also discussed in Chapter 3. He directed the St. Stanislaus Kostka Parish Dramatic Circle and also founded three Polish American Companies which presented plays in downtown theaters of Chicago. He attempted to establish a permanent theater in Chicago in 1915. In the amateur dramatic circles, he staged Shakespearean plays in Polish: *Hamlet, The Merchant of Venice, Othello, Romeo and Juliet, Julius Caesar,* and *King Lear.* He was the first lecturer on Poland at Northwestern University. He was the author of several books of poetry, drama, and history, and wrote a series of textbooks for Polish parochial schools. Miecislaus Haiman, "The Poles in Chicago," in *Poles of Chicago: A History of One Century of Contributions to the City of Chicago, Illinois, 1837–1937,* ed. Polish Pageant, Inc. (Chicago: By the Author, 1937), pp. 69–70.

[7]*Album Pamiątkowy Złotego Jubileuszu Parafii Świętego Stanisława Kostki, 1867–1917* [A Commemorative Album of the Golden Jubilee of St. Stanislaus Kostka Parish, 1867–1917] (Chicago: 1917), p. 362; and Raniszewski, p. 107.

[8]Jay P. Dolan, *The American Catholic Experience: A History from Colonial Times to the Present* (Garden City, New York: Doubleday and Company, Inc., 1985), p. 287.

[9]*Golden Jubilee, 1909–1959, SS. Peter and Paul's Catholic Church* (Spring Valley, Illinois: 1959), p. 50.

[10]Father Spetz is referring to the Reverend John Kosinski, CR. He was stationed at St. Stanislaus College from 1899 to 1909. Father Kosinski was a noted church orator and public speaker in both the Polish and English languages.

[11]Father Spetz is referring here to St. Vincent's Orphan Asylum.

[12]*Letters from America,* vol. 10, 1893–1912, Letter from the Reverend Andrew Spetz, CR, to Brother Stanislaus, 2 December 1901 (Archives of the Congregation of the Resurrection, Rome, Italy).

[13]Matka M. Teresa Dudzik, "Kronika Sióstr Franciszkanek pod opieką Św. Kunegundy w Chicago, Illinois" [The Chronicle of the Franciscan Sisters under the patronage of St. Kunegunda in Chicago, Illinois] Unpublished manuscript, 1910 (Chicago, Illinois, AFSCL), p. 73.

[14]Raniszewski, p. 110.

[15]*Golden Jubilee: SS. Peter and Paul's Catholic Church,* p. 50.

[16]Wacław Kruszka, *Historya Polska w Ameryce* [History of the Poles in America], 13 vols. (Milwaukee: Kuryer Press, 1905), 10:177.

[17]The houses were named in honor of particular saints. This house was named in honor of St. Joachim, the name traditionally given to the father of the Blessed Virgin Mary. Born in Nazareth, St. Joachim married St. Anne at a youthful age. Nothing is known of him except what is told in apocryphal literature.

[18]Dudzik, p. 77.

[19]Raniszewski, p. 110.

[20]Sister M. Aloysia Holysz, OSFK, "Franciscan Sisters of St. Kunegunda Chronicle" (Chicago, Illinois: AFSCL, 1894–1922. Manuscript).

[21]Secretaries General, *Community Chronicle,* p. 5 (AFSCL).

[22]*Book of Correspondence:* Letter from Mrs. Marie Pyka, sister of Sister M. Grace Kujawa, containing her father's recollections of the period, to author, 26 October 1975 (AFSCL).

[23]In a letter to the author from the Honorable William J. Wimbiscus, circuit judge, Spring Valley, January 14, 1976, he states: "Because of some friction and differences in both SS. Peter and Paul Church and that of St. Ann, there was mention from time to time of things not running smoothly. There was talk of two or three priests being difficult, causing members to join other parishes. I could go into this in detail and at length, but as I am already into the fifth page, I'd better forego this subject. It could be that one or more of these incidents were termed 'riots.'" The friction might have also been sparked by the antagonism existing between the Poles and the Lithuanians as is evidenced further in the text. *Book of Correspondence:* Letter from the Honorable William J. Wimbiscus, circuit judge, Spring Valley, Illinois, to author, 14 January 1976 (AFSCL).

[24]*Book of Correspondence:* Letter from Sister M. Carolyn Wruk, OSF, to author, 11 February 1976 (AFSCL).

[25]*Minutes of General Council Proceedings, 1910–1934,* 9 April 1910 (AFSCL).

[26]*Book of Correspondence:* Letter from the Reverend Joseph Cieśla to Mother M. Anna Wysinski, 1 May 1911 (AFSCL).

[27]*Book of Correspondence:* Letter from the Reverend Anton Deksnis to Mother M. Anna Wysinski, 8 May 1912 (AFSCL).

[28]*Minutes of General Council Proceedings, 1910–1934,* 7 July 1917 (AFSCL).

[29]*Minutes of General Council Proceedings, 1910–1934,* 13 August 1917 (AFSCL).

[30]In a letter sent to Mother M. Aloysia Holysz dated June 3, 1918, in which she submitted a report of what had transpired during her visitation, Sister M. Clara made a sentimental observation. She recalled that she had been among the pioneer Sisters who opened the mission in 1901, and now, seventeen years later, she was announcing its closing. *Book of Correspondence:* Letter from Sister M. Clara Ogurek to Mother M. Aloysia Holysz, 3 June 1918 (AFSCL).

[31]*Book of Correspondence:* Letter from the Honorable William Wimbiscus, circuit judge, Spring Valley, Illinois, to author, 14 January 1976 (AFSCL).

[32]Sister M. Grace died on June 20, 1979. In her ministry at St. John Regional Medical Center in Huron, South Dakota, she earned the distinction of being the first Sister pharmacist in the state of South Dakota. See Chapter 49.

[33]For a long time, this sparsely settled rural area west of Avondale made little or no progress because of its long distance from the city and the resultant lack of proper communication. In 1884, it had a population of two hundred, one general store, two schools, and three saloons. The Cragin Brothers' hardware factory had located nearby giving the area its name. Development of the Cragin area followed directly upon the northwest extension of the Chicago Street Railways. Earl H. Reed, "Belmont-Cragin, Montclare and Hermosa, Community Areas Nos. 18, 19, and 20," *Forty-Four Cities in the City of Chicago* (Chicago: The Chicago Plan Commission, 1942), p. 85.

[34]Among Poles, devotion to St. Stanislaus Bishop and Martyr (1030–1079) is widespread, especially in his native city of Cracow, whose bishop he was and where his relics are kept in the cathedral. Born in Szczepanów on July 26, he was educated at Gniezno, became a canon at the Cathedral of Cracow, and eventually a bishop in 1072. He was particularly distinguished by his love for the poor.

Stanislaus incurred the great displeasure of Boleslaus II, King of Poland, when the saint reprimanded the king for his savage cruelty and injustice toward his subjects, and especially for his notorious abduction of the wife of one of his noblemen. When Stanislaus was finally forced to excommunicate the king, Boleslaus, enraged, invaded the chapel where Stanislaus was celebrating mass and beheaded him with his own sword. Boleslaus was driven out of Poland, and Pope St. Gregory VII placed the country under an interdict. St. Stanislaus, patron of Cracow and symbol of her unity, was canonized by Pope Innocent IV in 1253. Many Polish churches in America are named after this noble saint. John Coulson, ed., *The Saints* (New York: Guild Press, 1957), p. 696.

[35]John J. Iwicki, *The First One Hundred Years: A Study of the Apostolate of the Resurrection in the United States, 1866–1966* (Rome: Gregorian University Press, 1966), p. 98.

[36]Kruszka, p. 125; and *St. Stanislaus Bishop and Martyr Church: Anniversary 1893–1968* (Chicago: 1968), p. 33.

[37]The Reverend John Obyrtacz, CR, was a respected advisor and faithful promoter of Catholic and social interests of Polish-American immigrants. Born in Poland in 1873, he was ordained at St. Stanislaus Kostka Church in 1895. He was stationed at several parishes served by the Congregation of the Resurrection in Chicago. Appointed pastor of St. Stanislaus Bishop and Martyr Church in 1901, he served in that capacity until 1909. He was chaplain at St. Joseph Home for the Aged from 1931 to 1933. He was very active in the affairs of the Polish Roman Catholic Union, and was a noted literary contributor. Father Obyrtacz died in Chicago in 1935. Edward T. Janas, CR, *Dictionary of American Resurrectionists, 1865–1965* (Rome: Gregorian University Press, 1967), p. 46.

[38]Dudzik, p. 82.

[39]Raniszewski, p. 111.

[40]Rosalie Pinkowski, who had entered the community on December 8, 1904, was the postulant. In religion, she was called Sister M. Stephanie. Dudzik, p. 84.

[41]In addition to the name of Sister M. Philipine which is linked to the parish of St. Stanislaus Bishop and Martyr, the names of Sister M. Mirone Koziol and Sister M. Epiphany Gorski are likewise historically important. Sister M. Mirone served the parish for thirty-one years until her death on January 28, 1980. Sister M. Epiphany has been stationed there for forty years.

This parish was the source of twenty-eight vocations to the Franciscan Sisters of Chicago. The parish merits the distinction of having the largest group of family-related vocations. The Madaj family was represented by Sister M. Ottilia, Sister M. Cherubim, Sister M. Theodore, and Sister M. Celine, all of whom are deceased. The Jakubski family was represented by Sister M. Scholastica and Sister M. Aquiline, both deceased. The Lewandowski family was represented by Sister M. Cyprian, deceased, and the former Sister M. Remigia; the Swiech family by Sister M. Bogumila and Sister M. Leontia, both deceased. The Rokicki family is represented by Sister M. Carmel and Sister M. Virginette who are stationed at St. Anthony Medical Center in Crown Point, Indiana.

[42]Raniszewski, p. 111.

[43]Ibid., p. 112.

[44]Ibid., p. 113.

[45]The large hall, known later as Humboldt Hall, was located at 1196 N. 53rd Court which today is 2159 N. Lorel Avenue. It was owned by Stephen Sergot, a very active and generous parishioner. He allowed the hall to be used without any financial remuneration. When Sergot died in 1908, Father Obyrtacz praised him in his eulogy for Sergot's generosity. Information concerning the address was secured from the Municipal Library, Civic Center, Chicago, Illinois, 1975. *The Fiftieth Anniversary of St. Stanislaus Bishop and Martyr Church* (Chicago: 1943), p. 31.

[46]Ibid.

[47]Ibid.

[48]Raniszewski, p. 113.

[49]The Reverend Stanislaus Świerczek, CR, was born in 1873 in the Galician Region of Poland. He studied philosophy and theology in Rome where he was ordained in 1904. He was

stationed at St. Stanislaus Kostka Church in 1906 and served as an assistant at St. Hyacinth's Church from 1906 to 1909. In 1909, Father Świerczek was appointed the pastor of St. Stanislaus Bishop and Martyr Church where he served until 1926 when he received an appointment as pastor of St. Hyacinth's Church. He was assigned to St. Joseph Novitiate House in Chicago where he served as superior and novice master from 1940 to 1945. From 1945 to 1946, he wrote a regular column, "Readings for Our Times," for the *Dziennik Chicagoski* [The Chicago Daily News]. He retired in 1961 and died on November 8, 1969, at the Resurrectionist novitiate in Woodstock, Illinois. Janas, pp. 154–155.

[50]The parish grew to such an extent that in 1914 Archbishop Quigley established the neighboring parish of St. James in Hanson Park. Iwicki, p. 99.

[51]*Archdiocese of Chicago, 1920* (Chicago: 1920), p. 562.

[52]*The Fiftieth Anniversary of St. Stanislaus Bishop and Martyr Church,* p. 38.

[53]Raniszewski, p. 114.

[54]The Reverend Francis Kubiaczyk served at St. Stanislaus Bishop and Martyr Church as pastor from 1928 to 1932. He died in Chicago on May 12, 1933, while stationed at St. Stanislaus Kostka Church. Janas, p. 35.

[55]When the energetic and zealous Reverend Jerome Fabianski, CR, was installed as the new pastor in 1936, he began an active program of improvements and beautification of parish buildings and grounds. In 1942, in the large vacant area adjacent to the Sisters' convent, the beautiful "Garden of Graces" was constructed. A statue of Our Lady of Grace was installed surrounded by a great variety of flowers, lawns, shrubbery, small firs, and six ponds. The sight was most beautiful, particularly at night when the entire garden was illuminated by artistically arranged color light reflectors.

An imposing statue of the Sacred Heart of Jesus was erected on Long Avenue when the entire parish was consecrated to the Sacred Heart in a special ceremony on September 18, 1938, by the Most Reverend Bernard Sheil, auxiliary bishop of Chicago. *The Fiftieth Anniversary of St. Stanislaus Bishop and Martyr Church,* p. 43.

[56]*St. Stanislaus Bishop and Martyr House Journal* (AFSCL).

[57]A name which is associated with the school band is that of Sister M. Consolata Markowicz who served as band moderator for eighteen years. As moderator, she also directed the band during rehearsals for the lavish musical concerts and performances which were presented annually in the school auditorium. Sister M. Consolata was also most diligent in teaching band beginners even during her free time.

[58]*St. Stanislaus Bishop and Martyr House Journal* (AFSCL).

CHAPTER 14

Growth and Expansion

On June 19, 1902, the young community received its official "Document of Erection." This document made mention of the prior "Document of Approbation" which had been granted in 1899 by the Most Reverend Patrick Feehan, archbishop of Chicago. It read:

> By this present Document we, on our own initiative, again approve the Congregation of Sisters of the Third Order of St. Francis under the patronage of Saint Cunegunda, [sic], founded back in 1899 in our Archdiocese with our permission by the Reverend Fathers of the Congregation of the Resurrection, and we ordain it be regarded as canonically established.

Issued from our Archiepiscopal Residence June 19, 1902

> \+ P. A. Feehan
> Archbishop of Chicago

With this official "Document of Erection," the small community continued to increase in its number of novices and postulants.[1] This generally meant an equal growth in the number of aged and orphans admitted as well. The lack of proper accommodations for the Sisters as well as for the resident aged and orphaned was increasingly apparent and called for immediate attention. In 1903, shortly after the start of the new year, an opportunity arose to secure five frame houses on Ridgeway Avenue, directly in back of St. Joseph Home for the Aged and Crippled and St. Vincent's Orphan Asylum on Hamlin Avenue. In spite of the Sisters' good fortune in learning of the availability of the houses, they were painfully aware that they lacked the necessary funds to purchase them. Through continued sacrifice and frugality, however, they finally saved enough money to buy two houses.[2] The first house, blessed shortly after its purchase and called St. Joachim Home,[3] was meant for the use of the aged. The second house, named St. Theresa Home, was blessed in March and housed the novices and postulants who, in this way, were separated from the professed Sisters for the first time as was advocated by Canon Law. Sister M.

Anna and Sister M. Theresa wanted to purchase the third house as well, but the owner steadfastly refused to sell the building for the price the Sisters could afford. In fervent prayer, the Sisters implored St. Joseph for help, and in a matter of weeks, the owner relented. This house, called St. Anne's Infirmary, became a hospital for the Sisters and the orphans. The last two houses on the block had a selling price of $1,000 each. As eager as the Sisters were to obtain these houses, they lacked the money to purchase them. Sister M. Theresa, however, wrote in her "Chronicle" of an unusual happening in the midst of all their financial problems:

> After some time, God sent us a benefactor[4] who, to this day, remains unknown. One day a man appeared at the door [of St. Joseph Home] and handed Sister M. Colette a map globe of the world. A small box was attached to it. Upon opening the box, Sister M. Anna found one thousand dollars.[5]

Several days later, Sister M. Anna found another little box on a table in the guest parlor. A note attached to the box read: "To be used as Sister Superior sees fit." Upon opening the box, Sister M. Anna again found the sum of $1,000. With the $2,000, the Sisters purchased and renovated the last two houses on Ridgeway Avenue. Since there were so many postulants now, they occupied one of the houses; the fifth house was occupied by aged women residents.[6]

Frame houses which served as temporary dwellings to alleviate crowded conditions in the original St. Joseph Home for the Aged and Crippled pictured in the background. The small houses were eventually razed and the present St. Joseph Home of Chicago was built on that site.

Father Spetz continued to exercise his solicitous care over the Sisters' spiritual life. In 1901, he had made it possible for the Sisters to begin the recitation of the *Little Office of the Blessed Virgin Mary,* a short form of the *Breviary* which consisted of psalms, lessons, and hymns in honor of the Mother of God.[7] Until September 8, 1901, when the Sisters began the recitation of the *Little Office,* they had remained faithful to praying the customary tertiary prayers and the "Little Hours of the Blessed Virgin Mary" called *Godzinki.* Sister M. Theresa expressed the sentiments of the Sisters when in her "Chronicle" she wrote: "It seemed as if a new life was begun when we adopted the *Little Office of the Blessed Virgin Mary.* At first, when we tried to recite it in common, it was rather difficult, but later we became quite proficient."[8]

On August 2, 1902, the Sisters received the privilege of having the Portiuncula Indulgence[9] attached to their modest chapel.[10] Their joy was unbounded when in 1903, one of the Church's best-loved devotions, the Forty Hours Devotion, was introduced into the community through the efforts of Father Spetz. The Forty Hours Devotion, the solemn exposition of the Blessed Sacrament for the time of forty hours for three separate days, was held yearly in the Motherhouse at the conclusion of the annual novena to the Blessed Virgin Mary preceding the feast of her Immaculate Conception on December 8.

With the permission of the Most Reverend James E. Quigley,[11] who had succeeded the Most Reverend Patrick A. Feehan as archbishop of Chicago, the Franciscan Sisters of Chicago agreed to staff a third parochial school in 1903. The sensitive and ingenious Archbishop Quigley was deeply concerned for the welfare and faith of the immigrant Catholics. Thoroughly convinced that the future of the Church was dependent on the Catholic School, he encouraged the young community of Franciscan Sisters to direct their services to the hearts and minds of children through parish schools, even though they might be outside his archdiocese.[12] The Sisters, therefore, agreed to staff St. Casimir's School in the Diocese of Cleveland which, after Chicago, was to prove a fertile ground for much of the congregation's future ministry. As the history of the congregation's successful efforts in Ohio reveals, and particularly in the number of vocations fostered,[13] it would be difficult to find fault with a state that has as its official motto, "With God, all things are possible."[14]

St. Casimir's School was located in the northeastern part of Cleveland called *Kaźmierzowo*[15] or *Poznań*[16] within the East 79th Street, St. Clair, and Superior Avenue districts, which had early been settled chiefly by immigrants from the vicinity of Poznań, Poland. This area, strong in national pride and buoyant of spirit, had been established by the Most Reverend Ignatius F. Horstmann, bishop of Cleveland, in 1891, as the third parish in Cleveland to meet the spiritual needs of the Poles.[17] On a large piece of land donated by a German Catholic, a brick combination church and school was built on East 82nd Street and Sowinski Avenue in 1892, under the supervision of the Reverend Benedict Rosinski, the pastor of St. Adalbert's Church in Berea.[18] In July 1893, the Reverend Peter

St. Casimir Convent
Cleveland, Ohio

Cerveny was appointed the first resident pastor, but his pastorate was short-lived, for in 1894, the Reverend Stanislaus Woźny replaced him. St. Casimir's School opened that year with sixty-one pupils under the direction of a lay teacher.[19] In 1900, during the pastoral tenure of the Reverend Constanty Łazinski, four Sisters of the Congregation of the Sisters of St. Felix of Cantalice (Felicians) from Livonia, Michigan, came to administer the school whose enrollment was increasing slowly but steadily. The Felician Sisters remained until 1903. At the invitation of still another pastor, the Reverend Ignatius Piotrowski, Sister M. Anna was asked for Sisters to replace the Felicians whose reason for withdrawal is not known.[20] Sent to St. Casimir's School on October 18 were Sister M. Clara Ogurek as superior and principal, Sister M. Seraphine Zamrowski, Sister M. Agnes Roszak, and Frances Blazek, a postulant.[21] For almost three years, the Sisters lived in the most dire poverty.[22] Their quarters consisted of two inadequate classrooms in the church-school combination. One room was used as the Sisters' sleeping quarters while the other served as the kitchen, refectory, study hall, living room, or oratory depending on what was occurring in the room at the time.[23] The impossible living arrangements plus a series of misunderstandings between the pastor and the Sisters made Sister M. Anna and her advisory council seriously consider withdrawing from the school.[24] Finally, in 1909, an ample and suitable home was built to serve as the convent, and the school enrollment, rising to 716 students by 1915, gave the Sisters good reason to remain.[25]

In 1914, an unfortunate incident occurred at the mission. Sister M. Gonzaga Raniszewski, in her brief history of the congregation relates the near disaster:

The celebration of the feast of St. Casimir, which that year fell on a Saturday, was postponed to Sunday. The church was beautifully decorated for the occasion and the Masses were all celebrated with great solemnity. The next day after school, several Sisters went to church to help the Sister-sacristan put away the decorations after the feastday. After completing their work, the Sisters returned to the convent and were at their customary evening meal at six o'clock when a woman rang their doorbell shouting: "Fire! Fire! There's a fire in the church!" Upon reaching the church, the Sisters saw the flames rising near the altar area. Parishioners were attempting to put out the flames with buckets of water. Having already notified the Fire Department, Sister M. Aloysia, the superior, proceeded to direct the men to carry out articles from the sacristy which was as yet untouched by the flames. It was determined that the fire had started from crossed electrical wiring in the wall behind the altar. Because the pastor was not at home, Sister M. Aloysia carried the Blessed Sacrament to the Sisters' convent. The firemen were able to contain the flames and save the church from irreparable damage.[26]

In 1918, a large, imposing, brick Romanesque church was constructed during the pastorate of the Reverend Charles Ruszkowski, and the old school-church combination became the school. Although there had been a frequent change of administration at St. Casimir's Church through the years, the parish grew remarkably. It reached its greatest heights with the appointment on July 4, 1924, of the Reverend Andrew Radecki, a priest of unusual vigor and insight, and a staunch, devoted advocate and benefactor of the Franciscan Sisters of Chicago.[27] By 1930, there were 1,122 students in the school. Because

St. Casimir School
Cleveland, Ohio (1903–1976)

166

of the needs of the large number of Sisters on the staff, the convent was remodeled and extended to include a second house in 1934. By the 1940s, however, the enrollment dropped to 624 with a staff of seventeen Sisters.[28]

Even with the drop in enrollment, Monsignor Radecki saw the need for better accommodations for the students and erected a modern eleven-room school which was dedicated by the Most Reverend Edward F. Hoban, archbishop-bishop of Cleveland, on July 4, 1949.[29] It was at this time that Monsignor Radecki indicated his desire to have the Franciscan Sisters of Chicago initiate a high school at St. Casimir's Parish. His wish was that the ninth grade open in September of 1949, and an additional grade each year thereafter. Mother M. Jerome Dadej alerted him to the fact that she could not supply qualified Sisters at the time, but she indicated a genuine willingness to prepare Sisters for the teaching of secondary school in the future.[30] For reasons unknown, the plan for St. Casimir's High School never materialized.

For years, St. Casimir's School continued to be one of the most stable and successful parish missions of the Franciscan Sisters of Chicago. Academically, the school ranked as one of the finest in the Diocese of Cleveland. With a "look to the future," a beautiful new convent was erected in 1956. By the late 1960s, however, a radical change occurred in the neighborhood's racial, ethnic, and economic composition. The growth of the black population and the subsequent loss of the white population left the school enrollment practically depleted. In 1973, Sister M. Hugoline Czaplinski, the superior general, informed the Right Reverend Monsignor William Novicky, superintendent of education in Cleveland, that the Franciscan Sisters of Chicago would be withdrawn from St. Casimir's School at the end of the school year. She did agree, however, to allow Sister M. Clemensa Klepek and Sister M. Daniel Gach to remain at the parish to maintain charge of the church sacristy, to visit the aged and sick in their homes, and to conduct religious education classes according to the wishes of the pastor, the Reverend John Bryk. Before such an agreement could be finalized, the newly appointed pastor of St. Casimir's, the Reverend Leo Telesz, asked that the school continue and the Sisters remain on the staff. With the permission of the diocesan school board, Sister M. Hugoline and the general council allowed the two Sisters to remain as teachers.[31] A third Sister, Sister M. Celeste Walkowski, was appointed to reside at St. Casimir's Parish while teaching at the Congregation's SS. Philip and James School on the West Side of Cleveland. At the close of the 1975–1976 school year, the futility of keeping St. Casimir's School open was obvious because of the continued low enrollment. When the school closed in 1976, Sister M. Clemensa and Sister M. Daniel remained at the parish as sacristans and parish visitors. Sister M. Celeste was appointed to the teaching staff of St. Leo the Great School in Parma, Ohio, when the Franciscan Sisters of Chicago withdrew from SS. Philip and James School in 1982. The Franciscan Sisters of Chicago continued to live, to pray, and to minister to the people of St. Casimir's Parish with the same compassion and dedication which fired the pioneer Sisters until 1986, the year in which the congregation found it necessary to withdraw from the mission permanently.

GROWTH AND EXPANSION

[1]On October 4, 1903, six more postulants were admitted to the novitiate. They were: Frances Kielpinski (Sister M. Susanna); Katherine Osinski (Sister M. Antonina); Marianne Nawracaj (Sister M. Margaret); Martha Barczewski (Sister M. Hyacinth); Sophie Scibior (Sister M. Louis); and Rosalie Makowski (Sister M. Dominic).

On December 8 of that year, four Sisters were admitted to first profession of vows: Sister M. Colette Nowak, Sister M. Francis Drufke, Sister M. Leona Pochelski, and Sister M. Magdalen Schreiber. *Spis Sióstr* (AFSCL).

[2]Siostra M. Gonzaga Raniszewski, OSFK, *Rys historyczny Zgromadzenia Sióstr Franciszkanek Błogosławionej Kunegundy. Część pierwsza, 1860–1910* [A historical survey of the Franciscan Sisters of Blessed Kunegunda. Part one, 1860–1910] (Chicago: By the Author, 1947), p. 100.

[3]The first persons to live there, it will be recalled, were the Sisters who had returned from SS. Peter and Paul School in Spring Valley, Illinois, when the school was ordered closed in 1903 because of a contagious disease. See Chapter 13 for more details.

[4]Although the "anonymous benefactor" who had twice come to the Sisters' rescue financially has never been identified, some Sisters believed that it was the Reverend Adalbert Furman, who was a personal friend of Sister M. Anna, and was thus aware of the community's financial woes. *Interview* with Sister M. Martha Bywalec and Sister M. Cecilia Janicki, 7 November 1975 (AFSCL).

Father Furman was born in Bruss, Poland, the birthplace of Sister M. Anna, on April 2, 1866. He received his elementary education partly in his native country and partly at St. Stanislaus Kostka School in Chicago where his family had settled. He graduated from St. Jerome's College, Kitchener, Canada. His philosophical and theological courses were taken in Kankakee, Illinois, and St. Mary's Seminary in Baltimore. On March 18, 1883, he was ordained. His first assignment of six months duration was as assistant at St. Josaphat's Church in Chicago. He became pastor of St. Casimir's Church on Chicago's Southwest Side in 1893. Because of failing health, he resigned his pastorate on January 31, 1922. He remained pastor emeritus until his death on December 20, 1929, at sixty-three. *St. Casimir Parish: Diamond Jubilee, 1890–1965* (Chicago, Illinois, 1965), p. 23. It was Father Furman who preached a very moving eulogy at the funeral of Mother M. Anna on January 27, 1917, although it was often historically inaccurate.

[5]Matka Maria Teresa Dudzik, "Kronika Sióstr Franciszkanek pod opieką Św. Kunegundy w Chicago, Illinois" [The Chronicle of the Franciscan Sisters under the patronage of St. Kunegunda in Chicago, Illinois] Unpublished manuscript, 1910 (Chicago, Illinois, AFSCL), p. 77.

[6]Ibid.

[7]Father Spetz had made arrangements for the *Little Office of the Blessed Virgin Mary* to be printed by the Polish Publishing Company founded by Father Vincent Barzynski in 1887 for the publication of Polish newspapers, periodicals, books, and pamphlets in the United States. Edward T. Janas, CR, *Dictionary of American Resurrectionists, 1865–1965* (Rome: Gregorian University Press, 1967), p. 8.

[8]Dudzik, p. 75.

[9]The Portiuncula is the chapel of St. Mary of the Angels near Assisi given to St. Francis by the Benedictines. The ruined chapel, rebuilt by St. Francis, is historically the birthplace of the Franciscan Order.

The name lends itself to the Portiuncula Indulgence or the Pardon of Assisi which is a plenary indulgence which may be gained for the dead when one visits the chapel on August 2. Eventually the Portiuncula Indulgence was extended to all Franciscan and other churches throughout the world. The Portiuncula Indulgence may be gained by the faithful who meet the usual conditions: confession and Holy Communion, and six Our Fathers, Hail Marys, and Glorys for the intention of the Holy Father. Donald Attwater, ed., *A Catholic Dictionary* (New York: The MacMillan Co., 1961), p. 390.

[10]Dudzik, p. 79.

[11]Born in Oshawa, Ontario, Canada, on October 15, 1854, James Edward Quigley was brought to the United States when a child. He graduated from St. Joseph's College in Buffalo, studied at Our Lady of Angels Seminary there, at Innsbruck in Austria, and at the Propaganda College in Rome where he was ordained in 1879. He served as pastor in several churches in New York. In 1897, he was consecrated bishop of Buffalo. Pope Leo XIII selected him as the archbishop of Chicago in 1903, upon the death of Archbishop Feehan. During his administration, the Catholic Church in Chicago made remarkable progress.

Although his administration lasted only thirteen years, Archbishop Quigley was known as a peacemaker and a builder. He founded seventy-five new churches in Chicago due mainly to the influx of foreign-born Catholics into the Midwest. He was especially interested in Italian immigrants and erected twenty churches for their benefit. It was during his administration that the first Polish bishop in the United States, the Most Reverend Paul P. Rhode, was consecrated in 1907. Archbishop Quigley aided in preserving the religious fervor of the Poles in Chicago and almost doubled the number of parishes to serve them. He also expressed great concern for the outcome of social welfare projects of special interest to the Poles. Because he was convinced that the future of the Catholic Church lay with the children, parochial schools were constructed whenever a new church was planned. As a consequence, he erected ninety new schools. The various religious orders in Chicago found the archbishop most sympathetic to their aims.

He organized the Cathedral College in 1905, which was the seed of the present archdiocesan seminary. Loyola and De Paul Universities were opened during his tenure. He was particularly interested in the needy, the exceptional and homeless child, and the deaf. For the latter, he founded the Ephpheta School for the Deaf which the Franciscan Sisters of Chicago purchased in 1951 and renamed Madonna High School. He also founded the Catholic Church Extension Society for the home missions.

He died on July 10, 1915. His body rests in the same mausoleum that contains the remains of Archbishop Feehan. It could truly be said of him: "Archbishop Quigley was a ruler who knew how to be silent with his tongue and how to speak in his deeds." Andrew M. Greeley, "Catholicism in America: Two Hundred Years and Counting," *The Critic* (Summer 1976): 14–47; 54–70; Reverend Joseph Thompson, ed., *Diamond Jubilee of the Archdiocese of Chicago, 1920* (Des Plaines, Illinois: St. Mary's Training Press, 1920), pp. 73–85; John Iwicki, CR, *The First One Hundred Years, 1866–1966* (Rome: Gregorian University Press, 1966, p. 101; Reverend M. J. Madaj, *The New World,* 16 August 1974, sec. 2, pp. 7–8; John J. Delaney and James Edward Tobin, *Dictionary of Catholic Biography* (New York: Doubleday and Company, Inc., 1961).

[12]Siostra M. Gonzaga Raniszewski, OSFK, *Rys historyczny Zgromadzenia Sióstr Franciszkanek Błogosławionej Kunegundy. Część pierwsza, 1860–1910* [A historical survey of the Franciscan Sisters of Blessed Kunegunda. Part one, 1860–1910] (Chicago: By the Author, 1947), p. 105.

[13]St. Casimir's Parish is represented by twenty-two members in the congregation. Sister Martha Joan Sempolski, who served as superior general from 1978 to 1983, entered the congregation from this parish.

[14]Kay Sullivan, *The Catholic Tourist Guide* (New York: Meredith Press, 1967), p. 178.

[15]As is so often the case, the name of the neighborhood is called by the church's name. *Kaźmierzowo,* therefore, was the name given to the St. Casimir's (Kaźmierz) Church area.

[16]The area called *Poznań* among the Clevelanders of Polish origin was distinguished from *Warszawa* (Warsaw), a Polish colony in the East 55th and Broadway section of Cleveland. The Sisters would eventually staff Sacred Heart of Jesus parish in that area in 1912.

[17]Mary Assumpta Pogorzelski, "A Historical Study of Religion and Education as

Underlying Influences in the Localization of the Poles of Cleveland up to 1915" (M.A. thesis, St. John's College of Cleveland, 1951), p. 58.

[18]Michael J. Hynes, *History of the Diocese of Cleveland* (Cleveland: World Publishing Co., 1953), p. 255.

[19]Pogorzelski, p. 59.

[20]*Book of Correspondence:* Letter from Sister M. Consuela, CSSF, provincial vicar, Felician Sisters, Livonia, Michigan, to author, 13 May 1976 (AFSCL).

[21]Frances Blazek became Sister M. Bonaventure in religious life. *Spis Sióstr* (AFSCL).

[22]The deposition of Sister M. Zita Kosmala states that she was sent as a candidate for two months in 1904 to be of assistance to the Sister who attended to household duties. Sister M. Zita revealed that she had to sleep on a mattress on the floor since the pastor did not want to buy a bed because she would not remain at the parish for very long. *Book of Depositions* (AFSCL).

[23]Raniszewski, p. 78.

[24]A move to leave the school had been contemplated as early as April 1909. Because of an indiscretion committed on the part of Sister M. Stanislaus Reich, Sister M. Theresa, at that time the mother superior, and her advisory council were forced to recall Sister M. Stanislaus from the school where she had served as superior and principal from 1904 to 1909. In July of 1909, she was appointed the mistress of novices. Because she did not wish to serve in that capacity, Sister M. Stanislaus left the community and returned to Cleveland. Her actions caused much unpleasantness for everyone concerned. On November 29, 1910, however, she was readmitted to the community. For the next forty-eight years she worked diligently in the Church Vestment Workshop and from 1946 to 1958 she served as its supervisor. She died at the Motherhouse on April 27, 1958. She was seventy-nine years old and had been in the congregation for fifty-nine years. *Spis Sióstr* (AFSCL).

[25]*Minutes of General Council Proceedings, 1910–1934* (AFSCL).

[26]Raniszewski, p. 128.

[27]The Right Reverend Monsignor Andrew A. Radecki was born in Poland on October 15, 1885. He emigrated to America where he studied for the priesthood in the Cleveland diocese. He took great pride in being one of the first American-instructed Polish priests in Cleveland. Ordained by the Most Reverend John P. Farrelly in St. John's Cathedral, Cleveland, on June 4, 1910, Monsignor Radecki had a long and distinguished priestly career. His first assignment was as an assistant at St. John Cantius Church in Cleveland. In 1912, he was appointed administrator of the financially troubled Nativity of the Blessed Virgin Mary Church in Lorain, Ohio. By 1914, when Bishop Farrelly appointed him pastor, Father Radecki had saved sufficient funds to build a lovely Gothic church and a two-story brick school. In 1924, he was called upon to rescue another parish facing bankruptcy and parish factions. This was St. Casimir's Church in Cleveland where he served with distinction until his death on March 9, 1969. Monsignor Radecki's generosity and graciousness to the Franciscan Sisters of Chicago ensure him a permanent memory in the annals of the congregation. Information received from Chancery Office, Diocese of Cleveland.

[28]Raniszewski, p. 120.

[29]*Minutes of General Council Proceedings, 1934* (AFSCL).

[30]*Book of Correspondence:* Letter from Mother M. Jerome Dadej to the Right Reverend Monsignor Andrew Radecki, 14 April 1949 (AFSCL).

[31]*Book of Correspondence:* Letter from Sister M. Hugoline Czaplinski to the Reverend Leo Telesz, 24 January 1974 (AFSCL).

CHAPTER 15

Progress in Early Ventures

Early in June of 1904, Sister M. Anna fell seriously ill. While she recuperated for nearly two months in St. Anne's Infirmary, Sister M. Theresa assumed the duty of mother superior in Sister M. Anna's place. In addition to this added responsibility, Sister M. Theresa continued to serve as mistress of novices and postulants. She also maintained supervision of the laundry and continued to assist the aged residents and orphans with loving maternal care.[1]

During the month of June, the Sisters returned from their teaching assignments and took part in the annual retreat. On July 27, at the conclusion of the retreat, nine postulants were admitted to the novitiate.[2] The following day was another day of jubilation for the Sisters, the aged residents, and the orphans. The newly installed archbishop of Chicago, the Most Reverend James E. Quigley, who had set for himself the task of visiting all the parishes and institutions of the burgeoning archdiocese in order to better acquaint himself with his flock, visited St. Joseph Home for the Aged and Crippled and St. Vincent's Orphan Asylum.[3] Archbishop Quigley was warmly greeted by the orphans in their dining room with songs and verses. After the enthusiastic welcome, he imparted his blessing to the aged residents who had gathered in the chapel to greet him. Archbishop Quigley looked at every room in the orphanage and the home for the aged. Upon learning of Sister M. Anna's illness, Archbishop Quigley visited the infirmary where Sister M. Anna greeted her distinguished visitor with genuine surprise and joy.[4] He spoke with her regarding various matters pertaining to the community and gave her his episcopal blessing. He also presented Sister M. Anna with a gift offering of $200 to be used for the support of the orphans. Before Archbishop Quigley left St. Joseph Home, promising to return in six years, he held a Benediction Service in the chapel.[5]

The monetary offering which Archbishop Quigley had presented to Sister M. Anna was genuinely welcome and essential. There were, at this time, eighty-six orphans in St. Vincent's Orphan Asylum and fifty-three aged residents in St. Joseph Home.[6] With the constant, but certainly welcome increase in the number of women who asked for admittance to the religious community, the need for more room was obvious. Sister M.

Anna and Sister M. Theresa consulted with Father Spetz, and, as a consequence, construction was begun in October on a new building which could accommodate the novices and postulants. By January of 1905, the new novitiate house, built to the left of St. Joseph Home for the Aged and Crippled and connected to it by a corridor, was ready for occupancy. The large first floor of the building was designed to serve as a much-needed laundry, where to Sister M. Theresa's great relief, the old washing machines and several new ones were placed.[7] The second floor consisted of six rooms. Five of the rooms were used as sleeping quarters accommodating at least thirty novices and postulants, while the sixth room was designated as a community workroom.[8] An addition to the novitiate house, in the form of a third floor, was completed in the summer of 1909.[9] The novices moved to the third floor while the postulants retained their quarters on the second floor. The laundry remained on the first floor. At the same time, Sister M. Theresa and her advisory council agreed on an addition to St. Anne's Infirmary.[10] A wall surrounding the community's entire complex was also built at this time.[11]

On October 26, 1904, the mother of Sister M. Theresa, Agnes Dudzik, who for over ten years had watched her daughter's noble work unfold, died after a brief illness in the institution built by her daughter.[12] Her funeral mass and burial ceremony from the chapel of St. Joseph Home were held on October 28 after which she was laid to rest in St. Adalbert's Cemetery.[13]

St. Michael School and Convent Berlin, Wisconsin (1904–1907)

Outside of a single entry in the "Chronicle" of Sister M. Theresa, there are only scant details concerning the Sisters' expanded teaching ventures into the state of Wisconsin in 1904. In her "Chronicle," Sister M. Theresa had written simply that "a mission had been accepted in Berlin," then in the Diocese of Green Bay.[14] On September 18, 1904, Sister M. Rose Gorski, as the superior and principal was accompanied by Sister M. Salomea Grabowski and Sister M. Francis Drufke to begin operation of St. Michael's School in Berlin, a little town west of Oshkosh with a large Polish population. A month later, Sister M. Louis Scibior, newly professed, was sent to attend to household duties.[15]

The Reverend Januarius Czarnowski of St. Stanislaus Church in nearby Berlin had helped organize St. Michael's parish in 1885.[16] On a lovely site that had formerly been an apple orchard, a wooden church had been constructed at West Franklin and Grove Streets for which the parishioners, chiefly Kashubes,[17] had willingly mortgaged their own property. In a large wooden building directly west of the church, a parochial school had existed since 1895 under the direction of two lay people. In September of 1904, a modern brick building was erected by the pastor, the Reverend John Bieniarz, who invited the Franciscan Sisters of Chicago to take charge of the school. When the Sisters arrived, therefore, they taught in the new school, and several rooms in the school building were designated as their living quarters.[18]

By 1907, however, severe financial reverses made it impossible for the parish to support the Sisters, and, very reluctantly, the small band of pioneer Franciscans in Wisconsin was forced to leave St. Michael's School.[19] The same spirit of integrity, progress, and cooperation which led the first determined settlers to undertake the building of St. Michael's Church and School, compelled the parishioners to overcome the financial crisis which threatened them at the time. By 1909, members of the Congregation of the Sisters of St. Joseph of the Third Order of St. Francis from Stevens Point, Wisconsin, were obtained to reopen the school.[20] When the Sisters of St. Joseph were recalled by their religious superior in 1915, the Congregation of the Sisters of St. Felix of Cantalice (Felicians) accepted the school and have remained to the present day.[21]

In addition to St. Michael's School which the Franciscan Sisters of Chicago had accepted in 1904, they also accepted a second school in Wisconsin in 1905.

Poles had begun to settle in Oshkosh, seventy-five miles north of Milwaukee after 1870. After the destructive fires which occurred in 1874 and 1975, the rebuilding and expanding of the city of Oshkosh created labor opportunities for the incoming Poles.[22] In the beginning, two Catholic churches served the spiritual needs of the Poles; however, the Reverend Theophilus Malkowski, a visiting priest who assisted the Poles at nearby St. Mary's Church in Oshkosh by hearing confessions and giving conferences in their native language, urged the Polish settlers to establish a church of their own. In 1895, a committee purchased land in the northern section of the city on Walnut Street but met with great difficulty when they attempted to secure a Polish priest to organize the parish.[23] When the committee learned of the success of the Reverend Wacław Kruszka in organizing St. Wenceslaus Parish in Ripon, Wisconsin, they appealed to the Most Reverend Sebastian Messmer, bishop of Milwaukee, to obtain Father Kruszka's help.[24] Bishop Messmer most obligingly authorized Father Kruszka to take charge as pastor of organizing a Polish parish in Oshkosh and of building a church. In spite of obstacles, Father Kruszka worked with zeal to establish a church for the Poles. On January 30, 1898, the new church was dedicated by Bishop Messmer and was called St. Josaphat, the name the bishop himself had suggested. The parish had at least fifty families at this time.[25]

St. Josaphat School
Oshkosh, Wisconsin (1905–1911)

Before the zealous Father Kruszka resigned his pastorate at St. Josaphat's Church that same year, he established a one-room school in the basement of the church and hired a layman as organist and teacher. The school continued to be conducted by laymen until it closed in 1903.[26] When the sixth pastor of St. Josaphat's Church, the Reverend Francis Własłowski, declared his intention to reopen the school in 1904, he petitioned Sister M. Anna Wysinski for teachers. On September 18, 1905, Sister M. Gerard Gorzkowski was sent as the superior and principal. She was joined by Sister M. Patricia Eiress,[27] who was assigned to household duties, and by a postulant who was assigned to teach.[28] The Sisters made their home in a little house next to the school.[29]

Through the efforts of Father Własłowski, a two-story brick building was erected in 1910, a rare and monumental achievement in the early days of the little parish. The building contained two classrooms, and the other two rooms in the new school served as the Sisters' living quarters. The parishioners offered special fervent petitions to St. Joseph for needed financial assistance, and when such assistance was received, the grateful parishioners voted to call the school St. Joseph's while the church retained its original name of St. Josaphat's.[30]

Information concerning this mission is very scarce. The records of the congregation, however, indicate that on July 21, 1909, Sister M. Theresa Dudzik, who had been reappointed mother superior of the community, and her advisory council[31] voted to make known to the pastor the "various difficulties and shortages" which existed at St. Joseph's School. While the records are not clear in regard to particular problems, it is obvious that the apparent lack of adequate classroom space and appropriate living quarters for the Sisters were the "difficulties and shortages" to which the records referred. As a consequence of the handicaps with which the Sisters were faced, an attempt was made to relinquish the school at the end of the 1909 school year. A subsequent decision was made to send the Sisters back for another "trial" year. By December 1909, Sister M. Theresa once again planned to remove the Sisters in June of 1910. Father Własłowski pleaded for the Sisters to remain, and for the second time, Sister M. Theresa reversed her decision to withdraw the Sisters.[32] The problems existing at the mission, however, proved insurmountable. Consequently, Sister M. Jerome Dadej, Sister M. Michaeline Tabor, and Sister M. Anastasia Halcerz made their final departure in 1911. Father Własłowski succeeded in obtaining the Congregation of the Sisters of St. Joseph of the Third Order of St. Francis from Stevens Point, Wisconsin, to staff the school. The Sisters remained until 1974 when a decision was made to close the school when only eighty pupils out of a possible three hundred were enrolled for the new school year.[33]

As for the Franciscan Sisters of Chicago, their next venture into Wisconsin would take place twenty-three years later, but in circumstances and in an apostolate not related to teaching.

PROGRESS IN EARLY VENTURES

[1]Matka Maria Teresa Dudzik, "Kronika Sióstr Franciszkanek pod opieką Św. Kunegundy w Chicago, Illinois" [The Chronicle of the Franciscan Sisters under the patronage of St. Kunegunda in Chicago, Illinois] Unpublished manuscript, 1910 (Chicago, Illinois, AFSCL), p. 88.

[2]The postulants were Anna Wojciechowski (Sister M. Hugoline); Frances Blazek (Sister M. Bonaventure); Joanne Nowak (Sister M. Jolanta); Eve Stefanski (Sister M. Bernice); Marianne Gorzkowski (Sister M. Gerard); Lauretta Eiress (Sister M. Patricia); Sophie Tabasz (Sister M. Cajetan); Marianne Grochola (Sister M. Barbara); and Anna Marszalkowski (Sister M. Philomena). *Spis Sióstr* (AFSCL).

[3]Siostra M. Gonzaga Raniszewski, OSFK, *Rys historyczny Zgromadzenia Sióstr Franciszkanek Błogosławionej Kunegundy. Część pierwsza, 1860–1910* [A historical survey of the Franciscan Sisters of Blessed Kunegunda. Part one, 1860–1910] (Chicago: By the Author, 1947), p. 105.

[4]Dudzik, p. 80.

[5]Sister M. Gonzaga states that Archbishop Quigley always showed the community genuine paternal concern. He truly wanted to "look after this community" and even expressed himself in this fashion on several occasions. Unfortunately, his early death in 1915 kept him from influencing the community to an even greater degree. Raniszewski, p. 106.

[6]The following statistics appeared in *Sierota* magazine, 5 March 1905, edited by Stanislaus Siatka, CR:

> From the Home of the Orphans and the Aged: In the last year twenty-six boys were admitted; of them, eighteen left and one died; presently there remain forty-nine boys. Twenty-three girls were admitted last year; twelve left and presently there remain thirty-seven girls. The number of all the orphans in the home in Avondale is eighty-six.
>
> There were fourteen aged men accepted that year; five of them left the home and four died; presently there remain twenty-four aged men. Thirteen aged women were accepted; four left and seven died; there are presently twenty-nine aged women. The home for the aged now shelters fifty-three residents.

[7]Dudzik, p. 83.

[8]Ibid.

[9]Raniszewski, p. 139.

[10]*Minutes of General Council Proceedings, 1910–1934* (AFSCL).

[11]Ibid., 29 March 1909.

[12]Stanley T. Kusper, Jr., County Clerk, *Bureau of Vital Statistics, Undertaker's Report* (Chicago: Department of Health, 1976), 1 April 1976.

[13]Dudzik, p. 81.

[14]Ibid.

[15]Ibid.

[16]"St. Michael's Souvenir Dedication Number," *Berlin* (Wisconsin) *Evening Journal,* 26 October 1927, sec. 4, pp. 1–6.

[17]The Kashubes, a most distinct folk group, were members of a Slavonic Pomeranian people who lived west of the Vistula River. Their Germanization produced their distinct Slavonic dialect. While closely allied to the Polish language, it still remains the subject of controversy among linguists. The Kashubes began emigrating to the United States increasingly after 1848.

[18]Harry H. Heming, *History of the Catholic Church in Wisconsin* (Milwaukee: Catholic Historical Publishing Co., 1895–98), p. 605.

[19]Dudzik, p. 90.

[20]*Book of Correspondence:* Letter to author from Sister M. Dulcia Wanat, Sisters of St. Joseph of the Third Order of St. Francis, South Bend, Indiana, 6 January 1976 (AFSCL).

[21]*Book of Correspondence:* Letter to author from Sister M. Monica, CSSF, provincial secretary, Our Lady of Good Counsel Convent, Chicago, Illinois, 20 November 1975 (AFSCL).

[22]*Our Golden Jubilee 1897–1947: St. Josaphat's Catholic Church* (Oshkosh, Wisconsin, 1947), no pagination.

[23]Among the slate of officers in the committee was the treasurer Martin Tadych. In 1909, his daughter Rose entered the Franciscan community and was named Sister M. Josephata in honor of the parish patron. Her sister, Gertrude Tadych, entered in 1925, and became Sister M. Antoinette. Both Sisters are now deceased. They were the only two entrants to the congregation from this pioneer mission.

[24]For a more detailed history of the Reverend Wacław Kruszka and his influence among the Poles, see Chapter 3.

[25]*Our Golden Jubilee*, p. 5.

[26]*Our Golden Jubilee*, pp. 3–4.

[27]Sister M. Patricia Eiress stayed until November. She was replaced by a postulant, Rosalie Kunkiel, who remained until March 30, 1906, when she, in turn, was replaced by Sister M. Jolanta Nowak. *Spis Sióstr* (AFSCL).

[28]The postulant, Agnes Kosmowski, who as a novice was called Sister M. Cecilia, did not remain in the community. *Spis Sióstr* (AFSCL).

[29]*Our Golden Jubilee*, p. 7.

[30]Ibid.

[31]The advisory council at that time consisted of Sister M. Vincent Czyzewski, Sister M. Angeline Topolinski, and Sister M. Aloysia Holysz. *Minutes of General Council Proceedings, 1910–1934* (AFSCL).

[32]Ibid.

[33]*Interview* with the Reverend Harold A. Beerntsen, pastor of St. Josaphat's Church, Oshkosh, Wisconsin, 15 November 1975 (AFSCL).

CHAPTER 16

St. Elizabeth's Day Nursery

Six more Sisters were admitted to their first profession of vows on October 4, 1904.[1] The eager young women were sorely needed for the expanding works of the community which, that year, had included the bold venture into the State of Wisconsin with the acceptance of two new elementary schools, St. Michael's and St. Joseph's. Another new apostolate which the Sisters embraced in 1905 was the very fertile field of maintaining a day nursery for the children of employed parents, most of whom were to be found among the working poor of Chicago. A period of large-scale immigration especially from Southern and Eastern Europe had begun in 1880 and had accelerated through the ensuing years. Once in America, most of the immigrants were forced to work or starve thus leaving the small children of poor families in perilous and hazardous conditions while both parents attempted to earn a livelihood.[2] This state of affairs led to the rise of badly needed day-care centers for infants and children.

In early 1904, the Congregation of the Resurrection had purchased a two-story frame building known as the Judge Schoenewald House, located at the southwest corner of Ashland Avenue and Blackhawk Street.[3] The Resurrectionist Fathers had also purchased two adjoining houses called the North Building, a rear two-story frame house facing Blackhawk Street and the South Building, a rear two-story red brick building which faced Ashland Avenue. The aim of the Resurrectionist Fathers was to remodel the private residences into a nursery complex for children below school age whose mothers were forced to work because of insufficient family income. When Father Spetz was appointed by his congregation as the guardian of this new charitable institution, which they named St. Elizabeth's Day Nursery, he asked Sister M. Anna Wysinski for Sisters to undertake the care of the children during the working day.[4] In August of 1904, Sister M. Anna appointed Sister M. Angeline Topolinski to serve as the superior and administrator of St. Elizabeth's Day Nursery. She was assisted by Sister M. Clara Ogurek, Sister M. Hyacinth Barczewski, and Sister M. Felixa Karwata.[5] The Sisters maintained living quarters in the Schoenewald House and slept in the small attic which was very inconvenient especially when the number of Sisters increased.[6]

St. Elizabeth's Day Nursery
Chicago, Illinois (1904–1915) (1920–1959)

When St. Elizabeth's Day Nursery opened, from sixty to sixty-five children attended daily. Even some infants as young as four months of age were boarded for the day. A fee of $0.10 a day per child was charged, and two hot meals were served to the children at no additional cost.[7] Besides operating the day nursery, the Sisters held catechism classes three times a week for the children who attended public schools and prepared them for the reception of their First Holy Communion. The Sisters also visited lapsed Catholics in their homes in the hope of bringing them back into the Church. Sister M. Veronica Maka,[8] in particular, visited the sick and infirm in their own homes providing them with both spiritual and material assistance. She also prepared neglected children in the local Polish parishes for First Holy Communion which they received in the Motherhouse chapel.[9] In the evening, the Sisters held classes for young girls and married women who learned cooking, sewing, crocheting, and other useful household arts. Sister M. Anselma Pasternacki was especially instrumental in organizing these valuable and practical programs.[10] She also supplied the needy people of the vicinity with clothing which she had obtained. To meet the expenses of operating the day nursery, the Sisters solicited alms. They also depended on the income they derived from the sale of fancywork which they themselves made. To supplement the meager income of the day nursery, Sister M. Angeline Topolinski sewed liturgical articles for priests at neighboring parishes in the evening.[11]

In 1911, through the efforts of Father Spetz, a free health clinic was opened on the first floor of the Schoenewald House. It was open daily, except Sundays, from ten o'clock in the morning until twelve o'clock noon, and from two o'clock to four o'clock in the afternoon. As many as fifty to sixty patients were treated daily. For those who could afford it, $0.10 was charged for medicine and general treatment.[12] The medical staff secured by Father Spetz consisted of fourteen doctors who donated their services.[13] He also obtained the help of the Rush Medical College[14] which offered services free of charge.[15] Minor operations were performed at the clinic while patients in need of more serious surgery were generally sent to Columbus Extension Hospital where medical services were rendered for a very nominal fee.[16] Sister M. Ladislaus Wroblewski, the superior and administrator of St. Elizabeth's Day Nursery from 1910 to 1915, who was also a registered nurse, provided invaluable assistance to the doctors.[17] Sister M. Boleslaus Nagorski, who had been sent to St. Elizabeth's Day Nursery in 1911, remained there until December of 1912. At that time, suffering from a heart ailment, she was sent back to the Motherhouse. She contracted pneumonia and died at the Motherhouse on December 13, 1918.[18]

The first floor of the South Building was used as a clinic for tubercular cases.[19] At first, the Municipal Tuberculosis Dispensary was connected with it. When this agency transferred to a new location, however, the city of Chicago ceased support of the South Building Branch. This proved unfortunate since St. Elizabeth's Day Nursery was deprived of a source of needed funds.

Father Spetz and the Sisters were also interested in the plight of the newly arrived immigrant women who were often exposed to the moral dangers found in a large city such as Chicago. As a consequence, St. Margaret's Maternity Home was opened in 1910 in one of the buildings where unwed expectant mothers and their infants could be provided for.[20]

An added benefit of St. Elizabeth's Day Nursery was the Infant Welfare Station where mothers were instructed in the proper nourishment and suitable care of their children. In the summer, on the vacant lot near the free health clinic, a tent was raised where nurses fed milk to the infants, bathed the babies, and taught the mothers how to dress their infants to keep them well during the various seasons.[21] All these aids significantly reduced infant mortality in the densely crowded neighborhood of St. Stanislaus Kostka Parish.[22]

In the early part of 1914, various financial difficulties which had quietly plagued the day nursery became crucial. In May of that year, Father Spetz was transferred by his superiors to St. Mary's College in St. Mary, Kentucky. This action, of course, further dispirited the Sisters who had come to depend upon his advice and support for over ten years at the day nursery.[23] Before Father Spetz left Chicago, however, he met with Archbishop Quigley who advised the Sisters to take St. Elizabeth's Day Nursery completely under their care and to operate it independently of the Resurrectionist Fathers. Archbishop Quigley also recommended that the Sisters approach the pastors of nearby parishes whose parishioners utilized the services of the day nursery to make donations for its upkeep.[24] *The Journal of St Elizabeth's Day Nursery* does not indicate what further disposition was made of the suggestions. The *Journal* does indicate, however, that by December 27, 1914, Mother M. Anna and her general council agreed to close the nursery for lack of funds. When the St. Elizabeth's Ladies' Auxiliary asked the Sisters to keep it open and promised to pay the Sisters a stipend,[25] the Sisters agreed to stay. By April 1915, however, the Ladies' Auxiliary revealed that they could not pay the Sisters' stipend and meet various other financial demands.[26] Unfortunately, St. Elizabeth's Day Nursery was forced to close its doors on April 30, 1915, and the property was sold to private owners.[27] This was a terrible blow to the working mothers of the vicinity who had depended so much on this assistance. Mother M. Anna, seeing their disappointment and obvious need, suggested that the day nursery continue to operate temporarily in one of the five cottages the Sisters owned on Ridgeway Avenue in the Avondale area.[28] After several months, however, continued financial difficulties and the attendant lack of children applying because of the distance to Avondale caused the Sisters to close the day nursery in January of 1916.[29]

The Reverend Louis Grudzinski,[30] pastor of St. John of God Church on Chicago's Southwest Side and well known among the Poles of Chicago for his philanthropic activities, had already successfully established the Guardian Angel Day Nursery in the Town of Lake district on Chicago's Southwest Side in 1912. When he heard of the closing of St. Elizabeth's Day Nursery, he arranged to purchase the homes from the private owners. He then proceeded to remodel the nursery and make various other improvements including a chapel for the Sisters. The duties of the chaplain were performed by the priests of the Congregation of the Resurrection.[31]

In 1920, the day nursery reopened and Father Grudzinski asked the Franciscan Sisters of Chicago who also staffed his Guardian Angel Day Nursery to once again take responsibility for its operation. On November 23, 1920, Sister M. Francis Drufke assumed the duties of superior and administrator. She was assisted by Sister M. Cecilia Janicki, Sister M. Borromea Stryjewski, and three postulants.[32] Neither the free health clinic nor St. Margaret's Maternity Home reopened. This did not prevent the Sisters from visiting the sick children and the sick mothers of the area to whom the Sisters brought food and clothing. Frequently, widows were supplied with needed medication. In some instances, the Sisters interceded for poor families, and thus, many doctors' fees were either reduced or cancelled.[33] All available space in the new St. Elizabeth's Day Nursery was intended for the harboring of children whose mothers were forced to work or whose illness prevented the children from being cared for properly at home. Even children of school age were admitted for noon meals as well as after school, on Saturdays, on holidays, and during the summer. With the passing of the years, the neighborhood had gone through various ethnic changes, and children of all nationalities were being accepted.

By 1940, the St. Elizabeth's Day Nursery had begun again to accept infants, and the roster indicates that approximately thirty-five children and fifteen infants were being cared for daily by six Sisters. When the beloved Father Grudzinski died in 1948, he left the day nursery to the Sisters in his will. On October 9, 1952, the St. Elizabeth's Day Nursery officially became the property of the Franciscan Sisters of Chicago.

During the early 1940s, efforts were being made by Sister M. Anselma Pasternacki, then the superior and administrator, to build a new day nursery.[34] It was not until 1956, however, that Mother M. Jerome Dadej gave permission to Sister M. Praxeda Ostrega, the superior and administrator, to collect funds for a new structure since the original buildings were now over one hundred years old. To aid the building fund, the Sisters at the day nursery planned to solicit funds from the pastors of Polish churches nearby such as St. Stanislaus Kostka, Holy Trinity, and Holy Innocents.[35] A new society, Our Lady of Grace, was begun in 1956 to help gather funds; the society's plans included maintaining one floor for widows and unmarried women in the new structure.[36] The responsibility for raising the necessary funds fell solely to Sister M. Praxeda, the Sisters on the staff, and the Our Lady of Grace Society. Mother M. Jerome declared that because the congregation was building a new Madonna High School on the city's Northwest Side, it could not be actively engaged in raising funds for the construction of a new day nursery.

While plans continued to be formulated for the erection of a new St. Elizabeth's Day Nursery, the *Journal* of the institution reveals that by 1958, only thirty-eight children could be accommodated daily by order of the Chicago Department of Health. At this time, parents paid $2 a day, and three hot meals were included. The children arrived at seven o'clock in the morning and left at six-thirty o'clock in the evening.[37] That same year, one of the most heartbreaking disasters occurred that was destined to change the future of many institutions in Chicago. On December 1, 1958, a tragic fire struck Our Lady of the Angels School on Chicago's West Side.[38] Because of this disaster, rigid and detailed inspections of schools and institutions were stepped up. As a result of these intensified inspections, many schools and institutions, failing to meet safety requirements or shown to contain positive fire hazards, were ordered abandoned or razed by order of the Chicago Fire Department. Because the defects at St. Elizabeth's Day Nursery were found to be beyond correction, Mother M. Jerome and her general council voted to close the day nursery in February of 1959.[39] The Schoenewald House could have remained open, but the remodeling and renovative costs were prohibitive, and in the end, only fourteen children could have been accommodated. Because of the lack of funds and the small number of children attending the day nursery at the time, Mother M. Jerome and her councilors cancelled any further plans to build a new St. Elizabeth's Day Nursery. In April, the day nursery was sold to a private couple and became their property officially on June 7, 1960. Long before that, on April 3, Sister M. Praxeda Ostrega, Sister M. Germaine Moson, and Sister M. Isidore Wilkos left St. Elizabeth's Day Nursery where the Franciscan Sisters of Chicago had labored for over fifty-five years.

ST. ELIZABETH'S DAY NURSERY

[1]Admitted to their first profession were: Sister M. Susanna Kielpinski, Sister M. Antonina Osinski, Sister M. Margaret Nawracaj, Sister M. Hyacinth Barczewski, Sister M. Louis Scibior, and Sister M. Dominic Makowski. *Spis Sióstr* (AFSCL).

[2]Reverend Monsignor Harry C. Koenig, STD, ed., *Caritas Christi Urget Nos: A History of the Offices, Agencies, and Institutions of the Archdiocese of Chicago,* 2 vols. (Chicago: New World Publishing Co., 1981) 2:852:853.

[3]The small two-story building occupied by the St. Elizabeth's Day Nursery was a notable Chicago residential landmark. Built in 1858, the unique house stood in the center of a sparsely settled neighborhood of German immigrants. Its owner, Judge Jacob A. Schoenewald, was regarded by historians as the "Father" of Chicago's once large German-American settlement and a leader in the city's civic and political affairs.

After the death of Judge Schoenewald in 1882, the house was in the possession of several owners until 1904 when it was purchased by the Congregation of the Resurrection who intended to convert the house and two nearby buildings into a nursery for children whose mothers were compelled to work. In the meantime, factories and tenements arose in the district, and the area became part of the crowded Polish-American neighborhood of St. Stanislaus Kostka.

The little, old-fashioned house, an example of pre-Civil War domestic architecture, was identified by its decorative trim, high-arched windows and doors, and a gabled roof edged with ornate cornices. A porch covered the entire front, and the square columns supporting it were likewise highly ornamented. In later years, when Ashland Avenue was raised to a higher level, a brick basement was built under the house. A pleasant anecdote is associated with this residence. Years ago, Judge Schoenewald's granddaughter visited the St. Elizabeth's Day Nursery. "I was born in that room where you now have the sanctuary," she informed the Sisters. "I am sure that my grandfather would be highly pleased if he knew that his home was now a Catholic institution. All his life he had been a devout Catholic." John Drury, "Chicago Homes" *Chicago Daily News,* 12 April 1940.

[4]"A Brief History of St. Elizabeth's Day Nursery" (AFSCL).

[5]Siostra M. Gonzaga Raniszewski OSFK, *Rys historyczny Zgromadzenia Sióstr Franciszkanek Błogosławionej Kunegundy. Część pierwsza, 1860–1910* [A historical survey of the Franciscan Sisters of Blessed Kunegunda. Part one, 1860–1910] (Chicago: By the Author, 1947), p. 123.

[6]Air conditioners were finally installed in 1956 according to the *Report* submitted by Sister M. Praxeda Ostrega, superior and administrator, to Mother M. Jerome Dadej on June 18, 1958.

[7]Raniszewski, p. 123.

[8]Sister M. Veronica, born in Poland, entered from St. Stanislaus Kostka Parish in 1899 at the age of thirty-four. According to the *Spis Sióstr* [Registry of Sisters] (AFSCL), the former Louise Maka had been a postulant in the Congregation of the School Sisters of Notre Dame for approximately three weeks. The *Registry of Sisters* also states that she had entered another congregation which is simply listed as "Sister Servants of the Lord," where she remained for six years. Dispensed from her vows in that congregation, she entered the Franciscan community on August 12, 1899. She was received into the novitiate on June 4, 1900, and made her first profession of vows on June 6, 1901. On December 8, 1909, she made her perpetual profession.

For most of her religious life, Sister M. Veronica resided at the Motherhouse. There she performed various light duties and took care of the sick. From 1908, she spent time visiting the sick in their homes, offering them spiritual and material assistance. After 1916, she chiefly assisted the aged residents who were ill at St. Joseph Home for the Aged and Crippled. In addition, she was in charge of the local collections for the maintenance of the home. Sister M. Veronica died on October 31, 1934, at the Motherhouse. She was sixty-nine years old and had been in the congregation for thirty-five years.

[9]Secretaries General, *Community Chronicle,* p. 32 (AFSCL).

[10]Siostra M. Gonzaga Raniszewski, OSFK, *Echo Avondalskie* [Avondale Echo], January 7, 1983 (AFSCL).

[11]Raniszewski, *Rys,* p. 123.

[12]"A Brief History of St. Elizabeth's Day Nursery" (AFSCL).

[13]Some of the names in *St. Elizabeth's Day Nursery Record Book* are Dr. William Swift, Dr. John Graham, Dr. Stephen Piotrowicz, Dr. Wayne, Dr. Clark, and Dr. Roller.

[14]Today, this is Rush-Presbyterian-St. Luke's Hospital.

[15]*Pamiętnik Jubileuszowy ku czci Ks. Ludwika Grudzinskiego, Proboszcza Parafji Św. Jana Bożego, 1903–1928* [A Jubilee Souvenir in Honor of the Reverend Louis Grudzinski, Pastor of St. John of God Church, 1903–1928] (Chicago, Illinois, 1928), p. 15.

[16]This is Columbus Hospital today.

[17]See Chapter 27.

[18]Sister M. Boleslaus was born in Chicago. She entered from St. Vincent's Orphan Asylum in Avondale. She began her postulancy on October 4, 1905, and was admitted to the novitiate on October 8, 1906. Sister M. Boleslaus made her first profession on December 10, 1907, and her perpetual vows on August 15, 1916.

After her first profession of vows, she served at St. Vincent's Orphan Asylum. In 1911, she was sent to St. Elizabeth's Day Nursery. She died at the Motherhouse on December 8, 1918, and was buried on the next day by order of the City Ordinance. Having had heart trouble since she was a child, she could not handle the added burden of pneumonia. She was thirty years old and had been in the community for thirteen years. Raniszewski, *Rys,* p. 153; and *Spis Sióstr* (AFSCL).

[19]Dr. Stephen Piotrowicz offered his free service to patients afflicted with this disease. "A Brief History of St. Elizabeth's Day Nursery" (AFSCL).

[20]The "Brief History of St. Elizabeth's Day Nursery" found in the archives of the congregation states that expectant mothers were placed in the "tender care" of Miss Amelia McDonald. Actually, the name is O'Donnell. Dominic A. Pacyga, "Villages of Packinghouses and Steel Mills: The Polish Worker on Chicago's South Side" (Ph.D. dissertation, University of Illinois at Chicago Circle, 1981), no pagination.

After the establishment of the Associated Catholic Charities in 1918, Archbishop Mundelein allocated a modest amount of support for the operation of the program. Three years later, Misericordia Hospital and Home for Infants was established to aid women who intended to keep their children but needed financial and material assistance. Koenig, p. 1100.

[21]"A Brief History of St. Elizabeth's Day Nursery" (AFSCL); and Raniszewski, *Rys,* p. 35.

[22]Theodore Roemer, OFM, Cap., *The Catholic Church in the United States* (St. Louis: B. Herder Book Co., 1950), p. 211.

[23]"A Brief History of St. Elizabeth's Day Nursery" (AFSCL).

[24]*Minutes of General Council Proceedings, 1909–1934,* 28 August 1914 (AFSCL).

[25]Ibid., 27 December 1914.

[26]Ibid., 25 April 1915.

[27]Secretaries General, *Community Chronicle* (AFSCL).

[28]*Minutes of General Council Proceedings, 1919–1934,* 9 May (AFSCL).

[29]Ibid., 19 January 1916.

[30]Reverend Louis Grudzinski was born in Lwów, Poland, on August 2, 1878. His parents emigrated to America when he was seven months old. They settled in Chicago in St. Adalbert's Parish, then the hub of Polish religious, cultural, and civic activity on Chicago's Near West Side. He studied for the priesthood at SS. Cyril and Methodius College in Detroit, and completed his theological studies at St. Francis Seminary in Milwaukee. After his ordination in 1903, he was assigned to Immaculate Conception Church in South Chicago. In 1909, he was appointed pastor of

St. John of God Church in the Town of Lake area on Chicago's Southwest Side and held that position for thirty-eight years until his death on September 23, 1948.

Father Grudzinski was vice-president of the Polish Council of Social Welfare and president of the Educational Department of the Polish Roman Catholic Union of America. He was a member of the Pontifical Academy in Rome, Italy, in 1928. For services rendered to the cause of Poland's independence, he was decorated by the Polish government with the medal "Polonia Restituta." He is considered an outstanding leader of Polish immigration in the United States. Francis Bolek, ed., *Who's Who in Polish America: A Biographical Directory of Polish American Leaders and Distinguished Poles Resident in the Americas,* 3rd ed. (New York: Harbinger House, 1943; Arno Publishers, 1970), p. 147.

In *Pamiętnik Jubileuszowy ku czci,* p. 63, the editor states: "He [Father Grudzinski] is widely-known and highly respected not only in this city but throughout the United States for his efficient assistance to the poor and needy, his love for the land of his fathers, and his intense patriotism and loyalty to the United States."

[31] Siostra M. Gonzaga Raniszewski, OSFK, *Zarys Półwiecza Zgromadzenia Sióstr Franciszkanek Bł. Kunegundy* [Sketch of the fifty-year history of the Congregation of the Franciscan Sisters of Bl. Kunegunda] (Chicago: By the Author, 1944), no pagination.

[32] The postulants were Helen Markowicz (Sister M. Consolata) and Estella Klepek (Sister M. Alice). The third postulant, Victoria Ignatowski (Sister M. Ludgarda) did not remain in the congregation.

[33] "A Brief History of St. Elizabeth's Day Nursery" (AFSCL).

[34] *Book of Correspondence:* Letter from Sister M. Anselma Pasternacki to Mother M. Antonina Osinski, 12 May 1940 (AFSCL).

[35] *St. Elizabeth's Day Nursery House Journal* (AFSCL).

[36] *Book of Correspondence:* Letter from Sister M. Praxeda Ostrega to Mother M. Jerome Dadej, 21 January 1958 (AFSCL).

[37] Ibid.

[38] The fire at the West Side parochial school struck without warning on Monday, December 1, 1958, and plunged the entire city into mourning. The disaster, called "Chicago's worst school fire in history," brought death to ninety-two children and three Sisters of the Congregation of the Sisters of Charity of the Blessed Virgin Mary. Many others were critically injured. The school blaze had the third highest death toll from a fire in Chicago's history.

Numerous investigations were launched into the possible origin of the fire. The Chicago Fire Department officials, determined to avoid such tragedies in the future, began the rigid enforcement of fire safety by means of thorough inspections. In the aftermath of the tragic fire, the Chicago Fire Department's inspections ultimately affected the original St. Joseph Home for the Aged and Crippled on Hamlin and Schubert Avenues which had also served as the Motherhouse for the Franciscan Sisters of Chicago.

[39] Secretaries General, *Community Chronicle,* 20 February 1959 (AFSCL).

CHAPTER 17

Undertakings in Missouri

Sister M. Anna continued to receive numerous requests from pastors who needed teaching Sisters. In 1905, she and her advisory council responded eagerly to the entreaties of pastors in two schools which were located in a diocese and in a state wholly new to the young community's parish school experience.

Towering over the waterfront of St. Louis today, the 630-foot-high Gateway Arch of stainless steel is a mute witness to westward expansion. Among the groups who had come to St. Louis as early as 1834 was a band of Poles whose numbers were relatively small when compared with the numbers who settled in cities such as Chicago or Milwaukee. After 1848, there was a small influx into St. Louis of Poles who had come up the river by steamboat from the port of New Orleans. The number of Polish settlers, however, never achieved any large proportions because they stayed for a brief period of time and then left St. Louis for other parts of the country.[1] In 1866, a Polish colony took root in Washington, Missouri, and it appears very likely that some settlers, attracted by the idea of a large city, eventually remained in St. Louis.[2] The Poles attended Catholic churches in their immediate neighborhoods, but feeling handicapped by language difficulties and wanting to worship in their own language, they decided to build their own church. They organized a parish in 1879, and by 1882, erected St. Stanislaus Kostka Church, destined to be the "Mother Church" of the Poles of St. Louis.[3]

The very rapid growth of St. Stanislaus Kostka Parish as well as the factors of distance and convenience soon made it obvious that the establishment of a second Polish church in St. Louis was a necessity. In October 1889, therefore, the Most Reverend John Kain, coadjutor archbishop of St. Louis, appointed the Reverend Francis X. Gnielinski to organize a new parish.[4] Father Gnielinski purchased and immediately proceeded to renovate a Protestant church which was located on Eighth and Mount Streets. The upper story of the building served as the church, while the basement was altered to serve as the school. One large classroom accommodated sixty pupils who were under the supervision of a lay teacher.[5] The church was dedicated to St. Casimir, one of the most beloved patron saints of Poland.

St. Casimir Church and School
St. Louis, Missouri (1905–1906)

The obvious need for larger accommodations became apparent with the progressive growth of St. Casimir's Parish. In 1894, Father Gnielinski erected a large and imposing two-story building on Eighth and Mullanphy Streets. As in the prior structure, the upper story served as a church and the lower story served as a school with four class-rooms.[6] The Congregation of the Sisters of the Most Precious Blood, who had been invited to staff the school in 1896, were housed in three rooms in the basement of the structure which also contained a small meeting hall.[7] Unfortunately, neither the church nor the school flourished as well as had been anticipated. By 1900, the parish claimed only 250 families.[8] An ongoing controversy involving St. Casimir's Parish and St. Stanislaus Kostka Parish generated a great deal of animosity. In addition, Father Gnielinski was not very successful at managing the parish. His idiosyncrasies annoyed many parishioners, and they were very vocal in their displeasure at the lack of an assistant priest to meet their needs.[9]

In 1903, Father Gnielinski suffered a nervous breakdown and took a leave of absence. The Reverend Theophil Pudłowski was then appointed the administrator, and a newly ordained priest, the Reverend Simon Żielinski, was named his assistant. In June of 1903, Father Gnielinski returned to St. Casimir's Parish, and during the course of the next two years, both Father Żielinski and the Reverend Stanley Wiśniewski served as his assistants respectively. Both priests remained for only a brief period of time, for once again, Father Gnielinski and his parishioners disagreed over the issue of the parish assistants. The opposition to Father Gnielinski became so intense that in 1905, he resigned his pastorate. At the time of his resignation, the Most Reverend John Glennon, archbishop of St. Louis, was out of the city. Father Gnielinski's unexpected departure from the parish during the absence of Archbishop Glennon further complicated matters and contributed greatly to the unpleasant circumstances which ultimately developed in the parish.[10]

It was during this period of agitation over Father Gnielinski's pastorate that the small band of Franciscan Sisters of Chicago received the invitation to staff the school. Sister M. Anna and her advisory council agreed to accept St. Casimir's School which had just witnessed the departure of the Sisters of the Congregation of St. Joseph of South Bend, Indiana, after only one year.[11] St. Casimir's School, with over three hundred children, was larger than any school the Sisters had accepted thus far. Sent to the community's mission in the Archdiocese of St. Louis were Sister M. Aloysia Holysz, superior and principal; Sister M. Francis Drufke; Sister M. Dominic Makowski; Sister M. Jolanta Nowak, Sister M. Barbara Grochola, assigned to household duties; and three postulants.[12] Several changes, however, occurred even that year. About the middle of November, one of the postulants returned to the Motherhouse to prepare for reception to the novitiate.[13] During the Christmas recess, Sister M. Aloysia and Sister M. Francis visited the Motherhouse to request that Sister M. Jolanta be replaced.[14] Since there was no other professed Sister available to replace her, Sister M. Chester Dziarnowski, a novice, was sent together with another postulant.[15] While at St. Casimir's School, the Sisters were housed in three rooms in the basement and the rear of the first floor of the church-school combination. The Sisters lived in the most abject poverty. Even more deplorable was the sight of sewer rats venturing into the Sisters' quarters through the pipelines during the night.[16] Regardless of the disagreeable physical living conditions in which the Sisters found themselves, they were not prepared for all of the great unpleasantness which followed the acceptance of this mission.

The Sisters had not been at St. Casimir's School very long when the pastor, Father Gnielinski, who had obtained them to staff his school, resigned his pastorate during the absence of Archbishop Glennon and left the city. Before Father Gnielinski left, however, a certain Reverend Stanislaus Plaza, young and eloquent, had arrived from Poland and had taken up residence at the rectory.[17] Upon Father Gnielinski's abrupt departure from the parish, Father Plaza unofficially assumed charge of it. When Archbishop Glennon returned to St. Louis, a parish committee, spurred by Father Plaza, petitioned the archbishop to appoint Father Plaza the permanent pastor. Since Father Plaza did not belong to the archdiocese and was certainly not known to Archbishop Glennon, the petition was refused. A Jesuit missionary, the Reverend Alexander Matauszak, was appointed instead, but he never took office, aware as he was of the dissatisfaction of the Poles over his appointment. Archbishop Glennon then assigned a former assistant, the Reverend Theophil Pudłowski, to serve as the new pastor.[18]

Before Father Pudłowski assumed his pastorate, however, Father Plaza had informed the worshippers at mass one day that since Archbishop Glennon had not confirmed his appointment as pastor, he was declaring St. Casimir's an "Independent" Church by renouncing the authority of the archbishop. After hearing Father Plaza's announcement, the Sisters who were present at the mass rose and left the church. A few days later, Sister M. Aloysia and Sister M. Francis met with Archbishop Glennon and informed him of the incident. He received the Sisters graciously, praised their conduct, and told them to remain in the parish and conduct the school as they had formerly. He forbade the Sisters to go into the church, attend mass, or receive Holy Communion at St. Casimir's Church during the week. On Sundays, they were to attend mass at a neighboring church.[19] The children were not to be restricted as to their attendance at mass. The Sisters obeyed the directives of Archbishop Glennon and allowed the children to go to St. Casimir's Church if they so desired. When the children saw that the Sisters were not going to church, none of them wanted to go either. The Sisters and children remained in their classrooms and recited the rosary aloud. Even the altar boys failed to appear to serve mass. Sometimes Father Plaza offered mass in an empty church, but he did not cause the Sisters any unpleasantness or indulge in recrimination against them.[20] Meanwhile, the Sisters informed their new mother superior, Sister M. Vincent Czyzewski, of the conditions under which they were working at St. Casimir's School. Father Andrew Spetz, as the Sisters' spiritual director, arrived in St. Louis in an attempt to reconcile Father Plaza to the Church and to prevent the growth of a schism. When Father Spetz arrived, the parishioners thought he was Father Żielinski, the former assistant at the parish, and attempted to keep him from entering the church. There was shouting and crude name-calling in the fracas which followed, and it was only when one of the Sisters recognized Father Spetz's voice and identified him to the crowd that he was left unmolested. The next day, Father Spetz persuaded the dissident Father Plaza to leave the parish and its people in peace. The parishioners were so impressed with Father Spetz's logic and conduct that they tried to persuade him to remain at St. Casimir's Church. Because of the discord and confusion at the parish, the Sisters left St. Casimir's School permanently at the close of the 1906 school year. In September of 1906, the newly founded Congregation of Franciscan Sisters of Our Lady of Perpetual Help of St. Louis arrived to staff the school.[21]

After Sister M. Vincent Czyzewski, the mother superior, recalled the small band of Franciscan Sisters of Chicago back to the Motherhouse, three more years of open contention and discontent prevailed at St. Casimir's Parish. Father Plaza, with the cooperation and support of the faction, organized a Polish National Church at Eleventh and Chambers Streets and became its pastor.[22] When in 1908, Archbishop Glennon officially excommunicated nine of the more active leaders of the schismatic church, most of the Poles returned to St. Casimir's Church.[23]

Through the untiring efforts of Father Theophil Pudłowski and subsequent pastors, St. Casimir's Parish had enjoyed its "Golden Age" from 1909 to 1919. With eight hundred families and over seven hundred children in school, it had become the largest parish in the city.[24] The parish's last banner year appeared to have been 1925 since subsequent years saw the decline of St. Casimir's Church and School. By 1951, most of the younger parishioners had moved to the suburbs, and the area began to take on a strictly commercial aspect. In 1957, the Mark Twain Expressway was built through the parish. That same year, the Most Reverend Joseph Ritter, archbishop of St. Louis, formed a new parish in the Hathaway Manor area of North St. Louis County and consented to name it St. Casimir the Prince thus carrying on the majestic name of the old church.[25]

St. Stanislaus Kostka Convent
St. Louis, Missouri

St. Stanislaus Kostka Church and School
St. Louis, Missouri (1906–1912)

When the Sisters withdrew from St. Casimir's School in 1906, Sister M. Vincent and her advisory council consented to accept the school connected with St. Stanislaus Kostka Church, the "Mother Church" of the Poles of St. Louis. The organization of the parish had begun in 1879, and by 1882, the church-school combination of St. Stanislaus Kostka had been erected. The church was located on the second floor of the structure while the first floor contained classrooms. The Reverend Sebastian Cebulla, OFM, was the pastor of the parish which Archbishop Glennon had placed under the supervision of the Franciscan Fathers. When the school opened in 1882, it was staffed by the Congregation of the Sisters of the Third Order of St. Francis of Oldenburg, Indiana, and a layman.[26]

In May 1885, the man who was to become the indisputable leader of the early Poles of St. Louis was appointed pastor. He was the Reverend Urban Stanowski, OFM, whose pastorate was to last for over forty years.[27] There were certain conditions existing at St. Stanislaus Kostka Parish which, from the beginning, created controversy. Firstly, a rather large debt still hung over the parish. Secondly, the fact that Father Stanowski resided in a Franciscan monastery rather than in the parish rectory proved irksome to many parishioners.[28] Father Stanowski, therefore, sought to be dispensed from his religious vows, and in 1892, the Most Reverend John Kain, archbishop of St. Louis, received him as a member of the secular clergy.[29] A builder and organizer, Father Stanowski formed numerous building and loan societies to help parishioners acquire homes near the church.[30] As the Poles swarmed into the neighborhoods, what formerly had been an "Irish Channel" now became a "Polish Corridor."[31] By 1892, a new church was built, the "architectural gem of St. Louis," and at its formal dedication, the Reverend Vincent Barzynski, CR, delivered the sermon.[32]

Earlier, Father Stanowski had encouraged three young women from St. Stanislaus Kostka Parish to enter the Congregation of the Sisters of St. Francis of Mary Immaculate of Joliet, Illinois. He then insisted that this congregation take charge of the school, and on September 4, 1888, the Joliet Franciscans arrived to staff it.[33] In 1901, Mother M. Alexandra, the superior general, informed Father Stanowski of her intention to withdraw the Sisters at the end of the school year. Mother Alexandra maintained that she could not comply with certain requests that Father Stanowski insisted upon concerning the staffing of the school in the future. Upon the advice of Father Stanowski and with the approbation of Archbishop Kain, the three young women who had entered the convent from St. Stanislaus Kostka Parish and were now professed members of the Joliet Franciscans, withdrew from the congregation and founded a new religious community at the parish.[34] This community, called the Congregation of the Franciscan Sisters of Our Lady of Perpetual Help, staffed the school until 1906.[35]

When this new community left the parish in 1906, Father Stanowski appealed to the little band of Franciscan Sisters from Chicago, who had, only the year before, agreed to staff the nearby St. Casimir's School. Sister M. Vincent and her advisory council accepted Father Stanowski's earnest invitation and appointed Sister M. Colette Nowak to serve as the superior and principal. To complete the staff were sent the following: Sister M. Bonaventure Blazek, Sister M. Zita Kosmala, Sister M. Bridget Czuj, Sister M. Barbara Grochola who was assigned to household tasks, and a postulant.[36] They taught in a large, four-story brick school building which had been erected to the left of the beautiful church. The Sisters lived in a most picturesque three-story dwelling at 1421 N. 20th Street which had been the "cradle" of the Congregation of the Franciscan Sisters of Our Lady of Perpetual Help.[37]

No explanation can be found in the records of the Franciscan Sisters of Chicago for the eventual withdrawal from the school of the Sisters in 1912. All available research indicates that in the early years of the twentieth century, St. Stanislaus Kostka Parish had reached the peak of its spiritual and material development. When the Sisters had arrived there in 1906, internal strife and discontent had enveloped the parish to such an extent that for the next three years, the activities of the parish were almost paralyzed. The parish was divided into two factions: one with the pastor and the trustees at the head; and the other, with several prominent parishioners who represented more than half the parish population. A great deal of controversy arose in 1908, ending with a crisis involving a civil suit. This was eventually concluded with a verdict which freed the pastor and the trustees of the charge of mismanagement of the corporation [St. Stanislaus Kostka Church and School], and thus the most dismal part of the parish history was over. The aftermath of this rift resulted in the transfer of many parishioners to St. Casimir's Church, and St. Stanislaus Kostka Parish found itself practically cut in half.[38]

The records of the congregation reveal that before the Franciscan Sisters of Chicago relinquished this parish, they had twice threatened to withdraw. The first of the departures had been ordered by Mother M. Anna, the superior general, when serious differences arose with Father Stanowski. The second attempt at departure was initiated by Father Stanowski himself when he had ordered the Sisters to leave.[39] When the Sisters did officially leave St. Stanislaus Kostka School, two other congregations staffed the school but eventually withdrew.[40] In 1920, and again in 1923, Father Stanowski begged the Franciscan Sisters of Chicago to return, claiming that he was making the appeal upon the insistence of his parishioners. Both times he was steadfastly refused by the superior general in office because of a lack of Sister-teachers.[41] In 1927, the Congregation of the Franciscan Sisters of Our Lady of Perpetual Help accepted the invitation to return to the school which they had left twenty-one years earlier. They remained until St. Stanislaus Kostka School closed forever in the advent of urban renewal.

Regrettably, the Franciscan Sisters of Chicago no longer have any ties with the proud old city of St. Louis, the "Rome of the West."[42]

UNDERTAKINGS IN MISSOURI

[1]Rev. John Myśliwiec, CR, "The History of the Catholic Poles of St. Louis" (M.A. thesis, St. Louis University, 1936) p. 3.

[2]Ibid., p. 4.

[3]Fenton J. Runge, "National Parishes in the City of St. Louis" (M.A. thesis, St. Louis University, 1955), pp. 41–42.

[4]Actually, the first Polish priest to come to St. Louis to work among the local Catholic Poles in 1875 was the ubiquitous Reverend Leopold Moczygemba. Myśliwiec, "Catholic Poles in St. Louis," p. 9.

[5]Myśliwiec, "Catholic Poles in St. Louis," p. 43.

[6]Ibid.

[7]*Official Catholic Directory,* 1896.

[8]Myśliwiec, p. 44.

[9]Ibid., p. 45.

[10]Ibid., p. 47.

[11]*Book of Correspondence:* Letter from Sister M. Dulcia Wanat, Sisters of the Third Order of St. Francis, St. Joseph Motherhouse, South Bend, Indiana, to author, 7 May 1976 (AFSCL).

[12]The postulants were Sophie Stasiek (Sister M. Theophila), Anna Antosz (Sister M. Innocenta), and Mary Janowiak (Sister M. Casimir). *Book of Annual Assignments* (AFSCL).

[13]The postulant was Mary Janowiak, Sister M. Casimir. *Spis Sióstr* (AFSCL).

[14]Sister M. Jolanta, who was experiencing some difficulty in managing a classroom, left the mission on January 3, 1906, and returned to the Motherhouse. *Spis Sióstr* (AFSCL).

[15]Josephine Witczak, called Sister M. Mercy, was sent along with Sister M. Chester. *Book of Annual Assignments* (AFSCL).

[16]The conditions were substantiated by a conversation the author had on July 27, 1976, with Sister M. Aloysius Kudłata whose congregation, the Franciscan Sisters of Our Lady of Perpetual Help, staffed the school after the small band of Franciscan Sisters of Chicago left. *Interview* with Sister M. Aloysius Kudłata, Franciscan Sisters of Our Lady of Perpetual Help, Ferguson, Missouri, 27 July 1976; also, Myśliwiec, p. 45 (AFSCL).

[17]*New St. Casimir, the Prince Church: Commemorative Book of Dedication* (St. Louis, Missouri, 1974), no pagination.

[18]Myśliwiec, p. 48.

[19]Siostra M. Gonzaga Raniszewski, OSFK, *Rys historyczny Zgromadzenia Sióstr Franciszkanek Błogosławionej Kunegundy. Część pierwsza, 1860-1910* [A historical survey of the Franciscan Sisters of Blessed Kunegunda. Part one, 1860–1910] (Chicago: By the Author, 1947), p. 111.

[20]Ibid., p. 112.

[21]Mother M. Theresa Dudzik, "Kronika Sióstr Franciszkanek, pod opieką Św. Kunegundy, w Chicago, Illinois" [The Chronicle of the Franciscan Sisters under the patronage of St. Kunegunda in Chicago, Illinois] Unpublished manuscript, 1910 (Chicago, Illinois, AFSCL).

[22]Sister M. Gonzaga Raniszewski relates this interesting turn of events in her brief history of the congregation: Years later, Sister M. Francis Drufke, who had been stationed at St. Casimir's parish during its time of unrest, was traveling through a small rural area of North Dakota. She discovered a Roman Catholic church there whose pastor was the Reverend Stanislaus Plaza. She met him and congratulated him upon his return to the Catholic Church. She was extremely moved when Father Plaza told her that the good example of the young Franciscan Sisters, who had so strongly

maintained their faith in the midst of the turbulence he himself had created at St. Casimir's Parish, had inspired him to reconcile with the Church. Raniszewski, p. 129.

[23]Myśliwiec, p. 48.

[24]*New St. Casimir,* no pagination.

[25]*St. Casimir's Catholic Church: Album Directory* (St. Louis, 1975), no pagination.

[26]*Złoty Jubileusz Parafji Św. Każimierza, 1889–1939* [Golden Jubilee: St. Casimir Church, 1889–1939] (St. Louis, 1939), p. 27.

[27]Father Stanowski was born in Opole, Poland, in 1856. He received his early education in his home town, and at sixteen, entered the Franciscan Order as a member of the Westphalian Province of the Holy Cross. He started his studies at Westphalia, but his stay there was shortened. In 1875, when the *Kulturkampf* in Germany was at its height, Father Stanowski fled to America. He settled in St. Louis and finished his studies there. He was ordained by the Most Reverend Patrick Ryan in 1880. His first assignment was at St. Michael's Church in Radom, Illinois. After five years, he was appointed pastor of St. Stanislaus Kostka Church in St. Louis. He died on January 23, 1927. Myśliwiec, p. 25.

[28]We have already seen how the issue of priest assistants and their function in a parish caused a major controversy in the case of St. Casimir's Parish in the same city.

[29]Myśliwiec, p. 19.

[30]In this, Father Stanowski bears a remarkable resemblance to the leader of Chicago's Poles, the Reverend Vincent Barzynski.

[31]William Barnaby Faherty, SJ, *Dream by the River: Two Centuries of St. Louis Catholicism, 1766–1967* (St. Louis: Piraeus Publishers, 1973), p. 104.

[32]Myśliwiec, p. 25.

[33]*Book of Correspondence:* Letter from Sister Elaine Kerscher, OSF, general secretary, Sisters of St. Francis, Joliet, Illinois to author, 1 February 1977 (AFSCL).

[34]Father Stanowski wrote to Mother M. Alexandra, the superior general of the Congregation of the Sisters of St. Francis of Mary Immaculate of Joliet, asking for more Sisters of Polish extraction. Mother M. Alexandra responded by informing Father Stanowski of her intention to withdraw the Sisters from St. Stanislaus Kostka School at the end of the school term. Three of the Sisters at the school who had entered the congregation from St. Stanislaus Kostka Parish agreed to remain at the school and form a new congregation devoted to educating the children of Polish immigrants. They were Sister M. Solana Leczna, Sister M. Ernestine Matz and her sister, Sister M. Hilaria Matz. They formed the nucleus of a new congregation in the Church, the Franciscan Sisters of Our Lady of Perpetual Help. The Reverend Urban Stanowski was named their spiritual director. With a growth in membership, the Sisters found it necessary to move to larger quarters. Father Stanowski purchased a private home adjacent to the school to serve as the convent. By 1906, however, the Sisters moved to a new home on Finney Avenue in St. Louis where the foundresses felt the need for an establishment independent of St. Stanislaus Kostka Parish. *Złoty Jubileusz Parafji Św. Każimierza,* p. 27.

Since 1957, the new Motherhouse of the congregation is located at Villa St. Joseph in Ferguson, a suburb of St. Louis. Today there are approximately 283 professed Sisters in the congregation. In Chicago, the Sisters staff St. Francis of Assisi School on West Walton Street.

The paths of the Franciscan Sisters of Chicago and the Franciscan Sisters of Our Lady of Perpetual Help crossed many times in the early histories of the congregations. From 1901 to 1912, both congregations had alternately staffed St. Stanislaus Kostka and St. Casimir Schools in St. Louis, and SS. Peter and Paul School in Spring Valley, Illinois. Sister M. Carolyn Mruz and *A Book of Celebration* Staff, Franciscan Sisters of Our Lady of Perpetual Help, 1901–1976 (Ferguson, Missouri, 1976), no pagination.

[35]*Book of Correspondence:* Letter from Sister M. Carolyn Mruz, OSF, Franciscan Sisters of Our Lady of Perpetual Help, to author, 11 February 1976 (AFSCL).

[36]Magdalen Pranke, the postulant, returned in 1909 as Sister M. Boniface.

[37]The convents at both 1401 N. 20th Street and 1421 N. 21st Street were in the process of being razed on July 26, 1976. The author, researching material pertaining to St. Stanislaus Kostka Church and School, happened to be on the scene and witnessed the historic dismantling.

[38]Myśliwiec, p. 28.

[39]*Minutes of General Council Proceedings, 1910–1934* (AFSCL).

[40]The Sisters of St. Francis of Sylvania, Ohio, staffed the school from 1921 to 1927. *Book of Correspondence:* Letter from Sister M. Augustine, Sisters of St. Francis, Sylvania, Ohio to author, 19 August 1976 (AFSCL). The other congregation could not be determined to this date.

[41]*Minutes of General Council Proceedings, 1910–1934* (AFSCL).

[42]Runge, p. 3.

CHAPTER 18

New Ways and New Works

The seventh year of Sister M. Anna Wysinski's leadership of the community was observed on October 4, 1905. Painfully aware of the fact that the budding community needed constant guidance, and often incapacitated by illness which she felt prevented her from being more effective, Sister M. Anna appealed to Father Spetz to relieve her of the office of mother superior. Father Spetz appointed Sister M. Vincent Czyzewski to serve in that capacity and Sister M. Theresa Dudzik to serve as her assistant. Father Spetz also appointed Sister M. Angeline Topolinski as second advisor and bursar, and Sister M. Rose Gorski was named third advisor and secretary.

When she assumed the duties of assistant superior, Sister M. Theresa was not relieved of her obligations as mistress of novices. She also continued to manage the laundry and to minister to the aged residents. As a consequence, it was not long before illness overtook her. While Sister M. Theresa recuperated, Sister M. Vincent, the newly appointed mother superior, assumed charge of the growing number of postulants. When Sister M. Theresa had sufficiently regained her health, she resumed her duties as mistress of novices, but she was relieved of her duties of managing the laundry and attending to the immediate needs of the elderly. The postulants, in the meantime, were placed in the care of Sister M. Hedwig Kubera who was destined to serve as directress of postulants in the congregation for seventeen years.

The former Rosalie Kubera was born in Poland in West Prussia on September 6, 1878. She came to the United States in 1881 with her parents, Jacob and Susanna Kubera, and settled in St. Stanislaus Kostka Parish. After a few months, they moved to South Chicago and became members of Immaculate Conception Church where she attended elementary school. After the death of her mother, she and her father moved back to Chicago and joined St. Hedwig's Parish. At sixteen, Rosalie secured employment as a dressmaker. She belonged to several religious societies at the parish and helped at bazaars and other entertainments for the benefit of the church. Here she became acquainted with the Sisters of the Congregation of the Holy Family of Nazareth and grew fond of them, especially Sister M. Hedwig, CSFN, who taught the fifth grade. Sister M. Hedwig was a friend of Rosalie Wysinski[1] who lived with her parents on Noble Street at that time.

A year later, Rosalie Kubera decided to enter religious life. When she revealed this desire to her pastor, the Reverend John Piechowski, he urged her to enter the Congregation of the Sisters of the Resurrection who were then planning to come to America from Poland. Rosalie Kubera preferred, instead, to enter a congregation that had been founded in America, and so Father Piechowski informed her of the newly established community on Hamlin Avenue in Avondale. Rosalie Kubera set out with her cousin, Marianne Pinkowski (later Sister M. Kunegunda), to see these new Sisters and was warmly welcomed by Sister M. Anna and Sister M. Theresa. In spite of objections from their families, Rosalie and Marianne were determined to become members of the little community of Franciscan Sisters in Avondale. Rosalie entered on June 29, 1899; two months later, she was joined by her cousin, Marianne.[2] During her postulancy and novitiate, Rosalie, now Sister M. Hedwig, worked at St. Vincent's Orphan Asylum. In 1905, she was named mistress of postulants, a position she held for three years. Later, she would be re-elected to this position for fourteen more years.[3]

From all accounts, Sister M. Hedwig was admirably suited to her task as postulant mistress. She was motherly, patient, and considerate to all the young women she directed. Warm and affable, she possessed a fervent religious spirit and was full of gentle sympathy toward her young charges. A very tall and stocky woman, Sister M. Hedwig was tenderly strong and humble.[4] For the brief time that the postulants spent with her before being assigned to a mission of the community, Sister M. Hedwig attempted to instruct and prepare the postulants as well as possible under the circumstances.[5]

In the summer of 1905 the Sisters returning to Chicago from St. Casimir's School in Cleveland for their annual retreat brought with them two new postulants, the first to enter the community from a city in which the Sisters conducted a school outside of the city of Chicago.[6] Anastasia Dukowski, who became Sister M. Ignatia, entered from St. Stanislaus Bishop and Martyr Church in Cleveland. The other postulant, who entered from St. Casimir's Parish in Cleveland, was received into the postulancy on July 16, 1905, but was dismissed in February of 1906.[7] Among the thirteen postulants[8] who received the habit of St. Francis on November 29, 1905, were also two novices, Sister M. Michael Sobieszczyk and Sister M. Augustine Malinowski who formerly had been professed members of the Congregation of the Sisters of the Holy Family of Nazareth. Both of the Sisters had received permission to withdraw from that congregation and join the Franciscan Sisters of Chicago on March 19, 1905.

Father Spetz was concerned with every aspect of the community and in 1905, recommended a bold move. Sensing the immediate need for nurses to minister to the Sisters who were ill, the aged, and the orphans, as well as foreseeing the eventual service of the Sisters to humanity in the field of medicine, he advised Sister M. Vincent to assign Sisters to be trained as nurses. As a result, Sister M. Antonina Osinski and Sister M. Bernice Stefanski[9] were sent to Mercy Hospital then located on Prairie Avenue and Twenty-sixth Street on Chicago's Far South Side. The two Sisters nursed the sick in St. Anne's Infirmary during the day and then traveled at least three hours each day to Mercy Hospital for classes, returning in late evening. All too often the inclement weather, especially in the winter, was a further burden for the young Sisters.[10] Sister M. Vincent and her advisory council decided, then, to have the Sisters train under more normal and beneficial circumstances. On October 30, 1905, therefore, Sister M. Antonina and a postulant, Frances Jakajtis, were sent to St. Elizabeth Hospital Training School for Nurses in Lafayette, Indiana, conducted by the Congregation of the Sisters of St. Francis of the Perpetual Adoration of Mishawaka, Indiana.[11]

In 1906, Sister M. Antonina returned to Lafayette, Indiana, to continue her training, and Frances Jakajtis entered the novitiate. Unfortunately, Sister M. Antonina contracted typhoid fever and was ill for more than two months. She was forced to return to the Motherhouse where she successfully combatted the dreaded disease. To recuperate, she was sent to St. Michael's School in Berlin, Wisconsin, for a year. After that time, she returned to the Motherhouse but never completed training as a nurse. Instead, she was assigned to take charge of St. Anne's Infirmary, where, with four other Sisters, she continued her training under the supervision of Dr. George Dohrmann, Sr., the house physician.[12] Frances Jakajtis, now Sister M. Benigna, returned to her studies in pharmacology at St. Elizabeth Hospital in Lafayette with two professed Sisters in January 1907. She returned to Chicago in 1908 where she continued her studies at the University of Illinois School of Pharmacy from which she graduated in June 1910.[13] Meanwhile, two professed Sisters, Sister M. Ladislaus Wroblewski and Sister M. Dionysia Kujanek,[14] were sent to St. Elizabeth Hospital where in 1911, they successfully completed their training thereby becoming the first registered nurses in the congregation.

Among the important events that transpired in 1905 was the visit of a most distinguished guest to St. Joseph Home for the Aged and the Crippled and St. Vincent's Orphan Asylum. He was Archbishop Albin Symon, whom Pope Pius X (now St. Pius X) had sent to America as his personal representative to investigate the conditions and grievances of the Catholic Poles in America. For several years there had been complaints among the Poles that American bishops were forcing "Americanization" upon them.[15] Other problems had centered around the schisms within parish churches, the relationship between the Church and secular organizations, the Polish seminary, and the Polish-American press.[16] One of the thorniest issues dealt with the lack of representation of the Polish clergy in the ranks of the American Catholic hierarchy.[17] Archbishop Symon visited 153 parishes, gave more than 350 speeches, and spoke to over seven thousand individuals in an attempt to obtain a correct evaluation of the situation concerning the Poles.[18] When, in July, Archbishop Symon visited St. Joseph Home for the Aged and Crippled as well as St. Vincent's Orphan Asylum, he was greeted with tremendous enthusiasm in the orphans' dining room. After delivering a brief address to the Sisters, the aged, and the orphans assembled there, he met with them in the chapel where he imparted his episcopal blessing before taking his leave. Parot states in *Polish Catholics, 1850–1920:*

> In his letter to the Vatican, Archbishop Symon called attention to the dedicated work performed by the Polish-based Orders of teaching nuns singling out for special commendation the efforts of the Resurrectionists, the Felicians, the Franciscans [of Blessed Kunegunda], and the Sisters of Nazareth. He was especially impressed by Polonia's social welfare contributions—the orphanages, the homes for the aged, hospitals, and immigrant homes.[19]

Three years later, the aforementioned visit of Archbishop Symon to America and to the city of Chicago in particular resulted in the appointment of the Reverend Paul Peter Rhode as the auxiliary bishop of Chicago. Formerly the pastor of St. Michael's Church in South Chicago, Bishop Rhode became the first American of Polish descent to become a bishop.[20] Since Bishop Rhode was a "son" of St. Stanislaus Kostka Parish, his elevation was greeted with enormous joy. He was consecrated a bishop on July 29, 1908, by Archbishop Quigley at Holy Name Cathedral. For the 3,500,000 Poles in the country and for the 300,000 Poles in Chicago the day of his consecration was a day of universal rejoicing, and, indeed, the Poles made it a national holiday. Bishop Rhode was installed not only as an auxiliary of Chicago, but also as the bishop for all the Poles in the United States. On the night of his installation, over thirty thousand people marched in a magnificent parade down Noble Street. There were three archbishops, twenty bishops, over seven hundred Polish priests from all over the United States, and hundreds of Sisters. Each of the thirty-two parishes in Chicago sent a delegation and delegates from scores of cities and states came to Chicago to honor him. Horse-drawn carriages, burning torches, and a vast array of societal banners and flags contributed to the splendor of the event. The color parade ended with a banquet in the auditorium of St. Stanislaus Kostka Church.[21] The next year, 1909, Marianne Kirschbaum, the niece of Bishop Rhode, entered the growing Franciscan community where she was professed as Sister M. Paul.

In the summer of 1906, the Sisters returned to the Motherhouse from six mission homes. Because of the ever-increasing number of Sisters, it was necessary to hold three retreats that year. From July through December, nineteen novices made their first profession of vows, and twenty-two postulants were received into the novitiate.[22] The new Sisters were all warmly welcomed, for the apostolates of the community were widening and Sisters were needed desperately.

An increasing number of requests were being directed to the Franciscan Sisters of

Chicago to undertake more elementary schools. By August of 1906, the Sisters had agreed to staff another school at the request of its pastor. Once again, it was located in an area which was to prove very fertile ground for the young community's future apostolates—the State of Indiana.

After the Civil War, Indiana's "Cities of the Calumet," namely, Gary, Hammond, and Whiting, gave rise to a great cluster of diversified industry. Whiting, birthplace of the Standard Oil Company of Indiana, was certainly one of the most uninviting portions of the Indiana area. Nevertheless, it attracted a great number of settlers who found steady employment in oil refineries and other factories.[23] By 1903, when Whiting was incorporated as a city, the Poles were among its chief settlers. Soon the Poles were the second largest nationality group in Whiting, and, characteristically, they yearned for a Catholic church in their area. A committee approached the Most Reverend Herman J. Alerding, bishop of Fort Wayne, who appointed the Reverend Peter A. Kahellek, pastor of St. Casimir's Church in Hammond, to direct the organization of the new parish. When the church, named in honor of St. Adalbert Bishop and Martyr was built on Indianapolis Boulevard, the Reverend Peter Budnik was appointed its first resident pastor.[24]

St. Adalbert's School, constructed in 1905, was a brick building consisting of four classrooms. Prior to the erection of the school, two dedicated laymen held classes in the back of the church. At the invitation of Father Budnik, who petitioned Sister M. Vincent Czyzewski, the mother superior of the Franciscan Sisters of Chicago, the school was

St. Adalbert School
Whiting, Indiana (1906–1913)

accepted in 1906. Assigned to St. Adalbert's School were Sister M. Aloysia Holysz as superior and principal,[25] Sister M. Francis Drufke as teacher, and Sister M. Cajetan Tabasz to household duties.[26] In January of 1907, Sister M. Clara Ogurek was added to the teaching staff. She likewise assumed the duties of organist and choir director. The Sisters made their residence in a modest home constructed diagonally opposite the church.[27] Both the school and the home were small and unimposing in appearance. The industrious and dedicated parishioners of St. Adalbert's Parish, nevertheless, were very pleased that their children were being raised in the Catholic tradition and were very supportive of the Sisters and their efforts.[28]

In 1911, the Reverend Julius Skrzypinski became the third pastor of St. Adalbert's Church. During his pastorate, he built an addition to the school, thereby enlarging it to its present size. That same year, Sister M. Hugoline Wojciechowski replaced Sister M. Aloysia Holysz as the superior and principal. On the school staff were Sister M. Emerentiana Sztuka, Sister M. Humilianna Lemanczyk, Sister M. Romualda Antkowiak, Sister M. Thecla Gawlowicz, and Sister M. Clothilde Stefiej who was assigned to household duties. When classes resumed in September of 1912, Sister M. Philomena Marszalkowski[29] replaced Sister M. Humilianna, and Sister M. Patricia Eiress took the place of Sister M. Clothilde.[30] The change on the staff at St. Adalbert's School, in retrospect, seems to have been a mistake, for before the close of the 1913 school year, Father Skrzypinski requested of Mother M. Anna, the superior general, that the Sisters not return to his school the following September. The apparent lack of tact and discretion on the part of some Sisters in their dealings with various school and conventual problems only added to the strained relations already existing between Father Skrzypinski and the Sisters.[31] The Sisters withdrew in June 1913, and Father Skrzypinski, with the aid of his friend, the Most Reverend Paul P. Rhode, the auxiliary bishop of Chicago, succeeded in obtaining the Congregation of the Sisters of the Holy Family of Nazareth to staff the school until it closed in 1977.[32]

The obvious lack of success with St. Adalbert's School in Whiting did not daunt the zeal of the Franciscan Sisters of Chicago. When, in 1907, a second school in Indiana was offered to them, Sister M. Vincent and her advisory council readily accepted the challenge. The new school was located in that part of the city along the lake known as Indiana Harbor. This industrial suburb, twenty miles southeast of the center of Chicago, remained unsettled until the last years of the nineteenth century. The expansion of the steel industry in the Chicago area was largely responsible for the industrial and real estate expansion of East Chicago. When, in 1901, the Indiana Steel Company located a plant in Indiana Harbor, European immigrants arrived in the city in great numbers seeking employment. The foreign-born constituted 43 percent of the population, and, of these, the Poles predominated.[33] To meet the spiritual needs of the numerous Polish settlers the Most Reverend Herman J. Alerding, bishop of Fort Wayne, granted approval to the Reverend

John Kubacki, pastor of East Chicago's St. Stanislaus Church, to organize a Polish parish in Indiana Harbor since Father Kubacki had already been ministering to the people of this area since 1903.[34]

The Reverend Peter Budnik of St. Adalbert's Church in Whiting, Indiana, replaced Father Kubacki in June of 1904. It was he who supervised the erection of the new St. John Cantius Church which was completed in the spring of 1906. The parish building, constructed of huge cement blocks, had two floors. The first floor was reserved as the school while two rooms on the second floor served as the pastor's quarters. The second floor contained the church. Although there is no recorded evidence, it appears that the Sisters' quarters were also located in the same building.[35]

The first permanent pastor of St. John Cantius Church was the Reverend Anthony Stachowiak who was appointed in 1906. It was at his invitation that the Franciscan Sisters of Chicago came to this parish.[36] On September 21, 1907, the following Sisters were sent to conduct St. John Cantius School: Sister M. Kunegunda Pinkowski, superior and principal; her cousin, Sister M. Stephanie Pinkowski; Sister M. Jolanta Nowak,[37] Sister M. Theophila Stasiek, and Sister M. Veronica Maka.[38] There were 127 pupils in the school that year. Before the Sisters arrived, the school had been under the supervision of one lay teacher who taught the initial twenty-six children who attended. In 1907, the pastor built a rectory which approximately five years later became the Sisters' convent. This building on Main Street, which served as the Sisters' home for all the years they remained in Indiana Harbor, had been enlarged, brick-veneered, and renovated.[39] There is no record of where the Sisters lived before the renovated rectory was given to them as a residence. Sister M. Gonzaga Raniszewski's brief account of this parish in her history of the congregation simply states:

> Like so many of our missions, [St. John Cantius School] was a difficult
> undertaking. Lack of space and other conveniences abounded. The Sisters
> tried to accommodate themselves to these insufficiencies until the parish
> could build a more comfortable school and home for the Sisters.[40]

By 1914, it was necessary to build an addition to the first church-school combination to accommodate the large number of students who enrolled.[41] In March of 1920, Sister M. Clemensa Steczko, who was on the teaching staff, left for the Motherhouse where she died in August of tuberculosis.[42]

Conditions became worse at the parish before they became better in regard to the church and the school. Father Stachowiak had proceeded to erect a new church in 1917. Because of the crisis brought about by World War I, only a substructure was built and placed under roof. In 1928, the new pastor, the Reverend Theophil Chemma, erected a large, new school building, "the pride of the parish," on Pulaski Street. The devastating Depression Era followed the school's completion, and a mortgage hung over the structure for twenty years. The parish of St. John Cantius had a very heavy debt to carry with a reduced and limited revenue.[43] The tireless effort of the Reverend Michael Petzhold, who

St. John Cantius Convent
Indiana Harbor, Indiana

became pastor in 1932, and the great generosity of the parishioners liquidated the debt in due time. Unfortunately, the church, so long desired, never rose above its original substructure, and so it remains to this day.[44]

The parish family was saddened in 1936 by the death of Sister M. Bonaventure Paprocki, the superior and principal, who died on August 18, at St. Margaret Hospital in Hammond, Indiana, following an operation.[45] She had just been appointed superior and principal in September of 1935.

During the early 1920s, the ethnic composition of Indiana Harbor had been rather stable with Poles comprising 21 percent of the population. Statistics indicate that in 1940, there were approximately 380 children in the school with thirteen Sisters on the staff. In 1955, there were approximately eight hundred families on the parish roster.[46] By the 1960s, however, ethnic and racial changes in the population of Indiana Harbor emerged. Blacks and Mexicans displaced the Poles. While St. John Cantius School maintained an ideal enrollment, several other Catholic parish schools in the city were understaffed, underattended, inadequate, and unable to meet the demands of modern education.[47] As a consequence, six Catholic schools in the diocese of Gary were consolidated in September of 1966,[48] and a new era for the Catholic school students of Indiana Harbor began. The consolidation permitted a standard of excellence of education that could never have been achieved in the smaller schools, and it strengthened the spirit of the entire Gary

St. John Cantius / Indiana Harbor Catholic Elementary School
Indiana Harbor, Indiana (1907–1979)

community. A $350,000 remodeling program rejuvenated the forty-year-old St. John Cantius School for use in the consolidation, and it emerged as the Indiana Harbor Catholic Elementary School, "The School That Cares."[49] As a result of the renovation program, the school could boast of sixteen classrooms, a gymnasium, a music room, a faculty lounge, a stage, a learning center, and a cafeteria.

The faculty of twenty was headed by the Reverend George B. Kashmer, assistant superintendent of Gary Diocesan Schools, and Mr. Hugh Huss, associate principal. Thirteen Sisters representing the Congregation of the Sisters of St. Casimir, the Sisters of the Holy Cross, and the Franciscan Sisters of Chicago were on the faculty. A Sister from each congregation was designated as assistant principal in order to have a voice in the administration of the school.[50] Representing the Franciscan Sisters of Chicago in this innovative program introduced in 1966 were Sister M. Arcadia Chmiel, assistant principal, teacher of grade five, and religious superior of the Sisters of St. John Cantius convent; Sister M. Purissima Babinski, grade one; Sister M. Robert Duda, grade two; and Sister Michael Marie Bysiek, grade six. Sister M. Zita Kosmala served as the church organist. There were approximately 640 students of various socioeconomic backgrounds and non-Catholics as well as Catholics in the school.

For years, the Indiana Harbor Catholic Elementary School continued to offer quality education to its diverse school population. In 1972, in order to meet the needs of the Mexican-American students who now comprised 65 percent of the enrollment and the needs of the community of East Chicago more adequately, Sister Marianne Kaplan, coordinator of the primary department of the school, attended the Universitas de Las Americas in Puebla, Mexico, with Sister M. Equitia Nawracaj of St. Hedwig's School in Gary.[51] In June of 1973, the Congregation of the Sisters of St. Casimir as well as the Sisters of the Holy Cross withdrew from their teaching assignments at the school. After much discussion, deliberation, and prayer, Sister Martha Joan Sempolski, the superior general, and her general council voted to withdraw the Franciscan Sisters of Chicago who remained on the staff of Indiana Harbor Catholic Elementary School. The decrease in vocations had left the school with only two Sisters on the staff, and the drain on parish finances in order to maintain the convent caused the congregation's administration to reevaluate the Sisters' mission in Indiana Harbor. After seventy-two dedicated and fruitful years of service to the people of St. John Cantius Parish and the community of Indiana Harbor, the Franciscan Sisters of Chicago left in 1979. The interest, understanding, and support of the parishioners of St. John Cantius Church as well as the community of Indiana Harbor made the Sisters' final departure a little easier. Years later, Sister Marianne Kaplan could still say: "The Sisters are terribly missed in Harbor!"[52]

In late October of 1906, Sister M. Theresa Dudzik was again stricken ill. She was admitted to St. Elizabeth's Hospital on North Claremont Street conducted by the Congregation of the Sisters, Poor Handmaids of Jesus Christ. She was diagnosed as having a fibroid uterus, and as a result, underwent a hysterectomy and salpingectomy. Her condition was pronounced good by her physician, Dr. Ernest Saurenhaus, when she left the hospital on March 6, 1907.[53] By November, however, Sister M. Theresa had suffered a relapse and was readmitted to the hospital where she was diagnosed as having an ovarian cyst. It was excised on November 22 by Dr. Saurenhaus who was assisted by Dr. W. C. Sanford. Eight days later, Sister M. Theresa was able to return to St. Joseph Home.[54]

On a happier note, twelve more postulants had been admitted to the novitiate on August 15, 1907,[55] while on December 10, twelve more novices made their first profession of vows.[56] The Reverend Ladislaus Filipski, CR,[57] celebrated the mass and delivered the sermon. Father Spetz, as was his custom, conducted the religious ceremonies and the Benediction of the Blessed Sacrament which followed.[58]

On December 13, 1907, at three o'clock in the afternoon, a statue of Blessed Kunegunda, a patroness of the community, was blessed for the chapel by the Reverend John Kasprzycki, CR, the superior general of the Congregation of the Resurrection. The Reverend Ladislaus Zapała, CR,[59] delivered a sermon to the assembled Sisters and their guests.[60]

Before the year 1907 came to an end, the Sisters accepted a parish school in a new diocese and a new area of Illinois. Asked to staff a school in East St. Louis, Sister M. Vincent Czyzewski and her advisory council responded with amazing zeal even though the number of Sisters in the community did not as yet allow for such continuing expansion into the apostolate of education.

East St. Louis, an old industrial town in southwestern Illinois, built on the east bank of the Mississippi River, was settled by Catholic Poles in the early 1900s when they were gainfully employed in the iron industry and the National Stock Yards. Their spiritual needs were attended to by the neighboring Polish parishes of St. Stanislaus Kostka and St. Casimir in the St. Louis metropolitan area. By 1904, the Reverend Julian Moczydłowski organized the fifty Polish families and over one hundred single men into St. Adalbert's Parish.[61] Upon the resignation of Father Moczydłowski, the Reverend Simon Nawrocki assumed the pastorate and remained at the parish until 1907. He, in turn, was succeeded by the Reverend Andrew Janiszewski under whose guidance the parish grew slowly but steadily.[62]

The parish school of St. Adalbert's, in the diocese of Belleville, was accepted by the Franciscan Sisters of Chicago in 1907 at the request of Father Janiszewski. The first Sisters arrived on September 7, and included Sister M. Salomea Grabowski, superior and principal; Sister M. Hugoline Wojciechowski, and Sister M. Leocadia Das who was assigned to household duties.[63] Like so many of the early school mission arrangements, the classrooms were located in the same building as the church. Initially, St. Adalbert's School opened with an enrollment of forty-eight students. For the first three years at St. Adalbert's, the Sisters suffered the gross inconvenience of living in very constrained quarters in the basement of the church-school combination. The pastor requested the services of a Sister-organist to play at all church services and to conduct two church choirs. In addition, the Sisters were assigned the care of altar boys and the church sacristy. For a number of years, the Sisters even had the somewhat dubious honor of getting the steam heat started in the church-school building on frigid winter mornings. The Sisters were also advised that the ringing of the church bells fell within the realm of their "duties." Fortunately, the latter two tasks were later assigned to the school janitor.[64]

In 1910, a small wooden house which had previously served as the rectory was given to the Sisters as their permanent residence. The Sisters' quarters in the basement of the church-school were then converted into classrooms. By 1914, the school population had risen to approximately 208 pupils with four Sisters on the staff. To minister more adequately to the needs of the growing enrollment, a two-room annex was erected in the Sisters' backyard in 1915. Two additional private houses were purchased and converted into classrooms during the next twenty years when the enrollment rose to five hundred pupils with eleven Sisters on the staff.[65] The "banner year" of St. Adalbert's School appears to have been 1930 when over 503 students were listed on the school roster. The number of Sisters stationed at St. Adalbert's School rose to thirteen. They now shared the cramped quarters which had only adequately housed four Sisters in 1910. For the next twenty years, what had been an impossible situation became intolerable.

In a letter to the pastor, the Reverend Anthony Żielinski, in January of 1948, Mother M. Jerome called attention to the deplorable situation:

> I would like to remind you of what I said to you last year when I was there, and that is, that you must secure better living accommodations for the Sisters. Under the circumstances in which they now work, the Sisters' health is impaired. It is my obligation, in conscience, to inform you of the existing circumstances because I intend to remove the Sisters from the mission unless we get better housing.
>
> I ask you, most sincerely, to alter the matter, for we cannot allow the Sisters' health to be endangered or to have them misuse or spend their energy unnecessarily if this can be avoided. I believe that acting in good will, something can be done. We have until vacation time to see how the matter will progress.[66]

In May of 1948, Mother M. Jerome proposed to her general council that the Sisters be withdrawn. The general council readily agreed. On May 11, 1948, Mother M. Jerome informed the Most Reverend Albert T. Zuroweste,[67] bishop of Belleville, of her decision.[68] In his reply, Bishop Zuroweste asked Mother M. Jerome to reconsider what he called her "sudden decision," and what he presumed to be short notice of the proposed withdrawal. He asked her to keep the Sisters at St. Adalbert's School until June of 1949.[69]

Mother M. Jerome agreed to Bishop Zuroweste's request not to withdraw the Sisters until that year. She did, however, make a stipulation:

> After having discussed this problem with my general council, we have agreed to leave the Sisters at St. Adalbert's School on condition that by September of this year, they live in a new house where, besides proper accommodations for the Sisters, a chapel could be arranged.

Her letter continued:

> As far as the Sisters are concerned, regarding their likes and dislikes of that place—I have never had any difficulties. They have never complained of the great discomfort they have had to endure. The only person who kept me informed of the conditions existing there was the superior who did this from a pure sense of duty.[70]

Mother M. Jerome also informed Bishop Zuroweste in her letter that the congregation was closing St. Philip of Jesus Community Center in Chicago which now gave her three additional Sisters she might assign to St. Adalbert's School if the conditions for renovation of the convent were met.[71]

On February 19, 1949, the situation seemed resolved with a letter from Bishop Zuroweste:

Dear Mother Jerome:

You, undoubtedly have been informed of the appointment of the Reverend Edward Borawski as pastor of St. Adalbert parish, East St. Louis.

During the administration of his predecessor, Monsignor Zielinski, you notified us that it would be necessary for you to remove the Sisters from St. Adalbert School. At that time I asked you to leave them there until September, 1949, which you graciously consented to do.

I am returning to you now, asking another favor. It is that you do not remove the Sisters but permit them to continue teaching at St. Adalbert's. I am confident that, under the pastoral care of Father Borawski, conditions which made it very difficult for the Sisters will be remedied, and the Sisters themselves will find much more pleasant surroundings in which to carry on their work.

I have not spoken to the Sisters at St. Adalbert's, but if you would inquire of them concerning the new pastor and his attitude towards their

St. Adalbert Convent
East St. Louis, Illinois

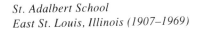

St. Adalbert School
East St. Louis, Illinois (1907–1969)

problems and the school, I am of the opinion they would be willing to remain to continue their splendid work.

If my memory is correct, the Sisters have been at St. Adalbert's for more than forty years during which time they have left their imprint upon the lives of many of the citizens of East St. Louis and to take them away now would be a terrific loss to the parish and to the Church.[72]

With the arrival of the Reverend Edward Borawski as pastor in 1949, plans were made to construct a convent. Forty-two years after the arrival of the first Sisters in East St. Louis, a new convent, complete with a chapel, was finally erected at 614 North Seventh Street. In 1952, a long overdue new school and gym were also built.

The turbulent 1960s made themselves felt in many distinct fashions in the cities, and East St. Louis did not escape change. In September of 1967, St. Adalbert's Parish was joined to the nearby Sacred Heart Parish; St. Adalbert's School remained open, but the parish had ceased to exist. Eventually the Sacred Heart School closed and the people of St. Adalbert's joined other parishes thereby causing a further decrease in the school enrollment at St. Adalbert's. By 1969, 52 percent of the population in East St. Louis was nonwhite.[73] There was now a pronounced increase of non-Catholics and blacks on the school roster. By 1968, there were only 151 students in four classrooms. The pastor, the Reverend Raymond Malec, maintained that St. Adalbert's School would remain open as long as the Sisters remained.[74]

In the reassessment of the congregation's apostolates at the First Extraordinary Chapter of Affairs held in 1968, many decisions were made regarding the schools staffed by the Franciscan Sisters of Chicago. The situation at each school was candidly studied and decisions were made no matter how painful. As a consequence, Mother M. Beatrice Rybacki notified Bishop Zuroweste that the Franciscan Sisters would withdraw from St. Adalbert's School in 1969. The reasons for that decision were now familiar ones: a lack of vocations to the congregation, a consequent lack of Sister personnel, the decrease in the number of Sisters actively staffing the schools, and the use of double grades which was not a desirable procedure to follow. Mother M. Beatrice was convinced that catechetical centers and nearby public schools could adequately meet the children's needs.[75]

When the official announcement to leave was made, the Franciscan Sisters of Chicago withdrew with regret leaving behind St. Adalbert's School which they had served for sixty-two years. Bishop Zuroweste arranged to have the Congregation of the Sisters Adorers of the Blood of Christ of Ruma, Illinois, staff the school.[76] The Sisters Adorers remained in the unstable area for four years. While East St. Louis had never been a preferred residential location due to its heavy industry, urban deterioration with the consequent encroachment of blight plagued the section as never before. It was only a matter of time before St. Adalbert's School ceased to be a school. In September of 1983, the Congregation of the Cordi-Marian Sisters from Mexico began operation of the Catholic Day Care Center in the building which had formerly served as St. Adalbert's School.[77]

NEW WAYS AND NEW WORKS

[1]*Spis Sióstr* (AFSCL).

[2]Ibid.

[3]In January of 1909, Sister M. Hedwig was named assistant to Sister M. Theresa who was then the mother superior. She was once again appointed mistresss of postulants from March 14, 1914, until 1916.

At the First General Chapter in 1910, she was elected second councilor for a term of six years. During this time, Sister M. Hedwig, an excellent seamstress, worked in the Church Vestment Workshop. At the Second General Council held in 1916, she was re-elected second councilor for another six-year term. In 1928, she was again appointed mistress of postulants and fulfilled this function until 1940.

[4]*Interview* with Sisters, April 1983 (AFSCL).

[5]*Book of Correspondence:* Letters from Sister M. Marinella Gubala and others, to author, 1976 (AFSCL).

[6]*Spis Sióstr* (AFSCL).

[7]On July 26, 1905, six postulants had been received into the novitiate. They were Frances Kosmala (Sister M. Zita); Anna Jagiello (Sister M. Bernarda); Victoria Czuy (Sister M. Bridget); Marianne Fidler (Sister M. Berchmans); Anna Polcyn (Sister M. Benedict); and Salomea Bobula (Sister M. Catherine).

The postulants received into the novitiate on November 29, 1905, were Martha Dziarnowski (Sister M. Chester); Anna Myszewski (Sister M. Delphine); Anna Scepuniak (Sister M. Rosalie); Eva Murdza (Sister M. Lucy); Honorata Makowski (Sister M. Alphonsa); Theophila Kostka (Sister M. Agatha); Marianne Janowiak (Sister M. Casimir); Marianne Wroblewski (Sister M. Ladislaus); Rosalie Pinkowski (Sister M. Stephanie); Antonina Das (Sister M. Leocadia); and Albina Scibior (Sister M. Angela), who left the congregation in 1907. She had been preceded in religious life by her sister, Sister M. Louis, who died in the congregation on September 9, 1960. *Spis Sióstr* (AFSCL).

[8]Both Sister M. Michael and Sister M. Augustine made their perpetual vows in the Congregation of the Franciscan Sisters of Chicago on July 27, 1915. Sister M. Michael died on October 15, 1934; Sister M. Augustine died on August 3, 1942. *Spis Sióstr* (AFSCL).

[9]After her initial introduction, Sister M. Bernice did not pursue further studies in nursing. After several years at St. Elizabeth's Day Nursery in Chicago, she was appointed to teach. Her later years were spent at the Motherhouse, Boys Town, and Mount Alverna Home in Parma, Ohio, where she died on March 16, 1956, at the age of seventy-three. *Spis Sióstr* (AFSCL).

[10]Siostra M. Gonzaga Raniszewski, OSFK, *Rys historyczny Zgromadzenia Sióstr Franciszkanek Błogosławionej Kunegundy. Część pierwsza, 1860–1910* [A historical survey of the Franciscan Sisters of Blessed Kunegunda. Part one, 1860–1910] (Chicago: By the Author, 1947), p. 130.

[11]Matka Maria Teresa Dudzik, "Kronika Sióstr Franciszkanek pod opieką Św. Kunegundy w Chicago, Illinois" [The Chronicle of the Franciscan Sisters under the patronage of St. Kunegunda in Chicago, Illinois] Unpublished manuscript, 1910 (Chicago, Illinois, AFSCL), p. 86.

[12]For over thirty years, Dr. George Dorhmann, Sr., gratuitously offered his services to the sick poor of St. Joseph Home and attended the Sisters beginning in 1898. Gratitude must also be expressed to other doctors who gave of their time and skill at St. Joseph Home for the Aged and Crippled. They are Dr. Leonard Sluzinski, Dr. Chester F. Pollowy, Dr. Stephen Czajkowski, and one whose name is most often listed with that of Dr. Dohrmann—Dr. Theodore J. Peterson. The doctors, many of whom were non-Catholic, esteemed the Sisters and their dedication and, therefore, offered their medical services generously. Dudzik, p. 89; Reverend Andrew Spetz, CR, "Annual Report to

the Board of State Commissioners of Public Charities of Springfield, Illinois," Chicago: 30 January 1908 (AFSCL); and Raniszewski, *Rys*, p. 38.

[13]The congregation lists four other Sisters who were trained pharmacists: Sister M. Grace Kujawa, Sister M. Tarcisia Bucki, Sister M. Antoniana Stanczak, and Sister M. Josepha Zwierzycki.

[14]Sister M. Dionysia Kujanek was born on October 7, 1889, in Chicago. She entered the postulancy from St. Stanislaus Kostka Church on June 19, 1905. On December 8, 1906, she entered the novitiate and made her first profession of vows on December 10, 1907. She made her perpetual vows on August 15, 1916. On January 11, 1908, Sister M. Dionysia was sent to St. Elizabeth Training School for Nurses in Lafayette, Indiana where she received her nursing diploma in 1911. The records of the congregation do not indicate why she did not serve as a nurse, but rather, as a teacher from 1911 to 1919. During the summer of 1919, she helped in the dispensary of the Guardian Angel Day Nursery. She asked for and received a dispensation from her vows on July 24, 1919. *Spis Sióstr* (AFSCL).

[15]The Poles were not unique in their clash with the American hierarchy. The Germans had expressed their discontent in the form of "Cahenslyism." Peter Paul Cahensly had organized the St. Raphael Society, a nineteenth-century Catholic lay organization to protect the religious, social, and material interests of German Catholics, as well as people of other nationalities who had emigrated to America. Essentially, the St. Raphael Society held that the Holy See should appoint bishops in the United States in accordance with the nationality of the faithful and even erect national churches staffed by priests who could communicate in the language of the immigrants. Of course the difficulties were due to a lack of understanding on both sides. The American bishops, most of whom were Irish or German, did not fully understand the spirit and the needs of the Polish Catholics. On the other hand, most of the Poles looked upon the American bishops as unsympathetic and repressive in regard to Polish nationalism, customs, and basic sense of identity. Reverend M. J. Madaj, "Chicago: The Polish Capital of the United States," *The New World,* 9 April 1971, p. 12.

[16]Frank Renkiewicz, *The Poles in America, 1608–1972, Chronology and Fact Book* (Dobbs Ferry, New York: Oceana, 1973), p. 15.

[17]The Reverend Wacław Kruszka, who rivaled Father Barzynski in his impact on American Polonia, was the main figure in the drive to present the plea of the Catholic Poles in America for the representation of Polish clergy in the ranks of the American Catholic hierarchy. He carried on the "fight" at two Polish Catholic Congresses and made two trips to Rome on that account. In Chicago, he was supported by most of the archdiocesan Polish clergy. Edward R. Kantowicz, "Polish Chicago: Survival Through Solidarity," in *The Ethnic Frontier,* eds. Melvin G. Holli and Peter d' A. James (New York: William B. Erdmanns Publishing Co., 1977), p. 197. When Archbishop Quigley was appointed to Chicago, Father Kruszka gained a real ally. Andrew M. Greeley, "Catholicism in America: 200 Years and Counting." *The Critic,* Summer 1976, p. 29.

Father Kruszka was born in Słabomierz, Poland, on March 2, 1868. His early education was obtained in Poland. He later studied in Jesuit colleges in Italy and Austria. In November 1893, he came to America and completed his studies at St. Francis Seminary in Milwaukee. On June 9, 1895, he was ordained by the Right Reverend John Vertin, bishop of Marquette, Michigan. He was then appointed by the Right Reverend Frederick X. Katzer as the assistant at St. Josaphat's Church in Milwaukee. In 1896, he helped to organize St. Wenceslaus Church in Ripon, Wisconsin, and in 1897, was sent by the Right Reverend Sebastian Messmer to erect St. Michael's Church for Poles in Oshkosh. From 1909 until his death in 1937, Father Kruszka was the pastor of St. Adalbert's Church in Milwaukee.

Deeply engaged in the religious and social life of Polish-Americans from his arrival in America, Father Kruszka was also a journalist and publicist of considerable talent. He was the first historian of Polish America, and at his death in 1937, he left behind him a number of important accounts and published works. He prepared the first comprehensive history of the Poles in America called *Historya Polska w Ameryce* [The History of the Poles in America] which appeared in thirteen small volumes between 1905 and 1908, and is still a standard reference work. As a historian, he is a rather controversial figure. He has frequently been criticized for his bias, inaccuracy, and misrepresentation of facts. His work is indispensable even if there are shortcomings. Right Reverend Monsignor Alexander Syski, STM, "The Nestor of Polish Historians in America: Reverend Wacław Kruszka," *Polish American Studies I* (1944): 14. See Chapter 15.

The whole issue of the efforts to obtain Polish bishops for the Polish Catholic community in America is a very detailed and sensitive one. The following sources are suggested for excellent reading on the subject: Borgia, Sister M. Francis. *He Sent Two.* Milwaukee: Bruce Publishing Co., 1965; Kantowicz, Edward R. "Polish Chicago: Survival Through Solidarity." In *The Ethnic Frontier,* pp. 180–209. Eds. Melvin G. Holli and Peter d' A. James. New York: William B. Erdmanns Publishing Co., 1977; Kruszka, Wacław. *Siedm Siedmioleci Czyli Pól Wieku Życia i Pamiętnik i Przyczynek do Historji Polskiej w Ameryce* [Seven times seven or the half century of my life; a memoir and aid to the history of the Poles in America]. 2 vols.; Kuzniewski, Anthony J., SJ. "The Catholic Church in the life of the Polish-Americans." In *Poles in America,* pp. 399–422. Ed. Frank Mocha. Stevens Point, Wisconsin: Worzalla Publishing Co., 1978; Madaj, Reverend M. J. "The Polish Immigrant, the American Catholic Hierarchy, and Father Wenceslaus Kruszka." *Polish American Studies,* 26 (1969): 16–29; Monzell, Thomas I. "The Catholic Church and the Americanization of the Polish Immigrant." *Polish American Studies,* 26 (1969): 1–18; Parot, Joseph J. *Polish Catholics in Chicago, 1850–1920.* (De Kalb: Northern Illinois University Press, 1981).

[18]Joseph J. Parot, *Polish Catholics in Chicago, 1850–1920* (De Kalb, Illinois: Northern Illinois University Press, 1981), p. 155.

[19]Ibid., p. 156.

[20]The Right Reverend Paul Peter Rhode, DD, was born in Wejherowo, Poland, on September 16, 1870. In 1879, he was brought to the United States by his widowed mother. He received his elementary education at St. Stanislaus Kostka Parochial School in Chicago. He attended St. Mary's College in St. Mary, Kentucky, and St. Ignatius College in Chicago. He studied philosophy and theology at St. Francis Seminary in St. Francis, Wisconsin, and was ordained on June 16, 1894, by the Most Reverend Frederick X. Katzer, archbishop of Milwaukee.

In the first two years of his priesthood, Bishop Rhode was an assistant at St. Adalbert's Church in Chicago. In 1897, Archbishop Feehan appointed him founding pastor of SS. Peter and Paul Church on Chicago's Southwest Side. After two years, he was assigned the pastorate of St. Michael's Church in South Chicago where he remained until 1915. He served as vicar general of the Archdiocese of Chicago from 1909 to 1915 when he was appointed bishop of Green Bay, Wisconsin. He served there until his death on March 3, 1945. A man of rare ability and intense energy, he was loved and admired by all who knew him regardless of nationality or creed. It was largely through his efforts that in 1910, St. Hedwig's Orphanage in Niles, Illinois, was founded. Throughout his lifetime, he was a loyal and patriotic American who was equally devoted to the causes and ideals of his native land. *Memorare: St. Mary's 1821–1971* (St. Mary, Kentucky, 1971), p. 40; and Reverend Joseph Thompson, ed., *Diamond Jubilee of the Archdiocese of Chicago, 1920* (Des Plaines, Illinois; St. Mary Training School Press, 1920), pp. 87–88.

[21]*Album Pamiątkowy Złotego Jubileuszu Parafii Świętego Stanisława Kostki, 1867–1917* [A Commemorative Album of the Golden Jubilee of St. Stanislaus Kostka Parish] Chicago, Illinois, 1917, p. 16; and Parot, pp. 158–159.

[22]On August 15, 1906, six novices were professed: Sister M. Benedict Polcyn, Sister M. Berchmans Fidler, Sister M. Bernarda Jagiello, Sister M. Bridget Czuj, Sister M. Catherine Bobula, and Sister M. Zita Kosmala.

On December 8, 1906, thirteen novices made their first profession of vows: Sister M. Leocadia Das, Sister M. Chester Dziarnowski, Sister M. Angela Scibior, Sister M. Lucy Murdza, Sister M. Agatha Kostka, Sister M. Casimir Janowiak, Sister M. Ladislaus Wroblewski, Sister M. Stephanie Pinkowski, Sister M. Michael Sobieszczyk, Sister M. Augustine Malinowski, Sister M. Rosalie Scepuniak, Sister M. Alphonsa Makowski, and Sister M. Delphine Myszewski. Ten postulants were received into the novitiate on July 26, 1906. They were Antonina Steczko (Sister M.

Clemensa); Katherine Prokuszka (Sister M. Ludwina); Anastasia Dukowski (Sister M. Ignatia); Sophie Stasiek (Sister M. Theophila); Marianne Swiszcz (Sister M. Helen); Anna Antosz (Sister M. Innocenta); Marianne Trojek (Sister M. Joanna); Anna Lemanczyk (Sister M. Humilianna); Angela Bywalec (Sister M. Pelagia); and Marianne Grott (Sister M. Walburga).

On December 10, 1906, twelve postulants were received into the novitiate: Agnes Kosmowski (Sister M. Cecilia); Cecilia Kujanek (Sister M. Dionysia); Angela Murdza (Sister M. Ursula); Martha Nagorski (Sister M. Boleslaus); Frances Jakajtis (Sister M. Benigna); Josephine Witczak (Sister M. Mercy); Rosalie Staszewski (Sister M. Julianna); Marianne Frankowski (Sister M. Monica); Catherine Tabor (Sister M. Michaeline); Angela Stozek (Sister M. Appolonia); Caroline Pelczar (Sister M. Sylvestra) and Antonina Ostrega (Sister M. Praxeda). *Spis Sióstr* (AFSCL).

[23]Millennium Committee, eds., *Poland's Millennium of Christianity: Indiana Observance Souvenir Book* (Hammond, Indiana: Klines Printers, 1966), no pagination.

[24]Ibid.

[25]Although Sister M. Aloysia Holysz had been elected to the general council as secretary general in 1910, she, nevertheless, remained at St. Adalbert's until August 1911, because of the lack of Sister-teachers. Secretaries General, *Community Chronicle, 1910–1934* (AFSCL), p. 9.

[26]Dudzik, p. 88.

[27]*Zarys Historyi Parafii Św. Wojciecha B. i M., 1902–1927, oraz szkice Towarzystwo. istniejących przy tej parafii* [Record of the history of St. Adalbert B. and M. Parish, 1902–1927, together with a sketch of the parish organizations] (Whiting, Indiana: 1927), no pagination.

[28]*Book of Correspondence:* Letter from Sister Rose Marie Machalski, CSFN, provincial secretary to author, 10 January 1976; *Enclosure:* Sketch of St. Adalbert's Parish: (St. Joachim's Home); History of the mission by Sister Hypolite, CSFN, first appointed superior of mission, written about 1945.

[29]At the end of the 1912–1913 school year, Sister M. Philomena returned to the Motherhouse where she died of tuberculosis on August 6, 1914. The former Anna Marszalkowski, who was born in Poland, entered from St. Vincent's Parish in Milwaukee. She was thirty-five years old and had been in the congregation for eleven years at the time of her death. She had been a teacher for all of those years. *Spis Sióstr* (AFSCL).

[30]Sister M. Romualda Antkowiak left the congregation on November 23, 1912. Sister M. Patricia Eiress, identified as the chief cause of the problems, was ordered to return to the Motherhouse on December 15, 1912. Sister M. Hugoline Wojciechowski, who had served as superior and principal for two years, left the congregation in July of 1913. *Book of Annual Assignments* (AFSCL).

[31]*Book of Correspondence:* Letter from Sister Rose Marie Machalski.

[32]Ibid.

[33]*Poland's Millennium of Christianity,* no pagination.

[34]*Album Srebrnego Jubileuszu Św. Jana Kantego, 1904–1929* [An Album of the Silver Jubilee of St. John Cantius Parish, 1904–1929] (Indiana Harbor, Indiana, 1929), p. 23.

[35]Ibid.

[36]Ibid.

[37]Sister M. Jolanta encountered various difficulties and remained until October 5 only.

[38]Sister M. Veronica Maka was sent there to recuperate from surgery. She was not a part of the staff.

[39]*St. John Cantius Church: Golden Jubilee Book, 1905–1955* (Indiana Harbor, Indiana, 1955), p. 16.

[40]Raniszewski, p. 133.

[41]*Album Srebrnego Jubileusza Św. Jana Kantego,* p. 15.

[42]Sister M. Clemensa was born in Poland. She entered from St. John Cantius Church in Chicago, on June 2, 1905. She was made a novice on July 27, 1906, and professed her first vows on July 27, 1907. She pronounced her perpetual vows on July 27, 1915.

Sister M. Clemensa was appointed to St. John Cantius School in 1918 and remained there until March 20, 1920, when she was taken ill. She died on August 11 of that same year at the Motherhouse. Only thirty-six years old, she had been in the congregation for fifteen years most of which were spent in the teaching field. *Spis Sióstr* (AFSCL).

[43]*St. John Cantius Church: Golden Jubilee Book,* p. 23.

[44]Ibid., p. 25.

[45]Sister M. Bonaventure, the former Rosalie Paprocki, was born in Duncan, Nebraska, in 1897, and entered from St. Stanislaus Kostka Church in that city. She entered the postulancy on October 4, 1914, and was received into the novitiate on July 27, 1916. She made her first profession of vows a year later, and pronounced perpetual vows on July 27, 1923. For all of her years in the congregation, she had served at six schools staffed by the Sisters. At the time of her death she had been in the congregation for twenty-two years and was thirty-nine years old. *Spis Sióstr* (AFSCL).

[46]*St. John Cantius Church: Diamond Jubilee Book, 1905–1955* (Indiana Harbor, Indiana, 1955), p. 26.

[47]*Hammond Times,* 2 October 1967.

[48]Included in the consolidation were St. John Cantius, St. Patrick, Assumption of the Blessed Virgin Mary, St. Francis, St. Jude, and Our Lady of Guadalupe Schools.

[49]*Indiana Harbor Catholic Elementary School Yearbook, 1976* (Indiana Harbor, Indiana, 1976), no pagination.

[50]Msgr. F. J. Melevage, Supt. of Schools, *Our Sunday Visitor* (Gary, Indiana: 1 May 1966).

[51]*Book of Correspondence:* Letter from Sister Marianne Kaplan, Franciscan Sisters of Chicago, to author, 6 May 1976 (AFSCL).

[52]*Book of Correspondence:* Letter from Sister Marianne Kaplan, Franciscan Sisters of Chicago, to author, 18 February 1980 (AFSCL).

[53]Gayle Soukup, RRA, Medical Records Department, St. Elizabeth's Hospital, Chicago, Illinois, Microfilm of Surgery Registers and Patient Registers, to author, 10 February, 1976.

[54]Ibid.

[55]On this day, the following were admitted: Anna Dadej (Sister M. Jerome); Leocadia Pasternacki (Sister M. Anselma); Veronica Moson (Sister M. Germaine); Magdalen Bywalec (Sister M. Martha); Marianne Ciurkot (Sister M. Sophie); Angela Halcerz (Sister M. Anastasia); Marianne Swiatowiec (Sister M. Genevieve); Sophie Tabor (Sister M. Raymond); Elizabeth Zynda (Sister M. Mechtilde); Sophie Stefiej (Sister M. Clothilde); Magdalen Pranke (Sister M. Boniface); and Anna Block (Sister M. Simplicia) who had withdrawn from the Franciscan Sisters of Lafayette, Indiana, and entered the novitiate on December 8, 1907. *Spis Sióstr* (AFSCL).

[56]The twelve novices admitted to the profession of first vows were Sister M. Cecilia Kosmowski, Sister M. Dionysia Kujanek, Sister M. Ursula Murdza, Sister M. Boleslaus Nagorski, Sister M. Benigna Jakajtis, Sister M. Mercy Witczak, Sister M. Julianna Staszewski, Sister M. Monica Frankowski, Sister M. Michaeline Tabor, Sister M. Sylvestra Pelczar, and Sister M. Praxeda Ostrega.

[57]The Reverend Ladislaus Filipski, CR, was an assistant at St. John Cantius Church from 1906 to 1909, and again from 1915 to 1920. He held positions as councilor general and assistant general in the Congregation of the Resurrection before his death in 1928. Edward T. Janas, CR, *Dictionary of American Resurrectionists, 1865–1965* (Rome: Gregorian University Press, 1967), p. 18.

[58]Dudzik, p. 91.

[59]The Reverend Ladislaus Zapała, CR, was one of the most distinguished members of the Congregation of the Resurrection. He was born in the Galicia region of Poland in 1874. In 1897, he was ordained in Rome. In 1900, he emigrated to the United States and labored at St. Stanislaus Kostka Church and served as rector of St. Stanislaus College.

A prolific writer, Father Zapała was the author of *A Grammar of the Polish Language* published in 1906 and *Dzieje Biblijne* [Bible Stories] published in 1912. He made literary contributions to the *Dziennik Chicagoski* [The Polish Daily News] and *Orędownik Językowy* [The Polish Language Advocate]. For many years, he was the editor of *Przegląd Kościelny* [The Polish Ecclesiastical Review]. Father Zapała was a staunch promoter of the Religious Sisters' Education Program at St. Stanislaus Church. He was a prominent member of the Polish Roman Catholic Union of America from 1904 to 1920. He was an ardent Polish patriot and promoter of Catholic Polish culture. A famous Polish orator in the United States for over forty years, he spoke at the funeral mass of Ignacy Jan Paderewski in 1941. Father Zapała was the superior general of the Congregation of the Resurrection from 1920 to 1926. Janas, pp. 71–75.

[60]Dudzik, p. 91.

[61]The original name of the parish was SS. Cyril and Methodius. The name was changed to St. Adalbert when the first mass was offered on March 12, 1905. *Srebrny Jubileusz Parafji Św. Wojciecha, 1905–1930* [Silver Jubilee: St. Adalbert Parish, 1905–1930] (East St. Louis, Illinois: 1930), p. 15.

[62]Reverend Frederick Beuckman, *History of the Diocese of Belleville, 1700–1914,* section one: St. Clair County (Belleville, Illinois: Buechler Publishing Co., 1914), p. 56.

[63]Raniszewski, p. 132.

[64]Ibid.

[65]*Srebrny Jubileusz Parafji Św. Wojciecha,* p. 18.

[66]*Book of Correspondence:* Letter from Mother M. Jerome Dadej to the Right Reverend Anthony Żielinski, 17 January 1948 (AFSCL).

[67]The Most Reverend Albert T. Zuroweste was the third bishop of Belleville. Born in East St. Louis in 1901, he was ordained to the priesthood in 1924. In 1948, he was appointed the bishop of Belleville. He retired on October 29, 1976.

[68]*Book of Correspondence:* Letter from Mother M. Jerome Dadej to the Most Reverend Albert T. Zuroweste, 11 May 1948 (AFSCL).

[69]*Book of Correspondence:* Letter from the Most Reverend Albert T. Zuroweste to Mother M. Jerome, 24 May 1948 (AFSCL).

[70]*Book of Correspondence:* Letter from Mother M. Jerome Dadej to the Most Reverend Albert T. Zuroweste, 2 February 1949 (AFSCL).

[71]Ibid.

[72]*Book of Correspondence:* Letter from the Most Reverend Albert T. Zuroweste to Mother M. Jerome Dadej, 19 February 1949 (AFSCL).

[73]*Illinois Guide and Gazetteer* (Chicago: Rand McNally and Co., 1969), p. 235.

[74]Special Chapter of Affairs, "Apostolate Commission Paper," December 1968 (AFSCL).

[75]*Book of Correspondence:* Letter from Mother M. Beatrice Rybacki to the Right Reverend Lawrence O'Connell, 18 March 1969 (AFSCL).

[76]*Book of Correspondence:* Letter from Sister Arlene, SSC, Provincial House, Adorers of the Blood of Christ, Red Bud, Illinois, to author, 1 December 1975 (AFSCL).

[77]*Interview* with Sister Gemma, Cordi-Marian Sisters, 25 June 1976 (AFSCL).

CHAPTER 19

Death and Life

On the last day of July 1908, death called the first member of the young Franciscan community. Sister M. Delphine Myszewski[1] died of tuberculosis at the Motherhouse on July 30, after an illness of three years. Sister M. Delphine, who was twenty-seven years old, had been in the community for only five years. Since all the Sisters were in residence at the Motherhouse during the summer months, the entire community was able to be present at her funeral. Father Spetz celebrated the Requiem Mass for the repose of her soul, and the eulogy was delivered by the Reverend Stanislaus Świerczek, CR, the assistant pastor of St. Hyacinth's Church. Sister M. Delphine was laid to rest in St. Adalbert's Cemetery in the first grave of the newly purchased plot of burial land for the Sisters of the community.[2]

The Sisters did not, as yet, have a resident chaplain at St. Joseph Home for the Aged and Crippled. Through the efforts of Father Spetz, the Reverend Victor Rodowicz was admitted to St. Joseph Home on July 17, 1908, at the age of seventy-three.[3] Sister M. Theresa recorded the event fondly in her "Chronicle":

> We received a resident chaplain in the person of the Reverend Victor Rodowicz who was over seventy years old. Until that time, we did not have daily Mass, only on Sundays and holydays, on some rare occasions, and during retreats. We missed it badly during the last few years. Although this priest was weak, especially in remembering, because he frequently made mistakes when he said Mass, nevertheless, for us it was a real joy since we now could have Holy Communion as often as we had permission to receive.[4]

Father Rodowicz rose each day at six o'clock in the morning happy that he could offer Holy Mass for the Sisters and the aged residents. He was eager to show his gratitude for the shelter the Sisters had extended to him. He fulfilled his priestly obligations from the time of his admittance until the three weeks immediately preceding his death on October 17, 1909. After Father Rodowicz's death, the Reverend Luke Świątkowski, CR,[5] was appointed the chaplain of St. Joseph Home. From the time of Father Świątkowski's appointment, the Congregation of the Resurrection has provided a resident chaplain for St. Joseph Home.[6] Since 1975, the ministering chaplain has resided at a nearby Resurrectionist mission house.

Because of the scarcity of teachers, the Sisters established only one mission in 1908. The frequent and urgent requests of the Reverend Florian Chodniewicz,[7] pastor of St. Florian's Church on Chicago's Southeast Side, persuaded Sister M. Vincent Czyzewski to send Sisters to staff the school in 1908.[8] Father Chodniewicz had been pastor of the nearby St. Columba's Church since 1900,[9] but with the large influx of Polish immigrants into the area called Hegewisch,[10] Archbishop Quigley appointed him to form a new parish. St. Florian's, the daughter parish of St. Columba's, therefore, had been formed in 1905 to serve the one hundred Polish families and more than two hundred single men who had settled in Hegewisch.[11]

In 1907, a solid three-story brick school at 12109 S. Houston had been built along Roman lines. It contained eight large and airy classrooms and a school hall on the first floor. Sister M. Colette Nowak was chosen the superior and principal. Assisting her in the school were Sister M. Chester Dziarnowski, Sister M. Boniface Pranke, Sister M. Barbara Grochola who was assigned to household duties, and a postulant.[12] There were approximately 360 children in four classrooms in grades two through six. Before the arrival of the Sisters, the children had attended the public school nearby. Because there had been no Catholic church or school in the area except for St. Columba's, the spiritual training of the children had been sorely neglected. In the sixth grade, taught by Sister M. Chester, there were pupils who ranged from fourteen to seventeen years of age. Some of the Sister-teachers were themselves not much older. The Sisters maintained three classrooms in the school building as their residence.[13]

Hegewisch was like an industrial satellite city. The area was separated from neighboring communities by vast stretches of vacant and undeveloped land; it was an extensive marshland with steel and industrial plants abounding.[14] When Hegewisch began to grow, St. Florian's Parish expanded rapidly. Because of the increasing number of pupils in the school, more Sisters arrived to staff it, and, consequently, they were badly in need of a larger residence. To meet their needs, Father Chodniewicz gave the Sisters a two-story frame residence, the former rectory built in 1913. The house soon earned the affectionate but aptly descriptive name of "Noah's Ark." Now the entire three-story school building was utilized for classes including the school hall which was divided into two classrooms by a curtain. Eventually, even the stage platform was used as classroom space.[15]

On January 27, 1922, tragedy struck the parish when its pastor, Father Chodniewicz, met his death at the hands of an unknown assailant who had come to rob the rectory. Chosen to succeed Father Chodniewicz was the energetic and zealous Reverend Vincent Nowicki. Shortly after his arrival, Father Nowicki purchased a small Lutheran church in the area and two more badly needed classrooms emerged from the church's renovation. By 1928, a new, spacious combination church and school was erected to accommodate the 870 students who attended the school. The church occupied the first floor while eight modern classrooms were located on the second floor. With the growth of the school enrollment, there was a corresponding growth of Sisters on the staff. Because of the shortage of space in "Noah's Ark," some of the Sisters assigned to St. Florian's had to occupy two classrooms in the new school as their sleeping quarters.[16] By 1929, there were approximately one thousand students in the school with twenty-two Franciscan Sisters of Chicago on the staff. Unfortunately, the Depression Era worked its havoc in Hegewisch; as a consequence, many of the residents were forced to leave the area in order to make a living, and the school enrollment declined drastically.[17]

With the appointment of the Reverend Francis Kulinski[18] as pastor in 1934, a new chapter of history began at St. Florian's Parish. In September of 1936, due to his efforts, a two-year commercial high school was initiated. The school was located in the building between the rectory and the church. The subjects taught in the area of commerce throughout the school's existence were shorthand, typing, bookkeeping, office practice, and commercial law. Sister M. Theophane Rakowski was the first teacher appointed to a class of twenty-seven students. She was joined the next year by Sister Bernice Marie Junio. In 1938, Sister M. Ancilla Janik replaced Sister Bernice Marie, and she remained on the staff until 1941. Both Sister M. Theophane and Sister M. Ancilla had as many as sixty students in the specialized commercial areas. In 1941, Sister M. Hildegarde Demps was appointed to teach English I and II, history, and algebra while Sister M. Doloretta Radzienda was assigned to teach the commercial subjects. By the 1942 school year, there were only eight students registered, and St. Florian's commercial high school closed the following year. The school's financial problems had been its downfall. During the years the high school had been in operation, the Reverend Stanley Shaw, an archdiocesan priest, taught the classes in Catholic doctrine.[19]

As early as 1939, Father Kulinski proposed to Mother M. Antonina Osinski that one of the Sisters on the staff teach without a monthly stipend since the parish was financially strapped, and St. Florian's elementary school had only 392 pupils enrolled.[20] In an effort to aid the parish, Mother M. Antonina and the general council agreed to Father Kulinski's proposal, and from September 1938 to June 1939, one of the fifteen Sisters on the staff served without financial remuneration. In the latter part of the year, Father Kulinski approached Mother M. Antonina with another proposition. Because St. Florian's parish was $5,673.95 in arrears for the Sisters' salary, he offered the congregation the St. Florian's Commercial High School building and suggested that the Sisters themselves equip it adequately and operate it as a four-year high school. Mother M. Antonina and the general council, realizing the problems inherent in a situation such as this and in dealing so closely with the volatile Father Kulinski, very judiciously rejected his offer.[21] As a matter of record, when Mother M. Antonina discussed Father Kulinski's proposal with George Cardinal Mundelein, the archbishop of Chicago, Cardinal Mundelein very strongly

St. Florian Convent
Chicago (Hegewisch), Illinois

suggested that she inform Father Kulinski that such matters were dealt with through the chancery office of the archdiocese.

In May of 1963, "Noah's Ark" was torn down to its very foundation. The Sisters moved into the old school building which had been selected by Father Kulinski as their new residence. Now the entire bulky structure, consisting of eight large classrooms, was their home. One classroom was converted into a chapel while a kitchen, refectory, recreation room, and study room were made of the other classrooms. Several classrooms were divided for use as the Sisters' sleeping quarters. In the ensuing years, the old school building grew neither in convenience nor practicality. Until 1965, when the new convent was constructed on East 131st Street, the Sisters did their very best to maintain a convent atmosphere in the massive, inconvenient, and grossly uneconomical old school building.[22]

St. Florian School
Chicago (Hegewisch), Illinois (1908–   )

219

In March of 1952, ground was broken for a youth center at the southwest corner of 130th and Houston Avenue. This large brick structure which contained a gym was dedicated on June 6, 1954, by Samuel Cardinal Stritch. Four years later, St. Florian's School celebrated its 50th anniversary of foundation. At that time there were 560 children enrolled in the school.

On November 5, 1963, Father Kulinski died, and the Reverend Chester Konsowski was appointed the pastor. It was under his leadership that ground was broken for a new convent and school on February 7, 1965. The new school was built at 13110 South Baltimore and housed the junior high school section. Grades two to five were located in the church building while the spacious gym structure contained the kindergarten and grade one.

In September of 1986, a nursery school for three-year-olds, two preschool classes for four-year-olds, and two full-day kindergarten classes for five-year-olds increased the school enrollment by 20 percent. This growth in the school population was due to its innovative principal, Sister Jeanne Marie Toriskie, who assumed the office in 1984. Today, this old but still developing community boasts 294 children enrolled in the school with four Sisters and fourteen lay teachers on the staff.

Beginning with 1944, the Sisters stationed at St. Florian's School ministered at Mother of God Church,[23] once a mission church for the Catholics of Burnham, a town near Hegewisch. The chapel was blessed on September 15, 1946. The Sisters taught Christian Doctrine classes, prepared the children for the reception of First Holy Communion and Confirmation, served as sacristans, maintained the chapel, and conducted a choir. In 1954, the Sisters discontinued their services to the Mother of God Church, resumed them in 1961, and finally in 1971, no longer ministered to the parish. As late as 1972, the pastor, the Reverend Sigismund Andryaszkiewicz petitioned Sister M. Hugoline Czaplinski, the superior general, for Sisters to teach CCD classes at Burnham saying that "the Sisters at St. Florian's have been doing wonderful work in teaching religion to the children of Burnham, and the parents are deeply appreciative of the work and sacrifice of the Franciscan Sisters."[24] Unfortunately, a reduction in the number of Sisters on the staff of St. Florian's School did not allow for the Sisters to minister at Mother of God Church as well.

DEATH AND LIFE

[1]The former Anna Myszewski was born in Poland in 1881. Her parents emigrated to the United States and settled in Manistee, Michigan. She entered the Congregation of the Sisters of St. Felix of Cantalice (Felicians) in Detroit, but withdrew to enter the small community of Franciscan Sisters of Chicago on July 13, 1903. She is listed as number forty-five among the early entrants. Her postulancy began on December 25, 1903. She entered the novitiate on November 29, 1905, and made her first profession of vows on December 8, 1906. In ill health since her entrance, her five years in the community were spent at the Motherhouse. Sister M. Delphine made her perpetual vows on her deathbed. Receiving her vows in the name of the Church was Sister M. Vincent Czyzewski, the mother superior. *Spis Sióstr* (AFSCL).

[2]*Spis Sióstr* (AFSCL).

[3]No further information was found concerning Father Rodowicz. A letter, received by the author and now in the archives of the congregation, simply states that Father Rodowicz served at Immaculate Conception (Lithuanian) Church in Sheboygan, Wisconsin, for one year prior to his coming to St. Joseph Home for the Aged. Since Father Rodowicz was not anywhere in the United States clergy listings prior to 1908, the assumption is that he was a foreign-born priest who served at an ethnic parish for a short time and when a diocescan priest could be found, he moved on to another field of priestly ministry.

[4]Matka Maria Teresa Dudzik, "Kronika Sióstr Franciszkanek pod opieką Św. Kunegundy w Chicago, Illinois" [The Chronicle of the Franciscan Sisters under the patronage of St. Kunegunda in Chicago, Illinois] Unpublished manuscript, 1910 (Chicago, Illinois, AFSCL), p. 93.

[5]The Reverend Luke Świątkowski, CR, served as chaplain at St. Joseph Home from 1909 to 1910. He was an author of several books and a contributor to the *Przegląd Kościelny* [The Polish Ecclesiastical Review], a monthly periodical devoted to the formation and education of clergy from 1915 to 1919. Edward T. Janas, CR, *Dictionary of American Resurrectionists, 1865–1965* (Rome: Gregorian University Press, 1967), pp. 59–60.

[6]The chaplains at St. Joseph Home of Chicago have included the following: Reverend Luke Świątkowski, CR, (1909–1910); Reverend Theophilus Szypkowski, CR, (1910–1912); Reverend John Kruszynski, CR, (1912–1914); Reverend Joseph Tarasiuk, CR, (1914–1931); Reverend John Obyrtacz, CR, (1931–1933); Reverend Joseph Baniewicz, CR, (1933–1934); Reverend John Drzewiecki, CR, (1935–1936); Reverend Joseph Baniewicz, CR, (1936–1953); Reverend Stanley Ziemba, CR, (1953–1964); Reverend Chester Norkiewicz, CR, (1964–1964); Reverend Joseph Samborski, CR, (1964–1975); Reverend Stephen Juda, CR, (1975–1977); and Reverend John Miles, CR, (1977–1985). Janas, pp. 15–16, 34–35, 46–47, 59–60, 61–62, 62, 63, 76, 161, 181–182, 195–196, and 208.

[7]Born in Poland in 1861, the Reverend Florian Chodniewicz emigrated to the United States as a cleric. He was ordained in 1889 in St. Vincent's Church in Detroit by the Right Reverend John Foley, bishop of Detroit, and began his priestly ministry in that city. He moved to Illinois and served at St. Mary of Gostyn Church in Downers Grove and St. Joseph's Church in the Town of Lake area on Chicago's Southwest Side before he became pastor of St. Columba's Church.

Father Chodniewicz, shot on the evening of January 27 by a thief he had startled in the rectory, died the next morning. For eighteen years, he had been the pastor of the church which bore the name of his patron saint. *Jubileusz 25cio-lecia Parafji Św. Florjana, 1905–1930; Księga Pamiątkowa* [A Dedication Book: Silver Jubilee of St. Florian's Parish, 1905–1930] (Hegewisch, Illinois, 1930), no pagination.

[8]Siostra M. Gonzaga Raniszewski, OSFK, *Rys historyczny Zgromadzenia Sióstr Franciszkanek Błogosławionej Kunegundy. Część pierwsza, 1860–1910* [A historical survey of the Franciscan Sisters of Blessed Kunegunda. Part one, 1860–1910] (Chicago: By the Author, 1947), p. 135.

[9]St. Columba's Church at 134th and Green Bay Avenue was established in 1884 as a mission of St. Kevin Church. The first resident pastor was the Reverend Francis Kroll who served there from 1896 to 1900. In 1900, Father Chodniewicz was appointed the pastor of this small congregation. When he began organizing the Polish parish of St. Florian's in Hegewisch in 1905, St. Columba's Church was entrusted to the care of the Carmelite Fathers who staffed St. Cyril College, now Mount Carmel High School. The Carmelite Fathers traveled to Hegewisch to celebrate mass for the English-speaking Catholics in the community. Reverend Monsignor Harry C. Koenig, ed., *A History of the Archdiocese of Chicago: Published in Observance of the Centenary of the Archdiocese, 1980,* 2 vols. (Chicago: The Archdiocese of Chicago, 1980), 1:203–205.

[10]Achilles Hegewisch planned to establish a workingmen's community in Hegewisch as George Pullman had in Roseland. The bright future predicted for the area failed to materialize. Hegewisch was originally populated by Poles, Swedes, Yugoslavians, Czechs, and Irish. By 1920, its population was 47 percent foreign-born of which the largest group was Poles. By 1930, 55 percent of the population was Polish, and they still remain the dominant group in the area today. Chicago Plan Commission, *Forty-Four Cities in the City of Chicago* (Chicago: City of Chicago, 1942), p. 55; and Evelyn M. Kitawaga and Karl E. Taeuber, eds., *Local Community Fact Book, Chicago Metropolitan Area, 1960* (Chicago: University of Chicago Press, 1963), p. 124.

[11]*Jubileusz 25cio-lecia Parafji Św. Florjana,* no pagination.

[12]The postulant was Antoinette Jasinski who became Sister M. Angela.

[13]Raniszewski, p. 136.

[14]Chicago Plan Commission, p. 55.

[15]Raniszewski, p. 136.

[16]Ibid., p. 137.

[17]Ibid.

[18]The Reverend Francis Kulinski was born in 1889 in Manistee, Michigan. He attended St. Stanislaus Kostka Elementary School and St. Stanislaus College in Chicago. He studied philosophy and theology in Orchard Lake, Michigan; and Ellenora, Ohio. Ordained on May 17, 1913, he celebrated his first mass at St. Stanislaus Kostka Church. Father Kulinski began his pastorate at St. Florian's Church in 1934 and remained there until his death in November 1963. *Book of Correspondence:* Report from the Archdiocese of Chicago to author, August 1978.

[19]*Minutes of General Council Proceedings, 1934–1956* (AFSCL).

[20]Ibid.

[21]Ibid.

[22]*St. Florian's House Journal* (AFSCL).

[23]Mother of God Church in Burnham, Illinois, was established in the 1940s as a mission church. Priests from neighboring parishes, especially St. Florian's Church—then located at 132nd and Houston Avenue—celebrated mass in a storefront for the small Catholic community. As the number of Catholic families increased, plans were formulated for the erection of a mission church of St. Florian.

Under the leadership of Reverend Francis A. Kulinski, pastor of St. Florian's, property at the corner of 142nd and Green Bay was purchased. On September 15, 1946, Samuel Cardinal Stritch dedicated Mother of God Church. In July of 1956, Reverend Paul A. Mytus, an assistant at St. Florian's Church, was named the first pastor of Mother of God Church. Reverend Sigismund Andryaszkiewicz came to Mother of God Church in March of 1961. When he became pastor emeritus in 1975, 350 families belonged to the parish. Because no parochial school was established, Catholic children in Burnham attended neighboring parishes or participated in the CCD program at Mother of God Church. Koenig, 11:1056–1058.

[24]*Book of Correspondence:* Letter from the Reverend Sigismund Andryaszkiewicz to Mother M. Hugoline Czaplinski, 19 August 1972 (AFSCL).

CHAPTER 20

Moving Toward the Future

Father Spetz had appointed Sister M. Vincent Czyzewski to succeed Sister M. Anna Wysinski to the office of mother superior of the community on October 4, 1905. Sister M. Vincent had served in that capacity for three years and three months when Father Spetz appointed Sister M. Theresa Dudzik to take her place on January 1, 1909.[1] As spiritual director of the community, Father Spetz was in the process of preparing the Sisters to hold their First General Chapter in 1909, an extraordinary page in the history of the young community. The general chapter, the first one ever to be held in the community, was to be a canonical meeting of elected representatives called delegates for the purpose of electing a superior general and a general council, and of making the laws and drawing up the articles of the Constitutions by which the congregation was to be governed. The Sisters were aware that the First General Chapter to be held in the community was destined to be a landmark, for it would remove them, thereafter, from the direct guidance and the jurisdiction of the Congregation of the Resurrection and establish them in self-government and self-accountability.

When Father Spetz appointed Sister M. Theresa to the office of mother superior in January of 1909, he had requested her to prepare a list of issues to be considered and acted upon by the delegates to the First General Chapter. Not surprisingly, the question naturally arises as to the reason why Father Spetz appointed Sister M. Theresa to assume the position of mother superior at this time. It is probably correct to surmise that Father Spetz believed that it would be in the best interests of the community if Sister M. Theresa, its foundress, were in the position of mother superior prior to and at the time of the First General Chapter. We can only speculate that Father Spetz presumed that with Sister M. Theresa at the helm of the community once again, the Sisters, and especially the Sister-delegates, would be inspired and invigorated by her spirit and dedication which had initially given birth to the Franciscan community. It would be Sister M. Theresa who would direct their hearts to the love of God and the steadfastness of Jesus Christ whom the Sisters had promised to follow in faith. "The Lord is my strength and my shield; in Him my heart trusts," the Psalmist prayed, and Sister M. Theresa would attempt wholeheartedly to imbue her Franciscan community with that ideal.[2] When Sister M. Theresa accepted the office of mother superior, Father Spetz also appointed a new advisory council to assist her. Assigned to aid Sister M. Theresa were Sister M. Hedwig Kubera, assistant superior and first advisor; Sister M. Angeline Topolinski, second advisor; Sister M. Aloysia Holysz, third advisor and secretary; and Sister M. Vincent Czyzewski, procurator. Sister M. Theresa's position as mistress of novices was unofficially undertaken by Sister M. Kunegunda Pinkowski[3] after Sister M. Theresa's last group of novices made their first profession of vows on July 16, 1909.[4] For the position of mistress of postulants, Sister M. Gerard Gorzkowski was chosen to replace Sister M. Hedwig.[5]

Early in January of 1909, Father Spetz met with Sister M. Theresa and her advisory council in regard to taking charge of a small nursery called St. Hedwig's Orphanage in the vicinity of St. Hedwig's Parish at 31 Coblentz Street.[6] The orphanage appears to have been meant solely to serve the needs of that particular parish, hence its name.[7] After a lengthy discussion, the Sisters voted unanimously to accept the orphanage and to begin working there immediately. The building which housed the orphans was to become the property of the Franciscan Sisters of Chicago for $3,000. It was assumed that all other expenditures connected with the purchase would also be met by the Sisters. At this meeting, Sister M. Josepha Suchomski was chosen the superior and administrator of the orphanage, and Sister M. Bernice Stefanski was assigned to assist her. After three weeks, however, the Sisters were recalled from the orphanage. There is no further information in the congregation's records concerning this undertaking.[8]

In the area of the teaching apostolate, two more schools were accepted in 1909. The first one was located in the newly formed Gary area and became the third school staffed by the Franciscan Sisters of Chicago in Indiana.

Gary, the second largest city in Indiana, about twenty miles southeast of Chicago's Loop, was founded in 1906, when the United States Steel Corporation began construction of its huge mills and various subsidiary plants at the southern tip of Lake Michigan. The prosperity of the citizens of Gary was determined by the great mills; therefore, it followed that the growth of Gary was rapid. The first Poles who came to the "City of Steel" to seek employment had settled on the "Sand Dunes," and in July 1907, a group of Poles met for the purpose of establishing a church and school to meet their particular needs. They agreed to build on the very site of their first meeting. In the meantime, the twenty-five families of the new parish attended church services in neighboring parishes in East Chicago, Hammond, and Indiana Harbor. The Reverend Anthony Stachowiak, the pastor of St. John Cantius Church in Indiana Harbor, aided the Poles in the organization of their proposed new parish and served the founding group of

St. Hedwig Convent
Gary, Indiana

Polish settlers for over two and one-half years. Fortunately, the Gary Land Company donated seven lots. As a result of door-to-door collections, picnics, and a number of other activities, the church was soon under construction. In July 1908, the Most Reverend Herman J. Alerding, bishop of Gary, blessed the new church which was placed under the patronage of St. Hedwig. The sermon for the occasion was preached by the Reverend Paul P. Rhode who, only days later, would become the auxiliary bishop of Chicago.[9]

In March 1909, the Reverend Peter Kahellek was appointed St. Hedwig's first resident pastor. It was at his urgent request that the Franciscan Sisters of Chicago arrived in September to staff the school.[10] The pioneer Sisters at the mission were Sister M. Jerome Dadej, superior and principal; Sister Mary Welter, teacher and organist; and two postulants.[11] In 1910, the parish school was constructed, and fifty pupils were enrolled. Like most ethnic parochial schools, St. Hedwig's flourished and the very next year showed an enrollment of two hundred students.[12] The Sisters occupied a few rooms on the second floor of the frame school building as their living quarters.[13] By 1913 the need for larger facilities for the Sisters was apparent, and a convent was built for them on Pennsylvania Street. One of the Sisters who pioneered at St. Hedwig's School was Sister M. Pelagia Bywalec who served at the school from September 1913 to February 1914. That year she returned to the Motherhouse because of illness. She pronounced her perpetual vows on September 8, 1914, and died on November 15, 1914. She was twenty-nine years old and had been in the congregation for nine years.[14]

In 1918, a large combination church and school was constructed. The top floor served as the church, and the lower floors were used as classrooms. In the latter part of the 1920s and the whole of the 1930s, enrollment at the school grew until it exceeded a thousand pupils. Of necessity, an addition was built to the convent in 1939 to accommodate the increasing number of Sisters who were assigned to St. Hedwig's School. With the erection of a large, beautiful new church in 1940, the combination church and school building was converted entirely into classroom space. A second sad occurrence relating to the Sisters in the parish's long history was the death of Sister M. Annunciata Klimasz[15] following an operation at St. Mary Mercy Hospital in Gary on July 5, 1934. Sister M. Annunciata, who was thirty-four years old, had been in the congregation for eighteen years.

As in every city in the United States, the Depression Era caused much hardship and poverty for the citizens of Gary. The severe drop in industrial output and consequent unemployment caused financial and social upheaval in the "Steel City." During these troublesome years, the pastors of many of the schools where the Franciscan Sisters of Chicago taught could not pay the Sisters' monthly stipend, and, in rare cases, some pastors

St. Hedwig School
Gary, Indiana (1909-1978)

did not feel the obligation to do so. Correspondence in the archives of the congregation pertaining to St. Hedwig's School reveals that such a situation existed there. A letter remains, written by Mother M. Aloysia in 1935 to Mother M. Antonina Osinski who had succeeded her as superior general in 1934.[16] Mother M. Antonina had evidently inquired of Mother M. Aloysia whether or not the superior at St. Hedwig's had signed a "contract" with the Most Reverend John F. Noll, bishop of Fort Wayne, to cancel any indebtedness to the Sisters in regard to their salaries. Mother M. Aloysia attempted to solve the dilemma:

> Dear Mother General:
>
> There was no "contract" from the bishop of Fort Wayne to sign. There was only a letter asking whether or not the Sisters would agree to work for whatever alms they could collect from the children and what the pastors would be able to pay the Sisters during the Depression. As for absolving the pastor of the debts which he owed the Sisters, there was never any talk. Every pastor knew that when times got better, the debt to the Sisters would be paid. I am surprised that Father Świątkowski[17] does not want to pay the debt. He was always conscious of any money he owed and strove to pay it back to the penny. If the bishop now tells them not to pay these debts, it would, indeed, be a grave injustice to the Congregation. No pastor can say that his debts to the Sisters can be cancelled. The superior, I am certain, would have been notified of this. If she knows nothing of it, then this proves that the claim is not true.
>
> I believe that the bishop is at fault here. We will make a novena to St. Joseph here for help in this matter.
>
> With best wishes,
The servant of the Lord,
Mary Aloysia[18]

It remained for Mother M. Jerome Dadej in 1953 to inform the Reverend Louis Michalski, pastor of St. Hedwig's Church, that out of sympathy for the parish, "the general council unanimously adopted the resolution to accept half of our dues as you had proposed and to have the other half cancelled."[19] The total debt of over $2,000 was finally settled for $1,127. The payment by Father Michalski on December 28, 1953, cancelled the parish's entire indebtedness to the Sisters.[20] This is a concrete example of how the Sisters aided financially strapped parishes during bleak times.

A census taken in Gary in 1910 indicated that 56 percent of the population of Gary were foreign-born with a preponderance of Poles. That same census showed the black population at only 2 percent. By 1960, the blacks had increased to 39 percent.[21] In 1951, St. Hedwig's School had an increased enrollment of over five hundred children; by 1964, the school enrollment had dropped to 147. Two new parishes had been formed in the residential suburbs of Gary, such as Glen Park, about five miles south of Fifth Avenue, thereby removing a substantial number of the student body.[22] In early 1961, the pastor of nearby St. Monica's Church asked St. Hedwig's Parish for assistance in accommodating the overflow of black students into his school. On September 4, 1961, seventy pupils from St. Monica's School, together with their teachers, two Sisters of the Congregation of the Sisters of the Blessed Sacrament, were warmly welcomed by the Franciscan Sisters of Chicago at St. Hedwig's School where two classrooms had been reserved for their use.[23]

With the continued growth of the black population and the continued white population loss to the suburbs, St. Hedwig's School vanished as an ethnic parochial school. The Franciscan Sisters of Chicago seriously contemplated relinquishing the school, but after much discussion, they agreed to remain in Gary and operate the biracial school. Within a short time, the school's entire student body was black. Just as the Sisters had committed themselves to working with the children of Polish immigrants more than fifty years before, they now committed themselves to working in what had become Gary's East Side black ghetto.[24] The school's 150 pupils, however, were being bused in from the city's more affluent West Side neighborhood. The majority of their parents were either professionals or semiprofessionals. In most cases, both parents worked and averaged two children per family. Catholic students comprised a mere 10 percent of the school's enrollment while the other 90 percent were either Baptists or Methodists. Because of these circumstances, serious discussions arose in the congregation in connection with its continued ministerial witness at the school. The congregation could not fully justify the existence of St. Hedwig's School as "Catholic" when it ministered to a select portion of Gary's black community, most of whom were not of the Catholic faith. The Sisters were willing to justify the school as "catholic" by continuing to give true Christian witness and quality education. The dedicated Sisters continued for several years in this capacity, but, by 1978, the congregation felt the need to consider seriously the conditions existing at St. Hedwig's School.[25] The staff of Sisters who had served so zealously and efficiently at the school gradually diminished in number, and regretfully, there were no Sisters to replace them. Eventually, there were only two Sisters on the staff living in a convent designed for as many as fifteen. Economically, the Sisters could not maintain themselves.[26] In June of 1978, the Franciscan Sisters of Chicago left St. Hedwig's School after sixty-nine years of service to the Gary faith community. The Sisters still look back fondly at their ministry at St. Hedwig's School which challenged their energies, both spiritual and scholastic, to fruitful ends. Today, only a remnant of Catholics from outlying areas who have cultural and ethnic ties to the parish return on Sundays and holydays for the liturgies. The school continues to function under a black administrator and faculty for a black student body.

Twelve years earlier, in June of 1966, the Reverend Casimir Senderak, the pastor of St. Hedwig's Church, had asked Mother M. Beatrice Rybacki to have the Franciscan Sisters of Chicago take charge of a proposed day nursery for black children in the neighborhood. Mother M. Beatrice informed Father Senderak of the serious lack of Sister personnel which would prohibit the congregation from staffing the nursery and nothing concrete ever evolved.[27]

The second school accepted in early February of 1909 was located in Youngstown, Ohio. Youngstown, once the fourth largest steel-producing area in the United States and located approximately sixty-eight miles southeast of Cleveland was settled by immigrant Poles who sought employment in the expanding iron and steel factories as early as 1902. With the pioneer settlement of eight families in the area, the ardent Polish countrymen petitioned the Most Reverend Ignatius F. Horstmann, bishop of Cleveland, for a priest to organize a Polish parish. Bishop Horstmann appointed the Reverend Charles Ruszkowski, pastor of the Nativity of the Blessed Virgin Mary Parish in Lorain, Ohio, in 1902. Father Ruszkowski aided the Poles until the appointment of the Reverend Ignatius Piotrowski as the first resident pastor of the newly erected church dedicated to St. Stanislaus Kostka on South Avenue.[28] In 1905, the Reverend Thomas Wilk assumed the pastorate. It was he who in 1909 invited the Franciscan Sisters of Chicago to accept their first school in what was later to become the Diocese of Youngstown. Until the arrival of the Sisters, the school had been conducted by the church organist.[29]

The Sisters who arrived on September 1, 1909, to teach at St. Stanislaus Kostka School were Sister M. Casimir Janowiak, superior and principal; Sister M. Seraphine Zamrowski; Sister M. Salesia Rzeszutko assigned to household duties; and a postulant.[30] Because the school enrollment had risen to 142 pupils, three classes were scheduled instead of the two which had been planned previously. Sister M. Salesia was removed from household duties and assigned to teach, and Sister M. Bridget Czuj, a new addition to the group, was sent to attend to household duties. The postulant remained at the mission only until December of that year. Where the Sisters lived from the time of their arrival in

St. Stanislaus Kostka Convent
Youngstown, Ohio

St. Stanislaus Kostka Church and School
Youngstown, Ohio (1909–1982)

Youngstown cannot be determined; it is presumed that they made their home in a private residence. During the tenure of the Reverend Francis Szydzik as pastor, from 1915 to 1917, two houses were purchased on South Avenue. One served as a convent for the Sisters while the other was used as classrooms.[31]

When the Reverend John Zeglen arrived in 1922 to assume his duties as pastor, the parish had grown so large that a decision was made to purchase a new site on Williamson Avenue for the proposed church and school. A beautiful new structure, Romanesque in style, containing the church, the school, and the auditorium, was completed in March of 1925 at a cost of $125,000. By 1927, the enrollment had surged to 616 students.[32] In 1929, Mother M. Aloysia Holysz informed her general council that because of the Sisters' successful work in the Cleveland and Youngstown schools, Father Zeglen had advised her to purchase available land between the two cities on which to build a future provincial house. No decision was made concerning the issue, and there are no records to indicate that it was ever brought up again.[33]

When the Reverend Dominic Mielcarek succeeded Father Zeglen as pastor in September of 1929, the zealous priest exerted all his energies to removing the parish debt, but the Great Depression, occurring as it did that year, resulted in a severe lack of employment. Consequently, the parish debt increased without the parishioners' monetary support. Unfortunately, in 1934, this state of affairs led to altercations between Father Mielcarek and Mother M. Antonina Osinski, the superior general, concerning the parish's neglect to pay the Sisters their salaries. While this kind of dispute was characteristic of other missions, the situation at St. Stanislaus Kostka School had an incongruity of its own. On December 31, 1934, Mother M. Antonina directed a letter to Father Mielcarek in which she stated the problem which existed:

> Dear Father Pastor:
>
> Not boldly and even with a certain amount of circumspection, a great need forces me to ask you to pay, if not all at once, at least a part of the overdue pension debt due to the Sisters.
>
> I am aware that there is some compensation due the Sisters for their work, even if a little, and despite the fact that they live frugally, they do not have enough to meet their obligations and they have the further duty of helping to support the Motherhouse.
>
> I beg you, Father Pastor, not to delay and to endeavor to pay the Sisters' pension.
>
> With deep respect,
> Mother M. Antonina
> Superior General[34]

Much correspondence passed back and forth between Father Mielcarek and Mother M. Antonina during the ensuing months. The gist of the matter appeared to be that Father Mielcarek proposed settling a $10,000 overdue debt dating from June 1931 to June 1937, for $2,000 cash. He further advised the Sisters to make voluntary house collections, sell existing books and school supplies, or hold a raffle from which all proceeds would accrue to the Sisters. Mother M. Antonina informed him that the general council did not approve of such an agreement, and, as a result, the matter was eventually referred to the Most Reverend Joseph Schrembs, archbishop-bishop of Cleveland, for settlement.[35]

Unfortunately, Father Mielcarek did not consider fully the Franciscan Sisters' demand for the justification of the parish's debt. Besides the monthly teaching salary that was due to the Sisters there were other areas where the Sisters contributed their services. They mended, laundered, and ironed the church linens including the church vestments and the priests' albs. The wafers for the hosts used during the celebration of Holy Mass were supplied by the Sisters. One Sister served as the church sacristan with all its attendant duties. The Sisters who taught in the school were obliged to support the superior, the cook, and the sacristan who were not salaried. Because the Sisters were not paid, they had contracted numerous debts themselves. For example, the tuition at Sisters College in Cleveland was unpaid; over $1,000 was left unpaid for the Sisters' clothing; board and retreat bills to the Motherhouse had not been paid for several years. Medical and dental bills were very seriously in arrears.[36]

With the death of Father Mielcarek in 1938, the Reverend John Grabowski was appointed the new pastor. Under his guidance and with the goodwill offerings of the parishioners, the Sisters' debt was settled amicably and the parish debt of $140,000 entirely liquidated by 1946. A renovation of the interior of the school also took place at this time.

In 1965, the Reverend Thaddeus Heruday was appointed the pastor by the Most Reverend Emmet M. Walsh,[37] the bishop of Youngstown. During Father Heruday's tenure as pastor, many improvements were made including a much-needed addition to the school. Many innovative and creative activities were introduced among which were the nongraded reading program, departmentalization of grades five to eight, and the establishment of a library in 1971. An instructional materials center was opened as well as a fully equipped science room. The science fair program at the school was coordinated with the Ohio Junior Academy of Science.[38] In keeping with the emphasis on Polish culture at St. Stanislaus Kostka School, Sister Clarent Marie Urbanowicz[39] held Polish classes on Saturdays for many years with the help of several lay persons. Among the special programs at St. Stanislaus Kostka was the Summer School Bible class for preschoolers. It was a two-and-a-half hour program for four- and five-year-olds which presented the children with a dynamic learning experience.

As in so many instances, the Sisters at St. Stanislaus Kostka School prepared children for the reception of First Holy Communion and conducted classes in religious education at St. Joseph's Church in Warren, Ohio, and St. Mary's Church in Orwell, Ohio. For many years the Sisters conducted religious education courses at St. John the Baptist School (now St. Joseph the Provider) in Campbell, Ohio. At all these parishes, the Sisters also managed the sacristy and trained the altar boys.

Having planted the seed of enduring faith more than seventy-three years before in the parish of St. Stanislaus Kostka, the Franciscan Sisters of Chicago found it necessary to withdraw in 1982, at the close of the school year. A very careful evaluation had been made prior to the school's closing which indicated that in spite of the Sisters' departure, the school would continue with a dedicated lay staff. A sad note of finality to the Sisters' leaving was added with the death of Sister M. Rosaline Lenart who succumbed to cancer upon her return to the Motherhouse in June. She had served as principal at St. Stanislaus Kostka School for twelve years with love, devotion, and dedication.

While the Sisters were accepting more and more schools and thus enlarging the apostolate of education, Sister M. Theresa and her advisory council, in 1909, grew more concerned with the care and maintenance of the elderly and the orphans. The Sisters were in dire need of money to maintain the orphans, the aged, and the membership. Three years earlier, in 1906, the magazine *Sierota* [The Orphan] had originally been started to raise funds, but it had now suspended publication. Another source of income was urgently sought in order to purchase the necessary staples such as clothing and medicine since food was easier to obtain by begging. In May of 1906, the Sisters decided to build and operate a greenhouse in the garden of St. Joseph Home for the Aged and Crippled near the corner of Schubert Avenue.[40] It was advertised locally as "St. Joseph's Home Florists—Fresh, Cut, and Artificial Flowers Furnished for All Occasions." When the greenhouse opened, the older orphans and some of the more able aged helped with the lighter work especially in the summertime. A small notebook in the congregation's archives gives an indication of the variety of flowers raised and the amount of income derived from their sales for a particular period:

Lilies of the valley	$6.25	Hyacinths	1.25
Hydrangea, geraniums	2.25	Chrysanthemums	1.00
Gerbera	1.40	Aspidistra	1.00
Ferns	3.00	Wreathesand palms	.40
Lilies	.50	Begonia	.50
Carnations, gladiolas	1.40	Cyclamen	1.00

A typical list of expenses included:

Transportation	$ .20	Paper	.25
Borrowing horses	20.00	Wire	.88
Repairs for wagon	2.50	Ink	.10
Repairs for stoves	41.88	Soil	.10
Repairing boilers	17.00	Vaughn Seeds, no price listed[41]	

On holydays of the Church, such as the Assumption of the Blessed Virgin Mary, the Sisters made floral bouquets which people purchased to be blessed after mass. Cut and potted flowers were sold at reasonable prices. For special occasions, such as weddings or funerals, beautiful floral arrangements were prepared by the Sisters. These floral pieces ranged in price from $0.50 to $4.25.[42] Flowers from the greenhouse were also purchased by several parishes such as St. Hyacinth, St. John Cantius, St. Stanislaus Bishop and Martyr, as well as by organizations like the St. Stanislaus Kostka Women's Rosary Society. Much of the revenue from the greenhouse came from the potted flowers which were sold from carts outside of St. Adalbert's Cemetery.[43] In many instances, some of the aged residents of St. Joseph Home were in charge of the wagons while the orphans sold the flowers. Among the Sisters who worked so diligently in the greenhouse were Sister M. Theresa Dudzik, who acted as the director; Sister M. Pascaline Dudek;[44] Sister M. Mathilda Szymoniak; Sister M. Martha Bywalec; Sister M. Gertrude Zimna; Sister M. Ernestine Radecki; and Sister M. Cyprian Lewandowski. Many of the orphans were also assigned to help the Sisters in the garden and the greenhouse.[45]

In spite of the Sisters' best efforts concerning the operation of the greenhouse, the derived income was not substantial enough. Sister M. Theresa and her council sought another avenue by which they could supplement the community income. They conceived the idea of engaging in an art directly related to the service of the Church—the sewing of church linens and church goods. Many of the Sisters were expert seamstresses who also

Church Vestment Workshop at St. Joseph Home for the Aged.

showed a pronounced artistic ability. Sister M. Theresa resolved, therefore, not to spare any effort in creating the Church Vestment Workshop. She succeeded in securing the services of Miss Theodosia Andrusiewicz, who, giving generously of her time and talent, taught the Sisters the needed skills in the art of gold and silver embroidery.[46] In November of 1909, the Church Vestment Workshop opened on the second floor of St. Vincent's Orphan Asylum. The entire operation was placed under the direction of Sister M. Hedwig Kubera and opened amid great difficulties owing to the lack of funds which were needed to purchase the necessary sewing machines, especially those imported from France. Through the efforts of Sister M. Antonina Osinski, the Reverend Albert Furman, the Sisters' staunch friend and benefactor, donated $350 for the installation of proper wiring and electrical fixtures in the workshop. The net worth of the Church Vestment Workshop at its beginning was approximately $6,000.[47]

With the passing of the years, the Church Vestment Workshop became firmly established and well known. When Sister M. Antonina Osinski was placed in charge in 1911, the project was opened on a wider scale. The Sisters designed, embroidered, hand and machine-stitched as well as painted. They hand-painted palls, burses, and altar linens. They produced lovely chasubles, copes, stoles, cassocks, and surplices for priests and altar boys. Beautiful Communion veils, processional canopies, banners, and flags as well as Church and societal ornaments and badges were created. The early Book of Customs pointed out the importance and dignity of that work stating that "a Sister should consider it an honor to make with her own hands Church ornamentations for her Spouse."[48] The Church Vestment Workshop continued successfully for many years drawing on the artistic creativity of many Sisters.[49]

With the transfer of the Motherhouse to Lemont in 1963, Mother M. Beatrice and the general council voted not to reopen the Church Vestment Workshop. The loss through the death of Sisters who were skilled in the art of embroidery, together with a decrease in the call for the type of articles produced, made it necessary to discontinue its operation.

From the time of her appointment as mother superior in January of 1909, Sister M. Theresa and her advisory council held regular monthly meetings to discuss matters pertaining to the community in order to prepare the agenda for the First General Chapter of Elections. For example, the Constitutions had to be studied and revised before being submitted to the delegates for final approval at the chapter. Until now, the Constitutions had seemingly lacked clarity, detail, and practicality in some instances. Father Spetz aided the Sisters in the revision of the Constitutions, and, when they were completed, presented them to Archbishop Quigley who granted the Constitutions the necessary approval. A copy of the religious Constitutions was given to each member of the community to determine whether or not they could be practiced and ultimately lived. A report would then be submitted to the delegates at the First General Chapter of Elections scheduled for August of 1909, indicating which articles of the Constitutions could be retained for permanent practice and which were to be rejected.[50]

In the latter part of April, Father Spetz was taken ill and was confined to his bed. He recovered sufficiently to celebrate the Silver Jubilee of his priesthood on May 4, 1909. On the day preceding his jubilee feast he left St. Joseph Home, where he had been confined since his illness, for St. Stanislaus Kostka Rectory.[51] Father Spetz celebrated his Jubilee Mass with great solemnity at St. Stanislaus Kostka Church assisted by his brother and two nephews who were also priests. Prior to the celebration of the mass, three little girls from St. Vincent's Orphan Asylum, dressed in white and adorned with wreathes, led Father Spetz to the altar from the rectory in a long procession. Many priests of the Congregation of the Resurrection, numerous Sisters, relatives, friends, and parishioners were present for the joyous occasion. On the day after the jubilee celebration, the children of the orphanage, with the aid of the Sisters, honored their "beloved Father Spetz" with a program filled with songs and original verses.[52]

Unfortunately, Father Spetz's health had been seriously endangered and his recuperation required more time than was previously estimated. Upon the advice of his physician, he took an ocean voyage to Europe in June. During his absence, Father Spetz placed the Franciscan Sisters of Chicago in the protective care of the Reverend Stanislaus Rogalski, CR,[53] the pastor of St. Stanislaus Kostka Church. Father Rogalski secured priests for the scheduled retreats and carried out the canonical examinations of the novices and postulants. The ceremonies of the investiture of novices and the first profession of vows which occurred that July were likewise conducted by Father Rogalski,[54] but the profession of perpetual vows which was to take place for the first time in the community in June was postponed until the return of Father Spetz. There was also the matter of the First General Chapter of Elections in the community for which the Sisters had been preparing.

Father Spetz returned from Europe at the beginning of November. The Sisters were overjoyed at his return because of the events which were scheduled to take place in the community in December. Nine years had elapsed since Sister M. Theresa, Sister M. Anna, and Sister M. Angeline had made their first profession of vows in the new community. In June of 1909, therefore, the Sisters were preparing to pronounce their perpetual vows—their spiritual consecration and surrender for life to the service of God and the Church. Because of Father Spetz's absence, the ceremony had been postponed, and the next group of Sisters preparing for the taking of perpetual vows was joined to the first, thereby bringing the number of Sisters to ten. With the return of Father Spetz from Europe, the Sisters began a retreat in December under the direction of the Reverend Francis Siara, CR.[55] It ended on December 8, 1909, the fifteenth anniversary of the community's foundation. In the early morning of December 8, Father Spetz celebrated a mass during which more than twenty Sisters renewed their temporary vows. The second mass that day, during which the Sisters made the first perpetual vows in the community, was celebrated by the Most Reverend Paul P. Rhode, auxiliary bishop of Chicago, with Father Spetz and the Reverend Francis Dembiński, CR, assisting him. During the Holy Sacrifice of the Mass, Sister M. Theresa Dudzik, Sister M. Anna Wysinski, and Sister M. Angeline Topolinski made their perpetual vows. The next group of Sisters, seven in number, pronounced their perpetual vows on the same day. They were Sister M. Clara Ogurek, Sister M. Elizabeth Baut, Sister M. Hedwig Kubera, Sister Mary Welter, Sister M. Andrea Zawadzki, Sister M. Kunegunda Pinkowski, and Sister M. Louise Maka.[56] During his inspiring sermon, Bishop Rhode spoke eloquently of the significance and of the obligations which the taking of perpetual vows imposed. In a brief ceremony following the mass, Bishop Rhode presented each Sister who had made her perpetual vows with a small wooden crucifix to be worn around the neck replacing the small silver one which each Sister had received at the time of her first profession. Bishop Rhode also placed a crown of thorns on the head of each perpetually professed Sister to remind her of her wholehearted offering of self to God and the service of his Church. At the conclusion of the Benediction of the Most Blessed Sacrament, Bishop Rhode confirmed two postulants. The first postulant was Mary Narozny, who had entered the community from Brenham, Texas, and was called Sister M. Bernadine after her reception into the novitiate. The second postulant was the bishop's cousin, Marianne Kirschbaum who became Sister M. Paul.

Father Spetz made St. Joseph Home for the Aged and Crippled his permanent residence from December 9 onward. There he continued to act as the Sisters' spiritual director and mentor. It was he who assigned Sister M. Theresa to work with an advisory council to prepare materials and finalize plans for the First General Chapter which, because of his illness, Father Spetz found necessary to postpone until August of 1910. Offering his invaluable spiritual insight and practical advice, Father Spetz had as his foremost goal to lead the young Franciscan community to autonomy, to inspire it to unity within, and to have it emerge as a viable, solidly established congregation in the Church.[57] As a consequence of the First General Chapter, a newly elected mother general would emerge who would govern the congregation with the advice of her general council. Together they would accept apostolates such as schools, and institutions devoted to the aged and the ill; they would select administrators for these schools and institutions; they would select local superiors and assign Sisters to the various mission homes; they would appoint the mistress of novices and postulants whose sole aim would be to guide and form worthy and dedicated religious. Rooted in the Gospel message of Jesus Christ:

> Remain united to me, and I will remain united to you. A branch cannot
> bear fruit by itself; it can do so only if it remains in the vine. In the same
> way, you cannot bear fruit unless you remain in me,[58]

the Sisters would bring faith, hope, and love to a suffering world. Having before them the good example of the Congregation of the Resurrection, their spiritual fathers, the Franciscan Sisters of Chicago would now repay their debt of gratitude to Father Vincent Barzynski, Father Andrew Spetz, and numerous Resurrectionist spiritual directors, by faithful ministry to Jesus Christ and to the People of God knowing that "in everything God works for good with those who love Him."[59]

MOVING TOWARD THE FUTURE

[1]This was Sister M. Theresa's second term as mother superior. She had been elected for the first time on December 23, 1894, and had served until October 4, 1898, when she was removed by Father Barzynski. This second appointment was to last until the community held its First General Chapter and a mother general would be elected, that is, until August 12, 1910.

[2]Ps. 28:7.

[3]See Chapter 21.

[4]The last group of novices under the care of Sister M. Theresa were the following: Marianne Pajor (Sister M. Felicita); Frances Gorski (Sister M. Wenceslaus); Genevieve Gawlowicz (Sister M. Thecla); Anna Molek (Sister M. Marcelline); Katherine Rzeszutko (Sister M. Salesia); and Katherine Wojcik (Sister M. Blase). *Spis Sióstr* (AFSCL).

[5]See Chapter 22.

[6]Coblentz Street was renamed Carver Street in 1918. In 1936, Carver Street was renamed McLean Avenue. Municipal Reference Library, City Hall, Chicago, Illinois.

[7]St. Hedwig's Parish grew rapidly. In 1909, there were 2,100 families; by 1911, this number had climbed to 2,729. The school was keeping pace. The total enrollment in 1911 equaled 1,800 pupils. There was, perhaps, good reason for an institution of this sort in the parish. *St. Hedwig Church: Diamond Jubilee, 1888–1963* (Chicago, 1963), p. 25.

[8]*St. Joseph Home for the Aged and Crippled House Journal* (AFSCL).

[9]*The Golden Jubilee Year of St. Hedwig's Parish 1908–1958* (Gary, Indiana, 1958), no pagination.

[10]Matka Maria Teresa Dudzik, "Kronika Sióstr Franciszkanek pod opieką Św. Kunegundy w Chicago, Illinois" [The Chronicle of the Franciscan Sisters under the patronage of St. Kunegunda in Chicago, Illinois] Unpublished manuscript, 1910 (Chicago, Illinois, AFSCL), p. 98.

[11]The postulant Stella Budka (Sister M. Virginia) was sent to teach; Frances Gemza (Sister M. Theodore) was sent to attend to household duties. Neither of the Sisters remained in the community. *Spis Sióstr* (AFSCL).

[12]*The Golden Jubilee Year*, no pagination.

[13]*Pamiętnik z Okazji Poświęcenia Nowego Kościoła Św. Jadwigi* [A Souvenir on the occasion of the Dedication of the new St. Hedwig Church] (Gary, Indiana, 20 September 1942), no pagination.

[14]Sister M. Pelagia Bywalec was born on June 5, 1885, in Poland. She entered from St. John Cantius Church in Chicago. Her postulancy began on September 8, 1905, and her novitiate on July 26, 1906. On July 27, 1907, she made her first vows. From 1908 to 1909, she remained at the Motherhouse. In 1909, she was sent to St. Stanislaus Bishop and Martyr School to attend to household duties. She returned in 1911 because of ill health. In 1913, she was sent to St. Hedwig's in Gary to teach, only to return in February of 1914. A victim of consumption, she made her perpetual vows on September 8, 1914, and died two months later. Sister M. Pelagia was the sister of Sister M. Martha Bywalec who died in 1976 in the seventieth year of her religious profession. *Spis Sióstr* (AFSCL).

[15]Sister M. Annunciata entered the congregation from St. Adalbert's Church in East St. Louis, Illinois, in 1916. Her novitiate began on July 27, 1918, and she made her first profession of vows on July 27, 1919. She professed perpetual vows on July 27, 1925. Sister M. Annunciata served as a teacher in the congregation for fifteen years. *Spis Sióstr* (AFSCL).

[16]At this time, Mother M. Aloysia was serving as superior and principal of St. Casimir's School in Johnstown, Pennsylvania.

[17]The Reverend Michael Świątkowski served as pastor of St. Hedwig's Church from 1929 until his death in 1947. *The Golden Jubilee Year*, no pagination.

[18]*Book of Correspondence:* Letter from Mother M. Aloysia Holysz to Mother M. Antonina Osinski, 15 May 1934 (AFSCL).

[19]*Book of Correspondence:* Letter from Mother M. Jerome Dadej to the Reverend Louis Michalski, 3 March 1953 (AFSCL).

[20]*Book of Correspondence:* Letter from Mother M. Jerome Dadej to the Reverend Louis Michalski, 29 December 1953 (AFSCL).

[21]Evelyn M. Kitawaga and Karl E. Taeuber, eds., *Local Community Fact Book, Chicago Metropolitan Area, 1960* (Chicago: Chicago Community Inventory, University of Chicago, 1963).

[22]*Franciscan Echo*, vol. 5 (Lemont, Illinois: 4 November 1963).

[23]Ibid.

[24]The Urban Apostolate of Sisters of Gary was formed in October 1965, to help acquaint the Sisters serving the black community with the common problems of prejudice, interracial justice, and culturally deprived adults and children. The Sisters at St. Hedwig's School were active members of the Urban Apostolate, and Sister Joan Klimek served as its treasurer. The Reverend Casimir Senderak, pastor of St. Hedwig's Church, served as the chaplain for the group. *Book of Correspondence:* Letter from Sister Joan Klimek to author, May 1977 (AFSCL).

[25]Sister Dolores Jean Molik, "The Black Non-Catholic Child in the Catholic School" Gary, Indiana 1978 (Typewritten).

[26]*Book of Correspondence:* Letter from Sister M. Alvernia Groszek, secretary general, to author, 7 January 1979 (AFSCL).

[27]*Book of Correspondence:* Letter from Mother M. Beatrice Rybacki to author, 29 March 1976; and 14 April 1981 (AFSCL); and *Minutes of General Council Proceedings, 1956–1970* (AFSCL).

[28]*Golden Anniversary of St. Stanislaus Kostka Church, 1902–1952* (Youngstown, Ohio, 1952), no pagination.

[29]*Minutes of General Council Proceedings, 1910–1934*, 13 February 1909 (AFSCL).

[30]The postulant was Salomea Bomba who later became Sister M. Eleanor.

[31]*75th Anniversary: St. Stanislaus Kostka Church, 1902–1977* (Youngstown, Ohio, 1977), no pagination.

[32]Ibid.

[33]*Minutes of General Council Proceedings, 1910–1934*, 28 July 1929 (AFSCL).

[34]*Book of Correspondence:* Letter from Mother M. Antonina Osinski to the Reverend Dominic Mielcarek, 31 December 1931 (AFSCL).

[35]*Minutes of General Council Proceedings, 1934–1956*, 11 May 1937 (AFSCL).

[36]*Book of Correspondence:* Letter from Mother M. Antonina Osinski to the Reverend Dominic Mielcarek, 27 September 1937; Letter from the Reverend Dominic Mielcarek to the Reverend George Whitehead, financial secretary of the diocese of Cleveland, 7 December 1937; Letter from Mother M. Antonina Osinski to the Reverend Dominic Mielcarek, 10 December 1937 (AFSCL); and *Minutes of General Council Proceedings, 1934–1956*, 11 May 1937 (AFSCL).

[37]Bishop Walsh became the second spiritual head of the diocese of Youngstown which was founded in 1943.

[38]Much of the credit for the educational improvements must go to Sister Jeanne Marie Toriskie who was missioned at the school at that time.

[39]Sister Clarent Marie has had a long and varied career in the congregation. Besides her numerous achievements in the congregation and in the field of education in general, her contributions in the field of Polish culture and language cannot go unrecorded. Sister Clarent Marie initiated a program of Polish studies at St. Stanislaus Kostka School in Youngstown for which texts were purchased with the assistance of the Polish American Congress. For ten years, she taught Polish

in the parish's Saturday school. While in Youngstown, she taught conversational Polish at adult evening classes at Youngstown State University and appeared on two television programs in that regard. She was instrumental in organizing the Youngstown Chapter of the Polish American Historical Association and served as its president for five terms. She served as co-chairperson of the Youngstown Diocese Polish Millennium Observance in 1966. Upon her transfer to Five Holy Martyrs School in Chicago in 1970, Sister Clarent Marie continued her efforts to propagate cultural pluralism and cultural awareness and to encourage bilingualism as a valuable asset. In 1974, she worked at the University of Illinois at Chicago Circle Campus in the capacity of Resource Materials collector on the Illinois/Chicago Project for Inter-ethnic Dimensions in Education funded by a $170,000 grant from the Ethnic Heritage Studies Branch of the U.S. Office of Education. Sister Clarent Marie was instrumental in helping to organize the Polish courses at the Maria Sklodowski Curie High School on Chicago's Southwest Side in 1973. She also led a petition to name the school in honor of the famed Polish scientist.

Sister Clarent Marie has served as the editorial secretary and the first, second, and third vice-president of the Polish American Historical Association. She gave devoted service for fourteen years as PAHA's treasurer. At the present time, she is an advisory board member. For the past several years, Sister Clarent Marie has taught English as a Second Language (ESL) to Polish-speaking students at Richard Daley College and Felician College in Chicago. She has had as many as 240 students in a semester. Sister Clarent Marie has been the recipient of numerous awards and honors for her very significant contributions to the Polish-American community in the promotion of Polish culture and language. She is indefatigable in her efforts to enhance self-esteem and group pride among all ethnic peoples. "Curriculum Vitae," Sister Clarent Marie Urbanowicz to author (AFSCL).

[40]Siostra M. Gonzaga Raniszewski, OSFK, *Rys historyczny Zgromadzenia Sióstr Franciszkanek Błogosławionej Kunegundy, Część pierwsza, 1860–1910* [A historical survey of the Franciscan Sisters of Blessed Kunegunda Part one, 1860–1910] (Chicago: By the Author, 1947), p. 131.

[41]*Rachunki z Oranżerii, l lipca 1915–8 Września 1917* [Greenhouse records, 1 July 1915–8 September 1917] (Lemont, Illinois, AFSCL).

[42]Ibid.

[43]*Book of Depositions:* Sister M. Isidore Wilkos and Sister M. Ladislaus Wroblewski (AFSCL).

[44]One of the orphans generally assigned to this task was Sophie Dudek. She was only twelve years old and the eldest of six children when her mother was killed by a train. In utter devastation, her father left all his children at St. Vincent's Orphan Asylum. Inspired by the fine example of Sister M. Methodia Pajdo, Sophie Dudek asked to join the community on November 6, 1909. She was received into the novitiate as Sister M. Pascaline on July 16, 1910, and made her first profession of vows on December 8, 1911. Her perpetual vows were made on August 15, 1919. Sister M. Pascaline taught in the schools of the congregation for twenty-two years. She ministered in Boys Town for fifteen years. In 1960, she was sent to St. John Regional Medical Center where she died on June 22, 1962, of cancer. She was sixty-two years old and had been in the congregation for fifty-three years. *Book of Depositions:* Sister M. Alexandra Jablonski; and *Spis Sióstr* (AFSCL).

[45]*Rachunki z Oranżerii.*

[46]Siostra M. Gonzaga Raniszewski, OSFK, *Zarys Półwiecza Zgromadzenia Sióstr Franciszkanek Bł. Kunegundy* [Sketch of the fifty-year history of the Congregation of the Franciscan Sisters of Bl. Kunegunda] (Chicago: By the Author, 1944), p. 37.

[47]Secretaries General, *Community Chronicle,* p. 9 (AFSCL).

[48]*Book of Customs of the Franciscan Sisters of Bl. Kunegunda,* Polish edition, pt. 9, p. 269 (AFSCL).

[49]Among the Sisters assigned were the talented artists Sister M. Anna Radzienda, Sister M. Clementine Ficek, Sister M. Helen Swiszcz, and Sister M. Sylvestra Pelczar.

The other gifted Sisters who gave of their artistic and sewing talent included Sister M. Alexandra Jablonski, Sister M. Alphonsa Makowski, Sister M. Antonina Osinski, Sister M. Barbara Grochola, Sister M. Boniface Pranke, Sister M. Bridget Czuj, Sister M. Casimir Janowiak, Sister M. Clara Ogurek, Sister M. Claudia Bomba, Sister M. Edmunda Siernicki, Sister M. Felixa Karwata, Sister M. Hedwig Kubera, Sister M. Herman Pieniazek, Sister M. Imelda Derbin, Sister M. Isidore Wilkos, Sister M. Ligoria Motyka, Sister M. John Barczak, Sister M. Joseph Suchomski, Sister M. Kunegunda Pinkowski, Sister M. Ladislaus Wroblewski, Sister M. Mechtilde Zynda, Sister M. Pius Wojcicki, Sister M. Philip Galinski, Sister M. Raphael Bogalecki, Sister M. Rosalie Scepuniak, Sister M. Scholastica Jakubski, Sister M. Salomea Grabowski, Sister M. Seraphine Zamrowski, Sister Sophie Marie Kierszke, Sister M. Stanislaus Reich, Sister M. Thecla Gawlowicz, and Sister M. Vincent Czyzewski.

[50]Dudzik, p. 95.

[51]Ibid p. 96.

[52]Raniszewski, p. 139.

[53]The Reverend Stanislaus Rogalski, CR, was among the eight aspirants who entered the Congregation of the Resurrection for American candidates established by the Reverend Vincent Barzynski, CR, in 1885, at St. Stanislaus Kostka Parish. Of the eight who entered, only two persevered. One of them, Stanley Rogalski, was sent to Rome to complete his novitiate training. He was ordained in Rome in 1895. Upon his return to the United States, he served as an assistant at St. Hedwig's Church. In 1902, he was appointed pastor of St. John Cantius Church where he remained until 1909. He served as pastor of St. Stanislaus Kostka Church from 1909 to 1912. He engaged in the congregation's apostolate in Vienna, Austria, and became the founding pastor of Sacred Heart Church in Kitchener (formerly Berlin), Ontario, Canada, where he remained for eighteen years. He died in Chicago in 1933. Edward T. Janas, CR, *Dictionary of American Resurrectionists, 1865–1965* (Rome: Gregorian University Press, 1967), p. 53.

[54]Dudzik, p. 96.

[55]The Reverend Francis Siara, CR, assisted at several Resurrectionist parishes in Chicago. He served at St. John Cantius Church from 1918 to 1920, and at St. Hedwig's Church from 1920 to 1922. He was assigned to the congregation's ministry in Poland where he died in 1945. Janas, pp. 54–55.

[56]Dudzik, p. 99.

[57]Raniszewski, p. 142.

[58]John 15:4–11.

[59]Romans 8:28.

Early Spiritual Directors

Rev. Joseph Gieburowski, CR

Rev. Stanislaus Rogalski, CR

Rev. Francis Dembinski, CR

Rev. Vincent Rapacz, CR

Rev. Stanislaus Siatka, CR

Rev. John Kasprzycki, CR

Rev. Joseph Zwierzycki, CR

Rev. Stephen Kowalczyk, CR

Rev. Joseph Tarasiuk, CR

Rev. Luke Swiatkowski, CR

Most Rev. Joseph Weber, CR

PART TWO

IT WAS I WHO CHOSE YOU TO GO FORTH AND BEAR FRUIT
1910–1946

CHAPTER 21

The First General Chapter:
Mother M. Anna Wysinski

The First General Chapter of Elections was scheduled to begin on August 12, 1910, on what was then the feast of St. Clare. In early March, therefore, Sister M. Theresa and her advisory council, under the capable and kindly direction of Father Spetz, held a number of preliminary conferences during which they discussed and prepared the material for the chapter. At one of the meetings, the Sisters agreed that the First General Chapter should be representative of all the Sisters. According to the Constitutions, one Sister was to be chosen as a delegate to the chapter from every ten members in the community. Each perpetually professed Sister was able to cast a vote. The result of the voting procedure yielded fourteen Sisters who constituted the delegation to the community's First General Chapter of Elections.[1] The following Sisters were the chosen delegates to this historic event: Sister M. Aloysia Holysz, Sister M. Anna Wysinski, Sister M. Clara Ogurek, Sister M. Elizabeth Baut, Sister M. Hedwig Kubera, Sister M. Josepha Suchomski, Sister M. Kunegunda Pinkowski, Sister M. Philipine Lama, Sister M. Salomea Grabowski, Sister M. Theresa Dudzik, Sister M. Leona Pochelski, and Sister M. Vincent Czyzewski.[2]

In compliance with the requirements of Canon Law and the Constitutions of the community, the ordinary of the place where the chapter was to be held was to preside in person or was to be represented by a delegate at the election of a superior general. The Sisters were overjoyed when they learned that the ordinary of the Archdiocese of Chicago, the Most Reverend James Quigley, had appointed Father Spetz to act as his delegate.

The First General Chapter of Elections met on August 12, 1910. The Sisters opened the chapter with the hymn, "Veni, Creator," invoking the Holy Spirit to enlighten them and begging for the gifts of faith, fortitude, and prudence in their deliberations. Father Spetz offered the Holy Sacrifice of the Mass after which the delegates proceeded to the room designated for the chapter sessions.

The first act of the assembled delegates was to choose a superior general. After the first secret balloting, Sister M. Anna Wysinski was elected the superior general by majority vote and was thus entitled to be called the mother general or superior general. The delegates next proceeded to vote for the Sisters who would form her general council.

The general chapter elected the following: Sister M. Vincent Czyzewski, assistant general and first councilor;[3] Sister M. Hedwig Kubera, second councilor;[4] Sister M. Andrea Zawadzki, third councilor; Sister M. Aloysia Holysz,[5] fourth councilor and secretary general; and Sister M. Salomea Grabowski, procurator general. The term of office for Mother M. Anna and her general council was six years. Conspicuously absent was the name of Sister M. Theresa Dudzik on the roster of council members.

When the results of the election were announced, there were many Sisters who were very disappointed that Sister M. Theresa Dudzik had not been chosen the superior general or had not even been elected to the general council. While most of the Sisters recognized Mother M. Anna Wysinski to be a gentle and loving person and were basically very happy with her election, many Sisters felt that Sister M. Theresa had been unduly overlooked, slighted, or worse, deliberately ignored. The Sisters felt that an injustice had been done to her, brought about, perhaps, by the hostility that had grown around her in the years prior to and certainly in the months directly preceding the First General Chapter. As a consequence of her not being elected to any office, Sister M. Theresa Dudzik exerted little or no influence on the active administration of the congregation she had founded except in an advisory capacity to her friend, Mother M. Anna. At the end of the First General Chapter, Sister M. Theresa was appointed by Father Spetz to head the Commission on Spiritual Affairs and to help formulate a Book of Customs. For the next eight years, she worked in the garden and the greenhouse, the laundry, and the sewing room. She accepted these duties with edifying humility. Thus the garden, the greenhouse, the laundry, and the sewing room became the witnesses of her life of intensive prayer and physical suffering. Until her death in 1918, she led a hidden life much like that of Jesus at Nazareth. She might have passed for the least important Sister in the congregation and, indeed, that was the impression she left on many of the young entrants. This situation existed for many years. It was not until the late 1930s that the Congregation of the Franciscan Sisters of Chicago would come to appreciate fully Sister M. Theresa Dudzik and the charism that had been given to her by God both for herself and her followers.

Mother M. Anna Wysinski, the woman destined to guide the growth and development of the young Franciscan community as its first elected superior general, was born in Bruss, near the city of Chojnice in West Prussia, Poland, on January 30, 1850. She was baptized Rosalie. Her parents, Peter and Kunegunda (née Platta) Wysinski,[6] were devoutly religious and industrious people who raised a son and four daughters in the strong tradition of the Catholic faith.[7]

After leaving Poland in 1873, the Wysinski family settled in Chicago on Chapin Street in St. Stanislaus Kostka Parish.[8] Shortly, thereafter, Rosalie's only brother, Eric, married as did one of her sisters.[9] Rosalie's youngest sister, Frances, joined the Congregation of the School Sisters of Notre Dame and was known in religion as Sister M. Andrea Bobola.[10] Her eldest sister, Matilda, who was unable to speak or hear, remained with her parents. Rosalie, an accomplished seamstress was given over wholeheartedly to the duties of her state of life and what she perceived as her obligation to her parents and her sister, Matilda. Rosalie was said to have had a gracious, warm personality and a tender heart.[11] Religious reverence and genuine piety were traits which seemed to be deeply stamped upon her noble character.[12]

Rosalie belonged to the first branch of the Young Ladies' Rosary Society and served as prefect from 1875 to 1898.[13] She also helped to organize the Archconfraternity of the Immaculate Heart of Mary along with Josephine Dudzik at St. Stanislaus Kostka Church.[14] Rosalie joined the Third Order of St. Francis as a tertiary and was one of the first members received into the novitiate, eventually serving as the group's first superior.[15]

Because of this mutual membership in parish organizations, Rosalie Wysinski and Josephine Dudzik became acquainted with each other and learned to love each other sincerely. Josephine recognized in this friend, who was ten years older than she, a person who was pious and faithful, a prudent woman who looked upon life soberly. Josephine often asked Rosalie's opinion about the leadership of the sodality and other matters, and she always received suitable and practical advice. It comes as no surprise, then, to learn that Josephine consulted Rosalie about her plans to organize the Franciscan tertiaries into a group to serve the poor, aged, homeless, and crippled of the neighborhood.

Mother M. Anna was described as being very amiable and compassionate. She seemed, in the opinion of many Sisters, to be "more approachable" in their dealings with her as contrasted with Sister M. Theresa who appeared somewhat "more reserved."[16] It was for these reasons, perhaps, that the Sisters wanted and welcomed Mother M. Anna as their superior general.[17] Mother M. Anna possessed a sympathetic understanding of the Sisters. She was gentle and affectionate and extremely beneficent to the Sisters who were ill.[18] Her personal integrity inspired her spiritual daughters to real piety and love of the interior life. The focus of her administration was the cultivation of the Sisters' spiritual life so that they would feel impelled to serve God with undivided hearts—in unity and mutual respect. The peace of Christ which filled her heart seemed to radiate from her very being and touched each member of the community. If the Sisters at times did not live up to their religious ideals, the fault did not lie with Mother M. Anna.[19]

After the death of Mother M. Anna in 1918, the Sisters recalled a conversation in which Father Spetz, having been her spiritual director for so many years, revealed that upon hearing the news of her death, he felt moved to pray *to* her rather than *for* her. He was convinced that such a soul could only go to God for a reward after death. A statement such as this by a person as close and trustworthy as Father Spetz proves an excellent indication of the spiritual stature of this quiet and humble Sister.[20]

A summary description by Sister M. Gonzaga in *Zarys Połwiecza Zgromadzenia Sióstr Franciszkanek Bł. Kunegundy* [Sketch of the fifty-year history of the Congregation of the Franciscan Sisters of Blessed Kunegunda] is a fine tribute to Mother M. Anna:

> Her refined manner, kindness, and capability in managing external affairs
> made her an excellent superior; her tender compassion made her a mother
> in the most beautiful sense of the word. Mother Anna loved her Sisters
> dearly; all enjoyed her full confidence. Patiently, without complaint, she

Mother Mary Anna (Rosalie Wysinski) 1850–1917
Co-Foundress of the Congregation of the Franciscan Sisters of Chicago
First Superior General, 1910–1916

inspired all with the utmost confidence she herself had in Divine Providence. The young community, encouraged by her example, bravely faced and weathered all the storms that beset it. In later years, she remarked on one particularly distressing occasion, "I know, dear Sisters, that I can do very little now, but after my death, I will be of much more use to you."[21]

As the first superior general of the Congregation of the Franciscan Sisters of Chicago, Mother M. Anna Wysinski would indeed leave a legacy of integrity, faithfulness, and perseverance to her spiritual daughters.

After the election of Mother M. Anna as superior general, the delegates at this First General Chapter of Elections proceeded to the election of her councilors. Chosen as the third councilor was Sister M. Andrea Zawadzki. Beginning with July 11, 1911, until September 12, 1912, Sister M. Andrea was also the local superior at the Motherhouse.[22]

Sister M. Andrea, the former Monica Zawadzki, was born in Poland, on July 4, 1874. She entered the community from Holy Trinity Church on July 5, 1899. On June 4, 1900, she was accepted into the novitiate and made her first profession of vows on June 6, 1901. On December 8, 1909, she made her perpetual vows. Sister M. Andrea's principal occupation after her first profession was the collecting of alms both in the city and outside it.[23] Though small in stature, Sister M. Andrea appeared a giant in the areas of fidelity to duty, consideration, and friendliness. She was especially loved by the novices and postulants for her kindness. One of the Sisters succinctly characterized her as being "of an open mind and an open heart."[24]

One of the congregation's most pleasant, prayerful, and understanding members was elected the general procurator at this chapter. Sister M. Salomea entered the congregation on November 21, 1899, from St. Hedwig's Church in Chicago. She was born Martha Grabowski on July 3, 1879, in Poland, in the section then under Prussian rule. She began her postulancy on December 8, 1899, and her novitiate on December 8, 1900. Her first profession of vows was made on December 15, 1901, and she was perpetually professed on August 12, 1910.

Sister M. Salomea was destined to have a varied and responsible role in the congregation. She served as a principal, superior, and teacher in schools in Wisconsin and East St. Louis, Illinois, before her election. While serving as general procurator, she also held the position of superior, teacher, and principal in schools in Chicago, East St. Louis, and Posen, Illinois; New Chicago, Indiana; Conemaugh, Pennsylvania; and Cleveland, Ohio.[25] She consistently proved to be a very able administrator, zealous teacher, and loyal member of the congregation, always faithful to the Rule and Constitutions which she had embraced while young.[26] Because of their importance in the congregation, the other councilors elected at this time, namely, Sister M. Hedwig Kubera, Sister M. Vincent Czyzewski, and Sister M. Aloysia Holysz will be discussed in later chapters.

Near the conclusion of the First General Chapter, Mother M. Anna and her general council made several appointments. Sister M. Clara Ogurek was chosen the superior of St. Joseph Home for the Aged and Crippled. Sister M. Kunegunda Pinkowski, who had served unofficially as mistress of novices in place of Sister M. Theresa Dudzik, was now officially appointed to that office. Sister M. Gerard Gorzkowski was assigned to serve as the mistress of postulants.

The congregation's second appointed mistress of novices, Sister M. Kunegunda, was born Marianne Pinkowski on December 18, 1880, in Poland. She came to the United States when she was one year old with her parents, and the Pinkowskis settled in St. Hedwig's Parish in Chicago. She entered the community on August 2, 1899, and was received into the novitiate on June 4, 1900. Her first profession of vows was made on June 6, 1901, and her perpetual vows were taken on December 8, 1909, at the same time Sister M. Theresa Dudzik, the foundress of the community, pronounced her vows.

Sister M. Kunegunda had served as the first superior and principal of SS. Peter and Paul School in Spring Valley, Illinois, in 1901. In 1903, she returned to the Motherhouse where she remained until 1907, when she was sent to St. John Cantius School in Indiana Harbor where she served as superior and principal until her appointment as mistress of novices in 1909.[27]

The new mistress of postulants was Sister M. Gerard, the former Mary Gorzkowski, who was born on February 25, 1880, in a small village in Tarnów, Poland. Her parents, Ignatius and Mary Gorzkowski, instilled in the hearts of their six children a deep faith and love of God. Later, four of them dedicated themselves to the service of God in the religious life.

Mary Gorzkowski attended elementary school in Poland. Because of her natural inclination toward learning, her parents made many sacrifices to allow her a higher education. At the age of eighteen, she graduated from the gymnasium and became a schoolteacher. Years earlier, her brother Stanislaus Gorzkowski had emigrated to America, had become a brother in the Congregation of the Resurrection, and was stationed at St. Stanislaus Kostka Church in Chicago. An older sister was also living in Chicago. Mary's brother made his first profession of vows in the Resurrectionist Order in 1899, the year she arrived in America. Realizing that both of his sisters were inclined toward the religious life, Brother Stanislaus directed them to the young community of Franciscan tertiaries under the leadership of Sister M. Theresa Dudzik. The older sister, however, decided to enter a convent in Poland. Mary Gorzkowski asked for permission to join the Franciscans but expressed a desire to return to Poland to bid her relatives a final farewell. She returned to America and entered the community on May 27, 1903. She was admitted to the novitiate on July 27, 1904, and made her first profession of vows on August 12, 1905. On August 15, 1913, Sister M. Gerard pronounced her perpetual vows.

After making her first vows in 1905, Sister M. Gerard was sent to St. Josaphat School in Oshkosh as superior, principal, teacher, and organist. A year later, she was transferred to St. Stanislaus Bishop and Martyr School in Chicago where she remained for two years. When Sister M. Theresa Dudzik was reappointed the mother superior of the growing community by Father Spetz in 1909 in preparation for the First General Chapter, Sister M. Gerard was appointed to take her place as postulant mistress in order to relieve Sister M. Theresa of some of her obligations.[28]

The First General Chapter of the congregation ended on the afternoon of August 17, 1910, with the singing of the "Te Deum." That same day, Archbishop Quigley arrived at St. Joseph Home for a canonical visitation which concluded with the Benediction of the Blessed Sacrament.[29]

During the deliberations in the five-day sessions of the First General Chapter of Elections, a number of corrections were made in the Constitutions. The following emerged as the most important:

1. The candidature would last for a whole year and might be lengthened by three months.

2. All the Sisters would attempt to receive Holy Communion on the First Friday of the month, on holydays, on the superior's feastday, on the confessor's feastday, the feast of one's patron saint, and on the anniversary of the consecration of the ordinary of the diocese.

3. The Sisters would be taught the fundamentals of the Catholic faith and should read spiritual books which the confessor or the spiritual director recommends or allows.

4. A general chapter would be convened every four years.[30]

5. The membership of the general chapter was stabilized and would include the following: superior general, council members, secretary general, procurator general, provincial general, provincial superiors, superiors of canonical houses, and Sisters after perpetual vows as special delegates who are elected by majority vote by the professed Sisters of such homes.[31]

Following the election of the superior general and her general council, Father Spetz had appointed Sister M. Theresa Dudzik, Sister M. Clara Ogurek, and Sister M. Leona Pochelski to head a Commission on Spiritual Affairs and to compile a Directory or Book of Customs, a practical and well-defined book of conventual regulations. At the sixth session of the First General Chapter, the Book of Customs [Regulamin] was read by Father Spetz and unanimously accepted by the Sister delegates. By 1916, each Sister received a personal copy of the Book of Customs and a compilation of the community's daily prayers in book form. Included in the Book of Customs was a formula for the profession of vows which indicated the special devotional bent of the Sisters and the saints under whose patronage the Sisters had placed the congregation:

I, Sister (N. N.), in the presence of Almighty God, Holy Mary, the Immaculate Conception; St. Michael the Archangel; St. John the Baptist, St. Joseph, the Holy Apostles, Peter, Paul and John; St. Kunegunda, our Holy Father St. Francis, the Angels and the Saints, and before you, Father, and before the entire Congregation of the Sisters of St. Francis, vow to God poverty, chastity, and obedience in this Congregation, for (one year, for life), according to its formulated Constitutions, according to the Rule of our Holy Father, St. Francis, ratified by the Most Reverend Archbishop of Chicago. So help me, Jesus Christ, Our Lord, His Holy Mother, the Immaculate Mary, and our Holy Father, St. Francis. Amen.

The Book of Customs finalized the following horarium at the Motherhouse:

5:00...................Rising
5:25...................Morning Prayer, Meditation, Holy Mass, Order in cell
7:15...................Breakfast
7:30-8:00...........Little Office of the Blessed Virgin Mary

8:00–11:00........ Duty

11:30–11:45...... Examen of conscience, Spiritual Communion

12:00................ Dinner

12:30–1:30........ Recreation

1:30–2:00.......... Vespers, Rosary Franciscan Crown (on Sundays)

2:00–3:30.......... Duty and Collation

3:30–5:15.......... Little Office, Spiritual Reading, Visit to the Blessed
Sacrament

5:15–6:00.......... Supper

7:00–7:45.......... Common Recreation

7:45–8:30.......... Catechism Lessons

8:30–9:00.......... Benediction of the Blessed Sacrament, Evening Prayers,
Evening Rest

At the conclusion of the First General Chapter, the Acts of the Chapter were sent to the mission homes. Of the 114 regulations enacted, these are sample illustrations of the often minor and disciplinary nature of the enactments:

1. No Sister may possess a clock.

2. Sisters may have visitors three times a year.

3. When leaving the convent house, Sisters are required to wear a top veil.[32]

4. From November to April, Sisters should return home by five o'clock in the evening; from May to October, before six o'clock.

5. Upon entering the chapel or a church, Sisters should kneel on both knees and make a profound bow. In the convent chapel, they sit in the pew assigned by the superior.[33]

Before the First General Chapter took place in August of 1910, it had become necessary to protect the growing work of the Franciscan community and secure its legal recognition as a duly authorized institution entitled to the privileges and the immunities of similar corporate bodies.[34] On March 24, 1910, therefore, proper registration of the corporation—the Sisters of the Third Order of St. Francis under the patronage of St. Kunegunda—was recorded in the State House at Springfield, Illinois, and the community received the State of Illinois Charter of Incorporation. The signers of this charter were Rosalie Wysinski (Sister M. Anna); Rosalie Kubera (Sister M. Hedwig); Marianne Pinkowski (Sister M. Kunegunda); Estelle Holysz (Sister M. Aloysia); and Marianne Czyzewski (Sister M. Vincent).[35] While the charter required the signatures of the administration of the community, it will be noted that the signatures of Sister M. Theresa Dudzik, the mother superior; and Sister M. Angeline Topolinski, the second advisor, were missing. According to Sister M. Gonzaga Raniszewski in her brief history of the congregation, each signee of the charter had to be an American citizen.[36] Because Sister M.

Theresa and Sister M. Angeline were not citizens of the United States, Sister M. Anna Wysinski and Sister M. Kunegunda Pinkowski signed the charter instead. In truth, Sister M. Gonzaga was erroneous in her view and in her explanation. According to a statement issued by the Reverend Robert L. Kealy, Ecclesiastical Notary of the Judge of the Metropolitan Tribunal, dated February 18, 1981:

> This is to certify that it has never been a requirement of the State of Illinois for an officer of an Illinois corporation to be an American citizen.
>
> I have verified this fact with the office of the Secretary of State of the State of Illinois, Corporations Division, and Professor Lawrence F. Daly who has been teaching law at De Paul University College of Law for fifty years, and has often taught the course in Corporations.
>
> Professor Daly and I are both members of the Bar of the State of Illinois as well as members of the Bar of the Supreme Court of the United States of America.[37]

Why, in effect, Sister M. Theresa and Sister M. Kunegunda did not sign the State of Illinois Charter of Incorporation is not known.

The Sisters had returned from eleven missions at the beginning of summer during which retreats were held. On July 15, 1910, five novices made their first profession of vows.[38] The next day, twenty-three postulants, a record number, were received into the novitiate.[39] The retreats were directed by the Reverend Paul Tudyka, CR.[40] On August 3, another retreat was held under the direction of the Reverend Francis Saborosz.[41] At the conclusion of the retreat, that is, on August 12, then the feast of St. Clare, seven Sisters made their perpetual vows. They were Sister M. Aloysia Holysz, Sister M. Vincent Czyzewski, Sister M. Josepha Suchomski, Sister M. Philipine Lama, Sister M. Agnes Roszak, Sister M. Salomea Grabowski, and Sister M. Seraphine Zamrowski.[42] On December 8, 1910, six Sisters pronounced their first vows in the congregation.[43]

That same summer, a benefactor, Mrs. H. Hanley, gifted the Sisters with a two-story home and two acres of land which contained an orchard of fruit trees in St. Joseph, Michigan. During the summer, the Sisters, especially the teachers, spent a few weeks there resting and enjoying the fresh air. In this healthful environment, they were able to study and prepare for the resumption of their apostolates.[44] In 1917, the general council discussed the matter of the property. They resolved that some Sisters should be assigned there permanently to maintain it. After a few years, however, because of its distance from the Motherhouse and because of the difficulty of maintaining the property and house in the winter, the land and house were sold on February 2, 1922.[45]

With the consistent growth in the number of Sisters as well as the number of aged residents and orphans, a decision was made in March to build a new, large chapel where everyone could be properly accommodated on Sundays and holydays.[46] The decision to build a chapel resulted in an entirely new wing attached to St. Joseph Home for the Aged and Crippled which, when completed in 1911, contained a large chapel, a kitchen, a refectory for the Sisters, rooms for a resident chaplain, a sewing room, and a recreation hall for the Sisters.[47] A campaign was launched to raise funds for the new addition which cost $6,650.[48] A new organ was purchased for the chapel by the Young Ladies' Rosary Sodality of St. Stanislaus Kostka Church.[49] The altars, the statues, and all the other materials needed for use in the chapel were gifts of generous benefactors. When the chapel was completed, Bishop Rhode officiated at its blessing on September 24, 1911. With the erection of the new chapel, the old chapel on the third floor of St. Vincent's Orphan Asylum was converted into sleeping quarters for the ever-increasing number of Sisters.

In May of 1911, a meeting of the general council was called by Mother M. Anna to elect a superior at the Motherhouse in place of Sister M. Clara Ogurek who had resigned. Sister M. Vincent Czyzewski, the assistant general, was appointed to take Sister M. Clara's place. Two months later, Sister M. Vincent asked to be relieved of the duty of superior pleading ill health. In an effort to restore her health in another climate, Sister M. Vincent left for Falls City, Texas, to assume the duties of superior and principal of the newly accepted mission of Holy Trinity School. Mother M. Anna and the general council then appointed Sister M. Andrea Zawadzki, the third councilor, to the position of the superior of the Motherhouse. In the meantime, Sister M. Hedwig Kubera, the second councilor, assumed the duties of Sister M. Vincent, the assistant general; Sister M. Antonina Osinski was appointed to supervise the Church Vestment Workshop which had been under Sister M. Hedwig's supervision.[50]

Sorrow came to the young congregation for the second time on July 6, 1911, with the death of Sister M. Ignatia Dukowski, who had been a member of the congregation for only six years. Sister M. Ignatia, at twenty-seven years of age, died of tuberculosis at the Motherhouse.[51] Only a few days prior to her death, Father Spetz had sent a letter from Rome to Mother M. Anna asking her to tell Sister M. Ignatia to "offer up one day of her sufferings for me." He had, in turn, promised to pray for her at the altar of St. Ignatius in Rome.[52]

With the passing of years, the number of orphans had increased to such an extent that St. Vincent's Orphan Asylum soon proved totally inadequate. As many as 117 orphans were now being accommodated in a structure originally built for sixty. The need for a new or larger institution was very apparent. Believing that it was the duty of the Poles to provide for their own neglected and dependent children so that the children would not be lost to their faith and culture, the Most Reverend Paul Rhode, the Polish auxiliary bishop of Chicago, summoned the pastors of all the Polish parishes in Chicago to a special meeting. After discussing the overcrowded conditions at St. Vincent's Orphan Asylum, he proposed the erection of a new institution to house Polish orphans, a project approved of and encouraged by the Most Reverend James A. Quigley, archbishop of Chicago.[53] A large site was selected on the northwestern outskirts of Chicago in what was then the "distant suburb of Niles." A plan was approved to assess taxes proportionately on all Polish parishes of the archdiocese to meet the expenses connected with the purchase of the land, the construction of the building, and the maintenance of the institution. It was to be called the Polish Manual Training School for Boys and St. Hedwig's Industrial School for Girls.[54]

The plan which had been devised to raise funds for the proposed St. Hedwig's Orphanage by means of assessing the Polish parishes in Chicago had dire effects on St. Vincent's Orphan Asylum which was, of course, still providing shelter for orphans until the completion of the new orphanage in Niles.[55] A letter to Monsignor Francis S. Rusch, the administrator of St. Hedwig's Orphanage in Niles from the Franciscan Sisters of Chicago indicated this:

> From the time the project of building the new Orphanage was begun, around 1907, the good-will offerings for supporting the orphans under our care have been reduced. Likewise, the offerings in parishes in which the Sisters collected previously have been affected; in fact, they have almost ceased. Still they [the pastors] maintain that they are not supporting the new Orphanage.
>
> In spite of these conditions, we had to provide food and clothing for over one hundred orphans who had to be supported all during this time. With the increase in the prices of food and clothing and the lack of support from the parishes, the upkeep of the orphans has weighed very heavily on us. It seems, from looking at the figures, that we are burdened with debts amounting to seven thousand dollars.
>
> We have hopes that the Reverend Pastors in the Polish parishes of the Archdiocese of Chicago will find a way to repay us the above-mentioned losses which are a large amount for a poor establishment like ours, and which, considering the number of parishes in general, should not be too much of a burden for them.
>
> With deep respect,
> Franciscan Sisters under the
> patronage of Blessed Kunegunda[56]

What had happened was unfortunate. As soon as the parishes heard about the proposed St. Hedwig's Orphanage in Niles, the offerings which had previously come to St. Vincent's Orphan Asylum from various societies and benefactors of Polish parishes ceased coming in and were now directed toward the new orphanage. This trend continued until St. Hedwig's Orphanage was built and the orphans moved there in 1911. The only aid extended to St. Vincent's Orphan Asylum at this time was that given by the Young Ladies' Rosary Sodality of St. Stanislaus Kostka Parish. Their contributions, however, barely covered the expense for the orphans. Except for a few for whom payments of $5 to $10 a month were made by relatives, all the other orphans had been admitted without payment.[57]

In order to help cover the expenses incurred for maintaining the orphans, the aged, and the Sisters themselves, the Sisters resorted to begging in areas where they conducted schools or institutions since they were no longer allowed to collect alms in those Chicago parishes which were now supporting St. Hedwig's Orphanage. Because these goodwill offerings were not adequate and because the Sisters did not want to refuse admittance to any aged person or orphan who asked for shelter or who was sent to them, the Sisters found it necessary to secure loans in an effort to supply their material needs. From the time the offerings from the parishes ceased, that is, about 1907, the Sisters were thousands of dollars in debt for food alone. There was an outstanding bill for $4,000 in a particular grocery store and an equally large indebtedness in a local bakery. The Sisters were warned that unless they paid a substantial part of the debt, the stores would refuse them any more credit. At one point creditors threatened to seize the five frame cottages on Ridgeway Avenue where some of the aged were housed. Under these perilous circumstances, the Sisters obtained a loan for $7,500 without interest from a "private citizen."[58] This rescued the Sisters from their creditors for a time.[59]

In 1915, however, this "private citizen," John Thym, demanded his loan of $7,500 to be repaid immediately and in full. No matter where the Sisters tried to secure another loan, they were refused. Unable to remit Mr. Thym's money at once as requested, the Sisters presented the entire matter to the Most Reverend James Quigley, archbishop of Chicago, who, after examining the reasons for the heavy debts, granted the Sisters a loan from the Chancery Office. Archbishop Quigley also concluded that, in justice, the Polish parishes should be taxed to obtain the money owed the Sisters for the years before St. Hedwig's Orphanage was built. Because he was leaving Chicago, Archbishop Quigley entrusted the entire matter to Bishop Rhode:

> My dear Bishop Rhode:
>
> I enclose a statement of the financial condition of the Franciscan Sisters, which I would like to have you look into and pass upon with a view of our doing something for them.
>
> They wish me to help them with Catholic Bishop endorsement so that they can borrow enough to pay a claim of the Resurrectionist Fathers— $10,000— and a note for a certain Mr. Thym for $7,500. These debts all were made for them through Reverend Andrew Spetz. The $10,000 is not pressing, but the Tym [sic] note is.
>
> Please read over the enclosed papers and report on them to me. Hoping you are well, I remain,
>
> > Yours truly in Xto,
> > Archbishop Quigley[60]

Unfortunately, many years later, Bishop Rhode was still urging pastors to send in their obligated sums to the Franciscan Sisters of Chicago.[61]

With the completion of St. Hedwig's Orphanage in Niles, sixty-three orphans were transferred from St. Vincent's Orphan Asylum on July 11, 1911. The Franciscan

Sisters had worked lovingly and tirelessly for twelve years to provide a home for over 542 orphans.[62] Of these, 479 had been placed in homes, adopted, or taken by relatives. Some of the orphaned girls asked to be accepted into the Congregation of the Franciscan Sisters of Chicago. The *Spis Sióstr* (Sisters' Registry, 1909–1919) lists the following: Sister M. Benigna (Frances Jakajtis), admitted to the orphanage on November 7, 1896, entered the community on October 4, 1905; Sister M. Boleslaus (Martha Nagorski), admitted January 17, 1899, entered October 4, 1905; Sister M. Mercy (Josephine Witczak), admitted May 6, 1891, entered October 4, 1905; Sister M. Pascaline (Sophie Dudek), admitted September 9, 1905, entered November 7, 1909. Four others had been accepted also but left the congregation after several years.[63]

When the last orphans had left St. Vincent's Orphan Asylum, the pastors of the Polish parishes suggested that the Franciscan Sisters of Chicago take charge of infants under two years of age since there were no provisions made for them at St. Hedwig's Orphanage. Mother M. Aloysia Holysz and the general council took up the matter of whether or not to reopen St. Vincent's Orphan Asylum for that purpose. The Sisters considered the proposal, but when they suggested that the Polish pastors provide adequate facilities and financial support for the care of the infants, the matter was dropped and never brought up again.[64]

With the transfer of the orphans to St. Hedwig's in Niles, some of the aged residents of St. Joseph Home now had sleeping quarters on the first floor of the empty St. Vincent's Orphan Asylum. The Church Vestment Workshop remained on the second floor while more sleeping quarters were made for the Sisters on the third floor of the orphanage and even in the attic of St. Joseph Home.

Throughout the course of the years, there had been various misunderstandings or disagreeable occurrences which had undermined the stability and peace of the young Franciscan congregation. One such incident erupted early in the administration of Mother M. Anna and threatened to have unfavorable consequences until it was properly rectified. In February of 1912, Mother M. Anna and the general council had declared that the Sisters involved in household duties, such as cooking, should be excused from praying the *Little Office of the Blessed Virgin Mary* with the other Sisters in the Motherhouse because of their numerous duties which sometimes prohibited them from being present in the chapel at the appointed time. It was the unanimous decision of the general council to allow the Sisters involved in domestic duties to pray the *Little Office* in private or to substitute the prescribed prayers of the Third Order.[65] As a consequence of this decision, a controversy arose involving the Sisters who served as cooks as well as some of the younger Sisters in the congregation. The Sisters who served as cooks wrongly assumed that they were to be completely excused from the obligation of praying the *Little Office*. The consequence of this action, they supposed, was to introduce the concept of choir and lay Sisters, the customary class systems prevalent in European convents and maintained in some

American ones. This meant the separation of the educated Sisters from those Sisters involved in household duties. In religious congregations which maintained the two choirs, the distinction was often indicated by some part of the religious garb or by the obligation to pray the *Little Office of the Blessed Virgin Mary* daily in choir. The ten young Sisters associated with creating the disturbance had encouraged the domestic Sisters in their erroneous view and even urged them to rebel. The Sisters were called to task by Mother M. Anna and Father Spetz. After the young Sisters gave their version of the way they had understood the matter, they realized that they had obviously been misinformed and had misconstrued the meaning of the domestic Sisters' exemption from choir recitation of the *Little Office*. Father Spetz reproved the young Sisters for their hasty judgments and warned them against such rash presumptions in the future concerning other areas of religious observance. Along with Mother M. Anna, Father Spetz reminded the Sisters that in the congregation every Sister was equal and no distinctions of social standing would ever exist. "As religious women," Father Spetz advised, "make distinctions among yourselves by the attainment of virtues—not by your wearing apparel."[66]

On Sunday, September 11, 1912, at three o'clock in the afternoon, the Most Reverend Paul Rhode, auxiliary bishop of Chicago, solemnly blessed a large bell which the Sisters had newly affixed atop the Motherhouse. At the blessing, the bishop was assisted by Father Spetz and the Reverend John Kruszynski, CR, chaplain of St. Joseph Home for the Aged. Numerous clergy participated in the moving ceremony. After the prescribed rituals, the bell—dedicated to St. Joseph, the Spouse, and St. Andrew, the Apostle—was rung for the first time. Its vibrant tones resounded throughout the entire garden where the solemn blessing took place.[67]

The bell, weighing over five hundred pounds, had been appropriately decorated by the Sisters for the occasion. Inscribed on it were the words "A.D. 1912—In Honorem Sti Josephi Sponsi et Sti Andreae Apostoli." The bell was presumably named by Sister M. Theresa Dudzik. Its historical worth was well expressed by Bishop Rhode in the sermon he delivered in the garden to the assembled Sisters concerning the role of bells in the Church's history. He pointed out how, characteristically, bells accompany a person from the cradle to the grave. He illustrated, in detail, how this particular bell would ring to call the Sisters to chapel for Holy Mass and other liturgical services. The bell would summon the Sisters to their duties of love and mercy. On a joyous note, it would announce the election of a new superior general and her council. Eventually, the bell of St Joseph and St. Andrew would toll for each Sister to announce her death and funeral. After the blessing of the bell, Bishop Rhode blessed two side altars in the convent chapel as well as a statue of St. Anne which stood in the corridor. At the conclusion of the Benediction of the Blessed Sacrament, there was a general visitation of the Sisters' lovely garden and their very productive Church Vestment Workshop.[68]

For fifty-two years the bell hung atop the Avondale Motherhouse. On May 12, 1964, it was brought to Lemont and erected on the grounds of the new Motherhouse near the Mother Theresa Museum.

THE FIRST GENERAL CHAPTER: MOTHER M. ANNA WYSINSKI

[1]It should be noted that there is no complete listing of delegates to the First General Chapter in the archives of the congregation. The names of the delegates were determined from the *Minutes of the First General Chapter Proceedings.*

[2]*Minutes of General Chapter Proceedings, 1910* (AFSCL).

[3]Sister M. Vincent will be discussed in Chapter 31.

[4]Sister M. Hedwig was discussed in Chapter 18.

[5]Sister M. Aloysia will be discussed in Chapter 25.

[6]Her father, Peter Wysinski, died on January 21, 1907. Kunegunda Wysinski died on November 23, 1923, at the age of ninety-seven. Both parents as well as Matilda Wysinski died at St. Joseph Home for the Aged and Crippled and were buried in St. Adalbert's Cemetery. St. Joseph Home for the Aged and Crippled, *Record Book* (Chicago, Illinois, 1894, AFSCL).

[7]Siostra M. Gonzaga Raniszewski, OSFK, *Rys historyczny Zgromadzenie Sióstr Franciszkanek Błogosławionej Kunegundy. Część pierwsza, 1860–1910* [A historical survey of the Franciscan Sisters of Blessed Kunegunda. Part one, 1860–1910] (Chicago: By the Author, 1947), p. 25; and *Zarys Półwiecza Zgromadzenia Sióstr Franciszkanek Bł. Kunegundy* [Sketch of the fifty year history of the Congregation of the Franciscan Sisters of Bl. Kunegunda] (Chicago: By the Author, 1944), p. 17.

[8]St. Joseph Home for the Aged and Crippled, *Record Book; Book of Deceased Sisters* (AFSCL); and *Spis Sióstr* (AFSCL).

[9]St. Joseph Home for the Aged and Crippled, *Book of Admittances,* January 1898–June 1920 (AFSCL), pp. 110–111.

[10]Frances Wysinski entered the Congregation of the School Sisters of Notre Dame on May 1, 1880, and was known in religion as Sister M. Andrea Bobola. She was "called" to the Motherhouse in June 1882, and received as a novice on August 22, 1882. She was professed on August 18, 1885, and made her perpetual vows on July 22, 1893. School Sisters of Notre Dame "Candidature Records, 1871–1800 and 1881–1890" (Motherhouse Archives, Mequon, Wisconsin). The *Obituaries, 1902,* by the School Sisters of Notre Dame, Mequon, Wisconsin, translated from the German by Sister M. Bonaventure, SSND, refer to Sister M. Andrea Bobola as a "good teacher in both Chicago and Milwaukee, who had a great love for children." Sister M. Andrea Bobola became ill in the middle of January 1902. She left the classroom hoping to return, but died on January 26, 1902, after a brief but intense illness. Two of her pupils were present at her funeral: the Reverend Joseph Kempa and the Reverend Paul Góra who worked in the Archdiocese of Milwaukee. Two blood sisters, her pupils whom she had left but two weeks earlier, and many members of the parish attended the services. She is buried in the congregation's cemetery (Section C, Row 2, Grave 1) at Elm Grove, Wisconsin. School Sisters of Notre Dame, *Obituaries, 1902* (Motherhouse Archives, Mequon, Wisconsin).

[11]Raniszewski, *Rys,* p. 17.

[12]Ibid.

[13]When she left office in 1898, the society had grown to over three hundred members.

[14]*Album Pamiątkowy Złotego Jubileuszu Parafii Świętego Stanisława* [A Commemorative Album of the Golden Jubilee of St. Stanislaus Kostka Parish] (Chicago: 1917), p. 112.

[15]Ibid., p. 126.

[16]*Book of Depositions:* Sister M. Chester Dziarnowski (AFSCL).

[17]*Interview* with Sister M. Cecilia Janicki (AFSCL).

[18]*Book of Depositions:* Sister M. Clavera Papiernik, Sister M. Fidelia Armatys, and Sister M. Cyprian Lewandowski (AFSCL).

[19]Raniszewski, *Rys*, p. 134.

[20]Secretaries General, *Community Chronicle, 1916–1934* (AFSCL).

[21]Raniszewski, *Zarys*, p. 18.

[22]In 1916, at the Second General Chapter of the congregation, Sister M. Andrea was re-elected third councilor and completed her term in 1922. When she died at the Motherhouse in 1929, she was fifty-five years old and had been in the congregation for thirty years. *Spis Sióstr* (AFSCL).

[23]*Spis Sióstr* (AFSCL).

[24]*Interviews* with Sisters, September 1983 (AFSCL).

[25]In 1922, Sister M. Salomea was re-elected to the general council as general procurator for another six years. From 1928 to 1934, she served as third councilor. Remembered as a trusting and prudent person, she was elected as second councilor in 1934 during the tenure of office of Mother M. Antonina Osinski. While acting as councilor, Sister M. Salomea was also appointed superior of Our Lady of Victory Convent in Lemont. Upon the death of Sister M. Innocenta Antosz, the vicar general, Sister M. Salomea assumed that position and completed the term in 1940. Her later years were spent at the Motherhouse, and in 1961, she retired to Our Lady of Victory Convent. On February 13, 1969, Sister M. Salomea died, a victim of cancer. She was ninety years old and had been a member of the congregation for seventy years. *Congregation Membership Records;* and *Spis Sióstr* (AFSCL).

[26]*Interviews* with Sisters, September 1983 (AFSCL).

[27]Sister M. Kunegunda was reappointed to another three-year term in 1913. At the conclusion of the term in 1916, she was elected superior of the Motherhouse by the general council. On November 18, 1919, Sister M. Kunegunda was relieved of this duty and until 1922, worked in the sewing room. In 1922, Sister M. Kunegunda was appointed mistress of postulants for three years, and at the conclusion of her term, was engaged as a teacher until 1932. That year she returned to the Motherhouse and remained there until 1937 when she was sent to Our Lady of Victory Convent in Lemont. When she returned to the Motherhouse in 1938, she was assigned to the Church Vestment Workshop until 1948 when she was appointed superior of the Motherhouse. At the conclusion of her term in January 1952, she returned to the Church Vestment Workshop until her death on January 27, 1958. At that time she was seventy-seven years old and had been in the congregation for fifty-eight years.

Sister M. Kunegunda was a cousin to Sister M. Stephanie Pinkowski and Sister M. Hedwig Kubera, also members of the congregation. *Spis Sióstr* (AFSCL).

[28]After the First General Chapter of 1910, Sister M. Gerard was reappointed the postulant mistress. The Second General Chapter of 1916 elected her mistress of novices for three years. At the end of that term, she became the superior of the Motherhouse from 1919 to 1922. The next ten years were spent at Five Holy Martyrs and St. Pancratius Schools in Chicago. In 1932, Sister M. Gerard was transferred to the Motherhouse where she taught Polish to the postulants and the young professed Sisters. In 1937, she was sent to Warsaw, Poland, with Sister M. Eymard Sanok, both recipients of one-year scholarships from the World Federation of Poles Abroad in conjunction with the University of Warsaw.

Upon her return from Poland, Sister M. Gerard remained at the Motherhouse. During all her religious life, Sister M. Gerard used her creative talent in composing poems for various occasions such as anniversaries of the priesthood or of marriage, feastday greetings, and holiday celebrations in honor of particular Poles visiting America. Such verses were in great demand by principals of schools who needed them for special events. She also wrote short plays in poetry form for children, especially in the primary grades, based chiefly on the love of God and loyalty to America and Poland. She strongly enriched her poetry with heartfelt thoughts of Polish culture and language. In addition, she contributed many articles and poems to the congregation's newsletter, *Echo Avondalskie* [Avondale Echo] from 1934 to 1940 and to the *Franciscan Echo.*

Sister M. Gerard died on February 2, 1964, at the new Our Lady of Victory Motherhouse in Lemont. She was eighty-four years old and had been in the congregation for sixty-one years. *Spis Sióstr* (AFSCL).

[29]Raniszewski, *Rys,* p. 128.

[30]It was later amended to read "every six years."

[31]*Minutes of General Chapter Proceedings, 1910–1934* (AFSCL).

[32]This was a large, thin, black over-veil worn when traveling, at exportations and funerals, and at mass outside the convent chapel. The second veil was sometimes called a "face" veil, but never in this congregation.

[33]*Chapter Decrees, 1910* (AFSCL).

[34]Prior to the incorporation of the community in Illinois, the legal and corporate name of the Association (St. Joseph Home for the Aged and Crippled and St. Vincent's Orphan Asylum) was the Congregation of the Resurrection, a corporation of Illinois. Incorporated under the laws of Illinois and commencing business on October 14, 1898, the officers were Very Reverend Francis Gordon, CR, president; Very Reverend Stanley Rogalski, CR, vice-president; Very Reverend John Kosinski, secretary; and the Reverend Andrew Spetz, treasurer and manager. The executive board or committee is listed as the Sisters of the Third Order of St. Francis under the patronage of St. Kunegunda, Sister M. Vincent, superior. "Annual Report to the Board of State Commissioners of Public Charities at Springfield, Illinois," 1907–1908 (AFSCL).

[35]Raniszewski, *Rys,* p. 143.

[36]Ibid., p. 194.

[37]Reverend Robert L. Kealy, Ecclesiastical Notary, Judge of the Metropolitan Tribunal, 18 February 1981. Received from Sister M. Alvernia Groszek, secretary general, 1981 (AFSCL).

[38]The Sisters were Sister M. Angela Jasinski, Sister M. Caroline Cabaj, Sister M. Cyril Gawlowicz, Sister M. Emily Kondziolka, and Sister M. Methodia Pajdo. *Spis Sióstr* (AFSCL)

[39]Received into the novitiate that day were Marianne Kirschbaum (Sister M. Paul); Katherine Zborowski (Sister M. Christine); Martha Olszewski (Sister M. Alexa); Leocadia Bogalecki (Sister M. Raphael); Thecla Klucznik (Sister M. Rufina); Thecla Mysliwiec (Sister M. Marcianna); Mary Szkutak (Sister M. Romana); Salomea Baron (Sister M. Kostka); Katherine Gazda (Sister M. Martina); Sophie Dudek (Sister M. Pascaline); Sophie Antkowiak (Sister M. Romualda); Caroline Pieniazek (Sister M. Herman); Mary Swiech (Sister M. Domicela); Salomea Szymanski (Sister M. Joachim); Mary Kopola (Sister M. Valentine); Martha Gorczynski (Sister M. Euphemia); Marianne Narozny (Sister M. Bernadine); Salomea Bomba (Sister M. Eleanor); Rose Tadych (Sister M. Josephata); Hedwig Partyka (Sister M. Lauretta); Estelle Budka (Sister M. Virginia); Frances Gemza (Sister M. Theodore); and Stephanie Oksiutowicz (Sister M. Natalie). *Spis Sióstr* (AFSCL).

[40]The Reverend Paul Tudyka, CR, was born in Silesia, Poland. He studied theology in Rome where he was ordained. He served as an assistant at St. Stanislaus Kostka Church from 1906 to 1914, and again from 1917 to 1921. Father Tudyka was the first editor of the United States edition of *Posłaniec Serca Jezusa* [Polish Sacred Heart Messenger] from 1915 to 1917 in Chicago. A frequent literary contributor to *Przegląd Kościelny* [The Polish Ecclesiastical Review], he was also the editor of the religious page in the *Dziennik Chicagoski* [Polish Daily News] in 1919 and the editor of several books of devotion for children. Father Tudyka was assigned to ministry in Poland in June 1921, but he died en route at sea. Edward T. Janas, CR, *Dictionary of American Resurrectionists, 1865–1965* (Rome: Gregorian University Press, 1967), p. 64.

[41] The Reverend Francis Saborosz, CR, arrived in the United States from Poland in 1901. After serving as an assistant at several Resurrectionist parishes in Chicago, he was appointed to St. Stanislaus Kostka Church in 1901 and remained until 1906. His last term at the parish was served from 1909 to 1911. Janas, p. 109.

[42]Three Sisters in the group had the taking of their perpetual vows postponed. They were Sister M. Rose Gorski, Sister M. Felixa Karwata, and Sister M. Gertrude Zimna. *Spis Sióstr* (AFSCL).

[43]Sister M. Albina Bieszczad, Sister M. Constance Pajdo, Sister M. Emerentiana Sztuka,

Sister M. Hilary Dadej, Sister M. Nicholas Poterek, and Sister M. Victoria Modelski pronounced their first vows on that day. *Spis Sióstr* (AFSCL).

[44]Secretaries General, *Community Chronicle, 1910–1934* (AFSCL).

[45]Ibid.

[46]*Minutes of General Council Proceedings, 1910–1934,* 5 March 1910 (AFSCL).

[47]*Community Chronicle,* p. 91 (AFSCL).

[48]Reverend Andrew Spetz, CR, "A Report to the Chicago Association of Commerce," Subscriptions Investigating Committee, 27 April 1911 (AFSCL).

[49]Existing records give much credit to a Miss Raczkowski from St. John Cantius Church in Indiana Harbor. She was a generous benefactor who helped to defray the costs of the organ.

[50]*Spis Sióstr* (AFSCL).

[51]Sister M. Ignatia was born in Poland on April 8, 1884. Upon her arrival in America, she settled in St. Stanislaus Bishop and Martyr Parish in Cleveland. She began her postulancy on July 16, 1905, and entered the novitiate on July 26, 1906. She made her first profession of vows on July 27, 1907. From May to June 1908, she taught at St. John Cantius School in Indiana Harbor. When she returned to the Motherhouse in June, she remained there until her death three years later. She pronounced her perpetual vows on her deathbed. *Spis Sióstr* (AFSCL).

[52]*Book of Correspondence:* Letter from the Reverend Andrew Spetz, CR, to Mother M. Anna Wysinski, 2 July 1911 (AFSCL).

[53]Sister M. Dulcissima Małolepszy, "A Historical Study of the St. Hedwig's Home, An Institution for the Care of Dependent Children, Archdiocese of Chicago" (M.A. thesis, Loyola University, Chicago, 1945), pp. 5–6.

[54]If the reader is inclined to wonder at the cumbersome title, there is an easy explanation for its usage. The institute was incorporated according to the Industrial School Act and Manual Training Act which were passed by the Illinois legislature in 1879 and 1881, respectively. In this way, the institution received some support from the county.

St. Hedwig's Orphanage, as it was more commonly referred to, was entrusted to the care of the Congregation of the Sisters of St. Felix of Cantalice (Felician Sisters) of the newly created Our Lady of Good Counsel Province in Chicago at the insistence of the Most Reverend Paul Rhode, auxiliary bishop of Chicago and with the approbation of Archbishop Quigley. According to Sister M. Dulcissima Małolepszy in her thesis entitled, "A Historical Study of the St. Hedwig's Home, An Institution for the Care of Dependent Children," Archbishop Quigley wanted to staff St. Hedwig's Orphanage with a congregation of Sisters who were already well established and well known among the Poles. He was acquainted with the work of the Felician Sisters in the Diocese of Buffalo where he had served as bishop before coming to Chicago.

A newly ordained priest, the Reverend Francis S. Rusch, was appointed administrator and chaplain of St. Hedwig's Orphanage. In 1910, only a modest three-story building was erected. Another three-story building, along with a separate power plant and laundry was built in 1915. A new dining room, a kitchen, storerooms, and a bakery were completed in 1919. By 1930, there were over eight hundred children at the orphanage under the loving and expert care of fifty-three Felician Sisters. The entire complex, consisting of ten buildings, evolved into a little town on the forty-three acre site. The orphanage thrived until 1961 when the last group of Sisters departed St. Hedwig's Orphanage and it became Niles College as a part of the new Chicago Archdiocesan Seminary System. *Diamond Jubilee, 1867–1942: St. Stanislaus Kostka Church* (Chicago, Illinois, 1942), pp. 762–763; and Sister Ellen Marie Ryba, CSSF, ed., in collaboration with Felician Sisters of American Provinces, *Response, 1874–1974* (Canada and Brazil: Felician Sisters, 1974), p. 63.

[55]When the decision was made by the pastors that a religious order undertake the management of the new St. Hedwig's Orphanage, it was suggested that the Franciscan Sisters receive the land and buildings as their own property. When the Felician Sisters agreed to take over this charitable work, however, they declined to have anything to do with the financial aspects of

maintaining the orphanage. The deed to the property, therefore, was made in the name of the Catholic Bishop of Chicago. The orphanage was supported by funds collected from the Polish parishes. Three committees were formed whose chief duty was to obtain the initial fund of $150,000 and additional subscriptions for the erection of the buildings. Małolepszy, p. 9.

[56]*Book of Correspondence:* Letter from the Franciscan Sisters to the Right Reverend Monsignor Francis Rusch, 8 May 1911 (AFSCL).

[57]Siostra M. Gonzaga Raniszewski, OSFK, "Rys historyczny Zgromadzenia Sióstr Franciszkanek Bł. Kunegundy. Część druga, 1910–1940" [A historical survey of the Franciscan Sisters of Blessed Kunegunda. Part two, 1910–1940] Unpublished manuscript (AFSCL), p. 130.

[58]Sister M. Gonzaga refers to Mr. John Thym simply as "this citizen" in "Rys," p. 132.

[59]Ibid., p. 131.

[60]Letter from the Most Reverend James E. Quigley to the Most Reverend Paul P. Rhode, 8 April 1915, Archives of the Archdiocese of Chicago, Mundelein, Illinois.

[61]Failure on the part of the pastors to live up to their promised monetary obligation was due to many reasons. They ranged from mere negligence on the part of the pastors to a lack of sympathy for the Franciscan Sisters of Chicago because of their affiliation with the Congregation of the Resurrection. The parishes of Holy Trinity and St. Adalbert which the Resurrectionists did not staff were especially noteworthy in this regard. *Book of Correspondence:* Letter from the Most Reverend Paul P. Rhode, auxiliary bishop of Chicago, to Polish pastors, 19 July 1915 (Copy in AFSCL); and Letter from the Most Reverend Paul P. Rhode to the Reverend Edward Hoban, 2 December 1916 (Copy in AFSCL).

[62]Sister M. Aloysia Holysz, OSFK, "Franciscan Sisters of St. Kunegunda Chronicle, 1894–1922," Unpublished manuscript (AFSCL).

[63]These included Sister M. Susanna (Frances Kielpinski), entered August 2, 1902, left August 20, 1913; Sister M. Hugoline (Anna Wojciechowski), entered August 26, 1902, left July 15, 1913; Sister M. Julianna (Rosalie Staszewski), entered October 4, 1905, left December 10, 1910; Anna Wojtynek, entered October 4, 1905, left in 1907. *Spis Sióstr* (AFSCL).

[64]*Minutes of General Council Proceedings, 1910–1934,* November 1929 (AFSCL).

[65]See Chapter 7.

[66]The reference to "wearing apparel" made by Father Spetz indicates what the author has stated, namely, that one of the general prerequisites for distinction in "choirs" was the wearing of an article of clothing which in some way indicated to the viewer the difference in "status." In some religious congregations, the distinction was sometimes indicated by a collar which the Sister wore. For instance, a choir Sister would wear a pleated collar while the lay Sister would wear a straight, unpleated one. Father Spetz's remark is so much more effective in the Polish. He said: *"Ne, ne . . . wyrównajcie się cnotami a nie szmatami."* Translated quite literally it means: "No, no, make distinctions among yourselves by the virtues you have acquired, not by the rags you wear!"

[67]*Dziennik Chicagoski,* 12 September 1912.

[68]Secretaries General, *Community Chronicle, 1910–1934* (AFSCL).

CHAPTER 22

From Illinois to Texas

Three new schools in diverse locations were welcomed by the Franciscan Sisters of Chicago in 1911. The first of these was twenty miles from Chicago's Loop, in the village of West Harvey, where large numbers of Polish, German, Italian, and Dutch families had come to work in Chicago's expanding plants and factories. When West Harvey's large population became predominantly Polish, the name of West Harvey was changed to Posen in tribute to the city of Posen (Poznań) from which most of the Polish residents had emigrated.[1]

In 1894, the Most Reverend Patrick A. Feehan, archbishop of Chicago, authorized the Reverend Stanislaus Nawrocki,[2] pastor of St. Mary of Perpetual Help Church in Chicago, to assist in organizing and building a church in Posen for which the Poles had petitioned. With the completion of the church structure in 1898, Father Nawrocki's assignment was finished, and he turned his attention once more to his own pastorate of St. Mary of Perpetual Help Church. Archbishop Feehan entrusted the new parish of St. Stanislaus Bishop and Martyr in Posen to the Congregation of the Resurrection. The Reverend Seraphim Cosimi, CR, was appointed its first pastor. He succeeded in building a rectory on South McKinley Avenue with several classrooms and a hall beneath it. He also secured laymen to staff the school. With the departure of Father Cosimi in 1902, St. Stanislaus Bishop and Martyr Church was once again placed in the care of the diocesan clergy.[3]

When in 1911 the Reverend John Robakowski was appointed the pastor, he appealed to Mother M. Anna Wysinski for Sisters to staff the school. She granted his request and assigned Sister M. Innocenta Antosz as superior and principal, Sister M. Josephata Tadych as teacher and organist, and Sister M. Ludwina Prokuszka to household duties. Sister M. Patricia Eiress was added to the teaching staff in February of 1912. There were, at the time, approximately forty-eight children enrolled in the small school. The parish grew rather slowly, and three years later, the enrollment still had not risen substantially.[4]

The struggles, burdens, and privations of the early settlers of Posen were exceedingly difficult, and the Sisters, undaunted, shared them all. There were at that time no roads, sewers, or running water in the vicinity.[5] From the time of their arrival, the

Sisters had living quarters consisting of two rooms in the school-hall combination. Finally, in 1917, a small, inadequate cottage was provided for them. The house, situated tightly between the church and the school, allowed for neither fresh air nor sunshine. Even worse, while the home already lacked running water, there was neither gas nor electricity.[6]

From all available resources studied, it is obvious that the Sisters in Posen were experiencing some unexpected and unwarranted difficulties more weighty than the lack of material necessities. The records of the congregation pertaining to this mission indicate that in the seven-year period in which the Franciscan Sisters of Chicago were in charge of the school, there were no less than nine superior-principals.[7] Six of them were transferred within a span of three years.[8] All correspondence directed to the Motherhouse indicates that the pastor's unbridled temper and generally insensitive attitude toward the Sisters finally proved intolerable, and the only recourse the Sisters had was to relinquish the school.[9]

St. Stanislaus Bishop and Martyr Church, School, and Convent
Posen, Illinois (1911–1918)

When Father Robakowski informed Mother M. Aloysia Holysz that he was determined to secure another congregation to staff his school, the Franciscan Sisters of Chicago withdrew at the end of June 1918. After their departure, Father Robakowski was unsuccessful in obtaining Sisters from any other congregation to conduct the school. In

1921, he appealed to Mother M. Aloysia to send the Franciscan Sisters of Chicago back.[10] His request was kindly but firmly denied, and for the next six years, St. Stanislaus Bishop and Martyr School remained closed. The children attended Parker Public School in the vicinity until 1923 when the new pastor, the Reverend Felix Kachnowski, invited to the Congregation of the Sisters of St. Felix of Cantalice (Felicians) to staff the school.[11] The Felician Sisters accepted the invitation and maintain this flourishing school in the colorful and historic Posen community to the present day.

The second school undertaken by the Franciscan Sisters of Chicago in 1911 was St. Roch's located in La Salle, an old city about a hundred miles from Chicago, situated on a hill overlooking the wide Illinois River. Named after the French Cavelier de La Salle, the city had grown to be a center of industry, notably the home of the "Big Ben" clock works and two famous zinc and cement factories employing scores of workers. There were also several coal mines which, throughout the years, had contributed much to the general economic instability suffered by the early settlers of La Salle.[12]

The first Slovenians came to La Salle in 1886. Their aim, like that of all immigrant ethnic groups, was to establish a church and a school which would serve their particular needs. In spite of many setbacks and hardships due to the lack of Slovenian priests in the United States, a young priest from Maribor, Slovenia, Austria, the Reverend Anton Podgorsek, volunteered to come to La Salle. As the first pastor of the newly established St. Roch's Parish in the Diocese of Peoria, he built a combination church and school in 1902 at Sixth and Crosat Streets. He designated three rooms on the second floor of the school section of the building as a temporary residence for the Sisters he hoped to obtain as teachers.[13]

In 1904, the Congregation of the Sisters of the Third Order of St. Francis of Assisi of Milwaukee was invited to staff St. Roch's School. The Sisters withdrew from the school two years later.[14] The Reverend Aloysius Kastigar succeeded Father Podgorsek as pastor in 1907. It was he who begged Mother M. Anna to send the Franciscan Sisters of Chicago to minister to the Slovenian people of La Salle. The Sisters who came to serve at St. Roch's were selected primarily for their ability to speak the Slovak language which is similar to Slovenian. Four Sisters arrived in La Salle in September 1911 to begin their mission: Sister M. Simplicia Bloch, superior and principal; Sister M. Anselma Pasternacki and Sister M. Marcelline Molek, teachers. Sister M. Blase Wojcik was assigned to household duties.[15] There were 136 pupils enrolled in the school.[16] The next school year, Sister M. Mercy Witczak replaced Sister M. Anselma, and Sister M. Clothilde Stefiej replaced Sister M. Blase.

At a meeting of the general council held in April of 1913, Mother M. Anna informed her councilors of the numerous problems existing at the mission of St. Roch's. There was a unanimous decision on the part of the general council to withdraw the Sisters in June of that year.[17] Whether or not the conditions for withdrawal were dependent upon

St. Roch School
La Salle, Illinois (1911–1913)

the closing of the coal mines that year is not known, but, historically, it appears that it was extremely difficult for the parishioners to maintain themselves and the Sisters whom they earnestly desired to keep.[18] There is no doubt whatsoever that serious problems concerning unemployment existed in the area. This led to acute financial problems in maintaining the school and supporting the Sisters.[19] Reluctantly, the Sisters withdrew.

All available historical records indicate that after the Franciscan Sisters of Chicago relinquished the school, it remained closed until 1917, when the Congregation of the Sisters of St. Francis of Christ the King of Lemont, Illinois, accepted the invitation to staff it. The Sisters remained until 1920.[20] The school closed again that year and when it reopened in 1922, St. Roch's School was under the supervision of the Congregation of the Benedictine Sisters of Nauvoo, Illinois.[21]

The third school to which Mother M. Anna sent the Franciscan Sisters of Chicago in 1911 took them to the South Texas prairies to a small Polish community in Karnes County called Falls City. The Sisters thus rendered service for the first time in a diocese which receives its name from one of the Sisters' favorite saints—San Antonio.

Five Franciscan Sisters of Chicago entered the Great Southwest in 1911 at the invitation of the pastor of Holy Trinity Church in Falls City, Texas. The booming state of Texas had welcomed among its numerous settlers a band of Silesian Poles who contributed in no small degree to its early development. This oldest permanent Polish settlement in Texas was that of Panna Maria in Karnes County, approximately fifty miles southeast of San Antonio.[22] In 1887, the San Antonio and Aransas Pass Railroad located a railway switch in Falls City near Panna Maria, and, as a consequence, Falls City became a thriving little town.[23] A number of Poles from other sections of Karnes County also moved to Falls City hoping to improve their economic conditions. Within a short time, Falls City had several stores, a cotton gin, a bank, and a number of saloons.[24] The settlers attended religious services at St. Boniface Church in nearby Hobson and the Nativity of the Blessed Virgin Mary Church in Cestohowa.[25] By 1902, there were seventy families living in the area. Under the guidance of the Reverend Stanislaus Przyborowski, the pastor of the church in Cestohowa, Holy Trinity Parish was organized in Falls City and a small church was built in 1905.[26]

There were many problems affecting the pioneer settlement of Falls City. Many of the early settlers did not have regular and adequate means of support because of unpredictable harvests and frequent crop failures. The ever-present problems of large, open prairies and dangers from the elements such as droughts, insects, and snakes also plagued the settlers. A problem of another nature was soon apparent. Unfortunately, from the very beginning of the settlement, a certain animosity had arisen among the parishioners. Hostile neighbors had branched off into two distinct groups—the "city people" versus the farmers or the "rural people."[27] This attitude was candidly revealed in a letter written by the Reverend John Karcz, the pastor of Holy Trinity Church in 1910, to the Most Reverend John William Shaw,[28] bishop of San Antonio. An excerpt reveals the bitterness existing between the two factions which had developed in Falls City:

> The Committee here consists of five men of whom three represent the farmers or the side favoring Father Frog[29] and two represent the city people. The farmers are hoping right along that Father Frog will come back and be the pastor here. The reason why Father Frog had such influence amongst the farmers is because he openly favored them . . . Moreover, he received their children to First Holy Communion after a few weeks of preparation without any consideration as to whether or not they were fit—and this the ignorant farmers like.
>
> This congregation has a school and a sisters' house on the premises. Here again, this was put up only by the city people, and the farmers would not take part in this at all; however, now they claim this is to be common property and insist upon having the same benefits as those who through their donations erected these buildings. Here again the latter demand that the farmers should put in their equal share if they intend to share the same benefits. Whether the farmers are obliged to join to do their equal share in this matter is also left up to Your Lordship's kind decision.[30]

Sadly, this hostility continued throughout the years and colored most of the history of this little Texas parish.

In September 1910, Father Karcz wrote to the Motherhouse of the Franciscan Sisters of Chicago requesting Sisters for his school. Holy Trinity School, built in 1905, was a frame building of one story which had been staffed by the Congregation of the Sisters of Charity of the Incarnate Word of San Antonio until they withdrew in 1909 for reasons which are not known.[31] Father Karcz had received the name and address of a Franciscan Sister of Chicago[32] from a resident of Falls City, and he set about the task of securing the Franciscan Sisters to come to Texas and take charge of the parochial school. To this Sister, whose name is unknown, he wrote:

> Reverend Sister:
>
> By chance, I received your address from Mrs. Kunegunda Krawiec[33] and I have taken the liberty to write to you in regard to a very important subject. Although I know that you are not the Superior General, I will, nevertheless, set forth my reason for writing.
>
> As pastor of the parish in Falls City for just a short time, I am aware that there is a very nice parochial school as well as a temporary home for the Sisters here. There is definitely a shortage of Sisters here. In view of the circumstances, that is, the great number of children and the warm feelings the parishioners have for the Sisters, their presence here is imperative. May I secure some help and advice from your Congregation? The conditions here are very good, and besides that, it is the wish of all Polish priests to assist your Congregation of Polish Sisters in the future. We need two Sisters, that is, one who speaks Polish, and another Sister who speaks English in view of the circumstances which exist here. I ask you, therefore, to honor us with an affirmative reply for which I thank you in advance.
>
> I remain,
A Servant in the Lord Christ,
Father John Karcz
>
> P.S. I beg you fervently that you put my request into the hands of your Reverend Superior General and I would be very happy if she would look upon my request favorably.[34]

On November 10, 1910, Father Karcz wrote to Bishop Shaw:

> My long efforts regarding the Sisters have been rewarded with the possibilities of getting them for this school year yet, and this is a fact that the "Franciscan Sisters of St. Kunegunda" of Chicago, Illinois, in a letter written to me, beg Your Lordship for permission [to work in the diocese of San Antonio]. As for whether or not the Sisters are necessary here,

there is no question. The Congregation also is willing to do its part. I beg, therefore, if possible, to send the permission for the above-mentioned Sisters to come and I hope to have them here soon.[35]

Mother M. Anna Wysinski responded affirmatively to Father Karcz's request on November 6 of that year. A few days later, he sent her a letter in which he thanked her for accepting the invitation and gave her additional details concerning the mission. Father Karcz informed her that there were approximately forty to fifty pupils in the school, and the parishioners were willing to pay the Sisters a monthly salary. He assured her that at the beginning it was not imperative for the Sisters to be highly qualified teachers. This could come later. He did request that one Sister teach in the Polish language only and one Sister be English speaking since there were two groups in Falls City who had indicated preferences for the languages being used. Father Karcz also asked that one of the Sisters be able to play the organ and conduct a church choir. He assured Mother M. Anna that the people of Falls City were generous and most anxious to welcome Polish Sisters. He even envisioned that the Franciscan Sisters of Chicago might someday have a province in the Southwest headed by a Sister, who, with the proper spirit and foresight, might bring this about. He spoke glowingly of the school and the people of Falls City, but because he wanted the Sisters to staff the school so badly, it is possible that Father Karcz was not entirely accurate in his appraisal of the actual conditions existing in his parish as the Sisters were to find out later.[36]

Holy Trinity Church, Convent, and School
Falls City, Texas (1911–1914)

In 1911, the Reverend Andrew Spetz, the spiritual director of the Congregation of the Franciscan Sisters of Chicago, paid a visit to Father Karcz in Texas regarding to the Sisters' proposed acceptance of the school.[37] That April, Father Karcz sent Father Spetz a letter which also contained a contract signed by the Church and School Committees and a sketch of the Sisters' proposed new residence. The contract, the first the Sisters had ever been offered upon taking charge of a school, read:

CONTRACT[38]

Between the Fall [sic] City, and Texas Catholic Congregation
and the Franciscan Sisters of St. Kunegunda of Illinois.

1. The Franciscan Sisters of St. Kunegunda will take charge of the parish school at Fall [sic] City in the month of September 1911.
2. They will teach all necessary branches as is the general custom in the parish schools of the country.
3. They will teach both the English and Polish language.
4. They will not teach more than ten months of the year, and in the same school during the full term.

1. The Congregation of Fall [sic] City will furnish the Sisters free rent-water heat-light-furniture-bedding-kitchen and dining room utensils.
2. The Congregation will pay all teaching Sisters an annual salary of two hundred and fifty dollars /$250.00/ each and will at least employ two Sisters from the beginning.
3. The Congregation will pay the expences [sic] for Extraordinary Confessor for the Sisters four times a year during the Ember Week, if any expense is connected with it.
4. If the priest should be absent for more than one Sunday in succession, the Congregation will provide transportation for the Sisters to the nearest church on such Sundays.
5. The Congregation will pay extra for services requested from the Sisters, except decorating the altar and preparing vestments for Divine Service.
6. The Congregation will pay the travelling [sic] expenses of the teaching Sisters from Chicago to Fall City.
7. The Congregation will provide living-room [sic] for at least five Sisters and increase same if more Sisters are required for the service in the parish.
8. The Sisters will have the privileges of procuring and furnishing the school books and stationery to the children at retail prices . . . subject to future regulations that will be made in the diocese.

Congregation of Holy Trinity

Church Committee	School Committee
Reverend John Karcz	Frank A. Pawelek
Peter Kowalik	A. F. Toman
J. W. Moczygemba	J. W. Szalwinski
R. J. Byrish	

Franciscan Sisters of St. Kunegunda.

Mother Anna, Sup.

Sister M. Alojza, Sec.[39]

Another Agreement was sent on June 5, 1911, and its contents read:

COPY OF AGREEMENT[40]

Falls City, Texas June 5th, 1911

We, the undersigned, members of the Falls City Catholic Congregation, agree and oblige ourselves freely to fulfill the following conditions to wit:

FIRST. To pay for the Railway tickets for two Sisters from Chicago to Falls City.

SECOND. To pay for all the expenses and cost of the new Sisters' residence on the parochial premises, accordingly to requirements and necessity. Furthermore, we agree to furnish it with the necessary furniture, and household utensials, [sic] all in compliance with the contract, being in force with the Franciscan Sisters of Chicago. Ills. [sic]

THIRD. To maintain the Sisters a general fund, i.e. through a tax imposed upon individual families without any regard how much such individual family will share the benefit of it or not, i.e. whether such family has any school children or not.

FOURTH. This Agreement shall be in force from the above date, and is strictly binding. The School Trustees consisting always of three active members of the congregation are authorized by the congregation to manage and transact all financial affairs in regard to maintenance the Sisters [sic] as also the school, with mutal [sic] understanding with the Pastor, and are hereby authorized to enforce the contents of said agreement.

FIFTH. In case of not acknowledgeing [sic] this Agreement, the Polish congregation of Falls City, shall be deprived of Sisters, and parochial school from their own fault.

SIXTH. This Agreement shall be forever in the archives of the congregation to manifest the action undertaken by the members of Holy Trinity Catholic Congregation of Falls City, Texas.

Rev. John Karcz

1. A. F. Toman
2. Frank A. Pawelek
3. John W. Szalwinski
4. Peter Kowalik
5. John W. Moczygemba
6. John Szczepanik
7. Alex Gabrysch
8. Urban Kocur
9. Ignatius Lyssy
10. Alex Pollok
11. Louis W. Lyssy
12. Peter Manka
13. Domen Gabrysch
14. Aug. D. Gabrysch
15. John L. Brander
16. Paul Pollok
17. Joseph N. Lyssy

18. Peter Niestroj
19. Albert F. Pawelek
20. Frank P. Moczygemba
21. John G. Schulz
22. Anton Richter
23. Frank Gabrysch
24. Frank Nieschweitz
25. Lorence E. Siwerc
26. August Winkler
27. Vecent S. Szczepanik
28. Paul Korzekwa

(Witness his signature:
Frank A. Pawelek
A. F. Toman
John Szalwinski)

29. Emanul M. Esparsza
30. Prosper W. Nieschwietz
31. Chas. Pawelek
32. Joseph Swierc
33. Adam Esparsza[41]

In the meantime, Mother M. Anna had written to Father Karcz regarding to the necessary textbooks and other requirements demanded by the Diocese of San Antonio. Father Karcz, in his reply, maintained that there had been no specific regulations or directions in regard to the manner of conducting the school. He assured her that when the Sisters arrived in Falls City, they would be able to determine their needs and those of their students. As for the textbooks, he advised the Sisters to bring Polish books from Chicago since they were not available in Falls City. Father Karcz reassured Mother M. Anna that the Sisters would not regret having agreed to staff Holy Trinity School.[42] A few days later, another letter from Father Karcz advised Mother M. Anna to send the Sisters at the end of August, since the new convent would not be completed until that time. He assured her that the convent was being built according to the plans submitted by Father Spetz. Father Karcz stressed the size and convenience of the convent which he presumed would someday serve as the central house of the Franciscan Sisters of Chicago in the Southwest.[43]

To serve as principal and superior of the mission, Mother M. Anna assigned Sister M. Vincent Czyzewski her assistant superior general. Sister M. Vincent, who was in ill health, took the assignment with the understanding that if her health improved in the Texas climate, she would resign her office and remain in Texas. In the meantime, Sister M.

Hedwig Kubera took over Sister M. Vincent's duties as assistant superior general and first councilor. Sent to Falls City along with Sister M. Vincent were Sister M. Raphael Bogalecki and Sister M. Paul Kirschbaum, who, besides teaching regular classes, was to teach music and, additionally, to play the organ at all church services.[44] Sister M. Nicholas Poterek was assigned to household duties. Sister M. Bonaventure Blazek, who suffered from tuberculosis, was sent to Falls City to recuperate in the mild Texas climate. There were sixty-six pupils in Holy Trinity School when classes began in September 1911.[45]

Less than two months after the arrival of the Sisters in Texas, two members of the Holy Trinity Catholic Parochial School Committee, at the request of several members of the Falls City community, wrote to Bishop Shaw describing what they termed the "sad conditions that exist here at present." They asked Bishop Shaw to look into the matter of children who were being prepared for Confirmation without having been adequately instructed in their religion by the parish priests.[46] Some parishioners resented the fact that they carried the additional financial burden of a ten-month school while some parishioners were sending their children to the public school in the area. As a matter of fact, these same parishioners now expected their children to be confirmed without having had proper religious instruction. The two members of the Holy Trinity Church, therefore, were dismayed and wondered what action, if any, they should take.[47]

The proof that intense strife existed between the pastor and the people of Holy Trinity Church is the fact that twenty-three priests were listed as having worked in the parish in a period of twenty-five years.[48] Indeed, ten of them had preceded Father Karcz. In early February of 1912, it seemed apparent to the Sisters that Father Karcz was going to be replaced. The Sisters, justifiably alarmed, directed a letter to Bishop Shaw. The letter stated that the parishioners had expressed angry sentiments against Father Karcz and warned that the Sisters "may leave this parish at the same time the pastor does, because they [the parishioners] will not try to support the school and pay the salaries of the Sisters." One parishioner who belonged to the School Committee asked the Sisters outright whether or not they would remain under such circumstances. The Sisters asked Bishop Shaw what course of action they should take:

> Now we kindly beg Your Grace to advise us. Should we write to our Mother General telling her we cannot stay here in the South and must come home to Chicago? Or is it possible for Your Grace to place us at some other Polish school so we need not be a burden to these people here who are, at the present time, so irritated? Or shall we leave the South altogether?[49]

Clearly, it was all a matter of finances. Many parishioners continued to be stubborn and refused to pay their share according to the agreement they had signed. There were those parishioners who did not sign the agreement and did not see any obligation to pay. Two parish members were finally delegated to solicit donations and to induce others to pay.[50] On March 21, 1911, the Alamo Lumber Company wrote to Bishop Shaw informing him that the bill for lumber used in constructing the parochial school was not yet paid. In an effort to avoid litigation, the Alamo Lumber Company asked the bishop to intervene in the situation where "the people can't seem to get together" and where "the Polanders won't keep their contract."[51] By May, with the bill still unpaid, Bishop Shaw was forced to address the parishioners with a stern reproof:

> To Our Beloved Children of the Holy Trinity Parish, Falls City,
> Greetings:
>
> We have on several occasions visited your parish to restore peace and harmony among you all, and to impress upon you the necessity of laying aside all differences and of working together for the welfare of your parish. We are very much grieved to see that our efforts have not been attended with that success that we had reason to hope for. Unfortunately, the spirit of dissension and discord still prevails among you all with the sad result that our holy Religion is suffering. This disunion has become a real scandal, and unless those who are disturbing the peace of the parish quickly realize the harm they are doing to the fair name of the Church, they will have to render a severe account to Him Whose prayer was for unity among His brethren. Their conduct is also disrespectful to the authority of the Bishop of the diocese. The Bishop is bound at all costs, regardless of consequences, to uphold the dignity and authority which the Church has placed in his charge.
>
> We have learned that many promised to contribute towards the building of the new school, and have not done so though they could easily have done their duty. Others again, well able to help, have shown a disposition and a determination to give no assistance towards paying the heavy debt that has been incurred for the building of the new school. It is very embarrassing for your Bishop to receive letters from the Company which furnished the material for the building, asking that some arrangements be made for the settlement of their claim, which is acknowledged to be just and is now overdue. I have, as you well know, done all in my power to help you in the matter of a new school, and I expected each and every family in the parish to do likewise. I regret to see my confidence in your hearty cooperation and loyalty and appreciation has been misplaced. It is true indeed, that some of the parishioners have responded nobly to the call of duty and for such noble-minded and generous children of the Church I have only words of praise. I sincerely hope that all from this time forth will work together under the direction of their good Pastor, and like the early Christians be of one

heart and mind. We, therefore, ask those who promised to donate money for the school to give their offerings or their notes as soon as possible; and all others who have done nothing up to the present to come forward and do their duty. We also request the Pastor and the Trustees to arrange in what way they think best for the payment of the lumber bill and for the money that was borrowed for the building of the school.[52]

Strangely enough, amid all the internal strife and confusion over old debts, a new frame school had been erected in 1911, "beyond the river," about six miles northwest of Falls City. Called St. Stanislaus Kostka School, this "mission school" of Holy Trinity was begun by Father Karcz on land donated by C. Bodden of Falls City and Frank Moy of St. Stanislaus Kostka Parish. The establishment of the school was due to several reasons. The distance to Holy Trinity was too great especially for the younger children. When frequent floods occurred, the children who lived "across the river" found the roads impassable, and attendance at school was irregular. Another pertinent reason which led to the erection of St. Stanislaus Kostka School was the fact that the people in that area wished to retain more of their Polish language and culture and were in favor of having Polish-speaking Sisters.[53]

Bishop Shaw had directed a letter to the new and twelfth pastor of Holy Trinity Church, the Reverend Arthur Hubsch, in September of 1912. An excerpt from Bishop Shaw's letter indicates the disturbing state of affairs still existing in Falls City:

> I was a little disappointed that you did not say something about the school question in Falls City. What arrangements have been made between the two factions about the Sisters teaching in both places? Have they [the parishioners] made up their minds to pay the debt on the school building?[54]

A week later, Father Hubsch informed Bishop Shaw that he had had a meeting with all his parishioners and both factions had agreed to pay the debt and to have the Franciscan Sisters of Chicago teach at both Holy Trinity and St. Stanislaus Kostka Schools.[55] Father Hubsch admitted that he was proceeding very slowly in this complicated matter "the spirit being on both sides super-irritated."[56] On November 25, 1912, the Franciscan Sisters of Chicago took charge of St. Stanislaus Kostka School with its enrollment of fifty-three children. Sister M. Benedict Polcyn was assigned to teach at the school and Sister M. Emily Kondziolka, sent basically as a companion to Sister M. Benedict, attended to household duties. Only one classroom in the school building was designated as the Sisters' living quarters. Sister M. Benedict and Sister M. Emily lived there all week but traveled to Holy Trinity Parish convent for Sundays and holydays.

At the mission school of St. Stanislaus Kostka, the Sisters were offered a contract to teach only five months of the year; they could extend this time to seven months if they so desired as outlined in their contract:

CONTRACT[57]

Between St. Stanislaus Kostka School Committee and
The Franciscan Sisters of St. Kunegunda of Illinois

1. The Franciscan Sisters of St. Kunegunda will take charge of the St. Stanislaus Kostka School on the twenty-fifth (25) of November 1912.
2. They will teach both the English and the Polish language.
3. They will teach five months of the year, and in the same school during the full term, but will prolong same to seven months, if desired.
4. It is customary with the Sisters to have three Sisters residing at one place; however, permission for two Sisters has been granted by the Reverend Mother, for this term only.

1. The St. Stanislaus Kostka School Committee will furnish the Sisters free rent-water-heat-light-furniture-bedding-kitchen and dining room utensils.
2. The St. Stanislaus Kostka School Committee will pay all teaching Sisters a monthly salary of twenty-five dollars (25) each.
3. The St. Stanislaus Kostka School Committee will furnish the Sisters free transportation between the City and the School, whenever requested by the Sisters.
4. The St. Stanislaus Kostka School Committee will pay extra for services requested from the Sisters, except decorating the altar and preparing vestments for Divine Service.

> St. Stanislaus Kostka School Committee
>
> Joe Swierc
>
> Willy Moczygemba
>
> Stanik Kollodziej

Approved: Falls City, Texas   +J. W. Shaw
          November 24, 1911   Bishop of San Antonio

Rev. Arthur A. Hubsch, Ph.D.
(Record of the Holy Trinity Church)

In September of 1913, with the start of the new year at Holy Trinity School, Sister M. Colette Nowak replaced Sister M. Vincent as superior and principal. Sister M. Bonaventure returned to Chicago where she died of tuberculosis on November 10.[58] Sister M. Emily was transferred from St. Stanislaus Kostka School to Holy Trinity where she continued to attend to household duties while Sister M. Marcianna Mysliwiec arrived in Texas to replace Sister M. Emily at St. Stanislaus Kostka convent. On September 26, 1913, the Sisters once again were forced to inform Bishop Shaw of some unpleasant happenings:

Dear Reverend Bishop:

We have been informed by our Pastor that one of the committee men told him that the congregation [of Falls City] will not have the Sisters and intend "to chase them away."

Under the circumstances, we are at a loss as to what to do; therefore, we kindly beg Your Grace for advice, whether we should write our Mother General to take us back to Chicago or whether we should continue to work here.

Commending ourselves to the prayers of Your Grace and humbly begging an early reply, we remain,

Your spiritual daughters in Christ,
Franciscan Sisters[59]

Bishop Shaw was quick to reply to the confused and intimidated Sisters:

Dear Sisters in Christ:

Your letter came to hand during my absence from the city. I think that you have attached entirely too much importance to the rumor. I was not aware that there was any dissatisfaction with your Community teaching the parish school. Besides, the people have nothing to say in this matter for it rests entirely with the Bishop of the diocese to decide what Sisters shall teach the parish schools of the diocese. As you well know, no one, not even the Bishop, escapes criticism. This fact should make us all the more careful to avoid everything which could provoke criticism. Your pastor did not mention the rumor to you to insinuate that he was not pleased with you, but on the contrary, he appreciates the good work that you have done and are doing for the children of the parish.

With kindest regards and best wishes, and a blessing on you and your companions, I am yours sincerely in Xto,

John W. Shaw[60]

At a meeting with the general council in April 1914, Father Spetz discussed the various problems confronting the Sisters at Falls City and suggested that they withdraw from the schools. He reminded the Sisters that they had accepted Holy Trinity School with the intention of teaching Polish and this condition was being disregarded.[61] It appeared that only English-speaking Sisters were now requested at the mission. Then in a letter to Bishop Shaw, Father Spetz tried to make his position clear in regard to the Sisters:

Right Reverend Bishop:

When the Franciscan Sisters of St. Kunegunda accepted the invitation of Father Karcz to come to Falls City, the understanding was that they were to teach Polish and for that reason they were desired there.

Now things have changed and it seems that only English-speaking Sisters are desired. To teach English only is a hardship for the Sisters as we are short of English teachers in our other missions and if only English is needed, your Diocesan Sisters are better qualified to do that work than ours. For this reason, I would wish to withdraw the Sisters from your diocese and employ them in purely Polish parishes where they will be able to do more good and where other Sisters cannot take their place. However, I would not wish to do anything in this matter if you find that my reasons are not important enough to take this step.

Father Spetz[62]

In June, Mother M. Anna informed the general council that it was Bishop Shaw's desire that all the Sisters return to the Motherhouse for retreat that summer. She added that since there was serious consideration about closing the mission, the Sisters were to bring their trunks and belongings with themselves.[63] On July 11, 1914, the Sisters sent a letter to the pastor, Reverend Arthur Hubsch confirming their actions:

Reverend and dear Father:

There are difficulties with the Texas mission which makes the stay of our Sisters there next to impossible and too burdensome for us. For this reason, we have decided to withdraw the Sisters and ask you to please provide otherwise for your school for next term.

We wished to notify you before this, but wrote to the Most Reverend Bishop about this matter. As a month has elapsed, his silence is his consent, but we lost so much time on this account.

With the same mail we sent the Sisters the order to come for retreat and to bring their effects with them. Hoping that this will not cause you much trouble.

Yours very respectfully,

Franciscan Sisters of St. Kunegunda[64]

On July 17, 1914, Bishop Shaw replied to Father Spetz's letter, upbraiding him for aiding in the decision to remove the Sisters from the Texas missions. Bishop Shaw's letter adamantly stated:

I cannot understand why Father Karcz should have stipulated that only Polish was to be taught in the school . . . our Polish people understand very well the importance of having their children learn English. It was not necessary that all the Sisters should be Polish-speaking nor all English. A few of each would suffice.[65]

Father Hubsch wrote to the bishop once more. He informed Bishop Shaw that the Franciscan Sisters were leaving Falls City permanently:

Several families were discontented with them [the Franciscan Sisters] and the rest had to be—with very few exceptions—always compelled to pay for their salary. The San Antonio Sisters[66] collect [money] themselves, and the people who know and like them so well will support them generously. Four Sisters, two English and two Polish—even three English, and one Polish—would do for both schools.[67]

As far as Bishop Shaw was concerned, however, the matter had ended earlier. In a letter to Father Spetz, Bishop Shaw concluded:

However much the Reverend Mother [Mother M. Anna] may express the hope that her action did not cause the pastor much trouble, I must say that it caused a great deal of trouble to him and annoyance to me . . . As far as I am concerned, the matter is closed.[68]

Matters were not destined to remain calm in Falls City. Further dissension followed and in late July of that year, Bishop Shaw was forced to send a notice to the School Committee of Holy Trinity Parish:

Gentlemen:

As all Church property, of whatever kind, in the diocese is vested in the Bishop of the diocese, who holds the same in trust for the different parishes, and as the Bishop is represented in the parishes by the Reverend Pastors, I now, in virtue of the authority given me by the Holy See as the Bishop of the diocese of San Antonio, direct and command that you put your Reverend Pastor—the Reverend A. A. Hubsch, DD—in full possession of the Parish School in Falls City by surrendering the keys of the same to him without further delay as becomes loyal and obedient children of the Church.

The question of procuring suitable teachers for the school is one that concerns the Bishop who is charged with the task of supervising Christian Education in the diocese. We are making every effort to provide Sisters for the coming school year.

We regret to tell you that the debt on the school building still remains unpaid. As this debt could have been paid easily long ago, it is unfair to your Bishop who went your security on the Note to oblige him to humble himself by asking the bank for an extension of time. I have had to do this already several times, and I am pained to know that I must do it again on the 8th of August. As the interest in the past year is due then also, you must take means to send me the interest before that date, as I do not feel under any obligation to pay the debts of your parish. In this matter, the good name and reputation of the parish is at stake, to say nothing of the honor due to your Bishop.

In writing to you, Gentlemen, this letter, I have no intention to question your motives, but I have felt that it was my duty to remind you of your obligations as children of the Church. Your ready compliance with the command of your Bishop will prove your loyalty and reverence for authority.

Assuring you, Gentlemen, that I have for you and the parish only the kindliest feelings, I am yours sincerely,

J. W. Shaw

Bishop of San Antonio[69]

Shortly after the departure of the Franciscan Sisters of Chicago and in the midst of Holy Trinity parish's "standoff" with its pastor, Father Hubsch, a deplorable incident occurred. Father Hubsch was dragged from a train and whipped by members of the Holy Trinity School Committee. Some parishioners blamed him for the Sisters' leaving. Other parishioners were angered over the supposition that Father Hubsch had spoken out against some of the relatives of the School Community in a sermon. Many unfounded reasons and arguments were offered. Others were spreading foolish and scandalous tales about Father Hubsch. The truth of the matter was that the incessant quarreling among the residents of Falls City had never ceased thereby giving rise to all its attendant problems. In all actuality, Mother M. Anna Wysinski had recalled the Sisters from Falls City after prudently analyzing the situation with her general council and with Father Spetz. The archives of the congregation contain letters to support this position. Again, the parishioners' attitude toward their legitimate pastors and their appointed bishop was less than edifying. As a consequence of the deplorable whipping incident concerning Father Hubsch, seven men of the parish were eventually excommunicated. The pastor, Father Hubsch, was removed and the church and school were closed until it could be proven to the bishop that the whole parish and those excommunicated had repented for their odious conduct. An emissary from Bishop Shaw was sent to inform the parishioners of the action that the bishop was obliged to take in the parish of Falls City much "to his great sorrow":

> I must tell you that there has been a great deal of trouble in Falls City with the priests in the past and also that some of the people have not treated the Bishop with proper respect. The Bishop knows very well that many of the people, perhaps most of them, are good and pious and obedient children of the Church; for these he is sorry but he feels that the whole parish must learn that he will not stand for any priest or Sister to be put in danger of their lives as is the case with Father Hubsch. The Bishop, therefore, wishes me to tell you that he is sorry but he is obliged to close the church and school until further notice.[70]

The Franciscan Sisters of Chicago left Texas in 1914, and the parish schools in Falls City were not in operation for twelve years after the Sisters departed. In 1924, however, the Congregation of the Sisters of Charity of the Incarnate Word and Blessed Sacrament reopened the school. St. Stanislaus Kostka School closed permanently in 1940, and Holy Trinity remained open until 1944.[71]

According to the *Community Chronicle*, the Reverend Joseph Szymanski, the pastor of Holy Trinity Church in 1918, had written to Mother M. Aloysia Holysz, the superior general at that time, requesting the Franciscan Sisters of Chicago to return to his parochial school. The request was refused and the only missionary venture of the Franciscan Sisters of Chicago in Texas truly became a part of the congregation's fruitful and grace-laden past.

FROM ILLINOIS TO TEXAS

[1]*Commemorative Book: The Diamond Jubilee of St. Stanislaus Parish* (Posen, Illinois: St. Stanislaus Parish, 1970), p. 12.

[2]The Right Reverend Monsignor Stanislaus Nawrocki was a secular priest associated with the ministry of the Congregation of the Resurrection in the United States. Born in Poland, he studied theology in Rome and Baltimore, Maryland. He was ordained in Chicago in 1887. His ordination mass was held at St. Stanislaus Kostka Church where he worked for three months after which he was assigned to St. Mary of Perpetual Help Church in the area known as Bridgeport.

In 1866, the Reverend Vincent Barzynski and the Reverend John Radziejewski were instrumental in establishing St. Joseph's Church on the Southwest Side of Chicago in the area known as Town of Lake. Because of a shortage of Resurrectionist clergy, Father Nawrocki was appointed its first permanent pastor in 1889. He served in this capacity until 1891. In May of that year, he returned to St. Mary of Perpetual Help Church at the suggestion of Father Barzynski and assumed the pastorate. Under his direction, St. Mary of Perpetual Help Church experienced phenomenal growth and became one of the largest parishes in the archdiocese. During his tenure as pastor, Father Nawrocki was also instrumental in establishing St. Stanislaus Bishop and Martyr Church in Posen, Illinois, in 1895. In 1917, he was elevated to the rank of domestic prelate by Pope Benedict XV in recognition of his pastoral work. Father Nawrocki remained pastor of St. Mary of Perpetual Help Church until his death in 1921. John J. Iwicki, CR, *The First One Hundred Years: A Study of the Apostolate of the Congregation of the Resurrection in the United States 1866–1966* (Rome: Gregorian University Press, 1966), pp. 78, 104.

[3]Ibid., p. 104.

[4]*Minutes of General Council Proceedings,* 10 January 1915 (AFSCL).

[5]*Golden Jubilee Book of St. Stanislaus Parish* (Posen, Illinois, 1944), no pagination.

[6]It may be difficult to believe, but the renovated convent building was first provided with running water in 1938 according to Siostra Maria Cyryla, CSSF, *Wśród Dusz Dla Dusz 1910–1953: Dzieje i Dorobek* (Chicago: Nakładem Sióstr Felicjanek, 1953), p. 52.

[7]See Appendix H.

[8]*Book of Annual Assignments* (AFSCL).

[9]*Book of Correspondence:* St. Stanislaus Bishop and Martyr School, Posen, Illinois, Letters from Sister M. Dominic Maka to Mother M. Anna Wysinski, 11 February 1916; to Mother M. Aloysia Holysz, 11 June 1916 (AFSCL).

[10]*Minutes of General Council Proceedings, 1910–1934* (AFSCL).

[11]*Interview* with Mr. Albert Chohrek, Trustee, Village of Posen, 22 November 1975 (AFSCL).

[12]*Złoty Jubileusz Parafii Św. Jacka* (La Salle, Illinois: St. Hyacinth Press, 1925), p. 8.

[13]*St. Roch's Diamond Jubilee* (La Salle, Illinois: St. Roch's Parish, 1975), no pagination.

[14]*Book of Correspondence:* Letter to author from Sister M. Alacoque, Sisters of St. Francis of Assisi, Milwaukee, Wisconsin, 11 February 1976 (AFSCL).

[15]Siostra M. Gonzaga Raniszewski, OSFK, *Rys historyczny Zgromadzenia Sióstr Franciszkanek Błogosławionej Kunegundy. Część pierwsza, 1860–1910* [A historical survey of the Franciscan Sisters of Blessed Kunegunda. Part one, 1860–1910] (Chicago: By the Author), p. 136.

[16]*Book of Closed Schools and Institutions* (AFSCL).

[17]*Minutes of General Council Proceedings,* 27 April 1913 (AFSCL).

[18]*Interview* with the Reverend Michael Zeleznikar, pastor of St. Roch's Church, La Salle, Illinois, 26 October 1976 (AFSCL).

[19]*St. Roch's Diamond Jubilee,* no pagination.

[20]*Book of Correspondence:* Letter to author from Sister M. Denise, secretary, Mount Assisi Convent, Lemont, Illinois, 6 April 1976 (AFSCL).

[21]*Book of Correspondence:* Letter to author from Sister M. Charlotte Conklin, OSB, La Salle, Illinois, 23 May 1976 (AFSCL).

[22]See Chapter 3 for the settlement of Panna Maria.

[23]T. Lindsay Baker, "The Early History of Panna Maria, Texas," (Ph.D. dissertation, Texas Tech University, 1975), p. 54.

[24]Reverend Edward Dworaczyk, *The First Polish Colonies in Texas* (San Antonio: The Naylor Co., 1936).

[25]Cestohowa is the Anglicized spelling of Częstochowa, the village in Poland where the famous shrine of the patroness of the Polish people, Our Lady of Częstochowa, is located and after which the settlers named their village in Texas.

[26]Wacław Kruszka, *Historya Polska w Ameryce,* tom VI [The History of the Poles in America, vol. 6] (Milwaukee: Kuryer Press, 1905), p. 150.

[27]*Interview* with Mrs. Rose Esparza, wife of Adam Esparza, president of the Church Committee of Holy Trinity Church, Falls City, Texas, January 1976 (AFSCL).

[28]The Most Reverend John William Shaw, bishop of San Antonio, was appointed the coadjutor bishop of San Antonio on February 10, 1910. He succeeded to the See of San Antonio on March 11, 1911. At this time in history, the diocese was still largely a missionary one. Bishop Shaw left San Antonio in 1918 to become archbishop of New Orleans. He labored there until his death on November 2, 1934. *Archdiocese of San Antonio, 1874–1974* (San Antonio, 1974), pp. 183–184.

[29]Reverend S. Frog served as pastor of Holy Trinity Church until 1910. He was replaced by the Reverend John Karcz who served from 1910 to 1912. Reverend Edward Dworaczyk, *The First Polish Colonies in Texas* (San Antonio, The Naylor Co., 1936), p. 144.

[30]*Book of Correspondence:* The Reverend John Karcz to the Most Reverend John Shaw, 3 October 1910 (Archives of the Archdiocese of San Antonio; AFSCL).

[31]*Archdiocese of San Antonio: Diamond Jubilee, 1874–1949* (San Antonio, 1949), p. 253.

[32]While the letter can be found in the archives of the Franciscan Sisters of Chicago, it is not addressed to a particular Sister. The salution is simply "Reverend Sister." *Book of Correspondence:* Letter from the Reverend John Karcz to an unknown Franciscan Sister of Chicago (AFSCL).

[33]The Krawiec family was one of the pioneer families of Cestohowa, Texas. Three daughters had even entered the Congregation of the Sisters of Charity of the Incarnate Word in San Antonio. No doubt it was Father Felix Zwiardowski (see Chapter 3) who supplied Mrs. Krawiec with the name of a Franciscan Sister of Chicago since Father Zwiardowski knew the Sisters very well. In "The History of Cestohowa Parish," *Centennial History of the Founding of the Nativity of the Blessed Virgin Mary Parish in Częstochowa, Texas, 1873–1973,* no pagination, the name is spelled *Krawietz.*

[34]*Book of Correspondence:* Letter from the Reverend Karcz to an unknown Franciscan Sister of Chicago (AFSCL).

[35]*Book of Correspondence:* Letter from the Most Reverend John Karcz to the Most Reverend John Shaw, 10 November 1910 (Archives of the Archdiocese of San Antonio; AFSCL).

[36]*Book of Correspondence:* Letter from the Reverend John Karcz to the Reverend Andrew Spetz, 14 October 1910 (AFSCL).

[37]*Book of Correspondence:* Letter from the Reverend John Karcz to Mother M. Anna Wysinski, 17 March 1911 (AFSCL).

[38]The original Contract is reproduced here with all its errors.

[39]*Book of Correspondence:* Letter from the Reverend John Karcz to the Reverend Andrew Spetz, 9 April 1911 (AFSCL).

[40]Once again, the Agreement is reproduced here with all its errors.

[41]*Book of Contracts:* (Archives of the Archdiocese of San Antonio, 5 June 1911; AFSCL).

[42]*Book of Correspondence:* Letter from the Reverend John Karcz to Mother M. Anna Wysinski, 9 July 1911 (AFSCL).

[43]*Book of Correspondence:* Letter from the Reverend John Karcz to Mother M. Anna Wysinski, 31 July 1911 (AFSCL).

[44]On a visit to Falls City in January of 1976, the author spoke with Mrs. Bernice Huehlefield who had been a pupil at Holy Trinity School. Mrs. Huehlefield recalled both Sister M. Paul Kirschbaum and Sister M. Bonaventure Blazek, in particular, as "wonderful Sisters." *Interview* with Mrs. Bernice Huehlefield, former pupil at Holy Trinity School, Falls City, Texas, January 1976 (AFSCL).

[45]*Book of Annual Assignments* (AFSCL).

[46]Father Karcz himself had complained to Bishop Shaw on December 28, 1910, in regard to families who wanted their children to receive Holy Communion "without having had any knowledge of religion whatsoever." *Book of Correspondence:* Letter from the Reverend John Karcz to the Most Reverend John Shaw, 28 December 1910 (Archives of the Archdiocese of San Antonio; AFSCL).

[47]*Book of Correspondence:* Letter from J. W. Szalwinski, secretary, and F. A. Pawelek, treasurer of the Holy Trinity Catholic Parochial School Committee to the Most Reverend John Shaw (Archives of the Archdiocese of San Antonio; AFSCL).

[48]Jacek Przygoda, *Texas Pioneers from Poland: A Study in Ethnic History* (De Kalb, Illinois: Northern Illinois University Press, 1981), p. 54.

[49]*Book of Correspondence:* Letter from Sister M. Vincent Czyzewski to the Most Reverend John Shaw, 26 February 1912 (AFSCL).

[50]*Book of Correspondence:* Letter from J. G. Schulz, Schulz Mercantile Co., Falls City, Texas, to Mrs. S. W. Huddleston, Cuaro, Texas, 11 March 1912 (Archives of the Archdiocese of San Antonio; AFSCL).

[51]*Book of Correspondence:* Letter from Alamo Lumber Co. to the Most Reverend John Shaw, 21 March 1911 (Archives of the Archdiocese of San Antonio; AFSCL).

[52]*Book of Correspondence:* Letter from the Most Reverend John Shaw to the parishioners of Holy Trinity Church, May 1911 (Archives of the Archdiocese of San Antonio; AFSCL).

[53]*Interview* with Mrs. Rose Esparza, January 1976.

[54]*Book of Correspondence:* Letter from the Most Reverend John Shaw to the Reverend Arthur Hubsch, 11 September 1912 (Archives of the Archdiocese of San Antonio; AFSCL).

[55]*Book of Correspondence:* Letter from the Reverend Hubsch to the Most Reverend John Shaw, 17 September 1912 (Archives of the Archdiocese of San Antonio; AFSCL).

[56]Ibid.

[57]*Book of Contracts:* (Archives of the Archdiocese of San Antonio, 24 November 1911; AFSCL).

[58]Sister M. Bonaventure Blazek was born on July 31, 1886, in Chicago. She was a member of the St. Stanislaus Kostka Church when she was admitted to the postulancy on July 2, 1903. She was accepted into the novitiate on July 27, 1904, pronounced her first vows on August 2, 1905, and made her final profession during her illness on October 31, 1912.

In persistent ill health, Sister M. Bonaventure was sent to recuperate at St. Joseph Sanatorium and Hospital in Alburquerque, New Mexico, conducted by the Congregation of the Sisters of Charity of Cincinnati, Ohio. She remained there from October 1905 until August 1906. Upon her return to the Motherhouse in Chicago, she was sent to St. Casimir's School in St. Louis, Missouri, where she taught from 1906 to 1907. She entered the St. Joseph Sanatorium again in 1909 and returned to Chicago a year later. In 1911, she was assigned to Holy Trinity School, not as a member of the staff, but to recuperate in the healthful climate. At her death, Sister M. Bonaventure was twenty-seven years old and had been in the community for ten years. *Spis Sióstr* (AFSCL).

[59]*Book of Correspondence:* Letter from the Franciscan Sisters of Chicago to the Most Reverend John Shaw, 26 September 1913 (AFSCL).

[60]*Book of Correspondence:* Letter from the Most Reverend John Shaw to the Franciscan Sisters of Chicago, 29 September 1913 (AFSCL).

[61]*Minutes of General Council Proceedings,* 27 April 1914 (AFSCL).

[62]*Book of Correspondence:* Letter from the Reverend Spetz to the Most Reverend John Shaw, 11 June 1914 (AFSCL).

[63]*Minutes of General Council Proceedings,* 14 June 1914 (AFSCL).

[64]*Book of Correspondence:* Letter from the Franciscan Sisters to the Reverend Arthur Hubsch, 11 July 1914 (AFSCL).

[65]By August of 1914, Bishop Shaw had reached his "breaking point" with the parishioners who insisted on having Polish Sisters at the parish. He sent a letter to Father Hubsch which indicated his sentiments: "If the Polish parishes are so insistent on having Polish Sisters, why do they not give some of their daughters to the religious life? It would be well for you to speak of this matter to the people when the occasion offers itself." *Book of Correspondence:* Letter from the Most Reverend John Shaw to the Reverend Arthur Hubsch, 19 September 1914 (Archives of the Archdiocese of San Antonio; AFSCL); *Book of Correspondence:* Letter from the Most Reverend John Shaw to the Reverend Andrew Spetz, 17 July (AFSCL).

[66]Here Father Hubsch is no doubt referring to the Congregation of the Sisters of Charity of the Incarnate Word and Blessed Sacrament whose Motherhouse was located in Victoria, Texas, but who, nonetheless, labored in apostolates in the Diocese of San Antonio.

[67]*Book of Correspondence:* Letter from the Reverend Arthur Hubsch to the Most Reverend John Shaw, 16 July 1914 (Archives of the Archdiocese of San Antonio; AFSCL).

[68]*Book of Correspondence:* Letter from the Most Reverend John Shaw to the Reverend Andrew Spetz, 14 July 1914 (AFSCL).

[69]*Book of Correspondence:* Letter from the Most Reverend John Shaw to the School Committee of Holy Trinity Parish, Falls City, Texas, 31 July 1914 (Archives of the Archdiocese of San Antonio; AFSCL).

[70]*Book of Correspondence:* Address of Emissary of the Most Reverend John Shaw to the parishioners of Holy Trinity Parish, 1914 (Archives of the Archdiocese of San Antonio; AFSCL).

[71]*Archdiocese of San Antonio,* p. 176.

CHAPTER 23

School Apostolate Extension

The new year, 1912, opened with the death on January 24 of Sister M. Bernadine Narozny who had spent only three years in the congregation.[1] The year was to end with the death on November 10 of Sister M. Bonaventure Blazek who succumbed to tuberculosis.[2] In the interim, the congregation continued to grow in membership and to expand its teaching apostolate.

Several appeals from concerned pastors to staff their schools arrived in 1912, and, whenever possible, no appeal was left unanswered by Mother M. Anna Wysinski. The first of three schools undertaken by the congregation that year was Five Holy Martyrs on the Southwest Side of Chicago in the area known as Brighton Park. This was the Sisters' first educational venture into that particular section of the city, and it proved to be one of its most fruitful and rewarding.

During the first quarter of the twentieth century, the village of Brighton Park[3] grew from flooded prairies and clay holes to a community of great industrial and residential proportions. The steady influx of Poles, Lithuanians, and Italians in the older sections of the area displaced the Germans and the Irish who were moving to communities farther south. By 1930, Brighton Park's population had reached a peak wherein 37 percent of its residents were Poles.[4]

In November 1908, the Reverend John Kruszka, pastor of St. Mary of Gostyn Church in Downers Grove, Illinois, was authorized by the Most Reverend James E. Quigley, archbishop of Chicago, to organize a parish for the Polish-speaking Catholics[5] of Brighton Park in the specific vicinity of 41st Street and Archer Avenue.[6] Since there was discord among the parishioners over the central location of the church, Father Kruszka, upon assuming the pastorate, changed the location to west of Kedzie Avenue on 41st Street. By May of 1909, a combination church and school dedicated to the Five Holy Martyrs[7] was blessed by the newly consecrated auxiliary bishop of Chicago, the Most Reverend Paul P. Rhode. The parish, at that time, consisted of ninety-five families.[8] The school, with forty students, was staffed by lay teachers until the arrival of the Franciscan Sisters of Chicago who responded to Father Kruszka's earnest request to take charge.[9] Sent to Five Holy Martyrs School for the pioneer term of 1912–1913 were Sister M. Clara Ogurek, superior, principal, and teacher of grades three, four, and five; Sister Mary Welter, teacher of grades one and two; and Sister M. Anastasia Halcerz who was assigned to household duties. The rear section of the first floor of the school served as the Sisters' living quarters.[10] At the Silver Jubilee banquet of Five Holy Martyrs Church celebrated in 1937, Father Kruszka, the founding pastor, related to the assembled guests the difficulties he had had in securing Sisters for his school. He recalled that he had made his request of many congregations and they had refused him citing the lack of Sisters as the reason. Finally, he had made an appeal to Mother M. Anna Wysinski, who, moved by his touching plea in regard to the young children whose religion was being neglected, promised to send him three Sisters no matter what difficulties the congregation might encounter. At the banquet, Father Kruszka commended the pioneer Sisters and recalled the many hardships they had endured. In spite of these trials, the Sisters had carried on their apostolate with courage, sacrifice, and inexhaustible confidence in the Providence of God.[11]

For the first five years, the parish grew slowly. The rise of new industrial enterprises, however, particularly the Crane Company Plant at 41st Street and Kedzie Avenue, directly across the street from Five Holy Martyrs Church, brought thousands of workingmen, especially Poles and their families, to the Southwest Side community. By 1916, 308 children were enrolled in the school. As Brighton Park grew with the influx of new families into the neighborhood and as the business district shifted to Archer Avenue, it soon became evident that Five Holy Martyrs Church was not centrally located. It was in a location favorable to the parishioners who lived south of Archer Avenue; others had a considerable distance to walk to church. In addition, parents feared the hazards of sending their children such long distances to school with the necessity of crossing "busy" Archer Avenue.[12] To add to those inconveniences, the noise from the Crane Company combined with the noise of the streetcars on Kedzie Avenue proved to be a great distraction at church services.

It was very apparent that a more suitable plot of land had to be purchased and the entire church and school relocated. At the command of the Most Reverend George Mundelein, archbishop of Chicago, Father Kruszka secured a square block of property bounded by 43rd and 44th Streets, Richmond Street, and Francisco Avenue. The spacious area was ideal for growth and wide expansion. Father Kruszka set about once again to build a new church and a separate school consisting of twelve classrooms on 43rd and Richmond Streets.[13] When completed, the church and school were blessed and dedicated by Archbishop Mundelein on October 31, 1920.[14] In his address at the dedication, Archbishop Mundelein said quite prophetically: "My only regret today is that we did not make your new school twice as large as we have built it, for we will soon need it all."[15]

When Father Kruszka was transferred to St. Ann's Church on South Leavitt Street, the Reverend James J. Strzycki became the pastor of Five Holy Martyrs Church in April of 1921. Sister M. Benigna Jakajtis, the superior and principal who had been appointed in 1919, was scheduled to attend The Catholic Sisters College in Washington,

Five Holy Martyrs Convent
Chicago, Illinois

Five Holy Martyrs School
Chicago, Illinois (1912–   )

DC, in 1921, as a full-time student. Since he was newly appointed, Father Strzycki begged her to stay at Five Holy Martyrs Parish; with permission she remained until 1925. In his thirty-five year pastorate, Father Strzycki proved to be an indefatigable worker, concerned as much over the material growth of the large parish as well as with its spiritual welfare. His first years were marked by the immediate building of key parish facilities. He erected a badly needed rectory for the parish priests who were still living in the cramped quarters in the school. Immediately thereafter, he directed construction of the spacious and practical convent with the familiar frosted glass windows. With the erection of the convent, the Sisters were no longer forced to commute each day from their living quarters in the old church building on 41st Street near Kedzie Avenue. That had proved to be vastly inconvenient and time consuming. When the new Five Holy Martyrs Church and School were relocated at 43rd and Richmond Streets, the original building at 41st Street and Kedzie Avenue continued to be used as a parochial hall and temporary auxiliary school. In 1924, when St. Pancratius Parish was established to serve the Polish families who had settled in the area north of Archer Avenue, the old Five Holy Martyrs church-school combination at 41st Street and Kedzie Avenue was given over to the new parish. As a consequence, a new addition to Five Holy Martyrs which provided a parish hall for recreational, social, and cultural activities was built on Francisco Avenue. It was dedicated by the newly appointed Cardinal Mundelein on May 17, 1925. For the many young people of the parish Father Strzycki provided, in the basement of the Francisco Avenue Building, what must have seemed revolutionary at the time and was certainly not to be had in any other parish in the archdiocese—a bowling alley with eight lanes. To continue to meet the needs of the children of the parish and to keep them from engaging in juvenile pranks, Monsignor Strzycki established a recreation center which was dedicated on July 17, 1938. The athletic field included baseball diamonds, a boxing ring, and ample playground space. One of the principal speakers at the dedication ceremony was the Honorable Edward J. Kelly, the mayor of Chicago.[16]

Enrollment in Five Holy Martyrs School continued to surge. By the 1928–29 school year, approximately 1,780 students were enrolled with a faculty of thirty Sisters. In 1930, the school reached its peak enrollment with 1,847 students and a staff of thirty-three Sisters. In order to accommodate all those who desired to be enrolled, an addition of four classrooms was made to the Francisco Avenue Building, and, finally, a four-room building, commonly referred to as the "Bungalow," was erected between the rectory and the Francisco Avenue Building.[17] That same year, the death of Sister M. Chrysostom Keller occurred.[18] Sent to Five Holy Martyrs School in October of 1927, she remained until February of 1930 at which time she returned to the Motherhouse. She died there on June 27, 1930, of tuberculosis in the twelfth year of her religious profession.

When adequate facilities for the large parish had been constructed, Father Strzycki looked to the spiritual and social welfare of his parishioners with extraordinary zeal. Civic, social, and religious organizations and societies were promoted. Girl and Boy Scouts, the CYO (Catholic Youth Organization), the Brighton Park Civic and

Improvement Association were all eagerly supported by Father Strzycki. The St. Cecilia Choir, with juvenile and adult divisions under the direction of Mr. Clarence Rybowiak, became popular. The St. James Athletic Club, named after Father James Strzycki, was famous throughout the city.[19] During the worst years of the nation's Depression, Father Strzycki proved himself a champion of the poor. He opened a free employment bureau and went to the heads of over seventy industries soliciting work for his people. He obtained employment for over three hundred of his parishioners and even employed some parishioners to landscape the parish grounds at the rate of thirty cents an hour.[20]

On November 19, 1934, in the year of the Silver Jubilee of the parish, George Cardinal Mundelein dedicated the "chapel" addition to Five Holy Martyrs Church and invested Father Strzycki as a papal chamberlain with the title of Very Reverend Monsignor. That year, the school enrollment was 1,497 with thirty-five Sisters in residence. Once again death reached out to touch the staff at Five Holy Martyrs School and claimed the life of Sister M. Ignatia Hodkiewicz[21] who died on September 5, 1934, at St. Mary of Nazareth Hospital in Chicago following an operation. Sister M. Ignatia who had been in the classroom for less than a week had just been transferred to Five Holy Martyrs from Sacred Heart Parish in Cleveland where she had completed a year as superior and principal. Another death occurred in 1937, when Sister M. Dominic Makowski died on February 10 at St. Mary of Nazareth Hospital also following an operation.[22]

On July 28, 1956, Monsignor Strzycki, the "Champion of Youth," died.[23] At that time more than 2,500 families belonged to Five Holy Martyrs Parish. Five months after Monsignor Strzycki's death, the Reverend Edward A. Maday[24] was appointed the new pastor. Armed with pastoral and administrative ability, Father Maday directed an extensive program of renovation during which most of the parish buildings were updated. The no-longer serviceable bowling alley was converted into a modern social hall. The abandoned "Bungalow" was made into a recreational hall and the Sisters' convent was moderately renovated. When Five Holy Martyrs Parish celebrated its Golden Jubilee in 1959, there were 3,800 families on the parish roster and 918 children in the school. Father Maday received permission to remodel and enlarge the church in 1963. The nave of the church was lengthened, and a new sanctuary was constructed as part of the modernization program. In July of 1968, Father Maday asked permission to resign his pastorate because of ill health. He died two months later on September 5, 1968. By that time, Five Holy Martyrs Parish had seen the deaths of several unselfish and dedicated women who had gone to their eternal reward while ministering to the needs of the parish and its youth. They were: Sister M. Monica Frankowski (May 16, 1953);[25] Sister M. Bibianna Wiza (February 26, 1960);[26] and Sister M. Cyprian Lewandowski (January 24, 1964);[27] and Sister M. Conrad Kempisty (January 4, 1967).[28] The last Sister to die while missioned at Five Holy Martyrs School was Sister M. Eugenia Detlaf who expired on May 25, 1973.[29]

On June 15, 1968, the same day as his appointment by Pope Paul VI as auxiliary bishop of Chicago, the Most Reverend Alfred L. Abramowicz[30] was named pastor of Five Holy Martyrs Church. During his pastorate, he concluded the renovation program begun by his predecessor. The school buildings were refurbished, and the hall of the Francisco Avenue Building was made into a gymnasium. The chapel, dining room, kitchen, and laundry of the convent were also completely renovated.

In 1979, the world learned that Pope John Paul II planned to visit several cities in the United States.[31] The parishioners at Five Holy Martyrs were overjoyed when it was announced that their parish had been selected as the site of an open-air mass to be celebrated by the Holy Father on Friday, October 5, 1979, as part of his three-day visit to Chicago. Pope John Paul II was no stranger to Chicago or to Five Holy Martyrs Parish for that matter. As the archbishop of Cracow, he had visited Chicago in 1969 and again in 1976, America's Centennial Year. On both occasions, he slept in the rectory of Five Holy Martyrs Parish. In preparation for the Pope's visit to Brighton Park in 1979, parishioners and home-owners decorated their homes with papal posters and other signs of welcome. More than 17,500 persons representing predominantly Polish parishes, organizations, and institutions of the Archdiocese of Chicago participated in the special mass which was held in the large parking lot of Five Holy Martyrs Parish. A history of the parishes in the Archdiocese of Chicago records the event:

> Speaking in his native tongue, the Pope told the assembled crowd that their offertory gifts represented "all the contributions that the sons and daughters of our first homeland, Poland, have made to the history and to the life of their second homeland across the ocean."[32]

To commemorate the visit of the Holy Father to Five Holy Martyrs Parish, Jane Byrne, then the mayor of Chicago, sponsored the proposal of the Democratic Committeeman, Theodore Swinarski, to have the name of West 43rd Street changed to West Pope John Paul II Drive. The street name change was enacted in the City Council, and as of January 16, 1980, that portion of West 43rd Street which extends from Kedzie to Western Avenue bears the name of the beloved first Polish pope.

As in all the schools conducted by the Franciscan Sisters of Chicago, the Sisters' total involvement in the parish ministry oftentimes extended beyond the classroom. Among the many activities performed by the Sisters at Five Holy Martyrs Parish throughout the years have been caring for the sanctuary and the sacristy in the church, training the altar boys, and conducting both the children's and the young ladies' choirs. As an adjunct of their teaching apostolate, the Sisters have provided catechetical instruction for public school children by means of the Confraternity of Christian Doctrine (CCD) classes, and the preparation of public school children for the Sacrament of Reconciliation and of the Holy Eucharist. In Five Holy Martyrs School itself, the Sisters had always encouraged the pursuit of the arts, and to that effect, had presented the school children in many and varied dramatic and musical entertainments. For many years, the Sisters also provided opportunities for the pupils of Five Holy Martyrs School to enhance their musical ability by providing instruction on the piano and other musical instruments, and particularly by forming the famed Five Holy Martyrs Band.

Five Holy Martyrs School has always cared about academic excellence. This excellence was the result of fine teachers and teaching methods. Sister M. Alvernia Groszek, who was stationed at the school, held the office of president of the Chicago First Grade Organization (CFGO) from 1950 to 1953, the aim of which was to unify and solidify the first grade teachers in the Archdiocese of Chicago. On April 21 to 23, 1950, a convention arranged with expertise by Sister M. Alvernia was held in Chicago for kindergarten teachers. In 1951, St. Joseph School in Wilmette, Illinois, was the locale of a demonstration of the Chicago First Grade Association. Mother M. Jerome and her general councilors were in attendance together with numerous Sisters from Chicago and Indiana schools. Samuel Cardinal Stritch, the archbishop of Chicago, addressed the association urging the members to continue their excellent work. Among the Sisters who took part in the special program were Sister M. Crescentine Oszuscik, St. Stanislaus Bishop and Martyr School, "First Phonics Demonstration, the Alphabet"; Sister M. Rosaline Lenart, St. Mary School, Hammond, Indiana, "Second Phonics Demonstration, the Vowels"; Sister M. Agnella Sieja, Five Holy Martyrs School, "Third Phonics Demonstration, Consonants, Blends, and Digraphs." In August of 1951, the program was demonstrated at St. Joseph and St. Anne School, Chicago, with hundreds of Sisters from various congregations in attendance. A highly successful physical education workshop was presented at Five Holy Martyrs School by Miss Louise Curtiss, a physical education expert. The workshop, held on August 25, 1951, had as "pupils" such persons as Mother M. Jerome Dadej, Mother M. Antonina Osinski, Sister M. Gonzaga Raniszewski, and more than one hundred Sisters.

Since 1970, the Franciscan Sisters of Chicago stationed at Five Holy Martyrs School have been engaged in works which are new to the congregation. Two Sisters who are actively engaged in ministerial service to the parish outside the classroom are Sister Clarent Marie Urbanowicz and Sister M. Rosalima Sierocki. Since 1975, Sister Clarent Marie has taught English as a second language to scores of newly arrived immigrants in the evening division at Richard Daley College. For many years, Sister M. Rosalima has given excellent service as Elderly Group Aide for the City of Chicago in the Department of Aging and Disability.

Five Holy Martyrs Parish has always been vitally alive with missions, novenas, penitential services, and various liturgies designed to meet the spiritual needs of its parishioners. It is also one of the parishes which has provided the Archdiocese of Chicago with many priests and religious Sisters and Brothers.[33]

Brighton Park continues to be a community of upwardly mobile ethnic groups. Because of the large influx of Polish immigrants into the area within the last fifteen years, Bishop Abramowicz has stressed the ethnicity of Five Holy Martyrs Parish. The Polish language is taught in the parish school and traditional Polish customs on Sundays and weekdays. During the last ten years, however, the Spanish-speaking groups have also begun to move into this area. Today, Five Holy Martyrs School has an enrollment of approximately five hundred pupils under the direction of seven Sisters and sixteen lay teachers who continue to provide the finest apostolic witness to Catholic education.

After agreeing to staff Five Holy Martyrs School in Chicago, the Sisters next turned their apostolic attention to the first of several schools which they were to staff eventually in Pennsylvania.

As early as 1880, the Pennsylvania coal region had a Polish population of 1,900. Twenty years later, the population had soared to nearly thirty thousand.[34] Located in the iron-rich Conemaugh Valley at the foot of the Allegheny Mountains, the "new, rough and busy" town of Johnstown in Cambria County welcomed the influx of Poles who arrived at the turn of the century to seek employment and establish homes.[35]

The early settlers of Johnstown worshipped at St. Stephen's Slovak Church, but in 1892, the Polish immigrants formed St. Casimir's Lodge which had as its aim the establishment of a parish for Polish-speaking people. After the establishment of the Diocese of Altoona[36] in 1901, the Poles petitioned the Most Reverend Eugene Garvey, the first bishop of Altoona, for permission to establish a church. On May 20, 1902, the Reverend Bronislaus Dembinski arrived from the Diocese of Scranton, and a month later, construction of the basement church and a rectory was begun. By August of 1907, the upper church structure was completed.[37]

In January of 1903, St. Casimir's Parochial School was opened in a section of the basement separated from the church by a partition. The organist, Mr. Szymanski, served as the first schoolteacher. For the next ten years, the school existed under the tutorship of dedicated lay people. In the early part of 1912, however, Father Dembinski set about to engage a congregation of Polish-speaking Sisters who would assume supervision of the school. His initial attempts all ended in failure. Finally, he wrote to the Most Reverend Paul P. Rhode, the auxiliary bishop of Chicago, for assistance, and following his instructions, Father Dembinski dispatched a letter to Mother M. Anna Wysinski petitioning for the services of the Franciscan Sisters of Chicago and giving her a vivid description of the area:

> Reverend Mother:
> I ask you cordially to accept our school in September. At the beginning I would need five Sisters and a cook. The parish is not old, only about ten years. Presently there are many youths here, about seven hundred, who came here four to six years ago. From time to time, I will need more Sisters. Presently there are in school about 250 to 275 pupils. Our town is the largest in the diocese, although the Cathedral is in Altoona. This is a factory town about a two-hour drive east of Pittsburgh. Here are located the steel works of the Cambria Steel Company, owned by the Pennsylvania Railroad and employing about twenty-two thousand workers. We have smaller factories also. The work is steady and the

parish grows year by year. To the Sister-teachers, I will give my rectory as a home which has many conveniences, twenty-five dollars a month, the Koleda[38] from Christmas which brings in about $150 to $200, for which the Sisters will provide wafers for the altar and take care of the altars, and, at the end of the year, one of the house collections. Presently, I am building a new rectory and the present one will be available for occupancy on September 1.

Please answer.

Your servant in Christ,
Father B. Dembinski[39]

A week later, Father Dembinski sent another letter to Mother M. Anna assuring her that "you will not be sorry if you take this school."[40] On April 30, 1912, he received a special delivery letter from Mother M. Anna with an affirmative response to his plea. That same day, Father Dembinski rushed to reply:

> I received your letter "Special Delivery" today for which I heartily thank you. I have hopes that Reverend Mother will settle the matter. I am willing to settle for four Sisters for the first year if I have to instead of five Sisters. I will wait with pleasure for a week or ten days for your decision.[41]

The first Sisters arrived in September of 1912, and occupied the old rectory on Power Street vacated by Father Dembinski.[42] The Sisters sent to St. Casimir's School were Sister M. Chester Dziarnowski, superior and principal; Sister M. Dionysia Kujanek, Sister M. Angela Jasinski, and Sister M. Salesia Rzeszutko. Sister M. Lauretta Partyka, who was sent to attend to household duties, remained only until November 12. Because of illness, she was replaced by Sister M. Isidore Wilkos.[43] When the Sisters arrived, classes were still being conducted in the basement of the church and consisted of six grades with two hundred students enrolled. Through diligent efforts on the part of the parishioners and the pastor, a new six-room school was completed at Chestnut Street and Fifth Avenue in September of 1913.[44] One of the Sisters who arrived in 1916 as part of the teaching staff was Sister M. Theodore Laski. At the end of the school year in June of 1918, she was forced to return to the Motherhouse in Chicago where she died on August 17 of tuberculosis.[45]

By 1921, there were 575 pupils in the school. In order to accommodate the growing student enrollment, a second story was added to the school in 1925 during the pastorate of the Reverend Ladislaus Finke. As late as 1928, there were still over five hundred children enrolled.[46]

A great disaster befell Johnstown on March 17, 1936. A flood occurred which made the city of Johnstown national news.[47] The Johnstown area had been buried in heavy snowfalls throughout most of the winter. It rained heavily for weeks in the spring. The

*St. Casimir Convent
Johnstown, Pennsylvania*

*St. Casimir / West End Catholic
Consolidation School
Johnstown, Pennsylvania (1912–1982)*

Conemaugh River and Stony Creek, taxed beyond their capacity to contain the surging waters, overflowed their contents throughout the Conemaugh Valley. Consequently, many boroughs in Johnstown were hit by the flooding. It appears that Cambria City, where St. Casimir's parish was located, received the full brunt from both rivers and took what can best be described as a "terrible beating." It is estimated that thirty lives were lost and property damage was listed at $40 million.[48]

The Sisters stationed at St. Casimir's lived through the devastating flood and its tragic aftermath. A letter sent to Mother M. Antonina Osinski from Mother M. Aloysia, the superior and principal of St. Casimir's School, contained the sad details:

Reverend Mother General:

Without a doubt, you have already learned what has happened here. God has protected us and we are well enough. Although the people here are in a bad way themselves, their generous hearts are concerned about us and what they can do to keep us from hunger.

On Tuesday, March 17, at one o'clock in the afternoon, the sky darkened and the foreboding of disaster was felt. In town, some streets were already drenched with rain. In this area, the water had already covered the grass. Quickly, we sent the children home. We then began to take foodstuffs to the attic and other articles we could save. We never realized things could get so bad. Almost everything is destroyed. The "ice box" is overturned as are the chapel organ, piano, and even the altar. The religious statues, except that of the Blessed Virgin Mary, are broken. The water rose in the convent basement to the level of sixteen feet. On the first floor, the water rose six feet high. By seven o'clock in the evening, the flood waters had reached the convent porch and were pouring into the convent. I took the Blessed Sacrament to the second floor of the convent and there at two o'clock in the morning we waited and prayed. Finally, it stopped raining and about two-thirty o'clock we noticed that the water was receding and rather quickly at that. We began to remove some of the mud and slime the waters had left behind when about noon, an alarm was sounded. We were warned to head for higher areas. At once, from all sides, the good people offered us shelter in their homes. A farmer took six of the Sisters on a truck to his home; two Sisters were sheltered in another family's home; finally, four Sisters took shelter in a home across the river from the convent. The convent stood deserted with all its doors ajar.

Today is Saturday. Now there are four of us in Morrellville which is some distance from us but still in our parish; two Sisters are with another family, and Father Chraca[49] took four Sisters to Conemaugh. Everyday some of us returned to the convent to tidy up with some of the women of the parish. We cannot live there, however, because the gas and electricity are gone. The boiler was flooded and the coal was soaked. The telephone service is gone, the post-office is destroyed, and the trains are being re-routed. I wanted to call from a neighbor's phone during the flood, but it's a good thing I didn't go because I don't think I would have made it back. There are practically no people left on our street. They cannot live in their present homes so they were forced to move. Mrs. Kon came to ask for shoes because she was left shoeless as a result of the flood. Now she has moved away from us. Our church was saved, so on Thursday, a Mass was celebrated. Other churches are badly ruined. People are not allowed into Johnstown unless they have a "Pass" or are coming in to aid the victims of the flood.

None of our parishioners drowned but there are many who are seriously ill. The interior of the rectory is badly ruined like our convent. It rained practically all last night and today almost three inches of snow have fallen. Again there will be poverty and pain because now almost no one is working in this town. Please pray for all of us. With greetings to Reverend Mother and all the Sisters from all of us,

> Sincerely in the Sacred Heart,
> Your spiritual daughter,
> Mother M. Aloysia[50]

The Sisters lived through the ordeal of wreckage, ruin, mud, and demolished property. But the imminent fear of more flooding prevailed. A few days later, Mother M. Aloysia once again wrote to Mother M. Antonina:

Dear Mother:

After the "St. Patrick's Flood," the sky is almost continuously overcast. Sometimes the sun shines, but in a little while it is again overcast. Today we had a lot of rain during the night, and thus the day is again overcast. It is sad on the earth.

When Sister M. Theresia [the superior and principal at the Assumption of the Blessed Virgin Mary School in Conemaugh] received a letter from Reverend Mother and I found out that Reverend Mother did not have any information from us, I phoned you immediately. I thank you for your prayers. There are not recurring heavy rains. After all, it could have been worse. They say that there could still be another flood because there is a lot of snow in the mountains. God preserve us from that misfortune!

On Thursday, after phoning you, I went to Johnstown and I sent Sister M. Rosalie and Sister M. Hubert to [the convent of St. Stanislaus Kostka School] Youngstown. I wanted to send Sister M. Josephata and another Sister to Sacred Heart Parish in Cleveland or to Youngstown, but they did not want to leave. I sent Sister M. Ludmilla to Central City where her parents live. Sister M. Josephata, Sister M. Therese Agnes, and Sister M. Theophane went to parishioners in near-by Morrellville. To Conemaugh went Sister M. Clothilde, Sister M. Leontina, Sister M. Salesia and I.[51]

School will reopen after Easter. On Thursday, it was warm in the convent and in some bedrooms so we stayed overnight and tried to put the convent in order. Then we left for Conemaugh again. The streetcars still do not run nor is there any electricity. Our home is standing open because the doors expanded from the flood waters and cannot close. The Sisters are well and in somewhat good spirits. The people work everyday to remove the mud from the streets but it hasn't improved much. It is sad in Johnstown—you cannot see the children around. Everyone you meet is sad and weeping. O God, such desolation!

On Sunday, the pastor did not take up a collection—he told the parishioners to buy bread. He did not have a sermon because he felt like crying when he looked at the suffering people he later told us.

Your spiritual daughter,
Mother M. Aloysia

P.S. Our Beloved also hid from the flood. When we were wading in the water in the chapel, there was no alternative but to run to the second floor for safety. My heart was pounding—will the water run that high? I took the Blessed Sacrament upstairs with a prayer—"Jesus, forgive me, but at the same time, I beg You to protect us and keep us alive"—and through the water I took the Blessed Sacrament to the second floor near the statue of St. Francis and this was His throne during the night. Six candles and two vigil lights were constantly burning. The people could see this through their windows and they were happy thinking that this was a chapel and the Sisters were praying for them which, indeed, we were.

I am sorry that Reverend Mother did not receive our letters because this letter which I write is the third. Please excuse my errors—my thoughts run in all directions.

With sincere greetings,
Your spiritual daughter,
Mother M. Aloysia[52]

Although death overlooked the Sisters in Johnstown during the flood, it came, nevertheless, to the well-loved Sister M. Salesia Rzeszutko on February 1, 1937.[53] Sister M. Salesia, one of the pioneer Sisters sent to St. Casimir's School in 1912, died of pneumonia at Mercy Hospital in Johnstown. Her death was both beautiful and unusual.[54] Funeral services for the former teacher and organist were held in St. Casimir's Church and attended by a large group of Sisters and parishioners. Her body was then sent to the Motherhouse in Chicago where it was interred in St. Adalbert's Cemetery.

In 1940, there were only 227 children in the school. During the tenure of St. Casimir Parish's third pastor, the Reverend Casimir Ossowski, the school population maintained an even balance until the late 1960s.[55] With the entire Catholic school enrollment in Johnstown in gradual decline and in an effort to maintain quality Catholic education, St. Casimir's School became one segment of a consolidation of neighboring schools effected in the diocese in 1967. The consolidation, known as the West End Catholic Consolidation School, produced the following merger: grades one and two were to be taught at St. Rochus (Croatian); grades three and four at St. Casimir (Polish); grades five and six at St. Stephen (Slovak) while grades seven and eight were to be taught at St. Columba's on Chestnut Street.[56]

On July 19, 1977, "flood-free" Johnstown was visited by a destructive flood for the third time.[57] The town in 1977 saw a phenomenal amount of rainfall. Nearly twelve inches of rain in five hours pounded the Conemaugh Valley on July 19 and 20. Six dams scattered throughout the area failed, and, once again, Johnstown was paralyzed with swirling, muddy floodwaters. The loss of lives totaled seventy-three and property damage was estimated at $300 million.[58] At the parish of St. Casimir, the flood caused damage estimated at more than $150,000 to the church, school, rectory, and convent. Basements in all of the buildings were flooded causing extensive damage to the heating systems, school cafeteria, and church hall.[59] Sister M. Evelyn Furman and her sister, Sister M. Seraphinia, natives of Johnstown, were at home for their annual visit when the tragedy struck. Sister M. Evelyn submitted the following memo of their traumatic experience to the congregation's newsletter:

> The night of July 19 will never be forgotten at our homestead. Sister Seraphinia and I . . . enjoyed a short visit in our happy family circle; then a tragic evening came. The unusual storm was raging all night. It settled in Johnstown and the near-by area for many hours; somehow, it never moved on till dawn.
>
> We prayed and kept vigil throughout the darkness of the night which was illuminated with endless lightning and roaring thunder. No one slept in our little neighborhood. People stood on their porches and watched the raging flood waters make a river on the street and the premises. In some near-by sections of the city, however, the people slept unaware that the water was reaching the first floor of their homes. Shortly after midnight, all the church bells rang to give warning of the impending danger. Rescue trucks, equipped with special wheels, drove the victims to the hills and to the incline.
>
> From time to time we would look outdoors to see the destructive water. The full force of the water came from the hillside like a roaring lion, devastating anything in its path. When the dam broke free, its torrents ran wild. People fought for their lives. We saw our neighbor drowning. Our peaceful street and surroundings turned into a swift and raging river, with chunks of rock, automobiles, and rooftops swiftly passing before our very eyes.

In the early morning hours, all of us stood outdoors in the dirty, heavy mud which came up to our knees. Everyone was silent, deep in thoughts and prayers, thanking the good Lord for life. The flood waters were still running wildly down one street, a path was made through the heavy mud, and with the help of snow shovels, much of the mud was thrown into the river. Work in every home was performed almost at an inch-by-inch pace. Before the National Guard and the Army personnel came into the city, many priests and sisters came to the rescue scenes first. They opened centers where food and clothing were given to the needy flood victims. We also put on work clothes as did all the nuns in the city in order to help the unfortunate infants, children, and the aged. Somehow we found time, despite the digging out of the mud, to visit some of the sick and helpless people and bring them the necessities from various centers. Walking in the streets in the neighborhood with mud almost up to our knees was a common sight—it was a common bond to clasp our hands and hope for the best. Many communities of Sisters came from various parts of Pennsylvania to give a helping hand. The Sisters of Mercy opened a center in my sister's backyard for the distribution of goods to those who were unable to receive provisions because of the lack of transportation.

On the first two Sundays after the flood, Holy Mass was celebrated on lawns, in private homes, in the open streets, and wherever the place was cleaned up for the Lord. We would sing the praises of thanksgiving with the helicopters above and the National Guard making its rounds throughout the city. Generators were coughing and chugging over the sounds of our voices as we triumphantly followed the intonation of "Glory to God in the highest."[60]

After the catastrophic flood, St. Casimir's School could no longer be used because of the extensive damage done to it. Only St. Stephen's and St. Columba's Schools, with a total enrollment of 455 pupils, were to be used for classes. From 1977 to 1978, St. Casimir's School served the needs of the Flood Relief Program. In 1979, the United States Government leased the school building and remodeled two classrooms for use by the Operation Head Start Program. Two other classrooms are being used as offices for two Diocesan Reading Coordinators.[61]

In June of 1982, the Franciscan Sisters of Chicago withdrew from this parish, ending the first and strongest of parish commitments in the state of Pennsylvania.

Mother M. Anna Wysinski and her general council also voted in 1912 to accept St. Casimir's "sister-school," the Assumption of the Blessed Virgin Mary, in the borough of East Conemaugh. Located at the far end of the giant Bethlehem Steel Mills that begin in Johnstown and end in Franklin borough, the town sprawls out and up from the banks of the Conemaugh River, dotting the hillside with modest homes, small stores, and churches. The early residents of Conemaugh reflected largely Central Eastern Europe with a mixture of Poles, Czechs, Serbs, Croats, and people from the Ukraine who labored in the steel mills and the coal mines in Cambria City.[62]

The Assumption of the Blessed Virgin Mary Parish began as a "mission church" of St. Casimir's Church in Cambria City. Because of the time and the distance involved in attending the church and school of St. Casimir in the days when automobiles were scarce and transportation was poor, the parishioners approached the Reverend Bronislaus Dembinski, the pastor of St. Casimir's Church, to aid them in building their own house of worship. Father Dembinski succeeded in purchasing property from the Cambria Steel Corporation on Main and Fifth Streets. A chapel was built there in 1910 and served a double purpose. It was used for church services on Sundays and holydays; during the week, it was converted into a schoolhouse. In 1912, Mother M. Anna appointed Sister M. Angela Jasinski to serve as the school's first teacher. She resided at St. Casimir's Convent in Johnstown and traveled each day to Conemaugh. For the next ten years, the Sisters appointed to teach at Assumption of the Blessed Virgin Mary School maintained their residence at St. Casimir's Convent and traveled daily to the classrooms at Conemaugh. Among the Sisters who were appointed to the school during this ten-year period were Sister M. Eugenia Detlaf, Sister M. Thecla Gawlowicz, Sister M. Bibianna Wiza, and Sister M. Annunciata Klimasz.[63]

In 1922, the Most Reverend John J. McCort, bishop of Altoona, raised the chapel from the status of a "mission church" to that of a parish. That same year, Bishop McCort appointed the Reverend Francis Pilz as the first resident pastor. Father Pilz purchased some land on Second Street and proceeded to erect a new church. Only the basement of the church was constructed, however, when the lack of laborers and materials prohibited further progress. In the same year, Father Pilz was able to purchase two additional homes

Assumption of the Blessed Virgin Mary Convent Conemaugh, Pennsylvania

on Second Street. One of them was designated as a home for the Sisters.[64] With a permanent convent in Conemaugh assured, a stable teaching staff was appointed to the school located in the latter half of the church. Sister M. Salomea Grabowski was appointed the first principal and superior. She was assisted by Sister M. Felicia Dolezych, who served as teacher and organist, Sister M. Julianna Kozaczka who attended to household duties, and a postulant.[65]

By May of 1924, however, the objectionable and inappropriate behavior of Father Pilz in regard to the Sisters caused Mother M. Vincent Czyzewski to make a decision to remove the Sisters from the school at the end of the school year. In June, therefore, the Sisters left for the Motherhouse in Chicago with the purpose of not returning to Conemaugh in September. Several attempts were made by both Father Pilz and the Parish Committee of the Assumption of the Blessed Virgin Mary School to persuade the Sisters to reconsider their decision, but Mother M. Vincent Czyzewski remained adamant in her refusal. In August, Bishop McCort asked Mother M. Vincent for a detailed explanation for her reluctance to send the Sisters back. In reply, Mother M. Vincent sent Sister M. Philipine Lama, the assistant superior general; and Sister M. Benigna Jakajtis, the third councilor, to Altoona to present the congregation's stand. The Sisters informed Bishop McCort that Mother M. Vincent was willing to return the Sisters to Conemaugh for one more year to enable Father Pilz to secure another religious community to assume charge of the school. Bishop McCort, however, advised the Sisters to remain in Conemaugh and added that, if necessary, he was prepared to remove the pastor.[66] The Sisters did return to the school in September of 1924, but with a whole new staff. It included Sister M. Eusebius Kolupka, as superior and principal; Sister M. Susanna Pietrzycki, as teacher and organist; Sister M. Fabian Owczarzak; and Sister M. Leontina Gawlik, who was assigned to household duties.[67] A year later, in 1925, attendance at Assumption of the Blessed Virgin Mary School reached its peak enrollment with 185 pupils. From that year on, however, a steady decline of pupil enrollment followed as the young people generally moved out of Conemaugh to larger cities where the opportunities for gainful employment were more favorable.[68]

The unfortunate matter of Father Pilz and the Sisters on the staff was not completely over in spite of the passage of time and the assignment of a totally new teaching staff. In October of 1928, Bishop McCort sent a letter to Mother M. Aloysia Holysz who had succeeded Mother M. Vincent Czyzewski in the office of superior general in July of that year. The letter revealed that Father Pilz had informed Bishop McCort that the Sisters were once again planning to withdraw from the school. In his letter to Bishop McCort, Father Pilz cited the "impoverished conditions of Conemaugh" as the reason for the Sisters' proposed withdrawal. Bishop McCort dispatched a letter to Mother M. Aloysia in which he sternly warned her that he would appeal to the apostolic delegate against the proposed act of removing the Sisters. In the opinion of Bishop McCort, "schools should be maintained for the young children at every sacrifice, and they shall never close when it is possible to continue them."[69] There is no evidence, however, in the congregation's

*Assumption of the Blessed Virgin Mary / Conemaugh Catholic Consolidation School
Conemaugh, Pennsylvania (1912–1979)*

archives to support Father Pilz's "presumed reasons" in regard to the Sisters' proposed
withdrawal. The entire matter was resolved in favor of the Sisters when Bishop McCort
transferred Father Pilz in 1928, and replaced him with the kind, considerate, and congenial
Reverend John Chraca.[70] When Father Chraca assumed the pastorate, he attempted to erase
the parochial debt, but because of the Depression which engulfed the entire nation, the
debt actually increased. Despite the financial difficulties which continued to plague the
parish, with the loyal support of the parishioners and with the aid of Most Reverend
Richard T. Guilfoyle, bishop of Altoona, a campaign was launched to complete the
basement church-school begun in 1922.[71]

Tragedy struck the area in 1936 when the Conemaugh River and Stony Creek
flooded their contents throughout the Conemaugh Valley thereby creating havoc. Present
at the Assumption of the Blessed Virgin Mary School during that perilous time were Sister
M. Theresia Rybak, superior and principal; Sister M. Innocent Smagacz, Sister Therese
Agnes Kniola, and Sister M. Bernarda Urbanski, who was assigned to household duties. In
the aftermath of the tragic flood, there were 114 children enrolled in the school with four
Sisters on the staff. In 1941, the school roster indicated only eighty-eight pupils, and by
1943, the enrollment had decreased to fifty-three.[72]

A thirty-three-year-old dream was realized when construction of a new church
above the old church-school combination was begun in 1955 during the pastorate of the

Reverend Walter Kurdziel. Church services were held in the neighboring parish of the Sacred Heart. While the new church was under construction, the school facilities were transferred to the parish hall on Fifth and Main Streets, the site of the former "chapel." With the start of the new school year in 1956, the Sisters and 109 pupils returned to the combination church-school foundation which had been renovated and converted entirely into classrooms.[73] After some delay, the new church, erected in the Gothic style, was dedicated on May 4, 1958, by the Most Reverend Howard J. Carroll, the bishop of Altoona-Johnstown.[74]

In September of 1967, because of continuing low enrollment patterns, the Reverend Thomas K. Mabon, superintendent of schools in the Altoona-Johnstown Diocese directed the merger of Conemaugh's two Catholic schools, that of the Assumption of the Blessed Virgin Mary and the Sacred Heart of Jesus. The Assumption of the Blessed Virgin Mary School, the nearby Sacred Heart School staffed by the Ursuline Sisters, and sixty pupils from Daisytown's St. Gregory School merged into the Conemaugh Catholic Consolidation School. In this manner, the best of personnel and the best of facilities would be shared.[75]

Once again, in 1977, a flood pounded the Conemaugh Valley and the area suffered unrelenting disaster. While some homes in Conemaugh suffered more serious damage, the convent of the Assumption of the Blessed Virgin Mary remained relatively undisturbed except for more than two feet of water which flooded the basement and brought with it inevitable food spoilage. The Conemaugh River Bridge suffered damage, and as a consequence, the children were bused to school on a longer route through the hills. [76]

The small community of Conemaugh indicated little possibility of growth in the 1970s. A steadily decreasing school enrollment coupled with a shortage of Sisters forced the painful decision to close the school in 1979. The community of Conemaugh paid the Sisters who had labored at the Assumption of the Blessed Virgin Mary School the highest compliment when the *Golden Jubilee Book* stated: "Praise, honor, and acknowledgement is accorded our Sisters for all their care, devotion, and sacrifice."[77]

SCHOOL APOSTOLATE EXTENSION

[1]Sister M. Bernardine was born in 1893 in Pittsburgh, Pennsylvania. She entered from Immaculate Conception Church in Brenham, Texas, on August 15, 1909. She became a postulant on September 8, 1909, and was received into the novitiate on July 16, 1910. Her first profession of vows was made on December 8, 1911; her novitiate was held back because she was not of legal age. A victim of rheumatic heart disease, Sister M. Bernardine died on January 24, 1912, pronouncing her perpetual vows on her deathbed to Mother M. Anna Wysinski, the superior general, who received them in the name of the Church. Sister M. Bernardine was only nineteen years old and had been in the community for three years. *Spis Sióstr* (AFSCL).

[2]See Chapter 22.

[3]Lovers of history might find it interesting to learn that Brighton Park received its name from the Brighton Park Race Track which was then located on Archer Avenue and Western, the present site of McKinley Park. Evelyn M. Kitawaga and Karl E. Taeuber, eds., *Local Community Fact Book, Chicago Metropolitan Area, 1960* (Chicago: Chicago Community Inventory, University of Chicago, 1963), p. 130.

[4]Ibid.

[5]As early as 1878, St. Agnes Parish had been founded by Irish Catholics of Brighton Park and in 1887, French Catholics established St. Joseph (now St. Joseph and St. Anne) Parish.

[6]*Five Holy Martyrs Church: Golden Jubilee Souvenir Book, 1909–1959* (Chicago, Illinois, 1959), no pagination.

[7]It has always been a source of historical concern that the names of the Five Holy Martyrs are shrouded in such obscurity. The names are herein presented for the scores of Five Holy Martyrs alumni, the author included, who graduated without knowing the names of the five gray-robed men in the distinctive painting which hung above the main altar in the church before its remodeling: Benedict, John, Isaac, Matthew, and Christian. While they were not blood brothers, they were members of the same Benedictine community. Neither were they all Poles. They did, however, meet their deaths at the hands of thieves who killed them with swords. The Five Holy Martyrs are said to be the first canonized saints of Poland and their commemorative feast is celebrated on November 12. *Dziennik Chicagoski*, 7 November 1959; and Five Holy Martyrs "Church Bulletin."

[8]Reverend Monsignor Harry C. Koenig, ed., *A History of the Archdiocese of Chicago: Published in Observance of the Archdiocese, 1980,* 2 vols. (Chicago: The Archdiocese of Chicago, 1980), p. 272.

[9]*Nasz Pamiętnik Parafjalny Wydanie Jubileuszowe z Okazji Uroszystośći Dwudziestopięcialecie Założania Parafji ŚŚ. Pięciu Braci Polaków i Męczenników* [Our Parish Record on the Occasion of the Silver Jubilee of Five Holy Martyrs—Poles and Martyrs Parish] (Chicago, Illinois, 1934), no pagination.

[10]*Golden Jubilee Souvenir Book,* no pagination.

[11]Siostra M. Gonzaga Raniszewski, OSFK, Echo Avondalskie [Avondale Echo], July–January 1938 (AFSCL).

[12]*Nasz Pamiętnik Parafjalny,* no pagination.

[13]One of the school's architectural distinctions is the fact that it has no front entrance—a rarity as schools go.

[14]A fact that the parishioners of Five Holy Martyrs Church have always been intrigued by is the noticeable difference in their church's physical structure as opposed to the "cathedral-like edifices" constructed on Chicago's Northwest Side, e.g., St. Stanislaus Kostka, St. John Cantius, St. Mary of the Angels, or even those on Chicago's South Side, e.g., St. Joseph, St. John of God, etc. The author, born and reared in the Brighton Park area, a parishioner of Five Holy Martyrs and a graduate of its school, recalls the answer almost always given when the style of architecture of the

Five Holy Martyrs Church was questioned: "Christ was born in a stable and Five Holy Martyrs Church is supposed to be an example of the poverty and simplicity of Jesus' birthplace." The author, while researching material at the archdiocesan archives at St. Mary of the Lake Seminary, Mundelein, Illinois, came across the sermon delivered by the Most Reverend George Mundelein, then archbishop of Chicago, at the dedication of the Five Holy Martyrs Church and School in 1920. It should settle all disparate views concerning the architectural design of that church. The sermon reads in part: "There are few churches in this city more attractive, more comfortable, more convenient, or more devotional than this new church of yours just dedicated. Perhaps it is hardly proper that I should be the one to praise it too highly; for some six years ago, I erected on the edge of the Atlantic Ocean one of the first of these churches in the style made famous by the Franciscan monks on the Pacific, and of which this is a replica on a somewhat larger scale." In another part of the sermon, he expressed his sentiments concerning the Sisters on the staff: "The fine churches can wait; the schools must come first. That is why I am insisting that your Sisters, hard workers as they are with crowded classrooms, be women of education." The Most Reverend George Mundelein, archbishop of Chicago, "Sermon" at the dedication of the Five Holy Martyrs Church and School, Chicago, 1920 (Archdiocesan Archives at St. Mary of the Lake Seminary, Mundelein, Illinois.)

[15]Ibid.

[16]Koenig, p. 273.

[17]*Five Holy Martyrs House Journal* (AFSCL).

[18]Sister M. Chrysostom was born in Poland and came to the United States in 1902 where her family settled in Sacred Heart Parish in La Porte, Indiana. She entered the congregation on July 17, 1918, and was made a postulant on August 15, 1918. She began her novitiate on July 27, 1919, made her first profession on July 27, 1920, and professed perpetual vows on July 16, 1926. Sister M. Chrysostom was thirty-four years old when she died. Her twelve years in the congregation had been spent chiefly in teaching. *Spis Sióstr* (AFSCL).

[19]*Golden Jubilee Souvenir Book,* no pagination.

[20]Koenig, p. 273.

[21]Sister M. Ignatia entered from the Nativity of the Blessed Virgin Mary Parish in Lorain, Ohio. She was admitted into the congregation on December 28, 1912, and was accepted into the novitiate on August 15, 1914. Her first profession of vows was made on August 15, 1915, and her perpetual vows were accepted on August 15, 1921. A teacher for most of her years in the congregation, she was forty-three years old and had spent twenty-two of them as a religious. *Spis Sióstr* (AFSCL).

[22]Sister M. Dominic was born in Poland and came to the United States in 1900. She entered from St. John Cantius Parish in 1902. She was a teacher for all of her convent life. At her death she was fifty-eight years old and had been in the congregation for thirty-five years. Sister M. Dominic was the older sister of Sister M. Alphonsa Makowski who died in the congregation in 1955 at the age of seventy-one. *Spis Sióstr* (AFSCL).

[23]*Golden Jubilee Souvenir Book,* no pagination.

[24]Father Maday was remembered by many parishioners as a young curate who had first come to Five Holy Martyrs Parish in 1929. The author was reminded that it was the same Father Maday who had baptized her in June of that same year.

[25]Sister M. Monica entered from Holy Trinity Church in Chicago on March 22, 1905, and was perpetually professed on August 15, 1916. She spent most of her years at the congregation's day care centers and as a sacristan. She was sixty-four years old and had been in the congregation for forty-eight years when she died of cancer. *Spis Sióstr* (AFSCL).

[26]Sister M. Bibianna entered from St. Mary of Perpetual Help Church in Chicago's Bridgeport area on May 15, 1912, and made her perpetual profession on August 15, 1921. She was sixty-eight years old and had been in the congregation for forty-eight years when she died. She had spent most of those years as a teacher in the congregation's schools in Indiana, Pennsylvania, Ohio, and Chicago. *Spis Sióstr* (AFSCL).

[27]A native of Chicago and a member of St. Stanislaus Bishop and Martyr Parish, Sister M. Cyprian entered on October 3, 1915. She made her perpetual vows on July 27, 1923. Sister M. Cyprian taught in the congregation's schools in Illinois, Indiana, and Ohio for forty-seven years. At her death, she was seventy years old and had been in the order for forty-nine years. *Spis Sióstr* (AFSCL).

[28]Sister M. Conrad was born in Poland and came to the United States in 1938. She entered from All Saints Church in Flint, Michigan, on July 12, 1942. Having spent most of her life engaged in household duties, Sister M. Conrad was sixty-eight years old when she died of cancer at St. Anthony Hospital in Chicago. She had been in the congregation for twenty-five years. *Spis Sióstr* (AFSCL).

[29]Born in the United States, Sister M. Eugenia was eighty years old and had been in the community for sixty-two years when she died. She had entered the congregation from St. Mary of Perpetual Help Church in Chicago on March 19, 1911, and made her perpetual vows on August 15, 1919. Sister M. Eugenia served at the congregation's schools in Pennsylvania, Indiana, Ohio, and Illinois at which she was also the principal and superior. She served in Boys Town for four years and as superior at St. Elizabeth's Day Nursery for six years. She was also the superior for two terms at Our Lady of Victory Convent in Lemont. Her last eight years were spent at Five Holy Martyrs Parish as the sacristan. *Spis Sióstr* (AFSCL).

[30]The Most Reverend Alfred L. Abramowicz was baptized in the original Five Holy Martyrs Church, and his family remained as parishioners until St. Pancratius Parish was organized in 1924. He attended St. Pancratius School and the archdiocesan seminaries. Samuel Cardinal Stritch ordained him to the priesthood on May 1, 1943. His first appointment after ordination was Immaculate Conception Parish in South Chicago, where he remained until 1948. In that year he was assigned to the Matrimonial Curia of the Chancery Office staff with residence at St. Helen's Parish. In 1949, he went to Rome to pursue postgraduate studies in Canon Law at the Gregorian University. Upon his return to Chicago in 1951, he was assigned to the Archdiocesan Metropolitan Tribunal with residence at Holy Name Cathedral. Bishop Abramowicz was named a papal chamberlain in 1959. In March, 1958, he was appointed an archdiocesan consultor. Bishop Abramowicz has been executive director of the Catholic League for Religious Assistance to Poland since July 4, 1960. He is the brother of Sister M. Antonella Abramowicz of the Franciscan Sisters of Chicago. *Book of Correspondence:* Report received by author from the Chancery Office, Archdiocese of Chicago.

[31]See Chapter 64.

[32]Koenig, p. 274.

[33]Among the young women who entered the congregation was Eleanor Strzycki who became Sister M. Marifilia. She was the niece of the Right Reverend Monsignor James Strzycki. See Chapter 49.

[34]Bessie Louise Pierce, *A History of Chicago,* vol. 3: *The Rise of a Modern City* (New York: Alfred A. Knopf, 1957), p. 16.

[35]David G. McCullough, "The Johnstown Flood," in *Reader's Digest Condensed Books* (Pleasantville, New York: 1960), p. 10.

[36]The Diocese of Altoona was redesignated the Diocese of Altoona-Johnstown in 1957.

[37]*Ave Maria: Pamiętnik Złotego Jubileuszu Parafii Św. Kazimierza, 1902–1952* [Golden Jubilee of St. Casimir's Parish, 1902–1952] (Johnstown, Pennsylvania: 1952), p. 12.

[38]The *kolęda* refers to a house-to-house distribution of the traditional Christmas wafer and the expression of Christmas and New Year's wishes. Recipients of the wafers and the wishes generally made a donation. As late as 1942, the Sisters were still plodding through the deep snow along the mountains distributing Christmas wafers with the ferocious winds slashing against their faces since the houses were far apart and the distances very long. *Book of Correspondence:* Letter from Sister M. Francesca Janowicz to author, 8 June 1978.

[39]*Book of Correspondence:* Letter from the Reverend Bronislaus Dembinski to Mother M. Anna Wysinski, 18 April 1912 (AFSCL).

[40]*Book of Correspondence:* Letter from the Reverend B. Dembinski to Mother M. Anna Wysinski, 25 April 1912 (AFSCL).

[41]*Book of Correspondence:* Letter from the Reverend B. Dembinski to Mother M. Anna, 30 April 1912 (AFSCL).

[42]This was a very frequent occurrence. All too often pastors would build new rectories or move into more adequate and convenient houses while assigning the old ones to the Sisters.

[43]Siostra M. Gonzaga Raniszewski, OSFK, *Rys historyczny Zgromadzenia Sióstr Franciszkanek Błogosławionej Kunegundy. Część pierwsza, 1860–1910* [A historical survey of the Franciscan Sisters of Blessed Kunegunda. Part one, 1860–1910] (Chicago: By the author, 1947), p. 136.

[44]*Ave Maria: Pamiętnik Złotego Jubileuszu Parafii Św. Każimierza,* p. 19.

[45]Sister M. Theodore was born in Duncan, Nebraska, and joined the Franciscan community in Avondale on September 21, 1912. She entered the novitiate on December 8, 1912, and made her first profession of vows on August 15, 1914. She made her perpetual vows on her deathbed to Mother M. Aloysia who received them in the name of the Church. Sister M. Theodore, who was only twenty-eight years old and in the community for six years, had previously spent seven years as a member of the Congregation of the Sisters of St. Francis of the Perpetual Adoration in Lafayette, Indiana. S*pis Sióstr* (AFSCL).

[46]Raniszewski, p. 137.

[47]Johnstown, a thriving town along the Conemaugh River, boasted a population of thirty thousand people in 1889. On May 31, 1889, a wall of water thirty to seventy feet high slammed into the city, killing an estimated 2,300 people and causing $22 million in damage. For a week before the tragedy, heavy rains had lashed the city. The reservoir, seventeen miles upriver, overflowed the seventy-two-foot-high South Fork Dam causing it to collapse. An estimated twenty million tons of water swept down the valley and the Johnstown Flood of 1889 became part of the American legend.

Another tragedy struck the town when on July 14, 1902, over forty members of St. Casimir's Parish perished in the disastrous Johnstown Mine explosion. *Chicago Sun-Times,* 1978.

[48]*Chicago Sun-Times,* 1978.

[49]The Reverend John Chraca was the pastor of the Assumption of the Blessed Virgin Mary Church in nearby Conemaugh where the Sisters also staffed the parochial school.

[50]*Book of Correspondence:* Letter from Mother M. Aloysia Holysz to Mother M. Antonina Osinski, 21 March 1936 (AFSCL).

[51]The listing of the Sisters indicates who was stationed at St. Casimir's School at the time of the disastrous flood: Sister M. Aloysia Holysz, superior and principal; Sister M. Josephata Tadych, Sister M. Theophane Rakowski, Sister M. Hubert Jasinski, Sister M. Rosalie Scepuniak, Sister Therese Agnes Kniola, Sister M. Ludmilla Fedak, Sister M. Salesia Rzeszutko, Sister M. Clothilde Stefiej, and Sister M. Leontina Gawlik. *Book of Annual Assignments* (AFSCL).

[52]*Book of Correspondence:* Letter from Mother M. Aloysia Holysz to Mother M. Antonina Osinski, 27 March 1936 (AFSCL).

[53]Sister M. Salesia was born in Poland in 1887. She entered the small community from St. John Cantius Parish in Chicago on February 2, 1907, and was received into the novitiate on July 16, 1906. She made her first profession of vows on July 17, 1909, and on July 17, 1917, she pronounced perpetual vows.

From 1909 to 1912, Sister M. Salesia attended to household duties at St. Stanislaus Kostka parish in Youngstown, Ohio. In 1912, she was transferred to St. Casimir's School in Johnstown where she remained until 1916 as a teacher. The next twelve years were spent at Five Holy Martyrs School in Chicago and St. Stanislaus Kostka School in Youngstown where she was a teacher and organist. Transferred again to St. Casimir's School in Johnstown in 1928, she remained there until her death. Sister M. Salesia was fifty years old and had been in the congregation for thirty years at the time of her death. *Spis Sióstr* (AFSCL).

[54]On the morning of January 28, Sister M. Salesia was in her classroom where she taught first grade. During the lunch hour, she felt strangely weak; nevertheless, she returned to class. When she felt worse, she asked Sister M. Ambrosia Tworek, her superior and principal, to be allowed to go home at two o'clock. When the Sisters returned to the convent after school, they saw Sister M. Salesia tidying up her bedroom. When the Sisters asked why she was not resting, she replied that she must leave everything in order because she was going to die. Because Sister M. Salesia possessed a gentle sense of humor, the Sisters did not take her seriously.

When the doctor was called to the convent, he diagnosed Sister M. Salesia's illness as influenza, and suggested she go to the hospital. She entered the hospital on the next day, January 29, which was her feastday. When the doctor paid her a visit on the morning of the next day, Sister M. Salesia again told him of her impending death. He summoned another doctor for consultation, and they both agreed that Sister M. Salesia was not in danger of dying. In spite of these reassurances, Sister M. Salesia asked for the pastor, Father Finke, so that she could make a general confession. Father Finke assured her that this was not necessary. Later in the day, feeling qualms of conscience for having refused her request, Father Finke asked two Sisters to accompany him when he returned to the hospital in the afternoon to hear Sister M. Salesia's confession. She persisted in her assertion that she would die. At about eleven o'clock that night, Sister M. Salesia ran a fever; She requested Extreme Unction. The chaplain brought her the Holy Eucharist at 12:45 o'clock in the morning. The Sisters at the hospital gathered at her bedside to pray. Sister M. Salesia asked for a candle. She grasped the lighted candle in her right hand with joy; in her left hand, she held a crucifix. She made the Sign of the Cross, kissed the crucifix, closed her eyes and lips, leaned back against the pillow and died. Raniszewski, p. 138.

[55]From 1953 to 1960, two classrooms at St. Casimir's School were used as an extension of the Johnstown Central Catholic High School. For seven years, two Franciscan Sisters of Chicago taught in the coeducational freshman section and maintained their residency at St. Casimir's convent. See Chapter 51.

[56]When classes began in September 1968, Sister M. Irmina Kon and Sister M. Angeline Kedzior taught grades three and four, respectively, at St. Casimir's School. A Sister of Mercy and a Franciscan Sister of Joliet, Illinois, also taught grades three and four at the same school. Sister M. Aurelia Zyla taught grade two at St. Rochus School and Sister M. Michael Siebab taught reading and math to seventh and eighth graders at St. Columba's School. *Franciscan Echo,* vol. 11 (Lemont, Illinois: December 1968).

[57]The Sisters who were stationed at St. Casimir's School during the ordeal of the third tragic flood were Sister M. Irmina Kon, Sister M. Lillian Szura, and Sister M. Hermenegilde Moszczynski.

[58]*Chicago Sun-Times,* 1978.

[59]*Johnstown Tribune-Democrat,* 7 December 1977.

[60]*Franciscan Echo,* vol. 25 (Lemont, Illinois: December 1977).

[61]*Book of Correspondence:* Letter from Sister M. Irmina Kon to author, 21 June 1980 (AFSCL).

[62]*Franciscan Echo,* vol. 19 (Lemont, Illinois: October 1976).

[63]*Assumption of the Blessed Virgin Mary House Journal* (AFSCL).

[64]*Assumption of the B.V.M. Church: Souvenir Book of Dedication* (Conemaugh, Pennsylvania, 1958), no pagination.

[65]The postulant was Josephine Nowak who became Sister M. Edward.

[66]Secretaries General, *Community Chronicle, 1957–1970* (AFSCL).

[67]*Assumption, B.V.M. House Journal* (AFSCL).

[68]Secretaries General, *Community Chronicle, 1957–1970* (AFSCL).

[69]*Book of Correspondence:* Letter from the Most Reverend John J. McCort to Mother M. Aloysia Holysz, 8 October 1928 (AFSCL).

[70]*Book of Correspondence:* Letters from Sister M. Basil Ochocinski, Sister M. Georgeann Kinel, and Sister M. Theresita Kuczmarski to author, 1978 (AFSCL).

[71]*Assumption of the B.V.M. Church, A Pictorial Directory: Golden Jubilee Year, 1922–1972* (Conemaugh, Pennsylvania, 1972), no pagination.

[72]Secretaries General, *Community Chronicle, 1957–1970* (AFSCL).

[73]*Assumption B.V.M. House Journal* (AFSCL).

[74]*Assumption Church Golden Jubilee,* no pagination.

[75]There were 339 children involved in the merger. Both the Assumption of the Blessed Virgin Mary School and the Sacred Heart School were used. Sister M. Aurelia Zyla was appointed principal of the Assumption of the Blessed Virgin Mary School which housed grades one through three. An Ursuline Sister taught grade one, and a lay teacher, the first in the history of the parish, taught grade two at Assumption of the Blessed Virgin Mary School. Sister M. Aurelia, the principal, also taught third grade. Sister M. Adelma Walkowski taught thirty-two children in grade six at Sacred Heart School. *Assumption B.V.M. House Journal* (AFSCL).

[76]*Franciscan Echo,* vol. 35 (Lemont, Illinois: December 1977).

[77]*Assumption Church Golden Jubilee,* no pagination.

CHAPTER 24

A Term Concluded

What began with the assassination of the Archduke of Austria-Hungary in June of 1914 led to the onset of hostilities which soon engulfed the whole world. By August of 1914, World War I had begun. The universal tragedy drew in nearly all of the world's nations including, eventually, the United States.

In the congregation, Father Spetz's days as spiritual director and advisor to the Franciscan Sisters of Chicago had, of necessity, come to an end. On February 27, 1914, he was transferred by his superiors to St. Mary's College in St. Mary, Kentucky.[1] The Sisters bade him farewell with genuine sorrow and deepest gratitude for his dedicated and noble efforts in fostering and promoting the good of the congregation. His farewell was made with the assurance that the Sisters were deeply rooted in the Church as a solid congregation and were now able to govern themselves.[2]

On June 14, 1914, Archbishop Joseph Weber, CR,[3] the superior at St. Stanislaus Kostka Church, visited St. Joseph Home for the Aged for the first time. The occasion of the visitation was to bless the new organ donated by the Young Ladies' Rosary Sodality of St. Stanislaus Kostka Church. As a consequence of this first visit, Archbishop Weber became genuinely interested in the young Franciscan congregation. He himself came to the Motherhouse every first Sunday of the month in order to give the Sisters conferences on the religious life, the attainment of spiritual perfection, and other topics related to the cultivation of the interior life and communal living. Upon the advice of Archbishop Quigley, Archbishop Weber appointed a new spiritual director for the Sisters to take the place of Father Spetz. He was the Reverend Joseph Zwierzycki, CR.[4] As the new spiritual director of the Franciscan Sisters of Chicago, Father Zwierzycki instructed them weekly in the *Catechism of the Vows*. The Reverend Francis Dembiński was assigned to teach the *Baltimore Catechism* to the Sisters on a weekly basis. Many Resurrectionist priests served the Sisters as weekly and extraordinary confessors and retreat masters. Among these were the Reverend Thaddeus Ligman, CR; the Reverend Francis Siara, CR; the Reverend Francis Pieczynski, CR;[5] the Reverend Francis Dembiński, CR; the Reverend Stephen Kowalczyk, CR; the Reverend Vincent Rapacz, CR; the Reverend Paul Sobczak, CR;[6] the

Reverend John Zdechlik, CR;[7] and the Reverend Adolph Drewniak, CR.[8] The Reverend Theophilus Szypkowski, CR,[9] and the Reverend John Kruszynski, CR, acted as the chaplains of St. Joseph Home for the Aged in addition to preparing novices and postulants for their apostolates. From April of 1914, the Reverend Joseph Tarasiuk, CR,[10] was appointed chaplain and served until 1931.

The only new school accepted in 1914 was St. Mary of Częstochowa in Hammond, Indiana, about twenty miles southeast of Chicago's Loop. Polish immigrants had come to work in the Standard Steel Company, and most of them employed there had come from Pennsylvania. They also worked at the George Hammond meat-packing plants in the city that bears his name. The Poles worshipped at St. Casimir's Church in Hammond, and in time, with the earnest cooperation of the Reverend Felix Seroczynski, its pastor, the Poles took steps to build a church on the east side of the city. In March of 1912, therefore, land was purchased for the new church of St. Mary under her title of Our Lady of Częstochowa. The first mass was joyfully celebrated on Christmas Day.[11]

In January of 1913, St. Mary's Church received its own pastor in the person of the Reverend Anthony Górek who remained at the parish until 1915. During his pastorate, the school building, a small, one-story wooden structure consisting of four classrooms was erected.[12] At the request of Father Górek, the Franciscan Sisters of Chicago consented to staff the 140-pupil St. Mary of Częstochowa School, their fourth school in Indiana. Sent to St. Mary's School on January 22, 1914, were Sister M. Gerard Gorzkowski as superior, principal, teacher, and organist. She was accompanied by a novice, Sister M. Febronia

St. Mary of Częstochowa Convent
Hammond, Indiana

St. Mary of Częstochowa School
Hammond, Indiana (1914–1970)

Morzych.[13] In September, Sister M. Gerard Moskal, Sister M. Raphael Bogalecki, and Sister M. Lauretta Partyka who was assigned to household duties arrived.[14] The Sisters lived in a small, one-story frame house close to the school without the convenience of a chapel.[15]

The Reverend John Chylewski succeeded Father Górek as pastor in 1915. His attention was focused mainly on the parish school which soon had an enrollment estimated at between two hundred and three hundred children.[16] Sister M. Josephata Tadych, the superior and principal during Father Chylewski's pastorate, applied herself especially to education and was the pastor's "right hand in the school."[17]

St. Mary of Częstochowa Parish, like many others, had numerous pastors. From 1931 to 1939, the Reverend Ladislaus Szczukowski served as the pastor. Sometimes it happened that pastors paid too much attention to the Sisters' private lives. While this was the case in some parish schools staffed by the Franciscan Sisters of Chicago it was very obvious at St. Mary of Częstochowa Convent where an irate Father Szczukowski often penned letters to the superior general in regard to the Sisters' conduct. Typical of his letters was one received by Mother M. Aloysia Holysz in March of 1934: ". . . Is it permissible for the Sisters to burn electricity and sit until 10:15 p.m. everyday?"[18] "What is happening here every night? . . . I ask you to call our Sisters' attention to this . . ."[19]

By 1939, there were 140 pupils in the school with five Sisters and a Sister-organist on the staff.[20] In July of that year, the Reverend Joseph Zobel was appointed pastor of St. Mary's. For the next twenty-three years until his retirement in 1962, the rapport between Father Zobel and the Sisters stationed at the school bordered on the precarious. While the parish showed extraordinary growth during his pastorate in the payment of outstanding debts, renovation of parish buildings, and guidance in the construction of a modern school building and auditorium, his unrelenting obstinacy in regard to improving the physical living conditions of the Sisters led to many unpleasant and unnecessary confrontations. A good indication of the conditions under which the Sisters were forced to work is contained in a letter sent to the Most Reverend John F. Noll, archbishop of Fort Wayne, by Mother M. Jerome Dadej in 1955:

> Your Excellency:
>
> It is with regret that I must report the poor living conditions of our Sisters at St. Mary's School in Hammond, Indiana. At present, there are seven Sisters living in a one-story family house which has a capacity for accommodating four adults. The facilities are very inconvenient and almost intolerable.
>
> When the parish was smaller, conditions were tolerable, but with the growth of the school enrollment, the number of Sisters has also increased. I had repeatedly requested Father Pastor to build the Sisters a new home after the new school was completed. He replied that an enlargement of the rectory was more urgent. Now he tells me that he has no funds for the Sisters' home because he is still in debt for the rectory.
>
> I am appealing, therefore, to Your Excellency, and presenting the situation to you. In case Father Zobel would not be able to remedy it, I will be obliged to remove two teachers from his school.
>
> Your humble servant in Christ,
> Mother M. Jerome[21]

After the construction of a modern and functional school which was built in the 1950s on Merrill Street, an addition was made to the convent by the purchase of the house adjacent to it. The two houses were later connected by a breezeway.

St. Mary of Częstochowa Parish in the late 1960s was undergoing the same changes which hammered away at so many of the other parishes in Indiana and elsewhere. The parish community was experiencing a decrease in the Catholic population and was being supported by many families living outside the parish boundaries. The lack of Sister personnel, the continued decrease in enrollment, and the attendant prohibitive costs of maintaining the school made it necessary for the Sisters to withdraw. With 135 pupils on the school's roster, Sister M. Consolata Markowicz, Sister M. Equitia Nawracaj, and Sister M. Sebastia Podraza reluctantly bade farewell to St. Mary's Parish and to its capable and sympathetic pastor, the Reverend Walter Mastey in June of 1970.[22]

The last mission accepted before the conclusion of Mother M. Anna's term as superior general was Sacred Heart of Jesus School in Tolleston, a suburb of Gary. The

Sacred Heart of Jesus Convent
Gary (Tolleston), Indiana

parish was begun in 1912 by immigrants from Poland who found the distance to St. Hedwig's Church in Gary a journey too lengthy for themselves and for their children.[23] The Reverend Peter Kahellek, pastor of St. Hedwig's Church, was placed in charge of founding the new parish and urged his parishioners to solicit donations for a speedy construction of a church for Tolleston. Fortunately, the new church was not long in coming because Sacred Heart of Jesus Church was one of the five recipients of land donated by the United States Steel Corporation for the building of ethnic parishes in Gary.[24]

In 1912, a frame church which contained a single classroom in the basement was built facing 15th Street. Because Sacred Heart Church was a "mission church" of St. Hedwig's in Gary and the Franciscan Sisters of Chicago had already been teaching at St. Hedwig's since 1909, the Sisters were asked to staff Sacred Heart of Jesus School also. In 1915, Sister M. Marcelline Molek was assigned there as a teacher and organist. She remained until 1917 when Sister M. Alphonsa Makowski replaced her as teacher, sacristan, and choir director. Like Sister Marcelline, Sister M. Alphonsa lived at St. Hedwig's Convent in Gary.[25] In 1918, as Sacred Heart of Jesus Parish developed and the school enrollment continued to climb, the Reverend Ignatius Gapczynski, the pastor, purchased a house for the Sisters next to the church so that they would no longer have to make the daily tedious trips to the parish by streetcar from Gary. During his pastorate, Father Gapczynski moved the church to face Taney Street and constructed three classrooms under the church. That same year, Sister M. Alphonsa assumed the full-time responsibility of superior and principal, Sister M. Regina Iwan was sent to teach, and Sister M. Blase Wojcik was assigned to household duties.[26]

There is evidence to indicate that the parish had financial difficulties during its formative years. An entry dated January 12, 1919, in the *Minutes of General Council Proceedings* indicates that Father Gapczynski was unable to pay the Sisters' salaries at that time.[27] The general council of the Franciscan Sisters of Chicago voted to "leave him in peace" until the parish developed along more stable lines. It is to the credit of the Sisters that a debt of more than $3,000 in Sisters' salaries was cancelled completely in 1954. This debt dated from the early days of the Depression Era and the consequent devastating effects it had produced on the finances of the parishioners of Sacred Heart Church.[28]

In 1929, the present church was built with the school above it. A church hall, which later served as classrooms, was also constructed at the same time. In 1945, Father Louis Michalski, the pastor, added two more classrooms to the hall. Earlier, in 1942, the Reverend Casimir Moskwinski, during his tenure as pastor, had built an addition to the convent.

The scant material in the congregation's archives concerning this mission reveals that the Sisters labored unselfishly and zealously at Sacred Heart of Jesus School, oftentimes under the most adverse circumstances. The "Half-Year Report of June, 1950" to Mother M. Jerome submitted by Sister M. Alberta Bialas, the superior and principal, indicates that each Sister was receiving $40 a month as her salary. It is important to remember that the Sisters maintained the sacristy without a salary, taught "drills" for the June graduation exercises, directed Polish and English choirs of women, and taught CCD classes on Sundays. Similar "Reports" in the following years indicate that, in addition, the Sisters taught CCD classes at Immaculate Heart of Mary Parish in Independence Hill,

Sacred Heart of Jesus Church and School
Gary (Tolleston), Indiana (1914–1968)

Indiana, on Saturdays.[29] As late as March 1955, Sister Bernice Marie Junio, then the superior and principal, was forced to inform the Most Reverend Leo A. Pursley, bishop of Fort Wayne-South Bend, of the unsuitable and inadequate state of the house in which the Sisters had been forced to live for so many years. The convent was woefully inadequate in terms of size and space for eight Sisters. There were six bedrooms, and in the winter, only two of them were heated. The sewerage system proved menacing and the electrical wiring was defective.[30]

As a consequence of the disclosures concerning the Sisters' living quarters, a new and spacious convent was built in 1957 at 1365 Taney Street. By 1967, the school enrollment indicated that of the two hundred pupils enrolled, more than one-half were black.[31] The Sisters continued to work in the racially changing neighborhood, but by 1968, Sacred Heart of Jesus School closed permanently. One of the reasons for its closing was the persistent lack of available Sister personnel. The more immediate cause, however, was the proposed consolidation of the school with the Cathedral of the Holy Angels School staffed by the Congregation of the School Sisters of Notre Dame. Three Franciscan Sisters of Chicago remained at Sacred Heart of Jesus Convent but taught at the Cathedral of the Holy Angels School for the 1968–1969 school year. They were Sister M. Gabriel Lazarski, Sister John Marie Foley, and Sister Rose Therese Bzibziak. For the 1969–1970 school year, Sister M. Celeste Walkowski replaced Sister John Marie. By 1970, Mother M. Beatrice Rybacki was forced to recall the three Sisters at the Cathedral of the Holy Angels and reassign them to schools staffed exclusively by the Franciscan Sisters of Chicago.[32] Even though the Sisters no longer taught at Sacred Heart School, they maintained their residence there, and when the decision was made to leave, the parishioners at Sacred Heart Church were very reluctant to see the Franciscan Sisters of Chicago depart. A School Sister of Notre Dame expressed the parishioners' true sentiments when the Franciscan Sisters left the Cathedral of the Holy Angels School to return to Chicago: "We felt bad to see all of them go. They were so dear!"[33]

Earlier, when Sacred Heart of Jesus School closed, a decision was made to have the Sisters who staffed the Blessed Sacrament School in Gary reside in the vacated Sacred Heart of Jesus Convent.[34] The parishioners of Sacred Heart Church continued to be gladdened by the Sisters' presence until July of 1986 when the Diocese of Gary voiced its intention to close Sacred Heart of Jesus Church and to sell the property for other purposes. The Sisters were relocated in the empty convent at St. Andrew's Parish in Merrillville, Indiana, where they continued to work in an atmosphere of faith, love, and concern.

A TERM CONCLUDED

[1]St. Mary's College, in St. Mary, Kentucky, was established in 1821 by the Reverend William Byrne during the episcopate of the Most Reverend Benedict Flaget, bishop of Louisville. In subsequent years, it was administered by the Society of Jesus and the diocesan clergy of Louisville. The Congregation of the Resurrection was invited to staff St. Mary's College in 1871 at the request of the Most Reverend William McCloskey, bishop of Louisville. In 1929, St. Mary's became a minor seminary for the education of candidates for the priesthood. The college prospered and attained an enviable reputation for educational and spiritual excellence. One of its greatest contributions is the more than five hundred men it has prepared for the priesthood. Beset by the attendant problems of the 1970s, however, St. Mary's College closed its seminary operation in July of 1976. John J. Iwicki, CR, *The First One Hundred Years: A Study of the Apostolate of the Congregation of the Resurrection in the United States 1866–1966* (Rome: Gregorian University Press, 1966), pp. 153–155.

[2]Siostra M. Gonzaga Raniszewski, OSFK, "Rys historyczny Zgromadzenia Sióstr Franciszkanek Bł. Kunegundy. Częsć druga, 1910–1940" [A historical survey of the Franciscan Sisters of Blessed Kunegunda. Part two, 1910–1940] Typewritten, unpublished manuscript (AFSCL), p. 130.

[3]The Most Reverend Archbishop Joseph Weber, CR, was born in Bukowina, Poland, in 1846. He studied for the priesthood and was ordained in 1873 for the Archdiocese of Lwów, Poland. From 1869 to 1873, while Joseph Weber was a seminarian at the Pontifical Polish College in Rome of which the Reverend Peter Semenenko, CR, co-founder of the Resurrectionist Fathers, was rector, he applied for admission to the Resurrectionist Congregation in fulfillment of a vow he had made during a serious illness as a seminarian. Following the counsels of his directors, the Reverend Jerome Kajsiewicz, CR, co-founder and superior general of the Resurrectionists, and the Reverend Peter Semenenko, he kept his vow in abeyance and was ordained a secular priest. He labored in Lwów as chancellor of the archdiocese and as spiritual father and rector of the seminary. He was consecrated auxiliary bishop of Lwów in 1895. Throughout all his labors, he was an ardent promoter of the Apostleship of Prayer and devotion to the Sacred Heart.

At the age of sixty and in his thirty-third year of priesthood, he finally obtained permission from Pope Pius X to enter the Congregation of the Resurrection. On June 24, 1906, he received the habit and began his novitiate in Rome under the guidance of his superior general, the Very Reverend John Kasprzycki, CR. He made his first and final profession of vows in the congregation on February 2, 1907, after receiving special permission to terminate his novitiate after seven months.

From 1909 to 1914, he served as novice master at the Canadian-American novitiate in Canada at which time he authored the *Catechism of the Constitutions and Vows of the Congregation of the Resurrection*. A member of the Congregation of the Resurrection Mission Band, he gave parish missions, Forty Hours' Devotion services, retreats, and conferences, especially to religious. From 1914 to 1918, he was superior at St. Stanislaus Kostka Church in Chicago. At the same time, he was elected general delegate of the Resurrectionist Fathers for the United States and Canada. Archbishop Weber founded and erected the Chicago Province of the St. Joseph Novitiate which opened in 1917. Because of his devotion to the Sacred Heart, he promoted the publication of the first United States' edition of the *Posłaniec Serca Jezusowego* [Polish Sacred Heart Messenger] for the Poles in the United States.

Archbishop Weber died on March 24, 1918, in Chicago, and is buried alongside the Reverend Vincent Barzynski and Reverend John Kasprzycki in the Resurrectionist Mausoleum in St. Adalbert's Cemetery, Niles, Illinois.

In 1930, the old St. Stanislaus College was renamed Weber High School in honor of this "great servant of God, proficient leader, spiritual advisor, and scholar who was zealous in preaching the Word of God and was trusted and respected by all—a truly religious person." Edward T. Janas, CR, *Dictionary of American Resurrectionists, 1865–1965* (Rome: Gregorian University Press, 1967), pp. 65–69; and *Weber's New Frontier: Souvenir Book of Dedication* (Chicago: 27 May 1962), no pagination.

[4]The Reverend Joseph Zwierzycki, CR, was a distinguished novice master at the Cracow novitiate in Poland from 1909 to 1913, and was so appointed in the Chicago Province of the Resurrectionist Fathers from 1914 to 1920. He served another term from 1925 to 1940. In the Chicago Archdiocese, he served as delegate to several congregations of religious women, including the Franciscan Sisters in Avondale from 1916 to 1922. He was also known as a retreat and conference master to religious women and served in that capacity to the Franciscan Sisters of Chicago from 1925 to 1940. Janas, p. 79.

[5]The Reverend Francis Pieczynski was born in Poland in 1872. Ordained in 1901 in Kitchener, Ontario, Canada, he served in Canada and Poland before his arrival in the United States in 1911. Father Pieczynski served as an assistant at several Resurrectionist parishes in Chicago. Appointed a councilor in the Congregation of the Resurrection, he left for Rome in 1929; in 1932, he became assistant general. Father Pieczynski continued to be actively involved in Resurrectionist labors in Poland until his death in 1952. Ibid., p. 49.

[6]The Reverend Paul Sobczak, CR, was born in Poland in 1875, and ordained in Rome in 1903. He was a temporary novice master of the Canadian-American novitiate in Kitchener. A missionary to the Poles in the mining region of Canada from 1904 to 1913, he also helped check the Independent Church Movement among the Poles in Canada. He served as assistant at St. Hyacinth, St. Hedwig, and St. John Cantius Parishes in Chicago until his death in 1922. Ibid., p. 56.

[7]The Reverend John Zdechlik was born and educated in Poland and ordained in Rome. He served as an assistant at several Resurrectionist parishes in Chicago, and, in 1915, was appointed pastor of St. Hyacinth's Parish whose magnificent church he built. He was a member of the general council of the Congregation of the Resurrection and at the time of his death in 1940 in Rome he was the master of novices. Ibid., p. 75.

[8]The Reverend Adolph Drewniak, CR, was born in Poland in 1877, and ordained in Rome in 1907. He labored in Europe for six years and upon his arrival in Chicago was stationed at St. Stanislaus Kostka Church at various intervals as well as at other parishes served by the Congregation of the Resurrection. Ibid., p. 15.

[9]The Reverend Theophilus Szypkowski, CR, was born in Poland in 1861. He entered the novitiate of the Resurrectionist Fathers in 1882 and studied philosophy and theology in Rome where he was ordained in 1887. After serving as an assistant at various parishes of the congregation, he was appointed chaplain of St. Joseph Home for the Aged from 1911 to 1912. He died in Chicago in 1930. Ibid., pp. 61–62.

[10]The Reverend Joseph Tarasiuk, CR, was stationed at St. Stanislaus Kostka Church from 1911 to 1912. He was then an assistant at several Resurrectionist parishes in Chicago and served as chaplain at several institutes in Poland and the United States. From 1913 to 1931, he was the chaplain of St. Joseph Home for the Aged. Ibid., pp. 62–63.

[11]*St. Mary of Częstochowa: 50th Anniversary* (Hammond, Indiana, 1963), p. 17.

[12]Ibid.

[13]Raniszewski, p. 146.

[14]*St. Mary's House Journal* (AFSCL).

[15]The chapel was finally built and the first mass celebrated on December 23, 1939. Raniszewski, p. 146.

[16]The estimate was difficult to arrive at. According to a letter to Sister M. Paul Kirschbaum from Sister M. Theresia Rybak, superior and principal, dated November 15, 1945, there were no records of students in the school prior to 1927.

[17]*Zarys Historyi Parafii Św. Wojciecha B. i M., 1902–1927, oraz szkice Towarzystw. istniejących przy tej parafii* [Record of the history of St. Adalbert B. and M. Parish, 1902–1927, together with a sketch of the parish organizations] (Whiting, Indiana, 1927), no pagination.

[18]While it is possible to sympathize with the pastor's dilemma, one has only to think of the many Sisters, who, through the years, taught school, participated in school-related activities,

supervised altar boys, served as sacristans, and even attended college—not to mention living their lives as religious—and all this before 10:15 p.m.!

[19]*Book of Correspondence:* Letter from the Reverend Ladislaus Szczukowski to Mother M. Aloysia Holysz, 14 March 1934 (AFSCL).

[20]Raniszewski, p. 146.

[21]*Book of Correspondence:* Letter from Mother M. Jerome Dadej to the Most Reverend John F. Noll, archbishop of Fort Wayne, 2 March 1955 (AFSCL).

[22]"St. Mary's Church Bulletin," Hammond, Indiana, 12 April 1970.

[23]An outline of the parish history, very short and sketchy, was sent to the author by Mrs. Julian (Cecilia) Jasiak of Sacred Heart of Jesus Church through the diligent efforts of Sister M. Deofilia Piaskowy in 1976. It constitutes the only available history on record.

[24]*Poland's Millennium of Christianity: Indiana Observance Souvenir Book* (Hammond, Indiana: Klines Printers, 1966), no pagination.

[25]Raniszewski, p. 147.

[26]*Sacred Heart Convent House Journal* (AFSCL).

[27]*Minutes of General Council Proceedings, 1910–1934* (AFSCL).

[28]*Book of Correspondence:* Letter from Sister M. Gonzaga Raniszewski to Sister Bernice Marie Junio, 18 November 1954.

[29]*Book of Correspondence:* "Half-year Report" from Sister M. Alberta Bialas to Mother M. Jerome Dadej, June 1950 (AFSCL).

[30]*Book of Correspondence:* Letter from Sister Bernice Marie Junio to the Most Reverend Leo A. Pursley, bishop of Fort Wayne-South Bend, 22 March 1955 (AFSCL).

[31]*Sacred Heart Convent House Journal* (AFSCL).

[32]*Book of Correspondence:* Letter from Mother M. Beatrice Rybacki to the Reverend Don C. Grass, 26 March 1970 (AFSCL).

[33]*Book of Correspondence*: Letter from Sister M. Rose, SSND, to author, May 1976 (AFSCL).

[34]*Minutes of General Council Proceedings, 1956–1970* (AFSCL).

CHAPTER 25

The Second General Chapter: Mother M. Aloysia Holysz

Six years had passed since the First General Chapter, and, thus, in 1916, the congregation was preparing for the Second General Chapter of Elections to take place. Because of Mother M. Anna's failing health, it was assumed that she would not seek re-election, and, therefore, the prospect of the selection of a new superior general presented itself. The First General Chapter had been held from August 12 to August 18, 1910, and now Mother M. Anna and her general council declared that the Second General Chapter would be held earlier so that matters such as retreats, profession of vows, reception to the novitiate, and other related activities could all be planned and executed expeditiously during the summer months. Consequently, the Second General Chapter was scheduled to last from July 20 to July 29. Special prayers were recommended by the general council so that the chapter would be carried out for the greater glory of God and the good of the entire congregation.[1] There were in the congregation, in 1916, one hundred-forty professed Sisters, eight novices, thirty-one postulants, and four aspirants. The Sisters were serving in fifteen schools, one home for the aged, and one day nursery.[2]

By March 19, 1916, voting for the delegates had been accomplished. Mother M. Anna and her general council were *ex-officio* delegates, that is, delegates by virtue of their office. The First General Chapter had determined that a religious house having ten members qualified as a canonical house. As such, one perpetually professed Sister was to be elected for every ten Sisters in that house. There were in the congregation at the time of the Second General Chapter three canonical houses.[3] Elected as representatives of these houses were Sister M. Clara Ogurek, Sister M. Leona Pochelski, and Sister M. Philipine Lama. Because the superiors of canonically erected houses were also chosen *ex officio*, Sister M. Chester Dziarnowski, Sister M. Innocenta Antosz, and Sister M. Zita Kosmala were automatically members of the delegation. At the Motherhouse, where twenty-eight Sisters in perpetual vows resided, two delegates, namely Sister M. Theresa Dudzik and Sister M. Kunegunda Pinkowski were chosen.

The Second General Chapter was preceded by a three-day retreat. On the morning of July 20, 1916, the election of the superior general took place. Presiding at the election as the delegate of the Most Reverend George Mundelein, archbishop of Chicago, was the Most Reverend Archbishop Joseph Weber, CR. Mother M. Anna, truly exhausted by ill health during most of her six-year tenure as superior general, was not able to be present in the chapter room. Two appointed Sisters were sent to the convent infirmary to obtain her vote. The results of the first voting revealed the names of four candidates for the office of superior general: Sister M. Theresa Dudzik, Sister M. Aloysia Holysz, Sister M. Leona Pochelski, and Sister M. Vincent Czyzewski. None of these Sisters received the necessary absolute majority,[4] so a second vote was necessary. This time, Sister M. Aloysia emerged as the leading candidate but still without the absolute majority required. A third balloting produced the same results. Because of the impasse reached in the voting, Archbishop Weber informed the delegates that the matter would have to be submitted to the ordinary, Archbishop Mundelein, who was authorized to settle the matter according to the Constitutions of the congregation.[5]

It was then that Sister M. Philipine Lama called the attention of Archbishop Weber to the fact that according to the Constitutions of the congregation, Sister M. Aloysia did not possess the required age in order to hold the office of superior general. According to the Constitutions, the superior general had to be at least forty years old and at least one year after perpetual profession.[6] Sister M. Aloysia was then thirty-seven years old and five and one-half years after perpetual profession.

It would appear that the Sister-delegates were aware of the fact concerning Sister M. Aloysia's age. Why they chose to proceed as they did in the election is not discernible from any material found in the congregation's archives. What is evident is that Sister M. Aloysia seemed to be the choice of the majority of the delegates. Now, armed with the knowledge that Sister M. Aloysia was not of age to assume the position of superior general, Archbishop Weber posed the question to the delegates: "Will you agree to take another vote to see if the results would be the same before I proceed to the ordinary?" The Sister-delegates agreed and once again the results of the voting revealed that Sister M. Aloysia had obtained the absolute majority. Archbishop Weber then informed the Sisters that he would seek permission from Archbishop Mundelein for a special dispensation allowing Sister M. Aloysia to accept the office.[7]

After consulting with Archbishop Mundelein, Archbishop Weber returned to the chapter room in the afternoon session with the announcement that the election of Sister M. Aloysia Holysz as the superior general was confirmed by Archbishop Mundelein who further stated that her election was to be looked upon "as the expressed Will of God."[8] With that announcement, the chapter delegates proceeded to make their act of obeisance to the new superior general.[9]

The chapter delegates next proceeded to the election of the members of the general council which resulted in the following: Sister M. Clara Ogurek, assistant general and first councilor; Sister M. Hedwig Kubera, second councilor; Sister M. Andrea Zawadzki, third councilor; Sister M. Philipine Lama, secretary general; and Sister M. Salomea Grabowski, procurator general.

Among the pioneer Sisters who influenced the congregation almost from the day of her entrance was the woman chosen to be its second superior general, Mother M. Aloysia. The former Estelle Holysz was born on October 25, 1879, in Chicago, thereby making her the first member of the congregation at that time to be born in America. The daughter of Casper and Theophilla (née Janke) Holysz, Estelle entered the young congregation from St. Hedwig's Church on Chicago's Northwest Side on August 15, 1899, and became a novice on August 8, 1900. She made her first profession of vows on December 15, 1901, and professed perpetual vows on August 12, 1910.

From the beginning of her active apostolate, from 1902 to 1905, she was stationed at St. Stanislaus Bishop and Martyr School in Chicago as principal and superior. On January 3, 1905, she returned to the Motherhouse because of illness. The following year she spent at St. Casimir's School in St. Louis, Missouri, where she again served as the superior and principal. In 1906, she was transferred to St. Adalbert's School in Whiting, Indiana, where she served as superior, principal, and substitute teacher until 1911.

In 1910, she was elected secretary general and served in that capacity until 1916. She remained at the Motherhouse for only two years and during that time, with Sister M. Philipine Lama, wrote "The Chronicle of the Franciscan Sisters of St. Kunegunda." She also kept a "Record" [*Notularz*] of monthly meetings held with the general council. Both of these records are invaluable contributions to the history of the congregation.[10]

When Mother M. Aloysia was elected superior general in 1916, she held that office until 1922. After spending the next six years as the superior and principal at Sacred Heart of Jesus School in Cleveland, she was destined to be elected the superior general for another six-year term in 1928.

Mother M. Aloysia is described as having been "much like Mother M. Anna in character and personality."[11] Tall and with a stately gait, she was endowed with intelligence, charm, and physical attractiveness. She appeared refined, almost aristocratic, with penetrating eyes that seemed to veil great feelings of compassion and concern. Reserved yet festive on occasion, Mother M. Aloysia emerged serious yet gentle.[12] That she was kind is borne out by numerous anecdotes revealed by the Sisters. An example of her zealous concern follows:

> I entered the community during Mother M. Aloysia's administration. As postulants and novices, we had little to do with her. One instance I remember where she showed concern for me and my family. My mother became very ill. I was the eldest; there was no one to take care of my mother because my sisters and brothers had to go to school. Mother M. Aloysia allowed me to go home for seven weeks as a second-year novice. This I will never forget.[13]

Mother M. Aloysia had special devotion to the Sacred Heart of Jesus, and during her term of office was responsible for the consecration of the entire congregation to the Most Sacred Heart. Her devotions were principally Eucharistic, Marian, and Franciscan.

She was said to have been a prayerful woman rather than a pious one.[14] She had great sympathy and love for the sick Sisters, and during her second term, she opened the infirmary for them in St. Joseph Home in 1930.

During her tenure of office, numerous candidates sought admission to the congregation. From 1916 to 1922 alone, seventy-five Sisters were admitted to the novitiate. In her second term of office, that is, from 1928 to 1934, novitiate ceremonies were held twice a year because of the large groups. The largest group of novices was received on August 15, 1931 when thirty-three young women entered the congregation.[15]

The only new member of the general council elected at the Second General Chapter was the secretary general Sister M. Philipine. Born on November 22, 1877, in Poland, the former Cecilia Lama came to the United States in 1883 and attended St. Hedwig's Church. She entered the small community on March 19, 1900, became a novice on July 27, 1901, and made her first profession of vows on August 2, 1902. Her perpetual profession was made on August 12, 1910.[16]

After making her first profession of vows, Sister M. Philipine was sent to St. Stanislaus Bishop and Martyr School where she served as teacher and superior until 1909. She next served at three different schools of the congregation as superior, principal, and teacher. Elected secretary general in 1916, she held the position until 1922. This was only the first of her many appointments to the general council.[17]

Sister M. Philipine was highly regarded as a good religious and fine teacher. She was dignified, articulate, and highly competent in many areas. Mature in judgment and amiable by nature, Sister M. Philipine was a good example of a religious committed to the Church and to the congregation.[18]

One of Mother M. Aloysia's first actions following her election was the naming of five special commissions to assist her in governing the congregation. The first of these, the Commission on Spiritual Affairs, was assigned to Sister M. Theresa Dudzik and Sister M. Andrea Zawadzki. The Commission on School Affairs was assigned to Sister M. Chester Dziarnowski, Sister M. Innocenta Antosz, and Sister M. Leona Pochelski. Sister M. Clara Ogurek, Sister M. Salomea Grabowski, and Sister M. Vincent Czyzewski were named to head the Sisters' House Affairs Commission. To the Commission on Novices and Postulants were appointed Sister M. Hedwig Kubera and Sister M. Kunegunda Pinkowski. Sister M. Salomea was also appointed to attend to the matters pertaining to the aged at St. Joseph Home for the Aged.

At a particular meeting held after one of the daily chapter sessions, the new general council met with Mother M. Aloysia to appoint Sisters to the local Motherhouse council. As a consequence of their deliberations, the following appointments were made: Sister M. Kunegunda Pinkowski, superior; Sister M. Theresa Dudzik, assistant superior; Sister M. Angeline Topolinski, secretary; and Sister M. Ladislaus Wroblewski, procurator. Appointed mistress of novices was Sister M. Vincent Czyzewski; Sister M. Zita Kosmala[19] was made her assistant. When the decision concerning her appointment was made known to her, Sister M. Vincent declined because of ill health. As a consequence, Sister M.

Gerard Gorzkowski[20] was chosen to replace her while Sister M. Zita remained as Sister M. Gerard's assistant.

On the evening of the sixth day of the general chapter, Mother M. Aloysia announced the selection of the local council to the Motherhouse Sisters. She began reading the list and had only announced the local superior and her assistant when Sister M. Theresa Dudzik raised her hand in objection. She voiced the opinion that the local house council had not been chosen according to the Constitutions of the congregation which stated: "The local superior is aided by three professed Sisters chosen by all the Sisters of the house having the right to vote and one of them is appointed the procurator."[21]

The objection, valid in essence, had to be considered. It was clear that the "Sisters of the house," meaning the Motherhouse in this instance, had not had a voice in selecting the three councilors mentioned in the Constitutions. Because of the lateness of the day, Mother M. Aloysia postponed the election by the Motherhouse Sisters to the next day. At the subsequent voting, Sister M. Colette Nowak was chosen secretary by majority vote thereby displacing Sister M. Angeline Topolinski. Sister M. Vincent Czyzewski was elected local procurator, but once again she declined and was replaced by Sister M. Ladislaus Wroblewski who had been appointed to that office originally. The Sisters at the Motherhouse had apparently also voted to retain the other Sisters appointed by Mother M. Aloysia and her general council.

The Second General Chapter ended officially on July 29. On that day, Archbishop Weber arrived at the Motherhouse to learn the results of the chapter deliberations. When Mother M. Aloysia assured him of the successful termination of the congregation's Second General Chapter, he asked that the convent bell be sounded to call the Sisters to chapel in thanksgiving. At the conclusion of the archbishop's insightful sermon, he extended good wishes to the congregation, the "Te Deum" was sung, and Benediction of the Most Blessed Sacrament followed.

Mother M. Aloysia and Sister M. Philipine paid a visit to Archbishop Mundelein[22] on August 21 in order to give him a report of the Second General Chapter. He received them with kindness, and, as was generally characteristic of him, soon put them at ease. He inquired as to the number of mission houses the congregation had in the city or near Chicago.[23] When he was informed of the number, he remarked: "I am surprised you have so few in Chicago. I promise to talk over these matters with local pastors." Archbishop Mundelein then inquired as to the "spirit" in the congregation. He urged the Sisters earnestly: "If you strive to keep a good spirit among you and you are faithful to your vows, everything else will come in time."[24] Upon returning to the Motherhouse, Mother M. Aloysia and Sister M. Philipine carried to the Sisters the welcome news of Archbishop Mundelein's great kindness and pastoral concern.

The official chapter decrees were read in the Motherhouse and in each mission house of the congregation on August 27. One of the main decrees provided for the recitation of the *Little Office of the Blessed Virgin Mary* in Latin. As a consequence, on November 1, the feast of All Saints, the Sisters began to pray the *Little Office* in Latin in order to unite themselves with the whole Church in the official language of the liturgy at that time. In this process, they were taught the pronunciation of the Latin and the accompanying rubrics by the Reverend Joseph Tarasiuk, CR, chaplain of St. Joseph Home for the Aged. The Sister delegates had also decreed that the morning and evening prayers, as well as the prayers before and after meals, be printed in both Polish and Latin and distributed to the Sisters. Besides the holydays designated by the Church, the Sisters also decreed to celebrate the following feasts with greater solemnity: Corpus Christi (then observed on the Thursday after Trinity Sunday); the Nativity of the Blessed Virgin Mary (September 8); St. Joseph (March 19); St. Francis of Assisi (October 4); Blessed Kunegunda (then celebrated on July 27); and Candlemas Day (Purification of the Blessed Virgin Mary, February 2). Certainly one of the chief decrees concerned the greenhouse.[25] It had been suggested at the chapter that the greenhouse be phased out slowly since it was not real and purposeful work for religious women. The chapter delegates voted to phase out the greenhouse in September of 1917.

Other decrees which emanated from the Second General Chapter concerned the following:

1. Sisters with a talent for art would be encouraged to study it.
2. Perpetual vows would to be made after six years rather than after eight years.
3. To keep within the confines of poverty, the amount of clothing possessed by each Sister would be regulated. Also, in keeping with simplicity, the tassels on the cords would be eliminated.

The Commission on Novices and Postulants made the following decisions during the chapter:

1. Under no circumstances would the novices to be engaged in secular study; only spiritual training would be provided.
2. Postulants giving definite signs of perseverance in the congregation would be professionally prepared for the teaching field after the conclusion of the novitiate.
3. In the summer, the postulants would wear white bonnets while at work; the black bonnet would be worn for chapel and upon leaving the house.

By November of 1916, Mother M. Aloysia and the general council decided that the postulants going into the novitiate should have their reception postponed until the summer vacation. It was often difficult to make changes at mission houses during the year, and the postulants had difficulty coming in for the retreat which preceded the taking of vows.[26]

Before the year came to an end, Archbishop Mundelein informed Mother M. Aloysia that a delegate for all female congregations in the Archdiocese of Chicago was being appointed. His duty would be to transact many of the matters pertaining to religious which, heretofore, Archbishop Mundelein himself had handled. The delegate named was the Right Reverend Monsignor Francis A. Rempe[27] who was called the vicar general for the women religious of the Archdiocese of Chicago.

On December 2, 1916, Monsignor Rempe held a canonical visitation at the Motherhouse of the Franciscan Sisters of Chicago. Privately, he received each member from the youngest postulant to Mother M. Aloysia, the superior general. At the conclusion of the visitation, Monsignor Rempe praised the congregation's life and spirit, giving special recognition to the novitiate. Monsignor Rempe assured Mother M. Aloysia that his report to Archbishop Mundelein concerning the Franciscan Sisters of Chicago would be highly commendatory since their spirit of poverty and dedication to duty had made a vivid impression on him.[28]

THE SECOND GENERAL CHAPTER: MOTHER M. ALOYSIA HOLYSZ

[1]Every general chapter of elections or chapter of affairs is preceded by a period of intense prayer and personal sacrifice, such as fasting, to implore the blessings of Almighty God on the deliberations of the delegates.

[2]Secretaries General, *Community Chronicle, 1910–1934* (AFSCL).

[3]St. Casimir Convent in Cleveland, St. John Cantius Convent in Indiana Harbor, and St. Casimir Convent in Johnstown qualified as canonical houses at this time.

[4]The term means one more than half of those eligible to vote.

[5]*Konstytucya Sióstr III Zakonu Św. Ojca Franciszka pod Wezwaniem Św. Kunegundy w Chicago, Illinois* (Chicago: *Dziennik Chicagoski*, 1909), p. 33.

[6]Ibid., p. 35.

[7]*Minutes of General Council Proceedings, 1910–1934* (AFSCL).

[8]*Minutes of General Chapter Proceedings, 1916;* and Secretaries General, *Community Chronicle* (AFSCL).

[9]The act of obeisance was a gesture of respect or reverence. At this time, it generally consisted of either kissing the hand or the sleeve of the habit of the new superior general.

[10]Sister M. Aloysia Holysz, OSFK, "Franciscan Sisters of St. Kunegunda Chronicle" (Lemont, Illinois: AFSCL, 1894–1922. Manuscript).

[11]*Interviews* with Sisters, 1983 (AFSCL).

[12]*Interview* with Sister M. Ferdinand Skiba and other Sisters, 1983 (AFSCL).

[13]*Book of Correspondence:* Letter from unidentified Sister to author (AFSCL).

[14]*Interview* with Sister M. Loyola Dymanowski and others (AFSCL).

[15]This was repeated for the second time in the history of the congregation when thirty-one young women entered in 1961.

[16]*Spis Sióstr* (AFSCL).

[17]In 1921, she attended The Sisters College of the Catholic University of America in Washington, DC. She received her bachelor's degree from De Paul University in Chicago. In 1922, she was elected vicar general and first council member. She served until 1928, but during that time she was also a teacher in the congregation's schools in Chicago. In 1933, she was appointed fourth council member upon the death of Sister M. Innocenta Antosz, a term which Sister M. Philipine concluded in 1938. Again, in 1940, Sister M. Philipine was elected to the general council. This time she was voted second councilor and served until 1946. She then spent five years as a superior at St. John Cantius School in Indiana Harbor. At the conclusion of her term as superior, she was sent to Our Lady of Victory Convent in Lemont to teach the postulants, a service she rendered from 1946 to 1949. That year she ceased teaching because of illness. Sister M. Philipine died of pernicious anemia on January 11, 1958, at Our Lady of Victory Convent. She was eighty years old and had been in the congregation for fifty-seven years. *Congregation Membership Records;* and *Spis Sióstr* (AFSCL).

[18]*Interviews* with Sisters, September 1983 (AFSCL).

[19]Sister M. Zita had been a religious for seventy years when she died on December 1974, at the Motherhouse. She had spent most of her life as a teacher and organist at the congregation's schools in Illinois and Indiana. A very sedate woman, Sister Zita cultivated a pleasant personality and possessed a deep spiritual life. *Congregation Membership Records;* and *Interviews* with Sisters (AFSCL).

[20]See Chapter 21.

[21]*Konstytucya,* p. 50.

[22]George W. Mundelein, "The First Cardinal of the West," was born in New York City on July 2, 1872. He studied at Manhattan College, St. Vincent Seminary in Latrobe, Pennsylvania, and the

Propaganda College in Rome where he was ordained in 1895. He became secretary to Bishop Charles McDonnell of Brooklyn and was appointed as chancellor of the diocese in 1897 only two years after ordination. He served there until he was appointed auxiliary bishop of Brooklyn in 1909.

In 1916, he was appointed archbishop of Chicago, one of the most important and desirable archdioceses in the United States. At forty-three, he was the youngest archbishop in the country. This energetic and brilliant churchman coordinated the various educational institutions into one uniform and efficient system by appointing three school supervisors. The result was a unification which included regular teacher meetings, unified methods of instruction, common exams, and anything relating to the school system. He founded and built Quigley Preparatory Seminary near Holy Name Cathedral. One of the major contributions to the archdiocese was St. Mary of the Lake Theological Seminary in Mundelein, Illinois, consisting of fourteen buildings in beautiful Georgian style.

During World War I, Cardinal Mundelein pledged the resources of the archdiocese to the government. For example, he allowed priests to volunteer for armed service chaplaincies, used his influence to support the American Red Cross, etc. At the end of the war, he actively supported relief to all the countries affected. In Chicago in 1918, he organized the charitable works of the archdiocese into the Associated Catholic Charities of Chicago. His accomplishments together with his personality put the Archdiocese of Chicago "on the map." A friend of the needy and the working man, he was a great humanitarian. He was a vigorous supporter of social reform and an early opponent of Nazism when it appeared in Europe. In the interests of the Church, he was a tough and relentless fighter. A very sophisticated person, he could be a very stern taskmaster.

Cardinal Mundelein died in Chicago on October 2, 1939, at his seminary residence. He is buried beneath the main altar of the Immaculate Conception Chapel at St. Mary of the Lake Seminary. In his lifetime, he had known many important people in lay and ecclesiastical circles. One of them, President Franklin D. Roosevelt, upon hearing of his death said: "He served his day and generation with unfailing fidelity to the highest principles of Christianity. I mourn the loss of a true friend." John J. Delaney and James E. Tobin, *Dictionary of Catholic Biography* (Garden City, New York: Doubleday and Company, Inc., 1961), pp. 833–34; *One Hundred Years: The Church of the Holy Name, the Chapel That Became a Cathedral, 1849–1949* (Chicago, Illinois), no pagination; and Reverend M. J. Madaj, *The New World,* 30 August 1974, sec. 2, p. 7.

[23]Besides the Motherhouse and St. Joseph Home for the Aged, the Sisters also conducted St. Elizabeth's Day Nursery. They taught at three schools: St. Stanislaus Bishop and Martyr, Five Holy Martyrs, and St. Florian's in Chicago. The other mission homes were in Spring Valley and East St. Louis, Illinois; Cleveland and Youngstown, Ohio; Indiana Harbor, Hammond, and Gary, Indiana; and Conemaugh and Johnstown, Pennsylvania.

[24]Secretaries General, *Community Chronicle, 1910–1957* (AFSCL), p. 33.

[25]*Minutes of General Council Proceedings, 1916* (AFSCL).

[26]Secretaries General, *Community Chronicle, 1910–1934* (AFSCL).

[27]The Right Reverend Monsignor Francis Rempe was named the first vicar general for the women religious of the Archdiocese of Chicago. Born in Aurora, Illinois, in 1874, he attended St. Francis Seminary in Milwaukee and the Franciscan Seminary in Teutopolis, Illinois. He was ordained by Bishop Feehan in 1897 in the private chapel of the archiepiscopal residence at 1555 N. State Parkway in Chicago. His first appointment was as an assistant at St. Boniface Church on Noble Street in the immediate vicinity of St. Stanislaus Kostka Church. In 1905, he was appointed by Cardinal Mundelein to found St. Clement's Parish on Deming Place. He died in Chicago in 1946. Report received from the Archdiocese of Chicago, 1976.

[28]Matka Maria Teresa Dudzik, "Kronika Sióstr Franciszkanek pod opieką Św. Kunegundy w Chicago, Illinois" [The Chronicle of the Franciscan Sisters under the patronage of St. Kunegunda in Chicago, Illinois] Unpublished manuscript, 1910 (Chicago, Illinois, AFSCL), p. 36; and Siostra M. Gonzaga Raniszewski, OSFK, "Rys historyczny Zgromadzenia Sióstr Franciszkanek Bł. Kunegundy. Część druga, 1910–1940" [A historical survey of the Franciscan Sisters of Blessed Kunegunda. Part two, 1910–1940] Typewritten, unpublished manuscript (AFSCL), p. 149.

CHAPTER 26

Expanding the School Apostolate

The only new commitment made in the field of education in 1916 was that in La Porte, in the northernmost part of Indiana. Poles were settling in this vicinity in 1855, and farming offered the immigrants a real livelihood. When the Planett Manufacturing Company relocated their Chicago-based factories in La Porte in 1903, the laborers they employed followed their move. From 1906 to 1907, many Poles came to La Porte and worked for the M. Rumely Company, makers of farm equipment. As a consequence of these labor opportunities, many families and single young men and women made their homes in La Porte.[1] The Polish settlers attended St. Joseph's (German) Church, and St. Mary's (Polish) Church in Otis, Indiana. When the population of La Porte increased overwhelmingly, steps were taken to organize a new Polish parish.

In 1913, the Most Reverend Herman J. Alerding, bishop of Fort Wayne, secured a Polish priest, the Reverend John Osadnik from Duluth, Minnesota, to assume the pastorate of the new Sacred Heart of Jesus Church in La Porte.[2] Much time and effort were expended in order to build the church, since at that time, many of the parishioners were suffering severe financial difficulties due to the country's declining economy. The dedicated pioneer members of the parish, however, bore the financial burden and even contributed their physical assistance in order to have their own church. On August 3, 1913, the dedication of the combination church and school building took place. The ceremony was conducted by the Most Reverend Paul P. Rhode, auxiliary bishop of Chicago, a personal friend of the pastor, Father Osadnik. The La Porte newspapers carried an account of a one-half mile procession that escorted Bishop Rhode from the train station to an altar arranged for the occasion near the church-school building to be blessed.[3]

Until 1916, the children of La Porte attended St. Joseph's School, St. Rose of Lima Academy, and the Maple Public School in neighboring areas. In 1916, however, Father Osadnik invited the Franciscan Sisters of Chicago to staff the school. With the consent of Mother M. Aloysia Holysz and her general council, he soon welcomed Sister M. Seraphine Zamrowski, superior and principal; Sister M. Ignatia Hodkiewicz, and Sister M. Nicholas Poterek, who was assigned to household duties. Five rooms were designated

Sacred Heart of Jesus
Church and School
La Porte, Indiana (1916–1969)

Sacred Heart of Jesus Convent
La Porte, Indiana

as classrooms in the combination church-school building. The Sisters made their home in the church-school building in a back room, wholly inadequate in size and lacking the basic facilities.[4]

The Reverend Ignatius Gapczynski succeeded Father Osadnik as pastor in 1920. During his pastorate, Father Gapczynski gave much consideration to establishing a high school to be staffed by the Franciscan Sisters of Chicago, but because of the financial burden it would have placed on the parishioners, the plan was soon abandoned.[5] That same year, Father Gapczynski purchased a charming, spacious, two-story house at 501 Park Street which, after renovation, served as the Sisters' convent.[6] Six years later, Father

Gapczynski was replaced by the Reverend Ladislaus Szczukowski. During the difficult years preceding the disastrous Depression of 1929, Father Szczukowski was forced to ask the superior general, Mother M. Aloysia Holysz, to lower the stipend paid to the Sisters for their teaching duties citing that "these are hard times in La Porte; the people are not working . . . and truly difficult times have arisen."[7]

During the worst days of the Depression Era, the Reverend Ignatius Gapczynski was reappointed as pastor. One of his first accomplishments in the more prosperous period that followed was the payment of all the past stipends which were rightfully due the Sisters but which the Sisters had voluntarily foregone during the time the parish was strapped for finances.[8]

The Sisters successfully conducted the Sacred Heart of Jesus School for fifty-three years. In 1969, at the conclusion of an in-depth study by the Apostolate and Education Committees at the First Extraordinary Chapter of Affairs, the school was designated to be closed. With 123 pupils listed on the school roster, the three remaining Sisers bade farewell to the Reverend Joseph Buczyna, the pastor, and they left La Porte in June of 1969 with extreme reluctance and truly heavy hearts—sentiments shared equally by the devoted parishioners of Sacred Heart of Jesus Church.

In 1917, during the second year of her term as superior general, Mother M. Aloysia, together with her councilors, voted to accept three schools in Pennsylvania, two in Illinois, and one in Indiana. Basically, they were in areas that were materially impoverished. The Sisters who were sent to these small missions often taught school with as many as seventy pupils in one grade; in other instances, three or four grades were often combined into one class. In addition, the Sisters were expected to maintain the altar and the sacristy, wash and repair church linens and vestments, conduct the parish choir, and arrange periodic entertainment by the school children in order to help the parish raise needed funds. Unfortunately, the inability of the parishioners of these small and indigent parishes to make a living and the consequent need to move to larger cities in order to survive were the reasons for much of the social and economic instability encountered in these areas.[9]

The first of the three Pennsylvania schools accepted by the Franciscan Sisters of Chicago was located in South Sharon, Pennsylvania, in the Shenango Valley which had attracted immigrant laborers for the steel mills in the early 1900s. The little "boom town" between the settled communities of Wheatland and Sharon existed as South Sharon until 1901 when it was incorporated as the city of Farrell.[10]

The Reverend Casimir Rybinski organized the parish of St. Adalbert[11] for the immigrant Poles in Farrell in 1910 and became its first pastor. By 1913, the cornerstone of the church had been laid. The school, completed in 1917, opened its doors to the first classes in September of that year. There are no records available which indicate under what circumstances the Franciscan Sisters of Chicago agreed to staff the school nor where they maintained their residence while teaching there. Since the Sisters already staffed schools in Johnstown and Conemaugh, Pennsylvania, however, there is little doubt that Father Rybinski appealed to Mother M. Aloysia Holysz to furnish Polish-speaking Sisters for his school.

The Sisters left for Farrell in early October of 1917. The school year began under unusually trying circumstances with Sister M. Francis Drufke as superior and principal, Sister M. Sophie Ciurkot assigned to household duties, and a postulant.[12] There were 116 children enrolled in the school on Fruit Street with the prospect of more to come when the Sisters arrived. Sister Mary Welter was sent to Farrell on October 25; unfortunately, she remained there only one week. Sister M. Francis herself remained as superior and principal for only two months, and from the correspondence directed to Mother M. Aloysia, it is relatively easy to discern why the Sisters' stays were of such short duration. After only one week of school, the pastor made no secret of his obvious displeasure with the Sisters. He criticized their classroom technique and even scolded them in public. Nothing they did seemed to please him.[13] The Sisters rose daily at five o'clock in the morning and taught until four o'clock in the afternoon. The pastor himself supervised the Sisters who were expected to perform janitorial services in the school at the conclusion of a busy day.[14] When Sister M. Francis could no longer accept the unstable conditions at the mission nor the animosity of the pastor, Sister M. Eugenia Detlaf was sent to replace her in December. She was not presumptuous in assessing the oppressive situation at St. Adalbert's School. In January of 1918, Sister M. Eugenia dutifully wrote to Mother M. Aloysia in earnest: "I have not cried over these series of events which I have outlined to you in this letter, but I have felt very bad. I still have hope, however, that I will become accustomed to all that is happening here."[15]

St. Adalbert School
Farrell, Pennsylvania (1917–1918)

St. Michael Church and School
Glen Campbell, Pennsylvania (1917–1928)

When in both March and April of that year, Sister M. Eugenia informed Mother M. Aloysia that she could "hardly wait for the school year to end because of the harsh conditions," the general council agreed with Mother M. Aloysia to recall the Sisters from St. Adalbert's School at the close of the school year in June of 1918.[16] Apparently, all the efforts of the Sisters had not been enough to overcome the difficulties which the pastor's shortsightedness had engendered. With the departure of the Franciscan Sisters of Chicago, the Congregation of the Sisters of the Holy Family of Nazareth of the Pittsburgh Province came to serve the people of Farrell and remained until 1960.[17]

The second and third schools in Pennsylvania to which the Franciscan Sisters of Chicago turned their attention were St. Michael the Archangel in Glen Campbell and SS. Peter and Paul in Arcadia.

When the indigent Polish and Slovak immigrants had settled in Glen Campbell, the nearest churches were in Punxsutawney and Spangler. Because of the distance involved in seeking a place in which to worship, the settlers of Glen Campbell met in private homes for prayer services. Eventually they succeeded in securing a priest from Punxsutawney to visit once a year to enable them to fulfill their Easter duty.[18]

In 1900, the immigrant settlers constructed a church. The first floor of the presently existing structure was the original church which the parishioners named in honor of St. Michael the Archangel. Three years later, the Reverend John Rokosz became the permanent pastor. He succeeded in erasing the debt on the church and proceeded to remodel the church into classrooms. A second floor was added to the original structure to serve as the new church.[19] The Franciscan Sisters of Chicago came to Glen Campbell in 1917 at the request of Father Rokosz. Arriving at St. Michael's School on August 13 were Sister M. Boniface Pranke, superior and principal as well as teacher and organist; Sister M. Joanna Trojak who was sent to attend to household duties and a postulant.[20] There were approximately eighty children enrolled in the school.[21]

The experience of arriving at the new mission was vividly recalled by Sister M. Boniface in a letter to Mother M. Aloysia written on the day the Sisters had finally settled down in the former rectory which now served as their convent:

> Reverend Mother General:
>
> We have successfully arrived at our farm mission. The hills are so very high, and I was practically out of breath already in Cresson. I hoped Glen Campbell would not be the same. We left Chicago at 10:40 p.m. and arrived in Youngstown, Ohio at 12:50 p.m. At 3:35 p.m., we took the train to Pittsburgh and arrived at 5:45 p.m. We took a bus to get to another station. From 6:00 p.m. to 4:30 a.m., we waited at the station. At 4:30 a.m. we took the train from Pittsburgh to Cresson. At 10:10 a.m., we took the train from Cresson to Glen Campbell. We were astounded at the large mountains we saw as we rode on the train. We arrived at Glen Campbell at 1:30 p.m. We were met by the pastor who took us to Arcadia for supper.
>
> On Sunday, I had to play at both churches and such hymns were sung that I had never heard of. Neither did I have time to practice. But all went well. The people were turning around and staring at us in church as though they couldn't believe their eyes!
>
> Our home is not finished yet. The pastor says it will take about three weeks to complete because he cannot get laborers in spite of the fact that he is willing to pay fifty cents an hour.
>
> In closing, let me repeat how happy the pastor is that you have sent the Sisters. If things remain this way, all will be well.
>
> Sister M. Boniface Pranke[22]

Unfortunately, all did not remain well for very long. The economic conditions in Glen Campbell were uncertain and insecure. There was little work to be had[23] and by 1924, the area, long-plagued by strikes, saw the closing of the coal mines which had provided employment for almost all the residents of the little town.[24] As a result, the residents of Glen Campbell began to leave the troubled area. During this unsettling period, the Reverend Marion Rosenthal was appointed the new pastor of St. Michael's Church. He was also appointed the pastor of the "mission church" of SS. Peter and Paul in nearby Arcadia which had been organized in 1905 as a "sister parish" to St. Michael's.[25] The

SS. Peter and Paul Church and School
Arcadia, Pennsylvania (1917–1928)

Franciscan Sisters of Chicago had also undertaken the staffing of SS. Peter and Paul School in Arcadia on August 13, 1917. Sister M. Dionysia Kujanek, the superior and principal, was joined by Sister M. Methodia Pajdo who was sent to teach but who remained only until March of that year. Two postulants were also sent.[26] The 129 pupils were accommodated in two classrooms made in the convent while one classroom was used in the nearby public school.[27] In 1921, the enrollment reached its peak with 189 children.[28]

When the economic conditions in Glen Campbell and Arcadia became oppressive because of the lack of employment and the departure of the residents from that area, Father Rosenthal saw how adversely the conditions had affected the maintenance of the two schools connected with the parishes of which he was pastor. He resolved to keep St. Michael's School in Glen Campbell open, but to close SS. Peter and Paul School in Arcadia which still listed 107 pupils on its roster.[29] Sister M. Bonaventure Paprocki, the superior and principal; Sister M. Crescencia Chmiel and Sister M. Vincenza Lech, therefore, were forced to return to the Motherhouse in Chicago. The parishioners of SS. Peter and Paul Church vigorously protested the closing of their parish school while that of St. Michael's remained open. As a consequence, both schools were closed in 1928 with the hope of reopening them when the economic situation would change for the better.[30]

At the closing of St. Michael the Archangel School, there were still sixty-two pupils in attendance. In a letter to Mother M. Aloysia in 1929, Father Rosenthal sadly expressed his inability to reopen St. Michael's School and doubted whether it would ever be opened again.[31] Eventually, the convent in Glen Campbell was torn down, but the lovely little church-school combination still stands today amid gigantic trees on a beautiful elevation. The church, completely renovated, is administered by a zealous pastor and enthusiastic parishioners who are proudly dedicated to their "Parish on a Hilltop."[32]

For many years after its official closing, SS. Peter and Paul School in Arcadia, the "sister school" to St. Michael's, was used for Confraternity of Christian Doctrine (CCD), classes during the summer. Two Sisters of the Congregation of St. Felix of Cantalice (Felicians) of Coraopolis, Pennsylvania, taught these classes until 1963 when they withdrew permanently.[33]

SS. Peter and Paul School, which had been used as a church hall after 1963, was eventually razed. The convent, now a privately owned home, is located directly across the road from the little white church. It has been extensively renovated throughout the years and still stands amid the lush greenery of the Pennsylvania hills in the town of Arcadia, the name given to a place the poet Virgil called "a home of pastoral simplicity and happiness." The vibrant faith of the people of Arcadia nurtured many vocations to the religious life, among them eight Franciscan Sisters of Chicago.[34]

The first of the two schools accepted in modest and poor sections of Illinois was that of St. Casimir's in Streator about fifty miles northeast of Peoria. Its founding pastor, the Reverend Wenceslaus Szalewski had petitioned Mother M. Aloysia for Sisters.[35] Sister M. Antonina Osinski was appointed the superior and principal and also taught grades five to eight. Sister M. Bridget Czuj was assigned to teach grades one to four. Because of the number of children, the classes were handled in double sessions. Sister M. Clothilde Stefiej was sent to aid the Sisters by managing the household.[36]

Streator, the "Glass Container Capital of Illinois," owed its highly industrial character to its great shale, clay, and sand deposits and to extensive coal mining which began there in 1872.[37] Many Polish immigrants settled in Streator in the early part of the nineteenth century and found gainful employment in the mines and many local industries. As had already occurred in so many other settlements, a committee of Polish men proposed the establishment of a church and the encouraging response led to the formation of St. Casimir's Parish.[38] The founding group searched for an available building to serve as a house of worship, and eventually the Beulah Baptist Church was purchased. The church was originally a gift from the Czar of Russia to Chicago's World Columbian Exposition held in 1893, and, as such, typified the Russian Orthodox architecture of that era. At the conclusion of the Columbian Exposition, the dismantled building was sent to Streator, reassembled at 401 South Illinois Street, and used by a Russian Orthodox congregation until 1910. It was then sold to the Baptist congregation, and they, in turn, sold it to the Poles who were seeking a suitable structure for the establishment of St. Casimir's Catholic Church.[39] After an extensive renovation of the building, the first mass was celebrated on Christmas Eve, 1916. An addition to the church provided two classrooms which now allowed the children to attend their own school. A house adjacent to the church served as the Sisters' convent.[40] It was here that the Sisters arrived on January 29, 1917, to begin their mission in Streator. Having had no prior opportunity to acquaint themselves with their new circumstances, Sister M. Antonina wrote to Mother M. Aloysia of the predicament the Sisters faced as the school year began:

> Dear Mother Superior:
>
> I bring you the news that we have arrived safely at the mission about 12 o'clock noon. The Reverend Pastor was not expecting us to arrive so early, but in a short time, a dinner was prepared for us. The next day, we ate breakfast and dinner at the rectory. Our lunch today was truly Franciscan because we are first going to get our dishes later in the day. Tomorrow there is a meeting concerning our classes and our classwork. Today we are beginning to clean and put our house in order since on the day after the meeting, we must begin teaching.
>
> Sincere greetings to you, Reverend Mother Superior, and to all the Sisters from all of us. In the love of the Sacred Heart of Jesus, I remain,
>
> > Your spiritual daughter,
> > M. Antonina
> > Praised be Jesus Christ.[41]

St. Casimir Church and School
Streator, Illinois (1917–1924)

Records regarding this mission are scarce, but by 1922, it became quite evident that conditions in Streator were not conducive to a fruitful apostolate. The working relationship with the pastor was steadily declining,[42] and when the newly appointed pastor, the Reverend William Woźniak arrived in March 1924, he was informed that the Sisters were relinquishing the school in June.[43] The school remained closed until 1926 when the Benedictine Sisters came to staff it.[44] After their departure in 1931, the school was discontinued and the parish itself was attended to by the clergy from the neighboring parish of St. Anthony's. Restored to the status of a parish in 1953, St. Casimir's Church today boasts a modern and functional house of worship. The one tangible remembrance of the Franciscan Sisters' apostolate in Streator is Sister M. Bronisia Kapusnik, the sole vocation to emerge from that mission.

Across the Mississippi River in Missouri, the famous Gateway Arch distinguishes the city of St. Louis. On the Illinois side, five miles north of East St. Louis, lies the little village of Madison. The area grew rapidly with the erection of the Merchants Bridge, and when the American Car and Foundry Company began operating in 1891, a giant influx of Europeans, notably Poles, settled in Madison. In 1912, in order to meet their spiritual needs, the Most Reverend James Ryan, bishop of Alton, appointed the Reverend William Woźniak to the pastorate of the newly created parish of St. Mary of Częstochowa. A two-story frame building was constructed with the church on the second floor and two classrooms and a parochial residence on the first floor. St. Mary of Częstochowa opened formally on Christmas Day, 1912, with sixty families on the parish roster.[45]

St. Mary of Częstochowa Church and School
Madison, Illinois (1917–1920)

In 1913, the Congregation of the Franciscan Sisters of Our Lady of Perpetual Help of St. Louis took charge of the school. They resided in a small house located across the street from the church-school combination. From sheer necessity, the Sisters conducted grades six through eight in the living room of their modest home.[46] Because of the increasing number of children and the lack of proper accommodations, the school was closed after a few years and all the children attended public school.[47]

The records concerning St. Mary of Częstochowa School are very scarce, and only a brief entry in the minutes of the secretary general reveals that on September 4, 1917, "a new mission was accepted by the Franciscan SS. of St. Kunegunda in Madison."[48] Three Sisters were appointed to staff the school. They were Sister M. Euphrosine Tryjanowski, teacher, superior and principal; Sister M. Sabina Bujak and Sister M. Bernadette Kowalski who was assigned to household duties. On the day following their arrival at St. Mary's, Sister M. Euphrosine and Sister M. Sabina took charge of ninety-nine pupils.[49] The following year, Sister M. Susanna Pietrzycki replaced Sister M. Sabina.[50]

In February of 1919, Sister M. Euphrosine fell ill and found it necessary to be relieved of her teaching duties. A postulant was sent to take her place in the classroom.[51] In April, Father Woźniak requested a reduction in the monthly salary paid to the Sisters from $25 to $20. These two occurrences are significant when attempting to discern the reason for the Sisters' eventual departure in June of 1920 from St. Mary of Częstochowa School.[52]

In June of 1919, Father Woźniak left for Europe to visit his parents. The visit proved to be an indefinite absence from the parish.[53] The Sisters, at the request of Mother M. Aloysia and the general council, packed their meager belongings and returned to the Motherhouse at the termination of the school year in June of 1920 with the intention of withdrawing permanently. The Reverend John Turek, OFM, who was left in charge of St. Mary's Church at the time of Father Woźniak's departure, wrote to Mother M. Aloysia and asked her to reconsider her decision not to send the Sisters back:

> The parish is what it is because of the Venerable Sisters . . . Father Woźniak should not have mixed in with the Venerable Sisters' private affairs. I agree with you fully, that it was his mistake, but I must say he is a young priest, inexperienced in this regard and he should be told at first not to meddle in the private affairs of the Venerable Sisters before any further move is made . . . perhaps the lack of a suitable school and proper living accommodations can be remedied.[54]

Father Turek's letter reveals the apparent problems existing at this mission. A study of the records which pertain to the parish indicates that the relationship between the Sisters and the "absent" Father Woźniak had deteriorated and could not be resolved.

With the Sisters' withdrawal from St. Mary of Częstochowa School in 1920, it remained closed for the next four years. In March of 1924, Father Woźniak once again petitioned for the return of the Franciscan Sisters of Chicago.[55] He was refused by Mother M. Vincent Czyzewski, the superior general. That same year, Father Woźniak resigned his pastorate.[56] He was succeeded by the Reverend David Scully, who, realizing the need for a parochial school, had plans drawn up immediately for a new building. Upon its completion in 1925, he secured the Congregation of the Sisters of Divine Providence to staff it.[57]

The last school undertaken by the Franciscan Sisters of Chicago in 1917 was located in East Chicago, Indiana. At the close of 1915, a determined group of Polish families living in the eastern section of the city proper approached the Reverend Peter Budnik, pastor of St. Stanislaus Church, about establishing a parish in their vicinity. In August of 1916, Father Budnik presented the proposed plan to the Most Reverend Herman J. Alerding, bishop of Fort Wayne, who appointed the Reverend Joseph Żielinski to be the founding pastor. Several lots were purchased in the "Calumet" area, as it was also known, and by October 1917, a church which also served as a school was erected on Kennedy Avenue and dedicated to St. Joseph.[58] Father Żielinski, hearing of the success of the Franciscan Sisters of Chicago at St. John Cantius School in Indiana Harbor, was determined to secure the Sisters to staff his school. He directed a petition to Mother M. Aloysia which she answered affirmatively.

As early as April 1917, a postulant Anna[59] was sent to teach all the combined grades in St. Joseph's church-school, and Sister Mary Welter was assigned the duty of church organist. Both Sister Mary and the postulant traveled to St. Joseph's Church every day from Indiana Harbor where they lived with the Sisters at St. John Cantius Convent.[60]

With the approach of the school year in September of 1918, Sister M. Berchmans Fidler was appointed the first superior and principal of St. Joseph's School. The same postulant Anna, and two new postulants were sent to assist Sister M. Berchmans.[61] From September to October, Sister M. Berchmans and the postulants lived at St. Florian's Convent in Hegewisch and traveled to Calumet daily. Finally, at the end of October, a small flat was made available to the Sisters in a large home with three other families several blocks from St. Joseph's Church.[62] When the postulant Anna left the congregation in November, Sister Mary Welter replaced her in the school while maintaining her duty as parish organist. In early March Sister Mary was taken ill, and Sister M. Theresia Rybak traveled daily to St. Joseph's Parish from St. Florian's School in Hegewisch to play the organ for all church services. To aid with household duties, Sister M. Gertrude Haniewicz[63] had been appointed to Calumet in October of 1918. On April 10, 1919, she died of pneumonia at St. Mary Mercy Hospital in Gary, a victim of the influenza epidemic of 1918. She was only thirty-one years old and had been in the congregation for four years. Her body was taken to the Sisters' home in Calumet. On the next day, she was exported to the church where the Solemn Vespers for the Dead were sung. On the following day, her remains were taken to the Motherhouse for services and burial. Sister M. Adolpha Waranowski was sent to replace Sister M. Gertrude in attending to household duties at St. Joseph's Parish.

At some time before 1923, Father Żielinski had secured a small frame house to serve as the Sisters' official convent. With his departure in 1923, the Reverend John Biernacki assumed the pastorate of St. Joseph's Church and proved to be extremely kind

*St. Joseph Convent
East Chicago, Indiana*

*St. Joseph School
East Chicago, Indiana (1918–1968)*

and accommodating to the Sisters who ministered at his school.[64] During his term as pastor, Father Biernacki succeeded in erecting a new school consisting of four classrooms. His successor, the Reverend August Kondziela, built an addition to the Sisters' overcrowded convent in 1927. In 1939, when the Reverend Edward Wroblewski became pastor, he launched an improvement program in which the church, school, hall, and convent were remodeled.[65]

The sixth pastor, the Reverend Joseph Buczyna was appointed in 1953. During his tenure as pastor, the school building and classrooms were modernized. It was he who in 1958 directed a letter to Mother M. Jerome Dadej which was an indication of the family spirit existing at St. Joseph's Parish:

Reverend and dear Mother:

I have a great favor to ask and I hope that it will be granted. The Most Reverend Andrew A. Grutka, bishop of Gary, as well as the superior general of the neighboring orphanage,[66] ask that we accept about thirty-five orphan girls to our school in September. The school which they attend is closing, and we have an empty classroom. It would be too much work, however, if only our three Sisters taught them. We have, until now, 145 children in school. With the girls from the orphanage, we would have close to two hundred. Can you, Reverend Mother, send just one more Sister to us? I ask you this sincerely, for I would like to honor the request of the bishop but it will be difficult if we lack enough teachers. I thank you from the bottom of my heart and wish you all God's blessings. I will remember you in my prayers.

I remain, with affectionate greeting,

In Christ the Lord,
Father Joseph Buczyna[67]

Mother M. Jerome responded enthusiastically a few weeks later:

Reverend and dear Father:

I am sorry that I did not answer sooner but I could not do so until I found a way to grant your request for another Sister for next year. It appears to me that I will be able to help you. I will try to send another teacher at the end of August or at the beginning of September. In the meantime, another classroom may be prepared.

I thank you for your prayers, and I commend myself and the entire Congregation to your priestly prayers with a promise to remember you in ours.

With deep respect,
Mother M. Jerome
Superior General[68]

St. Joseph's School eagerly accepted the orphan girls from St. Joseph's Home for Girls each year until 1968 when the school closed. The Calumet area, like so many localities during the 1960s, underwent an ethnic and racial change. All efforts to keep St. Joseph's School open despite financial difficulties and a drop in enrollment proved futile. Eventually, the lack of available Sister personnel brought matters to a crucial stage. In 1968, the Reverend Gerald Sroka, the superintendent of Catholic Schools in Indiana, deemed it feasible to close the school. On June 23, 1968, Sister Marianne Kaplan, Sister M. Eymard Sanok, and Sister M. Gabriel Lazarski reluctantly withdrew.[69] There were new challenges now facing the parish and the Calumet area. To meet them, the Sisters' former convent became the headquarters for the Catholic Family Center, and St. Joseph's School was utilized by the Cursillo Movement.[70]

EXPANDING THE SCHOOL APOSTOLATE

[1]*Ksiązka Pamiątkowa z Okazji Upomiątnienia Srebrnego Jubileuszu Polskiej Parafii Najsłodszego Serca Jezus* [A Silver Jubilee Book: Sacred Heart of Jesus Parish] (La Porte, Indiana: 1938), no pagination.

[2]*Dedication Book of the New Sacred Heart of Jesus Church* (La Porte, Indiana: 1971), p. 17.

[3]A few years later, during the height of World War I, this vibrant and enthusiastic ethnic parish had the unique distinction of meeting the world-famous Polish pianist, Ignacy Paderewski. He passed through La Porte and spoke to the Poles from the platform of the New York Central train urging them to support freedom for Poland. *Dedication Book of the New Sacred Heart of Jesus Church,* p. 17.

[4]Siostra M. Gonzaga Raniszewski, OSFK, *Rys historyczny Zgromadzenia Sióstr Franciszkanek Błogosławionej Kunegundy. Część pierwsza, 1860–1910* [A historical survey of the Franciscan Sisters of Blessed Kunegunda. Part one, 1860–1910] (Chicago: By the Author, 1947), p. 155.

[5]*Book of Correspondence:* Letter from Sister M. Martha Bywalec to Mother M. Antonina Osinski, 29 June 1938 (AFSCL).

[6]*Dedication Book of the New Sacred Heart of Jesus Church,* p. 17.

[7]*Book of Correspondence:* Letter from the Reverend Ladislaus Szczukowski to Mother M. Aloysia Holysz, 18 November 1930 (AFSCL).

[8]*Book of Correspondence:* Letter from Mother M. Antonina Osinski to the Reverend Ignatius Gapczynski, 14 May 1936 (AFSCL).

[9]Raniszewski, p. 156.

[10]*Farrell Golden Jubilee Book* (Farrell, Pennsylvania, 1951), p. 9.

[11]The congregation's archives contain the listing of a St. Casimir's School in Farrell, Pennsylvania, as having been accepted in 1917. All efforts to secure any information on the part of the author concerning this school were fruitless. In June 1977, however, the author made a trip to Farrell in an effort to locate St. Casimir's School which even the Diocese of Erie and the Diocese of Youngstown had disclaimed after numerous inquiries were made. A chance stop at St. Adalbert's Rectory proved that the "illusive" St. Casimir's School was in reality named St. Adalbert's. *Book of Closed Schools and Institutions.* (AFSCL).

[12]The postulant, Mary Wasik, later became Sister M. Philomena. *Spis Sióstr* (AFSCL).

[13]*Book of Correspondence:* Letter from Sister M. Francis Drufke to Mother M. Aloysia, 22 October 1917 (AFSCL).

[14]*Book of Correspondence:* Letter from Sister M. Francis Drufke to Mother M. Aloysia, 20 November 1917 (AFSCL).

[15]*Book of Correspondence:* Letter from Sister M. Eugenia Detlaf to Mother M. Aloysia, 13 January 1918 (AFSCL).

[16]*Book of Correspondence:* Letters from Sister M. Eugenia Detlaf to Mother M. Aloysia, 9 March 1918; 27 April 1918 (AFSCL).

[17]*Book of Correspondence:* Letter from Sister M. Daniel, provincial secretary of the Sisters of the Holy Family of Nazareth, Torresdale, Philadelphia, to author, 18 May 1978 (AFSCL).

[18]*Commemorative Booklet: St. Michael and SS. Peter and Paul, 145 Years of Faith* (Glen Campbell and Arcadia, Pennsylvania, 1975), no pagination.

[19]Ibid.

[20]The postulant was Angela Dzierwa who became Sister M. Leonarda. *Spis Sióstr* (AFSCL).

[21]*Book of Closed Schools and Institutions* (AFSCL).

[22]*Book of Correspondence:* Letter from Sister M. Boniface Pranke to Mother M. Aloysia Holysz, 13 August 1917 (AFSCL).

[23]*Minutes of General Council Proceedings, 1910–1934* (AFSCL).

[24]*St. Michael and SS. Peter and Paul, 145 Years of Faith,* no pagination.

[25]Ibid.

[26]Josephine Ochocinski, who became Sister M. Basil, was sent along with Magdalen Kolodziej who received the name Sister M. Angela. *Spis Sióstr* (AFSCL).

[27]*Book of Correspondence:* Letter from Sister M. Dionysia to Mother M. Aloysia, 12 August 1917 (AFSCL).

[28]*Book of Closed Schools and Institutions* (AFSCL).

[29]*Minutes of General Council Proceedings, 1918–1934* (AFSCL).

[30]*St. Michael and SS. Peter and Paul, 145 Years of Faith,* no pagination; *Interview* with Sister M. Crescencia Chmiel, 11 September 1977 (AFSCL).

[31]*Minutes of General Council Proceedings, 1910–1934* (AFSCL).

[32]The town of Glen Campbell, always a center of religious and faithful Catholics, produced eight vocations to the congregation in the short time of the Sisters' service there. They are Sister M. Alice Klepek, Sister M. Beata Klecha, Sister M. Callista Gach, Sister M. Clemensa Klepek, Sister M. Daniel Gach, Sister M. Eulalia Sierocki, Sister M. Michael Siebab, and Sister Maryanne Pawlikowski.

[33]*Book of Correspondence:* Letter from Sister M. David, CSSF, Coraopolis, Pennsylvania to author, 9 February 1976 (AFSCL).

[34]Sister M. Consolata Markowicz, Sister M. Dorothea Tomon, Sister M. Humilia Proc, Sister M. Innocentia Sierocki, Sister M. Julianne Markowicz, Sister M. Ludmilla Fedak, Sister M. Rosalima Sierocki, and Sister M. Venantia Rec entered the congregation from Arcadia. Author's visit to Arcadia, Pennsylvania, June 1977.

[35]*Book of Correspondence:* Letter from the Reverend Wenceslaus Szalewski to Mother M. Aloysia, 5 January 1916 (AFSCL).

[36]Raniszewski, p. 155.

[37]*Illinois Guide and Gazetteer,* p. 493.

[38]*St. Casimir's Church: Golden Jubilee, 1916–1966* (Streator, Illinois, 1966), p. 13.

[39]Ibid.

[40]Ibid., p. 14.

[41]*Book of Correspondence:* Letter from Sister M. Antonina Osinski to Mother M. Aloysia, 30 January 1917 (AFSCL).

[42]The Sisters had done everything possible to meet with the approval of the pastor. This included accepting a drop in their monthly stipend from $30 to $25 because the pastor was experiencing difficulty in paying them during this critical period. *Minutes of General Council Proceedings, 1910–1934* (AFSCL).

[43]This was the same Reverend William Woźniak who had been the pastor of St. Mary of Częstochowa Church in Madison, Illinois, where the congregation also served from 1917 to 1920.

[44]*Official Catholic Directory, 1925.*

[45]*The Western Catholic Supplement* (Souvenir Number, 25 April 1924).

[46]*Interview* with Sister M. Blandine Mainus, OSF, Our Lady of Perpetual Help Convent, Ferguson, Missouri, 27 June 1976; *Interview* with Mr. Joseph Kula, Custodian, St. Mary of Częstochowa Church, Madison, Illinois, 25 June 1976 (AFSCL).

[47]*Dedication of the New St. Mary Church* (Madison, Illinois, 25 November 1954), no pagination.

[48]*Minutes of General Council Proceedings, 1910–1934* (AFSCL).

[49]*Book of Correspondence:* Letter from Sister M. Euphrosine Tryjanowski to Mother M. Aloysia, 20 September 1917 (AFSCL).

[50]*Book of Closed Schools and Institutions* (AFSCL).

[51]Elizabeth Bojanowski, who became Sister M. Dolorosa, replaced her. *Spis Sióstr* (AFSCL).

[52]*Minutes of General Council Proceedings, 1910–1934* (AFSCL).

[53]*Book of Correspondence:* Letter from the Reverend Charles Schaefer to Mother M. Aloysia, 24 July 1920 (AFSCL).

[54]*Book of Correspondence:* Letter from the Reverend John Turek, OFM, to Mother M. Aloysia, 14 June 1920 (AFSCL).

[55]*Minutes of General Council Proceedings, 1910–1934* (AFSCL).

[56]*Golden Jubilee of St. Mary's Church, 1912–1962* (Madison, Illinois, 1962), no pagination.

[57]*Book of Correspondence:* Letter from Sister M. Catherine, Sisters of Divine Providence, Normandy, Missouri to author, 24 March 1976 (AFSCL).

[58]*A Memento of the 50th Anniversary of the Church of St. Joseph* (East Chicago, Indiana, 1967), no pagination.

[59]Any further information concerning this postulant could not be determined.

[60]*St. Joseph Home Journal* (AFSCL).

[61]A postulant, Helen Owczarzak, who became Sister M. Fabian, was sent there from April to May. Another postulant, Helen Rochowiak, who remained there from March to June, did not enter the novitiate. *Spis Sióstr* (AFSCL).

[62]*St. Joseph Home Journal* (AFSCL).

[63]Sister M. Gertrude entered from St. Stanislaus Church in Cleveland on May 14, 1915. She became a novice on July 27, 1916, and made her first profession of vows on July 27, 1917. Her perpetual vows were made on April 8, 1919, on her deathbed. *Spis Sióstr* (AFSCL).

[64]*St. Joseph Home Journal* (AFSCL).

[65]*A Memento of St. Joseph Church,* no pagination.

[66]Father Buczyna was referring to St. Joseph's Home for Girls on Grasselli Avenue conducted by the Carmelite Sisters of the Divine Heart of Jesus.

[67]*Book of Correspondence:* Letter from the Reverend Joseph Buczyna to Mother M. Jerome Dadej, 6 May 1958 (AFSCL).

[68]*Book of Correspondence:* Letter from Mother M. Jerome to the Reverend Joseph Buczyna, 14 June 1958 (AFSCL).

[69]*Interview* with Sister Marianne Kaplan, 19 May 1976 (AFSCL).

[70]*Visitation* by author, 1976.

CHAPTER 27

Guardian Angel Day Care Center

The acceptance of St. Elizabeth's Nursery on Chicago's Northwest Side in 1904 had proved to be a most rewarding new apostolate for the congregation. In 1917, therefore, when an opportunity arose to assume administration and staffing of the Guardian Angel Day Nursery and Home for Working Girls on the Southwest Side of the city, Mother M. Aloysia and her general council responded with characteristic interest and zeal.

The Guardian Angel Day Nursery and Home for Working Girls grew out of an inspired plan by a charitable and humanitarian priest to help Polish immigrants in the crowded Town of Lake section before World War I. The area, principally industrial and commercial, was the famed "Back of the Yards" situated south and west of Chicago's Union Stock Yards.

The first settlers of the area were generally Irish, Germans, Scandinavians, Bohemians, Lithuanians, and even some blacks.[1] Moved by the plight of the new Slav immigrants, chiefly Poles, who settled in the area to work in the "Yards" or the packing plants nearby, and in a determined effort to alleviate the poverty generally associated with Town of Lake, the Reverend Louis Grudzinski,[2] the pastor of nearby St. John of God Church,[3] proposed the establishment of a social center to meet the varied needs of the Polish residents. In 1912, he enlisted the aid of two neighboring pastors, the Reverend Stanislaus Cholewinski,[4] pastor of St. Joseph's Church, and the Reverend Francis Karabasz,[5] pastor of Sacred Heart of Jesus Church, to help him in his ambitious undertaking. They joined in a venture which resembled a modified example of Hull House, the famed social settlement initiated by the altruistic Jane Addams on Chicago's West Side.[6] As the guiding spirit behind the project, Father Grudzinski planned Guardian Angel Day Nursery and Home for Working Girls with four sections: a day care center for children whose mothers were forced to work; a temporary or permanent shelter for young Polish immigrant women who worked in "Packingtown"; an assembly hall for meetings, banquets, and even weddings;[7] and, finally, a health clinic or dispensary which would provide medicine and medical care free of charge to the truly needy. It also provided such activities as arts and crafts and naturalization classes in the evenings.[8] It is no wonder then that a Chicago daily paper writing about this haven called it the "ideal for the Poles of America and the pride of the Poles living in Town of Lake."[9]

The venture, which began in 1912 in a small, leased house, grew so rapidly that in 1915, the three priest-founders purchased land and erected a large, triangular structure at the junction of 46th Street and Gross Avenue (now McDowell Avenue)[10] at the cost of $65,000. Called the Guardian Angel Day Nursery and Home for Working Girls, it became one of the largest charitable institutions in the Town of Lake area, eventually serving all ethnic groups residing there. It is estimated that, by 1928, approximately twenty infants and eighty-five children were sheltered each day, and an average of thirty-eight women lived there on a daily basis. Between 1,400 and 1,500 people received medical treatment annually. In the summer, the number of children cared for often reached 150.[11]

When the project first began in 1912, Father Grudzinski secured the Sisters of the Congregation of St. Felix of Cantalice (Felicians) of the newly formed Chicago Province to staff the institution. By September of 1917, however, Father Grudzinski wished to relieve them of this responsibility. Scrupulously devoted as he was to the idea and the "ideal" of the Guardian Angel Day Nursery and Home for Working Girls, he believed he was defending a "principle and not anything else" when he asked the Felician Sisters to leave the

Guardian Angel Day Care Center
(Formerly Guardian Angel Day Care Center and Home for Ladies)
Chicago, Illinois (1917–   )

institution because "they had become unmindful of the purpose of his home," and in some instances, had attempted to govern the home for working girls by rules of convent life.[12]

Because the Franciscan Sisters of Chicago staffed St. Elizabeth's Day Nursery on the Northwest Side of Chicago, Father Grudzinski petitioned Mother M. Aloysia Holysz for the services of the Sisters at the Guardian Angel Day Nursery and Home for Working Girls. Knowing that the change in religious congregations at the institution was supported by Archbishop Mundelein, Mother M. Aloysia gladly complied with Father Grudzinski's request.[13] Within days the change in the religious congregations was pleasantly effected, and on September 28, 1917, the Franciscan Sisters of Chicago officially took charge of the institution. Sister M. Ladislaus Wroblewski, imbued with the spirit of Father Grudzinski's love and pride in the Guardian Angel Day Nursery and Home for Working Girls, undertook the administration of the institution and also served as the superior.[14] The pioneer staff also included Sister M. Ludwina Prokuszka, Sister M. Monica Frankowski, Sister M. Imelda Derbin, and several postulants.[15] At first some Sisters were sent to Guardian Angel Day Nursery for short periods of time. Sister M. Eusebius Kolupka lent her assistance from September to October. She was then replaced by Sister M. Gertrude Haniewicz who remained until January of 1918. After a few days, Sister M. Valerie Szkutak was sent as her replacement. In April of 1918, Sister M. Clemensa Steczko arrived and remained until August.

From the very beginning, the four-point plan as envisioned by Father Grudzinski met with great success. In the day nursery, located in large classrooms on the second floor, the Sisters cared for infants as young as one month old through children six years of age. A rudimentary daily program was established consisting of adequate time for play, sleep, meals, and instruction. In time, however, the age limit for children attending the day nursery was changed, and only children from the ages of two through seven were accepted. Working mothers dropped off youngsters on their way to work anywhere from six o'clock to nine o'clock in the morning. Parents were advised to pick the children up by five-thirty o'clock in the evening, but sometimes they failed to arrive until eight o'clock because of overtime at the "Yards."[16]

The home for working girls located on the third floor of the large, imposing structure provided modest but comfortable sleeping quarters in three large dormitories. In time, the dormitories were converted into twenty-two private rooms and three semiprivate rooms. A family atmosphere was encouraged by the Sisters, and the clean, pleasant home provided meals, laundry service, and medical care at moderate rates for the self-supporting women. No applicant was turned away if she were unable to pay. Records indicate that by 1957, more than two thousand women had resided at the home.[17]

Perhaps Father Grudzinski's most energetic enterprise was the well-equipped and ably conducted free medical dispensary established in September of 1914 under the supervision of Dr. Stella Napieralski.[18] It gained recognition as one of the foremost clinics in the city. In its early years, the clinic treated over 1,500 people per year.[19] The clinic was located in the basement of the institution and consisted of a large reception room, an X-ray

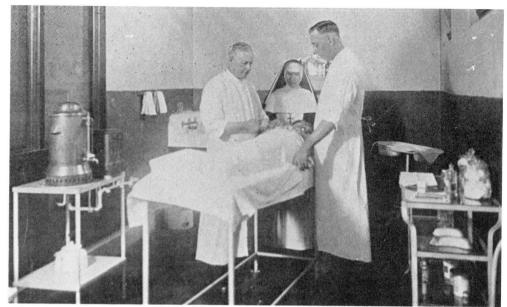

Free clinic attached to the Guardian Angel Day Care Center and Home for Ladies, c. 1917–1922

room, two consultation rooms, an operating room, and a pharmacy.[20] It was equipped to handle all ordinary cases including minor operations. Cases necessitating X-ray treatment were handled with the aid of a large and modern X-ray machine. The staff included three physicians, two pharmacists, and an optometrist all of whom maintained offices in the neighborhood and who volunteered their services. Assisting the doctors were the Franciscan Sisters of Chicago. Dr. W. J. Schneider, who was the general physician in charge of the dispensary in 1928, made this assessment of the Sisters' work in "True Christian Charity Knows No Race or Creed" appearing in a souvenir booklet commemorating the twenty-fifth anniversary of the priesthood of Father Grudzinski:

> The entire part of the building devoted to the care of the patients is kept scrupulously clean and in the most sanitary condition by the Sister in charge who deserves much credit for the excellent manner in which the dispensary is managed.[21]

According to the records of the congregation, Sister M. Ladislaus Wroblewski was assigned to the dispensary from 1927 to 1928, and Dr. Schneider's excellent appraisal of her dedication was well merited. Throughout its existence, the dispensary was under the supervision of various doctors and was open every day, except Sundays, from six-thirty o'clock in the morning until twelve o'clock noon. No one was ever denied medical aid because of creed, race, or ethnic origin. An incalculable number of patients was treated as a consequence of accidents, particularly at the "Yards."[22] During the time the dispensary was in operation, it is estimated that over 25,000 individuals were given free treatment. The figures do not represent the number of patients who were able to pay a slight fee.[23] It is generally concluded that one consequence of the establishment of the dispensary was the improvement in hygienic conditions in the Town of Lake area, especially in regard to the care of children below school age.[24]

During the epidemic of influenza which raged in 1917–1918, the members of the staff were taxed beyond their strength. Through the first third of this century, the death rate from tuberculosis was staggering and ranked as one of the highest causes of death in this area. The mortality rate was especially high for the children below the age of five years. All schools were closed as part of a desperate struggle to check the progress of the dreaded disease. The Sisters stationed at the Guardian Angel Day Nursery as well as the Felician Sisters at St. John of God School nearby aided the afflicted residents of the area while themselves braving the dangers of sickness and death. At times the Sisters remained at the homes of patients who had no one to help them. To the names of the pioneer Sisters who arrived in 1917, and who so heroically ministered to the sick and dying must be added the names of the Sisters who were stationed at Guardian Angel Day Nursery in 1918, and who, likewise, braved death in serving the residents of the troubled area: Sister M. Barbara Grochola, Sister M. Anselma Pasternacki, and Sister M. Caroline Cabaj. Sister M. Antonina Osinski stayed from March through September with four postulants.[25] It is estimated that about five thousand cases were taken care of at that time.[26] Two of the Sisters stationed at Guardian Angel Day Nursery during the severe epidemic themselves succumbed to tuberculosis a short while later. Sister M. Gertrude Haniewicz, thirty-one, died on April 10, 1919.[27] Sister M. Clemensa Steczko died on August 11, 1920, at the age of thirty-six.[28] Sister M. Caroline Cabaj, who was among those sent to the Guardian Angel Day Nursery in 1918, died of cancer two years later at the age of forty-one.[29]

During the height of the Depression years, notably 1931–1932, the Guardian Angel Day Nursery and Home for Working Girls cared for over eight hundred children who represented 413 families. Of these, only one-half paid $0.15 a day while the others were admitted free of charge. In the home for working girls, ninety-three women were provided with room and board, laundry services, and medical care. It is estimated that a significant number of the women did not pay any fees during these years. In the dispensary, over 4,151 patients were treated and paid a nominal fee while more than 10,444 received free medical attention.[30]

As late as 1942, during the worst days of World War II, Guardian Angel Day Nursery helped solve the same social problems which brought about its foundation in 1912. The work schedule at the institution was unduly taxing because of the shortage of Sister personnel. Approximately seventy-five children whose mothers went to work in defense plants, factories, and mills arrived at six o'clock in the morning and remained in the care of the Sisters until five-forty-five o'clock in the evening. There were about ten or twelve young working women living in the residence at that time who paid $6 a week for a comfortable room and a home-cooked meal. In 1937, Sister M. Dionysia Baron had arrived to take charge of the working women and remained at the institution for thirty-four years.[31] The statistics for the dispensary were also impressive. Health care services and medical examinations, with minor surgery performed twice weekly, were still being provided to more than four thousand residents of the area at little or no cost.[32] Approximately ten Sisters had the task of cleaning, cooking, educating, and ministering to the various needs of the children, the working women, and any needy persons who sought the services of the institution. Operational costs at the Guardian Angel Day Nursery and Home for Working Girls would have been higher during this period except for the surplus commodities provided by the United States government and the generosity of individual donors. The institution's chief sources of income were the Catholic Charities and its annual Associated Catholic Charities tag-day, the Back of the Yards Neighborhood Council, and an annual collection at Back of the Yards churches. As the years passed, however, and the city of Chicago's free clinics broadened their services to the public, the role of the dispensary and the services of the volunteer staff diminished. In 1952, the once-flourishing dispensary closed. The following year, Sister M. Praxeda Ostrega, the superior and administrator, approached Mother M. Jerome Dadej with the idea of transforming the institution into an orphanage because of the newly acquired space of the closed dispensary. Mother M. Jerome and the general council voted against any change or broadening of the original aim of the Guardian Angel Day Nursery and Home for Working Girls.[33] The clinic rooms were then converted into additional sleeping quarters for the women.

From its very foundation, the Guardian Angel Day Nursery and Home for Working Girls was the property of its three founders—Father Grudzinski, Father Karabasz, and Father Cholewinski. In time, however, they became increasingly less involved in the actual day-to-day operation of the institution. Because of commitments to their parishes as pastors, together with their advancing age, the priest-founders were not in a position to give the institution the attention it required. Throughout the years, the administration of the Franciscan Sisters of Chicago had petitioned the priest-founders to transfer ownership of the institution to the Sisters. The priests would thus be relieved of their responsibility and the Sisters could assume stricter control and greater freedom in the administration of the institution. As early as 1939, Mother M. Antonina Osinski had called Father Grudzinski's attention to the fact that besides staffing and administering the Guardian Angel Day Nursery and Home for Working Girls, the Franciscan Sisters of Chicago had borne the institution's financial and physical maintenance burdens as well. The congregation itself often bore the heavy responsibility for meeting the mounting costs of operating the institution and arranging for its basic repairs. It was mainly through the arduous and dedicated labor of the Sisters, which included the solicitation of funds and food by Sister M. Dosithea Ruz,[34] that the institution continued to meet its operational costs without a corresponding increase in fees for both the resident women and the children. Mother M. Antonina suggested to Father Grudzinski that he either assume greater financial liability for the institution or turn it over to the Sisters as their property and responsibility. Father Grudzinski assured her that the institution would someday become the property of the Franciscan Sisters of Chicago; until then, it would remain in the possession of its priest-founders.[35]

By 1945, both Monsignor Cholewinski and Monsignor Karabasz willingly and gladly turned over their respective one-third ownership of the institution to the Franciscan Sisters of Chicago for the services that they had rendered for almost thirty years. Father Grudzinski steadfastly refused to do so and offered no reason for his refusal. During the administration of Mother M. Jerome Dadej which began in 1946, Father Grudzinski was again approached in regard to relinquishing his share of the day nursery. Although Father Grudzinski was truly appreciative of the services which the Sisters offered at Guardian Angel Day Nursery and Home for Working Girls as well as at St. Elizabeth's Day Nursery on the Northwest Side of the city,[36] he informed Mother M. Jerome that only after his death would the congregation assume ownership of his one-third of the institution.[37]

Father Grudzinski, the guiding spirit of the Guardian Angel Day Nursery and Home for Working Girls, died on September 23, 1948. The congregation, aware that two-thirds of the day nursery was already its property, assumed that Father Grudzinski's one-third ownership would also become its property according to the contents of his will. Acting on the assumption that the Guardian Angel Day Nursery and Home for Working Girls would now belong to the Franciscan Sisters of Chicago, the superior and administrator of the institution, Sister M. Martha Bywalec, proceeded to make necessary improvements and renovations in the building in 1949. This action necessitated more financial burden on the part of the Sisters.[38] When the contents of Father Grudzinski's will were disclosed, it was revealed that the whole of his personal estate consisted of the Guardian Angel Day Nursery and Home for Working Girls, St. Elizabeth's Day Nursery, and some lots. After payment of funeral expenses and certain personal debts as specified in his will, it was revealed that Father Grudzinski made provision for legacies of $5,000 and $25,000, respectively, to private heirs. His will further stipulated that Dr. Stella Napieralski, who had directed the dispensary from its beginning in 1914 until its close in 1952 with only intermittent pauses, was to be provided with free room and board in the Home for Working Girls for twenty years after his death, in which case, the institution would then become the sole property of the congregation.[39] In November 1951, the congregation, which for over thirty years had faithfully supplied the institution with Sisters and had exercised financial responsibility for its existence, was advised to retain legal counsel to obtain possession of the Guardian Angel Day Nursery and Home for Working Girls rather than to wait the stipulated twenty years. The congregation, thus advised, paid all consequent court costs plus certain outstanding debts which were still incumbent on St. Elizabeth's Day Nursery. In September of 1952, therefore, both institutions became the property of the Franciscan Sisters of Chicago with the stipulation that Dr. Napieralski was to be provided with free room and board in the Home for Working Girls. An agreement was made to support Dr. Napieralski at the institution, but her untimely death occurred within weeks after the settlement of the legal action.[40] As a consequence, the Guardian Angel Day Nursery and Home for Working Girls was officially declared the property of the Franciscan Sisters of Chicago on October 9, 1952.[41]

For thirty-two years, the Sisters at the day nursery were without the benefit of a suitable chapel. A part of the day nursery's renovation in 1949 included the construction of a chapel from the large assembly hall which, until 1934, had been used for social functions. Besides the chapel, two sacristies and another room were made. The old and inadequate chapel and sacristy were then converted into private bedrooms for the Sisters. On May 15, 1949, the blessing of the newly erected chapel took place. The Right Reverend Monsignor Stanislaus Cholewinski imparted the blessing assisted by the Right Reverend Monsignor Francis Karabasz. The Reverend F. Bardel from SS. Cyril and Methodius Seminary in Orchard Lake, Michigan, a personal friend of the departed Father Grudzinski, delivered a sermon in Polish. The Reverend Angelo Zwiesler, OFM, the superior of the Franciscan Fathers at St. Augustine's Friary nearby, spoke in English. The Franciscan Sisters' Choir, under the direction of Sister M. Charitas Gajdzinski, sang selected hymns.[42] From the earliest years of the institution, the chaplaincy for the Sisters was the responsibility of the priests from St. John of God Parish. Since 1929, the chaplaincy for the Sisters has been the responsibility of the Franciscan Fathers at St. Augustine's Friary. The Reverend Albert J. Nimeth, OFM, who began his dedicated service to the Guardian Angel Day Nursery and Home for Working Girls in 1949, remained as chaplain until his transfer in 1980.

Throughout the years, one of the day nursery's greatest needs was a suitable playground for the children. At first, the roof of the institution had been converted into a playground by constructing a floor, and fencing and screening the roof. The Sisters already had possession of two lots which had been donated to the day nursery as the site of a future playground. Early in 1956, Sister M. Dionysia Baron, the superior and administrator, bought two more lots across the street from the day nursery for $2,000.[43] Finally, through the kindness and intercession of the Reverend Mark Hegener, OFM, of St. Augustine's Friary, the corner lot on which the St. Philip of Jesus Community Center had formerly stood was made available to the Sisters.[44] By the latter part of 1956, a lovely and suitable playground was constructed directly across the street from the day nursery. Through generous benefactors, a statue of Our Lady of Fatima was enshrined, and a grotto was erected to beautify the playground. The statue was blessed in a special ceremony on September 8, 1957, by the Reverend Marion Matlak, chaplain of the Queen of Angels Society, whose aim it was to provide financial and material assistance to the institution. A large statue of St. Joseph, the gift of a grateful benefactor, was also erected on the playground and blessed on June 22, 1958, by Monsignor Cholewinski. The Benediction which followed was conducted by Monsignor Henry Jagodzinski, the pastor of St. John of God Church, who was assisted by Monsignor Karabasz.

On the feast of Christ the King, October 31, 1965, the Guardian Angel Day Nursery and Home for Working Girls celebrated its Golden Jubilee. A Solemn High Mass was offered at St. Joseph's Church on South Hermitage Avenue by the Reverend Louis Nowak, pastor of St. John of God Church. The only living priest-founder of the institution, the Right Reverend Monsignor Francis Karabasz, was present. Monsignor Cholewinski, who was scheduled to attend the mass and banquet, had died in his sleep on October 20,

1965, eleven days before the event. The Very Reverend Monsignor Alfred L. Abramowicz of the Archdiocesan Chancery Office officiated at the celebration and the Reverend Albert J. Nimeth, OFM, the chaplain of the institution, delivered the sermon. More than one hundred Sisters were in attendance including Mother M. Beatrice Rybacki and the general council. In the evening, a banquet was held in St. Joseph's Church auditorium. Because the commemorative events of the Golden Jubilee might have proved too exhausting for him, Monsignor Karabasz was not present at the evening celebration. The keynote speaker at the event was Joseph Meegan,[45] the executive secretary of the Back of the Yards Neighborhood Council,[46] who was always one of the day nursery's greatest champions and most ardent benefactors. In conjunction with the Golden Jubilee of the institution, the Silver Anniversary of the founding of the Queen of Angels Society was also commemorated. The society, founded in 1940 by Mrs. Rose Chrobak, was an invaluable source of material aid to the institution.

At the First Extraordinary Chapter of Affairs held in the congregation in 1968, the position paper concerning the Guardian Angel Day Nursery and Home for Working Girls attested to the fact that after fifty years the institution was still providing a most valuable service, and, therefore, continued support of this ministry was highly recommended by the chapter delegates. A Great Depression, two World Wars, increased family mobility, a steady rise in the employment of women outside the home, and single-parent homes contributed to the necessary existence of the day care center. The Guardian Angel Day Nursery also extended its care to the children of parents undergoing marital stress, separation, divorce, and illness. Parents continued to rely on the institution to provide a religious atmosphere for their children even if they themselves did not provide it.

In 1973, a decision was made to change the name of the Guardian Angel Day Nursery and Home for Working Girls to the Guardian Angel Day Care Center and Home for Ladies. Under the new name as under the old, the institution continued its quality care, and in 1979, a third classroom was opened on the first floor across from the chapel to accommodate the sixty-five children whose ages ranged from two and one-half to six. In addition, the Home for Working Girls continued to serve the needs of approximately twenty resident women.

By 1983, however, it was becoming increasingly obvious that the ministry to the residents of the House for Ladies would have to be re-examined. The historical reasons for its foundation and the original purpose of the Home for Ladies had changed drastically. State laws regarding such homes, together with the changing times of society and its particular problems, led to the decision to phase out this aspect of the institution. The rooms that the ladies formerly occupied were renovated to provide further and more excellent service to the children in the day care center. In September of 1983, a kindergarten was opened, thereby increasing the enrollment in the day care center from sixty-five to ninety children.

The Back of the Yards area, always a large receiver for the foreign-born, saw the influx of Mexicans during World War I and the early 1920s. By 1928, approximately three thousand Mexicans lived in Back of the Yards.[47] As a consequence, Guardian Angel Day Care Center through the years has provided a much-needed service in the multi-ethnic but now largely Hispanic area of Town of Lake.

Today, under the guidance and supervision of the director, Sister Marianne Kaplan, the Guardian Angel Day Care Center, licensed by the State of Illinois and the City of Chicago, strives to provide a rich program of diversified activities, professional services, and most importantly, a pleasant environment for each child every working day from six-thirty o'clock in the morning until five-thirty o'clock in the evening. The Sisters[48] and the lay women on the staff continue to heed the Gospel message that originally inspired its three priest-founders: "Let the little children come to me; do not stop them; for it is to such as these that the kingdom of God belongs."[49]

GUARDIAN ANGEL DAY CARE CENTER

[1]Edward R. Kantowicz, *Polish-American Politics in Chicago. 1888–1940* (Chicago: The University of Chicago Press, 1975), p. 21.

[2]For a biography of Father Louis Grudzinski, see St. Elizabeth's Day Nursery in Chapter 16.

[3]St. John of God Church at 52nd and Throop Street on the South Side of Chicago was organized in 1906 to serve Polish families. Father Grudzinski began his thirty-nine year pastorate in June 1909. By 1922, it is estimated that 2,400 families belonged to the parish.

[4]St. Joseph Church at 48th Street and Hermitage Avenue on the South Side of Chicago was founded in 1886 to serve the Polish families who had settled southwest of the Union Stock Yards in old Town of Lake. Later this area became loosely defined as the "Back of the Yards."

Reverend Stanislaus Cholewinski was appointed the pastor of St. Joseph Church in 1910. Born in Poland, Father Cholewinski came to America when he was five years old. His family settled in the Bridgeport area where he attended Our Lady of Perpetual Help School and St. Ignatius High School. He entered St. Francis Seminary in Milwaukee and was ordained in 1902 by Archbishop Feehan. In 1941, Father Cholewinski established the St. Joseph coeducational high school of which the author is a proud 1948 graduate. In 1946, Father Cholewinski was named a Domestic Prelate with the title of Right Reverend Monsignor. After serving as pastor for fifty-five years, he retired in 1965 and died eight months later at the age of ninety. Reverend Monsignor Harry C. Koenig, ed., *A History of the Parishes of the Archdiocese of Chicago: Published in Observance of the Centenary of the Archdiocese, 1980*, 2 vols. (Chicago: The Archdiocese of Chicago, 1980), 1:518. One of the congregation's outstanding benefactors, Monsignor Cholewinski deserves to be remembered for his extraordinary generosity to the Franciscan Sisters of Chicago in their many times of need.

[5]In 1910, Archbishop Quigley appointed the Reverend Francis J. Karabasz to organize a parish for six hundred Polish families who lived near the Union Stock Yards on the South Side of Chicago. This was the beginning of Sacred Heart Church on Wolcott Avenue just south of 46th Street. The new parish was formed from the Polish parish of St. Joseph which had been established in 1886. By 1925, parish membership numbered more than 1,400 families. In the 1960s, many Polish families moved away from the neighborhood, and as a result, student enrollment dropped to 319. Today, there are about 750 families, mostly recent immigrants from Poland. Father Karabasz was a leader among the Polish immigrants and their American-born children. In recognition of his outstanding accomplishments, Pope Pius XII named him a Domestic Prelate with the title of Right Reverend Monsignor in June 1954. Father Karabasz died in the Sacred Heart Parish rectory on December 7, 1972, at the age of ninety-one. Koenig, pp. 872–873.

[6]See Chapter 6 for more details.

[7]By 1934, the assembly hall was no longer used for social functions. It was proven, in time, that the weddings, banquets, and dances conducted there proved incompatible with the general aim of the institution and the religious spirit of the Sisters. *Minutes of General Council Proceedings*, 6 August 1934 (AFSCL). To make matters worse, the Sisters also had the unpleasant task of cleaning up the debris and scrubbing the floors after many of the gala events held on the weekends in order to return the institution to "working order" for the coming week. The assembly hall was eventually converted into a lovely chapel in 1949. *Book of Correspondence:* Letter from Sister M. Dosithea Ruz to author, July 1980 (AFSCL).

[8]Secretaries General, *Community Chronicle*, 4 September 1917 (AFSCL).

[9]*St. John of God: Golden Jubilee Book, 1907–1957* (Chicago, 1957), no pagination.

[10]McDowell Avenue, which intersects 47th Street and Ashland Avenue, is named for Mary McDowell, "the Jane Addams of the Stockyards," the head resident at the University of Chicago Settlement House. At the intersection of McDowell, Laflin, and 46th Street was the notorious Whiskey Point, so called because each of the six corners at the intersection held a saloon, and more of them jutted out along each street. Eventually, two of these corners were taken over by the Guardian Angel Day Nursery and Home for Working Girls. Dominic A. Pacyga, "Villages of

Packinghouses and Steel Mills: The Polish Worker on Chicago's South Side" (Ph.D. dissertation, University of Illinois at Chicago Circle, 1981), p. 124.

[11]*Pamiętnik Jubileuszowy ku czci Ks. Ludwika Grudzinskiego, Proboszcza Parafji Św. Jana Bożego, 1903–1928* [A Jubilee Souvenir in honor of the Reverend Louis Grudzinski, Pastor of St. John of God Church, 1903–1928] (Chicago, 1928), p. 14.

[12]*Book of Correspondence:* Letter from the Reverend Louis Grudzinski to the Most Reverend George W. Mundelein, 9 September 1917 (Archives, Archdiocese of Chicago, Mundelein, Illinois; AFSCL).

[13]*Minutes of General Council Proceedings,* 4 September 1917 (AFSCL).

[14]Father Grudzinski was so pleased with the service and dedication of Sister M. Ladislaus that at the termination of her assignment in 1922, he came to the Motherhouse to request that she be sent back. Sister M. Ladislaus did not return at that time due to the fact that she was assigned to the Motherhouse infirmary. She returned in 1927 and resumed her invaluable work in the dispensary. In 1928, she was again assigned to the Motherhouse.

Sister M. Ladislaus was born Mary Wroblewski on March 16, 1881, in Kwierzno, Poland, the daughter of Joseph and Frances Wroblewski. The family arrived in America in 1890 and settled in St. Stanislaus Kostka parish. On the advice of her confessor, the Reverend John Obyrtacz, CR, she joined the small Franciscan community on December 7, 1904. She became a novice on November 29, 1905, and made her first profession of vows on December 8, 1906. She made her perpetual vows on July 27, 1915. In 1907, Sister M. Ladislaus was sent to St. Elizabeth's Hospital in Lafayette, Indiana, (1908–1911) to train as a nurse. From 1911 to 1915, she served as the superior and administrator of St. Elizabeth's Day Nursery. In 1915, she returned to the Motherhouse where she was assigned to the pharmacy and also worked in the infirmary. In 1917, she was appointed superior and administrator of Guardian Angel Day Nursery where she remained until 1922. In that year, she returned to the Motherhouse where she was assigned to the infirmary until 1927. Sister M. Ladislaus returned to the Guardian Angel Day Nursery in 1927 to work in the dispensary. At the conclusion of that assignment, she returned to the Motherhouse where she worked in the Church Vestment Workshop. In 1933, she was appointed the first superintendent of St. Joseph Home for the Aged. In later years, she held a variety of occupations at the Motherhouse. Finally, in 1962, she retired to Our Lady of Victory Convent where she died on March 20, 1965. Sister M. Ladislaus was eighty-four years old and had been in the congregation for sixty-one years. *Spis Sióstr* (AFSCL).

[15]The postulants were Ladislava Klimasz (Sister M. Annunciata); Mary Szczurek (Sister M. Pelagia); Stephanie Romanowski (Sister M. Adelle); Mary Repinski (Sister M. Assumpta); Hedwig Kujawa (Sister M. Grace); and Helen Kawczynski (Sister M. Longina). Mechtilde Raniszewski, a younger sister of Sister M. Gonzaga Raniszewski who served as the secretary general of the congregation for almost twenty-five years, left a month later because of ill health. Ibid.

[16]Pacyga, p. 124.

[17]*St. John of God: Golden Jubilee Book,* no pagination.

[18]Dr. Napieralski was herself a Polish immigrant. She had worked in Poland during the First World War treating wounded soldiers. She came to America after the War and was persuaded by Father Grudzinski to set up and manage the clinic in 1914. Sister M. Dosithea Ruz called Dr. Napieralski a "wonderful person who really took good care of the people."

[19]Pacyga, p. 126.

[20]Even a dental department was envisioned for the clinic but it never materialized. *Pamiętnik,* p. 63.

[21]Ibid.

[22]*Guardian Angel Day Nursery and Home for Working Girls House Journal* (AFSCL).

[23]*Pamiętnik,* p. 63.

[24]Ibid.

[25]Aiding the Sisters at the institution in 1918–1919 were Elizabeth Kulesza (Sister M.

Nepomucene); Josephine Olszewski (Sister M. Balbina); Thecla Lech (Sister M. Vincenza); and Angela Bidus (Sister M. Ildephonsa). *Spis Sióstr* (AFSCL).

[26]*Pamiętnik*, p. 63.

[27]For further details, see Chapter 18.

[28]For further details, see Chapter 27.

[29]Sister M. Caroline was born in Poland and came to the United States in 1903. She entered the congregation from St. John Cantius Parish in Chicago on November 9, 1907. She began her postulancy on November 10, 1907, and was received into the novitiate on July 15, 1910. She was perpetually professed on July 15, 1918. Sent to the Guardian Angel Day Nursery in 1918, she returned to the Motherhouse in 1919. Sister M. Caroline died on November 18, 1920. She had been in the congregation for thirteen years. *Spis Sióstr* (AFSCL).

[30]*Guardian Angel Day Nursery and Home for Working Girls Sheet of Statistics* (AFSCL).

[31]Sister M. Dionysia entered from St. Hyacinth's Church in Chicago on August 7, 1922. After teaching for fourteen years, she was sent to the Guardian Angel Day Nursery and Home for Working Girls. In 1955, she was named the superior and administrator and served in that capacity until 1961. In 1967, she was again named the superior and administrator. Sister M. Dionysia remained at the institution until her retirement to Lemont in 1971. She died there on May 21, 1981, at the age of ninety after fifty-nine years in the congregation. *Congregation Membership Records* (AFSCL).

[32]*Chicago Tribune*, 1942.

[33]*Minutes of General Council Proceedings*, 28 February 1953 (AFSCL).

[34]Sister M. Dosithea entered the congregation from St. Stanislaus Kostka Parish in Youngstown, Ohio, in 1929. She was assigned to the Guardian Angel Day Care Center and Home for Ladies in 1933. Except for the years in formation, she has spent her entire religious life in the Back of the Yards community. In 1985, Sister M. Dosithea celebrated fifty-two years of service at Guardian Angel Day Care Center. Her many years of dedication are well known to the Back of the Yards community and she is known to the merchants and residents of the area alike. *Spis Sióstr* (AFSCL).

[35]*Minutes of General Council Proceedings*, July 1939 (AFSCL).

[36]St. Elizabeth's Day Nursery closed in January 1916, and the property was sold to private owners. Father Grudzinski repurchased the home, made various improvements and renovations, and asked the Franciscan Sisters of Chicago to reopen the day nursery in 1920. See Chapter 16.

[37]Secretaries General, *Community Chronicle, 1947* (AFSCL).

[38]Secretaries General, *Community Chronicle*, May 1949 (AFSCL).

[39]Mother M. Jerome Dadej, *Chapter Report, 1952* (AFSCL).

[40]A short time later, after the conclusion of the legal affairs, a tragedy occurred. While she raking and burning leaves at her sister's residence, Dr. Napieralski's dress caught fire. After several days of intense suffering, she died as a result of burns. Secretaries General, *Community Chronicle*, 31 October 1965 (AFSCL).

[41]Secretaries General, *Community Chronicle*, 9 October 1952 (AFSCL).

[42]Ibid.

[43]Secretaries General, *Community Chronicle*, 31 October 1955 (AFSCL).

[44]For details concerning the Center, see Chapter 48.

[45]The Guardian Angel Day Nursery owes a large debt of gratitude to Joseph Meegan, the executive secretary of the Back of the Yards Neighborhood Council. A very successful organization founded in 1939, it is still an important factor in the Town of Lake community's life today. Mr. Meegan has been active in the prevention and treatment of juvenile delinquency and has engaged in community organization programs of health, education, housing, neighborhood conservation, recreation, business, industry, labor, senior and junior citizens, and all facets relating to community

life. He was chosen by the Jesuits of Chicago as one of "One Hundred Outstanding Chicagoans" and in 1969 was named "Chicagoan of the Year" by the Chicago Press Club. *Resume* received from the office of Joseph Meegan, executive secretary of the Back of the Yards Council, 8 September 1980 (AFSCL).

[46]In 1939, the Most Reverend Bernard J. Sheil, auxiliary bishop of Chicago; social activist Saul Alinsky; and local leader Joseph Meegan organized the Back of the Yards Neighborhood Council in an attempt to have the Town of Lake community solve its own problems. The Neighborhood Council was organized with the cooperation of local businesses, churches, and the CIO United Packinghouse Workers. The Yards model was used by Saul Alinsky to form similar organizations in other parts of the country. Pacyga, p. 124.

[47]Glen E. Holt and Dominic A. Pacyga, *Chicago: A Historical Guide to the Neighborhoods, the Loop and South Side* (Chicago: Chicago Historical Society, 1979), p. 243.

[48]Besides Sister M. Dosithea Ruz and Sister M. Dionysia Baron who served at the institution for fifty-two and thirty-four years, respectively, three other Sisters have also rendered dedicated and valuable service at the Guardian Angel Day Care Center and Home for Ladies. They are Sister M. Vincent Swies, twenty-nine years; Sister M. Ursula Murdza, twenty-seven years; and Sister M. Germaine Moson, eighteen years.

The institution's *Annals* also list six young women who entered the congregation through the inspiration of the dedicated Sisters: Sister M. Hedwinette Burliga, Sister Juanita Marie Drechny, Sister M. Laverne Rzonca, Sister M. Regina Krolak, Sister Susan Catherine Bayliss, and Sister M. Valery Ann Granat. *Guardian Angel Day Care Center and Home for Ladies House Journal* (AFSCL).

[49]Mark 10:13–16.

CHAPTER 28

Victory in Death

In 1917, while World War I still raged in Europe, Mother M. Anna Wysinski, the co-foundress of the Franciscan Sisters of Chicago, died. All her life, as we have seen, Mother M. Anna had been in precarious health. By Christmas Day of 1916 she was no longer able to leave her bed. Although her death was expected, the Sisters were most reluctant to part with her. Finally, on January 27, 1917, Mother M. Anna fell asleep in the Lord surrounded by a large group of grieving Sisters who knelt in prayer around her bed. Now the Sisters had just the fond memory of a good woman whose piety, prudence, and humility served as a splendid example to all of them.[1] They would always remember her quiet, simple, amiable, and modest nature which had made her so loved and respected.[2]

The remains of Mother M. Anna were taken to the Motherhouse chapel on Wednesday, January 31, 1917, at four o'clock in the afternoon. Preceding her coffin in the procession was a large number of Sisters from the Motherhouse and the mission homes, each holding a lighted candle. The procession included the Reverend John Kruszka, pastor of Five Holy Martyrs Church, in the company of the Reverend Joseph Tarasiuk, CR, chaplain of St. Joseph Home for the Aged; the Reverend Paul Sobczak, CR, assistant at St. Hedwig's Church; the Reverend Joseph Knapik, CSSR;[3] and the Reverend Joseph Monczynski. Once in the sanctuary, the priests sang the Solemn Vespers for the Dead.

On the cold but brightly shining Thursday morning of February 1, the funeral of Mother M. Anna Wysinski, the first superior general of the Franciscan Sisters of Chicago, took place. A Requiem Mass was offered at the main altar in the chapel of the Motherhouse early in the morning by the Reverend Joseph Tarasiuk, CR. The Reverend Joseph Monczynski, the Reverend John Osadnik, pastor of Sacred Heart Church in La Porte, Indiana; and the Reverend Joseph Żielinski, pastor of St. Joseph Church in East Chicago, Indiana, offered Low Requiem Masses at the side altars.

Following the mass in the chapel, the exportation of the remains of Mother M. Anna to St. Hyacinth Church took place at ten o'clock in the morning. Participating in this ceremony were the Reverend Paul Sobczak, CR; the Reverend John Kruszka; the Reverend Joseph Knapik, CSSR; the Reverend Stanislaus Świerczek, CR, pastor of St. Stanislaus

Bishop and Martyr Church in Chicago; and the Reverend John Chelewski, pastor of St. Mary of Częstochowa Church in Hammond, Indiana. The church was overflowing with relatives and friends of Mother M. Anna who had come to know her and to love her. At the church, the coffin was placed before the main altar on the catafalque,[4] where it was surrounded by six candles. In pews near the coffin sat those Franciscan Sisters of Chicago who were able to attend. Present also were many Sisters representing various congregations; numerous clergy were in attendance as well.

In the sanctuary of St. Hyacinth's Church was the Most Reverend George Mundelein, the archbishop of Chicago, who presided over the funeral ceremony. Present also in the sanctuary were the Right Reverend Monsignor Francis Rempe, vicar general for the women religious of the Archdiocese of Chicago, and the Reverend Dennis Dunne, vice-chancellor of the archdiocese. At the main altar, the Reverend John Zdechlik, CR, pastor of St. Hyacinth's Church, offered a Solemn Requiem Mass. He was assisted by the Reverend Stanislaus Świerczek, CR, as deacon, and the Reverend Francis Dembiński, CR, pastor of St. Stanislaus Kostka Church, as subdeacon. The master of ceremonies was Mr. H. Schultz, a cleric. Offering Low Requiem Masses at the side altars were the Reverend John Kruszka and the Reverend Joseph Knapik, CSSR. The organ was played by Mr. Karczynski while a quartet of organists, Messrs. Kowalski, Wiedemann, Bolewski, and Borowinski from neighboring churches, sang.

The Reverend Adalbert Furman,[5] pastor of St. Casimir's Church in Chicago, a very dear friend of Mother M. Anna and a generous benefactor to the congregation, delivered the eulogy. Father Furman, very generous in his accolades, bid Mother M. Anna farewell in the name of all those who were close to her. He begged his listeners to remember her goodness and to be concerned about the goals and services for which the congregation existed and to which Mother M. Anna had devoted her life. An eloquent speaker, Father Furman moved the mourners to tears in many instances. The *Dziennik Chicagoski* [The Polish Daily News], on the day of Mother M. Anna's funeral, carried Father Furman's eulogy. Although it was subsequently shown that his eulogy contained some historical inaccuracies concerning the life of Mother M. Anna,[6] his personal statements concerning her were undeniably true:

> Mother M. Anna was always happy, gracious to the Sisters, and truly maternal; she united the hearts of all those who knew her . . . everyone respected her . . . she was a beautiful example of a soul consecrated to God and doing God's work.[7]

After the eulogy, the choir sang, "My Soul, Praise God," during which time Archbishop Mundelein gave the final absolution. The six oldest members of the congregation carried the remains of Mother M. Anna from the church while the other Sisters walked behind the clergy. After a brief snack for the clergy at St. Hyacinth's rectory, the funeral cortege, led by Joseph Kowaczek, the director, left for the cemetery at about one o'clock in the afternoon. Present at the cemetery were the Reverend Joseph

Osadnik; the Reverend Paul Sobczak, CR; the Reverend John Piechowski, CR; the Reverend Stanley Świerczek, CR; the Reverend John Kruszka; the Reverend Joseph Knapik, CSSR; the Reverend Joseph Tarasiuk, CR; and the cleric. At the cemetery, in the section belonging to the congregation, Mother M. Anna was laid to rest while the mourners sang a traditional and touching funeral hymn, *"Witaj, Królowo Nieba,"* [Hail, Queen of Heaven]. The ceremony at the graveside was short because the weather had suddenly turned bitterly cold.[8]

For over four years—from 1914 to 1918—the leading nations of the world engaged in a struggle of death and destruction with their empires in ruins. Finally, Germany who had instigated the horror of World War I signed the terms of the Allied Armistice, and the long and torturous war came to an end. Firing ceased at eleven o'clock in the morning of November 11, 1918.

In the Congregation of the Franciscan Sisters of Chicago, a great sorrow had occurred just two months earlier. Sister M. Theresa Dudzik, the foundress of the congregation succumbed to cancer on September 20, 1918. The announcement of the passing of this gentle spirit appeared in an obituary editorial which was printed on September 21, 1918, in the *Dziennik Związkowy* [*Polish Daily News*] under the headline: "Of Holy Memory, Sister Mary Theresa":

> Yesterday, on the 20th of September, at 2:25 a.m., one of the oldest and most respected Sisters of the Congregation of the Franciscan Sisters of St. Kunegunda—Sister M. Theresa—died at St. Joseph Home in Avondale. After a long and painful illness, and after a lifetime of dedicated labor, she closed her eyes leaving behind her the respect and reverence of all who knew her and genuine sorrow in the hearts of the Sisters of the Congregation.[9]

After the death of her beloved friend and confidante, Mother M. Anna, Sister M. Theresa's health had seriously begun to decline. Her attacks became more frequent and her pain so intensified that she was hospitalized in March of 1918. According to her physician, Dr. Ernest Saurenhaus, Sister M. Theresa was diagnosed as having a malignant cancer. After a stay of nearly a month at St. Elizabeth's Hospital—from March 24 to April 22, 1918—Sister M. Theresa returned to her beloved St. Joseph Home.[10] Back at the convent, Sister M. Theresa was confined to her bed. It has been attested to by Sister M. Gonzaga Raniszewski in her unpublished manuscript, "Rys, Part two," that Sister M. Theresa suffered unbearable pain in the last months of her life. The depositions of Sister M. Pius Wojcicki and Sister M. Andrea Zawadzki who tended to the needs of Sister M. Theresa in the days before she died also testify to this. Sister M. Gonzaga states that the Sister M. Theresa bore her illness and the humiliations associated with it with her characteristic benevolent smile and gracious nature. She edified the Sisters by her abandonment to the Divine Will and bore her pain heroically saying from time to time: "Let all this suffering be for God."[11] Sister M. Gonzaga further records that Sister M. Theresa's chief concern, even in her intolerable pain, was not herself but her congregation. How she prayed that the congregation would bring glory to God by walking with him in the closest union! Now, nearing eternity, Sister M. Theresa could look back and thank God for the number of Sisters in the congregation—125 professed Sisters, fourteen novices, and twenty-one postulants—the 160 members of the Franciscan Sisters of Chicago in 1918.[12]

Without offering any further physical resistance, Sister M. Theresa died on Friday, September 20, 1918, at two-twenty-five o'clock in the morning after having received the last rites of the Church. According to the testimony of Sister M. Hedwig Kubera, Sister M. Theresa closed her eyes in death surrounded by the Sisters who had gathered at her bedside in prayer. Sister M. Theresa was fifty-eight years old and had been a religious for twenty-three years. The certificate of death, listing her cause of death as cirrhosis of the liver, was signed by Dr. George Dohrmann who had for over thirty years gratuitously offered his services to the sick poor at St. Joseph Home for the Aged as well as to the Sisters who were ill.[13]

The exportation of the body of Sister M. Theresa to the chapel of the Motherhouse of St. Joseph Home for the Aged took place on Sunday, September 22, 1918, at five o'clock in the evening. The chaplain of St. Joseph Home, the Reverend Joseph Tarasiuk, CR, led the procession and was assisted by the Reverend Paul Sobczak, CR; the Reverend Theophil Szypkowski, CR; the Reverend John Drzewiecki, CR;[14] the Reverend Francis Dembiński, CR; the Reverend Bronislaus Lazarowicz, CR; and the organist from St. Hyacinth's Church, Charles Borowinski. After the remains of Sister M. Theresa were brought to the chapel, Father Tarasiuk led the recitation of Solemn Vespers for the Dead.[15] The modest funeral of Sister M. Theresa took place on September 23, 1918, in the chapel of St. Joseph Home. A Solemn Requiem Mass was offered by the Right Reverend Monsignor Stanislaus Nawrocki, pastor of St. Mary of Perpetual Help Church in Bridgeport. He was assisted by the deacon, the Reverend John Piechowski, CR; and the subdeacon, the Reverend Stephen Kowalczyk, CR. The master of ceremonies was the Reverend Joseph Tarasiuk, CR, chaplain of St. Joseph Home. The Right Reverend Monsignor Francis Rempe, the vicar general for the women religious of the Archdiocese of Chicago was present in the sanctuary as the delegate of the Most Reverend George Mundelein, archbishop of Chicago. At the side altars, Low Requiem Masses were offered by the Reverend Joseph Zwierzycki, CR, and the Reverend John Drzewiecki, CR. Once again, Mr. Charles Borowinski played the organ and sang. There were numerous priests of the Congregation of the Resurrection present in the sanctuary, and in the chapel were representative members of the Congregations of the School Sisters of Notre Dame, the Sisters of the Holy Family of Nazareth, and the Sisters of the Resurrection.[16]

After the Requiem Mass, the funeral cortege left the chapel for St. Adalbert's Cemetery in Niles. At the cemetery lots, designated for the burial of the Franciscan Sisters of Chicago, the Right Reverend Monsignor Stanislaus Nawrocki conducted the burial services and preached a very poignant sermon.[17] Sister M. Theresa was laid to rest on the left side of a cemetery marker. On the right side lay her friend, Mother M. Anna Wysinski.[18] Many relatives and friends, both of Sister M. Theresa and of the congregation were present. Fathers Piechowski, Tarasiuk, Sobieszczyk, and Drzewiecki were also at the cemetery along with Charles Borowinski, the organist. Eight city aldermen representing wards near the Avondale area had supplied cars for the Sisters who accompanied the remains of Sister M. Theresa to the cemetery.

The following is the end of the article which appeared on the editorial page printed on September 21, 1918 in the *Polish Daily News,* written as it were, in a prophetic vein:

> Sister M. Theresa, living her quiet convent life—perhaps was less known than others to the larger segment of society—but those people with whom she dealt, found her work to be of great worth and her virtues truly Christian. They valued this steadfast and persevering worker in Christ's vineyard, who took care of the poor—such as abandoned orphans—and who, through selfless dedication, gave them a home and a family. For all her works and for her total commitment—her memory will remain— gracious and staunch . . . and her name will be honored for many years to come.[19]

To all appearances, the work of Sister M. Theresa Dudzik was finished. To her could now apply the words of St. Paul: "For you have died and your life is hidden with Christ in God."[20] But it was not destined to remain thus! By the late 1930s, the Congregation of the Franciscan Sisters of Chicago would come to acknowledge the holiness of their foundress and by the 1960s, she would be called the Servant of God, Mother M. Theresa Dudzik, a candidate for sainthood.

Three months after the death of Sister M. Theresa Dudzik, the congregation was saddened to learn of the death of their former spiritual director, Father Andrew Spetz, who died on December 6, 1918, in St. Louis, Missouri. From the time he had left Chicago in 1914 for St. Mary's College in St. Mary, Kentucky,[21] Father Spetz returned to visit the congregation twice. The first time was in November of 1917 when St. Stanislaus Kostka Parish was celebrating the Golden Jubilee of its foundation. Father Spetz had come from St. Mary, Kentucky, for the occasion and had taken the opportunity to spend two days at the Motherhouse with the Sisters. He visited principally with Mother M. Aloysia and the general council to whom he gave insightful and valuable advice and direction. He visited the Sisters again on July 27, 1918, on the feast of Blessed Kunegunda, when he participated in the ceremonies of reception into the novitiate and the first profession of vows; he remained for the breakfast following the ceremonies. On this occasion, Father Spetz wrote into his notebook the names of all the new Sisters in the congregation. Every day before saying mass he would glance at his notebook to see which Sister's feast fell on that day so that he could commend her to God during the mass he offered.[22]

Father Spetz remained in Chicago for a few days after the ceremonies and then left for St. Louis where he was to assume his position as rector of the newly established St. John Cantius Seminary, the major seminary for the priests of the Congregation of the Resurrection. Scarcely had Father Spetz begun his new office in August of 1918, when he died on December 6 just as he was preparing to celebrate mass.[23] When the news of his death spread throughout the congregation, a genuine sorrow overtook the Sisters. The older members who had known him personally recalled for the young professed Sisters, the novices, and the postulants Father Spetz's affection for and devotion to the young Franciscan congregation.

This noble and respected priest, the "Father of Orphans and Guardian of the Aged,"[24] was buried on December 10, 1918, from St. Stanislaus Kostka Church in Chicago. The Most Reverend George Mundelein, archbishop of Chicago, was present at the funeral together with a great number of clergy and lay persons. The Solemn Requiem Mass was celebrated by the brother of the deceased, the Reverend Theobald Spetz, CR; his nephew, the Reverend George Spetz, CR;[25] and the Reverend John Sobieszczyk, CR.[26] The Reverend Francis Gordon, CR, delivered the eulogy. Father Spetz was laid to rest in the mausoleum of the Resurrectionist Fathers in St. Adalbert's Cemetery in Niles, Illinois.

The lives of Sister M. Theresa Dudzik, Mother M. Anna Wysinski, and Father Andrew Spetz, interwoven in life, were thus also interwoven in death. Joined by a common purpose and sustained by an uncommon faith, hope, and charity, they left a legacy of service to the Church and to the People of God. The lives of Sister M. Theresa, Mother M. Anna, and Father Spetz echoed the words of St. Francis of Assisi who on his deathbed had uttered: "I have done my part. May Christ teach you yours."[27] This was the challenge they now left to every Franciscan Sister of Chicago.

There were as many Sisters present at the funeral of Father Spetz as had been possible under the circumstances. Unfortunately, the scourge of influenza was raging and more than half of the Sisters at the Motherhouse had fallen victim to its effects. The worldwide influenza outbreak of 1918–1919 was the third most devastating epidemic of all times after the bubonic plague. As many as fifty million people were killed by virulent strains of the disease that circled the world several times. This influenza (sometimes called "consumption") epidemic reached Chicago with devastating results. From September to November of 1917, there were 37,921 cases of influenza and 13,109 cases of pneumonia reported.[28] The horror of World War I was over but it was replaced by the influenza epidemic which medical science was not able to prevent. This menace did not escape the early Sisters, and tuberculosis and influenza claimed the lives of many of them. At the Motherhouse, those Sisters who were not ill ministered to those Sisters who were stricken. Much credit is due to Sister M. Antonina Osinski who, as the charge nurse, followed the directions of the congregation's benefactor, Dr. George Dorhmann, Sr., and unselfishly dedicated herself to the needs of the Sisters. Unmindful of her exhaustion, Sister M.

Antonina walked indefatigably from bed to bed ministering to the suffering Sisters and benefiting them with her skillful and efficient aid thereby earning the gratitude of the entire congregation.

During the worst days of the influenza epidemic, almost all of the schools staffed by the Sisters were closed. The Sister-teachers cared for the ill of the parishes with great dedication. Each day they went from house to house to minister to the sick. Many times, after several days of such service, the Sisters themselves fell victim to the disease. They, in turn, would be nursed back to health by other Sisters. The Sisters eagerly served the ill even if it resulted in their own deaths. Unfortunately, during the frightful months of contagion, the congregation lost several Sisters to the dreaded disease. Among them were Sister M. Theodore Laski, Sister M. Boleslaus Nagorski, Sister M. Gertrude Haniewicz, Sister M. Clemensa Steczko, and Sister M. Joseph Suchomski.[29] When finally the epidemic passed, the Sister-teachers returned to their reopened schools.[30]

VICTORY IN DEATH

[1]Secretaries General, *Community Chronicle,* p. 38 (AFSCL).

[2]*Book of Depositions:* Sister M. Martha Bywalec and Sister M. Paul Kirschbaum (ASFCL).

[3]The Reverend Joseph Knapik, CSSR, was a cousin to Mother M. Anna Wysinski. Although technically a professed member of the Baltimore Province of the Redemptorist Fathers from 1906 to 1918, he was a Canadian and made his novitiate and theological studies in Canada. In 1918, he became a member of the newly established Province of Toronto. Later, he became a member of the Redemptorist Province of Edmonton, Canada.

Father Knapik was born on August 31, 1885, in Bruss, Poland, then called West Prussia. He was baptized in All Saints Church on September 6, 1885, in Montreal, and was ordained to the priesthood by Archbishop Gauthier in Ottawa on September 11, 1911. He died on December 30, 1967, in Vancouver, British Colombia and is buried in Edmonton.

Father Knapik was fluent in many languages and so was "on the go" over a wide range of territory preaching missions to all kinds of ethnic groups. This mission work even brought him to the church of St. Joseph and St. Anne founded in 1899, principally for the French-speaking people of Brighton Park on Chicago's Southwest Side. The eventual fame of this humble parish lay in the annual novena in honor of St. Anne held yearly from July 17 to 26. Thousands of pious pilgrims have sought temporal and spiritual favors at its shrine which contains a relic sent in 1919 from the Shrine of St. Anne d'Apt in the Diocese of Avignon, France. People of various nationalities attended the novena but the greatest number of the petitioners were Polish. They came in pilgrimages from South Chicago and Indiana to hear this eloquent preacher. It became so difficult to accommodate all who wished to participate and especially to attend to the specific needs of the Polish people assisting at the service, that the pastor had a special novena in the Polish language scheduled for the Polish people in October. The Reverend Joseph Knapik conducted the first novena services and years later, when the novena was expediently moved to August, the piety and enthusiasm of Father Knapik so captivated the people that they requested his return yearly. He was known to have conducted over twenty-five Polish novenas by 1939. Father Knapik also conducted retreats at the Motherhouse of the Franciscan Sisters of Chicago for several years. *Book of Correspondence:* Letter from the Reverend Barnabas D. Hopkins, CSSR, provincial archivist to author, 8 October 1975 (AFSCL); *Book of Correspondence:* Letter from the Reverend Klennert Johnson, CSSR, Redemptorist provincial residence, Toronto, Canada, to author, 29 December 1975 (AFSCL); *Golden Jubilee of St. Joseph and St. Anne Church, 1899–1939* (Chicago, Illinois, 1939), pp. 27–33; and *Interview* with Sister M. Kingnetta Szczypula, January 1976.

[4]The catafalque is the platform used before the sanctuary to receive the coffin of a deceased person.

[5]See Chapter 14.

[6]For example, Father Furman stated that Mother M. Anna was born on December 31, 1850, and came to America in 1878. Historical records indicate that she was born on August 30, 1850, and came to America in 1873. That he gave credit to Mother M. Anna as having conceived the idea of the community and that the growth of the community "fell entirely upon the shoulders of Mother M. Anna" is inaccurate. In all justice, it is inconceivable that the title of "Foundress" can be applied to anyone but Sister M. Theresa Dudzik as this history solidly records. *Dziennik Chicagoski* [The Polish Daily News], 2 February 1917.

[7]Reverend Adalbert Furman, *Dziennik Chicagoski,* 1 February 1917.

[8]*Dziennik Chicagoski,* 2 February 1917; and Secretaries General, *Community Chronicle,* p. 38 (AFSCL).

[9]*Dziennik Związkowy,* 21 September 1918.

[10]Gayle Soukup, RRA, Medical Records Department, St. Elizabeth's Hospital, Chicago, Illinois, Microfilm of Surgery Registers and Patient Registers to author, 20 February 1976 (AFSCL).

[11]*Book of Depositions:* Sister M. Elizabeth Baut, Sister M. Alexandra Jablonski, Sister M. Hedwig Kubera, and Sister M. Clara Ogurek (AFSCL).

[12]*Spis Sióstr* (AFSCL).

[13]Edward J. Barrett, county clerk, State of Illinois, certificate of death #24434, photocopied from the original (AFSCL).

[14]The Reverend John Drzewiecki, CR, was stationed at St. Stanislaus Kostka Church after his ordination in 1909. He served at several Resurrectionist parishes in Chicago and in 1929 was appointed pastor of St. Stanislaus Church where he served until 1935. He served as chaplain at St. Joseph Home for the Aged from 1935 until his death in August of 1936. Edward T. Janas, CR, *Dictionary of American Resurrectionists, 1865–1965* (Rome: Gregorian University Press, 1967), pp. 15–16.

[15]Secretaries General, *Community Chronicle,* p. 43 (AFSCL).

[16]Ibid., p. 44.

[17]Siostra M. Gonzaga Raniszewski, OSFK, "Rys historyczny Zgromadzenia Sióstr Franciszkanek Bł. Kunegundy. Część druga, 1910–1940" [A historical survey of the Franciscan Sisters of Blessed Kunegunda. Part two, 1910–1940] Typewritten, unpublished manuscript (AFSCL), p. 151.

[18]On September 9, 1918, the remains of Mother M. Anna Wysinski were reburied on the right side of the monument in St. Adalbert's Cemetery. On the left side, the open grave was left for Sister M. Theresa who at this time was very ill and for whom the doctors held little hope for recovery. The Sisters do not remember why this was done. *Book of Depositions:* Sister M. Clara Ogurek and Sister M. Pius Wojcicki; and Secretaries General, *Community Chronicle,* p. 38 (AFSCL).

[19]*Dziennik Związkowy,* 21 September 1918.

[20]Col. 3:3.

[21]Father Spetz worked at the college from 1914 to 1917. From 1917 to 1918, he served as a missionary among the Poles in the mountains of Tennessee and Kentucky with the Reverend Michael Jagłowicz, CR. Father Spetz also labored as a missionary among the black people in St. Monica's Parish in Lebanon, Kentucky. They had become so fond of him that they cried when he was transferred to St. Louis as rector of St. John Cantius House of Studies.

Father Jagłowicz, the beloved "mountain missionary," was president of St. Mary's College in St. Mary, Kentucky, for twenty-five years. He was, however, the only priest in Kentucky and Tennessee who could speak Polish and hear the confessions of the Slavic peoples living there. Because of this, he made numerous missionary journeys to the Catholics in the mountains of Kentucky and Tennessee. Father Jagłowicz held the office of superior general of the Congregation of the Resurrection from 1932 to 1943. John J. Iwicki, CR, *The First One Hundred Years: A Study of the Apostolate of the Congregation of the Resurrection in the United States, 1866–1966* (Rome: Gregorian University Press, 1966), p. 129.

[22]Raniszewski, "Rys, Part two," pp. 150–152.

[23]Iwicki, p. 185.

[24]Siostra M. Gonzaga Raniszewski, OSFK, *Zarys półwiecza Zgromadzenia Sióstr Franciszkanek Bł. Kunegundy* [Sketch of the fifty-year history of the Congregation of the Franciscan Sisters of Bl. Kunegunda] (Chicago: By the Author, 1944), p. 31.

[25]The Reverend Theobald Spetz, CR, and the Reverend George Spetz, CR, were members of the Ontario-Kentucky Province of the Congregation of the Resurrection. The Reverend Theobald Spetz, in particular, was a recognized leader in local historical circles of the province and authored the valuable *History of the Catholic Church in Waterloo County* in 1916. The *Dziennik Chicagoski,* on the occasion of the 100th Anniversary of the foundation of the Congregation of the Resurrection, called Father Spetz's book a "gem."

[26]The Reverend John Sobieszczyk, CR, born in Poland in 1879, was ordained in Rome in 1903. He served at various Resurrectionist parishes in Chicago and served as pastor at St. Hyacinth's Church in Chicago from 1920 until his death in 1926. He was a popular speaker at church and patriotic celebrations. Edward T. Janas, CR, *Dictionary of American Resurrectionists, 1865–1965* (Rome: Gregorian University Press, 1967), p. 57.

[27]James Meyer, OFM, *The Words of St. Francis* (n.p., n.d.), p. 236.

[28]Department of Health of the City of Chicago, "Report on an Epidemic of Influenza in Chicago Occurring During the Fall of 1918," in *Report and Handbook of the Department of the City of Chicago for the Years 1911–1918, Inclusive* (Chicago: House of Severinghaus, 1919), p. 40.

[29]Sister M. Josepha Suchomski, a native of Poland, entered from St. Hedwig's Church in Chicago on November 21, 1899, as one of the pioneer Sisters of the community. On December 8, 1900, she became a novice under the direction of Sister M. Theresa Dudzik and made her first profession of vows on December 15, 1901. Her perpetual vows were made on August 12, 1910. Sister M. Josepha was in charge of the orphans at St. Vincent's Orphan Asylum from 1902 until February of 1908, when she was sent as the superior to the orphanage established in St. Hedwig's parish. She returned to the Motherhouse after three weeks when the orphanage closed. In 1911, she was assigned to the Church Vestment Workshop. In January of 1914, Sister M. Josepha was appointed mistress of candidates. Two months later, she was removed because of illness. Continuously in ill health, Sister M. Josepha was forty-two years old and had been in the congregation for nineteen years at the time of her death on August 30, 1918. *Spis Sióstr* (AFSCL).

The deaths of the other Sisters mentioned are in the histories of their respective missions.

[30]Raniszewski, "Rys, Part two," p. 153.

CHAPTER 29

The Spirituality of Sister M. Theresa Dudzik

When Sister M. Theresa died, she left very little which a biographer could explore in the light of her interior life. Outside of her "Chronicle," there are really no other written sources by which we might form a picture of Sister M. Theresa's spiritual life. Although she had, on occasion, written letters offering spiritual direction to some Sisters, none of these letters have been preserved.[1] What little else we have learned of her character and spirituality we have learned through the depositions collected by the postulator for the cause of her beatification.[2] These depositions are the testimonies of Sisters who had been her novices or of other Sisters in the congregation who had had personal contact with her. Very little fact, then, is known of the interior life of Sister M. Theresa, and it is, therefore, a very formidable task to write of her spirituality. But from what we have seen in this history thus far and later from the depositions of the Sisters, it is possible to construct a "spiritual portrait" of this noble and compassionate woman.

In her pious fervor, Sister M. Theresa drew on the rich storehouse of doctrine found in the works of two great masters of the schools of spirituality: St. Francis de Sales and St. Francis of Assisi.

The first of these, St. Francis de Sales,[3] was a principal contributor to the history of spirituality. As we have seen thus far, the Reverend Vincent Barzynski, CR, and the Reverend Andrew Spetz, CR, had served as spiritual directors to Sister M. Theresa and her pioneer community. Both Father Barzynski and Father Spetz, as members of the Congregation of the Resurrection, were deeply filled with the Salesian spirit, the legacy of their Resurrectionist founders. There can be little doubt, then, that St. Francis de Sales, the "Gentleman Saint," deeply influenced Sister M. Theresa.

If St. Francis de Sales was a good instructor in the school of spirituality, Sister M. Theresa was a good pupil. From his masterpieces of spiritual guidance, Sister M. Theresa learned that love is the apex of the Salesian spirit. To love God who loves humanity is the goal of perfection and the way that leads to this good.[4] Basically, the spirituality of St. Francis de Sales is positive and optimistic and not simply a list of prohibitions and negations.[5] Penance has value insofar as it enables one to grow in charity. Instead of concentrating, as did so many spiritual masters, on the advice of "being humble, poor, temperate, and mortified," he urges souls to "cultivate love and let it take root in order to grow strong." He was convinced that love generates virtue.[6]

One of St. Francis de Sales's principal contributions to the school of spirituality which impressed Sister M. Theresa was the belief that holiness is connected with the loving daily practice of the duties of one's state of life. Each person must excel in his profession: the worker must be a good worker, the soldier a good soldier, and the Sister must be a good Sister.[7]

Another basic teaching of St. Francis de Sales was his belief that souls should not ask for suffering but welcome it when it does come. He considered self-imposed penances such as fasting very commendatory, but he thought it even better if penance that had been sent by the Divine Will were borne generously and patiently. It is abandonment to Divine Providence that is important, a lesson that Sister M. Theresa learned early in life.[8]

For St. Francis de Sales, Christianity was always human. It was the flowering of the human person since theology teaches that the supernatural builds on the natural. As a consequence, he understood all forms of affection especially friendship. God's love possessed St. Francis de Sales so completely that he wished others to possess it as he did; consequently, he excluded no one from his personal love.

As far as prayer was related to the spiritual life, St. Francis de Sales considered mental prayer or contemplation the way to grow in love. Nevertheless, he also attached great merit to vocal and ejaculatory prayer which he called "exercises in devotion." He did not believe in wearisome vocal prayer but advocated instead always "to pray with ardor."[9] Each day he recited the rosary, and he had great devotion for the Divine Office which he believed should be recited correctly and devoutly so that its beautiful thoughts could develop to their full effect.

This noted theologian was among those who had done most to restore the practice of frequent and even daily Holy Communion. In his famous treatise, *The Introduction to a Devout Life*, St. Francis de Sales recommends Holy Communion— "to the strong that they will not become weak, and to the weak so that they become strong." By holding this theory, he reacted vigorously to the powerful and rigorous opinions held by the Jansenists[10] whose viewpoints, unfortunately, persisted even in the early 1900s.

Overflowing with good nature, kindness, generosity, and compassion, St. Francis de Sales was a saint whose natural virtue was vivified by grace. To him is attributed the famous lightsome quotation which so characterized his life: "You will catch more flies with a spoonful of honey than with a hundred barrels of vinegar." All during his lifetime, he stressed God's mercy, goodness, and love.[11] This was the alpha and omega of all his spiritual teachings which became deeply rooted in the soul of Sister M. Theresa.

If one were to read *Franciscan Perfection* by Cesaire De Tours, it is not surprising to learn:

> But for greater variety we have not hesitated to draw on the rich store of
> doctrine found in the works of certain masters of spirituality, such as St.

Francis de Sales, Bossuet, and Fenelon, who though not members of the Franciscan Order, are linked to the Franciscan family in thought or teaching. The doctrine of these men confirms and at times completes the teachings of the Doctors and the Fathers of the Franciscan Order.[12]

The doctrine of St. Francis de Sales did indeed link him to the Franciscan Order, and so it is not surprising that Sister M. Theresa also found inspiration for her life in the ideals of the founder of the Franciscan Order, the Seraphic St. Francis of Assisi.[13] When Sister M. Theresa, as Josephine Dudzik, was enrolled in the Third Order of St. Francis at St. Stanislaus Kostka Parish, she early acquired his special spirit and expressed that spirit in works of piety and charity. Since the first members of the original foundation group were also tertiaries, Josephine Dudzik and the women who joined her to devote themselves to the service of the poor, aged, and crippled eagerly accepted the Rule of the Third Order of St. Francis and attempted to embrace its Franciscan life and spirit.

In all actuality, Franciscan spirituality holds all practices and principles in common with other schools of spirituality. But St. Francis of Assisi was unique insofar as he understood his personal vocation to be a call to the exact imitation of Jesus Christ, and his particular vocation was to spread his own ideal among people.[14] When Francis turned to Christ, he discovered a new meaning in his life:

> Christ is living. He loves us. Let us believe in him. Let us imitate him and
> we will find that we are transformed into him. Therefore, let us observe
> his Gospel to the letter and without any additions.[15]

Indeed, the Franciscan Rule opens with the words:"The form of life of the members of the Order of St. Francis is to observe the Holy Gospel of Our Lord Jesus Christ living in obedience, in chastity, without owning anything of their own." Franciscanism is the imitation of Jesus based on his words and example. The formula that sums up Franciscan spirituality is this: "I live now, not I, but Christ lives in me."[16]

In *Some Schools of Spirituality* edited by Jean Gautier, the Reverend Valentin Breton, OFM, discusses the school of Franciscan spirituality the principles of which guided Sister M. Theresa throughout her religious life. Summarily, Father Breton emphasizes the Franciscan's conviction that he is guided by the spirit of Jesus and, so, zealously yearns to give himself in loving service to God and neighbor. In seeking the Kingdom of God like Christ, there are certain basic devotions that are a part of the Franciscan spiritual life. In substance they are: 1) the Holy Eucharist, a vital symbol of the union with Christ; 2) the imitation of Christ, the result of a deep and personal love for him; 3) the Holy Spirit, the author of the living transformation in Christ, the ultimate goal of the Franciscan; 4) the Blessed Virgin Mary, since she is Christ's Mother by God's own choice; and 5) the Mystical Body of Christ, which provides doctrine and sacraments to the Church to which the Franciscan owes love and obedience.[17]

The Franciscan, according to Father Breton, knows that the Liturgy of the Eucharist, meditation, and prayer are essential means of union with Christ. Since the world belongs to Jesus Christ, the world is good and to be made holy. All created things are revered since they come from God and human beings more than all others since all are brothers and sisters.

According to St. Francis of Assisi, the foundation stones of the Franciscan way of life are humility, simplicity, and poverty. Penance is welcomed by the Franciscan because it means a change of mind and heart under the inspiration of the Holy Spirit. For St. Francis, to be obedient to God is to be totally united to the Father's will producing a kind of radiant joy that cannot be destroyed.[18] Zeal and compassion in the apostolic life means desiring to help one's neighbor especially the poor and disadvantaged since all are created in the image of Christ, a belief held sacred by Sister M. Theresa.

One hallmark of spirituality which identifies St. Francis of Assisi is his role as a messenger of peace and nonviolence. There is also his spirit of fraternity—the "family spirit"—which he emphasized for his Francisan Order. Another of his beliefs is that the Vicar of Christ as the visible head of the Church is deserving of deep loyalty. St. Francis' own love for the Church and the priesthood is legendary.

Perhaps the virtue most often associated with St. Francis of Assisi is poverty. In its Franciscan context, however, poverty is much more than the essential deprivation of material goods. This virtue becomes the means of union and transformation in God because it recognizes the creature's dependence on his Creator and the need to rid oneself of all that is not of God. The ultimate goal is to achieve a true inner poverty. The humble soul, stripped of itself, is reduced to essential poverty sometimes called "seraphic" poverty, since it proceeds from intense love. This condition, in turn, makes room in the soul for fervent charity, the highest virtue to be sought.[19]

Several aspects of Sister M. Theresa's life in the spirit according to the examples of St. Francis de Sales and St. Francis of Assisi become very evident. These salient features formed the basis of her own spirituality and clearly served to identify her as a pattern for imitation.

Both St. Francis of Assisi and St. Francis de Sales had preached that the religious life was built on prayer as the foundation stone. Sister M. Theresa, as their fervent disciple, exhibited a devout and sincere prayer life. Her calm, humble exterior so revelatory of interior peace was the result of her spirit of and love for prayer. She always showed the greatest reverence during the Holy Sacrifice of the Mass and while reciting the *Little Office of the Blessed Virgin Mary*,[20] both of which she regarded as privileged moments. The other Franciscan or traditional forms of prayer or worship such as the rosary, visits to the Blessed Sacrament, meditation, spiritual reading, the daily examen, the Way of the Cross, the Rosary of the Seven Joys of the Blessed Virgin Mary known as the Franciscan Crown, litanies, novenas, and holy hours were all practiced by Sister M. Theresa herself and encouraged in the congregation in an effort to live the Gospel message to serve God and his people in holiness.

As a consequence of her fervent prayer life, it follows that the spirituality of Sister M. Theresa was rich in the love of the Blessed Sacrament. Her "Chronicle" clearly reveals her attitude toward the Eucharist: "At times, I felt such a great yearning for Jesus in the Blessed Sacrament, that I was ready to run to the church at any time, even late in the evening" . . . "I could not contain my joy at the thought that from this day forward, we would have the Blessed Sacrament in our small chapel" . . . "The longing for Jesus in the Blessed Sacrament returned again and again." It would appear, then, that the Holy Eucharist was the basis and center of her life. In her worship of the Holy Eucharist, the Liturgy of the Eucharist naturally held the most important place. Consequently, a characteristic outgrowth of her participation in the Eucharist was her devotion to Christ in the Blessed Sacrament. It was only natural, then, that in the congregation's daily spiritual exercises, a Eucharistic visit preceded the recitation of the *Little Office of the Blessed Virgin Mary*, and spiritual communion was always a part of the self-examen performed at noon. Benediction of the Most Blessed Sacrament and Adoration of the Blessed Sacrament before the First Fridays of the month were also a part of the Eucharistic devotion fostered by Sister M. Theresa. Being a woman of reflection and perception, she was well aware, however, that devotion and celebration of the Eucharist, to be genuine and complete, should lead to charity and mutual understanding as well as to greater apostolic activity and Christian witness.

St. Francis of Assisi had great reverence for the Holy Eucharist and a reverence for churches. Upon entering any church, he immediately prayed: "We adore you, Most Holy Lord Jesus Christ, here and in all your churches throughout the world, and we bless you because by your Holy Cross you have redeemed the world." Since the foundation of the congregation the Franciscan Sisters of Chicago have, therefore, begun and ended all their communal prayer exercises with this invocation.[21]

Devotion to the Blessed Virgin Mary had always been an integral part of Josephine Dudzik's spiritual life. Her membership in the Young Ladies' Rosary Sodality and the Archconfraternity of the Immaculate Heart of Mary at St. Stanislaus Kostka Parish had vastly strengthened her Marian devotion. When Josephine and the Franciscan tertiaries anticipated living in common to pray and to work as the outward sign of their commitment to the aged and the poor, they made a novena to the Blessed Virgin Mary in order to discern the Will of God regarding their decision. From its very beginning the congregation was placed under the patronage of Mary, the Immaculate Conception, and December 8 was designated as the official date of its foundation. In her "Chronicle," Sister M. Theresa speaks of the gratitude due to the Mother of God in the actual foundation of the congregation, and she calls the feast of the Immaculate Conception "the feast that I loved best in the whole year." Sister M. Theresa's interior life also revealed her love for the rosary and for the *Little Office of the Blessed Virgin Mary*. Among the Marian features in the congregation was the addition of the name *Mary* as a part of each Sister's name in religion. The Sisters wore the Franciscan Crown—the chaplet of the Seven Joys of the Blessed Virgin Mary—and were encouraged to recite it daily. The congregation's commitment to the Marian ideal is signified by the letter *M* and the Madonna lily, symbol of the Immaculate Conception, which is embossed on the ring received at the time of

Mother Mary Theresa Dudzik (a later portrait)

perpetual profession. This symbol also forms an integral part of the emblem of the Franciscan Sisters of Chicago.[22] Today, in the formula used for the profession and renewal of vows, the Franciscan Sisters of Chicago add as part of the formula, " . . . and I entrust my vows to the Blessed Virgin Mary."

While reading her "Chronicle" and the depositions of the pioneer Sisters, one cannot overlook the fact that Sister M. Theresa's spiritual life included an intense devotion to St. Joseph. Sister M. Theresa notes in her "Chronicle" that from the very beginning of the congregation, St. Joseph was chosen as one of its singular patrons and the host of all its institutions. The congregation's first institution for the aged was called St. Joseph Home. Sister M. Theresa often refers to St. Joseph as "the patron and master of our home" and in her "Chronicle" she writes: "St. Joseph heard my prayers and help came" . . . "He always gives help to anyone who asks" . . . "St. Joseph always remembers us, for in spite of all our hardships, we are never really abandoned." There are many examples in this history and in the depositions of the Sisters which tell of the numerous ways—both spiritual and material—in which St. Joseph came to the aid of the congregation, especially in its formative years. One of the most memorable examples is contained in the deposition of Sister M. Alexandra Jablonski:

> A group of novices was preparing to make their first profession in 1916. Because of the war in Europe, it was very difficult to obtain material for their new habits. The novices were reconciled to wearing their old, mended habits when, just prior to the day of profession, the new material arrived. Sister M. Theresa put aside her other duties and working arduously and tediously into the night, sewed a habit for each of the novices. The habits fit perfectly without having been measured. When the novices thanked Sister M. Theresa, she replied with a smile: "St. Joseph managed to send the material on time."[23]

Sister M. Theresa's life, both in the world and in religion, was ordinary. Her abandonment to Divine Providence and her complete conformity to God's Will in all the events of her life, however, were extraordinary. Herein she followed the doctrine of both St. Francis de Sales and St. Francis of Assisi who preached the blessedness of doing God's Will. Early in her "Chronicle" she states: "In spite of my adversities, I maintained my happy disposition since I saw the Will of God in all life's events" . . . "I submitted to God's Will" . . . and again, "I knew He would bless me if I cooperated with His grace." On other occasions she wrote, "My doubts disappeared after I submitted myself to the Will of God" . . . "I only wished that God's Will be done. I allowed him to do with me as he wanted." These statements are all indicative of her profound trust in God.

Sister M. Theresa was a model of boundless confidence in Divine Providence. While enduring years of suffering and obscurity, hard labor and physical illness, she bore herself with quiet dignity. The disappointments and vexations which threatened the very existence of the community she had labored so zealously to establish might have caused another person to sink beneath the burden, but Sister M. Theresa, recalling her promise to Father Barzynski to sustain the community at any price and to persevere in it, accepted the pain and contradiction she encountered as a manifestation of God's Holy Will. Even when she was deposed from the office of mother superior by Father Barzynski, she said to the Sisters: "This is what God wants of me." Overlooked for a position of authority at the Second General Chapter of Elections held in 1916, and in rapidly declining health, she was relegated to arduous labor in the garden and greenhouse. Yet she could pray with the Psalmist: "Behold, Lord, I come to do your Will."

While Sister M. Theresa did not speak of reparation as the aim of the community she founded, this aspect of penance is indispensable to a religious, who, in the spirit of St. Francis of Assisi, is lovingly drawn to Christ Crucified. Penance and atonement, therefore, were very visible in her life. For Sister M. Theresa, penance did not mean merely fasting, mortification, and discipline but a *metanoia,* a conversion of life, an ongoing process of directing oneself to the Lord, exemplified by self-denial. Sister M. Theresa did not practice nor prescribe bodily austerities or penances for her followers. Her "Chronicle" speaks for itself. On more than one occasion, she writes: "This act required much self-denial" . . . "I often chose the hardest tasks. I say this not to praise myself, but to admit God's ready assistance" . . . "When it was necessary to sacrifice myself in order to bring about peace among the Sisters, I did not hesitate" . . . "I desired to bear more so long as God was not offended" . . . "When something occurred to make me unhappy, I offered it to Jesus and hoped for the best." In a spirit of penance and renunciation, she accepted physical pain, mental and emotional stress, material poverty and discomforts, and even the animosity of others. She welcomed insult and persecution and rejoiced in suffering although these were repugnant to her. In her "Chronicle," she states: "After God and the Mother of God, I owed the greatest gratitude to him [Father Barzynski]. My success was due to his directing me on the road to self-denial." She realized that God does not demand extraordinary mortification but the deepest denial of one's self. Perhaps that is why Sister M. Theresa loved and had a devotion to the Holy Face. Such a devotion was a means for making reparation to Christ for all the insults and irreverences which he endured for sinners and by which Sister M. Theresa hoped to console him.

When Sister M. Theresa consented to take upon herself the burden of organizing the community, Father Barzynski had exacted a promise from her "to care for the community in times of difficulty as well as in times of prosperity." She writes in her "Chronicle": "The thought that I had freely agreed upon this undertaking for the love of Jesus Christ sustained me . . . " "I resolved not to lose heart in adversity, but to labor all the more energetically for the survival of the community" . . . "I would," she stated, "consider it even great happiness to be able to suffer for the greater glory of God and the good of this community." Quietly and unobtrusively, she worked to maintain the community materially by the labor of her hands. Sister M. Theresa knew that community was people. She understood that to choose God in religious life meant to accept the Sisters in community life. She believed in the force and the merit of the Rule and the

Constitutions to promote living in harmony and mutual support. With unwavering firmness, she always insisted on regular observance. Oftentimes, she upheld the Rule and Constitutions at the risk of incurring the rancor and disfavor of others. In her charity, however, she embraced all the Sisters, even the most curt and insensitive. She endured severe superiors and surly Sisters. Despite the suffering caused her by particular Sisters, as we have noted, she did not exclude them from her kindness.

Sister M. Theresa was sensitive to the needs of the Sisters, and she was admirably sensitive to the sick. She was especially delighted when new members joined the congregation. One of her most charming characteristics was the hospitality that she showed guests. She loved to welcome the guests of the postulants, novices, and Sisters and to refresh them with cake and coffee while conversing with them. Always amiable herself, she urged the Sisters to remain hospitable and to be particularly grateful and gracious to all benefactors whom she truly considered a blessing to all the community.

In the midst of community, friendship had its place. Both Sister M. Theresa and Mother M. Anna recognized the role of affectionate esteem and mutual understanding in their lives. They showed the fullness of personal enrichment which is a part of friendship—appreciation, loyalty, forbearance. Before they began their lives in common with the founding of the community, Sister M. Theresa and Mother M. Anna were known as the "pious ladies of St. Stanislaus Kostka Parish." In later years, when Sister M. Theresa related the beginnings of the community to the novices and postulants, she never failed to give credit to Mother M. Anna for her faithful support and early financial aid. "If it were not for Mother M. Anna," she would say, "we could never have done this [built St. Joseph Home for the Aged and Crippled]." Sister M. Theresa also valued the friendship of Father Vincent Barzynski, and at his death, she wrote in her "Chronicle": "My grief was greater than when my parents died—whom I loved dearly." She likewise considered Father Andrew Spetz a blessing to the community.

The physical aspects of poverty, so central to the Franciscan spirit, are apparent on nearly every page of the congregation's early history. The material want and the dependence on the charity and goodness of others are indelibly recorded. But Sister M. Theresa lived a much broader aspect of poverty, that is, she lived as a pilgrim en route to her Father's house. Therefore, she could say in her "Chronicle": "I could not live in comfort while others suffered" . . . "I felt the misery and sufferings of others" . . . "I was preoccupied with the thought of how I could be of service to the poor and the needy." She had mercy and compassion on the poor and yearned to relieve their suffering in some practical manner. She realized, however, that poverty meant more than "doing without." The spirit of true poverty meant availability, the use of one's time, knowledge, and talent for others. People who lacked certain abilities, religious consciousness, proper dispositions toward life, and perhaps even the simple courtesies of everyday living, whether they were people in the world or Sisters in the community, were also classified as needy, and as such, were benefactors of her kindness. This point is best illustrated in *Go to My Brethren: A Spiritual Document for Apostolic Communities of Franciscan Women:*

Blessed and confident in God's provident care, members of the Franciscan Gospel Brotherhood [Sisterhood] regard all things, persons, fortunes—both good and ill—as gifts to be gratefully, generously shared. But the thrust of poverty lies in the giving away of ourselves, sensitive to the Lord as he points out the truly needy.[24]

Franciscan joy was evident in the life of Sister M. Theresa—not forced or artificial cheeriness or unseemly laughter, but the joyous countenance and the kind tongue.[25] She wrote in her "Chronicle": "I possessed a happy disposition and I loved to sing very much. I did not like gloominess or tears." Many Sisters testify that nothing pleased Sister M. Theresa more than to see the Sisters happy and content. Like a true Franciscan, she was always a messenger of peace. In her conduct, she might be said to represent the peace and goodness of God.

In choosing the Way of St. Francis of Assisi as the expression of their consecration, the Franciscan Sisters of Chicago adopted the Franciscan coat-of-arms as the central portion of the emblem of the congregation and the motto, "My God and My All"— St. Francis' frequent aspiration and ideal.

No spiritual portrait of Sister M. Theresa would be complete without mention of a most pertinent characteristic: her love for and fidelity to the Catholic Church, which in essence we have seen, emerges as her distinct charism as a person and as a foundress. After the example of St. Francis of Assisi, Sister M. Theresa was obedient to the laws of the Church, to the Holy Father, and to its duly authorized bishops. Like St. Francis, she had a deep reverence for the priesthood.[26] Throughout her religious life, Sister M. Theresa was herself obedient and encouraged obedience to those within the community who exercised authority. In the old *Franciscan Ceremonial* at the taking of perpetual vows, the Sisters regarded as their ideal the sacrifice of self to Christ "as a holocaust for the Church and the salvation of souls."[27] Because of her love for the Church, Sister M. Theresa used the resources of her mind, body, and will to respond to the Church's needs. To minister to the People of God, she dedicated herself in joyful service to the Church and expected no less from her spiritual daughters.

During the archdiocesan process for the beatification of Sister M. Theresa, her novices' depositions presented a picture of a warm and loving novice mistress who displayed a mother's love and concern. She urged the young Sisters to persevere in spite of any hardships they might encounter. The advice she gave them was typical of her: "You must have a spirit of prayer, or you will find it hard to persevere."[28] She always presented the spiritual life as a simple but sincere effort: "Pray with great faith and God will take care of everything."[29] To a group of novices about to make their first profession, she said: "My children, think carefully about making your profession. It is better to leave the convent than to make vows and not keep them."[30] Her uplifting words brought strength and reassurance to the Sisters: "Give yourself to Jesus. Let Jesus teach you."[31] Her patience and kindness were obvious. She frequently addressed her novices and postulants affectionately calling them "my dear children," *"dziecko"* [child], or "my beloved children."[32]

From the depositions provided by other Sisters, it appears that Sister M. Theresa practiced as many virtues as circumstances necessitated. Most of the Sisters described her as diligent in the daily work surrounding the care of the aged and orphaned. She labored quietly and unobtrusively always taking upon herself the most fatiguing tasks.[33] Certainly one of the most impressive virtues attributed to Sister M. Theresa was her humility. Numerous Sisters attest to the fact that when she related the beginnings of the community to the novices or the professed Sisters, she spoke in such a way that they did not know that she had founded the community. She praised Mother M. Anna Wysinski and the pioneer Sisters for their zeal and steadfastness in times of trial but she never mentioned herself.[34] Other Sisters emphasized her unyielding faith, quiet fortitude, and gracious but modest manner. Collectively, these virtues produced in Sister M. Theresa a kind of magnanimity, a generosity of heart and elevation of soul. Cardinal Newman in his *Parochial and Plain Sermons* wrote: "What is more elevating and transporting, than the generosity of heart which risks everything on God's word!"

At the First Extraordinary Chapter of Affairs held in the congregation in 1968, the Sister-delegates saw the need to revise and update the Constitutions of the Franciscan Sisters of Chicago in the light of the post-Vatican era. The chapter produced the Interim Constitutions, the first section of which included a Spiritual Document meant to capture the essence of the congregation and to reveal the charism of Sister M. Theresa Dudzik—to be subservient to the Church and ever aware of her needs. A charism, by definition, is a personal gift or grace given by the Holy Spirit for the good of the Church.

It would be accurate to say that Josephine Dudzik had early perceived the needs of the people she felt called to serve. She attempted to understand the plan of Divine Providence drawing her to what she felt was a new and greater service to her neighbor, and she responded to it. It was Josephine's overflowing love of God and her compassion for the aged, crippled, and poor that prompted her commitment to the exercise of the spiritual and corporal works of mercy, and as Sister M. Theresa, to the establishment of the Congregation of the Franciscan Sisters of Chicago. She had received from God the grace for a particular way of life and a specific ministry within the Church. Her charism, passed on to her followers, has determined the congregation's identity, way of life, spirit, spirituality, structures, and mission.

In her humility, Sister M. Theresa was conscious of her lack of formal education and adequate theological training. She acknowledged that there were those who were her intellectual and cultural superiors. Even in this she resembled St. Francis of Assisi who used to call himself "a little unlettered man" but who, in reality, revealed himself to be a brilliant theologian "who attended no school of prayer and who knew no master but the Crucifix."[35] The biographers of St. Francis tell us that he did not intend, at least in the beginning, to create a particular movement or to establish a new religious order. He simply wanted to live according to the Gospel of Jesus Christ.[36] Because he was God's instrument, however, St. Francis of Assisi was able to create a tremendous and vital movement in the

Church. His first companions joined him because they had been attracted primarily by his example, by his simply "being what he was."[37]

Perhaps that is the secret of Sister M. Theresa Dudzik's interior sanctity of spirit and the blessed success of the initital grace accorded her by God which led eventually to the formation of the Congregation of the Franciscan Sisters of Chicago. It was what she *was* that made what she *did* worthwhile. As we have seen, Sister M. Theresa Dudzik did not leave behind numerous manuscripts or literary documents which could bear witness to her teachings or ideals. She simply left the example of her own life and work. With St. Paul she could say: "By the grace of God I am what I am and his grace in me has not been in vain."

THE SPIRITUALITY OF SISTER M. THERESA DUDZIK

[1]*Book of Depositions:* Sister M. Alexandra Jablonski and Sister M. Humilianna Lemanczyk (AFSCL).

[2]These depositions were secured by the Reverend Henry Malak, the archdiocesan postulator for the cause of beatification of Mother M. Theresa Dudzik, over a period of several years notably 1959 to 1964.

[3]Born of an aristocratic family in the Duchy of Savoy in 1567, Francis de Sales was destined by his father to be a lawyer. Instead, he revealed plans for entering the priesthood to his parents and was firmly opposed. Developing into a devout and intelligent preacher, Francis was ordained and elected provost of the Diocese of Geneva which was then a center of heretical Calvinists. By his amiable serenity and Christian meekness, coupled with his lucid and masterful eloquence in the pulpit, Francis succeeded in winning over seventy thousand of the Calvinists back to the Catholic faith. The success of his labors and the holiness of his life led to his appointment as bishop of Geneva.

St. Francis de Sales wrote profusely and brilliantly. His best-known works are *Introduction to a Devout Life* and *A Treatise on the Love of God.* With St. Jane de Chantal, he established the Sisters of the Visitation and the Salesian Fathers. On December 28, 1622, he died in Lyons at the age of fifty-six and was declared a Doctor of the Universal Church by Pope Pius IX in 1877. His feast is celebrated on January 24. Jacques Douillet, *What Is a Saint?* (New York: Hawthorn Books, 1958), p. 18.

[4]Msgr. Francis Vincent, "The Spirituality of Saint Francis of Sales," in *Some Schools of Catholic Spirituality,* ed. Jean Gautier (New York: Desclee Co., 1959), p. 255.

[5]Ibid., p. 256.

[6]Ibid., p. 259.

[7]Ibid., p. 264.

[8]Ibid., pp. 261, 266.

[9]Ibid., pp. 276, 283–84.

[10]Jansenism was a body of erroneous teaching developed by Cornelius Jansenius (1585–1638), the bishop of Ypres, Belgium, after the Reformation. Likened to "Catholic Puritans," Jansenists were austere, sullen, and pessimistic. They believed that human nature was utterly corrupted by original sin, and Christ died only for those predestined for heaven. One of the unfortunate results of its teachings was that it discouraged frequent Holy Communion. It looked upon Holy Communion as a reward rather than a remedy; therefore, children were not admitted to Holy Communion and even devout Catholics did not receive the Eucharist frequently because they felt unworthy. This false reverence was eventually attacked by St. Pius X who in 1906, made it possible for children who reached the age of reason to receive Holy Communion and for frequent and even daily Communion for all Catholics. Jansenism also attacked matters concerning the sacraments and the liturgy. It advocated a very rigorous code of morals and asceticism which affected the Catholic Church for many years despite its condemnation by several Popes. *New Catholic Encyclopedia,* 1963 ed., s.v. "Jansenism."

[11]Vincent, p. 252.

[12]Cesaire De Tours, OFM, Cap. *Franciscan Perfection,* trans. Paul Barrett, OFM, Cap. (Westminster, Maryland: Newman Press, 1956) p. 43.

[13]St. Francis of Assisi, the patron saint of the Third Order, is a saint who for over eight hundred years has attracted the love and admiration of people of all faiths. Both Catholics and non-Catholics alike have loved and admired "everybody's St. Francis," as he is often lovingly called.

Francis was born in Assisi in Umbria in the year 1181 or 1182, the son of Pietro and Pica Bernardone. His father, a wealthy cloth merchant, traded much with France and perhaps for this reason the child was called Francisco although he had been baptized John. High-spirited and adventurous as a youth, Francis reveled with his friends taking little interest in his father's business. It was the age of chivalry, and Francis was thrilled by the songs of the troubadors and the deeds of knights. At the age of twenty, Francis set out to win glory as a knight but fell seriously ill. While he was recuperating, a voice seemed to tell him to turn back and to "serve the Master rather than man."

Francis decided to change his life and after a pilgrimage to Rome, devoted himself exclusively to the poor and the sick. One day, the crucifix at the humble Church of San Damiano where he was praying said to him: "Francis, go and repair My house which you see is falling to ruin." Taking the message literally, he devoted himself to repairing ruined churches. During this time he was denounced by his father. He retired to a little chapel called the Portiuncula, two miles below Assisi, where he began his life of poverty. Soon he attracted followers and in 1209, the date of the founding of the Friars Minor [Fratres Minori], he went to Rome and succeeded in obtaining verbal approval from Pope Innocent III for his Rule, patterned after the gospel. The "Lesser Brothers," as his followers were called, devoted themselves to prayer, manual labor, and preaching the gospel in the effort to restore the Catholic Church. Poverty was the fundamental ideal. The new order grew quickly. By 1212, St. Clare became one of his most ardent admirers and followers and the foundress of the "Poor Ladies of San Damiane" [the Poor Clares].

In the years following the foundation of the Friars Minor, Francis traveled to Syria and attempted to reach Morocco to preach to the Mohammedans. Once again illness caused him to return to Italy. By this time the order had become so large that it was necessary to organize provinces. In 1217, the First General Chapter was held at the Portiuncula with approximately five thousand friars in attendance.

In 1221, Francis drew up a Rule for lay men and women who wished to associate themselves with the Friars Minor but who remained "in the world." They were called Franciscan tertiaries, Third Order members, or as they are known today, Secular Franciscans. Recognizing that the order needed more active leadership than he was able to provide, Francis resigned as head in 1220. He then set about to revise the Rule and in 1223 the final Rule was approved by Pope Honorius III. His health severely undermined and going blind, Francis returned to Mount Alverna in 1224, and there on September 14, he received the Stigmata, the marks of Christ's wounds on his hands, feet, and side. On the evening of October 3, 1226, he died in Assisi at the age of forty-four or forty-five. He was canonized in 1228 by the former Cardinal Ugolina who was now Pope Gregory IX. Reverend Joseph Vann, ed., *Lives of the Saints,* with an Introduction by the Reverend Thomas Plassmann (Roslyn, New York: W. J. Black, 1953), pp. 234–247.

[14]Valentin Breton, OFM, "Franciscan Spirituality," in *Some Schools of Catholic Spirituality,* ed. Jean Gautier (New York: Desclee Co., 1959), p. 49.

[15]Ibid., p. 52.

[16]Ibid., p. 64.

[17]Ibid., pp. 69–71.

[18]Cajetan Esser, OFM, *The Order of St. Francis,* trans. Ignatius Brady, OFM (Chicago: Franciscan Herald Press, 1959), p. 37.

[19]Breton, p. 73.

[20]After the Second Vatican Council, the *Little Office of the Blessed Virgin Mary* was replaced by the *Liturgy of the Hours*, the public prayer of the Church.

[21]Albert Paul Schimberg, *The Larks of Umbria* (Milwaukee: Bruce Publishing Co., 1942), p. 51.

[22]See Appendix C.

[23]*Book of Depositions:* Sister M. Alexandra Jablonski. (AFSCL).

[24]Federation of Franciscan Sisters of USA, *Go To My Brethren: A Spiritual Document for Apostolic Communities of Franciscan Women* (Pittsburgh: Federation of Franciscan Sisters of USA, 1969), pp. 33–34.

[25]Boniface Hanley, OFM, and Salvator Fink, OFM, *The Franciscans: Love at Work* (Paterson, New Jersey: St. Anthony's Guild, 1962) p. 172.

[26]St. Francis always showed esteem and great consideration to priests. In them he saw the Son of God and those who in this world minister the Eucharist to the People of God since priests alone consecrate the Body and Blood of the Lord. English-Speaking Conference of the Order of Friars Minor, *I Have Done My Part; May Christ Teach You Yours* (Pulaski, Wisconsin: Franciscan Publishers, 1981), p. 19.

[27]*Franciscan Ceremonial* (AFSCL).

[28]*Book of Depositions:* Novices of Sister M. Theresa Dudzik (AFSCL).

[29]*Book of Depositions:* Sister M. Ludwina Prokuszka (AFSCL).

[30]*Book of Depositions:* Sister M. Martha Bywalec (AFSCL).

[31]*Book of Depositions:* Sister M. Chester Dziarnowski (AFSCL).

[32]*Book of Depositions:* Novices and Postulants of Sister M. Theresa Dudzik (AFSCL).

[33]*Spis Sióstr, 1909–1919* (AFSCL).

[34]*Book of Depositions:* Sisters (AFSCL).

[35]Breton, pp. 53, 55.

[36]Arnoldo Mondadori, *The Life and Times of St. Francis* (Philadelphia and New York: Curtis Publishing Co., 1967), p. 26.

[37]Esser, p. 41.

CHAPTER 30

A Milestone Reached

In September of 1918, the Franciscan Sisters of Chicago took charge of another school in Indiana. Before the Assumption of the Blessed Virgin Mary Parish was organized, the pioneer Poles in New Chicago, Indiana, attended St. Bridget's Church in Hobart. Anxious to have a parish of their own, thirty-three families resolved to form a Polish parish in 1917.[1] With the permission of the Most Reverend Herman Alerding, bishop of Fort Wayne, the Assumption of the Blessed Virgin Mary Parish was the result. The Reverend Peter Kahellek, pastor of St. Hedwig's Church in Gary, offered the first mass on the first Sunday of Advent in 1917 in an old, abandoned school building. In May of 1918, the Reverend Ignatius Gapczynski was appointed pastor of the Assumption of the Blessed Virgin Mary Church and the Holy Family Church in Tolleston as well. Seven months later, the Reverend Anthony Górek assumed the role of permanent pastor of the Assumption of the Blessed Virgin Mary Church and remained until 1921. During his tenure of office, the first frame church building was blessed in May of 1921.[2]

During Father Górek's pastorate, the Franciscan Sisters of Chicago ministering at St. Hedwig's Parish in Gary were requested to maintain the choir and sacristy at the Assumption of the Blessed Virgin Mary Parish on Sundays. Sister M. Wenceslaus Gorski was sent as the organist and choir director while Sister M. Patricia Eiress fulfilled the duties of sacristan. In September of 1918, the Assumption of the Blessed Virgin Mary School opened with forty children in grades one through eight. The children were all in one class held in the church and under the supervision of Sister M. Zygmunta Zebracki. Sister M. Zygmunta who also served as the organist after the departure of Sister M. Wenceslaus traveled daily from St. Hedwig's convent in Gary. Later, to spare herself the inconvenience of traveling, Sister M. Zygmunta was able to secure sleeping quarters in a parishioner's home.[3]

When the school year began in September of 1919, three Sisters were assigned to the Assumption BVM School. Sister M. Dominic Makowski served as superior, principal, and teacher of grades one through three. Sister M. Theresia Rybak, in addition to teaching grades four through eight, was also the organist. Sister M. Irene Stojak was assigned to household duties. The Sisters made their home in a rented house located about a half-block from the church. Fortunately, the basement of the Sisters' house was capable of being utilized as a classroom for Sister M. Dominic's pupils while Sister M. Theresia conducted her classes in the church.[4] In the meantime, Father Górek was in the process of having a house built for the Sisters on Arthur Street, closer to the church.

When the school year ended in June of 1920, the Sisters were determined not to return in September because of a pronounced disagreement between Sister M. Dominic and Father Górek. At his earnest entreaties, however, the Sisters resolved to try again. In September of 1920, Sister M. Salomea Grabowski, although the procurator general of the congregation at this time, arrived to assume the additional assignment of superior-principal. Sister M. Blandine Orlowski replaced Sister M. Irene Stojak in the domestic department. Only Sister M. Theresia Rybak remained of the original group sent to staff the school.[5] By this time, the Sisters were living in their newly constructed residence. Meanwhile, classes for the children continued in the church and in the basement of the Sisters' new home.

Within a few months, dissension arose again between the Sisters and Father Górek. Mother M. Aloysia Holysz and her general council resolved not to allow the Sisters to return to the Assumption BVM School for the 1921–1922 school year. When they learned, however, that the Reverend Michael Gadacz had been assigned to replace Father Górek, the Sisters promised to return. An entirely new group of Sisters was sent to the school in September. The group included Sister M. Genevieve Swiatowiec, superior and principal; Sister M. Fabian Owczarzak, teacher; and Sister M. Borromea Stryjewski who was assigned to household duties.[6] That same year a parish hall was built which was later remodeled into badly needed classrooms for grades one through six. Classes were held for grades seven and eight in a nearby store which had previously served as a bakery and which had been converted into classrooms.[7]

Assumption of the Blessed Virgin Mary School and Hall
New Chicago, Indiana (1919–1969)

Assumption of the Blessed Virgin Mary Convent
New Chicago, Indiana

The Sisters stationed in New Chicago underwent numerous hardships. In April of 1935, for example, during the later stages of the Depression Era, Sister M. Josephata Tadych, the superior-principal; her sister, Sister M. Antoinette Tadych; and Sister M. Felicissima Wierciak[8] were receiving partial relief from Hobart Township. The Sisters were informed by the County District Supervisor that it was impossible for them to receive any more aid and that they should seek all aid from "their own organization."[9] Hardships such as this, however, were easy to accept when the difficulties of the 1940s are considered.

In July of 1939, the Reverend Valerian Karcz was appointed the new pastor of the Assumption BVM Church. Almost immediately, he set about building a new church-school combination which was completed by 1940. Although in 1930 the school roster had indicated fifty-seven children, by 1941, there were 150 listed. Father Karcz added classrooms and modernized the school facilities.[10] In terms of the Sisters' convent, however, the conditions were less than favorable. In 1942, a letter directed to the Most Reverend John F. Noll, bishop of Fort Wayne, Indiana, revealed that problems existed at the mission which made life for the Sisters barely tolerable:

Your Excellency:

May I take the liberty to express my surprise and dismay at the contents of Your Excellency's recent letter concerning New Chicago, Indiana. Not once had I even as much as mentioned a new home for the Sisters to Father Karcz, and as far as I could ascertain, neither have the Sisters residing there demanded this. One very just complaint the Sisters have made, namely, the lack of water in the house. The Sisters are compelled to beg and carry water from the neighbors. These people do not seem to mind when the Sisters request enough for drinking purposes only, but when larger quantities are necessary, it is frequently refused them because the electricity used to pump this water is an added expense. The janitor is supposed to see to the supply of water which must be carried from the school building at times, but he is either usually too busy with other chores, so he claims, or else, he is unable to do so on account of his condition. Father Karcz promised to remedy this three years ago. The Sisters are still waiting.

Mother M. Mechtilde[11]

In 1952, ten years after Mother M. Mechtilde's letter to Bishop Noll, an addition was made to the Sisters' convent which helped to alleviate the previously cramped conditions. The ever-present problem of securing water was also finally resolved.

As a consequence of the First Extraordinary Chapter of Affairs held in 1968, a decision to close several schools was made by the delegates after a thorough study of the apostolate of education in the congregation. The Assumption of BVM School was one of them. There were 122 children in the school when it closed in June of 1969. Sister Ann Rose Mroz, the principal and sister-in-charge; Sister Marianne Kaplan; and Sister M. Celeste Walkowski returned to the Motherhouse to be reassigned. The Franciscan Sisters of Chicago accepted the decision to leave the school in which for fifty years they had cultivated the Catholic faith and solid academic achievement.[12]

In 1919, the Franciscan Sisters of Chicago made only one foundation, namely, Sacred Heart of Jesus School in Cleveland. The Sisters agreed to staff the school at the request of the pastor who had been favorably impressed by the work done at St. Casimir's School which the Sisters had undertaken in 1903 in Cleveland.

Cleveland, at that time the fourth largest city in America and one of the four largest sites of Polish settlements in the United States, welcomed Poles in 1872 when the immigrants sought employment at the Graselli Company and the Newburgh Steel and Wire Company. Since the majority of the settlers worked at these factories, the pioneer Cleveland Poles settled in the southeastern part of the city near their places of employment.[13]

The first settlers, faithful to their Roman Catholic tradition, established St. Stanislaus Bishop and Martyr Church, the "Mother Church of the Poles in Cleveland," near Forman and Broadway in what was called the *Warszawa* neighborhood. By 1915, ten new parishes had been established and four principal Polish sections had developed.[14] The first division of St. Stanislaus Bishop and Martyr Parish, occurring in 1890, had resulted in the creation of the new parish of Sacred Heart of Jesus in what was called the *Sercowo* or *Kraków* district from East 71st Street to Harvard Avenue and then to the city limits.[15] The reasons for the emergence of the new section were valid. The long distance from St. Stanislaus Bishop and Martyr Church prohibited the parishioners from sharing fully in parish life. Many older members complained that they could not attend mass or church devotions, particularly during the winter, because of the distance. Children of school age found difficulty in regular attendance at school for the same reason. Because of its proximity to the *Warszawa* district where most of the city's Poles had been centered for half a century, the *Kraków* community seemed to be always at a disadvantage as far as cultural and social activities were concerned. The parishioners of *Sercowo,* therefore, petitioned the Most Reverend Richard Gilmour, bishop of Cleveland, for their own church and pastor; he assigned the Reverend Anthony Kolaszewski, pastor of St. Stanislaus Bishop and Martyr Church, to supervise the formation of the new parish. In the latter part of 1891, Bishop Gilmour appointed the Reverend Marion Orzechowski to serve as the first permanent pastor of Sacred Heart Church.[16] In the summer of 1889, a frame combination church and school was built at East 71st Street and Kazimier Avenue. The cornerstone was laid on September 29, 1889, and on Christmas Day, Father Orzechowski celebrated mass for the first time in the new structure. The church was located on the second floor of the building; the first floor was divided into four classrooms. In the spring of 1890, the school opened with fifty students under the supervision of the church organist who now assumed the role of teacher as well. In 1892, the Congregation of the Sisters of St. Felix of Cantalice (Felicians) were invited to staff the school.[17] The enrollment increased rapidly and by 1900, the school had 195 pupils under the direction of two Felician Sisters and a lay teacher.

With the continued growth in parish membership, larger accomodations were necessary. In 1908, the Reverend Victor Szyrocki, the fourth pastor of Sacred Heart Church, initiated construction of a new church in a lovely area completely surrounded by an orchard of fruit trees which, even today, retains the title of *Ogrodowa,* the "Orchard." The orchard was cut down in 1908 when the digging for the basement of the new church was begun. The new structure, standing fourteen feet from the ground, was covered with what was believed to be a temporary flat roof. All services were held in the basement of the structure which now served as the church. The parish census at this time listed approximately eight hundred families totaling nearly five thousand people.[18] The steady growth continued, and by 1915, there were 522 pupils and seven Felician Sisters.[19] Further construction of the church was delayed because of a lack of funds. Optimistically, the parishioners looked forward to the church's completion within the next ten years, but instead, it did not occur until almost fifty years later.[20]

In the meantime, the rapid increase in school enrollment demanded a new school. Opposing views held by the parishioners over whether the building of a church or school should receive priority resulted in a complete standstill on completion of the church. With the arrival of another new pastor, the Reverend John Czyżak in 1916, the decision to build the school prevailed. Construction of a twelve-room, red brick, two-story building facing East 71st Street began in the summer of 1916. By 1918, the faculty consisted of eighteen Felician Sisters with a school attendance of 860 pupils.[21] The old church was then remodeled into a parish hall.

Sacred Heart of Jesus School
Cleveland, Ohio (1919–1979)

The Franciscan Sisters of Chicago had first come to Cleveland in 1903 when they accepted the invitation to staff St. Casimir's School in the city's *Kaźmierzowo* or *Poznań* district. In 1918, Sister M. Innocenta Antosz was principal and superior of that school. In a series of letters addressed to Mother M. Aloysia Holysz, the superior general, Sister M. Innocenta related numerous inquiries that Father Czyżak had made regarding the Franciscan Sisters of Chicago and whether or not they were available to staff the school of a "certain" priest who was in dire of teachers. Sister M. Innocenta surmised, and future events proved her assumption correct, that Father Czyżak was actually speaking of himself. When he referred to a "certain" priest who was in extreme need of teachers, he himself was in the process of attempting to replace the Felician Sisters who had served faithfully at the parish for almost twenty-seven years and with whom he was undergoing a crisis. In further correspondence, Sister M. Innocenta acquainted Mother M. Aloysia with the benefits of accepting Sacred Heart School: "Once again, I beg you, Reverend Mother, if he [Father Czyżak] writes for Sisters, please do not refuse him. The pastor is very kind, the school is beautiful, and the classes are not overcrowded. "[22]

At the beginning of June 1919, the Felician Sisters "with sorrow and regret left a beloved parish."[23] The misunderstanding between the pastor and the Sisters was never clearly explained and caused more misunderstanding among the parishioners.[24] In a series of letters, Father Czyżak prevailed upon Mother M. Aloysia to send the Franciscan Sisters of Chicago to staff the school. In September of 1919, the following Sisters began their duties at Sacred Heart of Jesus School: Sister M. Innocenta Antosz, superior and principal; Sister M. Jolanta Nowak; Sister M. Methodia Pajdo; Sister M. Domicela Swiech; Sister M. Thomas Halgas; Sister M. Seraphia Bejrowski; Sister M. Bernadine Ostrega; Sister M. Philomena Wasik; Sister M. Blanche Bartkowski; Sister Bernice Marie Junio; Sister M. Grace Kujawa; Sister M. Celestine Potwora; and Sister M. Petronella Kuta. Six postulants were also sent.[25] The next year, eight new Sisters were added to the staff. They were Sister M. Kostka Baron, Sister M. Isidore Wilkos, Sister M. Pauline Dydo, Sister M. Sebastianna Nowak, Sister M. Sylvia Lewandowski, Sister M. Ildephonsa Bidus, Sister M. Seraphine Zamrowski, and Sister M. Romana Szkutak. Three of the pioneer Sisters, namely, Sister M. Jolanta Nowak, Sister M. Domicela Swiech, and Sister M. Petronella Kuta were transferred. Because of the large number of pupils, two postulants were also needed.[26] Sorrow overtook the parish that year, however, when Sister M. Methodia Pajdo died of postoperative complications at St. Alexis Hospital on March 23, 1921, at the age of thirty-three.[27]

In 1922, the Reverend John Młotkowski assumed the pastorate of Sacred Heart of Jesus Church. Unfortunately, he met with the same serious financial problems which had plagued his predecessors for so many years. Clearly the bond of social cohesion and parish loyalty and support were sorely lacking in the parish.[28] In 1926, there were 1,013 children in the school. By 1931, enrollment had dropped to 825. During the next five years, the enrollment plunged to 412 pupils. During this time, the Reverend Joseph Kocinski became the seventh pastor of Sacred Heart Church. Even with his arrival, however, the parish could not extricate itself from the apathy which enveloped it. As a consequence, many families joined neighboring parishes, and, eventually, only two hundred families remained on the parish roster.[29]

In June of 1927, the Most Reverend Joseph Schrembs, archbishop-bishop of Cleveland, appointed the Reverend Stanislaus Rybacki the new pastor of Sacred Heart Church. The history of the parish is forever intimately associated with the colorful, enigmatic Father Rybacki.[30] Upon his arrival and during the first years of his tenure as pastor, he succeeded in rekindling love, loyalty, and pride in the parish. After attending to the parish's spiritual needs, Father Rybacki turned his attention to its very apparent material needs.[31] Enthusiastically the parishioners paved the schoolyard—a virtual sea of mud—with bricks. The seventy-five-year-old schoolhouse, remodeled and serving as the Sisters' chapel, was repaired. The Sisters' residence, a private house located two blocks away from the church, was renovated and painted.[32] A proper heating system was installed. For these and many other necessary repairs the parishioners volunteered their services wholeheartedly thereby creating a genuine spirit of loyalty and pride which eventually became a characteristic of the Sacred Heart Parish family.

On May 6, 1951, a long-awaited event took place. An imposing stone church in Modern Gothic with a unique facade and seating one thousand people was built under the direction of Father Rybacki and was dedicated by the Most Reverend Edward Hoban, archbishop-bishop of Cleveland. The new church was erected above the original basement structure which had been built forty-three years before.[33]

As early as 1935, there had been some consideration given to beginning a high school at the parish. A letter in the archives of the congregation testifies to the fact that Mother M. Antonina Osinski had written a letter to the Reverend Joseph Kocinski in which she replied to his inquiries regarding the establishment of a high school. Mother M. Antonina was quick to indicate her feelings about the matter:

> Dear Father Pastor:
>
> I received a letter from Sister M. Herman[34] [Pieniazek] in the matter of opening a high school in your parish.
>
> It appears to me that under the present circumstances, it would be very difficult. Children are not paying their tuition, even if the amount is small, and I doubt that they will want to pay a dollar a month when they can receive their subject matter and books in a public high school free of charge.
>
> I fear that Father Pastor will only get into more debt in order to equip the classes properly and then the children might not enroll. As far as I know, there are in Cleveland many elementary schools and the city is not, at this time, building any high schools. Also, the Sisters who teach in high schools receive a larger pension and here, at this parish, it is so difficult to obtain even the small tuition.
>
> I hope that you will reconsider this matter. We do have qualified Sister-teachers to teach in high school. Whatever you decide to do, please let me know and I will try to satisfy you.
>
> With deep respect,
Mother M. Antonina
Superior General[35]

In view of the chaotic state of affairs at the parish, the entire matter relating to a high school was dropped. The question did come up again in 1956, when Mother M. Jerome Dadej informed the Reverend Francis Szczepanski, Father Rybacki's successor, in part:

> After long deliberation, I have arrived at the conclusion that it is impossible for me to give you any high school teachers. Since our new high school in Chicago will be opened in September of 1957, I shall need more teachers.[36]

In 1956, during the pastoral tenure of Father Szczepanski, a lovely new convent structure was built which displaced the former large and rambling thirty-room convent which consisted of two private homes.

As in so many other parishes with which the Franciscan Sisters of Chicago were associated, the Sisters stationed at Sacred Heart Parish conducted Confraternity of

Sacred Heart of Jesus Convent
Cleveland, Ohio

Christian Doctrine (CCD) classes and prepared children for the reception of the sacraments for many years at St. Mary's Church in Orwell, Ohio.[37] The Sisters were in charge of the sanctuary and sacristy in the church, the training of altar boys, and the conducting of both a Children's and a Young Ladies' Choir. In addition, Sacred Heart School presented the children in many and varied dramatic and musical entertainments as taught by the Sisters and lay musical directors.

In a survey of the congregation's schools made in 1970, Sacred Heart of Jesus Parish was listed as an aging community with strong national ties. Younger members were moving outside the parish area more and more. As early as 1973, a letter had been sent to the superior-principal informing her that the 1973–1974 school year would be its last. Nothing came of this.[38] Finally, in 1979, Sister Martha Joan Sempolski, the superior general, and the general council voted to have the Sisters withdraw from Sacred Heart School. The Sisters left the beloved parish at the close of the school year, and the Congregation of the Sisters of St. Joseph of the Third Order of St. Francis of Cleveland took charge of the school. There is a distinct sadness in any decision to close a mission at which the Sisters had labored for so many years. There was a great deal of sadness at the Franciscan Sisters' leave-taking from Sacred Heart of Jesus Parish where they had served unselfishly and zealously for more than sixty years.

There was cause for a genuine, albeit modest, celebration in the congregation on December 8, 1919, when the Sisters commemorated the 25th Anniversary of their foundation by Mother M. Theresa. A Mass of Thanksgiving was offered by the Reverend

Joseph Tarasiuk, CR, the chaplain of St. Joseph Home for the Aged. The Benediction of the Most Blessed Sacrament followed the mass during which the Sisters sang the "Te Deum" in gratitude for the graces and favors the congregation had received since its humble foundation and the substantial achievements which marked the first twenty-five years of the congregation's history.

Amid all the rejoicing at this time, the congregation suffered a loss with the death of a novice in 1920, the first Sister to die in religious formation. Sister M. Melanie, the former Joan Stoinski, was born in Chicago on March 5, 1893. She entered the congregation from St. John of God Church on Chicago's Southwest Side. Received into the postulancy on March 9, 1918, she became a novice on July 27, 1919. As a postulant, she was sent as a substitute teacher to St. Florian's School from March 10 to June 24, 1918. She was assigned to St. Florian's again in September and remained there until June of 1919. Upon her return to the Motherhouse, she began her novitiate on July 27. Her death occurred less than a year later on July 3, 1920, at St. Mary of Nazareth Hospital in Chicago. Before her death, Sister M. Melanie pronounced her perpetual vows. The cause of her death was listed as cancer of the stomach. She was twenty-seven years old and had been in the congregation for only two years.[39]

A MILESTONE REACHED

[1]*Poland's Millennium of Christianity: Indiana Observance Souvenir Book* (Hammond, Indiana: Klines Printers, 1966), no pagination.

[2]*Polish American Encyclopedia*, p. 308.

[3]*Book of Correspondence:* Letter from Sister Theresia Rybak to author, 1976 (AFSCL).

[4]Ibid.

[5]Ibid.

[6]*Minutes of General Council Proceedings, 1910–1934* (AFSCL).

[7]*Book of Correspondence:* Letter from Sister M. Theresia Rybak to author, 1976 (AFSCL).

[8]Sister M. Felicissima's name was later shortened to Sister M. Felicia.

[9]*Book of Correspondence:* Letter from Wesley W. Icenogle, Hobart Township, Lake County, Hobart, Indiana, to author, 26 April 1935 (AFSCL).

[10]*Polish American Encyclopedia*, p. 308.

[11]*Book of Correspondence:* Letter from Mother M. Mechtilde Zynda to the Most Reverend John F. Noll, bishop of Fort Wayne, 3 September 1942 (AFSCL).

[12]*Book of Closed Schools* (AFSCL).

[13]*Księga Wspomńien Parafii Najsłodszego Serca Jezus, 1891–1941* [Book of Memories: Sacred Heart of Jesus Parish, 1891–1914] (Cleveland, Ohio, 1941), p. 82.

[14]Sister M. Assumpta Pogorzelska, "A Historical Study of Religion and Education as Underlying Influences in the Localization of the Poles of Cleveland up to 1915" (M.A. thesis, St. John's College of Cleveland, 1951), p. 55.

[15]Ibid.

[16]*Księga Wspomńien Parafii Najsłodszego Serca Jezus*, p. 82.

[17]*Book of Correspondence:* Letter from Sister M. Emilita, provincial secretary, Livonia, Michigan, to author, 24 September 1975 (AFSCL).

[18]*Księga Wspomńien Parafii Najsłodszego Serca Jezus*, p. 80.

[19]Ibid., pp. 82–85.

[20]Pogorzelska, p. 58.

[21]*Księga Wspomńien Parafii Najsłodszego Serca Jezus*, p. 86.

[22]*Book of Correspondence:* Letter from Sister M. Innocenta Antosz to Mother M. Aloysia Holysz, 15 June 1918 (AFSCL).

[23]*Księga Wspomńien Parafii Najsłodszego Serca Jezus*, p. 86.

[24]Ibid.

[25]Of the six postulants, only two remained in the congregation. They were Rosalie Dadej, who became Sister M. Theresa, and Bernice Florek, who was given the name of Sister M. Claudia. *Spis Sióstr* (AFSCL).

[26]Mary Klepek (Sister M. Clemensa) and Mary Dolezych (Sister M. Felicia) were sent. *Book of Annual Assignments* (AFSCL).

[27]Sister M. Methodia, born in Poland, entered the congregation from St. John Cantius parish in Chicago in 1908. Actively engaged in the teaching apostolate for eleven years in both Chicago and Arcadia, Pennsylvania, she had been in the congregation for thirteen years. *Spis Sióstr* (AFSCL).

[28]*Księga Wspomńien Parafii Najsłodszego Serca Jezus*, p. 88.

[29]Ibid.

[30]Father Rybacki remained as pastor emeritus until his death on January 12, 1967.

[31]At this critical time in the parish's history, Father Rybacki turned to Our Sorrowful Mother for help. Under his leadership and with the approbation of the Servite Fathers in Chicago, the first novena to Our Lady of Sorrows was conducted in the Polish language in the United States in 1938. *Księga Wspomńien Parafii Najsłodszego Serca Jezus,* p. 90.

[32]*Księga Wspomńien Parafii Najsłodszego Serca Jezus,* p. 91.

[33]Michael H. Hynes, *History of the Diocese of Cleveland* (Cleveland: World Publishing Co., 1953), p. 420.

[34]Sister M. Herman served as the principal and superior at Sacred Heart School from 1934 to 1935.

[35]*Book of Correspondence:* Letter from Mother M. Antonina Osinski to the Reverend Joseph Kocinski, 10 July 1935 (AFSCL).

[36]*Book of Correspondence:* Letter from Mother M. Jerome Dadej to the Reverend Francis Szczepanski, 10 December 1956 (AFSCL).

[37]Siostra M Gonzaga Raniszewski, OSFK, *Rys historyczny Zgromadzenia Sióstr Franciszkanek Błogosławionej Kunegundy. Część pierwsza, 1860–1910* [A historical survey of the Franciscan Sisters of Blessed Kunegunda. Part one, 1860–1910] (Chicago: By the Author, 1947), p. 175.

[38]*Book of Correspondence:* Letter from Sister M. Hugoline Czaplinski to Sister M. Thaddea Duran, March 1971 (AFSCL).

[39]*Spis Sióstr* (AFSCL).

CHAPTER 31

The Third General Chapter:
Mother M. Vincent Czyzewski

On the feast of St. Joseph, March 1922, voting took place among the Sisters for the twenty-nine delegates[1] to the congregation's Third General Chapter of Elections which was swiftly approaching. A three-day retreat preceded the chapter which began on July 20. On the morning of that day, Holy Mass was offered by the Reverend Casimir Stuczko, CSC, pastor of Holy Trinity Church. He had been chosen to preside over the chapter representing the Right Reverend Monsignor Francis Rempe, the vicar general for the women religious of the Archdiocese of Chicago.[2] After the solemn intonation of the "Veni, Creator," Father Stuczko read the names of the eleven pioneers of the congregation who had already entered into eternity, among them the foundress and co-foundress of the congregation, Sister M. Theresa Dudzik and Mother M. Anna Wysinski. The "De Profundis" was also recited for the repose of the souls of the congregation's principal spiritual directors, the Reverend Vincent Barzynski, CR, and the Reverend Andrew Spetz, CR, who had been ordained by Divine Providence to play such a vital role in the foundation and growth of the Franciscan Sisters of Chicago.

Father Stuczko advised the delegates to attend to all chapter matters before voting for a superior general and her general council. The first act of the chapter delegates, therefore, was the creation of three committees.

The first committee was designated as the Committee on the Constitutions. Elected to serve on that committee were Sister M. Vincent Czyzewski, chairperson; Sister M. Benigna Jakajtis, secretary;[3] Sister M. Emily Kondziolka; Sister M. John Barczak; Sister M. Hedwig Kubera; Sister M. Kunegunda Pinkowski; Sister Mary Welter; Sister M. Sylvestra Pelczar; and Sister M. Zita Kosmala. The chief function of this committee was to study and revise the Constitutions in accordance with the Code of Canon Law, effective as of 1918, as it applied to religious. The committee was to make any necessary corrections or additions to the Constitutions after which they were to be sent to the Most Reverend George Mundelein, archbishop of Chicago, for approval. The final step was to direct them to the Sacred Congregation for Religious Affairs in Rome for papal approbation. Because of its importance, this matter is treated in great detail in Appendix A of this book.

The second committee appointed was the Committee on Finances. Sister M. Angeline Topolinski was elected as chairperson, while Sister M. Ladislaus Wroblewski was to serve as secretary. The other members were Sister M. Andrea Zawadzki, Sister M. Anselma Pasternacki, Sister M. Clara Ogurek, Sister M. Hyacinth Barczewski, Sister M. Marcelline Molek, and Sister M. Salomea Grabowski. Their main function was to examine and verify the accuracy of the financial accounts of St. Joseph Home for the Aged and all the other institutions belonging to the congregation.

The third committee was the Committee on Discipline and Education comprised of the following: Sister M. Gerard Gorzkowski, chairperson; Sister M. Leona Pochelski, secretary; Sister M. Seraphine Zamrowski; Sister M. Helen Swiszcz; Sister M. Hilary Dadej; Sister M. Innocenta Antosz; Sister M. Domicela Swiech; Sister M. Eugenia Detlaf; and Sister M. Euphrosine Tryjanowski. This committee made a number of suggestions and regulations regarding the preservation of convent discipline and the spirit of conventual life. One of the areas which received special attention was the training of future teachers for the schools of the congregation. The Committee on Discipline and Education considered it imperative that a plan be formulated and followed for assigning Sisters to the teaching apostolate and for providing for their education and pedagogical training.

At the completion of basic chapter matters, the delegates to the Third General Chapter next attended to the voting for a new administration. On July 25, 1922, in the balloting for the superior general, the delegates chose Sister M. Vincent Czyzewski. Sister M. Philipine Lama[4] was elected assistant general and first councilor. Sister M. Andrea Zawadzki received an absolute majority for the office of second councilor, but she adamantly refused to accept the position. In a subsequent vote, Sister M. Sylvestra Pelczar was elected second councilor. Sister M. Benigna Jakajtis was elected third councilor and secretary general, the first time the two offices were combined. Sister M. Seraphine Zamrowski was elected fourth councilor, and for procurator general, the delegates chose Sister M. Leona Pochelski.[5]

The new superior general was a woman of simplicity and deep faith. Mother M. Vincent, the former Mary Czyzewski, was born on August 17, 1875. She came to America with her parents, Valentine and Julia (née Urbaniak) arriving in 1888. The family settled in St. Hedwig's Parish in Chicago. On November 1, 1899, Mary Czyzewski entered the small community of Franciscan tertiaries and was received into the novitiate on December 8, 1900. She made her first profession of vows on December 15, 1901, and professed her final vows on August 12, 1910.

On October 4, 1905, Sister M. Vincent was appointed the mother superior replacing Sister M. Anna Wysinski who was ill. She served in this capacity until January 1, 1909. In 1910, she was elected the assistant general and first councilor by the First General Chapter. Always frail of health, Sister M. Vincent was sent to Falls City, Texas, in 1911, to recuperate from a recurring illness, but she also served as superior and principal of Holy Trinity School there. Her health somewhat restored, she returned to the Motherhouse where she was appointed the superior, a position she held for four years. At the conclusion of her term of office, she worked in the Church Vestment Workshop until she was elected the superior general at the Third General Chapter.[6]

Mother M. Vincent's administration, for the most part, was marked by what could be called the perfect extension of the gentle, loving spirit of Sister M. Theresa Dudzik.[7] Like Sister M. Theresa, Mother M. Vincent was a prayerful, charitable, and joyful person and was considered saintly by most of the Sisters who knew her. Worldliness, impatience, and harshness were entirely foreign to her character or interior life.[8] A conscientious woman dedicated to the spirit of St. Francis, she loved the congregation and was zealous in the observance of the Rule and Constitutions which she enforced with loving care.[9] It has been broadly hinted that as a superior general, she somewhat lacked administrative ability. While that might have been true to some extent, Mother M. Vincent was prudent and efficient in her dealings with many issues which originated during her tenure of office.[10] She has been characterized quite candidly and very nearly perfectly by one of the Sisters:

> Mother M. Vincent was modest, yet strong; simple, yet wise; humble yet courageous. She was interested in an increase of vocations to the congregation and was always gentle and sympathetic to those whom she considered unsuitable for religious life. She was always concerned and considerate toward the sick Sisters while she herself suffered from heart trouble and severe headaches.[11]

Physically, the new superior general was at least five feet, five inches tall and quite stately. She had a quiet, clear, and pleasant voice. While her appearance was dignified, even serious, she possessed a lively sense of humor. Meticulous and orderly by nature, she bordered on being a perfectionist regarding her room, books, and notes. Characteristically Franciscan, she loved the feast of Easter above all others and gloried in nature.[12]

One of the congregation's most artistically creative persons was elected second councilor at this chapter. Sister M. Sylvestra, the former Caroline Pelczar, was born on June 20, 1888, in Poland. While still a child, she was taken by her parents to America where they settled in St. John Cantius Parish in Chicago. Here she became acquainted with the Franciscan Sisters of Chicago and joined them on December 7, 1905. She was admitted to the novitiate on December 8, 1906, and made her first profession of vows on December 10, 1907. On August 15, 1916, she made her final profession.

For fifteen years, Sister M. Sylvestra taught in the schools of the congregation. At the Third General Chapter of 1922, she was elected the second councilor and completed her term in 1928. Even as second councilor, she returned to teaching in 1924 and labored diligently.[13]

Sister M. Sylvestra has been described as an efficient, understanding, and humble woman. She was excellent in art and was most zealous in sharing this gift with the congregation in the Church Vestment Workshop. Prudent and likable, she was a very selfless individual given to acts of charity.[14] Sister M. Sylvestra was the niece of a candidate for sanctity, the Most Reverend Sebastian Pelczar, auxiliary bishop of Przymysł, Poland. She was the aunt of Sister M. Agnes Zywiec, also a member of the Franciscan Sisters of Chicago.

Elected third councilor and secretary general was Sister M. Benigna, the former Frances Jakajtis, who was born in Szaki, Lithuania, in 1889. She came to America in 1896. Frances Jakajtis entered the community from its St. Vincent's Orphan Asylum in 1905. On December 8, 1906, she was admitted to the novitiate and made her first profession on December 10, 1907. On August 15, 1916, she was perpetually professed.

As a postulant, Sister M. Benigna was sent to St. Elizabeth's Hospital in Lafayette, Indiana, to study pharmacy. She continued her studies at the University of Illinois School of Pharmacology from which she graduated in June of 1910. She also received a bachelor's degree from Loyola University of Chicago. Sent to St. Stanislaus Bishop and Martyr School in Chicago as a teacher in 1910, she was appointed superior and principal in 1913, a position she held until 1919. She next served as teacher, superior, and principal at Five Holy Martyrs School until 1925, even as she served as third councilor and secretary general.[15]

There is no Sister among the oldest members who will not testify to the scholarly bent of Sister M. Benigna. She was a diligent and devoted student of Latin and Greek. Sister M. Benigna possessed a sharp intellect and used it with great generosity in all her dedicated service to and in the congregation. Generally described as fearless and out-spoken, she was a prudent and thoughtful woman who combined professionalism with deep spirituality.[16]

Sister M. Seraphine, the fourth councilor, was born Martha Zamrowski in the United States. She attended St. Hedwig's Church in Chicago before her entrance into the community on July 2, 1900. She entered the novitiate on July 27, 1901, and made her first profession of vows on August 2, 1902. Eight years later, on August 12, 1910, she made her perpetual profession.

From the time of her first profession until her election as fourth councilor, Sister M. Seraphine labored in the congregation as a superior, principal, and teacher in schools in Spring Valley, Illinois; Cleveland and Youngstown, Ohio; La Porte, Indiana; and Oshkosh, Wisconsin. During her term as fourth councilor, she was also a teacher at Five Holy Martyrs School in Chicago.[17]

For all of her religious life, Sister M. Seraphine was considered very prudent and trustworthy, qualities which enabled her to serve well as councilor. She is said to have exhibited great faith and recollection in prayer.[18]

The new procurator general, Sister M. Leona Pochelski was born in Poland, came to the United States at fourteen, and made her home in St. Hedwig's Parish in Chicago. She entered the small community as a postulant on September 17, 1901, and became a novice on December 8, 1902. Her perpetual profession was made on July 27, 1912, during the administration of Mother M. Anna Wysinski.[19] In 1904, Sister M. Leona was sent to St. Casimir's School in Cleveland where she remained until 1912. She served in Illinois,

Indiana, and Pennsylvania as superior and principal.[20]

A pleasant, kind-hearted, and dedicated religious, it is said that children loved her exceedingly. Sister M. Leona was noted for her love of community and its welfare for which she was always genuinely and prayerfully concerned.[21]

Following the conclusion of the general chapter, Mother M. Vincent and her general council voted for the members of the Motherhouse house council: Sister M. Martha Bywalec, superior; Sister M. Ludwina Prokuszka, assistant superior; and Sister M. Mathilda Szymoniak, secretary and procurator. Sister M. John Barczak was appointed the mistress of novices, and Sister M. Kunegunda Pinkowski became the mistress of postulants.

The new novice mistress was a gentle woman of a distinctly patient and unassuming manner. Sister M. John, a native of Poland, emigrated to the United States with her family in 1905 and settled in St. Mary of the Angels Parish. She entered the congregation on November 19, 1910, and on December 8, 1911, was admitted to the novitiate. She made her first profession of vows on December 8, 1912, and her perpetual vows on August 15, 1919. Sister M. John had served as mistress of postulants from 1919 to 1922. In 1922, this simple, devout, and conscientious religious was chosen to serve as mistress of novices. She completed her term in 1928.[22] It has been said of Sister M. John that she taught "by word and example."[23] Many Sisters considered Sister M. John a saint. A zealous religious, she served equally well as a council member in the congregation she loved.[24]

The fruitful six-year term of Mother M. Vincent and her general council brought many important introductions and significant changes to the congregation. Thanks to the vision and merit of Mother M. Vincent, the need to update the Constitutions and to secure papal approval of the congregation was recognized and realized. By 1925, the congregation also received the long-desired *Decree of Aggregation* which Mother M. Vincent had labored so earnestly to secure and which now associated the congregation to the First Order of Franciscans.

When the congregation began to implement the revised Constitutions and because of the *Decree of Aggregation* to the First Order of Friars Minor, there was a strong emphasis placed on the development of Franciscan spirituality and devotions. As a result, the devotion of the Way of the Cross, introduced in 1900, was cultivated and encouraged. The congregation also sought to encourage more Franciscan priests in conducting retreats and in giving monthly conferences to the Sisters. Books written by Franciscans and the lives of Franciscan saints were read aloud during the spiritual reading in the chapel and in the dining room during meals.

As a consequence of the revised Constitutions, a two-year novitiate was initiated in July of 1925, in accordance with the wishes of the Church for a firmer spiritual foundation for religious. The postulancy was arranged to last six months with an extension of time if necessary. In keeping with the new regulations, perpetual vows were to be made after three years instead of after six.[25] As a result, in July of 1926, for the first time, forty-five Sisters forming two groups made perpetual vows after three years of temporary vows. One group, consisting of twenty-one Sisters, made perpetual vows on July 16, the feast of Our Lady of Mount Carmel, after a ten-day retreat conducted by the Reverend Walter Jakowski, a member of the Congregation of Marian Fathers. The Reverend Thomas Bona conducted the religious ceremonies. On July 27, the feast of St. Kunegunda, twenty-four Sisters made perpetual vows and one Sister made her first profession. Their retreat had been conducted by Father Jakowski with the Right Reverend Monsignor Francis Rempe officiating at the ceremonies.

Another of Mother M. Vincent's chief priorities during her term of office was the education of the Sisters assigned to teaching in the schools of the congregation as proposed at the general chapter by the Committee on Discipline and Education. In order to accomplish this aim, she appointed a five-member committee to head the Education Commission of the Franciscan Sisters as directed by the chapter decrees. The Sisters appointed to the Education Commission were Sister M. Philipine Lama, Sister M. Benigna Jakajtis, Sister M. Paul Kirschbaum, Sister M. Josephata Tadych, and Sister M. Sylvestra Pelczar, who replaced Sister M. Jerome Dadej when the latter was appointed superior and principal of St. Casimir's School in Cleveland in 1925. At that time, Mother M. Vincent appointed Sister M. Benigna Jakajtis the chairperson of the Education Commission and the supervisor of schools.[26] The aims of the Education Commission were defined as follows:

1. To learn of the teacher qualifications as well as the educational status of each Sister-teacher in the community.
2. To give the Sisters Superior practical advice and guides in regard to further education of the Sister-teachers who were already teaching but did not have a diploma from Normal School or at least a high school diploma.
3. To strive not to use Sister-teachers for manual labor during the vacation period, but to send them for courses.
4. To inform the superior general and the general council as to the best methods and ways of preparing future teachers.
5. To work on a compact course of studies for elementry and secondary school Sister-teachers.
6. To submit names of qualified Sisters who would be trained at the university level as teachers.[27]

As a direct result of the Education Commission's program, there was a positive advancement in the area of education and teacher preparation. Until 1918, the Sister-teachers had been prepared for their teaching apostolate by the older, more experienced professed Sisters. After that year, the Sisters engaged in teaching began to attend courses on Saturdays and during the summer at St. Stanislaus College founded by the

Congregation of the Resurrection in 1890.[28] By 1920, there were twenty Sisters enrolled. There were approximately eight Sisters enrolled at De Paul University in Chicago. Because great emphasis was placed on the pre-teaching preparation of candidates for religious life and young professed Sisters, the Catholic Church in 1911 established The Catholic Sisters College, an undergraduate division of The Catholic University of America. Sent to The Catholic Sisters College in 1921 were Sister M. Philipine Lama and Sister M. Paul Kirschbaum although they received their degrees from De Paul University. Sister M. Antonina Osinski received her bachelor's degree from The Catholic Sisters College in 1925 and her master's degree from The Catholic University in 1926. She, therefore, became the first Sister in the congregation to earn a master's degree. Every summer, Sisters were sent to Washington, DC, for summer courses. The first Sisters sent there were Sister Bernice Marie Junio, Sister M. Laurentine Trocki, Siater M. Regina Iwan, and Sister M. Ignatia Hodkiewicz.

As the number of Sisters who had received their degrees increased, Mother M. Vincent and the general council decided to provide the prospective Sister-teachers with the necessary educational background which would be supplied by the degreed members of the congregation. In 1924, therefore, a convent high school or preparatory school was opened for aspirants, postulants, second-year novices, and professed Sisters under the direction of Sister M. Benigna Jakajtis who was later succeeded by Sister M. Paul Kirschbaum and Sister M. Antonina Osinski, each bringing an area of expertise to her position. The classes were held on Saturday mornings at the Motherhouse or at a parish school such as Five Holy Martyrs.[29] After a larger number of professed Sisters had received their decrees, the Our Lady of Victory High School, affiliated with The Catholic Sisters College of The Catholic University of America in Washington, DC, and De Paul University in Chicago, was opened at the Motherhouse in 1924 with the Franciscan Sisters of Chicago themselves on the staff.[30]

The first faculty at Our Lady of Victory High School and the subject matters they taught consisted of Sister M. Benigna Jakajtis, Latin; Sister M. Philipine Lama, English; Sister M. Gerard Gorzkowski, Polish; Sister M. Sylvia Lewandowski, religion; Sister M. Crescencia Chmiel, mathematics; and Sister M. Helen Swiszcz, art.[31] Through the years, the course offerings were enlarged and the members of the staff changed. In 1938, the novices' refectory in the old St. Vincent's Orphan Asylum was remodeled and opened as a chemistry laboratory. As many as twenty-six Sisters were enrolled in the class at a time. Sister M. Grace Kujawa taught chemistry as well as religion, history, and mathematics. A large hall which had served as the novices' recreation room was divided by erecting a wall. One room became a classroom while the other room served as the library for which several hundred books were obtained. The library, science laboratory, and classrooms were blessed in a special ceremony by the Reverend Vincent Nowicki, pastor of St. Pancratius Church, on July 26, 1938. Typing and shorthand were taught to the postulants by Sister M. Doloretta Radzienda. Science was taught by Sister M. Josepha Zwierzycki. English teachers included Sister M. Pancratius Pankowski, Sister M. Paul Kirschbaum, Sister M.

Benigna Jakajtis, and Sister M. Crescencia Chmiel. The Reverend Joseph Baniewicz, CR, taught religion. Our Lady of Victory High School more than adequately met the educational needs of the Sisters at this time.

Eventually the congregation made provisions for a high school which was intended solely for aspirants to the congregation. Each aspirant followed a standard high school curriculum. As a resident student, the aspirant to the religious life lived in an atmosphere permeated by the spirit of the congregation. The new high school was called Madonna High School with Sister M. Crescencia Chmiel at its helm as the principal. This school was the forerunner of the present Madonna High School, one of the congregation's treasures which is discussed at great length in Chapter 51.

The Second General Chapter had advocated that those Sisters with a talent for art should be encouraged in its study. Mother M. Vincent and her general council, therefore, enrolled Sister M. Helen Swiszcz, Sister M. Mechtilde Zynda, and Sister M. Sylvestra Pelczar as pupils of the noted artist, Sister Stanisia of the Congregation of the School Sisters of Notre Dame. Sister Stanisia, a former student at the Art Institute of Chicago and a painter of renown, worked from her studio at the Academy of Our Lady in the township of Longwood in Chicago from 1900 to 1960.[32]

Many Sisters who possessed a talent in music were likewise encouraged to pursue its study. Three postulants studied piano and harmony with Professor Marion S. Rozycki at the Illinois College of Music and Dramatic Arts. Sister M. Martha Bywalec, the superior at the Motherhouse, took up the study of the violin, and Sister M. John Barczak, the mistress of novices, undertook the study of the piano. By 1927, the first group of Sisters began studies at the De Paul School of Music in Chicago. Some Sisters were sent to the American Conservatory of Music.[33]

That the congregation was successful in its efforts to prepare the Sister-teachers for the classroom is evident from letters such as the following which Mother M. Vincent received:

Reverend and dear Mother,

I feel that I should convey to you the deep sentiments of appreciation which the school authorities of the Diocese of Pittsburgh feel for the advances which the teaching Communities are making in the normal training of the Sisters. We are not unaware of the sacrifices which this additional training entails nor of the fresh burden which it casts on the various Sisterhoods. Its effects upon Catholic elementary schools will be far-reaching and lasting. The enthusiasm and generosity with which the teaching Communities have shouldered the burden are certain to draw down upon them the choice blessings of heaven. I feel that I would be recreant in my duty if I did not make this acknowledgment and add the prayer that the noble work might continue and increase.

I wish again to express my appreciation of the great work you are undertaking in the field of teacher preparation and to assure you that its successful accomplishment will be the greatest safeguard our schools can have in days of criticism and bigotry.

Respectfully yours,

R. L. Hayes

Superintendent of Parish Schools

Pittsburgh, Pennsylvania[34]

By 1926, the congregation staffed nineteen schools, many of them with large faculties. In schools where there were formerly three Sisters, five or ten teachers were now needed. Five Holy Martyrs School, for example, had at this time forty Sisters stationed there.[35] Because of the obvious need for Sisters to serve in the teaching apostolate, permission was granted the congregation from Monsignor Rempe to send the second-year novices to teach.[36] In August of that same year, Mother M. Vincent and Sister M. Benigna visited Monsignor Rempe to ask for permission to prolong the time of the postulancy so that even the postulants could be used in schools because of a shortage of Sister-teachers. In 1925, according to the Constitutions, a two-year novitiate had been initiated with a postulancy of six months. Monsignor Rempe refused the request concerning the postulants, but he gave Mother M. Vincent permission to send some of the second-year novices, the newly received postulants, and all the Sister-councilors to the classroom. He strongly warned Mother M. Vincent that in the forthcoming year no novices or postulants were to be sent to teach. Yet when the next year arrived, Monsignor Rempe was asked again by Mother M. Vincent for permission to send the novices to teach in the classrooms. He very reluctantly agreed to let the novices teach in 1927, but made it absolutely clear that it would be the last time. In 1928, Monsignor Rempe resigned his position as vicar general for the women religious of the Archdiocese of Chicago. The next year, the second-year novices were again sent to teach because many of the professed Sisters were ill.[37] So many times, then, in spite of her better judgment and the best interests of the Sisters, Mother M. Vincent was forced to assign the Sisters to staff schools where their services were so badly needed. The dedication and perseverance of these young Sisters under the most trying circumstances was indeed commendable.

Perhaps as a result of the Finance Committee's suggestions at the Third General Chapter, one of the thorniest problems facing the Franciscan Sisters of Chicago was somewhat resolved during the term of Mother M. Vincent. This was the state of the congregation's financial difficulties.

Throughout the years since its foundation, the support of the residents and the maintenance of St. Joseph Home for the Aged and Crippled had been increasingly critical and uncertain. It was becoming more apparent that a new home for the aged was rapidly emerging as an urgent issue. From the earliest days of the home's foundation, the Polish pastors of several local churches in Chicago had maintained a benevolent interest in St. Joseph Home and the selfless services of the Franciscan Sisters of Chicago. In April of 1920, the Reverend Casimir Stuczko, CSC, the pastor of Holy Trinity Church, and the Reverend Louis Grudzinski, the pastor of St. John of God Church, had been chosen by the Polish pastors of the local churches as their representatives to a meeting with the Sisters to discuss the matter of enlarging and improving the home. The pastors presented several proposals including a suggestion to build a new St. Joseph Home for the Aged and Crippled in an entirely new location or to allow the home to become the property of the Archdiocese of Chicago in an effort to spare the Sisters any further financial strain. The Sisters objected vehemently to any proposal to divest them of St. Joseph Home, the site which Mother M. Theresa Dudzik had once referred to as "chosen by God Himself." They also rejected any proposal to abandon the apostolate to which both she and the founding Sisters had so devotedly dedicated their lives. Eventually, the Sisters agreed to accept only needed financial aid and material assistance from the Polish pastors.[38] At the same time, the Sisters staunchly upheld their decision to maintain the policy of keeping St. Joseph Home open to the aged, poor, and disabled of all ethnic backgrounds since for many years the Sisters had accepted people from such diverse parishes as St. Alphonsus, St. Boniface, St. Aloysius, Maternity of the Blessed Virgin Mary, St. Thomas, St. Patrick, St. Gertrude, and St. George which represented Germans, Irish, Lithuanians, and other nationalities.[39] As a consequence of the Finance Committee's presentation at the general chapter, the delegates voted to turn to the Catholic Charities of the Archdiocese of Chicago for financial assistance. Its director, the Reverend Moses Kiley, came to the aid of the Sisters in an advisory as well as a financial capacity thus enabling the congregation to be relieved of the constant uncertainty of obtaining funds to maintain St. Joseph Home for the Aged and Crippled.[40]

THE THIRD GENERAL CHAPTER: MOTHER M. VINCENT CZYZEWSKI

[1]See Appendix K.

[2]Monsignor Rempe could not officiate because he did not know the Polish language.

[3]Originally, Sister M. Benigna was appointed the secretary of the Discipline and Education Committee. However, it was necessary to transfer her to the Committee on the Constitutions since she was fluent in English and would be able to translate the Canon Law into Polish.

[4]See Chapter 25.

[5]Secretaries General, *Community Chronicle, 1894–1957* (AFSCL).

[6]*Spis Sióstr* (AFSCL).

[7]*Interview* with Sister M. Loyola Dymanowski, September 1983 (AFSCL).

[8]*Interviews* with Sisters, September 1983 (AFSCL).

[9]*Interview* with Sister M. Ferdinand Skiba, September 1982 (AFSCL).

[10]*Interviews* with Sisters, September 1983 (AFSCL).

[11]*Interview* with Sister M. Loyola Dymanowski, September 1983 (AFSCL).

[12]*Interviews* with Sisters, September 1983 (AFSCL).

[13]Sister M. Sylvestra was appointed the superior of Our Lady of Victory Convent in Lemont in 1938. In 1940, she returned to the classroom and taught until 1949, at which time she became ill with tuberculosis. After serving as superior at St. Anthony's Home for the Aged in Crown Point for six years, she returned to the Motherhouse where she died of cancer on January 10, 1956. She was sixty-eight years old and had been in the congregation for fifty-one years. *Spis Sióstr* (AFSCL).

[14]*Interviews* with Sisters, September 1983 (AFSCL).

[15]In 1928, Sister M. Benigna was elected vicar general and first councilor. At the conclusion of her six-year term, she served for twelve years as a teacher at the congregation's schools in Ohio, Indiana, and Pennsylvania until her appointment as the superior and administrator at Mount Alvernia Convent in East Cleveland in 1946. In 1955, she was appointed to teach Latin at Madonna High School in Chicago. Her last assignment was at St. Anthony's Hospital in Martin, South Dakota, in 1964. She was sent to St. John's Hospital in Huron, South Dakota, where she served until she returned to the Motherhouse in 1968. She died there of cancer on March 16. *Congregation Membership Records;* and *Spis Sióstr* (AFSCL).

[16]*Interviews* with Sister M. Loyola Dymanowski and Sisters, September 1983 (AFSCL).

[17]Sister M. Seraphine served as fourth councilor until 1928. At the fourth general chapter of 1928, she was elected second councilor and served until 1934. At the end of her term, she lived at the Motherhouse and devoted her time to sewing. When she died on September 7, 1949, she was sixty-seven years old and had been in the congregation for forty-nine years. *Congregation Membership Records;* and *Spis Sióstr* (AFSCL).

[18]*Interviews* with Sisters, September 1983 (AFSCL).

[19]*Spis Sióstr* (AFSCL).

[20]Sister M. Leona served in the general council until 1934. In 1937, she, who had suffered medical problems all her life, was sent to Our Lady of Victory Convent in Lemont. She died there on October 23, 1954, at the age of seventy-nine. Sister M. Leona had been in the congregation for fifty-three years. *Congregation Membership Records;* and *Spis Sióstr* (AFSCL).

[21]*Interviews* with Sister M. Loyola Dymanowski and Sisters, September 1983 (AFSCL).

[22]From 1934 to 1940, she served as superintendent of St. Joseph Home for the Aged. In 1940, she was elected fourth councilor and served in that capacity until 1946 when she was elected second councilor. At the same time she was in charge of the Church Vestment Workshop at the Motherhouse. Her term of office as second councilor ended in 1952. That year, Sister M. John

devoted much of her time to sewing habits for the Sisters. After an illness of approximately one year, she died on December 11, 1955, at the Motherhouse. She was sixty-seven years old and had been in the congregation for forty-five years. *Congregation Membership Records;* and *Spis Sióstr* (AFSCL).

[23]*Interview* with Sister M. Loyola Dymanowski, September 1983 (AFSCL).

[24]*Book of Correspondence*: Letters from Sisters to author, September 1983; and *Spis Sióstr* (AFSCL).

[25]*Minutes of General Council Proceedings, 1910–1934;* and Secretaries General, *Community Chronicle,* p. 85 (AFSCL).

[26]Siostra M. Gonzaga Raniszewski, OSFK, "Rys historyczny Zgromadzenia Sióstr Franciszkanek Bł. Kunegundy. Część druga, 1910–1940" [A historical survey of the Franciscan Sisters of Blessed Kunegunda. Part two, 1910–1940] Unpublished manuscript (AFSCL), p. 168.

[27]*Minutes of General Council Proceedings, 1910–1934* (AFSCL).

[28]The Reverend Thaddeus Ligman, CR, headed the religious Sisters' education program at St. Stanislaus College and gave Saturday and summer courses to thousands of Sisters to better prepare them as teachers in parochial schools. Father Ligman was a noted clergyman, educator, and editor. Born in Poland in 1880, he came to the United States in 1884. He attended St. Stanislaus College in Chicago. In 1901, he entered the Congregation of the Resurrection. He was ordained in 1908, returned to Chicago and pursued his studies of sciences at the University of Chicago. He was appointed to St. Stanislaus College in Chicago from 1920 to 1923 and again, from 1925 to 1931. He was elected general delegate for the congregation in the United States in 1931 and again in 1938. He wrote numerous articles on social, educational, religious, and scientific subjects for *Dziennik Chicagoski* and in 1932 became the paper's general manager. Edward T. Janas, CR, *Dictionary of American Resurrectionists, 1865–1965* (Rome: Gregorian University Press, 1967), pp. 42–44.

[29]*Book of Correspondence:* Letter from Sister M. Marinella Gubala to author, September 1976 (AFSCL).

[30]Raniszewski, p. 154. 31 *Echo Avondalskie* [Avondale Echo], 1934–1940 (AFSCL).

[32]Sister M. Stanisia, SSND, was an outstanding American portrait and mural artist. She believed that portraiture was the most enviable and the most noble of all the art forms and preferred it to the creation of landscapes and still life subjects. She saw, in each face, "the hidden soul as it will appear on the Morn of Resurrection," since "it is the most noble of all branches of graphic arts because it comes in contact with human nature, just as Man is in the highest form and is given preeminent place."

Sister M. Stanisia began the art department at Longwood Academy and Mount St. Mary College in Milwaukee. She was overjoyed when she received the commission to paint several religious murals for churches. Her original murals of startling power, rich in design, of exquisite loveliness and deep spirituality adorn the walls of sixteen churches in the United States. She was commissioned by George Cardinal Mundelein himself to paint his portrait which hangs in the gallery of American Cardinals in Washington, DC. Among the other famous celebrities she painted are Governor Henry Horner of Illinois, Mayor Kelly of Chicago, Bishop Fulton J. Sheen, actor Charles Coburn, and many others. She was commissioned by the Reverend James Keane, SM, of "Novena Notes" fame to paint her concept of the *Pieta* which appeared on the cover and elicited much favorable comment from Catholics and non-Catholics alike. *Book of Correspondence:* Academy of Our Lady (Chicago) to author, September 1980; and Reverend Monsignor Harry C. Koenig, STD, ed., *Caritas Christi Urget Nos: A History of the Offices, Agencies, and Institutions of the Archdiocese of Chicago,* I (Chicago: New World Publishing Co., 1981), p. 413.

[33]Raniszewski, p. 154.

[34]*Book of Correspondence:* Letter from R. L. Hayes, Office of Superintendent of Parish Schools, Pittsburgh, Pennsylvania, to Mother M. Vincent Czyzewski, 8 December 1923.

[35]Raniszewski, p. 168.

[36]*Minutes of General Council Proceedings, 1910–1934* (AFSCL).

[37]Ibid.

[38]*Minutes of General Council Proceedings, 1910–1934* (AFSCL).

[39]*St. Joseph Home for the Aged House Journal* (AFSCL).

[40]*Minutes of General Council Proceedings, 1910–1934* (AFSCL).

CHAPTER 32

Woodland Park: Our Lady of Victory Convent

When Mother M. Vincent assumed her duties as superior general in 1922, she and her new general council were soon involved in plans to secure property on which to build a new Motherhouse. The old Motherhouse on Hamlin Avenue, originally a part of St. Joseph Home for the Aged and Crippled, was severely overcrowded. While it was true that some of the residents had their sleeping quarters in one of the five frame cottages on Ridgeway Avenue, yet their dining room, kitchen, and workroom were in the main building of the Motherhouse, thereby creating numerous problems. Since the function of St. Joseph Home was to house the elderly and the crippled, it was imperative that the congregation now find or build a separate dwelling to serve as the Motherhouse for the Sisters. There was the obvious need for more room for the Sisters when they returned to the Motherhouse to make their annual retreat. The successful Church Vestment Workshop was expanding and there was the necessity of increasing the number of Sisters who worked there. Some of the older Sisters, as indeed some of the younger ones, often were ill and in need of an environment conducive to healing and recuperation. Whenever a Sister in the active apostolate became seriously ill and required a longer convalescence or more attentive care, she was sent to the Motherhouse where the space was so limited. There was also the fact that the Right Reverend Monsignor Francis Rempe, the vicar general for the women religious of the Archdiocese of Chicago, had advised Mother M. Vincent to search for an appropriate location, preferably beyond the city, to establish the novitiate since according to Canon Law[1] the novices were to be separated from the professed Sisters. In view of this situation, Mother M. Vincent and her general council began the search for a suitable site on which to build a new convent.[2] Various places were proposed. Among the sites viewed and considered seriously were the area of Belmont and Cumberland Avenues in Chicago and places in Brookfield, Hinsdale, Arlington Heights, and Mount Prospect, all in Illinois. Eventually, the choice was made for a land site and a large abandoned mansion in Lemont, a charming little village in northern Illinois.

Earlier, in 1918, the Reverend Louis Grudzinski,[3] the pastor of St. John of God Church in Chicago and one of the founders of the Guardian Angel Day Care Center and

Home for Working Girls, in an effort to express his gratitude to the Sisters who served at the Day Care Center, took them to the little town of Lemont, Illinois, for a day of rest and recreation. Once at their destination, the Sisters were introduced to George Walker[4] who owned the Lemont property, the site of the Sisters' recreational tour, and who, on a previous occasion, had informed Father Grudzinski of his desire to sell the property and the large abandoned mansion which stood on the site. Built in 1868, the house was a faithful reproduction of a type of mansion generally found in Leeds, England. At the conclusion of the day's outing, Sister M. Ladislaus Wroblewski, the superior and administrator of the Guardian Angel Day Nursery and Home for Working Girls, contacted Mother M. Aloysia Holysz, the superior general at that time, and told her of Mr. Walker's proposal to dispose of all his property. Sister M. Ladislaus indicated that the property was located near a highway and in the immediate vicinity of several other religious institutions. With the town and shopping areas only two miles away, the house, property, and location seemed ideal. A few days later, Mother M. Aloysia and the general council went to Lemont to view the property in the company of Father Grudzinski. While the Sisters believed the site was extremely suitable for their needs and the property most desirable, the cost at that time seemed prohibitive. Mother M. Aloysia and her council decided to postpone purchasing the Lemont property with the hope that Mr. Walker would eventually lower the cost. As a consequence, the entire matter lay dormant for several years.[5]

When Mother M. Vincent Czyzewski assumed her duties as the third superior general of the congregation, the matter of acquiring a new Motherhouse loomed paramount. At one of the meetings of the general council, the Walker home and property in Lemont, Illinois, were recalled as being particularly advantageous. Because of the severe financial problems which engulfed the congregation, several years were allowed to elapse before any decisive action was taken concerning the acquisition of the Lemont property. On July 27, 1925, the feast of Blessed Kunegunda, Monsignor Rempe came to the Motherhouse to participate in the ceremonies on the occasion of the profession of perpetual vows. Mother M. Vincent took advantage of the opportunity to discuss the purchase of the Walker home and land in Lemont. Having readily secured Monsignor Rempe's permission, the congregation purchased the Walker home and property called "Woodland Park" on August 20, 1925, for $100,000. The entire transaction was handled by Leonard Schuetz of the Schuetz Construction Company on behalf of the Sisters. The Sisters paid the sum of $80,000 from a fund which they had formerly set aside specifically for the purchase or construction of a new Motherhouse.[6]

Lemont, "Village of Faith,"[7] was a truly colorful and charming village of canals and prairies set in a historic river valley in Cook County in Northern Illinois. Nestled in the hills surrounding the Des Plaines River valley, the area was named *le mont,* "the mountain," by the French explorer, Louis Joliet. Lemont was about twenty miles southwest of Chicago and ten miles northeast of Joliet. Refreshingly novel, Lemont had picturesque streets, steep hills, historical sites, and many fine buildings, especially churches, constructed of massive quarry stone. The rich heritage of the quaint city of

Lemont gave it a character and charm all its own.[8] With its added advantages of good water, healthful climate, fine building sites, and clean industry, Lemont was truly a lovely town in which to locate the Motherhouse.[9]

The Walker property consisted of 155 acres which extended on both sides of Archer Avenue, reaching out south and east past McCarthy Road on Highway 4A. The southern part consisted of eighty acres with a farm and five frame houses in which the former employees of the Walker family had lived. To the east, the large garden surrounding the Walker house included beautiful, strong, and various species of trees, arranged in a harmonious and artistic manner. In the center of the garden stood a two-story stone and brick mansion which had been abandoned for a number of years. In spite of the mansion's majestic outward appearance, its interior was completely in ruins. The windows were broken, the locks were torn from the doors, and the roof leaked profusely. As a consequence, the walls and the floors of the mansion were rotting. It was obvious from the holes in the walls and the floors that rats and mice lived there in abundance. Not far from the Walker home stood an eight-room frame house that previously had been the quarters of the servants in the employ of the Walker family.

In May of 1926, $20,000, the remainder of the cost of purchase, was paid. Shortly after the property was bought, however, there appeared to be some inaccuracies in the sale and in the past taxes paid, so that the land lying north of Archer Avenue was considered separate from the property which was originally purchased. This left the congregation with 120 acres of land and the buildings on the property.[10]

As soon as the property was acquired, the Sisters set about repairing the homes and especially the Walker mansion in order to make them habitable. The Sisters also saw the necessity to work the soil, and fruits and vegetables needed to be picked and canned. Because the workers whom the Sisters had employed were not reliable, the work progressed slowly. Mother M. Vincent resolved to send several Sisters to Lemont to reside there even though the work on the Walker mansion was far from completed. On September 1, 1926, therefore, Sister M. Mechtilde Zynda, Sister M. Mathilda Szymoniak, and Sister M. Ludwina Prokuszka arrived in Lemont. Until this time, a Mr. Murawski had guarded the house while workers from the Schuetz Construction Company made the necessary repairs. Also sent at this time to lend some assistance to the Sisters and especially to provide security during the night was "Alojzy," a resident from St. Joseph Home for the Aged in Chicago. In truth, he seemed even more afraid of the night than the Sisters, so that Mr. Schuetz sent his own brother who stayed for two weeks.

The Sisters lived in Lemont under very severe hardships. They rose daily at four-thirty o'clock in the morning after a night's sleep that was frequently interrupted by scurrying mice that often came to the Sisters' very beds in the spacious house. The Sisters attended mass daily at St. Mary's Seminary, the Motherhouse of the Franciscan Fathers of the Custody of the Holy Cross,[11] a distance of approximately one and one-half miles which they walked even on the coldest days of winter. After breakfast, some Sisters walked to the farm to attend to their duties while the others gathered fruits and vegetables to be canned,

The Walker Mansion, first home of the Franciscan Sisters of Chicago in Lemont, Illinois, c. 1936

and raked the huge expanse of lawn. The worst hardship the Sisters endured was the lack of water which they were forced to carry from a neighbor from September until November 20, when the well on their own property was finished. Sometimes, when Mr. Malinowski, the farm supervisor, was ill, the Sisters had to attend to the farm chores which included feeding and tending thirteen cows, four horses, one sheep, and some chickens and pigs.

In October 1926, permission was granted by Cardinal Mundelein to open a chapel in the Walker house. The chapel had been fashioned from the living room, and a porch was added to make the chapel larger. On October 26, Sister M. Pauline Dydo was sent to Lemont to replace Sister M. Mathilda Szymoniak while Sister M. Imelda Derbin came to replace Sister M. Ludwina Prokuszka.[12]

One of the reasons which had led to the search for a new site for a Motherhouse was the fact, according to Canon Law, that the novitiate had to be separated from the professed Sisters. The purchase and the renovation of the Walker mansion, therefore, were now looked upon as solutions to this particular problem. After the Walker mansion was restored adequately, Mother M. Vincent asked Cardinal Mundelein for permission to have the novitiate transferred from Chicago to Lemont. On August 9, 1926, the permission was granted, and the novitiate was established in Lemont. The postulants who had been accepted to the novitiate on December 2, 1926, at the Motherhouse in Chicago were now brought to Lemont to complete their canonical year.[13] The novices were Sister M. Louise Bastasich, Sister M. Borgia Lesiak, Sister M. Theophane Rakowski, Sister M. Alcantara Ochwat, Sister M. Doloria Ostrega, Sister M. Priscilla Korc, and Sister M. Louise Nowicki.

Great joy lay in store for the Sisters when on Christmas Eve, 1926, the Holy Sacrifice of the Mass was offered for the first time in the chapel by the Reverend Joseph Tarasiuk, CR, who came from St. Joseph Home for the Aged with Mother M. Vincent and several Sisters. They cried from joy for all they saw. From the dilapidated, abandoned Walker mansion, the Sisters had created a home and a chapel with the Blessed Sacrament reserved in the tabernacle. Father Tarasiuk blessed the entire house, and the Sisters dedicated it to the Blessed Virgin Mary under the title of Our Lady of Victory.[14] On Christmas Day, however, Sister M. Mechtilde, Sister M. Imelda, and Sister M. Pauline walked to St. Mary's Seminary to attend mass since a priest could not come to the convent on that busy day. They also heard mass at St. Mary's Seminary on January 1, 1927.

The second mass celebrated in the chapel of Our Lady of Victory Convent by a Franciscan priest from St. Mary's Seminary was on January 2, 1927, then the feast of the Epiphany. The Franciscan Fathers agreed from that day on to celebrate mass for the Sisters in the chapel during the week. On Sundays and holydays, the Sisters still walked to St. Mary's Seminary. It was not until July 10, 1927, that the Franciscan Fathers from St. Mary's Seminary began to celebrate mass in the chapel on Sundays as well as during the week.[15]

On February 2, 1927, eleven postulants arrived from the Motherhouse in Chicago to reside in Lemont under the supervision of Sister M. Raphael Bogalecki, their postulant directress. These postulants were received into the novitiate at the Motherhouse in Chicago on July 16, 1927, and returned to Lemont on August 3, 1927. The novices were Sister M. Lucille Klockowski, Sister M. Alberta Bialas, Sister M. Canisia Niemiec, Sister Ann Rose Mroz, Sister M. Hugoline Czaplinski, Sister M. Virginette Rokicki, Sister M. Clarissa Kolupka, Sister M. Serafica Kwasniewski, Sister M. Justine Sierputowski,[16] Sister M. Gregoria Klimowski,[17] and Sister M. Eymard Sanok.[18]

With the permission of Cardinal Mundelein, Adoration of the Blessed Sacrament was held from March of 1927 on every First Friday of the month at Our Lady of Victory Convent.

In September of 1927, because of the dire need of Sisters in the schools and institutions of the congregation, the second-year novices were sent to minister at the mission houses. The first-year novices, according to Canon Law, remained enclosed at Our Lady of Victory Convent. All the novices were under the supervision of Sister M. John Barczak, their mistress of novices. That same month, Sister M. Mechtilde Zynda was named superior of the professed Sisters and the novices at Our Lady of Victory Convent.

Statue of Our Lady of Victory—a cherished item in the history of the Franciscan Sisters of Chicago—which occupied a prominent place in the original Motherhouse. It is now in the Mother Theresa Museum

The first Our Lady of Victory Convent, formerly the Walker Mansion, Lemont, Illinois; Novitiate House of the Franciscan Sisters of Chicago from 1927 to 1931 and from 1937 to 1963; since 1963, the Mother Theresa Museum

She also acted as assistant to Sister M. John. Because the Walker mansion was the home of the white-veiled novices, Our Lady of Victory Convent was often referred to as the "White House."[19] Mother M. Vincent Czyzewski, the superior general, and Sister M. Benigna Jakajtis, the third councilor, visited Monsignor Rempe on September 26, 1927. They requested permission to have the Franciscan Fathers of the Assumption Province from Pulaski, Wisconsin, give weekly conferences to the first-year novices and the professed Sisters. The permission was granted, and from March 1929 the Reverend Dionysius Babilewicz, OFM, was sent as the ordinary confessor to the Sisters at Our Lady of Victory Convent. Father Babilewicz also gave conferences to the Sisters and novices after they had received the sacrament of Penance.[20]

With the approach of June 1928, the postulants and the second-year novices who had been actively engaged in works of the apostolate returned to the novitiate. Once again there was an acute lack of room in the "White House." The postulants, therefore, slept in a two-story frame house on the premises. It was called St. Francis Home to differentiate it from Our Lady of Victory Convent. The second floor of St. Francis Home served as the postulants' sleeping quarters. The first floor served as storage space for the Sisters' trunks and various items such as habit material and other articles of clothing.

The retreat for the postulants and the novices was held that year from July 7 to 16, 1928. The retreat master was the Reverend Arcadius Krzywonos, OFM, of Pulaski, Wisconsin. On July 16, the feast of Our Lady of Mount Carmel, in the chapel of Our Lady of Victory Convent, for the first time since its foundation were held the novitiate and first profession ceremonies. The celebrant of the mass on that day was the Right Reverend Monsignor Stanislaus Bona, vicar general for the women religious of the Archdiocese of Chicago. Father Krzywonos performed the investiture and first profession ceremonies. The novices who made their first vows were Sister M. Donata Klepek,[21] Sister M. Dorothea Tomon, Sister M. Liliosa Hoinski, Sister M. Doloretta Radzienda, Sister M. Antoinette Tadych, Sister M. Evelyn Furman, Sister M. Edwina Wilk, and Sister Clarent Marie Urbanowicz. The postulants admitted to the novitiate were Sister M. Aloysetta Ciezadlo, Sister M. Norberta Haas, Sister M. Teresita Kuczmarski, Sister M. Bernarda Urbanski, Sister M. Ernestine Radecki, Sister M. Edith Dolasinski,[22] Sister M. Theresilla Ignasiak, Sister M. Julianna Pabian,[23] Sister M. Lillian Szura, Sister M. Leonia Mszanski, and Sister Helen Marie Zasadzinski.

Her term as superior general having ended in June, Mother M. Vincent Czyzewski was appointed the new superior of Our Lady of Victory Convent in August of 1928. Sister M. Mechtilde now served as the assistant superior and also remained the assistant to Sister M. Gonzaga Raniszewski who had been named mistress of novices. Sister M. John Barczak, the former mistress of novices, returned to the Motherhouse in Chicago to serve as the local procurator. Sister M. Gonzaga, however, did not remain long at her new assignment. The Constitutions of the Franciscan Sisters required that the novice mistress be thirty-five years of age and ten years after first profession of vows. Because Sister M. Gonzaga was only thirty-one years old and nine years after first profession, she was relieved of caring for the novices in September. She returned to the Motherhouse in Chicago where she waited until November 22, 1928, for her dispensation to arrive.[24] During this time, Mother M. Vincent Czyzewski served as mistress of novices. Having received the necessary dispensation, Sister M. Gonzaga returned to Our Lady of Victory Convent on December 1, 1928, in time to prepare a group of novices who were about to make their retreat before taking their first vows. The retreat was conducted by the Reverend Aloysius Staśkiewicz, OFM, from Pulaski, Wisconsin. The ceremonies were conducted by the Right Reverend Monsignor Stanislaus Bona on December 31, 1928. Once again, because of the shortage of Sisters, the second-year novices were sent to the active apostolate. The first year novices continued their study of the vows and the spiritual life with the Reverend Dionysius Babilewicz, OFM, who continued to serve as the Sisters' weekly confessor.[25]

By 1929, the membership in the congregation had risen to 271 professed Sisters, twenty-five novices and eighteen postulants. The Sisters who were ill were in need of an infirmary, and the postulants and novices required more adequate living quarters. In 1928, Mother M. Vincent Czyzewski had been replaced by Mother M. Aloysia Holysz as the superior general. Mother M. Aloysia and her general council concluded that only a new convent in Lemont would be the solution to the constant problem of accommodations for the membership.

To help the congregation achieve its long-range goal to build a Motherhouse in Lemont, the friends and relatives of the Sisters organized the Our Lady of Victory Society in 1929. Founded by Mrs. Anna Pejor and Mrs. Jane Karłowicz together with eighteen women from St. John Cantius Church in Chicago, the society pledged itself to support the work of the Sisters.[26] Because the ladies of the Our Lady of Victory Society were so dedicated to the goal of helping the Sisters raise funds, the Sisters felt that the women should have the opportunity of enjoying the benefits of the Lemont countryside. The Sisters, therefore, invited the ladies of the Our Lady of Victory Society, their families, relatives, and friends to hold an outing in Lemont. The members and their families took advantage of the opportunity to relax and recreate in the fresh air. This first outing was held in 1930, became an annual event until the late 1960s, and was held only intermittently after that time.

There were other outings held in Lemont in the late 1930s which were more spiritual in nature and were referred to as pilgrimages. The "pilgrims" came to visit the many shrines of St. Francis as well as the shrine dedicated to the Blessed Virgin Mary. Generally hundreds of men, women, and children came to Lemont from Chicago, its surrounding areas, and even Indiana. Once the pilgrims arrived in Lemont, a High Mass was celebrated and visits made to the chapel and shrines. After the religious services, luncheon was provided. In the afternoon, the Way of the Cross and Solemn Benediction usually took place. The Blessed Sacrament was carried in procession, and in a giant outpouring of faith, the pilgrims followed, praying and singing hymns. The procession with the Blessed Sacrament traveled from the chapel to an outdoor altar in the wooded area

Procession at Our Lady of Victory Convent, Lemont, Illinois, c. 1940

near the St. Francis grottoes. A sermon was always delivered by a priest in the group. A typical procession, for example, consisted of the Our Lady of Victory Society members and officials, the Sisters, the choir of St. Florian parish, the altar boys from St. Pancratius parish, and the faithful from Chicago and nearby areas often totaling as many as six hundred people. After the Benediction service, under the warm sun and on the open expanse of fertile land amid the sheltering trees and carpets of green grass, the pilgrims refreshed themselves and spent the remainder of the day in pleasant repose and visitation with the Sisters and priests. Oftentimes, the Sisters combined the religious pilgrimage with a small bazaar. They made handiwork and by its sale sometimes raised as much as $1,000.[27] The pilgrimages to Lemont were numerous from 1934 until 1940 when the Second World War drastically affected all civilian travel.

On January 29, 1930, due to the carelessness of one of the employees at Our Lady of Victory Convent, the St. Francis Home burned down. Much of the material for habits and other clothing stored on the first floor of the home was destroyed. With the destruction of their sleeping quarters, the postulants were forced to return to the Motherhouse in Chicago where they were placed under the direction of Sister M. Hedwig Kubera.

On April 13, 1930, Mother M. Aloysia informed her general council that Monsignor Bona had visited Cardinal Mundelein at which time he reminded the Cardinal of the Sisters' request for permission to build a Motherhouse. Mother M. Aloysia notified her council that Monsignor Bona had also said that the Sisters should keep to the prescription of Canon Law and have the second-year novices, who were working beyond the Motherhouse, come back to the novitiate house for two months before making their first profession.[28] In May, Cardinal Mundelein gave the Sisters permission to go forward with the matter of building a new convent in Lemont. Mother M. Vincent and the general council were to have plans drawn up and presented to the Cardinal at the nearest opportunity.

When the summer approached, two tents were erected in place of the St. Francis Home that had burned down. The novices were housed in the tents since they could not be accommodated in the Our Lady of Victory Convent where the professed Sisters took up the major part of the building. During the winter months, when the second-year novices were sent to minister in the schools and institutions of the congregation, the two groups of first-year novices lived in Our Lady of Victory Convent where sixteen of them slept in the attic. Because of the overcrowded and inconvenient conditions in Lemont, Monsignor Bona received permission from the Holy See in Rome to have the novitiate moved back to the Motherhouse in Chicago in May of 1931. Once again the novices lived in the old novitiate house as well as on the lower floors of the old St. Vincent's Orphan Asylum. The permission secured from Cardinal Mundelein was considered temporary, that is, until the Sisters could build a new Motherhouse in Lemont. Because these were the years of the Depression Era, however, the building of a new Motherhouse in Lemont became a remote possibility, and, indeed, did not occur for many years.

On July 19, 1931, a large bronze statue of the Sacred Heart[29] was erected on a pedestal before the front entrance to Our Lady of Victory Convent and was blessed by the Reverend Walter Bartylak, CR, the pastor of St. John Cantius Church in Chicago, who after the blessing delivered an appropriate sermon. During a huge procession, the Blessed Sacrament was placed on an altar prepared for it on the stairs of the convent. The Reverend James J. Strzycki, the pastor of Five Holy Martyrs Church, celebrated the Benediction service after which the people visited with the Sisters and recreated in the convent gardens until nightfall. Originally there had been a large bed of flowers in front of the Walker mansion. At each of the four corners marking off the mansion, there were four giant granite pots in which stood a statue representing a season of the year. When the Sacred Heart statue was placed in front of the mansion—now Our Lady of Victory Convent— these seasonal monuments were removed, but the pots containing beautiful flowers remained and can still be seen today. A large cross, visible from a distance, was placed atop the convent roof.

After the novices left the Motherhouse and returned to take up residence in Lemont in April of 1926, the first floor of the previous novitiate house in Chicago was converted into sleeping quarters for the postulants and the second floor was reserved for the Sisters who were ill. The superior and administrator at this time of transition was Sister M. Martha Bywalec,[30] who with special attention took care of the ninety aged residents and established the horarium which directed the work of the Sisters. She became increasingly aware of the fact that the five small frame cottages in which some of the residents were housed were no longer serviceable, and prudence seemed to dictate that it would be a waste of money to attempt to renovate them. Besides, the critical lack of space for the professed Sisters, the novices, and the aged residents was becoming more and more evident especially with more aged persons asking to be admitted to St. Joseph Home. Sister M. Martha informed Mother M. Vincent and her general council of her findings and suggested that instead of having the cottages repaired, a new, large home for the aged should be constructed on or near the site of the cottages. Mother M. Vincent and her general council were in complete agreement with Sister M. Martha's suggestion and were determined to build a new home for the aged rather than a new Motherhouse for the Sisters which was also desperately needed.

Mother M. Vincent met with Cardinal Mundelein in order to obtain the necessary permission to build a new home for the aged. He arranged for a $300,000 loan from the Holy See.[31] Sister M. Martha also secured financial aid from the Benevolent Aid Societies of St. Joseph at St. Joseph Home for the Aged and the Associated Catholic Charities of the Archdiocese of Chicago. In 1927, the building of the new St. Joseph Home for the Aged began on Ridgeway Avenue, the former site of the five frame cottages. Since St. Joseph Home for the Aged was built and completed in the next six years, it will be discussed further in Chapter 35.

WOODLAND PARK: OUR LADY OF VICTORY CONVENT

[1]Canon Law is defined as the whole body of rules which forms the legal system by which the Church governs its life and that of its members. It is Church law as distinguished from moral law and from the enactments of civil authority. All the rules and laws of the Church pertaining to faith, morals, and discipline are known as Canon Law.

[2]Siostra M. Gonzaga Raniszewski, OSFK, "Rys historyczny Zgromadzenia Sióstr Franciszkanek Bł. Kunegundy. Część druga, 1910–1940" [A historical survey of the Franciscan Sisters of Blessed Kunegunda. Part two, 1910–1940] Unpublished manuscript (AFSCL), p. 196.

[3]For further information concerning Father Grudzinski, see Chapter 27.

[4]The Walker family has been associated with Lemont since the Civil War years. Edwin Walker, the first Walker to settle in Lemont, was born in England and emigrated to the United States in 1856 with his wife. After spending one year in Philadelphia, the couple moved to Chicago. A building contrator by occupation, Edwin Walker purchased land in Lemont and quarried limestone for use in his business and for sale to other contractors. He gained fame as the contractor who built the old Chicago Water Tower and the Illinois State Capitol at Springfield. After the Civil War, with quarrying demanding more of his time and attention, he settled his family in Lemont. Today, only two descendants of the Walker family are identified with the Lemont area. Barbara Buschman, ed., *Lemont, Illinois: Its History in Commemoration of the Centennial of Its Incorporation, 1873–1973* (Des Plaines, Illinois: King/Mann Yearbook Center, 1973), pp. 185–186.

[5]*Minutes of General Council Proceedings, 1919–1934* (AFSCL).

[6]Secretaries General, *Community Chronicle*, p. 86 (AFSCL).

[7]In 1973, on the 100th anniversary of its foundation, Lemont adopted the slogan, the "Village of Faith" and with little wonder. In its vicinity are four Roman Catholic churches, two Protestant community churches, and four Protestant denominational churches. There are three religious schools: Mount Assisi Academy, St. Vincent de Paul High School Seminary, and De Andreis Seminary. There are these religious institutions: Mother Theresa Home, Alvernia Manor, St. Mary's Seminary and Retreat House, the Motherhouse of the Franciscan Fathers of the Custody of the Holy Cross, the Motherhouse of the Congregation of the Franciscan Sisters of Christ the King, and the Motherhouse of the Congregation of the Franciscan Sisters of Chicago. The "Summer Bulletin" of St. Patrick's Church in Lemont drew this observation from its pastor, the Reverend Edward Fitzgerald in 1976:

> In Lemont on this coming Saturday at De Andreis Seminary, many men besides our respected Vincentians will be ordained priests. In the convents on Main Street each year, there are young women who consecrate their whole being to God. One would not be surprised to learn that more have received the sacrament of Holy Orders or have professed Religious vows in our small village of Lemont than in cities which are many times its size.

[8]In the 1700s, the area attracted the Potawatomi Indians. The first *plat* of what today is Lemont was named Keepataw in honor of the Indian chief who ruled the valley tribe. Arrowheads and other Indian artifacts have been discovered in Lemont, and it is generally believed that most of the village of Lemont and its surrounding areas were at one time the site of an Indian village. After the Black Hawk War in 1832, most of the Indians had to surrender their land in Illinois by the Treaty of Chicago. In April of 1850, the name Keepataw was changed to Palmyra, and on May 30, 1850, the name of the town became Lemont. Buschman, p. 3.

As early as 1833, Jeremiah Luther became the first permanent settler in Lemont Township. Soon after, many of the earliest settlers, generally immigrants, were attracted to Lemont because of the building of the Illinois and Michigan Canal. Other settlers came because of the work offered in the numerous limestone quarries in the area for which Lemont became famous. The huge stones can be seen along Lake Michigan on Chicago's Outer Drive as well as the stones of the Old Chicago Water Tower and the Illinois State Capitol at Springfield. The city of Lemont has numerous examples of buildings made of its well-known limestone. Lemont was incorporated in 1873 and its population at that time was approximately 3,000. There are now about 5,600 in the village itself while the township has 8,850 residents. *Chicago Sun-Times,* 18 October 1985. If nothing else had put Lemont on the map, there is the added fact that the Argonne National Laboratory, researching peacetime uses of atomic energy, is at Lemont's doorstep. Buschman, p. 8.

[9]Buschman, p. 12; and *Illinois Guide and Gazetteer* (Chicago: Rand McNally and Co., 1969), no pagination.

[10]Siostra M. Gonzaga Raniszewski, OSFK, *Zarys Połwiecza Zgromadzenia Sióstr Franciszkanek Bł. Kunegundy* [Sketch of the fifty-year history of the Congregation of the Franciscan Sisters of Bl. Kunegunda] (Chicago: By the Author, 1944), p. 38.

[11]The Franciscan Fathers came to Lemont in 1924 and settled on property on Main Street. They built the temporary Motherhouse of the Slovenian Franciscan Friars of the Custody of the Holy Cross and called their headquarters St. Mary's. A school of theological studies for the students of the Custody, and a novitiate for new candidates entering the Franciscan Order was also erected. A new and permanent seminary and monastery were dedicated by Samuel Cardinal Stritch in 1940. From the time of their arrival in the Lemont area, the Franciscan Fathers have ministered at the parishes in the immediate vicinity. The priests and brothers of the Order expanded their work to include retreats, missions, publishing, and pilgrimages. They also ministered to convents and homes for the aged in the Lemont area. St. Mary's, the "good neighbor" of the Franciscan Sisters of Chicago, is a religious and national center particularly for people of Slovenian descent. In 1946, a guest house was built to accommodate persons participating in pilgrimages from distant cities. The guest house was also used for many years to accommodate the parents, relatives, and guests of the Franciscan Sisters of Chicago who came to Lemont to witness the investiture and profession ceremonies at Our Lady of Victory Convent before 1963. The grounds of St. Mary's are beautifully landscaped. The Franciscan Fathers themselves have deftly erected the Stations of the Cross, the Lourdes Grotto, the Rosary Valley, and the Fatima Shrine, as well as a park named in honor of Bishop Frederic Baraga, the "Snowshoe Priest," a Slovenian missionary to the Indians of Michigan and Wisconsin. On a hillside beneath the Lourdes Grotto and the Bled replica of the famous lake in Slovenia, Yugoslavia, lies the cemetery where many of the Franciscan Fathers who served the Sisters at Our Lady of Victory Convent so zealously as ministers of the Sacred Liturgy, confessors, teachers, and friends are buried. Buschman, pp. 115–116.

[12]Sister M. Ludwina returned to Our Lady of Victory Convent in 1928 and was assigned to the kitchen. Except for three months in 1934, when she was sent to Our Lady of Spring Bank Abbey in Oconomowoc, Wisconsin, she spent thirty-four years as the head cook at Our Lady of Victory Convent for the Aged and Infirm Sisters. Sister M. Ludwina, the beloved and colorful "taskmaster" of young novices who worked under her direction in the kitchen, died on August 18, 1974. She was ninety years old and had been in the congregation for sixty-nine years. *Congregation Membership Records;* and *Spis Sióstr* (AFSCL).

[13]According to the Constitutions of the congregation, the novitiate lasted for two years. For its validity, it was required that at least the first year be spent entirely and continuously in the house of the novitiate itself. During the first year of the novitiate, the novices could not be employed in performing the external works of the congregation, nor could they devote themselves to regular courses of studies of literature, sciences, or the arts. During the second year of the novitiate, if necessary, the novice could be employed in the works proper to the congregation.

[14]See Chapter 11.

[15]Secretaries General, *Community Chronicle,* p. 98 (AFSCL).

[16]Sister M. Justine left the congregation at the expiration of her temporary vows in July of 1932. *Book of Departures.* (AFSCL).

[17]Sister M. Gregory left the congregation in July of 1940. Ibid.

[18]Secretaries General, *Community Chronicle,* p. 98 (AFSCL).

[19]*Our Lady of Victory House Journal* (AFSCL).

[20]*Minutes of General Council Proceedings, 1910–1934* (AFSCL).

[21]On November 30, Sister M. Donata left the congregation. *Book of Departures* (AFSCL).

[22]Sister M. Edith Dolasinski left the congregation on July 3, 1938. Ibid.

[23]At the expiration of her temporary vows, Sister M. Julianna Pabian left in July of 1933. Ibid.

[24]A dispensation is an act whereby the lawful superior grants relaxation from the existing law. It is only the lawgiver, his delegate, or his successor who can dispense a person from observing a law. The law itself is not changed or altered but the operation of the law is suspended in a given case.

[25]In 1938, the Franciscan priests from the Sacred Heart Province of St. Louis at St. Roch's Friary Oak Forest, Illinois, served as confessors.

[26]Raniszewski, *Zarys,* p. 47.

[27]Secretaries General, *Community Chronicle,* p. 109 (AFSCL).

[28]*Minutes of General Council Proceedings, 1934–1956* (AFSCL).

[29]The statue was the gift of a woman who preferred to remain anonymous.

[30]Sister M. Martha, the former Magdalen Bywalec, was born in Poland and came to the United States in 1904. She entered the community on August 15, 1906, from St. John Cantius Church in Chicago. On August 15, 1907, she became a novice. A year later, on August 15, 1908, she pronounced her first vows and on August 15, 1916, was admitted to perpetual vows.

Sister M. Martha had a varied and colorful apostolic life. She served as a teacher in Cleveland and Youngstown, Ohio; and East Chicago and La Porte, Indiana. She served as mistress of postulants from 1917 to 1919. From 1920 to 1928, she was stationed at St. Joseph Home for the Aged and served as superior and administrator. She was also the organizer of lay advisory groups of men and women who aided the home financially. For six years she was missioned at St. Anthony's Home in Crown Point. For five years she was stationed at Guardian Angel Day Nursery and Home for Working Girls in Chicago. Later in life, Sister M. Martha was sent to Boys Town, Nebraska, where she remained for sixteen years in charge of outfitting the Boys Town Choir for all of their singing tours. Retiring to the Motherhouse in Lemont in 1973, she died on March 2, 1976 at the age of eighty. She had been in the congregation for sixty-nine years. *Spis Sióstr* (AFSCL).

A woman more wholeheartedly dedicated to God and her congregation than Sister M. Martha could not be found. A woman of prayer, she accepted life with all its sufferings and joys. She labored for the good of the congregation and immersed her own heart in God, a splendid example of a religious in old age. Interviews with Sisters, 1983 (AFSCL). Her sister, Sister M. Pelagia Bywalec, also a Franciscan Sister of Chicago, died in 1914.

[31]*Minutes of General Council Proceedings, 1910–1934;* and Secretaries General, *Community Chronicle,* p. 102 (AFSCL).

CHAPTER 33

Final Events

Mother M. Vincent accepted only one school during her term as superior general. The staffing of St. Pancratius School in 1924, a daughter-school to Five Holy Martyrs in Brighton Park, was a distinctly advantageous and apostolically rewarding action.

When the new Five Holy Martyrs Church and School were relocated in 1919 at 43rd and Richmond Streets, the original building on 41st Street and Kedzie Avenue was used as a parochial hall and a temporary auxiliary school. The Catholic Poles who lived north of Archer Avenue, close to the original church, wanted a church of their own. They cited two excellent reasons for this demand. Firstly, Five Holy Martyrs Church had become overly crowded; and secondly, the people living north of Archer Avenue did not want their children to cross that busy thoroughfare in order to attend school.[1] More than 773 families signed a petition to the Most Reverend George Mundelein, archbishop of Chicago, for permission to establish a new parish in their area. At first, Archbishop Mundelein was reluctant to form a new ethnic parish, but when he learned of a plan to form a Polish National Church in the neighborhood, he decided to establish a Roman Catholic Church for the Poles in order to thwart the dissidents. In March of 1924, therefore, he announced the organization of the new St. Pancratius Parish, the first parish he established after being named to the College of Cardinals. He assigned the Reverend Stanislaus Radniecki to organize it.[2]

The first mass at the new St. Pancratius Church was offered on March 9, 1924, in the two-story structure on 41st Street which had formerly served as the church, school, and hall for Five Holy Martyrs Parish. The first floor of the building was used as a school and rectory while the second floor served as a temporary church. The Franciscan Sisters of Chicago, who had promised to staff St. Pancratius School, lived in the convent of Five Holy Martyrs Parish until the new school and convent could be completed. The Sisters who traveled from Five Holy Martyrss to St. Pancratius School were the following: Sister M. Josepha Zwierzycki, Sister M. Scholastica Jakubski, Sister M. Gerard Gorzkowski, Sister M. Theodore Madaj, Sister M. Florentine Karasek, Sister M. Felicia Dolezych, and a postulant.[3] Sister M. Sylvestra Pelczar was appointed the superior and principal.

The Sisters' newly built convent was ready for occupancy on April 1, 1925. Leaving the hospitality of Five Holy Martyrs Convent and Parish, the Sisters assigned to St. Pancratius School moved to the spacious three-story structure erected on West 40th Place in late June of 1925. With the beginning of school in September of 1925, there were 865 pupils enrolled. They were met by the following Sisters: Sister M. Sylvestra Pelczar, superior and principal; Sister M. Gerard Gorzkowski, Sister M. Thomas Halgas, Sister M. Desideria Grendys,[4] Sister M. Felicia Dolezych, Sister M. Theodore Madaj, Sister M. Bertha Kaminski, and Sister M. Adolpha Waranowski who attended to household duties.[5] There were also two postulants sent.[6]

Within a matter of months, a new three-story brick school building which contained sixteen classrooms and an auditorium was constructed next to the convent on West 40th Place. When it was dedicated by the Most Reverend Edward F. Hoban, auxiliary bishop of Chicago, on May 9, 1926, there were more than nine hundred children enrolled.[7]

By 1927, a large debt faced the parish of St. Pancratius because of its numerous building projects. The hard-working parishioners believed the debt would be eradicated through generosity and determination. With the stock market crash of 1929, and the attendant Depression Era which engulfed the entire nation, it was impossible for the parishioners to pay their debts and build a new church which they so ardently longed to do. The school enrollment had reached its peak in 1933 with 1,100 pupils and a staff of twenty-seven Sisters which included a sacristan, a laundress, an organist, and a household manager.

St. Pancratius Convent
Chicago, Illinois

St. Pancratius School
Chicago, Illinois (1924–   )

In 1934, Father Radniecki was transferred and his successor was the Reverend Vincent Nowicki[8] who was responsible for a complete renovation of the interior of the church and its facade. During his pastorate, St. Pancratius School rose to new heights of scholastic excellence. By 1937, there were 750 children and twenty-three Sisters. Unfortunately, as the years passed, there was a decrease in enrollment and by 1940, there were only 517 children on the school's roster.[9]

With the death of Father Nowicki in 1955, the Reverend Robert Niec[10] was appointed the new pastor. He set about executing Father Nowicki's plans for a new house of worship. Additional land had been purchased directly across the street from the school on the southeast corner of 40th Place and Sacramento Boulevard, and ground-breaking ceremonies were held in 1957. On Sunday, August 9, 1959, the new church opened for public worship. The parishioners were overjoyed when St. Pancratius Church was dedicated on May 8, 1960, by Albert Cardinal Meyer, archbishop of Chicago. On July 29, 1960, a stained-glass window portrait of Mother M. Theresa Dudzik was installed in the new church as a gift from the schoolchildren.

In January of 1970, the Reverend Walter Stefanski succeeded Father Niec who had reached retirement age. When St. Pancratius Church celebrated its Golden Jubilee in 1974, the Most Reverend Alfred L. Abramowicz, auxiliary bishop of Chicago and pastor of Five Holy Martyrs Church, was the principal celebrant. The choice was appropriate since Bishop Abramowicz was himself an alumnus of St. Pancratius School.[11]

In the late 1930s and early 1940s, St. Pancratius School had been designated a "model school." It was visited by the elementary school principals and teachers of the Archdiocese of Chicago as a model of operation and performance. The school was lauded as well by the Reverend Stanley Stoga and the Reverend John Kozlowski, the archdiocesan school supervisors. Many demonstrations of innovative teaching methods were presented under the direction of Sister M. Blanche Bartkowski, the congregation's supervisor of schools. Demonstrations at Teacher Institute Days were conducted by Sister M. Alberta Bialas, Sister M. Charitas Gajdzinski, Sister M. Maristella Skrzynski, and Sister M. Dorothy Szostak for the benefit of the congregation's members as well as for the Sisters of other religious congregations.

The stabilized enrollment at St. Pancratius today is listed at approximately two hundred pupils with five Sisters and five lay teachers on the staff. The daughter-school of Five Holy Martyrs continues its efforts to increase the faith of its pupils, and to stir up zeal for quality education.

Before the year 1925 ended, a very distinguished guest visited St. Joseph Home for the Aged. This was the Most Reverend John B. Cieplak,[12] archbishop of Vilna, Poland, who had come to the United States to visit all Polish parishes and institutions at the request of Pope Pius XI. After World War I, the fiery spirit of Polish independence was again expressing impatience with what the Poles believed was a lack of appreciation of Polish-Catholic needs by a non-Polish hierarchy.[13] Archbishop Cieplak was called upon by Pope Pius XI to study and remedy the situation in the United States.

When Archbishop Cieplak arrived at St. Joseph Home for the Aged, Mother M. Vincent and the general council greeted him at the door. He was taken to the chapel where the chaplain of the home, the Reverend Joseph Tarasiuk, CR, greeted him in the name of the assembled Sisters and the residents. In the common recreation hall, the archbishop greeted all who were present individually. One of the residents gifted the archbishop with a beautiful spiritual bouquet on behalf of the aged at the home. Archbishop Cieplak inquired about the apostolates of the congregation, and when informed as to the missions and ministries of the Sisters, urged their fervent continuation and progress especially in the care of the aged. He departed after giving his blessing to all assembled. A few weeks later, the Sisters and the residents who treasured the memory of his warm paternal visit, were saddened to hear that Archbishop Cieplak had died unexpectedly at St. Mary's Hospital in Passaic, New Jersey, on February 17, 1926, while making preparations for his return to Poland.

The year 1926 was a memorable one for Chicago because of the XXVIII International Eucharistic Congress which opened on June 20.[14] Long known in Europe, this Eucharistic Congress was the first to be held in the United States. The huge manifestation of faith drew three bishops, fifty-seven archbishops, twelve cardinals, priests, Sisters, and hundreds of thousands of lay people to the many services in the city's massive Soldier Field as well as to the expansive grounds of the archdiocesan's St. Mary of the Lake Seminary in Mundelein, Illinois. The Holy Father, Pope Pius XI, sent Giovanni Cardinal Bonzano,[15] as the papal legate who was cordially received wherever he appeared.[16]

There was a Polish Section Program conducted on Sunday, June 20, at two o'clock in the afternoon. The opening address was given by the Right Reverend Monsignor Thomas Bona.[17] The chairperson of the sessions was the Reverend Paul Sapiecha, and speeches were presented by three bishops from Poland.[18] According to the program booklet distributed at the Eucharistic Congress, August Cardinal Hlond gave an address on Men's Night [*Wieczor mężczyzn*] at the Eucharistic Congress on Tuesday, June 22, 1926.

The Congress ended on June 24 with a solemn procession in Mundelein, Illinois, on the grounds of St. Mary of the Lake Seminary. Almost one million people participated.

All the Franciscan Sisters of Chicago, encouraged by Mother M. Vincent, participated in this public profession of faith, the greatest religious spectacle witnessed in the United States to that time. On the day following the conclusion of the Eucharistic Congress, the three bishops from Poland who had been guest speakers at the Polish session of the Congress visited St. Joseph Home for the Aged. They were the Most Reverend Henryk Przeździecki, bishop of Podlaski; the Most Reverend Stanisław Łukomski, auxiliary bishop of Poznan; and the Most Reverend Teodor Kubina, bishop of Częstochowa.[19] The Sisters extended their warmest hospitality to the Church dignitaries as well as to the many clergy who accompanied them on the visit. The Sisters and the residents of St. Joseph Home for the Aged were very happy with the spontaneous visit of these amiable, distinguished guests.[20]

In 1928, at the end of her term of office, Mother M. Vincent assumed the position of superior of Our Lady of Victory Convent in Lemont. She served in this capacity until 1935. In poorer health than at any other time in her life, she returned to the Motherhouse in Chicago where she died on April 22, 1942 of a cerebral embolism and endocarditis. She was buried on April 25 from the chapel of St. Joseph Home for the Aged. Mother M. Vincent was sixty-seven years old and had been in the congregation for forty-three years.[21]

FINAL EVENTS

[1]Monsignor Harry C. Koenig, ed., *A History of the Parishes of the Archdiocese of Chicago*, 2 vols. (Chicago: The New World Publishing Co., 1980) 1:745.

[2]Ibid.

[3]The postulant was Julia Duszynski who became Sister M. Richard.

[4]Sister M. Desideria spent forty-nine years of her religious life in service at this parish. From 1924 to 1932, she was a teacher at the school. From 1932 she served as sacristan at St. Pancratius Church until her retirement at the Motherhouse in 1973. She died there on September 30, 1978. *Spis Sióstr* (AFSCL).

[5]*Five Holy Martyrs House Journal* (AFSCL).

[6]The two postulants were Sophie Walkowski who became Sister M. Benilda and Rose Podraza who became Sister M. Sebastia.

[7]Koenig, p. 747.

[8]The Reverend Vincent Nowicki was born in 1889 in South Chicago. He received his seminary training in St. Francis, Wisconsin, at St. Francis Seminary where he was ordained on June 1, 1912. He served as pastor at St. Florian's Church from 1922 to 1934. In 1934, he was transferred to St. Pancratius Church where he served as pastor until his death on September 6, 1955. Francis Bolek, ed., *Who's Who in American Leaders and Distinguished Poles Resident in the Americas*, 3rd ed. (New York: Harminger House, 1943; Arno Publishers, 1970), p. 323.

[9]*St. Pancratius Church Dedication Book* (Chicago: 8 May 1960), no pagination.

[10]Father Niec had served as assistant at St. Pancratius Church from 1934 to 1941, and again from 1947 until his formal appointment as pastor in January of 1956. He was named pastor emeritus on December 22, 1969.

[11]See Chapter 23.

[12]Born in Dombrova, Russia (later Poland) on August 17, 1857, John Cieplak was ordained a priest in 1881. For the first twenty-five years of his ministry, he was a priest and teacher laboring under the rule of autocratic Orthodox Russian Czar. In 1908, he was appointed Suffragan Bishop of Hohilev, Russia, by Pope Pius X and made an archbishop in 1919. When the Bolshevik Revolution broke out, he remained to continue his ministry, all the while an ardent foe of Communism. He was tried in Moscow in 1923 with fourteen other priests for an alleged crime. Death sentences were pronounced for him and a Monsignor Budkiewicz; the other priests received prison sentences. Monsignor Budkiewicz was executed at once; Archbishop Cieplak was imprisoned for a year and then expelled to Poland. It is the general impression that outraged protests from the United States and other countries all over the world caused the Bolsheviks to commute his death sentence.

Archbishop Cieplak came to America at the request of Pope Pius XI to visit all Polish parishes and institutions. He visited four hundred Polish churches, 25 dioceses, 375 parishes, and 800 institutions in ninety-two days, and delivered over eight hundred sermons. He was greeted enthusiastically everywhere in America. Joseph Ledit, SJ, *Archbishop John Baptist Cieplak* (Montreal: Palm Publishers, 1963) no pagination; and "Arcybiskup Jan Cieplak," *The New World*, 27 February 1976.

[13]This movement which had been strong in the last part of the 1800s and the early 1900s flared up again. See Chapter 18.

[14]Eucharistic Congresses are public demonstrations of faith in the Holy Eucharist. They combine liturgical services, other public ceremonies, and various kinds of instructional and inspirational elements united by central themes which serve to increase understanding of and devotion to Christ in the Holy Eucharist. The aim is to relate this liturgy of worship and witness to daily life. International Congresses, of course, include clergy, religious, and lay persons from countries and national and international Catholic organizations. *Catholic Almanac*, 1980.

[15]Giovanni Bonzano (1867–1927) was named Apostolic Delegate to the United States in 1912, and a cardinal in 1922. He was named Papal Legate to the Eucharistic Congress at Chicago in 1926. He died in Rome on November 26, 1927. *Dictionary of Catholic Biography*, p. 160.

[16]John Cogley, *Catholic America* (New York: The Dial Press, 1973), p. 87.

[17]The Right Reverend Monsignor Thomas Bona was a consultor in the Archdiocese of Chicago. He was also chairman of the Archdiocesan School Board. He served as pastor of St. Mary of Perpetual Help parish in Chicago from 1921 to 1950. Advisor to the Polish Social Welfare for the Archdiocese of Chicago, he was also appointed Director of American Relief for Poland in 1939. He died on June 28, 1950, in Chicago. He was a brother to the Most Reverend Stanislaus Bona, bishop of Green Bay, Wisconsin. Reverend Monsignor Harry C. Koenig, ed., *A History of the Archdiocese of Chicago: Published in Observance of the Centenary of the Archdiocese, 1980,* 2 vols. (Chicago: The Archdiocese of Chicago, 1980), 1:607.

[18]XXVIII Międzynarodowy Kongres Eucharystyczny w Chicago, Illinois, 20–24 June 1926, *Program Polskiej Sekcji Kongresu* [XXVIII International Eucharistic Congress, Chicago, Illinois, 20–24 June 1926, *Program of the Polish Section of the Congress*] (Niles: St. Hedwig's Orphanage Printery, 1926), p. 19.

[19]Ibid.

[20]Siostra M. Gonzaga Raniszewski, OSFK, *Rys historyczny Zgromadzenia Sióstr Franciszkanek Błogosławionej Kunegundy. Część pierwsza, 1860–1910* [A historical survey of the Franciscan Sisters of Blessed Kunegunda. Part one, 1860–1910] (Chicago: By the Author, 1947), p. 167.

[21]*Spis Sióstr* (AFSCL).

CHAPTER 34

The Fourth General Chapter: Mother M. Aloysia Holysz

Early in 1928, with Mother M. Vincent Czyzewski's term as superior general drawing to a close, preparations were made for the Fourth General Chapter of Elections which was to begin on June 29. At the beginning of June, the Right Reverend Monsignor Francis Rempe informed Mother M. Vincent that he would be unable to preside at the congregation's Fourth General Chapter as the delegate of Cardinal Mundelein.[1] On June 20, Cardinal Mundelein sent Mother M. Vincent a letter in which he informed her that Monsignor Rempe had resigned his position as vicar general for the women religious of the Archdiocese of Chicago and the Reverend Stanislaus Bona was to serve as his successor.[2]

The Fourth General Chapter of Elections convened on June 29, 1928, and lasted for ten days. On July 2, the election of the superior general and the general council took place with the newly appointed Father Bona presiding. Mother M. Vincent Czyzewski secured an absolute majority in the voting and was thus elected to a second term. In spite of this show of support, Mother M. Vincent refused to accept the office of superior general again. She remained steadfast in her sheer unwillingness to assume another term pleading ill health. The casting of votes resumed, and after the fourth balloting, Mother M. Aloysia Holysz who had already served as superior general from 1916 to 1922 was once again elected to that office. The delegates elected Sister M. Benigna Jakajtis the assistant general and first councilor; Sister M. Seraphine Zamrowski, second councilor; Sister M. Salomea Grabowski, third councilor; Sister M. Innocenta Antosz, fourth councilor and secretary general; and Sister M. Leona Pochelski, procurator general.[3]

The only Sister elected to the general council for the first time was the fourth councilor, Sister M. Innocenta. Born in 1887 in Galicia, Poland, Sister M. Innocenta came to the United States in 1900. Entering the community from St. John Cantius Parish in Chicago on August 1, 1905, she was accepted into the novitiate on July 26, 1906, and made her first profession of vows on July 27, 1907. Her perpetual profession was made on July 27, 1915.

Sister M. Innocenta spent most of her religious life as a teacher and superior in the schools of the congregation. For six years, from 1922 to 1928, she served as the administrator and superior of Guardian Angel Day Nursery and Home for Working Girls. At this Fourth General Chapter, she was elected fourth councilor and secretary general for a six-year term which ended in 1934.[4] At the congregation's Fifth General Chapter held in 1934, Sister M. Innocenta was elected assistant general and first councilor for a term of six years. In the fourth year of her term, much to everyone's sorrow, Sister M. Innocenta was stricken with cancer and died at the Motherhouse on March 6, 1938. A tall, dignified, and personable woman, Sister M. Innocenta was recognized as being very prayerful, strong of faith, and full of compassionate understanding.[5]

On the day after the elections, Mother M. Aloysia distributed to the delegates a copy of the Rule of the Third Order of St. Francis which was to be placed in the Constitutions according to the custom of all Franciscan congregations. Mother M. Aloysia's next act was to appoint three commissions to study and make suggestions pertaining to the issues connected with those commissions. Because there were thirty-four delegates, she divided the Sisters into three groups: the Constitutions Commission consisted of Sister M. Benigna Jakajtis, Sister M. Seraphine Zamrowski, Sister M. Salomea Grabowski, Sister M. Innocenta Antosz, Sister M. Leona Pochelski, Sister M. Angeline Topolinski, Sister M. Martha Bywalec, Sister M. Francis Drufke, Sister M. Antonina Osinski, and Mother M. Vincent Czyzewski. The Finance Commission consisted of Sister M. Hyacinth Barczewski, Sister M. Gerard Gorzkowski, Sister M. Zita Kosmala, Sister M. Berchmans Fidler, Sister M. Chester Dziarnowski, Sister M. Stephanie Pinkowski, Sister M. Helen Swiszcz, Sister M. Ursula Murdza, Sister M. Sylvestra Pelczar, Sister M. Jerome Dadej, and Sister M. Mechtilde Zynda. The Discipline and Education Commission had as its members Sister M. Felicita Pajor, Sister M. Salesia Rzeszutko, Sister M. Hilary Dadej, Sister M. Herman Pieniazek, Sister M. Paul Kirschbaum, Sister M. Raphael Bogalecki, Sister M. Euphrosine Tryjanowski, Sister M. Eugenia Detlaf, Sister M. Ottilia Madaj, Sister M. Brunona Szwagiel, and Sister M. Immaculate Matuszewski.

A few days after the election, the following appointments were made by Mother M. Aloysia and her general council: Sister M. Chester Dziarnowski, superior of the Motherhouse; Sister M. Stanislaus Reich, assistant superior; Sister M. Gonzaga Raniszewski,[6] mistress of novices; and Sister M. Mechtilde Zynda, the assistant to Sister M. Gonzaga and the mistress of postulants.[7]

The decrees stemming from the Fourth General Chapter dealt with elements of Franciscanism in prayer and spirit. As a result of this chapter, the first uniform community prayer book, *Kocham Chrystusa, Oblubienica Przed Obliczem Boga, książka do Nabozeństw Sióstr Franciszkanek pod wezwaniem Bł. Kunegundy,* [Amo Christum, I Love Christ, the Spouse Before the Face of God, a Book of Devotions of the Franciscan Sisters under the patronage of Blessed Kunegunda], was published in 1932 and distributed in January of 1933 to each Sister. The prayer book was largely the compilation of Mother M. Aloysia Holysz. In the choice of prayers, she was advised by the Franciscan Fathers of the Assumption of the Blessed Virgin Mary Province of Pulaski, Wisconsin.

The Franciscan Fathers were becoming increasingly more involved in giving retreats and instructing the Sisters in regard to their religious obligations. With the help of the Reverend Arcadius Krzywonos, OFM, of Pulaski, Wisconsin, the Sisters were introduced to the practice of "Cross Prayers." Said during the Adoration of the Blessed Sacrament which preceded the daily evening recitation of the *Little Office of the Blessed Virgin Mary,* the Cross Prayers consisted of six Our Fathers, six Hail Marys, and six Glory Be's said with outstretched arms. This penitential form of prayer was adopted to petition God for earnest and generous vocations to the congregation.

The religious ceremonies connected with the reception of the habit and the first and perpetual profession of vows were to be based on the format suggested in the *Franciscan Ceremonial,* a book of religious procedures generally used by Franciscan congregations. The new ceremonies based on the *Franciscan Ceremonial* were introduced into the congregation in December of 1930.

Many of the Fourth General Chapter decrees issued had to do with the Sisters' apparel. There was a move initially to change the style of the religious habit in order to provide for a removable scapular. The delegates, however, voted to keep the same habit pattern. The prior general chapter, held in 1922, had proposed that the material and cut of the mantle worn during the winter be changed because the mantle in use did not offer enough protection from the cold. The measure passed but for some reason or other the new style of mantle was first adopted in 1932.

The delegates also voted to change the wooden crucifixes the Sisters wore to nickel-plated ones suspended from a brown tape around the neck. The wooden crucifixes had been imported from Europe and in 1928, in the midst of the widening insecurities concerning the impending World War II, were difficult to obtain. The nickel-plated ones were made in America. The Sisters began to wear the new crucifixes on the feast of Christ the King, October 30, 1932.

Some of the other decrees of the Fourth General Chapter were of rather minute consequences and resulted in these prescriptions:

1. In the future, as was presently the case, Sisters would observe the twenty-fifth anniversary of religious life from the day of entrance into the congregation. The Sisters would celebrate this joyous occasion at the mission or home where they were stationed at the time; the Golden Jubilee would be celebrated as a group at the Motherhouse.

2. Every Sister would be permitted to visit her parents for two weeks every five years.

3. The Sisters would title the superior general "Reverend Mother" or "Mother General" not "Mother Superior."[8] The assistant general would now be called "Sister Vicar" or "Vicar General."

One of the chief topics of discussion during the Fourth General Chapter was the matter of wearing rings to represent a Sister's perpetual commitment to Jesus Christ.

While the matter was introduced at the chapter, no decision was made. Just before leaving office in 1928, Mother M. Vincent had interviewed the Sisters during her final visitation in regard to their feelings concerning the wearing of rings. It was determined that 163 Sisters were against the proposal while 79 Sisters seconded it. The reason for the Sisters' adverse reaction to the ring of perpetual profession seems to have been based on a false assumption which they propagated among themselves. It appears that someone had informed the Sisters erroneously that with the acceptance of the ring as a part of perpetual commitment to the congregation came the obligation to practice the public chapter of faults[9] and external penances. Again, according to a vote taken by Mother M. Vincent, only fifty-five Sisters were in favor of public chapter of faults while 187 were against it. The congregation never accepted the public chapter of faults nor did it accept extraordinary penances. It was not until thirty-six years later, in 1964, that the congregation gladly approved and accepted the beautiful custom of the bestowal of rings as a sign of lifelong commitment to Christ and service to the Church.

Of meaningful significance occurring at this time was the transfer of the celebration of the feast of Blessed Kunegunda to July 24 from July 27 in accordance with the Roman and the Franciscan Missal. In another instance, the congregation reflected its growing devotion to Christ the King by replacing the Sacred Heart statue on the main altar of the Motherhouse chapel with one of Christ the King.

During the second term of Mother M. Aloysia, there were other occurrences which were of importance. In 1930, great joy came to the congregation when, after four years of waiting, the Constitutions of the congregation were approved and ratified for a seven-year probation period by Pope Pius XI on December 9, 1930.[10]

The accent on education was enhanced by the fact that approximately eighty-one Sisters were attending Normal School or a university and fifty or more were finishing their high school education.[11] Sister M. Antonina Osinski was selected to succeed Sister M. Benigna Jakajtis as the school supervisor for the congregation's schools. During this administration, the Sisters began nurses' training and educational courses to prepare them for their work in the health apostolate. In 1934, three Sisters were sent to St. Joseph School of Nursing in Joliet. They were Sister M. Leonilla Stogowski, Sister M. Laurentine Trocki, and Sister M. Antonina Waloch. The emphasis on music education initiated by Mother M. Vincent Czyzewski was encouraged by Mother M. Aloysia who arranged to have many Sisters enroll in the Progressive Series School of Music in St. Louis, Missouri. A number of Sisters attended the course offerings in the summers from 1929 to 1932. In March of 1931, Mother M. Aloysia attempted to rescind the contract made with the Progressive Series School of Music because of the Depression Era but the School of Music held the Sisters to the contract.[12] Among the Sisters who participated in the Progressive Series School of Music were Mother M. Aloysia Holysz, Sister M. Adelle Romanowski, Sister M. Alberta Bialas, Sister M. Bibianna Wiza, Sister M. Benigna Jakajtis, Sister M. Consolata Markowicz, Sister M. Crescencia Chmiel, Sister M. Edmunda Siernicki, Sister M. Euphemia Switalski, Sister M. Henrietta Machowski, Sister M. Humilia Proc, Sister M.

Hugoline Czaplinski, Sister M. Ignatia Hodkiewicz, Sister M. Josephata Tadych, Sister M. Loyola Dymanowski, Sister M. Mercy Witczak, Sister M. Methodia Ryzner, Sister M. Paul Kirschbaum, Sister M. Remigia Lewandowski, Sister M. Philomena Wasik, Sister M. Rosalima Sierocki, Sister M. Theresia Rybak, and Sister M. Zygmunta Zebracki.

THE FOURTH GENERAL CHAPTER: MOTHER M. ALOYSIA HOLYSZ

[1]Monsignor Rempe resigned his office on July 1, 1928.

[2]*Minutes of General Chapter Proceedings, 1910–1940* (AFSCL).

[3]Ibid.

[4]*Spis Sióstr* (AFSCL).

[5]*Interviews* with Sisters, September 1983 (AFSCL).

[6]Sister M. Gongaza is discussed at greater length in Chapter 47.

[7]*Minutes of General Chapter Proceedings, 1910–1940* (AFSCL).

[8]The title, "Mother Superior," was used in other congregations to signify local superiors or provincials.

[9]A chapter of faults was an exercise carried out in some religious congregations at regular intervals during which the religious confessed known faults and transgressions of the Rule (not sins) publicly and received suitable penance from her religious superior. In some religious houses members accused one another of faults, but generally counter-accusations were not allowed. The exercise was conducted in the spirit of charity and came about as a result of tradition in long-established congregations and orders.

[10]See Appendix A.

[11]Secretaries General, *Community Chronicle*, p. 109 (AFSCL).

[12]*Minutes of General Council Proceedings, 1910–1934* (AFSCL).

CHAPTER 35

Added Blessings

At the end of the Fourth General Chapter in July of 1928, Mother M. Aloysia Holysz, together with her councilors, resolved to carry through the plans undertaken by her predecessor, Mother M. Vincent Czyzewski, in the matter of building a new St. Joseph Home for the Aged. In March of 1928, the congregation had received permission from Cardinal Mundelein to build a new residence for their beloved aged. To defray the costs of the building venture, he helped the Sisters to secure loans from the Holy See and the Associated Catholic Charities of the Archdiocese of Chicago. The Benevolent Aid Societies of St. Joseph Home for the Aged, organized in 1917, lent their most valuable assistance.[1] Cardinal Mundelein also gave the Sisters[2] permission to conduct a "drive" to collect funds for the proposed new building:

> Reverend and dear Mother Superior:
>
> I am pleased to grant you permission, subject in all instances to the consent of the respective pastors, to solicit and receive the contributions of the friends and well-wishers of St. Joseph's Home for the Aged under the care of the Sisters of St. Kunegunda in the Archdiocese of Chicago towards the new buildings you are now erecting to take care of the old people in your care. Surely this is a work of great charity, which appeals in a particular way to our people, and I am happy to give you my blessings and the encouragement you desire in this work to which your Sisters in a special way have dedicated their lives.
>
> Wishing you all success, I am,
>
> > Sincerely yours in Christ,
> > George Cardinal Mundelein
> > Archbishop of Chicago[3]

In addition, a general committee was formed to aid in the construction of St. Joseph Home for the Aged. This committee comprised prominent Chicago citizens such as the following: Jane Addams; Anton J. Cermak, mayor of Chicago; the Reverend Francis

Earlier St. Joseph Home, Chicago, Illinois, c. 1931

Gordon, CR; the Right Reverend Monsignor Thomas Bona, Judge Edmund K. Jarecki, Judge Stanley Klarkowski, Judge J. P. McGoorly, and Nikodem Piotrowski among others.

Planned by architects Slupkowski and Piontek, the building operations, under the direction of the L. W. Schuetz Construction Company, began in September of 1928 on the southwest corner of Ridgeway and Schubert Avenues, the site of the five small frame cottages which had been razed. On September 12, 1928, the Reverend Francis Gordon, CR, pastor of St. Mary of the Angels Church, blessed the ground for the new structure and delivered a sermon for the occasion. The mass and benediction which preceded the blessing were celebrated by the Reverend John Kasprzycki, CR, superior general of the Congregation of the Resurrection.

The work of laying the foundation went so quickly that on the afternoon of Thanksgiving Day, November 29, 1928, the setting of the cornerstone took place. The cornerstone bore an appropriate inscription from Ecclesiastes: "Deposit generosity in your storerooms, and it will release you from every misfortune."[4] The ceremonial blessing was administered by the Right Reverend Thomas Bona, pastor of St. Mary of Perpetual Help Church. The Reverend John Obyrtacz, CR, pastor of St. Mary of the Angels Church, read aloud to the assembled priests, Sisters, and guests the document which had been placed in the cornerstone.

When the decision to build the new St. Joseph Home had been made, it had become necessary to plan for the furnishing of rooms and other vital purchases for such a large institution. Because the costs could not be met with the aid of even the most generous benefactors, the Sisters found it necessary to seek another loan for $15,000 from the Associated Catholic Charities. The task of furnishing and preparing the home for occupancy lasted until the autumn of 1929. Much of the success of the entire project was due to Sister M. Chester Dziarnowski,[5] the administrator and superior of the home, who with her managerial skill and efficiency was able to bring the project to a successful conclusion. As for the original St. Joseph Home for the Aged and Crippled, it was now called St. Francis Home and was converted into offices for the superior general and some members of the general council.

The records of St. Joseph Home for the Aged indicate that approximately 20 percent of the residents brought to the home some monetary compensation at the time of their admittance. The other 80 percent of the residents were entirely dependent upon the home for their support and, eventually, their funeral expenses. The needs of the indigent elderly were met by donations from the friends of St. Joseph Home, funds raised by auxiliary and volunteer organizations, and alms collected by the Sisters. The Sisters were also grateful for the continued aid that they received from the Associated Catholic Charities of Chicago. Medical care was very often given gratis to the residents by generous and caring physicians.

The Sisters at St. Joseph Home and at all the missions did what they could to aid the home financially. It must be remembered, however, that a sudden and disastrous drop in the stock market rocked the American economy in 1929 and continued through the 1930s ushering in the Great Depression. As a consequence, bank failures, factory shutdowns, and widespread unemployment were rampant. The new St. Joseph Home for the Aged was a victim of these circumstances.

By 1929, nonetheless, the new St. Joseph Home was completed. Now the Franciscan Sisters had beautiful and adequate facilities for the aged, the ailing, and the bedridden. It was truly a splendid example of a modern institution. The four-story brick and reinforced concrete structure was located on quiet, residential, tree-lined Ridgeway Avenue. The spacious St. Joseph Home was built to offer sheltered care and limited nursing care to almost two hundred residents. It offered private, semiprivate and ward rooms, an infirmary with full accommodations, and a doctor's reception and examination room with a small pharmacy. There was a large and lovely chapel. The home contained a two-room suite with bath for the resident chaplain, his dining room, and two suites with bath for guests. Arranged accordingly were a wake room and parlor for mourners, a two-room office, a large parlor, dining rooms—one for two hundred guests and one for the Sisters—separate community and sewing rooms for the Sisters and the residents, a lounging and smoking room for residents and visitors, a library, a solarium, and a kitchenette with a small dinette on each floor. An auditorium was built to accommodate three hundred persons. A modern, fully equipped kitchen, special storage and service rooms, a large pantry, a walk-in cooler, a carpenter shop, a laundry room, and a fully equipped power house rounded out St. Joseph Home's facilities. There was an elevator for the residents and a large service elevator and an intercommunication system on each floor.

Because of the large number of Sisters at the Motherhouse, a wing on the third floor was designated as their sleeping quarters.[6]

The elderly had the services of a resident chaplain, a member of the Congregation of the Resurrection, who met their spiritual needs. He offered Holy Mass daily, and Benediction of the Most Blessed Sacrament was also held at eight-fifteen o'olock each evening. Every afternoon the rosary was prayed, and the sacraments of Penance and Extreme Unction were always available.[7]

The blessing of the new St. Joseph Home for the Aged by George Cardinal Mundelein, the archbishop of Chicago, had been scheduled for October 20, 1929. He had graciously accepted the invitation to bless the home but asked the Sisters to postpone the blessing until the spring when the weather would be more favorable. In the meantime, a private blessing of the home took place on November 29, 1929, by the chaplain, the Reverend Joseph Tarasiuk, CR.[8] With the arrival of spring, Mother M. Aloysia requested Cardinal Mundelein to set a date for a formal blessing. While Cardinal Mundelein did not decline her invitation, he informed her that he was shortly expecting the visit of the Primate of Poland, August Cardinal Hlond.[9] Cardinal Mundelein suggested to Mother M. Aloysia that Cardinal Hlond be given the honor of blessing the St. Joseph Home thereby leaving a beautiful memory of his visit for the Franciscan Sisters and the residents. The Sisters were overjoyed with the Cardinal's plan, but unfortunately Cardinal Hlond never came to America, and, consequently, St. Joseph Home was never publicly blessed.[10]

Because the new St. Joseph Home was now able to minister to approximately two hundred elderly, Mother M. Aloysia and the general council voted to separate the offices of superior and administrator. On August 16, 1933, therefore, Sister M. Ladislaus Wroblewski was appointed the administrator of St. Joseph Home, and Sister M. Bogumila Swiech served as the religious superior.

In the late 1930s, the chaplain, the Reverend Joseph Tarasiuk, CR, landscaped the grounds near St. Joseph Home and succeeded in creating a lovely garden where the Sisters and the residents could sit and recreate in the summer. By planting trees, bushes, and flowers, he created the image of a small city park. On June 3, 1940, the Reverend Wenceslaus Cich, OFM,[11] from Pulaski, Wisconsin, blessed the outdoor Stations of the Cross which had been renovated and placed in new frames during the landscaping.[12]

In the years that followed, St. Joseph Home for the Aged had a bed capacity of 163 and maintained full occupancy at all times. It provided full-time housing, nursing care, and medical attention. Extensive repairs and renovations were undertaken in 1956. However, an event occurred in 1959 which altered the history of St. Joseph Home. Shortly after the tragic fire which claimed so many lives[13] at Our Lady of the Angels School on Chicago's West Side, the Chicago Fire Department ruled that the original St. Joseph Home for the Aged and Crippled (also the Motherhouse) and St. Vincent's Orphanage adjoining it were no longer safe or habitable. Because of this ruling, the original buildings were razed, and a new Motherhouse was built in Lemont, Illinois in 1963.[14] To provide the necessary living quarters for the Sisters who remained on the staff of St. Joseph Home, an addition was erected over the garages and storage rooms facing Hamlin Avenue. The addition was blessed at a special ceremony on May 30, 1970, by the Most Reverend Alfred L. Abramowicz, auxiliary bishop of Chicago.[15]

St. Joseph Home celebrated its Diamond Jubilee with a concelebrated liturgy at the home on Saturday, October 27, 1973. John Cardinal Cody, archbishop of Chicago, was the main celebrant with the Most Reverend Alfred A. Abramowicz, auxiliary bishop of Chicago; the Most Reverend Aloysius Wycislo, bishop of Green Bay; the Reverend Francis Grzechowiak, CR, and the Reverend Stanley Rokocinski as co-celebrants. The Reverend Edmund Raczka, CR; provincial of the Congregation of the Resurrection, delivered the homily.

In 1976, the name, St. Joseph Home for the Aged, was changed to St. Joseph Home of Chicago, and with that change a $1 million massive renovation of the interior took place. After careful and lengthy consideration of the residents of and applicants to the home, the congregation determined that these elderly were generally in need of intermediate care, that is, care for those who were unable to live independently but who required less than continuous nursing service on a twenty-four-hour basis. Since only twenty-two beds in the infirmary were so licensed, the home underwent extensive renovation to meet local, state, and federal standards. The interior reconstruction of the sturdy institution began on February 9, 1976.[16] Most private rooms gave way to double rooms, and new plumbing, sprinklers, wiring, and smoke detectors were installed; ceilings were lowered, and doors were widened. A year later, a virtually "new" facility emerged from the old.

Dedication of the renovated St. Joseph Home of Chicago took place at a Mass of Thanksgiving and Blessing on March 19, 1977, at three o'clock in the afternoon at which John Cardinal Cody was the principal celebrant. Concelebrating with the cardinal were the Reverend Francis Rog, CR, provincial of the Resurrectionist Fathers; the Right Reverend Monsignor Thomas Holbrook, director of Catholic Charities for the Archdiocese of Chicago; the Reverend Francis Grzechowiak, CR, pastor of St. Hyacinth Church; the Reverend Walter Zmija, pastor of St. Ladislaus Church; the Reverend Stephen Juda, CR, chaplain of St. Joseph Home of Chicago; and the Reverend John Rolek, the master of ceremonies. The residents and staff of St. Joseph Home plus approximately one hundred invited guests attended. An open house was held on March 20 from one to four o'clock in the afternoon for the general public.

The history of St. Joseph Home contains the names of dedicated women who have served as administrators, superiors, and ministers to the elderly. One of the many qualified and generous Sisters who served in this capacity was Sister M. Agnes Zywiec, who guided the home during its turbulent renovation. Appointed in 1960, Sister M. Agnes served intermittently as administrator-superior for sixteen years. A tribute, well deserved, was accorded her in October 1968 when she was presented with the St. Bridget Award for outstanding service to humanity through her work with the aged for almost all of her religious life. Sister M. Agnes was the first American woman to receive the award

Present St. Joseph Home of Chicago
Chicago, Illinois

presented to her by Colonel Frank Chesrow, a papal chamberlain, at the Executive House in Chicago.

Today, St. Joseph Home of Chicago is under the administration of Mr. Joseph Bonnan. It is staffed by twelve Franciscan Sisters and 116 full-time and 47 part-time employees. The staff is augmented by an active group of volunteers. The central aim of the St. Joseph Home administration and staff in its present and projected services is to enhance the quality of life of its residents who are in the "vespertide of life,"[17] by providing them with a home that feels like a home and with supportive services that promote the highest level of loving care in an environment that fosters dignity and respect for each person.

St. Joseph Home of Chicago meets the standards of quality health care as prescribed and legislated by the State of Illinois Department of Public Health and the City of Chicago Department of Public Health. It is a member of the Illinois Association of Homes for the Aging and the Catholic Health Association. It welcomes residents of all religious, national, racial, social, and economic backgrounds.

With a chapel for quiet devotion, meditation, and inspiration, the home provides excellent opportunities for spiritual activities. A nonresident chaplain, the Reverend John

Miles, CR, ministers to the spiritual needs of the residents, a service the Congregation of the Resurrection has provided for St. Joseph Home of Chicago since 1909. Residents may participate daily in the celebration of the Sacred Liturgy, the reception of the Holy Eucharist, the daily recitation of the rosary, as well as Benediction of the Most Blessed Sacrament on the First Friday of each month. The Sacrament of Reconciliation and the Sacrament of the Anointing of the Sick are made available to Catholic residents. Non-Catholics are welcome to receive visits from their ministers or rabbis. The Department of Pastoral Care was initiated in August of 1985 by Sister Martha Joan Sempolski, Sister M. Crescentine Oszuscik, and Sister M. Francesca Janowicz. In 1986, Sister M. Antonissima Jamruk, a certified pastoral minister, assumed supervision of the department. The Department of Pastoral Care addresses the emotional, social, and spiritual needs of the residents of the home, their families, and those of the employees as well.

By 1983, more physical changes took place at the home. A new heating, ventilating, and air-conditioning system was installed. A new physical therapy room was developed, and a redecoration of the interior of the facilities was also completed. The final touches to the exterior of the home took place in 1985 when the lobby renovation project was completed. The front entrance to the home was revamped to include the installation of a very functional elevator, a new reception section, a security area, and a ramp to accommodate wheelchair residents.

Chapel, St. Joseph Home of Chicago, c. 1960

During the 1980s, the home had been shifting from an intermediate care center to a more expanded skilled-care facility. The expansion of the medical services included the addition of many staff professionals such as registered nurses, licensed practical nurses, and an increase in the total number of support staff.[18] By March of 1987, St. Joseph Home of Chicago was licensed solely as a skilled-care nursing facility. Twenty-four-hour professional nursing care is provided, and patient conferences are held weekly to ensure the best possible physical and psychological progress of each resident. While the home provides twenty-four-hour physician care, many residents maintain a private physician. Dental, podiatry, optometric, and psychiatric consultants are available. A social worker conducts the social service program and directs the various departments towards attaining total patient care.

Delicious, well-balanced meals are served each day in a cheerful and comfortable dining-room. Some residents prefer to enjoy the tray service which is also provided. Special diets are attended to by a competent dining room and kitchen staff.

In order to help residents strengthen their sense of socialization, the home provides beauty and barber shops. There are comfortable and attractive activity rooms, TV rooms, and lounges offering pleasant areas where residents may meet to visit, play cards and games, or simply to watch TV. A full-time activities director supervises a varied and interesting program planned around the special needs of the residents. The choices include movies, sing-alongs, discussions, arts and crafts, bingo, exercises, poetry classes, newspaper reading, and musical programs. There are celebrations on such days as birthdays, Christmas, New Year's Eve, Thanksgiving, Halloween, St. Valentine's Day, and the feast of St. Joseph. Every third Sunday of the month throughout the year, the St. Vincent de Paul Society makes person-to-person visits. The residents are frequently entertained by different community organizations. Parties, concerts, plays, movies, and bingo games are organized for the residents' enjoyment. Annually the residents take part in the Golden Olympics held at Maryville Academy in suburban Des Plaines. A newspaper for and about the residents and staff is published monthly. Begun in 1961, it is presently called the *St. Joseph Journal*. The home also has a Resident Council which meets once a month to voice the problems, concerns, or recommendations of the residents. Provisions for letter writing and letter reading are made by the Sisters.[19]

St. Joseph Home of Chicago has been a true home to many aged men and women. Attuned to the Gospel concept of the corporal and spiritual works of mercy, the home provides medical, spiritual, and protective care to the aged in the vision and tradition of Mother M. Theresa Dudzik, the foundress of St. Joseph Home of Chicago and of the Franciscan Sisters of Chicago who have ministered there for over ninety years.

One of the new apostolates to which Mother M. Aloysia and her general council gave wholehearted assent in the summer of 1929 was the catechetical mission or the religious vacation school as it was commonly called. In a number of rural areas and in small towns where children were unable to attend parochial schools, religious education programs were conducted by the Sisters to provide instruction in Christian doctrine and to prepare children for the reception of the sacraments. Another notable aim, often achieved, was to encourage the faith of lapsed Catholics—families as well as individuals. This special catechetical work was performed by Sisters who throughout the year had already carried a full teaching load.

The first known summer catechetical assignment was made in 1929 when Sister M. Carmel Rokicki and Sister M. Consolata Markowicz were sent to Holy Rosary Parish in Fairmont City, Illinois. Sister M. Carmel wrote of her experience:

> All the children, parents, and the pastor lined up in front of the church to greet us. The people were very happy to have the Sisters there even if it were for only one summer. As the parents greeted us, they kissed our hands. Imagine! Sister Consolata and I were only twenty-four years old and here we were being greeted by older people in that way. Something I'll never forget is that one little girl ran home every day during recess and brought us a basket with cookies and a jar of milk.[20]

That summer proved to be the small beginning of a wider and a more fruitful involvement in rural catechism work. No records exist, however, of home mission activities again until 1931 when several Sisters whose names are not recorded were sent to St. Michael's Church, Perronville, Michigan; St. Joseph's Church, Foster City, Michigan; and St. Mary's Church, Orwell, Ohio.[21]

In 1932, Sister M. Euphemia Switalski and Sister M. Marcelline Molek were sent to Perronville, Michigan, a happy obligation various Sisters assumed for the next nine years. The Reverend Thomas A. Drengacz, the pastor of St. Michael's Church in Perronville, wrote to Mother M. Aloysia Holysz that year:

> Dear Reverend Mother Aloysia:
>
> I suppose you have wondered whether I have forgotten about you or not, being that I have not written anything all this time. Nevertheless, I have been sending prayers to Almighty God for your generosity and kind-heartedness towards me in sending these good nuns to me for the summer. Words fail me in trying to tell you how I feel at this moment, as they are doing splendid work here. The children and the parents are already showing the fruit of the Sisters' labor and any sacrifice that I have made in their coming to my parish, or any sacrifice you have made, dear Mother Aloysia, in sending them here, has been worth it many times over.
>
> The children seem to be different now. Parents can't keep them home. Now it's a cry to go to Sisters' school. You can't call it by any other name either. It's "Sister this," and "Sister that." Even I don't rate around here so much. The Sisters come first, and thanks be to God for the inspiration of asking you for the Sisters.

Thanks be to God for the fulfillment of that since it's the saving thing for these poor starved souls. At last they have someone who takes more interest in them than before. The parents are so taken up with the Sisters that it has been told to me that they are circulating a petition begging to be able to keep at least two Sisters here continually. And, of course, I need not speak for myself, how I feel about it. I don't know how I ever managed without them and I know I'll never fill their place when they go. It seems I have a different parish now. You remember I said: "I'd like to reach the parents through the children." Well, I have already. I have more people to Mass on Sunday than I ever had before. That fact alone speaks volumes. Adding to that, the behavior in church of the children and parents has been marked, too. The singing is angelic. In fact, my power of composing this letter in praise of the work of the Sisters here is very limited for I would need the pen of Sienkiewicz and the ardor of Skarga in the telling. Sufficient it is to say that I am pleased beyond words at the work of the Sisters and I don't know how I will ever be able to repay you for your kindness. I pray daily for you, Mother, and your kind Sisters that God may shower His choicest blessings on you and your Community. May God bless you always.

> Your sincere and humble debtor,
> Fr. Drengacz[22]

Because he was so pleased with the work of the Sisters, Father Drengacz, with the permission of the Reverend Joseph C. Plagens, auxiliary bishop of Marquette, Michigan, petitioned Mother M. Mechtilde Zynda in 1940 for three Sisters to teach religion on Saturdays in Wakefield and Ramsey. He also requested that they take charge of the choir and do sacristy work on a permanent basis.[23] Mother M. Mechtilde was advised by the Right Reverend Monsignor John Mielcarek, the vicar general for the women religious of the Archdiocese of Chicago, to refrain from sending Sisters to the Marquette Diocese at that time. It appeared that there was not enough work for three permanent Sisters and certainly one Sister could not be sent. According to the conditions laid down by Father Drengacz, the Sisters hardly would be able to support themselves.[24]

That same year, Sister M. Blanche Bartkowski and Sister M. Chester Dziarnowski were assigned to St. George's Church in Bark River, Michigan, where the Sisters served for five consecutive summers. St. Joseph's Church in Foster City, Michigan, was also staffed for nine years.

The Sisters' catechetical teaching consisted of Christian doctrine, Bible history, and Church history. Special classes such as the First Holy Communion class and the Confirmation class were conducted. Efforts were made to initiate the children into an intelligent participation in liturgical functions, especially the mass. Various hymns and prayers were also taught. In addition, the Sisters at almost every summer catechetical mission cared for the sanctuary and the sacristy, kept the religious vestments in repair, and visited the sick and the aged in their homes. In some instances, the Sisters also taught Polish to the school children.

Generally, the Sisters received a stipend of some sort from the pastor of the parish for their services, but, in many instances, the only material compensation was travel fare plus room and board. In many of the parishes, it was necessary for the Sisters to live in secular homes. Sister M. Esther Obuchowski recalls another example:

> Neither of the priests (Father Krysty of Perronville nor Father Breault of Bark River) was able to pay us for the work, so at the end of the summer school, we had to have an entertainment with the children and all proceeds were sent to the Motherhouse.[25]

Most often, the eager enthusiasm and appreciation on the part of the children, parents, and pastor were ample thanks for the Sisters. The Sisters taught more by example than by doctrine, and the unbounded love and genuine affection shown the Sisters were evidence of the worth of this apostolate. There was sincere regret at seeing the Sisters leave at the end of the summer catechetical session.

Regular summer catechetical centers also functioned for years in Menominee, Wakefield, Schaffer, Stephenson, Ramsey, and Ironwood in Michigan; Orwell, Campbell, Warren, Parkman, and Sheffield in Ohio; Madison, Illinois; Fish Lake, Rolling Prairie, and Independence Hill in Indiana; Osceola, Nebraska; Spooner, Lublin, Shell Lake, Iron Belt, Hurley, and Saxon in Wisconsin; and South Heart, Medora, Belfield, Scranton, Gaylor, and Amidon in North Dakota.

Canada welcomed the Franciscan Sisters in 1963 when Sister M. Innocent Smagacz and Sister M. Consilia Przybyl went to Holy Trinity Parish in Windsor where they taught religion and Polish. In the afternoon, the Sisters visited the sick and aged in hospitals, nursing homes, and at their homes. The Sisters maintained the sacristy and decorated the altars for liturgical functions. In the summer of 1964, Sister M. Victoria Valerie Smagacz joined her sister, Sister M. Innocent, in Windsor, Chatham, and Woodstock for six weeks. The next summer, Sister M. Innocent and Sister M. Adelma Walkowski went to Holy Trinity Parish in Windsor while Sister M. Hildegarde Demps and Sister M. Donald Urban were sent to Woodstock and Chatham.[26]

From June to August of 1973, Sister M. Claudiana Jachimowicz worked with her sister, Sister M. Pascaline Jachimowicz, a member of the Congregation of the Sisters of St. Felix of Cantalice (Felicians), in Carlsberg, Germany, at the *Kinderheim Marianum,* a home for dependent and neglected refugee children. As late as June 1976, Sister M. Francine Labus and Sister M. Crescentine Oszuscik taught religion at St. Raphael the Archangel Parish in Raleigh, North Carolina.[27]

Among the Sisters who had been in the foundation group of the congregation was Sister M. Angeline Topolinski. Of the eight original members who began the small community with Sister M. Theresa Dudzik and Sister M. Anna Wysinski, only Sister M. Angeline persevered with them in overcoming all the hardships and crises which threatened the community's very existence. On December 4, 1930, Sister M. Angeline was called to her eternal rest.

Sister M. Angeline was born on October 11, 1856, the daughter of Simon and Mary (née Mindykowski) Topolinski, near Poznań in Western Prussia. She came to America with her parents in 1889 and settled in St. Stanislaus Kostka Parish. Constance Topolinski, as she was known before her entry into the community, was a talented seamstress and was engaged to sew in private homes of women customers frequently for weeks at a time.[28]

As an active member of St. Stanislaus Kostka Parish, Constance Topolinski belonged to the Third Order of St. Francis, but because of the nature of her work, she seldom attended the meetings. She had been present at the meeting on November 24, 1894, however, when Josephine Dudzik presented her plan to the assembled tertiaries for the organization of a charitable group of women to serve the poor, and she asked to be permitted to join them. At thirty-eight, she was one of the oldest volunteers in the group.

Having been accepted as a member, Constance was also present at the Third Order's fourth and final meeting with Father Barzynski on December 12, 1894, at which time the aspiring members were to take up residence at Josephine's home. Constance arrived at the home on Chapin Street on December 20, and her postulancy is subsequently listed as having begun on December 22, 1894. Like the others, Constance chose to be called by her tertiary name, Sister Angeline. Her novitiate, first profession, and perpetual profession were all shared with Sister M. Theresa Dudzik and Sister M. Anna Wysinski as outlined earlier.

Sister M. Angeline served the small community as procurator from 1899 to 1905, a position to which she had been appointed by Father Spetz. From 1905 to 1910, she was also a member of the advisors under the mother superior, Sister M. Anna. At the same time, she was the superior and administrator of St. Elizabeth's Day Nursery from 1905 to 1911. She returned to the Motherhouse in 1911 where she sewed and did splendid handicraft which contributed financially to the congregation. She was occupied in this capacity when she died of pneumonia. Her remains were taken to the convent chapel on December 8 at five o'clock in the evening. The exportation ceremonies were conducted by the Reverend Joseph Tarasiuk, CR, chaplain of St. Joseph Home, assisted by the Reverend Stephen Kowalczyk, pastor of St. Hyacinth Church; the Reverend Theodore Klopotowski, CR, the Reverend Jerome Fabianski, CR, and the Reverend Walter Baron, CR.[29]

The next day at nine-thirty o'clock in the morning, a Solemn Requiem Mass was celebrated in the convent chapel by the Reverend John Kasprzycki, CR, the superior of St. Joseph Novitiate for the Resurrectionist Fathers in the Cragin area. Assisting him were the Reverend Francis Uzdrowski, CR, and the Reverend Joseph Samborski, CR. The master of ceremonies was the Reverend Joseph Tarasiuk, CR, and the Reverend John Obyrtacz, CR, delivered the sermon. At the side altars, Low Masses were offered by the Reverend Giles

Strub, OFM, and the Reverend John Wisniewski, assistant at Five Holy Martyrs Church. Many other priests participated in the funeral as well. Present also were members of the Congregation of the Sisters of the Holy Family of Nazareth and the Congregation of the Sisters of the Resurrection. All of the superiors of the mission homes of the Franciscan Sisters of Chicago, many Sisters of the congregation, and relatives of the deceased were also in attendance. Sister M. Angeline was laid to rest at St. Adalbert's Cemetery. At her death, Sister M. Angeline was seventy-four years old and had served in the congregation for thirty-six years.[30]

At the Tenth General Chapter of Elections held in 1964, it was decreed to bestow upon Sister M. Angeline the title of "Mother" for her perseverance, fortitude, and generosity in light of the founding of the congregation. There is not a great deal of material to be found by which to characterize this staunch pioneer Sister. The *Spis Sióstr* [Sisters' Registry] contains this simple statement which, without a doubt, sums up the thrust of Sister M. Angeline and is responsible for the ultimate compliment of calling her Mother. The statement reads simply—"She was liked by the community; she loved it, and was dedicated to it."[31]

Sister M. Angeline was the superior of Sister M. Praxeda Ostrega in 1906 when the latter was stationed at St. Elizabeth's Day Nursery. Of Sister M. Angeline, Sister M. Praxeda remembers fondly:

> Sister M. Angeline lived a life of sacrifice, dedication, and hard work. Although she was choleric by temperament, she possessed a heart of gold. She had great faith in the Providence of God and she seemed to repeat it in so many instances of her life by her favorite saying: "God has more good gifts than he has yet distributed to us. Let us ask him for them."[32]

A great honor was bestowed upon the Poles of Chicago when a new bishop of Polish descent, the Most Reverend Stanislaus Bona, was named by Pope Pius XI.[33] The Polish Sisterhoods rejoiced in particular since Bishop Bona had served as a member of the board of delegates for religious communities of Polish women. As a delegate, he had been known for his prudence, sincerity, kindness, and justice when rendering counsel to an individual Sister or to a congregation.

Bishop Bona visited the Motherhouse of the Franciscan Sisters on March 5, 1932, at which time the Sisters offered him their sincerest congratulations on his appointment. They also expressed their gratitude to him for the many services he had rendered. Bishop Bona offered Holy Mass and Benediction of the Most Blessed Sacrament for the intention of the congregation and gave a sermon in which he extolled the life of dedication and service to the aged led by the Franciscan Sisters of Chicago.[34] After breakfast, a farewell program was presented in the social hall of St. Joseph Home for the Aged by the novices.

Mother M. Aloysia, the superior general, on behalf of the congregation, offered him a gift of $25 and three surplices made by the Sisters in the Church Vestment Workshop. The Sisters were genuinely sorry to see Bishop Bona leave the Archdiocese of Chicago for the Diocese of Grand Island, Nebraska.

Another area to which Mother M. Aloysia and her general council turned their attention was the matter of retreats for lay people. The Church has always placed great emphasis on retreats or days of recollection, those days of prayer when a person withdraws from daily life or occupation in order to pray, meditate, or receive instruction in the spiritual life, usually under the direction of a retreat master. For this reason, the Franciscan Sisters of Chicago initiated one-day retreats and days of recollection each quarter of the year for young men and women from Chicago and the immediate vicinity. The first retreat was held on September 10, 1933, with a large number of participants under the direction of the Reverend Aloysius Staśkiewicz, OFM.[35] The retreat or day of recollection generally began with Holy Mass at ten o'clock in the morning and ended with Benediction of the Most Blessed Sacrament at five o'clock in the afternoon. The program for the rest of the day usually consisted of several conferences, meditation, spiritual reading, common prayer, and meals. The conferences were delivered in the convent chapel of St. Joseph Home for the Aged by the missionary priest who conducted the retreat.[36]

At the expiration of her term of office in 1934, Mother M. Aloysia was assigned to St. Casimir's School in Johnstown, Pennsylvania, as the superior and principal. She remained there until 1936 when she returned to the Motherhouse in ill health. In 1939, she was assigned to St. John Cantius School in Indiana Harbor, Indiana, as superior and principal. Still in poor health, she was forced to return to the Motherhouse in 1940, where she remained for the next two years. Afflicted with acute arthritis, she retired to Our Lady of Victory Convent for the infirm Sisters of the congregation in 1942. She became seriously ill on March 9, 1955, and was taken to St. Joseph Hospital in Joliet, Illinois, where she died on March 18 at ten-fifty o'clock in the morning. She was seventy-six years old and had been a religious for fifty-six years. She was laid to rest at St. Adalbert's Cemetery on March 22 on what has been described by some Sisters as a particularly wintry and snowy day, which led, consequently, to a small and unpretentious funeral.[37] At the time of Mother M. Aloysia's death, there were 354 Sisters in the congregation with forty-two novices and thirteen postulants.

ADDED BLESSINGS

[1]To a large extent, St. Joseph Home for the Aged was sustained financially in these trying times by a society of men under the patronage of St. Joseph called St. Joseph's Benevolent Society which was organized in 1917. Its aim was to offer financial aid to the Sisters and recreational programs to the residents. Later that same year, the Ladies Aid Society of St. Joseph Home for the Aged was organized. Both societies joined in 1935 to become the Friends of St. Joseph Home. *St. Joseph House Journal* (AFSCL).

[2]These Sisters were especially singled out for their success in raising donations: Sister M. Rudolpha Trytek, Sister M. Honorata Makowski, Sister M. Siegfrieda Scensny, Sister M. Jolanta Nowak, and Sister M. Ligoria Motyka. *St. Joseph House Journal* (AFSCL).

[3]*Book of Correspondence:* Letter from George Cardinal Mundelein, archbishop of Chicago, to Mother M. Aloysia Holysz, March 1928 (AFSCL).

[4]Eccles. 29:12–15.

[5]Born in Chicago in 1886, Sister M. Chester, the former Martha Dziarnowski, attended St. Mary of the Angels Church. She entered the community on October 3, 1904, became a novice on November 29, 1905, and professed her perpetual vows on July 27, 1915. For over thirty years, she served as a teacher and principal at several of the congregation's schools in Chicago, East St. Louis, and Streator in Illinois; Cleveland, Ohio; Johnstown, Pennsylvania; and New Chicago, Indiana. She also served as the superior and administrator of St. Joseph Home for the Aged from 1928 to 1931, and Mount Alvernia Home in East Cleveland, Ohio, from 1936 to 1937. In 1948, she acted as the business manager of St. John's Hospital in Huron, South Dakota, and was later transferred to the business office at Boys Town, Nebraska. She spent 1949 to 1958 at Our Lady of Victory Convent for the aged and infirm Sisters as the organist. In 1958, she was sent to St. Anthony's Hospital in Martin, South Dakota, to assist clerically in the office. She died there on January 19, 1963, of heart disease at the age of seventy-seven. *Congregation Membership Records;* and *Spis Sióstr* (AFSCL).

[6]*Book of Correspondence:* Letter from Neri, Spooner, and Sit, Inc. to Mother M. Beatrice Rybacki, 8 September (AFSCL).

[7]If at any time since Sister M. Theresa Dudzik first initiated her labor of love to the aged the Sisters felt overwhelmed by the circumstances in which they found themselves, they had letters such as the following to pick up their spirits and make all their sacrifices worthwhile. It was written by John Czekala, alderman of the 16th Ward on February 21, 1922. It read: "Dear Sisters: This letter will be handed to you by W. Zembal. He is seventy years of age. I want to send him to the Oak Forest Home, but he says he wants a church where he can pray. If you can help him, it would be greatly appreciated."

Needless to say, Mr. Zembal was accepted into St. Joseph Home where he could pray, and more than that, he had the assurance and example of the daughters of Sister M. Theresa who on one occasion had entered in her "Chronicle": "My greatest joy was kneeling to say the evening prayers and rosary with the residents. I rejoiced when I saw how fervently and willingly they prayed." And again she wrote: "It seemed to me that God received glory from the prayers of the residents, and knowing that many of them had reconciled with God, now gave me great hope." Matka Maria Teresa Dudzik, "Kronika Sióstr Franciszkanek pod opieką Św. Kunegundy w Chicago, Illinois" [The Chronicle of the Franciscan Sisters under the patronage of St. Kunegunda in Chicago, Illinois] Chicago, 1910 (Unpublished manuscript, AFSCL.), p. 27; and *Book of Correspondence:* Letter from Mr. John Czekala to Franciscan Sisters at St. Joseph Home, 21 February 1922 (AFSCL).

[8]Secretaries General, *Community Chronicle,* p. 121 (AFSCL).

[9]August Cardinal Hlond was born in Breckowicz, Poland, in 1881. He studied at Don Bosco, Turin; and the Gregorian, Rome, and was ordained in 1905. As a Salesian, he directed their institutes in Poland, Austria, Hungary, and Germany. In 1922, he was named bishop of Silesia; in 1926, he was named the archbishop of Gniezno and the primate of Poland. He was appointed a

cardinal in 1927. He cooperated with selected sociologists to change farming and industrial conditions, and he labored to bring forced ecclesiastical taxation to an end. He sought to prevent the outbreak of war between Germany and Poland in 1939, and in that same year was forced into exile and was made a prisoner by the Germans. He returned to Poland in 1945 when the Communist government renounced the Concordat with the Vatican. When the new borders were imposed upon Poland by the Russians, he objected bitterly. He remained an ardent foe of Communism and his nine-year struggle with totalitarian governments ended only with his death in Warsaw on October 22, 1948.

According to the program booklet at the Eucharistic Congress, Cardinal Hlond gave an address during *Wieczor Mężczyzn* [Mens Night] at the 28th Eucharistic Congress on Tuesday, June 22, 1926. *Dictionary of Catholic Biography*, p. 565.

[10]*Minutes of General Council Proceedings, 1910–1934* (AFSCL).

[11]The Reverend Wenceslaus Cich, OFM, was born in Omaha in 1894, and was educated at St. Joseph Seraphicate in Teutopolis, Illinois, and St. Bonaventure Minor Seminary in Pulaski, Wisconsin. In 1913, he entered the novitiate in Pulaski and was ordained in Green Bay, Wisconsin, in 1920. Father Wenceslaus taught at St. Bonaventure Minor Seminary from 1921 to 1939. He also served as rector from 1926 to 1928, and again from 1934 to 1937. In 1939, Father Wenceslaus was appointed guardian of St. Mary of the Angels Monastery and lector in theology in Green Bay, Wisconsin. He died at fifty years of age in October 1943. Archives of the Franciscan Fathers of the Assumption of the BVM Province, Pulaski, Wisconsin, 16 October 1943.

[12]Siostra M. Gonzaga Raniszewski, OSFK, "Rys historyczny Zgromadzenia Sióstr Franciszkanek Bł. Kunegundy. Część druga, 1910–1940" [A historical survey of the Franciscan Sisters of Blessed Kunegunda. Part two, 1910–1940] Unpublished manuscript (AFSCL), p. 134.

[13]See Chapter 16.

[14]See Chapter 58.

[15]*Minutes of General Council Proceedings, 1970* (AFSCL).

[16]About fifty residents had either been transferred temporarily to other facilities or were taken home by their relatives during this period.

[17]Dedication of St. Joseph Home of Chicago, Homily by John Cardinal Cody, 19 March 1977 (AFSCL).

[18]*St. Joseph House Journal*, February 1984 (AFSCL).

[19]*Interview* with Sister Eleanor Marie Jadrych, March 1987 (AFSCL).

[20]*Book of Correspondence:* Letter from Sister M. Carmel Rokicki to author, 9 May 1978 (AFSCL).

[21]*Summer Catechetical Mission Report* (AFSCL).

[22]*Book of Correspondence:* Letter from the Reverend Thomas Drengacz to Mother M. Aloysia Holysz, 25 July 1932 (AFSCL).

[23]Secretaries General, *Community Chronicle*, July 1940 (AFSCL).

[24]*Minutes of General Council Proceedings*, 6 September 1940 (AFSCL).

[25]*Book of Correspondence:* Letter from Sister M. Esther Obuchowski to author, 1976 (AFSCL).

[26]*Record of Summer School and Catechetical Centers* (AFSCL).

[27]*Book of Correspondence:* Letter from Sister M. Francine Labus to author, 21 September 1976 (AFSCL).

[28]*Spis Sióstr* (AFSCL).

[29]Secretaries General, *Community Chronicle*, p. 126 (AFSCL).

[30]*Spis Sióstr* (AFSCL).

[31]Ibid.

[32]*Book of Depositions:* Sister M. Praxeda Ostrega, 4 August 1964.

[33]The Most Reverend Stanislaus V. Bona was born on October 1, 1888, the son of immigrant parents. He studied at St. Stanislaus College in Chicago and was sent to the North American College in Rome for his philosophical and theological studies. He was ordained to the priesthood in 1912 in Rome and was appointed to serve as assistant at St. Barbara's Church in Chicago from 1912 to 1916. After serving as resident chaplain at the House of Corrections in Chicago for six years, he was appointed professor of Latin, mathematics, and Polish at Quigley Preparatory Seminary. He was named pastor of St. Casimir's Church in Chicago in 1922, and served there until 1932. Appointed papal chamberlain in 1931, he was also a member of the board of delegates for religious communities of Polish women. He was appointed bishop of Grand Island in 1932, and upon the death of the Most Reverend Paul P. Rhode in 1945, succeeded him to the Diocese of Green Bay. Bishop Bona died in 1967. *Polish American Encyclopedia,* pp. 443–444; and Reverend Joseph Thompson, ed., *Diamond Jubilee of the Archdiocese of Chicago, 1920* (Des Plaines, Illinois: St. Mary Training School Press, 1920), p. 546.

[34]John Bona, the father of the Most Reverend Stanislaus Bona and the Right Reverend Monsignor Thomas Bona, was a widower when he was admitted to St. Joseph Home for the Aged on May 16, 1938. He remained in the care of the Franciscan Sisters until his death on November 6, 1939. *Book of Admittances, St. Joseph Home for the Aged and Crippled, Chicago, Illinois, 1898–1920* (Lemont, Illinois: AFSCL).

[35]The Reverend Aloysius Staśkiewicz, OFM, was born in 1893 in Chicago. He was ordained in 1918 in Green Bay, Wisconsin, by the Most Reverend Paul P. Rhode. From 1919 to 1938, he was a professor in the provincial schools of Pulaski and Sturtevant, Wisconsin. In 1938, he was assigned to St. Anthony Friary, Pittsburgh, where he zealously carried out his missionary and pastoral assignments. He was greatly dedicated to the spreading of Marian devotions, Eucharistic assemblies, and night adoration. He also took an active and zealous interest in social concerns. He died on December 10, 1968, at seventy-five years of age and was buried next to his parents in a family plot in Omaha. Archives of the Franciscan Fathers of the Assumption of the BVM Province, Pulaski, Wisconsin, 1975 (AFSCL).

[36]Raniszewski, p. 180.

[37]*Interviews* with Sisters, 1983 (AFSCL).

CHAPTER 36

The Fifth General Chapter:
Mother M. Antonina Osinski

On June 29, 1934, the feast of SS. Peter and Paul, the Fifth General Chapter of Elections began under the direction of the Right Reverend Monsignor John Mielcarek,[1] who had succeeded the newly elevated bishop, the Most Reverend Stanislaus Bona, as vicar for religious communities of women in the Archdiocese of Chicago. Three days later, on July 2, the feast of the Visitation, voting for the superior general and the general council took place. At a session presided over by Monsignor Mielcarek, the thirty-seven delegates[2] chose as the fourth superior general of the congregation the spirited, prudent, and dedicated Sister M. Antonina Osinski. Sister M. Innocenta Antosz was elected vicar general and first councilor, Sister M. Salomea Grabowski became second councilor, and Sister M. Stephanie Pinkowski was elected third councilor. Chosen as fourth councilor and secretary general was Sister M. Jerome Dadej while Sister M. Raphael Bogalecki became the procurator general. Because she was not a member of the chapter, Sister M. Jerome Dadej was summoned by the chapter body and took her place as a delegate on the next day.

The General Chapter of 1934 produced a wonderfully gifted superior general, Sister M. Antonina Osinski, a religious whose deep spirituality, keen intellect, persuasive leadership, and forceful personality caused her to emerge as one of the most central figures in the history of the congregation. With Mother M. Antonina as its superior general from 1934 to 1940, the Congregation of the Franciscan Sisters of Chicago entered into what might be called its most fruitful era.

Sister M. Antonina, the former Catherine Osinski, was born on October 17, 1877, in Biskupin in Prussian Poland. The daughter of Thomas and Barbara (née Nowakowski) Osinski, she came to America with her parents when she was eight years old. They settled in St. Joseph's Parish on the Southwest Side of Chicago in the Town of Lake area. She attended St. Joseph's School and planned to enter the Congregation of the Sisters of St. Felix of Cantalice (Felicians) after graduating from the eighth grade. Forbidden by her father to enter the convent at such an early age, Catherine Osinski took up dressmaking as an occupation. Her mother died prematurely, and not long after, her father remarried, and Catherine moved to St. John Cantius Parish on the Northwest Side of Chicago to live with relatives. Through Sister M. Veronica Maka, who had stopped at Catherine's home when collecting alms, she learned of the young band of Franciscan Sisters in Avondale. Catherine's confessor, the Reverend Vincent Rapacz, CR, had been urging her to enter the Congregation of the Sisters of the Resurrection, who, at this time, were en route to America to staff an elementary school in Chicago. But Catherine had already made up her mind to be a Franciscan and on September 17, 1902, joined the Franciscan Sisters of Chicago where she was welcomed by Sister M. Theresa Dudzik and Sister M. Anna Wysinski. Because of Catherine's great love for St. Francis of Assisi, Sister M. Theresa had urged Catherine to enter on that day, the feast of the Stigmata of St. Francis.

After her first profession of vows, Sister M. Antonina was sent to St. Michael's School in Berlin, Wisconsin, where she remained until October of 1905. That year, at the suggestion of Father Andrew Spetz, she was sent to Mercy Hospital in Chicago with Sister M. Bernice Stefanski to study nursing. Since the Sisters could not be accommodated for lodging there, it was necessary for them to travel daily. After a few months of this inconvenience, the Sisters transferred to St. Elizabeth's Hospital in Lafayette, Indiana, but after two years, Sister M. Antonina became ill with typhoid fever. Upon learning of her illness, Sister M. Theresa Dudzik visited Sister M. Antonina and arranged to have her return to the Motherhouse for an extended rest. As a consequence, Sister M. Antonina never finished her nursing studies. She remained at the Motherhouse from 1906 to 1909, attending to the needs of the Sisters and the aged residents who were ill.[3]

In 1910, she was sent to Cleveland where she taught for one year at St. Casimir's School. Returning to the Motherhouse in 1911, she served as the directress of the Church Vestment Workshop until 1915. That year, she returned to teaching and was assigned to St. John Cantius School in Indiana Harbor. In 1916, she was appointed superior, principal, and teacher at St. Stanislaus School in Youngstown, Ohio. She remained there until December of that year when she was sent to St. Casimir's School in Streator, Illinois, serving in the same capacity until 1918. In 1918, Sister M. Antonina was stationed at Guardian Angel Day Care Center in Chicago. The next year, she was sent to St. John Cantius School in Indiana where she remained until 1922.

From 1922 to 1926, Sister M. Antonina was stationed in Washington, DC, at The Catholic Sisters College where she earned her Teacher's Normal Certificate in February of 1924, and her bachelor of arts degree on February 2, 1925. On June 6, 1926, she received her master's degree from The Catholic University of America.[4]

Sister M. Antonina returned to teaching after her graduation, and in 1927, served as superior and principal at St. Florian's School in Chicago. While at St. Florian's, she was also acting supervisor of the congregation's schools in Chicago; from 1930 to 1934 she supervised the congregation's schools in Indiana. On the fateful day of July 2, 1934, Sister M. Antonina was elected superior general of the congregation for a term of six years.

In appearance, Mother M. Antonina was a petite, frail, and attractive woman. Her complexion was somewhat dark, and her eyes were bright and alive. Genuinely refined by nature, she possessed a dignified posture and gait. Although she often appeared stern and on occasion proved to be, she was a kind, prayerful, and truly inspiring person.[5]

During her term, Mother M. Antonina stressed the spiritual progress of the congregation. She insisted that great effort be exerted by the Sisters to affirm the dignity of the religious state and its consequent obligations. Because of this conviction, she was a staunch promoter of vocations to the religious life in general and to the Congregation of the Franciscan Sisters of Chicago in particular. She did everything in her power to encourage the Sisters to give testimony to the presence of God in their lives so that young women might be drawn to the religious life. A letter found in the archives and addressed to the Sisters concludes with her constant theme: "The good of the congregation and its growth lie in my heart."[6]

While Mother M. Antonina had devotion to several saints, she especially loved St. Francis of Assisi and her own namesake, St. Anthony of Padua, the fervent disciple of the Seraphic St. Francis. Her devotion to the Sacred Heart of Jesus was well known but she was particularly drawn to Christ the King. As the superior general, she always saw that this feast was celebrated in a most fitting and festive manner. Correspondence in the archives indicates that Mother M. Antonina frequently sent letters to the Sisters at the mission houses on holydays and specifically on the feasts of Christ the King and St. Francis of Assisi.[7] She loved the feast of the Immaculate Conception and cultivated a special devotion to the Holy Face of Jesus. All the spiritual exercises of the religious life, most notably attendance at the Sacred Liturgy, the recitation of the *Little Office of the Blessed Virgin Mary,* and daily adoration before the Blessed Sacrament were her great and immediate concern.

Through the kindness of the Reverend Richard Bakalarczyk, a member of the Congregation of the Marian Fathers of the Immaculate Conception of the Blessed Virgin Mary,[8] Mother M. Antonina was able to secure spiritual books for the congregation. Several copies of each book printed and published by the Jesuits of Cracow, Poland, were dispatched to the congregation, and, as a result, the library in the Motherhouse held hundreds of translations of French, English, and Spanish spiritual classics. Mother M. Antonina continued to purchase these books until World War II made it impossible.

Whether as a young temporarily professed religious, a perpetually professed Sister, or the superior general, the keeping of the three religious vows was for Mother M. Antonina a most sacred commitment. She believed with all her heart that being faithful and observant of the Rule, the Constitutions, and the Book of Customs was the way to religious perfection. As a consequence, she could be very firm and legalistic concerning conventual observances.[9] She believed solidly in community life and worked diligently to ensure it. While she was motherly, with a gracious concern and a deep respect for the personality and talents of each Sister, she was a strict disciplinarian and absolute obedience was demanded by her even if this meant running the risk of her being feared or disliked. She made visitations to the convent mission homes at least once a year if not more often and took these opportunities to correct or admonish the Sisters if necessary, a task she neither feared nor avoided. To some Sisters, Mother M. Antonina appeared tactless at times, and her penances and restrictions seemed out of proportion to the offenses. Perhaps in her enthusiasm to succeed at the task of guiding the entire congregation, she dismissed many Sisters whom she deemed unfit for religious life.[10] As a result, twenty-six Sisters, both in perpetual and temporary vows, either left the congregation or were asked to leave during her term. Some members of the congregation were inclined to believe that Mother M. Antonina acted imprudently or too hastily in many instances thereby forfeiting many vocations.[11] Even Sister M. Gonzaga, her trusted private secretary, personal friend, and great admirer would say of her: "Mother M. Antonina was energetic, inventive, and choleric by nature. Consequently, she was very rigorous in her attitude toward the duties and responsibilities of the religious life."[12]

Probably because of her own precarious health, Mother M. Antonina was truly compassionate to the Sisters who were ill and needed medical attention. Concerned not only about the Sisters' illnesses, she was also an avid promoter of physical fitness and preventive medicine. She was especially concerned about the infirm and the elderly members and during her term initiated construction of Our Lady of Victory Convent in Lemont for the aged and the infirm Sisters.[13]

Among the other Sisters elected at the chapter to the new general council was the third councilor, a very prayerful and conscientious woman. Sister M. Stephanie, the former Rosalie Pinkowski, was born in America in 1887. She entered the community from St. Hedwig's Parish in Chicago on December 8, 1904, and began her novitiate on November 29, 1905, making her first profession on December 8, 1906. She made her perpetual profession of vows on August 15, 1915.[14]

Sister M. Stephanie was a teacher, superior, and principal in various schools of the congregation for twenty-seven years. As third councilor, she served until 1940 during whch time she was also appointed the superior at the Motherhouse.[15]

Characterized as tall and stately, Sister M. Stephanie's calm dignity of manner was indicative of her deep and vibrant spirituality. An excellent role model for young religious, she was well liked by all the members of the congregation.[16]

Sister M. Raphael, appointed the procurator general at the fifth general chapter, was born on July 11, 1888, in Poland. In 1890, the former Leocadia Bogalecki came to America with her parents who settled in St. Stanislaus Bishop and Martyr Parish in Chicago. She entered the postulancy of the community on December 8, 1909, and became a novice on July 16, 1910. Her first profession of vows was made on August 15, 1911, and she was perpetually professed on August 15, 1919.[17]

After her first profession of vows, Sister M. Raphael was sent to Holy Trinity School in Falls City, Texas, where she remained until 1914. The next fourteen years she spent teaching in various schools of the congregation. From 1925 to 1927, she served as the mistress of postulants, and at the conclusion of her term, she was appointed principal and superior of St. Adalbert's School in East St. Louis, Illinois. For the next three years, from 1931 to 1934, she served as superior and administrator of St. Elizabeth's Day Nursery.[18]

Always zealous for God and the congregation, Sister M. Raphel was a hard-working and circumspect woman who was very dedicated to her duty. Patient, mild, and prayerful, Sister M. Raphael was an exemplary religious.[19]

At the Fifth General Chapter, the Sister-delegates discussed the Rule, the Constitutions, and the Book of Customs. Most of the Sister-delegates were of the mind that conventual observance and discipline had to be reinforced, and as such, the following directives were among the more important ones issued:

1. A Sister would always be accompanied by another Sister when leaving the house.
2. No home visits were allowed. Sisters were not allowed to attend First Holy Communion receptions, Confirmation ceremonies, or graduations.
3. Sisters who were born in Poland could not return there for home visits.
4. The home visits every five years which were voted in at the last chapter were now cancelled.
5. The Sisters were to date their twenty-fifth anniversary from the year of their first profession of vows rather than from the day of entrance as had been the custom. They were to celebrate the Silver Jubilee as a group at the Motherhouse.
6. The veil would be worn in four folds representing the last four ends of life: death, judgment, heaven, and hell. The first fold was formed from right to left with the first pin twenty-two inches from the top; the second pin six inches from the top of the head and the third pin placed one inch from the border.
7. The cords would have five turns representing the five wounds of Jesus Christ; the three knots represented the three vows of poverty, chastity, and obedience.

At a session of the general council held on August 8, 1934, the following appointments were made: Sister M. Paul Kirschbaum, superior of the Motherhouse; Sister M. Seraphine Zamrowski, assistant superior; and Sister M. John Barczak, superintendent of St. Joseph Home for the Aged. Chosen as the new novice mistress was Sister M. Mechtilde Zynda.[20] Her selected assistant was Sister M. Rosaria Frodyma.[21] A novel appointment was that of Sister M. Gonzaga Raniszewski who was chosen by Mother M. Antonina to serve as her personal secretary and the congregation's first historian.[22]

Mother M. Antonina embarked upon the task of superior general full of vigor and energy, good judgment, and prudent foresight. She saw the great needs of the young congregation and full of confidence in God, she set out to meet them.

Many prospects were presented to her, and in anticipation of spreading the Kingdom of God and alleviating suffering, she turned to the area of the health care services. She encouraged the Sisters to enter schools of nursing. Those who completed their courses and achieved nursing licensure were encouraged to take on specialties in various fields of medicine. Because of this foresight, qualified Sister personnel were prepared for the opening of the congregation's St. John Hospital and School of Nursing in Huron, South Dakota, in 1947.

Among the pioneer Sisters who began nurses' training during the term of Mother M. Antonina were Sister M. Paul Kirschbaum, Sister M. Innocentia Sierocki, and Sister Eleanor Plocki who were sent to St. Mary's Hospital in St. Louis, Missouri in 1935. In 1939, Sister M. Leonia Mszanski and Sister M. Eucheria Obara were sent to St. Joseph's Hospital School of Nursing. They were accompanied by Sister M. Amabilis Bellock, Sister M. Aloysilla Kedzior, and Sister M. Ruth Wojtowicz. In 1941, the congregation's first registered pharmacist, Sister M. Josepha Zwierzycki, entered the Illinois College of Pharmacy, graduating in 1943. Earlier, in 1942, Sister M. Aquinas Rosky and Sister M. Natalie Uscinowicz had embarked on their nursing degree courses at St. Joseph's Hospital School of Nursing.[23]

To extend the works of the apostolate, to provide meaningful and necessary service to the Church, and to have the Sisters preach in these apostolates by the example of their fervent spiritual lives, Mother M. Antonina also engaged the congregation in works devoted to the area of domestic service. Thus, scores of Sisters gave witness at such varied apostolic posts as Boys Town, Nebraska; Our Lady of Spring Bank Abbey, a Cistercian monastery in Oconomowoc, Wisconsin; and Brady Hall at The Catholic Sisters College of The Catholic University of America in Washington, DC.[24]

To Mother M. Antonina might be applied the words of Sirach: "Learning to the prudent is an ornament of gold, and like a bracelet upon his right arm."[25] She was a wise and prudent administrator whose innate wisdom and foresight made her aware of the need for educational proficiency. Because educational requirements were becoming ever more demanding, it was imperative that the congregation concentrate on the continuing education of its membership. At the congregation's Our Lady of Victory High School, 102 Sisters finished their courses. The professional training initiated under previous administrations was intensified and expanded under Mother M. Antonina's leadership as more than 140 Sisters pursued their degrees at De Paul University, St. Louis University, John Carroll University, Sisters' College of Cleveland, The Catholic University of America, and the American Conservatory of Music. Mother M. Antonina also encouraged and inspired the Sisters in securing teacher certification at state normal schools particularly for states such as Ohio which maintained stringent teacher certification requirements. It was she who initiated the strict supervision of the congregation's school system and introduced many progressive and experimental school innovations. She arranged institutes and meetings for superiors, teachers, and nurses in order to unify techniques and methods of procedure and to raise the educational and intellectual level of the membership. She was adamant in her demands regarding class preparation and encouraged the Sisters to be strict and orderly in the classrooms. So that the Sisters might be more adequately prepared for their classes, she demanded that they write lesson plans and experiment with new methods and techniques of teaching. She insisted on the administration of examinations to monitor pupil progress and recommended that results be charted and graphed especially in the areas of English, spelling, and mathematics. Whenever possible, she recommended the study of music. She commissioned Sister M. Gonzaga Raniszewski to write a booklet called *Politeness* which was distributed to the school children and which was highly praised and recommended by members of the Archdiocesan School Board for use in the schools.

During her administration, Mother M. Antonina appointed Sister M. Blanche Bartkowski[26] the supervisor of schools for grades four to eight. Sister M. Eymard Sanok[27] was appointed supervisor of grades one to three. When Sister M. Eymard went abroad in 1937 to study at the University of Warsaw, Sister M. Blanche assumed sole charge of all the schools staffed by the Franciscan Sisters. Sister M. Blanche proved to be most creative and supportive both as a person and as a supervisor.

Drawing on the procedures and techniques that she had seen used in the model school at The Catholic Sisters College in Washington, DC, Sister M. Blanche arranged workshops and demonstrations at various schools staffed by the congregation.[28] She initiated and encouraged the "open house" at the congregation's schools to which parents of the pupils as well as any other parishioners were invited. Producing good readers was one of her chief aims, and she urged the Sisters to encourage their pupils to read by means of classroom libraries and reading charts. She promoted activities such as mapmaking, art work, model plane construction, units on various subjects, the keeping of scrapbooks, and the making of aprons by hand. Much of this work was put on exhibition at the respective schools and especially at St. Joseph Home for the Aged auditorium where exhibits were generally held in May and June. Often, the Reverend David Fulmer, the Reverend John Kozlowski, and the Reverend Stanley Stoga, assistants to the Very Reverend Monsignor Daniel Cunningham, the superintendent of schools in the Archdiocese of Chicago, attended.[29] These same kinds of works were exhibited at St. Casimir's School in Cleveland which represented the Ohio center for educational methods. Many Sisters, parents, and pupils visited these exhibits. Sister M. Blanche also promoted field trips to the post office, department stores, and museums. She did much to feature entertainment and "drills" participated in by almost every student in the school. These presentations were well liked by the boys and girls and most welcomed by enthusiastic and proud parents.

In her efforts to raise the educational standards of the teaching Sisters, Sister M. Blanche issued a "Teachers' Bulletin" devoted to curriculum and pedagogy every two months. She stressed the need for and required attendance at monthly house meetings for the Sister-teachers. In all of her educational endeavors she was firmly supported by Mother M. Antonina. As a direct consequence of their dedication and growing efficiency and professionalism in classroom techniques, the Franciscan Sisters of Chicago rendered excellent service to their pupils and the Sisters' administrative abilities and educational talents achieved exceptional results in the classroom. They were, as well, gaining professional recognition from the members of their own congregation and the Sisters of other congregations.

Perhaps one of Mother M. Antonina's most valuable contributions to the congregation was her effort to have the saintly Mother M. Theresa Dudzik proclaimed the foundress of the congregation and raised to the altar as a saint. Since Mother M. Antonina had been a novice under Mother M. Theresa, she was familiar with the foundation of the congregation and knew that Mother M. Theresa was the true foundress and not Mother M. Anna Wysinski as some Sisters erroneously maintained or had been led to believe. Elected the superior general only sixteen years after the death of Mother M. Theresa, Mother M. Antonina was determined to keep alive the memory and influence of Mother M. Theresa. For that purpose, Sister M. Gonzaga Raniszewski was commissioned to write the first history of the congregation which resulted in the *Rys historyczny Zgromadzenia Sióstr Franciszkanek Błogosławionej Kunegundy. Część pierwsza, 1860–1910* [A historical survey of the Franciscan Sisters of Blessed Kunegunda. Part one, 1860–1910] based on the "Chronicle of Mother M. Theresa Dudzik." To Mother M. Antonina, the Congregation of the Franciscan Sisters of Chicago owes a debt which cannot be repaid. A further discussion of Mother M. Antonina's contribution to the cause for beatification of Mother M. Theresa Dudzik is found in Appendix B.

During the summer of 1934, sorrow came to the congregation in the form of death to five Sisters. They were Sister M. Angela Kolodziej,[30] Sister M. Rufina Klucznik,[31] Sister M. Ignatia Hodkiewicz,[32] Sister M. Annunciata Klimasz,[33] and Sister M. Veronica Maka.[34] This was the first time in the history of the congregation that five Sisters died in one year.

The year 1934 ended with the visit to St. Joseph Home for the Aged and to the Motherhouse by the distinguished Dr. Waclaw Gawronski: diplomat, journalist, and consul general of the Republic of Poland in which capacity he served for several years in Chicago. He made his visit on December 30, 1934, accompanied by other notable heads of large institutions whose aim it was to acquaint themselves with the operation of St. Joseph Home. Upon their arrival, a postulant greeted the consul general and the other guests in the name of all the Sisters and the residents of the home.[35]

Before the visitation, the Reverend Ladislaus Bartylak, CR, of St. John Cantius Church, celebrated the Holy Sacrifice of the Mass and delivered a sermon after which the delegation visited the home and the convent. Following a luncheon, several guests delivered brief speeches praising the dedication of the Sisters to the apostolate of the aged and infirm.[36]

The residents of St. Joseph Home for the Aged, in turn, were very pleased to meet Dr. Gawronski and had earnestly prepared for the meeting for a week. One of the residents, Mr. John Motyka, delivered a poem of welcome which he himself composed and which particularly moved the consul general. Later Dr. Gawronski visited the Church Vestment Workshop with special interest. During the speech which he delivered at dinner that evening, he spoke of the ministries and dedication of the Franciscan Sisters and promised to visit again as a private citizen.

At the conclusion of the visit, Mother M. Antonina thanked the guests for their presence, and in outlining the works of the congregation, referred to the absolute need for a new convent for the Sisters in order to enable them to continue to exercise the corporal and spiritual works of mercy more effectively.[37]

A year later, on July 26, 1935, St. Joseph Home for the Aged welcomed as a guest the Most Reverend Joseph Gawlina, bishop of Warsaw and military vicar of the Polish Armed Forces.

During her tenure of office, Mother M. Antonina, eager to share the matters of the congregation with the membership, initiated the publication of a community newsletter called *Echo Avondalskie* [Avondale Echo]. From January 1935 to 1940, the newsletter, written in Polish, was issued twice a year. Edited by Sister M. Gonzaga Raniszewski, Mother M. Antonina's private secretary, the *Avondale Echo* reflected the activities of the entire congregation. It consisted of news and special reports of the Sisters' activities at their mission homes. All mission personnel, notices of Sisters who were ill, and brief biographies of those who had died were listed. Announcements of forthcoming community events, community celebrations and anniversaries, and any special Motherhouse bulletins were printed. One of the publication's most appealing features was its section of original poetry, prose, and short plays written principally by Sister M. Gerard Gorzkowski.[38] Spiritual reflections and meditative essays appeared as well, and a bit of humor always concluded the issue. The typing and mimeographing of the material, as well as the cover illustrations, were done by Sister M. Blanche Bartkowski and Sister M. Crescencia Chmiel. The newsletter, extremely well received by all the Sisters, succeeded in its primary aim as envisioned by Mother M. Antonina—to issue a publication which recognized the activities of the entire congregation with the hope of leading to a sincere pride in and appreciation of each Sister's efforts. It achieved its goal of engendering mutual love and support for each Sister and encouraging the feeling that each one was contributing to the growth of the "still budding" congregation. The archives of the Motherhouse contain a compilation, approximately four hundred pages, of the *Avondale Echo*, a valuable historical document attesting to the administration of Mother M. Antonina Osinski. In 1940 Mother M. Mechtilde Zynda succeeded Mother M. Antonina as superior general. During the tenure of office of Mother M. Mechtilde, the *Avondale Echo* was discontinued, and no apparent reason was given for this action.

In 1935, the World Federation of Poles Abroad, in conjunction with the University of Warsaw in Poland, funded a scholarship program conducted by the faculty of the University and other prominent educators for young Polish Americans. The stipend was extended to include Polish American Sisters who were teachers. The scholarship program consisted of religion, language, history, geography, literature, and educational courses combined with lecture tours and visits to museums, historical buildings, and institutions of higher learning and culture. Educational lecture excursion tours were taken to Częstochowa, Lwów, Poznań, Kraków, and other famous Polish cities.[39]

The first recipients of the one-year scholarship granted in 1936 were Sister M. Beatrice Rybacki and Sister M. Bogumila Swiech. In October of 1937, Sister M. Eymard Sanok and Sister M. Gerard Gorzkowski were recipients of the scholarship to the University of Warsaw. Before their return in June of 1938, the Sisters made pilgrimages to Rome, Assisi, Padua, Florence, and Pompeii. They were also present for the canonization ceremonies of St. Andrew Bobola in Rome that year.[40]

The Sisters selected to be the recipients of the scholarship in 1938 were Sister M. Dolorosa Bojanowski and Sister M. Edward Nowak. That year, however, Mother M. Antonina and the general council came to the conclusion that because of an acute shortage of teachers and because of financial encumbrances, the congregation would not participate in the scholarship program.[41] The decision proved to be a propitious one. In September of 1938 Prime Minister Neville Chamberlain of Britain waved a copy of an agreement with Hitler and Mussolini and claimed: "This is . . . peace with honor. I believe it is peace in our time." Yet a brief year later, on September 9, 1939, Germany invaded Poland and Hitler's troops, tanks, and severe air attacks devastated Poland and engulfed humanity in a fierce global war.

At the end of her term of office in 1940, Mother M. Antonina presented her report to the Fifth General Chapter. She concluded her report by saying: "I accepted this heavy duty of being the superior general with the thought that with the grace of God, trust in the Sacred Heart, the aid of the Immaculate Conception, and the patron saints of the Congregation—St. Francis and Blessed Kunegunda—and all my Sister-councilors, I would try as hard as I could to work for the glory of God and the spiritual and material good of the Congregation." It is safe to say that by her piety, intelligence, and goodness, Mother M. Antonina succeeded.

THE FIFTH GENERAL CHAPTER: MOTHER M. ANTONINA OSINSKI

[1]The Right Reverend Monsignor John Mielcarek, born in Poland, emigrated to Chicago at an early age. He received his early education at St. Mary of Perpetual Help School and St. Ignatius College and completed his studies for the priesthood at the North American College in Rome where he was ordained in 1911.

Returning to Chicago, he served as an assistant at St. Joseph and St. Anne's Church before his appointment to the staff of Quigley Preparatory Seminary in 1916. He taught at Quigley until 1931 when he was named pastor of St. Mary Magdalen Parish. In 1936, he was appointed the pastor of St. Casimir's Church where he remained for twenty-five years. Just four months short of his 50th anniversary of priesthood, he died in Chicago on July 7, 1961. Report from the Chancery Office; Archdiocese of Chicago, August 9, 1982.

[2]See Appendix K.

[3]*Spis Sióstr* (AFSCL).

[4]Ibid.

[5]*Interviews* with Sisters, September 1983 (AFSCL).

[6]*Book of Correspondence:* Letter from Mother M. Antonina Osinski to the congregation, 22 May 1937 (AFSCL).

[7]*Book of Correspondence:* Letter from Mother M. Antonina Osinski to the congregation (AFSCL).

[8]See Chapter 37.

[9]Mother M. Antonina's fastidiousness even extended to the Sisters' personal appearance. She was concerned about their sitting and walking posture. She did not hesitate to measure with a ruler the pinning of the veil and cap when she believed a Sister was not keeping the regulation concerning these items of apparel. *Interviews* with Sisters, 1983 (AFSCL).

[10]*Interviews* with Sisters, 1983 (AFSCL).

[11]Ibid.

[12]*Book of Depositions:* Sister M. Gonzaga Raniszewski (AFSCL).

[13]*Spis Sióstr* (AFSCL).

[14]Ibid.

[15]*Congregation Membership Records* (AFSCL).

[16]In 1940, Sister M. Stephanie was appointed mistress of postulants. Upon the death of Sister M. Francis Drufke in 1940, she was again elected to serve as superior of the Motherhouse. After completing her term in 1948, she was elected superior of St. Anthony Home in Crown Point, Indiana, where she served for the next two years. In January of 1950, she entered St. Mary's Mercy Hospital in Gary and died there on February 17, a victim of cancer. She was sixty-three years old and had been in the congregation for forty-six years. She was a cousin to Sister M. Kunegunda Pinkowski. *Congregation Membership Records* (AFSCL.)

[17]*Spis Sióstr* (AFSCL).

[18]Ibid.

[19]Sister M. Raphael served two terms and was re-elected to the office of procurator general for a third term from 1946 to 1952. The years preceding her death were spent at the Motherhouse in the Church Vestment Workshop. She died on November 7, 1959, at the age of seventy-one and had been in the congregation for fifty years. *Congregation Membership Records* (AFSCL); *Interviews* with Sisters, 1983 (AFSCL).

[20]See Chapter 42.

[21]Sister M. Rosaria Frodyma, born in Tarnów, Poland, came to the United States in 1915.

She was one of the few Sisters who entered from the parish of St. Adalbert in East St. Louis. Sister M. Rosaria taught in various schools of the congregation for sixteen years before being appointed assistant to the novice mistress for two years. Her later years were spent at Boys Town and St. Joseph Home for the Aged in Cleveland. In 1952, she was sent to Alvernia Rest Home (now Mount Alverna Home) in Parma, Ohio, where conscious of the dignity and needs of the aged, she gave dedicated service for twenty-seven years. Of happy disposition and sacrificial spirit, Sister M. Rosaria retired to the Motherhouse in 1980. *Congregation Membership Records;* and *Spis Sióstr* (AFSCL).

[22]See Chapter 47.

[23]*Congregation Membership Records* (AFSCL).

[24]See Chapter 37.

[25]Sirach 21:21.

[26]Sister M. Blanche, the former Wanda Bartkowski, was born on September 4, 1901, in Poland. Her family emigrated to the United States in 1902 and settled in St. Hedwig's Parish in Gary. She entered the postulancy on June 23, 1917, and was received into the novitiate on July 27, 1918. Sister M. Blanche professed her first vows on July 27, 1919, and was perpetually professed on July 27, 1925. After her first profession in 1919, she taught at Sacred Heart School and St. Casimir's School in Cleveland, Sacred Heart School in La Porte, Indiana, and St. Florian's School in Chicago. She obtained a bachelor of science degree in education from De Paul University in Chicago. At the conclusion of her six-year term as supervisor in 1940, Sister M. Blanche returned to teaching at St. Stanislaus Kostka School in Youngstown, and later at St. Casimir's School in Cleveland. From 1943 to 1946, she served as superior and principal of St. Peter Claver School in Mobile, Alabama. In 1946, she was appointed superior and principal of St. Stanislaus Bishop and Martyr School in Chicago.

In March 1951, Sister M. Blanche went to St. John's Hospital in Huron, South Dakota, as a patient and remained until January 28, 1952. She returned to Chicago and was sent to Five Holy Martyrs School where she remained for only two months. In December of 1953, she left again for St. John's Hospital as a patient. By May, she was well enough to do light office work. When she died at the hospital on February 12, 1959 of heart disease, she was fifty-eight years old and had been in the congregation for forty-two years. *Congregation Membership Records* (AFSCL).

[27]Sister M. Eymard, the former Thecla Sanok, was born on July 17, 1909, in Footedale, Pennsylvania. She entered the congregation from St. Hedwig's Church in Gary on July 16, 1926, and was received into the postulancy on September 3, 1926. Welcomed into the novitiate on July 16, 1927, she made her first profession of vows on July 17, 1932. She received her bachelor's degree from De Paul University in Chicago where she had also studied the violin. In 1934, she was appointed supervisor of the primary grades in the congregation's schools. In 1937, she was the recipient of a scholarship to study at the University of Warsaw in Poland for one year. As a teacher, Sister M. Eymard was assigned to various schools in Chicago; Cleveland and Campbell, Ohio; Conemaugh, Pennsylvania; New Chicago and East Chicago, Indiana. At many of the missions, she was also the organist and director of women's choirs. In 1978, Sister M. Eymard left the teaching ministry and was assigned to the Motherhouse. *Congregation Membership Records* (AFSCL).

[28]*St. Stanislaus Bishop and Martyr House Journal,* Chicago, April–May 1929; *Assumption BVM House Journal,* Conemaugh, Pennsylvania, 1938; and *St. Pancratius House Journal, Chicago,* 1940 (AFSCL).

[29]*Minutes of General Council Proceedings, 1934–1940* (AFSCL).

[30]Sister M. Angela Kolodziej entered from St. John Cantius Church in Chicago. She died on April 28, 1934, after eighteen years in the congregation. She was thirty-eight years old and had been a homemaker in convents in Ohio and Indiana. *Spis Sióstr* (AFSCL).

[31]Sister M. Rufina performed household duties at several convents of schools in which the Sisters taught. Ill for most of her religious life, Sister M. Rufina died at St. Mary's Hospital in

Chicago after an operation. She entered from St. Mary of Perpetual Help Church in Chicago and served in the congregation for twenty-five years before her death at fifty-eight. *Spis Sióstr* (AFSCL).

[32]See Chapter 23.

[33]See Chapter 20.

[34]See Chapter 16.

[35]The postulant was Frances Piaskowy who became Sister M. Deofilia. Sister M. Deofilia was quick to recall that she greeted Dr. Gawronski in the Sisters' parlor in the old Motherhouse and that the consul general kissed her on the forehead. *Book of Correspondence:* Letter from Sister M. Deofilia Piaskowy to author, 23 September 1982 (AFSCL).

[36]Secretaries General, *Community Chronicle,* p. 160 (AFSCL).

[37]Siostra M. Gonzaga Raniszewski, OSFK, "Rys historyczny Zgromadzenia Sióstr Franciszkanek Bł. Kunegundy. Część druga, 1910–1940" [A historical survey of the Franciscan Sisters of Blessed Kunegunda. Part two, 1910–1940] Unpublished manuscript (AFSCL), p. 184.

[38]This poem, written by Sister M. Gerard, expresses her wonderment at being inspired by the Holy Spirit to join the band of poor Franciscan Sisters at Avondale:

> Czemu pominęłam zakon Sióstr Św. Ducha?
> Czemu na głos SS. Służebniczek pozostałam głucha?
> Czemu nie poszłam do zgromadzenia SS. Felicjanek,
> Zmartwychwstanek, Nazaretanek albo Notredamek?
> Czemu? choć w tej myśli wszędzie zaglądałam
> Ubiór tychże i ducha bardzo ciekawie badałam?
> Dlaczego do tych biednych Franciszkanek nabrałam ochoty
> Jakież w tych zakonnicach znęciły mię cnoty?
> Czemu? czemu się tak stało . . . ?
> Że własńie ten klasztor me serce wybrało!
> Jakaż mię tu służyc Bogu znęcila robota? . . .
> Spodobał mi się pokutniczy habit—i Sióstr założycielek
>   serdeczna prostota.
> One mię swem obejściem miłem niejako wołały:
> "Pójdz! przyłacz się do nas—będziem cię kochały!"
> Ich ubóstwo, duch pokuty, serce moje ujmowało . . .
> Znać się Bogu w tym Zakonie mieć mię podobało.
> Jeszcze mi dziś te drogie Siostry stoją przed oczyma:
> Matka M. Anna, S. M. Teresa, S. M. Angelina.
> Pamiętam, gdym przed wstąpieniem do Polski jechała
> Jak ta "Trójka" o mój powrót szczerze się troskała.
> One, te poczciwe dusze, one wymodliły,
> Że ten Klasztor Avondalski stał się dla mnie i drogi i miły.
>   O święty Franciszku, Serafinie Boga
>   Wspieraj! niech wiernie stąpa w Twe ślady Two
>   pupiłka droga.

The following is a translation of the Polish poem. As in most literal translations, much of the rhyme and rhythm are lost.

> Why did I overlook the Congregation of the Sisters of the Holy Spirit?
> Why did I remain deaf to the voices of the Sisters Servants?
> Why did I not enter the Congregation of the Felician Sisters,
> The Sisters of the Resurrection, of Nazareth, or Notre Dame?
> Why? in this frame of mind I searched everywhere—
> The habits of each and the spirit of each Congregation I examined carefully—

Why to these poor Franciscans did I gather enthusiasm?
What kinds of virtues in these Sisters attracted me?
Why? Why did it happen thus . . . ?
That my heart chose this convent?
To serve God, what work attracted me here?
I liked their penitential habit—and the sincere simplicity
    of the Sister foundresses.
They were calling me, as it were, with their very conduct!
"Come, join us—we will love you!"—
Their poverty, their spirit of penance, tugged at my heart . . .
To be known by God in this Community appealed to me.
Even today these dear Sisters stand before my eyes:
Mother M. Anna, Sister M. Theresa, Sister M. Angeline.
I remember when before I entered I went to Poland
How this "Trio" sincerely worried about my return.
They, these noble souls, prayed,
That this convent in Avondale, became dear and lovable to me.
    O St. Francis, Seraph of God,
    Help me! let your dear pupil walk faithfully
        in your steps.

Sister M. Gerard Gorzkowski, "Private Notebook," Chicago, 1911 (AFSCL).

[39]Sister M. Gonzaga Raniszewski, *Zarys Półwiecza Zgromadzenia Sióstr Franciszkanek Bł. Kunegundy* [Sketch of the fifty-year history of the Congregation of the Franciscan Sisters of Bl. Kunegunda] (Chicago: By the Author, 1944), pp. 66–67.

[40]St. Andrew Bobola was born in 1591 of an illustrious family in Sandomierz, Poland. He became a Jesuit in 1619, and for a number of years fulfilled the tasks of a parish priest. During the Cossack invasion of Poland, he went to Polesie in Eastern Poland where savage fighting raged. His ministry there was most fruitful among the faithful members of the Church, but he was fiercely hated by its confirmed enemies. On May 16, 1657, he was captured by a band of wild Cossacks who killed him in a public slaughterhouse by the most barbarous methods. He was burned, flayed, and lacerated. He was buried in the Jesuit church at Pinsk, where after temporary obscurity, a miraculous incident uncovered his gravesite. When after the tragic Second Partition of Poland in 1793, the Jesuit church at Pinsk was in the hands of Russian Orthodox monks, the body of St. Andrew Bobola was transferred to the parish church in Polock. Consequently, he was beatified by Pope Pius X on July 5, 1853. In June of 1922, irreligious Reds removed the body and transported it to the Medical Museum on the Petravka in Moscow. Pope Pius XI pleaded with the Soviet government for the restoration of the precious relics. Finally, the incorrupt body of the martyred Bobola was brought to the Jesuit church of the Gesu in Rome. On Easter Sunday, 1938, Pope Pius XI solemnly proclaimed him a saint of the Universal Church. The sacred remains of St. Andrew Bobola are now interred in Warsaw. *Polish American Encyclopedia*, 1954 ed., s.v. "Bobola, St. Andrew."

[41]*Minutes of General Council Proceedings, 1938* (AFSCL).

CHAPTER 37

Areas of Domestic Service

While advances were being made in the areas of elementary education and homes for the aged, Mother M. Antonina was being besieged on all sides for Sisters to enter the area of domestic service, a steadily growing apostolic work among women religious. Many of these requests came before and during World War II when many women were working in defense plants leaving open the fields of domestic service. As early as 1911, the Franciscan Sisters of Chicago received a request from the Sacred Heart High School and College in Detroit, Michigan. In 1920, the Reverend Anthony Kłowo asked for eight Sisters to take charge of the household duties at SS. Cyril and Methodius Seminary in Orchard Lake, Michigan.[1] Soon requests poured in from all over the United States asking the Sisters to staff the domestic departments of seminaries or residences of bishops. Letters of request came from such places as St. Louis, Missouri; Milwaukee, Wisconsin; Fort Wayne, Indiana; Kenmore and Lacey, Washington; Bloomfield, Connecticut; Dayton, Ohio; New Orleans and Alexandria, Louisiana; Erie, Loretto, Coraopolis, and Hollidaysburg, Pennsylvania; Kansas City, Kansas; and Minneapolis and Winona, Minnesota. Pleas for domestic aid came from such institutions as St. Mary's College conducted by the Christian Brothers in Moraga (near Oakland), California; and the Jesuit Novitiate of St. Stanislaus in Stockbridge, Massachusetts. There was even a request, in 1947, to staff the domestic department in St. Stephen's Seminary in Honolulu, Hawaii.[2]

Mother M. Antonina's first official act after her election as superior general in July of 1934 was to present a plea to her general council from the Right Reverend Thomas A. Roos, prior of a Cistercian monastery in Oconomowoc, Wisconsin. The prior requested six Sisters to attend to domestic work all-the-year-round at the Abbey called Our Lady of Spring Bank and during the summer, at the Manor,[3] the Abbey's vacation home for priests.[4] When the general council agreed to accept the challenges of this new apostolate, Mother M. Antonina made several trips to Oconomowoc. Perhaps because the Abbey was close to Chicago, Mother M. Antonina was happy with the conditions as they presented themselves. After one of these trips, she met with the vicar general for women religious of the Archdiocese of Chicago, the Very Reverend Monsignor John Mielcarek, to request his permission to accept this new extension of Franciscan service to the Church. Monsignor Mielcarek offered no objections to the proposed acceptance of the Cistercian Abbey apostolate but, rather, was genuinely pleased that the congregation was continuing to expand its corporal works of mercy.[5]

Our Lady of Spring Bank, the Cistercian Abbey, was located in Wisconsin on a large tract of land on Lake Okauchee in Oconomowoc, chiefly a resort village. The abbey's surroundings, truly remarkable with various flowers and trees, lent to the area an aura of peace and tranquility which the Sisters who were stationed there truly cherished.[6]

On July 12, 1934, eight Franciscan Sisters of Chicago began their new apostolate at Our Lady of Spring Bank Abbey with their appointed superior, Sister M. Humilianna Lemanczyk. The pioneer Sisters included Sister M. Amabilis Bellock, Sister Emily Kowal, Sister M. Genevieve Swiatowiec, Sister M. James Rucinski, Sister M. Ludwina Prokuszka, Sister M. Nepomucene Kulesza, Sister M. Pontiana Nowakowski, and Sister M. Theresilla Ignasiak.[7] Two members of the general council, Sister M. Salomea Grabowski and Sister M. Stephanie Pinkowski, were also sent to provide any needed guidance in assuming this new apostolate.[8] When the first Sisters arrived to begin their work, they were forced to sleep on mattresses on the floor because no proper sleeping accommodations had been provided for them. Some Sisters were appointed to aid the cook, a layman. Instead, he resigned, leaving the Sisters to prepare all the meals. This included meals for the priests, the clerics, the manor guests, and the Sisters themselves.[9] By the end of the summer,

Our Lady of Spring Bank Manor
Okauchee, Wisconsin (1934–1942)

Sister M. Salomea, Sister M. Stephanie, Sister M. Ludwina, and Sister M. Pontiana, having completed their assignments, all returned to the Motherhouse. Sister M. Nepomucene departed in October. In the meantime, Sister M. Humilianna, the superior, informed Mother M. Antonina that all had gone well during the Sisters' first days there. She did find it necessary to point out, however, that a kind of "confusion" existed among those in authority at the Abbey.[10] This observation made by Sister M. Humilianna was all too soon confirmed, and its consequences had a serious effect on the conditions in which the Sisters attempted to exercise their new apostolate.

During the 1935–1936 year of service, six of the Sisters were reappointed to the Abbey. They were Sister M. Humilianna, Sister M. Genevieve, affectionately termed the "Little Spider" by the Cistercian monks because of her smallness and orderliness,[11] Sister M. Emily, Sister M. Amabilis, Sister M. James, and Sister M. Theresilla. In October of 1935, however, when Mother M. Antonina visited Our Lady of Spring Bank, Sister M. Humilianna returned to the Motherhouse with her. Existing records do not indicate the reason for Sister M. Humilianna's departure at that time, but Sister M. Gonzaga Raniszewski was temporarily appointed to serve as the superior. On February 3, 1936, Sister M. Ottilia Madaj was sent to assume that position and Sister M. Gonzaga returned to the Motherhouse.[12] At some point during the next two years, the prior, the Right Reverend Thomas Roos, who had been instrumental in securing the Sisters for the Our Lady of Spring Bank mission, was succeeded by the Right Reverend Romuald Pecasse. While the *Our Lady of Spring Bank House Journal* does not record any events of particular significance for the next two years, a change in the office of superior occurred in December of 1938.[13] Sister M. Hyacinth Barczewski was appointed to succeed Sister M. Ottilia whose relationship with the prior, Father Pecasse, as well as with the Sisters stationed at the Abbey, had slowly deteriorated.[14] Several of the Sisters serving at Our Lady of Spring Bank during those two years characterized Father Pecasse as "difficult," somewhat unsympathetic, and largely unrealistic as to the real amount of work required of the Sisters at the Abbey.[15] With the coming of the new year and the appointment of Sister M. Hyacinth Barczewski as superior, five new Sisters were assigned to Our Lady of Spring Bank. They: were Sister M. Concepta Makarowski, Sister M. Felicia Wierciak, Sister M. Lucille Klockowski, Sister M. Pulcheria Mikolajczyk, and Sister M. Redempta Demski.

In the summer of 1938, for the first time in the history of the Cistercian Abbey, the students from Milwaukee's Seminary of St. Francis de Sales, the highly reputable "Salesianum," arrived to spend the entire month of August on vacation from their studies. Because of the need for more Sisters to handle the additional duties connected with caring for the seminarians, Sister M. Ligoria Motyka, Sister M. Carmelita Szczypanski, and Sister M. Perpetua Sulski were sent to Our Lady of Spring Bank to help at the Manor. Sister M. Donald Urban was appointed to serve as the chief chef during the month of August. As many as eighty seminarians arrived. The Sisters cooked, baked, served in the dining rooms, did occasional laundry, and cleaned the sleeping quarters for the Cistercian monks, the brothers, and the vacationing seminarians at the Manor.[16] At the close of the vacation period, the seminarians departed, and the Sisters who had been added to the staff temporarily returned to the Motherhouse for reassignment. Sometimes as many as three or four Sisters were added to the staff during the summer.

The conditions at Our Lady of Spring Bank were frequently reviewed during the meetings of the general council especially during the last year of Mother M. Antonina's administration. She herself had been a frequent visitor at the Cistercian Abbey. A very close examination of the apostolate at Our Lady of Spring Bank was made in July 1940, and valid and cogent reasons were presented for the proposed withdrawal of the Sisters in December of 1941. The general council agreed that the workload was unduly burdensome for the small number of Sisters on the permanent staff. The summer demand for additional Sisters created problems in personnel assignment, since by this time, more and more Sisters were actively engaged in pursuing academic studies in the summer. Sister M. Lucille Klockowski indicates an aspect of the problems facing the Sisters:

> Sister M. Redempta [Demski] worked in the office. She was the prior's secretary and also served the evening meal to the priests in the dining room. Sometimes, late in the evening, a carful of priests would pull up and all of them had to be served dinner on short notice. These and similar experiences made the first three to five months very trying for us . . . Sister M. Hyacinth [Barczewski] was the superior of the Sisters and she also did all the laundry by hand since there were no washers or dryers at that time. How she did it we can't imagine, yet it got done.
>
> I stayed in Okauchee for three and a half years. These were difficult times but our strength was, I am sure, somehow daily replenished by the moments spent in adoration before the Blessed Sacrament.[17]

On June 29, 1940, the Sixth General Chapter elected Mother M. Mechtilde Zynda to succeed Mother M. Antonina. Mother M. Mechtilde was made aware of the problems existing at Our Lady of Spring Bank, and as a consequence, took firm action in 1942 when Prior Pecasse suggested still another full-time duty for the already overburdened small staff of Sisters. Mother M. Mechtilde's reply was quick and decisive:

> Dear Reverend Father Prior:
>
> For obvious reasons, our Sisters at Okauchee cannot be permitted to take over the laundry as you recently requested them to do. Furthermore, they will be recalled at the close of July, their services being needed for other duties in the community.
>
> I do think that the time for the recall of the Sisters has already been

extended beyond reasonable expectation and I cannot accept a request for further extensions of time.

Respectfully yours,
Mother M. Mechtilde
Superior General[18]

In May, Father Pecasse informed Mother M. Mechtilde that he had arranged for the Sisters of St. Elizabeth of Hungary, whose chief mission was domestic service, to take charge of Our Lady of Spring Bank. Subsequently, on June 1, 1942, Sister M. Hyacinth Barczewski, Sister M. Marietta Dadej, Sister M. Theodosia Biss, and Sister M. Francesca Janowicz returned to the Motherhouse ending the years of service at Spring Bank.

Because the records concerning Our Lady of Spring Bank are so scarce, the full particulars concerning this mission will, perhaps, never be known. Nonetheless, the contributions of the Franciscan Sisters of Chicago to this mission are sincerely and humbly expressed in a letter to the author from the Right Reverend Joseph van Grevenbroek, SO Cist., Abbot of Spring Bank, in February of 1975:

> It was a nice surprise to hear from you as one of the beloved Sisters of years ago. For the time that the Sisters were here, I was connected with them every day. I had care of the garden and the farm and kitchen where the Sisters did their superb work.
>
> I always appreciated their great courage in doing all that hard work for us. They were really mothers, everyone of them, and if Reverend Pecasse was sometimes critical about them, as a historian, you have to know that there is always a human side to everything and God's plans are insoluble. We often regretted that Reverend Pecasse treated the Sisters that way. Everyone else in the monastery had the greatest praise for them. Many times I think back to all that work they performed, especially in the month of August with all the seminarians of St. Francis at the place.
>
> I hope your Congregation prospers spiritually and also in numbers. Believe me, I remember you in all my prayers. I am the only one left here who knew the Sisters . . . in case you need more information, please write and I will try to help you. Greetings to all the Sisters and remember us all in your prayers.
>
>
>
> All yours in Christ,
> Joseph, Abbot[19]
>
>

Perhaps an excerpt from the letter of Sister Marianne Kaplan to the author provides an explanation for the Sisters' devotedness to duty as "Marthas and Marys" while at Our Lady of Spring Bank: "I really and truly felt privileged that I could help the seminarians on their way to ordination. I felt that I was sharing in the priesthood."[20]

Anthony Brady Memorial Hall at The Catholic Sisters College
The Catholic University of America
Washington, DC (1938–1946)

The initial attempt of the Sisters to serve in the area of domestic service was supported prayerfully and enthusiastically by Mother M. Antonina and her general council. It was in this frame of mind that Mother M. Antonina received and responded to another call for involvement in the field of domestic service in 1938. She eagerly accepted a petition to staff the domestic department at one of her favorite institutions of learning— The Catholic Sisters College of The Catholic University of America in Washington, DC.

The Catholic University of America in Washington, DC, the national university of the Catholic Church in the United States, opened in November of 1889 with forty-six students, all of them priests or clerics. In time, eighty-seven religious houses of study representing fifty-six communities of men and twenty-one of women appeared on campus.[21] The Catholic Sisters College, on 8th and Varnum Streets, opened as an undergraduate division of The Catholic University of America in 1911 through the efforts of the Reverend T. Shields.[22] It had as its chief function to provide advanced training for teaching Sisters. There were seven residence halls for religious women on the campus open to graduate and undergraduate students. One of these, the Anthony Brady Memorial Hall, was under the direct supervision of The Catholic Sisters College administration. From 1918, the Congregation of the Sisters of the Precious Blood from Dayton, Ohio, had charge of the domestic work at The Catholic Sisters College.[23] After twenty years of service, the Sisters withdrew in 1938. The successor of Father Shields, the Right Reverend Monsignor Edward B. Jordan,[24] sent a telegram to Mother M. Antonina on May 24, 1938, asking the Franciscan Sisters of Chicago to consider taking charge:

Mother M. Antonina:

Would you consider having your Community take charge of the domestic department of The Sisters College beginning August First STOP We should like to have from six to nine Sisters STOP Wire collect.

Catholic Sisters College

Edward B. Jordan, Dean[25]

Mother M. Antonina and her general council, ever intent on widening the areas of service to the Church, voted to accept the invitation to staff the domestic department of The Catholic Sisters College and quickly dispatched a telegram to Monsignor Jordan which read tersely but fervently: "Yes, we will take charge!"[26] The Catholic Sisters College was no stranger to the congregation, for Mother M. Antonina had already received her bachelor's degree from The Catholic Sisters College and her master's degree from The Catholic University of America. Several other Sisters had been students there as well. By the end of May, Mother M. Antonina had another letter from Monsignor Jordan:

My dear Mother Antonina:

I cannot tell you how pleased I am to know that your Community will take charge of our domestic department. The Sisters of the Precious Blood are withdrawing because they have not enough Sisters to provide for the various houses under their control. As far as I know this is the only reason for terminating their contract.

I said in my telegram that we could use from six to nine Sisters. A word with regard to the work that is expected of them. The Sisters will have charge of the kitchen, dining room, and chapel, and the superior will have supervision over Brady Hall generally. We do not require the Sisters to do any janitorial work as the students take care of their own rooms, and the corridors, etc., are kept in order by the janitors. The laundry is sent out so that the only washing the Sisters would have to do would be their own. We generally serve about one hundred forty-five in the dining room. We have a trained dietitian, whom we must retain as this is the wish of the Board of Trustees. She plans the meals and orders the food. Her relations with the Sisters of the Precious Blood have been wholly pleasant and I am sure that the superior you send will find her willing to cooperate in every way. As for accommodations, I can let you know the number of rooms that will be available for your Sisters when you let me know how many Sisters you can send. We shall provide a community room and a private dining room.

We have been accustomed to pay the Precious Blood Sisters $30.00 per month for each Sister in addition to providing her with room and board. I hope that this figure will be satisfactory to you. We have always allowed the Sisters to take a vacation of two weeks in addition to the time that they require for their regular retreat.

If you desire any further information let me know. I should be very pleased to have you come out and look over the situation at your convenience.

Very sincerely yours,
Rt. Rev. Edward B. Jordan, Dean[27]

On June 9, the Very Reverend Michael J. Curley, archbishop of Baltimore, granted permission for the Sisters to work in the Archdiocese of Washington. On July 30, 1938, the assigned Sisters arrived to staff the new mission. They were Sister M. Felixa Jorz, the superior; Sister M. Honoria Urbaniak; Sister M. Callista Gach; Sister M. Norberta Haas; Sister M. Theresilla Ignasiak; and Sister Louise Ann Glowacki.[28] On August 1, they took charge of the kitchen, dining room, sacristy, and chapel while Sister M. Felixa supervised Brady Hall in general. Because of the beautiful statue of the Blessed Virgin Mary, under her title "Sedes Sapientiae," on the grounds, the Sisters called their convent "Seat of Wisdom Home." On August 24, after making their perpetual profession of vows, Sister M. De Chantal Mazuryk, Sister M. Melita Wiacek, and Sister M. Theodosia Biss also joined the staff at The Catholic Sisters College.[29] That year, Monsignor Jordan wrote to Mother M. Antonina and stated in part:

> I take this occasion to tell you how well-pleased we are with your Sisters. Everyone connected with the College is loud in their praise. It is my earnest hope that our association will be long and pleasant.[30]

Monsignor Jordan's words were an addition to the kind words expressed in the bulletin of The Catholic Sisters College called "The Sisters College Messenger," appearing in October of 1938:

A Word of Welcome

On July 31 the College had the happiness of welcoming six members of the Franciscan Sisters of St. Kunegunda, Chicago, Illinois, who have taken over the work of the domestic department of the College. On August 25, three Sisters were added to the staff, which is under the direction of Sister Felixa . . . the College is extremely grateful to Mother Antonina for her kindness in acceding to our request for Sisters to take charge of the household and we trust that both she and her Community will find their relation with the College not only satisfactory but also pleasant as well. The students of the College join with the Administration in welcoming the new Sisters and in assuring them that they may depend upon the wholehearted cooperation of all those whom they have come to serve.[31]

That same year, the Reverend Richard Bakalarczyk[32] of the Congregation of the Marian Fathers at the Marian House of Studies in Washington, DC, was appointed confessor to the Sisters.[33] This initial encounter was the beginning of a spiritual liaison with the Franciscan Sisters of Chicago which spanned several years. In May of 1939, The Catholic Sisters College was host to a most distinguished visitor in the person of the apostolic delegate to the United States, Archbishop Amleto Cicognani. He celebrated Holy Mass, had breakfast with the Sisters in their private dining room, and then visited the Sisters' home. At the conclusion of his visit, he expressed great satisfaction with the work of the Sisters' administration of Brady Hall. According to the *House Journal* of the Seat of Wisdom mission, life at The Catholic Sisters College had an essence all its own. The feast of St. Francis, celebrated for the first time in the nation's capital by the Sisters was a very touching occasion. The Holy Sacrifice of the Mass was offered by a Capuchin priest who was assisted by a Capuchin brother. Many Sisters, representing the various congregations present on the campus, attended the mass celebrated by the Franciscans and sang hymns in honor of the Blessed Sacrament and the Blessed Virgin Mary. According to the *House Journal,* the only item missing to make the Sisters' joy complete was a statue of St. Francis of Assisi in the chapel. Sister M. Honoria, in charge of the kitchen, baked special bread and cookies for all the Sister-students in Brady Hall.[34] Besides a statue of St. Francis, the chapel at the college lacked many other necessities. Eventually, altar linens, stoles, and vestments for the clergy made by the Franciscan Sisters of Chicago in the Church Vestment Workshop at the Motherhouse in Chicago were sent to Washington, DC, by Mother M. Antonina. Monsignor Jordan responded:

> My dear Mother Antonina,
>
> I wish to thank you most sincerely for the beautiful vestments which you sent for the College Chapel. Some good angel,[35] whose name I think I know, must have whispered in your ear that our supply of vestments was deficient. I hope that Our Lord will bless you and your Community in return for your kind remembrance.
>
> Very sincerely yours,
Msgr. Jordan, Dean[36]

The Sixth General Chapter of the congregation was held on June 28, 1940. Sister M. Felixa, the superior, left for Chicago to serve as a delegate to the general chapter and never returned to The Catholic Sisters College. The general chapter had elected her the mistress of novices and she now took up her assignment at the novitiate of Our Lady of Victory Convent in Lemont.[37] Sister M. Mechtilde Zynda was chosen the new superior general to succeed Mother M. Antonina Osinski. Mother M. Antonina, in turn, was now selected to take the place of Sister M. Felixa Jorz at The Catholic Sisters College as the superior. Mother M. Antonina left for Washington, DC, in July to assume her new obligation. Assisting her at The Catholic Sisters College were Sister M. Aurea Cybert, Sister M. Carol Rychlicki, Sister M. Casimir Janowiak, Sister M. De Chantal Mazuryk,

Sister M. Edna Perciach, Sister M. Honorata Makowski, Sister M. Honoria Urbaniak, Sister Louise Ann Glowacki, and Sister M. Norberta Haas. Among the distinguished visitors at The Catholic Sisters College in 1942 was the extraordinary Father Flanagan of Boys Town who played a large role in the apostolic history of the Franciscan Sisters of Chicago. He spent some time with the Sisters and expressed his delight with their service and dedication.[38] It had been only two years since he had requested the Sisters to assist him in the tremendous and rewarding apostolate at Boys Town. During the year of Father Flanagan's visitation, the staff at The Catholic Sisters College remained basically the same: Mother M. Antonina, Sister M. Honorata, Sister M. Honoria, Sister M. Edna, Sister M. Carol, Sister M. De Chantal, and Sister Louise Ann. Sister M. Theresilla Ignasiak returned to the college after a brief absence, and new to the staff were Sister M. Ambrosia Tworek and Sister M. Theodosia Biss.[39] In August, Mother M. Antonina was reappointed as superior while continuing as dietitian at The Catholic Sisters College.[40]

In 1943, Sister M. Euphrosine Tryjanowski, Sister M. Narcissa Skomski, Sister M. Olga Kulik, and Sister M. Generose Siepak were sent to The Catholic Sisters College in place of Sister M. Theresilla, Sister M. Carol, and Sister Louise.[41] By 1944, the staff decreased when only eight Sisters were appointed to Washington, DC. Mother M. Antonina, in her fondness for The Catholic Sisters College, requested of Mother M. Mechtilde that more Sisters be sent to the mission. Neither Mother M. Mechtilde nor the general council shared Mother M. Antonina's over-all enthusiasm concerning this apostolate. They were of the opinion that the labor exacted from the Sisters at Brady Hall of The Catholic Sisters College bordered mainly on the physical and was of a very strenuous nature. Mother M. Mechtilde and the general council began to question seriously the relevance of such service by dedicated religious women.[42] As a consequence, a letter was directed to the Reverend Frank P. Cassidy, who had succeeded Monsignor Jordan as dean of The Catholic Sisters College, announcing plans for the withdrawal of the Sisters.[43] The matter was subsequently discussed fully by Mother M. Mechtilde and her general council, and a definite proposal to withdraw the Sisters was made. The general council, believed that if the Sisters were recalled from The Catholic Sisters College, where the domestic activities were becoming more demanding and increasingly janitorial,[44] other apostolates conducted by the congregation might benefit. Because the congregation was actually in the process of opening St. John Hospital and School of Nursing in Huron, South Dakota, trained Sister personnel were needed. In addition, Father Flanagan's Boys Town was more and more in need of Sisters to handle all the aspects of work associated with that world-famous institution.[45] In January of 1946, Mother M. Mechtilde once again took up the matter of withdrawal of the Sisters in a letter to Dean Patrick O'Connor:

> Dear Reverend Father O'Connor:
> Since my return from Washington, we have discussed and thoroughly gone over the matter of withdrawing our Sisters from the domestic department of Sisters College.

As you know, the Sisters are relating that the work is too strenuous although I realize that you have made every effort to ease it. Perhaps if it were possible for us to supply more Sisters, this unpleasant situation could be avoided. But as it is, with the present shortage of vocations, we find it impossible to supply the demand for Sisters in our own establishments. Reverend Father, you will better appreciate our cause for worry and for taking this step when I tell you that there is only one novice to be professed this summer![46]

I regret sincerely that we will have to withdraw our Sisters at the close of the academic year in June.

Sincerely in Christ,
Mother M. Mechtilde[47]

Most graciously, Father O'Connor replied:

Very Reverend and dear Mother:

I am in receipt of your letter of January 29, 1946 in which you state that it will be necessary to withdraw the Sisters from the work here at the College at the end of the school year. Needless to say, I am deeply sorry that such a move is necessary, but I also want to say how deeply grateful I am to you for your kindness and understanding in this matter that is such a weighty one for me. I can readily understand your great problem with so few in the novitiate, and I know, too, to what lengths you have had to go to satisfy the needs of so many.

Be assured of our deep gratitude to you and the Franciscan Sisters of Blessed Kunegunda. Their contribution to the work here at Catholic Sisters College has been a notable contribution and we will ever be deeply indebted to your Sisters for all that they have done. Be assured, too, of our prayers for the success of your work and may Almighty God bless you and yours abundantly.

In accordance with your letter, I understand that the Sisters will leave at the end of the scholastic year.

Believe me to be

Sincerely in Christ,
(Rev.) P. J. O'Connor[48]

In March of 1946, Mother M. Mechtilde died and was succeeded by Sister M. Jerome Dadej, the assistant general. Mother M. Antonina, having been elected third councilor at the general chapter held in July of 1946, attempted once again to have the new administration reconsider the withdrawal of the Sisters from The Catholic Sisters College. In a letter to the Very Reverend Gerald Ryan, vice-dean of The Catholic Sisters College, Mother M. Antonina revealed her sentiments:

Thank you again for your thoughtfulness as well as your generous compliments. Please accept my apology for keeping you in suspense [as to whether or not the Sisters would remain at the College].

In regard to the help that you are looking forward to, I would be willing to help in any way. The Catholic Sisters College always brings sweet memories of my stay there. Nevertheless, because of the shortage of help, especially with the hospital in full bloom, our Mother General is prevented from answering your fervent desires. I did present your petitions, but I want to be frank with you. The chances are few as to any help from us.

I will pray fervently in your behalf to ease your burdensome task. May Our Lord grant your urgent desires in the nearest future. For my part, I will try to send you some information in this regard as soon as results are available.

Yours in Christ,
Mother M. Antonina[49]

The acute shortage of Sisters did not diminish. The concentration on Sister personnel for the proposed new hospital apostolate in South Dakota plus the widening scope of Father Flanagan's Boys Town office and domestic departments made the general council's decision final. On June 24, 1946, the Franciscan Sisters of Chicago left The Catholic Sisters College after eight years of service. The Congregation of the Sisters of St. Felix of Cantalice (Felicians) of the Immaculate Conception Province of Lodi, New Jersey, responded affirmatively to an invitation extended by the procurator of The Catholic Sisters College, the Reverend Patrick O'Connor, to staff Brady Hall. The Felician Sisters remained until 1958, when they, too, withdrew.[50] The last Sister-tenant of Brady Hall at The Catholic Sisters College left in the early 1970s. Few religious congregations remain on the campus today, and these with a skeleton population. The upper floors of Brady Hall are now used to house students of the Model Secondary School for the Deaf of Gallaudet College. The basement of Brady Hall houses an annex of the archives of The Catholic University of America.[51]

The association of The Catholic Sisters College in Washington, DC, and the Franciscan Sisters of Chicago came to an end in 1946. In an issue of the congregation's newsletter, *Avondale Echo,* published in 1938, Sister M. Gonzaga Raniszewski had announced the undertaking of The Catholic Sisters College mission and stated: "To have our own 'place' in the capital of the United States is a rare privilege."[52] That is precisely how the Franciscan Sisters of Chicago have always looked upon their eight years of service at The Catholic Sisters College in our nation's capital.

As late as May 1951, the Most Reverend Stanislaus Bona, bishop of Green Bay, asked for four Sisters to undertake the domestic department of the Sacred Heart Diocesan Minor Seminary in Wisconsin. In 1961, the Franciscan Sisters of Chicago were requested to supply Sisters for St. Mary Seminary (now Niles College of Loyola University) in Niles, Illinois. The Congregation of the Resurrection, associated with the Franciscan Sisters of Chicago since their foundation, invited the Sisters to staff the domestic department of St. John Cantius Minor Seminary in St. Louis, Missouri. All these requests were refused on the grounds that the apostolate of domestic service was not among the chief aims of the congregation.[53] Because the Sisters were now being educated at the university level and were being professionally prepared for the work of their apostolates, there were fewer Sisters to assign to strictly domestic work. There was much importance attached to the fact, also, that the area of strictly domestic service was recognized as being less in keeping with the focus of dedicated religious women in the Church.

AREAS OF DOMESTIC SERVICE

[1]Secretaries General, *Community Chronicle,* p. 51 (AFSCL).

[2]*Book of Letters of Request* (AFSCL).

[3]The Manor was built by a Mr. Parker, a sea captain from Scotland, who had settled in Oconomowoc and proceeded to erect for himself an elegant estate. *Book of Correspondence:* Letter from the Right Reverend Joseph van Grevenbroek, SO Cist., abbot of Spring Bank Cistercian Abbey, Oconomowoc to author, 1975 (AFSCL).

[4]*Interview* with the Right Reverend Joseph van Grevenbroek, SO Cist., abbot of Spring Bank Cistercian Abbey, Oconomowoc, 16 November 1975 (AFSCL).

[5]*Minutes of General Council Proceedings, 1934–1956* (AFSCL).

[6]*Book of Correspondence:* Letter from Sister Marianne Kaplan to author, 3 December 1975 (AFSCL).

[7]*Our Lady of Spring Bank House Journal* (AFSCL).

[8]*Minutes of General Council Proceedings, 1934–1956,* 10 July 1934 (AFSCL).

[9]*Book of Correspondence:* Letter from Sister M. Emily Kowal to author, 26 January 1976 (AFSCL).

[10]*Minutes of General Council Proceedings, 1934–1956,* 19 July 1934 (AFSCL).

[11]*Interview* with the Right Reverend Joseph van Grevenbroek, SO Cist., abbot of Spring Bank Cistercian Abbey, Oconomowoc, 16 November 1975 (AFSCL).

[12]*Our Lady of Spring Bank House Journal* (AFSCL).

[13]Ibid.

[14]Ibid.

[15]*Interviews* with Sisters formerly stationed at Our Lady of Spring Bank, 1976 (AFSCL).

[16]*Book of Correspondence:* Letter from Sister M. Lucille Klockowski to author, 8 December 1975 (AFSCL).

[17]Ibid.

[18]*Book of Correspondence:* Letter from Mother M. Mechtilde Zynda to the Right Reverend Romuald Pecasse, 20 April 1942 (AFSCL).

[19]*Book of Correspondence:* Letter from the Right Reverend Joseph van Grevenbroek, SO Cist., abbot of Spring Bank Cistercian Abbey, Oconomowoc, to author, 22 February 1975 (AFSCL).

[20]*Book of Correspondence:* Letter from Sister Marianne Kaplan to author, 3 December 1975 (AFSCL).

[21]Kay Sullivan, *The Catholic Tourist Guide* (New York: Meredith Press, 1967), p. 78.

[22]*Book of Correspondence:* Photocopy from Sister M. Harriet, provincial secretary, Immaculate Conception Province, Lodi, New Jersey, to author, 29 November 1975 (AFSCL).

[23]*Book of Correspondence:* Letter from Mother M. Magna, superior general of the Sisters of the Precious Blood, to the Right Reverend Monsignor Edward B. Jordan, 16 March 1937 (Copy in AFSCL).

[24]The Right Reverend Monsignor Edward B. Jordan came to Washington, DC, in 1921 as an instructor in the Department of Education at The Catholic University of America. He became head of the department in 1941. He was appointed vice-rector of The Catholic University and held that position until his death on July 19, 1951 at the age of sixty-six. Monsignor Jordan exerted salutary influence on his students and emerged as an educational leader by his stress on the importance of Catholic principles involved in the educational process at a time when John Dewey and his school were influencing American education. *New Catholic Encyclopedia,* vol. 7 (New York: McGraw-Hill Book Co., 1967), pp. 1100–1101; and the Catholic Education Press, *The*

Catholic Educational Review 89 (September 1951): 433.

[25]*Book of Correspondence:* Day letter from the Right Reverend Monsignor Edward B. Jordan, dean of The Catholic Sisters College, to Mother M. Antonina Osinski, 24 May 1938 (AFSCL).

[26]*Book of Correspondence:* Western Union Telegram from Mother M. Antonina Osinski to the Right Reverend Monsignor Edward B. Jordan, dean of The Catholic Sisters College, 24 May 1938 (AFSCL).

[27]*Book of Correspondence:* Letter from the Right Reverend Monsignor Edward B. Jordan to Mother M. Antonina Osinski, 27 May 1938 (AFSCL).

[28]*The House Journal of the Franciscan Sisters of Chicago at The Catholic Sisters College* (AFSCL), p. 1.

[29]Ibid.

[30]*Echo Avondalskie* [Avondale Echo], vol. 9 (Chicago: July–January 1938). Excerpt from letter to Mother M. Antonina Osinski from the Right Reverend Monsignor Edward B. Jordan, 1938 (AFSCL).

[31]Ibid., pp. 7–9.

[32]The Reverend Richard Bakalarczyk was a member of the Congregation of the Marian Fathers of the Immaculate Conception of the Blessed Virgin Mary. He served as a missionary and spiritual director to many congregations. Born in Poland in 1885, he was ordained at Włocławek, Poland in 1912. He spent several years as an assistant in the Włocławek Diocese before he entered the Congregation of Marian Fathers. In 1922, he came to the United States and was a missionary throughout Polish settlements until he enrolled in the School of Canon Law at The Catholic University in Washington, DC. In 1927, he received his doctorate. He was one of the founders of the Marian House of Studies in Washington, DC. Father Bakalarczyk also became one of the founders of the Secretariate for the Enthronement of the Sacred Heart in homes for Poles in the United States and Canada. He was instrumental in the publishing of the Apostolic Work, Inc. which printed and edited *Przegląd Katolicki* [The Catholic Review], the official organ of the Polish Roman Catholic Union of the clergy in the United States.

Father Bakalarczyk specialized in conducting retreats for Sisters and thus became widely respected as a spiritual advisor to many Sisterhoods. He authored a treatise on the religious novitiate called "De Novitiatue." He died in Stockbridge, Massachusetts in 1948. *Book of Correspondence:* Letter from the Congregation of the Marian Fathers of the Immaculate Conception to author, 4 August 1978 (AFSCL).

[33]*Book of Correspondence:* Letter from the Reverend Joseph Luniewski, MIC, to the Right Reverend Edward B. Jordan, 4 August 1938 (Copy in AFSCL).

[34]*The House Journal of the Franciscan Sisters of Chicago at The Catholic Sisters College,* p. 2 (AFSCL).

[35]Monsignor Jordan is referring to Mother M. Antonina herself.

[36]*Book of Correspondence:* Letter from the Right Reverend Monsignor Edward B. Jordan to Mother M. Antonina Osinski, 11 June 1940 (AFSCL).

[37]*The House Journal of the Franciscan Sisters of Chicago at The Catholic Sisters College,* p. 6 (AFSCL).

[38]Ibid., p. 13.

[39]Ibid., p. 19.

[40]Ibid.

[41]Ibid., p. 20.

[42]*Minutes of General Council Proceedings, 1934–1956,* 24 September 1944 (AFSCL).

[43]Ibid.

[44]This had also been the complaint of the Sisters of the Precious Blood who had staffed The Catholic Sisters College prior to the coming of the Franciscan Sisters of Chicago. *Book of Correspondence:* Letter from Mother M. Magna, superior general of the Sisters of the Precious Blood to the Right Reverend Monsignor Edward B. Jordan, 16 March 1937 (Copy in AFSCL).

[45]See Chapter 43.

[46]The novice was Sister M. Frances Swider.

[47]*Book of Correspondence:* Letter from Mother M. Mechtilde Zynda to the Reverend Patrick J. O'Connor, dean of The Catholic Sisters College, 29 January 1946 (AFSCL).

[48]*Book of Correspondence:* Letter from the Reverend Patrick J. O'Connor, dean of The Catholic Sisters College, to Mother M. Mechtilde Zynda, 15 February 1946 (AFSCL).

[49]*Book of Correspondence:* Letter from Mother M. Antonina Osinski to the Very Reverend Gerald Ryan, vice-dean of The Catholic Sisters College, 11 May 1947 (AFSCL).

[50]*Book of Correspondence:* Letter from Sister M. Harriet, provincial secretary, Immaculate Conception Province, Lodi, New Jersey, to author, 29 November 1975 (AFSCL).

[51]*Book of Correspondence:* Letter from Anthony Zito, assistant archivist, The Catholic University of America, Washington, DC, to author, 4 February 1976 (AFSCL).

[52]*Echo Avondalskie* [Avondale Echo], 1938.

[53]*Book of Refused Requests* (AFSCL).

CHAPTER 38

Our Lady of Victory Convent for the Aged and Infirm Sisters

Shortly after her election in 1934, Mother M. Antonina presented to her general council the urgent necessity of providing more facilities to accommodate the Sisters who were infirm or aged. She also reminded the council that at the end of the General Chapter of 1934, the Right Reverend Monsignor John Mielcarek, the vicar general for the women religious of the Archdiocese of Chicago, had reminded her of the prescription of Canon Law which stressed that the novices should be separated from the professed Sisters as soon as possible after being invested with the habit. This prescription obviously applied to the novices who were now living at the Motherhouse in Chicago. Monsignor Mielcarek also stated that the novices should spend their two-year formation period strictly in the novitiate because of their youth and also because of their lack of solid preparation for the apostolate, especially that of teaching.[1] Though money was very scarce, the new convent was urgently needed. To solve the problem, Mother M. Antonina proposed to her general council the addition of two wings to the existing Our Lady of Victory Convent in Lemont. She suggested that perhaps one wing of the addition could be used as a shelter for the large number of Sisters who were suffering from tuberculosis, while the second wing could be used to accommodate the aged and infirm Sisters thereby relieving the crowded conditions at the Motherhouse in Chicago. At this time, the matter of building an entirely new Motherhouse in Chicago was also considered but discounted early in the planning. The general council, together with Mother M. Antonina, came to the conclusion that it would be more feasible to build in Lemont an entirely new convent whose sole purpose would be to provide the aged and infirm Sisters with a peaceful and restful environment in their senior years.[2] The old Our Lady of Victory Convent could then be reserved for the exclusive use of the novices.

On January 7, 1935, Mother M. Antonina and her vicar general and first councilor, Sister M. Innocenta Antosz, visited Cardinal Mundelein to obtain his permission to secure a loan for the construction of a new convent in Lemont. After guaranteeing the Sisters a loan and the necessary authorization to build, Cardinal Mundelein urged them to discuss all further details with Monsignor Mielcarek. On January

20, Mother M. Antonina and Sister M. Innocenta met with Monsignor Mielcarek at which time he heartily approved of the proposed project, and as a matter of record, urged Mother M. Antonina to change the novitiate back to Lemont from Chicago where it had been forced to move in 1931. It was agreed at the meeting, therefore, that the aged and infirm Sisters would make their home in the convent to be constructed, and the novices would make their home in the original Our Lady of Victory Convent, the "White House."[3]

In the early part of 1935, sixty-eight acres of additional land were purchased on the southwest corner of Joliet and Walker Roads in Lemont. Monroe E. Sandel, the architect, was engaged to design the new convent. A look at the original architectural plan published in *Przegląd Kościelny* [The Polish Ecclesiastical Review] in 1933, shows how narrowly the Sisters had to scale down the proposed structure in order to keep it in line with their available finances. To secure the necessary funds, each Sister was encouraged to sell at least twenty-five "bricks" at $5 each among her family, relatives, and friends.[4] Mother M. Antonina and the general council agreed to have masses offered for all of the congregation's benefactors until the next general chapter to be held in 1940. There would be a mass for the living offered one month, and the next month, the mass would be offered for all deceased friends and benefactors of the congregation. The offerings for the masses were to be sent to the Bernardine Fathers in Lwów, Poland.[5] From this time also arose the practice in the congregation of offering Holy Communion and the rosary for all benefactors, both living and deceased, every Wednesday of the week.

At a private ceremony held on April 20, 1936, the first spadeful for the foundation of the new convent was turned by Mother M. Antonina after the land had been blessed by

Our Lady of Victory Convent for the Aged and Retired Sisters,
Lemont, Illinois, (1936–1963)
Presently, Mother Theresa Home

the Reverend John Drzewiecki, CR, the chaplain of St. Joseph Home for the Aged. The general council, several Sisters, and a number of lay people were present.

Construction of the new Our Lady of Victory Convent for the retired and infirm Sisters began early in May 1936. The convent, 180 feet by 79 feet in size, of yellow face brick with a slate roof, stood three stories high with an attic. On the first floor, the building contained a kitchen, laundry room, ironing room, and individual dining rooms for the Sisters, novices, chaplain, guests, and the custodians. It also contained five storage rooms and an auditorium which could hold approximately three hundred people. On the second floor, there was a foyer, a reception hall, a two-room guest suite, an office and reception room combination, a recreation room seating fifty Sisters, a fully equipped kitchenette, a dining room for convalescent Sisters, and twenty-three single bedrooms. A lovely chapel with a seating capacity for one hundred fifty persons was also on this floor along with two sacristies. All corridor floors were of ceramic tile while selected oak floors and trim were used in the other rooms. In addition, there was one open and one closed porch on the north side of the building. The third floor consisted of a choir loft for twenty-five people, a fully equipped pharmacy, a doctor's examining and waiting room, a music room, a large sewing room, a kitchenette, a dining room for eight Sisters, twenty-two single rooms and ten rooms with connecting baths. The third floor also had an open and a closed porch on either side. The attic, with large dormers, could accommodate sixty beds with room left for storage space. The complete structure was evaluated at $159,141.[6]

On July 12, 1936, the cornerstone for the new Our Lady of Victory Convent was blessed at three o'clock in the afternoon by the Right Reverend Monsignor Thomas Bona, archdiocesan consultor and pastor of St. Mary of Perpetual Help Church in Chicago. He was assisted by the Reverend Vincent Nowicki, pastor of St. Pancratius Church, and the Reverend John Kozlowski, pastor of St. Mary Magdalen Church. The Reverend Jerome Fabianski, CR, the pastor of St. Stanislaus Bishop and Martyr Church, delivered the sermon. He also read the document which was placed in the cornerstone of the building along with the "time capsule" which contained some very interesting mementoes. The document placed in the cornerstone read:

> In the Year of the Lord, 1936, July 12 at 3 p.m. during the reign of Pope Pius XI; the Archbishop of Chicago, George Cardinal Mundelein; the President of the United States, Franklin D. Roosevelt; the Governor of Illinois, Henry Horner; the Mayor of the City of Chicago, Edward J. Kelly; the Mayor of the Village of Lemont, Roy McCarthy; the President of the Polish Republic, Ignatius Moscicki; the Superior General of the Congregation of the Franciscan Sisters of Blessed Kunegunda, Mother M. Antonina Osinski, and her General Council; Sister M. Innocenta Antosz, Assistant General; Sister M. Salomea Grabowski, Sister M. Stephanie Pinkowski, Sister M. Jerome Dadej, Secretary General; Sister M. Raphael Bogalecki, Procurator General, was accomplished the Act of Blessing of

the Corner Stone by Monsignor Bona assisted by the Reverend John Kozlowski and the Reverend Vincent Nowicki for the convent building bearing the name of Our Lady of Victory Convent in Villa St. Francis, Lemont, Illinois. An appropriate sermon was delivered by the Reverend Jerome Fabianski, CR. This convent is intended for the sick and the aged Sisters of the Congregation—the Franciscan Sisters of Blessed Kunegunda—before the following witnesses:

> Mother M. Antonina Osinski
> Sister M. Innocenta Antosz
> Sister M. Salomea Grabowski
> Sister M. Stephanie Pinkowski
> Sister M. Jerome Dadej
> Sister M. Raphael Bogalecki[7]

The following items were also sealed in the cornerstone: a brief history of the congregation in both English and Polish; a copy of three Polish dailies, the *Dziennik Zjednoczenie, Dziennik Chicagoski,* and *Dziennik Związkowy,* all of which bore the date of July 12, 1936; a paper dollar, a fifty-cent piece and a twenty-five-cent piece dated 1935; and a dime, a nickel, and a penny dated 1936.

Under the direction of Mr. Adalbert Misiura, the St. Cecilia Choir of St. Stanislaus Bishop and Martyr Church sang at the blessing of the convent and the Benediction of the Most Blessed Sacrament which followed. Although the day was unusually warm, the happy occasion drew more than twenty priests and over five hundred people to Lemont.

On August 23, 1936, at two o'clock in the afternoon, two grottoes dedicated to St. Francis of Assisi were blessed by the Right Reverend Monsignor James J. Strzycki, pastor of Five Holy Martyrs Church, who was assisted by the Reverend Francis Lapinski, CR, assistant at St. Hyacinth's Church in Chicago, and the Reverend Michael Świątkowski, pastor of St. Hedwig's Church in Gary, who also delivered the sermon. After the blessing of the grottoes, a procession with the Blessed Sacrament took place on the convent grounds. The procession ended at the shrine of St. Francis, depicting him in repose in his grave, over which an altar had been improvised.[8] The area selected for the grottoes was a wooded area on a ridge placed on a little hill behind a rivulet. The site had originally been wild, but with the addition of selected and rare species of trees arranged artistically on the property, the entire area took on the aspects of a lovely park. White gravel roads as well as paved sidewalks were added around the property. As many as twenty-six fruit trees were planted. The maintenance of the beautiful grounds was the responsibility of Sister M. Felicita Pajor.[9] The flowers, trees, grounds, and gardens were always at the height of their beauty because of her vigilance and loving attention. A shrine, depicting St. Francis with the Wolf of Gubbio,[10] was placed at the beginning of the convent park area. Close to the areas of the grottoes were built the Stations of the Seven Sorrows of the Blessed Virgin

*Shrine of St. Francis of Assisi and the Wolf of Gubbio at the entrance to the Stations of
the Cross, Our Lady of Victory Convent, General Motherhouse, Lemont, Illinois*

Mary which were cast in cement and whose base construction was tufa, a porous
limestone. The stations were blessed by the Reverend Raymond Zock on October 4, 1938.
In 1939, the Stations of the Cross were erected near the original Our Lady of Victory
Convent, now the novitiate house. These stations were also made of tufa and stood twenty-
two inches wide and thirty-two inches high. All the stations were individual donations by
benefactors in memory of deceased loved ones. A cement crucifix, ten feet in height,
bearing the corpus of Christ, also of cement, stood a few feet from the entrance to the
Stations of the Cross. Erected at the entrance was an impressive arch, also made of tufa,
standing nine feet by eight feet, with the words, *Wieczny Odpoczynek,* [Eternal Rest]
across the top. This arch and the Stations of the Cross were erected in memory of deceased
Sisters by generous benefactors and blessed on June 2, 1940, by the Reverend Wenceslaus
Cich, OFM, of Green Bay, Wisconsin. At two-thirty o'clock in the afternoon, a procession
from the chapel to the shrine took place. Father Cich blessed the Stations of the Cross and
then led the crowd in praying them. They returned to the chapel for the Blessed Sacrament
which was carried in procession outdoors where benediction took place. Father Cich
delivered a sermon on the meaning of the Stations of the Cross in everyday life and
encouraged the people to pray them often.

  The official blessing of the new Our Lady of Victory Convent took place on
Sunday, July 18, 1937. Guests came from Chicago and the surrounding areas to participate

in the event. Chartered buses brought guests from as far as La Porte and Gary in Indiana and East St. Louis, Illinois where the Sisters staffed schools. The Right Reverend Monsignor Thomas Bona[11] performed the blessing and was assisted by the Reverend Vincent Nowicki and the Reverend Hipolit Górski.[12] The dedicatory sermon was delivered by the Reverend Jerome Klingsporn, CR. Once again, the St. Cecilia Choir of St. Stanislaus Bishop and Martyr Church sang under the direction of Mr. Adalbert Misiura. The St. Stanislaus Bishop and Martyr School Band, under the direction of Mr. Richard Mau, performed for the guests.[13] From morning until dusk, the assembled visitors enjoyed themselves on the spacious convent grounds of St. Francis Villa as the convent and grounds came to be called.

Four days before the blessing of the new convent took place the Sisters had received permission to transfer the novitiate back to Lemont from the Motherhouse in Chicago. When the infirm and retired professed Sisters[14] vacated the original Our Lady of Victory Convent on July 28, the convent underwent extensive renovation in preparation for the exclusive use of the novices. The novitiate house, or the "White House," as it was fondly called, contained a chapel and a classroom each seating approximately thirty Sisters. In addition, on the first floor were found the sacristy, reception room, a priest's dining room, and a sewing room. The second floor had two single bedrooms and several dormitories. There was a large dormitory on the attic floor and even the quaint tower had sleeping space. A utility kitchen and dining room were located in the basement. On September 23, 1937, the novitiate of the Franciscan Sisters of Chicago officially moved to Lemont where it remains to the present day. The postulants, meanwhile, remained at the Motherhouse in Chicago where they attended the congregation's Our Lady of Victory High School. The postulants occupied the first floor of the former novitiate left vacant by the novices who had moved to Lemont while the second floor was now occupied by the professed Sisters.

While the novices spent a great deal of time in the novitiate house, all the main religious services, including daily Holy Mass took place at the chapel in the new Our Lady of Victory Convent. In addition, the novices also took their main meals in the refectory designated for their exclusive use at the new convent. At least six times daily, the novices took the ten-minute walk from the novitiate house to the new Our Lady of Victory Convent in all the beauty, warmth, and icy cold of the changing seasons of the year. With the novices lived Sister M. Mechtilde Zynda who had been appointed the mistress of novices in 1934 and her assistant, Sister M. Rosaria Frodyma. The Holy Sacrifice of the Mass was offered for the first time in the novitiate house on January 22, 1938, with the Reverend Benignus Snoj of nearby St. Mary's Seminary in Lemont as the celebrant. By August 18, the Blessed Sacrament was reserved in the novitiate house and mass was offered there once a week.

Only three days before, on August 15, 1938, the ceremonies of the reception into the novitiate of nine postulants and the first profession of vows of ten novices took place for the first time in the new Our Lady of Victory Convent chapel.[15] The mass and the religious ceremonies were conducted on that day by the Right Reverend Monsignor James J. Strzycki, the pastor of Five Holy Martyrs Church.[16] The Sisters' guests who arrived from out of town were lodged in the houses belonging to the congregation on Archer Avenue while some guests chose to go to a rooming house in Lemont.

In March of 1937, a relic of Blessed Kunegunda had been received as a gift from the Congregation of the Poor Clares of Stary Sącz, Poland. Sister M. Beatrice Rybacki and Sister M. Bogumila Swiech brought it to the United States upon their return from Poland in 1937 after completing their studies at the University of Warsaw. The relic was placed under the main altar in the convent chapel of Our Lady of Victory Convent for the aged and infirm Sisters. Below the altar, a replica of the body of Blessed Kunegunda on her deathbed was fashioned.

On Sunday, April 14, 1940, at two-thirty o'clock in the afternoon, the Reverend Joseph Baniewicz, CR,[17] the chaplain of St. Joseph Home for the Aged, blessed the symbolic grave of Blessed Kunegunda. After the blessing, Father Baniewicz spoke to the assembled crowd of her life and virtues. Following the Benediction of the Most Blessed Sacrament, Father Baniewicz presented the relic of Blessed Kunegunda for veneration to the guests who had participated in the ceremony. This visit to the shrine of Blessed Kunegunda became a yearly event for many persons who had cultivated a devotion to the popular saint.[18]

A fierce storm occurred in Lemont on May 15, 1941. At approximately nine-twenty o'clock in the morning a tornado passed through and destroyed at least thirty-seven trees. The benches in the garden of the grottoes were broken and tossed about. A part of the roof of the convent was destroyed and many windows were broken in the chapel. The awnings were completely destroyed and rain poured into all the bedrooms on the south side of the convent.[19] Fortunately, the Sisters themselves were not victims of the tornado's dire effects.

A double ceremony took place for the first time at Our Lady of Victory Convent on August 15, 1943. Received into the novitiate that day were Sister M. Conrad Kempisty, Sister M. Veronica Blaszkiewicz, Sister M. Regina Krolak, Sister M. Roberta Duda, and Sister M. Renata Krukowski. They were joined by Sister M. Rose Ann Zmich, Sister Victoria Valerie Smagacz, Sister M. Jeannette Golojuch, Sister M. Agatha Walerski, Sister M. Celeste Walkowski, Sister M. Dorothea Micek, Sister M. Judith Kwiatkowski, and Sister M. Noel Janicki who made their first profession of vows. The celebrant was a prominent preacher and missionary, the Very Reverend Michael Kolbuch, MS, the provincial of the Missionaries of Our Lady of La Salette at Olivet, Illinois.[20]

With the grottoes on the grounds of the convent dedicated to St. Francis, the Sisters now wished to dedicate one to the Blessed Virgin Mary under her title of the Immaculate Conception, the patroness of the congregation. Through the generosity of Sister M. Praxeda Ostrega, the administrator and superior of the Guardian Angel Day Nursery and Home for Working Girls, a replica of the grotto at Lourdes was constructed on the grounds between the new Our Lady of Victory Convent and the novitiate house.

Shrine of Our Lady of Lourdes, Our Lady of Victory Convent, General Motherhouse, Lemont, Illinois

Most of the rock shrine was painstakingly erected by Sister M. Brunona Szwagiel.[21] For many years, Sister M. Brunona devoted much time and energy to beautifying and maintaining the grotto in excellent condition. On October 13, 1946, a large group of Sisters, friends, and guests gathered for the blessing of the grotto by the Reverend Jerome Fabianski, CR. Led by altar boys and the children from St. Stanislaus Bishop and Martyr School, a procession with the Blessed Sacrament began from the convent chapel to the grotto. The talented and reliable St. Cecilia Choir of St. Stanislaus Bishop and Martyr Parish again provided the singing. A sermon was delivered by the Reverend Stanislaus Fiołek, CR, the principal of Weber High School in Chicago.

In 1950, Mother M. Jerome Dadej and her general council considered moving the novitiate into the Our Lady of Victory Convent and using the novitiate house, the "White House," for another purpose. This finally occurred in 1963 when the new Motherhouse was built and the novices moved into the section reserved for them. The novitiate house was then converted into the Mother Theresa Museum which contains the memorabilia of Mother M. Theresa Dudzik. It holds numerous artifacts, period furniture, and historical information concerning the beginning of the congregation. The Mother Theresa Museum is listed in the National Register of the American Association of Museums in Washington, DC, with Sister M. Venantia Rec named as its director.

To aid the Franciscan Sisters of Chicago financially in maintaining the chapel at the Motherhouse in Chicago and at Our Lady of Victory Convent in Lemont and to honor the Blessed Virgin Mary under her beloved title of Our Lady of Częstochowa, Mother M. Antonina supported the organization of the Our Lady of Częstochowa Society in 1936.[22] The society owes its origin to Mrs. Sophie Pawelczyk who served as the chairperson at the first meeting which was attended by forty equally zealous women on October 18, 1936. At this meeting, Mrs. Pawelczyk was chosen the president and proceeded to present her basic idea which was the erection of a shrine dedicated to the renowned image of Our Lady of Częstochowa to which pilgrimages could be made on the convent grounds in Lemont. Mrs. Pawelczyk presented her plan, which the members of the society had voted upon favorably, to Mother M. Antonina Osinski who greeted it with great enthusiasm and gratitude. She informed the society, however, that the erection of such a shrine was not in the congregation's foreseeable future. The icon could be purchased, but it would be enshrined temporarily at a side altar in the chapel of the Motherhouse at St. Joseph Home for the Aged.[23] Chester Nowicki, a dealer in religious goods in Częstochowa, Poland, was commissioned to have the icon painted at the shrine in Jasna Góra, Poland. Specific instructions for the execution of the famed image of Our Lady of Częstochowa were relayed to Mr. Nowicki by Mother M. Antonina.[24]

The beloved "Black Madonna" arrived at the Motherhouse on June 18, 1937. The icon, duplicated from the original image, was approximately five feet by three feet in size and encased in a gold frame. It was beautifully carved in wood, gilded with gold, and richly studded with imitation stones. It had been blessed by the Pauline Fathers before the miraculous image of Our Lady of Częstochowa and solemnly touched to the original painting at Jasna Góra. On July 4, 1937, the Reverend Stanislaus Rozak, a member of the Chicago Archdiocesan Mission Band, unveiled the icon in a special chapel ceremony in the presence of the Sisters and the members of the Our Lady of Częstochowa Society. On August 1, Father Rozak returned to bless the icon in a chapel overflowing with members and friends of the society.[25]

When Mrs. Angela Ciura was elected president of the Our Lady of Częstochowa Society in 1937, the society took as its project the installation of a suitable altar in the Motherhouse chapel to complement the icon. On October 23, 1938, at two-thirty o'clock in the afternoon, a beautiful altar shrine and gold capula, executed by the Da Prato Art Firm in Chicago at a cost of $2,934 was blessed by Father Rozak. When permission had been received from the chancery office of the Archdiocese of Chicago for the consecration of the altar, Mother M. Antonina had also asked for permission to hold a weekly public novena in the chapel which was granted.[26]

In 1954, Mrs. Alyce Pociask became the third president of the Our Lady of Częstochowa Society.[27] The indefatigable Mrs. Pociask maintained the society's aim of financial assistance to the Franciscan Sisters of Chicago and labored unselfishly for that cause until her death in 1982.

After the new Our Lady of Victory Convent Motherhouse in Lemont was

Altar of Our Lady of Częstochowa, Sacred Heart Chapel, Our Lady of Victory Convent, General Motherhouse, Lemont, Illinois

completed in 1963, the beloved Our Lady of Częstochowa icon was transferred to Lemont by the Reverend Joseph Samborski, CR, chaplain of St. Joseph Home, in the company of a large number of members of the society. On October 10, 1965, the icon was enshrined in a rear niche of the Sacred Heart Chapel. Once again, plans for a public shrine to Our Lady of Częstochowa on the convent grounds in Lemont were discussed, and the firm of Pirola and Erbach was consulted in regard to its erection. When the circumstances of the ensuing years proved the plan unfeasible, the project was dropped.[28]

In 1925, the congregation purchased the Walker mansion and 155 acres of land which included 120 acres of desirable farmland and a farmhouse.[29] The farm also had thirteen cows, four horses, one sheep, some chickens and some pigs, one lamb, seven geese, and numerous pigeons. Simon Malinowski, a hired hand placed in charge of the farm, was helped by several other men including some residents of St. Joseph Home for the Aged in Chicago. Because the workers were elderly, the greatest amount of work fell to the appointed Sisters who, each day, walked to the farm after breakfast to attend to their many chores. The circumstances at the farm produced innumerable hardships and difficulties, the biggest by far being the lack of water which forced the Sisters to carry buckets of water from a neighboring farm until November when a well was completed on the Sisters' farm. Hay, fruits, and vegetables lay rotting in the fields because of neglect. In the stable, there was the urgent need for repairs so that the cattle would not freeze to death.[30]

When Mr. Malinowski became seriously ill and left the farm, the other hired farmhands proved most unreliable thus forcing the Sisters to perform the most arduous farm chores including the care of the animals. There were days when the Sisters returned to Our Lady of Victory Convent soaked to the skin and utterly exhausted. Frequently they did not have enough time to fulfill their religious obligations.[31] To aid the Sisters, three new men were hired in September of 1926. From that day on, a Sister went to the farm only to supervise the workers. The first Sister appointed to this supervisory duty was Sister M. Pauline Dydo who was in charge from October 1926 to March 1927.[32]

Throughout the years, there were various repairs and improvements made on the farm, but more changes were made in the farm workers, who more often than not, still proved to be transient and unreliable. Finally, with the arrival of the trusted and diligent Mr. Felix Tworek who came from Duncan, Nebraska, to take charge of the farm, an

The farm in Lemont, Illinois, purchased by the Congregation in 1925 and maintained until 1953

atmosphere of stability and productivity resulted. Mr. Tworek, who gave many years of dedicated service to the congregation long after the farm was sold, was the brother of Sister M. Ambrosia Tworek, a member of the Franciscan Sisters of Chicago since 1914. From December 1, 1938, with the efficient Mr. Tworek in charge, the Sisters attended to light duties at the farm such as cooking for the farm workers and taking care of the chickens.[33]

In November of 1940, the administration of the congregation became concerned over the farm and the expenditures which were proving to be large and burdensome. The Sisters recognized more and more that this labor was not in keeping with religious life, and any reason for it no longer existed. There was also no apparent income to be derived from the farm at any time in the future. The administration of the congregation was determined to sell the farm if a suitable offer were presented.[34]

The Seventh General Chapter of Elections held in 1946 further studied the question of the farm and its promises for the future. At the chapter, Sister M. Eugenia Detlaf, the superior of Our Lady of Victory Convent at that time, presented to the Sister-delegates solid evidence for its sale: there were not enough qualifed workers; there was a need for better machinery; and the need for a new barn was urgent. There was also no revenue being derived from the farm; the Motherhouse paid for most of the workers' salaries and other expenditures. Mother M. Jerome Dadej and many of the delegates felt, however, that a good landlord and good workers could still save the farm. By unanimous vote, therefore, it was agreed not to sell the farm, but instead, to improve its overall condition.[35]

Less than four years later, Mother M. Jerome and her general council thought seriously of renting the farm to some interested party. At a meeting with Sister M. Martha Bywalec, the superior of Our Lady of Victory Convent, and her house council, Sister M. Felicita Pajor, Sister M. Chester Dziarnowski, and Sister M. Edmund Siernicki, a vote was taken against renting the farm.[36] The Sisters all agreed that it should be sold as quickly as possible.

When the Eighth General Chapter of Elections convened in 1952, the general administration was thoroughly convinced of the need to dispose of the property. During the chapter a commission, dealing exclusively with the farm issue, reported its decision to sell the farm which was now valued at $40,000. The reasons to sell were essentially the same given in 1946: the work was inappropriate for religious women; there was a continued lack of revenue; the farm was too costly to maintain; repairs of any kind were expensive; and finally, reliable and steady workers were not readily available. The delegates voted unanimously to sell the farm with its proceeds going to the building of the new Alvernia Rest Home in Parma, Ohio. Sister M. Edmund Siernicki, the local treasurer of Our Lady of Victory Convent, was placed in charge of the sale of the livestock and the farm equipment.[37]

In April 1953, a request was sent to the Holy See in Rome for permission to sell the farm.[38] On June 16, 1953, the Sisters received the needed permission,[39] and on

December 19, 1953, the farm was sold to a private party.[40] Thirty-four acres of land from the original purchase in 1925 were left to the Sisters. This included the Our Lady of Victory Convent, the novitiate house, the workers' house near the novitiate buildings, and a large garden.[41]

At the time of the original purchase of the Lemont property, there were five frame houses on Archer Avenue that were a part of the sale. At first, they were used to house the workers on the farm in Lemont, and later, some of the houses were rented to private parties. By 1951, the houses were either razed, dismantled, or sold to eager buyers.[42]

Among the Sisters who had been assigned to the farm in a supervisory capacity or who attended to domestic duties throughout the years were Sister M. Pauline Dydo, Sister M. Ludwina Prokuszka, Sister M. Mathilda Szymoniak, Sister M. Imelda Derbin, Sister M. Julianna Kozaczka, Sister M. Pius Wojcicki, Sister M. Thomas Halgas, Sister M. Bernarda Urbanski, Sister M. Herman Pieniazek, Sister M. Blase Wojcik, Sister M. Clavera Papiernik, Sister M. Raymond Tabor, Sister M. Edmunda Siernicki, and Sister M. Humilianna Lemanczyk.[43]

OUR LADY OF VICTORY CONVENT FOR THE AGED AND INFIRM SISTERS

[1]*Minutes of General Council Proceedings, 1934* (AFSCL).

[2]Siostra M. Gonzaga Raniszewski, OSFK, "Rys historyczny Zgromadzenia Sióstr Franciszkanek Bł. Kunegundy. Część druga, 1910–1940" [A historical survey of the Franciscan Sisters of Blessed Kunegunda. Part two, 1910–1940] Unpublished manuscript (AFSCL), p. 185; and Secretaries General, *Community Chronicle*, p. 167 (AFSCL).

[3]Secretaries General, *Community Chronicle*, p. 167 (AFSCL).

[4]*Interview* with Sister M. Martha Bywalec, 22 July 1975 (AFSCL).

[5]*Minutes of General Council Proceedings, 1910–1934;* and Secretaries General, *Community Chronicle*, p. 91 (AFSCL).

[6]*Minutes of General Council Proceedings, 1934–1956* (AFSCL).

[7]Copy of Cornerstone Document (AFSCL).

[8]*Minutes of General Council Proceedings, 1934–1956* (AFSCL).

[9]Sister M. Felicita was born in Poland and entered the congregation in 1906 where she served as a teacher and religious superior for many years. From 1937 to 1940, she was the superior of Mount Alvernia Home in East Cleveland, Ohio. Transferred to Lemont, she resided there for thirty-two years until her death on April 26, 1972, at the age of eighty-two. She had been in the congregation for sixty-six years. The novices of Sister M. Doloretta will always recall the kind and jolly Sister M. Felicita with the stern face, who, the novices were warned, should never catch them using the lawn for "short cuts" from the White House to the Big House, that is, the Our Lady of Victory Convent. *Congregation Membership Records;* and *Spis Sióstr* (AFSCL).

[10]A huge, monstrous wolf was terrorizing the town of Gubbio in Italy. One day, St. Francis called the wolf to himself. It came bounding at him, poised to kill. The saint raised his hand and the wolf stopped. "Brother Wolf," St. Francis said, "it is wrong to kill. Leave these people alone and they will get you all the food you need." The wolf approached St. Francis who patted him on the head. A pact was sealed. Some historians regard this story as a myth, a mere legendary interpretation of St. Francis' peacemaking efforts.

[11]The convent was to have been blessed by the Most Reverend William O'Brien, auxiliary bishop of Chicago, but on that day he was called to the bed of a very sick relative and did not officiate at the blessing. Siostra M. Gonzaga Raniszewski, OSFK, *Rys historyczny Zgromadzenia Sióstr Błogosławionej Kunegundy. Część pierwsza, 1860–1910* [A historical survey of the Franciscan Sisters of Blessed Kunegunda. Part one, 1860–1910] (Chicago: By the Author, 1947), p. 189.

[12]Father Górski was a secular priest associated with the apostolate of the Congregation of the Resurrection.

[13]Raniszewski, *Rys,* p. 189.

[14]After the blessing of the new Our Lady of Victory Convent, the first Sisters arrived to take up permanent residence. They were Sister M. Salomea Grabowski, superior; Mother M. Aloysia Holysz, Sister M. Adelaide Szyper, Sister M. Apolonia Stozek, Sister M. Barbara Grochola, Sister M. Basil Ochocinski, Sister M. Clavera Papiernik, Sister M. Colette Nowak, Sister M. Gabriela Moskal, Sister M. Imelda Derbin, Sister M. Genevieve Swiatowiec, Sister M. Humilianna Lemanczyk, Sister M. Leona Pochelski, Sister M. Kunegunda Pinkowski, Sister M. Loyola Dymanowski, Sister M. Raymond Tabor, Sister M. Ludwina Prokuszka, Sister M. Sophie Ciurkot, Sister M. Virginia Minta, Sister M. Lucille Klockowski, Mother M. Vincent Czyzewski, Sister M. Augustine Malinowski, Sister M. Brunona Szwagiel, Sister M. Clara Ogurek, Sister M. Chester Dziarnowski, Sister M. Elizabeth Baut, Sister M. Cyprian Lewandowski, Sister M. Henrietta Machowski, Sister M. Jolanta Nowak, Sister M. Julianna Kozaczka, Sister M. Louis Scibior, Sister M. Lauretta Partyka, Sister M. Pius Wojcicki, Sister M. Romana Szkutak, Sister M. Margaret

Nawracaj, Sister M. Symphorosa Pisula, Sister M. Urban Klimek, and Sister M. Leocadia Das. Siostra M. Gonzaga Raniszewski, OSFK, *Echo Avondalskie* [Avondale Echo], July–January 1938 (AFSCL).

[15]The postulants invested with the habit were Sister M. Francesca Janowicz, Sister M. Vincentine Szczepanek, Sister M. Clarissima Zielaskiewicz, Sister M. Antonissima Jamruk, Sister M. Kingnetta Szczypula, Sister M. Purissima Babinski, Sister M. Albertine Schab, Sister M. Teresanna Bartuszewski, and Sister M. Dominic Plizga.

Novices professing first vows were Sister M. Gemma Stanek, Sister M. Praesentia Grzybowski, Sister M. Cundette Minczuk, Sister M. Antonella Abramowicz, Sister M. Deofilia Piaskowy, Sister M. Generose Siepak, Sister M. Reginalda Siminski, Sister M. Laetitia Kolczak, Sister M. Concordia Lawrence, and Sister M. Dulcissima Kaczmarek.

[16]*Our Lady of Victory House Journal* (AFSCL).

[17]The Reverend Joseph Baniewicz, CR, ordained in 1932, was a native of Chicago. He served as assistant novice master from 1933–34 after which he served in several Resurrectionist parishes. He was chaplain of St. Joseph Home for the Aged from 1936 to 1951. He died in Crown Point, Indiana, on July 21, 1968, at St. Anthony Home operated by the Franciscan Sisters of Chicago. Edward T. Janas, CR, *Dictionary of American Resurrectionists, 1865–1965* (Rome: Gregorian University Press, 1967), p. 161.

[18]*Minutes of General Council Proceedings, 1934–1956* (AFSCL).

[19]In 1976, another devastating storm hit Lemont, but no damage was sustained by the convent or its grounds.

[20]Secretaries General, *Community Chronicle*, p. 212 (AFSCL).

[21]Sister M. Brunona was born in Poland and came to America in 1912. She entered from St. Stanislaus Kostka Parish and was received into the postulancy on December 25, 1914. For most of her life she attended to household duties at convents of schools of the congregation, the Guardian Angel Day Care Center and Home for Working Girls, at the Motherhouse, and Our Lady of Victory Convent. She was admitted to the infirmary in 1969 and died on April 9, 1970. She was seventy-five years old and had been in the congregation for fifty-six years. *Spis Sióstr* (AFSCL).

[22]The Polish people best know and love the Blessed Virgin Mary under the title of Our Lady of Częstochowa. This miraculous image has been preserved for centuries at the National Shrine of Jasna Góra in Częstochowa approximately 120 miles southwest of Warsaw and 70 miles northwest of Cracow. The origin and early history of this painting is based on facts transmitted by popular belief and tradition among the faithful. It has been the occasion of very great devotion because of the numerous miracles attributed to it. Our Lady of Częstochowa is for the Poles what Our Lady of Lourdes is for the French, and Our Lady of Guadalupe is for the Mexicans. According to tradition, the picture of Our Lady of Częstochowa was painted by St. Luke the Evangelist at the request of the first Christians in Jerusalem. It was painted on the top of a cypress table built by St. Joseph in the Holy Family's home at Nazareth, and as such, remains one of the first portraits of Our Lady. The picture remained in Jerusalem until 326 when it was discovered by St. Helena, the mother of Constantine the Great, who brought it to Constantinople where it remained for approximately five hundred years. In the ninth century, the Emperor of Constantinople gave the picture to Charlemagne, who, in turn, presented it to Prince Leo of Ruthenia who had requested it to repel the attacks of Tartar invaders in his homeland. It remained in Ruthenia in the castle at Belz, north of Lwów, for another five hundred years. During the fourteenth century, Prince Ladislaus of Belz, fearing the onslaught of the Tartars once more, and deeply devoted to the Blessed Virgin Mary, attempted to transfer the icon to his castle in Upper Silesia to a district called Opole. According to legend, the wagon bearing the picture reached Częstochowa, the site of Jasna Góra, when the horses, drawing the wagon, refused to go any further. Accepting this as a sign that the Blessed Virgin Mary wished to remain at this site, Prince Ladislaus erected a church to hold the precious relic. The church and subsequent monastery were placed in charge of the Pauline Fathers who had come to Poland from

Hungary at the request of the Prince. Because the mountaintop where the picture was enshrined gleamed white in the sunlight, he named it Jasna Góra which means, "Hill of Light," or "Bright Mountain." From the year 1382, the remarkable history of this miraculous picture begins. On several occasions, it proved the defense against the enemies of Poland and the Church. In 1430 the Bohemian Hussites plundered the monastery and attempted to steal the icon. The picture refused to leave Jasna Góra; the cart in which it was placed refused to move. In their rage, the baffled invaders threw the picture to the ground leaving unharmed only the faces of the Madonna and Child. Another plunderer struck the right cheek of the Madonna twice with his saber. After the desecration of the picture by the Hussites, it was restored but the saber cuts remain to this day. In another formidable battle, two hundred monks and knights held Jasna Góra against the attacks of nine thousand Swedish troops in 1655. As a result of this memorable victory, King Casimir V accorded the title "Queen of Poland" to the Blessed Mother of God. Our Lady of Częstochowa (which translated literally means Our Lady "who hides often") played an important part in the famous Battle of Vienna in 1683 in which sixty-seven thousand men under King Sobieski of Poland defeated two hundred thousand Turks who were threatening Christendom. In 1920, the Russians threatened to attack Warsaw. According to legend, the Madonna appeared in the clouds above Warsaw on September 15, the feast of Our Lady of Sorrows. This day proved to be a turning point in the war. In Polish history, this victory is called the "Miracle of the Vistula."

The icon is about five feet by three feet in size and encased in a gold frame. Against a green background, Our Lady is pictured in half-figure holding the Christ Child in her left arm. She is clothed in a black mantle lined with crimson and edged with gold. The Christ Child, in full figure, is robed in red with a gold-band edging. He holds a four-cornered object in his left hand while his right hand is raised in blessing. Both are adorned with heavy crowns of gold, studded with jewels and supported by angels. Both have overdresses of precious pearls, diamonds, rubies, and emeralds. At the time of the restoration of the icon, the background was covered by thin plates of fine silver on which are engraved several scenes from the lives of Christ and his Mother. Because of its dusky faces, the picture is sometimes called the "Black Madonna." While some legends have it that the painting was set afire by infidels in the fifth century and smoke darkened the faces, a more common explanation is that the faces of the Virgin and Child have been darkened through the centuries by smoke from candles and incense. The Madonna of Częstochowa is intimately connected with Polish history and its miracles have often provided themes in Polish literature. The picture inspired a moving poem by the English writer, Hilaire Belloc, entitled, "Ballade to Our Lady of Częstochowa," a portion of which reads:

> The Battler's and the World's reply
> You shall restore me, O my last Ally
> To vengeance and the glories of the bold
> This is the faith that I have held and hold
> And this is that in which I mean to die.

The feast of Our Lady of Częstochowa is observed annually on August 26. Several churches in the United States are dedicated to Mary under this title. "Częstochowa: National Shrine of Poland," *The Grail*, March 1945, pp. 83–86; "The Miraculous Our Lady of Częstochowa," *Naród Polski*, August 1966, p. 7; and Ruth Oswald, "Our Lady of Częstochowa," *Action Now*, April 1951, pp. 1–3.

[23]Siostra M. Gonzaga Raniszewski, OSFK, *Echo Avondalskie* [Avondale Echo], July–January 1938 (AFSCL).

[24]*Book of Correspondence:* Letter from Mother M. Antonina Osinski to Mr. Chester Nowicki, 9 January 1937 (AFSCL).

[25]*Minutes of General Council Proceedings, 1934–1956* (AFSCL).

[26]*Book of Correspondence:* Letter from Mother M. Antonina Osinski to the Very Reverend Monsignor George Casey, 20 October 1938 (AFSCL).

[27]Mrs. Alyce Pociask was well known since she was the vice-president of the Avondale Savings and Loan Association on Milwaukee Avenue in the Avondale district for many years. Mrs. Pociask also proved to be a generous benefactor to the congregation and especially to Madonna High School whose educational goals she supported wholeheartedly.

[28]*Book of Correspondence:* Letter from Mrs. Alyce Pociask to the members of the Our Lady of Częstochowa Society, October 1964 (Copy in AFSCL).

[29]*Our Lady of Victory House Journal, 1925* (AFSCL).

[30]Ibid.

[31]Ibid.

[32]*Spis Sióstr* (AFSCL).

[33]*Minutes of General Council Proceedings, 1948* (AFSCL).

[34]Ibid.

[35]*Minutes of General Council Proceedings, 1946* (AFSCL).

[36]*Our Lady of Victory House Journal, 1951* (AFSCL).

[37]*Our Lady of Victory House Journal, 1952* (AFSCL).

[38]Secretaries General, *Community Chronicle*, p. 337 (AFSCL).

[39]*Minutes of General Council Proceedings,* 14 June 1953 (AFSCL).

[40]*Minutes of General Chapter Proceedings, 1943–1964* (AFSCL).

[41]Ibid.

[42]*Our Lady of Victory House Journal*, p. 37 (AFSCL).

[43]*Book of Annual Assignments* (AFSCL).

CHAPTER 39

Mount Alvernia Convent

In 1934, during the first year of her administration, Mother M. Antonina made an official visit as superior general to Cleveland, Ohio. Aware as she was of the wholly inadequate facilities at the Motherhouse for the steadily increasing number of Sisters, she thought it expedient to establish a home for the congregation nearer to the Sisters who worked in the East and thus alleviate the overcrowded conditions at the Motherhouse in Chicago.[1] In January of 1936, approximately two years later, Mother M. Antonina, Sister M. Jerome Dadej, Sister M. Innocenta Antosz, Sister M. Salomea Grabowski, and Sister M. Stephanie Pinkowski journeyed to Cleveland to view several homes and pieces of property under consideration for purchase.[2] A great deal of time and effort was spent in an endeavor to find a suitable location. The credit for the eventual discovery, selection, and purchase of a house and property must be attributed to Mother M. Antonina who had been aided in her search by Sister M. Chester Dziarnowski and Sister M. Sylvestra Pelczar.[3] Thus, on February 28, 1936, an agreement was signed by Mother M. Antonina and witnessed by Sister M. Chester and Mrs. L. H. Monter for the purchase of a large residence and property at 15850 Terrace Road in East Cleveland, Ohio, from Mr. Michael Gleason for the sum of $43,500.[4]

Located in a strictly residential area, the property was approximately thirty-five miles from Greater Cleveland. The spacious residence stood imposingly on a hill with sixty-seven stairs leading to its entrance. Adjacent to the residence were two large garages. An immense garden with shrubbery and flowers of varied hues were part of the purchase. The "bonus" to this extraordinary property was an orchard which contained over one hundred fruit trees. The gracious and roomy "Home on a Hilltop" was designated to serve the congregation as a center for retreats for the Sisters in the East. The home was also to serve as a house of studies for Sister-students who eventually would attend the Sisters' College of Cleveland (later St. John College of Cleveland).[5] In truth, it was the cherished dream of Mother M. Antonina to make the "Home on a Hilltop" the headquarters of the congregation's proposed Cleveland province.

Before the home could be ready for occupancy, however, it was in dire need of

Mount Alvernia Convent
East Cleveland, Ohio (1936–1952)

cleaning and repairing. The Sisters in the East, together with the aid of the members of the Our Lady of Victory Societies of the parishes where the Sisters taught, accomplished this feat. In an effort to meet the financial payments, the societies conducted "card parties" and other fund-raising activities. The Sisters accepted donations from interested patrons, and the gracious pastors of the Cleveland area contributed gladly at the urgent request of Mother M. Antonina. Sister Sophie Marie Kierszke, Sister M. Leontia Swiech, and Sister M. Ernest Blazonczyk were especially instrumental in collecting funds in Cleveland specifically for the purchase of the Terrace Road property and home.[6]

While it appeared that the house and the locality were perfect, the circumstances of purchase fell short of being ideal. Some property owners on Terrace Road opposed the purchase of the Gleason House by the Franciscan Sisters of Chicago on the grounds that East Cleveland was rigidly defined as a residential area, and, consequently, no corporation could establish itself there. The East Cleveland Zoning Board of Appeals ruled against the use of the property as a convent, but the city commissioners overruled the Zoning Board upon the representation by Judge Stanton Addams of Michael Gleason, the former owner.[7] The East Cleveland property owners now opposed the permit on the grounds that the Sisters might want to expand or use the house for purposes other than merely residential, and the East Cleveland residents feared that their property might be devaluated by this action. At a subsequent confrontation, John Chamberlain, the former city commissioner, successfully led the fight for the permit arguing that the East Cleveland neighborhood had outlived its usefulness as a strictly residential district, and the purchase of the Gleason house and property by the Franciscan Sisters of Chicago was permitted.[8]

On May 1, 1936, the Sisters took up residence in the house now officially named Mount Alvernia Convent.[9] It was formally opened by Monsignor Andrew Radecki, the pastor of St. Casimir's Church in Cleveland. Mother M. Antonina was among the numerous Sisters and priests present for the occasion.[10] At first, five Sisters took up residence there: Sister M. Chester Dziarnowski, Sister Sophie Marie Kierszke, Sister M. Leontia Swiech, Sister M. Ernest Blazonczyk, and Sister Louise Ann Glowacki.[11] On June 16, 1936, Sister M. Chester was appointed the superior of the group. After that date, Sister M. Josephine Penza and Sister M. Angela Jasinski were also officially assigned to Mount Alvernia Convent.[12]

On June 26, 1936, a private blessing of the chapel and the altar took place after which Monsignor Radecki offered Holy Mass for the first time at the altar which he himself had donated.[13] The official blessing and dedication of Mount Alvernia Home occurred in a ceremony on Sunday afternoon, June 28, during which the Most Reverend Joseph Schrembs,[14] bishop of Cleveland, who in speaking to the gathered crowd, called Mount Alvernia Convent "another advance in the progress of the Diocese of Cleveland."[15] He further stated that, "somehow or other it seems that the finger of God pointed to this place as it has been under consideration from time to time by other religious communities."[16] The Reverend John Hagan, superintendent of schools in the Cleveland Diocese, delivered a sermon in English; Monsignor Radecki preached the sermon in Polish and was celebrant of a Solemn Benediction which was conducted at an improvised altar on the spacious lawn. At the conclusion of the religious functions, a bazaar was held on the grounds.[17] Mother M. Antonina was also present on this joyous occasion accompanied by six Sisters from Chicago.

Garden at Mount Alvernia Convent
East Cleveland, Ohio

As early as August 1936, Mount Alvernia Convent housed twenty-seven Sisters for their annual retreat. After that date, the Sisters from Ohio and Pennsylvania came to this home annually for several years to fulfill their retreat obligation. The home was also prepared to house the many Sisters who attended the Sisters' College of Cleveland in pursuit of their undergraduate degrees.

That same year, plans were discussed for a separate chapel to be built near the convent on Mount Alvernia. Because the projected cost was prohibitive and the remaining debt on the Terrace Road property was already a burden, the plans were summarily dismissed.[18] By 1937, however, six lots were purchased for $9,971.64 for the purpose of future expansion[19] and the house was remodeled extensively. A part of the veranda was made into a sacristy. A refectory was made from the rest of the veranda, and a library was constructed from the previous refectory. Two years later, the empty land was cleared and fenced in by hedges for which Sister M. Leontia Swiech and Sister M. Marietta Dadej had personally collected funds, A statue of the Blessed Virgin Mary and a grotto dedicated to St. Francis of Assisi were the additional donations of Monsignor Radecki, always a generous benefactor, to further beautify the grounds.[20] These improvements were all made during the superiorship of Sister M. Felicita Pajor.

In June of 1938, Mother M. Antonina wrote the following letter to Bishop Schrembs:

> Your Excellency:
>
> The realization of a fond hope cherished by our community has been made possible through Your Excellency's kindness to us—our new home at 15850 Terrace Road, East Cleveland, Ohio. Will Your Excellency extend Your benevolence a little further to aid us?
>
> It is our wish, with Your Excellency's consent, to erect upon our premises, a home for the convalescent, infirm, and aged. Already applications requesting admission have been received, but the lack of sufficient funds at this time prevents us from setting up a new building.
>
> We have thought that, in the meantime, a section of our present home—which is quite spacious and in which only a small number of Sisters reside—could be temporarily devoted to this purpose. Besides providing the nuns with a means of support, this occupation would constitute a step towards the proposed project.
>
> We had written to Bishop McFadden, at the time of Your Excellency's late illness, asking for leave to collect funds for this purpose. We have not as yet received word to this effect.
>
> We humbly beg Your Excellency to grant us the permission to carry out this plan and, in order that our wish—The Home—may the sooner become a reality, to give us a written permit to collect the necessary funds.

Thanking Your Excellency for the past, kind consideration and begging to remain

Respectfully yours in the Sacred Heart,

Mother M. Antonina
Superior General[21]

The letter, written innocently enough, was the beginning of a controversy leading to the Sisters' eventual withdrawal from the Mount Alvernia Convent several years later. Bishop Schrembs, in his response to Mother M. Antonina, informed her that he had discussed the matter with the Most Reverend James McFadden, auxiliary bishop of Cleveland, and they were both firm in denying permission for the erection of a home for the aged by the congregation at Mount Alvernia Convent. Bishop Schrembs reminded Mother M. Antonina that the Sisters had received permission to buy the Terrace Road property on condition that it would be used as a residence for Sisters. Any other plans the Sisters might have for the property would now be understood by the bishops and the public as having been withheld by the Sisters at the time of purchase. Under these circumstances, it was obvious that the Sisters would never have received permission to buy the property. While Bishop Schrembs believed that a home for the aged was a real necessity in the diocese, he remained adamant in his refusal to give permission to the Sisters to build a home for the aged in the East Cleveland area and declared the matter laid to rest.[22]

In January of 1943, however, the Most Reverend Edward Hoban[23] was appointed coadjutor bishop of Cleveland with all the rights and powers needed for the direction and administration of the diocese because of Archbishop Schrembs' long-standing ill health. At a visit to Mount Alvernia on October 12, 1943, in the company of other clergy, Bishop Hoban suggested, and the others agreed, that a hospital or convalescent home should be built at the Terrace Road location.[24] Bishop Hoban was aware early in his episcopate of the needs of the aged who had difficulty in securing suitable care and living quarters in the Diocese of Cleveland. For the next three years, however, matters remained at a standstill until February 1946, when a tragic fire in Cleveland destroyed the Jennings Home for the Aged conducted by the Congregation of the Missionary Sisters of the Holy Ghost. Upon the request of Bishop Hoban and Monsignor Albert Murphy, the director of Catholic Charities, the Franciscan Sisters of Chicago were asked to shelter eight aged women from the Jennings Home at Mount Alvernia Convent. Eventually the Sisters made room for fourteen elderly women.[25] In April of 1946, Bishop Hoban wrote to Mother M. Jerome Dadej, at this time the superior general of the Sisters. He concluded his letter stating: "It seems that our hearty approval was given to your proposed building for convalescents on Terrace Road, but never put in writing. I take this occasion to enclose a written approval with the hope and prayer that you will be able to develop this home in the near future."[26]

Three years later, in spite of Bishop Hoban's long-awaited blessing upon the housing project for the aged, Sister M. Benigna Jakajtis, the superior-administrator at Mount Alvernia Convent, informed Mother M. Jerome, in April of 1949, that any further plans to remodel Mount Alvernia Convent would have to be abandoned since after an extensive evaluation, building a new structure was deemed more advisable. Sister M. Benigna added that Bishop Hoban was extremely anxious to offer financial assistance in the building of a new home for the aged, but because she was unaware of the terms,[27] she urged Mother M. Jerome to come to Cleveland to consult with him.

In January of 1950, Mother M. Jerome, acting on Sister M. Benigna's advice, informed Bishop Hoban that she and her general council had agreed that a one-hundred-bed convalescent home should be built at the Mount Alvernia Convent site. If material aid could be obtained from the Diocese of Cleveland, a wing specifically equipped for retired priests would be added.[28]

With Sister M. Hilary Dadej, the superior-administrator of Madonna Hall for Women in Cleveland, acting as liaison, a plan of action concerning the funding of the Mount Alvernia project evolved. Since the congregation was already in debt in connection with St. John's Hospital in Huron, South Dakota, the Sisters would be unable to secure permission from the Holy See to contract a sizable new debt. Bishop Hoban promised to loan the congregation $5,000. Mother M. Jerome suggested that the Diocese of Cleveland pay all the costs connected with the construction of the building and retain the right of ownership. The Sisters would try to raise funds to equip the institution. When the institution was in operation, the congregation would reimburse the Diocese of Cleveland according to the income derived. Once the congregation made its last payment, the Diocese of Cleveland would transfer the title of ownership to the congregation. This transaction would be protected by drawing up an agreement in which the diocese would not sell the property to anyone else if the Sisters were unable to make the payments. The interest on the money would be considered a donation to the institution.[29] Bishop Hoban, after consultation with the diocesan council, agreed to all the conditions and told the diocesan bursar, the Reverend Monsignor George Whitehead, to write an official letter to Mother M. Jerome confirming the plans.[30]

In June of 1950, Mother M. Jerome went to Cleveland to consolidate the plans for building a home for the aged in East Cleveland. She returned to Cleveland in July with Sister M. Gonzaga Raniszewski, Sister M. Hilary Dadej, Sister M. Virginia Minta, and Mother M. Antonina Osinski to examine the plans submitted by the architectural firm of Stickle, Kelly, and Stickle. It was at this time that Mother M. Jerome proposed calling the new institution Mount Alvernia Rest Home.

In the midst of the abundant goodwill and excellent progress being made in regard to the proposed new structure, the matter of the East Cleveland Zoning Ordinance which had first been encountered in 1936 prohibiting the use of the property for institutional buildings in a residential area seemed distant or forgotten. When the residents of East Cleveland, however, learned of the renewed plans for the construction of a home for the aged in their area, they sent letters to Bishop Hoban and Sister M. Benigna Jakajtis, the superior-administrator of Mount Alvernia Convent, informing them of their displeasure. Any plans to build a home for the aged at Mount Alvernia Convent on Terrace Road were brought to a final standstill on September 20, 1950. The city manager, Charles A. Carran, wrote to Sister M. Benigna and emphasized the position of the city of East Cleveland in regard to the Sisters' last appeal for permission to construct a home for the aged on the property in East Cleveland. He reminded her that the motions passed by the Zoning Board and the City Commission of 1936 allowed the Sisters to use the Gleason residence as a home for Sisters only and did not permit the use of the residence or the rest of the property for a school, a home for the aged, a hospital, or convalescent home. It was with this specific understanding that the permission had been granted in 1936. If any other use of the property had been brought out in 1936, the appeal at that time would undoubtedly have been refused. Mr. Carran reminded Sister M. Benigna:

> With this background, the Zoning Board of Appeals finds several of the same property owners still opposing the proposed change in zoning and stating that they are of the definite opinion that such a change in zoning would seriously injure the value and use of their property. The Zoning Board now has before it, in writing, requests from owners . . . in the area designated . . . that the Board refuse you your appeal. The Board of Zoning Appeals has given this matter very careful consideration, and under the circumstances, are unanimous in their opinion that your appeal cannot possibly be granted. It is their feeling [the five city commissioners] and that of the Board, that zoning ordinances were created for the protection of the adjacent property as well as the welfare of the public in general, and that considerable weight must be given to the opinions of adjacent property owners as to whether or not any proposed new use would be detrimental to their properties.[31]

The sale of Mount Alvernia Convent on Terrace Road was now imminent. The refusal by the Zoning Board to accept the Sisters' proposed expansion of their apostolate by means of a home for the aged, and the large expenditures associated with the maintenance of the Mount Alvernia Convent with little income derived and no visible means of support in the future were sufficient reasons for Mother M. Jerome and her general council to vote to sell the Mount Alvernia Convent property. Thus, the house and property on Terrace Road were eventually sold for $37,000. A loss was sustained on the sale of the property because it was difficult to find a buyer for such a large estate at that time.[32] The Sisters left Mount Alvernia Convent with their possessions on March 20, 1953. The last to leave were Sister M. Angela Jasinski and Sister M. Imelda Derbin.

With the permission to build a home for the aged at Mount Alvernia Convent irrevocably denied and with the consequent sale of the Terrace Road propery, Bishop Hoban met with Mother M. Jerome in Cleveland at which time he suggested a new and bold course of action.[33] The result of that action was the eventual construction of a beautiful and modern haven for the aged called Alvernia Rest Home in Parma, Ohio. It will be discussed further in Chapter 53.

MOUNT ALVERNIA CONVENT

[1]Siostra M. Gonzaga Raniszewski, OSFK, *Zarys Połwiecza Zgromadzenia Sióstr Franciszkanek Bł. Kunegundy* [Sketch of the fifty-year history of the Congregation of the Franciscan Sisters of Bl. Kunegunda] (Chicago: By the Author, 1944), p. 40.

[2]Sister M. Ralph Stawasz, "Summary of Activities of Corporation," (Photocopy], Alvernia Rest Home Parma, Ohio, 5 October 1960 (AFSCL).

[3]Siostra M. Gonzaga Raniszewski, OSFK, *Echo Avondalskie* [Avondale Echo], January–July, 1936, p. 3 (AFSCL).

[4]Stawasz, "Summary of Activities."

[5]St. John College of Cleveland, formerly known as the Sisters' College of Cleveland, opened in 1928. The Sisters' College combined the efforts of the previous nine separate Normal Training Schools which were maintained in the Diocese of Cleveland by many different religious communities to provide effective and efficient teachers for the elementary schools of the diocese. St. John College, tuition-free, was incorporated under the laws of the State of Ohio and was empowered to grant the degree of bachelor of science in education. In 1939, the college was empowered to grant the master's degree in education for high school teachers, principals, and supervisors. St. John College, unfortunately, terminated all of its academic programs in August of 1975. *Book of Correspondence:* Report from Chancery Office, Diocese of Cleveland to author, 1976 (AFSCL).

[6]Raniszewski, *Echo Avondalskie.*

[7]*Catholic Universe Bulletin,* 22 May 1979.

[8]Ibid.; and Raniszewski, *Echo Avondalskie.*

[9]Mount Alvernia is a variant spelling of Mount Alverno, the name of an isolated mountain peak among the Tuscan Apennines, rising above the valley Casentino, in Italy. A solitary mountainous spot, it was selected by St. Francis himself as living quarters for his followers. It was here that St. Francis received the stigmata, the impression of the Sacred Wounds of Christ, on his own body. The feast of the Impression of the Stigmata on St. Francis is celebrated on September 17.

[10]*Minutes of General Council Proceedings, 1934–1956,* 14 April 1956 (AFSCL).

[11]Raniszewski, *Echo Avondalskie.*

[12]Stawasz, "Summary of Activities."

[13]Secretaries General, *Community Chronicle,* p. 171 (AFSCL).

[14]The Most Reverend Joseph Schrembs, archbishop-bishop of Cleveland, was born in 1866 in Ratisbon, in Bavaria, Germany. His family emigrated to America in 1877, and he began his studies for the priesthood at St. Vincent College in Beatty, Pennsylvania; Laval University and the Grand Seminary, Montreal. Ordained for the Diocese of Grand Rapids, Michigan, in 1889, he engaged in pastoral work in Michigan and was appointed vicar-general of Grand Rapids in 1903. He was appointed auxiliary of Grand Rapids in 1911, and became the first bishop of Toledo later in the same year. In 1921, he was appointed bishop of Cleveland, and created Our Lady of the Lake Seminary to prepare Cleveland candidates for the priesthood. In 1929, he was made an archbishop. He paid special attention to the needs of the immigrants and created over eighty new parishes by 1936. He died on November 2, 1945, leaving most of his estate to the Sisters' College of Cleveland which educated teachers for the diocesan schools. Biographical sketch received from the Chancery Office, Diocese of Cleveland.

[15]"Klasztor SS. Franciszkanek Błogosławienstwo," *Polish Daily,* 28 June 1936.

[16]Ibid.

[17]Raniszewski, *Echo Avondalskie.*

[18]*Minutes of General Council Proceedings, 1934–1956,* 29 August 1936 (AFSCL).

[19]Ibid.

[20]Stawasz, "Summary of Activities."

[21]*Book of Correspondence:* Letter from Mother M. Antonina Osinski to the Most Reverend Joseph Schrembs, archbishop-bishop of Cleveland, 8 June 1938 (AFSCL).

[22]A letter in the archives of the Motherhouse from an unsigned party to Mother M. Antonina dated July 24, 1939, reveals an additional reason for Bishop Schrembs' and Bishop McFadden's dismissal of any plan to house the aged on Terrace Road. While Bishop Schrembs admitted that an institution of that kind was needed in the vicinity, he recommended that the congregation seek to build such an institution strictly among Poles. There were pastors of two parishes in East Cleveland who resented the Sisters' presence in the locality. The letter states clearly that the bishops were under the impression that the two pastors were very adamant about "not having any Poles here."

[23]Bishop Edward Hoban was a native of Chicago having been born there on June 27, 1878. He attended St. Columbkille's elementary school and St. Ignatius High School and College. Ordained in 1903 in Chicago, he was sent to the Gregorian University in Rome for advanced studies. Upon his return, he was appointed to the staff of the Quigley Preparatory Seminary in Chicago. In 1909, he was named chancellor of the Archdiocese of Chicago and in November 1921, he was appointed auxiliary bishop.

Before his appointment as coadjutor bishop of Cleveland in 1942, he was bishop of Rockford, Illinois from 1928. Upon the death of Bishop Schrembs in 1945, Bishop Hoban became the sixth bishop of Cleveland. At once he turned his attention to the needs of the aged, the handicapped, troubled children, and religious education. He infused new life into all departments of the Church's work.

Before his death on September 22, 1966, Pope Pius XII had conferred upon him the title of archbishop in 1951. See also Chapter 53. Biographical sketch received from the Chancery Office, Diocese of Cleveland.

[24]Stawasz, "Summary of Activities."

[25]Ibid.

[26]*Book of Correspondence:* Letter from the Most Reverend Edward Hoban, bishop of Cleveland to Mother M. Jerome Dadej, 3 April 1946 (AFSCL).

[27]*Minutes of General Council Proceedings, 1934–1956,* 27 March 1949 (AFSCL).

[28]*Book of Correspondence:* Letter from Mother M. Jerome Dadej to the Most Reverend Edward Hoban, bishop of Cleveland, 19 January 1950 (AFSCL).

[29]*Book of Correspondence:* Letter from Mother M. Jerome Dadej to the Most Reverend Edward Hoban, bishop of Cleveland, 27 April 1950 (AFSCL).

[30]Secretaries General, *Community Chronicle,* p. 256 (AFSCL).

[31]*Book of Correspondence:* Letter from Charles A. Carran to Sister M. Benigna Jakajtis, 20 September 1950 (AFSCL).

[32]*Minutes of General Council Proceedings, 1934–1956,* 28 February (AFSCL).

[33]Secretaries General, *Community Chronicle,* p. 337 (AFSCL).

CHAPTER 40

St. Anthony's Home

One of the world's worst calamities occurred on September 1, 1939, when Adolf Hitler's German forces invaded Poland. Two days later, Great Britain and France declared war on Germany, and World War II, the most widespread, costly, destructive, and massive conflict in history erupted.

That year also saw the beginning of the nineteen-year pontificate of Pope Pius XII, the former Eugenio Cardinal Pacelli, who had been elected on March 2. It was he who greatly relaxed the old rules governing the time of mass and the fast necessary to receive Holy Communion. In the congregation, the Franciscan Sisters of Chicago were slated to begin one of their most blessed and fruitful apostolates.

In the bound copies of the *Echo Avondalskie* [Avondale Echo], the community newsletter dating back to 1934, an article appears concerning the acquisition of property and a house which the Franciscan Sisters of Chicago had opened in 1939, as St. Anthony's Home for the Aged in Crown Point, Indiana. The first sentence of the article reads "As often happens, big things come from small beginnings, and so it is with St. Anthony's Home. A real beginning is being made there."[1] Sister M. Gonzaga Raniszewski, the author of the article, did not know at the time how prophetically she wrote. Twenty-seven years later, St. Anthony Home in the St. Anthony Medical Complex in Crown Point is living proof that her prediction materialized with truly remarkable results.

The story of the acquisition of the house and property in Crown Point and the foundation of St. Anthony Home is truly a story of steadfast faith and perseverance as manifested by the Franciscan Sisters of Chicago. Before 1939 the St. Joseph Benevolent Society of Gary, Indiana, long operative at St. Hedwig's Parish, had worked diligently to support St. Joseph Home for the Aged in Chicago where many of the parishioners eventually came to place their aged parents. After a number of years, some of the members spoke of withdrawing their charitable support of St. Joseph Home for the Aged in Chicago on the grounds that housing their aged in Chicago constituted a distinct hardship because of the distance and the time it took to travel to that city. The president of the St. Joseph Benevolent Society of Gary maintained that a home for the aged somewhere in Indiana would be an answer to their prayers. This suggestion was brought to the attention of Mother M. Antonina who, in turn, presented the idea to her general council and then to the community-at-large. Almost immediately, Sister M. Marcelline Molek and Sister M. Genevieve Swiatowiec[2] volunteered to go to Indiana and search for a suitable site. At first the Sisters lived at St. Hedwig's Convent in Gary while they canvassed various areas in La Porte. While they were greatly encouraged by the pastor of Sacred Heart Parish in La Porte, the Reverend Ignatius Gapczynski, the Sisters were not successful in finding a suitable place there. When the Most Reverend John Noll, bishop of Fort Wayne, came to administer the sacrament of Confirmation at Sacred Heart Church in Gary, Sister M. Marcelline and Sister M. Genevieve obtained permission from the bishop to continue their search for a site in that city and in nearby areas and to solicit alms for the proposed project.[3] Disappointment followed disappointment as the Sisters were unable to find a suitable location for a home for the aged. The Sisters then turned in the direction of Crown Point in South Lake County. While begging for alms in the vicinity of St. Mary's Church whose administrator was the Reverend Joseph Hammes,[4] the Sisters met a Mrs. Clausen who, in turn, informed them of Michael Williams, a widower, who was anxious to dispose of his house and property. Advanced in age and unable to exercise proper care of his house and land, Mr. Williams' only stipulation in selling his property was that the homestead pass into the hands of a Catholic party.

Sister M. Marcelline and Sister M. Genevieve invited Mother M. Antonina to Crown Point to examine the property. She eagerly made the trip accompanied by the members of the general council. They were all very impressed with the site and indicated great interest in the property especially since it presented a wonderful opportunity for expansion.

The sturdy farmhouse, set back in a small forest of trees, was a white frame two-story building with ten large rooms and a veranda that wrapped around the front and east side of the house.[5] Located near Fancher Lake,[6] the site lay just beyond the Lake County Fairgrounds on the Crown Point-Cedar Lake Road, presently the southeast corner of South Court Street and Franciscan Road. Called "Fairview Farm," the white frame house with the clapboard siding was a familiar sight to local residents and travelers alike.[7]

In addition to the house, the property consisted of forty acres of land with an orchard, poultry house, stable, kitchen garden, and garage. Included in the proposed sale of the property were four cows, two calves, two horses, and about thirty pigs.[8] The price requested by Mr. Williams was an incredibly low $1,000. Mother M. Antonina was quick to take advantage of the splendid opportunity and arranged for the purchase of the Crown Point house and property on June 20, 1939. By August 16, the Franciscan Sisters of Chicago had received the deed to the property from Lake County. While the Williams' homestead was indeed a most prudent purchase, the house and land were in extreme disorder for they had long been neglected. Two weeks after the purchase, Mother M. Antonina advised Sister M. Marcelline and Sister M. Genevieve to discontinue their solicitation of alms in the Indiana area and to take up residency at the farmhouse since Mr.

Original St. Anthony's Home
Crown Point, Indiana (1939–1974)

Williams had become seriously ill and was unable to continue to maintain the homestead. Sister M. Marcelline and Sister M. Genevieve, therefore, left St. Hedwig's Convent in Gary, which they had kept as their home base in Indiana, and journeyed to Crown Point to prepare the unkempt house and grounds for occupancy by the Sisters. About a month after the purchase of the Williams' homestead, Mother M. Antonina paid Sister M. Marcelline and Sister M. Genevieve a visit. She brought with her Sister M. Imelda Derbin and Sister M. Sigfrieda Scensny[9] who remained in Crown Point. On August 20, Mother M. Antonina visited again and this time brought with her Sister M. Olga Kulik and Sister M. Emily Kowal.[10] On October 1, 1939, Sister M. Marcelline was appointed the superior and future administrator of the Williams' homestead which the Sisters now affectionately called St. Anthony's Home in honor of the holy Franciscan priest and doctor. The Sisters at St. Anthony's Home spent many months painting, cleaning, and remodeling the homestead in preparation for its future residents.

The renovations of the home were extensive. A stucco exterior was used to cover its wood frame and clapboard siding. The huge veranda that wrapped around the front and east side of the house was enclosed to provide space for four bedrooms. An open-air porch was built on the second story of the east side only. An enclosed vestibule was added to the north side where originally stairs had been located. Walls were moved and replaced, although much of the woodwork, the mantel, and the fireplace remained. A chapel was fashioned from one of the rooms, and an altar was obtained from the Motherhouse. The sacristy was remodeled to serve as a recreation room and a workroom while the coal bin was made into a pantry for canned goods and other staples. One of the rooms was tranformed into a dining room for the Sisters. Laboring arduously and often far into the night, the Sisters wished to have as much work completed as possible. The Sixth General Chapter was scheduled to be held in July of 1940, and the Sisters feared that the next administration might not share the same zeal and interest for St. Anthony's Home as Mother M. Antonina had exhibited.

As the new year of 1940 approached, the Sisters' dining room was not yet completed, the laundry room was disorganized, and the heating system was still not installed. In addition, the Sisters had to clear the land of tree stumps and rubbish before they could cultivate it. At first they worked in the garden, in the fields, and tended the animals themselves. Eventually, however, the Sisters gave refuge to two men who then proceeded to attend to the grounds, the chickens, and the cattle. Nevertheless, the Sisters still mended and sewed, pasteurized the milk, and made their own cheese. In all of this labor and sacrifice, the Sisters were aided and supported by the Sisters on the staff of the congregation's nearby schools in Gary, Hammond, East Chicago, La Porte, and New Chicago. Sister M. Zita Kosmala, the superior and principal of St. Hedwig's School in Gary, was especially helpful in meeting the needs of the pioneer Sisters at St. Anthony's Home, and several Sisters came from the Motherhouse in Chicago to be of assistance. Chief among them were Sister M. Bernice Stefanski, Sister M. Hyacinth Barczewski, and Sister M. Gonzaga Raniszewski. Sister M. Donald Urban, it is noted, almost single-handedly painted the house's interior.[11] Even though the house was not yet officially opened as a refuge for the aged, a poor and homeless wanderer, Benjamin A. Patten, was brought to the Sisters by the Crown Point police who were seeking shelter for him. Thus, on December 4, 1939, he became the first resident of St. Anthony's Home.[12]

On May 30, 1940, St. Anthony's Home was blessed and dedicated by the Reverend Edward Mungovan, vicar general of the Diocese of Fort Wayne. After the blessing, the Blessed Sacrament was carried in procession throughout the home and then to an improvised altar on the grounds. The Reverend Joseph Hammes greeted the Sisters and the guests and in a brief sermon expressed his joy at the opening of St. Anthony's Home and wished it growth. The Reverend Ambrose Poznanski, OFM, spoke to the guests in Polish, using as his theme the beatitude: "Blessed are the merciful, for they shall obtain mercy." Benediction of the Blessed Sacrament followed with music by the choir of Franciscan clerics from Our Lady of Lourdes Franciscan Retreat House in Cedar Lake. At the conclusion, the Honorable Vincent Youche, the mayor of Crown Point,[13] expressed his joy and satisfaction in the completed project and added that he lived in the hope that someday a much-needed hospital would be built in the area by the Sisters. This voiced hope became a reality thirty-four years later.

On the feast of St. Theresa of Avila, October 15, 1940, the first mass was celebrated in the newly constructed chapel. The celebrant, the Reverend John Szot of St. Mary's Church, served as the temporary chaplain celebrating mass on Sundays and holydays and occasionally during the week. Later, the Franciscan priests from Our Lady of Lourdes Retreat House at Cedar Lake celebrated daily mass and administered the sacraments.

The St. Joseph Benevolent Society of Gary again became deeply involved in helping the Sisters complete the home. They sponsored "tag days" which enabled the Sisters to buy a washing machine and a mangle for the laundry. A generous donor supplied the Sisters with a car, and Sister M. Marcelline learned to drive. Raffles, bingos, and card parties were all introduced to secure needed funds. Just before Christmas, Sister M. Thecla Gawlowicz arrived to serve as organist and sacristan. The first Midnight Mass was celebrated by the Reverend Alexander Karcz of Our Lady of Lourdes Retreat House who brought with him the Franciscan clerics who sang with the help of the Sisters stationed at St. Hedwig's School in Gary. Present also in the small and overcrowded chapel at the three masses of praise and thanksgiving allowed the celebrant on Christmas Day were many friends of the Sisters from Gary.[14]

In January 1941, the first residents arrived. They were indeed of infinite variety. Among them were two aged people from Whiting, Indiana; a one-hundred-year-old woman from Gary; a forty-year-old semi-retarded man who kept running away and needed constant supervision; and a seventeen-year-old girl who was found to be somewhat mentally disturbed. Two men from Chicago also applied. Within a year, one of them, Mr. Biernicki, died peacefully in the arms of Sister M. Marcelline. By the end of the month, St. Anthony's Home was filled to its capacity of eighteen residents. Seven beds were placed in the large basement for the newly arrived male residents. The women were housed on the second floor.[15] Sister M. Leonilla Stogowski, a registered nurse, was sent to minister to the residents. During the foundation years, Sister Eleanor Plocki, Sister M. Basil Ochocinski, and Sister M. Teresanna Bartuszewski were sent to provide nursing care.

The *Minutes of the General Council Proceedings* for October 8, 1941, reveal an entry which sheds much light on the conditions prevailing at St. Anthony's Home. Sister M. Paul Kirschbaum, the newly elected secretary general and third councilor, was sent to observe first-hand the success or failure of the congregation's new mission. She provided a report which gave an index of the conditions: the residents consisted of nine men and nine women in constant need of the Sisters' services. Two women residents were in their twenties. They had been expelled from their parental home because of what their parents considered their daughters' immoral lives. They were brought to St. Anthony's Home by a public health nurse from Gary who insisted the women were "incorrigible" and required sterilization. They were received warmly by the Sisters and every attempt was made to shelter them until their case was successfully concluded. In making her report to Sister M. Paul, Sister M. Marcelline justified this very personal ministry saying: "Our Constitutions say that we are to minister to such people who desperately need our care." Sister M. Paul noted that Sister M. Sigfrieda still faithfully solicited alms while the other Sisters stationed at St. Anthony's Home, besides attending to the residents, continued to work in the fields digging potatoes and harvesting corn and soybeans.[16]

By April of 1942, Sister M. Marcelline was in very poor health due to over-exhaustion. On a cold day, she had gone outdoors to work in the garden. As a consequence, she was hospitalized at St. Mary's Hospital in Gary. Although her condition improved enough to enable her to return to St. Anthony's Home, she again fell gravely ill after several weeks and died on July 7, 1942.[17]

During the war years, providing food was no problem since St. Anthony's Home raised animals which were slaughtered when needed and kept in a city refrigeration system for $12 a month. Chickens supplied the breakfast eggs; the gardens supplied the noon vegetables; and bread was collected by Sister M. Sigfrieda and refrigerated for future use. The only expenses were for home necessities and renovation. Since the roads were torn up and worn, gravel and sand were supplied by the congregation. Water was a constant source of worry because the well had been dug for the needs of a small family only. Rusty well-water from an old-fashioned, failing pump posed a major problem. When faced with a scarcity of water, the Sisters asked Mayor Youche who had promised to resolve the matter if they could obtain water from the city by purchasing pipes to tie into the municipal system. The mayor declined citing that he did not have enough pipes for the city's need and expressed doubts over whether or not pipes could be obtained due to the shortage of steel during World War II. Undaunted, Sister M. Sigfrieda contacted Mayor Edward J. Kelly of Chicago. He called Washington, DC, and obtained a carload of pipes once intended for use in Chicago. The 1,700 feet of water main, instead, went to the Sisters at St. Anthony's Home. The installation of the pipes began on November 20, 1943, and by March 20, 1944, city water was available to the home.[18]

There were no significant changes at St. Anthony's Home in the years that followed the end of World War II. Early in the 1950s, however, the need for more rooms and services to the residents became very pronounced. Every foot of the farmhouse, the veranda, and the basement was being used. There were nineteen residents and six Sisters who continued to live in conditions which were not conducive to exercising the works of mercy most effectively. Not only was there a serious lack of conveniences but also of necessities for both the residents and the Sisters at the home. The future of St. Anthony's Home, in those circumstances, became the matter of much discussion by Mother M. Jerome Dadej and her general council at their sessions. At one particularly spirited session, Mother M. Antonina Osinski, the third councilor, pleaded: "Do not sell the [Crown Point] property . . . there is a future there . . . if nothing else, leave conditions as they are until we are in a better position to do something more constructive."[19] Mother M. Jerome Dadej reiterated the fact that indeed "nothing can be done for a few years."[20] It was agreed, therefore, not to sell the Crown Point property and in the ensuing years, the little white house sheltered its eighteen residents and staff of Sisters under very trying circumstances. When the Eighth General Chapter convened in 1952, a lengthy discussion arose over what course of action to take concerning St. Anthony's Home. The Sister-delegates were informed that the State of Indiana forbade the housing of bedridden residents on the second floor of the home. The space on the first floor for such residents was inadequate. In addition, as in every school and institution of the congregation, the shortage of Sister personnel was evident. As a consequence, the delegates voted to keep St. Anthony's Home but not to accept bedridden patients. In view of the shortage of Sisters on the staff of the home, the delegates voted against the further admittance of any new residents unless lay personnel were hired to asssist the Sisters. In the meantime, the "waiting list" for St Anthony's Home grew longer and longer.

Finally, in November 1958, Mother M. Beatrice Rybacki who had succeeded Mother M. Jerome Dadej as superior general, Sister M. Gonzaga Raniszewski, and Sister M. Ottilia Madaj met with the Most Reverend Andrew Grutka,[21] bishop of Gary, to discuss the matter of building a new home for the aged. He promised to help the Sisters select an architect and made various suggestions concerning the plans. Financially, the Diocese of Gary could not offer any assistance except to furnish two suites for use by retired priest residents. Bishop Grutka advised the Sisters to turn to a Polish fraternal organization to secure material assistance. The Sisters declined any such suggestion and worked even harder to secure funds for a new home. At first it was arranged to get a government loan; however, the federal loan upon which the Sisters were depending was not actualized. The government's proposition—the leasing or the renting of apartments to residents rather than the building of a conventional home for the aged—was not acceptable to the Sisters. As a congregation of religious women, the Sisters desired to care for the aged in a loving and family atmosphere rather than merely to provide living quarters.[22] The Sisters were forced to contend with another issue. This was the fact that very little help could be expected from the Motherhouse because of the debt of nearly $1 million which still remained on the new Motherhouse under construction in Lemont.[23] It seemed that the Sisters would have to depend on their own resources without any financial aid from the congregation.

Although the Sisters at St Anthony's Home had labored diligently for years to raise funds for a new home, under the leadership of the zealous and dedicated Sister M. Cherubim Madaj,[24] who had been appointed superior and administrator in July of 1962, the Sisters renewed their vigor. With fervor they continued to work, sacrifice, and save funds for a new building. They held summer festivals in their lush groves alongside the home. The Sisters and some of the residents provided handknitted and crocheted items to be sold. Sister M. Emily Kowal baked cakes, cookies, and as many as five hundred loaves of "St. Anthony's Bread."[25]

Eventually, the Sisters collected over $300,000, and private loans worth over $1 million were to be acquired for building the home. Bishop Grutka promised the Sisters a loan from the Diocese of Gary. Yet actual construction of the new St. Anthony's Home was hindered by intermittent delays. Problems arose in the architectural planning and financing. Further problems with the city were encountered with extending Main Street and hooking up to municipal sewers and water mains. The delays did not dampen the spirits of the Sisters; rather, the delays seemed to add fuel to their endeavors. The Sisters continued to work, sacrifice, and save for the single purpose of building a new nursing home. Finally, ground-breaking ceremonies were held on July 1, 1962, for the new structure. Bishop Grutka officiated at this long-awaited ceremony. The plans for the new home, drawn up by the architect William M. Butoric of Munster, were now near completion, but it was not until July of 1964 that the R. T. Milord Company of Chicago actually began construction. The new St. Anthony Rest Home, as it was now called, was built on forty acres of land on Main Street, near the south end of the Lake County Fairgrounds. It was equipped with all the most modern facilities and afforded the residents superior nursing care. This home and its expansion will be further discussed in Chapter 59.

The activities of the year 1939 were brought to a climax on December 8 when the congregation celebrated its 45th Anniversary. In the morning, the Reverend Joseph Baniewicz, CR, the chaplain of St. Joseph Home for the Aged, offered a Mass of Thanksgiving in the chapel of the Motherhouse. The Benediction of the Most Blessed Sacrament followed at ten o'clock in the morning. At the conclusion of the benediction service, the Sisters, singing hymns, walked in procession from the chapel to the garden where Father Baniewicz blessed the grotto of Our Lady of Lourdes which had been erected in honor of the anniversary. The grotto was built on the right side of the convent door entrance on Hamlin and Schubert Avenues. While not very large, it could be seen above the wall which surrounded the garden and the entire St. Joseph Home for the Aged and the Motherhouse. The grotto made from stones of various colors had a stream running down its stone crags. At its steps, the figure of St. Bernadette knelt in the midst of many trees and bushes. The grotto's constuction, while beautiful and inspiring, proved to be of only slight cost to the congregation since all of the materials, outside of the statues, were donated by generous benefactors.

On the evening of the 45th Anniversary celebration, Mother M. Antonina read aloud to the Sisters the first part of the brief history of the congregation written by Sister M. Gonzaga Raniszewski entitled *Rys historyczny Zgromadzenia Sióstr Franciszkanek Błogosławionej Kunegundy. Część pierwsza, 1860–1910* [A historical survey of the Franciscan Sisters of Blessed Kunegunda. Part one, 1860–1910]. The Sisters listened to the reading with extraordinary interest for well over one hour. At the conclusion of the reading, the Sisters begged Mother M. Antonina to continue on another day since many of them were not actually aware of the congregation's real beginnings and of the numerous people who helped in its initial founding. Because of this interest, Mother M. Antonina and the general council were very eager for the book to be printed and distributed to each Sister.

For the anniversary celebration, Sister M. Donald Urban baked a cake decorating it with figurines of Mother M. Theresa Dudzik, Mother M. Anna Wysinski, and Sister M. Angeline Topolinski. Sister M. Donald's crowning achievement was a miniature sugar representation of the Motherhouse which topped the cake.

At the time of the celebration of the congregation's 45th Anniversary, there were 388 professed Sisters, twenty novices, and thirteen postulants and aspirants.[26]

Before Mother M. Antonina's term of office officially came to an end, an important change which was unprecedented took place in the administration of the congregation. The death of Sister M. Innocenta Antosz had occurred on March 6, 1938. At the Fifth General Chapter she had been elected vicar general and first councilor for a term of six years. In the fourth year of her term, she was stricken with cancer. According to the Constitutions of the congregation, the remaining councilors each stepped up into the next position. Sister M. Innocenta's place as vicar general and first councilor was taken by Sister M. Salomea Grabowski; Sister M. Stephanie Pinkowski became the second councilor; and Sister M. Jerome Dadej became the third councilor. Sister M. Philipine Lama was selected by Mother M. Antonina and the general council to the office of fourth councilor while Sister M. Raphael Bogalecki remained as the procurator general.

A visit by the mayor of Chicago to St. Joseph Home for the Aged occurred in December of 1938. The Honorable Edward J. Kelly[27] visited the home at the invitation of the St. Joseph Home Auxiliary Society who had sponsored their annual Christmas party for the residents. Since this was the mayor's first visit to St. Joseph Home, Mother M. Antonina welcomed him with gracious hospitality:

> Your Honor:
> This institution exists because of the good will offerings of charitable people who are sympathetic toward it. With unshaken faith in God's Will, we expect to maintain ourselves indefinitely. On the occasion of your first visit to our modest institution, I greet you in the name of the Congregation of the Franciscan Sisters, as well as in the name of the elderly placed in our care, with the custom-honored gifts of bread and salt, symbols of Polish hospitality and friendship.[28]

Following another time-honored Polish custom, Mother M. Antonina invited the mayor to partake of the blessed Christmas wafer and cordially exchanged greetings with him. On March 15, 1939, Mayor Kelly wrote to Mother M. Antonina:

> It was indeed a privilege to visit your wonderful Home and I was especially impressed by the happiness and contentment which were so evident among the residents of your institution. After such a visit, one can readily understand why you and your company in the Home have built up such admiration and gratitude for your splendid work on behalf of the aged.
> I wish you all God's blessings and every possible measure of happiness and continued achievement in your glorious work.
> With kindest regards, I am,
>
> Sincerely yours,
> Edward J. Kelly, Mayor[29]

At the conclusion of her term as superior general in 1940, Mother M. Antonina was sent to The Catholic Sisters College in Washington, DC, to serve as the superior at Brady Hall, the house of studies for Sister-students. She remained there until 1946 when she was elected the third councilor during the term of Mother M. Jerome Dadej. During this time she also served as superior and principal at Five Holy Martyrs School. In 1948, she was appointed the superior and administrator of St. John's Hospital in Huron, South Dakota, where she remained until 1952 when she was elected to the office of vicar general to Mother M. Jerome. At the conclusion of her term in 1958 and displaying the energy and desire to be of further service, she was made the superior of Our Lady of the Sandhills Hospital in Atkinson, Nebraska, where she remained until 1962. That year she returned to the Motherhouse in Chicago for the observance of her Diamond Jubilee—a total of sixty years of devoted service in the congregation. After the ceremonies held on July 24, Mother M. Antonina never returned to Atkinson. Instead, she remained at the Motherhouse where, at the age of eighty and sapped of her strength, she still kept busy folding laundry on washdays and helping Sister M. Aloysetta Ciezadlo, the procurator general. The leukemia which finally weakened her was aggravated by an attack of the flu. A hacking cough racked her tiny body day and night. At those times she was heard to say slowly and reverently: "Jesus, Mary, Joseph, I love you. Save souls."[30] Her death was expected.

Mother M. Antonina surprised all the Sisters when in the middle of February, she was up and about and even came to the refectory for her meals on several occasions. Those were to be her final visits with the community for her condition worsened and she was anointed on February 25, 1963. In the early hours of the morning of May 4, the night nurse, Sister M. Ernest Blazonczyk, while making her rounds, summoned Sister M. Venantia Rec, the vicar general, and other Sisters who slept nearby. While the assembled Sisters prayed, Mother M. Antonina died at three-thirty o'clock in the morning. When death came, she had reached the age of eighty-six; sixty-one of these years had been spent in religious life. She had borne "the burden and the heat of the day" in the congregation's pioneer stage and had left to the members of the community a splendid example of holy zeal, abiding faith, and perseverance in good.[31]

The Solemn Requiem Mass on the day of her funeral was celebrated by her cousin, the Reverend Vincent Nowakowski of Evanston. He was assisted by another cousin, the Reverend Stanley Nowakowski of Benson, Michigan, and the Reverend Walter Szczypula of Chicago, a brother to Sister M. Kingnetta of the Franciscan Sisters of Chicago. The Reverend John Mysliwiec, CR, delivered the eulogy. Mother M. Antonina was interred on May 7, 1963, at St. Adalbert's Cemetery. She was laid to rest in the burial site she had requested—between the graves of Mother M. Anna Wysinski and Mother M. Theresa Dudzik.

ST. ANTHONY'S HOME

[1]Sister M. Gonzaga Raniszewski, OSFK, *Echo Avondalskie* [Avondale Echo], July–January 1939–1940 (AFSCL).

[2]Sister M. Genevieve was born in Poland and entered the community from St. John Cantius Church in Chicago on September 7, 1906. She made her perpetual vows on August 15, 1916. She served as a teacher for almost sixteen years, and after a brief illness engaged in domestic activities at such missions as Madonna Hall in Cleveland; Boys Town, Nebraska; Our Lady of Spring Bank Abbey in Wisconsin; and St. Anthony's Home in Crown Point. In 1963, she was transferred to the Motherhouse. Sister M. Genevieve is distinguished by the fact that in 1983 she reached her one-hundredth birthday, the congregation's only member to do so. *Congregation Membership Records;* and *Spis Sióstr* (AFSCL).

[3]"The Founding of St. Anthony's Home for the Aged." Crown Point, Indiana (AFSCL).

[4]Father Hammes is retired and living in Crown Point. He has taken an active role in all the celebrations in connection with St. Anthony Home.

[5]The farmhouse, built in 1912, is rich in historical background. It was built by the Reverend Maurice J. Dorney, first pastor of St. Gabriel's Church in Chicago. He commissioned Joseph McCarthy, a contemporary of Frank Lloyd Wright and an architect of some prominence, to design the house for Johanna and Michael Williams, Father Dorney's sister and brother-in-law, as a vacation home. Joseph McCarthy had also graduated from St. Gabriel's High School built by Father Dorney in 1901. Father Dorney was also a close friend of Will J. Davis who owned the Iroquois Theater in Chicago, and had purchased land adjacent to the Williams' site. The adopted daughter of Will J. Davis is the well-known Crown Point family physician, Dr. Mary Davis Carroll, who was the first medical director of the new St. Anthony Home. (It might be recalled here that the Iroquois Theater in Chicago achieved its inglorious fame during a fire in 1903, when 588 people died in less than half-an-hour during a gala Christmas holiday matinee performance.)

When the Williams' home was being built, Father Dorney is quoted as saying: "A religious is building this house and I hope that religious would live here in the future." For twenty-seven years, Father Dorney's wish was a fact when the needs of the aged of Crown Point and nearby areas were met in a spirit of love and compassion by the Franciscan Sisters serving them in the venerable white house known as St. Anthony's Home. Sister M. Gonzaga Raniszewski, OSFK, *Echo Avondalskie* [Avondale Echo], June–July 1939–1940 (AFSCL).

[6]Fancher Lake emerges historically as a landmark known to the Pottawatomie Indians. Timothy Ball's *History of Lake County* states that sick Indians were restored to good health in Crown Point. The founder of Crown Point, Solon Robinson, was informed by the Indians themselves that many of them were brought to Crown Point "to be benefited and cured." Clean air, rest, and the waters of Fancher Lake were the necessary ingredients for a return of good health. The Williams' farm, it is said, was crossed by several Indian trails and a number of early pioneer roadways are believed to have formed the five-point intersection now bordering the property on two sides. Originally, the acreage was presumed to be part of an extensive federal land grant given in 1832 to a female Pottawatomie half-chief. The Williams' home, the original St. Anthony's Home, is being nominated for listing in the National Registry for Historical Places. Dolores Fetcko, "St. Anthony Vital Part of Area History," *Northwest Indiana Post-Tribune,* 26 July 1981.

[7]Fetcko, 26 July 1981.

[8]*Minutes of General Council Proceedings, 1934–1957* (AFSCL).

[9]Sister M. Sigfrieda was one of the Sisters who came to Crown Point in 1939 to staff the nursing home as the receptionist and remained until her death on January 26, 1975. *Congregation Membership Records;* and *Spis Sióstr* (AFSCL).

[10]Several Sisters rendered long terms of service to St. Anthony Home. Among them are Sister M. Sigfrieda Scensny, thirty-six years; Sister M. Cherubim Madaj, thirty years; and her sister,

Sister M. Ottilia Madaj, sixteen years. *Congregation Membership Records* (AFSCL).

[11] "The Founding of St. Anthony's Home."

[12]Siostra M. Gonzaga Raniszewski, OSFK, *Zarys Połwiecza Zgromadzenia Sióstr Franciszkanek Bł. Kunegundy* [Sketch of the fifty-year history of the Congregation of the Franciscan Sisters of Bl. Kunegunda] (Chicago: By the Author, 1944), p. 83.

[13]The Honorable Vincent Youche served as mayor of Crown Point from January 1930 to December 1946.

[14] "The Founding of St. Anthony's Home."

[15]Ibid.

[16]*Minutes of General Council Proceedings,* 8 October 1941 (AFSCL).

[17]Sister M. Marcelline, born in Poland, entered from St. John Cantius Church in Chicago on December 7, 1906, and made her perpetual vows on July 17, 1917. She served as a teacher in various parishes for seven years and later attended to household duties both at the Motherhouse and at Five Holy Martyrs Convent. From 1930 to 1934, she collected alms for the community in Gary while based at the Motherhouse. She was fifty-four years old and had been in the congregation for thirty-six years when she died. *Spis Sióstr* (AFSCL).

[18]"Brief Report" received from Sister Frances Szczur (AFSCL).

[19]*Minutes of General Council Proceedings, 1934–1957* (AFSCL).

[20]Ibid.

[21]The Most Reverend Andrew G. Grutka, bishop of Gary, born in Joliet, Illinois, was ordained in Rome on December 5, 1933. After serving as a pastor in several parishes in Indiana, he was chosen as the first bishop of the newly created Diocese of Gary in 1956. Bishop Grutka attended all four sessions of the Second Vatican Council. He has long been an advocate of world peace, youth, and is renowned for his denunciation of racial discrimination. Biographical sketch received from Chancery Office, Diocese of Gary.

[22]Secretaries General, *Community Chronicle, 1957–1975* (AFSCL).

[23]Ibid.

[24]Sister M. Cherubim Madaj was born on Chicago's Northwest Side on May 6, 1897. She entered the congregation from St. Stanislaus Bishop and Martyr Church in Chicago on December 8, 1915, and made her perpetual vows on July 27, 1924. For twenty-two years she was stationed at Five Holy Martyrs as a teacher and later, as a household Sister. In 1942, she was sent to St. Anthony's Home. She remained for thirty years and died there on February 29, 1972. She was seventy-five years old and had been in the congregation for fifty-seven years. Sister M. Cherubim had three blood Sisters in the congregation: Sister M. Ottilia, Sister M. Theodore, and Sister M. Celine, all now deceased. *Congregation Membership Records;* and *Spis Sióstr* (AFSCL).

[25]*St. Anthony's Home Journal* (AFSCL).

[26]*Minutes of General Council Proceedings, 1949* (AFSCL).

[27]The Honorable Edward J. Kelly was born in Chicago on May 1, 1876. He was appointed mayor of Chicago in 1933 to fill the unexpired term of Mayor Anton J. Cermak who had been assassinated. Mayor Kelly was elected to office in 1935 and re-elected in 1939 and 1943.

[28]Siostra M. Gonzaga Raniszewski, OSFK, "Rys historyczny Zgromadzenia Sióstr Franciszkanek Bł. Kunegundy. Część druga, 1910–1940' [A historical survey of the Franciscan Sisters of Blessed Kunegunda. Part two, 1910–1940] Typewritten, unpublished manuscript (AFSCL), p. 230.

[29]*Book of Correspondence:* Letter from the Honorable Edward J. Kelly to Mother M. Antonina Osinski, 15 March 1939 (AFSCL).

[30]*Interviews* with Sisters, September 1983 (AFSCL).

[31]Ibid.

[32]*Book of Depositions* (AFSCL).

CHAPTER 41

The Franciscan Sisters in North Dakota

Only one school was accepted during the tenure of office of Mother M. Antonina. North Dakota, "The Gateway to Canada and the Heart of the Old West," welcomed the Franciscan Sisters of Chicago in 1939. In April of that year, the Reverend Felix Andrzejkiewicz,[1] pastor of St. Mary's Church in South Heart, ten miles from the larger town of Dickinson, North Dakota, wrote to Mother M. Antonina requesting Sisters to staff the South Heart Public School. Prior to his request, the Sisters had already been active at St. Mary's Church in South Heart where they had conducted catechism classes in the summer from 1936 to 1938.[2]

On April 27, 1939, Father Andrzejkiewicz happily announced to Mother M. Antonina:

> Reverend and dear Mother General:
>
> It gives me great pleasure to announce sad and joyful news. Sad because I will not be able to have the Sisters teach catechism during the summer vacation . . . Now for the good news. It took a lot of convincing, but finally the school board has decided to get Sisters to teach in our public school. I spoke to Reverend Mother concerning this matter some three years ago, and at that time I received an assurance that you would be able to supply three qualified Sisters for the grades, one for the high school, and one to do the housework. I am hoping that this offer still holds good. So far, I have assured the school board that I am able to get qualified Sisters who will meet every demand of the State. Reverend Mother, you cannot disappoint me now. I have also assured the Board that I can get the Sisters to teach for thirty dollars a month in the grades and sixty dollars in the high school (for nine months of the year only). That is the salary of all Sisters teaching in schools in this vicinity, so I took for granted that that would also be the salary of our Sisters. Another reason is that that was the most convincing argument. All schools out

here are in a very bad shape due to the constant droughts, and if there is any way that a school can be run cheaper, they want it. The schools are operated with money from the taxpayers, but no one, or at least very few, have been paying their taxes in the last years. The South Heart School is fortunate, however, in receiving a certain amount of utility tax from the railroad, power, light, sales tax, etc.

It is also understood that the school board will buy and furnish suitable quarters. In time, when we get some kind of a crop, then, perhaps, they can somewhat raise the salaries.

This whole business has gone only as far as the school board. What we must do next is call a meeting of all taxpayers in this district and take a vote on it. Therefore, I'd like to have Reverend Mother write me a positive letter that I can read to the public at this meeting, stating that you will supply the Sisters, their qualifications, and that the salary will be satisfactory. We'll meet the opposition and we must be ready for it, but the community is so predominently Catholic (about 98%) that we shouldn't have much trouble.

After this meeting, which will be held in about a week or ten days when the farmers are all through working, I would like to have Reverend Mother come out here and make definite arrangements.[3]

In May of 1939, Mother M. Antonina replied affirmatively to Father Andrzejkiewicz's request. A month later, she wrote to the Right Reverend Monsignor John Mielcarek, the vicar general for the women religious of the Archdiocese of Chicago, informing him of her proposed plans and asking him for permission to accept the school.[4] A month later, a letter addressed to Monsignor Mielcarek from the Right Reverend Monsignor George Casey, chancellor of the Archdiocese of Chicago, resolved the issue:

I am returning herewith the letter addressed to the Mother Superior of the Franciscan Sisters of St. Kunegunda. His Eminence[5] was loath to put his stamp of approval on the idea of Catholic nuns teaching in public schools. However, His Eminence realizes that there may be conditions existing in North Dakota of which he is not cognizant. Therefore, His Eminence suggests that the matter be referred to the bishop of the diocese there, and whatever the bishop decides to do will be satisfactory to His Eminence.[6]

Assured that the Sisters were coming to North Dakota, Father Andrzejkiewicz wrote to Mother M. Antonina informing her of the particular qualifications required of the Sisters. The county superintendent had specified a bachelor's degree for the high school teacher, and a standard certificate, that is, at least two years of college for the grade school teachers. The certificates would have to be obtained in the state of North Dakota which

South Heart Public School
South Heart, North Dakota (1939–1941)

meant that the Sisters would have to fill out applications and present their credits. Father Andrzejkiewicz contended that much unnecessary formality and a little red tape were connected with obtaining the certificates, but in the end, everything would certainly be satisfactory.[7]

In June of 1939, Mother M. Antonina herself went to South Heart to determine the particular circumstances of the Sisters' apostolate there. South Heart, so-called because of its location south of the Heart River, was a straggling farm region ten miles from Dickinson, a large town of six thousand residents. South Heart District School Number Nine was a public school with eight grades and a secondary division. North Dakota permitted religious Sisters to teach in public schools provided that they would not interfere with the regular public school curriculum. Religion was not taught during regular school hours, but there was nothing to prevent the Sisters from teaching it for a half-hour before or after school. Since parishes were not able to have parochial schools, the next best thing was to have the Sisters teach in the public schools. Father Andrzejkiewicz was to serve as the principal.[8] The bishop of Bismarck, the Most Reverend Vincent Wehrle, OSB, was most pleased that the Sisters had accepted the invitation to come to North Dakota.[9]

During Mother M. Antonina's visit, a home for the Sisters was selected. In July of 1939, Father Andrzejkiewicz informed the Sisters that the house purchased for them was "practically the prettiest in the whole town," and was ready to receive them.[10] He did ask, however, that the Sisters furnish their own towels, bed sheets, pillowcases, and woolen blankets for North Dakota's vigorous winters for at least the initial year. Father Andrzejkiewicz and C. J. Perdaems, the president of the school board, had already spent

$500 for furniture and furnishings, and, at this point, could not afford to spend any more.[11]

Father Andrzejkiewicz wrote to Mother M. Antonina in the latter part of July, offering her some "last minute" reassurance:

Reverend and dear Mother:

From all appearances it seems that your trip to North Dakota was not in vain. I hope that you have acquired the rest that was so necessary for you after a year of hard work. Furthermore, we can all relax a little because everything came out just the way we planned it. Everything is all fixed and you can start making definite arrangements.

The Thursday after your departure, the school board held its meeting at which I was also present. Everything was considered and reconsidered and it all pointed towards one thing; namely, to buy Becker's house. Finally, at 11:30 p.m., a motion was made, seconded and carried. There was a little opposition on the part of one of the taxpayers who is also the county commissioner, but this was all due to a misunderstanding. After it was all explained to him then the matter was settled. I didn't dare to write any sooner until the whole deal was closed, because otherwise anybody could start a campaign against it although it would be of no avail because the school board was acting in its capacity.

South Heart Public School Convent
South Heart, North Dakota

Our main difficulty was, that in order for us to buy Mr. Becker's house and get a loan on it, he had to buy that bank building, which he was good enough to do. As the deal stands now, the Sisters will have to be here at least five years because otherwise the district would lose money. So there is no fear that the Sisters will only be here a year or two. I'm sure it will be permanent unless the community should become non-Catholic in its majority which is almost impossible.

Most sincerely yours in Christ,
Felix J. Andrzejkiewicz[12]

On September 1, 1939, South Heart Public School opened classes on the elementary school level and on the secondary level with the following staff: Sister M. Bogumila Swiech, superior of the convent and teacher of grades 9 through 12 with twenty-eight students; Sister M. Hildegarde Demps, fifteen pupils in grades 7 and 8 and teacher of Algebra I; Sister M. Remigia Lewandowski, with twenty-eight students in grades 5 and 6 and the church organist; and Sister M. Doloretta Radzienda, grades 1 through 3 with thirty-one students and two classes of typing in the secondary division. Sister M. Assumptiana Rosinski was sent to manage the household.[13] To get to the school, the Sisters had to travel by bus.[14] The Sisters, North Dakota's newest residents, sent a spirited letter to Mother M. Antonina which was printed in the *Echo Avondalskie* [Avondale Echo], the congregation's bulletin:

The highlight of North Dakota's bleak beauty lies in its skies and its cloud formations. Indeed, one has to acknowledge the hand of God in creation and his majesty is reflected in North Dakota's stark nature.

South Heart is a small place. We live a block away from the church which is truly pretty, surrounded as it is by small trees and pretty flowers. There is a cemetery near the church, a rectory, a restaurant, a post office, a grocery store, two other homes, and another store. There are a few homes near us. This is the town of South Heart!

We have a wide view from our house and it is easy to see the farmers' homes in the distance as well as our school since it stands on a hill. It is the only brick building in South Heart and has a side wall made of scoria, a loose, red-burned coal like cinder which is found in great abundance in South Heart. The school is about fifteen minutes away from our home if you travel on foot. It is surrounded by beautiful trees.

We have ninety-seven children in the elementary and high school divisions. Father Andzrejkiewicz is our principal and teaches three subjects in the high school. The children are of various nationalities, especially Czech and Dutch. There are hardly any Poles. Almost all are Catholic. We teach religion every day from 8:30 a.m. to 9:00 a.m. We teach until 3:45 p.m. daily. We teach so long because we end the school year in May. It is too far to go home for lunch so we eat in school. The janitor maintains the school; we have nothing to do with its cleaning. We do not ask for tuition because the check arrives regularly the first of every month—these are the advantages of teaching in public school!

The children are good. They are real farmers. It is funny to hear their excuses for being late, for example: "I had to husk the corn"; "I had to milk the cows"; "Our pigs ran away and I had to chase after them."

We feel this is real mission work—we need not go to China or Africa. The people are poor, but good-hearted. They often bring us sausage and marinated pork, etc. For Christmas, we had so much meat we could not eat everything.[15]

So successfully did the first school year progress that at its conclusion, Mother M. Antonina received the following letter from G. J. Perdaems, president of the South Heart School Board:

Dear Reverend Mother General:

Now that the early summer work is over, I have time to write you a few words thanking you for past favors.

We have been most pleased with the Franciscan Sisters we have had in our school during the past year and the benefits derived by the children . . . We are proud of the growing boys and girls, who all, without exception, liked the Sisters very much.

In the name of all the parents of this community, I with to thank you for giving us the splendid Sisters and we hope to have them back again in the fall.

Sincerely yours,
G. J. Perdaems, President
South Heart School Board[16]

With the arrival of the 1940–1941 school year, there were 104 children in the elementary school and twenty-eight students in the secondary division. Sister M. Bogumila returned as the superior and secondary school teacher. Sister M. Hildegarde and Sister M. Doloretta were also reassigned to South Heart. Sister M. Bernadette Uzdrowski was sent as the organist and household manager. In December, however, she was replaced by Sister M. Honorata Makowski.[17] Sister M. Remigia was not reassigned to South Heart that year and Sister M. Fabian Owczarzak was sent in her place. Quite unexpectedly, Sister M. Fabian was changed in December of that year and replaced by Sister M. Edmunda Siernicki. All these changes in Sister personnel had serious repercussions insofar as they displeased Father Andrzejkiewicz.[18] He was even more agitated when in February of 1941, Sister M. Bogumila was hospitalized, and Mother M. Mechtilde Zynda, who had replaced Mother M. Antonina Osinski as the superior general in 1940, informed him that she was unable to send a replacement for Sister M. Bogumila. In this emergency, Mother M.

Mechtilde sent a letter to Father Andrzejkiewicz offering a solution:

> Reverend and dear Father:
>
> I regret this very much, but it is impossible for me to send a Sister to teach high school. In an emergency like this, I can only suggest that you secure a lay teacher, either a grade or high school teacher if Sister Hildegarde cannot handle the high school subjects herself.
>
> May I mention here, that I believe it would be to our mutual advantage for you to do everything possible to secure teachers from a local Community of Sisters, who, perhaps would not experience a difficulty in supplying teachers when they are demanded.
>
> We wired our answer to your telegram. Please secure a lay teacher until such time as Sister Bogumila will be able to resume her duties. When she leaves the hospital, she will take this matter up with you, and I am certain some definite arrangements can be made.
>
> Again, may I please request your kind cooperation in the matter? With kindest respects, I am,
>
> Respectfully yours in Christ,
> Mother M. Mechtilde[19]

Father Andrzejkiewicz's reply foreshadowed the beginning of the end of the congregation's apostolate in North Dakota. Hurt and angry, he accused Mother M. Mechtilde of not consulting him in regard to any decision to leave South Heart. In response to Mother M. Mechtilde's advice to seek a local community to take over South Heart Public School, Father Andrzejkiewicz wrote in part:

> . . . I don't know in what proportion you are using the word "local." If you mean the state of North Dakota, then I must inform you that we have no Religious Community within the state, either large enough or established to meet the requirements of the State Board of Education.
>
> I might mention also that I had a definite purpose in getting your Sisters to North Dakota. I knew Mother M. Antonina and many other Sisters and *we* thought it would be quite an asset to the Order if they got another mission. I still think that it is, because what else can the Sisters in South Heart ask for?
>
> I don't know, nor can I figure out what advantage you will have by not supplying the Sisters for South Heart. As for my mutual advantage, I can't see any. In the first place, I was instrumental in getting Sisters to teach, mind you, in a public school. It wasn't easy; we had to fight opposition. The community has spent a lot of money providing adequate living accommodations; it is making supreme efforts to keep the Sisters here. They appreciate the work the Sisters are doing, realizing that if not

for the Sisters, we would be left without a high school and only two lay teachers in the grades due to the poor conditions in the state. All this was done because of an assurance that the Sisters would stay at least five years or longer. It was a condition whereby Mother M. Antonina agreed to send the Sisters. At that time, no one gave a thought to the fact that a priest and Sisters must make a written contract in order to have it binding.[20]

In conclusion, let me add the following: give me a definite reason, based on the verbal agreement that we made, why you don't want to send Sisters to South Heart next year. I will present it to the bishop of Bismarck and if he approves of it and tells me to look for some other Order to take your place, I will do so. If not, then you will have to take the matter up with him. Remember, all we are asking for is five good Sisters. Just give us that and you won't have to worry about them for nine months of the year. We had no trouble whatsoever last year, and there is no reason why we should in the future.

Kindly give this letter your serious reconsideration.

Father Andrzejkiewicz[21]

Mother M. Mechtilde answered quickly but remained unswerving in her decision. She regretted that Father Andrzejkiewicz had misunderstood the tone of her letter, but she was adamant in maintaining that the Sisters would be removed from the school. She cited the lack of Sister personnel and especially, the lack of qualified teachers at that time who were available to teach in a public school. In her conscience, she could not countenance sending a Sister who was not academically prepared. Another valid reason was the fact that an ex-member of the congregation who took up residence in South Heart after her dispensation was creating a misunderstanding and maintaining an adverse effect among the Sisters. As early as 1939, when Mother M. Antonina had learned of the situation concerning the ex-member's presence in South Heart, Mother M. Antonina had informed Father Andrzejkiewicz that she did not approve of it and was convinced that "it would cause misunderstanding in the future."[22] Eventually, Mother M. Antonina's worst fears were realized and the ex-member in question disrupted the peace and harmony of the South Heart School mission.[23] Mother M. Mechtilde, meanwhile, continued steadfastly to maintain that she had no qualified Sisters available for the South Heart mission and termed the decision to withdraw from the school "unfortunate but necessary."[24] Before the Sisters left South Heart for good, Mother M. Mechtilde sent a letter to the president of the South Heart Public School Board:

Dear Mr. Perdaems:

It is with much regret that I am compelled to inform you that our community of Sisters will not be with you next fall. While we appreciate all the kindness and courtesies shown the Sisters, we have found it very difficult to supply the teachers, and also it is inconvenient on account of the great distance from our Motherhouse.

I suppose Reverend Father Andrzejkiewicz has taken this matter up with you, for I understand he has secured a different community of Sisters to take over the school. This being the case, the children will not be deprived of the good influence of a Catholic school.

Please be assured that nothing on the part of the good people and children of South Heart has influenced us in this matter. We are sincerely grateful for the kind attention the Sisters have received during their brief stay with you. I am positive that the members of the school board and the community have left nothing undone to make them happy and comfortable, and in return, the Sisters will bring home very pleasant memories of your hospitality and thoughtful attentions.

With best wishes and the grateful prayers of our congregation for your continued temporal and spiritual success, I am,

Respectfully yours,

M. M. Mechtilde Zynda[25]

Even before the Franciscan Sisters of Chicago left South Heart on June 30, 1941, Father Andrzejkiewicz had set about securing another religious congregation to staff the school. He succeeded in obtaining the Sisters of the Congregation of the Holy Family of Nazareth. The Sisters served the community of South Heart for eighteen years. In 1948, however, the state legislature of North Dakota, influenced by the strong anti-Catholic sentiments of its members, enacted the North Dakota Anti-garb Act.[26] This drastic legislation was directed at the Sisters teaching in the public schools of North Dakota. It required the Sisters to wear a secular outfit while teaching instead of the religious habit. The Sisters of the Holy Family, desiring that the mission of South Heart not be lost to the Church, met the Anti-garb Act agitation by changing into secular dress for classes and wearing the religious garb in the convent.[27] After ten years, when the Anti-garb Act was not repealed, the Sisters informed the Most Reverend Hilary Hacker, bishop of Bismarck, of their desire to relinquish the South Heart Public School. The huge volume of correspondence that passed between the administration of the Sisters of the Holy Family of Nazareth and the school and governmental bodies of the state of North Dakota indicates that the Sisters' withdrawal from South Heart was a slow and painful process which actually took fifteen years.[28]

THE FRANCISCAN SISTERS IN NORTH DAKOTA

[1]The Reverend Felix Andrzejkiewicz, who later changed his name officially to the Reverend Felix Andrews, served the Diocese of Bismarck at St. Mary's Church in South Heart, North Dakota, from June 1937 to May 1944. A native Chicagoan, Father Andrews was ordained to the priesthood in 1935 for the Diocese of Bismarck. After he left St. Mary's Church in South Heart he became a chaplain in the United States Army from 1944 to 1946 and again from 1951 to 1954. He was later pastor of several small churches in North Dakota. Finally, he was pastor of Little Flower Church in Minot, North Dakota from 1954 until 1974 at which time he retired. *Book of Correspondence:* Report from the Diocese of Bismarck to author 15 January 1976 (AFSCL).

[2]In 1937, Sister M. Philomena Wasik, Sister M. Louise Nowicki, and Sister M. Aloysetta Ciezadlo were assigned to teach catechism in South Heart. Sister M. Louise and Sister M. Philomena returned in 1938 for three weeks. Two additional weeks were spent in Amidon, North Dakota and one week in Medora, North Dakota. In 1947, Sister M. Louise and Sister M. Aloysetta returned to South Heart to teach catechism for several weeks. *Book of Annual Assignments* (AFSCL).

[3]*Book of Correspondence:* Letter from the Reverend Felix Andrzejkiewicz to Mother M. Antonina Osinski, 27 April 1939 (AFSCL).

[4]*Book of Correspondence:* Letter from Mother M. Antonina Osinski to the Right Reverend Monsignor John Mielcarek, 14 June 1939 (AFSCL).

[5]Monsignor Casey is referring here to George Cardinal Mundelein, the archbishop of Chicago.

[6]*Book of Correspondence:* Letter from the Right Reverend Monsignor George Casey to the Right Reverend Monsignor John Mielcarek, 27 June 1939 (AFSCL).

[7]*Book of Correspondence:* Letter from the Reverend Felix Andrzejkiewicz to Mother M. Antonina Osinski, 13 June 1939 (AFSCL).

[8]*Book of Correspondence:* Letter from the Reverend Felix Andrzejkiewicz to Mother M. Antonina Osinski, 22 June 1939 (AFSCL).

[9]*Book of Correspondence:* Letter from the Most Reverend Vincent Wehrle, OSB, to Mother M. Antonina Osinski, c. 1939 (AFSCL).

[10]*Minutes of General Council Proceedings,* 1934–1956 (AFSCL).

[11]*Book of Correspondence:* Letter from the Reverend Felix Andrzejkiewicz to Mother M. Antonina Osinski, 14 August 1939 (AFSCL).

[12]*Book of Correspndence:* Letter from the Reverend Felix Andrzejkiewicz to Mother M. Antonina Osinski, 26 July 1939 (AFSCL).

[13]Sister M. Assumptiana Rosinski left the congregation on April 19, 1941, dispensed from her religious vows. In her eleven years in the congregation, she had been stationed at nine different missions. After she left South Heart in 1940, she was sent to St. Adalbert's School in East St. Louis, Illinois, which she left without finishing the school year. *Spis Sióstr* (AFSCL).

[14]*Book of Correspondence:* Letter from Mr. Peter Kuntz to author, 7 June 1976 (AFSCL).

[15]*Echo Avondalskie* [Avondale Echo] July–January 1939–1941 (AFSCL).

[16]*Book of Correspondence:* Letter from Mr. G. J. Perdaems to Mother M. Antonina Osinski, 1 July 1940 (AFSCL).

[17]Sister M. Bernadette Uzdrowski returned to the Motherhouse and was dispensed from her religious vows on 5 June 1941. *Book of Departures* (AFSCL).

[18]*Book of Correspondence:* Letter from Mother M. Mechtilde Zynda to the Reverend Felix Andrzejkiewicz, 11 March 1941 (AFSCL).

[19]*Book of Correspondence:* Letter from Mother M. Mechtilde Zynda to the Reverend Felix Andrzejkiewicz, 7 February 1941 (AFSCL).

[20]While it is true that no contracts existed between the Sisters and the pastors in the schools undertaken by the congregation, a written contract did exist, for example, between the Falls City, Texas, Catholic Congregation of Holy Trinity and the Franciscan Sisters of St. Kunegunda in Chicago as early as 1911. See Chapter 22.

[21]*Book of Correspondence:* Letter from the Reverend Felix Andrzejkiewicz to Mother M. Mechtilde Zynda, 26 February 1941 (AFSCL).

[22]*Book of Correspondence:* Letter from Mother M. Antonina Osinski to the Reverend Felix Andrzejkiewicz, 11 August 1939 (AFSCL).

[23]The ex-member of the congregation responsible for most of the misunderstanding at the mission was neither Sister M. Assumptiana nor Sister M. Bernadette, but a third member who had left the congregation in 1938. She had actually never been stationed at South Heart during her years in the congregation, but she did take up residence there after she was dispensed from her vows.

[24]*Book of Correspondence:* Letter from Mother M. Mechtilde Zynda to the Reverend Felix Andrzejkiewicz, 11 March 1941 (AFSCL).

[25]*Book of Correspondence:* Letter from Mother M. Mechtilde Zynda to Mr. C. J. Perdaems, 26 May 1941 (AFSCL).

[26]The anti-garb agitation in North Dakota, stirred up particularly by a group called "Protestants and Other Americans United for the Separation of Church and State," was part of a nationwide attack to arrest the progress of the Catholic Church and to hamper it in its work. The group had as its aim to drive the Catholic Sisters out of public schools. The general idea prevailed that the religious habit worn by a Sister teaching in a public school was a sign of religious witness and therefore, a violation of the strict nonsectarian education required by the Constitution. It is to the credit of the Most Reverend Vincent J. Ryan, bishop of Bismarck, that he met the action by having the Sisters remove their religious habits and change into secular clothes in order to continue teaching in the public school. When, however, this legislation proved to be of longer duration than anticipated, the Sisters chose to withdraw from the school. Correspondence between the administration of the Sisters of the Holy Family of Nazareth and the school and governmental bodies of the state of North Dakota (copies in AFSCL); and Sister M. De Chantal, CSFN, *Out of Nazareth, A Centenary of the Sisters of the Holy Family of Nazareth in the Service of the Church* (New York: Exposition Press, Inc., 1974), p. 244.

[27]De Chantal, p. 244.

[28]*Book of Correspondence:* Letter from Sister Rose Marie Michalski, CSFN, to author, December 1975 (AFSCL).

CHAPTER 42

The Sixth General Chapter:
Mother M. Mechtilde Zynda

The tenure of office of Mother M. Mechtilde occurred during a grave time in our country's history. A surprise attack by the Japanese on the American naval base at Pearl Harbor in the Hawaiian Islands took place on December 7, 1941. The sudden destruction of the military units in the fleet and the naval base plunged the United States into a state of hostility when on December 8, Congress declared war with Japan. On December 11, 1941, Germany and Italy declared war on the United States. Thus, the war in the Pacific and the war in Europe merged into a global holocaust destined to last until 1946. The war had its inevitable effect on the congregation especially regarding its membership and its expansion of pressing apostolic works.

The Sixth General Chapter of Elections was held in 1940 from June 29 to July 7. On July 2, at six-thirty o'clock in the morning, a mass was offered by the Reverend Joseph Baniewicz, CR, the chaplain of St. Joseph Home for the Aged, for the intention of the delegates to the general chapter. At ten o'clock in the morning after the singing of "Veni, Creator" in the chapel, the thirty-six delegates[1] walked in procession to the room where the voting for the superior general and her council was to take place. The Right Reverend Monsignor James J. Strzycki presided during this election as a representative of the Most Reverend Samuel Stritch, archbishop of Chicago.

In the first balloting, Sister M. Mechtilde Zynda was elected the superior general by majority vote. The other members of the general council elected that day were Sister M. Jerome Dadej, vicar general and first councilor; Sister M. Philipine Lama, second councilor; Sister M. Paul Kirschbaum, third councilor and secretary general; Sister M. John Barczak, fourth councilor; and Sister M. Raphael Bogalecki, procurator general. Because Sister M. John was not a delegate, she was summoned to the chapter immediately thereby raising the number of delegates to thirty-seven.[2]

Mother M. Mechtilde, the daughter of Leo and Mary (née Jaske) Zynda,[3] was born Hedwig Zynda on November 19, 1889, in Berent, West Prussia. She came to the United

States in July of 1905 with the intention of joining the small Franciscan community which her cousin, Mother M. Anna Wysinski, had helped establish.[4] Mother Mechtilde entered from St. Stanislaus Kostka Church in Chicago on October 3, 1906, was invested with the habit on August 14, 1907, and a year later, on August 15, 1908, professed her first vows. Her perpetual vows were pronounced on August 15, 1916.[5]

After her first profession of vows in 1908, Sister M. Mechtilde was sent to St. Casimir's School in Cleveland where she remained until 1912. She returned to the Motherhouse that year and was assigned to the Church Vestment Workshop where she worked until 1926. That year, she was transferred to Our Lady of Victory Convent in Lemont where from 1927 to 1928 she served as the superior. At the expiration of her term, she was engaged in various duties at Our Lady of Victory Convent.[6]

Prior to her election as superior general, Mother M. Mechtilde had served as the mistress of novices from 1934 to 1940. Her maternal love, her understanding of young people, her solicitous and kind nature together with her solid spirituality aided her in the difficult task of forming the hearts and minds of the novices in the spirit of St. Francis of Assisi whom she dearly loved. Sister M. Mechtilde knew how to blend firmness with gentleness. She corrected the novices at the right time and in the right place with the mildness, serenity, and gentleness which were a part of her genuine character. Her judgment regarding the dismissal of unsuitable candidates was free from prejudice and suspicion. She exerted no favoritism toward the novices but was considerate and understanding toward all. One of her unfailing characteristics was her love of the congregation, a trait she attempted to instill in her novices. Possessed of a truly compassionate nature, she was always especially kind and considerate towards the Sisters who were ill. Her ideal of combining a deep prayer life with apostolic action taught her spiritual daughters to cling to God in mind and heart while spreading the kingdom of God. Unfailing in her sincerity and amiability, she showed these endearing characteristics first of all to her novices, then to the entire congregation when she was elected its superior general.[7]

Mother M. Mechtilde, the congregation's fifth superior general, was in person much like her photographs depict her. Tall and slender, she had a kind and pleasant face with penetrating eyes and a very enchanting smile. She radiated a personal calm giving her a degree of poise and serenity which manifested itself throughout her life. At first glance, she might have appeared austere. To have known her, however, was to have known a woman who was gentle, joyful, compassionate, and prayerful.[8]

As attested to by her former novices, Mother M. Mechtilde was a rather remarkable woman. A highly intelligent person, she read profusely and was able to quote many religious authors. She kept herself aware of city, national, and world affairs. A lover of nature, she could readily identify all trees, shrubs, and plants growing near Our Lady of Victory Convent in Woodland Park in Lemont. Mother M. Mechtilde was meticulous in caring about the orchards, fruit trees, and the birds, making her indeed, a Franciscan forerunner of the ecologist of today.

Attracted by all things beautiful, Mother M. Mechtilde had a deep appreciation of the fine arts. She had studied painting with the well-known artist, Sister Stanisia, SSND,[9] and ever after retained a delicate sense of color and line. She made a valuable contribution to the Church Vestment Workshop by designing, painting, and embroidering vestments, banners, altar linens, and religious pictures.

As the superior general, Mother M. Mechtilde exerted every effort to foster a deep spirituality in the membership. Because she had a deep reverence for and devotion to the Holy Eucharist, she encouraged Night Adoration of the Blessed Sacrament during her administration. Night Adoration was held for the first time in the Motherhouse on Holy Thursday in April of 1943. A few weeks later, on May 6, the entire congregation was accepted into the Society of Night Adoration as a means of reparation to the Sacred Heart, to beg for world peace, and to ask for an increase of vocations to the congregation:[10] This devotion was spread by the Reverend Mateo Crawley-Boevey, SSCC, the apostle of the Sacred Heart who furthered the cause of the Enthronement of the Sacred Heart.[11] During the congregation's Golden Jubilee Year celebrated in 1944, Mother M. Mechtilde initiated daily adoration before the Blessed Sacrament at the Motherhouse from eight o'clock in the morning until six o'clock in the evening.

The Blessed Virgin Mary was also beloved by Mother M. Mechtilde. When as a novice mistress she would accompany the novices on their daily trek from Our Lady of Victory Convent to the novitiate house, she would most enthusiastically enjoin them: "Come, let us sing to the Mother of God!"[12] Out of her great devotion to the Blessed Virgin Mary, she aided Sister M. Brunona Swagiel in building the Lourdes grotto on the grounds of Our Lady of Victory Convent in Lemont.

During her administration, Mother M. Mechtilde was highly supportive of all the Sisters' efforts in the area of education. There were 129 Sisters studying at De Paul University, Loyola University, the University of Illinois, The Catholic University of America, Alverno College of Music in Milwaukee, Gregg Business College, the Chicago Art Institute, and Duquesne University. There were twenty-nine part-time and nine full-time Sisters attending the Sisters College in Cleveland. Five Sisters were enrolled at St. Joseph's Hospital Training School in Joliet. In 1945 alone, there were sixty-one Sisters taking courses during the school year while more than sixty-seven Sisters were enrolled in summer school at various colleges and universities.[13]

As inspiring as she was in devoting her spiritual and physical energies to the advancement of the congregation, Mother M. Mechtilde appears to have been remiss in two areas. Firstly, there are indications that in many instances she depended too much upon the advice of her council members thereby abdicating some of her power and influence. One of the councilors who appears consistently as having affected Mother M. Mechtilde's decisions, sometimes adversely for the congregation, was Sister M. Paul Kirschbaum, her enterprising secretary general and first councilor. Secondly, during her tenure of office she did little or nothing to encourage the recognition of Mother M. Theresa Dudzik as foundress of the congregation preferring instead to present Mother M.

Anna Wysinski as foundress whenever the opportunity arose.[14]

At the Sixth General Chapter, the Sister elected to the general council for the first time was Sister M. Paul, the former Maryann Kirschbaum, who became the third councilor and secretary general. Born in Chicago on February 22, 1883 she entered the community from St. Michael's Church in South Chicago on November 21, 1909, after having studied at a business college and having worked in a business office for a time. She was received into the novitiate on July 16, 1910, and made her final profession on August 15, 1919.[15]

Sister M. Paul had a varied background in the congregation. At first she taught in schools staffed by the congregation in Texas, Ohio, and Illinois. From 1921 to 1922, she was a day student at The Catholic Sisters College of The Catholic University in Washington, DC. For the next several years, she served as a superior, teacher, and organist at schools in Ohio, Pennsylvania, Indiana, and Illinois. From 1934 to 1935, she served as superior at the Motherhouse. From 1935 to 1938, she was in nurses' training at St. Mary's Hospital in St. Louis where she received her nursing certificate.[16] She also received a bachelor's degree from De Paul University.

The Sisters have characterized Sister M. Paul as talented and inventive. She was a fine nurse, an excellent stenographer, a dynamic teacher, and a good musician. A very intelligent woman, she was well spoken and well versed in writing. Self-assured and strong-willed, with vision and perception, Sister M. Paul was a person who used her spiritual and material gifts for the honor and glory of God and the good of the congregation.[17]

It was also necessary to select a new mistress of novices to take the place of Sister M. Mechtilde who had been elected the superior general. The Sister chosen for this important duty was Sister M. Felixa Jorz.

A woman of great strength of soul and character, Sister M. Felixa, the former Josephine Jorz, was born on September 11, 1903, in Pniewo, Poland. The daughter of Stanislaus and Stanisława Jorz, she came to the United States in 1907 and settled in St. Casimir's Parish in Cleveland, Ohio. Josephine entered the postulancy on December 13, 1919, and was received into the novitiate on July 27, 1921. She made her first profession on July 28, 1922, and her perpetual profession on July 27, 1926.[18]

A solemn but gracious person, Sister M. Felixa began her active apostolate in the congregation at St. Adalbert's School in East St. Louis, Illinois. In 1928, she was transferred to Sacred Heart School in Cleveland. In September of 1933, she was assigned as a day student at The Catholic Sisters College of The Catholic University of America in Washington, DC, where she received her bachelor's degree. She spent the next two years as a teacher and in 1938, she was appointed the superior of the Franciscan Sisters of Chicago stationed at The Catholic Sisters College where the congregation had undertaken the supervision of a residence hall for Sister-students. In 1940, she received her unexpected appointment as mistress of novices.[19]

From the beginning of her religious life, Sister M. Felixa was looked upon as a model of religious fervor. She bore herself with calmness and self-control almost bordering on the aloof. She was always insistent on the strict observance of the Rule, Constitutions, and the Book of Customs. Very faithful of their observance herself, she was sometimes stern and rigid with her novices and their failings. Faithful to her conservative ideals, Sister M. Felixa is remembered as a faithful, loving, and dedicated member of the congregation.[20]

Chosen to act as an associate to Sister M. Felixa was the intensely devout and kind Sister M. Isabel Sutor. Born in Spytkowice, Poland, on July 5, 1890, she came to the United States in 1901, and lived in the vicinity of St. Stanislaus Kostka Parish. On April 17, 1910, she entered the postulancy and was received into the novitiate on May 30, 1911. Her first profession of vows was made on July 27, 1912, and she made her perpetual profession on August 15, 1919.[21]

Sister M. Isabel spent the years from 1913 to 1936 mainly in Indiana in schools of the congregation. From 1936 to 1940, she was stationed at the Guardian Angel Day Nursery and Home for Working Girls. In 1940, she moved to Our Lady of Victory Convent in Lemont when she was appointed assistant to Sister M. Felixa.[22]

Sister M. Isabel was an accomplished seamstress and one of her duties was to teach the novices to sew. It was she who made the new habits for the novices about to make their first profession. In the twenty-five years that Sister M. Isabel served as assistant to the novice mistresses, she was loved and cherished by scores of novices because of her affability, warmth, and holiness. Her genial laughter, pleasant demeanor, and most of all, her devout religious example spoke a quiet sermon to the numerous young women with whom she came in contact in the novitiate.[23]

The decrees which proceeded from the Sixth General Chapter pertained generally to communal observance and discipline. One of the significant decrees was the resolution, proposed by Sister M. Raphael Bogalecki, that Sister M. Theresa Dudzik be accorded the title of "Mother" and, thereafter, be referred to as Mother M. Theresa Dudzik. The motion was unanimously approved with the condition that all past and subsequent superiors general be called "Mother" and retain the title even after leaving office.

It was also decided that the white cords worn by the Sisters were to be shortened and would consist of three turns instead of the customary five. A further discussion took place to determine whether or not the habit should be altered in form so as to eliminate an excess of difficult-to-obtain material, but the delegates did not pursue the topic.[24]

The congregation celebrated the Golden Jubilee of its foundation on Friday, December 8, 1944. Although the *Book of Leviticus* states: "This fiftieth year you shall make sacred. It shall be a Jubilee,"[25] yet because of the war, the celebration of the event, while solemn and festive, was relatively modest. It emphasized the aspects of gratitude and thanksgiving to God and his Mother for the blessings showered upon the congregation for fifty years. At the Motherhouse, on the feast of the Immaculate Conception, patroness of the Congregation, a Solemn Pontifical Mass was celebrated by the Most Reverend

Stanislaus Bona, the newly appointed coadjutor bishop of Green Bay, while the Most Reverend Samuel A. Stritch, the archbishop of Chicago, presided. He delivered the sermon in which he praised the important contributions of religious communities of women, and more specifically, the Congregation of the Franciscan Sisters of Chicago. Many priests, friends, and benefactors were present on that joyous and grace-filled occasion.

The next day, the Most Reverend William D. O'Brien was the celebrant at a Pontifical Mass for all the Franciscan Sisters of Chicago, members of other religious communities, and the laity. Bishop O'Brien delivered a sermon in English and was followed by the Reverend Isidore Cwiklinski, OFM, who addressed himself to the Polish-speaking guests.

The third day's celebration was a mass offered by the Very Reverend Monsignor James J. Strzycki, the pastor of Five Holy Martyrs Church, for the members of the various Ladies' and Men's Auxiliaries associated with the congregation. A stirring sermon was delivered by the Reverend A. Piorkowski.[26]

To commemorate this happy occasion, Mother M. Mechtilde designed and supervised the repainting and decorating of the sanctuaries of the chapels in the Motherhouse and Our Lady of Victory Convent in Lemont. Especially beautiful was the sanctuary arch in the Motherhouse chapel which was embellished with the Franciscan crest and motto, "Deus Meus et Omnia," [My God and My All].

A commemorative booklet entitled *Zarys Półwiecza Zgromadzenia Sióstr Franciszkanek Bł. Kunegundy* [Sketch of the fifty-year history of the Congregation of the Franciscan Sisters of Blessed Kunegunda] was prepared by Sister M. Gonzaga Raniszewski, the secretary general, on the occasion of the Golden Jubilee. Sister M. Paul Kirschbaum wrote *The Congregation of the Franciscan Sisters of Blessed Kunegunda: A Sketch of Its Foundation and Progress, 1894–1944.* Both publications are invaluable today because they remain among the chief sources of information pertaining to the congregation.

Even though the congregation rejoiced on the occasion of its Golden Jubilee of foundation, there was some element of sadness present based on more than the war which engulfed the entire world. The fact of the matter was that the congregation was suffering from a crucial lack of vocations. Only one postulant, Mary Swider, who became Sister M. Francis, had been received into the novitiate. For the first time in the history of the congregation, there was no novice ready to pronounce her vows; therefore, there was no profession ceremony in 1944.[27] With the reduction of tensions surrounding world events, the Franciscan Sisters of Chicago began to address themselves to the problem of a lack of vocations which had made itself seriously felt since the war years had begun.

In keeping with the original aim of Mother M. Theresa and the pioneer Sisters and in the spirit of the Golden Jubilee Year, it was most appropriate that Mother M. Mechtilde and the general council voted to accept the invitation of the Most Reverend Edward F. Hoban, archbishop-bishop of Cleveland, to staff St. Joseph Home for the Aged in that city.

*St. Joseph Home for the Aged
Cleveland, Ohio (1943–1966)*

A native of Chicago and an auxiliary bishop of Chicago from 1921 to 1928, Bishop Hoban was well acquainted with the work of the Sisters at St. Joseph Home for the Aged in Chicago.[28]

The Diocese of Cleveland had purchased the buildings which comprised the St. Joseph Home for the Aged from the Society of the Daughters of the Heart of Mary who had formerly operated them as St. Joseph's Orphanage for Girls.[29] The original solidly built brick structure at 6431 Woodland Avenue near St. Edward's Church was erected in 1879, and a similar three-story structure was erected alongside it in 1894.[30] As part of the expansion and reconstruction of the institutes of charity for the aged during Bishop Hoban's tenure as bishop of Cleveland, the Diocese of Cleveland acquired the buildings, thoroughly renovated them and modernized them to accommodate more than 110 aged men and women.[31]

On December 6, 1943, at five o'clock in the afternoon, four Franciscan Sisters arrived from Mount Alvernia Convent on Terrace Road in East Cleveland to undertake the supervision of St. Joseph Home for the Aged. The first Sisters assigned to the institution were Sister M. Hilary Dadej, who was appointed superior and administrator; Sister Sophie Marie Kierszke; Sister M. Beata Klecha; and Sister M. Stella Szczepanik.

On February 1, 1944, Sister M. Virginia Minta replaced Sister M. Hilary as superior and administrator. On the morning of October 4, Monsignor Albert G. Murphy, director of Catholic Charities, came to see the progress of the renovation.[32] Bishop Hoban was also a very frequent visitor.[33] While the first male resident had been admitted on January 7, 1944, as an emergency case, St. Joseph Home for the Aged was far from completed. Because of World War II, there was a serious shortage of materials and labor. Emergency admissions continued, however, and by the time St. Joseph Home for the Aged was dedicated on February 18, 1945, it was almost filled to its capacity of 110 residents.[34] That same month, Sister Sophie Marie Kierszke and Sister M. Stella Szczepanik returned to Mount Alvernia Convent on Terrace Road. On March 1, Sister M. Clarissa Kolupka and Sister Louise Ann Glowacki arrived from Chicago to take their places. Two days later, Sister M. Illuminata Szczepanski and Sister M. Pulcheria Mikolajczyk arrived to become part of the staff at St. Joseph Home.[35]

After diligent and dedicated service of twenty-two years duration by the Franciscan Sisters of Chicago, the Right Reverend Monsignor Michael Ivanko, Diocesan Director of Catholic Charities, announced in 1965 that St. Joseph Home for the Aged was closing. The home and the adjoining property had been purchased by the Cleveland Metropolitan Housing Authority as part of the Dike Park Project. St. Joseph Home was slated to be demolished for a fifty-acre low-rent housing project. When the last resident had been transferred to another home in the area, St. Joseph Home was officially closed on January 31, 1966. Shortly before that date, however, the Most Reverend Clarence G. Issenman,[36] bishop of Cleveland, paid St. Joseph Home a visit and later expressed his feelings in a letter to Mother M. Beatrice Rybacki:

> Dear Mother Beatrice:
>
> I have just visited for what most probably is the last time St. Joseph's Home for the Aged here.
>
> The three remaining guests will be transferred within a few days. The Sisters have done an admirable job in packing and preparing whatever may be of use in other institutions, under Monsignor Ivanko's direction.
>
> The six Sisters will be ready to leave as soon as these movable furnishings are carried away to the respective recipients. According to expectations, all this should be accomplished within a week.
>
> Of course, the Sisters are welcome to stay at St. Joseph's without rushing to leave. They know that they are all to return to the Motherhouse. It is a good plan to give them all a little respite after these past strenuous months of closing St. Joseph's.
>
> Words do not adequately say the thanks that Archbishop Hoban and I and all the Diocese extend to you and your Community and to the Sisters, every one of them whom you had assigned to care for our aged at St. Joseph's. It was a work of dedication and an unselfish service of love. The sadness filling the hearts of all is the best evidence of the place of

esteem in which St. Joseph's is held. It is the Sisters who gave the spirit of Christlike charity to St. Joseph's.

I know that you have many places for the Sisters. I trust that you will send as many as you can spare to your other houses in our Diocese, and I prayerfully hope that you and your Council will be receptive to a future St. Joseph's in our midst, though at the moment I can't predict other than it will be as quickly as additional funds may increase the amount of the sale of St. Joseph's. With my blessing, I am

Clarence G. Issenman
Coadjutor Bishop[37]

The last Sisters left Cleveland's St. Joseph Home for the Aged on February 11, 1966, and returned to the Motherhouse for reassignment. Sister M. Colombiere Piotrowski, superior and administrator; Sister M. Rita Schmitt; Sister M. Carol Rychlicki; Sister M. Ernestine Radecki; Sister M. Simon Glowacki; and Sister M. Joseph Grochowski had the sad duty of closing St. Joseph's Home for the Aged which had proved such a protective and loving haven for their beloved aged.[38]

The Second World War which had raged from September 1939 to August 1945 finally came to an end. In May of 1945, the Germans surrendered to the Allies ending the hostilities in Europe. By August 14, 1945, the Japanese surrendered to the American forces. By September 2, the official end of the Second World War, so long hoped and prayed for, became an actuality.

THE SIXTH GENERAL CHAPTER: MOTHER M. MECHTILDE ZYNDA

[1] See Appendix K.

[2] *Minutes of General Chapter Proceedings,* 1936 (AFSCL).

[3] Sister M. Mechtilde's mother, Mary Zynda, was the daughter of Lucy Platta, a sister to Mother M. Anna Wysinski. Both Mary Zynda and her daughter, Clara, were admitted to St. Joseph Home for the Aged and Crippled on August 13, 1911, and lived there until their deaths. Leo Zynda, the father of Sister M. Mechtilde, had died in Poland. St. Joseph Home for the Aged and Crippled, *Book of Admittances* (Chicago, Illinois), pp. 12–13.

[4] Sister M. Paul Kirschbaum, OSFK, ed., *The Congregation of the Franciscan Sisters of Bl. Kunegunda: A Sketch of Its Foundation and Progress* (Niles: St. Hedwig Printery, 1944), p. 220.

[5] *Spis Sióstr* (AFSCL).

[6] Ibid.

[7] *Book of Correspondence:* Letter from Sister M. Alvernia Groszek and other Sisters to author, September 1983 (AFSCL).

[8] *Book of Correspondence:* Letters from Sisters to author, September 1983 (AFSCL).

[9] See Chapter 31.

[10] Secretaries General, *Community Chronicle,* p. 212 (AFSCL).

[11] The Sacred Heart Enthronement was an acknowledgment of the sovereignty of Jesus Christ over the Christian family expressed by the installation of an image or picture of the Sacred Heart in a place of honor in the home and accompanied by an Act of Consecration to the Sacred Heart by the entire family.

[12] *Book of Correspondence:* Letter from Sister M. Alvernia Groszek to author, September 1983 (AFSCL).

[13] *Book of Annual Assignments* (AFSCL).

[14] Annual Report sent to the Right Reverend Monsignor Whitehead, Diocese of Cleveland, January 1942–1943; and *Interview* with Sisters, September 1983 (AFSCL).

[15] *Spis Sióstr* (AFSCL).

[16] After her six-year term as third council member and secretary general, she was sent to Boys Town where she remained for six years. The next three years she spent as superior and administrator at St. Anthony's Hospital in Martin, South Dakota. She returned to Boys Town in 1955 and remained there until February 4, 1961. At that time, she learned that she had cancer and was sent to St. John Hospital in Huron where she died on March 13. After her death, Sister M. Paul was taken to Boys Town where a funeral service was held. She was buried from the Motherhouse four days later. At her death, Sister M. Paul was sixty-eight years old and had been in the congregation for fifty-one years. *Congregation Membership Records;* and *Spis Sióstr* (AFSCL).

[17] *Interviews* with Sisters, September 1983 (AFSCL).

[18] *Spis Sióstr* (AFSCL).

[19] At the Seventh General Chapter, she was elected vicar general to Mother M. Jerome Dadej. During this time, she also served as superior at the Motherhouse. At the conclusion of her term in 1952, Sister M. Felixa returned to Cleveland and for the next seventeen years served as a teacher. In 1969, she began her apostolate to the young men of Boys Town, but, unfortunately, she died on March 20, 1970. She was sixty-seven years old and had been in the convent for fifty-one years. *Congregation Membership Records;* and *Spis Sióstr* (AFSCL).

[20] *Interviews* with Sisters, 1983 (AFSCL).

[21] *Spis Sióstr* (AFSCL).

[22] Sister M. Isabel was retained as the assistant to Sister M. Doloretta Radzienda when she succeeded Sister M. Felixa as novice mistress. Sister M. Isabel remained in this position until she

became ill in August of 1965. She died on November 18, 1966, of congestive heart failure at the Motherhouse. At her death, Sister M. Isabel was seventy-six years old and had been in the congregation for fifty-six years. *Congregation Membership Records* (AFSCL).

[23]*Interviews* with Sisters, September 1983 (AFSCL).

[24]*Minutes of General Chapter Proceedings, 1936* (AFSCL).

[25]Lev. 24:10–11.

[26]Secretaries General, *Community Chronicle,* p. 216 (AFSCL).

[27]This state of events repeated itself in 1983 when there were no novices for first profession nor any postulants entering the novitiate.

[28]*Minutes of General Council Proceedings,* 21 October 1943 (AFSCL).

[29]The girls were transferred to a new group of cottages for the care of orphans called Parmadale, the "Children's Village," in Parma, Ohio.

[30]*Book of Correspondence:* Report from the Diocese of Cleveland, Chancery Office to author, 26 January 1976 (AFSCL).

[31]Michael J. Hynes, *History of the Diocese of Cleveland* (Cleveland: World Publishing Co., 1953), p. 401.

[32]From 1939 to 1950, Father Murphy served as the Director of Catholic Charities in Cleveland. He was very concerned with the plight of the lonely aged who had previously been ignored. He was instrumental in planning and starting several homes for the aged. *Book of Correspondence:* Report from the Diocese of Cleveland, Chancery Office to author, 26 January (AFSCL).

[33]*Book of Correspondence:* Letter from Sister M. Virginia Minta to Sister M. Paul Kirschbaum (AFSCL).

[34]St. Joseph Home, "Candle," vol. 13, no. 1 (Cleveland, 1966).

[35]*Book of Correspondence:* Letter from Sister M. Virginia Minta to Sister M. Paul Kirschbaum (AFSCL).

[36]The Most Reverend Clarence G. Issenman, bishop of Cleveland, was named coadjutor bishop and apostolic administrator of the Cleveland diocese on October 7, 1964. He succeeded to the Cleveland See on September 22, 1966. Bishop Issenman suffered a severe illness in July of 1972 which prompted his resignation in 1974. On July 16, 1974, the Most Reverend James Hickey succceeded him as the Cleveland Ordinary. *Book of Correspondence:* Report from the Diocese of Cleveland, Chancery Office to author, 26 January 1976 (AFSCL).

[37]*Book of Correspondence:* Letter from the Most Reverend Clarence G. Issenman, coadjutor bishop of Cleveland, to Mother M. Beatrice Rybacki, 28 January 1966 (AFSCL).

[38]*Book of Annual Assignments* (AFSCL).

CHAPTER 43

Boys Town, Nebraska

Shortly before Mother M. Antonina Osinski's term of office had come to an end in July of 1940, she had received a letter which launched the congregation on one of its longest and most rewarding commitments to social service. The letter she received stated in full:

> Very Reverend and dear Mother:
>
> Would it be possible for me to get some Sisters from your great Order for our Domestic Department? We are completing a new dining hall and kitchen at Boys Town, and we would like very much to have Sisters conduct that Department. I would appreciate very much, dear Mother, if you could help me. Our poor boys need this encouragement. If you think there is any hope of securing Sisters, I would come down immediately to discuss the matter with you. A note, written to me, personally, will be deeply appreciated. Thanking you, dear Mother, and wishing you God's blessing, I remain
>
> Yours most sincerely,
Reverend E. J. Flanagan[1]

Boys Town had been founded by the charismatic Right Reverend Monsignor Edward J. Flanagan, better known throughout the world as "Father Flanagan of Boys Town," as a home and school for abandoned, neglected, and underprivileged boys regardless of color or creed.[2] Father Flanagan had said, "There's no such thing as a bad boy," and immortalized himself. This gentle man, with his revolutionary concept concerning the young rebels whom society did not understand, was born in County Roscommon, the sheep country of Ireland, on July 13, 1886. He studied at Summer Hill College at Sligo, and it is said that his passionate hatred of reform schools came from memories of Sligo.[3] In 1904, he sailed for America to study for the priesthood and took up studies at Mount St. Mary's College, Emmitsburg, Maryland. He attended the Gregorian University in Rome and the University of Innsbruck in Austria where he was ordained in 1912. Upon his return to America, he did parish work at St. Patrick's Church in Omaha.

Confronted with jobless harvest workers, Father Flanagan organized "The Workingmen's Hotel," a refuge for down-and-out men whose jobs proved disheartening and unrewarding. After an exhaustive study of over two thousand men at the "Hotel," he realized that the lives of the men had been wrecked in boyhood. He was determined to prevent any further waste of mankind.[4] He closed the "Hotel" and received consent from his superiors to move into a drafty Victorian mansion at 25th and Dodge Streets in Omaha with five boys—three from a juvenile court and two homeless newsboys. The date was December 10, 1917. When these quarters became overcrowded, another move was made to the German-American Home on South 13th Street where one hundred fifty boys were cared for. By 1921, this home was also outgrown and the third and last move was made to the 160-acre Overlook Farm, ten miles west of Omaha. By this time, the population had grown to over two hundred boys. In 1934, Boys Town[5] became an official municipality with its own post office. Boys Town continued to grow and with each phase of its growth, thousands upon thousands of new friends were won to the new community and public support abounded. The vision and faith of Father Flanagan were rewarded. His sincere conviction that most of the homeless boys could be helped by providing a home like atmosphere, complete with love and trust, proved true.[6]

As touched as Mother M. Antonina was by the sincere pleas of Father Flanagan to have the Franciscan Sisters of Chicago conduct the domestic department at Boys Town, she was forced to refuse his request. She informed Father Flanagan that while she wished to "take up more missions, especially among the poor, forlorn, and needy, it was just impossible for the congregation to accept more places at the present time." Mother M. Antonina regretted the fact that "vocations are not more numerous since work such as yours would answer our purpose very nicely."[7]

Father Flanagan persisted in his entreaties. On March 23, 1940, he informed Mother M. Antonina that "we are completing a building project here at Boys Town of four apartment buildings, and a dining hall and kitchen that will care for five hundred boys." He specifically asked that Mother M. Antonina supply him with Sisters to take charge of the domestic department by August 15.[8] At the end of March 1940, he repeated his request and stated his willingness to come to Chicago to speak with her in person. After his visit to the Motherhouse in Chicago in the latter part of May, he directed another plea to Mother M. Antonina:

> My dear Mother Antonina:
>
> I need not tell you, dear Mother, how heartbroken I was when I heard you state that there might be some difficulty in securing the Sisters that you and I talked about at your Motherhouse. I have built so much on getting your wonderful Sisters because I know of their value. Only yesterday, Bishop O'Brien,[9] the auxiliary bishop of Chicago, was here to visit me while I was at a council meeting in Omaha, and he came out to Boys Town in the afternoon, and he was so intensely interested when I

told him of my difficulties regarding the Nuns. And this is what he said: "If you can get the Polish Sisters, you will have a prize." I did not tell him of my heartache at the moment, because I still have hopes of getting even a few of your Sisters.

Dear Reverend Mother, we talked in terms of twenty Sisters. Perhaps you could give me five or ten, for just the dining room and kitchen. We are moving tomorrow into our dining room and kitchen, which is a beautiful set-up. I have held out so long, hoping that perhaps I might be able to get the Sisters in time before moving in. But we have to move now, because our present building is going to be changed into a high school and grade school, as I outlined to you, and this work must be started immediately in order to be finished by September. Perhaps, dear Mother, you could give me five or ten Sisters—this is all I would ask for the present time—just to take care of that department, and the other Sisters will do the work that they have been doing.[10] We could house your Sisters in one of the apartments in the new buildings, where they would be completely apart and separated from all the rest of the apartments. This would only be a temporary arrangement, until I could build the proper Convent for them. Perhaps you could take a run down here to see my place before you make a decision in the negative.

Wishing you God's choicest blessings, and hoping, dear Mother, that you can give me some little encouragement, and will you please acknowledge this letter at your earliest opportunity, I remain,

Yours most sincerely,

Rt. Rev. Msgr. E. J. Flanagan[11]

On June 20, 1940, Mother M. Antonina and Sister M. Jerome Dadej, the secretary general and fourth councilor, went to Boys Town to examine the prospects for the new undertaking. After meeting with Father Flanagan and observing the ripe field of apostolic activity present there, Mother M. Antonina committed the congregation to accepting the apostolate at Boys Town. Upon her return to the Motherhouse, she thanked Father Flanagan for his hospitality in a letter in which she confessed that "words cannot express" how both she and Sister M. Jerome felt about what they had witnessed:

My dear Rt. Rev. Monsignor:

We wish to thank you, Rt. Rev. Monsignor, for the hospitality shown to us. Words cannot express what we saw. It was not only a visit but also a treat for us. May Almighty God bestow His choicest blessings upon you, Rt. Rev. Msgr. and upon your great undertaking which you so nobly conduct. May God reward you a hundredfold.

We shall not take the Wayne Hospital;[12] instead, we shall work for the homeless and abandoned boys. Only a little patience—our general chapter starts on June 29. The election of the superior general takes place on July 2, hence the delay. Besides, many of the Sisters are in summer school and some are taking care of a Retreat Summer House.[13] I really must wait for some of those appointed Sisters to return in order to send them to your place.

So have hope, Rt. Rev. Msgr., that your pleading is not in vain.

We are now awaiting permission from His Excellency, Archbishop Samuel A. Stritch. With kindest regards, I remain,

> Very respectfully yours in the Sacred Heart,
> Mother M. Antonina,
> Superior General[14]

On July 2, during the course of the Sixth General Chapter of Elections, Mother M. Mechtilde Zynda was elected the new superior general, thereby replacing Mother M. Antonina. Mother M. Mechtilde was quick to inform Monsignor Flanagan that the general council supported and confirmed the previous administration's commitment to Boys Town. The Franciscan Sisters of Chicago, she assured him, would now take over not only the domestic department, but also all the other departments which were being served by the Congregation of the School Sisters of the Third Order of St. Francis of Savannah, Missouri,[15] who had staffed Boys Town since 1930.[16] All that now remained to be settled was the number of Sisters to be sent. In a long letter to Mother M. Mechtilde, Monsignor Flanagan outlined his plans:

> My dear Mother Mechtilde:
>
> Your kind letter received this morning, and I want to thank you from the very bottom of my heart for its encouraging contents.
>
> The number of Sisters that would be needed here would depend entirely upon what your Superior here would consider necessary. For instance—I could not state whether ten Sisters would be necessary for the dining room and kitchen, or eight, or seven Sisters. That would depend entirely upon the Sister's own judgment. However, this estimate will give you some idea. The same would be true with the laundry—perhaps four Sisters would do the work, and perhaps six Sisters would be needed. Of course, we will furnish a man for the machines, and occasional boys. Sewing and housekeeping of the four apartment buildings, I would judge, would require about eight Sisters. The sewing Sisters, two in each building, would be housekeepers—by that I mean—they would have charge of the boys who do the cleaning up and keeping the buildings in the fine condition in which they are now, and being new—it should not be difficult to do this, for they will have everything to do this with. Therefore, let us say eight Sisters for the sewing and housekeeping of four apartment buildings. There would be one Sister in the infirmary, who

should be a registered nurse.[17] I would say that six Sisters would be needed for the office, on an average; perhaps at Christmas time we might need a little extra help there in opening the mail.

The Sisters in the office have nothing to do with the answering of the mail—merely opening it and taking care of the money and accounts. We work in close connection with them on all these matters. The fifth and sixth grades will be taught by the Sisters, as is being done now, except that the Sisters have been teaching up to the eighth grade at the present time. But we are establishing a Junior High School and the Brothers will take over, therefore, the seventh and eighth grades, which were originally taught by the Sisters. This will leave the fifth and sixth grades to be taught by the Sisters.[18] As our enrollment is increasing right along—it may be necessary to divide up those two classes and make four of them. This, I do not know for sure, as yet, and therefore, would say that four teachers would be needed for teaching them.

I thought that our beautiful church should have proper supervision, and that possibly two Sisters would be needed for that, with the boys' help, of course, and maybe those two Sisters could keep house for me at my own house. They would not be kept busy all of the time and could easily take care of the new church and help in the sewing department. This, of course, would be entirely up to you, Reverend Mother.

I think this is about all, and I will now leave the matter to your judgment. I have merely outlined the work of the Sisters as I see it.

I spoke to Bishop Ryan last night when he was out to see me, and he was very happy to know that you are going to help me. I will secure from you, today or tomorrow, the necessary letter for you from him. I am also grateful that Archbishop Stritch has given you the necessary permission.

Thanking you again, dear Reverend Mother, and wishing you God's choicest blessings, I remain,

Yours most sincerely,
Rt. Rev. Msgr. E. J. Flanagan[19]

On July 10, Mother M. Mechtilde received a most welcome confirmation from the Bishop of Omaha:

Dear Mother Mechtilde:

Monsignor Flanagan informed me that your Community is able to send the required number of Sisters to Boys Town to take charge of the domestic department as well as the other departments now in charge of the Sisters.

I am pleased to give you my permission to come to the Diocese of
Omaha to take over the assigned work at Boys Town, and I welcome you.
With every good wish, I am,

Yours sincerely in Christ,
Most Reverend James H. Ryan, STD
Bishop of Omaha[20]

Mother M. Mechtilde happily informed Monsignor Flanagan in July that he might
expect twenty Sisters or more after August 15. Before that date, however, Monsignor
Flanagan and his cousin, Patrick Norton, came to the Motherhouse again where they
requested three additional Sisters for the business office. Mother M. Mechtilde now
promised thirty Sisters altogether to the apostolate at Boys Town.[21]

Mother M. Mechtilde and Sister M. Paul Kirschbaum, the newly elected secretary
general and third councilor, left for Boys Town on August 6 in the company of Sister M.
Innocentia Sierocki, Sister M. Gonzaga Raniszewski, and Sister M. Electa Rytel, who
were appointed to serve as bookkeepers in the business office. Ten days later, a group of
twelve Sisters arrived. They were Sister M. Athanasia Murzyn, Sister M. Bertille Geffert,
Sister M. Epiphany Gorski, Sister M. Eugenia Detlaf, Sister M. Laetitia Kolczak, Sister M.
Laurentine Trocki, Sister Marianne Kaplan, Sister M. Nepomucene Kulesza, Sister M.
Placidia Rzonca, Sister M. Susanna Pietrzycki, Sister M. Simon Glowacki, and Sister M.
Vincentia Wszolek. On August 21, a second group of Sisters arrived to join the staff:
Sister M. Andrea Puchalski, Sister M. Bronisia Kapusnik, Sister M. Herman Pieniazek,
Sister M. Leona Watroba, Sister M. Pascaline Dudek, Sister M. Peter Ostrega, Sister M.
Praesentia Grzybowski, Sister M. Rosaria Frodyma, and Sister M. Theresine
Wojciechowicz. Sister M. Leonilla Stogowski, a registered nurse assigned to the
infirmary, arrived on November 26, 1940. Each Sister was to receive twenty-five dollars a
month together with room and board.[22]

Father Flanagan and the Sisters celebrating their first Christmas at Boys Town in 1940

Sister M. Innocentia, the newly appointed superior proceeded to assign the Sisters to their various duties. Seven Sisters took charge of the boys' apartments, six Sisters worked in the kitchen, three Sisters attended to the laundry, while one Sister was appointed to the sacristy, infirmary, and Monsignor Flanagan's rectory, respectively.[23] Before long, Monsignor Flanagan requested a Sister to cook for the Brothers of the Christian Schools but Mother M. Mechtilde was quick to respond:

Dear Monsignor Flanagan:

I regret exceedingly that it is absolutely impossible to comply with your request for a Sister to do the cooking for the good Brothers at dear Boys Town.

At present I am trying to replace three Sisters who have cooked in our own houses for many years and now are in ill health and need a long rest. This shortage of cooks has become a serious problem and I really don't know what I should or can do about it. To make matters worse, it seems that vocations are at a standstill. The boys of Boys Town must help us with their fervent prayers for more Sisters.

I sincerely hope that the good Brothers will be able to make some other satisfactory arrangement.

With kindest regards, begging a prayer for myself and community,

Sincerely yours,
Mother M. Mechtilde[24]

When the Sisters first arrived at Boys Town, some of them lived in the convent formerly occupied by the School Sisters of the Third Order of St. Francis. The others lived in the school building where hasty accommodations made for them. On April 16, 1941, the Sisters who had lived in the school building moved into the new addition that had been

Immaculate Conception Convent
Boys Town, Nebraska

built onto the old convent. A blessing of the new convent wing and the boys' infirmary took place on May 1, 1941, with the Reverend L. J. Demers officiating.[25] The residency was called the Immaculate Conception Convent. The one sad note in the whole proceedings was the death of Sister M. Peter Ostrega[26] who died of pneumonia after an operation on June 3, 1941, at St. Catherine's Hospital in Omaha. She was forty-eight years old and had been in the congregation for thirty years. The boys were said to have wept unashamedly at her funeral services which were held in the Boys Town chapel.[27]

The addition to the convent had been built in time to house three more Sisters who were due to arrive on August 31. They were Sister M. Callista Gach, Sister M. Fidelia Armatys, and Sister M. Pulcheria Mikolajczyk. In 1944, Monsignor Flanagan, happy with the state of affairs at Boys Town, sent the following letter to Mother M. Mechtilde which read in part:

> I am very grateful for the fine service your Sisters render to the boys at Boys Town. It is heartening to see such a spirit of unselfishness in these days of of selfishness and greed, and were it not for their cooperation and the splendid type of work they are doing, it would be impossible for me to carry on. I assure you, dear Mother, I am grateful beyond any expression of words; particularly is your Sister Superior[28] here an example of real Christian womanhood and leadership.[29]

In 1945, Monsignor Flanagan expressed a desire to open a one-room classroom for the children of the employees of Boys Town.[30] The facilities in the local country school were seemingly inadequate, and provision could not be made for the ever-increasing number of students. Monsignor Flanagan and Sister M. Innocentia agreed upon the establishment of a classroom in the building formerly used by the Brothers of the Christian Schools who had withdrawn, somewhat abruptly, from their teaching post at Boys Town.[31] Mother M. Mechtilde was asked by Monsignor Flanagan to supply a Sister for the ten to fifteen children from kindergarten to third grade who were enrolled in the school.[32] Classes began for grades one through four on September 10, 1945, under the direction of Sister M. Simplicita Mruczkowski, who remained only until September 28. On October 1, Sister M. Agnes Zywiec arrived to take her place.[33]

The day-to-day apostolate of Boys Town continued for six years with relative success. But in early 1946, several dormant problems surfaced. The dining room and kitchen service were among them. As early as January of 1941, Sister M. Innocentia, the superior, had written to Mother M. Mechtilde stating her fears that some Sisters were doing the labor of two in the kitchen because of the large amount of work and the insufficient number of Sisters available.[34] In March of 1946, Mother M. Jerome Dadej, who had succeeded Mother M. Mechtilde as superior general upon the latter's untimely death, was prevailing upon Monsignor Flanagan to hire a food service to take over the kitchen, thereby releasing some of the overworked Sisters from the long and arduous work associated with an institutional dining room and kitchen. By September of that year,

Monsignor Flanagan assured Mother M. Jerome that he had been successful in obtaining the services of a "fine Catholic man" who had asked only that three of the Sisters remain in the kitchen, at least in a supervisory capacity, because of the "reliability and the conscientious approach on the part of the Sisters toward food in general and their abhorrence against waste." That same letter revealed these further thoughts of Monsignor Flanagan: "I have just learned that our dietitian here has thrown away a regular day's unused food from the day before because it did not fit into her menu for that particular day. To me this is very sinful with so many poor human beings suffering from starvation in Europe and the Orient."[35] Mother M. Jerome, of course, was only too happy to comply with Monsignor Flanagan's request for three Sisters to remain in the kitchen. After the abrupt departure of the Brothers of the Christian Schools in 1947, Monsignor Flanagan requested that the Sisters conduct the elementary school, grades one through six. Mother M. Jerome declined his request on the grounds that there were no Sisters available to assume this additional undertaking. She informed him, instead, that because of the scarcity of vocations to the Sisterhood and the number of Sisters required to staff the existing missions, there arose an immediate need to remove a number of Sisters from Boys Town in the near future. Six Sisters would still remain in the main kitchen and one Sister in the laundry. These Sisters would operate in a supervisory capacity only, and, therefore, lay personnel would have to be secured. The other departments would remain untouched for the time being. In January of 1948, Mother M. Jerome found it necessary to inform Monsignor Flanagan that she found it imperative to remove more and more Sisters for other missions where they were just as badly needed, and especially at St. John's Hospital and School of Nursing in South Dakota. Earlier, perhaps in a conciliatory effort to meet the needs of Boys Town, Monsignor Flanagan had asked for, and received, written consent from Mother M. Jerome to secure another community of Sisters to come to Boys Town and work alongside the Franciscan Sisters who "were not in a position to supply the required number of Sisters any longer."[36] Despite this concession, Mother M. Jerome received a letter from Monsignor Flanagan a few days later which, in part, underlined his general dissatisfaction with the existing situation:

> Your letter of January 19 received last Saturday upon my return from my Te Deum Lecture Tour and it is, of course, a great shock to me and to those around me who are deeply interested in the well-being of Boys Town. I do not know why Boys Town has been picked out to suffer the inconvenience of having to give up our best Nuns for other places, except that it might be because we are the latest institution which your Community has taken over. . . .[37] I think that you know that all of us do appreciate the Sisters very much at Boys Town. They have been wonderful—and I am going to ask you to reconsider your letter of January 13, and at least leave the Sisters here until such time as I can see my way of supplying the places of those that you now intend to take out

at this time. I am referring to the six Sisters ordered to leave on February 10, according to your letter of January 13.[38]

It is an unfortunate decision for us, Mother, since we have had no advance notice of your intention and certainly less than a month is not considered a sufficient amount of time for me to secure help in these days . . . the Sisters were placed here in good faith by you and your predecessor—and they have done magnificent work. They are certainly doing God's work here[39]—there is no doubt about that.[40]

The Sisters were removed in February of 1948, nevertheless, and were replaced by lay personnel in the main kitchen for the boys, the boys' dining room, the laundry, and Monsignor Flanagan's residence. The Sisters remained in the following areas: the sacristies, the boys' chapel, the tailor shop, the infirmary, the dentist's office, the school for the children of employees of Boys Town, and the four apartment buildings for boys. The bookkeeping, Boys Town campaign, and mail duties in the business department which included taking care of the payroll, were still being handled by the Sisters. Once again, in February of 1948, Mother M. Jerome related to Monsignor Flanagan the needful circumstances which demanded the presence of more Sisters at the congregation's new hospital in Huron, South Dakota, and of the financial crisis which existed at the hospital which did not allow for the hiring of more lay personnel at that time. She repeated the fact that many Sisters were overtaxed at some missions because of the lack of Sister personnel and their health had to be considered. Sadly, she closed her letter:

Since we should see the Will of God in all circumstances of our lives, we are accepting the lack of vocations in the spirit of submission to Almighty God, though I realize that it harms the institutions such as yours, Monsignor. We can only ask you to pray for the improvement of this situation.[41]

Monsignor Flanagan had made a trip to Japan and Korea in 1947 to study child welfare problems at the invitation of General Douglas MacArthur and the United States War Department. In the spring of 1948, at the request of President Harry S. Truman, Monsignor Flanagan left for Austria and Germany to perform a similar mission. The whole world was saddened by the news that Monsignor Flanagan died of a heart attack in war-ravaged Berlin on May 15, 1948.[42] The round of conferences, lectures, interviews, inspections, and discussions had taken their toll. Monsignor Flanagan was buried in the Dowd Memorial Chapel on the Boys Town campus. His tomb bears the inscription:

Father Flanagan, Founder of Boys Town
Lover of Christ and Man
July 13, 1886 – May 15, 1948[43]

An important page in the history of Boys Town was written with the appointment of the Right Reverend Monsignor Nicholas H. Wegner as the next director of Boys Town on September 15, 1948. Born in Humphrey, Nebraska, on July 16, 1898, he attended high school and college at St. Joseph Seminary, Teutopolis, Illinois. He studied philosophy and theology at St. Paul Seminary, St. Paul, Minnesota, and the Gregorian University in Rome. He studied Church Law at The Catholic University of America in Washington, DC. Father Wegner was ordained a priest on March 7, 1925, in Rome, and was assigned to St. Cecilia's Cathedral in Omaha. He was promoted to chancellor of the Archdiocese of Omaha in 1939, and held that position until he was named director of Boys Town succeeding the beloved Father Flanagan. Under Monsignor Wegner, Boys Town continued to grow in size, population, and influence.

Shortly after he became the director, Monsignor Wegner wrote to Mother M. Jerome to tell her how pleased he was with the Sisters. He admired their willingness to cooperate with the new administration but wished he had "about thirty more Sisters to help along with the very important work on behalf of the younger boys."[44] Mother M. Jerome did grant permission for the Sisters to teach catechetics to the boys in the lower grades at Monsignor Wegner's request.[45] Although the priests who worked with Monsignor Wegner at Boys Town desired more Sisters to be in charge of catechetics, Mother M. Jerome and the general council were adamant in refusing this request, which in effect, meant sending more Sisters to Boys Town.[46] As a matter of record, several overtures were made to Monsignor Wegner by Mother M. Jerome at this time to terminate the services of all the Sisters at Boys Town since the congregation was hard-pressed to supply Sisters. Finally and decisively Mother M. Jerome and her general council informed the Most Reverend Gerald T. Bergan, archbishop of Omaha, and Monsignor Wegner of their decision to withdraw all the Sisters from Boys Town in June of 1953.[47] A plea arrived from Monsignor Wegner requesting at least seven Sisters to remain in the business department and in the sacristy for one more year so that he could secure another community of Sisters. Mother M. Jerome acceded to his request, but, nevertheless, made one point perfectly clear. She informed Monsignor Wegner that the occupations of business clerks, sacristans, and domestic service were not outlined as the aims of the Franciscan Sisters of Chicago as expressed in their Constitutions. While she understood, therefore, the need for Sisters in those positions, those services were not the Sisters' first priority. At missions where the Sisters could be spared, or where such services accompanied the general ministries, these types of services were permitted. With the scarcity of vocations, however, it was imperative that the Sisters be sent to schools, homes for the aged, and the field of nursing.[48] Monsignor Wegner never desisted from his course. He was back in 1955 with a new plea:

> I wish you to know that I appreciate very much the wonderful work your Sisters are doing at Boys Town, and also your kindness in leaving the Sisters here. The only regret I have is that there is not a sufficient number of Sisters at Boys Town to do the work that is required of them, but somehow even with these few—the work assigned to them gets done.

It would really be a Godsend to us if you would assign a Sister to administer our new hospital and clinic.[49]

Mother M. Jerome was forced not only to refuse any further requests from Monsignor Wegner for Sisters but also to remove six Sisters from Boys Town in 1956. Ten more Sisters were withdrawn in 1959.[50]

On June 30, 1958, Mother M. Beatrice Rybacki was elected the new superior general of the congregation replacing Mother M. Jerome. Monsignor Wegner approached Mother M. Beatrice in 1962 with a new phase of the apostolate at Boys Town to which she responded with concern and approval. Monsignor Wegner had revealed to her his intention of opening a school for retarded boys on the Boys Town campus with the completion date set for late 1965.[51] He requested that the Sisters assume this responsibility and proposed that some Sisters be trained in preparation for this new field. Mother M. Beatrice selected Sister M. Georgeann Kinel to be sent to Cardinal Stritch College in Milwaukee in pursuit of a master's degree in special education. Mother M. Beatrice selected Sister M. De Sales Wyszynski and Sister M. Bonaventure Nagrocki to be in charge of the material welfare of the boys and the maintenance of the school for the handicapped. Unfortunately, the apostolate of working with the handicapped boys never reached fruition. The project had begun with much enthusiasm with a ground-breaking ceremony attended by Hubert H. Humphrey, the vice-president of the United States, and his wife. Sister M. Georgeann had received her master's degree in Special Education in 1964, but because of the conditions which prevailed at Boys Town at that time, the entire project was abandoned. Sister Georgeann remained at Boys Town for the next six years, nevertheless, as the religious superior and a teacher in the elementary school.

Although the project for the education of the handicapped boys did not materialize, other changes did occur. Under Monsignor Wegner's direction, the campus expanded physically with the addition of a new grade and middle school, renovation of the high school and grade school gyms, and an addition to the vocational career center. A new warehouse, a fire station, a civil defense center, the Nativity chapter for non-Catholic boys, the building of the Boys Town PhilaMatic Center adjoining the Visitor's Center, and new offices for the social services department were also erected. Like his predecessor, Monsignor Wegner aided in establishing international counterparts of Father Flanagan's Boys Home in Monterey, Mexico, and also a Boys Town in the Philippines.[52]

During the First Extraordinary Chapter of Affairs held in 1968, an assessment of the entire apostolate at Boys Town was made. While all the Sister-delegates were most enthusiastic about this ministry, they were surprised to learn the number of Sisters working there had dwindled to eight. Four Sisters taught religion in the grade school and four Sisters were housemothers on a part-time basis. One of the Sisters was still the sacristan in three chapels on the campus. In addition, every Sister supervised some work assignment of the boys.[53] A careful and sensitive evaluation was given to the ministry at Boys Town, and the Sister-delegates were of the mind that the time had come for a change in direction on the part of the congregation. A change did occur five years later, and when it did, it was literally overwhelming.

On September 15, 1973, Monsignor Wegner retired as the director of Boys Town. His successor was the Reverend Robert P. Hupp. Father Hupp came at what he termed "an agonizing time for the institution."[54] Only several months earlier, newspapers had revealed assets of more than $200 million in Boys Town. It remained for Father Hupp to look about for ways to put Boys Town's wealth into operation. The result was "a transformation so vast in scope, that the very concept of the institution, at least as had been known in the last twenty years, was being challenged."[55] Father Hupp began a massive reorganization of Boys Town. Soon many innovative and dynamic projects were underway. According to Father Hupp, "The people running Boys Town felt it no longer was good enough to offer boys custodial care, to take them in, feed them, house them, and turn them loose after graduation."[56] Among the many changes taking place in Boys Town, two dramatic developments in 1972 were initiated by Father Hupp. The Boys Town Institute for Communication Disorders in Children was created to incorporate a clinical, diagnostic, and rehabilitative center and a preschool language and learning center with home units for communicatively handicapped boys and girls requiring extended language training. It was built close to Creighton University Medical Center in Omaha. The Boys Town Institute for the Study of Youth Development was also established. Its headquarters were on the Boys Town campus with regional research complexes at Stanford University in Palo Alto, California, and at The Catholic University of America in Washington, DC. The administration of Boys Town anticipated further growth which continued to broaden the application of Father Flanagan's goals first established over sixty years ago. New programs for the boys were being formulated and new projects were in the planning and early implementation stages. Grade school children now lived in four attractive apartments, while the high school students resided in twenty-five cottages on the campus with house parents or child-care workers. In line with the idea of providing a family-style setting for the boys, the cafeteria and laundry on the campus ceased to exist.[57]

In the midst of the colossal changes taking place at Boys Town, the Sisters still continued to serve in their traditional roles. Sister M. Equitia Nawracaj, Sister M. Kinga Repinski, and Sister Ann Rose Mroz were assigned to the religion department in the school while Sister M. Angelica Seidl, Sister M. Richard Duszynski, and Sister M. Theophane Rakowski worked in the business office. Sister M. Praesentia Grzybowski continued to serve as the sacristan. In April of 1976, Sister M. Hugoline Czaplinski, who had succeeded Mother M. Beatrice Rybacki as superior general, regretfully notified Father Hupp of a decision, which, in view of the changes and controversy occurring on the Boys Town campus, seemed inevitable. The Franciscan Sisters of Chicago were to leave Boys Town for good. The *Chicago Sun-Times* tersely summarized the situation at Boys Town in an opening paragraph of an article appearing in December of 1976, which stated, "Spencer Tracy and Mickey Rooney wouldn't recognize the old place anymore. It's grown. It's changed."[58] Indeed, the structural and philosophical changes in the operation of Boys

Town combined with the moving of the business office to Downtown Omaha made the decision to remove the Sisters easier to arrive at and finally, irreversible. On June 14, 1976, Sister M. Equitia, the superior; and Sister M. Praesentia, the sacristan, were the last Sisters to leave Boys Town to return to Chicago.

The congregation's records indicate that from September of 1940 until June 14, 1976, over seventy-five Sisters had contributed 540 years of dedicated service to the needy, troubled, and underprivileged boys by serving them in the capacity of teachers, counselors, office clerks, seamstresses, sacristans, infirmarians, cooks, laundresses, and housemothers. Some of the Sisters achieved a notable record in the number of years spent in service: Sister M. Gracianne Fibich, 33; Sister M. Theophane Rakowski, 22; Sister M. Norberta Haas, 20; Sister M. Electa Rytel, 19; Sister M. Ambrosia Tworek, 17; Sister M. Hyacinth Barczewski, 17; Sister M. Martha Bywalec, 17; Sister M. Pascaline Dudek, 15; Sister M. Praesentia Grzybowski, 15; Sister M. Humilia Proc, 14; Sister M. Agnes Zywiec, 14; and Sister M. Simon Glowacki, 13. In addition, many Sisters in the congregation rendered service at Boys Town during the summer months when they were free from classroom or other obligations.[59]

Earlier in 1972, when the Right Reverend Monsignor Francis Schmitt, the founder of the Boys Town Music Department and the Boys Town Concert Choir,[60] had heard that the Sisters might be leaving, he addressed this letter to Sister M. Hugoline, the superior general, which best expressed the true nature of the Sisters' dedication:

> My dear Mother General,
>
> I have been at Boys Town for almost as long (June 1941) as the Franciscan Sisters of Chicago, so I trust that you will find my observations seasoned, true, and sincere.
>
> Through all of those years the Sisters have formed a most important part of the warp and woof of our organization. Indeed, I don't know what we would have done, would do, without them. There were many times in the old days (still are, for that matter), when there was no one but the nuns one could call on when a boy, or a group of boys, needed some particular help, some special service. This might have involved the convent, the chapel, the school, the kitchen, the fiscal office, or any one of the numerous areas in which the Sisters gave service.
>
> I certainly do not mean to imply that it was necessary to call upon them. Whenever situations have arisen where they could be of help, that help was automatic. The late Dr. Plewa and I often talked about how the most important work done for the boys was not so much by dint of high organization, but by their casual association with people of character, moral power, religious example, and love. The Sisters figured very eminently in these conversations.
>
> Getting down to the specifics of your apostolate at Boys Town: I am sure that we should soundly welcome whatever special expertise the

Sisters might bring to their tasks, whether it be training in religious education, welfare work or whatever. Incidentlly, I do not personally feel that their work, e.g. in religious education—need be confined to the elementary level. I have known a good many of our nuns over the years who could handle the roughest hombres we had—sometimes when a lot of others couldn't. Work as educators, housemothers, etc. aside, I carry the conviction that the really most important part of the Sisters' apostolate at Boys Town is their mere *presence* here. The more so as we, with the rest of the world, become more secular.

And so I hope and pray that in the Providence of God, and in the judgments of your evaluation, you will see fit not only to continue, but possibly amplify your successful, and I trust, rewarding, apostolate at Boys Town.

> In Our Lord and St. Francis,
> Rev. Msgr. Francis Schmitt[61]

On March 18, 1976, Monsignor Wegner died after a lengthy illness. He had served as director of Boys Town for twenty-five years. When he retired in 1973 the *Omaha World-Herald* wrote of him: "Boys Town is as much a monument to Monsignor Wegner's direction and singleness of purpose as it is to Father Flanagan's vision."[62] With this assessment of Monsignor Wegner, the Sisters had seen Boys Town grow until it comprised over 1,475 acres of land, one thousand of which were used for farming and more than fifty buildings on campus. On June 13, 1976, the day before the Sisters left Boys Town for good, the Dowd Memorial Chapel "Bulletin" contained a tribute to the Franciscan Sisters of Chicago. It was a modest, heartwarming, and to all appearances, correct evaluation of the Sisters' presence on the Boys Town campus:

> This weekend, the last of the Franciscan Sisters will be leaving the Boys Town campus to return to their Motherhouse in Lemont, Illinois. With their leaving, a very long and self-sacrificing chapter in the history of Boys Town will come to an end.
>
> Father Flanagan personally obtained the help of the Sisters in 1940. The first Sisters came to Boys Town in June of that year. At one time, thirty-six Sisters were co-workers with Father Flanagan in every aspect of the Home. When the Sisters first came, they were the housemothers of the four buildings, they taught the school, they cooked all the meals, they did all the laundry, they were the only secretaries and office workers in the promotion department. THEY WERE THE HEART AND SOUL OF THE BOYS TOWN COMMUNITY.
>
> During the summer months, many times Sisters from various other apostolates would come to Boys Town to help with the campaigns to obtain funds for its survival. Without the donation of their talents at very

meager salaries, without their total dedication to a task that was not popular at the time, without their joy, interest, and love BOYS TOWN AS WE KNOW IT SIMPLY WOULD NOT EXIST. WE OWE THEM A GREAT DEBT OF GRATITUDE.

The first Sister Superior at Boys Town was Sister Innocentia, who died just a few weeks ago.[63] To a great extent the thrust of the Sisters' dedicated work on this campus was due to her vision and spirit.

As the Sisters leave, they say that the living memory they cherish most is the wonderful spirit of family that existed in those early days. Father Flanagan and the priests would hold recreation with the Sisters and the other staff each evening. Many times the boys would join in. All that happened during the day was shared and so-called problems were handled in a family manner. Each boy was appreciated for the person God had made him and EACH BOY FOUND IN ONE OF THE SISTERS THE MOTHER HE LONGED FOR.[64]

The motto on the famous "Two Brothers" statue associated with Boys Town—"He ain't heavy, Father . . . he's m'brother," had been taken literally by all the Sisters stationed at Boys Town in whatever capacity they had served.

BOYS TOWN, NEBRASKA

[1]*Book of Correspondence:* Letter from the Right Reverend Monsignor Edward J. Flanagan to Mother M. Antonina Osinski, 10 August 1939 (AFSCL).

[2]Clifford Stevens, "The Founder of Boys Town," *Catholic Digest,* May 1972, pp. 37–42.

[3]Ibid.

[4]Ibid.

[5]The Boys Town name became prominent in 1938 when actor Spencer Tracy immortalized Father Flanagan in the motion picture, *Boys Town.* That year, Tracy received the Academy Award for his sensitive portrayal of Father Flanagan. Mickey Rooney, a favorite of American moviegoers, played Boys Town's toughest enrollee in the same movie. The second Boys Town film produced in 1941 called *Men of Boys Town* made this "City of Little Men" even more popular. Both Tracy and Rooney appeared in the sequel.

Boys Town became a part of America's history and was widely imitated in other parts of the world. Today, an astounding number of tourists visit Boys Town each year. *Boystown: Memories and Dreams* (Boystown, Nebraska, 1976), no pagination.

[6]Ibid.

[7]*Book of Correspondence:* Letter from Mother M. Antonina Osinski to the Right Reverend Monsignor Edward J. Flanagan, 5 September 1939 (AFSCL).

[8]*Book of Correspondence:* Letter from the Right Reverend Monsignor Edward J. Flanagan to Mother M. Antonina Osinski, 23 March 1940 (AFSCL).

[9]The Most Reverend William O'Brien served as the auxiliary bishop of Chicago from 1934 to 1962. Bishop O'Brien was also instrumental in encouraging Mother M. Jerome Dadej to establish an academy for young women in 1945. The result of this encouragement was the founding of Madonna High School in 1949. *Minutes of General Council Proceedings,* 29 January 1945 (AFSCL).

[10]Father Flanagan is referring here to the Congregation of the School Sisters of the Third Order of St. Francis of Savannah, Missouri, who had come to Boys Town at his request in 1930. *Book of Correspondence:* Letter from Sister M. Annunciata, secretary general, School Sisters of the Third Order of St. Francis, La Verna Heights, Savannah, Missouri to author, October 1978 (AFSCL).

[11]*Book of Correspondence:* Letter from the Right Reverend Monsignor Edward J. Flanagan to Mother M. Antonina Osinski, 12 June 1940 (AFSCL).

[12]Mother M. Antonina is referring to a hospital in Wayne, Nebraska, which the congregation was asked to staff in 1940.

[13]The reference here is to Our Lady of Spring Bank, a Cistercian Abbey and Summer Retreat House located in Oconomowoc, Wisconsin, on Lake Okauchee. The Sisters worked here from 1934 to 1942.

[14]*Book of Correspondence*: Letter from Mother M. Antonina Osinski to the Right Reverend Monsignor Edward J. Flanagan, 29 June 1940 (AFSCL).

[15]See footnote number 10.

[16]*Book of Correspondence:* Letter from Mother M. Mechtilde Zynda to the Right Reverend Monsignor Edward J. Flanagan, 3 July 1940 (AFSCL).

[17]The first registered nurse to serve in the infirmary was Sister M. Leonilla Stogowski. After several years, Sister M. Aquinas Rosky was sent to replace her. When Mother M. Jerome informed Monsignor Flanagan of her intention to remove Sister M. Aquinas and send her to the congregation's newlybuilt St. John Hospital and School of Nursing in Huron, South Dakota, Monsignor Flanagan wrote to Mother M. Jerome: "Sister M. Aquinas has rendered excellent service . . . her work has been most satisfactory and she loves the work and loves the boys and we think a great deal of her." *Book of Correspondence:* Letter from the Right Reverend Monsignor Edward J. Flanagan to Mother M. Jerome Dadej, 2 November 1946 (AFSCL).

[18]Monsignor Flanagan arranged, however, to have the Brothers of the Christian Schools teach in both the grade and junior high school, i.e., from grades five to eight. *Book of Correspondence:* Letter from the Right Reverend Monsignor Edward J. Flanagan to Mother M. Mechtilde Zynda, 17 July 1940 (AFSCL).

[19]*Book of Correspondence:* Letter from the Right Reverend Monsignor Edward J. Flanagan to Mother M. Mechtilde Zynda, 5 July (AFSCL).

[20]*Book of Correspondence:* Letter from the Most Reverend James Ryan, bishop of Omaha, to Mother M. Mechtilde Zynda, 10 July 1940 (AFSCL).

[21]*Minutes of General Council Proceedings,* 21 July 1940 (AFSCL).

[22]*Book of Annual Assignments* (AFSCL).

[23]*Boys Town Annual* (AFSCL).

[24]*Book of Correspondence:* Letter from Mother M. Mechtilde Zynda to the Right Reverend Monsignor Edward J. Flanagan, 4 August 1941 (AFSCL).

[25]A letter written by Chaplain L. J. Demers on October 19, 1943, from Indiantown Gap, Pennsylvania, to Mother M. Mechtilde states in part:

> Your Sisters, as I have observed, have always done marvelous work at Boys Town. When I was there last there were about 250 boys. Now it seems that there are 450. This increase in numbers plus the difficulty of securing civilian employees for various departments of the Home because of the war means as Monsignor Flanagan wrote to me rather recently, that everyone there is doing double duty . . . I agree perfectly with the Christian Brothers who visited you . . . Boys Town could not exist without the Sisters to do the domestic work.

Book of Correspondence: Letter from Chaplain L. J. Demers, Indiantown Gap, Pennsylvania, to Mother M. Mechtilde Zynda, 19 October 1943 (AFSCL).

[26]Sister M. Peter Ostrega was the sister of Sister M. Bernadine Ostrega who died in the congregation on December 8, 1972.

[27]*Spis Sióstr* (AFSCL).

[28]The Sister Superior to whom Monsignor Flanagan had reference was Sister M. Innocentia Sierocki who served at Boys Town from 1940 to 1946 and endeared herself to everyone who knew her.

[29]*Book of Correspondence:* Letter from the Right Reverend Monsignor Edward J. Flanagan to Mother M. Mechtilde Zynda, 17 October 1944 (AFSCL).

[30]Sister Kathleen Melia, a member of the congregation, attended the school.

[31]*Boys Town Annual* (AFSCL).

[32]*Book of Correspondence:* Letter from the Right Reverend Monsignor Edward J. Flanagan to Mother M. Mechtilde Zynda, 24 July 1945 (AFSCL).

[33]*Boys Town Annual* (AFSCL).

[34]*Book of Correspondence:* Letter from Sister M. Innocentia Sierocki to Mother M. Mechtilde Zynda, January 1941 (AFSCL).

[35]*Book of Correspondence:* Letter from the Right Reverend Monsignor Edward J. Flanagan to Mother M. Jerome Dadej, 14 September 1946 (AFSCL).

[36]*Book of Correspondence:* Letter from Mother M. Jerome Dadej to the Right Reverend Monsignor Edward J. Flanagan, 13 January 1948 (AFSCL).

[37]Boys Town was not the latest place the Sisters had accepted. After 1940, the Sisters staffed St. Peter Claver School in Mobile, Alabama; St. Joseph the Provider School, Campbell, Ohio; St. Joseph Home for the Aged and Madonna Hall for Women in Cleveland, Ohio. Of course, the Sisters' most ambitious undertaking in building and staffing was St. John Hospital and School of Nursing in Huron, South Dakota; and Madonna High School in Chicago.

[38]The Sisters slated to leave Boys Town were Sister M. Aquinas Rosky, Sister M. Fidelia Armatys, Sister M. Bertille Geffert, Sister M. Laetitia Kolczak, Sister M. Theresilla Ignasiak, and Sister M. Theresine Wojciechowicz. *Book of Annual Assignments* (AFSCL).

[39]In reading the histories of all the missions mentioned in footnote 37, it must be noted that all of them were undertaken at the specific requests of bishops or under circumstances that warranted their acceptance at that time. Monsignor Flanagan himself states in his letter regarding the apostolate at Boys Town: "They [the Sisters] are certainly doing God's work here." This could be applied to all the other missions which the Sisters accepted.

[40]*Book of Correspondence:* Letter from the Right Reverend Monsignor Edward J. Flanagan to Mother M. Jerome Dadej, 19 January 1948 (AFSCL).

[41]*Book of Correspondence:* Letter from Mother M. Jerome Dadej to the Right Reverend Monsignor Edward Flanagan, 17 February 1948 (AFSCL).

[42]The May 30, 1976 issue of the Dowd Memorial *Bulletin* contained an article entitled "Father Flanagan's Secret" written by Mitt Stoffel on the occasion of Father Flanagan's anniversary. The last paragraph is recorded here:

> Father [Flanagan] was not in the best of health and while the rigorous life he had led in his crusade for youth had taken its toll, it was the opinion of close friends and confidants that he actually died of a broken heart because of the appalling conditions he experienced in the tormented cities of Western Europe.

Dowd Memorial Chapel, *Bulletin,* 30 May 1976 (AFSCL).

[43]Stevens, pp. 37–42.

[44]*Book of Correspondence:* Letter from the Right Reverend Monsignor Nicholas H. Wegner to Mother M. Jerome Dadej, 16 May 1949 (AFSCL).

[45]*Book of Correspondence:* Letter from the Right Reverend Monsignor Nicholas H. Wegner to Mother M. Jerome Dadej, September 1949 (AFSCL).

[46]*Minutes of General Council Proceedings,* 14 September 1949 (AFSCL).

[47]*Book of Correspondence:* Letter from Mother M. Jerome Dadej to the Right Reverend Monsignor Nicholas H. Wegner, 15 October 1952 (AFSCL).

[48]*Book of Correspondence:* Letter from Mother M. Jerome Dadej to the Right Reverend Monsignor Nicholas H. Wegner, 11 May 1953 (AFSCL).

[49]*Book of Correspondence:* Letter from the Right Reverend Monsignor Nicholas H. Wegner to Mother M. Jerome Dadej, 11 January 1955 (AFSCL).

[50]In the spring of 1955, the Alexian Brothers were asked by Monsignor Wegner to take over administration and operation of the new forty-bed hospital at Boys Town. The Alexian Brothers installed an administrator of the Boys Town Hospital on August 20, 1955. The Brothers remained there for twenty years. When the new administration of Boys Town in 1975 indicated that the services of the Brothers would be dispensed with in view of the new administration's policies regarding the boys' health care, the Alexian Brothers elected to transfer their services and left Boys Town in 1976. Rev. Msgr. Harry C. Koenig, STD. *Caritas Christi Urget Nos, A History of the Offices, Agencies, and Institutions of the Archdiocese of Chicago,* 2 vols. (Chicago: The New World Publishing Co., 1981), 2:997.

[51]*Minutes of General Council Proceedings,* 27 January 1962 (AFSCL).

[52]*Boys Town Times,* 12 October 1973.

[53]"Apostolate Commision Paper," Extraordinary Chapter of Affairs, December 1968 (AFSCL).

[54]David Carmichael, *Our Sunday Visitor,* 1974.

[55]Ibid.

[56]Ibid.

[57]*Boys Town: Memories and Dreams,* no pagination.

[58]*Chicago Sun-Times,* 19 December 1976.

[59]*Book of Annual Assignments* (AFSCL).

[60]The Boys Town Choir is known nationally and internationally. The choir, on its annual concert tours, has been heard in every section of the United States, in Cuba, Japan, and five Canadian Provinces. It has also been heard on radio and television. Under the guidance of Monsignor Francis P. Schmitt, the founder of the Boys Town Music Department, the Boys Town Concert Choir has maintained a tradition of excellence for over thirty-five years. When Monsignor Schmitt retired in 1973, the assistant director of the Boys Town Concert Choir and a former Boys Town student himself assumed the position as director.

[61]*Book of Correspondence:* Letter from the Right Reverend Monsignor Francis Schmitt to Sister M. Hugoline Czaplinski, 24 February 1972 (AFSCL).

[62]*Omaha World Herald,* 1973.

[63]Sister M. Innocentia Sierocki died on April 15, 1976.

[64]Dowd Memorial Chapel *Bulletin,* 13 June 1976 (AFSCL).

CHAPTER 44

The Franciscan Sisters in the Southland

The Franciscan Sisters of Chicago made their first and only settlement in the "Heart of Dixie" in 1943 when Mother M. Mechtilde and her general council agreed to staff St. Peter Claver School in Mobile, Alabama. Mobile, a commercial city and seaport in the southwestern corner of Alabama, was the first permanent white settlement established by the French in 1711. For years the Most Reverend Thomas J. Toolen,[1] bishop of Mobile, had been especially concerned with bringing the Church into rural districts and had been deeply affected with the welfare of the black residents in his diocese.[2] He sent his representative, Monsignor Harold Purcell, to the Motherhouse of the Franciscan Sisters of Chicago in July of 1943 to secure at least three Sisters to staff St. Peter Claver School.[3]

St. Peter Claver Church[4] in the southern section of Mobile at Dearborn and Palmetto Streets was purchased and opened for the exclusive use of the blacks by the Most Reverend Edward P. Allen, bishop of Mobile, in 1911. It was known as the "Downtown" black parish. The black Catholics in this section south of Government Street had previously attended the Cathedral of the Immaculate Conception, St. Vincent de Paul Church, or the Church of the Most Pure Heart of Mary. Most of the black Catholics were Creoles[5] and did not take too well to the separate black Church.[6] St. Peter Claver Church, which had formerly served a white Baptist congregation, was placed in the care of the Josephite Fathers.[7] Since the church structure consisted of an upper and lower level, and building a new church was an impossibility, the Reverend William Reichmeyer, SSJ, pastor of St. Peter Claver Parish, remodeled the lower level of the church and partitioned it into five classrooms.[8]

In October of 1911, at the invitation of Bishop Allen, the Congregation of the Sister-Servants of the Holy Ghost and Mary Immaculate came to Mobile to staff the school.[9] The Sisters began the school with ninety-five pupils, and at its highest enrollment, the number reached 175.[10] The Sisters remained at the school for over thirty years until they withdrew completely from the Diocese of Mobile in 1943. After the Sisters relinquished the school, an intense search was begun for another congregation to take its place. When Monsignor Purcell, therefore, presented his ardent request for Sisters to

Mother M. Mechtilde on behalf of Bishop Toolen, she consented to send the Franciscan Sisters of Chicago to Mobile after having received permission from Samuel Cardinal Stritch, the archbishop of Chicago.[11] Mother M. Mechtilde and her council accepted St. Peter Claver School in Alabama as the congregation's first real "missionary" venture with the hope that the congregation would be blessed with many vocations.[12] For the first year, at least, the staff was comprised of Sisters who had volunteered to go "to the South," to a city and to a people with whom the Sisters had had little or no experience. Unlike the Sisters in other parishes and institutions, the Sisters at St. Peter Claver School would not receive a salary but would be dependent on the goodwill offerings of the benefactors of the Josephite Fathers who conducted the parish. The Reverend Edwin F. Youngkin, SSJ,[13] the pastor of St. Peter Claver Church, was overjoyed when he wrote Mother M. Mechtilde:

> Dear Mother,
>
> I was delighted to hear from Bishop Toolen that you have kindly consented to send us Sisters for this mission.
>
> I am very sorry to hear you can send but three teachers as we need four. It is impossible to get a lay teacher here as all the girls are receiving

St. Peter Claver Church and School
Mobile, Alabama (1943–1949)

large salaries for war work. The population jumped from 85,000 to over 200,000. The salaries are very high and some high school teachers are now doing war work.

Mother, will you please, in the name of God, do everything possible to send four teachers? I am sure God will bless you and the Community for this kindness and you will have my ever-lasting appreciation and prayers.

Yours sincerely in Christ,
Edwin F. Youngkin, SSJ[14]

In September, five Sisters arrived to staff the school. Sister M. Blanche Bartkowski was appointed the superior, principal, and teacher of grades five and six; Sister M. Richard Duszynski was appointed to teach grades three and four; Sister Therese Agnes Kniola was slated for grades one and two; and Sister M. Therese Grajek was assigned to teach grades seven and eight and maintain the sacristy. Sister M. Praesentia Grzybowski assumed the household duties. There were approximately 120 to 150 children enrolled in the school.[15]

Once again, the enthusiastic Father Youngkin's joy knew no bounds when he sent the following letter of appreciation to Mother M. Mechtilde:

Dear Mother:

First allow me to thank you for the fifth Sister that you so kindly sent me.

The Sisters are doing wonderful work and the people of the parish are delighted with them and are trying to help them all they can.

The discipline and general order of the school is nothing short of a miracle. Your Sisters here are hard-working Sisters and are led by Sister Blanche who never seems to tire.

They cooperate with me and I with them, and the whole place just hums with work being well done and blessed by God. May God bless you and your Sisters for this noble undertaking and may He increase your Community a hundredfold is my prayer in appreciation for what you have done for St. Peter Claver.

Yours sincerely in Christ,
Edwin F. Youngkin, SSJ[16]

The house in which the Sisters took up residence had originally belonged to a Baptist minister. It was unlike any house the Sisters had ever lived in before. The lovely, two-story frame house painted white both inside and out stood next to the church and school. The house had no foundation as such, but was supported by square beams made of brick, and where there were cracks in the floor, the ground underneath could be seen.[17] Sweet honeysuckle and azaleas grew along the filigreed ornamentation of the spacious front porch. At the back of the comfortable and adequate home, near the kitchen, grew an abundantly overflowing pecan tree.[18]

St. Peter Claver Convent
Mobile, Alabama

If the house was unlike any the Sisters had lived in before, so were their experiences here so charmingly recounted by Sister Marie Francis Moson:[19]

> The climate of Mobile was humid and very difficult to adjust to since we wore our heavy woolen habits. We were very warm all day, sticky and clammy because there was no such thing as air conditioning. Oh, yes, I forgot the ever-present ant who was our guest at all times. Everything had to be kept in tightly sealed jars or else we had a trail of ants. Even the flowers on the altar were not safe from these marauders.

> Christmas was so different from the ones we knew in the North. We beat soap flakes to make suds to put on the Christmas trees in the church and at home. It was so much fun and work that there were more suds on us than on the trees. I remember taking the trees out in the backyard as

the sun shone brightly and placing them among the poinsettias growing there. These are things I'll never forget.

What memories we have of the Mardi Gras! It was a gala affair for the whites as well as for the blacks. We watched the Mardi Gras parade of the blacks and we had fun. What goodies were thrown to us as we watched from the veranda of the Dominican Sisters! It lasted a whole week and we had two days off before Ash Wednesday. Or our field day sponsored by the Catholic School Board! A picnic was arranged for all school children both black and white. Each separate, of course. Food, transportation, and beverages were supplied free-of-charge to the students. What fun! And the climax—a free day after the picnic to recuperate from all the exertion.

The one summer we did not come up North we spent at St. Mary's College in New Orleans, attending Loyola University. I shall never forget the incredulous stares of the Southerners as they caught sight of us in our heavy brown habits and cornets walking down St. Charles Avenue. They turned twice to look at us. The weather was unbelievable. It always rained at noon as we left school. It was only a short shower and then the sun would come out. We met a young lady who took us sightseeing. We rode the ferry across the muddy Mississippi River. How fascinated we were by the cemeteries and the mansions. Such memories!

We spent ten days in retreat with the Visitation Nuns.[20] It was an unforgettable experience. It was rather eerie to find yourself locked in with no doorknobs on the inside. We slept in beds on straw mattresses and with net curtains to keep out the night bugs. The tower clock chimed the quarter hour and we slept across from the art room with shrouds covering statues and other art easels. Needless to say, we were petrified! Whenever we moved, the straw crackled. We couldn't wait to leave. The Sisters, however, were most cordial. The retreat master we had was also very kind. Later he became the personal chaplain of Prince Rainier of Monaco.

Then there were the train rides. We generally traveled twenty-six hours by train to Mobile or Chicago so we traveled Pullman. That was fun!

I shall never forget my first sight of the Gulf of Mexico. A Josephite missionary and our pastor took us out for a ride to the missionary's home and from there we went to see the Gulf. Miles and miles of beautiful sand and blue water. Unforgettable!

These are some of my memories. Some I have forgotten but one I shall never forget . . . the picnic we had with the first and second graders. Sister M. Rosaline and I took our students on a picnic out in the country to a black mission school. It was the first time some of these children had ever been out in the country. We had some minor problems like the bus breaking down and not enough seats on the bus, but the children took turns sitting on my lap and for them that was an unforgettable experience. It was worth all the melted ice cream, bugs, etc. when one little girl said she would remember this for the rest of her life. We were heartbroken when the decision was made to close St. Peter Claver School.[21]

While at this time Mobile was the gracious South of mansions and magnolias, it was also, to a large extent, the South of poverty, prejudice, and segregation. The Sisters shared many of the unhappy experiences associated with the racial bigotry which, unfortunately, existed in so much of the South prior to the momentous Supreme Court Decision of May 17, 1954, which ushered in the integrated system of American education, and eventually, the integration of the whole social and economic structure.[22]

At the end of the first school term in 1944, Father Youngkin wrote to Mother M. Mechtilde:

Reverend dear Mother:

What a wonderful gift you sent me for my jubilee celebration. It is beautiful and all the more appreciated because I did not look for or expect any gift from you.

Believe me, Mother, it was one of the high spots in the celebration. Your Sisters were delighted that you had sent it. Let me assure you that you and your Sisters will be remembered among my benefactors at my Masses, not only for this gift but the great gift of five good Sisters. You have been kind to me and I remember how you sent me the extra teacher.

Mother, the work of these dear Sisters is proclaimed by the entire parish. We all love them for their self-sacrificing service. My earnest prayer and the desire of these people and children is that you please return all five of the Sisters to us. I have never asked you for anything yet that you have not granted me. Please do not let me down now.

Yours sincerely in Christ,
Edwin F. Youngkin, SSJ[23]

All the Sisters returned in September of 1945, but a year later, changes did occur on the staff. Sister M. Blanche, Sister M. Richard, and Sister Therese Agnes did not return to Mobile. Sister M. Therese Grajek was appointed the superior and principal and kept her previous assignment as teacher of grades seven and eight. Sister M. Rosaline Lenart was assigned to grades one and two; Sister M. Vincentine Szczepanek was put in charge of grades three and four, while Sister Dorothy Joan Lagocki took over grades five and six. At the end of September, Sister Marie Francis Moson was sent to replace Sister M. Vincentine.[24] Writing in *Our Colored Missions* at the end of that school year, Father Youngkin stated:

This year we have about 198 children in the school and had to add one more Sister to the teaching staff. We also had to raise the Sisters' salaries to thirty-five[25] dollars so that makes the bill $175 a month. We have Franciscan Sisters here who are sure doing fine work with the school children.[26]

Mother M. Mechtilde, who had been very supportive of the Mobile mission, died unexpectedly on March 16, 1946. Her successor was Mother M. Jerome Dadej, who, at a session of the general council in September of 1948 confronted the Sisters with what she termed a problem. Because of the increase in the number of schools through the years and the obvious lack of Sister personnel to staff the schools to which the Sisters were already committed, Mother M. Jerome was thinking seriously of withdrawing the Sisters from the Mobile area in order to bring them closer to the schools the Sisters staffed in Chicago and nearby areas.[27] Sister M. Gonzaga Raniszewski, the secretary general, was vocal in her defense of retaining St. Peter Claver School. She was, nevertheless, requested to send a letter to Bishop Toolen informing him that the Sisters would leave at the close of the school year. The letter read:

> Your Excellency:
>
> It is not easy for me to write a letter like this one to Your Excellency, but I am compelled to do so under the present circumstances.
>
> During the last few years, our Community has been suffering a great shortage of Sisters. On the average, we receive only three vocations a year. This small number does not meet with the ever-increasing number of Sisters we lose by death, illness, and old age.
>
> In order to keep the schools closer to the Motherhouse, we must close some schools which are farther away. At the last meeting of the general council, it was decided to close several schools among which is St. Peter Claver.
>
> I have not yet informed Father Youngkin of this decision. I shall do so after receiving Your Excellency's consent to remove the Sisters at the end of the school year in June of 1949.
>
> Thanking you for all the kindnesses extended to our Order by Your Excellency, I beg to remain,
>
> A humble servant in Christ,
> Mother M. Jerome[28]

A week later, Bishop Toolen replied to Mother M. Jerome's unwelcome letter:

> Dear Mother,
>
> If it was not easy for you to write your letter, it was much harder for me to get the news.
>
> I realize that all our Communities are suffering a great shortage, but, as you know this school is a real missionary work, and I do believe that

our Communities should make a greater effort to take care of these schools than those in more Catholic centers. We are not too far away from Chicago.

I do believe that taking your Sisters out of the school would mean closing the school, and though I do not know just how many children they have this year, they had around 160. I am sure that you would not want to deprive this large number of children, many of them non-Catholics, of an opportunity to know, love, and serve God.

I hope, Mother, that you will have another meeting of your Council and you will find a way to allow these Sisters to remain at St. Peter Claver's. It would be a calamity to take them away. They have done most excellent work in this school and have given it a standing it never had before. I do hope and pray that you will not take the Sisters from us. We will pray together for more vocations to make up for the number that are at St. Peter Claver's.

Asking God to bless you, and with all good wishes and prayers, I am,

> Sincerely in Christ,
> Thomas J. Toolen
> Bishop of Mobile[29]

Mother M. Jerome replied a week later:

Your Excellency:

Despite my earnest efforts to leave the Sisters at St. Peter Claver's School, I just cannot see how I could manage to do it. I feel that God does not demand the impossible from us.

My greatest difficulty presently is to staff a 150-bed hospital, our property, which is burdened with a heavy debt.[30] Due to the shortage of Sisters, a high salary must be paid to the lay help. Recently it has been very difficult to obtain lay nurses. Consequently, the Sisters must work from twelve to sixteen hours daily. I fear that their health is tremendously impaired and will not stand such a strain much longer.

There are some teachers here[31] who would be most willing to change their teaching position for that of nursing if they could be replaced in schools by the Sisters from St. Peter Claver's and those of St. Adalbert's of East St. Louis, Illinois, another school which we must close at the end of this scholastic year for the same reason.[32]

Hoping that Your Excellency would see my extreme need of those Sisters, I am,

> Humbly in Christ,
> Mother M. Jerome
> Superior General[33]

Bishop Toolen, undaunted, wrote to the Most Reverend Samuel Stritch, archbishop of Chicago, asking his intercession. Archbishop Stritch responded on December 30, 1948, by urging Mother M. Jerome to "reconsider your decision and find a way to consider teaching the school."[34] Once again, Mother M. Jerome repeated her reasons for withdrawing the Sisters from the school to Archbishop Stritch. She pleaded the scarcity of vocations, the overworked Sisters at the new hospital in Huron, South Dakota, and Boys Town, Nebraska, and the desire to locate the Sisters closer to the Motherhouse. Two trips to Chicago by Father Youngkin and Monsignor Leo Byrne, the superintendent of schools at Mobile, to convince Mother M. Jerome to change her decision proved fruitless. The school was closed on June 3, 1949. There were 215 students at St. Peter Claver's School when the Sisters withdrew.[35] Sister M. Therese Grajek and Sister M. Praesentia Grzybowski were the last two Sisters to leave. Prior to the Sisters' leaving, Bishop Toolen had come to the convent to bid farewell personally to each Sister.[36]

Without exception, the Sisters who ministered in Mobile all look upon their time of service there as one of the happiest and most rewarding experiences of their religious lives. Sister M. Rosaline Lenart tried to put her feelings into words: "My fondest memories still lie with the Southern mission of Mobile. To me, Mobile was a real mission. Away from family and community, I had a feeling of really giving my life and work to the Lord . . . what made our work beautiful and our home great were the lovely Sisters who helped build community so far away from everyone."[37] Sister M. Praesentia Grzybowski who was one of the last Sisters to leave Mobile made her strong statement: "We did not suffer too many inconveniences (except ants that got into everything) because the pastor was so good to us and the people would have given us their last crumb!"[38] All the Sisters missioned at St. Peter Claver School unanimously agree on the sadness they felt when the congregation chose to withdraw from this apostolate. The Sisters who were stationed at St. Peter Claver School, unfortunately, were themselves unaware of the actual plans for withdrawing the Sisters until the very end.[39] They lament the fact that neither Mother M. Jerome nor any member of the general council had ever visited Mobile to appraise the situation. To this day, regrets are still voiced over the decision to leave Mobile.[40] In all fairness to Mother M. Jerome and her councilors, it must be pointed out that Sister-nurses were needed at the congregation's newly opened St. John Hospital and School of Nursing in Huron, South Dakota. In 1942, for the first time in its history the congregation had no postulants. So pressed was Mother M. Jerome for Sisters that she continued the policy of sending the second-year novices to teach in the schools staffed by the congregation.

St. Peter Claver School remained closed until 1950 when it was reopened by the Congregation of the Sisters Servants of the Immaculate Heart of Mary of Monroe, Michigan. A new school was built in 1955, but the old church, rectory, and convent were demolished with the advent of urban renewal. In 1970, the Sisters Servants became increasingly aware of the fact that despite all efforts, they could not maintain quality education in the situation as it existed. After much negotiation, the Most Reverend John L. May, bishop of Mobile-Birmingham, decided to close St. Peter Claver School. The students and all the resources went to St. Matthew's School. St. Peter Claver Church merged with St. Vincent's Church, and the joint merger was called Prince of Peace Church. St. Peter Claver School became the home of the Catholic Department of Education.[41]

Thus, the first real "missionary" venture of the Franciscan Sisters of Chicago into the Southland ended after six brief years. None of the Sisters who ministered to the people of Mobile, Alabama, would ever deny that those six years were years filled with grace, love, and benediction.

THE FRANCISCAN SISTERS IN THE SOUTHLAND

[1]The man whom Governor George C. Wallace of Alabama called an outstanding churchman from whom "all Alabamians have to some degree profited by his leadership and the splendid example of his life and work," was born Thomas J. Toolen on February 28, 1886, in Baltimore, Maryland. He was ordained on September 27, 1910, in Baltimore by James Cardinal Gibbons. On February 28, 1927, Pope Pius XI named him the sixth bishop of Mobile, and in October of 1949, Pope Pius XII bestowed on him the title of archbishop.

The building record of Archbishop Toolen is phenomenal. A total of 709 buildings were built in the diocese: 189 churches and chapels, 95 grade schools, 17 high schools, 119 rectories, 112 convents, 104 parish halls, 23 hospitals and nursing homes, and 50 other buildings. A total of eighty parishes were established from the time he assumed office. He brought thirty-four religious communities of women into the diocese in his forty years and eleven communities of men.

In 1927, when Bishop Toolen came to the Diocese of Mobile, there was a Catholic population of just about 1 percent where forty-nine counties out of seventy-seven did not have a Catholic Church. When he retired, there were only seventeen counties without at least one Catholic mission chapel.

Archbishop Toolen retired in October of 1969 as bishop of Mobile-Birmingham when it was divided into two dioceses. He died in 1976. *Solemn Observance of the Fortieth Episcopal Anniversary of the Most Reverend Thomas J. Toolen, DD, LLD, Litt. D. Archbishop-Bishop of the Diocese of Mobile-Birmingham,* 25 October 1967; *Mobile-Birmingham Diocesan Record Sheets* (AFSCL).

[2]Bishop Fulton J. Sheen called Archbishop Toolen, "the defender of the socially disinherited." Bishop Toolen's zeal for the blacks in his diocese was well known. Realizing that the diocese offered a fertile field for the black apostolate, Bishop Toolen steadily fostered and advanced black education. He erected numerous and modern schools. The Diocesan School Report for 1947 reveals the following statistics for black schools: 20 elementary with 3,000 pupils and 77 religious; and 5 high schools with 443 pupils and 20 religious. The Franciscan Sisters of Chicago were proudly listed among the fifteen communities of religious women represented in the diocese at that time.*The Catholic Week,* 9 May 1947, p. 52; 21 October 1960, p. 11.

[3]*Minutes of General Council Proceedings,* July 1956 (AFSCL).

[4]St. Peter Claver (1581–1654) was a Jesuit who did missionary work for forty-four years among the black slaves at Cartagena in Central America. The Church has declared him special patron of all Catholic missions among black people. A. J. M. Mausolff and M. K. Mausolff, *Saint Companions for Each Day* (St. Paul: St. Paul Publications, 1954), no pagination.

[5]Creoles are generally persons of black descent who were born in the Americas. They are descended from or culturally related to the original French settlers of the Gulf States. The first permanent white settlement was established at Mobile by the French in 1711. Kay Sullivan, *The Catholic Tourist Guide* (New York: Meredith Press, 1967), p. 68.

[6]"A Brief History of St. Peter Claver Church, Mobile, Alabama," 6 June 1953. (Typewritten).

[7]The St. Joseph's Society of the Sacred Heart, popularly called the Josephites, have the specialized purpose of working for and among the blacks in the United States.

[8]*Fiftieth Anniversary of St. Peter Claver Church, 1911–1961* (Mobile, Alabama, 1961), no pagination.

[9]The congregation was founded in San Antonio in 1893 by Mrs. Margaret Mary Healy-Murphy, the devout widow of the former mayor of Corpus Christi. She was extremely interested in the needy and neglected children of the black race. She realized the need for a religious community of women to carry out the mission to which she had dedicated herself. *Archdiocese of San Antonio, 1874–1974* (San Antonio, 1974), p. 291.

[10]*Book of Correspondence:* Letter from the Sisters-Servants of the Holy Ghost and Mary Immaculate to author, 4 December 1975 (AFSCL).

[11]*Minutes of General Council Proceedings, 1934–1956* (AFSCL).

[12]*Book of Correspondence:* Letter from Sister M. Praesentia Grzybowski to author, 24 May 1978 (AFSCL).

[13]The Reverend Edwin F. Youngkin, SSJ, spent his entire missionary career in the Josephite missions in Alabama, Florida, Louisiana, Mississippi, and Tennessee. Born in Brooklyn, New York, in January of 1889, he joined the Josephites filled with a desire to spend his life in the special cause of black America. He served as pastor of St. Peter Claver parish from 1939 until 1950. He died in Baltimore in 1966 after a prolonged illness. *The Josephite Harvest* 78 (July–August 1966): 11.

[14]*Book of Correspondence:* Letter from the Reverend Edwin F. Youngkin, SSJ, to Mother M. Mechtilde Zynda, 12 August 1943 (AFSCL).

[15]*Book of Correspondence:* Letter from Sister M. Therese Grajek to author, 6 February 1975 (AFSCL).

[16]*Book of Correspondence:* Letter from the Reverend Edwin F. Youngkin, SSJ, to Mother M. Mechtilde Zynda, 7 October 1943 (AFSCL).

[17]*Book of Correspondence:* Letter from Sister Marie Francis Moson to author, 30 December 1975 (AFSCL).

[18]*Book of Correspondence:* Letters from the Sisters Servants of the Immaculate Heart of Mary to author, 14 November 1975 (AFSCL).

[19]Sister Marie Francis Moson withdrew from the congregation in the early 1970s and joined the Congregation of Franciscan Sisters, Daughters of the Sacred Hearts of Jesus and Mary.

[20]The Sisters had a convent at 2300 Springhill Avenue in Mobile.

[21]*Book of Correspondence:* Letter from Sister Marie Francis Moson to author, 30 December 1975 (AFSCL).

[22]*Book of Correspondence:* Letters from Sisters Servants of the Immaculate Heart of Mary to author, 1975 (AFSCL).

[23]*Book of Correspondence:* Letter from the Reverend Edwin F. Youngkin, SSJ, to Mother M. Mechtilde Zynda, 17 June 1944 (AFSCL).

[24]She replaced Sister M. Vincentine Szczepanek who was sent to St. Stanislaus Bishop and Martyr School in Chicago. Sister M. Vincentine left the congregation in May of 1952.

[25]It should be recalled that the Sisters were not to receive a salary as such, but instead would depend upon the goodwill offerings of benefactors of the Josephite Fathers. Writing to the readers of *Our Colored Missions,* he states: "Your check received and I am indeed glad to receive it, as it will enable me to pay the Sisters for the complete year." Again in 1946: "Your check received for the support of our school Sisters." *Our Colored Missions,* 27; 32; 33 (February 1941); (March 1946).

[26]*Our Colored Missions,* 33 (March 1947): 44.

[27]*Minutes of General Council Proceedings, 1934–1956* (AFSCL).

[28]*Book of Correspondence:* Letter from Mother M. Jerome Dadej to the Most Reverend Thomas J. Toolen, 15 September 1948 (AFSCL).

[29]*Book of Correspondence:* Letter from the Most Reverend Thomas J. Toolen to Mother M. Jerome Dadej, 21 September 1948 (AFSCL).

[30]Mother M. Jerome has reference here to St. John Hospital and School of Nursing which the Sisters opened in November of 1947 in Huron, South Dakota.

[31]One of the Sisters, Sister Dorothy Joan Lagocki, did change to the nursing field.

[32]The general council had decided to close St. Adalbert's School in East St. Louis, Illinois. Unlike the actual closing of St. Peter Claver School in 1949, however, St. Adalbert's School

remained open for several more years. *Minutes of General Council Proceedings, 1934–1956* (AFSCL).

[33]*Book of Correspondence:* Letter from Mother M. Jerome Dadej to the Most Reverend Thomas J. Toolen, 29 September 1948 (AFSCL).

[34]*Book of Correspondence:* Letter from the Most Reverend Samuel Stritch to Mother M. Jerome Dadej, 30 December 1938 (AFSCL).

[35]*Book of Correspondence:* Letter from the Reverend William Friend, Vicar for Education, Catholic Department of Education, Mobile, Alabama, to author, 5 November 1975 (AFSCL).

[36]*Book of Correspondence:* Letter from Sister Marie Francis Moson to author, 30 December 1975 (AFSCL).

[37]*Book of Correspondence:* Letter from Sister M. Rosaline Lenart to author, 13 December 1975 (AFSCL).

[38]*Book of Correspondence:* Letter from Sister M. Praesentia Grzybowski to author, 24 May 1978 (AFSCL).

[39]Sister M. Praesentia had received a letter from Sister M. Athanasius Murzyn telling her that the East St. Louis mission (St. Adalbert's) and Mobile were closing. That was the first time the Sisters heard of the decision to withdraw the Sisters from Mobile. *Book of Correspondence:* Letter from Sister M. Praesentia Grzybowski to author, 24 May 1978 (AFSCL).

[40]*Book of Correspondence:* Letters from the Sisters Servants of the Immaculate Heart of Mary to author, 24 May 1978 (AFSCL).

[41]*Book of Correspondence:* Letter from Sister Gail Stackpole, IHM, assistant archivist to author, 14 November 1975 (AFSCL).

CHAPTER 45

Towards New Horizons

To minister to the needs of the sick and the incapacitated has always been a goal of the Franciscan Sisters of Chicago. The Constitutions and the Directory of the Sisters testify to this worthy service:

> We recognize the care of the sick and the aged as an authentic Christian commitment, relevant to the saving mission of Christ and the Church. In imitation of St. Francis and Mother M. Theresa, our service should be one of love and simplicity. By our good example, loving care, and visible Christian witness, we are that leaven which transforms all in Christ.[1]

While the administration and staffing of elementary schools appeared to be the increasingly dominant mission of the congregation, service to those who were ill developed as a strong secondary apostolate. It will be remembered that as far back as 1905, the Reverend Andrew Spetz, CR, the congregation's spiritual director, had advised the Sisters to prepare for this special ministry. It was decided at that time that as many Sisters as possible would obtain nurses' training for this unselfish and courageous work made meritorious by the words of Christ: "As long as you did it to one of these, the least of my brethren, you did it to Me."[2] The Sister-nurses in the congregation were to perceive in those committed to their care the Person of the Savior who always manifested the greatest compassion toward the sick.[3] Although the superiors general attempted to send Sisters to train as nurses, the immediate need was for their services in homes for the aged and as teachers in elementary schools. As a consequence, only a few Sisters could be spared to enter the hospital ministry at the congregation's beginning.

The earliest recorded request for Sisters to enter the hospital ministry was received in 1921 from Dr. Louis Georgi for at least four Sisters to assist him in opening a hospital in Gary, Indiana. At that time, Mother M. Aloysia Holysz was forced to refuse his request because of a lack of sufficiently trained Sister-nurses.[4] Two years later, a new petition to staff St. Anthony's Hospital on Wabash and Ann Streets in Michigan City, Indiana, was presented by Mother M. Vincent Czyzewski, the new superior general, to her council. They voted to accept the staffing of the hospital and appointed Sister M. Antonina Osinski and Sister M. Ladislaus Wroblewski to this duty. The Reverend Monsignor Francis Rempe, vicar general for the women religious of the Archdiocese of Chicago, however, advised against taking the hospital. Following the advice of Monsignor Rempe, Mother M. Vincent refused any further requests from St. Anthony's Hospital.[5]

A new offer to staff a hospital was received in 1928 from the Right Reverend Monsignor William O'Meara, the pastor of Immaculate Conception Church in Watertown, South Dakota. He requested that the Franciscan Sisters of Chicago take charge of the forty-five-bed Barton Hospital. Both Dr. Barton and the mayor of Watertown came to Chicago to ask Mother M. Vincent to undertake the staffing of the hospital for a period of two years. If after that time the Sisters were not happy with the arrangements, they would be free to leave. In May of 1928, Sister M. Antonina Osinski and Sister M. Benigna Jakajtis paid a visit to Watertown and returned to Chicago with excellent reports.[6] Mother M. Vincent and her general council voted to accept the Watertown Hospital, but when Mother M. Vincent approached the Most Reverend George Mundelein, archbishop of Chicago, for permission, he did not sanction the Sisters' staffing the Barton Hospital. As a result, the Sisters refused any further offers from Watertown.

In 1937, a newspaper clipping concerning a hospital in Gettysburg, South Dakota, was brought to the attention of Mother M. Antonina Osinski. The article read:

Sisters Needed for New Dakota Hospital

The Reverend P. P. Meyer, pastor of Sacred Heart Church here, is seeking an Order of Sisters to take charge of a proposed hospital in the city. The hospital is to be a county project of the WPA and is to cost $40,000. There are two Orders of Sisters working in the territory but both are short of nuns to accept the offer.[7]

Having seen the announcement, Mother M. Antonina reacted favorably to Father Meyer's request. A week later, Father Meyer thanked her for her interest in the Gettysburg Memorial Hospital and promised to keep her informed.[8] According to the *Community Chronicle,* the question of the acceptance of the hospital, however, was shelved for the next ten years. In February of 1947, another request came to take over the administration of the thirty-bed hospital. The superior general and her general council were in favor of accepting the Gettysburg Memorial Hospital when a conflict of interests arose with another religious congregation concerning the hospital. The Franciscan Sisters of Chicago terminated the tentative agreement they had entered into with the Gettysburg Hospital.[9]

A new hospital offer appeared in January of 1939. Mother M. Antonina Osinski presented to her general council the offer of a new hospital in Webster, South Dakota, by a Dr. Peabody who offered to sell it to the Franciscan Sisters of Chicago for $40,000. Mother M. Antonina declined the offer and next turned her attention to a proposal to purchase the Belmont Community Hospital on Karlov and Melrose Avenues in Chicago.[10]

To that end, Mother M. Antonina visited Cardinal Mundelein and disclosed to him the Sisters' intention of buying the hospital, expressing the congregation's deep desire to enter the health apostolate. Cardinal Mundelein refused to grant permission to Mother M. Antonina to purchase the Belmont Community Hospital citing the fact that there was a sufficient number of Catholic hospitals in Chicago.[11] He urged Mother M. Antonina to accept a hospital out of the city or even out of Illinois.[12]

In the meantime, the Right Reverend Monsignor Andrew Radecki, pastor of St. Casimir Church in Cleveland, Ohio, and a good friend of the Franciscan Sisters of Chicago, informed Mother M. Antonina of an opportunity to take charge of St. Joseph Hospital and School of Nursing in Lorain, Ohio. Mother M. Antonina and Sister M. Jerome visited the Lorain hospital, but because of the complications concerning the debt on the institution, the Sisters decided not to pursue further consideration of the hospital.[13]

Strangely enough, at a general council meeting on April 8, 1940, Mother M. Antonina informed her councilors that there had been several announcements in the Crown Point, Indiana, newspapers concerning a hospital to be built there by the Franciscan Sisters of Chicago.[14] This came as a surprise to the councilors since they had never discussed such a possibility. It appeared that officials of Crown Point had issued statements regarding the great need for a hospital. Lacking the necessary funds, however, the city officials wanted the Sisters to undertake the project. What is startling and prophetic about the offer is that in 1974, thirty-four years later, the Franciscan Sisters of Chicago would actually build and staff the beautiful St. Anthony Medical Center in Crown Point!

On July 2, 1940, Mother M. Mechtilde Zynda was elected the superior general. After her election, she visited Samuel Cardinal Stritch, the new archbishop of Chicago, and informed him of the congregation's desire to undertake the staffing of a hospital. Cardinal Stritch warned Mother M. Mechtilde not to purchase an old hospital but instead to build a new one once World War II was over.

Four years later, in 1944, the Franciscan Sisters of Chicago received a request to undertake the Sprague Hospital and School of Nursing in Huron, South Dakota. The time had finally come for the Sisters' ministry in the health field to begin. That year, several civic-minded leaders, namely, the Reverend John J. O'Neil, the pastor of St. Martin's Church in Huron; Robert D. Lusk, the publisher of the Huron city newspaper; and Dr. J. C. Shirley, the president of the Huron Clinic and the Sprague Hospital staff, appealed to Mother M. Mechtilde to send the Franciscan Sisters of Chicago to manage the Sprague Hospital and School of Nursing in Huron. The request for the services of the Sisters became an urgent plea when it was realized that the school of nursing which had been in operation for twenty-three years would have to close due to the shortage of qualified personnel. Mother M. Mechtilde and the general council agreed to comply with the request and selected Sister M. Leona Mszanski and Sister Eleanor Plocki to spearhead the congregation's newest ministry. The undertaking of the Sprague Hospital and School of Nursing eventually led to one of the congregation's most salutary and rewarding apostolic missions—the foundation of the St. John Hospital and School of Nursing, later called St.

John Regional Medical Center, in Huron. Because of its importance, St. John's establishment and ministry will be discussed at length in Chapter 49.

Two more requests were received in 1948. One came from Gregory and the other from Chamberlain, both in South Dakota. Mother M. Antonina and Sister M. Felixa Jorz were sent to view the two hospitals and their reports concerning both were very favorable. Mother M. Jerome, the superior general, and the general council determined that the Gregory Hospital and its location were preferred. The Sisters voted to undertake the staffing of the Gregory Hospital in October of 1948 with four Sisters. Learning of Mother M. Jerome's affirmative reply, the Most Reverend William Brady, bishop of Sioux Falls, responded in part: "I am sure you will make no mistake in accepting the offer of the bishop of Rapid City to accept the hospital at Gregory."[15] The account of the Sisters' ministry in Gregory, South Dakota, is discussed in a subsequent chapter as will be the matter of the Our Lady of the Sandhills Hospital (Atkinson Memorial Hospital) in Atkinson, Nebraska, which was accepted in 1952.

At a meeting of the general council in 1950, the offer of a hospital in Winner, South Dakota, was discussed. The town of Winner was situated between Gregory and Martin, South Dakota, where the Franciscan Sisters of Chicago had already accepted the administration and the staffing of two hospitals. The general council voted to accept the hospital in Winner and a letter was sent to the Reverend Charles Virnig from whom the request to take charge of the hospital had come, outlining the conditions under which the Franciscan Sisters of Chicago would agree to undertake the hospital. A letter was sent to the Most Reverend William T. McCarty, bishop of Rapid City, stating that the Sisters were prepared to accept the hospital in Winner whenever it was feasible.[16] On July 8, 1950, Mother M. Jerome received a letter from Bishop McCarty in regard to the Winner Hospital. In it, Bishop McCarty stated: "It would be a great boon for Winner if your Sisters could take the hospital."[17] The matter lay dormant until 1953 when the Reverend Charles Virnig again contacted Mother M. Jerome informing her of the availability of the Winner hospital.[18] Mother M. Jerome advised Father Virnig that there were no Sisters available since, by this time, the Sisters were already in charge of four hospitals and a school of nursing. She did tell him, however, that the Sisters at St. Anthony Hospital in Martin, South Dakota, could be transferred to Winner since they were undergoing numerous hardships due to the lack of an adequate hospital in which to function. As a matter of fact, the Martin community had been informed that unless it started building the proposed new hospital, Mother M. Jerome would be forced to withdraw the Sisters.[19] Conditions did change for the better in Martin, however, and the Sisters were not removed. By the middle of April, Mother M. Jerome was forced to admit to Father Virnig that because of the pressing demand for nursing Sisters in the congregation's homes for the aged, the Franciscan Sisters of Chicago could no longer accept the Winner Hospital.[20] Father Virnig continued his pleas through much correspondence and even made a visit to the Motherhouse. Letters in the archives of the congregation indicate that the matter of the Winner Hospital was put on reserve. It was not until five years later, in November of 1958, that Bishop McCarty raised the issue of the hospital again. He received a reply from Mother M. Beatrice Rybacki, who in June of 1958, had succeeded Mother M. Jerome Dadej as superior general, stating in part that "conditions have changed considerably since the time Mother M. Jerome had planned to take over the Winner hospital. Now we have the opportunity to build a hospital on our own property in Lemont, and the Winner proposition can no longer be considered."[21]

The matter of a hospital in Lemont was a long and drawn-out affair. As far back as 1947, a small group of doctors had begun to explore the possibilities of a hospital for the Lemont area and had approached Mother M. Jerome Dadej. The idea of a hospital in Lemont appeared advantageous to the congregation since Our Lady of Victory Convent for the aged and infirm Sisters and the novitiate were located there. Two doctors from Lemont, Dr. Bruce Brown and Dr. Ernest Blondis, suggested to Mother M. Jerome that instead of building an entirely new hospital, the Our Lady of Victory Convent could be converted into a fifty- to sixty-bed hospital. Dr. Brown was prepared to give the Franciscan Sisters $300,000 to help equip the proposed hospital. At a session of the general council, the councilors voted to reject Dr. Brown's suggestion for valid reasons.[22] Firstly, there was no other place to house the aged and infirm Sisters and Our Lady of Victory Convent had been erected specifically for that purpose. Secondly, any renovation and remodeling would be expensive and at that specific period of time, the congregation had large debts and financial worries concerning St. John Hospital and School of Nursing, their newly built institution in Huron, South Dakota. While the Sisters were not totally adverse to a hospital on the grounds in Lemont, they were not in a position to undertake its financing at that time.[23]

Dr. Brown returned to Mother M. Jerome in January of 1949 after having discussed the matter of the hospital with doctors in the village of Lemont and its surrounding communities: Downers Grove, Westmont, Lockport, Orland Park, and Willow Springs. All the physicians consulted were strongly interested in the erection of a hospital in Lemont. Dr. Brown also insisted that he had the support of groups such as the Lemont Chamber of Commerce, the American Legion, and the Veterans of Foreign Wars.[24]

The matter of the hospital did not surface again until 1958. Both Dr. Blondis and Dr. Brown continued to present to the congregation the merits of Lemont and Our Lady of Victory Convent as the perfect hospital location. Letters such as the following were meant to support their position:

> Reverend Mother:
>
> I am addressing this letter to you as president of the Lemont Chamber of Commerce to bring to your attention a project which, I can assure you, is close to the hearts and wishes of a great many people in Lemont.
>
> I have reference, Reverend Mother, to the possibility of converting facilities at Our Lady of Victory Convent, which your Order conducts, into a hospital for Lemont and its surrounding area.

The need for such hospital facilities to serve the Greater Lemont area is graphically demonstrated by statistics which showed that more than 1,000 residents of the village of Lemont alone were patients at St. Joseph's and Silver Cross Hospitals in Joliet last year.

I know I speak for the business community—and Lemonters generally—when I say they would welcome the opportunity to assist in such a project as the conversion of Our Lady of Victory Convent into a hospital to provide badly needed facilities here.

May I have the honor of an appointment with you in the near future to explore the possibilities of such a project?

Thank you very kindly for your attention in this matter.

Respectfully,

Harry Witkoski

President, Chamber of Commerce[25]

Mother M. Beatrice authorized Sister M. Gonzaga Raniszewski, the secretary general, to confer with the Very Reverend Monsignor John W. Barrett,[26] the director of hospitals in the Archdiocese of Chicago, concerning a hospital in Lemont. Father Barrett informed Sister M. Gonzaga that a hospital was not needed in the village of Lemont since there were two excellent hospitals in Joliet, namely, St. Joseph Hospital and Silver Cross Hospital, only fourteen miles away.[27] Furthermore, at a council meeting held in May of 1961, Mother M. Beatrice informed her general council that a survey indicated that the Lemont community could not raise the necessary funds no matter how badly the Chamber of Commerce wanted a hospital on the grounds of the Franciscan Sisters of Chicago. Another effort was made by Dr. Brown regarding the hospital by offering to give the congregation some land worth $25,000 near his clinic in downtown Lemont. The councilors examined the property and confirmed that the place was not suitable for use as a hospital. Another doctor, Dr. Charles Kallick, had even brought a sketch of the proposed renovation of the Our Lady of Victory Convent into a hospital to persuade Mother M. Beatrice and the general council to his point of view. The doctors were willing to supply funds totaling $200,000 and the Sisters were asked to supply the remainder. Mother M. Beatrice hastened to inform the doctors of the futility of any plans to build a hospital in Lemont since the congregation was planning to build a new Motherhouse there soon.

Evidence is found in the archives of the congregation to indicate that, throughout the years, many other requests came from hospitals in various areas seeking the services of the Franciscan Sisters of Chicago. These included Evanston, Joliet, and Peoria in Illinois; Donaldson, Elkhart, Evansville, Logansport, and Mishawaka in Indiana; Aberdeen, Sioux Falls, Redfield, Britton, Webster, Tyndall, and Hoven in South Dakota; Wayne, Nebraska; Louisville, Kentucky; Dillon, South Carolina; and Estherville, Iowa. Each request was validly considered in the light of the congregation's personnel and on the advice of ecclesiastical authority.

TOWARDS NEW HORIZONS

[1]*Constitutions and Directory of the Franciscan Sisters of Chicago,* Article 56 (Lemont, Illinois, 1975), pp. 25–26.

[2]Matt. 25:40.

[3]*Constitutions of the Congregation of the Sisters of Bl. Kunegunda of the Third Order of St. Francis,* Article 194 (Chicago, Illinois, 1954), p. 40.

[4]Secretaries General, *Community Chronicle, 1910–1957,* 26 February 1922 (AFSCL).

[5]*Minutes of General Council Proceedings, 1910–1934,* 12 May 1923 (AFSCL).

[6]Secretaries General, *Community Chronicle, 1910–1957,* p. 105 (AFSCL).

[7]*Gregory (South Dakota) Times-Advocate,* 23 June 1937.

[8]*Book of Correspondence:* Letter from the Reverend P. P. Meyer to Mother M. Antonina Osinski, 18 May 1937 (AFSCL).

[9]*Minutes of General Council Proceedings, 1934,* 29 March 1947 (AFSCL).

[10]The hospital is two blocks north of Madonna High School and a mile away from St. Joseph Home of Chicago.

[11]The Sisters also had an opportunity to secure a hospital in Rogers Park but once again Cardinal Mundelein vetoed it saying it was too close to St. Francis Hospital in Evanston.

[12]Secretaries General, *Community Chronicle,* p. 189 (AFSCL).

[13]*Minutes of General Council Proceedings, 1934,* 28 July 1939 (AFSCL).

[14]According to an old newspaper clipping published in 1939, Sister M. Marcelline of St. Anthony's Home in Crown Point, was quoted as saying that "within the next two years the Sisters hope to build a hospital for Southern Lake County residents on the same site as the home." She said: "We hope to be able to start this hospital movement as soon as possible. For a good many sick and accident cases, it is a long distance to take patients to Hammond and Gary."

[15]*Book of Correspondence:* Letter from the Most Reverend William Brady to Mother M. Jerome Dadej, 25 June 1948 (AFSCL).

[16]*Minutes of General Council Proceedings, 1934,* 12 July 1950 (AFSCL).

[17]*Book of Correspondence:* Letter from the Most Reverend William T. McCarty to Mother M. Jerome Dadej, 8 August 1950 (AFSCL).

[18]*Book of Correspondence:* Letter from the Reverend Charles Virnig to Mother M. Jerome Dadej, 9 January 1953 (AFSCL).

[19]*Minutes of General Council Proceedings, 1934,* 28 February 1953 (AFSCL).

[20]*Book of Correspondence:* Letter from Mother M. Jerome Dadej to the Reverend Charles Virnig, 16 April 1953 (AFSCL).

[21]*Book of Correspondence:* Letter from Mother M. Beatrice Rybacki to the Most Reverend William T. McCarty, 6 December 1958 (AFSCL).

[22]*Minutes of General Council Proceedings, 1956,* 31 December 1948 (AFSCL).

[23]Secretaries General, *Community Chronicle,* p. 236 (AFSCL).

[24]*Book of Correspondence:* Letter from Dr. Bruce Brown to Mother M. Jerome Dadej, 26 January 1949 (AFSCL).

[25]*Book of Correspondence:* Letter from Mr. Harry Witkoski to Mother M. Beatrice Rybacki, 4 June 1959 (AFSCL).

[26]Father Barrett was the archdiocesan director of hospitals from September of 1931. For thirty-five years, he was a leader in hospital and health fields on the national level. He died in Chicago on November 21, 1966. Biographical sketch from the Chancery Office, Archdiocese of Chicago.

[27]Secretaries General, *Community Chronicle,* 25 January (AFSCL).

CHAPTER 46

Meeting Apostolic Needs

While the congregation had taken a serious turn toward the ministry of health care services, an increasing number of requests continued to be directed to Mother M. Mechtilde urging her to undertake the staffing of more parochial schools. During her administration, she and her general council agreed to accept only one school in addition to that of St. Peter Claver in Mobile, Alabama. The new school, accepted in 1944, was that of St. John the Baptist, later renamed St. Joseph the Provider, located in East Youngstown, now called Campbell, Ohio.

Polish immigrants had settled in East Youngstown early in 1906. Several years before World War I, a Polish colony was firmly grounded in the area near the City Hall and the present Waterworks Building. In order to worship, the Poles were forced to travel to St. Stanislaus Kostka Church in Youngstown, a distance of approximately four miles. In 1919, the Most Reverend John P. Farrelly, bishop of Cleveland, appointed the Reverend Joseph Rojewski to the pastorate of a new church to serve the 145 families who had requested permission to form a new Polish parish. Severe economic hardships plus the entrance of the United States into World War I impeded the progress of the building program undertaken by the parishioners. In August of 1920, however, a modest church named in honor of St. John the Baptist was formally dedicated in Campbell.[1]

In 1925, the Reverend Lawrence Budny became pastor of St. John the Baptist Church. During his administration, a parish hall was built. Once again, the parish had financial difficulties due to the Depression of 1929 and frequent changes in the parish administration. Finally, in 1940, with the appointment of the Reverend Thaddeus Heruday as pastor, the parish assumed a more positive prospect for the future.[2]

The Franciscan Sisters of Chicago stationed at nearby St. Stanislaus Kostka School in Youngstown had begun as early as 1931 to teach religion and Polish to the children of St. John the Baptist Church on Saturdays. The appointed Sisters, Sister M. Edwina Wilk and Sister M. Amata Holub, also performed the sacristy duties. Finally, in 1944, Father Heruday addressed a letter to Mother M. Mechtilde:

Dear Venerable Mother:

The Franciscan Sisters stationed at St. Stanislaus Parish in Youngstown have been helping our parish on Saturdays, especially with catechism and sacristy work. They indeed proved themselves a blessing to this small parish and the children love them dearly.

Beginning with this semester, because of various tasks and doubling of classes, although willing, they find it too difficult to come to Campbell. The Superior[3] feels (and rightly so), that an overworked Sister will become a sick Sister. She is willing but does not want to overburden the Sisters.

If the mission fields need Sisters, we need them even more. A young generation is growing up right in our midst without a sufficient knowledge of God. I wish we could do more to save the souls of these little ones.

May I make a suggestion? I would be willing to pay for the upkeep of one Sister who could stay at St. Stanislaus Parish during the week and help there, and come here [Campbell] on Saturdays and Sundays.

I sincerely hope, Venerable Mother, that you find a way to assist us in this little problem, so that we too can do more for the Sacred Heart and extend His love in the hearts of the little ones.

Sincerely yours in Christ,

Reverend Thaddeus Heruday[4]

Mother M. Mechtilde responded to Father Heruday's request by sending Sister M. Theresa Dadej to Youngstown on October 4, 1944. Sister M. Theresa lived with the Sisters at St. Stanislaus Kostka Convent in Youngstown and commuted to Campbell on weekends to teach catechism to approximately sixty-four children. As early as 1940, Father Heruday had initiated a survey in the parish to determine whether or not a parish school was needed. World War II forced him to postpone further planning, but in 1945, he was able to arrange for the purchase of a house on Ninth Street below Reed Avenue, approximately two and one-half blocks from the church. He informed Mother M. Mechtilde that he was in the process of starting a Catholic Social Mission House and was in need of three Sisters. He requested an organist, a kindergarten teacher, and a Sister to teach religion and conduct a study club for high school boys and girls.[5] Mother M. Mechtilde complied with his request by sending Sister M. Euphrosine Tryjanowski as the sacristan, part-time kindergarten teacher, and superior. Sister M. Theresa Dadej was appointed nursery and kindergarten teacher, while Sister M. Francesca Janowicz served as the organist. On August 31, 1945, Sister M. Theresa and Sister M. Francesca moved into the seven-room house on Ninth Street. With the arrival of Sister M. Euphrosine on September 6 from Mount Alvernia Convent in East Cleveland, St. John's Mission House was officially established.[6] Two rooms in the house were used as classrooms for the children in the nursery and kindergarten classes which were conducted daily from ten o'clock in the morning until twelve-fifteen. On Saturdays, the Sisters taught catechism to public school children from nine-thirty o'clock in the morning until twelve o'clock noon. Sister M. Euphrosine taught Polish classes on Tuesdays and Thursdays from four o'clock to five-fifteen o'clock in the afternoon. During the summer vacation, the Sisters conducted a mission school for children who wished to attend, regardless of nationality, color, or creed. The Sisters also visited the parishioners especially the members of the Polish National Church[7] in the hope of bringing them back into the Catholic Church and of sending their children to religion classes. An entry in the *House Journal of St. John the Baptist Convent* sums up the Sisters' challenge and response: "We have before us a great and difficult field of labor, securing these souls for Christ. But with the goodness and grace of God, we believe our efforts will not be in vain."[8]

On August 27, 1946, Sister M. Euphrosine was replaced by Sister M. Theresia Rybak as superior. She also served as sacristan, organist, and teacher of catechism to the younger children. Sister M. Theresa Dadej continued to conduct the kindergarten classes in addition to holding catechism classes for the older boys and girls. Sister M. Francesca was replaced by Sister M. Claudia Bomba who attended to household duties. In October, Father Heruday requested that Sister M. Theresia and Sister M. Claudia begin an intensive canvass of parish homes to determine the interest in a parish school.

With the coming of the 1947 school year, Sister M. Theresia returned to St. John's Mission House as the superior. Joining her that year were Sister M. Seraphia Bejrowski and Sister M. Ephrem Soprych. The canvass undertaken by Sister M. Theresia of parishioners interested in a parish school had indicated strongly that there was a genuine need of and desire for a school, and as a consequence, she advised Father Heruday to lose no time in starting one.[9] On September 2, 1947, St. John the Baptist School opened in two classrooms in the remodeled parish hall with more than seventy pupils. Sister M. Theresia had eighteen children in pre-kindergarten classes and thirty-two children in the

St. Joseph the Provider School
Campbell, Ohio (1944–1987)

St. Joseph the Provider Convent
Campbell, Ohio

kindergarten. Sister M. Seraphia taught twenty-four children in grades one and two. On Saturdays, the Sisters continued to teach catechism to public school children. As for the school, when the need arose additions were built to the original hall. By 1949, the Sisters had relocated to 102 Warhurst Road in a home which was located closer to the church.[10] Eventually, the enrollment reached 160 in 1954 with a kindergarten and eight grades.

A long-cherished dream was realized on August 4, 1963, when a new church was dedicated. Built about a mile away from the old site, the new church also had a new name. At the suggestion of Father Heruday, the forty-three-year-old St. John the Baptist (Polish) Church was renamed St. Joseph the Provider. The parishioners who had sacrificed and labored to make the new church possible felt very comfortable with the name of the saint of family life and laborers. On a practical level, the name change ended the confusion of having three churches in Campbell named in honor of St. John the Baptist.[11]

In May of 1964, the Reverend Leon Dobosiewicz succeeded Monsignor Heruday aa pastor. When the new rectory was completed, the Sisters moved from their house at 102 Warhurst into the old rectory at 85 Warhurst. In August of that year, ground-breaking took place for a new convent and school. The two-story school and gym built at the rear of the church was occupied on February 24, 1965. The convent on Sanderson Avenue into which the Sisters moved on April 14, 1966, was joined to the church on the south side of the altar boys' sacristy. The entire parish plant, striking in its modernity and compactness, occupied an entire beatifully landscaped block in Campbell's northeast residential area. The exterior beauty and preciseness of the parish plant was symbolic of the interior beauty of the parish through its commitment to Christ and his teachings coupled with the constant emphasis on academic excellence.

In 1987, after long and serious study and prayerful reflection regarding the Sisters' apostolic commitment at St. Joseph the Provider School, Sister Joseph Marie

Zenda, the superior general, and her general council informed the pastor and parishioners of the necessity to withdraw the Franciscan Sisters of Chicago at the close of the school year. Once again, the scarcity of new vocations and a concerned attention to the health and retirement needs of the Sisters had prompted the withdrawal.

A further challenge to the apostolic zeal of the Franciscan Sisters of Chicago presented itself in the summer of 1945 and along with the proposed commitment, a very special kind of obligation. The challenge called for Sisters of good will and of equally good physical stamina to participate in a varied and stimulating program of supervised park recreation for thousands of Chicago's underprivileged youngsters who would, otherwise, dread a long summer filled with "nothing to do." The Catholic Youth Organization, commonly referred to as the CYO, provided the park program for nearly fifteen thousand children regardless of race, color, or creed in some fifty-four strategic locations in the Archdiocese of Chicago.

At the request of the Most Reverend Bernard J. Sheil,[12] auxiliary bishop of Chicago, Mother M. Mechtilde appointed four Sisters to this pioneer park work conducted mainly in overcrowded neighborhoods of the city. In June of 1945, the field supervisor for the CYO Vacation School, as it was called, informed Sister M. Blanche Bartkowski and Sister M. Hildegarde Demps of their assignments to the Hamlin Park Center on Chicago's Northwest Side. Sister M. Esther Obuchowski and Sister M. Xavier Wroblewski were assigned to Humboldt Park, one of the city's four major parks on the West Side.[13]

Constructive courses in recreation for more than 180 park leaders were presented at the Sheil School of Social Studies.[14] These courses were designed to teach the fundamental techniques for successful work with the children. Once at their designated sites, the assigned leaders directed games and sports, taught useful arts and crafts, choral speaking, folk dances, and the art of story-telling. They held creative drama classes, arranged talent contests, and provided field trips to the forest preserves, museums, and the zoo. Each day at noon they distributed free milk to the children. The park program operated from nine o'clock in the morning until twelve o'clock noon from Monday through Friday for six weeks.

In 1946, Sister M. Dorothy Szostek and Sister M. Maristella Skrzynski were assigned to Hardin Square, the area centered on Cermak Road and Wentworth Avenue on the Southwest Side in what is popularly known as Chicago's Chinatown.[15] The next year, Sister M. Ferdinand Skiba, Sister M. Hildegarde Demps, Sister M. Julitta Szczepanik, and Sister M. Xavier Wroblewski eagerly accepted their assignments to the same area.[16] In 1948, four more Sisters were assigned to Hardin Square; and again in 1949, four Sisters were firmly committed to this summer service to the young.[17]

In 1950, Bishop Sheil's letter to Mother M. Jerome Dadej renewed the CYO Vacation School's challenge to its Sister participants:

The year 1950 seems to be particularly significant. On the positive side, it is pleasant to reflect upon the fact that the Vacation Centers have been in operation for twenty years. Their growth from one center in the Chicago area to fifty centers, and the fact that they annually serve the leisure time needs of some 15,000 children speak for the necessity of such a program. Responsible for these statistics are the years of hard work, the patience and the selflessness of the Sisters who have helped to make this program possible.

It is imperative that this work continue. In Chicago, particularly in the neighborhoods where the Centers operate, there is a constant increase of unemployment among unskilled workers. We have a special obligation to the children of these families. The want and the despair which unemployment causes, can and does bring an appalling increase in delinquency. Petty thievery may be the result of actual physical hunger. Insecurity within the family can cause a child to commit crimes against society which would not occur in ordinary times.

We must, with your assistance, during the summer months, offer a program of prevention, unparalleled in excellence. Therefore, I am asking you to assist me by appointing Sisters to the Hardin Square.[18]

Encouraged by the bishop's letter of appreciation and once again recognizing his plea for continued participation in the program, Mother M. Jerome assigned Sisters to the CYO Vacation School. For the next five years, undaunted by the hot Chicago summers, the Sisters gave eagerly of their time, talent, and energy at the Hardin Square to which they were assigned and which remained geographically convenient for them. The enthusiasm and resourcefulness displayed by the first Sisters assigned there were matched with equal vigor by the Sisters assigned to the Vacation School each year until 1955, the last summer in which the congregation participated in the program.[19] While in complete agreement with the goals of the park work, Mother M. Jerome was forced to refuse further requests for the Sisters' services. While the congregation in general continued to be affected by the lack of Sister personnel, other immediate and equally valid reasons for withdrawing were present. Many Sisters were on college campuses in pursuit of their basic education or in universities pursuing higher degrees. A large group of Sisters was engaged in teaching at remedial reading centers in a program sponsored by the Archdiocese of Chicago. Even more significantly, the Government of the United States was now granting stipends to parishes, which in turn hired lay people to staff the CYO Centers. Heretofore, the CYO had paid the Sisters $1.50 per day for their services. Finally, the Chicago Park District began its own day camp programs for youth.[20]

For the most part, the CYO Vacation Centers provided a necessary social service at the time. While the Vacation School proved taxing, and at times, was seemingly unproductive of the desired results in spite of the Sisters' best efforts, the Sisters were quick to agree that the rewards for participating were undeniably present. According to Sister M. Ferdinand Skiba:

> While all the youngsters were not Catholic, they respected and obeyed the Sisters . . . Though the routine was sometimes tiresome, especially in the hot, humid summer, we truly enjoyed the work.[21]

In another instance, Sister M. Maristella Skrzynski wrote:

> As the time for terminating the Vacation School approached, we were surprised a few times by groups of children who walked from 22nd and Wentworth to our convent on 43rd and Francisco just to see us again. I must confess that I grew quite attached to my Vacation School children, and I was sad when the time came to say goodbye.[22]

Of course, the prime reason for the Sisters' dedication to the CYO Vacation School was best summarized by Bishop Sheil himself in a letter to Mother M. Jerome: "The welcome accorded the children of Chicago's depressed areas makes it more evident every year that this is a greatly needed and truly Christ-like work."[23]

Although after 1955 the Franciscan Sisters of Chicago were no longer an integral part of the CYO Vacation School, the program continued under the auspices of the CYO and the Catholic Charities. Today, hundreds of archdiocesan employees and volunteers continue to make summer "fun" for thousands of children, and in an expanded program, for senior citizens who also have become special victims of modern urban problems.[24]

Early in January of 1946, Mother M. Mechtilde had paid a visit to the Sisters at St. John Hospital in Huron, South Dakota. Before she left for Chicago, the Sisters begged her to return to Huron soon. At the Sisters' earnest inquiries as to when she might return, Mother M. Mechtilde smiled widely and replied, "In the springtime, I shall be as happy as a *przepiórka* [partridge]." Since Mother M. Mechtilde's term as superior general was to end in June of 1946, the Sisters believed that she was expressing delight at that prospect. By March 16, 1946, less than two months after her visit to Huron, Mother M. Mechtilde was dead.[25]

Mother M. Mechtilde died on Saturday, March 16 at seven o'clock in the evening. She had not been in good health for some time, and finally, she entered Augustana Hospital in Chicago on February 18, 1946, after she could no longer bear the pain she had endured for many months. Mother M. Mechtilde had never complained and no one realized the severity and degree of her affliction.[26] She submitted to exploratory surgery which was performed by the eminent Dr. Nelson Percy on March 5. The procedure revealed that Mother M. Mechtilde was suffering from cancer of the pancreas and liver. Her condition was so advanced that Dr. Percy was unable to operate. Mother M. Mechtilde left the hospital and was brought to the Motherhouse by ambulance. The next day, her condition worsened. The Reverend Joseph Tarasiuk, the former chaplain of St. Joseph Home for the Aged, visited her in the morning and the Reverend Joseph Baniewicz, the chaplain of St. Joseph Home for the Aged, along with many Sisters, was at her bedside when she fell asleep in death.

The exportation of her body to the chapel of St. Joseph Home took place on Tuesday, March 19, at four-thirty o'clock in the afternoon. There were nine priests, three organists from neighboring parishes, including the well-known Mr. Adalbert Misiura[27] from St. Stanislaus Bishop and Martyr Church, and many Sisters present. On the night before her funeral, the Vespers of the Dead were sung in the chapel of the home. There were forty-three priests present, all the superiors of the congregation and many other Sisters and lay persons.

A Solemn High Funeral Mass was sung for the repose of the soul of Mother M. Mechtilde at ten o'clock in the morning on March 20. The celebrant of the mass was the Reverend Casimir Gużiel, CR, the provincial of the Congregation of the Resurrection. The Reverend Bruno Lazarowicz, CR, the pastor of St. Stanislaus Kostka Parish, served as deacon; the Reverend Jerome Fabianski, CR, pastor of St. Stanislaus Bishop and Martyr Church, served as the subdeacon. The Reverend Stanley Fiołek, CR, principal of Weber High School in Chicago delivered the eulogy in which he stressed Mother M. Mechtilde's virtuous life—her charity, patience, and conformity to God's Will. Forty-six priests attended her funeral along with scores of Sisters and lay persons.

After her death, Mother M. Mechtilde received that which she had shunned during her lifetime–honor and recognition in a solemn and splendid funeral. She was laid to rest in St. Adalbert's Cemetery in a grave next to that of her cousin, Mother M. Anna Wysinski. Mother M. Mechtilde was fifty-six years old and had been in the congregation for thirty-nine years.

Three days later, the congregation received a letter from Cardinal Stritch:

My dear Sisters:

I am very sorry to learn on return home from a recent trip to the South of the death of your good Mother General. I knew her and esteemed her. She was a good religious and sought only the honor of God in all her work. I join with you in your sorrow, and I shall join with you in your prayers for her.

Sincerely yours in Christ,
Samuel Cardinal Stritch
Archbishop of Chicago[28]

Mother M. Mechtilde's kind heart had always drawn others to herself. Cardinal Stritch's message of sympathy to the congregation at the time of her death summed up the life of this fine woman with the sentence: "She was a good religious and sought only the honor of God in all her works."

MEETING APOSTOLIC NEEDS

[1]*St. Joseph the Provider: Dedication Book* (Campbell, Ohio, 4 August 1963), no pagination.

[2]The Franciscan Sisters of Chicago were acquainted with the Reverend Thaddeus Heruday who had served as the assistant at Sacred Heart Church in Cleveland where the Sisters staffed the school. He was appointed pastor of St. John the Baptist Church in Campbell in September 1940. He was invested as monsignor on May 28, 1961.

[3]The superior at St. Stanislaus parish in Youngstown at that time was Sister M. Bogumila Swiech.

[4]*Book of Correspondence:* Letter from the Reverend Thaddeus Heruday to Mother M. Mechtilde Zynda, 16 September 1944 (AFSCL).

[5]Ibid., 4 August 1945.

[6]*St. Joseph the Provider House Journal* (AFSCL).

[7]As early as December 8, 1917, Sister M. Bernice Stefanski, superior and principal of St. Stanislaus Kostka School in Youngstown, had written a letter to Mother M. Aloysia Holysz pointing out that the church was actually a Slovak church but that many Poles belonged to it probably as a matter of convenience. The Reverend Michael Konwinski, who served as pastor of St. John the Baptist Church in Campbell from 1931 to 1940 observed during this period: "The people here are completely given over to Polish nationalism. They are more Polish than Catholic. Therefore, there is a great deal of effort to enkindle in them a religious attitude. I imagine that through hard work and patience, in the future we will have a parish school." *Book of Correspondence:* Letter from Sister M. Bernice Stefanski to Mother M. Aloysia Holysz, 8 December 1918 (AFSCL).

[8]*St. Joseph the Provider House Journal* (AFSCL).

[9]*Book of Correspondence:* Letter from Sister M. Theresia Rybak to author, 27 September 1978 (AFSCL).

[10]*St. Joseph the Provider House Journal* (AFSCL).

[11]*St. Joseph the Provider: Dedication Book* (Campbell, Ohio, 4 August 1963), no pagination.

[12]The Most Reverend Bernard J. Sheil, DD, was born on February 18, 1888, in St. Columbkille's Parish on Chicago's West Side. At an early age, he became aware of the difficulties and problems presented by a congested big city. Educated at St. Viator's College in Bourbonnais, Illinois, he took an active part in school athletics, becoming a star baseball and football player. Rejecting an offer to play for the Cincinnati Reds, he entered St. Viator's Seminary. At the conclusion of his studies he was ordained to the priesthood by the Most Reverend James E. Quigley, archbishop of Chicago, in the Cathedral of the Holy Name on May 21, 1910. While an assistant at the Cathedral, he was at the same time the chaplain at the old Cook County Jail. Here the serious problem of juvenile delinquency first presented itself in all its ugly aspects. He saw in many inmates the results of poverty and of broken homes. Bishop Sheil conceived the idea of a character-building organization for youth when a prisoner waiting to be hanged told him of his sordid family background and lack of opportunity. This gave him the incentive to dedicate his priestly labors to the causes of youth. After his consecration as auxiliary bishop of Chicago on May 1, 1928, and with the blessing of George Cardinal Mundelein, he created the Catholic Youth Organization (CYO) in 1930, which eventually spread its influence throughout the United States, Canada, and Hawaii. He developed the four-point program which constitutes the basis of the CYO: religion, athletics, education, and social service. Out of the social service program came the CYO Vacation School. Chicago rightly mourned Bishop Sheil as the revered "Apostle of Youth" when he died on September 13, 1969, at Tucson, Arizona, where he had been living in retirement. *Chicago Daily News,* 2 September 1954; 19 September 1969.

[13]*CYO Vacation School Records* (AFSCL).

[14]More than five hundred Sisters and lay people were taking courses arranged by a staff of volunteer instructors. Specialists in the field of group work lectured on the art of leadership. *The New World*, 3 March 1944.

[15]*Five Holy Martyrs House Journal* (AFSCL).

[16]*CYO Vacation School Records* (AFSCL).

[17]The Sisters who gave service in those years included Sister M. Alcantara Ochwat, Sister M. Aloysetta Ciezadlo, Sister M. Dorothy Szostek, Sister M. Equitia Nawracaj, Sister M. Julitta Szczepanik, Sister M. Louise Nowicki, Sister M. Tyburcia Sliwa, and Sister M. Xavier Wroblewski.

[18]*Book of Correspondence:* Letter from the Most Reverend Bernard J. Sheil, bishop of Chicago, to Mother M. Jerome Dadej, 24 March 1950 (AFSCL).

[19]The participating Sisters were Sister M. Adelma Walkowski, Sister M. Aloysetta Ciezadlo, Sister Ann Rose Mroz, Sister M. Antoinette Tadych, Sister M. Antonia Polcyn, Sister M. Charitas Gajdzinski, Sister M. Concordia Lawrence, Sister M. Cyprian Lewandowski, Sister M. Damian Graczyk, Sister M. Edwinette Wisz, Sister M. Francis Swider, Sister M. Julitta Szczepanik, Sister Marianne Kaplan, Sister M. Narcissa Skomski, Sister M. Pachomia Rychlicki, Sister M. Ralph Stawasz, and Sister Rose Therese Bzibziak.

[20]*Book of Correspondence:* Vacation Center Report from the Reverend Raymond A. Pavis, archdiocesan director of CYO, to author, 5 May 1976 (AFSCL).

[21]*Book of Correspondence:* Letter from Sister M. Ferdinand Skiba to author, 5 September 1976 (AFSCL).

[22]*Book of Correspondence:* Letter from Sister M. Maristella Skrzynski to author, 5 September 1974 (AFSCL).

[23]*Book of Correspondence:* Letter from the Most Reverend Bernard J. Sheil to Mother M. Jerome Dadej, 5 February 1947 (AFSCL).

[24]*The New World*, 23 July 1971.

[25]*St. John's Hospital Home Journal*, 20 January 1946 (AFSCL).

[26]*Interview* with Sister Eleanor Plocki, 1981 (AFSCL).

[27]Mr. Misiura played at the funerals of the Franciscan Sisters at the Motherhouse for over twenty-five years entirely gratis.

[28]*Book of Correspondence:* Letter from Samuel Cardinal Stritch to the Franciscan Sisters of Chicago, 23 March 1946 (AFSCL).

Former Superiors General of the
Franciscan Sisters of Chicago

Mother M. Aloysia Holysz
Second Superior General
1916–1922
1928–1934

Mother M. Vincent Czyzewski
Third Superior General
1922–1928

Mother M. Antonina Osinski
Fourth Superior General
1934–1940

Mother M. Mechtilde Zynda
Fifth Superior General
1940–1946

Mother M. Jerome Dadej
Sixth Superior General
1946–1952
1952–1958

Mother M. Beatrice Rybacki
Seventh Superior General
1958–1964
1964–1970

Sister M. Hugoline Czaplinski
Eighth Superior General
1970–1974
1974–1978

Sister Martha Joan Sempolski
Ninth Superior General
1978–1983

PART THREE
AND YOUR FRUIT MUST ENDURE

1947-1987

CHAPTER 47

The Seventh General Chapter:
Mother M. Jerome Dadej

When the Seventh General Chapter of Elections convened on June 29, 1946, it was the first time in the history of the congregation that a chapter was not presided over by a superior general. The delegates met that day in the summer of 1946, coming together to fill the place left vacant by the untimely death on March 16, 1946, of the superior general Mother M. Mechtilde Zynda. For the three-month interim between the death of Mother M. Mechtilde and the assembling of the general chapter, the duties of the superior general had been performed by her vicar general and first councilor, Sister M. Jerome Dadej.

When the forty delegates[1] assembled at the Motherhouse, Sister M. Jerome read the customary general report listing the accomplishments of the administration from 1940 to 1946. She reminded the delegates that there were now in the congregation 355 Sisters in perpetual vows and twenty-seven Sisters in temporary vows, a total of 382 professed members. There were five novices, four postulants, and two aspirants. Unfortunately, twenty-nine Sisters had left the congregation in the last six years, and thirteen Sisters had died. At the end of her presentation, Sister M. Jerome urged the delegates to work at solving a problem that she believed to be of prime importance—the growth of the membership. She asked the delegates to analyze, during the chapter, the reasons for the lack of new members since it was obvious that there were now fewer Sisters than when the last general chapter had been held in 1940.[2]

On July 2, 1946, the Reverend Raymond Zock,[3] delegate for communities of religious women, having been appointed by Samuel Cardinal Stritch, archbishop of Chicago, presided over the elections during which Mother M. Jerome Dadej was chosen the sixth superior general of the congregation. She accepted her election with grace and humility as she addressed the delegates:

> I know that neither you nor any other members of the congregation
> consider me infallible. I am weak and I see in myself more ill than good. I
> feel my weakness because I am only human. I will try, however, to follow
> the Master and do that which God and the congregation demand of me. I

ask, therefore, for earnest prayer and cooperation. What God demands of me, I am prepared to do.[4]

Elected to the office of vicar general and first councilor was Sister M. Felixa Jorz, the mistress of novices.[5] Because Sister M. Felixa was not a chapter delegate, she was summoned to the Motherhouse from the novitiate in Lemont. In further elections, Sister M. John Barczak was chosen second councilor, and Mother M. Antonina Osinski, who had previously served as superior general from 1934 to 1940, was chosen third councilor. Sister M. Gonzaga Raniszewski was elected fourth councilor and secretary general, a position she would maintain for the next twenty-four years.[6] Chosen as procurator general for a third term was Sister M. Raphael Bogalecki.

The determined and pragmatic new superior general, Sister M. Jerome, the daughter of Frank and Mary (née Witek) Dadej, was born Anna Dadej on November 10, 1888, in Bielcza (Galicia), Poland. In 1899, her parents joined the numerous immigrants seeking a new home in America. Upon their arrival, the Dadej family settled in St. John Cantius Parish on Chicago's Northwest Side.[7]

Anna Dadej entered the young community of Franciscan Sisters on February 2, 1906, and was received into the novitiate on August 15, 1907, at which time she received the name Jerome. Originally, she had intended to become a School Sister of Notre Dame since she had become acquainted with those Sisters at St. John Cantius School. She was inspired to join the Franciscan Sisters of Chicago, instead, by a parishioner, Sister M. Cajetan Tabasz, who, in turn, had been drawn to the small community by her friend, Sister M. Bernarda Jagiello. After her first profession of vows on August 15, 1908, Sister M. Jerome was assigned to St. Stanislaus Kostka School in St. Louis, Missouri. From the very beginning of her religious life, Sister M. Jerome was appointed to various responsible positions in the congregation. In 1909, when only twenty-one years of age, she was assigned as superior, teacher, and principal of St. Hedwig School, Gary, Indiana. The next year, she was sent to St. Josaphat School in Oshkosh, Wisconsin, to serve in the same capacity. She returned when the mission closed in 1911, and was reassigned to St. Casimir's School in Cleveland as a teacher.[8]

From 1913 to 1916, she taught at St. Casimir's School in Johnstown, Pennsylvania. Transferred to Five Holy Martyrs School, she served as superior, teacher, and principal for three years. At the end of that period, she was elected mistress of novices. Because Sister M. Jerome was only thirty-one years of age and in the congregation for only thirteen years at that time, it was necessary to obtain a special dispensation for her to accept the office.

In 1922, Sister M. Jerome was assigned to Sacred Heart School in Gary (Tolleston), Indiana, as superior, teacher, and principal. Three years later, she was appointed superior and principal of St. Casimir's School in Cleveland where she remained until 1931. From 1931 to 1934, she was a teacher, superior, and principal of Sacred Heart School in La Porte, Indiana.

In 1934, Sister M. Jerome was elected fourth council member and secretary general. At the conclusion of her term in 1940, she was elected vicar general to the superior general, Mother M. Mechtilde Zynda. It was at the Seventh General Chapter of Elections held in 1946 that she became the sixth woman to lead the congregation as superior general.[9]

If one word could be used to describe Mother M. Jerome's particular physical characteristics, it would be her "regal" bearing. She had about her an air of staid dignity that aroused reverence if not fear. Of average weight, tall, with piercing brown eyes, a pleasant face, a very firm chin, and a dignified gait, Mother M. Jerome's appearance personified the very element of religious decorum. It appeared that every movement and action was performed in a very disciplined and reserved manner. Her smile sometimes seemed to mask her inner feelings. While Mother M. Jerome could be extremely pleasant and joyful, at times she appeared austere and overbearing.

In many aspects, Mother M. Jerome was an exemplary religious and was interested in promoting the spiritual welfare of the congregation. In her letters, conferences, and addresses to the Sisters, she always stressed charity, self-respect, and conformity to the Will of God. Faithfully observant of the Holy Rule and the Constitutions herself, she stressed their importance to the Sisters and the value of silence as a means of interior peace. She had a particular love for Jesus in the Blessed Sacrament, for the Blessed Virgin Mary, and St. Joseph. Her favorite dictum for religious living was: "In all things, consider your last end."[10]

For the most part, Mother M. Jerome had the support and loyalty of the congregation. Always most respectful herself, she commanded the respect of the Sisters and the laity. She had reverence for the clergy and was always most hospitable to them. Aware of the needs of the sick Sisters, she did her best to have the congregation meet their special requirements. Because she recognized the lack of growth in membership, she was very vocation conscious and was extremely grateful to the Sisters who were dedicated to and extended themselves in the matter of the growth and progress of the congregation. There were those Sisters, however, who felt that Mother M. Jerome did not exercise the most pleasant rapport with particular Sisters and may have been inclined toward favoritism.[11]

Mother M. Jerome loved laughter and conviviality. She especially loved to hear anecdotes as related by the Sisters, and she reveled in telling them herself. Because she truly loved life, the Sisters could always be assured of a happy recreation when Mother M. Jerome was present or at the time of her visitation to the mission homes.

While lacking educational and professional training herself, Mother M. Jerome was a very wise and energetic woman with a good sense of business. She exercised tact in management and made prudent judgments in matters pertaining to the physical expansion of the congregation and its institutions. Because Mother M. Jerome was a very strong and assertive leader, however, she appeared at times to be rigid and even oppressive.[12] The educational status of the Sisters was important to her, and she was interested in educating Sisters for the future. She encouraged professional preparation and attendance at meetings of professional organizations. Unfortunately, she was rather selective in assigning Sisters to the pursuit of academic studies, and much potential was wasted because the education of some Sisters was delayed or neglected.[13]

When Mother M. Jerome assumed her office, there was much to be done, but her faith and courage were equal to the task. Throughout her two terms of office, the congregation passed through prodigious expansion and growth in apostolates. She possessed a zeal to keep alive the spirit of the congregation. To the office of superior general, she brought the fruits of a sound interior life and preserved the spirit and dedication she had witnessed in the lives of the foundress, Mother M. Theresa Dudzik, and the pioneer Sisters.

Sister M. Gonzaga Raniszewski
Mistress of Novices (1928–1934)
Secretary General (1946–1970)

At this Seventh General Chapter, one of the finest, most influential, and exemplary religious in the congregation was elected the fourth councilor and secretary general. She was Sister M. Gonzaga, the former Estelle Raniszewski, who was born on March 6, 1897, in Myszyniec, Poland, not far from Warsaw. She arrived in the United States in July of 1913 and settled with her parents in St. John Cantius Parish in Cleveland, Ohio. After a year, they moved to St. Stanislaus Bishop and Martyr Parish in that city. Here the Franciscan Fathers from St. Louis were in charge of the church and the Reverend Cyril Mitera[14] became her spiritual director.

Before her entrance into the congregation, Sister M. Gonzaga had been employed as a seamstress. She became a postulant on July 16, 1917, and a novice on July 27, 1918. Her first profession of vows was made on July 27, 1919, and she bound herself perpetually to the congregation on July 27, 1925.[15]

After her first profession of vows, Sister M. Gonzaga taught at St. Florian's School in Chicago for eight years and Sacred Heart of Jesus School in La Porte, Indiana, for one year. During this time, she attended St. Stanislaus College, De Paul University, and Chicago Normal College. In 1928, she was appointed mistress of novices. Her deep spirituality, absence of pride or self-assertion, and her warmly human and compassionate nature made her extremely suitable for the position. Because Sister M. Gonzaga was only thirty-one years of age and nine years after her first profession of vows, it was necessary to obtain a special dispensation for her to accept the office which she held until 1934. That year, Mother M. Antonina Osinski was elected the superior general and chose Sister M. Gonzaga to be her private secretary. Her special service ended in 1940 when Mother M. Antonina's term as superior general came to an end. At that time, Sister M. Gonzaga was sent to Boys Town where she was engaged in clerical work.[16]

At the Seventh General Chapter of Elections, Sister M. Gonzaga was voted fourth councilor and secretary general. In 1952, at the Eighth General Chapter of Elections, she was elected third councilor and secretary general. She was subsequently re-elected third councilor and secretary general in 1958 and 1964 thereby making her the secretary general for twenty-four years when her last term of office ended in 1970.[17]

The congregation is forever indebted to Sister M. Gonzaga. Extremely knowledgeable in matters pertaining to religious life, especially Canon Law, Sister M. Gonzaga was a distinct asset to every superior general with whom she served. The congregation is grateful to this sincere and conscientious woman, who, possessed of quiet dignity and a gentle and loving disposition, emerged as the congregation's first historian. She lent her writing talent and gentle insight to the brief history of the congregation called *Rys historyczny Zgromadzenia Sióstr Franciszkanek Błogosławionej Kunegundy. Część pierwsza, 1860–1910* [A historical survey of the Franciscan Sisters of Blessed Kunegunda. Part one, 1860–1910] and the unpublished "Rys historyczny Zgromadzenia Sióstr Franciszkanek Błogosławionej Kunegundy. Część druga, 1910–1940" [A historical survey of the Franciscan Sisters of Blessed Kunegunda Part two, 1910–1949] wherein she depicted the joys, sorrows, frustrations, and victories of the congregation from the time of its foundation by Mother M. Theresa Dudzik.

The Seventh General Chapter of Elections ended on July 7, 1946, after thirteen sessions during which several resolutions were passed. One of the most significant was the change in the form and style of the religious habit worn by the Sisters since their foundation. Traditionally, they had always worn the long, brown, one-piece habit with four deep pleats in the front and in the back, folded in such a way that the top pleat formed a scapular. The Sisters voted to depart from tradition and by 1951, had developed and adopted a new habit consisting of a long, simple, brown tunic over which a shorter, narrow piece of cloth, about the width of the shoulders and reaching the ankles, was worn. This scapular[18] was to be worn over the tunic and separate from it. It was to be worn at all times except when the Sisters were doing manual labor. Since no part of the religious garb could be changed without the explicit permission of the Holy See, a letter was sent to Rome on November 28, 1951, requesting the change. On June 1, 1952, on the feast of Pentecost, the Sisters wore the new form of the habit for the first time. For all practical purposes, the Sisters had converted their old habits to the new style when possible.[19]

Other parts of the religious garb taken under consideration were the cornets and collars which the Sisters working in the hospitals were particularly anxious to modify by making them shorter and narrower. Two of the delegates demonstrated a newly designed cornet and collar which were quickly met with approval. Mother M. Jerome asked that the older Sisters who resided at the Motherhouse be consulted about the matter before a final vote was taken. The majority of the older Sisters voted for the change, and, as a consequence, the cornets were shortened to vary from thirty-six inches to thirty-two inches in length and only six inches in width. The collars were altered to match the cornets and the new set was worn for the first time on December 8, 1946.[20]

Among the other resolutions emanating from the Seventh General Chapter were two that pertained to conventual discipline. The first specified that the 25th and 50th anniversaries of religious life were to be calculated from the day of entrance into the congregation. The Sisters were to celebrate the anniversary as a group at a ceremony in the Motherhouse rather than individually at their mission homes. Since for the first time in the congregation two Sisters had attained their 50th anniversaries, an appropriate ceremony for the occasion was formulated, and on April 17, 1947, Sister M. Clara Ogurek and Sister M. Elizabeth Baut celebrated this achievement with great joy. The second resolution restored a home visit every three years for one week. A home visit every five years had been cancelled at the time of the General Chapter of 1934.[21]

Several vital issues were discussed at great length during the Seventh General Chapter. Mother M. Jerome presented the need for a new Motherhouse to the delegation citing many reasons which by now were obvious to every member of the chapter. At this time, some property which the congregation had purchased on Higgins Road in Chicago in 1937 during the tenure of office of Mother M. Antonina Osinski was suggested as a good site. At the end of the chapter, one of the delegates suggested that Mother M. Jerome, the general council, and the delegates view the property with the intention of building a Motherhouse there if the conditions were appropriate.[22] The subject of the congregation's farm in Lemont arose for discussion also. At this chapter, it was agreed to keep the farm and to make certain adjustments.[23]

The new general council held its first session on July 16, the feast of Our Lady of Mount Carmel. After a preliminary prayer, Mother M. Jerome expressed her deep faith in the councilors and urged them toward unity and mutual respect. Speaking in the name of

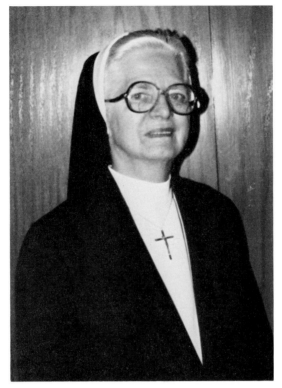

Sister M. Doloretta Radzienda
Mistress of Novices (1946–1968)

the council members, Mother M. Antonina assured Mother M. Jerome of their prayers, support, and cooperation.

Among the important matters to be settled at the session was the selection of a mistress of novices to replace Sister M. Felixa. The names of several exemplary and dedicated Sisters were submitted by the council members. Fully aware of the fact that the future and the spirit of the congregation depended, to a large degree, on the training given the novices, Mother M. Jerome and her general council sought to find the Sister most suitable to serve as the novice mistress in place of Sister M. Felixa Jorz who had been elected vicar general at the chapter. This tremendous responsibility called for a woman who not only exemplified sacrifice, dedication, and religious commitment, but who was also a well-balanced, competent, and holy religious. With confidence and resoluteness in their decision, Mother M. Jerome and her councilors selected the tranquil, affable, and deeply spiritual Sister M. Doloretta Radzienda who began her term on July 23, 1946.[24] Tender, pious, humble, blessed with good judgment and a keen discernment of character, Sister M. Doloretta was the perfect choice.

Sister M. Doloretta, the former Angela Radzienda, the daughter of Louis and Helen (née Snieg) Radzienda, was born in Chicago on August 3, 1906. She entered the congregation from St. Joseph's Church on Chicago's Southwest Side, on August 15, 1925.

She began her novitiate on April 16, 1926, and made her first profession of vows on July 16, 1928. On July 26, 1931, she professed her perpetual vows.

After her first profession of vows, Sister M. Doloretta was assigned to the congregation's schools where she taught for eighteen years. Always an exemplary religious and a zealous educator, she was missioned at Sacred Heart of Jesus School, Cleveland, from 1928 to 1936; St. Pancratius School, Chicago, from 1937 to 1939; South Heart Public School, South Heart, North Dakota, from 1939 to 1941; and lastly, St. Florian Elementary and High School, Chicago, from 1941 to 1946.[25]

Seemingly stern and of a serious outward demeanor, Sister M. Doloretta combined firmness with gentleness and a motherly solicitude which endeared her to all her novices. Most essentially, it can be said that she practiced what she herself preached heeding the words of St. Paul: "I do not run like a man who loses sight of the finish line. I do not fight as if I were shadowboxing. What I do is discipline my own body and master it, for fear that after having preached to others, I myself should be rejected." [26]

A woman of solid personal spirituality, she urged her novices to prayerfulness. She encouraged them to be kind, courteous, and forgiving, especially to the older Sisters. She urged the novices to assume their work in joyful obedience and to perform their duties conscientiously and happily. Fidelity to the Rule and the Constitutions together with observance of the religious vows, she taught, would naturally result in loyalty to the Church and to the congregation. When her novices were overcome by loneliness, as sometimes occurred, she always encouraged them to pray for the grace of perseverance reminding them to cherish their calling as "daughters of St. Francis." As for herself, her own sufferings were never made visible.[27]

Sister M. Doloretta possessed a gentle sense of humor. She frequently entertained the novices and the postulants with simple stories during recreation. Many of them were anecdotes connected with her early experiences in the classroom, but very often they were the reflections of a novice mistress who had encountered her eager and obedient novices in humorous situations. Indeed, the recital of the anecdotes was often reminiscent of the spirit of the first Franciscans and of the lively and errant Brother Juniper in particular.[28]

Because proper religious formation in the novitiate had always been emphasized, Sister M. Doloretta, during her years as mistress of novices, set about to secure zealous priests who were qualified to teach theology, especially Franciscan theology, and to provide conferences and spiritual guidance to the novices and the postulants. For this purpose, she secured the services of the Reverend Cyril Shircel, OFM, who served as counselor to the novices and taught classes in Franciscanism and the spiritual life from 1952 to 1956.[29] The Reverend Aloysius Madic, OFM, taught Franciscan Spirituality in the novitiate from 1951 to 1952 and again from 1956 to 1958.[30] The Reverend Sergius Wroblewski, OFM, served for eleven years as the spiritual director and the instructor of theology to the novices. His subjects included the Spiritual Life, the Old and the New Testaments, Franciscanism, and the Pauline Epistles.[31]

Another priest held in high esteem by Sister M. Doloretta and her novices was the outstanding benefactor, the Right Reverend Monsignor Stanislaus Cholewinski, the pastor of St. Joseph Church in Chicago's Town of Lake area. He was a sincere patron of the novitiate during the term of Sister M. Doloretta and was instrumental in helping to defray the costs of many of the projects connected with the former novitiate house in Lemont.[32]

No length of office for the mistress of novices had ever been established in the congregation, and as a consequence, Sister M. Doloretta M. Radzienda was appointed to the position of novice mistress for seven consecutive terms, a total of twenty-two years. The superiors general and their councils showed their confidence in and support of her by repeatedly selecting her for the office. Eventually, however, the responsibility for fostering and stimulating the development of the novices—each with a unique personality and character development—and the attendant physical and psychological demands exacted upon her resulted in illness for the gentle and kind Sister M. Doloretta. Perhaps the departure of many Sisters after the Second Vatican Council contributed to her illness. Acting on her doctor's orders, Sister M. Doloretta resigned her position as mistress of novices in 1968.

In July of 1968, Sister M. Doloretta was assigned to Boys Town, Nebraska, where she served as a part-time counselor and religion teacher. She pursued her new assignment with her proverbial reliance and dedication. Her last assignment, in 1973, transferred her to St. Anthony's Home in Crown Point, Indiana. [33]

In December of 1946, Mother M. Jerome received a letter from Samuel Cardinal Stritch in which he notified her that he had been contacted by the Sacred Congregation for Religious Affairs concerning the congregation's "Five-year Report on the State of the Congregation." Cardinal Stritch informed Mother M. Jerome that the Franciscan Sisters of Chicago were highly praised by the Sacred Congregation, but that it advised the Sisters to use all sources and resources to obtain more vocations and to pray ardently for this specific intention.[34] Mother M. Jerome, therefore, summoned all the Sisters from Illinois and Indiana to attend a meeting at the Motherhouse where they learned of the Seraphic Society for Vocations. According to authors Masseron and Habig in *The Franciscans,* the Franciscan Order had established this special Seraphic Society for fostering vocations. It was founded in 1944 in the United States and was organized on a large scale. Later, the Seraphic Society for Vocations was joined to the Pontifical Organization for Religious Vocations. The members of the Seraphic Society had a share in the spiritual benefits which the Holy See had granted to the Pontifical Organization. The requirements for admission into the Seraphic Society were to pray three Hail Marys each day for vocations, to offer one day a week for the intention of vocations, and to offer all suffering for that cause.[35]

Earlier in 1946, Mother M. Jerome and her general council had explored the idea of bringing to Chicago several young women who had been born in Poland but who had been displaced after World War II. These young women had indicated a desire to enter the religious life. The War Relief Services of the National Catholic Welfare Conference under the leadership of the Reverend Aloysius J. Wycislo, was most anxious to bring the Polish orphans to the United States from all the outlying countries where they had been displaced, India being one of them.[36] A chaplain at an orphanage in Bombay had sent the names of thirty Polish orphaned girls who desired to become Sisters to the Reverend Casimir Bobrowski of SS. Cyril and Methodius Seminary in Orchard Lake, Michigan. At first, Mother M. Jerome and the general council were reluctant to accept the young women because the congregation did not have a high school or academy wherein the young women could complete their secondary education at that time. Eventually, however, they decided to accept eight of them from the ages of eighteen to twenty-five.[37]

It was agreed that the travel expenses from India to Chicago and all expenses for the girls' upkeep and education would be supplied by the congregation. After much deliberation, the general council overturned their original decision to accept the young women, but in 1947, the Reverend Edward Flanagan, the beloved "Father Flanagan," agreed to pay the fare for the eight young women and then deduct it from the Sisters' monthly stipend at Boys Town.[38] Sister M. Bogumila Swiech, the superior at Boys Town, came to Chicago to discuss the matter and to formulate plans with Mother M. Jerome. Sister M. Ambrosia Tworek was assigned as the directress of the eight young women.[39] It was only a matter of weeks, however, before the entire matter was dismissed as unfeasible since the United States Government had ruled that visas for the displaced young women could be secured only if they were entering the United States as students. Thus the entire plan for accepting the eight Polish young women into the congregation was rejected.

The Seventh General Chapter of Elections had recognized Mother M. Theresa Dudzik as the foundress of the congregation and recommended that the *Rys*, written by Sister M. Gonzaga Raniszewski during Mother M. Antonina's tenure as superior general, be published. The brief history was meant to revive the spirit of the congregation and especially, to set before the young Sisters the example of the dedication and perseverance of the pioneer Sisters in the midst of adversity.

On November 22, 1939, Mother M. Antonina sent a letter to the Reverend Isidore Cwiklinski, OFM, requesting him to have a priest read the *Rys* and comment on it. Father Cwiklinski assigned the Reverend Ferdinand Pawłowski, OFM, the editor of the *Miesięcznik Franciszkański* [Franciscan Monthly] to review and add corrections to the book. In a letter to Sister M. Gonzaga dated June 1, 1940, Father Pawłowski wrote that he found the manuscript "pure, clear, and beautifully written, containing interesting facts and interestingly told." In his letter, Father Pawłowski also wished the "Venerable Sister Authoress the attainment of her goal of publishing the book and continued energy and success in the field of literature."[40] In September of 1947, therefore, Mother M. Jerome Dadej ordered the book to be printed and distributed to each Sister. In June of 1948, one thousand copies of the *Rys* were printed at a cost of $616.00.[41]

A review of Sister M. Gonzaga's book appeared in *Polish American Studies* in the January–June issue of 1952. The reviewer, a member of the staff of SS. Cyril and Methodius Seminary in Orchard Lake, Michigan, wrote in part:

> A worthwhile addition to the story of Polish American Sisterhoods is this work under consideration . . . The story of this Sisterhood is well told by the author. Simply, yet convincingly, she describes the noble work of the Sisters in the field of humanitarian as well as educational service. Her tale makes for inspiring reading and should also be told in English. The book contains valuable pictures which add to the historical worth of the brochure.[42]

Part Two of the *Rys,* containing the history of the congregation from 1910 to 1940 was also written by Sister M. Gonzaga, but because of World War II, was never published. The original manuscript is reserved in the archives of the congregation.

During the First General Chapter of Elections held in 1910, a set of Customs [Regulamin] had been read and accepted. After the Second General Chapter of 1916, each Sister received a copy of the Customs, but it was not until 1934, at the Fifth General Chapter, that the thought of compiling an official Book of Customs was voiced. The idea was generated by Mother M. Antonina Osinski who commissioned Sister M. Gonzaga Raniszewski to compile the Customs of the congregation in effect from 1934 to 1940, that is, the practices governing the conduct and observances of the Sisters. At the Sixth General Chapter of 1940, however, Sister M. Gonzaga was not a delegate, and so her progress in the compilation of the Book of Customs was impeded. When at the Seventh General Chapter of 1946 Sister M. Gonzaga was elected the secretary general, she continued to work on the Book of Customs with the help of the Reverend Francis Cegiełka, a Pallotine priest and a good friend of the congregation.[43]

In January of 1950, Mother M. Jerome and the general council examined and approved the Directory or Book of Customs written by Sister M. Gonzaga. On October 27, 1951, each Sister received a copy. At its publication, the Polish version of the *Book of Customs* was translated into English by Sister M. Dolorosa Bojanowski.[44] Throughout the ensuing years, there were no notable changes in the *Book of Customs* until after the First Extraordinary Chapter of Affairs held in 1968.

THE SEVENTH GENERAL CHAPTER: MOTHER M. JEROME DADEJ

[1]See Appendix K.

[2]*Minutes of General Chapter Proceedings, 1946* (AFSCL).

[3]In addition to his service as parish priest and pastor, the Right Reverend Monsignor Raymond Zock served as archdiocesan vicar for religious communities of women from 1940 to 1949. He was named pastor emeritus of Our Lady of Victory Church, Chicago, in 1973. He later retired to Las Vegas where he died.

[4]*Minutes of General Chapter Proceedings, 1946* (AFSCL).

[5]In addition to having been elected vicar general and first councilor, Sister M. Felixa Jorz was also appointed superior of the Motherhouse on December 1, 1947, after having received permission from the Reverend Casimir Guźiel, CR, delegate to communities of religious women, to assume this added responsibility. Less than a year later, however, Sister M. Kunegunda Pinkowski was selected to take Sister M. Felixa's place since her principal duties as vicar general prohibited her from effective leadership as the local superior. *Congregation Membership Records* (AFSCL).

[6]Sister M. Gonzaga served as secretary general from 1946 to 1970.

[7]*Spis Sióstr* (AFSCL).

[8]Ibid.

[9]Ibid.

[10]*Interviews* with Sisters, September 1983 (AFSCL).

[11]Ibid.

[12]Ibid.

[13]Ibid.

[14]See Appendix A.

[15]Sister M. Gonzaga had two sisters who had also entered the congregation. Apolonia, who was born in 1894, entered on September 5, 1915. She left on September 28, 1915, because of illness. On August 25, 1916, she reentered and left again on August 30, 1916.

Another sister, Mechtilde, born in 1899, entered on June 8, 1917. She left on October 12, 1917, because of chronic illness. *Spis Sióstr* (AFSCL).

[16]*Spis Sióstr* (AFSCL).

[17]*Congregation Membership Records* (AFSCL).

[18]The scapular was adopted and retained because of the traditional belief, wherein, through St. Simon Stock, the Blessed Virgin Mary added a scapular to the Carmelite habit. To the wearing of this scapular was attached the Sabbatine Privilege and many indulgences. The Sabbatine Privilege is defined as the belief that those who wear the scapular of Our Lady of Mount Carmel, who observe chastity according to their state, abstain from meat on Wednesdays and Saturdays and daily recite the *Little Office of the Blessed Virgin,* and who otherwise lead a virtuous life, will upon death be a special object of the intercession of the Blessed Virgin Mary.

[19]*Minutes of General Council Proceedings, 1934–1956* (AFSCL).

[20]Ibid.

[21]Ibid.

[22]Ibid.

[23]See Chapter 58 for a fuller discussion of the farm problem.

[24]*Minutes of General Council Proceedings, 1934–1956* (AFSCL).

[25]*Congregation Membership Records;* and *Spis Sióstr* (AFSCL).

[26]I Cor. 9:26.

[27]*Interviews* with Sisters, September 1983 (AFSCL).

[28]Ibid.

[29]The Reverend Cyril A. Shircel, OFM, was born in Sheboygan, Wisconsin and received his early education at St. Peter Claver School and SS. Cyril and Methodius Schools in that city. His seminary training was received at St. Joseph's in Teutopolis, Illinois. At St. Mary's Seminary, Lemont, Illinois, as a member of the Order of Friars Minor, Custody of the Holy Cross, he entered the novitiate on September 8, 1930, and made his solemn profession of vows on September 10, 1934. He was ordained to the priesthood on May 16, 1937. Father Shircel pursued graduate studies at De Paul University in Chicago and The Catholic University of America in Washington, DC, where he received his Ph.D. in 1942. He was a professor of philosophy at St. Mary's Seminary in Lemont for five years after which he became professor of religion and philosophy at St. Francis College in Joliet, Illinois from 1950 to 1959. Father Shircel aided in the establishment of the Seraphic Theological Institute for Sisters at St. Francis College in 1954.

To aid him in his most effective ministry of counseling in the 1950s, Father Shircel did postgraduate work in psychology at Loyola University in Chicago. During this time, he was active in the Franciscan Education Conference which began in 1952. Father Shircel died on October 17, 1959, after a long and painful struggle with cancer. Biographical sketch from the Reverend Blase Chemazar, OFM, Custos, St. Mary's Friary and Retreat House, Lemont, Illinois, 15 November 1975 (AFSCL).

[30]The Reverend Aloysius Madic, OFM, a classmate of Father Shircel, was born in Chicago. He entered the novitiate as a member of the Order of Friars Minor, Custody of the Holy Cross, on September 8, 1934. After his ordination in May of 1937, he served assistantships and pastorates at parishes in Chicago, Illinois; Johnstown, Pennsylvania; and Willard, Wisconsin. Father Madic served as guardian at St. Mary's Seminary in Lemont, as retreat master at St. Mary's Retreat House attached to the seminary, and teacher of religion at Mount Assisi Academy, also in Lemont. Father Madic died in September of 1979. Ibid.

[31]The Reverend Sergius Wroblewski, OFM, is a member of the Assumption Province of the Order of Friars Minor whose headquarters are in Pulaski, Wisconsin. Father Wroblewski was ordained in 1946 in Green Bay, Wisconsin. His provincial appointments have included: professor and master of clerics and retreat master at Lourdes Retreat House in Cedar Lake, Indiana, and theology professor at Christ the King Seminary in West Chicago, Illinois. In 1960, he was appointed by the minister general to the Franciscan National Marian Commission. He was instrumental in establishing the Chicago Inner City Apostolate in 1969.

Father Wroblewski's activities have further included retreat work for priests, religous, and lay people. He has served as professor at the Seraphic Theological Institute for Sisters at St. Francis College in Joliet, Illinois. A staunch promoter of Franciscanism, Father Wroblewski has served as a member of a commission for renewal and as a lecturer on Franciscanism especially in the service of the Federation of Franciscan Sisters in Pittsburgh. He has given workshops on Franciscanism all over the country and has served as a faculty member at the Franciscan Institute at St. Bonaventure University in St. Bonaventure, New York. In addition, he has written prolifically on Franciscan topics.

From 1959 to 1965, Father Wroblewski taught religion at Madonna High School owned and operated by the Franciscan Sisters of Chicago. He also served as the spiritual director to Tau House and St. Paul Mission, the Franciscan Sisters' experimental houses for small-group living established in the early 1970s. Biographical sketch from the Assumption Province of the Order of Friars Minor, Pulaski, Wisconsin (AFSCL).

[32]See Chapter 27.

[33]*Congregation Membership Records* (AFSCL).

[34]Secretaries General, *Community Chronicle, 1934–1957* (AFSCL).

[35]Alexandre Masseron and Marion A. Habig, OFM, *The Franciscans* (Chicago: Franciscan Herald Press, 1959), p. 145.

[36]*Book of Correspondence:* Letter from the Reverend Aloysius J. Wycislo to Mother M. Jerome Dadej, 22 May 1947 (AFSCL).

[37]*Minutes of General Council Proceedings, 1934–1956* (AFSCL).

[38]Ibid.

[39]Ibid.

[40]*Book of Correspondence:* Letter from the Reverend Ferdinand Pawłowski, OFM, to Sister M. Gonzaga Raniszewski, 1 June 1950 (AFSCL).

[41]*Minutes of General Council Proceedings, 1934–1956* (AFSCL).

[42]Al T. Kulik, "A Review of *Rys historyczny Zgromadzenia Sióstr Franciszkanek Błogosławionej Kunegundy. Część pierwsza, 1860–1910*" [A historical survey of the Franciscan Sisters of Blessed Kunegunda. Part one, 1860–1919], *Polish American Studies* 9 (January–June 1952).

[43]See Appendix B.

[44]*Minutes of General Council Proceedings, 1956–1970* (AFSCL).

CHAPTER 48

Developing Missions

Two further developments of significance marked the beginning of Mother M. Jerome's time in office. One was the acceptance of a home exclusively for aged women in Cleveland, Ohio; the second was the entrance into an area of social service entirely new to the congregation in the vicinity of the Guardian Angel Day Care Center and Home for Working Girls in Chicago where the Sisters had served since 1917.

Madonna Hall, on East 82nd Street near Euclid Avenue in Cleveland, had been operated by the Society of the Daughters of the Heart of Mary from December 18, 1926, as a home for professional and business women. From the time of its foundation, it had served a distinct need. Many young women had come to Cleveland seeking employment opportunities, and the Church had been concerned over their welfare.[1] In 1945, Madonna Hall fell victim to a changing culture when working women no longer sought a group home. On April 3, 1946, the Most Reverend Edward F. Hoban, bishop of Cleveland, informed Mother M. Jerome that the diocese had purchased Madonna Hall. Aware of the desperate need for homes for the aged, the diocese had slated Madonna Hall to be converted into such a home. After extensive enlargement and renovation, Madonna Hall opened as a home exclusively for aged women.[2] Bishop Hoban asked Mother M. Jerome to have the Franciscan Sisters of Chicago assume charge of Madonna Hall with its proposed capacity of 112 residents.[3] The Sisters would operate the institution, and ownership would remain with the Diocesan Catholic Charities Bureau.[4]

In May of 1946, the decision to accept the supervision of Madonna Hall was announced and the home for aged women opened officially on September 1, 1946, with the following Sisters on the staff: Sister M. Redempta Demski, Sister M. Olga Kulik, Sister M. Norberta Haas, Sister M. Francis Swider, Sister M. Francesca Janowicz, Sister M. Judith Kwiatkowski, and Sister M. Laetitia Kolczak. In December, Sister M. Laetitia was replaced by Sister M. Rose Ann Zmich. Sister M. Hilary Dadej, who had just completed her six-year term as superior of Mount Alvernia Convent on Terrace Road in East Cleveland, was selected by the general council to be the superior and administrator of the

Madonna Hall
Cleveland, Ohio (1946–1970)

newly acquired institution.[5] The Sisters made their home on the second floor of the attractive four-story building until an adjoining residence could be renovated into a convent. A separate chapel, a lovely structure of brick and stone seating 125 persons, was dedicated to the Immaculate Conception by Bishop Hoban on June 26, 1948. On the following day, he blessed the residence hall itself which was connected with the chapel and the Sisters' home by a covered gallery.[6]

Although the Sisters served with love and dedication, in the wake of a thorough study made by the Congregation at the First Extraordinary Chapter of Affairs of 1968 in regard to the assignment of Sister personnel, a decision was made to leave the highly praised institution since the congregation was no longer in a position to staff it. The Sisters left after twenty-two years of service, anxious to respond to other needs as discerned by the superior general and her councilors. A few years later, Madonna Hall was closed due to the changing ethnic and racial patterns in the area.

In May of 1947, the Reverend Philip Marquard, OFM, stationed at St. Augustine's Friary in the Back of the Yards District on Chicago's Southwest Side, and whose Franciscan Order[7] served the needs of the Guardian Angel Day Nursery and Home for Working Girls, asked Mother M. Jerome Dadej for two Sisters to undertake a special aspect of social work at the St. Philip of Jesus Community Center. Located at 46th, Laflin, and McDowell Streets,[8] the social center, a renovated tavern located directly across the street from the Guardian Angel Day Nursery, was under the direction of Father Marquard who was assisted by the Reverend Mark Hegener, OFM, and the Reverend Albert Nimeth, OFM.[9] The center had been established by the Franciscan Fathers to meet the religious and social needs of the Mexican youth in the area although all the young people in the vicinity were welcomed. St. Philip of Jesus Community Center, since the summer of 1945, had been conducted by two Sisters of the Congregation of the Poor Handmaids of Jesus Christ who staffed the nearby St. Augustine's School.[10]

Earlier in 1946, Sister M. Praxeda Ostrega, who had served as the administrator and superior of the Guardian Angel Day Nursery since 1940, learned that the Poor Handmaids would be leaving the center. Sister M. Praxeda was extremely anxious to see the St. Philip of Jesus Community Center in the hands of the Franciscan Sisters of Chicago. She communicated this zeal and desire to Sister M. Martha Bywalec who had succeeded her as superior and administrator of Guardian Angel Day Nursery and Home for Ladies in early August of 1946.[11] Although the congregation was suffering from a serious lack of Sister personnel, Sister M. Martha heartily supported Father Marquard's petition to Mother M. Jerome. Before the departure of the Poor Handmaids on August 8, 1947, Sister M. Martha committed herself to the release of one Sister from the Guardian Angel Day Nursery to serve at St. Philip of Jesus Community Center if Mother M. Jerome would provide the second Sister who was needed. As a consequence, Sister Victoria Valerie Smagacz was released from her duties at the Guardian Angel Day Nursery and was joined by Sister M. Celine Madaj on August 30, 1947, in order to begin the congregation's new apostolate among the youth of the Back of the Yards area.[12]

The Sisters' tasks, for which they were basically unprepared, were many and varied. Sister Victoria Valerie was placed in charge of the small children who assembled daily at St. Philip of Jesus Community Center from three o'clock to five o'clock in the afternoon where they played games, sang songs, and engaged in various learning activities. Besides being instrumental in introducing the Brownie and Girl Scout organizations, Sister Victoria Valerie established a library in a nearby garage. Sister M. Celine, on the other hand, was actively engaged with the teens who assembled daily from approximately seven o'clock to eleven o'clock every evening. She taught arts and crafts to the young girls and supervised the games and sports activities of the young men. The teens also played cards, listened to the jukebox, and danced until the center closed. On days when the children and youths were free from public school classes, the Sisters taught religion and prepared children and young adults for the reception of the sacraments. Unfortunately, Sister Victoria Valerie fell ill in December. She was replaced by Sister M. Mildred Bieda. Two months later, in February of 1948, Sister M. Theresine Wojcie-chowicz was recalled from Boys Town and appointed to St. Philip of Jesus Community Center to replace Sister M. Celine who had been transferred.[13]

Under the supervision of the newly assigned Sisters, St. Philip of Jesus Community Center continued to operate daily providing many and varied services. These duties included instructing public school children who were being especially prepared for the reception of First Holy Communion,[14] conducting meetings for Boy Scouts and Girl Scouts of whom Sister M. Theresine was in charge,[15] providing recreational activities for the younger children in the basement of the center, and supervising the games and evening dances for the teens. The Sisters made visits to the poor and the sick in the neighborhood bringing with them baskets of food supplied by the Sisters at the Guardian Angel Day Nursery. Occasionally, temporary lodging was provided at the Guardian Angel Day Nursery for women and children who had been evicted from their homes or who had left during a family dispute. At Christmas and Easter, parties were held for the children with gifts provided by students from neighboring high schools. Midnight Mass was celebrated on Christmas Eve at the center by either Father Mark or Father Philip.[16] Because St. Philip of Jesus Community Center was affiliated with the Catholic Youth Organization (CYO), the Sisters, with the help of the seminarians from the Quigley Archdiocesan Seminary, kept the children off the streets in the summer by providing classes in arts and crafts, physical education, and brief excursions to worthwhile places.[17]

While the Sisters were in charge of St. Philip of Jesus Community Center, they lived in three rooms on the second floor of the wooden building with only a gas range to provide heat during the winter. They were forced to maintain their residence at the center chiefly because of the late hours at which the teen socials ended. In addition, the Blessed Sacrament was reserved in the tiny chapel and the Sisters did not wish to leave it unattended.[18] The Sisters took all their meals and performed their religious exercises in common with the Sisters at the Guardian Angel Day Nursery.[19]

Left: St. Philip of Jesus Community Center
Right: Guardian Angel Day Care Center
Chicago, Illinois (1948–1951)

By February of 1949, Mother M. Jerome was made aware of the general feeling of unrest existing at the center as communicated to her by the Sisters working there. At a meeting of the general council, Mother M. Jerome outlined the various problems encountered at the center. Chief among them was the evening socials which the Sisters were forced to supervise without the lay adult chaperones which had been promised them. This was one of the situations which forced the Sisters to stay overnight at the center, a matter which greatly interfered with their health especially during the cold winter months. Another problem which surfaced was the fact that Sister M. Theresine received neither salary nor financial support from any source during her first year of service.[20] The general council agreed with Mother M. Jerome's suggestion that the Sisters leave this area of activity. She sent a letter, therefore, to the director of St. Philip's Center, the Reverend Mark Hegener, which stated in part:

> After a thorough investigation of the work performed by the Sisters at the center, I have decided to withdraw them. While I realize the benefits of social work involved here, I do not feel it becoming for a nun to supervise dances. The council, therefore, has decided that the Sisters will be withdrawn on June 1, 1949. Beginning with March 2 of this year, the Sisters will no longer supervise the evening dances.[21]

On receiving the letter, an appeal was made immediately by the Franciscan Fathers to Cardinal Stritch to prevent Mother M. Jerome from putting her proposed plan into action. Cardinal Stritch summoned Mother M. Jerome to the Chancery Office in April, and after a discussion of the situation at St. Philip of Jesus Community Center, he secured her promise to keep the Sisters there until he had time to study the matter.[22]

Cardinal Stritch appointed the Right Reverend Monsignor Vincent Cooke, the archdiocesan supervisor of Catholic Charities, to study the state of affairs at the center. In his account to Cardinal Stritch, Father Cooke emphasized the immense good the Sisters were doing. It was decided, then, that the Sisters would remain only on the conditions outlined by Mother M. Jerome, which were that the cleaning and maintenance of the center would no longer be the responsibility of the Sisters; that the Sisters would not be required to sleep overnight and maintain their residence at the center; that they would leave the center at nine o'clock in the evening daily; that they would conform to the already existing program, but in certain areas, lay people would be recruited to aid them; and lastly, that the two Sisters would receive $1,200 for their upkeep and for the use of materials which were sorely needed at the center.[23] In a letter directed to Mother M. Jerome, Monsignor Cooke outlined the terms of agreement and presented a positive picture of the nature and scope of the work of the Sisters at the Center:

> Dear Mother Jerome:
>   Having returned from my visit . . . and having cleared up the majority
> of unfinished business, I am finally getting down to drawing up the

agreement concerning the two Sisters who will work at St. Philip of Jesus Community Center.

After consideration of the splendid work already done and the possibilities of even greater work in the future on behalf of Christ's poor, I think the following is a just and equitable agreement:

1. The Sisters will be relieved of the responsibility of remaining overnight in the Community Center.

2. Arrangements shall be made to have the cleaning and scrubbing of the Center done by lay people and relieve the Sisters of this responsibility.

3. The following shall be the program to be followed in the Center:

   a) Summer School: June 30 to August 15

9 A.M. – 12 P.M.	Follow CYO program. One full period in the morning devoted to religious instruction; other periods for crafts and skills; art craft, leather craft and woodwork.
1 P.M. – 5 P.M.	Twice a week during the Summer School period the Sisters will arrange for outings with the children to various parks and places of interest in the city.
7 P.M. – 9:15 P.M.	Center open daily, except Sunday evening. Program arranged for each evening.

Afternoons on which there is no special activity should be devoted to preparing for the classes and art work and to visiting homes of youngsters attending the summer school.

   b) During the Year: The Center is open daily from:

3 P.M. – 5:15 P.M.	For children of grade-school age. The Brownies have their regular meeting one afternoon a week during this period. On Wednesday afternoon from 2 P.M. to 3 P.M. religious instruction given to Catholic public school children availing themselves of the "released time" period. On other afternoons, programs to be arranged by the Sisters.
7 P.M. –9:15 P.M.	Beginning in September, the main room or "store" will be reserved for the following activities:

Monday evening:	Girl Scouts
Tuesday evening:	Cub Scouts
Wednesday evening:	Crafts. These craft classes will be conducted by young Third Order members under the supervision of the Sisters.
Thursday evening:	Boy Scouts
Friday evening:	Teen agers. For this group there will be a short period of religious instruction conducted by one of the Fathers.

On the First Friday of each month: Holy Hour

Saturday evening: Confessions and Senior-teens

While these activities are going on in the main room, the Sisters should be attending children in the library and television room. During the year, the mornings should be devoted to preparing for the afternoon and evening programs and to a certain amount of home visitation to get acquainted with home conditions of children availing themselves of the center's facilities.

4. Fifty dollars a month shall be paid to Angel Guardian Day Nursery [*sic*] for[24] the services of two Sisters working in the settlement. This amount shall also pay for a limited amount of craft materials ($1,200 per year).

5. This payment of $100.00 per month shall be made retroactive to January 1, 1949.

6. The spirit of the Charity of Christ, rather than strict adherence to rights and duties, will permeate all our actions on behalf of the poor of Christ in this project. The spiritual advancement and happiness of both the children and their parents shall be our paramount concern.

Prayerfully awaiting an early happy reply to this request in order to start the program at the earliest possible date, I remain, dear Mother,

Sincerely yours in Christ,

Vincent Cooke

Archdiocesan Supervisor of Charities[25]

On August 20, 1949, Sister M. Placidia Rzonca replaced Sister M. Mildred.[26] Both Sister M. Placidia and Sister M. Theresine wholeheartedly devoted themselves to the plan proposed by Monsignor Cooke, but in the "Half-yearly Report" submitted to Mother M. Jerome by Sister M. Praxeda, who had been reappointed the superior and administrator of the Guardian Angel Day Nursery, it was obvious that the plan did not have the cooperation of all the parties involved. Once again, Sister M. Praxeda pointed out the fact that while the Sisters were doing a tremendous amount of good, the whole burden for the success of the program seemed to rest on the two Sisters.[27] By April of 1951, conditions proved so unfavorable that Mother M. Jerome ordered Sister M. Placidia and Sister M. Theresine to come to the Motherhouse to present an accurate account of the situation to the general council.[28] At the conclusion of the general council session, the basis of the complaints of the Sisters was the matter of a letter which Mother M. Jerome sent to Monsignor Cooke on April 21, 1951:

> Right Reverend Monsignor:
>
> Referring to your letter of June 16, 1949, in which a program had been outlined for St. Philip of Jesus Community Center at 46th and South Laflin, I must report the following:
>
> Since that time, for only two months, has the program been followed . . . by giving the Sisters some aid in cleaning the building and in supervising the social activities in the evenings. Then the heavy burden of it all was left entirely to the Sisters. Frequently, boys got into fights and there was no one to help the Sisters maintain order. There was even an incident when a boy almost killed another . . . Sister Placidia threw herself between them and although she was hurt and splashed with blood, she saved the life of one and the reputation of the other.
>
> The repeated complaints and requests . . . remain unheeded. Sister Theresine, one of the Sisters working at the Center . . . feels that St. Philip of Jesus Center does not get the attention it needs to function properly.
>
> The equipment such as is found at other social centers is lacking thereby causing difficulties for the Sisters. In addition to that, the poor heating system and dampness due to the frequently flooded basement after heavy rain make the building unhealthy to stay in. The Sisters sometimes wear galoshes all day to keep warm. I have just received a statement from Dr. Mace Gazda to transfer Sister Theresine because the dampness is affecting her health. Recently a notice was received stating that the building is condemned. Due to these conditions I have resolved to withdraw the Sisters from St. Philip of Jesus Center in August.
>
> As far as the welfare of the under-privileged children is concerned, I have learned that several parishes in that neighborhood have started to conduct their own youth centers.[29] Among those there is one only two or three blocks away from St. Philip's.
>
> Hoping this is a clear presentation of the facts prompting me to withdraw the Sisters, I am
>
> > Sincerely yours in Christ,
> > Mother M. Jerome[30]

Monsignor Cooke urged Mother M. Jerome to make no move to withdraw the Sisters until such time as he could discuss the matter with the director of St. Philip of Jesus Community Center to determine what could be done.[31] In her reply to Monsignor Cooke, Mother M. Jerome advised him that she was determined to remove the Sisters after consulting with Cardinal Stritch. She also informed Monsignor Cooke that she had consulted the Reverend Francis Cegiełka, a member of the Society of the Catholic Apostolate (Pallotines), as well as the Reverend Raymond Zock, the vicar general for the women religious of the Archdiocese of Chicago, who agreed with her decision.[32] Having prevailed in her determination, Mother M. Jerome withdrew the Sisters from St. Philip of Jesus Community Center on June 16, 1951, in an aura of good will.[33] The Congregation of the Daughters of Charity of St. Vincent de Paul were secured to continue working at St. Philip's Center but their stay was of a very brief duration. The building, condemned in time by the Chicago Fire Department, was razed and in its place a playground was made for the children at Guardian Angel Day Nursery in 1956.[34]

Many requests for the services of the Sisters had been received by the superiors general since the congregation's founding. To respond affirmatively to all requests received from bishops, pastors, and priests was not an easy task since the requests for the services of the Sisters were not in proportion to the number of Sisters available. The superiors general charitably and prudently examined each request before accepting or declining an invitation. Requests came for Sisters to undertake domestic work, to care for seminaries, and to staff hospitals. Most of the requests, by far, were from pastors begging the Sisters to accept the administration and staffing of schools, especially elementary ones. Beginning with 1911, requests came in from practically every state: Michigan, Nebraska, Pennsylvania, Texas, Minnesota, Ohio, South Dakota, Missouri, Massachusetts, New Jersey, Wisconsin, Indiana, Colorado, Illinois, California, Washington, Mississippi, Connecticut, Oklahoma, Iowa, Montana, Arizona, New Mexico, Utah, New York, Tennessee, North Dakota, and Florida. Requests came from places with such intriguing names as Hallsapple, Pennsylvania; Pawhoska, Nebraska; Pisek, North Dakota; Orient, South Dakota; St. Michael, Arizona; Maximo, Ohio; Opa-locka, Florida; Dos Palos, California; Davant, Louisiana; Sleepy Eye, Minnesota; Carpinteria, California; Kileen, Texas; and Coal City, Illinois. As early as 1937, a request came for missionary Sisters to be sent to Shasi, China, a city approximately eight hundred miles west of Shanghai. Other requests came from Brazil, Hawaii, India, Australia, Thailand, and Canada.[35]

Perhaps one of the saddest letters to come to the attention of Mother M. Jerome and her general council was the following received in the spring of 1946:

Dear Reverend Mother:

I am almost frantic. We shall have an 8-room school ready for September 1946. God was good. We got three surplus government

buildings enough for eight classrooms and kindergarten and a Sisters'
house. We need Sisters. Can you possibly help us?

We have over 1,000 children in our area. Many of them of Mexican
parentage are poor, and most poorly instructed. We just must have
Sisters. I promise them it will be grand work—I do not doubt vocations
will come, too.

To date we have refusals from exactly 110 Religious Superioresses.
Please help us for the love of God.

> Sincerely yours in St. Francis,
> Rev. Eustace Struckhoff, OFM[36]

Unfortunately, the answer to that letter and scores of others was the same as the
one given by Father Spetz to a letter received in 1913:

My dear Father Spetz:

I cordially recommend Father Klonowski's[37] case to your kind
attention. If you can induce the Franciscan Sisters of St. Cunegunda [*sic*]
to take his school in Chicago Heights, you will have done a great work of
religion.

> Yours truly in Xto.,
> Archbishop J. E. Quigley[38]

Father Spetz, the spiritual director of the congregation at the time, responded on
August 24, 1913, sadly but tersely: "It is impossible. There are no Sisters."[39]

DEVELOPING MISSIONS

[1]*Book of Correspondence:* Letter from Lucille Le Vay, archivist, Society of the Daughters of the Heart of Mary to author, 18 February 1976 (AFSCL).

[2]Michael J. Hynes, *History of the Diocese of Cleveland* (Cleveland: World Publishing Co., 1953), p. 401.

[3]*Book of Correspondence:* Letter from the Most Reverend Edward Hoban, bishop of Cleveland to Mother M. Jerome Dadej, 3 April 1946 (AFSCL).

[4]Ibid.

[5]*Book of Annual Assignments* (AFSCL).

[6]Hynes, p. 401.

[7]The Franciscan Fathers at St. Augustine's Friary publish the *Franciscan Herald* magazine and operate the Franciscan Herald Press at 51st and Laflin Streets. The Franciscan Fathers, under the jurisdiction of the Sacred Heart Province, are in charge of the popular and well-attended St. Peter's Church on Madison Street in Downtown Chicago.

[8]*Minutes of General Council Proceedings,* 17 April 1947 (AFSCL).

[9]Father Nimeth served as chaplain at Guardian Angel Day Nursery and Home for Ladies from 1949 to 1980.

[10]Two Sisters worked at the center during the summer of 1945. They moved from St. Augustine's Convent to the community center in October 1945. In 1946, they were joined by a third Sister who assisted with the summer program. *Book of Correspondence:* Letter from Sister M. Joette, PHJC, provincial secretary, Donaldson, Indiana, 11 May 1978 (AFSCL).

[11]*Book of Correspondence:* Letters from Sister M. Theresine Wojciechowicz to author, June 1975; and Sister Victoria Valerie Smagacz, 7 May 1978 (AFSCL).

[12]*Minutes of General Council Proceedings, 1934–1956* (AFSCL).

[13]*Book of Correspondence:* Letter from Sister Victoria Valerie Smagacz to author, 7 May 1978 (AFSCL).

[14]A poignant entry is found in the *Guardian Angel Day Nursery Home Journal* on page 58 entered on June 4, 1950: "Thirteen children received First Holy Communion from Father Albert Nimeth, OFM, during Holy Mass at St. Philip of Jesus Community Center. Benefactors provided clothes for those children who did not have parents." *Guardian Angel Day Nursery Home Journal* (AFSCL).

[15]Sister M. Theresine was the first Sister to take a correspondence course in scouting. She passed with "flying colors" and was officially granted permission to be in charge of the Boy Scouts and Girl Scouts at the Center. *Book of Correspondence:* Letter from Sister M. Theresine Wojciechowicz to author, 1975 (AFSCL).

[16]*Book of Correspondence:* Letter from Sister M. Placidia Rzonca to author, 1978 (AFSCL).

[17]*Book of Correspondence:* Letter from Sister M. Theresine Wojciechowicz to author, June 1978 (AFSCL).

[18]Ibid.

[19]Ibid.

[20]Ibid.

[21]*Book of Correspondence:* Letter from Mother M. Jerome Dadej to the Reverend Mark Hegener, OFM, 28 February 1949 (AFSCL).

[22]Secretaries General, *Community Chronicle,* 13 March 1949 (AFSCL).

[23]Secretaries General, *Community Chronicle,* 22 May 1949 (AFSCL).

[24]There was an Angel Guardian Child and Family Center at 2001 West Devon. Monsignor Cooke's reference was directed to Guardian Angel Day Nursery, the institution being discussed.

[25]*Book of Correspondence:* Letter from the Right Reverend Monsignor Vincent Cooke to Mother M. Jerome Dadej, 16 June 1949 (AFSCL).

[26]Although Sister M. Mildred was very happy in her work at the center, she withdrew in order to study nursing at the congregation's St. John Hospital and School of Nursing in Huron, South Dakota.

[27]*Guardian Angel Day Nursery House Journal,* 3 January 1950 (AFSCL).

[28]*Minutes of General Council Proceedings, 1934–1956* (AFSCL).

[29]Mother M. Jerome probably had reference here to the Immaculate Heart Community Center at 45th and Ashland which was successfully operated for many years by the Claretian Fathers, that is, the Missionary Sons of the Immaculate Heart of Mary, founded by St. Anthony Mary Claret in 1849.

[30]*Book of Correspondence:* Letter from Mother M. Jerome Dadej to the Right Reverend Monsignor Vincent Cooke, 21 April 1951 (AFSCL).

[31]*Book of Correspondence:* Letter from the Right Reverend Monsignor Vincent Cooke to Mother M. Jerome Dadej, 2 May 1951 (AFSCL).

[32]*Book of Correspondence:* Letter from Sister M. Theresine Wojciechowicz to author, June 1968 (AFSCL).

[33]*Minutes of General Council Proceedings, 1934–1956* (AFSCL).

[34]*Guardian Angel Day Nursery and Home for Girls: Golden Jubilee Souvenir Book, 1915–1965* (Chicago, 31 October 1965), no pagination.

[35]Siostra M. Gonzaga Raniszewski, OSFK, *Echo Avondalskie* [Avondale Echo] January–July, 1936; and *Minutes of General Council Proceedings, 1934–1956; 1956–1975* (AFSCL).

[36]*Book of Correspondence:* Letter from the Reverend Eustace Struckhoff, OFM, to the Franciscan Sisters of Chicago, 27 April 1946 (AFSCL).

[37]Historically, there is no Father Klonowski associated with this parish in 1913 or at any other time. St. Casimir Church in Chicago Ridge was founded as a national parish serving Lithuanian Catholics. Archbishop Quigley had appointed a Reverend Joseph Kleinauskas to organize the parish. Father Kleinauskas served as pastor until 1916. Reverend Monsignor Harry C. Koenig, ed., *A History of the Archdiocese of Chicago: Published in Observance of the Archdiocese, 1980,* 2 vols. (Chicago: The Archdiocese of Chicago, 1980), 2:1078.

[38]*Book of Correspondence:* Letter from the Most Reverend James E. Quigley, archbishop of Chicago, to the Reverend Andrew Spetz, CR, 7 August 1913 (AFSCL).

[39]*Book of Correspondence:* Letter from the Reverend Andrew Spetz, CR, to the Most Reverend James E. Quigley, archbishop of Chicago, 24 August 1913 (AFSCL).

CHAPTER 49

St. John Hospital and School of Nursing

The city of Huron, in South Dakota, is chiefly a farming and cattle community located in the east central part of the state. South Dakota's history and legends are replete with names like General Custer, Wild Bill Hickok, the Badlands, and Mount Rushmore. To this "land of infinite variety" the Franciscan Sisters of Chicago came in 1944 by way of the old "400 Dakota" train to lay the groundwork for their hospital ministry.

As early as 1937, Mother M. Antonina Osinski, the fifth superior general of the congregation, expressed a desire that the congregation enter the area of health care. She was eager to secure a hospital where the Sisters might begin their proposed apostolate to the sick. In 1938, she received a request from the Reverend Francis Cronin,[1] pastor of St. Bernard's Church in Redfield, South Dakota. He wanted to establish a hospital in that city and planned to initiate a campaign for funds. He asked Mother M. Antonina to come to South Dakota to select an appropriate site for the hospital. As a consequence, Mother M. Antonina and Sister M. Paul Kirschbaum visited Redfield late in 1938.[2] Because the population of Redfield was largely non-Catholic, a major part of the community did not support the idea of a hospital administered and staffed by Catholic Sisters, and the bond issue, proposed to support the funding of the hospital, failed. Father Cronin and the Sisters accepted the existing situation and withdrew plans for the foundation of a hospital in that city. Two years later, however, Father Cronin had occasion to meet with the Reverend John J. O'Neill, the dynamic pastor of St. Martin's Church, the only Catholic Church in Huron. Father O'Neill was equally eager to secure a Sisterhood to undertake a hospital project in Huron. Father Cronin, therefore, informed Father O'Neill of the Franciscan Sisters of Chicago who were seeking to minister in hospital health care.[3]

In June of 1940, Mother M. Mechtilde Zynda had been elected to succeed Mother M. Antonina Osinski as superior general of the Franciscan Sisters of Chicago. In August of 1940 and again in February of 1941, Father O'Neill visited Mother M. Mechtilde at the Motherhouse in Chicago to present to her the urgent need and the obvious benefits of a Catholic hospital for the Huron community.[4] Father O'Neill also came as the representative of Robert D. Lusk,[5] publisher of the *Huron Daily Plainsman*, and Dr. J. C. Shirley,[6] president of the Sprague Hospital and the Huron Clinic. These men were quick to recognize the need for a modern, independent hospital for the city of Huron.

To understand more fully what was to happen at St. John Hospital thirty years later, it is necessary to establish more precisely the conditions which existed when the Franciscan Sisters of Chicago came to Huron.

In 1910, Dr. B. H. Sprague began the Huron Hospital[7] at 70 Seventh Street; in 1915, he built the Sprague Hospital[8] at 450 Dakota Street. He was joined by Dr. J. C. Shirley, Dr. Harry Sewell, Dr. William Griffith, Dr. W. H. Saxton, and later, by Dr. Howard L. Saylor, Sr. The outpatient department of the hospital was usually referred to as the Huron Clinic.[9] Two houses adjacent to the building were used to house the students of the Sprague Hospital School of Nursing which had opened in 1921. Throughout the years, the Sprague Hospital was maintained by the group of Huron physicians and surgeons who were part of the Huron Clinic. Meanwhile, in 1923, Dr. John S. Tschetter established the Huron Sanitorium[10] at 720 Dakota Street. It was destroyed by fire in December of 1943. In the mid-40s, Dr. Tschetter and his colleagues formed the Tschetter-Hohm Clinic and established the Samaritan Hospital. Physicians in Huron who were not affiliated with either of the two groups practiced independently or in smaller clinics. [11]

In a hospital survey conducted by Dr. A. B. Price of the United States Public Health Service, District Number 7, on December 10, 1943, the statistics revealed the threatening medical shortages existing in Huron.[12] According to Dr. Price, up to and during World War II, it was obvious that Huron was seriously deficient in hospital facilities. The two existing "semi-hospitals" and clinics, namely, the Sprague Hospital and Huron Clinic and the Samaritan Hospital and Tschetter-Hohm Clinic, were not meeting the needs of the Huron community for hospital facilities nor did they meet the requirements for modern hospital services. Dr. Price's survey revealed the following: 1) there were only 78 hospital beds in the Huron, South Dakota area representing the total facilities for over 76,000 people; 2) the facilities in existence were below standard; 3) the city of Huron constituted the medical center for the surrounding country, as indicated by the lack of hospital facilities and the source of hospital patients in and from an area within a radius of forty miles of the city; 4) there was a need for 125 to 130 additional hospital beds in the Huron area; 5) lastly, the Huron area was engaged in a substantial amount of industry which contributed directly or indirectly to the conduct of World War II. According to the survey, Dr. Price concluded that consideration be given to the construction of a 125-bed hospital in Huron.[13]

The requests of the Sprague Hospital and Huron Clinic doctors and the civic-minded leaders of the city for the services of the Franciscan Sisters of Chicago intensified when they learned that the Sprague Hospital School of Nursing would have to close because of a shortage of qualified personnel due to staffing difficulties resulting from the wartime conditions of the 1940s.[14] The Franciscan Sisters of Chicago, the Huron representatives maintained, could begin their ministry of healing in Huron by staffing the Sprague Hospital and at the same time, assuming responsibility for continuing the program in nursing education at the Sprague Hospital School of Nursing.

In March of 1943, the Most Reverend William O. Brady,[15] bishop of Sioux Falls, and a committee from Huron came to the Motherhouse to meet with Mother M. Mechtilde and her general councilors. They urged the Sisters to accept the invitation to staff the Sprague Hospital and to administer its school of nursing, and once in Huron, to formulate plans for the construction of a new hospital to meet the needs of the Huron community. The Sisters were informed that a campaign for funds had already started with an initial yield of $26,000 and with the support of the medical staffs of both the Sprague Hospital and the Samaritan Hospital.[16] In order to keep the Sprague Hospital and its school of nursing functioning, and to minister to the health needs of the Huron community, with the prospect in mind of someday building a new hospital, Mother M. Mechtilde and her general councilors, after prayer and discernment, made the decision to send the first Franciscan Sisters of Chicago "out West" to Huron.

On October 15, 1944, on the feast of St. Teresa of Avila, the patroness of Mother M. Theresa Dudzik, two Franciscan Sisters of Chicago arrived in Huron to begin the congregation's hospital apostolate. The pioneer Sisters appointed by Mother M. Mechtilde and her council were Sister Eleanor Plocki[17] and Sister M. Leonia Mszanski.[18] They were met at the train by Father O'Neill and several leaders of the Huron community. Father O'Neill drove the Sisters to St. Martin's, his parish church, where he celebrated mass to thank God for the Sisters' safe journey and to invoke God's blessing upon their noble efforts in the West. Sister M. Leonia and Sister Eleanor were warmly welcomed by the Sisters of the Congregation of the Presentation of the Blessed Virgin Mary who conducted St. Martin's School. Of necessity, Sister M. Leonia and Sister Eleanor had to make their home in the rectory since there were no other quarters available at the time. The next day, Father O'Neill pointed out the corner of 4th and Iowa, SE, to the Sisters and predicted that "someday a Catholic hospital would stand there."[19] At the time, the Washington Public School, vacant for several years and surrounded by tall grass and a high wire fence, occupied the site.[20]

Father O'Neill proceeded to take the Sisters to the Sprague Hospital where they were introduced to the physicians and the hospital personnel. A patient at the hospital, Judge Tegwell Simmons, was overjoyed at the sight of the Sisters and in greeting them remarked: "It does my heart good to see you. The [new] hospital is now not only a budding hope but a blossoming reality."[21]

On the following day, Sister M. Leonia was appointed the assistant director of nurses, and Sister Eleanor assumed the responsibility of supervisor of the medical floor at the Sprague Hospital. Both Sisters were also appointed instructors at the Sprague Hospital School of Nursing. The nurses, unaccustomed to the Sisters, looked upon them with curiosity. When the Sisters ventured into the downtown area several days later, a group of lads greeted them with cries of: "Oh, look, the hospital Sisters are here!"[22] For the most part, it appeared to the Sisters that the people of Huron were rather reserved in response to them. Before long, however, patients at the hospital were spreading the good news concerning the arrival of the Sisters and the efficiency of the services at the "Sisters'

Hospital." Although only 20 percent of the city of Huron was Catholic, the Huron community eventually grew very fond of the Sisters and respected their dedicated service and genuine concern for each patient as a person.[23]

When the Sisters began ministering to the physical needs of their patients, they soon realized that, oftentimes, the spiritual life of their patients had been sorely neglected. Most of the people who came to the hospital were farmers and their families who came from the territory covering a radius of about sixty miles. Many of the patients had formerly been Catholic but had abandoned their faith when they married or when they settled on farms that were a long distance from St. Martin's Church. Father O'Neill often repeated to the Sisters: "God has a plan for you Sisters here—many of his children need you, and it is in the hospital where they begin again to think of God and want to come back."[24]

The Huron Clinic had arranged to purchase a small house for the Sisters on Fifth Street for use as a convent. Philip Crowlie, the business manager of the Huron Clinic, accompanied the Sisters when they viewed it for the first time. Upon seeing it, Sister Eleanor exclaimed: "Oh, my, Noah's Ark!"[25] It was a long, one-story structure with seven small rooms. There were no walks on the sides of the house and the yard had been sadly neglected. The interior of the house was in disrepair. The plaster had fallen off the walls in many rooms, and dirty rags were stuffed in the empty spaces. The floors were made of wide, rough boards. There was no sink in the kitchen; rather, the dishes had been washed in the bathroom by the previous occupants. Because of the condition of the house, the Sisters continued to live at the rectory while the house was being remodeled. Each morning they walked to the convent of the Presentation Sisters[26] to attend mass after which they hurried off to the Sprague Hospital where they changed into white habits, ate breakfast, and attended to their nursing duties. They remained at the hospital until five o'clock in the evening and after taking supper at St. Martin's rectory, they concluded the day with communal prayer at the church.[27]

Perhaps one of the nicest gestures directed toward the Sisters at this time was performed by Dr. J. C. Shirley, the president of the Huron Clinic, who was always very kind and solicitous about the Sisters' welfare. When he realized that on December 8, the Franciscan Sisters of Chicago would celebrate the 50th Anniversary of their foundation, he urged the Sisters to return to Chicago for the celebration . Mother M. Mechtilde also requested the Sisters to return for this significant day, and once at the Motherhouse, Sister M. Leonia and Sister Eleanor, amid tears of joy and gratitude, related their experiences in South Dakota—the "distant outpost" of the congregation's many ministries.[28]

On December 20, 1944, the Sisters, aided by the Altar Society of St. Martin's Church, left the rectory for their renovated home on Fifth Street. When Father O'Neill announced to his parishioners on Christmas Eve[29] that the Sisters had moved into their convent but lacked many necessities, the bell never stopped ringing with well-wishers—a woman with a box full of items that she thought the Sisters could use; a little boy bearing a tray of cookies; a girl with a jar of preserves; another parishioner with curtains, towels, pots, and pans. Now the little convent consisted of more than two beds, two rockers, a coal stove, a table, and two kneelers. Father O'Neill's joy was unbounded when he visited the Sisters' refurbished home and saw the results of his parishioners' kindness.

On January 12, 1945, Mother M. Mechtilde Zynda and Sister M. Paul Kirschbaum, third councilor and secretary general, arrived in Huron to discuss the preliminary plans for the construction of the new hospital. Present at the meeting were Dr. J. C. Shirley; Dr. W. H. Saxton; Mr. Philip Crowlie; Mr. Robert Lusk; Mr. Harry Liem, then the acting mayor of Huron; the Reverend John O'Neill; Sister M. Leonia; and Sister Eleanor.[30]

Two weeks later, the first official meeting of the Board of Directors took place at which time the Articles of Incorporation were drawn up and submitted to the state of South Dakota for approval. In the meantime, permission was sought from the United States Government to build the hospital. A survey of the Huron community was made by the United States Public Health Service, and the War Production Board was asked that priority be granted for the construction of the hospital because of the urgent need for such a facility in Huron.[31]

On March 1, 1945, Sister M. Amabilis Bellock[32] arrived in Huron to assume the position of director of education and instructor of nursing at the Sprague Hospital School of Nursing. That same day, the Kobel Company demolished the old public school which stood on the proposed site for the new hospital at 4th and Iowa Streets. To Father O'Neill was given the honor of unloading the first cart of concrete into the foundation after the excavation had begun on March 3.[33] At this time, it was decided to name the new hospital in honor of St. John of God, the patron saint of hospitals, of nurses, and of the sick.[34]

On May 9, 1945, the firm of Magney, Tusler, and Setter, architects and engineers from Minneapolis, began construction of the new hospital. Unfortunately, the building proceeded very slowly from the onset because of the shortage of qualified laborers and the difficulty of obtaining materials. The project was plagued by labor-management problems and at times, by a sluggish working crew.[35]

Among the happy events that occurred in the midst of all the setbacks was the addition of two more Sisters to the staff of the Sprague Hospital and School of Nursing. On March 24, 1945, Sister M. Natalie Uscinowicz,[36] who would give dedicated service for twenty-seven years as an instructor and eventually as the second director of the St. John School of Nursing, arrived in Huron. She was followed on August 17, 1945, by Sister M. Aloysilla Kedzior,[37] who began her fruitful thirty-three year apostolate in Huron. Sister M. Aloysilla was assigned the duty of head nurse at Sprague Hospital and surgical nursing instructor at the school of nursing. With four Sisters now missioned in Huron, Sister M. Leonia Mszanski was named the superior on October 15, 1945.

On March 10, 1946, Sister Eleanor Plocki undertook the organization of the St. John Hospital Auxiliary. A nucleus of four grew to 156 active members by the end of the year. The auxiliary aided the hospital from the very beginning by sponsoring fund-raisers and by sewing needed items for the institution.

With great sorrow the Sisters learned of the death on March 16, 1946, of their superior general, Mother M. Mechtilde Zynda. Her commitment to the establishment of the hospital was continued by Sister M. Jerome Dadej, the assistant general, who now served as the interim superior general. In April, Sister M. Jerome and Sister M. Paul Kirschbaum visited Huron to view the progress of the hospital. While in Huron, Sister M. Jerome arranged for the purchase of a second house, called "St. Francis Villa," on Fifth Street to accommodate several Sisters who were assigned to Huron that year, namely, Sister M. Basil Ochocinski,[38] a nursing supervisor who remained for twenty-five years; Sister M. Antonita Waloch, a nurse who served for four years; and Sister M. Chester Dziarnowski,[39] who arrived in May to oversee the construction of the hospital which was still proceeding much too slowly. Sister M. Jerome, while on her visit to Huron, had been surprised to discover the slow and unsteady progress of the hospital which was generally attributed to the inability to obtain certain building materials. She was extremely disappointed to learn, instead, that one of the doctors on the staff, not wanting the hospital project to succeed, had a lobbyist in Washington, DC, who opposed the granting of the St. John Hospital priority every time the matter came up for discussion.[40]

During Sister M. Jerome's visit to Huron as interim superior general, she presented Sister M. Innocentia Sierocki as the administrator of the proposed new St. John Hospital and the religious superior of the Sisters. Sister M. Innocentia was the first of the administrators of St. John Hospital who would provide competent leadership in bringing excellent Christian medical care to the sick and the injured of the Huron community.

Born in Barnesboro, Pennsylvania, on October 11, 1905, Sister M. Innocentia entered the congregation from SS. Peter and Paul Church in Arcadia, Pennsylvania, on October 16, 1920. She became a postulant on June 26, 1921, received the habit of St. Francis on July 26, 1922, and made her first profession of vows on July 27, 1923. On July 27, 1927, she was perpetually united to the congregation.

She began her life of service as a Franciscan Sister of Chicago in the elementary schools of the congregation. In 1935, however, she entered St. Mary's Unit of St. Louis University School of Nursing in St. Louis from which she received her diploma. She spent two years as the administrator and religious superior at the Guardian Angel Day Care Center and Home for Working Girls and the next six years as the religious superior at Boys Town, Nebraska. In 1946, she came to Huron, South Dakota, to supervise the construction of St. John Hospital and to help organize its various departments. As the newly appointed administrator, she would ultimately be responsible for the smooth and orderly transition from the Sprague Hospital to the new hospital. Sister M. Innocentia was destined to leave St. John Hospital in 1948; she returned in 1952, and remained until 1967, serving the Huron community and the surrounding areas with the highest level of commitment for seventeen years.[41]

On March 8, 1947, Father O'Neill blessed the cornerstone of the hospital on the feast of St. John of God. Expressive of St. John Hospital's pursuit of health care excellence in the spirit of Christ, the Master Healer, the cornerstone boldly proclaimed its mandate: "For God and Humanity."

Several days later, the Sisters conferred with their neighbors, the Mahaffeys, in regard to purchasing their large, three-story, sixteen-room house as a convent.[42] Anticipating the opening of the new hospital, the Sisters, by now, had added twelve new members to the staff: Sister M. Marifilia Strzycki,[43] medical records librarian who served for twenty-three years; Sister M. Grace Kujawa,[44] chief pharmacist who remained for twenty-five years; Sister Martha Joan Sempolski,[45] dietitian who also served at the hospital for twenty-five years; Sister Leona Watroba,[46] X-ray technician student who after her training served for twenty-one years; Sister M. Eucheria Obara,[47] an anesthetist for fifteen years; Sister M. Lucille Klockowski,[48] food service attendant for nineteen years; Sister M. Theophane Rakowski,[49] who served a total of fourteen years in the business office; Sister M. Laurentine Trocki,[50] a nurse for nine years; Sister M. Felicia Wierczak, who served in central supplies for four years; and Sister M. Simplicita Mruczkowski, who remained at the hospital for five years as an X-ray technician. Sister Josephine Marie Haske and Sister M. Gerardette Molda came to Huron as the first members of the congregation to enter what would become the St. John School of Nursing.

In late August, Dr. J. C. Shirley and Mr. Warren Darling visited Mother M. Jerome at the Motherhouse in regard to the sale of the northwest corner of the block on which the hospital stood. Dr. Shirley and the Huron Clinic group, who owned the property, intended to build a new clinic there someday. Mother M. Jerome saw the wisdom of purchasing this lot for the expansion of the hospital and at the meeting persuaded Dr. Shirley to sell it to the Sisters. Dr. Shirley and his group agreed to build their clinic on the opposite street corner. Now, with the exception of one house, the Sisters were in possession of three-fourths of the city block. St. Martin's Church and its rectory occupied the other fourth of the block.

Although the building was far from completed, St. John Hospital was blessed and dedicated by the Most Reverend William O. Brady, bishop of Sioux Falls, on September 28, 1947. The Reverend John O'Neill served as master of ceremonies. Mother M. Jerome, now the superior general, and Sister M. Felixa Jorz, the vicar general, were among the two thousand people who came to witness the ceremony. An account of this historical event written in the *St. John Hospital Journal* contained a line which is very significant. It indicates the climate of "unrest" which existed in the Huron hospital community and which affected the Franciscan Sisters of Chicago's ministry in Huron. The line read: "Perhaps the greatest thrill for the Sisters as well as for everyone concerned was the fact that the rival doctors of both clinics sat side by side on the platform and all pledged support of the new hospital."[51]

Despite the fact that the chapel was not finished, the first mass was offered by Father O'Neill on the day after the dedication of the hospital. The second mass that day was celebrated by the Reverend Jerome Fabianski, CR, pastor of St. Stanislaus Bishop and Martyr Church in Chicago, who had accompanied Mother M. Jerome and her general councilors to Huron for the event.

With the dedication of St. John Hospital finally accomplished, the Sprague Hospital School of Nursing was taken over in its entirety, and through a transfer of title, became the St. John Hospital School of Nursing. A brief account of the school of nursing is found at the end of this chapter.

On November 19, 1947, Mother M. Jerome, who had chosen to remain in Huron to oversee the completion of the hospital project personally, and Sister M. Gonzaga, the secretary general, happily sat down to breakfast with the entire group of Sisters now stationed at St. John Hospital. It was a time of gentle rejoicing and prayerful thanksgiving in preparation for the opening day of the hospital which was to occur on November 21. Historically, another event took place which was of paramount importance and which, twenty-six years later, would involve St. John Hospital in a lawsuit.

On that fateful afternoon of November 19, Mother M. Jerome and the Board of Trustees met with all of the physicians in the city who had been invited to this organizational meeting, and the bylaws of St. John Hospital were presented. From the time the Franciscan Sisters of Chicago had come to Huron, that is, in 1944, it was obvious to the Sisters on the staff that an ongoing conflict existed among the physicians in Huron. They were basically divided into three groups, namely, the Huron Clinic group, the Tschetter-Hohm Clinic group, and the independent physicians who were not affiliated with either of the two groups. The roots of this conflict had been growing long before the Sisters arrived or St. John Hospital had been planned.[52] When it had been announced that the Huron Clinic physicians supported the building of a new hospital in cooperation with the Franciscan Sisters of Chicago, the Tschetter-Hohm Clinic and the independent physicians feared they would lose patients to the larger Huron Clinic.[53] Consequently, they began to formulate plans for another hospital complex in connection with a Lutheran health care organization. When a "Certificate of Need" could not be obtained from the state of South Dakota for the second hospital, the Tschetter-Hohm group and the independents agreed to become a part of St. John Hospital's medical staff.[54]

At the strategic November 19 meeting, Dr. Shirley was voted the president of St. John Hospital's medical staff; Dr. Buchanan, the vice president; and Dr. H. P. Adams, the secretary. Since Dr. Shirley and Dr. Adams were members of the Huron Clinic and Dr. Buchanan was an independent, it was obvious that the Tschetter-Hohm group had been overlooked in the nominations. Because Mother M. Jerome was extremely anxious for St. John Hospital to serve the entire community of Huron and because she wanted to achieve harmony among the physicians and the hospital, Mother M. Jerome and the Board of Trustees sought what they considered a workable solution to the situation with which they were faced. They allowed a compromise from the hospital in regard to the wording of the medical staff bylaws—the rules, regulations, and guidelines established to control the scope of activities by the physicians within the medical staff of the hospital. As a result, the original bylaws, as amended and accepted by both the medical staff and the Board of Trustees, included two provisions which in 1973 would create dissension and lead to legal action. Basically, the provisions were: 1) in the election of medical staff officers, the presidency would be rotated; on even-numbered years the presidency would go to a physician from the Huron Clinic; on odd-numbered years, to a representative of the

Tschetter-Hohm Clinic or a physician practicing independently in the community; 2) the original bylaws as amended would not be further changed for at least one year following approval by the Board of Trustees.[55] For the sake of cooperation and with the assumption that the passage of years would alleviate the inter-clinic rivalry and lead to a normal, mutually respecting physician-hospital relationship, the Board of Trustees (then consisting entirely of the Franciscan Sisters of Chicago) consented to the Tschetter-Hohm Clinic's wishes. The stage was set for greater difficulties and more than twenty-five years later, they did occur.[56] The years that followed the opening of St. John Hospital seemed relatively peaceful, but in reality, a basic dissension still existed among the three groups of physicians and the hospital as they continued to meet the health care needs of Huron and the surrounding area.

The long-awaited day of the opening of St. John Hospital took place on the feast of the presentation of the Blessed Virgin Mary, November 21, 1947. The day before, the city had experienced a mild fall day which had been preceded by weeks of very good weather. On November 21, however, the people of Huron awoke to a cold, snowy, wintry day and a blinding snowstorm which soon turned into a full-blown blizzard. Sister M. Chester prevailed upon the officials of the city of Huron to clear the streets and alleys for the transfer of seventy patients by car and ambulance from the Sprague Hospital to St. John Hospital. Thirteen babies were also transferred; both Mother M. Jerome and Sister M.

*St. John Regional Medical Center (originally St. John Hospital and School of Nursing)
Huron, South Dakota (1947–1978)*

Innocentia cradled premature babies in their arms while being driven to the hospital by Dr. W. H. Saxton. The first baby born that day in the new hospital was a girl. On the following day, twenty-nine patients were transferred from the Samaritan Hospital thereby making a total of ninety-nine patients.

At its completion, St. John Hospital was a fine, five-story general comprehensive hospital excellently equipped with the most modern conveniences, facilities, and instruments in all of its well-defined departments. It was able to accommodate 150 patients and 20 bassinets. Each department was under the direction of qualified and experienced registered nurses who acted as supervisors and head nurses. All the facilities offered exceptional opportunities for clinical nursing practice. When the hospital opened its doors, it welcomed the admission of patients regardless of age, race, creed, or economic status.

When the hospital was first planned in 1944, construction was estimated at $450,000. The total cost, however, rose to more than $1.2 million with the decision to add a fifth floor and fifty more beds. The planning committee of the hospital had hoped initially to receive assistance from the federal government. When it did not, the actual cost of the hospital was borne by the Franciscan Sisters of Chicago.[57] Late in 1946, Mother M. Jerome had requested and received a loan from Samuel Cardinal Stritch, the archbishop of Chicago, to cover part of the expenditures.[58] Eventually, the entire cost was covered by donations and through fund-raising campaigns held by the Sisters. Because of the support and generosity of their families, friends, and benefactors, the entire debt was covered. The Franciscan Sisters of Chicago were able to overcome the financial problems and burdens of constructing St. John Hospital and School of Nursing by displaying great courage, a spirit of sacrifice, and unlimited confidence in the Providence of God.

St. John Hospital had, since its opening, been fully accredited by the Joint Commission on Accreditation of Hospitals and its member organizations. It was also a member of the American Hospital Association, the Catholic Hospital Association of the United States and Canada, the South Dakota Hospital Association, and the Associated Hospitals Service, Inc. St. John Hospital was approved by the South Dakota State Department of Health, the Council on Medical Education and Hospitals of the American Medical Association, the South Dakota Board of Nursing, and the National League for Nursing.

In July of 1948, the Franciscan Friars of the Assumption of the Blessed Virgin Mary Province of Pulaski, Wisconsin, accepted the chaplaincy of the hospital. The Reverend Fidelis Filipek, OFM,[59] was appointed to serve as the chaplain at the hospital and as an instructor in psychology and ethics at the St. John Hospital School of Nursing. Six more Sisters were added to the staff in 1948: Sister Frances Szczur[60] who arrived as a student nurse and eventually served as a medical nursing instructor for nineteen years; Sister M. Redempta Demski[61] who was a part of the business staff; Sister M. Fidelia Armatys[62] and Sister M. Theresilla Ignaszak[63] who worked in central supplies; Sister M. Bertille Geffert[64] who served as a laboratory technician; and Sister M. Leonilla Stogowski, floor nurse who remained at the hospital for a period of five years.

In 1948, an epidemic of poliomyelitis, commonly referred to as "polio," struck South Dakota. The disease was a merciless crippler and killer of children and young adults. Because of St. John Hospital's central location and the size of the facility, the hospital became a polio treatment center. Over a relatively short period of time more than 697 victims were treated at St. John Hospital. The American Red Cross supplied additional nursing personnel and the Huron American Legion raised funds for the construction of a treatment pool. Beds were even placed in the halls of the 150-bed hospital. At one time, as many as nine iron lungs were in use. As a consequence of the excellent treatment and tireless efforts of all the hospital personnel, only nine patients were lost to the disease. Because of the remarkable recovery rate of the polio victims, St. John Hospital received special recognition from the National Polio Foundation.[65]

Following the rapidly paced activity at St. John Hospital during the polio epidemic, the growth and development of the hospital returned to a more organized and normal pattern. In October of 1948, Sister M. Innocentia, the hospital's first administrator, was transferred to Gregory, South Dakota, to assume the administration of the old Mother of Grace Hospital; she eventually supervised the construction of the new hospital of the same name in that city.[66] She was succeeded as administrator at St. John Hospital by Mother M. Antonina Osinski who had served from 1934 to 1940 as the fifth superior general of the Franciscan Sisters of Chicago. Mother M. Antonina brought to her appointment a wide range of experience in administration and a vast knowledge of health care services.

Four more Sisters arrived at the hospital during this period: Sister M. Vincentia Wszolek,[67] a laboratory technician who gave twenty-three years of faith-filled service, and Sister M. Aquinas Rosky, a supervisor of nurses who remained for three years. Sister Dorothy Joan Lagocki and Sister M. Mildred Bieda both arrived to enter the St. John Hospital School of Nursing.

The start of the year 1951 brought along its own note of sadness. Early in January, the Sisters and the staff of St. John Hospital mourned the death of their beloved benefactor, protector, and director, the Right Reverend Monsignor John J. O'Neill, who died at the hospital which he largely inspired and helped to build. Without a doubt, his determination, enthusiasm, support, and love had been key ingredients in the success of the hospital.[68]

A happy note was added to the events at St. John Hospital in 1952 when Sister M. Innocentia returned as both administrator and religious superior replacing Mother M. Antonina Osinski, who had been elected assistant superior general to Mother M. Jerome Dadej at the Eighth General Chapter of Elections held that year. Along with Sister M. Innocentia, a number of Sisters arrived who served at the hospital throughout the 1950s. They were Sister Jean Adamczyk,[69] an instructor at St. John School of Nursing who with great zeal devoted twenty-seven years of service; Sister Dorothy Joan Lagocki,[70] an operating room supervisor; Sister M. De Chantal Mazuryk,[71] a sacristan; Sister M. Dorothea Micek,[72] an anesthetist; Sister M. Antonissima Jamruk,[73] who worked in obstetrics and later, as director of nursing services; Sister M. Agatha Walerski[74] and Sister M. Blanche Bartkowski,[75] who served in the business office; and Sister M. Noel Janicki, who worked in the area of dietetics for three years. Admitted to St. John Hospital School of Nursing were Sister M. Clare Brunkala and Sister M. Francis Ann Saliwanchik.

In 1953, the Sisters on the nursing staff of St. John Hospital adapted their traditionally styled habits to their working situation. As a result, their white religious garb, worn while on duty, underwent a change. From December 8, the Sisters adopted a modified white habit with a detachable scapular, a white cotton Franciscan cord, and a small, black Franciscan chaplet.

The Reverend Fidelis Filipek, OFM, was transferred in 1957. His successor was the Reverend Norman Maras, OFM,[76] who served as chaplain at the hospital and instructor in ethics at the school of nursing.

Through the years, the Franciscan Sisters of Chicago increased their numbers on the staff and improved their services at St. John Hospital. The statistics of 1957 concerning the hospital reflected its growth and progress. The construction that year of the more than $1 million St. John Hospital School of Nursing and Residence helped serve to establish Huron as an important medical center. With the completion of the nurses' large new residence at 4th and Kansas Avenue, the Sisters sold the Mahaffey house, which had been their living quarters, and moved into the former residence for nurses at 5th and Iowa Avenue on February 17, 1958.[77] A month later, on March 2 the Reverend Theophane Kalinowski, OFM, blessed the convent home in a private ceremony.

In 1958, Mother M. Jerome Dadej had just concluded her second term as superior general of the Franciscan Sisters of Chicago. She was appointed the religious superior at St. John Hospital in October of that year. Sister M. Innocentia Sierocki remained the administrator.

Along with Mother M. Jerome, Sister M. Maurita Wszolek,[78] arrived in Huron to take up her duties at the St. John Hospital School of Nursing where she remained for sixteen years as librarian and instructor of rhetoric and composition. Another addition to the school of nursing faculty was the Reverend Howard Stunek, OFM,[79] as a full-time instructor in the medical sciences. In 1961, when Mother M. Jerome left St. John Hospital, Sister M. Innocentia became both administrator and superior.

Perhaps one of the most poignant events occurring at St. John Hospital took place on February 12, 1959. In the evening of that day, Sister M. Blanche Bartkowski, who had served at the hospital for five years, passed away while at evening prayer in the chapel. She had been the reader in the refectory that week and had read to the Sisters at breakfast that very morning: "How thoroughly the Savior, our Divine Representative, has sanctified and conquered all the extreme bitterness of death, so that now our own death may be even sweet and peaceful."[80]

A Requiem High Mass was celebrated the next morning by the Reverend Norman Maras, OFM, the hospital chaplain, for the repose of the soul of Sister M. Blanche. Her body lay in state in the chapel until seven-thirty o'clock in the evening when it was removed in preparation for transportation to the Motherhouse the next morning. Mother M. Jerome Dadej, the superior; Sister M. Basil Ochocinski; and Sister M. Grace Kujawa accompanied the remains of Sister M. Blanche to the Motherhouse in Chicago.

By 1965, St. John Hospital had noted eighteen years of service. It recognized that it had worked diligently to meet the continuing challenges of growth both in services and in programs. There had been some amount of remodeling and renovating through the years to meet the growing need for more adequate and modern hospital facilities. In 1965, the hospital records showed 82,963 patient admittances and the birth of 13,198 children. The immediate Huron city was not alone in receiving valuable services from the hospital. An average of 2,500 admissions per year from farm area towns outside Huron.[81]

Among the two hundred persons committed to rendering quality health care at St. John Hospital in the 1960s were several new religious staff members including Sister M. Olimpia Wroblewski,[82] Sister M. Mildred Bieda,[83] and Sister M. Renata Krukowski.[84] A number of Sisters rendered short terms of service during this period. These included Sister M. Humilia Proc, Sister M. Laetitia Kolczak, Sister M. Judith Webster, Sister M. Dianne Kiernicki, Sister M. Peter Ann Przeniczny, Sister M. Kenneth Mulcahy, Sister M. Electa Rytel, Sister M. Christine Brzozowski, and Sister M. De Sales Wyszynski. Sister M. Maxencia Pozniatowski[85] was appointed to St. John Hospital in 1968 where she served as librarian for three years. That same year, the Reverend Albert Nienart, OFM, was named the chaplain; he left after a three-year appointment.

In 1967, Sister M. Innocentia left St. John Hospital as administrator after seventeen years of faithful and compassionate service.[86] Assigned to succeed her as administrator was Sister M. Amabilis Bellock. The Sisters, medical staff, and hospital personnel expressed gratitude-filled goodbyes to Sister M. Innocentia who had guided St. John Hospital expertly and favorably through its formative and challenging years. Under her leadership, St. John Hospital had played a vital role in the quality of health care administered to the people of Huron and its surrounding areas. While the administrator, she had served as president and as treasurer of the South Dakota Hospital Association for many years. An active member of the South Dakota Nurses' Association, she had received the "Outstanding Nurse of the Year Award" in 1948.[87]

Sister M. Innocentia's unquestionably efficient management of the hospital together with her natural ability to help others created a positive attitude that was reflected in the Sisters, patients, medical staff, and employees.[88] As a religious, she was truly exemplary. A warm, sensitive woman, she radiated an inner joy which was reflected in her sincere smile and pleasant disposition. She had that rare ability to "really listen" to people and to be genuinely concerned about their well-being. As woman, nun, nurse, and administrator, Sister M. Innocentia inspired hope and a heartfelt joy in living, loving, and serving others.[89]

During the years that Sister M. Innocentia ministered at St. John Hospital, there had been thousands of persons served: 14,185 babies born; 61,922 persons treated as outpatients; 18,211 major operations and 27,779 minor operations performed; 697 polio patients treated; and 1,084 patients admitted under the new Medicare program. Almost half of the patients had come from Huron—although the hospital served the residents of the Huron trade area and its rolls listed persons from every county in the state, from forty other states, the District of Columbia, and Canada.[90] One of Sister M. Innocentia's last works of mercy before her departure was to cooperate with the Catholic Social Services of the Diocese of Sioux Falls, South Dakota, in providing shelter and employment for unwed mothers.[91]

In 1968, the Congregation of the Franciscan Sisters of Chicago, in keeping with the mandate issued by the Second Vatican Council, held its First Extraordinary Chapter of Affairs.[92] During this strategic and historic chapter, a comprehensive study was made of all the congregation's corporate apostolates. Every school and institution owned and operated by the Franciscan Sisters of Chicago was studied and evaluated in the light of the needs of the times and of the Church as expressed in the Pastoral Constitution on the Church in the Modern World as well as the Decree on Adaptation and Renewal of the Religious Life.[93] As a consequence, the delegates to the First Extraordinary Chapter of Affairs held in 1968 passed a decree which stated: "We continue to own and operate hospitals as long as the Church and the congregation see this as a relevant response to the needs of the times in the health care apostolate."[94] The delegates confirmed their belief that the continuing influence of the Catholic Church in the health field was highly desirable and contributed substantially to the public good. They believed and affirmed that Sisters in the Catholic-sponsored health care facilities bear witness to Christ and foster the charism of Mother M. Theresa Dudzik.

One of the immediate results of the chapter deliberations was the introduction of lay administrators into the congregation's schools and institutions. Consequently, the year 1969 marked the beginning of a new era at St. John Hospital. On January 5, 1969, Mr. Lawrence T. Filosa was named the president. In addition, he was also appointed the Executive Director of Health Facilities for the Franciscan Sisters of Chicago.[95]

After his appointment, Mr. Filosa continued to expand and improve the hospital's services. Under his direction, St. John Hospital became St. John Regional Medical Center in 1972, thus recognizing the hospital's role in providing quality patient care and health career education not only in Huron but in a large portion of central South Dakota. In the course of entering its third decade of health care services, St. John Hospital had grown from the precious dream of a few determined and courageous persons to the vivid reality of an important medical center.

In August of 1972, Mr. Filosa was appointed to St. Anthony Medical Center in Crown Point, Indiana, a new hospital whose foundation had been undertaken by the Franciscan Sisters of Chicago. He was placed in charge of the construction of the hospital and was to assume the presidency of St. Anthony Medical Center at its completion. In September of 1973, therefore, with his permanent residence now in Crown Point, Mr. Filosa named R. Hannan Jones the president of St. John Regional Medical Center. Along with Mr. Jones, four more Sisters were welcomed to the staff: Sister M. Alacoque

Czartoryski, director of the dietary department; Sister M. Ephrem Soprych, director of housekeeping; Sister M. Olga Kulik, who worked in central supply; and Sister M. Arcadia Chmiel, a member of the hospital's office staff.

Other additions to the religious staff of St. John Regional Medical Center in the 1970s were the following: Sister M. Theresia Rybak, Sister M. Theodosia Biss, Sister M. Antoniana Stanczyk,[96] Sister Lois Marie Rossi, Sister Michelle Marie Golaszewski, Sister Victoria Valerie Smagacz, Sister M. Carol Rychlicki, Sister Marie Dominic Wyza, Sister Paula Frances Howard, Sister M. Tarcisia Bucki, Sister M. Bronisia Kapusnik, Sister M. Angelica Seidl, Sister M. Virginette Rokicki, and Sister Isabel Mendez, who had entered the congregation from Carupano, Venezuela.

There were also several assignments of the clergy as chaplains in the hospital and instructors in the school of nursing during this period. The Reverend Myron Lowisz, OFM,[97] served from 1971 to 1974. The Reverend Richard Evenson, the Reverend Robert Flannery, and the Reverend Joseph Murphy served on the staff from 1974 to 1975. In 1975, the Reverend Rembert Badarzynski, OFM, was appointed to minister to the spiritual needs of the patients at St. John Regional Medical Center.

Fully aware that a hospital has an obligation to commitment to excellence not only in dispensing medical care but also in meeting the emotional, social, and spiritual needs of its patients, St. John Regional Medical Center made provisions to establish a Department of Pastoral Care. Sister Bernice Marie Junio initially began her service as a Sister-visitor in October of 1970. Father Badarzynski continued to serve as hospital chaplain. Sister Jean Adamczyk, in addition to continuing her duty as an instructor at the hospital's school of nursing also served as a part-time pastoral minister.

On Sunday, September 24, 1972, St. John Regional Medical Center celebrated its Silver Jubilee of foundation. More than five hundred persons were present for the Liturgy of the Eucharist which was celebrated at St. Martin's Church. The Most Reverend Lambert A. Hoch,[98] bishop of Sioux Falls, was the celebrant and preached the homily. A reception was held in the Huron College Campus Center after the liturgy of praise and thanksgiving.

St. John Regional Medical Center had weathered many storms since the day it first opened on November 21, 1947, to an actual surprise blizzard, but none like the storm that engulfed it in 1973.

Earlier, in 1972, the hospital administration had proposed a comprehensive new set of medical staff bylaws to replace the bylaws that dated back to 1947.[99] These changes were not acceptable to the physicians on the medical staff. On November 24, 1972, the Board of Directors of St. John Regional Medical Center adopted bylaws for the medical staff to become effective on January 1, 1973. The date was later extended to July 11, 1973. These bylaws were not approved by the members on the medical staff. A dispute arose between the hospital administration and the medical staff, the principal issue being that the medical staff maintained that the bylaws issued in 1947 did not give the governing body of the hospital any power to change or even introduce any changes in the medical staff bylaws.

As a consequence of the various attempts to correct the medical staff bylaws, dispute at St. John Regional Medical Center, fifteen Huron physicians joined in action as plaintiffs against the medical center and four other local doctors. The fifteen doctors maintained that the hospital administration adopted the medical staff bylaws on July 11, 1973, without the approval of the doctors. The medical staff went to court, and on March 4, 1975, the Circuit Court ruled in favor of the medical staff. The hospital administration appealed to the South Dakota Supreme Court and in September of 1976, the Supreme Court upheld the medical staff's position on the bylaws.

In the midst of the strife occurring at St. John Regional Medical Center, R. Hannan Jones, the administrator, resigned in March of 1974. Sister M. Aloysilla Kedzior was appointed the acting president of St. John Regional Medical Center. It was she who was responsible for keeping the medical center functioning in spite of the controversies that raged around and within it. Under her guidance, development in several departments continued. Major improvements were made in I.C.C.U., Surgery, Obstetrics, Radiology, and Nuclear Medicine. Many renovations were made to keep the hospital in compliance with various state and federal regulations that govern health care facilities and contribute so much toward the cost of treatment. St. John Regional Medical Center continued as a modern, well-equipped, and well-staffed total health care facility where quality health care services were offered to the people of the Huron community and beyond.

Sister M. Aloysilla, a native of Chicago, entered the congregation from St. Pancratius Church in 1932. She was received into the novitiate on August 15, 1933, and made her first vows on August 16, 1935. Her perpetual commitment to God and to the congregation was made on August 16, 1938.

Her early service in the congregation was in the elementary schools for a period of four years. In 1941, she graduated from St. Joseph Hospital School of Nursing in Joliet, Illinois, and received her bachelor's degree in nursing from Loyola University of Chicago. She served as general staff nurse at St. Joseph Home for the Aged in Chicago for four years. In August of 1945, she was transferred to the Sprague Hospital in Huron, South Dakota, where she assumed the roles of head nurse and surgical instructor. When the St. John Hospital School of Nursing opened in 1947, she was operating room and pharmacology instructor for the next ten years. At this time, she received a master's degree from Marquette University in Milwaukee.

Sister M. Aloysilla served as a member of the Board of Trustees of St. John Regional Medical Center from 1970–1978, and as vice chairperson of St. John Regional Medical Center from 1973–1974. In 1974, she was appointed to the Board of Trustees of St. Anthony Medical Center, Crown Point, Indiana. She was chairperson of the Health Care Facilities of the Franciscan Sisters of Chicago from 1972–1974. She served as president, board member, and secretary of the 13th District of the South Dakota Nursing Association of Huron from 1950–1959; and from 1954–1957, she was elected president of the South Dakota Operating Room Association. From 1960–1973, Sister M. Aloysilla was St. John Hospital and School of Nursing photographer in Huron. During her many years of service, she also conducted seminars and programs, wrote articles for publication, arranged for and presented workshops, and often counseled students and faculty members.[100] Sister M. Aloysilla has been described as a firm administrator whose devotion to duty was outstanding. Inspiring, self-sacrificing, and generous, she was highly regarded as a religious woman, hospital nurse, and administrator.[101]

After the South Dakota Supreme Court had ruled in favor of the medical staff in the matter of the lawsuit which the medical staff initiated in 1973, St. John Regional Medical Center, under the leadership of Sister M. Aloysilla Kedzior, continued to provide the same quality health care services it had provided through the years. When the conflict begun by the lawsuit did not resolve itself but became, instead, an issue involving the governor, the mayor, and the Huron community, a momentous decision was made by the Franciscan Sisters of Chicago.[102] In an open letter to the public, the Sisters informed the Huron community through the *Huron Daily Plainsman* on Sunday, February 26, 1978, that they were terminating their services at St. John Regional Medical Center. On July 1, 1978, the Sisters sold the hospital to a private corporation, which, in turn, sold it to the Huron community. The hospital was renamed the Huron Regional Medical Center.

The profound words of the *Book of Ecclesiastes* were not lost on the part of the Sisters: "There is an appointed time for everything, and a time for every affair under the heavens; a time to uproot the plant . . . a time to tear down . . . a time to weep . . . a time to cast away." The Franciscan Sisters of Chicago had often prayed the words of the Psalmist, and without a doubt, had believed what they prayed. Now the Sisters were forced to live the words. As God continued to be their shelter and their strength, the Franciscan Sisters of Chicago left Huron, South Dakota, and turned with renewed love and dedication to pressing health care ministries outside that city.

In 1983, the Franciscan Sisters of Chicago were invited to attend the centennial celebration on October 22 and 23 at St. Martin's Church in Huron, South Dakota. Representing the congregation at this festivity were Sister M. Aloysilla Kedzior, Sister M. Amabilis Bellock, Sister M. Basil Ochocinski, Sister Jean Adamczyk, Sister Martha Joan Sempolski, and Sister M. Natalie Uscinowicz. On October 23, a Liturgy of Thanksgiving was celebrated by the Most Reverend Paul F. Anderson, bishop of Sioux Falls, and the Most Reverend Lambert Hoch, the retired bishop of Sioux Falls, together with the former pastors of St. Martin's Church. While at the celebration, the Sisters had the opportunity to visit with many of the parishioners of St. Martin's Church, the employees of the former St. John Regional Medical Center, and the former students of St. John Hospital School of Nursing. The Sisters were received warmly and with great gratitude. The *Post-Tribune* put it aptly: "The Sisters are remembered kindly in Huron."[103]

A lovely and sincere tribute was paid to the Franciscan Sisters of Chicago on August 10, 1984, when the Huron Regional Medical Center presented a special gift to the Sisters in the form of a stained glass window taken from the former St. John Regional Medical Center chapel. The frame surrounding the window read: "Presented by the Huron community to the Franciscan Sisters of Chicago for their many years of service in providing health care to the people of Eastern South Dakota."[104] Historically, it had been forty years since the Franciscan Sisters of Chicago had begun their hospital ministry by going to Huron. Now, in a gesture of gratitude and good will by the Huron community, a piece of Huron had come to the Sisters.

The history of St. John Hospital School of Nursing must necessarily begin with the Sprague Hospital School of Nursing. It will be recalled that the Sprague Hospital School of Nursing had been organized by a group of doctors who owned the Sprague Hospital. There is evidence to believe that the "training school for nurses" was begun as early as 1917; it was certainly in existence by 1921.[105] The Sprague Hospital School of Nursing continued to operate successfully until it encountered difficulties resulting from the wartime conditions of the 1940s when many nurses were called to or volunteered for active duty with the armed forces. As a consequence, the Sprague Hospital School of Nursing, in operation for twenty-three years, was in danger of closing. In 1944, therefore, the Franciscan Sisters of Chicago finally acceded to the repeated requests of the Reverend John J. O'Neill, Dr. J. C. Shirley, and Mr. Robert Lusk to manage the Sprague Hospital and School of Nursing. In October of 1944, Sister M. Leonia Mszanski and Sister Eleanor Plocki arrived in Huron, South Dakota, to pioneer this movement of the Franciscan Sisters of Chicago into the health apostolate.

At the Sprague Hospital School of Nursing, Sister M. Leonia assumed the position of assistant director of nurses and instructor of nursing while Sister Eleanor served as supervisor of the medical floor in the hospital and as an instructor. Virtually all the courses were taught by the two Sisters and Miss Bertha Boekelheide, the director of the Sprague Hospital School of Nursing, with the assistance of several doctors who aided because of the acute shortage of instructors. Fortunately, in May of 1945, Sister M. Amabilis Bellock arrived in Huron to assume the position of director of education and instructor of nursing at the Sprague Hospital School of Nursing. In August of that year, Sister M. Aloysilla Kedzior was appointed head nurse at the Sprague Hospital and surgical nursing instructor at the school of nursing. One year later, Sister M. Natalie Uscinowicz became a part of the teaching staff which was increasing with lay instructors as well.[106]

With the construction of St. John Hospital in 1947, the Sprague Hospital School of Nursing was taken over in its entirety, and through a transfer of title, became St. John Hospital School of Nursing. The first classes were held on September 7, 1947. Included among the students were two Franciscan Sisters of Chicago, namely, Sister Josephine Marie Haske and Sister M. Gerardette Molda.

On February 2, 1948, Sister M. Amabilis was appointed the first director of the St. John Hospital School of Nursing. Sister Eleanor Plocki, in turn, was appointed the director of education at the school succeeding Sister M. Amabilis. That same year, Sister M. Grace Kujawa was added to the faculty of the nursing school where she remained for the next fifteen years as a part-time instructor in pharmacology and chemistry. In September of 1948, the Reverend Fidelis Filipek, OFM, was appointed chaplain of St. John Hospital and joined the staff of the school of nursing as an instructor in ethics and psychology.

The woman selected to serve as the first director of the St. John Hospital School of Nursing, Sister M. Amabilis, entered the congregation from St. Casimir Church in Cleveland, Ohio, on January 31, 1931. She was received into the novitiate on January 6, 1932, and made her first profession of vows on January 8, 1934. She pledged herself perpetually to God and to the congregation on August 16, 1938.

Sister M. Amabilis began her training at St. Joseph Hospital School of Nursing in Joliet, Illinois, in 1938, and received her diploma in 1941. She completed her under-graduate work in nursing education at Loyola University of Chicago in 1944. In 1960, she obtained her master's degree in nursing education from St. Louis University.[107] A woman of gentle demeanor and firm principle, Sister M. Amabilis showed great devotion to duty. An excellent teacher and friend to all the students and staff, Sister M. Amabilis was well chosen for her position as director.[108]

When the Sprague Hospital School of Nursing became the St. John Hospital School of Nursing, thirty-three students made the transfer.[109] The senior group of eleven students became the first graduates of the school on June 13, 1948. The commencement exercises were held in the chapel of St. John Hospital. The Reverend Dennis Donovan of St. Patrick's Church in Cavour, South Dakota, gave the graduation address, and a reception in the hospital cafeteria followed the graduation exercises.[110] The school of nursing, which provided a three-year diploma program, continued to prosper. The program of basic nursing required one hundred fifty-six weeks to complete. It offered instruction in the five usual services: medical, surgical, obstetric, pediatric, and psychiatric; the last two were taught by affiliation. In the latter part of 1948, the school of nursing received approval from the South Dakota Board of Nurse Examiners to accept males into the student nursing program.[111]

At the outset of the school of nursing program, provisions had been made for the students to live in leased quarters on the second and third floors of the Sprague Hospital. Classes were held on the fifth floor of the hospital, but all meals were served in the cafeteria of St. John Hospital. Early in June of 1949, it was learned that the student nurses would have to vacate their living quarters by December of that year.[112] This announcement made it imperative for the Franciscan Sisters of Chicago to begin immediate construction of a nurses' temporary residence. Although the Sisters had envisioned building a new and large school and residence for nurses, sufficient funds were not available for the Sisters to undertake such a costly project at that time. They did succeed, however, in obtaining the services of a local contractor, a parishioner of St. Martin's Church, who agreed to build a small residence for the nurses at a cost of approximately $75,000. All attempts to obtain federal aid to help in the construction of the nurses' temporary home were unsuccessful, and the cost of the proposed construction had to be borne by the congregation.[113]

On July 11, 1949, the building site at 5th and Iowa Avenue was blessed and the ground broken by the Reverend John J. O'Neill with Mother M. Jerome Dadej, the superior general of the congregation, present at the ceremony. A few days later,

Nurses Home (later, the Sisters' residence)
St. John Hospital School of Nursing
Huron, South Dakota

construction of the nurses' residence began in earnest. Besides providing sleeping quarters for fifty students, it also contained offices for the instructors, a small living room which could be enlarged by opening the partition which separated it from the library, a small chemistry laboratory, and a classroom. All during the time of construction, classes for the nurses were conducted at St. John Hospital.

One of the worst blizzards ever to hit the state of South Dakota occurred on March 7, 1950. Amid this natural disaster, preparations were being made for the dedication on the next day of the nurses' new residence. Despite all the difficulties engendered by the inclement weather, the Most Reverend William Brady, bishop of Sioux Falls, dedicated the St. John Hospital School of Nursing Residence on March 8, the feastday of the patron of the hospital. At the ceremony, Bishop Brady was assisted by the Reverend John J. O'Neill and the Reverend Fidelis Filipek, OFM. Although the storm kept many out-of-towners from participating in the joy of the dedication, there were many friends of the hospital present on this long-awaited day. However, Mother M. Jerome, the superior general, who had so looked forward to this day had been stranded in Sioux City and arrived a day late for the dedication.[114]

The new building, however serviceable and attractive, soon proved vastly inadequate. To accommodate the increased number of student nurses making application, a private residence called Madonna Hall, facing Kansas Avenue, was purchased for the third-year students. In addition, some of the students, as well as a few Sisters, had to be housed in the south wing of the second floor of the new St. John Hospital.[115]

On April 24, 1950, the St. John Hospital School of Nursing Alumni Association was formed.[116]

The first graduating class of the new St. John Hospital School of Nursing held their commencement exercises on June 11, 1950. Among the graduates were Sister Josephine Marie Haske[117] and Sister M. Gerardette Molda[118] who had successfully concluded their studies and became, therefore the first two members of the Franciscan Sisters of Chicago to receive their nursing diplomas from the St. John Hospital School of Nursing. At an impressive ceremony held in the hospital chapel, the Reverend Paul F. Anderson addressed the graduates and presented them with their diplomas. The Reverend Fidelis Filipek, OFM, pronounced the invocation and the benediction. Both Sister Josephine Marie and Sister M. Gerardette were added to the staff of St. John Hospital after graduation. When the new class opened on June 14, 1950, there were eleven prospective nurses including two males. There was also a new full-time instructor of nursing on the staff, Sister Jean Adamczyk, who dedicated the next twenty-seven years of her religious life to the inspiring task of preparing student nurses for their careers of service to humanity.

In the next few years, St. John Hospital School of Nursing followed modern trends in nursing and expanded its educational opportunities. The first pediatric affiliation had been established in 1943 at St. Mary's Hospital in Rochester, Minnesota. It was terminated, however, in 1955, and an affiliation was made with Children's Hospital in Denver, Colorado. Later, an affiliation was made with Children's Hospital in Milwaukee, Wisconsin, and a final affiliation was made with the Cook County Children's Hospital in Chicago. Earlier, in 1950, arrangements had been made for a thirteen-week course in psychiatric nursing in Moose Lake State Hospital in Moose Lake, Minnesota. When in 1953 a program was arranged for affiliation at Yankton State Hospital in Yankton, South Dakota, the psychiatric affiliation was transferred to that facility.[119]

In October 1952, on the basis of its qualified faculty, curriculum, teaching facilities, and affiliating programs in pediatric and psychiatric nursing, St. John Hospital School of Nursing was temporarily accredited for a period of five years by the National Nursing Accrediting Service. In 1955, the school received praise from the National Nursing Accrediting Service who stated that they considered St. John Hospital School of Nursing to be "one of the 'strong' schools in the state."[120] In 1960, St. John Hospital School of Nursing was approved by the South Dakota State Board of Nursing and accredited by the National League for Nursing. This status was maintained through the years and confirmed at the last National League for Nursing survey in 1974. In addition, St. John Hospital School of Nursing was a member of the Council of Diploma Schools, the National League for Nursing, the American Hospital Association, and the Conference of Catholic Schools of Nursing.

St. John Hospital School of Nursing graduated two more Franciscan Sisters of Chicago in 1952, namely, Sister Dorothy Joan Lagocki and Sister M. Mildred Bieda. The year before, Sister Frances Szczur had also successfully completed her training and received her diploma in nursing.

On June 27, 1954, for the first time in the history of St. John Hospital School of

Nursing, the Most Reverend William Brady, bishop of Sioux Falls, was the guest speaker at the commencement exercises held at St. Martin's Church. Among the twenty-one graduates that year was a male nurse.[121]

The problem which continued to confront the Sisters, however, was the very apparent need of constructing a new and larger school of nursing and a residence. The students and some of the religious staff were housed on the second floor of St. John Hospital in rooms which were needed for patients. Mother M. Jerome and her general council, therefore, granted permission to the hospital administration to plan the building of a large and modern facility as soon as possible in spite of the fact that, financially, it would present a major problem to the congregation.[122]

In the midst of the planned construction of a new St. John Hospital School of Nursing, Sister M. Natalie Uscinowicz was appointed the new director succeeding Sister M. Amabilis.[123] During her tenure as director of the school of nursing, Sister M. Amabilis had succeeded in placing the school of nursing on a very firm foundation causing it to be one of the first schools of nursing in South Dakota to receive national accreditation. She had participated willingly and actively in all the studies and surveys necessary to project the school into national focus.[124] Always very active in professional organizations, Sister M. Amabilis was appointed a member of the South Dakota Board of Nursing and later served as its president. She was elected chairperson of the Curriculum Committee of the South Dakota League of Nursing and was the only woman to be appointed to a committee investigating the Yankton State Hospital in 1957. In addition, she served as a guest speaker, lecturer, and panel participant on numerous occasions. It was generally agreed that her intellectual curiosity, religious spirit, warm personality, and sincere compassion for the ill were traits characteristically identified with her.[125]

In welcoming Sister M. Natalie as its second director of nursing, St. John Hospital School of Nursing welcomed a woman of notable talents and deep devotion to duty. Sister M. Natalie, born in Cleveland, Ohio, entered the Congregation of the Franciscan Sisters of Chicago from St. Casimir Church. Her postulancy began on February 2, 1932, and her novitiate commenced on January 6, 1933. On August 16, 1935, she made her first profession of vows and on August 12, 1941, she professed perpetual vows.

Sister M. Natalie spent her first four years of service in the congregation as an elementary school teacher. In 1939, she entered St. Joseph Hospital School of Nursing in Joliet, Illinois, and received her diploma in nursing in 1942. For the next three years, she was engaged in nursing duties at the Motherhouse, but in March of 1946, she was sent to St. John Hospital. Returning to Chicago, she attended De Paul University. Once again assigned to St. John Hospital in 1947, she remained there until 1951. That year she obtained a bachelor's degree in nursing from Loyola University of Chicago. She returned to St. John Hospital School of Nursing in 1955 with a master's degree from the Catholic University of America in Washington, DC, and remained at St. John Hospital for the next eighteen years.[126] Sister M. Natalie proved to be an untiring, conscientious director with professional competence and a wonderful ability to relate to the student body.[127] As a

St. John Hospital School of Nursing
Huron, South Dakota

religious, she was a heartwarming inspiration to students and staff alike.

The plans and architectural sketches for a new and larger school of nursing and residence had been made known to the general public in November of 1954. Due to a continual lack of available funds, construction could not begin on the classroom and residence complex in spite of the urgent need for it. In 1955, however, St. John Hospital received a $67,000 grant from the Ford Foundation for the expansion and improvement of hospital services.[128] This initial sum was an answer to the Sisters' prayers. For the remainder of the cost of the structure, the Sisters requested the Most Reverend William O. Brady, the bishop of Sioux Falls, to negotiate a loan from the Holy See. Eventually, the loan would be repaid by St. John Hospital itself; in the meantime, the congregation struggled to cover the cost of the construction.[129] As a result, excavation for the new facility began in May of 1956 at 4th Street and Kansas Avenue. Construction proceeded so well that the blessing of the cornerstone was able to take place on November 21, 1956— the ninth anniversary of the dedication of St. John Hospital. The cornerstone of the new edifice proudly bore the motto of the St. John Hospital School of Nursing and its highest aspiration: "For God and Humanity."

Along with the good news of the progress in the construction of the school of nursing was the appointment of several more Sisters to the faculty. Sister M. Dorothea Micek had joined the staff in 1954 as a part-time instructor in post-anesthesia nursing. She was followed in 1955 by Sister Martha Joan Sempolski who served as part-time nutrition and diet therapy instructor for sixteen years. Sister Frances Szczur arrived in 1956 to serve as medical nursing instructor and remained for the next seventeen years.[130] The St. John Hospital School of Nursing community rejoiced when three more Sisters received their diplomas. They were Sister M. Bertille Geffert, Sister M. Clare Brunkala, and Sister M. Francis Ann Saliwanchik.

An administrative change took place on October 7, 1957, when the first layman, Edward Fuss,[131] was engaged as assistant educational director to Sister Eleanor Plocki, the educational director of the school of nursing. Along with Mr. Fuss, two more Sisters joined the teaching staff. Sister M. Antonissima Jamruk served as a full-time instructor in obstetrics; Sister Josephine Marie Haske served for five years as an instructor of nursing. That same year, the Reverend Norman Maras, OFM, arrived in Huron to serve as chaplain at St. John Hospital and instructor at the school of nursing.[132]

In 1958, on the feast of St. John of God, March 8, the St. John Hospital School of Nursing and Residence complex was formally dedicated. The new structure when completely furnished represented an investment of more than $1 million.

The Most Reverend Lambert A. Hoch, who had succeeded the Most Reverend William O. Brady as bishop of Sioux Falls, had been scheduled to bless and dedicate the nursing complex. He was, however, unable to attend because of illness. Acting for Bishop Hoch was the Reverend Paul Anderson, editor of the *Bishop's Bulletin* and administrator of St. Catherine Church in Oldham, South Dakota. He was assisted by the Reverend Norman Maras, OFM, and the Reverend Gary Nolt of St. Martin's Church. At the ceremonies preceding the open house that same day, Robert D. Lusk, the editor and publisher of the *Huron Daily Plainsman,* had called the school of nursing and residence "an act of faith." That theme was also the focus of the address of Sister M. Innocentia Sierocki, the administrator of St. John Hospital, when she spoke to the guests at the ceremony:

> Today's occasion is one of special joy as we find ourselves in the midst
> of friends with whom we are able to share the happiness of our new
> accomplishment. This new edifice represents their dedication, too, to the
> ideals of serving God and humanity. Directly and indirectly, materially or
> morally, our many friends continually promote the welfare of the hospital
> in their midst, realizing Christ's great commandment of love.[133]

As part of the St. John Hospital complex, the new St. John Hospital School of Nursing and Residence was an impressive sight. It was a five-story brick and steel structure of modern design with a two-story wing which served as the school proper. Brightly lit, with cheerful and well-equipped classrooms plus attractive, comfortable living quarters, the building could accommodate 150 students. Each of the four upper floors of the residence had twelve double rooms, one private room, and a comfortable and spacious lounge with kitchenette facilities. The bathrooms on each floor included a shampoo sink, a hair dryer, bath and shower facilities, and sinks with overhead fluorescent lighting. A house telephone and a pay phone booth were located on each floor. The well-furnished bedrooms had desks with overhead bookshelves, a chest of drawers, and built-in wardrobes of blond oak finish. On the first floor of the residence, a huge lobby with picture windows facing the courtyard created a lovely entranceway. The offices for the staff, a library, and a beautiful and functional auditorium with seating for three hundred persons were located on the first floor. Leading out of the tower section was a two-story structure, the school of nursing itself. It contained three large and attractive lecture halls, one very large and well-equipped science room, and a small dietary unit. The east hall on the first floor had separate living accommodations for six male students of nursing. The school of nursing was connected to the hospital by means of a breezeway.

Early in February of 1958, preparations had begun for the Sisters who staffed St. John Hospital to move into the now vacated former nurses' residence. Although all the renovations for its use as a convent were not as yet complete, the Sisters moved into their new and permanent home on February 17. Some Sisters lived in the nurses' new residence where they served as prefects or house mothers.[134]

In 1959, Sister M. Maurita Wszolek arrived in Huron to serve as librarian in the St. John Hospital School of Nursing and also as an instructor in English. Joining her was Sister Dorothy Joan Lagocki who for the next twelve years served as operating room instructor. Another welcome addition to the faculty was the Reverend Howard Stunek, OFM, who served until 1962 as a full-time instructor in the medical sciences.

The next several years saw the appointment of more religious and lay staff members. In 1961, Sister M. Francis Ann Saliwanchik served as a nurse at St. John Hospital and as a part-time instructor at the school of nursing. In 1962, Sister M. Vincentia Wszolek became a part-time instructor in microbiology. The Reverend Bede Joseph Hepnar, OFM, was a full-time instructor, who, however, remained for only one year. By 1963, St. John Hospital School of Nursing had seventy-four students enrolled, thirty of whom were non-Catholic. In 1966, Sister M. Peter Ann Przeniczny and Sister M. Kenneth Mulcahy were added to the staff as full-time instructors. Two more Franciscan Sisters of Chicago received their diplomas in nursing in 1967, namely, Sister Margaret Mary Peckenpaugh and Sister Therese Wegiel. In 1968, the Reverend Albert Nienart, OFM, was added as a part-time instructor; in 1970 the Reverend Myron Lowisz, OFM, joined the staff. By 1974 three members of the clergy shared part-time positions as instructors: the Reverend Joseph Murphy, the Reverend Richard Flannery, and the Reverend Richard Evenson, a Protestant minister. The last priest to serve as instructor was the Reverend Rembert Badarzynski, OFM, who came to Huron in 1975.

On August 1, 1971, Sister M. Maurita who had held the position as librarian at St. John Hospital School of Nursing for fourteen years[135] and had served as a part-time instructor in English for nine years, was appointed dean of students.

In 1973, Sister M. Natalie Uscinowicz, the director of the school of nursing was transferred to the congregation's new St. Anthony's Hospital in Crown Point, Indiana. During her eighteen-year tenure as director, Sister M. Natalie had upheld the fine standards early established for the school of nursing and had definitely left the mark of her fruitful and forceful leadership on the institution.[136] While director, she had served as vice president of the South Dakota Nurses Association in the 1960s and had been a member of the board of directors. She had also been a member of the Board of Directors of St. John Hospital, a board member of the South Dakota League of Nursing and had served as chairperson of the State Convention of the South Dakota League for Nursing. She had often served as guest lecturer and panel participant. Sister M. Natalie was long recognized as a woman of abiding faith, devotion to duty, and sincere cordiality—an admirable combination of nun and nurse.[137]

Throughout the years, St. John Hospital and School of Nursing had been staffed by the Franciscan Sisters of Chicago and lay men and women. The qualifications of the administration and staff were equal to or better than those of the average school of nursing of similar enrollment in the area. But early in 1968, the Huron community was informed that the St. John Hospital School of Nursing was slated to be closed. After five years of intense study and evaluation, in January of 1973, the Board of Directors of St. John Regional Medical Center (as it was now known) announced that the school of nursing would not admit a freshman class in August of 1974. The school of nursing was scheduled to close permanently with the graduation of the class of 1976. At this strategic time in the history of the institution, Sister M. Aloysilla Kedzior was appointed the third director of the school of nursing.[138]

The reasons given for the closing of the school of nursing were logical and crucial. With each passing year, it had become decidedly more difficult to secure qualified and experienced nursing instructors at the master's degree level.[139] There was even a serious lack of qualified faculty that could be recruited to South Dakota. The medical center had no resources to upgrade audiovisual aids and other teaching materials necessary for educational instruction. The depth of medical specialties, that is, exposure in all areas in which the student could practice was not at a level which would offer the nursing student maximum benefits and an excellent education. The students saw a very narrow spectrum of diseases and pathology within the confines of St. John Medical Center. The hospital did not have the specialties to give a well-rounded experience in medicine and surgery. Part of this was due to the shorter lengths of stays of patients who were admitted, leaving the student with a shorter time to observe the patient clinically and to develop an in-depth knowledge of the disease processes.[140] Finally, the high cost of operating the school of nursing and maintaining the nurses' residence was prohibitive.[141] St. John Regional Medical Center could no longer afford the $315,000 a year needed to support the school of nursing. Only a third of the cost of the program was paid by tuition and other school-generated money. The remaining $210,000 had to be made up from funds furnished by St. John Regional Medical Center and by increased patient costs. Although various community interests had been approached for financial support, none were gathered; no personal or group donations were ever received. To compound the problem, few graduates of the school of nursing returned to St. John Regional Medical Center as employees.[142]

There were many plans outlined for the school of nursing facilities once the St.

John School of Nursing was closed. In view of the fact that the members of the medical staff at the hospital were aging, there was a need to recruit a younger, more aggressive, and more progressive medical staff. One of the primary uses of the school of nursing would be the creation of doctors' offices in the building which would facilitate both inpatient and outpatient care. With the recruitment of needed specialists, St. John Regional Medical Center would be able to expand its ancillary services. A portion of the building would be allocated toward an in-service education program to upgrade the skills of the practicing nurses and all other hospital personnel. Other space in the building would be utilized to coordinate the Allied Health Organizations such as the Heart Association, the Mental Health Center, the Muscular Dystrophy Association, and many others. The closing of the St. John School of Nursing would not end the hospital's commitment to health education. All the hospital's priorities would attempt to remain within the realm of excellence in patient care.[143]

Sister M. Aloysilla Kedzior had served only one year as director of the school of nursing when on March 18, 1974, she was elected president of St. John Regional Medical Center replacing Mr. R. Hannan Jones. Sister M. Maurita Wszolek, in turn, was appointed the acting director of the school of nursing until it closed.

The last class of the St. John School of Nursing graduated in May of 1976. The total number of graduates throughout the school's notable history had been 602. Of these, fourteen were men and twelve were Sisters. The last Franciscan Sister of Chicago to receive her nursing diploma was Sister Lois Marie Rossi who graduated in 1975.

For nearly thirty years, the St. John Hospital School of Nursing had attempted to offer the best quality of health care instruction to its student nurses. The administration and staff had taught their students, by word and example, how to minister to the spiritual and physical needs of the sick and injured. The school's motto had been the incentive for their splendid endeavor—"For God and Humanity."

ST. JOHN HOSPITAL AND SCHOOL OF NURSING

[1]The Reverend Francis A. Cronin was appointed to St. Bernard's Church in Redfield in June 1937. In 1945, he was transferred to St. Leo's Parish in Tyndall, South Dakota. He died there on March 9, 1965. See Chapter 50. *The Bishop's Bulletin,* published monthly by the Diocese of Sioux Falls.

[2]*Minutes of General Council Proceedings, 1938* (AFSCL).

[3]"Brief History of St. John Hospital," Huron, 1947. (Mimeographed).

[4]*Minutes of General Council Proceedings,* 22 August 1940; and 25 February 1941 (AFSCL).

[5]Mr. Lusk joined with Father O'Neill and Dr. Shirley in support of the proposed new hospital. Through his newspaper and particularly his editorials, he sought to unite the community of Huron in supporting the proposed hospital by pointing out the need and the advantages of its construction. With the death of Mr. Lusk in 1962, St. John Hospital lost a powerful patron and friend. St. John Regional Medical Center, *St. John Reports, 30th Anniversary Issue,* (Huron, South Dakota, 1977), p. 40.

[6]Dr. J. C. Shirley had been a prominent physician and surgeon in Huron. In 1920, he formed a partnership with Dr. William Saxton, which led, in 1922, to the formation of the Sprague Hospital and School of Nursing and the Huron Clinic. At the time of his death, in 1948, Dr. Shirley was chief of the medical staff at St. John Hospital and chief of staff at the Huron Clinic.

His partner, Dr. Saxton, was also a pioneer physician and friend of St. John Hospital. He was one of the original members of the group of physicians and citizens to recognize the need for a modern independent hospital in Huron, and very active in the planning and development stages of St. John Hospital. He served as a charter member of St. John's medical staff. After retiring from active practice in January of 1977, he died on December 4 of that same year. Ibid., p. 3.

[7]The Huron Hospital was purchased in 1915 by Dr. Tillson J. Wood, who used it as a private home. *Huron Daily Plainsman,* 23 October 1985.

[8]A brick and frame building, the Sprague Hospital was a three-story general hospital with 51 beds and 9 bassinets. It was owned by Dr. J. C. Shirley, a general surgeon; Dr. W. H. Saxton, an obstetrician and gynecologist; and Dr. H. L. Saylor, an ear, nose, and throat specialist. The hospital was very unpretentious in appearance and rather poorly located. The first floor was used for offices and outpatient clinic facilities. Hospital beds, operating rooms, and one office were located on the second floor. On the third floor were additional rooms and beds and the delivery room and nursery. The basement contained the kitchen, dining room, heating unit, storage space, and two classrooms for the nursing school program. Several minor additions to the hospital had been built through the years, but a shortage of space for proper accommodations existed in almost every department. The hospital had a closed staff of six doctors, all partners of the Huron Clinic. It was registered by the American Medical Association.

The Sprague Hospital also maintained a three-year nursing school program with twenty-one women enrolled in the Nursing Cadet Corps. The nursing personnel were housed in two old, hazardous, dilapidated private dwellings of wood frame construction situated on the hospital grounds. Surgeon A. B. Price, *Hospital Survey, South Dakota,* 10 December 1943, Kansas City; U.S. Public Health Service District Number 7, pp. 1–11.

[9]When the Sisters arrived in Huron, the members of the Huron Clinic were Dr. J. C. Shirley, president; Dr. William H. Saxton; Dr. H. L. Saylor, Sr.; Dr. B. T. Lenz; Dr. Hans Jacoby; Dr. B. H. Sprague; Dr. H. D. Sewell; and Dr. H. P. Adams who was in the Armed Forces. Warren Darling, the manager and superintendent of the Huron Clinic, was also in the service. Mr. Philip Crowlie was the acting manager in the absence of Mr. Darling. These men were all very staunch promoters of the new hospital. *Huron Daily Plainsman,* 23 October 1985; and *St. John Hospital House Chronicle,* 17 October 1944 (AFSCL).

[10]When the Huron Sanitorium burned down, the patients were moved into a house at 267 East Third Street which had previously served as the Welter Funeral Home. Thirty beds were installed and six bassinets were provided. Although the patients received good medical care, the hospital and medical facilities could not be considered consistent with modern standards. The Huron Sanitorium, unlike the Sprague Hospital, was not registered with the American Medical Association. Price, p. 4.

Because this temporary hospital was inadequate, the Tschetter-Hohm group purchased the three-story Costain Apartment complex at Fifth and Dakota South and converted it into the 35-bed Samaritan Hospital. The majority of patients were private patients referred to the hospital from the practice of the owners. Other cases were referred to the hospital by physicians practicing in the surrounding area. St. John Regional Medical Center, *Open Letter from the Board of Trustees of St. John Regional Medical Center to the Concerned People of Huron and Vicinity,* Huron, 15 September 1976; and Price, p. 5.

[11]*St. John Reports,* 1977, p. 18.

[12]Price, pp. 10-11.

[13]Ibid., p. 11.

[14]*St. John Hospital House Journal* (AFSCL).

[15]The Most Reverend William O. Brady, bishop of Sioux Falls, South Dakota, was born in Fall River, Massachusetts, on February 1, 1899. Ordained on December 21, 1923, he was appointed bishop of Sioux Falls on June 10, 1939. Appointed archbishop of St. Paul on October 11, 1956, he died on October 1, 1961. *Book of Correspondence:* Letter from the Archdiocese of St. Paul-Minneapolis to author, September 1977 (AFSCL).

[16]*Minutes of General Council Proceedings,* 21 March 1942 (AFSCL).

[17]Sister Eleanor entered from St. Adalbert's Church in South Bend, Indiana, in 1930. She graduated from St. Mary's Unit of St. Louis University School of Nursing in 1938, and took postgraduate courses in surgery at St. Francis Hospital in Evanston, Illinois. While stationed at the Motherhouse as a nurse, she attended Loyola University of Chicago from which she received a bachelor's degree in nursing. Originally sent to Huron in 1944, she left in 1947 for the Motherhouse in Chicago; a year later she returned to St. John Hospital and remained until 1958. She was reassigned to the hospital in 1964 and remained until 1969. Her next years were spent in various areas of service to the congregation. Retiring to the Motherhouse in 1983, she died in 1984 at the age of seventy-two. She had been in the congregation for fifty-four years.

During her years at St. John Hospital and School of Nursing, she was often a guest lecturer on various topics ranging from nursing education to hospital administration. She gave demonstrations in procedures in nursing education, civil defense, and Red Cross nursing. She served as secretary and historian of the South Dakota Catholic Hospital Association, chairperson of the South Dakota Conference of Catholic Schools of Nursing, secretary of the South Dakota Joint Commission for the Improvement of the Patient, and chairperson of the South Dakota Catholic Nurses Association. *Congregation Membership Records* (AFSCL).

[18]Sister M. Leonia, a native of Youngstown, Ohio, entered from St. Stanislaus Kostka Church in that city in 1927. In 1936, she was sent to St. Joseph Hospital School of Nursing in Joliet, Illinois, where she obtained a nursing diploma. She took postgraduate courses in obstetrics at St. Francis Hospital in Evanston, Illinois. After nine years of service at St. John Hospital, she was missioned at St. Joseph Home in Chicago; Atkinson Memorial Hospital in Atkinson, Nebraska; and Mother of Grace Hospital in Gregory, South Dakota. The last ten years of her religious life were spent as part of the infirmary staff at the Motherhouse and in retirement. She died on July 25, 1977, one week after celebrating her 60th anniversary as a Franciscan Sister of Chicago. Ibid.

[19]*St. John Hospital House Journal* (AFSCL).

[20]When the school was demolished, the land was purchased by the Huron Clinic doctors and the deed donated to the Sisters. *Minutes of General Council Proceedings, 1945* (AFSCL).

[21]*St. John Hospital House Journal* (AFSCL).

[22]Ibid.

[23]Ibid.

[24]Ibid.

[25]Ibid.

[26]On the Feast of the Presentation, the Sisters were invited to partake of a pheasant dinner. This could only happen in South Dakota. After dinner, the Sisters played bridge and Sister M. Leonia and Sister Eleanor left the Presentation Convent with salt and pepper shakers, napkin rings, wash clothes, and other kitchen materials. Ibid.

[27]Ibid.

[28]Ibid.

[29]The first Christmas Eve in Huron was never to be forgotten. A package arrived from the Motherhouse that day with wonderful contents. After supper, the Sisters sat opposite each other at the table opening their Christmas mail. Two tiny artificial Christmas trees decorated the table and the manger was a large Christmas card sent by Sister M. Immaculate Matuszewski, depicting Christ surrounded by angels. Late in the night, the strains of "Silent Night" were heard and the Sisters were surprised to see the pupils from St. Martin's School on the convent porch. After Midnight Mass, Sister Eleanor wrote in the house journal: "Our hearts overflowed with love and gratitude." Ibid., 24 December 1944.

[30]Ibid.

[31]*St. John Hospital House Journal*, January 1945; and 21 February 1945 (AFSCL).

[32]Sister M. Amabilis is discussed later in the chapter.

[33]*St. John Hospital House Journal*, 2 April 1945 (AFSCL).

[34]The patron of the new hospital was St. John of God, a famous Portuguese penitent canonized in 1690. At about the age of forty, he decided to serve others in earnest. He rented a house where he could tend the abandoned sick, and for the remaining ten years of his life he was a perfect example of selfless charity supported by humility, prayer, and self-denial. He died at fifty-five and his followers, called the Brothers Hospitalers, drew up the rules of the order after his death and eventually took vows. John Coulson, ed., *The Saints* (New York: Guild Press, 1957), p. 86.

[35]*St. John Hospital House Journal*, 2 December 1954 (AFSCL).

[36]Sister M. Natalie is mentioned at greater length later in the chapter concerning the St. John Hospital School of Nursing.

[37]Sister M. Aloysilla is mentioned at greater length later in the chapter.

[38]Sister M. Basil was born in Johnstown, Pennsylvania, and entered from St. Casimir Church. She spent fifteen years as a teacher in the congregation's elementary schools after receiving her degree from De Paul University. In 1937, she received her diploma in nursing from St. Joseph Hospital School of Nursing in Joliet, Illinois. As a registered nurse, she was stationed at St. Joseph Home of Chicago and St. Anthony Home in Crown Point, Indiana, before her assignment to the Sprague Hospital in Huron. She trained as an anesthetist at St. Luke's Hospital in Aberdeen, South Dakota, and returned to St. John Hospital where she remained until 1976. That year she was transferred to St. Joseph Home of Chicago where she served as a staff nurse for eight years. In semi-retirement from 1984 to 1986, she was missioned at Madonna High School. In 1986, she retired to the Motherhouse. *Congregation Membership Records;* and *Spis Sióstr* (AFSCL).

[39]Born in Chicago in 1886, Sister M. Chester attended St. Mary of the Angels Church before she entered the congregation on October 3, 1904. For more than thirty years, she served as a teacher and principal at several of the congregation's schools. She also served as the superior and administrator of St. Joseph Home from 1928 to 1931 and Mount Alvernia Convent in East Cleveland, Ohio, for one year. After serving as business manager of St. John Hospital for two years,

she was transferred to the business office of Boys Town, Nebraska. From 1949 to 1958, she was the organist at Our Lady of Victory Convent for the Aged and Infirm Sisters in Lemont. In 1958, she was appointed to St. Anthony Hospital in Martin, South Dakota, where she served as part of the office staff. She died there on January 19, 1963, at the age of seventy-seven. She had been in the congregation for fifty-nine years. Ibid.

[40]*St. John Hospital House Journal,* 12 February 1945 (AFSCL).

[41]*Congregation Membership Records* (AFSCL).

[42]On October 15, 1949, the Sisters moved into the Mahaffey house having left their two small one-story residences called "St. Francis Villa" and the "Motherhouse." In time, however, the Mahaffey house also proved inadequate for the growing number of Sisters on the hospital staff. There was no room for a chapel, so the Sisters continued to attend St. Martin's Church for mass and daily communal prayer.

[43]Sister M. Marifilia entered from Five Holy Martyrs Church in Chicago. After her religious profession, she was sent to St. Elizabeth Hospital School of Nursing in Chicago to become a medical librarian. Appointed to St. John Hospital in 1947, she served as a medical librarian until 1970. In 1973, she received a diploma in nursing from St. Joseph Hospital School of Nursing in Joliet, Illinois. When the congregation's new St. Anthony Hospital opened in Crown Point, Indiana, she was appointed to pediatrics. Later, she served as director of the Quality Assurance Program.

She was a charter member of the group that organized the South Dakota Association of Medical Record Librarians and served several terms as its president, vice-president, secretary, and treasurer. She served on various committees of that association and as a faculty member at two regional institutes conducted by the American Association of Medical Records Librarians; in 1972, she was a member of the special committee of the SDAMRL working on a guide for release of information from medical records. For seventeen years, she was a member of the Board of Trustees of St. John Hospital and the vice-president of the corporation from 1969–1970. She also served as a member of the Board of Trustees of St. Anthony Medical Center. *Congregation Membership Records* (AFSCL).

[44]Sister M. Grace entered the congregation from SS. Peter and Paul Church in Spring Valley, Illinois. After her formation period, she served in the congregation's schools in Ohio, Indiana, and Illinois. She was also a teacher of chemistry, religion, and mathematics at Our Lady of Victory Convent High School in Chicago for several years. She received a bachelor of philosophy degree from De Paul University and a bachelor of science in pharmacy degree from the University of Illinois. Sister M. Grace held the position of part-time registered pharmacist at St. Joseph Hospital in Joliet, Illinois; St. Anthony Hospital, Chicago; and St. Joseph Home for the Aged in Chicago. She also served as chief pharmacist at McKennan Hospital in Sioux Falls, South Dakota, and the Sprague Hospital. Upon the completion of St. John Hospital, Sister M. Grace took charge of the pharmacy department and became instructor of pharmacology and chemistry at St. John Hospital School of Nursing, a position she held for twenty-five years. Sister M. Grace was an active member of the American Pharmaceutical Association, the American Society of Hospital Pharmacists, and a member of the South Dakota State Pharmaceutical Association. In 1962, the students of nursing at St. John's acclaimed her an "Outstanding Teacher and Friend." Sister M. Grace had the distinction of being the first Sister pharmacist in the state of South Dakota. She left St. John Hospital in 1972 for the Motherhouse where she continued to work in the infirmary. She died in 1979 at the age of seventy-nine after serving in the congregation for sixty-two years. Ibid.

[45]See Chapter 63.

[46]A native of Hammond, Indiana, Sister Leona entered the congregation from St. Mary's Church in that city. Prior to her assignment to St. John Hospital, she served at St. Casimir School in Johnstown, Pennsylvania, and Boys Town, Nebraska. Upon her arrival at the hospital in 1947, she was sent to Mount Marty College and later, to the Sacred Heart Hospital in Yankton, South Dakota, to become a radiologist, a position she held for twenty-one years. In 1971, she left St. John Hospital

and was assigned to St. Joseph Home of Chicago where she served as an administrative assistant and religious superior. In 1983, she was transferred to the Motherhouse where she serves as the Motherhouse treasurer. *Congregation Membership Records* (AFSCL).

[47]Sister M. Eucheria came to the congregation from St. Casimir Church in Johnstown, Pennsylvania. She taught for four years at St. Stanislaus Bishop and Martyr School in Chicago before she entered St. Joseph Hospital School of Nursing in Joliet, Illinois, in 1935, and earned a nursing diploma. She studied anesthesia at St. Francis Hospital in Peoria, Illinois, and St. Francis Hospital in Evanston, Illinois. During this period she also received her bachelor's degree from De Paul University. Sister M. Eucheria was appointed to St. John Hospital in 1947 as an anesthetist and remained until 1954. The next ten years she spent at the community's hospitals in Gregory and Martin, both in South Dakota. She returned to St. John Hospital in 1957 and remained until 1965. In 1975, she retired to the Motherhouse after aiding in various apostolates. Ibid.

[48]Sister M. Lucille entered from Five Holy Martyrs Church in 1909. She spent almost all of her religious life as a food supervisor in the congregation's institutions. From 1947 to 1961, she served at St. John Hospital; she returned in 1968 and served to 1973, a total of nineteen years. In 1973, she was transferred to St. Anthony Medical Center in Crown Point, Indiana, remaining there until she retired to the Motherhouse in 1985. Ibid.

[49]Sister M. Theophane entered from St. Joseph Church in East Chicago, Indiana. She served as a teacher for the first fourteen years of her religious life. When she left St. John Hospital in 1961, she labored in Boys Town for the next fourteen years and Mother of Grace Hospital in Gregory, South Dakota, for eight years. She died at the Motherhouse in April of 1982. Ibid.

[50]Sister M. Laurentine joined the community from Holy Family Church in Ashland, Wisconsin. In 1933, she enrolled at St. Joseph Hospital School of Nursing in Joliet, Illinois, from which she graduated in 1938. She was appointed to Boys Town, Nebraska, and then to St. Joseph Home of Chicago as a night nurse. In 1947, she came to St. John Hospital where she remained for nine years before being transferred to Our Lady of Victory Convent for the Aged and Infirm Sisters where she died in 1959. Ibid.

[51]*St. John Hospital House Journal* (AFSCL).

[52]*Minutes of General Council Proceedings,* 19 November 1947 (AFSCL); and *St. John Reports, 1977.*

[53]*St. John Reports, 1977.*

[54]Ibid.

[55]*Open Letter, 1976.*

[56]*St. John Reports, 1977.*

[57]*Open Letter, 1976.*

[58]Secretaries General, *Community Chronicle,* 16 August 1946 (AFSCL).

[59]A native Chicagoan, Father Filipek received the Franciscan habit in 1934, and was ordained a priest in 1942. He served as an instructor at Our Lady of Lourdes Seminary in Cedar Lake, Indiana, before his appointment to St. John Hospital. During his stay in Huron, Father Fidelis was licensed by the Federal Communications Amateur Radio Operation. In 1956, he received a Public Service Award by the American Radio Relay League, Inc. in "consideration of meritorious work in connection with a snow and freezing rain emergency in South Dakota." Presently, he is a chaplain at St. Mary's Hospital in Livonia, Michigan. *Book of Correspondence:* Letter from the Reverend Richard Tulko, OFM, provincial secretary, Franciscan Friars, Assumption BVM Province, Pulaski, Wisconsin, to author, 27 October 1987 (AFSCL).

[60]Sister Frances was born in Bayonne, New Jersey, and entered from Our Lady of Mount Carmel Church in that city. After receiving her diploma from St. John Hospital School of Nursing, she served at Mother of Grace Hospital in Gregory, and St. Anthony Hospital in Martin, both in South Dakota. She attended Creighton University in Nebraska and returned to St. John Hospital in

1956 where for nineteen years she served as nurse and instructor at the school of nursing. In 1973, she was assigned to St. Anthony Medical Center in Crown Point, Indiana. Ten years later, she was appointed director of the infirmary at the Motherhouse. In 1986, she returned to St. Anthony Medical Center.

While at St. John Hospital she served as secretary and board member of the American Nurses Association of South Dakota. She was the recipient of a scholarship for cancer nursing at New York Nursing Hospital in 1957 and often served as guest lecturer. *Congregation Membership Records* (AFSCL).

[61]Sister M. Redempta came to the congregation from St. Stanislaus Kostka Church in Chicago. Prior to her service at St. John Hospital she was an office clerk at St. Joseph Home, Our Lady of Spring Bank Cistercian Monastery, and Boys Town. She was also an admitting clerk at Mother of Grace Hospital in Gregory, South Dakota; and Atkinson Memorial Hospital in Atkinson, Nebraska. After seventeen years of service at St. John Hospital, she retired to the Motherhouse where she died in 1973. Ibid.

[62]A native of Omaha, Nebraska, Sister M. Fidelia entered from Immaculate Conception Church. She remained at St. John Hospital for nineteen years as director of laundry services. She died at the Motherhouse in 1980. Ibid.

[63]A native of Chicago, Sister M. Theresilla joined the congregation from Five Holy Martyrs Church. Her many years in religious life were spent in various apostolates of the congregation. She was assigned to St. John Hospital twice for a total of ten years. Presently she is in retirement at the Motherhouse. Ibid.

[64]Sister M. Bertille, born in Avonmore, Pennsylvania, entered from Assumption of the Blessed Virgin Mary Church in Conemaugh. In 1948, she came to St. John Hospital as a laboratory technician; in 1955, she graduated from St. John Hospital School of Nursing. She served at hospitals in Martin, South Dakota; and Atkinson, Nebraska, before her appointment to the infirmary at the Motherhouse. Returning to St. Anthony Hospital in Martin in 1966, she served as the administrator and superior for several years. Her other appointments were at Mother Theresa Home in Lemont and St. Joseph Home of Chicago. For two years she was a member of the St. Francis House of Prayer in Lemont, and, later, she served as superior at the Motherhouse from 1984 to 1987. She is presently the school nurse at St. Florian School in Chicago. Ibid.

[65]*Franciscan Echo*, Vol. 10, No. 3, March 1968; and *St. John Reports, 1977.*

[66]In 1947, the Franciscan Sisters of Chicago had agreed to accept the administration and staffing of the small Mother of Grace Hospital which the Benedictine Sisters of Yankton were in the process of relinquishing. See Chapter 50 for further details.

[67]Sister M. Vincentia entered from St. Florian Parish in Chicago in 1933, and professed perpetual vows in 1942. After serving at Boys Town, Nebraska, for six years, she attended Creighton University in Omaha. Appointed to the St. John Hospital staff in 1949, she was also an instructor at the school of nursing from 1962 to 1968. She was elected president of the South Dakota Medical Technologists and state delegate to the national convention. Having long harbored thoughts of a cloistered religious vocation, Sister M. Vincentia transferred to the Congregation of the Franciscan Nuns of the Most Blessed Sacrament in Portsmouth, Ohio, in 1972. *Congregation Membership Records* (AFSCL).

[68]Sister Jean Adamczyk and Sister M. Aloysilla Kedzior, eds., *St. John School of Nursing: Graduates 1948–1976,* Special edition (Huron, South Dakota: St. John School of Nursing, 1976).

[69]Sister Jean, the former Sister M. Seraphica, was born in Chicago and entered the congregation from St. Pancratius Church. She taught in the elementary schools of the congregation for twelve years before attending St. Joseph Hospital School of Nursing in Joliet, Illinois, where she secured her diploma in 1950. She also did postgraduate work at St. Louis University. Assigned to St. John Hospital School of Nursing, she was an inspiring and dedicated instructor of nursing for twenty-nine years. While at the hospital she was the recipient of a scholarship awarded by the

American Cancer Society. Throughout her long years of service at the school of nursing, she served as guest lecturer, published articles especially relating to the treatment of cancer, and held offices in professional organizations such as the South Dakota League for Nursing. In 1978, she was transferred to St. Anthony Medical Center in Crown Point to the Department of Pastoral Care. *Congregation Membership Records* (AFSCL).

[70]A native of Chicago, Sister Dorothy Joan entered from Five Holy Martyrs Parish. She taught for eight years before beginning nurses training in 1949. After graduating, she was assigned to St. Anthony's Hospital in Martin, South Dakota, and Our Lady of Sandhills in Atkinson, Nebraska. In 1959, she returned to St. John Hospital as the operating room supervisor. She graduated from Creighton University with a master's degree in nursing education in 1963, and remained on the staff of St. John Hospital until 1971. She is presently a clinical instructor at St. Anthony Medical Center in Crown Point, Indiana. Sister Dorothy Joan has the distinction of having been the congregation's only public health nurse. Ibid.

[71]Sister M. De Chantal, born in Montreal, Canada, entered from St. Florian Church in Chicago. She remained at the hospital until 1960 at which time she was transferred to Boys Town. Since 1963, she has been stationed at the Motherhouse. She has spent most of her religious life as a sacristan in the institutions of the congregation. Ibid.

[72]Sister M. Dorothea came to the congregation from Immaculate Conception Church in Omaha, Nebraska. She received her diploma from St. Joseph Hospital School of Nursing in 1950. The next year was spent at Sacred Heart Hospital in Yankton, South Dakota, where she received training as an anesthetist. In 1954, she was appointed to St. John Hospital where as anesthetist and part-time instructor at the school of nursing, she remained for ten years. She left the hospital only to return in 1971. During her years of service at St. John Hospital, she was president of the South Dakota Association of Nurse Anesthetists in 1955. For several years she served as staff nurse at Archbishop Bergan Mercy Hospital in Omaha, Nebraska; and Palos Community Hospital in Palos Heights, Illinois. After graduating from Sangamon State University in Springfield, Illinois, she served as administrator and superior of Mother Theresa Home in Lemont. Ibid.

[73]Sister M. Antonissima is mentioned in Chapter 61.

[74]Sister M. Agatha Walerski, a native of Hamtramck, Michigan, entered from St. Florian's Church in that city. She rendered nine years of service at the hospital. Presently missioned at St. Anthony Medical Center in Crown Point, Indiana, she had also been stationed at Boys Town, Nebraska, and St. Anthony Hospital in Martin, South Dakota. *Congregation Membership Records* (AFSCL).

[75]See Chapter 36.

[76]Father Maras, a native of Cleveland, was received into the novitiate of the Assumption of the Blessed Virgin Mary Province of Pulaski, Wisconsin, in 1932. He was ordained a priest in 1942. Prior to his appointment to St. John Hospital, he was rector of St. Bonaventure Minor Seminary and High School in Sturtevant, Wisconsin. When he left Huron, he was sent as a missionary to Samar in the Philippine Islands. Today, he resides at St. Mary's Home in Manitowoc, Wisconsin. *Book of Correspondence:* Letter from the Reverend Richard Tulko to author, 27 October 1987 (AFSCL).

[77]Secretaries General, *Community Chronicle, 1957–1970* (AFSCL).

[78]Sister M. Maurita entered from Sacred Heart of Jesus Church in Gary (Tolleston) Indiana. She was received as a postulant in 1930, entered the novitiate in 1931, and made her first profession in 1933. In 1937, she professed perpetual vows.

Earning her bachelor's degree from De Paul University in Chicago, she taught in the elementary schools of the congregation for over twenty years. After obtaining her master's degree in library science from Rosary College in River Forest, Illinois, she was sent to St. John Hospital School of Nursing. She left the hospital for a period of three years during which she served as a principal at Blessed Sacrament School in Gary (Glen Park) Indiana, returning in 1971. When the school of nursing closed, she was sent to St. Anthony Medical Center in Crown Point, Indiana, where she served as overseer, researcher, and librarian of the Health Science Library. *Congregation Membership Records* (AFSCL).

[79]Father Stunek was born in Cleveland and attended John Carroll University and Western Reserve University in Cleveland before his entry into the Franciscan Friars at Pulaski, Wisconsin, in 1951. He was ordained a priest in 1957. His first assignment was on the staff of Bishop Neumann High School in Philadelphia after which he came to St. John Hospital. After three years as instructor at the school of nursing, he taught at St. Francis College in Burlington, Wisconsin. In 1968, he was sent to Kowloon, Hong Kong, to serve as vice-principal of Nq Wah College. Returning in 1981, he was assigned to Crown Point, Indiana, as part of the pastoral ministry team at St. Anthony Medical Center. In 1984, he was transferred to Parma, Ohio, where he serves as chaplain at Mount Alverna Home. *Book of Correspondence:* Letter from the Reverend Richard Tulko to author, 27 October 1987 (AFSCL).

[80]*St. John Hospital House Journal* (AFSCL).

[81]*Minutes of General Council Proceedings, 1965* (AFSCL).

[82]Sister M. Olimpia was born in Milwaukee, Wisconsin, and entered from Holy Family Church in Cudahy, Wisconsin. She served at St. Joseph Home of Chicago from 1946 to 1960; from 1953 to 1958, she acted as the administrator. She served at the hospital for sixteen years in the central supplies department. Her remaining years were spent at the Motherhouse where she died in 1981. *Congregation Membership Records* (AFSCL).

[83]Sister M. Mildred entered from St. Florian's Church in Chicago. In 1952, she graduated from St. John Hospital School of Nursing. She served at the congregation's hospitals in Martin and Gregory, South Dakota, and Alvernia Rest Home in Parma, Ohio, before being assigned to St. Joseph Home in 1962. Upon her departure in 1968, she was assigned to St. Anthony Home in Crown Point, Indiana, and later to Mother Theresa Home in Lemont as director of nursing services. Since 1978, she has devoted herself to the parish community outreach program at St. Rose of Lima Parish on Chicago's South Side. Ibid.

[84]Sister M. Renata entered from St. Casimir Church in Cleveland. After attending Marquette University in Milwaukee and Loyola University of Chicago, she spent eight years at St. John Hospital as a bookkeeper. She also served at Mother of Grace Hospital in Gregory, South Dakota. For the past seventeen years, she has been financial supervisor at St. Joseph Home of Chicago. Ibid.

[85]A native of Chicago, Sister M. Maxencia joined from Five Holy Martyrs Church. A graduate of De Paul University, she taught in the elementary schools of the congregation for sixteen years. She earned a master's degree in library science from Rosary College in River Forest, Illinois, and in the summer of 1951, was assigned to Madonna High School as librarian and teacher. She remained there for thirteen years. In 1968, after successfully recovering from a stroke, she was assigned to St. John Hospital School of Nursing where she replaced Sister M. Maurita Wszolek, the librarian, for a period of three years. She was last assigned to St. Florian's School in Chicago where she remained for six years until her death on July 23, 1977. Ibid.

[86]Sister M. Innocentia was transferred to the Motherhouse in 1967 where she served as head nurse in the infirmary. In 1971, she was appointed the superior of the Motherhouse and held that position for four years. She died on April 15, 1976, at St. Anthony Medical Center in Crown Point, Indiana. She was seventy-one years old and had been a member of the congregation for fifty-six years. She was survived by her sister, Sister M. Rosalima Sierocki, also a Franciscan Sister of Chicago. Ibid.

[87]*Minutes of General Council Proceedings,* 30 May 1958 (AFSCL).

[88]*St. John Reports, 1977.*

[89]*Interviews* with Sisters, 1985 (AFSCL).

[90]*Franciscan Echo,* Vol. 10, No. 3, March 1968.

[91]The young women were often provided with suitable employment in one of the many hospital departments. While awaiting delivery, the women lived in the St. John Hospital School of Nursing. *Interview* with Sister Leona Watroba, November 1987 (AFSCL).

[92]See Chapter 60 for the full meaning and impact of this historic meeting of Sister-delegates at the First Extraordinary Chapter of Affairs.

[93]*Chapter Decrees, 1970,* p. 103.

[94]Ibid., p. 112.

[95]*Book of Correspondence:* Letter from Mother M. Beatrice Rybacki to Lawrence T. Filosa, executive director of the health facilities for the Franciscan Sisters of Chicago, 11 November 1968 (AFSCL).

[96]Sister M. Antoniana entered from St. Florian's Church in Chicago. She received her bachelor's degree from De Paul University and taught at elementary schools in the congregation for thirteen years before she was sent to Creighton University in Omaha. Graduating as a pharmacist, she spent the next ten years at the Motherhouse in Chicago as the chief pharmacist. In 1959, she was appointed to the staff of Madonna High School where she taught general science and health for twelve years. Transferred to St. John Hospital in 1971, she served as the pharmacist until 1978. That year she was transferred to St. Anthony Home in Crown Point, Indiana, where she remained until 1985. She is presently stationed at the Motherhouse. *Congregation Membership Records* (AFSCL).

[97]A native of Chestnut Ridge, Pennsylvania, the Reverend Myron Lowisz, OFM, entered the Franciscan Order in 1951 and graduated from St. Francis College in Burlington, Wisconsin. In 1956, he entered Christ the King Seminary in West Chicago and was ordained to the priesthood on February 2, 1960. In June of 1965, he received a doctorate in theology, and taught at the seminary until 1971. After three years as chaplain at St. John Hospital, he was assigned to St. Anthony Medical Center in Crown Point, Indiana, where he assumed the position of Director of Pastoral Care. He has thus been associated with the Franciscan Sisters of Chicago for the past sixteen years. *Book of Correspondence:* Letter from the Reverend Richard Tulko to author, 27 October 1987 (AFSCL).

[98]The Most Reverend Lambert A. Hoch, the fifth bishop of Sioux Falls, was born in 1903 in Elkton, South Dakota. He was ordained a priest on May 30, 1928. On March 25, 1952, he was ordained the bishop of Bismarck, South Dakota. Appointed the bishop of Sioux Falls on December 5, 1956, he retired in June of 1978. *Book of Correspondence:* Letter from Chancery Office, Sioux Falls, South Dakota to author, September 1986 (AFSCL).

[99]*St. John Reports, 1977;* and *Open Letter, 1976.*

[100]*Congregation Membership Records* (AFSCL).

[101]*Interviews* with Sisters, 1987 (AFSCL).

[102]*Post-Tribune* (Crown Point, In.), 5 June 1983.

[103]*Post-Tribune* (Crown Point, In.), 23 October 1983.

[104]*Franciscan Echo,* Vol. 23, No. 1, September 1984.

[105]Sister Jean Adamczyk and Sister M. Aloysilla Kedzior, *St. John School of Nursing: Graduates 1948–1976. Special Edition* (Huron, South Dakota, 1976) p. 3.

[106]*Book of Annual Assignments* (AFSCL).

[107]*Congregation Membership Records* (AFSCL).

[108]*Interviews* with Sisters, 1987 (AFSCL).

[109]Among the students was the first foreign student nurse who came from Barranquilla, Colombia, South America.

[110]*St. John Hospital House Journal* (AFSCL).

[111]The first male student nurse was a native of South Dakota.

[112]*Minutes of General Council Proceedings,* 7 June 1949 (AFSCL).

[113]*St. John Hospital House Journal,* 30 July 1947 (AFSCL).

[114]Secretaries General, *Community Chronicle*, p. 218 (AFSCL).

[115]Adamczyk and Kedzior, *Special Edition*, p. 4.

[116]Ibid.

[117]The only Sister to join the congregation from Detroit, Michigan, entered on November 25, 1915, from St. Thomas the Apostle Church in that city. The first six years after profession, Sister Josephine Marie, the former Sister M. Humiliata, rendered service at Guardian Angel Day Nursery and St. Joseph Home of Chicago. After she received her diploma in nursing, she was assigned to the staff of St. John Hospital and School of Nursing in 1957. In 1962, she was assigned to Atkinson Memorial Hospital in Atkinson, Nebraska, where she served for seven years. Upon returning to Chicago, she was appointed to St. Joseph Home. After four years, she was assigned to the newly built St. Anthony Medical Center in Crown Point, Indiana. Since 1978, she has ministered to the Sisters in the Motherhouse infirmary. See Chapter 53. *Conregation Membership Records* (AFSCL).

[118]A native of Decatur, Illinois, Sister M. Gerardette entered from Holy Trinity Church in Chicago on February 1, 1940. Her first areas of service were St. Elizabeth Day Care Center and St. Joseph Home of Chicago. After she professed perpetual vows on July 24, 1947, she was sent to St. John Hospital School of Nursing. After receiving her diploma, Sister M. Gerardette joined the staff of St. John Hospital and remained for two years. The next four years were spent at St. Anthony Hospital in Martin, South Dakota. She returned to St. John Hospital in 1956 and was a staff member until her death from cancer on June 7, 1959. Sister M. Gerardette has been characterized as a gentle, kind, and loving religious. *Congregation Membership Records;* and *Interviews* with Sisters, 1986 (AFSCL).

[119]Adamczyk and Kedzior, *Special Edition*, p. 4.

[120]Ibid.

[121]In July, 1957, the policy was changed regarding male students and they were no longer accepted. This order was rescinded in November 1968. *Minutes of General Council Proceedings*, 23 November 1968 (AFSCL).

[122]Secretaries General, *Community Chronicle*, 27 February 1954; and *Minutes of General Council Proceedings*, 28 February 1954 (AFSCL).

[123]In her twenty-two years of service to the Huron community, Sister M. Amabilis also held the position of education director of St. John Hospital School of Nursing from 1960 to 1967. She became acting administrator of St. John Hospital and served well in this capacity until 1969. She also served as administrator of Atkinson Memorial Hospital in Atkinson, Nebraska, and St. Michael Hospital in Tyndall, South Dakota, a hospital staffed by the Benedictine Sisters of Yankton, South Dakota. After 1975, Sister M. Amabilis rendered service at Mount Alverna Home in Parma, Ohio, and St. Joseph Home of Chicago. She is presently on the staff of St. Anthony Medical Center in Crown Point, Indiana. *Congregation Membership Records* (AFSCL).

[124]*Diaconian, III* (Spring 1963), p. 10.

[125]*Interviews* with Sisters, 1985–1987 (AFSCL).

[126]*Congregation Membership Records* (AFSCL).

[127]*Interviews* with Sisters (AFSCL).

[128]*Minutes of General Chapter Proceedings*, 1958 (AFSCL).

[129]Secretaries General, *Community Chronicle*, 4 January 1956; and 14 March 1956 (AFSCL).

[130]*Congregation Membership Records* (AFSCL).

[131]Mr. Edward Fuss held this position until 1960 at which time he was succeeded by Sister M. Amabilis Bellock.

[132]Father Maras remained on the staff for ten years.

[133]*Huron Daily Plainsman*, 8 March 1958.

[134]Sisters who served as prefects at St. John Hospital School of Nursing Residence through the years included Sister M. Natalie Uscinowicz, Sister Dorothy Joan Lagocki, Sister Frances Szczur, Sister Leona Watroba, Sister M. Vincentia Wszolek, Sister Jean Adamczyk, and Sister M. Aloysilla Kedzior.

[135]For the brief term of three years, that is, from 1968 to 1971, she had been replaced by Sister M. Maxencia Pozniatowski, a former librarian at Madonna High School. See Chapter 51. *Congregation Membership Records* (AFSCL).

[136]In 1980, she was transferred to Mount Alverna Home in Parma, Ohio, where she remains today as the director of nursing. *Congregation Membership Records* (AFSCL).

[137]*Interviews* with Sisters, 1985, 1987 (AFSCL).

[138]Sister M. Aloysilla was mentioned more specifically in her role as president of St. John Regional Medical Center earlier in this chapter.

[139]Each Sister on the faculty had her master's degree.

[140]Another factor was the aging medical staff which was slowing down its practice of medicine. Significantly, no new medical staff members were being recruited into the Huron community. Report to the Franciscan Sisters of Chicago from the Board of Directors and President of St. John Regional Medical Center, 8 December 1973.

[141]The furniture and equipment used in the dormitories were due for replacement and these additional costs were also prohibitive.

[142]Report to the Franciscan Sisters of Chicago from the Board of Directors and President of St. John Regional Medical Center, 8 December 1973 (AFSCL).

[143]Ibid.

CHAPTER 50

The Growing Hospital Apostolate

In September of 1947, the Reverend Francis Cronin, the pastor of St. Leo Church in Tyndall, South Dakota, wrote to Mother M. Jerome with a request to have the Franciscan Sisters of Chicago assume charge of a small hospital which he intended to build in Tyndall. He also petitioned for several Sisters to staff his parish school. Mother M. Jerome agreed to accept the hospital in Tyndall where five or six Sisters were needed, but she refused the request to staff the school pleading a lack of teaching Sister personnel. When Father Cronin turned to the Most Reverend William Brady, bishop of Sioux Falls, in whose diocese the hospital was to be built, for permission to have the Franciscan Sisters of Chicago take charge of the hospital in Tyndall, Bishop Brady changed the entire plan of operation. Because Tyndall was hardly thirty miles from Yankton, South Dakota, where the Benedictine Sisters operated a 250-bed hospital, and because they had accepted the staffing of Tyndall's St. Leo School, Bishop Brady decided that it would be more feasible for the Benedictines to take charge of the hospital in Tyndall. The Franciscan Sisters of Chicago, Bishop Brady maintained, could accept the administration and staffing of the small Mother of Grace Hospital which the Benedictine Sisters were in the process of relinquishing in Gregory, South Dakota.[1]

Upon learning of the Benedictine Sisters' planned departure from Gregory, the Most Reverend William T. McCarty, CSSR,[2] bishop of Rapid City, South Dakota, happily extended an invitation to the Franciscan Sisters of Chicago to enter his diocese:

Dear Mother Jerome:

I am writing to you at this time, as will Father Frank Monighan,[3] the pastor, in regard to Mother of Grace Hospital at Gregory, South Dakota. Father Monighan will explain the case and our request to you in detail. The Benedictine Sisters of Yankton, South Dakota, have had charge of the hospital for the past ten years . . . I would like to inquire of you whether or not you would be in a position to take over Mother of Grace Hospital after the Benedictine Sisters withdraw. I assure you that if you act favorably on this request, I will welcome you to the diocese of Rapid City, and I will help you to get established at Gregory. Father Monighan has my permission to extend an invitation to you to come to Gregory and to take charge of the hospital there.

With kind regards and with a prayer to Our Lady that you will act favorably on this letter, I remain

Devotedly yours in Christ,
William T. McCarty, CSSR
Bishop of Rapid City[4]

Mother of Grace Hospital in Gregory, South Dakota, was located a few miles east of the Rosebud Indian Reservation. The seventeen-bed hospital, originally known as the Gregory Community Hospital, was begun in 1933 in a house once belonging to the Coulter family. From 1933 to 1936, the hospital was operated by a lay staff and a lay administrator. In 1936, however, the Benedictine Sisters of Yankton, South Dakota, were invited to manage the hospital which they promptly renamed Mother of Grace.[5] In 1938, in need of a larger hospital facility, the city of Gregory took over the Kleinfelter Funeral Home, a two-story family house, to serve as the new Mother of Grace Hospital.

At first, Mother M. Jerome hesitated to accept the Gregory Hospital, but the bishop would not be put off:

I have the greatest confidence that Our Lady of Perpetual Help will see some way that you will be in a position to take Gregory. I feel that God has added the extra burden of ailing Sisters, and of the crosses that come with such circumstances, in order to bless your work at Gregory. It is my firm belief that God never closes one door without opening another one for us. In the months that are ahead, I pray God and Our Blessed Mother that you will find some way to accept the invitation to come to the diocese of Rapid City and take the hospital at Gregory. I am going to ask you to reconsider the matter, take time to think it over and see if there is not some way you can adjust the replacement so that you can come to our diocese.[6]

In June of 1948, Sister M. Felixa Jorz, the vicar general, and Mother M. Antonina Osinski, the third councilor, were sent to Huron, South Dakota, by Mother M. Jerome to make the final inspection of St. John Hospital and School of Nursing then under construction. The Sisters took this opportunity to visit Gregory and also Chamberlain where the Sisters had been invited to administer that city's hospital. The Sisters were more favorably impressed with the Gregory location and once at home, advocated the undertaking of the Mother of Grace Hospital. The general council formalized plans for accepting the hospital by means of a five-year contract through which the hospital would be leased to the Franciscan Sisters of Chicago for one dollar a year. The cost of building and equipping the new hospital would be covered by the people of Gregory.[7]

On September 8, 1948, Sister M. Innocentia Sierocki arrived in Gregory to assume the administration of Mother of Grace Hospital. She was accompanied by Sister M. Andrea Puchalski and Sister M. Colombiere Piotrowski. A few days later, Sister Leona Watroba, Sister M. Felicia Wierciak, Sister M. Renata Krukowski, and Sister M. Antonita Woloch arrived in Gregory thus completing the pioneer band of Sisters. The grateful residents of Gregory arranged a reception on September 30 to bid the Benedictine Sisters farewell and to welcome the Franciscan Sisters of Chicago. Bishop McCarty, whom the Franciscan Sisters were meeting for the first time, addressed the group gathered to honor the Sisters in St. Joseph School Hall.[8]

On the morning of October 1, 1948, Bishop McCarty offered mass in the small chapel which the Sisters had set up in the hospital where they maintained their meager living quarters. Later that same day, Sister M. Simon of the Yankton Benedictines turned over the management of the Mother of Grace Hospital to Sister M. Innocentia. When the Franciscan Sisters of Chicago took up their new duties, the census at the seventeen-bed hospital was eleven adults and three infants. Sister M. Innocentia and Sister M. Felicia worked with medical patients on the first floor; Sister M. Antonita and Sister Leona worked in the maternity and nursery areas. Both Sister M. Andrea and Sister M. Renata were scheduled for night duty while Sister M. Colombiere served as the dietitian.[9]

The hardships which the patients and the Sisters endured in the small, inadequate hospital were many and varied calling for the practice of a great deal of understanding, patience, and physical stamina. For what now appeared a long period of time, there had been much talk and very little effort put forth in attempting to build a new and badly needed hospital. Sister M. Innocentia, who had undergone similar exasperating experiences in the construction of the new St. John Hospital and School of Nursing in Huron, South Dakota, determined to assume a more decisive role in encouraging the few but willing new hospital promoters. She proposed that the Sisters entertain the Board of Directors of the Gregory Hospital Association at a dinner on Sunday, December 5, 1948. The wives of the board members, as well as several of the doctors, were present. At the dinner, Sister M. Innocentia suggested that the women of the Gregory community form an auxiliary to gather funds for the proposed hospital. The suggestion was received very enthusiastically, and on December 10, a group of women in the Gregory community met at Mother of Grace Hospital and formed the Hospital Ladies' Auxiliary whose aim was to increase the hospital fund, and in particular, to raise money for hospital equipment. The Hospital Ladies' Auxiliary held their first meeting on January 14, 1949, at which time they elected their officers. Four days later, another meeting was held at which the enthusiastic women discussed the constitutions and bylaws of their organization.[10]

There was much progress made from the time of the first December meeting. While the Gregory Hospital Association was busy planning a campaign, the newly organized Hospital Ladies' Auxiliary also planned additional functions which would be of assistance in raising funds. The best news received, however, was the notice from Representative Francis Case of South Dakota, who informed the Gregory Hospital

Association that federal aid for the new hospital had been approved. At that time, the federal share in the proposed $210,050 hospital was to have been $70,000 or 33-1/3 percent. Later, even more fortunately, the share was raised to 50 percent or $105,000. The prospect of a new hospital seemed extremely promising.[11]

A questionnaire was distributed to the public on January 27, 1949, in an endeavor to pinpoint what the townspeople viewed as the most necessary improvement needed. Decisively, the citizens listed a "hospital" in the first place. To keep the need constantly before the public eye and to create enthusiasm for working toward a new hospital, weekly letters written by hospital personnel were sent to the newspaper encouraging the Gregory community to be generous in donations and service and pointing out the deficiencies of the old hospital structure.

At this point in time, the Gregory Hospital Association presented a petition to the Gregory City Council that the council submit to the voters the proposition of issuing bonds in the amount of $36,000 for the construction of the hospital. The hospital then would be turned over entirely to the city of Gregory to be managed and maintained by the city or leased. The issue received much publicity from the city attorney, the city's legal advisors, the city auditor, and from other important public officials. When the issue was presented to the public on April 19, 1949, however, it failed to pass because the margin for a majority vote was not large enough. It was obvious that the Gregory Hospital Association could not now look to the city government of Gregory for aid. To counter the situation, the Gregory Hospital Association resorted to raising the needed funds by soliciting the public. The solicitors, local men volunteers, were greatly encouraged by the popular sentiment of the people and their generous contributions. After ten days of visiting the rural and local people, the volunteers had collected $12,000. Through the untiring efforts of the hospital board, the contributions accumulated sufficiently, and on May 14, less than a month after the defeat of the bond issue, the architect, Walter J. Dixon, of Mitchell, South Dakota, prepared the plans and specifications for the new hospital.[12]

On June 25, 1949, Mother M. Jerome paid her first visit to Mother of Grace Hospital where she remained for three days. Bishop McCarty visited the hospital on August 11 and expressed his sincere appreciation for the work of the Sisters.[13]

The first anniversary of the Sisters' arrival in Gregory was celebrated on October 1, 1949. A report printed in the Gregory daily newspaper presenting the census at the hospital for the year read: patients admitted last year, 844; surgeries performed, 152; births, 143; and deaths, 31. The average per day number of patients in the hospital was sixteen. The need for a new and larger hospital was daily becoming more apparent. On December 21, 1949, just a little over a year since the Sisters' arrival, the one-thousandth patient was admitted to the hospital. The beds at the hospital were always occupied to capacity; frequently patients had to be turned away for lack of space.[14]

The Gregory Hospital Association had not been idle during the Christmas holidays. The architect had notified the association that the plans and specifications were ready to be presented for bids to the contractors. Bids were to be opened in late December

1949 at Mitchell, South Dakota. Members of the hospital board went to Mitchell to accept the bids but returned somewhat disappointed. The federal government agent informed the Gregory Hospital Association that the government would contribute 50 percent of the cost instead of 33-1/3 percent of the entire expense which had been previously announced, but the Gregory community would have to match the government share dollar for dollar in ready money which meant that Gregory's share would amount to $105,000 of which only $84,000 was on hand. The board was given until January 4, 1950, to raise the $21,000 needed. The hospital board began soliciting the necessary funds and on January 4, 1950, the contracts were signed. The weather now proved to be the only obstacle hindering immediate construction.[15]

On April 12, 1950, construction of the twenty-five bed hospital costing $210,000 began, and by June, the furnishings from the old hospital were disposed of by public auction. In October 1950, a very enthusiastic Mother M. Jerome wrote to Bishop McCarty concerning the Mother of Grace Hospital:

> Your Excellency:
>
> Your Excellency's letter reached me at St. John's Hospital of Huron where I have been attending its annual meeting of directors.
>
> I have also visited Gregory and I am quite pleased with the achievements accomplished there. The new hospital presents a very lovely sight. It also provides convenient living quarters for the Sisters. I was happy to see them all enthusiastic about the new hospital.
>
> Thanking Your Excellency for all your considerations and the great interest extended to our Congregation, and begging for His episcopal blessing, I have the honor to be, Your Excellency's
>
> > Humble servant in Christ,
> > Mother M. Jerome
> > Superior General[16]

On April 1, 1951, the grand opening and tour of the new hospital was held. The white-bound registration book presented to the hospital by the *Gregory Times-Advocate* contained the names of over 1,500 visitors from as far south as Omaha and as far west as the Black Hills and Rapid City. Two days later, seven patients were transferred from the old hospital to the new one.[17]

The Sisters signed a new contract on August 20, 1952, agreeing to operate and staff the hospital for ninety-nine years. The hospital was leased to them for one dollar a year. In case of unforeseen hardships, the Sisters would be able to leave the hospital, notifying the civil government sixty days before, and likewise, the reverse would occur if the city government wished to replace the Sisters. The general council agreed, and Mother M. Jerome and Sister M. Gonzaga signed the contract.[18]

On October 22, 1952, Sister M. Innocentia Sierocki, the superior and administrator of Mother of Grace Hospital, was sent to St. John Hospital and School of

Mother of Grace Hospital (Gregory Community Hospital)
Gregory, South Dakota (1948–1962)

Nursing in Huron, South Dakota, where she was assigned to serve in the same capacity. She was replaced by Sister M. Aquinas Rosky.[19]

For the next seven years, following the words of the Psalmist: "Our hearts have not shrunk back, nor our steps turned aside from your path,"[20] the Franciscan Sisters of Chicago devoted their service to God and their neighbor by responding with zeal, dedication, and compassion to the very apparent need for ministerial healing at Mother of Grace Hospital. In 1959, however, the small number of patients being admitted to the hospital caused the Sisters some consternation. The twenty-five bed hospital was occupied on the average of 54.8 percent. A census taken in June of 1959 revealed that the highest number of patients in the hospital on any given day was twenty; the lowest was four.[21] Unfortunately, it was revealed at this time that a doctor on the staff who was opposed to the Sisters encouraged his patients to enter hospitals other than Mother of Grace. Mother M. Beatrice Rybacki, who in 1958 had succeeded Mother M. Jerome Dadej as superior general, was made aware of the situation and felt that because of the small number of patients, the Sisters could be more effectively used elsewhere.[22] Consequently, by 1961, there was a concerted effort by Mother M. Beatrice and the general council to leave the Mother of Grace Hospital. Since the hospital was not the property of the congregation, but rather, belonged to the city of Gregory, it would be possible for the Sisters to leave after submitting a sixty-day notice. A letter was sent to J. J. Raymond, president of the hospital board, informing the city officials that the Sisters would withdraw after the next sixty days and would, therefore, be gone by the end of October 1961.[23]

On July 29, 1961, Mother M. Beatrice informed Bishop McCarty of her decision:

Your Excellency:

After due consideration, we have decided to withdraw our Sisters from the Mother of Grace Hospital of Gregory, South Dakota.

Since the death of the previous doctor, the number of patients there has been decreasing considerably. I can use the Sisters at Gregory elsewhere where their services are more urgently needed.

The hospital belongs to the local community and is leased to us with an option that either party may terminate the contract upon a sixty-day notice. We intend to issue such a notice to the Board of Directors of the Gregory Hospital so that within the next two months I may transfer the five Sisters who staff the hospital.

Your servant in Christ,
Mother M. Beatrice, Sup. Gen.[24]

The board members of the Gregory Hospital Association held a meeting in the hospital dining room on September 26, 1961, to determine the reason for the Sisters' leaving. While the board members demonstrated an amiable spirit, they were determined to know whether the idea of leaving Mother of Grace Hospital had originated with the Sisters on the staff or whether it was a directive from the Motherhouse in Chicago. The Sisters at the hospital admitted, in all honesty, that the idea of leaving the hospital had originated with the general council of the congregation in Chicago after responsible deliberation. The board members continued to be deeply concerned over the issue.[25]

The following day, J. J. Raymond, president of the board, spoke to Sister M. Colombiere Piotrowski, the administrator, indicating his wish to know what Mother M. Beatrice and the general council proposed to do concerning the hospital. There was now a Lutheran delegation that was interested in inspecting the hospital with a view to administering and staffing it.[26]

At a meeting of the general council in October, Mother M. Beatrice informed the Sisters of the situation in Gregory. They agreed that if the Franciscan Sisters of Chicago were to leave the hospital, they wished to leave it in the hands of another religious congregation. At this point, Mother M. Beatrice admitted that she was having difficulty finding another group of Sisters to staff the hospital. Finally, she resolved to go to Gregory herself to determine her mode of action. In late October, Mother M. Beatrice paid a visit to Gregory and conferred with the Sisters, the doctors, and the members of the board of hospital advisors. The physician who was particularly opposed to the Sisters indicated that he would send more patients to the hospital and cooperate more fully with the hospital administration. Because Mother M. Beatrice perceived that there were areas where the Sisters also needed to make concessions, she advised them to cooperate with the physicians for a more harmonious atmosphere. Mother M. Beatrice left Mother of Grace Hospital revoking her former decision to remove the Sisters.[27]

It was not long, however, before the decision to remain at the hospital was rescinded. After careful deliberation, Mother M. Beatrice informed the county office in February of 1962 that the Sisters would be leaving. Try as the Sisters might, there were simply not enough patients at any given time, and, consequently, the Sisters could not maintain the hospital financially. Mother M. Beatrice advised Sister M. Innocentia to secure a lawyer in South Dakota who would assist the congregation in its dealings with the Gregory community. Don A. Bierle, a legal consultant for the Catholic Hospital Association of South Dakota, was retained. Mr. Bierle personally made a visit to Gregory for the purpose of interviewing key citizens and hospital personnel regarding the advisability of continuing the administration of Mother of Grace Hospital by the Franciscan Sisters of Chicago. He came to the same conclusion: as the patient census averaged only 50 percent or less on the basis of a twenty-five bed capacity, it was not economically sound for the Sisters to continue maintaining the hospital. Even more, the situation at Gregory had become such that only one doctor remained in the city. Since he could treat only ten patients for in-hospital care, it appeared that the patient census was not likely to improve. Mr. Bierle believed that the prospects of continued administration by the Sisters did not appear bright.[28] Following Mr. Bierle's letter, Mother M. Beatrice and the general council gave Sister M. Innocentia the power to settle the matters in Gregory even if it resulted in closing the hospital. Her letter of March 28, 1962, to the Gregory Hospital Association pointed out in part:

> Our relationship over the years has been a most sincere and beneficial one and it is only for the reason that the hospital facilities cannot sustain its maintenance costs that such action must necessarily be taken. On behalf of Mother M. Beatrice, superior general, and the Franciscan Sisters of Chicago, I wish personally to express our appreciation to the Gregory Hospital Association for the past experience of working with and enjoying the people of the Gregory community and its surrounding area.
>
> I wish to assure the Board of Trustees of the Gregory Hospital Association that we shall cooperate in every respect in making the termination of our agreement most satisfactory to the Gregory Hospital Association.[29]

Mother of Grace Hospital was officially closed on May 30, 1962. Four Sisters remained on the staff at the hospital's closing and then left for the Motherhouse in Chicago: Sister M. Leona Mszanski, administrator and superior; Sister M. Simplicita Mruczkowski, Sister M. Lucille Klockowski, and Sister M. Redempta Demski. Sister M. Mildred Bieda had already been transferred to St. John Hospital and School of Nursing in Huron in March.[30]

Bishop McCarty bade the Sisters farewell with the same graciousness with which he had welcomed them:

Greetings, best wishes and thanks to all of you for the years of noble and dedicated service to the sick and afflicted in the Gregory area.

I am so very, very sorry to know that the good Sisters will leave Gregory in a day or so as they have been Angels of Mercy to us all, and surely the good they have done for souls can never be measured by the standards of this world. Their reward will be with God, and it will be infinite. My, how I dislike to know that these Sisters will actually and truly leave Gregory. I have been praying and praying that they would remain. God help us all![31]

On June 4, 1962, the Gregory Community Hospital reopened under the administration of the Lutheran Hospitals and Homes Society of America Inc. of Fargo, North Dakota. In reporting the departure of the Franciscan Sisters, the *Gregory Times-Advocate* stated:

Many hundreds have had occasion to avail themselves of the service of one of Gregory's most important institutions during the fourteen-year tenure of the Franciscan Sisters. Theirs has truly been a devoted and dedicated service that will ever be remembered by a grateful populace.[32]

The Lutheran Hospitals and Homes Society of America eventually built a new, larger hospital on another site in 1975, and the old Mother of Grace Hospital remained unoccupied.[33]

THE GROWING HOSPITAL APOSTOLATE

[1]Secretaries General, *Community Chronicle,* 1 October 1948 (AFSCL).

[2]The Most Reverend William T. McCarty, CSSR, bishop of Rapid City, South Dakota, was born in 1890 in Crossingville, Pennsylvania. In August, 1910, he was professed as a member of the Congregation of the Most Holy Redeemer. On June 10, 1915, he was ordained by John Cardinal Farley, archbishop of New York. From 1918 to 1926, he taught philosophy at Mount St. Alphonsus in New York. From 1930 to 1933, he was assistant rector at Our Lady of Perpetual Help Church in Roxbury, Massachusetts. He was rector of Mount St. Alphonsus from 1933 to 1939 when he was Provincial of the Eastern Province of the Redemptorists with headquarters in Brooklyn. During his term, fourteen new foundations were established in the United States, Puerto Rico, Brazil, and Paraguay. At the invitation of Archbishop Francis J. Spellman, Spanish-speaking American Redemptorists were assigned to work among the Puerto Ricans in New York. In the South, likewise, work among the blacks was developed as a new vice-province of the congregation was formed with headquarters in Richmond, Virginia. In 1943, he was named assistant bishop to Cardinal Spellman in charge of chaplains' affairs in the Armed Forces of the United States. Bishop McCarty was installed as the bishop of Rapid City on May 8, 1947. He retired in 1969. "Biographical Sketch" received from the chancery office, Rapid City, South Dakota, January 1976 (AFSCL).

[3]In 1944, the Right Reverend Monsignor Francis Monighan was appointed the chaplain of Mother of Grace Hospital and pastor of St. Joseph Church where he remained until his death in 1967. He spent his entire priestly career in the Diocese of Rapid City. In 1950, Monsignor Monighan requested that the Franciscan Sisters of Chicago also accept the staffing of St. Joseph School, but Mother M. Jerome Dadej denied his request citing the fact that no Sisters were available. "Biographical Sketch" received from the director of the Diocesan Office of Communication, Rapid City, South Dakota, January 1976 (AFSCL).

[4]*Book of Correspondence:* Letter from the Most Reverend William T. McCarty, CSSR, to Mother M. Jerome Dadej, 17 May 1948 (AFSCL).

[5]This is a special feast of Our Lady celebrated on June 9.

[6]*Book of Correspondence:* Letter from the Most Reverend William T. McCarty, CSSR, to Mother M. Jerome Dadej, 30 May 1948 (AFSCL).

[7]*Minutes of General Council Proceedings, 1934–1948,* 9 July 1948 (AFSCL); and Secretaries General, *Community Chronicle, October 1948* (AFSCL).

[8]"Short History of Mother of Grace Hospital" (AFSCL).

[9]*Book of Annual Assignments* (AFSCL).

[10]"Short History of Mother of Grace Hospital" (AFSCL).

[11]Ibid.

[12]Ibid.

[13]Secretaries General, *Community Chronicle, 1934–1957* (AFSCL).

[14]"Short History of Mother of Grace Hospital" (AFSCL).

[15]Ibid.

[16]*Book of Correspondence:* Letter from Mother M. Jerome Dadej to the Most Reverend William T. McCarty, CSSR, 17 October 1950 (AFSCL).

[17]"Short History of Mother of Grace Hospital" (AFSCL).

[18]Secretaries General, *Community Chronicle, 1934–1957* (AFSCL); and *Minutes of General Council Proceedings, 1934–1956* (AFSCL).

[19]*Book of Annual Assignments* (AFSCL).

[20]Ps. 43:19.

[21]"Short History of Mother of Grace Hospital" (AFSCL).

[22]Secretaries General, *Community Chronicle, 1957–1970* (AFSCL).

[23]Ibid.

[24]*Book of Correspondence:* Letter from Mother M. Beatrice Rybacki to the Most Reverend William T. McCarty, CSSR, 29 July 1961 (AFSCL).

[25]*Minutes of General Council Proceedings, 1956–1970* (AFSCL).

[26]Ibid.

[27]Ibid.

[28]*Book of Correspondence:* Letter from Mr. Don A. Bierle to Mother M. Beatrice Rybacki, 1 February 1962 (AFSCL).

[29]*Book of Correspondence:* Letter from Sister M. Innocentia Sierocki to the Gregory Hospital Association, Inc., 28 March 1962 (AFSCL).

[30]*Book of Annual Assignments* (AFSCL).

[31]*Book of Correspondence:* Letter from the Most Reverend William T. McCarty, CSSR, to Sister M. Innocentia Sierocki, 28 May 1962 (AFSCL).

[32]*Gregory Times-Advocate,* 7 June 1962.

[33]Author's visit to Gregory, South Dakota, June 1976.

CHAPTER 51

Madonna High School

The congregation began its fifty-first year of existence in an environment of mixed historical tensions. On April 12, 1945, President Franklin Delano Roosevelt, who had guided the United States through one of its most perilous times in history, died at Warm Springs, Georgia. While the country grieved the passing of its president, still the spirits of the American people, as well as those of the entire world anxious for peace, were lifted by the events which followed. On May 7, 1945, representatives of the German High Command surrendered unconditionally to Allied officers at Reims; on May 8, V-E (Victory in Europe) Day was announced, thus proclaiming the end of the war in Europe.

Meanwhile in the Pacific, the Americans were poised to invade the home islands of Japan by the summer of 1945. In August, the United States dropped the first atomic bomb on Hiroshima, Japan. Another atomic bomb was dropped on Nagasaki. On August 14, 1945, the eve of the feast of the Assumption of the Blessed Virgin Mary, Japan surrendered. On September 1, V-J (Victory in Japan) Day, Japan's delegates surrendered unconditionally in a formal ceremony on board the *USS Missouri* anchored in Tokyo Bay. The horrendous war had finally come to an end.

With the easement of the tensions surrounding these historical events, the Franciscan Sisters of Chicago began to face the problem which had made itself seriously felt during the war years, namely, the lack of vocations to the congregation.

In January of 1945, Mother M. Jerome and the general council met for what they considered a routine session. Instead, during the meeting, the growth of the congregation became the central topic. Mother M. Jerome announced to her councilors that she believed the time was ripe for the expansion of the congregation's educational apostolate into the area of the secondary school. She was firmly convinced that an academy or high school for girls might be a potential mainspring for vocations to the Franciscan Sisters of Chicago. She, therefore, proposed the establishment of a high school where young girls might enter the convent as aspirants after having completed elementary school, and, where, reared in a religious atmosphere, they might be attracted to the religious life. Mother M. Jerome was quick to point out the success which seminaries had achieved in preparing young men for the priesthood. Mother M. Jerome and her councilors left the meeting determined to do something about the fact that the congregation needed a vibrant program for its aspirants and postulants.[1]

With the supportive consent of the general council, Mother M. Jerome met with Samuel Cardinal Stritch,[2] the archbishop of Chicago, in August of 1946. At that time, she presented to him her dream of opening a boarding school or high school where religious vocations might be fostered. At that meeting, she also informed Cardinal Stritch of the proposal she had received from the Reverend Jerome Fabianski, CR, the pastor of St. Stanislaus Bishop and Martyr Church in the nearby area of Cragin, to accept five lots opposite the church on which the Franciscan Sisters of Chicago might build a high school. While Cardinal Stritch saw the obvious need for a high school in that area, he urged Mother M. Jerome to reject Father Fabianski's offer since the area was really inadequate.[3] Because the cardinal's consent for the congregation to move into the apostolate of secondary education was encouraging, Mother M. Jerome was very determined to exert all her energy and talent toward the establishment of a girls' high school for which she foresaw a great future.

In 1947, Mother M. Jerome learned that the Society of the Daughters of the Heart of Mary,[4] who conducted the Ephpheta School for the Deaf on Belmont Avenue and Pulaski Road, wished to sell some of the property adjacent to their school. The Sisters' entire property consisted of ten acres of land which included a very large boarding school, a very ample recreational field, and acres of open land. The Daughters of the Heart of Mary desired to sell at least four and one-half acres of the land connected with the Ephpheta School. When Mother M. Jerome and her general council examined the property, it seemed ideal for the proposed high school, and they were overjoyed at the prospect of securing the land. Mother M. Jerome contacted Cardinal Stritch for permission to buy the land on which to erect a high school for girls in the near future. She also admitted to him, quite reluctantly, that the Franciscan Sisters of Chicago were not in a position to build the proposed high school for several years because most of the congregation's funds were invested in the construction of St. John Hospital and School of Nursing in Huron, South Dakota, another project close to the hearts of the Franciscan Sisters of Chicago.[5]

As early as 1936, Mother M. Antonina Osinski, the superior general and Sister M. Jerome Dadej, the secretary general, had had an audience with George Cardinal Mundelein during which time the Sisters informed him of their intention to purchase thirty acres of land on Higgins Road in Chicago where they had hoped someday to build either a hospital or a Motherhouse. At that time, Cardinal Mundelein had agreed that the land would indeed be suitable for those purposes or even a high school and advised them to proceed with the purchase. On May 3, 1937, the Sisters received the deed to the Higgins Road property.[6] Now, in 1947, in order to cover the purchase of the Ephpheta School land, Mother M. Jerome and the general council proposed selling most of the Higgins Road holdings.[7]

Having obtained the necessary permission from Cardinal Stritch to buy the Ephpheta School property, the formalities connected with the sale of the land were undertaken. On May 10, 1948, the following resolution was approved and signed:

> To Whom It May Concern:
>
> I, Sister Mary Gonzaga, secretary of the Franciscan Sisters of St. Kunegunda, an Illinois corporation, do hereby certify that at a meeting of the Directors of said Corporation, duly called and held on May 10, 1948, the following resolution was duly adopted.
>
> Resolved, that the land for an academy be purchased from the Ladies of the Ephpheta School for the sum of $47,500.00 of which $4,750.00 has been paid as earnest money on the 2nd of March, 1948, and the balance in the amount of $42,750.00 is to be paid now at the expiration of a 60-day term since the contract has been made, and that Mother Mary Jerome, Superior General, and Sister Mary Gonzaga, Secretary General, are authorized to take all steps necessary to complete this purchase.

<table>
<tr><td>Mother Mary Jerome
Superior General</td><td>Sister M. Felixa
Vicar General</td></tr>
<tr><td>Sister M. Gonzaga
Secretary General</td><td>Sister M. Janina
Second Council Member</td></tr>
<tr><td></td><td>Mother M. Antonina
Third Council Member[8]</td></tr>
</table>

With this resolution, the land became the property of the Franciscan Sisters of Chicago. The people in the Belmont Gardens neighborhood, as the area was known, had long used the large, empty lots to raise vegetables. At their request, Mother M. Jerome allowed them to continue to use the land for this purpose rather than have it remain fallow. In addition, the large playground was used by the neighborhood Little League baseball teams every spring and summer.

To inform the Sisters of the proposed opening of a high school, Mother M. Jerome directed a letter to them written with deep sincerity and affection:

> Dear Sisters:
>
> I am convinced that the best method by which to foster vocations is to accept young girls after eighth grade. I ask you sincerely, therefore, to encourage young girls to try religious life.
>
> I do not have the intention of accepting the girls as postulants but as aspirants to whom we shall attempt to give the best education in "our high school" which will be accredited by the state just as soon as the courses are started and the requirements are met. If an aspirant wishes to

return to her home, she may do so without any problem. Other girls, who are already attending high school, will also be admitted and will be assigned the courses necessary for graduation.

If you know of any girls who are interested, please give them my name and address. Let them write to me as soon as possible, and I shall send them all the information they need.

I beg you to continue praying for vocations and encouraging young girls to enter. The bishops advise us to do so because many good vocations are lost when they are neglected. O, that Jesus, our Spouse, would call many souls to unite with Him in offering their lives to save the souls of sinners. Let every Sister remember that she did not come to the convent to save her own soul only—because that can be done in the world also—but she entered to help save souls by her own daily dedication.

Let the young girls be made conscious of this goal so that later when they become religious, they will understand that they are saving souls for Jesus. Do not be disturbed if, later, some of them leave. It can and it will happen, but, nevertheless, some will remain. And those who do leave— they will also benefit by having gotten to know God better and they will live their lives accordingly.

May the Immaculate Heart of Mary help us!

> Devotedly yours in Christ
> and St. Francis,
> Mother M. Jerome[9]

Although the continued lack of funds prohibited the Sisters from moving ahead with their plan to build a high school on the newly acquired property at that time, Mother M. Jerome and the general council arranged for the nucleus of the prospective high school to begin at a temporary location. The site selected was the former St. Vincent's Orphan Asylum, adjacent to the Motherhouse, and which, after the departure of the orphans in 1911, had been converted into living quarters for the Sisters. In four rooms on the first floor of the old orphan asylum on Hamlin and Schubert Avenues, the high school opened on September 8, 1949, with four aspirants.[10] They had arrived on August 8 in preparation for the school's September opening.

To differentiate it from the old Our Lady of Victory High School which the congregation had earlier established for its postulants and young professed Sisters in 1924, the new school was called Madonna High School. The name had been selected by Mother M. Jerome whose undaunted faith, vision, and spirit had called the school into existence. When the school opened, Sister M. Crescencia Chmiel served as its first principal. Much of the credit for the future success of the school was due to Sister M. Crescencia, an able and dedicated teacher and administrator, who proved equal to the enormous task imposed upon her by the congregation.

Born in Johnstown, Pennsylvania, on January 9, 1906, Sister M. Crescencia, the former Sophie Chmiel, entered the congregation from St. Casimir Church on August 2, 1922. She was received into the novitiate on July 26, 1923, and made her first profession on July 27, 1924. She professed perpetual vows on July 27, 1927.

Sister M. Crescencia attended De Paul University from which she received her bachelor's and master's degrees. She did postgraduate work at Loyola University of Chicago and Duquesne University in Pennsylvania. As a teacher, she ministered at various schools in Chicago, Illinois; Cleveland, Ohio; Johnstown, Pennsylvania; Gary, Indiana; and at Johnstown Central Catholic High School in Johnstown, Pennsylvania.[11] Earlier, from 1934 to 1940, she had taught the postulants at the Motherhouse in Our Lady of Victory Convent High School. A gentle, generous, and talented woman, Sister M. Crescencia provided for Madonna High School the firm leadership which was to become a distinct characteristic of the school.

The staff members and their subject offerings that first memorable year included the principal, Sister M. Crescencia Chmiel, who taught Latin, algebra, and geometry; Sister M. Therese Grajek, English and history; Sister M. Gerard Gorzkowski, Polish;[12] Sister M. Helen Swiszcz, art;[13] Sister M. Charitas Gajdzinski, piano and music appreciation; and Sister M. Dorothy Szostek, voice.[14] The Reverend Joseph Baniewicz, CR, the chaplain of St. Joseph Home for the Aged, was the religion instructor.[15] Sister M. Therese was selected to act as the directress of the aspirants.[16] A mass was offered by Father Baniewicz on September 12, 1949, in the chapel of St. Joseph Home to mark the opening of the school year.

Early in January of 1950, Mother M. Jerome jubilantly informed the general council that the Society of the Daughters of the Heart of Mary had revealed their intention to sell the Ephpheta School for the Deaf and relocate in a new and smaller center on Wellington Street. As a result of this decision, Mother M. Jerome and her councilors visited the school on January 11. The dignified building was a most impressive sight surrounded as it was by acres of open spaces. The school seemed perfectly suited to serve as a resident and day school for young women. The majestic old building, containing numerous rooms both large and small, was a massive four-story brick structure with a large dome and a gabled roof. Adjacent to the structure on the corner of Belmont Avenue and Pulaski Road was a one-story annex which contained a currency exchange and a hardware store.[17] The large areas of open acres provided much room for future expansion. Extremely pleased with what they saw, Mother M. Jerome and the councilors expressed their desire to purchase the Ephpheta School for the Deaf for $325,000. At a subsequent meeting with Cardinal Stritch on April 4, 1950, Mother M. Jerome received the necessary permission for the purchase after Cardinal Stritch expressed his wholehearted agreement with the Sisters' plans to convert the Ephpheta School into a resident and day school for young women.[18]

On May 26, 1950, the acquisition of the Ephpheta School from the Society of the Daughters of the Heart of Mary was finalized. When the contract was signed, a sum of

Original Madonna High School and Convent
The "Old Building"
Chicago, Illinois (1951–1974)

$50,000 was paid. The terms called for $50,000 to be paid in sixty days with the remainder of $225,000 to be paid when the Franciscan Sisters of Chicago took possession of the building, which according to the contract, was to occur no later than October of 1951.[19]

Soon after the Ephpheta School was purchased, the Sisters were approached by several friends of the congregation who offered to help conduct a fund-raising campaign for the high school. Mother M. Jerome, Sister M. Gonzaga, and the volunteer fund-raisers met with the Right Reverend Joseph Casey, vicar general of the Archdiocese of Chicago, who, in the course of the meeting, rejected any plans on the part of the congregation to accept the services of a fund-raising group. Monsignor Casey further informed his visitors that Cardinal Stritch had an explicit plan called the Catholic High School Building Fund which was directed to conducting a campaign in the parishes of the archdiocese with the specific intention of raising $10 million dollars for badly needed high schools. From this projected sum, ten religious congregations were to receive an outright gift of $1 million with which to build a new high school; later they could continue with their own particular fund-raising plans. At this meeting, Monsignor Casey could not assure Mother M. Jerome that the Franciscan Sisters of Chicago would be one of the congregations receiving the money. What was obvious, however, was that since Cardinal Stritch had definite plans for raising funds in the archdiocese at this particular time, Mother M. Jerome was expressly directed to refrain from any fund-raising campaign in the archdiocese conducted with the aid of lay people.

The day after the visit with Monsignor Casey, Mother M. Jerome directed a letter to Cardinal Stritch. She informed him, therein, that the Sisters thought it more advantageous to build an entirely new high school rather than to attempt to renovate the old Ephpheta School. Mother M. Jerome ended the letter with a sincere plea:

> It would be a privilege deeply appreciated, if our Franciscan Order, having been organized in Chicago, would be considered one of the recipients of the Catholic High School Building Fund monies. If some money could be advanced on a loan from the Archdiocese, we would start building this autumn.
>
> It was very encouraging when in one of my interviews, Your Eminence stated that a girls' high school had been very badly needed in the locality we had chosen by purchasing the land from the Daughters of the Heart of Mary. Having Your Eminence's approval to carry out my program, I have been preparing a high school staff by sending Sisters to various Catholic institutions to acquire their masters' degrees. At the present time, we have quite a number of Sisters who are academically prepared. I will have the proper personnel for each department ready for September of 1951.
>
> May I humbly beg for a reply and some advice in the matter presented above?
>
> Asking for the blessing of Your Eminence, I have the honor to be
>
> A humble servant in Christ,
> Mother M. Jerome
> Superior General[20]

While waiting to hear from the cardinal, the Sisters proceeded with the original plan of converting the Ephpheta School into a small high school facility. In the meantime, Madonna High School began its second year of operation at the original Motherhouse location. The sophomore and junior years were introduced with a total of twenty-one students among whom were eight aspirants. The thirteen day students came from St. Hyacinth and St. Stanislaus Bishop and Martyr Schools while the others were transfer students from Good Counsel, Cardinal Stritch, Lourdes, and Schurz Public High School. The aspirants came from St. John Cantius School, Indiana Harbor, Indiana; Sacred Heart and St. Hedwig School, Gary, Indiana; and St. Casimir School, Johnstown, Pennsylvania. The day students were attired in blue jumpers and white blouses while the aspirants wore navy blue uniforms with white collars and cuffs. This outfit replaced the black dresses and short veils which the aspirants had worn the year before.

The members new to the faculty included Sister M. Tarcisia Bucki, chemistry and general science;[21] Sister M. Lucretia Kot, glee club;[22] Sister M. Felixa Jorz, freshman religion;[23] Sister Eleanor Marie Jadrych, sewing and home economics;[24] and Miss Gerry Wright, who taught physical education at the nearby Kosciusko Park whose facilities Madonna High School utilized. The Reverend Joseph Baniewicz, CR, continued to teach religion on the sophomore and junior levels.

At the end of November 1950, Mother M. Jerome was pleased to receive a promise from Cardinal Stritch that some funds would be allocated from the Catholic High School Building Fund for a new Madonna High School.[25] In the meantime, four more acres belonging to the congregation on Higgins Road were sold for $10,000 to a land developer in an effort to raise money.[26]

In February of 1951, Mother M. Jerome sent a letter to Cardinal Stritch informing him of the necessity to act quickly in regard to the erection of a new Madonna High School. Her letter read in part:

> Last week I had a call from Alvernia High School inquiring whether or not we could accept one hundred students. Alvernia admitted 250 freshmen although 350 had applied. Cardinal Stritch High School asked us to take 60 students. We receive numerous calls from individual girls and their parents begging for admission. We cannot accept more than 34 girls this year.[27]

Happily, on February 4 of that year, four aspirants from Madonna High School were received into the postulancy.[28] The new postulants remained under the guidance of Sister M. Therese Grajek.

In early March, Mother M. Jerome and Sister M. Gonzaga met with Cardinal Stritch. In a most amiable mood, he gladly gave the Sisters permission to build a new high school while advising them to continue renovating the old Ephpheta School as had originally been planned. He suggested that Mother M. Jerome secure the architectural firm of W. F. McCaughey and Associates and the George Sollitt Construction Company as the general contractor to erect the new structure.[29] In April of that year, the Society of the Daughters of the Heart of Mary sold the remainder of the land they owned near the Ephpheta School to the Franciscan Sisters of Chicago for the sum of $46,252.95. A month later, McCaughey and Associates submitted the blueprints for the $1.2 million high school to be constructed. While Mother M. Jerome and the general council were extremely pleased with the architect's blueprints, it was obvious that Cardinal Stritch did not share their sentiments. In a letter directed to Mother M. Jerome in early June, the cardinal informed her that McCaughey and Associates had presented him their plans, but he found the cost of the building prohibitive. He also expressed his regrets at being unable, at that time, to make any donation toward the building of the new high school. Cardinal Stritch maintained that conditions in the archdiocese had thus far not allowed him to begin his proposed Catholic High School Building Fund.[30]

The Society of the Daughters of the Heart of Mary officially withdrew from the Ephpheta School on June 8, 1951. On July 31, at three o'clock in the afternoon, Mother M.

Jerome arrived at the school with a group of sixteen overjoyed Sisters to take possession formally of the building vacated by the Daughters of the Heart of Mary. The Franciscan Sisters of Chicago who accompanied Mother M. Jerome on this happy occasion were Sister M. Gonzaga Raniszewski, Sister M. Clara Ogurek, Sister M. Carmelita Szczepanski, Sister M. Salomea Grabowski, Sister M. Perpetua Sulski, Sister M. Eleanor Bomba, Sister M. Honoria Urbaniak, Sister M. Virginia Minta, Sister M. Isidore Wilkos, Sister M. Hedwinette Burliga, Sister M. Honorata Makowski, Sister M. Gerard Gorzkowski, Sister M. Stanislaus Reich, Sister M. Dorothy Szostek, Sister M. Alvernia Groszek, and Sister M. Joseph Grochowski.

The next day, August 1, the first mass was offered in the beautiful chapel by the chaplain of the old Ephpheta School, the Reverend James Lowney, CSV, a Viatorian.[31] After the mass, he spoke to the Sisters, warmly welcoming them to the house and offering congratulations on their new apostolate. The Sisters present at the mass that morning, some of whom had stayed overnight were Mother M. Jerome Dadej, Sister M. Gonzaga Raniszewski, Sister M. Clara Ogurek, Sister M. Salomea Grabowski, Sister M. Stanislaus Reich, Sister M. Gerard Gorzkowski, Sister M. Isidore Wilkos, Sister M. Virginia Minta, Sister M. Honoria Urbaniak, Sister M. Hedwinette Burliga, and Sister M. Joseph Grochowski. They were joined by Sister M. Felixa Jorz, Sister M. Innocentia Sierocki, Sister M. Therese Grajek, Sister M. Lucretia Kot, Sister M. Tarcisia Bucki, Sister M. Renata Krukowski, and several aspirants. After breakfast, many of the Sisters remained at the school to prepare it for its September opening. During the entire month of August, Sisters from nearby mission houses of the congregation also came to clean the many rooms and immense corridors of the spacious building. Living quarters on the third floor and several rooms on the second floor which were reserved for the Sisters on the faculty were also made ready for occupancy. Sister M. Virginia Minta served as the superior until August 11, when Sister M. Hilary Dadej[32] assumed her position as the first official superior at the new Madonna High School.[33]

In the old Ephpheta School building, Madonna High School opened for its third year on September 6, 1951, with a total enrollment of ninety-seven students. Of these, sixty-eight were freshmen, twenty-three were sophomores, and six were juniors. The Reverend Stanley Shaw, a member of the Chicago Archdiocesan Mission Band, offered mass in the chapel. By October 29, the number of students had risen to 102. The school opened with the following faculty: Sister M. Crescencia Chmiel, principal and teacher of Latin and mathematics; Sister M. Lucretia Kot, music and glee club conductor; Sister M. Tarcisia Bucki, religion, general science, and chemistry; Sister M. Maxencia Pozniatowski, librarian and history teacher;[34] Sister M. Felixa Jorz, religion; Sister Eleanor Marie Jadrych, home economics and sociology; Sister M. Alvernia Groszek, biology, physical education, and moderator of the Mothers' Club;[35] Sister M. Kingnetta Szczypula, religion, Polish, and commercial subjects;[36] and Sister M. Therese Grajek, English and directress of aspirants, postulants, and boarding students. Sister M. Josephine Penza, Sister Rose Ann Zmich, and Sister M. Sebastianna Nowak were assigned to household duties. Sister M. Francis Swider was appointed sacristan while Sister M. Virginia Minta served as portress.[37] Sister M. Felixa, Sister M. Lucretia, and Sister M. Tarcisia traveled to Madonna High School daily from the Motherhouse.

Prior to the opening of the 1952 school year, the Reverend James Lowney, CSV, who had served as chaplain of the Ephpheta School and as resident chaplain of Madonna High School, terminated his duties on August 31. Because the Viatorian Fathers were no longer in a position to provide a chaplain, Mother M. Jerome turned to the Reverend Stanley Fiolek, CR, the provincial superior of the Congregation of the Resurrection, requesting a chaplain. From September 1, 1952, until the present day, the Resurrectionist Fathers from nearby Weber High School celebrate the Liturgy of the Eucharist in the Sisters' convent chapel daily.

When school began in September of 1952, the enrollment had reached 269; consequently, four more Sisters were added to the staff. They were Sister M. Alberta Bialas, assistant principal;[38] Sister Clarent Marie Urbanowicz, history, Latin, vocation directress, and directress of boarding students;[39] Sister M. Dolorosa Bojanowski, English and French;[40] and Sister M. Dorothy Szostek, Spanish and drama.[41] Sister M. Lucretia Kot and Sister M. Tarcisia Bucki continued to commute daily from the Motherhouse. Sister M. John Barczak served as the seamstress for the Sisters at the high school.[42]

Less than three weeks after the semester had begun, the North Central Association of Colleges and Secondary Schools visited Madonna High School. On September 20, 1952, the team arrived for the purpose of determining the standards of the school and the qualifications of its teachers. Thus, while only in its third year of operation, the school was fully accredited by North Central and fully recognized and accredited by the Office of Public Instruction of the State of Illinois, an accreditation the school has merited successfully every seven years after undergoing intense self-evaluation.[43]

In October of 1952, Mother M. Jerome secured a meeting with Cardinal Stritch. Once again she reminded the cardinal of the congregation's desire to build a new school for approximately four hundred students. The cardinal promised to come to the aid of the congregation with a donation of $500,000. The remainder of the building costs, he emphasized, was to be raised by the Sisters' own efforts.[44] To that end, the last of the Higgins Road property was sold in December for $87,000 and the money was set aside for the high school building fund.

When, by April of 1953, no money had as yet arrived from the cardinal's office, Mother M. Jerome boldly addressed him:

> Your Eminence:
>
> It has been brought to our attention that a campaign for high school funds has been started among the parishes of the Archdiocese. If this is true, then I wish to renew my petition for help in financing our project of building a new high school for girls at Pulaski Road and Belmont Avenue.

We have been prompted to renew this petition by the requests of mothers whose daughters' admissions to our Madonna High School have been rejected because of lack of space. We were able to accommodate only 250 students this year while over 500 applied. Some parents even want to enroll their daughters two years before their completion of elementary school in order to make sure they will get into a Catholic high school. Generally we do not accept such applications, but we had no registration this year since all the places for September of 1953 were filled by the earlier applicants.

We are trying to save some of our earnings for our high school building project. If assistance is given to us, we should be ready to start building in 1954.

A grateful servant in Christ,

Mother M. Jerome

Superior General[45]

In the meantime, a change was made in the architect and in the construction company originally engaged to build the new school. On April 13, Mother M. Jerome and the faculty members met with the architect, C. I. Krajewski, and the general contractor of the J. J. Kinnare Construction Company that had been newly hired.

On May 31, 1953, the first commencement exercises of Madonna High School were held in the convent chapel of St. Joseph Home at three o'clock in the afternoon. The Reverend Stanley Stoga, assistant superintendent of schools in the Archdiocese of Chicago, officiated at the graduation ceremony at which he presented diplomas to ten graduates.[46] During his commencement address, he praised Mother M. Jerome for her extraordinary courage and laudable foresight in founding Madonna High School and added that he anticipated a great future for the high school.[47]

In June of 1953, Sister M. Alberta Bialas, the assistant principal, was appointed the new principal of Madonna High School. She succeeded Sister M. Crescencia Chmiel who was transferred to Johnstown Central Catholic High School in Johnstown, Pennsylvania. The faculty and students were saddened at the departure of Sister M. Crescencia who had contributed indispensably to the growth and expansion of Madonna High School by her deft organization of a program of studies and her expert teaching of subject matter in regular classes. She had added Spanish, office practice, bookkeeping, advanced clothing, and sociology to the curriculum. New and revised textbooks had been adopted and a variety of audiovisual materials had been acquired. In four years, Sister M. Crescencia had placed Madonna High School on a solid academic foundation.

Madonna's second principal, Sister M. Alberta, entered the congregation from St. Stanislaus Bishop and Martyr Church in Chicago on August 25, 1926. On July 12, 1927, she was invested with the habit of St. Francis and made her first profession of vows on July 17, 1929. She was perpetually professed on July 17, 1932. She received her bachelor's degree from De Paul University in Chicago and her master of arts degree from St. John College of Cleveland.

An innovative and skilled teacher, Sister M. Alberta had been equally efficient as an elementary school principal in schools in Chicago, Illinois; Cleveland, Ohio; and Gary, (Tolleston), Indiana. In 1952, she had been elected fourth councilor in the general administration of the congregation while still maintaining her role as a teacher of mathematics and religion at Madonna. In addition, she had been equally effective as the supervisor of schools for a number of years as well as directress of education for the Sister-teachers of the congregation.[48] A physically tall and imposing figure, she possessed a quiet dignity and efficiency which made her brief tenure as principal memorable. Pensive and sedate, Sister M. Alberta combined her gifts of piety, patient determination, and diligence to serve the young women at Madonna High School.[49]

Along with the appointment of a new principal came several new appointments of Sisters to the faculty in September of 1953: Sister M. Sponsa Bajorek, art, Polish, and religion;[50] M. Marinella Gubala, mathematics, religion, and English;[51] and Sister M. Maristella Skrzynski, appointed to teach religion and English while also succeeding Sister M. Therese Grajek as directress of aspirants and postulants.[52] Sister M. Leontia Swiech was appointed sacristan and chauffeur.[53] By this time, the school had tripled in size and now enrolled 322 students.

Much effort was exerted that year to beautify the grounds of Madonna High School. Mother M. Jerome appointed Sister M. Clarent Marie Urbanowicz to attend to the landscaping. She, in turn, secured the services of the City Forestry Department which proceeded to trim thirty-nine trees, cut down seven of them, and cure many more. In April of 1955, three more lots were purchased on Pulaski Road and Barry Avenue.

When the new school year began in September of 1954, Sister M. Seraphinia Furman was added to the faculty as a typing and religion instructor.[54] The faculty also welcomed Miss Frances Mazurek to the mathematics department and Miss Margaret Vello to the department of physical education. Sister M. Dolorosa Bojanowski was appointed the superior succeeding Sister M. Hilary Dadej.

With the steady rise in enrollment during the six years of Madonna High School's existence, the old Ephpheta School could no longer accommodate the many students who sought admission. Mother M. Jerome found it imperative to obtain permission from Cardinal Stritch to build an entirely new and large Madonna High School with adequate facilities for the hundreds of students from nearby parishes who applied for entrance. In late March of 1955, Mother M. Jerome directed another letter to Cardinal Stritch, asking for needed financial assistance. She stated that Madonna High School sorely lacked an adequate gym, auditorium, and cafeteria. The curriculum could not be expanded because of the lack of ordinary classroom space in the old Ephpheta Building:

> Taking all of this into consideration, we have been concentrating all
> of our efforts on the financial aspect of the school project. To that end,

the Old Building [the Ephpheta School] will remain a part of the school serving as a science building and a faculty residence. Our assets toward a new Madonna High School at present consist of $600,000 from a sale of land.[55]

Mother M. Jerome informed the cardinal that the projected cost of the new high school had been estimated at $2,279,000. Without financial assistance from the archdiocese, the Sisters would be unable to undertake the building of an entirely new Madonna High School. Once again she begged for a $1 million donation from the Catholic High School Building Fund and stated that the remainder of the cost of the high school would be covered by a loan which she hoped to secure from the Holy See. Mother M. Jerome assured the cardinal that the efforts of the entire congregation plus the help of the Mothers' Club and Auxiliary of Madonna High School would enable the congregation to meet the interest and gradually repay the principal.[56]

Mother M. Jerome was summoned to an audience with Cardinal Stritch as a result of her letter. At the meeting on April 5, he recommended that the gym and auditorium be combined so that the total cost of the high school would not exceed $2 million. Cardinal Stritch also met with C. I. Krajewski, the architect, and advised him to alter his blueprints accordingly. When the architect informed Mother M. Jerome of Cardinal Stritch's determination to combine the gym and auditorium and of the cardinal's orders to alter the blueprints, Mother M. Jerome was disheartened. She wrote the cardinal a few days later, begging him to reconsider the auditorium-gym combination which neither she nor the Sisters favored. His answer was not long in coming and when it did, it allowed no further room for discussion.[57] Cardinal Stritch firmly stated that since the congregation did not have adequate funds on hand for the building of the high school, it would be impossible for him to approve the desired petition to the Holy See for a loan if the Sisters did not agree to the lowered cost of an auditorium-gym combination.[58]

A few days later, Mother M. Jerome and the general council submitted to the cardinal's wishes:

> We feel deeply grateful for your kind letter in reference to the new Madonna High School. We must submit to the proposed plan of an auditorium combined with a gymnasium in order to decrease the cost of the entire project.
>
> This matter has been discussed with our architect who is willing to remake the plans so that the cost of the building with all its equipment will not exceed the sum of two million dollars. He will not start working on the altered plans, however, until we hear from Your Eminence.
>
> In further development of this project, we solely and trustfully depend on Your Eminence's decision as to the grant from the Catholic High School Building Fund and the loan which we wish to make.

Beseeching Your Eminence for support and paternal guidance, I remain,

Your obedient spiritual daughter in Christ,
Mother M. Jerome
Superior General[59]

In the midst of the ongoing discussions concerning the financial aspect of the construction of Madonna High School, the third commencement exercises took place on June 5, 1955, at St. Viator's Church on Addison Street. The Reverend Edwin Bak, CR, of Weber High School, presented diplomas to fifty-two Madonna seniors.

In September of 1955, two more Sisters joined the faculty: Sister M. Benigna Jakajtis[60] arrived to teach Latin, while Sister M. Alacoque Czartoryski took charge of the clothing department.[61]

Less than a month later, Mother M. Jerome directed a letter to the Sisters at the Motherhouse:

Dear Sisters:

Because the building of a new school is so dear to my heart, the Sisters at all the missions have made a wonderful surprise for me. I was presented with offerings in the sum of $14,050.00 for the new high school on my feastday. I am so pleased by this act of love which the Sisters have expressed for the good of all of us. Praise be to God! To me, this gesture is an incentive to work harder on this project.

I wish to thank you for your offering of $60.00. I know that more money will be realized when the lovely items which you made for me for my feastday will be used as the prizes for a ticket raffle. Right now it is very necessary to raise funds for the high school and I believe that you will all lend your efforts to do something in this regard.

I thank you sincerely for all your gifts, greetings, and prayers. Please continue to pray so that we are able to build as soon as possible. The best prayer is the offering of your daily work to God, especially to bear patiently the various crosses of life. For this kind of prayer, I humbly beg.

Sincerely devoted to the Heart
of Mary, Queen of the Holy Rosary,
Mother M. Jerome[62]

A few weeks later, Mother M. Jerome eagerly shared her good news with the entire congregation:

My dear Sisters,

For the past few years you have been splendidly responding to my plea for organizing a building fund for the new Madonna High School, and, no doubt, you are all eagerly looking forward to its realization. It is, therefore, my great joy and pleasure to announce to you, dear Sisters, that we have obtained His Eminence's approval to build. This means that the Cardinal has countersigned our request to the Holy See for permission to make a loan of one million dollars.[63] It will be a heavy load on our shoulders, but I earnestly desire and hope that this burden will be shared by all of us.

At this point, may I ask you, dear Sisters, to plan ways and means by which we will be able to make payments readily on this tremendous loan. We need to consider it now, because the time element is essential.

In this regard, I am sure that we can accumulate a considerable amount of money if we refrain from such things that are not essentially needed. Try to save on unnecessary articles, perhaps wearing your clothes a little longer or by using less expensive apparel. Sacrifice those things in the spirit of poverty for the good of our common goal, but likewise, do it all for God. Offer every sacrifice as a token of love for God, to gain His blessings for yourselves, the new project, and for your loved ones.

In the spirit of St. Francis, accept these suggestions and thus you will assist me in raising the necessary funds to meet the payments on the loan.

Sincerely yours in Jesus and Mary,

Mother M. Jerome[64]

From the very beginning, the financial burden for the maintenance of and improvements in the Ephpheta School and later for the construction of the new Madonna High School was very heavy. The cost of the new school rose to $2,386,121 with the cost of equipment at $242,715 for a total of $2,628,836.[65] In order to help the Sisters defray the huge debt, the Madonna High School Mothers' Club and Auxiliary had been founded on February 24, 1952, with the Reverend Walter Szczypula as chaplain, Sister M. Alvernia as moderator, and Sister M. Tarcisia Bucki as co-moderator. The club had as its aim "to bring into relation the home and school so that parents, teachers, and friends of the students might cooperate to secure for the girls the best spiritual, mental, moral, and physical education," and "to render to Madonna High School and faculty, such financial and physical assistance as shall be deemed necessary by the club."[66]

To obtain funds, the resourceful Sister M. Alvernia and Sister M. Hilary undertook the running of a carnival in 1953 on the empty grounds at Belmont and Karlov Avenues. This venture proved to be a tremendous financial success and, as a consequence, was continued for six more years until the new school was erected. Bingos were held at St. Joseph Home for the Aged and later at the completed high school to raise the needed funds. The Sisters also sold chance books in an effort to secure the money. In 1957, upon the advice of Miss Berenice Lesniak, a lawyer and devoted friend of the congregation, the Sisters sought a loan for $1 million trusting in Divine Providence that benefactors would be found. To achieve this end, Miss Lesniak proposed that the Sisters secure promissory notes from their families and friends in the sum of $500 or more for five to ten years without interest.[67] In this important undertaking and in all other activities sponsored for the new Madonna High School, the Franciscan Sisters of Chicago were consistently aided by the loyalty and support of their families, friends, and benefactors who watched the school's progress with fondness and concern. Without this aid and encouragement, it would have been exceedingly difficult, if not impossible, for the congregation to have financed the erection of the new school.

In a further endeavor to be of assistance to the school, the Madonna High School Fathers' Club and Auxiliary whose aims were consonant with those of the Mothers' Club came into existence on March 19, 1956. Sister M. Alberta Bialas was appointed its moderator, Sister M. Dorothy Szostek was designated its co-moderator, and the Reverend Andrew Kloska, CR, was named its chaplain. Both of these organizations have always been undeniably responsible for furthering the progress and development of Madonna High School by their characteristic loyalty and devotion to the school and the Franciscan Sisters of Chicago.[68]

A strategic change occurred at Madonna High School when on July 26, 1956, the dynamic and amiable Sister M. Hugoline Czaplinski arrived from Johnstown Central Catholic High School in Johnstown, Pennsylvania, to become the third principal of Madonna High School. When she assumed the position of principal, she headed a school which listed 395 students and a faculty roster of eighteen religious and two lay teachers.

When Sister M. Hugoline was appointed the principal, Sister M. Alberta, her predecessor, was named assistant principal and faculty coordinator of the new Madonna High School building program. As the second principal of the school, Sister M. Alberta had enriched the curriculum with a greater emphasis on art, language, dramatics, and with the latest audiovisual equipment and library materials. She had added French to the language curriculum and secured more and advanced equipment for the art and business departments. Sister M. Alberta had contributed to the advancement of Madonna High School by her steady and dependable leadership.

Scarcely had Sister M. Hugoline settled into her various duties as administrator when examiners from Springfield paid a visit to the school on September 5, 1956. Happily, Madonna High School, still located in the Ephpheta School building, was again fully accredited and the examiners conveyed their congratulations and expressed their satisfaction at the progress of the school.

Shortly thereafter, on Sunday October 21, 1956, the ground-breaking for the new Madonna High School took place on the northeast corner of Belmont and Karlov Avenues. The Right Reverend Monsignor Raymond Zock, vicar for religious communities of women, officiated at the ceremony during which Robert G. Hayes, the assistant county superintendent of public instruction of the state of Illinois, was the guest speaker.

In August of 1957, Sister M. Alberta was named superior of the religious faculty, a position she held for seven years. She remained on the faculty as a teacher of algebra and physics until 1970 when she was named apostolate coordinator as a member of the collegial board of the congregation at the Eleventh General Chapter of Elections.[69] That same year saw the return of Sister M. Crescencia Chmiel who was assigned to teach religion, algebra, and Latin. At the Ninth General Chapter of Elections held in 1958, she was elected the second councilor in the general administration of the congregation. She was also appointed the assistant principal of Madonna High School, served in that capacity for the next eleven years, and remains a part of the office staff today. Another new arrival in 1957 was Sister M. Albertine Schab who assumed the position of food service manager of the cafeteria where for thirty years she has rendered an invaluable service to the school.[70]

When September of 1957 arrived, the enrollment at the school had reached its capacity of 420 students. To everyone's joy and satisfaction, the blessing of the cornerstone for the new Madonna High School took place on Sunday, September 22, at three o'clock in the afternoon. The cornerstone, inscribed with the school's motto, "For Sanctity and Wisdom," was blessed by the Most Reverend Raymond P. Hillinger, auxiliary bishop of Chicago. The Franciscan Sisters of Chicago, the clergy, and the members of the Mothers and Fathers' Clubs together with students and friends of Madonna High School joined in a long procession leading from the old building on Pulaski Road and ending at Belmont and Karlov Avenues, the site of the proposed new school.

Mother M. Jerome and Sister M. Alberta found it necessary to meet with Cardinal Stritch again on March 26, 1958, to renew their oft-repeated request for a donation for the building of the new Madonna High School. At the meeting, they learned, instead, that Cardinal Stritch had been named pro-prefect of the Sacred Congregation for the Propagation of the Faith and would, of necessity, be moving to Rome permanently. A month later, Cardinal Stritch informed Mother M. Jerome that there was no more money left in the Catholic High School Building Fund. Mother M. Jerome was truly saddened at the cardinal's disclosure:

> I can assure you that later this year when payments have been made
> on the pledges we shall be glad to give you a substantial donation to help
> you pay the cost of the furnishings and equipment of your high school.
> Just at this time it is impossible for us to give you any financial help. . . . I
> am sorry but as I said in our conversation, we must look forward to what
> will come from the parishes in this next five-year period to give you some
> hope towards meeting your equipment and furnishings' costs.[71]

Regretfully, this was the congregation's last communication with Cardinal Stritch. He died in Rome on May 27, 1958.

In the shadow of the old Madonna High School—the Ephpheta School Building— the large and beautiful new high school slowly rose in the days and weeks that followed. The two-story structure of Roman brick, rectangular in shape, consisted of Buildings A and B. The section designated as Building A contained the science laboratories, the commercial department, and several standard classrooms. The home economics

Madonna High School
Chicago, Illinois (1958–   )

department complete with a model living room, dining room, bedroom, kitchen, and bath which adjoined the home management class, plus the student publication room were also in Building A. In Building B were located the administration offices, the art department, the library, an oratory, a visual-aid room, a large study hall, and a nurse's office. A Little Theater built to accommodate four hundred students for sectional assemblies, films, meetings, drama classes, and lectures was also found in this area. Adjoining both buildings was a large combination auditorium-gymnasium with a seating capacity of 1,500. To the rear of Building B was a two-story music department consisting of a band room, choral room, six music studios, and a large stagecraft room. Located in the basement were a bookstore, senior lounge, and a social hall. A beautiful and serviceable cafeteria, seating four hundred students and enclosed on three sides with glass walls, emerged as one of the school's unique features. Lastly, a spacious and lovely inner courtyard containing flagstone walks, flowers, bushes, two stone benches, and a statue of the Madonna joined Buildings A and B.

The lovely interior of the main entrance to the school was highlighted by a white marble statue of the Madonna imported from Italy. It was set against a background of two-inch-square mosaic tiles spotted intermittently with squares of gold. On both sides of the Madonna were marble slab pillars engraved with the letter *M*. Stone planters with potted foliage and terrazzo flooring completed the lovely and colorful main entrance.

A terra-cotta statue of the Madonna and Child, approximately nine and one-half feet tall, adorned the outside walls of the new school. The entrance to the school was distinguished by a large pylon column, fifty-four feet high and affixed with a nine-foot steel cross, set against the skyline and projecting prominently and significantly in the Belmont Gardens area.[72]

Acres of open space provided for a physical education field and a parking lot for more than one hundred cars. Recreational facilities included two tennis courts, a volleyball court, and a baseball diamond. Finally, more than 260 feet of beautiful overpass of glass and aluminum connected the new school to the old Madonna High School.

The workers labored diligently to finish the new facilities before the first official graduation in the new school. On June 1, 1958, the Reverend Stanley Stoga, assistant supervisor of schools in the Archdiocese of Chicago, granted diplomas to sixty-six young women, one of whom was a postulant. Father Stoga was assisted by the Reverend Walter Szczypula and the Reverend Norbert Zawistanowicz on this most memorable occasion.[73]

Three months later, on September 2, 1958, the first day of the new school year, eleven aspirants and 650 students crossed the threshold of the new Madonna High School. A Mass to the Holy Spirit was celebrated in the auditorium-gym two days later. There were three additional Sisters on the staff which now numbered twenty-six: Sister M. Charitas Gajdzinski,[74] Sister M. Christine Brzozowski,[75] both of the English Department; and Sister M. Esther Obuchowski, who was part of the office staff.[76]

The formal dedication of Madonna High School occurred on Sunday, April 26, 1959, at four o'clock in the afternoon. The Most Reverend Albert Gregory Meyer, the newly installed archbishop of Chicago, officiated at the dedication and blessing of the structure. He was assisted by the Reverend Andrew Kloska, CR, of St. Stanislaus Bishop and Martyr Church and chaplain of the Fathers' Club of Madonna High School; and by the Reverend Walter Szczypula, of St. Ladislaus Church and chaplain of the Mothers' Club. The master of ceremonies was the Right Reverend Monsignor James C. Hardiman. Members of the clergy under the direction of the Right Reverend Monsignor Joseph Mroczkowski performed as chanters. During the blessing of the school facilities, a musical program was held in the auditorium-gym during which Sister M. Lucretia Kot directed the Madonna High School Glee Club in several selections while Sister M. Charitas Gajdzinski accompanied them on the organ. The dedication concluded with the Solemn Benediction of the Most Blessed Sacrament. For this historic and blessed event, the overjoyed Mother M. Jerome Dadej traveled from St. John Hospital in Huron, South Dakota, where she was stationed after her term as superior general had expired.

A few weeks after the dedication, Sister M. Hugoline received a letter from the Very Reverend Monsignor William E. McManus,[77] superintendent of schools of the Archdiocese of Chicago, which summed up the good feelings of all those who had seen the new Madonna High School:

Dear Sister M. Hugoline:

This is a tardy note to thank you for your hospitality and gracious reception at the time of the beautiful dedication ceremonies of the new Madonna High School. It is a magnificent building, well planned and expertly constructed. All who had a hand in its development deserve to be congratulated most highly.

It was a real thrill to hear the Archbishop announce the glad tidings that Madonna High School has been granted accreditation by North Central Association. This recognition is a tribute to your brilliant leadership as principal of the school and to the generous cooperation of your dedicated and loyal faculty of Sisters and lay teachers.

It is true to say that inside and outside Madonna High School is in the best tradition of Catholic secondary education in our great Archdiocese.

God bless you.

Sincerely in Christ,
William E. McManus[78]

In September of 1959, when the school population rose from 654 to 892, the exploding enrollment demanded an increase in the number of faculty members, by now many of them dedicated lay women. Four more Sisters were assigned to the faculty that year: Sister M. Euphemia Switalski, music and piano;[79] Sister M. Tyburcia Sliwa; typing and bookkeeping;[80] and Sister M. Antoniana Stanczyk, science. Sister M. Ephrem Soprych was appointed to food management service.[81] Mrs. Wanda Rozmarek, who was hired to teach Polish, began her long association with the school.[82] Joining the staff as a part-time religion and guidance counselor was the Reverend Sergius Wroblewski.[83]

In September of 1960, Sister Bernice Marie Junio[84] joined the business department, Sister Helen Marie Mackowiak[85] was engaged as a guidance counselor and teacher of Polish, while Sister M. Antonella Abramowicz was welcomed into the history and religion departments.[86] As the era of the 1960s continued, the new school appeared to be outgrowing the accommodations which had seemed so adequate. By September of 1961, there was a student enrollment of 1,118 and the faculty rose to forty-one. Among the new Sisters at the high school were Sister Janice Piesko, sociology and religion; and Emily Lesniak, a postulant who taught religion. Sister M. Celestine Kobos was assigned to the food service department.[87]

A record enrollment was noted in 1962 when 340 freshmen were accepted and the entire student body numbered 1,165 with forty-four teachers. New to the faculty that year were Sister M. Concordia Lawrence, history; Sister M. Jude Kruszewski, English; and Sister M. Edward Nowak, who served as mistress of postulants and aspirants.[88]

Earlier in March of that year, Mother M. Beatrice Rybacki, who had succeeded Mother M. Jerome Dadej as superior general, presented to her councilors the matter of building a much-needed addition to Madonna High School. Twelve classrooms and a science laboratory were to be constructed at a cost of $340,000. The Archdiocese of Chicago promised the congregation $100,000 to aid in the building. Because the congregation was still in debt in the sum of $600,000, however, Mother M. Beatrice and the general council dismissed the plan as unfeasible at that time.[89]

With a growing school enrollment, several members were added to the faculty in 1963. They were Sister Marie Francis Moson, English and debate; Miss Wanda Baron, counselor, who had been an education consultant for Scott, Foresman, and Company for thirty-four years and had taught at De Paul University; and Sister M. Laetitia Kolczak who came to assist Sister M. Albertine in the food service department.[90]

When the 1964 school year began, there were several new additions to the staff: Sister Anne Marie Knawa, English; Sister Angela Marie Benedyk, mathematics; Sister Kathleen Melia, English, Latin, and journalism;[91] and Mrs. Barbara Davidson, English. As Madonna's longest-employed lay teacher, Mrs. Davidson is entering into her twenty-third year of service.

As the history of Madonna High School has thus far revealed, early in 1945, Mother M. Jerome Dadej had proposed to her councilors the creation of an academy or high school which might serve as a potential mainspring of vocations to the Franciscan Sisters of Chicago. From Madonna High School's foundation in 1949, it had indeed been the avenue through which the congregation was enriched with innumerable candidates to the religious life. There were substantial numbers of aspirants and postulants to the congregation from the high school in the 1950s and the early 1960s. In 1961 alone, for example, thirty young women entered the congregation.[92] In September of 1964, Sister M. Rosemary Ferus[93] was assigned to Madonna High School to head the guidance and counseling department. Additionally, she was appointed to continue the successful aspirancy and postulancy program begun so promisingly in 1949. By 1967, however, in the light of the changing religious, societal, and school climate, the aspirancy of the Franciscan Sisters of Chicago as it had existed for eighteen years was phased out. An additional consequence of this extraordinary period of change resulted in only two new religious faculty members, namely, Sister Joseph Marie Zenda, the assistant principal and teacher of religion; and Sister Timothy Marie Cieniewa, teacher of biology.[94] From this period on, there was an increased dependency on the laity to share in Madonna High School's educational ministry.

At the Eleventh General Chapter of Elections held in 1970, Sister M. Hugoline, the principal of Madonna High School, was chosen the eighth superior general of the Franciscan Sisters of Chicago. Although the Sisters, lay faculty, and students at the high school were truly sorry to see her leave, they were overjoyed at the honor which had come to her, and they shared her enthusiasm regarding her new role in the congregation. When Sister M. Hugoline had taken charge of the school in 1956, there were 395 students and twenty teachers in the Madonna High School community. At her departure fourteen years later, the school roster listed 1,120 students and forty-five faculty members.

In any assessment of Sister M. Hugoline as principal, there is no doubt whatsoever that she exerted a real and lasting influence on the school during the fourteen years of her tenure of office. It was a time of phenomenal growth, improvement, and prestige for Madonna High School resulting in its well-deserved reputation as one of the finest high schools on Chicago's Northwest Side. Besides being active in professional organizations and holding offices in the Archdiocesan High School Principals' Association, Sister M. Hugoline, in her day-to-day administration of the school, had a unique capacity for creating a genuine "esprit de corps" among the faculty and students. Combined with her good-natured disposition, this made her extremely effective as an administrator. A woman of broad intellect and keen vision, Sister M. Hugoline gained a notable record of achievement. She provided the school with a language laboratory and three resource centers, encouraged advanced work in the art department and solidly equipped it. Classes in advanced biology were opened, a special science research laboratory was built, and participation in the Illinois Junior Academy of Science Fairs was initiated and encouraged. The business department was expanded, and audiovisual material for all departments was purchased or updated. A journalism workroom was opened, a program of electives was added to the curriculum, and active participation in interscholastic symposiums, forums, and discussions was inaugurated. Summer school classes were conducted for students in need of remedial instruction. For the faculty, whose success she always encouraged, she advised postgraduate studies and she herself participated in various enrichment programs.

At her departure in 1970, Sister M. Hugoline was succeeded as principal by her assistant, Sister Joseph Marie Zenda. Throughout her thirteen-year tenure as principal, the varied orientations and competencies needed by a principal were expertly met by Sister Joseph Marie's vivacity and adept organizational skills. She was instrumental in providing guidance in existing programs and was quick to initiate and experiment with new ones. Circumspect, industrious, and prudent, Sister Joseph Marie introduced the following during her administration: modular scheduling; experimentation with large and small group instruction patterns and independent study; open laboratories in the science, art, and clothing departments; development of an eight-week orientation program for freshmen; adoption of data processing for student records and schedules; senior electives to improve the curriculum; electives in physical education; development of career education programs; adoption of the activity schedule to increase participation in school clubs; experimentation with the use of learning packets and behavioral objectives; mini-courses in a variety of interests for varied abilities; and Academic Olympics in areas of English, general knowledge, math, science, and social science for competing eighth graders.

Sister Joseph Marie encouraged involvement in the areas of the arts, speech, and in athletics by fostering membership in the Illinois High School Association (IHSA) which encourages competition between schools in both the private and public sectors. Greater opportunities were made available to high ability students with the introduction of the College Acceleration Program (CAP), Advanced Placement Courses, and the expansion of in-school curriculum programs. In April of 1981, she reintroduced the tradition of the annual spring musical production in conjunction with Gordon Technical High School.

Mindful of Madonna's responsibility to its religious mission, Sister Joseph Marie added a full-time chaplain, the Reverend Norbert Sharon, CMF, to the staff. Although there was an oratory where students might pray, the obvious need for a larger chapel became apparent. In 1979, the faculty room located on the first floor next to the main office was redesigned to serve as a chapel. On November 1, the feast of All Saints, the Mater Christi Chapel was dedicated by the Reverend Robert G. Darow, associate pastor of St. Cornelius Church. In 1982, the Office of Campus Minister was established to provide for a more vibrant spiritual and liturgical life for the students. The student retreat program was vastly improved and a sacramental program was introduced.

In addressing needs for students' services and long-range plans to ensure the future of Madonna High School, Sister Joseph Marie established an Office of School Development in 1982 with Ms. Mary Hafner of the school's athletic department a director. The purpose of the Office of Development was to promote an understanding of, participation in, and support for the high school. A newsletter called *Clarion 2* was begun to inform parents, friends, and alumnae of Madonna High School of how the "mission of Madonna" was progressing.[95] Sister Joseph Marie also provided for the reorganization and revival of the Alumnae Association.[96]

Many other major accomplishments and undertakings took place at Madonna High School during Sister Joseph Marie's years as chief administrator. She implemented changes in the curriculum which stressed an academic tradition and preparation for a new technological society. Because of the support of the students who participated in a walk-a-thon and the generosity of the Parents' Club, a student computer laboratory was installed. Equipped with sixteen Apple II microcomputers and disk drives, two printers, and the necessary software, the laboratory became operational at the beginning of the 1982 school year. Approximately one hundred juniors and seniors were enrolled in a first-year course in Computer Literacy and Computer Programming I under the direction of Sister M. Helene Galuszka. The computer lab was officially dedicated at a ceremony and reception held on September 16, 1982. The Reverend Norbert Sharon, the school chaplain, performed the blessing. Madonna High School's three former principals, namely, Sister M. Crescencia Chmiel, Sister M. Alberta Bialas, and Sister M. Hugoline Czaplinski were present. Also present to witness the dedication were the 30th District State Representative, the Honorable Ted Lechowicz; City Alderman George Hagopian; and a number of other community leaders.

Because of continuing patterns of high enrollment in the 1970s, the sophomores, juniors, and seniors attended classes in the new Madonna High School on Belmont and Karlov Avenues while the freshmen continued to occupy the old Ephpheta School affectionately referred to as the "Old Building" or the "Freshman Building." By 1972, however, it became increasingly obvious that the spiraling expense of operating and maintaining the "Old Building" was becoming cost prohibitive. The proud "Old Building" was razed in 1973 at which time the property from Belmont Avenue to Barry Avenue was sold to the Jewel Food Company who developed the land into a food service store and a

Madonna High School Convent
Chicago, Illinois

parking lot. Since the Sisters had maintained their residence on the entire third and a large part of the second floors of the dismantled building, an innovative, three-story religious faculty residence[97] was constructed on Karlov Avenue in 1973 with the funds which had come from the sale of the Pulaski Road property.[98] The freshmen classes, on the other hand, were accommodated in eight attractive ultramodern mobile units on the south side of the school.[99]

On November 5, 1972, the ground-breaking ceremony for the religious faculty house had taken place. The Reverend Dennis Sanders, CR, the assistant principal of Weber High School, officiated. Preceding the ground-breaking was a nine-thirty o'clock Liturgy of the Eucharist in the Little Theater for the Sisters and their guests at which the Reverend Edwin Karlowicz, CR, the superior of Weber High School religious faculty house, was the celebrant. A breakfast in the school cafeteria for friends, benefactors, and the construction personnel took place after the Liturgy.

In 1975, Madonna High School marked twenty-five years of ministry to the young women of the Archdiocese of Chicago. On April 27, a Liturgy of Praise and Thanksgiving was celebrated at St. Stanislaus Bishop and Martyr Church in the Cragin area. John Cardinal Cody, archbishop of Chicago, presided and delivered the homily at the Eucharistic Celebration at which the Most Reverend Alfred L. Abramowicz, auxiliary bishop of Chicago, was the celebrant. Immediately following the Liturgy of the Eucharist, an open house was held at the high school, thus giving students, teachers, friends, parents, and benefactors an opportunity to socialize and reminisce.

The culminating event of Madonna's Jubilee Year took place on June 15, 1975, when the Silver Anniversary Benefit Dinner was held in the beautiful Grand Ballroom of the Martinique Restaurant in Evergreen Park on Chicago's Far South Side.

During Sister Joseph Marie's administration, many of Madonna High School's facilities received major attention. In 1972, she authorized the organization of the Instructional Materials Center which is the center for all audiovisual materials and equipment as well as overnight circulating editions in a section of the large former senior lounge. In 1980, a new language laboratory was created in another section of the lounge. A third portion of that space was allocated for the student computer laboratory.

The school office was completely transformed in 1983 into a more modern, attractive, colorful, and efficient complex. The renovation resulted in a larger office for the principal, a private assistant principal's office, a larger business area, an attendance room, two counseling rooms, a conference room, and an alumnae and development office. Since earlier in the year computerization for all student records, report cards, scheduling, alumnae and development records were introduced, a room for these administrative functions was also provided.

In the auditorium-gym complex, electrically operated basketball goals were suspended from the ceiling and the main stage lighting system was upgraded. An excellent exercise room was outfitted by the Universal Equipment Company and opened in 1983. Basically used by the juniors and seniors, the splendidly equipped room was also used by the faculty and by some parents.

To make maximum use of Madonna High School and to build community involvement and support, Sister Joseph Marie opened the high school facilities to numerous and various community programs.

The emphasis on updating and renewal initiated by the Second Vatican Council, and the subsequent changes in religious life which occurred during the early 1970s affected the assignment of the Sisters to the religious faculty. Some Sisters appointed to the staff of Madonna High School during this period[100] chose to become involved in aspects of the ministerial life of the Church other than teaching and so requested transfers. In some instances, a few members on the staff chose to leave the Congregation of the Franciscan Sisters of Chicago. Among the Sisters who were assigned to Madonna High School in the 1970s, however, and who ministered or continue to minister today to youth on the secondary level are Sister M. Consolata Markowicz, Sister Jeanne Marie Toriskie, Sister M. Helene Galuszka, Sister Diane Marie Collins, Sister M. Monica Sendlosky, and Sister Lora Ann Slawinski.[101]

Like her immediate predecessor, Sister M. Hugoline, who had been elected superior general in 1970, Sister Joseph Marie was elected the superior general of the Franciscan Sisters of Chicago at the Fourteenth General Chapter held in 1983. Chosen as her successor at Madonna High School was Sister M. Alvernia Groszek, who, that year, had just completed a thirteen-year term as secretary general of the congregation. Sister M. Alvernia was no stranger to Madonna High School having served on the staff from 1951 to 1970 before her election to the congregation's administration.

Sister M. Alvernia entered the Congregation of the Franciscan Sisters of Chicago from St. Pancratius Church on June 27, 1935. She was received into the novitiate on August 15, 1937. On August 15, 1939, she made her first profession of vows and was perpetually professed on August 2, 1944.

She began her teaching career in 1938 at St. Hedwig's School in Gary, Indiana, and obtained her bachelor's degree from St. John College in Cleveland. After three years at St. Casimir School in that city, she was sent to Five Holy Martyrs School in Chicago where she remained for five years and distinguished herself as an excellent primary grade teacher. During this period, she received her master's degree from De Paul University in Chicago.[102]

In 1951, Sister M. Alvernia was sent to Madonna High School to teach biology and to head the science department. She achieved notable success in her nineteen years of dedicated service as has been outlined earlier in this chapter. In 1970, she left Madonna High School to assume her duties as the secretary general of the congregation.[103]

As Madonna High School's fifth principal, Sister M. Alvernia strove to support the excellent academic standards maintained so forcibly by Sister Joseph Marie who described her successor as "enthusiastic, intelligent, and personable."[104] Aware of the new orientations and competencies required by principals today, Sister M. Alvernia explored new ways toward instructional improvement and the updating of courses. While supporting the idea of strong academic basics in all the areas of instruction, new courses such as the following were introduced during her tenure as principal: Applied Economics, Computer Literacy, Advanced Nutrition, Child Care, Photography, advanced electives in Art, Honors Calculus and College Algebra, Symphonic and Intermediate Band, and World Affairs. She strove zealously to continue the pattern of firm leadership established by the past principals. At the Fourteenth General Chapter of Elections held in 1983, however, Sister M. Alvernia was elected to the new general administration of the congregation. Her numerous and expanded duties as second councilor conflicted with her duties as principal. The added fact that she was also experiencing increasing health problems caused her to submit her resignation as principal of Madonna High School in 1986. During the three-year administration of Sister M. Alvernia, only one religious was added to the faculty. Sister M. Julitta Szczepanik joined the department of English in 1986.[105]

With the departure of Sister M. Alvernia, the position of principal was assumed by Sister Carol Marie Schommer, herself a graduate of the class of 1961 of Madonna High School. Madonna's sixth principal entered the congregation from Our Lady of Grace Church in Chicago in January of 1961. She was accepted into the novitiate on August 11 of that year and made her first profession of vows on August 12, 1963. Her perpetual vows were taken on August 12, 1968.

For six years, Sister Carol Marie taught on the elementary school level in the congregation's schools. In 1970, she was appointed to teach science, physics, and algebra at Madonna. In 1974, she added chemistry to her expert range of subjects. Appointed director of curriculum and scheduler/programmer in 1985, she also became the assistant principal. She received a bachelor's degree in chemistry from the Illinois Institute of Technology and her master's degree in administration from Loyola University of Chicago.[106]

Early displaying organizational and management expertise, Sister Carol Marie served as the state president of the Illinois Junior Academy of Science from 1980 to 1982; treasurer of the Chicago Non-Public Schools Science Exposition from 1973 to 1979; and state judging chairperson for the Illinois Junior Academy of Science for five years. She has also served on four North Central Visiting Committees. Her numerous activities also include participation in various civic and neighborhood associations.[107]

Sister Carol Marie has been described as having a friendly, understanding, yet professional approach to her duties as principal. Concerned about the religious and educational welfare of the Madonna High School community, the enthusiastic, intellectual, and progressive Sister Carol Marie maintains a sense of purpose that promises to help the Madonna High School community grow in the spirit of Christian unity and educational endeavor during the years of her administration.[108]

Madonna High School has always provided and continues to provide an academically challenging curriculum with course selections in fine arts, business education, communication arts, foreign languages, home economics, mathematics, music, physical education, religion, science, and social studies. Guidance and counseling are an essential part of the program. Madonna High School offers a comprehensive curriculum geared to meet the varied demands of the times: a College Preparatory Program, which concentrates on college requirements and lays the foundation that will prepare for success in college; a Business Program, which prepares the more able student for solid business positions while providing minimum essentials for college entrance; a General Preparatory Program, which affords a general education with an area of specialization and grants a standard high school diploma. The students have more than one hundred courses to choose from to earn their minimum of twenty credits for graduation.

Madonna High School presents its students with splendid opportunities for involvement in numerous clubs as a means of enjoyment and service to their school. Throughout the years, these activities have included Active Artists, Aquatics, Band (Beginning, Intermediate, Jazz, Marching, and Symphonic), Badminton, Bits and Bytes Club, Business Honor Society, Candy Stripers, Challenge Club, Chess Club, CALM (Chicago Area Lay Movement), Chicago Interracial Club, Chorus (Beginning, Treble, Concert, and Choraleers), CISCA (Chicago Inter-Student Catholic Action), *Clarion* newspaper, Camera Club, Debate and Forensics, Drama Club, French Club, French Honor Society, Future Business Women, Future Nurses Club, Girls Athletic Association, Glee

Club, Guitar Club, Historically Speaking Club, Home Economics Club, Human Relations Club, Journalism Honor Society, Library Aides, Liturgy Planning Committee, Madonna's Lifesavers, *Madonnary*, Math Club, Mathematics Honor Society (Mu Alpha Theta), Mission Club, National Business Honor Society, National Honor Society, Piano, Political Science Club, Photography, Polish Arts Club, Polish Honor Society, Pom-Pon Squad, Pro-Life Club, Psychology Club, Quill and Scroll Society, Red Cross Society, Science Club, SDS (Supply the Demand for the Supply), Spanish Club, Spanish Honor Society, Stage Crew, Student Government, Table Tennis, Thespian Society, Tutoring, Video Crew, Vocation Awareness Club, and Volunteers for Human Services.

From its beginning, the school has provided extensive opportunities for the development of the students' religious interests in the form of the Sodality of the Blessed Virgin Mary, the Third Order of St. Francis, the Liturgical Sign and Symbol Club, and On-Campus and Off-Campus Retreats. In addition, the school has vigorous sacramental programs offering Baptism, First Holy Communion, Confirmation, and Reconciliation. The Mater Christi Chapel is available to students and faculty for private devotions as well as for homeroom or class liturgical or paraliturgical celebrations. All the religious activities are planned and coordinated by the campus minister, chaplain, and the members of the religion department.

Extracurricular activities are vitally integrated at the high school. These activities include the following: International Festival Day, Junior Ring Mass/Dance, Music Department Christmas and Spring Concerts, Annual Spring Musical Production with Gordon Tech High School, Senior Prom, Graduation, Freshman Initiation, Gym Show, Spirit Days, Mardi Gras, Ski Trips, and Student Tours.

The co-curricular program at the school has always been designed to provide enrichment experiences outside of the classroom. Throughout the years, the yearbook, the *Madonnary*;[109] *A Gathering*, a literary magazine; the *Senior Memory Book*; and the school newspaper, the *Clarion*[110] have been activities offered at the school. Madonna High School has never lacked spirited moderators and assistant moderators for its co-curricular clubs and activities because of its talented, generous, and genuinely concerned Sisters and lay teachers.

Nonathletic interscholastic competition takes place in the following areas: Forensics, Instrumental Music, Vocal Music, Science, Journalism, Mathematics, Social Studies, Art, and Foreign Languages. Other projects include student participation in the annual Illinois Junior Academy of Science Fair and the Metro Fair supported by the history department.

In addition, Madonnians regularly participate in community service projects such as the Red Cross Blood Drive, Right to Life, and the Muscular Dystrophy Association. The students aid various food pantries, nursing homes, hospitals, and day care centers.

Madonna High School is a member in good standing of the Illinois High School Association (IHSA) and the Girls' Catholic Athletic Conference (GCAC). Membership in these two organizations enables Madonnians to compete in interscholastic activities in the state of Illinois. Madonna participates in the following interscholastic sports: Varsity Volleyball, Junior Varsity Volleyball, Freshman Volleyball, Varsity Basketball, Junior Varsity Basketball, Freshman Basketball, Cross Country Track, Varsity and Junior Varsity Gymnastics, Track and Field, Softball, and Bowling. Activities related to athletics include the Flag Squad and Cheerleading, the Gym Show, and Pep Rallies.

For the first time in the history of the school, the 1980 census showed a decline in enrollment which could be attributed to three main factors: fewer students of high school age in the community; an urban flight to suburbia precipitated generally by changing racial and ethnic patterns, a fact readily confirmed by accumulated transfer data; and growing economic pressures placed on families and institutions. While the early records reveal the students as basically of Polish, Italian, German, Irish, and Ukrainian extraction, by 1980, approximately 30 percent of the students came from minority groups and 12 percent were not of the Catholic faith. There was an increase of black, Hispanic, Greek, and Oriental students with 13 percent of the student body coming from public schools.

In 1987, Madonna High School's enrollment was listed at 750 students with eleven Sisters and thirty-seven lay teachers on the staff. More than 50 percent of the students came from ethnic minority groups and 21 percent were not of the Catholic faith. Significantly, according to a survey taken that year, more than 50 percent of Madonna High School's graduates attended a college or university.[111]

The faculty of Madonna High School has always consisted of a competent staff of Franciscan Sisters of Chicago, Sisters of other religious congregations, and lay men and women whose Christian values and attitudes are embodied in Madonna's philosophy. The members of the faculty have studied at some of the most prestigious universities and colleges in the country and have held offices in various professional organizations. Postgraduate work is heartily encouraged, and attendance at various meetings and annual conventions is always supported by the administration. Throughout the years, priests from neighboring parishes, as well as priests belonging to religious orders, have rendered invaluable service to Madonna High School as teachers of religion, counselors, confessors, retreat masters, and celebrants of the Sacred Liturgy. Madonna High School has also enjoyed the benefits that come from a loyal and dedicated staff of office personnel and service employees.

Madonna High School is fully recognized by the Illinois Office of Education, the State Board of Education, and fully accredited by the North Central Association of Colleges and Secondary Schools. It is an institutional member of the National Catholic Educational Association and a member in good standing of the Illinois High School Association.

At Madonna High School, the threefold purpose of Catholic education is being solidly implemented. Because its goal of "message, community, and service" is vibrantly and steadfastly maintained, Madonna High School's administration, faculty, and student body are prepared to meet the challenges of the twenty-first century.

The Franciscan Sisters of Chicago remain committed to Madonna High School as they attempt, within the framework of their Franciscan philosophy of education and a society of expanding knowledge and specialization, to create a climate of love and concern for the special people of God—the young women of the archdiocese and the city of Chicago. Madonna High School has proudly graduated thousands of students since 1949 who have happily sung and truthfully acknowledged: "Mary, Madonna, you rule, Queen of our hearts and our school."[112]

MADONNA HIGH SCHOOL

[1] *Minutes of General Council Proceedings,* January 1945 (AFSCL).

[2] Born in Nashville, Tennessee, on August 17, 1887, Samuel Alphonsus Stritch studied at St. Gregory's, Cincinnati, and the North American College in Rome. He was ordained in Rome in 1910 and served in parishes in the Nashville diocese from 1909 to 1916. He served as chancellor of the diocese from 1911 to 1921, and as diocesan superintendent of schools from 1915. In 1921, he was consecrated bishop of Toledo; in 1930, he was named archbishop of Milwaukee.

Archbishop Stritch was installed as the fourth archbishop of Chicago on March 7, 1940. One of his first interests was the building of a strong and vigorous Catholic press; through his efforts, the circulation of *The New World* (now *The Chicago Catholic*), grew tremendously. He established the Confraternity of Christian Doctrine to meet the needs of Catholic children enrolled in public schools. He developed Catholic Charities and the Catholic Youth Organization. In 1940, he reorganized the Holy Name Society. He was instrumental in the formation of the Cana Conference, the Christian Family Movement, the Catholic Interracial Conference, the Young Christian Students, and Adult Education. Archbishop Stritch attacked materialism, worked for higher motion-picture standards, better social conditions for the blacks and Latins in urban centers, and better labor conditions. Deeply interested in liturgical music, he banned familiar popular songs for weddings and funerals.

In 1946, Archbishop Stritch was created a cardinal, thereby becoming the second cardinal of the Archdiocese of Chicago. During his tenure, he founded seventy new parishes in the city of Chicago and its suburbs.

On March 1, 1958, Cardinal Stritch was given charge of the mission of the Church as pro-prefect of the Sacred Congregation for the Propagation of the Faith, the first prelate born in the United States to be named to the Roman Curia. Shortly after his arrival in Rome, he suffered an occlusion of the main artery of the right arm which necessitated the amputation of the arm slightly above the elbow. He died on May 27, several days after suffering a severe stroke which paralyzed him. Reverend Monsignor Harry C. Koenig, ed., *A History of the Archdiocese of Chicago: Published in Observance of the Centenary of the Archdiocese, 1980.* 2 vols. (Chicago: Archdiocese of Chicago, 1980); Reverend Joseph Thompson, ed., *Diamond Jubilee of the Archdiocese of Chicago, 1920* (Des Plaines, Illinois: St. Mary Training School Press, 1920); Reverend Menceslaus J. Madaj, *The New World,* 13 September 1974, pp. 39–51.

[3] *Minutes of General Council Proceedings,* 18 August 1946 (AFSCL).

[4] The Society of the Daughters of the Heart of Mary commenced their work for the deaf in Chicago in 1884. In 1897, a four-acre site was purchased at the junction of Belmont Avenue and Crawford (presently called Pulaski Road) on which was erected the Ephpheta School for the Deaf. The school was formally opened in 1909.

The society was founded in 1790 by a young French noblewoman, Marie-Adelaide de Cice, and a Jesuit priest, the Reverend Pierre-Joseph de Cloriviere, with the purpose of saving religious life when its existence was threatened by the dissolution of religious orders in France during the French Revolution. The members of the society have never worn any distinguishing habit or uniform which could identify them as religious. While all the Sisters are involved in works of charity, some members live in their own homes while others live in community. The society has always moved freely among the people they serve according to the needs of the times under the approbation of the ordinary of the diocese.

The Society of the Daughters of the Heart of Mary are associated with the Franciscan Sisters of Chicago through the Ephpheta School for the Deaf in Chicago and Madonna Hall and St. Joseph Home for the Aged in Cleveland. *Careers with Christ,* April–May 1973.

[5] *Minutes of General Council Proceedings,* July 1947 (AFSCL).

[6] *Minutes of General Council Proceedings,* July 1937 (AFSCL).

[7]*Book of Correspondence:* Letter from Mother M. Jerome Dadej to Samuel Cardinal Stritch, 17 July 1947 (AFSCL).

[8]*Book of Contracts:* Resolution to purchase land from the Ladies of the Ephpheta School, 10 May 1948 (AFSCL).

[9]*Book of Correspondence:* Letter from Mother M. Jerome Dadej to the congregation, 22 March 1949 (AFSCL).

[10]The four aspirants were Irene Picklo from St. Casimir Church, Johnstown, Pennsylvania; Theresa Golaszewski from Five Holy Martyrs Church, Chicago, Illinois; Marianne Waksmundzka from Gobles, Michigan; and Frances Lelek from St. Hedwig Church, Gary, Indiana. After a few days in the aspirancy Frances Lelek chose to return home and was eventually followed by Marianne Waksmundzka. Today, none of the original aspirants remains. *Congregation Membership Records* (AFSCL).

[11]Ibid.

[12]See Chapter 21.

[13]Sister M. Helen, born in Poland, entered the congregation in 1905 from St. John Cantius Church in Chicago. After her profession, she served as a teacher in the congregation's elementary schools for fifteen years. For six years she served as a superior only at St. Stanislaus Bishop and Martyr School in Chicago. She was the supervisor of the Church Vestment Workshop for three years and worked there for more than thirty years. At her death on May 31, 1963, she was in the eightieth year of her life and in the fifty-eighth year of her service in the congregation. *Spis Sióstr;* and *Congregation Membership Records* (AFSCL).

[14]Both Sisters maintained their residence at Five Holy Martyrs Convent on the Southwest Side of the city and commuted to Madonna High School. Later, both Sisters were permanently assigned to Madonna and made their residency there. Secretaries General, *Community Chronicle,* p. 274 (AFSCL).

[15]See Chapter 38.

[16]Sister M. Therese, the former Helen Grajek, entered the convent from Sacred Heart Church in Cleveland in June of 1929. She began her novitiate on June 23, 1930, and made her first profession of vows on August 15, 1932. On August 15, 1935, she pronounced her perpetual profession. Sister M. Therese received her bachelor's degree from De Paul University. She taught at Five Holy Martyrs School in Chicago for thirteen years and at St. Peter Claver School in Mobile, Alabama, for six years. In 1949, she began her long association with Madonna High School where she taught for twenty-six years in the departments of history, religion, and English. From 1949 to 1953, she served as directress of aspirants. Sister M. Therese was a model of spiritual fervor and superb dedication to ministry. A more loving and spiritually oriented woman would have been difficult to find. Sister M. Therese left Madonna in 1975 to join the pastoral ministry team at St. Anthony Medical Center in Crown Point, Indiana. *Congregation Membership Records* (AFSCL).

[17]While the currency exchange and hardware store were means of extra revenue, in time their upkeep became an additional drain on Madonna's finances.

[18]*Minutes of General Council Proceedings, 1950* (AFSCL).

[19]Secretaries General, *Community Chronicle,* p. 285 (AFSCL).

[20]*Book of Correspondence:* Letter from Mother M. Jerome Dadej to Samuel Cardinal Stritch, 12 June 1950 (AFSCL).

[21]Sister M. Tarcisia entered the congregation from Five Holy Martyrs Church in 1929. After several years as an elementary school teacher, she attended the University of Illinois College of Pharmacy where she received her bachelor's degree. In later years, she did postgraduate work at Cornell and De Paul Universities. Her theological training was received at St. Francis College, Joliet, Illinois.

From 1950 to 1967 Sister M. Tarcisia taught chemistry and general science at Madonna and was also moderator of the extremely active Sodality of the Blessed Virgin Mary, the Third Order of St. Francis, and the Science Club.

Prior to and after her departure from Madonna High School, Sister M. Tarcisia has had a notable history in religious, professional, and educational work. In the health and geriatrics field, she worked as a pharmacist, consultant, and instructor in pharmacology and social service. Several years were spent in ministry at St. Joseph Home in Chicago as chief pharmacist. She also ministered at St. John Medical Center and St. Anthony Hospital in South Dakota; Our Lady of the Sandhills in Nebraska; and St. Anthony Medical Center in Crown Point, Indiana. She was active and held offices in numerous organizations. Founder and first president of the Midwest Association of Sister Pharmacists, she was also active in the Chicago Council for the Aged and the Catholic Charities Care of the Aged Council. She co-chaired the first Catholic Conference on the Aged in the United States at St. Joseph Home of Chicago. She has written articles and served as guest lecturer in addition to participating on many levels in interfaith seminars and conventions.

Her religious interests have inspired her to direct youth groups and to instruct the moderators of these groups. As a consequence, she has received the Peace Award for leaders of the Third Order of St. Francis, the Sodality Marian Award, and the Bishop Sheen Award for Missions. She has lectured on drug abuse to youth groups in the West and the Midwest and encouraged the importance of spiritual values in the lives of young people. From 1954 to 1968, she served as the congregation's vocation director and held offices in various vocation associations. In 1980, she asked to enter the congregation's St. Francis House of Prayer. She remained there until 1983 at which time she was appointed pharmacist and pastoral minister in the Motherhouse infirmary. *Congregation Membership Records* (AFSCL).

[22]Sister M. Lucretia, a native of Conemaugh, Pennsylvania, was an elementary school teacher for five years before graduating from Alverno College of Music in Milwaukee. She also attended many sessions at the University of Detroit and Creighton University in Omaha. For two years, she served as an organist at St. Stanislaus Bishop and Martyr Church in Chicago. In 1937, serious illness overtook her, and she returned to the Motherhouse where, while recuperating, she served as the organist and director of the community choir. In 1950, she was assigned to Madonna High School where she taught music, chorus, and was in charge of the Glee Club. She also directed scores of concerts and musical programs and was in charge of the chorus for the many musicals presented by Sister M. Dorothy Szostek and the drama department. She remained at Madonna for twenty-six years until she left in 1976 to become the organist at St. Joseph Home of Chicago. Sister M. Lucretia continued as community organist and director of the Franciscan Sisters of Chicago Choir until 1964. Her dedication to and love of music was apparent to everyone. In addition, she was also an expert philatelist. *Congregation Membership Records* (AFSCL).

[23]See Chapter 42.

[24]A native of Cleveland, Ohio, Sister Eleanor Marie, the former Sister M. Ignatius, was a teacher in the congregation's elementary schools for eleven years. A graduate of De Paul, she also attended Mundelein College and St. Louis University from which she obtained her master's degree. After thirty-two years of dedicated service, she left the high school in 1982 to pursue a degree in administration after which she assumed the position of assistant administrator of St. Joseph Home of Chicago. *Congregation Membership Records* (AFSCL).

[25]*Minutes of General Council Proceedings,* 27 November 1950 (AFSCL).

[26]Secretaries General, *Community Chronicle,* 19 January 1951 (AFSCL).

[27]*Book of Correspondence:* Letter from Mother M. Jerome Dadej to Samuel Cardinal Stritch, 19 February 1951 (AFSCL).

[28]The four postulants were Marie Frances Niecikowski and Therese Golaszewski from Five Holy Martyrs School, Chicago; Irene Picklo of St. Casimir School, Johnstown, Pennsylvania; and Elizabeth Watroba of Assumption Blessed Virgin Mary Church, Conemaugh, Pennsylvania. *Congregation Membership Records* (AFSCL).

[29]*Minutes of General Council Proceedings,* 12 February 1951 (AFSCL).

[30]*Book of Correspondence:* Letter from Samuel Cardinal Stritch to Mother M. Jerome Dadej, 12 June 1951 (AFSCL).

[31]The Clerics of St. Viator, popularly known as Viatorians, staff the nearby St. Viator's Church at 4170 W. Addison Street.

[32]Sister M. Hilary served as a teacher, superior, and principal at several elementary schools. She also served as superior and administrator at the congregation's nursing homes in Cleveland for ten years before her assignment to Madonna. Sister M. Hilary, who was the sister of Mother M. Jerome Dadej and Sister M. Celine Dadej, died in May 1967. *Congregation Membership Records* (AFSCL).

[33]*Madonna High School House Journal;* and Secretaries General, *Community Chronicle, 1894–1957* (AFSCL).

[34]Sister M. Maxencia was the first professionally degreed librarian in the congregation. She received her master of arts degree in library science from Rosary College in River Forest, Illinois. Besides serving on the faculty of Madonna High School for thirteen years, she pioneered the establishment of libraries in many of the elementary schools in the congregation. In addition, she organized a tape and record library at the Motherhouse in Lemont. A native of Chicago, Sister M. Maxencia entered the congregation in 1932 from St. Pancratius Church. She died on July 23, 1977. *Congregation Membership Records* (AFSCL).

[35]From the very beginning of her teaching apostolate, Sister M. Alvernia was characterized as a leader. Early in her teaching experience, she served as the president of the First Grade Association of the Archdiocese of Chicago. When she was assigned to Madonna in 1951, she served as moderator of various school organizations. She was always closely connected with the Catholic Youth Organization, and for many years, she was instrumental in promoting CISCA (Chicago Inter-Student Catholic Action). She served very ably as the dynamic and efficient moderator of the Madonna High School Mothers' Club for seventeen years.

From the time of her assignment to the high school, Sister M. Alvernia was extremely eager for Madonna's success and worked indefatigably to achieve it. In truth, most of the early credit for the outstanding work done in the field of science can be attributed to her. In 1954, she initiated the science fairs at Madonna High School to encourage a higher level of scientific literacy and student involvement. As a result, she served as coordinator, corresponding secretary, treasurer, chairperson, special awards and scholarship chairperson of the Illinois Junior Academy of Science from 1960 to 1967. From 1968 to 1970, she served as president of the academy with zeal and dedication. Through her inspiration and efforts, the Illinois Junior Academy of Science grew intellectually and geographically making it the largest of its kind in the United States. The Illinois Junior Academy has referred to her as "outstanding in any area to which she was assigned; she is most dedicated to the academy and worthy of the position [as president]." In gratitude to Sister M. Alvernia, the 1985 Illinois Junior Academy of Science Yearbook was dedicated to her. One of the biggest tributes to her expertise and zeal in the area of science has been her numerous grants from the National Science Foundation which allowed her to engage in postgraduate studies at summer institutes which have included, among others, the University of California at Berkeley; the University of Montana; Stephen College, Columbia, Missouri; Loyola University of Chicago; Illinois Institute of Technology; St. Mary's College, Winona, Minnesota; and the University of Colorado, Boulder, Colorado.

Sister M. Alvernia has held numerous memberships in professional organizations on the national, state, and local levels. She has participated in many professional and educational organizations as a guest lecturer, workshop sponsor, and panel member. *Congregation Membership Records;* and *Book of Correspondence:* Letter from Donald G. Hopkins to Sister M. Hugoline Czaplinski, principal of Madonna High School (AFSCL).

[36]Sister M. Kingnetta entered from Five Holy Martyrs Parish in Chicago. She taught in the congregation's elementary schools for twelve years during which time she graduated from De Paul

University. When she was assigned to Madonna, she continued her studies at The Catholic University of America in Washington, DC. Because of her wide experience, she served as president of the Greater Midwest Catholic Business Education Association from 1977 to 1978. In 1981, she was awarded the Enos C. Perry Service Award for outstanding service in the field of business education. In 1985, she became director of the Alumnae Association. To date, Sister M. Kingnetta has rendered thirty-six years of service to the high school. Her brother, "Father Wally," served as chaplain of the Madonna High School Mothers' Club for twenty-nine years. *Congregation Membership Records* (AFSCL).

[37]Sister M. Josephine retired to the Motherhouse after a year. Sister M. Rose Ann left after eight years to serve at the Guardian Angel Day Care Center and Home for Ladies. Sister M. Sebastianna, who left in 1954, died in 1978. Sister M. Francis departed in 1953 and died in 1977 after a long and painful illness. After two years, Sister M. Virginia left to serve in the apostolate to the aging and died in 1969. Ibid.

[38]Sister M. Alberta will be discussed later in the chapter.

[39]Sister Clarent Marie, born in Johnstown, Pennsylvania, entered the congregation in 1925 from St. Casimir Parish. She taught in the elementary schools of the congregation during which time she received her bachelor's degree from De Paul University in Chicago and her master's degree from St. John College of Cleveland. In 1952, she was assigned to Madonna High School where she taught religion, Latin, U.S. history, and debate. In 1957, she was transferred to Johnstown Central Catholic High School in Johnstown, Pennsylvania, where she remained until 1960. That year she was sent to St. Stanislaus Kostka School in Youngstown, Ohio, were she taught Polish and math. After serving as the principal of St. Stanislaus Bishop and Martyr School in Chicago for a year, Sister Clarent Marie was assigned to Five Holy Martyrs School in Chicago in 1970 were she taught Polish and math to the junior high school students for nine years. From 1979, she devoted her service to Adult Education at Richard Daley College where she remained on the staff until her retirement to the Motherhouse in 1988. *Congregation Membership Records* (AFSCL). See Chapter 20.

[40]A native of Cleveland, Sister M. Dolorosa entered from St. Stanislaus Bishop and Martyr Church in that city. She joined the congregation in 1918 and spent thirty years as an elementary school teacher after obtaining her degree from De Paul University. She served as superior and teacher of French at Madonna High School from 1954 to 1957 and as teacher only until 1966. At that time, she was assigned to St. Anthony Home in Crown Point, Indiana. She died in September of 1970. *Congregation Membership Records* (AFSCL).

[41]A native of Gary, Indiana, Sister M. Dorothy entered from St. Hedwig's Parish. She taught in the elementary schools of the congregation for twenty-one years and during that time she graduated from De Paul University and the University of Notre Dame with a master's degree.

From 1952 to 1976, the Drama Department at Madonna High School was under her very capable direction. She had studied drama at Quincy College in Illinois and The Catholic University of America. She participated in various Directors' Workshops and numerous Theater Conferences in addition to maintaining membership in professional theatrical organizations. Her musical productions were especially memorable because of their expert direction, exotic costuming, authentic sets, talented casting, and all-around professionalism. Among her outstanding productions were *Camelot, Song of Norway, The King and I*, and *My Fair Lady*. Especially unforgettable was the presentation of an original musical based on the "Chronicle of Mother M. Theresa" entitled *Somebody, Somewhere*, and presented in 1969 during the congregation's seventy-fifth Jubilee Year. After twenty-five years of dedicated service at Madonna, Sister M. Dorothy transferred to St. Anthony Medical Center in Crown Point in 1977. Ibid.

[42]Sister M. John remained for only one year after which she returned to the Motherhouse. She died there on December 11, 1955. Ibid.

[43]This evaluation of secondary schools as developed by the National Study of Secondary School Evaluation is based partly on the extent to which the needs of pupils enrolled in the school are being met. It is a self-evaluation carried out by the school staff to interpret the function of the

school to the parents, community, and alumni. The complete evaluation requires the services of a visiting committee whose ability and experience prove beneficial to Madonna High School in its sincere effort at a comprehensive view of the work of the school.

[44]Secretaries General, *Community Chronicle,* p. 294 (AFSCL).

[45]*Book of Correspondence:* Letter from Mother M. Jerome Dadej to Samuel Cardinal Stritch, April 1953 (AFSCL).

[46]Among the recipients was the postulant, Theresa Labus, who, as Sister M. Francine, has served the congregation as novice directress, superior, principal, teacher, and secretary general. Four novices received their diplomas in the novitiate: Sister Marie Frances Niecikowski, Sister M. Paulette Picklo, Sister Peter Marie Watroba, and Sister M. Seraphine Golaszewski.

[47]*Madonna High School House Journal* (AFSCL).

[48]*Congregation Membership Records* (AFSCL).

[49]*Interviews* with Sisters, September 1983 (AFSCL).

[50]Sister M. Sponsa entered from St. Pancratius Church in Chicago. After serving as an elementary school teacher for seventeen years, she came to Madonna where she taught Polish and religion in addition to art. From 1959, she taught art exclusively and continued for the next twenty-one years. She received her undergraduate degree at De Paul University and her master's degree in art from the University of Notre Dame. She also studied at the Cleveland Art Institute and Western Reserve University in Ohio. Besides being instrumental in compiling numerous dedication books for many of the congregation's institutions, she designed the community ring and the community logo. She has served as a judge in many art contests and as a member of evaluation teams at various schools. Ill health forced her to semi-retirement in 1980 with residence at the high school bringing her presence in the Madonna community to thirty-three years. *Congregation Membership Records* (AFSCL).

[51]A native of Youngstown, Ohio, Sister M. Marinella came to the congregation from St. Stanislaus Kostka Church. She taught for twenty-two years in the elementary schools of the congregation. She was a graduate of De Paul University from which she received both her graduate and undergraduate degrees. At Madonna High School, she taught various subjects among them algebra, United States history, religion, and English which she taught exclusively from 1956. Her extracurricular activities were numerous and efficiently coordinated. Her last contribution at Madonna High School was the revival of the Alumnae Association. In 1985, Sister M. Marinella chose to enter the pastoral care ministry at Mount Alverna Home in Parma, Ohio. She had served at Madonna for thirty-two years. Ibid.

[52]Perhaps one of the friendliest and gentlest women in the congregation was selected directress of postulants in 1953. Sister M. Maristella was born Rose Skrzynski in Youngstown, Ohio. She entered the congregation in 1931 from St. Stanislaus Kostka Church in that city. Received into the novitiate on January 6, 1932, she made her first profession on January 8, 1934, and her final profession on August 16, 1938. Sister M. Maristella received her bachelor's degree in education from De Paul University. She took postgraduate courses at St. John College of Cleveland and Loyola University of Chicago. She taught in the schools of the congregation for nineteen years before being transferred to Madonna High School. Earnest and enthusiastic as a teacher and directress, Sister M. Maristella had oneness of vision—to introduce young women to the joy of Jesus and community life. Her gravity of manner was always outshone by her kindness and good nature. In 1962, Sister M. Maristella was transferred to St. Stanislaus Bishop and Martyr School in Youngstown. Later as both superior and principal, she rendered service at SS. Philip and James School in Cleveland. After a few years at Sacred Heart of Jesus School in Cleveland, she was sent to St. Florian's School in Chicago in 1973. *Congregation Membership Records* (AFSCL); and *Interviews* with Sisters, September 1983 (AFSCL).

[53]Sister M. Leontia, the sister of Sister M. Bogumila, entered on May 3, 1919, from St. Stanislaus Bishop and Martyr Church in Chicago. She rendered service at various elementary

schools and at homes for the aged. She also served at Boys Town, Nebraska, and at St. John Hospital in Huron, South Dakota as well as at the Motherhouse as a chauffeur. After six years at Madonna, she left for the Motherhouse where she died on June 29, 1978.

[54]Sister M. Seraphinia was born in Johnstown, Pennsylvania, and entered from St. Casimir Church in that city. A graduate of St. John College of Cleveland, she taught at the elementary school level for eighteen years. After postgraduate courses at De Paul and Marquette, she was assigned to Madonna High School were she taught religion, typing, and shorthand. From 1958 to 1983, she served as the school treasurer and bookkeeper. During her thirty-two years at the high school, Sister M. Seraphinia was assistant moderator for the school newspaper and the yearbook for twelve years. Ibid.

[55]*Book of Correspondence:* Letter from Mother M. Jerome Dadej to Samuel Cardinal Stritch, 18 March 1955 (AFSCL).

[56]*Book of Correspondence:* Letter from Mother M. Jerome Dadej to Samuel Cardinal Stritch, 24 March 1955 (AFSCL).

[57]*Book of Correspondence:* Letter from Samuel Cardinal Stritch to Mother M. Jerome Dadej, 3 May 1955 (AFSCL).

[58]Ibid.

[59]*Book of Correspondence:* Letter from Mother M. Jerome Dadej to Samuel Cardinal Stritch, 14 June 1955 (AFSCL).

[60]Sister M. Benigna left Madonna High School in 1964 after nine years of service. She died on March 16, 1970. See Chapter 31 for a further biography.

[61]Sister M. Alacoque entered from St. Casimir Parish in Cleveland. She spent her earlier convent years as an elementary school teacher during which time she graduated from Mundelein College. With a master's degree from Northern Illinois University, she served at Madonna High School for eighteen years. In 1973, she studied dietetics at Augustana Hospital in Chicago and the following year was sent to St. John Hospital in Huron, South Dakota, as the chief dietitian. Except for the year of 1984–85 during which she returned to Madonna High School, Sister M. Alacoque has been stationed at Mount Alverna Home in Parma, Ohio, since 1977 as director of dietary services. *Congregation Membership Records* (AFSCL).

[62]*Book of Correspondence:* Letter from Mother M. Jerome Dadej to the Sisters, 5 October 1955 (AFSCL).

[63]This permission arrived officially on December 17, 1955. Secretaries General, *Community Chronicle*, p. 369. (AFSCL).

[64]*Book of Correspondence:* Letter from Mother M. Jerome Dadej to the Sisters, 28 November 1955 (AFSCL).

[65]*Madonna High School House Journal* (AFSCL).

[66]Constitutions and bylaws of the Mothers' Club and Auxiliary, Madonna High School, Art. II, adopted 11 June 1955 (AFSCL).

[67]*Minutes of General Council Proceedings, 1957,* 22 February 1957 (AFSCL).

[68]On April 28, 1981, the Mothers' Club and Auxiliary and the Fathers' Club and Auxiliary merged to form the Madonna High School Parents' Club under the moderatorship of Sister M. Rosemary Ferus and Sister Carol Marie Schommer. *Madonna High School House Journal* (AFSCL).

[69]At the conclusion of her term in 1974, Sister M. Alberta remained at the Motherhouse as the religious superior for one year. She was then assigned to St. Stanislaus Bishop and Martyr School in Chicago in 1975 as principal and remained in that capacity until 1979 when she returned to Madonna to teach mathematics. She died in 1983 just one day before the convocation of the Fourteenth General Chapter of Elections to which she was a delegate. *Congregation Membership Records* (AFSCL).

[70]Sister M. Albertine came to the community from St. Francis Parish in Omaha, Nebraska.

She was in charge of culinary duties at convents in Chicago, Gary, Hammond, and Cleveland. For three years she served at Boys Town, Nebraska, and in 1950, was sent to Mount Alverna Home in Parma, Ohio, where she remained until her assignment to the high school. Ibid.

[71]*Book of Correspondence:* Letter from Samuel Cardinal Stritch to Mother M. Jerome Dadej, 8 April 1958 (AFSCL).

[72]The pylon column was removed in November of 1975 because of deterioration.

[73]Secretaries General, *Community Chronicle, 1958* (AFSCL).

[74]Sister M. Charitas entered from St. Casimir Church in Cleveland, Ohio. Her elementary teaching experience totaled ten years. A graduate of De Paul University, she also studied music at Alverno College in Milwaukee, after which she was the organist, accompanist, and music teacher at Five Holy Martyrs School for fourteen years. She received her master's degree from St. Louis University and taught at Johnstown Central Catholic High School in Pennsylvania before being assigned to the new Madonna High School. In 1985, after twenty-seven years of service to the young women at the school, she was appointed assistant of the Health Science Library at St. Anthony Medical Center in Crown Point, Indiana. *Congregation Membership Records* (AFSCL).

[75]Sister M. Christine, a native of Cleveland, entered from St. Stanislaus Bishop and Martyr Church in that city. She obtained her bachelor's degree from De Paul University and taught in elementary schools in Chicago, Cleveland, and La Porte, Indiana, for more than eighteen years. She received her master's degree from John Carroll University in Cleveland and taught English and religion at Madonna High School for seventeen years. In 1976, she tranferred to St. Anthony Medical Center in Crown Point, Indiana, where she served as coordinator of admissions for seven years. In 1983, she was appointed director of the Holy Family Day Care Center in Crown Point. Ibid.

[76]Sister M. Esther entered the congregation from Sacred Heart Parish in Cleveland. After obtaining her bachelor's degree from De Paul University, she taught in the elementary schools of the congregation for over thirty years. After recovering from a very serious illness, she was assigned to Madonna where she served for twenty-two years attending to various duties. In 1985, she retired to the Motherhouse. Ibid.

[77]A noted Catholic educator, the Reverend Monsignor William E. McManus served as the archdiocesan superintendent of schools for many years. Later, he was appointed auxiliary bishop of Chicago and pastor of St. Ferdinand Church. In September of 1976, he was made bishop of the Fort Wayne-South Bend Diocese.

[78]*Book of Correspondence:* Letter from the Very Reverend Monsignor William E. McManus, superintendent of schools, Archdiocese of Chicago, to Sister M. Hugoline Czaplinski, May 1959 (AFSCL).

[79]A member of the congregation for fifty-eight years, Sister M. Euphemia served as teacher, principal, superior, musician, and organist during that time. She obtained her bachelor's degree from the American Conservatory of Music in Chicago. At Madonna, she was a member of the music department, and also gave private piano lessons. She died on April 26, 1978, in semi-retirement. *Congregation Membership Records* (AFSCL).

[80]Sister M. Tyburcia entered from St. Mary's Church in Hammond, Indiana. She served as an elementary school teacher for thirty years during which time she graduated from De Paul University. She obtained her master's degree in business education from The Catholic University of America. After twenty-one years at Madonna High School, she was transferred to St. Anthony Medical Center in Crown Point, Indiana, where she serves as the secretary of the Pastoral Ministry Department. Ibid.

[81]See Chapter 49 for Sister M. Antoniana who gave twelve years of service at Madonna. Sister M. Ephrem, after two years, left Madonna in 1961. Ibid.

[82]Mrs. Rozmarek had long been active in educational work, organizing, and conducting Polish classes on Saturdays in various parishes, teaching at Alliance College in Cambridge Springs, Pennsylvania, and teaching Polish at Wright College and Southwest College in Chicago. She was the

author of *Polish for Americans, Parts I* and *II.* Her husband, Charles Rozmarek, was a former president of the Polish American Congress and the Polish National Alliance of which she was also an active member. Mrs. Rozmarek gave unstintingly of her time and talent to Madonna for twenty-one years until her retirement in 1980. *Madonna High School Journal* (AFSCL).

[83]He remained on the staff until 1965. See Chapters 47 and 61.

[84]Sister Bernice Marie Junio, born in Braddock, Pennsylvania, entered from St. Hedwig Church in Gary in 1917. A graduate of De Paul University, she had a long and distinguished career in the congregation as a teacher, principal, and supervisor of schools. After ten years at Madonna High School, she left for St. John Hospital in Huron, South Dakota, where for seven years she served as a pastoral visitor. In 1977, she retired to the Motherhouse. *Congregation Membership Records* (AFSCL).

[85]Formerly known as Sister M. Antonima, Sister Helen Marie Mackowiak entered from St. Pancratius Church. She taught in the elementary schools of the congregation for many years before her assignment to Madonna High School. She received her bachelor's degree from De Paul University and her master's degree in guidance and counseling from Loyola University of Chicago. Her elder brother, the Reverend Joseph Mackowiak, died in 1978. Her younger brother, the Reverend Edward Mackowiak, is currently the pastor of St. Albert the Great Church in Burbank, a suburb of Chicago. Sister Helen Marie succumbed to cancer in 1982. Ibid.

[86]Sister M. Antonella Abramowicz, who entered from St. Pancratius Church, taught for twenty-three years in the elementary schools of the congregation during which time she obtained her bachelor's degree from De Paul University and her master's degree from John Carroll University in Cleveland. At Madonna, she taught religion, history, sociology, and debate. In 1971, she was named assistant principal. In 1984, she left Madonna to assume the duties of postulant and novice directress in place of Sister Joan Klimek who was taking special courses at St. Louis University. Sister M. Antonella, currently the principal of St. Pancratius School, is the sister of the Most Reverend Alfred L. Abramowicz, auxiliary bishop of Chicago. Ibid.

[87]Sister Janice Piesko remained at the high school for ten years; the postulant who became Sister Emilie Marie Lesniak, entered the novitiate the next year. Sister M. Celestine left after two years and was later reassigned for a brief period in the early 1970s. Ibid.

[88]Sister M. Concordia was born in Cleveland and joined the congregation from Sacred Heart of Jesus Church. Having obtained her undergraduate and graduate degrees from De Paul University, she taught in the elementary schools for more than twenty-five years and for three years at Johnstown Central Catholic High School in Pennsylvania before her assignment to Madonna High School where she remained for eight years. She later served as administrator of St. Joseph Home of Chicago and as principal of St. Pancratius School.

Prior to her assignment to Madonna High School Sister M. Jude taught in the elementary schools of the congregation for eleven years. An entrant from Sacred Heart of Jesus Church in Cleveland, she obtained her bachelor's and master's degrees from Loyola University of Chicago. In 1985, she marked her twenty-third year at the high school.

For further reference to Sister M. Edward see Chapter 52. Ibid.

[89]*Minutes of General Council Proceedings, 1962* (AFSCL).

[90]Sister Marie Francis, a niece of Sister M. Germaine Moson, who died in the congregation in 1973, entered from Holy Trinity Church in Chicago. She spent twenty years as an elementary school teacher. After graduating from Rosary College in River Forest with a master's degree in library science, she succeeded Sister M. Maxencia Pozniatowski as librarian at Madonna High School. She left the high school in 1977.

Sister M. Laetitia entered from Assumption Blessed Virgin MaryParish in New Chicago, Indiana. After leaving the high school in 1971, she rendered service at both St. John Medical Center in Huron, South Dakota, and St. Anthony Medical Center in Crown Point, Indiana. Ibid.

[91]Sister Kathleen, the former Sister M. Agnes Ann, entered from St. Patrick Church in Pueblo, Colorado. After serving as an elementary teacher in the congregation's schools, she was

assigned to Madonna High School. After ten years of service at the high school, she obtained a master's degree in social work from Loyola University. Since 1975, she has served as administrator of St. Joseph Home of Chicago and later at St. Anthony Home in Crown Point, Indiana. Ibid.

[92]This was the largest number of young women to enter the congregation since the 1930s. Ibid.

[93]A native of East Chicago, Indiana, Sister M. Rosemary entered the congregation on August 12, 1949. She became a postulant on February 2, 1950, and a novice on August 12, 1950. Her first profession was made on August 12, 1952, and she pronounced her perpetual vows on August 12, 1957. Sister M. Rosemary was assigned to SS. Philip and James School and St. Casimir School, both in Cleveland, for a period of twelve years. She received her bachelor's degree from St. John College of Cleveland. In 1964, she was transferred to Madonna High School where she served as director of guidance and counseling after obtaining her master's degree from Loyola University of Chicago. That same year, she became the directress of aspirants and postulants. In 1982, she was appointed assistant principal at Madonna. A year later, she was named directress of Sisters in temporary vows. Soft-spoken and gentle in approach, Sister M. Rosemary brought to the position of directress a quiet dignity and wholehearted dedication in the performance of her duties both religious and secular. Ibid.

[94]Sister Joseph Marie's contributions to Madonna High School are covered at length in this chapter. Sister Timothy Marie remained on the staff for two years.

Other members of the religious faculty who had arrived and departed from 1965 to 1970 included Sister M. Michelle Perlinski, religion, two years; Sister M. Luke Dohra, physical education, two years; Sister M. Francelle Labedz, (now deceased) religion, guidance and counseling, six years; and Sister Margaret Zulaski, religion, three years.

[95]Clarion 2, Vol. 1, No. 1, Fall 1982.

[96]Originally under the leadership of Sister M. Sponsa Bajorek, the Alumnae Association was disbanded in 1959. Sister M. Marinella Gubala reorganized it in 1982, and when she left in 1985, Sister M. Kingnetta Szczypula succeeded her.

[97]After much deliberation, it was decided to build an apartment structure rather than a standard convent residency since an apartment building would be easier to dispose of if the necessity arose for the Sisters to leave their ministry at Madonna High School. In January of 1974, the Sisters moved into their beautiful new residency which consisted of five apartments with approximately six Sisters living in each separate apartment. While each apartment was independent, the Sisters worshipped together daily in the lovely convent chapel. *Madonna High School House Journal* (AFSCL).

[98]Ibid.

[99]Due to a drop in enrollment, the mobile classrooms were dismantled and sold in 1987.

[100]During this period, the Sisters assigned to the high school were 1971, Sister M. Carol Rychlicki, one year; Sister M. Noel Janicki, one year; 1972, Sister M. Claudia Bomba, two years; Sister M. Aquiline Jakubski, one year; Sister M. Georgene Wilson, one year; Sister M. Francetta Glowacki, one year; Sister Dawn Louise Capilupo, one year; Sister Diane Przyborowski, one year; 1973, Sister Jane Madejczyk, one year; Sister Dorothy Joan Lagocki, two years; Sister Terri Slezak, seven years; 1974, Sister Theresa Mary Obremski, two years; Sister M. Francine Labus, one year; 1975, Sister Doloria Kosiek, one year; 1976, Sister Marie Frances Niecikowski, four years; Sister M. Symphorosa Goryszewski, one year; Sister M. Olga Kulik, four years; 1977, Sister M. Georgeann Kinel, four years; Sister M. Laurentine Michalowski, two years; Sister Joan Klimek, five years; Sister Dru Ann Freed, two years; and 1983, Sister M. Basil Ochocinski, two years. *Book of Annual Assignments* (AFSCL).

[101]Sister M. Consolata entered from SS. Peter and Paul Church in Arcadia, Pennsylvania. After serving as a teacher, organist and musical director for forty-six years, she came to Madonna High School to operate the bookstore. After sixteen years, she retired to the Motherhouse in 1984.

Sister Jeanne Marie entered the postulancy from St. Leo the Great Parish in Cleveland, Ohio. She received her undergraduate degree from Youngstown State University, a master's degree in library science from Rosary College, and a master's degree in administration from Loyola University of Chicago. Her professional activities include dedicated participation in the Illinois Junior Academy of Science. Her contributions to curriculum improvement both on the elementary and high school level have been most significant. In her eight years at Madonna High School, Sister Jeanne Marie taught German, English, and algebra. Presently she is the principal of St. Florian School and is also on the staff of Olive-Harvey Junior College on Chicago's Far South Side. She is also actively involved in the parish's liturgical life.

A native of Chicago and a graduate of Madonna High School, Sister M. Helene entered from St. Genevieve Church. She began her varied service in the congregation as an elementary school teacher. She received her undergraduate degree from the College of St. Francis in Joliet, Illinois, a master's degree in biology from St. Mary's College in Minnesota, and a master's degree in business administration from St. Louis University. In addition, she has been the recipient of numerous government grants. In 1974, she was assigned to Madonna where she taught science, chemistry, and biology. During her ten years at the school, she was also a member of numerous service organizations and directed many student activities. In June of 1986, she was appointed the director of fiscal services for the congregation and is a full-time employee of the Home Office located at the Motherhouse.

Born in Chicago, Sister Diane Marie entered from Sacred Heart of Jesus Parish in Gary (Tolleston), Indiana. The only graduate in the congregation of Marillac College in Normandy, Missouri, she was appointed to Madonna High School in 1973 where she taught English, speech, and forensics. She also moderated service organizations and student activities. She has always been particularly associated with religious vocation awareness. During her years at Madonna, she received a master's degree in English from De Paul University. In 1987 she obtained a master's degree from Loyola University of Chicago as a clinical social worker. She is the first staff member in the history of the high school to be so certified. See Chapter 52.

Sister M. Monica, a native of Johnstown, Pennsylvania, entered from St. Casimir Church in that city. She earned her bachelor's degree from Loyola University of Chicago and did postgraduate work at Loyola University and Felician College in Chicago and St. John College of Cleveland. A teacher in the congregation's elementary schools for more than twenty years, she has served as librarian and media coordinator at Madonna High School since 1976.

Sister Lora Ann entered the congregation from St. Casimir Church in Saginaw, Michigan. She obtained her bachelor's degree from Aquinas College in Grand Rapids, Michigan, a master's degree in pastoral studies from Loyola University of Chicago, and a master's degree in administration also from Loyola. She was assigned to Madonna High School in 1976 and taught religion, psychology, and developmental reading. Her professional and school activities for the eight years she had been missioned at Madonna were many and varied with an emphasis on activating a strong liturgical program. At her departure from the high school in 1985, she assumed the position of principal of St. Stanislaus Bishop and Martyr School on Chicago's Northwest Side. In addition, she serves as moderator, coordinator, director, or consultant to numerous professional and service organizations. *Congregation Membership Records* (AFSCL).

[102]Ibid.

[103]As secretary general, Sister M. Alvernia was efficient and devoted to her work. Always intensely loyal to the congregation, she exhibited much of the intrepid spirit of the congregation's foundress, Mother M. Theresa Dudzik, for whose beatification cause she has always been an outspoken advocate and adherent.

As the fifth principal of Madonna High School, Sister M. Alvernia was remembered as a kind, dedicated, and energetic woman and religious. *Interviews* with Sisters, September 1983; May 1985 (AFSCL).

[104]Sister Joseph Marie Zenda, *Clarion*, Vol. 33, No. 7, 25 May 1983.

[105]Sister M. Julitta entered from Assumption BVM Church in Conemaugh, Pennsylvania. A graduate of De Paul University, she served for more than fifty years as a teacher in the elementary

schools of the congregation before her assignment to Madonna High School as part-time reading instructor. *Congregation Membership Records* (AFSCL).

[106]Ibid.

[107]North Central Association Evaluation, School and Community, May 1987.

[108]North Central Association Self-Study Report from Staff and Administration Committee, November 1987.

[109]The school's first yearbook, the *Madonnary*, published in June 1953, had as its advisor, Sister M. Alberta Bialas. In 1954, Sister M. Sponsa Bajorek was designated the advisor. For fifteen years, Sister M. Sponsa produced with her student staff a yearbook of the highest excellence. She was most capably assisted by Sister M. Seraphinia Furman from 1954 to 1964 and by Sister M. Jude Kruszewski from 1965 to 1969. That year, the spiraling cost of producing the *Madonnary* coupled with the difficulty of securing students who could devote a large segment of time to quality production of the book led to its cancellation. In its place, the *Senior Memory Book*, aimed at and edited by the Seniors was published. Sister M. Jude served as advisor. In 1981, the *Madonnary* was reintroduced with Sister Lora Ann Slawinski as advisor. *Madonna High School Journal* (AFSCL).

[110]The paper began in 1949 as the *Madonna Monthly* with Sister M. Therese Grajek serving as advisor. Sister M. Kingnetta Szczypula and Sister M. Seraphinia Furman took charge of the paper in 1951. As the *Madonna Clarion*, the newspaper was raised to journalistic excellence. Other advisors who continued the pattern of literary excellence were Sister Kathleen Melia, Sister M. Jude Kruszewski, and Sister Anne Marie Knawa. The paper, today called simply, the *Clarion*, continues as an important medium of communication for the student body. Ibid.

[111]North Central Association Evaluation, School and Community, May 1987.

[112]The school song, "Madonna, Madonna, Dear Mother We Love," was written by the Reverend Daniel Lord, SJ, at the specific request of Madonna's administration. Father Lord was a very popular American Jesuit who authored hundreds of religious pamphlets and was associated with the staff of the *Queen's Work* from 1913 until his death in 1955.

CHAPTER 52

The Eighth General Chapter:
Mother M. Jerome Dadej

Thirty-nine delegates met at the Motherhouse on the feast of SS. Peter and Paul, June 30, 1952, at the convocation of the Eighth General Chapter of Elections. Although forty Sisters were to comprise the delegation, Mother M. Aloysia Holysz, hospitalized at the time, could not participate. Since she was an ex-officio member of the delegation, no substitute was required to take her place.

On July 2, Monsignor Raymond J. Zock, the delegate for the communities of religious women in the Archdiocese of Chicago and delegate of Samuel Cardinal Stritch, presided at the election of the superior general. By an absolute majority of votes, Mother M. Jerome Dadej was re-elected superior general for a second six-year term. When asked whether or not she would accept the office for a second term, Mother M. Jerome replied: "I accept only because I recognize this to be the Will of God." Chosen as vicar general and first councilor was Mother M. Antonina Osinski. Sister M. Edward Nowak was elected the second councilor. Elected to a second term as third councilor and secretary general was Sister M. Gonzaga Raniszewski. Sister M. Alberta Bialas was chosen fourth councilor and Sister M. Aloysetta Ciezadlo was elected procurator general. Since neither Sister M. Alberta nor Sister M. Aloysetta were members of the general chapter, they were summoned to the chapter at once, thereby increasing the number of delegates to forty-one.[1]

During Mother M. Jerome's second term as superior general, two Sisters were elected to the council for the first time. Sister M. Edward, elected second councilor, was the former Josephine Nowak who had a long history of service to the congregation. Born on the feast of St. Joseph, March 19, 1906, in Chicago, she entered the congregation from St. John Cantius Church on May 5, 1921. Her postulancy, begun on June 26, 1921, lasted two years because of her youth. She made her first profession of vows on July 27, 1924, and pronounced her perpetual vows on that same day three years later.[2]

After her first profession, Sister M. Edward was sent to St. Casimir's School in Cleveland where she taught from 1924 to 1936. That year, she was appointed a day student for one year with residence at the Motherhouse in Chicago. She returned to St. Casimir's School in Cleveland for the next three years. After her graduation from De Paul University in

1940, she taught at St. Stanislaus Kostka School in Youngstown, Ohio, for the next four years. She was appointed superior and principal of St. Adalbert's School in East St. Louis in 1945, and at the conclusion of her term in 1948, she was sent to Five Holy Martyrs School in Chicago. While serving there as superior and principal, she was elected second councilor. In addition, she was appointed supervisor for the congregation's Chicago schools.

When in 1956 the congregation accepted its first school in the Chicago suburbs, St. Louise de Marillac School in La Grange Park, Sister M. Edward was appointed its first principal and superior of the religious faculty. In July of 1958, she was elected fourth councilor at the congregation's Ninth General Chapter of Elections while still retaining her position at St. Louise de Marillac School. At the end of her tenure as principal, she was sent to Madonna High School where she served as mistress of postulants and aspirants for one year. Other appointments followed at St. Hedwig's School in Gary and St. Casimir's School in Cleveland. Her last active assignment was as assistant principal and coordinator of the learning center at St. Stanislaus Bishop and Martyr School in Chicago. In 1981, she was taken ill and was transferred to the Motherhouse infirmary where she has since resided.[3]

Short of stature and always rather robust, Sister M. Edward could be recognized easily by her sonorous voice and laugh. Amiable in nature, she believed wholeheartedly in the aim of community living and was a strict enforcer of convent horarium. Sensible and practical, she was an excellent and innovative teacher and administrator. Seemingly domineering at times because of her sense of order, Sister M. Edward coupled wise experience with true Franciscan fervor for the spiritual life.[4]

Sister M. Aloysetta,[5] the former Veronica Ciezadlo, elected to the office of procurator general, was born in Chicago on January 26, 1908. She entered the congregation on March 25, 1927, from St. Stanislaus Bishop and Martyr Church in Chicago's Cragin area. She became a novice on July 11, 1928, and made her first profession of vows on July 24, 1930. Her perpetual vows were made on the same day three years later.[6]

Her apostolate of teaching began when, as a second-year novice, she was assigned to Five Holy Martyrs School on Chicago's Southwest Side. Returning there after her first profession, she remained until 1940. For the next eleven years, she taught at St. Pancratius School. Sister M. Aloysetta served as superior and principal at Assumption of the Blessed Virgin Mary School in New Chicago, Indiana, for only one year when in 1952 she was elected procurator general at the Eighth General Chapter.[7]

After the election of the superior general and her general council, various commissions were formed to deliberate special topics. As a consequence, these resolutions were arrived at, albeit minor in nature:

1. Night Adoration would be abolished; instead, an Hour of Adoration would be held on the Thursday before the First Friday of the month from ten o'clock to eleven o'clock in the evening.

2. In the future, a one-day retreat for the delegates would precede the convocation of the general chapter.

3. In the novitiate and at the mission houses where the English language was prevalent, all prayers were to be said in the English language.[8]

4. The farm in Lemont would be sold.

5. For health and economy's sake, celluloid collars would now be worn.

6. White habits and veils would now be worn by all the Sisters in hospitals, homes for the aged, day nurseries, laundries, and kitchens. The cornets attached to the white veils were to be shorter, that is, twenty-two inches long and four inches wide.[9]

An ambitious building program was undertaken in almost every parish of every diocese in the United States in the 1950s. One of the main reasons for this tremendous expansion was the development of various suburbs on the outskirts of most big cities. A second valid reason was the "baby boom" which created the need for either more parish schools or larger ones. Both of these occurrences came at the conclusion of World War II and generated a climate of building—both parish plants that needed enlarging or the construction and formation of entirely new churches and schools. The teaching apostolate had evolved out of the needs of the parishes, and by the early 1950s, the original aim of the congregation—the care of the aged, crippled, and orphans—gave way to the teaching of pupils on the elementary and secondary levels. There were now over two hundred Franciscan Sisters teaching in twenty-four schools in the Archdiocese of Chicago and the Dioceses of Cleveland, Gary, Youngstown, Belleville, and Altoona-Johnstown.[10]

There were many Sisters who, while teaching full-time, simultaneously pursued a college degree at various universities such as Loyola, De Paul, and Mundelein in Chicago; Creighton in Omaha; and St. John's College in Cleveland. To keep abreast of the various trends and advances in education, the Sisters attended teaching institutes, conventions, and workshops held in their respective dioceses. The Sisters were motivated in their pursuit of academic and classroom excellence by the Constitutions of the congregation which stated:

> The Sisters, who are appointed by the superior general to teach in schools, shall undertake the charge with purity of intention and confidence in God, and cheerfully submit to the labor and fatigue associated with it. (Article 171)
>
> For the love of Jesus Christ, let them diligently prepare themselves for their work, that in the art of teaching they may become so proficient that they may be able to educate those committed to their care and trust to be useful members of society and faithful members of the Church. (Article 172)[11]

One of the new schools, SS. Philip and James, accepted before the beginning of Mother M. Jerome's second term, was established on Cleveland's West Side by the Most Reverend Edward Hoban, the archbishop-bishop. Organized on April 20, 1950, it drew approximately one thousand families from the parishes of St. Ignatius, the Annunciation, and St. Vincent de Paul. The Reverend James O'Brien,[12] the former well-known director of the Catholic Youth Organization (CYO) was appointed its pastor. At first the auditorium of Louis Agassiz Public School was used as a place of worship for the parishioners. On September 24, 1950, the cornerstone was laid for a lovely, T-shaped combination church and school of gray Ohio sandstone at Bosworth Avenue and Adeline Road. On Christmas Eve, mass was celebrated in the auditorium of the new school, the first building to be completed.[13]

In June of 1950, the general council of the Franciscan Sisters of Chicago had voted to accept SS. Philip and James School in Cleveland at the request of Archbishop Hoban.[14] The bishop expressed a need for eight Sisters to begin the operation of the school, but an agreement was reached to send four Sisters and to employ lay teachers to complete the staff.[15] In July of 1950, Father O'Brien made a trip to Chicago to meet Mother M. Jerome Dadej, Mother M. Antonina Osinski, Sister M. Gonzaga Raniszewski, and Sister M. Euphemia Switalski, principal of Sacred Heart of Jesus School in Cleveland, and drive them back to Cleveland to see the progress of the parish complex. When the Sisters returned from their visit, Mother M. Jerome assigned the following Sisters to staff the new mission: Sister M. Alberta Bialas, the superior and principal; Sister M. Esther Obuchowski, Sister M. Maristella Skrzynski, and Sister M. Pulcheria Mikolajczyk, who was assigned to household duties.[16]

SS. Philip and James Church and School
Cleveland, Ohio (1950–1982)

Because the school had not as yet been thoroughly completed, and there were no adequate living quarters for the Sisters in the parish, various accommodations had to be made. Sister M. Alberta and Sister M. Esther resided at Sacred Heart of Jesus School Convent on Cleveland's South Side, while Sister M. Maristella maintained her residence at St. Casimir's School Convent on Cleveland's East Side. From October of 1950, the Sisters traveled every Sunday to SS. Philip and James Parish where they conducted Confraternity of Christian Doctrine (CCD) classes after the nine o'clock mass. The classes were held in the Louis Agassiz Public School auditorium for all the students who were to enter the new SS. Philip and James School in January. Father O'Brien took upon himself the task of picking up the Sisters every Sunday in order to bring them to SS. Philip and James Parish. After the CCD classes and a light lunch, the Sisters were driven back to their respective convents. They continued in this fashion until December 22, 1950.[17]

On January 6, 1951, Sister M. Alberta and Sister M. Esther were finally able to move into a house which Father O'Brien had purchased at 10901 Adeline Road. While the rooms on the second floor of the house were being converted into sleeping quarters for the Sisters, Sister M. Alberta and Sister M. Esther occupied the first floor only, where they took their meals and prepared for class. Their sleeping quarters and chapel were in the old rectory at 11017 Oliver Road. Sister M. Pulcheria arrived to take up her duties on January 17, 1951, and Sister M. Maristella arrived eleven days later. By February 5, all the Sisters were able to move into the cozy, remodeled house on Adeline Road where Holy Mass was offered for the first time in the newly constructed chapel. In the meantime, additional remodeling of the entire first floor of the house continued.[18]

The beautiful SS. Philip and James School, which contained ten classrooms, opened on February 5, 1951, with 298 children in five grades. For a long period of time, the Sisters operated the school while walking under scaffolds, ladders, and over plaster bags while the workmen labored to complete the structure.[19] By September of 1951, when all eight grades were opened, the enrollment jumped to 430 in the school designed to hold 550 pupils. That same year, Sister M. Venantia Rec was added to the staff. In February of 1952, a "first" occurred for the SS. Philip and James School and parish community when a postulant was sent to teach grade four. She was accompanied by a second-year novice who had been transferred from Five Holy Martyrs School in Chicago to teach the fifth grade.[20] Since the number of Sisters on the staff was increasing, Father O'Brien acquired a house directly in back of the convent on Adeline Road. Because the Sisters took up residence there on February 6, the feastday of St. Agatha, the "extra" house was called "St. Agatha's Cottage." The cottage provided five more Sisters with sleeping quarters.

In 1953, a great tornado ravaged the West Side of Cleveland. The parish hall of SS. Philip and James was converted into a Red Cross shelter for three days during the disaster. Fortunately, neither the parishioners nor the Sisters suffered any great loss from the calamity.[21]

The school population continued to escalate for the next few years. In 1960, it reached its peak with 593 pupils. In these overcrowded conditions, for example, Sister

SS. Philip and James Convent
Cleveland, Ohio

Elizabeth Marie Jadrych taught seventy-two children in the first grade on the thirty-foot by forty-foot stage of the school auditorium. A much-needed second floor was added to the school and completed by January 30, 1956.

The Sisters maintained their residence on Adeline Road until 1964. On October 26 of that year, the Sisters moved into a large and beautiful new convent which Father O'Brien had arranged to have built for them on Oliver Street.

In 1978, a lay teacher was hired as the principal, another "first" in the history of SS. Philip and James School. The school roster that year listed 370 pupils. Three years later, only two Franciscan Sisters of Chicago remained on the teaching staff. In 1981, still another "first" occurred in the parish when a Sister of another congregation was hired to serve as the principal. She was Sister Julie Demchak of the Congregation of the Sisters of the Humility of Mary.[22]

After much discussion, deliberation and prayer, Sister Martha Joan Sempolski, then the superior general of the Franciscan Sisters of Chicago, and her general council recognized the necessity of withdrawing the last two Sisters from SS. Philip and James School. Both Sister M. Claudiana Jachimowicz and Sister M. Josetta Kuczmarski[23] departed in June of 1982, leaving SS. Philip and James School in the excellent and capable hands of the Sisters of the Humility of Mary of Villa Maria, Pennsylvania.

THE EIGHTH GENERAL CHAPTER: MOTHER M. JEROME DADEJ

[1]See Appendix K.

[2]*Congregation Membership Records* (AFSCL).

[3]Ibid.

[4]*Interviews* with Sisters, September 1983.

[5]The author is most pleased to report that Sister M. Aloysetta was her first grade teacher whom she loved. It is to dear Sister M. Aloysetta that the author is indebted for having learned to read—and to write—first the alphabet and then wonderful words and sentences and eventually—a history.

[6]*Spis Sióstr* (AFSCL).

[7]In 1958, she was re-elected for another six-year term. In 1964, she was re-elected for a third term and eventually served for a total of seventeen years.

[8]As a consequence, in August of 1952, the retreat for the Sisters preparing for the novitiate and first profession was conducted in English for the first time by the Reverend Arnold Rzatkiewicz (Radkie). The ceremonies on the day of investiture and first and perpetual profession were likewise in English. Secretaries General, *Community Chronicle, 1952* (AFSCL).

[9]*Minutes of General Chapter Proceedings, 1952* (AFSCL).

[10]*Congregation Membership Records* (AFSCL).

[11]*Constitutions of the Congregation of the Sisters of Blessed Kunegunda of the Third Order of Saint Francis* (Chicago, 1954), p. 36.

[12]The Reverend James O'Brien was raised in Blessed Sacrament Parish on the West Side of Cleveland and was a star athlete in his youth. At both St. Ignatius High School and John Carroll University, he was the mainstay of the baseball and basketball teams. Even in the seminary, studies did not interfere with his athletic interests. He helped organize recreational programs for Merrick House and Alta House in Cleveland while still a seminarian. One of his appointments after ordination was Ursuline High School where he taught religion and served as the athletic director. Father O'Brien founded the Catholic Youth Organization (CYO) and left it a strong and viable group in 1950, the year he was appointed the first pastor of SS. Philip and James Church. In ill health for the last decade of his life, he resigned his pastorate in 1974. He died in Cleveland on March 5, 1975. *Book of Correspondence:* Report from the Chancery Office of the Diocese of Cleveland, to author, 9 July 1975 (AFSCL).

[13]Michael J. Hynes, *History of the Diocese of Cleveland* (Cleveland: World Publishing Co., 1953), p. 414.

[14]Secretaries General, *Community Chronicle, 1950* (AFSCL).

[15]Ibid.

[16]*Congregation Membership Records* (AFSCL).

[17]*SS. Philip and James House Journal* (AFSCL).

[18]*Book of Correspondence:* Letter from Sister M. Esther Obuchowski to author, 1976 (AFSCL).

[19]*Book of Correspondence:* Letter from Sister M. Alberta Bialas to author, December 1975 (AFSCL).

[20]The postulant was Jean Knawa, who became Sister Anne Marie, the author of this history. The second-year novice was the former Loretta Ferus, Sister M. Rosemary.

[21]*SS. Philip and James: 25th Anniversary, 1950–1975* (Cleveland, 1975), no pagination.

[22]*SS. Philip and James House Journal* (AFSCL).

[23]Sister M. Josetta had been stationed at the school for twenty-three years.

CHAPTER 53

Expansion in Health Care Services

As the health care apostolate gained in importance in the congregation during the tenure of office of Mother M. Jerome Dadej, the Franciscan Sisters of Chicago accepted management of the Atkinson Memorial Hospital in Atkinson, Nebraska, in 1952.

Atkinson Memorial Hospital had its beginning shortly after World War II. The Atkinson community, with a population of approximately eighteen hundred had no health facility at that time. Fourteen married women, members of the Atkinson Veterans' Wives Club, decided to make the hospital their project in a nationwide community betterment contest sponsored by the Federated Women's Club. In 1948, the AVW Club formed a corporation to "provide the community with a hospital adequate to take care of local needs such as minor surgery, maternity cases, emergency medical and surgical care, and convalescence."[1] The articles of incorporation were drawn up by Attorney Charles E. Chace. The corporation, a nonprofit organization, was to "provide a memorial hospital in Atkinson to be a monument to the men and women of the Atkinson community who served in the Armed Forces of the United States during World Wars I and II."[2]

Having obtained an architect's estimate of approximately $25,000, the women asked the Farley-Tushla Post of the American Legion for $10,000 pledging that they themselves would raise the remainder. In June of 1949, the campaign to raise the money began, and by the first week in December, the goal was reached. Ten acres of land for the site were purchased from a private citizen for the construction of a one-story, full basement building. The women also purchased nineteen acres of land at the southwest edge of town. These acres were subdivided into twenty-one lots and sold to individuals to raise additional funds for the hospital, the cost of which had now risen to $35,000.[3] Ground-breaking took place in June of 1951, and, by November, the hospital building was near completion. An additional equipment fund campaign was launched when Ernest E. Gotschall, a prominent Atkinson rancher, accepted the post of general chairman of a campaign to raise $50,000. Local businessmen, farmers, ranchers, farm women, and Atkinson wives made a door-to-door canvass of the area to secure the necessary funds to equip the much-needed hospital for Atkinson and its surrounding communities.

The Reverend A. A. Lehmen, the pastor of St. Joseph's Church in Atkinson, had requested the services of the Benedictine Sisters of Yankton, South Dakota, to conduct the hospital and had made a trip to Yankton for that specific purpose. Father Lehmen was given little hope of acquiring the Benedictine Sisters, but while at the Sacred Heart Hospital, owned and operated by the Benedictine Sisters, he met Sister Leona Watroba, a member of the Franciscan Sisters of Chicago, who was studying X-ray technology there. Father Lehmen and Sister Leona discussed the possibility of the Franciscan Sisters staffing the hospital in Atkinson. When Father Lehmen returned to Atkinson, he wrote a letter to Mother M. Jerome Dadej, which she received on September 29, 1949, petitioning her for Sisters to staff the proposed Atkinson Memorial Hospital. Briefly, he informed her:

> Together with Sister Radegund [of the Benedictine Sisters], we talked over the possibility of you, Reverend Mother, sending us the required Sisters if Sister Jerome of Yankton finds it impossible to do so. The Sisters spoke of the possibility that you would perhaps withdraw your Sisters from Gregory[4] on account of insufficient accommodations there. In case you did so, would you, in your gracious kindness, consider sending us five or six Sisters?
>
> Mother, it would be most pleasing to both the Catholic and the non-Catholic people of Atkinson and community if you could give us the required Sisters to conduct the hospital.
>
> Will you kindly give our petition your most favorable consideration and give us the desired "yes" for an answer? As pastor of St. Joseph's Church of Atkinson, I know and realize the need of nursing care of the sick of this community. The care of the sick is appalling—falling on homes of a number of Catholic ladies, who, acting as practical nurses, give the best care they can both to medical and obstetrical cases. This situation should be remedied by a local hospital and a staff of good Sisters.
>
> We sincerely hope, Reverend Mother, that we can welcome your Sisters to our community of friendly people; we hope that we can furnish you with a profitable and happy place for your Sisters to live, work, and pray.
>
> May God's blessing descend upon you and your Community of good Sisters.
>
> Very sincerely in Christ,
> Father A. A. Lehmen[5]

Nothing of consequence occurred for two years. Then, on May 6, 1951, Sister Bertilla, OSB, a member of the staff of St. Joseph's School in Atkinson, sent a letter to Mother M. Antonina Osinski, the superior of St. John Hospital and School of Nursing in Huron, South Dakota, informing her of the opportunity offered by the Atkinson hospital:

Dear Sister Antonina,

By chance the other day, I was speaking to someone about getting Sisters to take over our hospital in Atkinson, when it was suggested to try the Sisters of your Community. If I am not mistaken, your Motherhouse is in Chicago. I am uncertain as to the address, so I am sending the letter to you and asking you to kindly forward it to your Reverend Mother.

Atkinson is a lovely town with a population of approximately 1,500. As it is in the midst of a ranching section and farms, there is a large part of the country to be served by this hospital. Father Lehmen, the pastor, claims between 800 and 900 souls. We have a good school here with about 180 enrolled in the high and grade school. The children and people are exceptionally lovely to deal with. These people would be very good to the Sisters. At present, the good ladies are busy getting the linens and all the furniture for the hospital.

The hospital is not yet completed, but the work will most probably be finished by mid-summer. It has a fine location a little more than a block from the church. It is in a quiet part of town and the building is surrounded by a lovely large plot of ground. There is plenty of room for expansion and I would not be surprised but an addition would be needed especially if the Sisters have charge of the hospital.

I am hoping that you will consider this hospital, for I assure you we are badly in need of one. We have two Catholic doctors and another expects to come in as soon as the hospital is ready. We are quite fortunate in having a number of Catholics in business here.

I am hoping to hear from you soon. In the meantime, we shall pray that your good Mother Superior will see fit to help the Atkinson people.

Yours in St. Benedict,

Sister Bertilla, OSB[6]

As a consequence of the letter, Mother M. Antonina Osinski and Sister M. Gonzaga Raniszewski were sent to Atkinson in September of 1951 to examine the hospital facilities and the accommodations for the Sisters. Upon their return, the Sisters gave a most satisfactory report to Mother M. Jerome concerning the hospital now near completion.[7] On October 5, Mother M. Jerome wrote to the Most Reverend Gerald T. Bergan, archbishop of Omaha:

Your Excellency:

The undersigned is humbly begging Your Excellency's permission to open a second religious house of the Congregation of the Franciscan Sisters of Chicago in the Archdiocese of Omaha. The first house was opened in 1940 at Boys Town, Nebraska, where our Sisters are in charge of the domestic and bookkeeping departments. The second one to be opened is in Atkinson where the wives of the war veterans have collected money and built a fourteen-bed hospital. They are willing to hand over the hospital completely furnished to the Sisters.

Since we operate two hospitals in South Dakota, namely, in Gregory and Huron, the people of Atkinson have sent a petition to our Congregation to take possession of their hospital. At the general meeting of the council, the members voted to accept the hospital and to operate it according to the standards of the Catholic Hospital Association provided we have Your Excellency's permission.

Begging this favor, I have the honor to be, Your Excellency,

A humble servant of Christ,

Mother M. Jerome

Superior General[18]

A few days later, Mother M. Jerome received a letter from Charles E. Chace, attorney-at-law in Atkinson, in which he expressed the joy of the Atkinson community upon learning that the Franciscan Sisters were coming to Atkinson. He further informed Mother M. Jerome that he had notified Sister Bertilla [of the Benedictine Sisters], the Reverend R. J. Parr, who had succeeded the Reverend A. A. Lehmen as pastor of St. Joseph's Church, and the hospital group about Mother M. Jerome's proposed visit in the middle of October.[9]

With the guarantee that the Franciscan Sisters of Chicago would administer and staff the Atkinson Hospital, an article appeared in the Atkinson paper, a brief excerpt of which is presented here:

> Trained personnel have already been obtained. Four Sisters of the Franciscan Order will take over the operation of the hospital as soon as it is ready to open. In this respect, Atkinson is most fortunate, as there is a dangerous shortage of trained hospital people throughout the country. The presence of the nuns will not make this a sectarian hospital. Atkinson Memorial Hospital will be a community hospital, open to all who need its care, regardless of race or creed. The nuns have been given a deed to the hospital with reservations. If, at any time, this institution is not run for the welfare of the entire community, then the deed reverts to the people of Atkinson and surrounding areas. In addition to operating the hospital, the Sisters are furnishing several items of equipment, among which will be a BMR machine and a completely equipped laboratory.[10]

When the general council of the Franciscan Sisters of Chicago voted to accept the hospital, Sister M. Antonita Waloch was appointed administrator and superior. She left Chicago on January 6, 1952, in the company of Sister M. Andrea Puchalski who was also assigned to the Atkinson Memorial Hospital.[11] On January 27, Sister M. Aquinas Rosky

Our Lady of the Sandhills (Atkinson Memorial Hospital)
Atkinson, Nebraska (1952–1972)

and Sister M. Felicia Wierciak joined the staff.[12] The hospital had full surgical, laboratory, and delivery room facilities with three physicians on the staff. Referrals were made to Omaha or other places if Atkinson Memorial Hospital was unable to handle certain cases.

On February 10, 1952, the Franciscan Sisters of Chicago assumed possession of the separately incorporated not-for-profit general hospital which they named the Atkinson Memorial Hospital under the protection of Our Lady of the Sandhills, a poetic reference to the undulating sand hills of Nebraska. It has been estimated that during the first two years of the operation of the hospital, the number of patients admitted was 1,673. These included 1,106 medical patients, 302 surgical patients, and 265 infants. During this time, the Sisters went about their work of caring for all their patients in a very edifying and efficient manner.[13]

On October 15, 1952, during a visit to Our Lady of the Sandhills Hospital, Mother M. Jerome was warmly received at a dinner given by the building committee. In the company of local dignitaries, Mother M. Jerome was presented with a warranty deed as a legal sign that the title of ownership had come into the hands of the Franciscan Sisters of Chicago. In order to keep the procedure legal, the building had to be purchased for at least one dollar. In a symbolic gesture of good faith, this sum was paid by one of the citizens of Atkinson at the dinner in honor of Mother M. Jerome. Because the hospital was not as yet completed, the committee promised to have the hospital finished and furnished without any financial obligation on the part of the Sisters.[14]

By 1956, the Sisters celebrated their 5th anniversary of health care ministry to the people of Atkinson. The hospital had grown steadily in providing services to the sick and injured of the area. During this five-year period almost 3,000 patients had been admitted to the hospital and nearly 700 babies had been born. That year, the administrative board voted to expand the hospital. The addition, which cost $50,000, more than doubled the size of the original building.[15] Connected to the east of the original building, the addition provided four private rooms and three semiprivate rooms for patients, a waiting room or visiting room for relatives and friends, a kitchen and dining room on the main floor to displace those rooms now in the basement, an X-ray room on the main floor, and a doctor's room for consultations and preparation for surgery.[16]

When the Sisters first arrived in Atkinson, they had lived in three cramped and inadequate rooms in the basement of the hospital. Now, quiet and cheerful living quarters for the Sisters were provided on the main floor complete with a chapel, a recreation room, and six private bedrooms. When Mother M. Jerome requested permission of Archbishop Bergan to build the addition, he had agreed and responded: "The Sisters have done excellent work under crowded conditions and there is a great need for enlargement."[17]

The new wing was constructed with money received as a gift from the Ford Foundation in the sum of $10,000. This amount was matched by another $10,000 gift from the Motherhouse of the Franciscan Sisters of Chicago. Approximately $4,500 was contained in the building fund from previous gifts, and for the balance, families in the Atkinson area were asked to contribute.[18] With the completion of the new addition on February 11, 1957, Archbishop Bergan assigned the Reverend R. J. Parr, the pastor of St. Joseph's Church, to bless the new wing of the hospital. On April 23, 1957, Mother M. Jerome was present for the simple religious ceremony and later examined the hospital's new addition.

For years, Our Lady of the Sandhills Hospital continued to function successfully. In 1963, the hospital was incorporated in the state of Nebraska, became an independent corporation, and was returned to the Atkinson community. Mother M. Jerome had arrived at this decision after consulting with legal counsel. Since the Sisters now only operated the hospital, this relieved them from any lawsuits or liabilities in the future.[19]

In 1968, the First Extraordinary Chapter of Affairs was held in the congregation. At this special chapter, the Sister-delegates were informed of the national studies made of small hospitals and of the congregation's own intensive self-study in an effort to determine the future of its health care services. At this First Extraordinary Chapter of Affairs, the decision was made by the chapter delegates to phase out all the congregation's small hospitals, Our Lady of the Sandhills among them. Hospital records reveal that the bed capacity at this time was eighteen with five Sisters[20] on the staff and twenty-two employees.[21] The target date for the Sisters' leaving was June of 1974, but they were determined not to leave the area before a larger Catholic hospital near by would agree to serve the people of Atkinson. The Congregation of the Franciscan Sisters of Penance and Christian Charity, who operated St. Anthony's Hospital at O'Neill, Nebraska, approximately fifteen miles from Atkinson, agreed to take over Our Lady of the Sandhills Hospital.

Sister M. Hugoline Czaplinski, the superior general elected in 1970 at the Eleventh General Chapter, announced that the Franciscan Sisters of Chicago would withdraw from the Atkinson hospital in June of 1974, and the Franciscan Sisters of Penance and Christian Charity from O'Neill would assume operation of the health facility. It was then decided that Lawrence T. Filosa, the newly appointed president and executive director of health services for the Franciscan Sisters of Chicago, would hire legal counsel to meet all the necessary requirements for withdrawing from Our Lady of the Sandhills Hospital. Only renovation projects and improvement expenditures necessary to keep the facility in good operating condition were to be made during the period of time preceding the withdrawal of the Franciscan Sisters of Chicago from the hospital. The Sisters at Our Lady of the Sandhills were instructed to continue, as they had always in the past, to build good public relations with local residents and those of the immediate surrounding area so that the transition in ownership to the Franciscan Sisters in O'Neill would be smooth, profitable, and positive in every aspect.[22] After serious deliberation, however, the Franciscan Sisters in O'Neill declined the offer to staff the hospital preferring instead to center their interests on their own community-owned hospitals.

Although the Franciscan Sisters of Chicago had decided that the hospital would have until 1974 to arrange the transition, Mr. Filosa informed the hospital's lay advisory board on July 18, 1972, that the congregation's governing body had made a decision to withdraw its staff within ninety days. Earlier in the month, Mr. Filosa had met with the hospital advisory board and had recommended that they form a governing board for the purpose of administering the hospital. He reasoned that by doing so it would be easier to update and modernize the hospital. While members of the local advisory board asked for time to make a study of needed improvements and requested that a team from the State Department of Health be asked to make such a study, Mr. Filosa announced that the Sisters would be leaving by October 31, 1972. Several problems existed. The advisory board was now confronted not only with what was needed to update the facility, but also with what might be required by the State Board of Health to keep the hospital in operation. After the State Board of Health would complete its planned study and present its recommendations to the advisory board of Our Lady of the Sandhills Hospital, the board would hold meetings to inform the public concerning the state's requirements, to what extent the people in the area wanted to go toward construction, and how to finance such construction. According to Mr. Filosa, the hospital was in excellent financial condition. He added that there would be no financial difficulty when a new governing board took over the administration of the hospital.[23]

Steps were taken by the advisory board of Our Lady of the Sandhills Hospital to hire an administrator before October 31, 1972, when the Franciscan Sisters of Chicago were slated to leave. Problems still existed. One of them was the necessity of obtaining a license from the Nebraska Department of Health. Specialists had come from the Department of Health by local request to inspect the building to determine if it could be used and how much would be needed to bring it up to state and federal requirements. Updating the existing complex, the inspectors contended, was extremely difficult because of the type of construction which made it impossible to remove walls. The inspector from the Department of Health promised to expedite the feasibility study because of the sixty-day deadline involved. He told board members that if the cost of building on to the Our Lady of the Sandhills Hospital totaled more than one-half of the cost of a new building, the state would probably recommend that a new building be constructed. In the meantime, the president of the advisory board received a letter from Mr. Filosa in which he affirmed that the Franciscan Sisters of Chicago would cease operation of Our Lady of the Sandhills Hospital after October 31, 1972. He urged that a local body be formed to assume management of the hospital after that date and stated terms which would be required for the transfer of administration. Mr. Filosa also stated in his letter that if a local governing board were not ready to assume operation of the hospital by October 31, the hospital would be closed.[24]

As the deadline approached, members of the advisory board filed a petition in Holt County District Court to prevent a loss of assets which they believed belonged to the residents of the Atkinson area. The court issued a temporary restraining order which prevented the Sisters from closing or ceasing operation of the hospital until both sides came to an agreement on an orderly transfer of property.[25]

After the agreement was reached, plans were put into motion and by December 31, 1973, Sister M. Amabilis Bellock,[26] the administrator and superior, and Sister M. Felicia Wierciak were the last to leave Atkinson. Sister M. Leonia Mszanski and Sister M. Tarcisia Bucki had left Our Lady of the Sandhills Hospital in early December. The Sisters were very sorry to leave the hospital and the Atkinson community was truly sorry to see the Sisters depart.[27]

With the departure of the Franciscan Sisters of Chicago, the hospital advisory board voted to build a new and larger facility several blocks away. The million–dollar replacement facility called the West Holt Memorial Hospital was dedicated on February 13, 1977. Our Lady of the Sandhills Hospital was then turned over to the newly formed West Holt Memorial Hospital which was then under the administration of Mr. J. M. McDonald who had succeeded Sister M. Amabilis.[28]

The Franciscan Sisters of Chicago undertook the operation of a second hospital in the diocese of Rapid City in 1952. St. Anthony's Hospital in Martin, South Dakota, was located between the Pine Ridge and the Rosebud Indian Reservations. The community of Martin, founded in 1912, consisted mainly of farmers. The Indians of the reservations, mostly Oglala Sioux, made up a large part of the population.[29]

In the early 1930s, Bennett Community Hospital, as St. Anthony's Hospital had been known originally, was a privately owned hospital built by Dr. Charles A. Swift of Martin. Purchased by Bennett County at a later date, the hospital was staffed by a religious congregation that left in 1949. From 1949 to 1952, the hospital, a very old two-story building with a basement and a bed capacity of fourteen and four bassinets,[30] was directed by a lay nurse.[31]

The matter of staffing the hospital was first brought to the attention of the Franciscan Sisters of Chicago when Mother M. Jerome received a letter from the Most Reverend William McCarty, CSSR, bishop of Rapid City, in 1949. At that time, he wrote:

Dear Mother Jerome:

Greetings from the Black Hills of South Dakota![32]

I am writing to you, at this time, to let you know that the Sisters in charge of the hospital at Martin, South Dakota, will have to return to their Motherhouse. This change is brought about due to a lack of vocations for this group of Sisters, and because it is not possible for them to bring new recruits from Europe.

I would like to extend an invitation to you to have your Sisters take over the hospital at Martin just as soon as the present Sisters leave. This will be within the next month or six weeks.

With kindest personal regards, and with every good wish, I remain,

Devotedly yours in Christ,

William T. McCarty, CSSR

Bishop of Rapid City[33]

Two years later on August 24, 1951, another letter arrived from Bishop McCarty which stated:

Dear Mother M. Jerome:

My heartfelt congratulations and best wishes on the new hospital at Gregory, South Dakota.[34] I was there yesterday. The Sisters are so happy and the care of the sick as well as the latest equipment is so complete that, I am sure, there is nothing better anywhere. I was most favorably impressed and pleased by everything.

I would like to renew my invitation to you to have your Sisters take charge of St. Anthony's Hospital at Martin, South Dakota. Since Gregory is comparatively close to Martin, I feel sure that it would be advantageous to your Community to have charge of the hospital there. It would please me very much if you would go with me to Martin the next time you come to Gregory and look over the place and see what is offered to you there. I pray God that you will be able to see your way clear to accept this invitation of mine to have your Sisters take charge of St. Anthony Hospital in Martin.[35]

Although she gave Bishop McCarty's letter serious consideration, Mother M. Jerome continued to refuse his requests. The shortage of Sister personnel and the distance of the Martin hospital in relation to the other hospitals maintained by the congregation prohibited her from accepting the invitation to staff St. Anthony's Hospital. Once again, in October of 1951, the undaunted Bishop McCarty contacted Mother M. Jerome:

Dear Mother Jerome:

It pleased me very much to be able to stop to see your good Sisters at Gregory yesterday. I blessed the Stations of the Cross for them. Your new hospital there is one of the finest I have ever seen. It is a real credit to all.

In my visit with Sister Innocentia she mentioned that you had said to her " . . . The bishop should forget what I said in my last letter to him about the distance between Gregory and Martin. That distance has diminished since I wrote."

I was delighted to hear this news. I would like to ask you once again if you would consider taking over the hospital at Martin, and by your charity bridge the miles between Gregory and Martin. With my kindest personal regards, and with a prayer for your continued success, I remain,

> Devotedly yours in Christ,
> Wm. T. McCarty, CSSR
> Bishop of Rapid City[36]

That same month, Mother M. Jerome visited Mother of Grace Hospital in Gregory, South Dakota. During her visit, the Right Reverend Monsignor Francis Monighan, chaplain at Mother of Grace Hospital, urged Mother M. Jerome to reconsider staffing St. Anthony's Hospital. Monsignor Monighan introduced her to Frank Roth, head of the committee which had organized in order to plan a new hospital for Martin. Mr. Roth assured Mother M. Jerome that the residents of Martin were so anxious to secure the Sisters that they were willing to build a new hospital on a more suitable site. Mother M. Jerome promised to reconsider Bishop McCarty's many invitations to staff the hospital. On October 27, 1951, she wrote to Bishop McCarty, an indication of the genuine good will which animated her decision making:

Your Excellency:

The distance between Martin and Gregory has been recently considerably diminished it is true, but there are two posts to be put up before the "bridge" can be materialized. These two posts are: a new site and a new hospital at Martin.

While in Gregory, I met Mr. Roth of Martin. He stated that the people of Martin would be willing to build a new hospital in a more suitable place. In that event, I would consider taking over the hospital. Thanking Your Excellency for all the kindness and prayers for us, I remain

> Humbly in Christ,
> Mother M. Jerome, Sup. Gen.[37]

On January 7, 1952, Mother M. Jerome informed Bishop McCarty that the Franciscan Sisters of Chicago had made a final decision to accept St. Anthony's Hospital. Twenty days later, the Sisters arrived in Martin and were eagerly welcomed by Bishop McCarty who had traveled to Martin to meet them.[38] The pioneer Sisters assigned to St. Anthony's Hospital were Sister M. Paul Kirschbaum, as superior and administrator; Sister Frances Szczur; and Sister M. Gerardette Molda. The Sisters were the only community of religious women in Bennett County which also boasted one Catholic Church and one Catholic priest. The Sisters made their home in an old house consisting of five rooms adjoining the hospital. Since there were no sidewalks or grass, the Sisters secured and laid two planks on the ground which enabled them to walk the approximately twenty-five feet from the house to the hospital. The furnishings in the house were less than adequate, consisting of old beds and a small dresser. There were no chairs in the bedrooms, so the Sisters used their trunks on which to sit. The recreation room had one sofa and one chair. There was no kitchen, and the dining room served as their laundry and storage space. The Sisters, who had arrived several days earlier in order to put the house in order, cleaned so thoroughly that at leave five rats were killed each day in the process.[39]

The Franciscan Sisters of Chicago began their ministry at St. Anthony's Hospital on February 1, 1952. A few days later, Sister M. Paul received a letter from Bishop McCarty which read in part:

> I would like to suggest, Sister, that you and the other Sisters lay the groundwork for the new building that must necessarily be planned and erected in the future. It may take a little time to get things moving in the right direction, but I know that you will have the cooperation of all in what you plan as time goes on. The people of Martin and vicinity have the will to see the hospital succeed one hundred per cent. It will be a gradual process, as I have said, but I know that your grand work will be the means of seeing all accomplished as you plan.[40]

A month later, Sister M. Paul sent a letter to Mother M. Jerome requesting a fourth Sister to be sent to the hospital to serve as the dietitian since Sister M. Paul had been unable to secure a suitable one. She further advised Mother M. Jerome that the Sisters were extremely exhausted from the excessive amount of work they performed in the old and inadequate hospital. According to Sister Frances Szczur, one room served as the admissions, surgery, emergency room, and nurses' station. Patients had to be carried via stairs. When surgery was performed, it was necessary for the participants to stand in one place because the room was too small. The delivery room table was an old bed with three mattresses piled on it for height.[41]

Mother M. Jerome addressed a letter to Mr. Roth in March of 1952, with a tone of keen disappointment and determined action:

> Dear Mr. Roth:
>
> After hearing the jubilant words in welcoming the Sisters to the hospital at Martin, the bare facts now reveal themselves.
>
> The hospital facilities are inadequate causing many difficulties and hardships for the Sisters. I am forced to send a fourth Sister to Martin to alleviate the heavy burden for the Sisters at the hospital.
>
> After due consideration of the many difficulties presented to us by

the present staff at St. Anthony's, we wish to inform you, Mr. Roth, and the Board of Directors of the Hospital, to have a new hospital built within a year. If nothing is done by that time, I will withdraw the Sisters.

Would you please take this matter up with the Board to make preliminary plans so that when I come to Martin toward the end of April, you can show me some definite steps taken in that direction.

> Sincerely yours,
> Mother M. Jerome[42]

Mother M. Jerome was determined that the Hospital Commission proceed with the promised new building. To that effect, she delivered a stern ultimatum to the Hospital Commission in early March of 1953:

> Taking into consideration the many requests for Sisters to take over hospitals which proposals we must turn down due to the shortage of Sisters, we have decided that if the construction of a new hospital in Martin is not started by April, we will withdraw our Sisters from St. Anthony's Hospital by the 15th of June of this year. Kindly reply to this notice as we would like to know what plans to make for the future.
>
> Franciscan Sisters of Blessed Kunegunda
> By: Mother M. Jerome
> Superior General[43]

Finally, by January of 1953, almost a year later, plans were activated to begin a campaign to raise funds for the construction of a modern hospital in Martin to serve the growing needs of the Martin community and its vicinity. A statement released to the press by the Sisters continued to underscore the dire situation which existed at the old hospital:

> Although our hospital was established in 1948, it is approved only for a temporary state license. It cannot possibly meet the requirements of the Commisson of Hospital Accreditation because the building has not the space for required facilities.
>
> There is no space for a medical laboratory, for an X-ray department, or for an admitting and records department. The maternity department is absolutely inadequate.
>
> The hospital today can offer only ten beds on the first floor, and three beds on the basement floor for adult patients. No private rooms are available.
>
> There are only two cribs on the basement floor for children, and there have been times when all five available bassinets were occupied by new-born babies.
>
> This is hardly a condition that should be permitted to exist in any hospital anywhere in this day and age. Science has made gigantic strides

in the field of medicine and surgery, but these advances are of limited practical value unless they can be applied.[44]

The campaign to build the hospital began in earnest when an area was chosen south of the town on Highway 73 on a donated site. Bennett County was on top of a list of areas of the state for allocation of 1953 federal-aid hospital funds that had just been granted the state by an appropriation of Congress. Funds were available as an outright grant to the Bennett County in the amount of 50 percent of any hospital they chose to build, so long as it met federal and state requirements. It was imperative that the hospital be operated on a nonprofit basis by a political subdivision of the state or by a religious or other nonprofit organization. The title to the property was to be held by such a subdivison or organization, and there could be no discrimination of patients as to race, color, or creed. In September of 1953, Mother M. Jerome again appealed to the County Board Commissioners to rush the building of the new hospital because of the deplorable conditions of the old one. "I dread," Mother M. Jerome stated, "to think of the Sisters going through this winter under the existing circumstances. I am even contemplating taking the Sisters home until a new hospital is built."[45]

Instead of making progress, however, the Bennett County Hospital Program struck a serious roadblock in October when a close examination of the books of Bennett County by an auditor revealed that the county actually had no money whatsoever to match the federal funds to build the hospital. The commissioners had previously appropriated $40,000 from Bennett County's general fund believing that $60,000 in government bonds represented an unearmarked surplus to aid in the construction of the hospital. Of this, $35,000 was to be put with the $65,000 bond issue authorized by the voters at the general election in November, and the other $5,000 was to be used to provide a site. But a thorough examination of the books revealed that the government bonds held by Bennett County did not represent a surplus at all but actually represented all the money the county had of its own for the operation of its various phases of government.[46]

By December, however, Mr. George Day, the state's attorney of Bennett County, informed Mother M. Jerome that a plan had been worked out to everyone's satisfaction. In a letter to Mother M. Jerome, he stated in part:

> The whole idea is for you people to have a solid right of possession in the old hospital while the new one is being built, and the Bishop wanted this in the form of a lease dated at least one day prior to his Deed, which he prepared . . . there is a further provision that in case the county fails for three years to build a hospital, the title to the old hospital property reverts back to the Diocese of Rapid City.
>
> As we are having good weather here, I see no reason why the contractor can't start putting material on the ground yet this winter with the idea of being ready to construct the building rather rapidly as soon as spring comes.
>
> George Day[47]

St. Anthony's Hospital
Martin, South Dakota (1952–1971)

The new St. Anthony's Hospital, built at a cost of $262,000, was dedicated on July 2, 1955, and officially opened on July 7. It was financed with only a $65,000 county-bonded indebtedness. Fortunately, more than $130,000 of federal matching funds had been made available to Bennett County.[48] The building was a medium-sized, modern, open staff hospital with a patient capacity of twenty-eight. The Sisters now made their home on the second floor of the hospital where they had private bedrooms, a recreation room, and a chapel.[49] The structure was lovely and functional with many conveniences. Sister M. Paul had worked diligently and successfully with the county auditor in planning the building.

While St. Anthony's Hospital was being built, the staff at the hospital consisted of Sister M. Paul Kirschbaum who served as superior and administrator; Sister M. Simplicita Mroczkowski; Sister M. Athanasia Murzyn; Sister Dorothy Joan Lagocki; and Sister M. Gerardette Molda. On September 18, 1955, however, Sister M. Bertille Geffert[50] arrived to succeed Sister M. Paul.[51]

On August 6, 1956, at seven-fifteen o'clock in the evening, a tornado struck Martin causing almost a $500,000 worth of damage to the town. The hospital sustained heavy water damage estimated at $100,000 after the twister peeled back the roof like a carpet and allowed the water to seep into the building.[52] The thirteen patients in the hospital at the time were evacuated to the safety of a corner of the basement. The Sisters walked in water up to their ankles carrying the patients to safety. After the storm, the patients were taken to private homes in the town. There were no casualties except for Sister Dorothy Joan Lagocki who was hit and bruised by hailstones as large as baseballs when she attempted to close a door.[53] In 1956, Sister M. Bertille proudly accepted the South Dakota Hospital Association Merit Award which read:

This Merit Award Certificate is presented to Sister M. Bertille, RN, Administrator, to the other Sisters, and to the Hospital personnel of St. Anthony's Hospital, Martin, South Dakota, for meritorious, courteous, and loving service to the patients and to their families under great stress, during and after a tornado seriously damaged their hospital and community on August 5, 1956.

> Horace E. Attking,
> President
> Zello C. Messner,
> Secretary

In 1958, the Sisters applied for and received permission to obtain a chaplain for the hospital. On November 14, 1958, a trailer was purchased and situated east of the hospital for the Reverend Benedict Determan, TOR, from Latrobe, Pennsylvania. Father Determan served as the chaplain until his death in 1965. After Father Determan's death, the chaplaincy was assumed by the pastor of the nearby church.[54]

By 1960, St. Anthony's Hospital welcomed a badly needed addition which increased the hospital's capacity to thirty beds and five bassinets. The hospital also contained clinic outpatient facilities. During the early 1960s, seven Sisters were stationed at St. Anthony's Hospital to meet the patients' needs.

By the late 1960s, however, there was a distinct climate of change at the hospital. Records indicate that there existed a lack of sufficient medical personnel, and, at times, there was no physician who was duly certified in attendance or even residing in town. A low patient census did not allow for future planning and implementation of technological advancement in the health care delivery field without the hospital's being a satellite facility. In 1968, the First Extraordinary Chapter of Affairs held in the congregation caused the Sisters to examine their hospital apostolate very carefully and to make major decisions regarding its future. After much study and reflection, Sister M. Hugoline Czaplinski, the superior general, and the collegial board decided to take steps to withdraw from the operation of St. Anthony's Hospital. Records indicate that in 1971, with a twenty-eight bed capacity, there were only 576 admissions with a daily census of nine and an occupancy percentage of 31.0. Five bassinets were available and only forty-seven babies were born.[55] Lastly, national studies indicated that adequate medical service in hospitals below a fifty-bed capacity was highly questionable.[56]

Consequently, in June of 1971, Sister M. Hugoline informed the Most Reverend Harold J. Dimmerling, bishop of Rapid City, of plans to withdraw the Sisters. Bishop Dimmerling was most gracious and understanding. Sister M. Hugoline next contacted the prioress general of the Benedictine Order in Yankton, South Dakota, in order to discuss the possibility of their taking over St. Anthony's Hospital as a satellite of their large hospital in Rapid City.[57] The Franciscan Sisters of Chicago wished to leave St. Anthony's Hospital in the hands of Sisters who were able to continue to serve the Martin community.

If the Benedictine Sisters were not available, the hospital would return to the administration of civic authority.

On September 14, 1971, Sister M. Hugoline and Lawrence T. Filosa, president and executive director of the health care facilities owned and operated by the Franciscan Sisters of Chicago, met with the Bennett County Commissioners. The county commissioners passed a resolution agreeing to release the Sisters from their lease effective September 30, 1971. The hospital had not actually been in operation since September 11, when the last patient had been dismissed. On October 8, 1971, Sister M. Bertille Geffert signed the building back to Bennett County. With the completion of all records, charts, and inventories, Sister M. Bertille, Sister M. Agatha Walerski, and Sister M. Celestine Kobos left Martin on November 1, 1971, with very heavy hearts.[58]

Prior to their departure, the Sisters were honored at a farewell open house on Sunday, September 26, 1971, at the local American Legion Hall. Included among the honored guests were Sister M. Bertille Geffert, Sister M. Antonita Waloch, Sister M. Felicia Wierciak, Sister M. Leonia Mszanski, Sister M. Agatha Walerski, and Sister M. Celestine Kobos. The Bennett County community expressed their sincere appreciation for the services the Sisters had rendered and sincere regret that the Sisters were leaving after nineteen years. Their sentiments were expressed very adequately in the farewell letter of Bishop Dimmerling received by Sister M. Bertille a month later:

> Dear Sister M. Bertilla [sic]:
>
> I am indeed aware that the Sisters are leaving St. Anthony's Hospital in Martin. I would have preferred that you could stay, but, at the same time, I understand your thinking and reasoning that has motivated your Community to leave.
>
> I wish at this time, to thank you and all the good Sisters who have worked at St. Anthony's Hospital since 1952. I am sure that your presence in the community has been an inspiration to all of the people, and that the loving care that you have given your patients has provided everyone with a beautiful example of Christ-like concern and compassion for the sick. I feel, likewise, that your presence there has also been a source of many graces and blessings for all of the members of the community. As you leave then, I wish to thank you again for your work, sacrifices and services and ask Almighty God that he will bless you and your work wherever you serve in the future.
>
> With kindest regards and sincere best wishes I am,
>
> > Devotedly yours in Christ,
> > Harold J. Dimmerling
> > Bishop of Rapid City[59]

Sister M. Bertille Geffert returned for six weeks in July of 1972 to help the Benedictine Sisters take over the hospital. Unfortunately, the Benedictine Sisters remained for a period of only ten months. After their departure, the Bennett County Community Hospital assumed its original name in April of 1973. As late as 1976, it was under the administration of a lay woman and continued to serve the health care needs of the people of Martin, South Dakota, who lived within a fifty-mile radius. It maintained a twenty-bed capacity with four bassinets and four pediatric beds. The rest of the hospital was used for the Martin clinic.[60]

The apostolate in health care service in hospitals had gained momentum in the congregation in the early 1950s, yet the continuing ministry to the aged was never overlooked and proved equally challenging. As chronicled earlier in Chapter 39, the Franciscan Sisters of Chicago had purchased Mount Alvernia Convent on Terrace Road in East Cleveland, Ohio, in 1936. Basically, the convent had functioned as a house of studies for Sister-students who attended St. John College of Cleveland and as a summer retreat center for the Sisters who were stationed in Ohio and Pennsylvania.

On February 15, 1946, a tragic fire destroyed Jennings Hall for the Aged in Cleveland. Upon the request of the Most Reverend Edward J. Hoban, bishop of Cleveland, the Franciscan Sisters of Chicago agreed to shelter fourteen aged women, former residents of Jennings Hall, at Mount Alvernia Convent. It was this state of affairs which inspired the Sisters to give serious consideration to the possibility of continuing their ministry to the aged by converting Mount Alvernia Convent into a home for the aged or building an entirely new home on the property. In 1950, when the Sisters announced plans to construct a new facility for elderly residents on their Terrace Road property, the East Cleveland Zoning Board emphatically denied them permission to do so. As a consequence, the Terrace Road convent and property eventually were sold.

The plan for building a home for the aged in Cleveland, however, was never abandoned either by the Franciscan Sisters of Chicago, or, as future events were to prove, by the bishop of Cleveland. Bishop Hoban met in Cleveland with Mother M. Jerome Dadej, the superior general, in October of 1950 and suggested a new course of action.[61] To the many religious, educational, and welfare programs which Bishop Hoban had initiated and developed in Cleveland during the first ten years of his tenure as bishop, he now proposed the addition of a new institution. Upon its completion, it would be the only one of its kind under Catholic auspices in the Diocese of Cleveland. The new institution being proposed was a combination home for the aged and convalescent. To encourage the Franciscan Sisters of Chicago to accept his proposal, Bishop Hoban informed Mother M. Jerome that the Diocese of Cleveland was prepared to donate the land necessary for the institution. He was also prepared to lend any financial assistance which the congregation might require for this project so very dear to his heart.[62] At Bishop Hoban's request, Mother M. Jerome; Sister M. Benigna Jakajtis, the superior of Mount Alvernia Convent in East Cleveland; and Sister M. Hilary Dadej, the superior and administrator of Madonna Hall on East 82nd Street, met on October 22 with Robert Stickle of the architectural firm of Stickle, Kelly, and Stickle to view several possible locations for the proposed new facility to be called Alvernia Rest Home for the Convalescent and Aged.[63]

Two very appealing sites, both belonging to the Diocese of Cleveland, emerged as ideal. They were both on State Road in Parma, a residential suburb eight miles south of Cleveland. The first area was the site of St. Edward's Orphanage and consisted of several buildings surrounded by large trees. The second site, directly across the street from St. Edward's Orphanage, was part of the beautiful grounds of an orphanage called Parmadale. It was this site which appealed to the Sisters. Mr. Stickle set about immediately to draw up plans indicating exactly where the new institution would stand. When Bishop Hoban met with Mother M. Jerome and the Sisters a few days later, he expressed his extreme satisfaction at the site they had selected. The Sisters were grateful beyond belief when Bishop Hoban informed them that he was offering them an additional seven and one-half acres so that someday they might be in a position to build a provincial house for the Franciscan Sisters of Chicago whom he was most anxious to see well established in his diocese.[64] Besides the donation of $400,000 made by the Diocese of Cleveland towards the construction of Alvernia Rest Home, Bishop Hoban also granted the Sisters an additional donation of $50,000, the bequest of a priest of the Diocese of Cleveland who had died in 1935 and had stipulated in his will that the money was to be used exclusively to build a home for the aged someday. The diocese further agreed to transfer the title to the home and the above-mentioned land to the Franciscan Sisters of Chicago. The Sisters, in turn, would be responsible for all costs in excess of the amount donated by the Diocese of Cleveland which might be incurred in completing and fully equipping Alvernia Rest Home.[65] Mother M. Jerome announced that the money which the Sisters received from the sale of Mount Alvernia Convent in East Cleveland would be used to furnish the new institution. The Franciscan Sisters of Chicago would make a contribution of $100,000 and the remainder of the money needed to complete the project would be obtained by securing a loan.[66]

On January 23, 1951, construction began of the first institution for the aged and convalescent under Catholic auspices in the Diocese of Cleveland. Mother M. Jerome appointed Sister M. Benigna Jakajtis to supervise the construction of the building which proceeded without any unaccountable delays.[67]

On Sunday, June 14, 1953, Bishop Hoban, now the archbishop-bishop of Cleveland, solemnly dedicated the new Alvernia Rest Home. Assisting him were the Right Reverend Monsignor Thomas Shannon, pastor of Christ the King Church, and the Right Reverend Monsignor Andrew Radecki, pastor of St. Casimir Church. Before the dedication ceremony, the archbishop blessed the cornerstone in the vestibule of the structure. The Right Reverend Monsignor John J. Krol,[68] chancellor of the Diocese of Cleveland, delivered a moving sermon. At the conclusion of the dedication, a Solemn Benediction of the Most Blessed Sacrament followed during which the Reverend Anthony Gawlik of Sacred Heart Church and the Reverend Thaddeus Michalski of St. Casimir Church, both assistant pastors of parish schools conducted by the Franciscan Sisters of

Chicago, assisted Archbishop Hoban. The St. Joseph Seminary Choir of the Blessed Sacrament Fathers sang. To conclude the grace-filled day, a dinner and open house followed the liturgical ceremonies.[69] The years were nostalgically telescoped for Archbishop Hoban when he dedicated the new Alvernia Rest Home. Monsignor Krol, in his dedication sermon, spoke of the "happy chain of circumstances" which brought Archbishop Hoban and the Franciscan Sisters of Chicago together in the fulfillment of this ministerial project. As a young boy, Archbishop Hoban had lived in the vicinity of St. Stanislaus Kostka Church in Chicago and had witnessed the works of mercy to which Sister M. Theresa Dudzik had devoted herself. He had been witness also to her founding of the St. Joseph Home for the Aged and Crippled which had been erected in the very neighborhood in which he had spent his early life. Until 1928, when he was transferred to the Diocese of Rockford, Illinois, Archbishop Hoban had seen the steady growth of the Congregation of the Franciscan Sisters of Chicago after its foundation by Sister M. Theresa Dudzik.[70] One of his early deeds as bishop of Cleveland had been to call upon the Franciscan Sisters of Chicago in 1946, to staff St. Joseph Home for the Aged on Woodland Avenue in Cleveland. He had likewise entrusted Madonna Hall for Women on East 82nd Street in Cleveland to the devoted care of the Sisters. It was he who urged the Sisters to house the homeless aged women at Mount Alvernia Terrace Convent on Terrace Road in East Cleveland after the Jennings Hall for the Aged had been destroyed by fire. His intense desire to help Cleveland's aged culminated in the dedication of the beautiful and spacious new Alvernia Rest Home. Because of Archbishop Hoban's gracious guidance, encouragement, and financial assistance, Alvernia Rest Home had been built. He had always been "a good Father" to the Franciscan Sisters of Chicago. In 1957, Mother M. Jerome wrote to Archbishop Hoban expressing her sentiments, which in this history, become a reality:

> I have no adequate words to express the sentiments of my heart towards Your Excellency, but I can assure you that in the history of our congregation the name of His Excellency, Archbishop Edward F. Hoban, will be inscribed in golden letters. It will be a perpetual remembrance to posterity to keep the name of the Beloved Shepherd in grateful reverence and prayerful memory.[71]

As originally constructed, Alvernia Rest Home was a beautiful, large, three-story H-shaped building in modern colonial architecture with a magnificent 255-foot frontage facing State Road. There were facilities for ninety-three aged residents and fifty convalescents. The aged persons were admitted on application to the administrator, and the convalescent patients were admitted on their doctor's recommendation.

The aged residents lived in private and semiprivate rooms and suites on the first and second floors. The top floor, set apart for the convalescence of men and women sixteen years and older, was equipped as an infirmary with a registered nurse on duty.

Each of the floors had a lounge with an open sun porch as well as an enclosed porch. A nurses' station and lounges were also located on each floor. Each of the three floors had its own serving kitchen. The food was prepared in the main kitchen and then sent on electrically heated lifts to the designated floor where it was then transferred to heated carts. The ground floor, practically below street level, had a recreation room, women's lounge, a smoking room, a billiard room, and a beauty and barber shop. A doctor's examination room was also located there. In addition, the ground floor contained the dining rooms and the main kitchen.[72] The lovely chapel on the first floor seated approximately 150 persons. Elegant stained glass windows and a Bottocino marble altar added to its beauty. The Holy Sacrifice of the Mass was celebrated every day in the chapel by the resident chaplain, the Reverend Charles A. Patrick, who attended to all of the other spiritual needs of the residents and convalescents.[73]

On March 20, 1953, prior to the dedication, three Franciscan Sisters of Chicago had taken up residence at Alvernia Rest Home. They were Sister M. Benigna Jakajtis, the superior and administrator;[74] Sister M. Rosaria Frodyma,[75] and Sister M. Albertine Schab.[76] Their living quarters were located in the east wing on the second floor of the home. With the arrival at a later date of Sister M. Ernestine Radecki, Sister M. Sylvia Lewandowski, Sister M. Leonia Mszanski, Sister M. Imelda Derbin, Sister M. Leontia Swiech, and Sister M. Regina Krolak, additional rooms in the east wing ordinarily occupied by residents were used, of necessity, to house the Sisters on the staff.

Alvernia Rest Home, built at a cost of more than $1 million opened officially with a rest home licensure on the feast of St. Francis, October 4, 1953. Prior to its formal opening, it had welcomed fourteen aged women whom the Sisters had sheltered at Mount Alvernia Convent on Terrace Road in East Cleveland.[77]

Early in 1955, Sister M. Benigna Jakajtis, the superior and administrator of Mount Alvernia Home, was replaced by Sister M. Philomena Wasik.[78] Sister M. Philomena had scarcely served a year when she died on March 31, 1956. Approximately two weeks earlier, Sister M. Bernice Stefanski,[79] who had served at the home for two years, had also passed away. Both Sisters had succumbed to heart disease. Chosen as the new administrator and superior was Sister M. Immaculate Matuszewski.[80]

Sister M. Immaculate's six-year term as superior and administrator ended in 1962. Appointed her successor was Sister M. Ralph Stawasz[81] who had come to Alvernia Rest Home in September of 1954 and for six years had served as treasurer. When in August of 1968, Sister M. Ralph was transferred to the Our Lady of Victory Convent Motherhouse in Lemont to assist the treasurer general, Sister M. Aloysetta Ciezadlo who was ill, the residents of Alvernia Rest Home were very reluctant to part with her. Judging from the petitions which had gone out from Alvernia Rest Home to the Motherhouse, the residents felt very strongly about the departure of their dear and capable administrator.[82] As a final gesture of gratitude, the residents moved to dedicate an outdoor shrine to the Blessed Virgin Mary in Sister M. Ralph's honor. A plaque posted on the shrine listed the names of all the living and deceased benefactors of the home.

Among Sister M. Ralph's unique accomplishments while administrator of

Alvernia Rest Home was the installation of an outdoor swimming pool and mobile home in 1966. The swimming pool was used rather infrequently by the residents and the staff. In the early 1970s, therefore, the pool and mobile home were designated as a summer home for the members of the Franciscan Sisters of Chicago who might choose to use the grounds and facilities as a vacation spot or for therapeutic purposes. In 1977, with the addition of more Sisters to the staff there was a dire need for living quarters. Fortunately, the mobile home, which contained three bedrooms, was now conveniently used to house three Sisters until a convent was eventually built.

The history of Alvernia Rest Home would be remiss if it did not specifically mention the long-term service rendered by Sister M. Aquinas Rosky,[83] who, in 1968, succeeded Sister M. Ralph Stawasz as administrator and superior. Sister M. Aquinas served in that capacity for two years and has remained on the staff for a total of twenty-seven years in devoted and selfless service. In 1970, Mother M. Beatrice Rybacki, at the conclusion of her second term of office as superior general, was appointed to Alvernia Rest Home and served as the administrator until 1979. That year, Sister M. Aloysilla Kedzior[84] arrived to succeed Mother M. Beatrice Rybacki who remains on the staff today.

From the time the Franciscan Sisters of Chicago had established Alvernia Rest Home, they had had no convent residence. It had been necessary for the Sisters to maintain their living quarters in a section of Alvernia Rest Home. By 1978, the rooms the Sisters occupied were urgently needed for incoming residents, and with the increase of Sisters on the staff, separate living quarters had become a real necessity. As a result, ground-breaking ceremonies were held for the construction of a convent, a new dining room for the residents, and a three-story addition called the "Annex." The Most Reverend Gilbert Sheldon, auxiliary bishop of Cleveland, officiated at the ceremonies at which Sister Martha Joan Sempolski, the superior general, and Sister M. Gabriel Lazarski, the apostolate coordinator, were present.[85]

During Mount Alvernia Home's preparation for expansion, it celebrated its 25th anniversary of foundation on October 8, 1978. The Liturgy of the Eucharist was celebrated by the Most Reverend James A. Hickey, bishop of Cleveland, in La Verna Chapel of the home, and the Reverend John Storey, the pastor of St. Mary's Parish in Bedford, Ohio, delivered the homily. The Franciscan Sisters of Chicago sang under the direction of Sister M. Celeste Walkowski. A banquet concluded the jubilee celebration.

On May 7, 1979, the old front entrance of Alvernia Rest Home was razed, and the beautiful Annex was attached to the main building on the State Road frontage. The Annex provided the ground floor with an enlarged lobby area, complete business and social services office, a large residents' dining room, a visitors' and employees' café seating approximately 150 persons, a central visiting area, an activities department, a beauty and barber shop, and a gift shop. The second and third floors of the Annex provided rooms for fifty more residents with a solarium and a nurses' station on each floor.

The blessing and dedication ceremony for the new convent took place in the La Verna Chapel of Alvernia Rest Home on Saturday, May 24, 1980. The ceremony began

Mount Alverna Home
Parma, Ohio (1952–   )

with the celebration of the Liturgy of the Eucharist at ten-thirty o'clock in the morning by the Most Reverend James Hickey, bishop of Cleveland, and seven concelebrants. The Reverend Edward Camille, diocesan director of Catholic Charities, delivered the homily during the Sacred Liturgy while the Franciscan Sisters of Chicago sang under the direction of Sister M. Celeste Walkowski. On Sunday, May 25, many other priests, religious, and laity were invited to tour the new convent.[86] Beautiful and most innovative, the convent with four large wings was located behind Alvernia Rest Home. It contained sixteen rooms for the Sisters, a chapel, a guest parlor, four bedrooms for guests, and a large community room with a library, reading area, and kitchen facilities. The Sisters were in their new convent by May 30, 1980.

The time had come for the Annex and the new dining room for the residents to be dedicated. On July 11, 1981, the Liturgy of the Eucharist was celebrated in La Verna Chapel of Alvernia Rest Home by the Most Reverend Anthony Pilla, bishop of Cleveland, who was also the homilist. Shortly before the dedication of the Annex, the name of the institution was changed from Alvernia Rest Home to Mount Alverna Home and the addition was called Mount Alverna Annex.[87]

Mount Alverna Home which had provided all the conveniences of a modern nursing home underwent even more changes in the 1980s. The heating, ventilating, and air-conditioning project and the laundry and the Sisters' dining room expansion were concluded. A new physical therapy room was developed and the redecorating of the interior of the facilities was also completed. As a consequence, the residents were now able to enjoy larger and more aesthetically appealing solariums on each floor, and the laundry personnel could perform their work more efficiently in an environment which was now well lighted, ventilated, and spacious. Most importantly, the residents could now enjoy the comfort of balanced temperature control throughout the year. The final touches to the exterior of the home took place in 1985 when the lobby renovation project was completed. The front entrance to the home was revamped to include the installation of a very functional elevator, a new reception section, a security area, and a ramp to accommodate wheelchair residents.

Sorrow came to Mount Alverna Home on August 17, 1984, when Sister M. Teresanna Bartuszewski who had been on the staff since 1970 succumbed to a heart attack. She had always served the residents with great devotion and her forty-seven years as a member of the Franciscan Sisters of Chicago had proved her to be an inspiring example of true compassion and dedication to duty.[88]

From 1953 to 1968, Mount Alverna Home had operated with a rest home license. From 1968 to 1981, it was licensed as both a rest home and an intermediate care facility. With the increase of applicants who required constant supervision and much nursing care, the license for a complete intermediate care facility was received in August of 1984. As a result, Mount Alverna Home and Annex is now fully licensed for 203 intermediate care beds.[89]

Because the spiritual as well as the bodily welfare of the residents is so important, Mount Alverna Home has an active Pastoral Care Program. The Reverend Howard Stunek, OFM, is the director of the Pastoral Care Department and is assisted by Sister M. Marinella Gubala and Sister M. Therese Grajek, both certified chaplain assistants. The Liturgy of the Eucharist is celebrated every day, and distribution of Holy Communion outside of the Eucharistic Liturgy takes place daily. Benediction of the Most Blessed Sacrament is held on Fridays at four o'clock in the afternoon, and communal Anointing of

Rear View of Mount Alverna Home and Convent
Parma, Ohio

the Sick takes place every two months. Other sacraments such as Baptism and the Sacrament of the Anointing of the Sick are available in time of need and upon request. On Wednesdays before the First Fridays of the month, as well as other days upon request, the Sacrament of Reconciliation is administered. The rosary is recited daily at four o'clock in the afternoon in the chapel or solariums. During Lent, the Stations of the Cross are a part of the paraliturgical services offered. Mount Alverna Home provides a Memorial Service for deceased residents once a year, and funerals for the residents are held in the chapel of the home when requested by the family. Protestant and other denominational services are conducted by local clergymen, and visits to the residents by their clergymen are encouraged. To this end, Mount Alverna Home conducts Ecumenical Prayer Services four times a year. The Department of Pastoral Care at Mount Alverna Home provides sacramental, pastoral, and counseling services to the residents and to their families as well.[90]

The residents of Mount Alverna Home are offered excellent medical care. The medical director is a licensed physician specializing in geriatrics. Approximately six other doctors visit the home on a regular basis. Of these, one is a dentist, one a podiatrist, and one an ophthalmologist. The medical director also does employee physicals on a monthly basis. Mount Alverna Home offers the services of a licensed dentist who visits the home on a biweekly basis and is also available on an on-call basis.

The nursing department offers twenty-four-hour professional nursing service with a staff of approximately twenty-four nurses, thirty-one LPNs and 119 nursing assistants. This department is headed by the director of nursing who works closely with her staff to meet the needs of all the residents.

Mount Alverna Home employs a full-time food service director, a part-time registered dietitian, and a staff of thirty-seven. Three basic meals, morning and evening snacks, nutritional intake, and lunch and dinner to the employees are served daily. This department also caters all business luncheons and special events.

The home employs a full-time social service director along with a social service designee. They are responsible for all admissions and discharges; they attend resident care conferences, and meet with residents and family members as requested or when necessary.

Specialized services are provided by Mount Alverna Home to meet the rehabilitative and functional needs of each resident as prescribed by a physician. A fully equipped physical therapy room is served by a licensed physical therapist and his assistant. Every effort is made to maintain and restore physical functioning, prevent physical and mental deterioration, and build and maintain morale.

The residents of Mount Alverna Home find companionship and friendship at the home. The Activities Department seeks to provide intellectual, physical, and social diversion throughout the day. There are many planned social activities such as birthday parties, carnival days, bowling, crafts display, movies, and slide presentations. Books and magazines are always available in the home library. The activities are based upon the needs and abilities of the residents. Besides the lounges which are located on all three floors providing pleasant areas where the residents may gather to visit, play cards, or watch television, there is a large variety of craft programs, exercise programs, and suitable sports activities. The residents are likewise entertained frequently by various community organizations. Among them are the Catholic Charities Group, the Catholic War Veterans, the Greenbriar Ladies Guild, the Singing Angels, the Boy and Girl Scouts, the Garfield Heights Mothers Singers, and the 60+ Club. One of the most enjoyable groups is the Animal Protective League that, with a program of pet therapy, comes to the home with a selection of puppies on a monthly basis to visit the residents.

Mount Alverna Home is recognized by and is a member of the American Association of Homes for the Aged, the Association of Ohio Philanthropic Homes and Housing for the Aging, the Catholic Health Association of the United States, the Federation of Catholic Community Services, and the Area Training Center Project at Menorah Park—Department of Health—State of Ohio.

In November of 1986, Mr. Mark A. Muzillo[91] was appointed the first lay president of Mount Alverna Home succeeding Sister M. Aloysilla Kedzior. Mount Alverna Home, the largest Catholic nursing home in the Diocese of Cleveland, has thirteen Franciscan Sisters of Chicago and 235 lay employees on its staff. They are aided by men, women, and youths who volunteer on a daily or monthly basis to be of service to Mount Alverna's residents. Mount Alverna Home has many immediate and long-range goals. They are being implemented at every opportunity and are all designed to offer its residents the very best in professional and dedicated service. Among the home's future plans are the construction of a retirement center for independent living and provisions for an adult day-care center. The ultimate aim is to build Mount Alverna Home into a campus thereby offering a wide spectrum of services to the aging of the Diocese of Cleveland.[92]

Mount Alverna Home has always been governed by the fundamental philosophy which governs the conduct of all Catholic nursing homes. Regardless of race, creed, social or financial status, Mount Alverna Home offers the total concept of human care which enhances the physical, emotional, social, and spiritual needs of its residents. Mount Alverna Home strives to promote genuine community and to enhance the dignity of its residents in a spirit of real love and concern on the part of the administration and staff. At Mount Alverna Home, "Caring" is what they are about.[93]

EXPANSION OF HEALTH CARE SERVICES

[1]*Atkinson Graphic,* 10 February 1977.

[2]Ibid.

[3]Ibid.

[4]The Sisters had accepted Mother of Grace Hospital in Gregory, South Dakota, in 1948. See Chapter 50.

[5]*Book of Correspondence:* Letter from the Reverend A. A. Lehmen to Mother M. Jerome Dadej, 22 September 1949 (AFSCL).

[6]*Book of Correspondence:* Letter from Sister M. Bertilla, OSB, to Mother M. Antonina Osinski, 6 May 1951 (AFSCL).

[7]Secretaries General, *Community Chronicle,* p. 312 (AFSCL).

[8]*Book of Correspondence:* Letter from Mother M. Jerome Dadej to the Most Reverend Gerald T. Bergan, archbishop of Omaha, 5 October 1951 (AFSCL).

[9]*Book of Correspondence:* Letter from Mr. Charles E. Chace to Mother M. Jerome Dadej, 6 October 1951 (AFSCL).

[10]*Atkinson Graphic,* 20 July 1972.

[11]"Brief History of Atkinson Memorial Hospital" (AFSCL).

[12]Secretaries General, *Community Chronicle,* p. 319 (AFSCL).

[13]"Report to the Members of the First Extraordinary Chapter of Affairs," 1968 (AFSCL).

[14]Secretaries General, *Community Chronicle,* p. 213 (AFSCL).

[15]*Atkinson Graphic,* 30 March 1956.

[16]The surgeons would now no longer have to change into their surgical gowns in a closet-sized room at the opposite end of the hospital from surgery.

[17]*Book of Correspondence:* Letter from the Most Reverend Gerald T. Bergan, archbishop of Omaha, to Mother M. Jerome Dadej, 5 October 1951 (AFSCL).

[18]Secretaries General, *Community Chronicle,* p. 372 (AFSCL).

[19]"Report to the Members of the First Extraordinary Chapter of Affairs," 1968 (AFSCL).

[20]Sister Josephine Marie Haske, administrator of Our Lady of the Sandhills Hospital from 1962 to 1969, was selected to appear in the 1968 edition of *Outstanding Personalities of the West and Midwest.* She had organized the Catholic Hospital Association in Nebraska and served as its president from 1963 to 1964. *Franciscan Echo,* Vol. 2 (Lemont, Illinois: October 1968). She was also the secretary and public relations chairperson of the South Dakota Nurses' Association.

[21]"Report to the Members of the First Extraordinary Chapter of Affairs," 1968 (AFSCL).

[22]*Book of Correspondence:* Letter from Mr. Lawrence T. Filosa to Sister M. Amabilis, administrator of Atkinson Memorial Hospital, 9 May 1972 (AFSCL).

[23]*Atkinson Graphic,* 20 July 1972.

[24]Ibid.

[25]Ibid.

[26]Sister M. Amabilis became the administrator of St. Michael's Hospital in Tyndall, South Dakota. The hospital, staffed by Benedictine Sisters, had thirty-two beds. Sister M. Amabilis had a one-year contract agreed upon by the president of the board of St. Michael's; Sister M. Hugoline Czaplinski, the superior general of the Franciscan Sisters; and Sister M. Amabilis.

[27]*Interview* with Gary Bieganski, administrator of West Holt Memorial Hospital and Mrs. Lawrence Kaup, director of nursing, 11 June 1976 (AFSCL).

[28]*Atkinson Graphic*, 21 December 1972.

[29]By 1975, the population was 1,285. Of these, one-third were the Oglala Sioux.

[30]Secretaries General, *Community Chronicle*, 1 February 1952 (AFSCL).

[31]*Book of Correspondence:* Letter from the Most Reverend William T. McCarty, CSSR, to Mother M. Jerome, 3 October 1950 (AFSCL).

[32]Martin is located 125 miles southeast of Rapid City, South Dakota. The Badlands are fifty miles north of Martin while the beautifully colored cliffs, ridges, and spires which make up South Dakota's Black Hills are 120 miles northwest.

[33]*Book of Correspondence:* Letter from the Most Reverend William T. McCarty, CSSR, to Mother M. Jerome Dadej, 9 July 1949 (AFSCL).

[34]The Sisters had accepted this small community hospital in 1948.

[35]*Book of Correspondence:* Letter from the Most Reverend William T. McCarty, CSSR, to Mother M. Jerome Dadej, 24 August 1951 (AFSCL).

[36]Ibid., 23 October 1951.

[37]*Book of Correspondence:* Letter from Mother M. Jerome Dadej to the Most Reverend William T. McCarty, CSSR, 27 October 1951 (AFSCL).

[38]*Book of Correspondence:* Letter from the Most Reverend William T. McCarty, CSSR, to Mother M. Jerome Dadej, 5 February 1952 (AFSCL).

[39]*Book of Correspondence:* Letter from Sister Frances Szczur to author, 24 May 1980 (AFSCL).

[40]*Book of Correspondence:* Letter from the Most Reverend William T. McCarty, CSSR, to Sister M. Paul Kirschbaum, 5 February 1952 (AFSCL).

[41]*Book of Correspondence:* Letter from Sister Frances Szczur to author, 24 May 1980 (AFSCL).

[42]*Book of Correspondence:* Letter from Mother M. Jerome Dadej to Mr. Frank Roth, 31 March 1952 (AFSCL).

[43]*Book of Correspondence:* Letter from Mother M. Jerome Dadej to the Martin Hospital Commission, 2 March 1953 (AFSCL).

[44]*Bennett County Booster*, Martin, South Dakota, 20 January 1953.

[45]*Book of Correspondence:* Letter from Mother M. Jerome Dadej to William A. Hauff, auditor and county board commissioner, Bennett County, Martin, South Dakota, 24 September 1953 (AFSCL).

[46]St. Anthony's Hospital, "Collection of Newspaper Clippings," October 1953 (AFSCL).

[47]*Book of Correspondence:* Letter from George Day, state's attorney of Bennett County, to Mother M. Jerome Dadej, December 1953 (AFSCL).

[48]Bennett County Community Hospital, "Short History," 27 August 1975 (AFSCL).

[49]*Book of Correspondence:* Letter from Sister M. Bertille Geffert to author, May 1983 (AFSCL).

[50]Sister M. Bertille served at St. Anthony's Hospital from 1955 to 1961 and again from 1966 until 1971. *Book of Annual Assignments* (AFSCL).

[51]Sister M. Paul was transferred to Boys Town in 1955. In February of 1961, she became ill and was taken to St. John's Hospital in Huron, South Dakota, where she died on March 13.

The March 1965 issue of of the *Franciscan Echo* reveals that a street in Martin, South Dakota, had been named in honor of Sister M. Paul for her efforts in building the new hospital. The new "Sister Paul Street" was located a short distance from the old hospital. Earlier, the *Bennett County Booster* had praised Sister M. Paul for her great skill, determination, tact, and diplomacy. *Congregation Membership Records* (AFSCL).

[52]*Bennett County Booster*, August 1956.

[53]Another tornado occurred on July 28, 1966, but, fortunately, it caused only broken windows in some areas of the hospital.

[54]*Book of Correspondence:* Letter from Sister M. Bertille Geffert to author, April 1976 (AFSCL).

[55]St. Anthony's Hospital, "Brief Report," 1971 (AFSCL).

[56]*Bulletin of the Superior General,* "From the Desk of Sister M. Hugoline Czaplinski," 21 May 1971 (AFSCL).

[57]Ibid.

[58]*St. Anthony's Hospital House Journal,* 8 October 1971 (AFSCL).

[59]*Book of Correspondence:* Letter from the Most Reverend Harold J. Dimmerling, 22 October 1971 (AFSCL).

[60]*Interview* with Roslyn Bolzer, administrator, 9 June 1976 (AFSCL).

[61]*Minutes of General Council Proceedings,* 17 October 1950 (AFSCL).

[62]Ibid.

[63]At this meeting also, Bishop Hoban, undaunted, urged the Sisters to build a high school on Terrace Road for which he was convinced he could get permission. Mother M. Jerome informed him that the congregation was already planning to build Madonna High School in Chicago, and could not possibly staff another one at that time. Secretaries General, *Community Chronicle,* 22 October 1950 (AFSCL).

[64]*Franciscan Echo,* May 1965; and *Minutes of General Council Proceedings, 1958–1964* (AFSCL).

[65]*Book of Correspondence:* Letter from the Most Reverend Edward F. Hoban, archbishop-bishop of Cleveland, to Mother M. Jerome Dadej, 16 February 1952 (AFSCL).

[66]Ibid.

[67]"Short History of Alvernia Rest Home," Parma, Ohio, 1950 (AFSCL).

[68]One of the leading figures of the Church and a friend of the Franciscan Sisters of Chicago is John Cardinal Krol. He served as auxiliary bishop of Cleveland from 1953 until his appointment as archbishop of Philadelphia in 1961. In 1967, he was named to the Roman Catholic College of Cardinals. Though there had been ten other Catholic American bishops of Polish ancestry before him, Cardinal Krol is the first to lead a major American Roman Catholic diocese. Biographical sketch received from the chancery office, Diocese of Cleveland.

[69]*Catholic Universe Bulletin,* 19 June 1953.

[70]Ibid.

[71]*Book of Correspondence:* Letter from Mother M. Jerome Dadej to the Most Reverend Edward F. Hoban, 14 December 1957 (AFSCL).

[72]Alvernia Rest Home, Archival Report, 5 October 1960 (AFSCL).

[73]Serving as resident chaplains after Father Patrick were the Reverend Ignatius Dembowski; the Reverend Julius Viglas; the Reverend Charles Kovari, SJ; the Reverend Leo Schumacher; and the Reverend Humilis Solond, OFM, who died on duty on June 15, 1984. Sister M. Gemma Stanek, a certified pastoral assistant, served with Father Schumacher.

[74]See Chapter 31.

[75]Sister M. Rosaria was sent to Alvernia Rest Home in 1952 and left in 1980 thereby giving a total of twenty-eight years of dedicated and loving service at the home. *Congregation Membership Records* (AFSCL).

[76]See Chapter 51.

[77]*Interview* with Sister M. Albertine Schab, November 1987 (AFSCL).

[78]Sister M. Philomena entered from St. Stanislaus Bishop and Martyr Church in Chicago in 1916. She made her perpetual profession in 1925. Her service to the congregation included teaching

at several schools and working with the children at St. Elizabeth's Day Nursery. A history of heart trouble at one point required that she have bed rest for two years at the Motherhouse. When she died, she was sixty-three years old and had served in the congregation for forty years. *Congregation Membership Records* (AFSCL).

[79]Sister M. Bernice entered from St. Stanislaus Kostka Church in Chicago and was one of the pioneer Sisters of the community having entered in 1903. She was perpetually professed in 1913 and her vows were accepted by Mother M. Anna Wysinski. For most of her convent life, she served as a teacher in the various schools of the congregation and in Boys Town. She was seventy-three years old at the time of her death and had been in the congregation for fifty-three years. *Congregation Membership Records* (AFSCL).

[80]Sister M. Immaculate entered from St. Stanislaus Bishop and Martyr Church in Cleveland in 1915. She made her perpetual profession in 1923. For over thirty-five years she served as a teacher, principal, or religious superior until her appointment to Alvernia Rest Home. At the conclusion of her six-year term as administrator and superior, she returned to the Motherhouse. On October 7, 1964, she left to visit her family in Cleveland where she suffered a heart attack and died in the emergency room of St. Alexis Hospital on October 24, 1964. She was sixty-six years old and had been in the congregation for forty-eight years. *Congregation Membership Records* (AFSCL).

[81]See Chapter 61.

[82]*Book of Correspondence:* Letter from Mother M. Beatrice Rybacki to the residents of Alvernia Rest Home, 9 August 1968; and *Catholic Universe Bulletin,* 17 August 1968.

[83]A native of Youngstown, Ohio, Sister M. Aquinas entered the congregation in 1927. Her early years were spent teaching in the elementary schools of the congregation. In 1942, she received a diploma in nursing from St. Joseph Hospital School of Nursing in Joliet, Illinois. Before her appointment to Alvernia Rest Home in 1960, she ministered at St. Anthony Home, Crown Point, Indiana; St. John Hospital, Huron, South Dakota; and Mother of Grace Hospital in Gregory, South Dakota. *Congregation Membership Records* (AFSCL).

[84]See Chapter 49.

[85]Secretaries General, *Community Chronicle, January 1978* (AFSCL).

[86]*Catholic Universe Bulletin,* 25 May 1980.

[87]*Minutes of General Council Proceedings, July 1981* (AFSCL).

[88]Sister M. Teresanna entered from St. Adalbert's Church in East St. Louis, Illinois, in December 1937, and was received into the novitiate on August 15, 1938. She made her first profession on August 15, 1940, and was perpetually professed on August 12, 1945. For all of her religious life, Sister M. Teresanna served the aged at St. Joseph Home in Chicago; St. Anthony Home in Crown Point, Indiana; and Mother Theresa Home in Lemont. *Congregation Membership Records* (AFSCL).

[89]*Profile,* "Mount Alverna Home," produced for television by the Diocese of Cleveland, 6 March 1988; and *Book of Correspondence:* Letter from Sister M. Aloysilla Kedzior to author, 1986 (AFSCL).

[90]*Book of Correspondence:* Letter from Mark Muzillo, president of Mount Alverna Home, Parma, Ohio, to author, 6 March 1988 (AFSCL).

[91]Mr. Mark Muzillo was installed as president on May 19, 1987.

[92]Profile, "Mount Alverna Home."

[93]Ibid.

CHAPTER 54

The Challenge of the Fifties

The International Congress on the State of Perfection met in Rome in November of 1950. Both before and after that time there were many things written and said about the adaptation of the religious life to modern conditions as proposed by the Holy Father, Pope Pius XII. In addition, during the International Congress of Mothers General held in September of 1952, the Holy Father issued a call to "renewal" and recommended prudent directions for adaptation which basically narrowed down to two very serious issues: providing young Sisters with a strong supernaturally motivated preservice education, and studying the cause of the lack of perseverance among postulants and novices. In the opening address of the Congress, Pope Pius XII said:

> For your part, this is what we counsel: Make sure that nothing in your Community customs, your manner of life, or your ascetical practices raises a barrier or causes loss of vocation. We have in mind certain usages, which were no doubt suited to the times and surroundings in which they were instituted, but are out of place today, so that even a good girl with courage would find it an obstacle in her vocation.[1]

The mothers general returned to their convents knowing that to carry out this huge task outlined by Pope Pius XII would require courage and resourcefulness. This meant that an examination of the Rule, the Constitutions, the Book of Customs, and the Sisters' manner of life would have to be made. The Holy Father was clear. While the Sisters must remain faithful to the "spirit" of their founders or foundresses, religious life would have to be revitalized.

Pope Pius XII had sounded the call to religious congregations to adapt to modern conditions, but in some religious congregations meaningful changes were already taking place. This was true of the Franciscan Sisters of Chicago. The changes and adaptations generally fell into the following basic areas:

1. Introducing more Liturgy and Scripture into the Sisters' prayer life.

2. Reducing vocal prayers with an emphasis on mental prayer.

3. Modifying the religious habit

4. Modifying the horarium: de-emphasizing punctuality as a virtue; waiving the custom of having spiritual exercises such as saying the rosary, visiting the Blessed Sacrament, reciting litanies, etc. in common; making flexible the hours for meals.

5. Updating spiritual reading with an individual choice of books.

6. Giving young Sisters preservice preparation and providing for growth on the spiritual, intellectual, social, and professional levels.

7. Revising the horarium in order to find more time for study and class preparation.

8. Permitting the Sisters to take a more active role in the life of the parish and to relate better to the laity.

9. Dispensing with spiritual reading during meals.

10. Increasing the time for relaxation or recreation.

Thus, the 1950s began the years of change and the Franciscan Sisters of Chicago, as well as religious of all congregations, experienced it in their spiritual, community, and professional lives. The transitions which provoked reactions on the part of the Sisters at this time, however, could not compare with the reactions which followed the convocation of the Second Vatican Council in 1959 which so drastically altered religious life, especially in the United States.

Early in 1952, aware of the need for the Sisters to be suitably prepared for growth in the spiritual life, the congregation enrolled several Sisters at St. Xavier College on Chicago's Far South Side to pursue courses in theology. Two very practical aims were at the root of the pursuit, namely, to prepare teachers adequately for Catholic schools at all levels, and to develop the personal spiritual life of the Sisters. St. Xavier College, in cooperation with the Dominican Fathers of the Province of St. Albert the Great, presented summer sessions at a theological institute for Sisters. Sixteen Sisters were enrolled in the basic program which extended through three summers and led to a certificate in theology.[2]

Beginning steps were also taken in the area of Franciscan spirituality. On November 28 and 29 of 1952, the First National Meeting of Franciscan Teaching Sisters was held at the College of St. Francis in Joliet, Illinois. Organized by the Reverend Pius J. Barth, OFM, president of the Franciscan Educational Conference at that time, the first national convention of some 450 representatives of thirty-two thousand Franciscan teaching and nursing Sisters met for the purpose of academic discussion and exchange of ideals, content, methods, and activities on an unprecedented scale among Franciscan primary, elementary, secondary, collegiate, and nursing educators.[3] At this initial meeting, many Sisters realized their need for a deeper understanding of Franciscan spirituality.

They believed that if they were taught in the light and spirit of the Franciscan Ideal, they could be more devoted and effective religious. They concluded that Franciscanism could provide them with the knowledge and motivation necessary for a deeper understanding of their lives as religious women, as Christian educators and nurses, and as recipients of the tradition of learning and sanctity in the Franciscan Order. Several Sister-delegates to the First National Meeting were imbued with the idea of developing an institute of theology for Franciscan Sisters. This idea was met with enthusiasm at the Second National Meeting of Franciscan Sisters at Alverno College in Milwaukee in 1953, when the subject of theology was discussed. Notable encouragement also came from a number of general and provincial superiors who expressed their willingness to enroll their Sisters in such an institute.

With the gracious consent of the board of directors under Mother M. Immaculate, OSF, then superior general of the Congregation of the Franciscan Sisters of Mary Immaculate of Joliet, Illinois, and with the approval and blessing of the Most Reverend Martin D. McNamara, bishop of Joliet, as well as the Seraphic Blessing of the minister general of the Order of Friars Minor in Rome, the Most Reverend Augustine Sepinski, OFM, the Seraphic Institute of Theology for Sisters was established at the College of St. Francis in 1954, the Marian Year. It was placed under the patronage of Mary Immaculate and St. Bonaventure, the seraphic doctor and cardinal of the Church.[4]

A large and enthusiastic group of Sisters of various Franciscan communities enrolled in the first class in June of 1954. Instructors in the institute were Franciscan Fathers who were authorities in their respective fields of dogma, spiritual theology, Sacred Scripture, and Canon Law. The Reverend Cyril Shircel, OFM, of St. Mary's Seminary, Lemont, Illinois, and chairperson of the Department of Philosophy at the College of St. Francis, was appointed director of the institute. With his help and the generous cooperation of the provincials of several Franciscan provinces, the first faculty was arranged. With the untimely death of Father Shircel in 1959, the Reverend Ernest Latko, OFM, a Franciscan priest of the Province of the Assumption of the Blessed Virgin Mary of Pulaski, Wisconsin, became the new director.[5]

In the summer of 1956, certificates in Sacred Doctrine were awarded to forty-two Sisters of the charter class of the Marian Year, 1954. Among them were three Franciscan Sisters of Chicago: Sister M. Charitas Gajdzinski, Sister M. Julitta Szczepanik, and Sister M. Tarcisia Bucki. Every year the congregation was able to send students to participate in this extraordinary program, and by 1964, Sister Cheryl Marie Piesko, Sister M. Concordia Lawrence, Sister M. Dolorosa Bojanowski, and Sister M. Therese Grajek had earned their certificates in theology. Some Sisters, who could not take advantage of the entire course of studies, registered as special students.[6] By 1971, however, the innovative and provocative Seraphic Institute of Theology which had made Franciscan history when it was initiated in 1954 was discontinued. The institute's original aims had been met but had been altered by the spirit of the Church "in change."[7]

At a meeting with her general council on May 9, 1953, Mother M. Jerome read a letter which she had received from Cardinal Valerio Valeri, prefect of the Sacred Congregation of Religious. The letter announced the opening, in a few years, of the Roman Institute of Sacred Studies at Rome called *Regina Mundi*. The institute was directed to selected members of every congregation and order of religious women, of societies without vows, of secular institutes, and, in general, to women dedicated to the pursuit of perfection and to apostolic works. The aim of the institute was to provide a thorough and complete training in Sacred Studies, and to prepare the participants either for the work of government and the guidance of others within their religious communities, or for apostolic labors outside. The letter further asked for a donation which each congregation might be prepared to make to support the *Regina Mundi* institute. Mother M. Jerome and the general council agreed to donate $500 to maintain the residence of the participants and a standard amount of $50 a year to maintain the institute.[8] At this meeting of the councilors, Mother M. Jerome proposed sending Sister M. Hugoline Czaplinski to The Catholic University at Washington, DC, in order to pursue a doctorate in philosophy. After having obtained it, Sister M. Hugoline was to be sent to the *Regina Mundi* institute. She had been accepted by The Catholic University as a doctoral candidate and had been making all the necessary preparations when Mother M. Jerome assigned her, instead, to the faculty of Johnstown Central Catholic High School in Johnstown, Pennsylvania, in September of 1953.[9]

The Sacred Congregation of Religious opened the Roman Institute of Sacred Studies at Rome on October 18, 1954, with the approval and blessing of the Holy Father, Pope Pius XII. In a letter dated September 6, 1955, Mother M. Jerome advised Samuel Cardinal Stritch that "although we have no students at *Regina Mundi* as yet, I am contemplating sending two Sisters in the near future."[10]

Several years elapsed, and on January 30, 1960, Mother M. Beatrice Rybacki, who had succeeded Mother M. Jerome, met with her general council. During the meeting, Sister M. Gonzaga Raniszewski, the secretary general, brought up the matter of the *Regina Mundi* institute. She stressed the wish of Pope Pius XII and of Cardinal Stritch to send a Sister from each congregation to participate in the institute. According to the ratio employed, the Franciscan Sisters of Chicago were allowed to send one Sister to study at the theological institute for three years without any payment of fees except room and board. Mother M. Beatrice, however, proposed that two Sisters be sent to the institute. While the congregation was not in a position to send two Sisters immediately, Mother M. Beatrice and her councilors agreed that the Sisters could be sent in a matter of a year or two when the large groups of novices would be professed, and it would be easier to release two professed Sisters to take advantage of the splendid opportunity offered by the *Regina Mundi* institute.[11] Unfortunately, the events of the next few years made participation in the program impossible.

On September 8, 1953, Pope Pius XII, issued the encyclical *Fulgens Corona*, a call for Catholics to celebrate the centenary of the promulgation of the doctrine of the Immaculate Conception of the Blessed Virgin Mary. As a consequence, the Franciscan National Marian Commission proclaimed December 8, 1953 to December 8, 1954, as a year of Franciscan tribute to Mary and called it the Marian Year. The Commission issued a letter to ecclesiastical dignitaries, eminent scholars, and members of the three Franciscan Orders to inform them of a Franciscan National Marian Congress to be held in May of 1954 in several cities in California. Fittingly, the congress was to hold its opening sessions in Los Angeles, the city named after Our Lady, Queen of the Angels, by the saintly Fra Junipero Serra, the Apostle of California. The closing ceremonies were to be held in San Francisco, named after the Seraphic Father of all Franciscans.

The Centennial Observance was hailed as a Franciscan triumph since the doctrine of the Immaculate Conception of the Blessed Virgin Mary had been championed against great odds by the illustrious Franciscan, Blessed Duns Scotus. The congress was determined to recall, during the Centennial Observance, what the Franciscan School had contributed to Mary's honor, giving special attention to the renowned proponents of the Immaculate Conception, namely, Duns Scotus and Fra Junipero Serra. A campaign was launched by the offices of the Franciscan National Marian Commission to promote an enthusiastic movement on a national, local, community, and individual scale.[12]

To arouse interest in the Immaculate Conception Centennial as advocated by the Franciscan National Marian Commission, Mother M. Jerome suggested to the congregation that each mission house submit a list of Marian activities to the Motherhouse detailing the projects to be carried out in that particular mission home as part of the Franciscan program honoring Our Lady. For example, the postulants who entered the novitiate in August of 1954 all took the name *Marie* as part of their names as religious.[13] At the congregation's St. John School of Nursing in Huron, South Dakota, a statue of Mary Immaculate was erected on the campus and dedicated publicly on May 1, 1954. At Madonna High School in Chicago, the dogmas related to the Blessed Virgin Mary were used as the theme for the school yearbook, the *Madonnary*. Many of the other Marian activities were spiritual or devotional by nature. Mother M. Jerome herself urged the Sisters to greater Marian devotion and imitation through prayer and penance in the spirit of the Mother of God.[14]

The statewide observance in Franciscan California began on Sunday, May 2, 1953, taking the form of a Marian Day to be celebrated in the Archdiocese of Los Angeles, beginning with a Solemn Pontifical Mass celebrated by the Most Reverend James Cardinal McIntyre. In the final moments of the Marian Congress, the Blessed Virgin Mary was outlined in a reverent pyrotechnic display over the waters of historic Monterey Bay.[15]

Representing the Franciscan Sisters of Chicago during those days of devotional, educational, and social functions at the Franciscan National Marian Congress were Mother M. Jerome Dadej, the superior general; Sister M. Hilary Dadej, the superior at Madonna High School; and Sister M. Gonzaga Raniszewski, the secretary general.

THE CHALLENGE OF THE FIFTIES

[1]Address of Pope Pius XII to the International Congress of Mothers General, Rome, September 1952.

[2]Enrolled in the basic program extending through three summers and leading to a certificate in theology were Sister Clarent Marie Urbanowicz, 1952; Sister M. Annuncia Milanowski, Sister M. Esther Obuchowski, Sister Maryanne Pawlikowski, Sister M. Archangela Tyranski, 1953; Sister M. Alphonsine Kobylinski, Sister M. Remigia Lewandowski, Sister M. Tyburcia Sliwa, 1954; Sister M. Petronia Budzinski, Sister M. Richard Duszynski, Sister Eleanor Marie Jadrych, Sister Helen Marie Mackowiak, Sister M. Dolorine Piwowarski, Sister M. Bibianna Wiza, 1955; Sister Therese Agnes Kniola, and Sister M. Dolores Radziwiecki, 1956. *Book of Correspondence:* Letter from the registrar, St. Xavier College to author, 12 November 1975 (AFSCL).

[3]Franciscan Educational Conference, Sisters' Division, *Franciscan Education, Report of the First National Meeting of Franciscan Teaching Sisterhoods* (Chicago: Franciscan Educational Conference, 1953), p. 7.

[4]Seraphic Institute of Theology for Sisters, "Bulletin of Information," College of St. Francis, Joliet, Illinois, 1959.

[5]Dacian Bluma, OFM, and Theophilus Chowaniec, OFM, comps., *A History of the Assumption of the Blessed Virgin Mary Province* (Pulaski, Wisconsin: Franciscan Publishers, 1966), p. 95.

[6]*Book of Correspondence:* Letter from Sister Margaret Duffy, OSF, registrar, College of St. Francis, Joliet, Illinois, to author, 14 November 1975 (AFSCL).

[7]*Telephone conversation:* Sister Margaret Duffy, OSF, registrar, College of St. Francis, Joliet, Illinois, with author, 29 October 1976.

[8]*Minutes of General Council Proceedings,* 9 May 1953 (AFSCL).

[9]*Interview* with Sister M. Hugoline Czaplinski, 1974 (AFSCL).

[10]*Book of Correspondence:* Letter from Mother M. Jerome to Samuel Cardinal Stritch, 6 September 1955 (AFSCL).

[11]*Minutes of General Council Proceedings,* 30 January 1960 (AFSCL).

[12]*Book of Correspondence:* Letter from the Reverend Alfred Boeddeker, OFM, national executive chairman of the Franciscan National Marian Commission to Mother M. Jerome Dadej (AFSCL).

[13]The group of novices bearing the name *Marie* were Sister Bernard Marie, Sister Juanita Marie, Sister John Marie, Sister Stanislaus Marie, and Sister Thomas Marie.

[14]*Marian Year File,* 1954 (AFSCL).

[15]*Book of Correspondence:* Letter from the Reverend Alfred Boeddeker, OFM, to Mother M. Jerome Dadej (AFSCL).

CHAPTER 55

Era of Growth and Transition

During the last five years of Mother M. Jerome's term, the congregation witnessed the expansion of the school apostolate in three areas. The first of these was on the secondary school level in Johnstown, Pennsylvania; the second, in Cleveland, Ohio; and the third, in La Grange Park, Illinois.

In early 1953, Mother M. Jerome Dadej received a letter from the Reverend Linford F. Greinader, the diocesan priest-principal of Johnstown Central Catholic High School in Pennsylvania. He informed Mother M. Jerome of the lack of adequate space at the senior high school located at 25 Osburn Street. In his letter to Mother M. Jerome, Father Greinader presented a plan to open a few classes for freshmen in various Catholic elementary schools in the Johnstown area. Father Greinader had scheduled two classes to open at St. Casimir's School on Power Street. Since both St. Casimir's School in Johnstown and the Assumption of the Blessed Virgin Mary School in Conemaugh were "feeder" schools to Johnstown Central Catholic High School and both were staffed by the Franciscan Sisters of Chicago, Father Greinader requested Mother M. Jerome to assign two Sisters to staff the proposed coeducational freshman branch at St. Casimir's School.[1] Mother M. Jerome and the general council gladly accepted the proposal and in September of 1953, sent Sister M. Crescencia Chmiel and Sister M. Hugoline Czaplinski. Sister M. Crescencia was assigned to teach Latin, algebra, and general science; Sister M. Hugoline was appointed to teach English, music, world history, and health. The Sisters joined the members of five other Sisterhoods who comprised the staff of Johnstown Central Catholic High School. Sister M. Crescencia and Sister M. Hugoline resided with the Sisters at St. Casimir's Parish convent.[2]

In 1956, Mother M. Jerome appointed Sister M. Hugoline the principal of the congregation's own Madonna High School in Chicago. Madonna High School, at that time, was undergoing tremendous growth in student enrollment, and in a matter of two years, would require the erection of a new school building to accept all the students who made application. Sister M. Hugoline was, therefore, replaced at Johnstown Central Catholic High School by Sister M. Charitas Gajdzinski who was scheduled to teach

English, communications, and Pennsylvania history. She remained on the staff until 1957, when both she and Sister M. Crescencia were sent to the new Madonna High School. Mother M. Jerome assigned Sister Clarent Marie Urbanowicz and Sister M. Concordia Lawrence to continue to represent the Franciscan Sisters of Chicago on the staff of Johnstown Central Catholic High School. Sister Clarent Marie taught Latin, algebra, health, mathematics, and Pennsylvania history. English, general science, and communications were assigned to Sister M. Concordia.[3] Soon, however, the matter of meeting the salaries of the increasing number of lay faculty members at Madonna High School saw the necessity of withdrawing the Sisters from their apostolate at Johnstown Central Catholic High School. Thus, at the conclusion of the 1959–1960 school year, Sister Clarent Marie and Sister M. Concordia returned to Chicago, and the Franciscan Sisters of Chicago withdrew from the staff of Johnstown Central Catholic High School.

In the early 1960s, Johnstown Central Catholic High School changed its name to Bishop McCort High School. An extensive complex was added to the original building thereby eliminating the branches at various elementary schools including that at St. Casimir's School.[4]

In the Diocese of Cleveland the Most Reverend Edward Hoban, the archbishop-bishop, established another parish, St. Leo the Great, whose school was accepted for staffing by Mother M. Jerome at the bishop's request. Located in the thickly populated Broadview-Schaff Road section near Parma, the parish was organized in October of 1948 by the Reverend Sylvester Lux. In the beginning, the Benjamin Franklin Public School auditorium was used as a chapel, but in 1950, construction of a brick combination church and school was begun on a site which allowed for expansion. In September of that year, four hundred students began their classes in nine rooms under the direction of the Congregation of the Vincentian Sisters of Charity of Bedford, Ohio. The church-auditorium, seating 750, was completed in time for the Christmas Day Masses. The church and school combination was dedicated by Bishop Hoban on June 3, 1951.[5]

When in June of 1955 the Vincentian Sisters of Charity relinquished the school,[6] the Franciscan Sisters of Chicago agreed to undertake its staffing. When it opened in September of 1955,[7] the Sisters at the mission were Sister M. Albertine Schab, Sister M. Alphonsine Kobylinski, Sister Anne Marie Knawa, Sister M. Claudiana Jachimowicz, Sister Helen Marie Zasadzinski, and Sister M. Maurita Wszolek. Sister M. Virgina Murawski was appointed the superior and principal.[8]

Some of the pioneer Sisters arrived in Cleveland a few days prior to the opening of the new mission and resided at Sacred Heart of Jesus Convent on East 71st Street. Mother M. Jerome accompanied the Sisters to Cleveland with the intention of remaining at St. Leo's School for a few days. On August 22, at that time the feast of the Immaculate Heart of Mary, Mother M. Jerome, Sister M. Alphonsine, Sister Anne Marie, Sister Helen Marie, Sister M. Maurita, and Sister M. Virgina arrived at the convent of St. Leo the Great.

St. Leo the Great School
Cleveland, Ohio (1955–   )

The women of the parish, anxious to welcome the new Sisters, prepared an enjoyable dinner in the convent dining room in the Sisters' honor and did their utmost to make the Sisters feel at home. The next day, August 23, Father Lux offered Holy Mass in the tiny chapel of the large, white, rambling frame house which had previously served as the rectory at 4865 Broadview Road.[9] The Sisters remained at this residence on the west side of Broadview Road for six years until Father Lux arranged for the construction of a large and beautiful convent on the east side of Broadview. Completed in December of 1961, the convent was built behind the school away from the heavy traffic of Broadview Road and was beautifully backgrounded by giant maple trees.

From the time of the Sisters' arrival at St. Leo's School in 1955, the superior and principal was also a full-time teacher. In 1969, however, Mother M. Beatrice Rybacki informed Father Lux that a full-time principal was a necessity because of the steadily increasing enrollment. To allow the principal to function even more fully, Sister M. Theresia Rybak was appointed the local superior, and Sister M. Eileen Kazmierowicz was designated the principal. After 1973, a lay principal headed the faculty and students.[10]

Throughout the years, particularly in the post-Vatican II period, the Sisters at St. Leo's also engaged in various activities outside the classroom. These activities consisted of renewal work in the parish, membership in the Sisters' Senate of Cleveland, religious education classes for public school children, active participation in the parish council, and visitation of the sick and the needy. From the very beginning of their work in the parish, the Sisters also attended to the sanctuary and sacristy duties.[11]

By 1973, a decrease in the number of Sisters on St. Leo's faculty led to an experiment in intercommunity living in order to make maximum use of the spacious convent. Several Sisters who were members of the Congregation of St. Joseph of Cleveland, the Congregation of the Dominican Sisters of the Most Holy Rosary (Adrian), and the Congregation of the Sisters of Charity of Cleveland made their residence with the Franciscan Sisters of Chicago. None of the Sisters of the other congregations who made their home at St. Leo's was on the teaching staff of the school. In this unique atmosphere, the Sisters shared their various ministries and enriched communal living. In September of 1982, however, with seven Franciscan Sisters of Chicago on the staff and one Sister a resident student, the convent was used by the Franciscan Sisters of Chicago only.

An important change occurred at St. Leo's in August of 1984. The number of Franciscan Sisters of Chicago on the staff was drastically reduced to three. When Sister Joseph Marie Zenda, the newly elected superior general, made her visitation at St. Leo's, the decision was made to relocate the three Sisters in a house near the school. As in other parishes where similar changes were made, the convent would now be used for parish meetings, retreats, renewals, and days of recollection. By September of 1984, Sister M. Dolorine Piwowarski, Sister M. Pachomia Rychlicki, and Sister M. Virgina Murawski were settled in their new home at 2415 Silverdale Avenue.

St. Leo the Great Parish continues to be a stable and vital community with an enrollment of over five hundred pupils served by three Sisters and fifteen lay teachers.

In June of 1955, Samuel Cardinal Stritch assigned the Reverend Cletus J. Lynch to organize a new parish in La Grange Park, a western suburb of Chicago. La Grange Park

St. Leo the Great Convent
Cleveland, Ohio

was a part of the "suburban boom" which had more than doubled that village's population in the 1950s. St. Louise de Marillac Church was one of five parishes formed outside of the city. The new parish was meant to serve approximately 750 Catholic families of northeastern La Grange Park and the northern section of Brookfield.[12] Before the new church could be built, however, Father Lynch offered Holy Mass on Sundays and holydays in the gym-auditorium of nearby Brook Park School. During the week, mass was offered in the "basement church" of Father Lynch's temporary rectory, a lovely tri-level duplex house at 1601 E. 31st Street. One of the priests who assisted Father Lynch in parish duties in the beginning and was so well liked by the Franciscan Sisters was the Reverend Daniel Kucera, OSB, president and later chancellor of St. Procopius College (now Illinois Benedictine College) in Lisle, Illinois. Today, he is the archbishop of Dubuque, Iowa.

Upon receiving notice to begin the new parish, Father Lynch directed requests to more than ninety-four religious Sisterhoods in the United States in the hope of securing a staff for the proposed parish school. Secretly desirous to see his parish in the hands of the Congregation of the Daughters of Charity of St. Vincent de Paul, Father Lynch named the new parish after their foundress, St. Louise de Marillac.[13] When his petition to the Daughters was refused due to the lack of available Sisters, Father Lynch turned to the *Catholic Directory.* Noting that the Franciscan Sisters of Chicago had their Motherhouse in Illinois, he dispatched a most engaging letter to Mother M. Jerome Dadej:

Dear Mother Superior:

I owe you an explanation. This morning in my meditation after Mass, I was presenting certain of my problems to Almighty God and I mentioned the fact that I was going to write to you. I begged Him to make you receptive to my plea and then I placed the whole matter in His Hands. Consequently, whatever happens now, I promised Him that I will accept it as mark of His favor.

You see, Mother, just a few short weeks ago, I experienced that great thrill of saying to 550 good Catholic families in the La Grange Park area, "My dear parishioners."

Yes, His Eminence, our beloved Cardinal, has made one-half of the dream of my priesthood come true. The other half is up to God . . . and to you. As pastor of the new parish, St. Louise de Marillac, I shall strive to minister to the needs of my parishioners. A new church, school and convent . . . these I am confident are within our capacity to achieve. Ready for use in 1956 . . . that is our goal. But whether or not they will be in use in 1956 depends upon whatever consideration Our Lord influences you to give to my plea.

My dear Mother Superior, I would that I could entrust the education of our children to the good nuns of your community. Now before you say, "It's impossible," let me caution you in that I have prayed to St. Rita. And before you say, "The situation is hopeless". . . I have prayed to St.

Jude, too. But most of all, I have prayed to the Sacred Heart, just as I'm sure you must have done so often, too, as you went "heavy-burdened" to seek the refreshment of His graces and help.

Please let me call your attention to the two parishes out of which our parish was formed: St. Barbara's in Brookfield and St. Francis Xavier in La Grange. Both have nurtured many vocations . . . the families average four to six children . . . and they harbor the European tradition of the hopes of a vocation in every family.

The gravity of the situation . . . yes, I appreciate it, Mother, but in spite of it, I can't help but feel that I stand with the children of my parish in the amphitheater. Thumbs up or thumbs down? . . . the education of these little ones rests upon your decision. Surely, it isn't wrong for me to pray that your answer will be identified with that quotation from Mark, voiced in Pope Pius XI's great encyclical on the Christian Education of Youth: "Whosoever shall receive one such child in My Name, receiveth Me."

Thank you so much, Mother, and be assured of a personal memento in my Mass on September 20, commemorating my 25th anniversary as His priest. May Our Blessed Mother watch over you at all times.

Sincerely,
Rev. Cletus J. Lynch[14]

Despite Father Lynch's ardent plea, Mother M. Jerome was forced to deny his request. She cited the fact that the congregation had only recently accepted the staffing of St. Leo the Great School in Cleveland, and, therefore, was not in a position to accept another school at that time.[15] A few months later, much to Father Lynch's pleasant suprise, Mother M. Jerome informed him that she had reconsidered the prospect of staffing St. Louise de Marillac School. She stated that while the congregation would experience some difficulty in assigning Sisters to the new mission in La Grange Park, it was judicious to branch out in an area which was so close to the Motherhouse. She promised that a sincere effort would be made to assign four Sisters to the school, and to that end, she had written letters to pastors whose schools maintained a kindergarten, informing them of her plan to withdraw the Sisters from these classes. The pastors had the option of closing the kindergarten or securing a lay teacher.[16] In this fashion, some Sisters would be available for St. Louise de Marillac School.

On Sunday, April 8, 1956, the ground-breaking ceremony for the proposed new St. Louise de Marillac School was held. Father Lynch officiated at the ceremony which marked the first step in the construction of a series of buildings designed to fulfill the needs of this rapidly growing parish. Mother M. Jerome was present to turn over a spadeful of dirt, as were ten other Sisters of the congregation. While the school was under construction, the four Sisters who had been assigned to staff St. Louise de Marillac School had taken up residence at St. Barbara's Parish in nearby Brookfield in the latter part of August of 1955.[17] Sister M. Edward Nowak, the superior and principal; Sister M. Agnella Sieja; Sister Margaret Mary Jakusz; and Sister M. Roberta Duda lived in four rooms on the second floor of the old St. Barbara's School. The four pioneer Sisters taught grades one through four in classrooms on the first floor of their living quarters. The Sisters took their meals and occasional recreation at the convent with the Congregation of the Sisters of St. Joseph of La Grange who staffed St. Barbara's School. The Sisters of St. Joseph had graciously agreed to extend their hospitality to the Franciscan Sisters for the nine months it took to construct St. Louise de Marillac School.[18]

With great jubilation, the Sisters and students moved into the new St. Louise de Marillac School consisting of fourteen ultramodern classrooms on April 26, 1957, the feast of St. Cletus, their pastor's patron. There were 148 children enrolled in the school at the time. The Sisters also moved into their own convent home, the beautiful tri-level duplex which previously had served as the rectory for Father Lynch and his assistants at 1601 A and 1601 B East 31st Street. In September of 1957, with the enrollment at 510 students, four additional Sisters were assigned to St. Louise de Marillac School: Sister M. Charitas Gajdzinski, Sister M. Francine Labus, Sister Anne Marie Knawa, and Sister Louise Ann Glowacki who was assigned to household duties.[19] Before long, a second addition of two classrooms was made together with the famed Colonnade Room, the parish's social hall. While the beautiful church of St. Louise de Marillac had been completed earlier, it was formally dedicated on April 20, 1958. A Solemn Mass of Thanksgiving was offered by the Most Reverend Raymond P. Hillinger, auxiliary bishop of Chicago, in the absence of Samuel Cardinal Stritch, who was then en route to Rome to take up his duties in the Roman Curia.

St. Louise de Marillac School
La Grange Park, Illinois (1956–1987)

St. Louise de Marillac Convent
La Grange Park, Illinois

The need for more adequate housing for the growing number of Sisters was now evident. On October 15, 1961, therefore, ground was broken at the corner of East 31st Street for a new convent. On the property east of the tri-level duplex residency, a lovely, spacious convent meant to accommodate eighteen Sisters was constructed. Father Lynch had overlooked nothing in planning a convent that was as serviceable as it was beautiful. The Sisters moved into their new home on November 16, 1962, and the convent was blessed by Albert Cardinal Meyer on April 29, 1963.[20] Already in September of 1962, another historical event was noted when Sister M. Edward Nowak, whose six-year term as superior and principal had ended, was replaced by Sister M. Louise Nowicki.

The third stage of St. Louise de Marillac School's building program reached completion in 1964. A junior high school wing containing seven classrooms, a spacious library, a science lab, and an audiovisual room was added to the original school plant. That year was additionally significant insofar as St. Louise de Marillac had reached its peak enrollment of 853 students with twelve Sisters and thirteen lay teachers on the staff.[21]

The St. Louise de Marillac Church community is active, interested, and sincerely involved in total parish commitment. The Sisters, in post-Conciliar years, have been involved in religious education for public school children, special sessions of religious education for retarded children (the SPRED Program), adult discussion groups, and visitation of the parish sick. With the emphasis on excellence a constant factor, the school, nevertheless, declined in enrollment. In 1974, the first lay principal took charge of the school.[22] A loss that the parish felt more keenly was the retirement of its founding pastor, Father Lynch,[23] who had guided the establishment of St. Louise de Marillac parish to spectacular growth and Christian dedication to education. He was succeeded by the

Reverend Edward J. Borisewicz in 1977, who in turn, was succeeded by the Reverend John Hergenrother in 1985.

By 1984, the religious faculty was reduced to three teachers. When the new superior general, Sister Joseph Marie Zenda, made her official visitation at the mission, the Sisters' residence was an important topic of discussion. The implausibility of housing three Sisters in a convent home meant for eighteen was obvious. The solution was to have the Sisters move back to 1601 A East 31st Street, occupying just one-half of the tri-level duplex house that the Sisters had first lived in twenty-two years earlier. The large convent became the new residence of the Comboni Missionaries of the Heart of Jesus. The three remaining Sisters on the staff of the school continued to minister to over two thousand active and dedicated families and approximately three hundred children who continued to be strengthened in their faith and urged to academic excellence by the dedicated faculty. In 1987, however, a decision was made to leave St. Louise de Marillac School because of a continued depletion of Sister personnel. The Sisters left La Grange Park, the "Village of Roses," after thirty-two years of truly fulfilling ministry.

Early in December of 1957, Mother M. Jerome Dadej received a letter from Samuel Cardinal Stritch concerning a Special Reading Program which was being introduced in the Catholic Schools of Chicago by the Archdiocesan Office of Catholic Charities. On December 30, Mother M. Jerome and Sister M. Alberta Bialas, the superintendent of primary grades in the congregation's schools, conferred with Cardinal Stritch at his office in regard to his letter. The cardinal informed Mother M. Jerome and Sister M. Alberta that the newly appointed archdiocesan supervisor of schools, the Reverend William McManus, had proposed to the cardinal that each congregation of Sisters working in the Archdiocese of Chicago submit the name of at least one qualified Sister to participate in a specialized Archdiocesan Reading Program which would eventually qualify her as a reading consultant. The Sister to be selected was to be sent to Cardinal Stritch College, long famous for its outstanding reading clinic in Milwaukee.[24] At the conclusion of her training, the reading consultant would receive a master of arts degree as a reading specialist and work in the Archdiocese of Chicago under the supervision of Father McManus. At the meeting on December 30, Mother M. Jerome was prepared to inform Cardinal Stritch that, together with the general council, she had selected Sister M. Virgina Murawski to train as the congregation's reading specialist.[25] As the reading consultant, Sister M. Virgina would serve as many children as possible in approximately twenty or thirty schools located in different areas of Chicago and its suburbs.[26]

From September of 1958 until May of 1959, Sister M. Virgina studied at Cardinal Stritch College. At the conclusion of her studies, she made her headquarters at St. Pancratius School where she took up residence on June 3. Sister M. Virgina had as her immediate duty to introduce and supervise the reading program in twenty-six schools in the Archdiocese of Chicago. Her function as a reading consultant included tutoring special students, conducting workshops for teachers, and administering both reading and intelligence tests at her assigned schools.[27]

During the vacation period from school, Summer Reading Programs were sponsored by the Archdiocesan School Board at twenty-eight schools in various areas of the city. In 1960, on Chicago's Southwest Side, St. Pancratius School staffed by the Franciscan Sisters of Chicago was selected as a Corrective Reading Center under the direction of Sister M. Virgina. Nine Sisters, whose salaries were paid by the Archdiocesan Office of Catholic Charities, were appointed to teach at the St. Pancratius Corrective Reading Center for six weeks to help students identify and overcome reading disabilities. Selected to teach at the St. Pancratius Center in 1960 were Sister M. Angeline Kedzior, Sister M. Consilia Przybyl, Sister M. Dolores Radziwiecki, Sister M. Edwina Wilk, Sister M. Eymard Sanok, Sister M. Maximina Pachut, Sister Therese Agnes Kniola, and Sister M. Xavier Wroblewski. From June 27 to August 5, 1960, in particular, Sister M. Roberta Duda was appointed by Mother M. Beatrice, at the recommendation of Sister M. Virgina, to teach methods in remedial reading to elementary school teachers. The location center was St. Gall School at 55th Street and South Kedzie Avenue, an easy distance from St. Pancratius School. Sister M. Roberta's proficiency in the reading and phonics program in the primary grades, her expert knowledge of constructing learning devices to encourage young readers, and her jovial personality made her ideal for the position.

In 1961, the following Sisters were appointed to the St. Pancratius Corrective Reading Center: Sister M. Claudiana Jachimowicz, Sister M. Dolores Radziwiecki, Sister M. Edwina Wilk, Sister M. Maxima Pachut, Sister Mary Kulik, Sister M. Roberta Duda, and Sister M. Thaddea Duran. For the 1962 summer session were chosen Sister M. Archangela Tyranski, Sister M. Claudiana Jachimowicz, Sister M. Consilia Przybyl, Sister M. Kinga Repinski, Sister Mary Kulik, Sister M. Maximina Pachut, Sister M. Petronia Budzinski, and Sister M. Thaddea Duran.[28] All the Sisters selected were proficient in identifying and overcoming reading disabilities and in offering remedial instructions. In addition, they possessed the patience, sensitivity, and gentle understanding necessary for success with children who had reading problems.

After serving conscientiously and proficiently as a reading consultant from 1960, Sister M. Virgina tendered her resignation in 1965.

At the expiration of her term of office as superior general in 1958, Mother M. Jerome served as superior at St. John's Hospital and School of Nursing in Huron, South Dakota, until 1961. She remained at the hospital until her retirement in 1966 at the Motherhouse in Lemont. She died there on the feast of All Saints, November 1, 1970, of cerebral thrombosis. The eldest of four daughters of the Dadej family, Mother M. Jerome had three sisters who were also members of the congregation. Sister M. Hilary Dadej died on May 3, 1967, after fifty-nine years as a religious; Sister M. Theresa Dadej passed into eternity on September 9, 1984, after having served for sixty-five years. The youngest, Sister M. Marietta Dadej, had earlier left the congregation.

ERA OF GROWTH AND TRANSITION

[1]*Minutes of General Council Proceedings,* 10 March 1953 (AFSCL).

[2]*Book of Closed Schools and Institutions* (AFSCL).

[3]Ibid.

[4]*Book of Correspondence:* Letter from the Reverend Monsignor Thomas K. Mabon, Superintendent of Schools, Altoona-Johnstown Diocese to author, 26 March 1976 (AFSCL).

[5]Michael J. Hynes, *History of the Diocese of Cleveland* (Cleveland: World Publishing Co., 1953), p. 415.

[6]*Book of Correspondence:* Letter from Sister M. Regis, Vincentian Sisters of Charity, Bedford, Ohio, to author, 10 January 1976 (AFSCL).

[7]Secretaries General, *Community Chronicle, 1955* (AFSCL).

[8]*St. Leo the Great House Journal* (AFSCL).

[9]Ibid.

[10]*Franciscan Echo,* vol. 18 (Lemont, Illinois: October 1975).

[11]*St. Leo the Great House Journal* (AFSCL).

[12]*Dedication Book: St. Louise de Marillac Church and School* (La Grange Park, Illinois, 1958), no pagination.

[13]*Interview* with the Reverend Cletus J. Lynch, 15 April 1974 (AFSCL).

[14]*Book of Correspondence:* Letter from the Reverend Cletus J. Lynch to Mother M. Jerome Dadej, 12 June 1955 (AFSCL).

[15]*Book of Correspondence:* Letter from Mother M. Jerome to the Reverend Cletus J. Lynch, 22 September 1955 (AFSCL).

[16]Secretaries General, *Community Chronicle, 1955* (AFSCL).

[17]This parish was originally founded as a mission of St. Francis Xavier in La Grange, Illinois, in 1912.

[18]*Book of Correspondence:* Letter from Sister M. Roberta Duda to author, 28 April 1974 (AFSCL).

[19]Sister Margaret Mary Jakusz was transferred to another mission at the close of the 1955–1956 school year.

[20]*Dedication Book: St. Louise de Marillac Church and School,* no pagination.

[21]*St. Louise de Marillac House Journal* (AFSCL).

[22]Ibid.

[23]Not the least of the things missing in the thriving, vibrant parish today is the resonant voice of Father Lynch singing the song he loved best at various parish functions and with which he is so easily identified—"Louise."

[24]Cardinal Stritch College is an accredited liberal arts college for women. This school offers programs for teachers of the mentally retarded and for reading specialists. Cardinal Stritch College was founded in Milwaukee under the name St. Clare College by the Franciscan Sisters of Penance and Charity of Milwaukee, Wisconsin.

[25]Secretaries General, *Community Chronicle, 1957* (AFSCL).

[26]*Book of Correspondence:* Letter from Sister M. Virgina Murawski to author, 3 May 1974 (AFSCL).

[27]*Book of Correspondence:* Letter from Sister M. Virgina Murawski to author, 28 May 1974 (AFSCL).

[28]*Book of Annual Assignments* (AFSCL).

CHAPTER 56

The Ninth General Chapter:
Mother M. Beatrice Rybacki

The Ninth General Chapter of Elections had the markings of what appeared to be another "first" in the congregation. One of the decrees of the Eighth General Chapter of 1952 had been to have a one-day closed retreat for the Sister-delegates. Thus, the thirty-nine delegates[1] to the Ninth General Chapter met on June 28, 1958, for a one-day retreat conducted by the Reverend Francis Domanski, SJ. The first general session of the chapter began the next day with a report by Mother M. Jerome. In her report to the delegates, she informed the Sisters of the congregation's membership. There were 362 Sisters in perpetual vows, twenty-five Sisters in temporary vows, ten novices, six postulants, and three aspirants—a total of 406 members. Mother M. Jerome explained to the delegates that the last years of her second term of office had indicated that the whole of religious life was perceived to be in a climate of change and that all congregations were experiencing "problems." In an attempt to meet the changing climate of religious life "head-on," the delegates were told, a federation called the Conference of Major Religious Superiors of Women had been formed in 1956.[2] The conference stressed the formation of young religious, and all congregations would have to address themselves to the introduction of a Sister Formation Program. The next administration, Mother M. Jerome stated, would have to direct its priorities to facing this issue.

On July 2, 1958, the chapter delegates met to elect a superior general and the general council. Mother M. Jerome Dadej had already served two consecutive six-year terms for a total of twelve years. There were those Sisters in the congregation and certainly in the chapter delegation itself who wished to see Mother M. Jerome elected to a third term, an event unprecedented in the history of the congregation. The chapter delegates were aware of the fact that for Mother M. Jerome to secure a third term, it would be necessary for her to receive a two-thirds vote from the delegation. If she were to receive the two-thirds vote, it would then be necessary for the congregation to postulate to Rome, that is, the congregation would have to submit a description of the election to the Holy See and give valid and cogent reasons for the re-election of Mother M. Jerome indicating that she was the most suitable candidate for the office of superior general.[3] The Sister-delegates proceeded to the election presided over by the Very Reverend Monsignor Raymond J. Zock, delegate of the ordinary of the Archdiocese of Chicago, the newly installed Albert Cardinal Meyer.

When the delegates cast their votes for the superior general, however, the majority vote went to Sister M. Beatrice Rybacki, thereby negating any attempted process to postulate to Rome for Mother M. Jerome. Sister M. Beatrice, who herself had been a novice under Mother M. Jerome, accepted the position with her characteristic simplicity and gentleness, declaring that she felt "like the Blessed Virgin Mary at the foot of the Cross on Mount Calvary."[4] Although Sister M. Beatrice was somewhat awed at the responsibilities associated with the position of superior general, she, nevertheless, accepted the will of the delegation, confident that her love and devotion to the Mother of God would sustain her in the days that lay ahead.

Elected vicar general and first councilor was Sister M. Venantia Rec, principal of SS. Philip and James School, Cleveland. Other newly elected councilors were Sister M. Crescencia Chmiel, second councilor, the assistant principal of Madonna High School;[5] Sister M. Gonzaga Raniszewski, third councilor and secretary general, a position she already had held for twelve years; Sister M. Edward Nowak, fourth councilor, principal of St. Louise de Marillac School, La Grange Park, Illinois; and Sister M. Aloysetta Ciezadlo, general bursar, elected to a second term as procurator general.

Mother M. Beatrice, the newly elected superior general, was born in Pakość, Poland on May 22, 1901. The eldest child of John and Agnes (née Dzwoniarek) Rybacki, she was given the name Helen at baptism. When she was one year old the family emigrated to America and made their home in St. Casimir's Parish in Johnstown, Pennsylvania. On May 3, 1919, she entered the congregation. Received into the novitiate on July 27, 1920, she was given the name Sister M. Beatrice. She made her first profession on July 27, 1921, and pronounced her final vows on July 16, 1926. Sister M. Beatrice received her degree from St. John College of Cleveland.[6]

After making her first profession, Sister M. Beatrice was assigned to St. Hedwig's School in Gary, Indiana, where she remained for six years. Transferred to St. Casimir's School in Cleveland, she taught there from 1927 to 1936. In that year, she received a scholarship—the aim of which was to foster cultural and artistic relationships among American Poles[7]—to study at the University of Warsaw in Poland. In 1937, after completing the year of study, she returned to St. Casimir's School where she served in the capacity of superior and principal until 1943. When she was sent to teach at St. Stanislaus Kostka School in Youngstown, Ohio, in 1946, she was also appointed superior and principal. In 1952, she was reassigned to St. Casimir's School in Cleveland as teacher, superior, and principal where she remained until her election as the congregation's seventh superior general.[8]

Mother M. Beatrice, of medium height and moderate weight, was a kindly, sympathetic, and refined woman. While reserved in demeanor, she possessed a quick, shy smile that dissolved any notion of fear and swiftly put one at ease. In her determined devotion to religious observance and duty, Mother M. Beatrice set a splendid example.

In governing the congregation, Mother M. Beatrice was always a keeper of a Sister's confidence which inspired great trust on the part of the membership. Reserved and a good listener, she was one in whom each Sister could easily confide. She never scolded or spoke harshly to any Sister who had occasion to deal with her. Always interested and sympathetic in regard to the welfare of the Sisters, she was genuinely concerned about those who were ill. She was also interested in the Sisters' education and encouraged them to prepare themselves academically and professionally. Never rash and always guided by a sense of integrity, she was conscientious and persevering in all her endeavors. Guided by a genuine spirit of poverty, she was circumspect in all her financial dealings.[9]

While Mother M. Beatrice cannot be characterized as a born leader, she did have the talent but not the striking ambition to lead. Under her benevolent and temperate guidance, however, two of the biggest achievements in the congregation took place, albeit during her second term of office. By far the crowning glory of Mother M. Beatrice's external accomplishments was the erection of the new Motherhouse in Lemont, Illinois, in 1963, an undertaking of absolute importance and necessity. The second important achievement during her tenure of office was her progressive and constructive community reforms in the wake of the Second Vatican Council. With complete absence of pride or self-assertion, but with deep spiritual insight and the unity and balance of her nature, Mother M. Beatrice assumed the responsibility and burden of leadership in a spirit of faith and trust in Divine Providence. As a consequence, Mother M. Beatrice emerges in the congregation's history as a pillar of strength, perseverance, and inspiration.

The new vicar general and first councilor was Sister M. Venantia, the former Mary Rec, who was born on August 28, 1905, in Poland. The daughter of Matthias and Agatha (née Malec) Rec, she came to the United States with her parents when she was one year old. Upon their arrival in America, the Rec family settled in Arcadia, Pennsylvania, where they belonged to SS. Peter and Paul Church. At the age of fifteen, Mary Rec entered the congregation on October 26, 1920. She was accepted into the postulancy on February 24, 1921, and was received into the novitiate on July 26, 1922. On July 27, 1923, she pronounced her first vows and on July 27, 1927, made her perpetual profession.[10]

After her first profession of vows, Sister M. Venantia was sent to St. Casimir's School in Cleveland where she remained for the next twenty-seven years teaching from grades eight to kindergarten and earning her bachelor's degree at St. John College of Cleveland. In 1950, she taught the primary grades at St. John the Baptist School (now St. Joseph the Provider) in Campbell, Ohio. When the congregation accepted the new SS. Philip and James School in Cleveland in 1951, Sister M. Venantia was assigned to teach the first grade. From 1952 to 1958, she was also the principal and superior.[11] At the Ninth General Chapter in 1952, Sister M. Venantia was elected vicar general and first councilor. In that capacity, she also served as the superior at the Motherhouse in Chicago.[12]

As diminutive in size as her patron St. Venantius, Sister M. Venantia was equally as fervent. She possessed a quiet and sincere demeanor which often made her appear shy.

As a religious superior, she was the epitome of kindness and understanding. A gentle, humble person, Sister M. Venantia's prayerfulness revealed a spirit of faith and recollection that was the envy of many.[13]

In the light of the transition occurring in the structure and practices of the religious life in the United States, many prescriptions were passed by the Sister-delegates at the Ninth General Chapter. Beginning with October 6, 1958, several changes went into effect in the congregation:

1. Because the stock of the congregation's official prayerbook, *Amo Christum,* was depleted, it was decided to use mimeographed copies of a shortened community prayerbook until the congregation had studied the changes which were anticipated in the recitation of vocal prayers.

2. The Sisters' daily rising time was changed from five to five-thirty o'clock in the morning.

3. Morning prayers were to be shortened and repetitive vocal prayers were to be omitted. Spiritual reading, now only at breakfast, was to be read either in English or Polish according to the discretion of the Sister-reader. All prayers said in common and those before and after meals were to be recited in Latin except at the Motherhouse.

4. Meditation could now be made privately using a book of one's own choice and not necessarily in the chapel.

5. A Holy Hour on the vigil of the First Friday was to be held from eight to nine o'clock on the Thursday preceding the First Friday of the month.

6. The Sisters could now study and prepare for class in their bedrooms rather than in the study hall.

7. The Sisters would observe their Diamond Jubilees as a group on the sixtieth anniversary of their entrance into the congregation.

8. The use of TV's was to be regulated by the superior and individual TV's or radios were strictly prohibited.

Many of the decrees passed at the Ninth General Chapter dealt with the religious garb. For the sake of simplification, modification, economy, health, and comfort, steps were taken at this time to change the headdress. The heavily starched linen cornet to which the veil was attached was now eliminated. A soft, loose-flowing veil held in place with several pins and attached to a small stiff band pinned to the sides of the coif was the result. Although the white coif was retained, the "new look" allowed for a greater freedom of movement and did away with the cumbersome cornets which actually curtailed vision to a large extent. The new veils were worn for the first time by all the Sisters on January 1, 1959. Because of the new veil, there was no longer a need for the "top veil"[14] and its use was discontinued. A resolution was passed concerning the white habits worn in the nursing field and by the Sisters engaged in domestic duties. The form of the habit was to remain the same as the brown one except that the white habits would have narrower sleeves and would close at the wrist with a snap for reasons of sanitation and efficiency. The use of raincoats was permitted. The Franciscan chaplet would now be attached to the cord by a round hook and be suspended from the cord whose substance was changed from wool to cotton for the sake of economy. The collar was to be shortened to measure no longer than eight inches.

Generally, only the second-year novices made a retreat prior to their profession of first vows. For the first time, a retreat was held for the first-year novices from February 2 to 11, 1958. Because one postulant had had her postulancy postponed and was to be received into the novitiate privately, it was imperative that she have a ten-day retreat before she was to be admitted. It was decided, therefore, that all the first-year novices would participate in the retreat. From that time on the retreat became a custom for all first-year novices.

In an effort to awaken within the Sisters-superior a heightened awareness of their obligations as religious leaders and to offer them guidance in the very apparent "climate of change," a retreat for Sisters-superior was initiated in 1959. The first one was held from December 27 to January 2, 1960, at the Motherhouse.

In September of 1958, when the newly elected Mother M. Beatrice took office, her administration voted to issue a quarterly in both the English and the Polish languages to be called *Echo Franciszkanski* [The Franciscan Echo].[15] Sister M. Gonzaga Raniszewski, the secretary general, served as its editor. By 1968, however, the pressing duties and responsibilities of her position, especially after the First Extraordinary Chapter of Affairs held that year, caused her to relinquish the additional duty of editing the newsletter. Sister Kathleen Melia assumed this responsibility in place of Sister M. Gonzaga and continued as the newsletter's editor until June of 1970.

To implement the directives of Mother M. Beatrice in regard to fostering vocations, a meeting was held at Madonna High School for all the Franciscan Sisters of Chicago stationed in Illinois and Indiana on November 1, 1958. The guest speaker was the Reverend Samuel Stanek, OFM, who was an experienced director of vocations. Sister M. Tarcisia Bucki served as chairperson. An election was held and the following Sisters were chosen to serve as the first officers of the soon-to-be-organized Mother Theresa Vocation Council: Sister M. Rosalima Sierocki, president; Sister M. Teresita Kuczmarski, vice-president; Sister M. Consilia Przybyl, secretary; and Sister M. Louise Nowicki, treasurer. Sister M. Tarcisia was elected director of vocations which she remained until 1968.

Some of the more meaningful changes occurred in the novitiate and postulancy. Heretofore, the novices were prohibited from having any guests. It had been a matter of penitential practice according to Canon Law that the novices have no contact with their families or friends during their two-year novitiate except for letters on occasions such as Christmas and Easter. In 1960, the general council voted to have the novices receive guests three times a year—on the first Sunday in September, the second Sunday in January, and the first Sunday after Easter. By 1962, the first-year novices also were allowed to write home once a month and receive guests on the fourth Sunday of January.[16]

*Reverend Henry M. Malak, Postulator for the Cause of the Beatification of
Mother M. Theresa Dudzik in the Archdiocese of Chicago.*

The delegates to the general chapter had voted to continue the matter of the cause of the beatification of Mother M. Theresa Dudzik. Several very strategic steps were taken during this administration to secure the oral testimony of more than 116 Sisters, among them Mother M. Theresa's former novices. With the permission of Albert Cardinal Meyer, archbishop of Chicago, pamphlets were printed with a prayer for Mother M. Theresa's beatification, and her biography was published in a brief form. The League of Mother M. Theresa was formed and a quarterly bulletin was sent to all subscribers. By 1963, the cause of Mother M. Theresa had matured to such a degree that a postulator for the cause of the beatification of Mother M. Theresa Dudzik, the Reverend Henry Malak, was appointed in the Archdiocese of Chicago. These happenings are dealt with in more detail in Appendix B.

THE NINTH GENERAL CHAPTER: MOTHER M. BEATRICE RYBACKI

[1]See Appendix K.

[2]This association of major superiors of religious communities of women whose purpose was promoting the spiritual and apostolic calling and works of Sisterhoods in the United States was organized in the late 1950s. It was approved by the Congregation for Religious and Secular Institutes on June 13, 1962. Its original name, changed in 1971, was the Conference of Major Superiors of Women. With its formerly affiliated Sister Formation Conference, the Major Superiors Conference inaugurated measures for the religious and professional development of Sisters and contributed to the renewal of religious life in the United States. It is now called the Leadership Conference of Women Religious (LCWR).

[3]*Book of Correspondence:* Letter from the Reverend John Mulvihill to Sister M. Antonissima Jamruk, 1974; and letter from Sister M. Francis Clare Radke, assistant superior general to author, October 1987 (AFSCL).

[4]*Minutes of General Chapter Proceedings, 1958* (AFSCL).

[5]See Chapter 51.

[6]*Spis Sióstr* (AFSCL).

[7]See Chapter 36.

[8]*Congregation Membership Records* (AFSCL).

[9]*Interviews* with Sisters, September 1983 (AFSCL).

[10]*Spis Sióstr* (AFSCL).

[11]Congregation Membership Records (AFSCL).

[12]See Chapter 58.

[13]*Interviews* with Sisters, 1983 (AFSCL).

[14]See Chapter 21.

[15]Secretaries General, *Community Chronicle, 1956–1970* (AFSCL).

[16]*Minutes of General Council Proceedings, 1956–1970* (AFSCL).

CHAPTER 57

In the Midst of Change

There were some events which occurred during the term of Mother M. Beatrice which were truly phenomenal. These occurrences were both of a spiritual and a temporal order and indeed evoked genuine wonder and ardent interest. Without a doubt one of the most significant events taking place in the Catholic Church in the twentieth century was the election in 1958 of Angelo Roncalli as Pope John XXIII. In his casual and patient way, Pope John XXIII embarked the Church on a spiritual and temporal journey in the building up of the Kingdom of God on earth with challenging and tumultuous results. He started processes that gradually came to infuse many Catholics with a new vision of their role in the Church and in the world. It is safe to say that Pope John XXIII ushered in a new era in the history of the Catholic Church. Rooted in the past but living in the present, a new spirit of Catholicism sought to revivify the Church and the world.[1]

On January 25, 1959, the feast of the Conversion of St. Paul, Pope John XXIII[2] announced to the world his intention of convoking the 21st Ecumenical Council in the history of the Catholic Church. Traditionally, an ecumenical council is an assembly of the college of bishops under the presidency of the Pope. This Council has supreme authority over the Church in matters pertaining to faith, morals, worship, and discipline. Thus, Councils have played a highly significant role in the history of the Church, and in general, have represented attempts on the part of the Church to mobilize itself in times of crisis for self-preservation, purification, and growth. The first council was the Council of Nicea held in 325; the last was Vatican I held from 1869–1870. Now, in 1959, Pope John XXIII planned to bring together the bishops and patriarchs of the international Church for an *aggiornamento*, an updating and renewal of the Catholic Church in the twentieth century.

In his opening address at the Second Vatican Council[3] to the assembled Council Fathers on October 11, 1959, Pope John XXIII emphasized that he aimed at the renewal and rebirth of the Church in today's world. Thus the Second Vatican Council would not convene to condemn heresies or pronounce "anathemas," but, in the words of the Pontiff, the council would meet to "open a window and let in a little fresh air" so that the light and air of modern times would permeate the ancient treasure houses of the faith.[4] Pope John

XXIII convoked and opened the first session of the council on October 11, 1959. It closed on December 8, 1962. The second session was held from September 29 to December 4, 1963, but, unfortunately, before the second session could be called, Pope John XXIII died on June 3, 1963. On September 14, 1963, his successor, Pope Paul VI, convoked the third session of Vatican II which lasted until November 21, 1964. The fourth and final session was held from September 14 to December 8, 1965. On December 8, 1965, at a mass in St. Peter's Square, Pope Paul VI adjourned the Council almost five years after its convocation. Pope John XXIII's *aggiornamento*—updating—had begun in earnest.

The Council Fathers studied the nature of the Church, Christian unity, the liturgy, mass communication, the role of Mary in the life of the Church, ecumenism, and other dimensions of doctrine and Christian life. As a result of the work of the council, there were sixteen documents formulated and promulgated. The documents with the most visible and pronounced effects were those on the liturgy, the Church, the Church in the world, ecumenism, the life and ministry of priests, and the lay apostolate. Among the important documents was *Perfectae Caritatis* [Decree on the Appropriate Renewal of the Religious Life] issued on October 28, 1965, which dramatically affected and changed religious life, especially in the United States. Its profound impact on religious life and that of the Franciscan Sisters of Chicago in particular will be examined in Chapter 60.

One of the most interesting elections for the presidency of the United States took place in 1960. By the closest race in history, John F. Kennedy, a Roman Catholic, became the youngest man ever to become President of the United States, and certainly, the first Roman Catholic to have been elected to the presidency. His youthfulness, intelligence, and vigor plus his magnetic personality made him one of the most popular presidents in history. The Catholic world rejoiced at the election because it proved that a Catholic could be President. But the many social and cultural changes in the United States through the years in the areas of war, race, feminism, the environment, and politics left a dramatic impact on American Catholics. Coupled with the "renewal" movement in the Church initiated by Pope John XXIII, the moral and religious tradition of American Catholics was being severely tested. In *The American Catholic Experience*, author Jay Dolan writes:

> Only against this backdrop of social and religious turbulence is it possible to understand the measure and meaning and significance of the changes that transformed Catholicism in the United States. Catholics not only had to cope with changes in American society, they also had to contend with changes initiated by the Second Vatican Council. The events from Dallas to Watergate rocked the nation and the churches; add to these the revolution sparked by Vatican II, and the result is a powerful one-two punch that sent American Catholics reeling.[5]

In the midst of a continuing stable educational climate, Mother M. Beatrice and the general council voted to accept the staffing of the congregation's twenty-second elementary school. Located in Gary, Indiana, Blessed Sacrament School opened on September 19, 1960.

Blessed Sacrament Church was organized in 1947 by the Reverend Louis Madejczyk on a ten-acre plot on 41st Street between Hayes and Garfield Streets. Prior to the opening of Blessed Sacrament School, the children attended Confraternity of Christian Doctrine (CCD) classes in the Ross Public School. The classes were conducted by the Sisters of the Congregation of the Poor Handmaids of Jesus Christ from St. Ann's Parish in Black Oak on Thursday mornings. After the celebrated McCollum Case which ruled against the use of public schools for "released time" instructions, the Franciscan Sisters of Chicago, stationed at nearby St. Hedwig's School in Gary, agreed to provide the children with regular religious instructions. The Sisters and the children met every Saturday in the community hall at 45th and Cleveland Streets.

In 1958, Father Madejczyk presented a request to Mother M. Jerome Dadej for Sisters to staff Blessed Sacrament School. About one hundred of his parish children were being bused daily to St. Hedwig's School in Gary. On March 2, 1958, Mother M. Jerome promised Father Madejczyk four Sisters for the opening of Blessed Sacrament School in September of 1960.[6] It had been necessary for Father Madejczyk to secure the commitment of the Franciscan Sisters of Chicago before he was given permission to build the school. He was ecstatic when he received a letter from Mother M. Jerome to that effect:

> Reverend and dear Father Madejczyk:
>
> I am pleased to inform you that on the 1st of March, 1958, at the regular meeting of the general council of our congregation, it was resolved to grant your request for teaching Sisters for your school.
>
> You may proceed, therefore, with your plans for building a school, and we shall be ready to give you four Sisters in September of 1960.
>
> Please continue remembering us in the Memento of your Holy Masses, and we will likewise remember you in our prayers.
>
> Sincerely yours in Christ,
Mother M. Jerome Dadej
Superior General[7]

Mother M. Beatrice Rybacki, who had been elected superior general in July of 1958 in place of Mother M. Jerome Dadej, agreed to honor Mother M. Jerome's promise to Father Madejczyk to supply Sisters for his school.

On August 21, 1960; Sister M. Theodore Madaj, the assigned principal; Sister M. Gabriel Lazarski; Sister M. Elaine Bartkowski; and Sister M. Laverne Rzonca arrived in Gary as the first Sisters to staff the beautiful new Blessed Sacrament School. An agreement was made for the Sisters to share living quarters with the Sisters at St. Hedwig's Convent in Gary. Sister M. Carmel Rokicki served as the superior of both

Blessed Sacrament School
Gary, Indiana (1960–1987)

groups of Sisters. Each day the Sisters traveled to Blessed Sacrament School where approximately 151 children were in attendance in grades one through four. Grades five to eight were still being conducted at St. Hedwig's School.[8] Blessed Sacrament Church and School were blessed and dedicated on Sunday, May 14, 1961. In September of 1961, all eight grades were in full session with an enrollment of 265 students.

In the meantime, the Sisters who taught at Blessed Sacrament School were waiting patiently for a convent. They were often exposed to inclement weather and other inconveniences in traveling back and forth to the school from St. Hedwig's Convent.[9] A solution was reached when the Sacred Heart School in Tolleston, approximately four miles away from Blessed Sacrament School and staffed by the Franciscan Sisters of Chicago, was closed leaving the convent empty. The Sisters staffing Blessed Sacrament School moved into the vacated convent and made excellent use of the ample facilities although they still drove to school every day.[10] At one point, Sister M. Claritta Warchalowski and Sister Doloria Kosiek, the religious education coordinators at St. Matthias Church in Crown Point, Indiana, resided there for a brief length of time.[11] In March of 1974, the Sisters welcomed Sister M. Bernadette Bajuscik of the Congregation of the Daughters of the Most Holy Savior as a resident teacher who joined the Franciscan Sisters of Chicago in June of 1976.[12]

The peak of Blessed Sacrament School's enrollment occurred in 1965 when 420 students were listed on the roster. Through the years, however, there was a steady decline in Sister personnel and pupils. By 1987, with approximately two hundred students, three

Sisters, and seven lay teachers on the staff, Sister Joseph Marie Zenda, the superior general, and her general council voted to withdraw the Sisters from Blessed Sacrament School, a closing which touched the hearts of the Sisters, pupils, and parishioners.

While it is true that religious life still flourished in the United States in the early 1960s, there had always been what has been termed a "Sister shortage." The ever-present Sister shortage had affected the Franciscan Sisters of Chicago through the years no less than it had many other congregations as we have already seen in the course of this history. One of the solutions to the problem of the lack of Sisters for the apostolates of the Church had been the practice, in almost every congregation, of sending Sisters who were just beginning their teaching careers or who were in their postulancy or the second year of their novitiate into the active apostolates. These Sisters lacked not only professional preparation but also a firm footing in the religious life. Sometimes overlooked, of necessity, was the matter of a Sister's essential adjustment to community life and faithfulness to a heavy schedule of spiritual exercises. Morever, the Sisters had to secure the necessary professional training under circumstances, which, more often than not, proved to be very arduous. All too often, problems befell the young professed Sisters who were sent into the active apostolates of their congregation without the time and training necessary to prepare them for the problems confronting them in religious life.

In an address in 1952 to the Roman Congress for Communities of Religious Women, Pope Pius XII had urged the adaptation of religious to the new social order and to responsibility for their work in the Church. He urged that Sisters be prepared for their profession and receive the necessary academic degrees demanded by the State. One of the consequences of the Pope's counsel was the organization of the Sister Formation Conference in 1954 under the leadership of Sister M. Emil, IHM, the first national chairperson of Sister Formation and later its first national executive secretary. The aim of the Sister Formation Program which the Sister Formation Conference engendered was the preservice training of every Sister which would include her spiritual, intellectual, social, and professional development so that a holy and effective religious would be the result.[13] It would make of the Sister, in short, "a better religious and a better professional person."[14] This period of full-time spiritual and professional training in an established house of formation under the direction of a mistress and a formation staff was called the juniorate. As outlined by the Sister Formation Conference, the juniorate would follow the novitiate and last for at least two years in the case of candidates who had entered religious life after graduation from high school and had had a two-year novitiate following the postulancy. The juniorate was not merely a word used to refer to Sisters in temporary vows, but rather a structured program in a house of formation. To aid in this process, many congregations established junior colleges allied with their own Motherhouses.[15]

In accordance with the wishes of the Sacred Congregation for Religious and the directives of the Sister Formation Program, the Franciscan Sisters of Chicago initiated the juniorate program in September of 1961. It had as one of its objectives to provide at least two or three years of professional education for the young Sisters before they were assigned to the active apostolate. Two newly professed Sisters that year plus a young professed Sister who was already active in the teaching apostolate were enrolled as full-time students at the College of St. Francis in Joliet, Illinois.[16] The three Sisters resided with the professed Sisters at Our Lady of Victory Convent in Lemont and had special classes in religious life with Sister M. Doloretta Radzienda, the novice mistress. Four other newly professed Sisters were sent to St. Francis Xavier Cabrini Hospital to become licensed practical nurses.[17] A seventh newly professed, Sister Cheryl Marie Piesko, had her undergraduate degree and was assigned to Madonna High School. In 1962, twelve newly professed Sisters resided at the Motherhouse in Chicago and attended Mundelein College on Sheridan Road. The juniorate at the Motherhouse was located in the "old postulancy" and was under the direction of Sister M. Crescencia Chmiel.

In September of 1963, Sister M. Venantia Rec, the vicar general, was appointed directress of the juniorate which had now been transferred officially to the new Motherhouse in Lemont.[18] The entire fourth floor of the A wing of the new Motherhouse was reserved for their exclusive use.

After the Tenth General Chapter of 1964, Sister M. Rosalima Sierocki, who had been elected the fourth councilor at the chapter, also assumed the position of juniorate directress. By 1965, the congregation's formation program was more clearly defined. The aspirancy began after the completion of the eighth grade. The aspirant would then attend Madonna High School for three years after which she entered the postulancy which lasted six months. This was followed by a two-year novitiate, the first year of which was canonical. The juniorate itself lasted for three years. This program allowed the young Sister a total of five and one-half years or more of spiritual and professional training before entering the area of apostolic works.[19] Early in 1967, however, the formation program was assessed by Mother M. Beatrice and her council. They decided in June of that year to drop the aspirancy program which existed at Madonna High School. After further deliberation and review, they also voted, in August of 1967, to discontinue the juniorate program as it existed. As a consequence, the two Sisters making their first vows in August of 1968, were assigned to the active apostolate.[20] Mother M. Beatrice and her councilors were aware that the First Extraordinary Chapter of Affairs was scheduled to begin in June of 1968, and that at the chapter, the entire formation program would be assessed in the light of the Second Vatican Council.

IN THE MIDST OF CHANGE

[1] Jay P. Dolan, *The American Catholic Experience: A History from Colonial Times to the Present* (Garden City, New York: Doubleday and Company, Inc., 1985), p. 425.

[2] Pope John XXIII was born Angelo Roncalli on November 25, 1881, at Sotto il Monte in Northern Italy. He was educated at the seminary of the Bergamo Diocese and the Pontifical Seminary in Rome, where he was ordained to the priesthood on August 10, 1904. He spent the first ten years of his priesthood as secretary to the bishop of Bergamo and as an instructor in the seminary there. During World War I he became Sergeant Roncalli of the medical corps and later Lieutenant Roncalli of the chaplains' corps. In 1925, Pius XI made him an archbishop and appointed him Apostolic Visitor to Bulgaria. He also served as Apostolic Delegate to Greece and Turkey where he distinguished himself. These years in the Near East enabled him to establish contacts with members of the separated Eastern Churches which gave rise to the urge to heal the sad break between Rome and so many Eastern Catholics. In 1953, at seventy-two years of age, Archbishop Roncalli was made a Cardinal and three days later was appointed Patriarch of Venice. He proved to be a people's patriarch, always accessible and kindly as he led his flock in the practice of Christian virtue.

In 1958, Cardinal Roncalli went to the conclave following the death of Pope Pius XII where he was elected to the papacy on October 28. Because Cardinal Roncalli was seventy-eight years old, the general attitude seemed to be that a "caretaker" Pope had been elected. John XXIII, as Roncalli chose to be called, at once adopted an energetic and forward-looking policy. He was a strong and vigorous Pope whose influence far outmeasured both his age and the shortage of his time in the Papacy which was filled with an energy, novelty, and humor hitherto unknown in a Pontiff.

Pope John XXIII will forever be remembered as the Pope of the Second Vatican Council. The council was announced on January 25, 1959, and met on October 11, 1962. From the beginning, Pope John XXIII declared that its purpose was ecumenical—a strong working for unity among Christians. As far as doctrine was concerned, nothing new was said but in its atmosphere and its general approach, this was the start of a new era in the Catholic Church. The ultimate aim of the council was unity. The method to be used to achieve it was the reform and renewal of the Catholic Church—"bringing up to date," as the Pope himself called it. To prepare the agenda for the council, committees of preparation were set up over the entire field of the Church's structure, life, and music.

Pope John's reign of five and one-half years succeeded in radiating his concrete and practical charity. His encyclical, *Pacem in Terris* (1963), was based on the idea of the dignity of the individual person. Men and women of different races are referred to as having equal rights. This encyclical created a stir throughout the world. The short reign of Pope John XXIII brought an emphasis on diversity, decentralization, and relaxation. Many of his closest advisors were in disagreement with his ecumenical stance, his desire to promote the vernacular of the liturgy, his calling of the council, and the detente with the Communist countries.

"Good Pope John" died on June 3, 1963, of stomach cancer. He had been truly a good pastor, especially as pastor of the Church. Pope John XXIII had succeeded in having Catholics look on other Christians as their brothers and sisters in Christ, children of a common Father, all members of the same *famiglia humana* as he himself often said. Eric John, ed., *The Popes: A Concise Biographical History*, I (New York: Hawthorn Books, Inc. 1964), pp. 473–477).

Author Betty Friedan, writing in *Parade* magazine of the *Chicago Sun-Times* on August 12, 1984, in an article entitled, "The Men I Most Admire," states:

> Pope John XXIII I admire for relocating the religious spirit by stressing our responsibility for this world. In his own metaphor, he blew open the windows of the Church. A compromise candidate for the papacy—short, 77, weighing 205 pounds, remarkable only for his warmheartedness, gusto and love of life—he was expected to protect the Church from the threat of change. Instead, he convened Vatican II, inviting Catholic bishops from all over the world (and for the first time Protestants, Jewish and Eastern Orthodox observers) to bring the Church up

to date with a changing secular society. Instead of seeing "truth" as something given once and for all, he embraced the *search* for truth as a living, never-ending process and the need for many opinions to exist in dialectical tension. He also emphasized that the human dignity inherent in each person becomes real only as his/her rights are demanded in human societies.

[3]The twenty-one ecumenical councils in the history of the Catholic Church were named after the places where they were held.

[4]Felician A. Foy, OFM, ed., *1971 Catholic Almanac* (Paterson, New Jersey: St. Anthony's Guild, 1971), p. 174.

[5]Dolan, p. 424.

[6]*In Commemoration of Blessed Sacrament Church and School: Blessing and Dedication* (Gary, Indiana: 14 May 1961) no pagination.

[7]*Book of Correspondence:* Letter from Mother M. Jerome Dadej to the Reverend Louis Madejczyk, 2 March 1958 (AFSCL).

[8]*In Commemoration of Blessed Sacrament Church and School.*

[9]*Book of Correspondence:* Letter from Mother M. Beatrice Rybacki to the Reverend Louis Madejczyk, 10 February 1957 (AFSCL).

[10]Secretaries General, *Community Chronicle, 1957–1970* (AFSCL).

[11]*Franciscan Echo,* Vol. 13, No. 5 (Lemont, Illinois: December 1971).

[12]*Blessed Sacrament House Journal, 1970–1971* (AFSCL).

[13]Sister Bertrande Meyers, DC, *Sisters for the 21st Century* (New York: Sheed and Ward, 1965), p. 119.

[14]Sister M. Emil, IHM, President of Marygrove College, *Sister Formation Bulletin, Supplement,* Detroit, Summer 1956, p. 1.

[15]In 1971, Sister Diane Marie Collins was sent to Marillac College in Normandy, Missouri. Conducted by the Congregation of the Daughters of Charity of the St. Louis Province, the college had been established as a liberal arts college exclusively for Sisters in keeping with the norms of the Sister Formation Program. A graduate of the class of 1973, Sister Diane Marie stated: "Marillac offered numerous challenges and experiences that could not be found elsewhere . . . there was a spirit that was uniquely Marillac." Unfortunately, due to insufficient funds and a decline in student enrollment, Marillac College closed in May of 1974. *Book of Correspondence:* Letter from Sister Diane Marie Collins to author, 1975 (AFSCL).

[16]The young professed Sisters were Sister Angela Marie Benedyk, Sister M. Claritta Warchalowski, and Sister M. Lenore Kuderka. They attended the College of St. Francis which had been established in 1920 by the Congregation of the Sisters of St. Francis of Mary Immaculate of Joliet, Illinois. *Book of Annual Assignments* (AFSCL).

[17]The Sisters were Sister Lois Marie Rossi, Sister Joan Klimek, Sister M. Stanislaus Grecznik and Sister M. Kunegunda Gwiazdzinski. *Book of Annual Assignments* (AFSCL).

[18]Sister M. Crescencia was then appointed directress of the aspirants and postulants at Madonna High School. She replaced Sister M. Edward Nowak who was transferred to St. Stanislaus Bishop and Martyr School. *Book of Annual Assignments* (AFSCL).

[19]Secretaries General, *Community Chronicle, 1952–1970* (AFSCL).

[20]They were Sister Margaret Mary Peckenpaugh and Sister Isabel Mendez of Carupano, Venezuela, the first Sister in the congregation to enter from South America. *Book of Annual Assignments;* and *Minutes of General Council Proceedings, 1956–1970* (AFSCL).

CHAPTER 58

Our Lady of Victory Convent: The New General Motherhouse

The year 1963 was truly extraordinary. A new pope, Cardinal Giovanni Montini, the archbishop of Milan, was elected on June 21, 1963, by the largest conclave of cardinals in the history of the Catholic Church. As Pope Paul VI, he was crowned on June 30 in solemn ceremonies in St. Peter's Square.

On September 29, 1963, Pope Paul VI carried on the work of his predecessor, Pope John XXIII, by opening the second session of the Second Vatican Council. The Catholic world rejoiced at this event, yet a few months later, was saddened and devastated by the tragic death of President John F. Kennedy, who was assassinated on November 22, 1963, while riding in an open presidential automobile in a motorcade in Dallas, Texas. Vice President Lyndon B. Johnson, who was touring with the Kennedy motorcade at the time of the assassination, took the oath of office as president.

In the congregation, the conditions and prospects for the future never looked brighter. In the memorable year of 1963, the number of Sisters in the congregation had risen to 441, the highest number since its foundation. There were thirty novices, the highest number since 1931. In the same wondrous year of 1963, the Franciscan Sisters of Chicago could finally look forward to moving into their new Motherhouse in Lemont, Illinois, sixty-nine years after their foundation by Mother M. Theresa Dudzik.

Because the congregation had grown in membership through the years, the lack of adequate housing and the genuine need for expansion at the Motherhouse in Chicago became more apparent. The congregation had long envisioned a Motherhouse where the sick and the aged Sisters might spend their retirement years in relative peace and quiet, where young women might be prepared for religious life and their eventual ministries in the Church, and where adequate accommodations for retreats during the summer months and other community functions such as anniversaries, reception, and profession ceremonies could be provided. In the early days of the congregation, the needs of the apostolate had always received first priority. Coupled with the acute financial difficulties the congregation had experienced at its foundation, any question of building a new Motherhouse had been, at best, unthinkable. The decision to build a new Motherhouse was literally forced upon the administration of the congregation when inspectors from the Chicago Fire Department ruled that the original Motherhouse on Hamlin Avenue was no longer safe and habitable in its condition. In December of 1959, after the tragic fire which had claimed so many lives at Our Lady of the Angels School, the Chicago Fire Department enforced rigid safety standards. The original St. Joseph Home for the Aged and the adjacent St. Vincent's Orphan Asylum, which together had served as a Motherhouse since the foundation of the congregation, were judged hazardous and beyond renovation.[1]

When it became apparent that the matter of a Motherhouse could no longer be postponed, the question arose as to a suitable location for a new one. Mother M. Beatrice secured the services of the firm of Neri, Spooner, and Sit, Inc., a noted planning, architectural, and engineering firm, to estimate the cost of renovating the existing Motherhouse facilities in order to meet the City Code requirements and to determine the degree of rehabilitation the buildings demanded. The estimated figure for renovation was $372,373. The firm made it clear that many of the problems of the existing facilities,[2] such as their high maintenance cost, poor air and heat circulation, and inefficient layout (since each unit represented an addition that was not originally planned), would be in need of replacement again in ten years or less. In view of the high cost of renovation and the limited benefits to be derived from this labor, the firm felt justified in recommending the razing of the old buildings and replacing them with an entirely new structure.[3]

In August of 1959, the administration of the congregation set about to select a suitable site for the new Motherhouse. The first plan was to raze the original St. Joseph Home for the Aged and the adjacent St. Vincent's Orphan Asylum and erect an L-shaped building in their place on the corner of Hamlin and Schubert Avenues.[4] The chapel in St. Joseph Home would then be enlarged to accommodate the Sisters. By October of 1959, the general council had come to the conclusion that the Hamlin-Schubert site was not the solution.[5] Another site was suggested on Belmont and Cumberland Avenues, but investigation proved that the property in question belonged to another religious congregation and was, therefore, not available. Other sites were either unsuitable for a Motherhouse or were prohibitive because of the cost of valuable Chicago city property.[6] Another possibility existed in building an addition to Our Lady of Victory Convent for the retired Sisters in Lemont. That plan, too, was rejected as being as costly as building an entirely new structure.[7] After much deliberation, the general council voted to erect a new Motherhouse in Lemont, Illinois. The new Motherhouse would be built on the property already owned by the congregation and on additional acres purchased from willing neighbors.[8] It would consist of a four-wing structure for three hundred Sisters with separate sections for the novitiate, the postulancy, the infirmary, and the administration. On October 12, 1960, Mother M. Beatrice and Sister M. Gonzaga visited Albert Cardinal Meyer, the archbishop of Chicago, to secure permission to build and to request a sizable loan from the Holy See. The general council also sought permission at this time to plan a

Our Lady of Victory Convent
General Motherhouse of the Franciscan Sisters of Chicago
Lemont, Illinois (1963–)

cemetery for the Sisters on the grounds of the Motherhouse.

The architectural firm of Pirola and Erbach of Chicago was selected by the general council to design the Motherhouse, and the R. T. Milord Company, also of Chicago, was hired to construct it. Mother M. Beatrice secured the advice of the Reverend Theophane Kalinowski, OFM, minister provincial of the Assumption Province of the Franciscan Fathers of Pulaski, Wisconsin, who offered many valuable suggestions.[9]

Ground-breaking for the new structure took place on Friday, December 8, 1961, on the 67th Anniversary of the congregation's foundation. The Reverend John Grabowski, CR,[10] provincial superior of the Congregation of the Resurrection and the vicar for religious communities of women in Chicago, officiated. More than one-hundred fifty Franciscan Sisters of Chicago were present. On the next day, construction began in earnest. In less than two years, the new Our Lady of Victory Motherhouse was completed at a cost of $2,800,000. For months before the completion of the Motherhouse, the Sisters from the convents in Chicago and Indiana had come on Saturdays to prepare the Motherhouse for occupancy. They spent many weekends in tedious and arduous cleaning chores. Their fatigue was balanced, however, by the joy and pride they felt in having a new Motherhouse.

On September 15, 1961, the cornerstone of the new convent was put in place. The massive building was a graceful structure of face brick with stone trim and lannon stone motif, practical as it was beautiful. The structure, more than six hundred feet in length, was built in the form of a modified cross on a beautifully landscaped twenty-acre site. It consisted of four wings, designated as A, B, C, and D which were centrally united at the heart of the structure, the chapel. The property, nearly 1,300 feet deep, rose approximately seventy-five feet above the highway offering an excellent view of the countryside from all parts of the building. The main entrance to the building led into a spacious foyer dominated by a marble statue of Our Lady of Victory, set majestically against a gold and pink mosaic panel. At the head of the terrazzo staircase leading to the Sacred Heart Chapel, a beautiful oil painting of the Crucifixion was suspended. More than three hundred sleeping rooms, accented by simplicity, were provided in addition to a solarium, recreation rooms, study rooms, storage rooms, and a library. Several attractive classrooms and the spacious and multipurpose Marian Hall were located on the main level. The front portion of the building, five stories high, contained a forty-eight bed infirmary, comfortable and well equipped, designed for direct access to the chapel balcony for the sick and infirm Sisters. A nurse's station, with a registered nurse at all times, made immediate contact with the infirmary possible. The spacious administrative quarters were located in this area on the main level. A large social hall, suitable for community meetings, social activities, and educational workshops, was located on the lowest level and was equipped with tables, chairs, and a large stage.

The words of the Psalmist proclaim: "How beautiful is your dwelling place, O Lord of Hosts. My soul is longing and yearning for the courts of the Lord." The Sacred Heart Chapel in the Motherhouse could truly elicit the Psalmist's ardent response, for it was a masterpiece of graceful design conducive to prayer and worship. Executed in the shape of a truncated "V," it was located at the center part of the main level, and was accessible from all parts of the building. It was finished in specifically selected brown wood veneers lending it an atmosphere of beauty and naturalness. The entire sanctuary was marble with the pews radiating in banks around it to seat four hundred fifty persons. The Greco Manufacturing Company, dealers in ecclesiastical furnishings, after consultation with the architects and Father Theophane Kalinowski, designed an altar suitable to conform to the new liturgical expression in worship. The altar, constructed of Imperial white marble was set on a tiered white marble predella in the center of the modified circular sanctuary. The sanctuary floor, laid in Italian Cremo and Botticino marble, was of a matching pattern and conveyed the impression of a halo or sunburst. An eight-point faceted glass window, directly over the altar radiated vibrant hues of reds, blues, and golds. On the wall, directly in back of the altar, a large, beautiful, and imposing figure of the Sacred Heart was depicted in a mosaic of Venetian glass. Stained glass windows, each illustrating an apparition of Our Lady, were found on either side of the altar. On the right and left sides of the altar, white Carrara statues of the Blessed Virgin Mary and St. Joseph were suspended. Two side altars contained white Carrara statues of St. Francis of Assisi and St. Anthony of Padua. In the rear of the chapel were two large niches. One held the large, beautiful portrait of Our Lady of Częstochowa which had once been enshrined in the chapel of the old Motherhouse. The other niche would eventually contain the remains of Mother M. Theresa Dudzik. The Stations of the Cross, carved in white Carrara marble, enriched the walls of the convent chapel. Most of the chapel and convent furnishings were gifts to the congregation from grateful and generous benefactors.

On June 20, 1963, with the permission of ecclesiastical authorities, Mother M. Beatrice, Sister M. Venantia, and all the Sisters assigned to live at the new Motherhouse left St. Joseph Home which had served as the Motherhouse for sixty-nine years. Two days prior to their leave-taking, Mother M. Beatrice had given "obediences" to the Sisters at the old Motherhouse. Seventeen Sisters were to remain and would constitute the staff of St. Joseph Home while thirty-four Sisters were assigned "obediences" to their new Motherhouse in Lemont.[11] On that same day, at seven-thirty o'clock in the evening, the Reverend Martin Stepanich, OFM, of St. Mary's Seminary in Lemont, transferred the Blessed Sacrament from the novitiate house to the new Motherhouse and made the memorable journey in the company of all the novices, their novice mistress, Sister M. Doloretta Radzienda; and her assistant, Sister M. Isabel Sutor. The novices and the postulants were assigned to occupy the C wing of the building which constituted the formation section. During the following week, the retired and infirm Sisters vacated the old Our Lady of Victory Convent which had served them since 1936 as a retirement home.

Sacred Heart Chapel, Our Lady of Victory Convent
General Motherhouse of the Franciscan Sisters of Chicago
Lemont, Illinois

Preparations were already underway to convert the retirement home into the Mother Theresa Home for the Aged.

Although the chapel was not as yet completed, the Holy Sacrifice of the Mass was celebrated for the first time in the new Motherhouse on June 21, 1963. The Reverend John Grabowski, CR, the provincial of the Chicago Province of the Congregation of the Resurrection, offered the mass at ten o'clock in the morning during which he delivered a sermon expressing gratitude to God for the bountiful blessing of the new Motherhouse. After the mass, he conducted a simple blessing of the building. More than 250 Franciscan Sisters of Chicago and numerous clergy and religious of other congregations were present.

The first conventual ceremonies were held at the new Motherhouse on July 24, 1963, when thirteen Sisters celebrated their jubilees of religious consecration.[12] The celebrant was the Very Reverend Monsignor Alfred L. Abramowicz of the archdiocesan chancery office and the brother of a silver jubilarian, Sister M. Antonella. The Reverend Sylvester Makarewicz, OFM, guardian of Christ the King Seminary in West Chicago, delivered the congratulatory homily.

The Motherhouse was dedicated by the Most Reverend Albert Cardinal Meyer[13] on Sunday, August 11, 1963, the vigil of the feast of St. Clare, a spiritual daughter of St. Francis. Cardinal Meyer was assisted by the Reverend Cletus J. Lynch, pastor of St. Louise de Marillac Church in La Grange Park, and the Reverend Anthony Laskowski, CR, pastor of St. Stanislaus Bishop and Martyr Church in Chicago. All of the schools and institutions staffed by the Sisters sent representatives. Scores of clergy, Sisters from various religious congregations, and lay guests joined in the jubilant celebration. While Cardinal Meyer erected a crucifix in the refectory and blessed the interior of the Motherhouse, the Reverend Ted Cocot, assistant at St. Pancratius Church in Chicago, explained the actions of the cardinal to the guests assembled in the chapel and read in English the prayers which the cardinal prayed in Latin. Upon his return to the chapel, Cardinal Meyer delivered a sermon to the guests in which he explained the real meaning of a Motherhouse from the Church's point of view. A letter addressed to Mother M. Beatrice earlier contained his main points:

> My dear Mother Mary Beatrice:
>
> The Dedication of the new Motherhouse of the Franciscan Sisters of Blessed Kunegunda on Sunday, August 11, 1963, will mark a very special event in the history of the order.
>
> A Motherhouse for Sisters is an important and necessary adjunct to a Sister's life. It is most likely here where her first contact with the order is made and where in all likelihood she will spend many days during the tenure of her religious life. It is home to the Sister; it is where she can return from her assignments and in serene and peaceful surroundings obtain and recapture the deep spiritual devotion that sometimes is not obtainable in the busy days of the various duties of her station in life.

I congratulate you and commend you for having made this beautiful new Motherhouse possible, and in offering it to Almighty God in the Dedication Ceremony, I am confident that great blessings will accrue to the Franciscan Sisters of Blessed Kunegunda.

Extending to you and to all the Sisters my very best wishes and blessings, I remain,

> Very sincerely yours in Christ,
> Albert Cardinal Meyer[14]

A Solemn Benediction followed the blessing of the Motherhouse during which the Sisters' choir sang under the direction of Sister M. Lucretia Kot. Immediately following the Benediction of the Blessed Sacrament, a dinner was served in the Sisters' refectory to the cardinal, clergy, religious, and special guests, with the Sisters of Madonna High School as the hostesses. All the other guests were served refreshments in the social hall, and before departing, were given a tour of the entire convent. The day was one of absolute rejoicing. Perhaps the one person whose heart literally overflowed with gratitude that day was Sister M. Clara Ogurek, the only surviving member of the foundation group who had witnessed the dedication of the old Motherhouse in 1898 in the company of Sister M. Theresa, Sister M. Anna, and Father Vincent Barzynski. The cornerstone inscription on the newly blessed Motherhouse read: "For Sanctity and Service." Sixty-five years had passed between the dedications of the two Motherhouses but their essential reason for coming into existence had remained the same.

On the next day, August 12, the ceremonies of Initiation, Reception, and First Profession took place for the first time in the new Motherhouse. Twenty-two young women took part in the lovely and meaningful ceremonies.[15]

Two months later, the first death occurred in the new Motherhouse in the person of Sister M. Immaculate Matuszewski who died on October 26, 1963.[16] She was buried in St. Adalbert's Cemetery in Niles while the congregation was in the process of developing a community cemetery on the grounds of the new Motherhouse.

On June 10, 1964, in the company of fourteen priests and numerous Sisters, the Most Reverend Aloysius Wycislo, auxiliary bishop of Chicago, consecrated all the altars in the Sacred Heart Chapel.[17]

Together with the construction of the huge Motherhouse, a private sewage plant, garages, parking area, and a tennis court were also provided. A lovely, small lake was developed on the grounds, and in 1966, a swimming pool was built behind the Mother-house. It was a gift of the Milord Company who had offered the construction of the pool as a donation and was influential in eliciting private donors to complete the project. Today, the Sisters avail themselves of this healthy exercise and have as their guests Sisters from various congregations stationed nearby. Per an agreement with the congregation, the children from the Lt. Joseph P. Kennedy, Jr. School for Exceptional Children in Palos Park also made use of the facility for several summers.[18]

With the new Motherhouse now situated in Lemont, Mother M. Beatrice and her general council continued discussions concerning a community cemetery on the grounds. To this end, a half-acre of land was purchased at the rear of the large Motherhouse structure in 1963.[19] Prior to this, the Sisters had been buried in St. Adalbert's Cemetery in Niles.[20] In October of 1966, Sister M. Venantia Rec, the vicar general, successfully concluded negotiations with the mayor of Lemont and the director of cemeteries of the Archdiocese of Chicago, the Right Reverend Monsignor Francis J. McElligott, to plan the proposed Our Lady of Victory Convent Cemetery.[21] In the meantime, the Sisters who died were temporarily interred in the Resurrection Mausoleum at Resurrection Cemetery in Justice, Illinois.[22]

Work on the community cemetery commenced on July 14, 1967. By August, the remains of all the former mothers general and twenty Sisters were transferred from St. Adalbert's Cemetery in Niles and reinterred at Our Lady of Victory Convent Cemetery in Lemont. By September 21, the transfer of the remains of 131 more Sisters to Our Lady of Victory Convent Cemetery was completed. The grave of Mother M. Theresa Dudzik at St. Adalbert's Cemetery, however, remained undisturbed as was Sister M. Chrysostom Keller's grave,[23] which adjoined that of Mother M. Theresa.

When the process of the beatification of Mother M. Theresa Dudzik was begun with the permission of John Cardinal Cody, the ordinary of the Archdiocese of Chicago, the remains of Mother M. Theresa were brought from St. Adalbert's Cemetery and interred on October 15, 1972, at the side altar in the rear of the Sacred Heart Chapel in the Motherhouse in a beautiful Botticino marble sarcophagus. In the meantime, a special grave

Community Cemetery, Our Lady of Victory Convent
General Motherhouse, Lemont, Illinois

site with a large memorial stone was constructed for Mother M. Theresa on the grounds of the community cemetery.

On May 10, 1968, Sister M. Rita Schmitt was the first Sister to be buried directly from the new Motherhouse in the congregation's lovely cemetery on the hill.

In the late 1970s, a Communications Media Library was opened on the first floor of the Motherhouse. It contained a large collection of records, tapes, and filmstrips which were made available to the Sisters, especially at the time of yearly retreats.

In 1976, in the year that marked the 750th Anniversary of the death of St. Francis of Assisi, and in the spirit of the 41st Eucharistic Congress held that year, the Chancery Office of the Archdiocese of Chicago heartily approved the Exposition of the Blessed Sacrament on each Thursday of the week. This practice began on October 7, 1976, and continues on each Thursday with the exception of the Thursday preceding the First Friday of the month. All-day Exposition of the Blessed Sacrament is still continued on the First Friday of the month.

In 1977, thirty rooms at the Motherhouse were reconstructed from typical one-bedroom sleeping units to two-room units consisting of sleeping quarters and a sitting room. In addition, more needed closet space was provided. The rooms occupied by the novices and the postulants, the infirmary, and the rooms generally occupied by the Sisters at the time of their annual retreat were not a part of the reconstruction.

The facilities of the Motherhouse have always been utilized advantageously. The Motherhouse hosts one-day retreats representing parishes, societies, students on all levels, and pilgrimages. The pilgrimages begin with the Liturgy of the Eucharist and a visit to the sarcophagus of Mother M. Theresa Dudzik at the rear of the Sacred Heart Chapel. A catered luncheon is served in the social hall and then a tour of the Mother Theresa Museum and Mother Theresa Home is conducted. A Benediction service follows after which the refreshed pilgrims enjoy a coffee break before departing. The guests at the Motherhouse, no matter what their purpose, never fail to express their pleasure at the opportunity of enjoying the beautiful Motherhouse grounds.

Our Lady of Victory Motherhouse and the Sacred Heart Chapel testify to the zeal and untiring efforts of Mother M. Beatrice Rybacki and Sister M. Venantia Rec, her assistant general, who planned and promoted its construction, and to the deep faith and self-denial of each Sister. The Motherhouse stands as a tribute to the sacrifice and loyalty of the congregation's families, friends, and benefactors whose financial aid allowed the project to become a reality.

For the Franciscan Sisters of Chicago, Our Lady of Victory Convent Motherhouse is what Albert Cardinal Meyer termed it in his congratulatory message to Mother M. Beatrice in May of 1963—"it is *home*." Here it is that the superior general and the general council, ecclesial women of faith, govern all ministries in the light of the Gospel. It is here that the novices and the postulants intensify their Baptismal consecration in a personal response to the call of Jesus. It is here that the senior Sisters draw forth inspiration and renewed courage after years of dedication to the Lord and his Church. Here it is that the ill and the retired Sisters undertake their special mission of prayer and suffering.[24] It is from here that those who have fallen asleep in the Lord are carried to their final resting place. It is at the Motherhouse of the Franciscan Sisters of Chicago in Lemont where the Sisters live and die according to the words of St. Paul: "I will make up in my body what is lacking in the suffering of Christ, for the sake of his Body, the Church."[25]

While the new Motherhouse was still under construction, Mother M. Beatrice and her general council discussed plans for the future use of the newly vacated Our Lady of Victory Convent at 1270 Main Street. When the convent had been erected in 1936, it had served as a home for the aged and infirm Sisters of the congregation. Now with more than ample room in the new Motherhouse to accommodate them and with the provision of an infirmary to care for the ill Sisters, the old Our Lady of Victory Convent was no longer necessary. At a session of the general council held on August 20, 1962, Mother M. Beatrice and her councilors settled on a plan to convert the convent into a home for the aged of Lemont and its surrounding communities.[26] In June of 1963, therefore, E. Benko, a general contractor from Chicago, was hired to make constructive changes in Our Lady of Victory Convent in order to meet the requirements as demanded by the federal government and the State of Illinois for a home for the aged. Late in October, the general council received copies of the blueprints prepared by the National Survey Service, Inc. in connection with the proposed conversion of the convent into a home for the aged. Copies of the proposals were sent to the Zoning Board and to Vincent Sill, the architect. On December 9, the vice–president of the Schirmer Engineering Corporation sent to Harry Hughes, the deputy state fire marshal, several drawings showing the gravity tank, yard mains, fire hydrants, automatic sprinkler installations in the basement and attic, and smoke detectors on the first and second floors. All the plans for the conversion of the old convent into a home for the aged were eventually approved by the deputy state fire marshal.[27]

On June 8, 1964, a public hearing, approved by the County Zoning Board of Appeals, was held in the Lemont Village Hall to request a special permit for the conversion of the former convent into a facility for the aged. At a later meeting held on July 30, 1964, the Board of Commissioners of Cook County agreed that the request for the proposed home for the aged should be granted since the Zoning Board had shown evidence of the need for such a facility in the Lemont area. With the aid of the Catholic Charities Bureau of the Archdiocese of Chicago, extensive remodeling and renovation of the convent took place under the strict supervision of Sister M. Virginia Minta.[28] While the impressive three-story, yellow-brick structure retained its original facade, the interior of the building was renovated in order to meet the stringent requirements demanded by the State of Illinois for homes for the aged. Over fifty private and semiprivate rooms for residents were constructed. The former auditorium which seated over three hundred persons was refurbished as a lovely dining room in Early American decor for the residents, and extensive colorful painting and decorating of the entire home's interior took place. This included the beautiful chapel which seats one hundred fifty persons.[29] After its renovation, the Our Lady of Victory Convent was renamed Mother Theresa Home in honor of Mother M. Theresa Dudzik.

Mother Theresa Home opened its doors to fifteen residents on June 18, 1964. Sister M. Virginia Minta, who had so carefully supervised the renovation of Mother Theresa Home and who had already served as the administrator of St. Joseph's Home for the Aged in Cleveland for nine and a half years, was appointed its first administrator. Besides Sister M. Virginia, the pioneer staff included Sister M. Febronia Morzuch, Sister Lois Marie Rossi, Sister M. Lucy Drozdz, Sister M. Pauline Dydo, and Sister M. Theresilla Ignasiak. The Sisters resided in the new Our Lady of Victory Convent Motherhouse where Sister M. Eugenia Detlaf served as their local superior.[30]

At a special ceremony held on October 15, 1964, the feast of St. Teresa of Avila, Mother Theresa Home was blessed and dedicated by the Reverend Henry M. Malak, the postulator for the cause of beatification of Mother M. Theresa Dudzik. A festive open house followed the paraliturgical celebration. On Sunday, November 22, 1964, the first mass for the residents was offered in the chapel of Mother Theresa Home by the Reverend Bertrand Kotnik, OFM, a member of the Franciscan Fathers of the Custody of the Holy Cross who staff St. Mary's Seminary and Retreat House in Lemont. Accompanied by Sister M. Amata Holub at the organ, the Sisters in the juniorate sang at the Liturgy of Thanksgiving.[31] The Franciscan Fathers, who had served the Sisters in Lemont since 1926, were requested to minister to the spiritual needs of the residents and staff of Mother Theresa Home, a service they continue to this day.

On March 29, 1965, the Franciscan Sisters of Chicago were informed by the State of Illinois Department of Health that Mother Theresa Home now met the requirements for a home for the aged. It received a license to operate and it officially opened on April 19, 1965. Mother Theresa Home reached its total capacity of fifty-seven residents in early 1967. At that time, Mother Theresa Home was licensed to provide intermediate care for five residents who were unable to live independently but required less than continuous nursing services on a twenty-four-hour basis. Residential or sheltered care was available to fifty-two residents who were able to maintain a more independent lifestyle not requiring constant supervision.[32]

At the end of July 1969, Sister M. Virginia, the administrator, was taken ill, and Sister M. Agnes Zywiec was chosen to replace her. In August of 1970, Mother Theresa Home became an "independent mission" at the Motherhouse, and Sister M. Agnes was appointed the superior of the Sisters who staffed the home. The Sisters who worked at Mother Theresa Home resided at the Motherhouse where they occupied a large section of the B wing on the third floor. This arrangement enabled the Sisters to develop a truly communal spirit which they were able to share with the residents and staff at Mother Theresa Home.

In the early part of 1981, the emphasis on the type of care offered at Mother Theresa Home shifted, and the administration petitioned the State of Illinois for a change in licensure. Mother Theresa Home was anxious to provide the added necessary care to the residents so that they would be able to remain in the home. To meet the new regulations and specifications for the change in licensure, a nurses' station and the necessary utility rooms were installed on the second floor. Call cords and hospital beds were also added to the residents' rooms. The State of Illinois granted the petition for the change in licensure, and since December 4, 1981, Mother Theresa Home has been licensed for forty-six intermediate care beds and eleven sheltered care beds for its total capacity of fifty-seven residents. The occupancy rate runs at one hundred percent and like most Catholic nursing homes today, Mother Theresa Home has a long waiting list.[33]

In February of 1981, Mother Theresa Home was asked by the sponsors of the "Meals and Services for the Homebound of Lemont" to provide meals for persons living in their own homes in the immediate vicinity of Lemont. The program provides an average of eight to fourteen meals daily for needy and housebound persons from Monday through Friday. A representative of Mother Theresa Home is a member of the Board of Directors of the program. The meals, both hot and cold, are cooked and delivered from the kitchen of Mother Theresa Home itself.[34]

Once described in the *Lemont Herald* as a "special little corner of the world,"[35] Mother Theresa Home strives to promote Christian community and enhance the dignity of persons in a spirit of love and concern regardless of race, creed, social, or financial status. To achieve this end, it provides a "homelike" atmosphere and personalized care. Optimal health care services and programs contribute to the well-being of its residents and the community of Lemont. Mother Theresa Home is served by a social worker and a social worker designee as required by the State of Illinois. Besides providing a doctor on call for twenty-four hours a day, Mother Theresa Home has the services of a dentist, a speech therapist, and a physical therapist. The home maintains consultant agreements with the Lemont Fire Department personnel, a dietitian, a podiatrist, and a registered pharmacist. A full-time activity director supervises a varied and interesting program planned around the needs of the residents. Each month the home publishes an interesting, informative newsletter called *The Villager*. Resident council meetings are held monthly and the residents may voice their problems and concerns. There is a variety of craft programs, exercise programs, and suitable sports activities. Provision for letter writing and letter reading for those whose vision is declining is made. The home provides opportunities for spiritual activities such as the daily Eucharistic Liturgy, the daily recitation of the rosary, and the yearly May Crowning of the Blessed Virgin Mary as well as other liturgical functions. The Reverend Reginald Maslinski, OFM, the chaplain at the Motherhouse, visits the residents twice a week, conducts Bible classes, and has the Benediction services on appointed days. The concepts of reality orientation and reminiscing are done daily. Perhaps one of the most important activities—simply sitting down, listening, and sharing with the residents in an unrushed manner—takes place.

Through the Catholic Charities of the Archdiocese of Chicago, captioned films for the deaf are shown. The New Life Lutheran Church Women's Club of Bolingbrook provides a weekly shopping cart whereby the residents can purchase small items. On Wednesdays, the St. Dominic/St. Francis Council of Catholic Women of Bolingbrook come to visit the residents. They usually bring along their small children who are always a joy to the residents. The St. Vincent de Paul Society of St. Odilo Parish in Berwyn provides a cash bingo twice a year. Each month in Westmont, a few of the residents attend the Knights of Columbus bingo during which a noon meal is served. The residents are likewise entertained frequently by many community organizations. A dance band appears at frequent intervals. Annually, Mother Theresa Home residents take part in the Golden Olympics held at Maryville Academy in suburban Des Plaines. During this event, the residents of the Catholic homes compete against each other in various sports. In 1981, Mother Theresa Home placed sixth among the thirteen homes represented, and one of its residents won the Gold Medal for his ability to outplay everyone in pool.

Mother Theresa Home, recognized by and a member of the Illinois Association of the Homes for the Aged, the American Association of Homes for the Aging, and the National Conference of Catholic Charities, presently ministers to its total capacity of fifty-seven residents. The administration of the Franciscan Sisters of Chicago has a long-range plan for the renovation of its present facilities and construction of another wing to expand its services to one hundred beds. Of these, twenty would be skilled–care beds and eighty would be intermediate-care beds with full ancillary services.[36]

In 1984, Sister M. Dorothea Micek was appointed to serve as the administrator of Mother Theresa Home. In addition to seven Franciscan Sisters of Chicago, the residents are served by fifty-seven full-time and part-time employees whose main object is to render service in the spirit and tradition of Mother M. Theresa Dudzik.

OUR LADY OF VICTORY: THE NEW GENERAL MOTHERHOUSE

[1]*Minutes of General Council Proceedings, 1956–1970*, 19 August 1959 (AFSCL).

[2]The facilities consisted of the original St. Joseph Home for the Aged and Crippled built in 1897, the convent annex building known as St. Vincent's Orphan Asylum built in 1899, the convent-laundry building built in 1911, and the convent-chapel building built in 1911.

[3]*Book of Correspondence:* Letter from Neri, Spooner, and Sit, Inc. to Mother M. Beatrice Rybacki, 8 September 1959 (AFSCL).

[4]*Minutes of General Council Proceedings, 1956–1970* (AFSCL).

[5]Secretaries General, *Community Chronicle, 1957–1970*, 25 October 1959 (AFSCL).

[6]Ibid., 24 April 1959.

[7]Ibid., 26 July 1960.

[8]For example, a neighbor, Mr. Kotlin, sold the Sisters thirty-seven and a half acres. Secretaries General, *Community Chronicle, 1957–1970*, July 1960 (AFSCL).

[9]The name of Father Kalinowski appears quite often in this history. A native Chicagoan, he entered the Order of Friars Minor of the Province of the Assumption of the Blessed Virgin Mary in Pulaski, Wisconsin. In the order, Father Kalinowski served as master of clerics and lector in philosophy and theology, teacher, missionary, and guardian. In 1945, he was elected minister provincial for a three-year term. After his term concluded, he became master of novices in Pulaski. He was re-elected provincial in 1951 and remained in office until 1960. After concluding his term as minister provincial, Father Kalinowski retained his office of delegate general and took up his residence in Lake Geneva. He had been instrumental in building Christ the King Seminary in West Chicago and was, therefore, very knowledgeable concerning the planning and building of Our Lady of Victory Convent. Biographical sketch from the Order of Friars Minor of the Province of the Assumption of the Blessed Virgin Mary, Pulaski, Wisconsin.

[10]Father Grabowski served as the provincial of the Congregation of the Resurrection of the Chicago Province from 1958 to 1964. He also served as the delegate to the communities of religious women of the Archdiocese of Chicago (Polish). He succeeded the Reverend Stanley Fiołek, CR, who died in December of 1958. Edward T. Janas, CR, *Dictionary of American Resurrectionists, 1865–1965* (Rome: Gregorian University Press, 1967), pp. 175–176.

[11]The following Sisters remained at St. Joseph Home: Sister M. Agnes Zywiec, superior and administrator; Sister M. Laurentia Owczarzak, assistant superior and receptionist; Sister M. Theodosia Biss, kitchen supervisor; Sister M. Generose Siepak, infirmary supervisor; Sister M. Kunegunda Pinkowski, sacristan; Sister M. Susanna Pietrzycki, organist; Sister M. Isidore Wilkos, dining room supervisor; Sister M. Irene Stojak, refectory supervisor; Sister M. Michaeline Tabor, laundry supervisor; Sister M. Ernest Blazonczyk, night supervisor; Sister M. Bruno Szwagiel, night duty; Sister M. Leonilla Stogowski, floor supervisor and registered nurse; Sister M. Angelica Seidl, bookkeeper and office; Sister M. Rose Ann Zmich, assistant cook; Sister M. Marcella Turlinski, assistant cook; Sister M. Bernadine Ostrega, floor supervisor; Sister M. Honorata Makowski, floor supervisor; and Sister M. Antoniana Stanczak, weekend pharmacist. *Minutes of General Council Proceedings, 1956–1970*, 10 June 1963 (AFSCL).

[12]The celebrants included Sister M. Jolanta Nowak and Sister M. Gerard Gorzkowski who were observing their 60th anniversary of religious life; Sister M. Desideria Grendys and Sister M. Eustace Borowski, fifty years; and the Silver Jubilarians: Sister M. Antonella Abramowicz, Sister M. Concordia Lawrence, Sister M. Cundette Minchuk, Sister M. Dulcissima Kaczmarek, Sister M. Deofilia Piaskowy, Sister M. Gemma Stanek, Siser M. Generose Siepak, Sister M. Laetitia Kolczak, and Sister M. Praesentia Grzybowski. In a break with community tradition, the jubilarians were able, for the first time, to eat lunch with their guests in the social hall in the new Motherhouse. *Minutes of General Proceedings, 1956–1970* (AFSCL).

[13]On November 16, 1958, Albert Gregory Meyer was named archbishop of Chicago and emerged as one of its best-loved churchmen. Born on March 9, 1903, in Milwaukee, he received his religious education at St. Francis Seminary in Milwaukee and the North American College in Rome where he was ordained in 1936. He was associated with St. Francis Seminary in 1931 where he served as professor of Greek, dogma, and scripture. In 1946, he was consecrated bishop of Superior, Wisconsin, and in 1953, archbishop of Milwaukee. In September 1958, he succeeded Samuel Cardinal Stritch as archbishop of Chicago, the center of the largest Catholic population in the United States.

Sixteen days after his installation, Archbishop Meyer was faced with one of the worst school disasters in the history of Chicago. Ninety-two children and three Sisters of Charity of the Blessed Virgin Mary were lost in the tragic fire at Our Lady of the Angels School on the city's West Side. As a consequence, Archbishop Meyer inaugurated an extensive program of school modernization and the construction of over sixty-nine new grade schools and fifteen high schools. One of the outstanding facilities erected during this time was Quigley Preparatory Seminary South on Chicago's South Side; the other was a Junior College division of the major seminary in Mundelein, was established in the former St. Hedwig's Orphanage in Niles, Illinois. During Archbishop Meyer's tenure of office, thirty parishes were established and enrollment in the archdiocesan schools was at its peak. On December 14, 1959, Pope John XXIII named Archbishop Meyer a cardinal. Because of his experience in the field of education dating from his service as a seminary professor and his interest in scriptural scholarship, Cardinal Meyer was an ardent participant in the Second Vatican Council and emerged as the leader of the American hierarchy. Cardinal Meyer emphasized the need for greater lay participation in the activities of the Church. He was also deeply interested in the ecumenical movement. Sensitive to the racial and ethnic changes taking place in Chicago parishes, he urged the integration of Catholic schools, hospitals, and other institutions. Cardinal Meyer has been characterized as a firm, sensitive, and deeply intelligent, down-to-earth yet totally spiritual giant of a man.

In early February of 1965, Cardinal Meyer entered Mercy Hospital where he underwent intercranial surgery for the removal of a tumor which was diagnosed as malignant. He died, never fully recovering consciousness on April 9, 1965. His death, occurring after his being only six and a half years in Chicago, was a loss to the universal Church as well as to the Church of Chicago. *The Catholic Encyclopedia* (New York: McGraw-Hill Book Co., 1965); and Reverend Menceslaus J. Madaj, "Third Cardinal of the Archdiocese of Chicago," *The New World,* 21 February 1975, sec. 3, pp. 7–10.

[14]*Book of Correspondence:* Letter from Albert Cardinal Meyer to Mother M. Beatrice Rybacki, 22 May 1963 (AFSCL).

[15]Received into the novitiate were Bernadette Foley (Sister M. John); Mary Granat (Sister M. Valerie Ann); Carol Gliwa (Sister M. Thaddeus Marie); Jeanette Cap (Sister M. Mark); Diana Galuszka (Sister M. Helene); Diane Przyborowski (Sister Anthony Marie); and Barbara Gill (Sister Eva Marie). Novices admitted to their first profession included Sister M. Luke Dohra, Sister Susan Catherine Bayliss, Sister Margaret Grempka, Sister Carol Marie Schommer, Sister M. Judith Webster, Sister M. Ann Francis Grosh, Sister Jeanne Marie Toriskie, Sister Frances Marie Cieniawa, Sister Chestine Bugay, Sister Therese Ann Wegiel, Sister M. John Sotiroff, and Sister Dolores Jean Molik. To perpetual vows were admitted Sister Joseph Marie Zenda, Sister M. Julianna Podraza, and Sister M. Victoria Bednara. *Minutes of General Council Proceedings, 1956–1970* (AFSCL).

[16]*Congregation Obituary Records* (AFSCL) and Secretaries General, *Community Chronicle, 1957–1970* (AFSCL).

[17]The relics in the main altar, facing the chapel, are those of St. Felix and St. Amata, Martyr, received from the Chancery Office of the Archdiocese of Chicago, and the relic of St. Stanislaus Kostka donated by Mother M. Beatrice Rybacki. The relics in the main altar, facing the sacristy, are those of St. Candida and St. Constance received from the Chancery Office, and of St. Beatrice donated by Mother M. Beatrice.

At the side altar of St. Francis of Assisi are relics of St. Justin and St. Cyreneus both provided by the Chancery Office; those of St. Francis and St. Clare were given to the congregation by Mother M. Beatrice. At the side altar of St. Anthony, the relics of St. Dylekta and St. Concordia were obtained from the Chancery Office; the relics of St. Anthony of Padua and St. Andrew Bobola were offered by Mother M. Beatrice. Secretaries General, *Community Chronicle, 1957–1970* (AFSCL).

[18]*Minutes of General Council Proceedings, 1956–1970;* and Secretaries General, *Community Chronicle, 1957–1970* (AFSCL).

[19]*Minutes of General Council Proceedings, 1956–1970,* 10 November 1963 (AFSCL).

[20]In a letter to the author from Mr. Anthony S. Urbanski, service representative of St. Adalbert's Cemetery, dated September 12, 1975, the burial plots in which the Franciscan Sisters of Chicago were interred were blocks *K, L, M, N,* and *O* of Section 49, and lots 6, 8, 10, 12, 14, and block *H,* section of St. Hedwig.

[21]*Minutes of General Council Proceedings, 1956–1970,* 27 October 1966 (AFSCL).

[22]The last Sister to be buried at St. Adalbert's Cemetery was Sister M. Eleanor Bomba who died on November 18, 1966. Four Sisters were interred in the Resurrection Mausoleum: Sister M. Ursula Murdza (December 6, 1966); Sister M. Conrad Kempisty (January 4, 1967); Sister M. Hilary Dadej (May 3, 1967); and Sister M. Hedwig Kubera (May 25, 1967) until the community cemetery was completed. *Congregation Obituary Records* (AFSCL).

[23]Sister M. Chrysostom was the last Sister to arrive at Our Lady of Victory Cemetery in Lemont. Her remains were reinterred in 1974. *Congregation Obituary Records* (AFSCL).

[24]Sister M. Jude Kruszewski, ed., *I Have Done My Part. May Christ Teach You Yours* (Marceline, Missouri: Walsworth Publishing Co., 1982), p. 48.

[25]Col. 1:24.

[26]Secretaries General, *Community Chronicle, 1957–1970,* 20 August 1962 (AFSCL).

[27]"History of Mother Theresa Home," 12 November 1973 (AFSCL).

[28]Secretaries General, *Community Chronicle, 1957–1970* (AFSCL).

[29]"History of Mother Theresa Home," 12 November 1973 (AFSCL).

[30]*Our Lady of Victory Convent House Journal* (AFSCL).

[31]Secretaries General, *Community Chronicle, 1957–1970* (AFSCL).

[32]"History of Mother Theresa Home," 12 November 1973 (AFSCL).

[33]Sister Margaret Mary Peckenpaugh, "Mother Theresa Home" talk delivered 17 April 1982, Lemont, Illinois.

[34]*Interview* with Sister M. Dorothea Micek, 26 September 1985 (AFSCL).

[35]*The Lemont Herald,* 27 February 1974, p. 8.

[36]*Interview* with Sister M. Dorothea Micek, 26 September 1985 (AFSCL).

CHAPTER 59

The Tenth General Chapter:
Mother M. Beatrice Rybacki

A "first" of another kind occurred in the new Motherhouse when the Tenth General Chapter of Elections convened on Monday, June 29, 1964. As in 1958, the chapter was preceded by a one-day retreat led by the Reverend Theophane Kalinowski, OFM. On July 2, with the Very Reverend Bernard Bak, CR, the delegate of the ordinary of the Archdiocese of Chicago, and Albert Cardinal Meyer presiding, the forty-three Sister-delegates[1] unanimously re-elected Mother M. Beatrice Rybacki as superior general to a second six-year-term. The delegates also re-elected Sister M. Venantia Rec[2] as vicar general and first councilor for a second term, while Sister M. Aloysetta Ciezadlo was re-elected to a third term as procurator general. Sister M. Gonzaga Raniszewski accepted a fourth term as secretary general and third councilor. The delegates voted for two new members of the general council. They were Sister M. Hugoline Czaplinski,[3] principal of Madonna High School, as second councilor; and Sister M. Rosalima Sierocki, superior and principal of St. Stanislaus Bishop and Martyr School on Chicago's Northwest Side, as fourth councilor.

Sister M. Rosalima, one of the two new members of the council, was a woman who, from the day of her entrance into the congregation, had embraced religious life zealously and wholeheartedly. Self-sacrificing and genuinely caring, she was always known for her disarming simplicity, amiability, and deep-seated love for God and the People of God.[4]

Sister M. Rosalima, the former Salomea Sierocki, was born in Barnesboro, Pennsylvania, in 1909. After a few years, the family moved to Dearborn, Michigan. She was received into the novitiate on August 15, 1931, and made her first profession of vows on August 15, 1933. On August 16, 1935, she professed perpetual vows.[5]

From the time of her first profession of vows, Sister M. Rosalima spent most of her religious life as a teacher and organist in the congregation's schools, particularly at St. John Cantius School in Indiana Harbor, Indiana, and St. Louise de Marillac School in La Grange Park, Illinois. Earlier, she had received her bachelor's degree from St. Francis College, Joliet. From 1960 until her election to the general council, she served as superior and principal at St. Stanislaus Bishop and Martyr School in Chicago. When elected as fourth councilor in 1964, she was also appointed juniorate directress, an appointment she met with her customary joy and forbearance.[6]

In a report of her administration from 1958 to 1964 delivered to the general chapter, Mother M. Beatrice admitted, in all humility, that she had not foreseen some of the very important decisions which had to be made during her first term as superior general. She had reference to the arduous and time-consuming task of building a new and spacious Motherhouse, the minute and meticulous care which the beatification process of Mother M. Theresa Dudzik required, and the conversion of Our Lady of Victory Convent for the Aged and Infirm Sisters to Mother Theresa Home for the Aged. Could Mother M. Beatrice, on resuming her office for another six years, have been allowed to see all the startling events which were to occur during her second term of office, she would have prayed, no doubt, to be delivered from them. As the matter stood, Mother M. Beatrice was called upon to exercise every ounce of vision, courage, and faith which she possessed in order to complete her second term.

The Tenth General Chapter of Elections revealed that in the seventieth year of its existence, the congregation consisted of 324 perpetually professed Sisters, thirty-five temporarily professed Sisters, and twenty-five novices. The climate of change initiated by the Second Vatican Council was already making itself felt in the congregation by the departure of eight Sisters who chose not to renew their vows. The attitude toward change and its consequences also made itself felt through many of the resolutions passed at the Tenth General Chapter.

The ordinances of the General Chapter of 1964 dealt with various matters, many of which, heretofore, had been strictly enforced through the Book of Customs or tradition. They offered significant directives in assorted categories, and at the same time, striking departures from previous customs or tradition. Chief among the new prescriptions were changes in the congregation's formation program. It was decided that aspirants would be considered resident students at Madonna High School. If a student entered the aspirancy directly after the eighth grade, she would remain an aspirant until her senior year at which time she would become a postulant. Postulants would reside at the Motherhouse in Lemont and complete their senior year under the supervision of the novice mistress.[7] Postulants who had already completed high school would also reside at the Motherhouse while they attended college. In the novitiate, first-year novices would now be permitted to have visits from relatives twice a year except during Advent and Lent; second-year novices were permitted three visits. In addition, the novices were allowed to correspond with their parents at least once a month.

A number of customs, many of which were common to other religious communities, were changed or discontinued. In the area of religious discipline, for example, the traditional chapter of faults[8] was cancelled and a private monthly interview with the superior was encouraged instead. The Sisters were allowed to visit the sick in their homes as well as in the hospital. Home visits scheduled once in three years for seven days remained in effect. The Sisters could now attend the jubilee celebrations of their parents, sisters, and brothers. Secular newspapers and magazines could now be read; wristwatches could be worn. In the convent dining room, the Sisters were not required to sit according to seniority. A new concept, the "day of grace," was introduced whereby one day a week, generally Saturday, a Sister need not strictly follow the horarium or order of the day thus giving her a margin of freedom.

There were some changes and adaptations in the prayer life of the Sisters as well. The monthly day of recollection could be held either on a Saturday or a Sunday. Since the congregation was awaiting the decision of Rome concerning the Divine Office, the general chapter had decreed that, in the interim, the Franciscan chaplet, prayed in common, should replace the traditional *Little Office of the Blessed Virgin Mary.*

Some other modifications to emerge from the Tenth General Chapter dealt with disparate items common only to the congregation:

1. It was determined that the mistress of novices would be a member of the general chapter by virtue of her office.
2. The annual retreat at the Motherhouse for the Sisters-superior at Christmastime would be discontinued.
3. After funeral services in the chapel for a deceased Sister, the "Magnificat" would be sung in Latin before her burial in the community cemetery.
4. The feastday of all the Sisters would be celebrated on September 12, the feast of the Holy Name of Mary.
5. Mother M. Theresa Dudzik's feastday would be celebrated in the congregation on September 20, the day of her death.
6. Because of her perseverance and faith experience with Mother M. Theresa Dudzik and Mother M. Anna Wysinski in the founding of the congregation, Sister M. Angeline Topolinski would be accorded the title of "Mother."[9]

Perhaps one of the most notable changes brought about by the Tenth General Chapter was the adoption of a ring to replace the traditional "larger crucifix" given to a Sister at the profession of perpetual vows.[10] The ring, made of white gold, was designed by Sister M. Sponsa Bajorek. It depicted the official emblem of the Franciscan Sisters of Chicago and consisted of the Chi-Rho, the crossed hands of Jesus and St. Francis, together with the curved *M,* the symbol of Mary. What remained to be done was to bestow the rings on the Sisters already in perpetual vows in a special ceremony. On December 8, 1964, on the 70th Anniversary of the foundation of the congregation, therefore, the Sisters in perpetual vows received their rings in a lovely ceremony in the Sacred Heart Chapel of the Our Lady of Victory Convent Motherhouse. A Mass of Thanksgiving was celebrated in the late afternoon by the Very Reverend Monsignor Alfred L. Abramowicz. The Reverend Bernard Bak, CR, delivered a most appropriate sermon after which he bestowed the ring upon each Sister at the altar rail. After the reception of the Holy Eucharist, the Sisters all renewed their vows. The Sisters from the Illinois, Indiana, and East St. Louis areas were present at the festive occasion. In Ohio and Pennsylvania, the Sisters received their rings from Mother M. Beatrice at Mount Alverna Home in Parma, Ohio, on Sunday, December 13. There the Mass of Thanksgiving was celebrated by the Right Reverend Monsignor Andrew Radecki, and the Reverend Francis Szczepanski delivered an inspiring sermon.

On December 8, 1964, the Sisters at St. John Hospital in Huron, South Dakota; St. Anthony Hospital in Gregory, South Dakota; and Our Lady of the Sandhills in Atkinson, Nebraska, received their rings from the Reverend Norman Maras, OFM, in a special ceremony in the chapel of St. John Hospital. In Boys Town, Nebraska, the formal bestowal of the rings was conducted by the Right Reverend Monsignor Nicholas Wegner in the main chapel of the Boys Town complex in the presence of all the residents.[11]

One year after Mother M. Beatrice's election, the congregation lost one of its youngest members with the death in 1965 of Sister M. Ann Francis. She had entered from St. Joseph Church in Strongsville, Ohio. Born Susan Mary Grosh in Cleveland, she was the first of nine children. While still a student at St. Joseph's Academy on Rocky River Drive in Cleveland, she had paid a visit to an aspirant friend at Madonna High School in Chicago during the Christmas recess. Instead of returning to Cleveland after her visit, Susan asked to be admitted to the postulancy of the Franciscan Sisters of Chicago. She was received on January 29, 1961, and in August of that same year, entered the novitiate. After her first profession of vows, a medical examination into her deteriorating health revealed the presence of an incurable cancer of the glands. Sister M. Ann Francis hid her pain and suffering with a smile and a pleasant disposition edifying all with whom she came in contact. Fully resigned to the Will of God, Sister M. Ann Francis died on May 10, 1965, and was buried on May 12 in the congregation's new cemetery in Lemont. She was twenty-one years old and had been in the congregation for only five years.[12]

A celebration of religious, social, and cultural importance took place in the summer of 1966 when the Millennium of Poland's Christianity was celebrated.[13] The 1000th Anniversary commemorated the Catholic baptism of Poland's first historical ruler which had set the stage for the entry of the Polish people into the Catholic Church.[14] The Millennium festivities were primarily a religious observance initiated by Stefan Cardinal Wyszynski, the primate of Poland. Polish Catholics of every city and state in the United States organized their own great and unique observance. The encomium given to Poland by the successors of St. Peter, "Polonia Semper Fidelis," [Poland always faithful] was richly deserved. The Polish Millennium, underscoring Poland's adherence to the Catholic faith and to the See of Peter amid wars and oppression of every kind, was a spectacular and joyous celebration. The Chicagoland Observance of Poland's one thousand years of Christianity was celebrated with great solemnity.

The Franciscan Sisters of Chicago joined in the joyous manifestation in numerous ways. They were represented in the Millennium Choir which sang at Chicago's huge Soldier Field on August 28, 1966. Sister M. Crescencia Chmiel and Sister Helen Marie Mackowiak were members of a committee which helped to plan the theme and to chose the saints to be depicted in the stained glass windows of the ten-thousand-crypt Resurrection Mausoleum which became an architectural landmark of the beautiful Resurrection Cemetery in Justice, Illinois. In Youngstown, Ohio, Sister Clarent Marie Urbanowicz served as co-chairperson of the Youngstown Diocese Polish Millennium Observance.

Stefan Cardinal Wyszynski was represented at the Millennium ceremonies in the United States by the Most Reverend Ladislaus Rubin, auxiliary bishop of Gniezno. On Sunday, August 20, 1966, a reception was held for him at Madonna High School from seven to ten o'clock in the evening during which more than two thousand people greeted him. Bishop Rubin was presented with ten albs and many amices, purificators, and finger towels which were all gifts of the Franciscan Sisters of Chicago. In addition, a large number of mass stipends was offered for the education of Polish student priests in Rome.

By the mid-sixties, change and renewal were the order of the day, yet the corporate apostolates of the Franciscan Sisters of Chicago not only continued but even grew. As chronicled earlier in Chapter 40, the Sisters, in June of 1939, had purchased in Crown Point, Indiana, a homestead which they had opened as St. Anthony's Home to serve the aged. For twenty-seven years, the needs of nineteen elderly men and women were met in the small house on the southeast corner of South Court Street and Franciscan Road until the urgent necessity for more rooms and services to the residents became very pronounced. In 1958, the Sisters resolved to build a new and larger home near that site for the aged. A federal loan which the Sisters had depended upon was not realized, however, and the general administration of the Franciscan Sisters of Chicago conceded that, financially, the congregation could help but little at the time. The administration and staff of St. Anthony's Home were determined to minister to the elderly in the area and labored diligently for years to raise the necessary funds. By 1962, the Sisters at St. Anthony's Home had raised enough capital to proceed in the construction of a new haven for their beloved aged. Consequently, ground-breaking ceremonies were held on July 1, 1962, for the proposed new facility. Because of numerous hindrances and delays, as recounted earlier, it was not until 1964 that actual construction began.

The impressive new structure rose with the same ministerial purpose but with a new name. Now called St. Anthony Rest Home, the $3 million institution opened officially on April 25, 1966, with the Sisters who had been on the staff of the old St. Anthony's Home.[15] They were Sister M. Cherubim Madaj, the superior and administrator; Sister M.

St. Anthony Home
Crown Point, Indiana (1974–)

Maxima Woznicki, Sister M. Sigfrieda Scensny, Sister M. Emily Kowal, and Sister M. Clare Brunkala. Sister Lois Marie Rossi and Sister M. Carol Rychlicki were newly added to the staff; Sister M. Athanasia Murzyn was appointed to lend temporary assistance. The residents of the old home were moved to the new facility by the auxiliary society of St. Anthony Rest Home. On April 26, the most Reverend Andrew Grutka, bishop of Gary, consecrated the altar in the lovely chapel located on the first floor of the new home and celebrated the home's first Liturgy of the Eucharist. Mother M. Beatrice Rybacki, the superior general, and her entire council were present along with the architect, William M. Butoric; the general contractor, of the R. T. Milord Company; and forty guests.[16]

For several weeks prior to the opening of the new home, many Sisters came from parish schools which they staffed in Indiana as well as from the Motherhouse in Lemont to help prepare the new St. Anthony Rest Home for its incoming residents. When the new home opened, the elderly whose names were on the home's "waiting list" were cordially welcomed. Before long, the home had still another expanding reservation list.

The new St. Anthony Rest Home, designed in the shape of a "T" and constructed of tan and red-blend bricks with cut stone sills and stoops, was a comprehensive, intermediate, and residential care facility. Two wings of the structure contained two floors, and one wing had three. There were forty-seven private rooms with connecting full baths and forty-six rooms with connecting half-baths. There were also four couple suites and two suites for retired priests. All the rooms were furnished and decorated tastefully.[17] There was a central air-conditioning and heating system, and for safety purposes, the home's fire alarm system was connected with that of the Crown Point fire station.

Immediately adjoining the attractive main lobby was a chapel with a seating capacity of 250. The chapel was decorated in a soft shade of celery, carpeted in gold, with an overhead light reflecting the exquisite granite altar. The area directly in back of the altar was constructed of washed marble in mosaic style with a large crucifix in the center. Beautiful stained glass windows depicted the seven corporal and the seven spiritual works of mercy. Designed by Mr. William M. Butoric, the windows were meant as a tribute to the generosity and dedication of the Franciscan Sisters of Chicago.[18]

An admitting office, a conference room, and several administrative suites were located on the main floor. The dining room, particularly attractive because of its Early American furniture and décor, was also on this floor. The adjoining kitchen area was thoroughly modern in concept and execution.

Drinking fountains and telephone books were placed in strategic areas and were accessible from wheelchairs; handrails throughout all the hall areas were added safety features. Each floor of the facility had an attractive lounge for residents and visitors. One of the home's loveliest features was a fountain surrounded by trees and blooming flowers in an enclosed courtyard where residents could relax and entertain their families and friends. Other facilities on the ground floor included a gift shop, a beauty and barber shop, and a cheery snack shop for residents, staff, and visitors. The first floor also contained rooms for medical consultation, examination, and treatment. Two workshops, a craft room, and a maintenance shop completed the floor. The laundry rooms were equipped with the most modern facilities for that department. In the basement, a large social hall was available for all types of recreation.

On the second floor of the residence, the rooms were decorated in surf green and tile. A laundry room equipped with a small washer and a dryer was found on each floor. The infirmary wing, located on this floor, included a nurses' station, a sterilization room, and a medication room. The third floor, in a yellow décor, basically carried out the same room arrangements as the second floor.

The new St. Anthony Rest Home was formally dedicated on Sunday, September 3, 1967. The solemn ceremony was performed by the Most Reverend Andrew Grutka, bishop of Gary, who was assisted by the Right Reverend Monsignor Leo Hildegrant of Griffith and the Very Reverend Monsignor Vincent Lengerich of Hammond. A ninety-five-year-old resident, Mr. Raney, was confirmed by Bishop Grutka on that day. Prior to the actual dedication, the bishop had written to the Sisters at the home:

> It is with the most delightful sentiments of appreciation that I join with you and your Community of Sisters, with your guests, your relatives and friends and with all your benefactors in the solemn dedication of St. Anthony Home.
>
> Credence in miracles is not very common these days, but anyone who views the new Home with all of its modern conveniences and compares it with the old one in all its simplicity, is forced to admit that wonderful things still happen. As wonderful as the new Home is, it, nevertheless, cannot overshadow the flaming faith of the small group of nuns whose virtue of charity and spirit of dedication founded it, whose cheerful sacrificing work maintained it, and whose unfaltering confidence and hope brought it to the glory of this day.[19]

When the new St. Anthony Rest Home was built, the Sisters on the staff resided in ten rooms on the second floor of the home. Because of the long waiting list of applicants to the home, however, the Sisters moved out of their quarters and back into the old St. Anthony's Home. By 1971, the Franciscan Sisters of Chicago had begun construction of St. Anthony Hospital,[20] adjacent to St. Anthony Rest Home. It was necessary for the congregation, therefore, to build a convent which could house the Sisters on the staffs of both the home and the new hospital. In December of 1969, the congregation had finalized the purchase of twenty more acres adjoining the home.[21] Early in 1973, a beautiful, one-story, Spanish-style convent was constructed facing Franciscan Road. The Sisters moved into the twenty-four room convent on July 6, 1973. It was blessed on August 7 by the Reverend James Verdick, chaplain of St. Anthony Home, as St. Anthony Rest Home was now called after its third name change. Appointed the first superior of the new St. Anthony Convent was Sister Frances Szczur. With the eventual increase in the staffs of the "Home" and the "Hospital," twelve more bedrooms were added. On September 12, 1977, the Reverend Myron Lowisz, OFM, the director of the Department of Pastoral Ministry at St. Anthony Medical Center, blessed the addition.

Even before the construction of the new convent, Sister M. Hugoline Czaplinski, the superior general; her collegial board; and the board of directors of St. Anthony Home had discussed a projected increase in the number of residents and the need for additional services. They voted unanimously to construct a 74-bed addition to the nursing home. This would increase the bed count to 209 comprehensive and intermediate-care beds.[22] As a consequence of the decision to expand St. Anthony Home, ground-breaking ceremonies were held for the proposed fourth wing of the nursing home on Sunday, October 12, 1975, at which Bishop Grutka officiated and delivered the main address. Local and state officials, including Otis Bowen, the governor of Indiana, and a number of religious dignitaries attended. Many of the Franciscan Sisters of Chicago were present to share the joy of the day together with the administrations, staffs, friends, and benefactors of the "Home" and the "Hospital."

At its completion, the major part of the new, three-story, multimillion-dollar fourth wing contained 68 private rooms. On each floor were also three suites of rooms containing a two-bed bedroom, bathroom, dining and living rooms, and a kitchenette. Additionally, there were lounges and private dining areas, nursing stations, an office and medication room, and utility rooms. The basement floor contained the employees' lounge, restrooms, four private offices, a conference room, two classrooms, and a storage area. In addition to the new wing, a fan-shaped pavilion was built specifically to be used for therapeutic, recreational, and social activities. Formerly called the occupational therapy pavilion, it was named the Mother Theresa Pavilion in September of 1985 in honor of the foundress of the Congregation of the Franciscan Sisters of Chicago.

The addition of the fourth wing, completing the intended architectural design of a "cross," enabled St. Anthony Home to accommodate 211 residents. Bishop Grutka privately blessed the new wing on January 9, 1977. By January 15, new residents filled the entire wing, and the home was functioning at one hundred percent occupancy. The grand dedication was held on Sunday, May 15, 1977. The Liturgy of the Eucharist was offered by Bishop Grutka at ten o'clock in the morning. At two o'clock in the afternoon, the official dedication took place. The Honorable Theodore Sendak, attorney general for the state of Indiana, delivered the keynote address. The Franciscan Sisters' choir sang under the direction of Sister Emilie Marie Lesniak.

Since the opening of the new St. Anthony Home in 1966, utilization of its facilities has grown rapidly. As might be expected, much of the growth occurred during its first few years of operation and was an apparent indication of the need that existed for a comprehensive and intermediate-care facility in South Lake County. Through the years, St. Anthony Home has rendered its residents excellent spiritual, medical, nursing, dental, dietary, social, rehabilitative, personal, and recreational services.

Perhaps the most fundamental and necessary services are performed by the members of the Pastoral Care Department of St. Anthony Medical Center who also provide assistance to the residents of St. Anthony Home. The Pastoral Care Department is under the direction of the Reverend Myron Lowisz, OFM, the Reverend Anthony Janik, OFM, and the Reverend Carmen Scuderi, OFM, all members of the Franciscan Fathers of the Assumption of the Blessed Virgin Mary Province of Pulaski, Wisconsin. At St. Anthony Home, Sister M. Louise Nowicki serves as coordinator of the Pastoral Care Department and is assisted by Sister M. Laetitia Kolczak and Sister M. Amabilis Bellock.[23] The Pastoral Ministry team addresses the spiritual, emotional, and social needs of the residents of St. Anthony Home as well as those of their families and of the employees of the home.

With a beautiful chapel for quiet devotion, meditation, and inspiration, St. Anthony Home provides many opportunities for a full spiritual life. The Liturgy of the Eucharist is celebrated every Sunday at nine o'clock in the morning and at four o'clock in the afternoon. From Monday through Saturday, the Eucharistic celebration takes place at nine o'clock in the morning. Distribution of Holy Communion outside the Liturgy takes place daily. On Fridays, Benediction of the Most Blessed Sacrament and Evening Prayer is conducted at five o'clock in the evening. In the skilled-care unit of the home, pastoral care is an integral part of the daily care of the patients. Communal anointing of the sick is held every few months. Other sacraments such as Baptism, the Sacrament of Reconciliation, and the Sacrament of the Anointing of the Sick are available in time of need and upon request. The rosary is recited every Monday and Wednesday at twelve-forty-five o'clock in the afternoon. Protestant and other denominational services are conducted by local clergymen and their visits to the residents are heartily encouraged. Approximately every three months, a Memorial Prayer Service is held in the chapel of St. Anthony Home to which families and friends of the deceased residents are invited.[24]

Since 1973, St. Anthony Home has been an integral part of St. Anthony Medical Center, a 411-bed hospital providing primary, secondary, and tertiary medical care. A staff of dedicated professionals, armed with the most sophisticated technological equipment, stands ready to serve the residents of the home. The health care of every resident of St.

Anthony Home is under the supervision of a licensed physician who is a member of the St. Anthony Medical Center medical staff. Residents may continue to consult a family physician, but they must select a local physician who will be available during emergencies. The attending physician establishes and maintains a schedule of visits appropriate to the needs and plan of care of the residents. The plan of care, including medication and treatment, is reviewed quarterly and revised as needed. Routine podiatry examinations are provided annually by a consulting podiatrist at the home. In the event of an emergency situation requiring immediate medical attention, the resident is transferred to the Emergency Room of St. Anthony Medical Center and provided with the medical care indicated by the patient's condition.[25]

Ideally, many programs and services are shared or, in some cases, purchased by the "Home" from the "Hospital." These programs and services include pharmacy, diagnostic radiology, clinical pathology, blood bank, physiological testing, respiratory therapy, physical therapy, occupational therapy, emergency services, social services, pastoral care, nursing administration, personnel recruitment, dietary, laundry, house keeping, materials management, plant maintenance, and engineering.[26]

Around-the-clock nursing is provided by a qualified staff headed by a professional nurse. A team of professionals dispenses medications, provides required treatments, and assists residents in the performance of daily activities. Highly trained, the nursing staff receives continual upgrading through attendance at an ongoing series of in-service educational programs. Most importantly, the nursing staff, composed of responsible and caring people who treat each resident with love and dignity, is dedicated to the philosophy that Christ is served through their devoted attention to the residents.

The Dietary Department at St. Anthony Home is responsible for regular and special diets with preparation and service to please the sight and the appetite. Dietetic counseling is available to every resident. Registered dietitians assess the nutritional requirements of each resident and prepare menus according to individual needs.[27]

St. Anthony Home furnishes specialized services in order to meet the rehabilitative and functional needs of each resident as prescribed by the attending physicians. All types of rehabilitative services are made available to assist in restoring residents to their highest level of functioning.

Another valuable department, that of social services, is available to assist the residents and their families during the transition to the lifestyle at St. Anthony Home. Within a resident's first week, a social history is obtained to develop an appropriate care plan. This comprehensive plan is built by the resident, the family, the nursing staff, the activities director, the physician, the pastoral care team, the medical director, the dietary department, and the social services department. A social worker is available to residents, and any resident with problems is encouraged to use the services of the Social Services Department. The social worker acts as a liaison, encouraging residents to maintain involvement in the community and with family members, thus helping the residents to sustain a well-rounded lifestyle.[28]

There are numerous recreational activities at St. Anthony Home which provide a sense of belonging and pride in one's accomplishments through active participation. A full schedule of activities is maintained, and outside groups provide entertainment on a regular basis. There are many community organizations involved with the residents at St. Anthony Home. Among them are the Lions' Club, the Rosary Sodality of St. Mary's Church in Crown Point, the Daughters of the American Revolution, and the Young Mens' Christian Association.

Many residents enjoy activities such as rug weaving, ceramics, leather and woodwork, knitting, crocheting, and painting. Others take enjoyment in making potholders, dolls and pillows, or working with plants. Those who enjoy cooking take part in the gourmet program. Bingo, bunco, and a variety of other games are regularly offered, and informal card games are a favorite. There are a specially designed bowling alley and a billiards table for the use of the residents. Social activities are a regular and welcome event. Twice a month administrative personnel join residents for a "Happy Hour," and birthday parties are scheduled every month. Ice cream socials are a favorite activity, and special events, such as the King and Queen Pageant and the Spring Carnival, are held annually. There are also movies, slide presentations, and frequent appearances by outside entertainers for the enjoyment of the residents. Trips to the theater, various sports events, parades, and picnics are also scheduled if any resident wishes to participate. A selection of books and magazines is readily at hand in the home library. A newsletter insert for the residents called "The Resident" is included in St. Anthony Medical Center's monthly newspaper and enjoyed by the residents and their family members as well.

The newest addition to St. Anthony Home was a $1 million 18-bed skilled-care unit completed in March of 1983. It is designed to serve the needs of the chronically ill and terminally ill patients who require twenty-four-hour nursing care at a level above that normally found in a nursing home, but below that provided at a hospital.[29]

St. Anthony Home added a new dimension in its services to the aged in 1984. The Respite Care Program was introduced, the aim of which is to give short-term relief to persons caring for elderly individuals at home. It allows such nonresidents to be admitted to temporary stays of one to six weeks in the nursing home. Through the Respite Care Program, family members are relieved of their ongoing care for a brief time thus encouraging them to keep their elderly relatives at home.[30]

Any history of St. Anthony Home, however brief, would be incomplete without particular mention of Sister M. Emily Kowal. Born in Elizabeth, New Jersey, she entered the Congregation of the Franciscan Sisters of Chicago from St. Adalbert Church in East St. Louis, Illinois, in 1929. After her initial formation and eight years in the area of domestic service in the congregation, she was appointed to the first St. Anthony's Home when it opened in 1939.[31] On July 22, 1984, in recognition of forty-five years of cheerful and conscientious devotion to her ministry as food service supervisor and in special recognition of her fifty-five years of religious life, the dining room of St. Anthony Home was dedicated in her honor. Thus, Sister M. Emily was publicly acknowledged as a kind and loving woman, who in 1989, will celebrate fifty years of outstanding dedication to duty at St. Anthony Home.[32]

St. Anthony Home is a member of the Indiana Association of Homes for the Aged, the National Geriatrics Society, the American Health Care Association, the Indiana Health Care Association, and the American Association of Homes for the Aging. In 1974, St. Anthony Home was awarded national accreditation by the Joint Commission on the Accreditation of Hospitals. It was the first long-term care facility in Lake County to be so distinguished.[33]

In June of 1986, Edward W. Koerner was appointed the first lay administrator of St. Anthony Home. He is in charge of a facility whose residents are proud to call "home." The residents are cared for by nine Franciscan Sisters of Chicago and 230 lay employees. The staff is aided by men and women of the St. Anthony Medical Center Auxiliary who volunteer thousands of hours each year to serve the residents and patients of St. Anthony Home and St. Anthony Medical Center. Other services are provided by junior volunteers from area high schools.

Since its humble beginnings in 1939 until the present day, St. Anthony Home exemplifies, by its very essence, the philosophy of a Catholic nursing home. In a friendly, cheerful, and Christian atmosphere with no restrictions as to color, creed, or residential area, it is a fitting residence for elderly men and women who wish to live in an adult community where they are treated with the utmost dignity and where they can make their own decisions regarding their personal lives. They are offered a beautiful home, clean and comfortable quarters, and the restorative services they need so much. The total concept of human care which embraces the physical, emotional, social, and spiritual needs of the elderly is met at St. Anthony Home by providing excellent health care in a loving and compassionate atmosphere.

THE TENTH GENERAL CHAPTER: MOTHER M. BEATRICE RYBACKI

[1]See Appendix K.

[2]In 1963, the new Our Lady of Victory Convent in Lemont was completed and the Motherhouse was then changed from Chicago to Lemont. When the juniorate was transferred to Lemont, Sister M. Venantia served as juniorate directress for one year. At the expiration of her term as vicar general in 1970, she devoted her time and energy exclusively to laboring for the cause of Mother M. Theresa. *Congregation Membership Records:* and *Spis Sióstr* (AFSCL).

[3]Sister M. Hugoline is discussed at greater length in succeeding chapters.

[4]*Interviews* with Sisters, September 1983 (AFSCL).

[5]*Spis Sióstr* (AFSCL).

[6]With the closing of the juniorate in 1967, Sister M. Rosalima was transferred to Five Holy Martyrs School. After having served as a teacher for many years, she undertook the duty of Elderly Group Aide for the City of Chicago in the Department of Aging and Disability, serving with her customary gentleness, sympathy, and understanding. Her sister, Sister M. Innocentia, died in the congregation on April 15, 1976. *Congregation Membership Records* (AFSCL).

[7]At the Period of Re-inspiration held in the summer of 1965, Sister M. Rosemary, the directress of aspirants, persuaded Mother M. Beatrice and the general council to allow the aspirants to wear the uniform of the students at Madonna High School and allow the aspirants to graduate before being accepted into the postulancy. Secretaries General, *Community Chronicle, 1957--1970,* 19 August 1965 (AFSCL).

[8]See Chapter 34.

[9]*Minutes of General Chapter Proceedings, 1958–1964* (AFSCL).

[10]The Sisters professing their perpetual vows in August of 1965 received rings for the first time in the ceremonies attendant with the profession of perpetual vows. A short addition to the formula of vows was made: "I take Jesus Christ for my Spouse, Whom alone I desire to love above all created beings. I promise to be faithful to him forever." *Book of Correspondence:* Letter from Mother M. Beatrice Rybacki to Pope Pius VI, 1965 (AFSCL).

Today, the celebrant at the ceremony of perpetual profession says to the Sister at the time of the presentation of the ring: "Receive this ring, for you are betrothed to the Eternal King; keep true faith with your Spouse, so that you may come to the wedding feast of eternal joy. Amen."

[11]*Franciscan Echo,* Vol. 9 (Lemont, Illinois: December 1968).

[12]*Congregation Membership Records* (AFSCL).

[13]Secretaries General, *Community Chronicle, 1957–1970* (AFSCL).

[14]Prior to 966, Poland was a pagan state. Archeological findings, however, indicate that Christianity had been practiced in Poland for at least a hundred years before, due to the missionary work of SS. Cyril and Methodius whose work in Czechoslovakia had influenced the people in the southern part of Poland. Dąbrowka, the daughter of King Boleslaus I of Bohemia, came to Poland in 965. She was responsible for the conversion of her husband, Mieszko I (963–992), the Duke of Poland, who was baptized in 966 A.D. As a consequence, Poland adopted the Western Christian culture of Rome over the Eastern Christianity of Byzantium, became Europe's easternmost outpost of Roman Catholicism, and won the cherished title of "Bulwark of Christianity." *Poland's Millennium of Christianity: Indiana Observance Souvenir Book* (Hammond, Indiana: Klines Printers, 1966), no pagination.

[15]*Franciscan Echo,* Vol. 8, No. 4, June 1966; and *Hammond Times,* 4 April 1966.

[16]Secretaries General, *Community Chronicle, 1957–1970* (AFSCL).

[17]Sharon Clawson, comp. *St. Anthony Medical Center, Inc.,* "The Nursing Home," Crown Point, Indiana, 15 May 1977, p. 5.

[18]Delores Fetcko, "St. Anthony—Vital Part of History," *Northwest Indiana Post-Tribune,* 26 July 1981.

[19]*Book of Correspondence:* Letter from the Most Reverend Andrew Grutka, bishop of Gary, to Sister M. Cherubim Madaj, 20 July 1967 (AFSCL).

[20]St. Anthony Hospital is discussed in Chapter 62.

[21]*Minutes of General Council Proceedings, 1950–1970* (AFSCL).

[22]St. Anthony Medical Center, Inc., "Summary, St. Anthony Home, Inc." Crown Point, Indiana, 27 January 1978.

[23]All the Sisters and priests in the Pastoral Care Department are members of the National Association of Catholic Chaplains.

[24]*Book of Correspondence:* Letter from Mrs. Mary Ashbaugh, Department of Pastoral Care, St. Anthony Medical Center to author, 1 February 1988 (AFSCL).

[25]St. Anthony Home, Inc. "Home Sweet Home," (Crown Point, Indiana, 1982).

[26]Ibid.

[27]Ibid.

[28]Ibid.

[29]*Hammond Times,* 24 February 1983; and "Home Sweet Home," no pagination.

[30]*Hammond Times,* 31 May 1984.

[31]*Congregation Membership Records;* and *Spis Sióstr* (AFSCL).

[32]In September of 1979, at the Recognition and Awards Day held at the Holiday Inn in Merrillville, Indiana, for the Sisters and employees serving at St. Anthony Home for five years or more, Sister M. Emily was singularly honored. She received the "Humanities Award" for her forty years of service to the elderly and in special recognition of her fifty years in religious life. See Chapter 40.

[33]"Summary: St. Anthony Home, Inc."

CHAPTER 60

The Winds of Change:
The First Extraordinary Chapter of Affairs

After a resolution was enacted at the Tenth General Chapter of Elections to drop the annual retreat generally held at Christmastime for the religious superiors, Mother M. Beatrice launched a Period of Re-inspiration or Renovation for them in the summer of 1965. From June 15 to July 3, therefore, under the direction of the Reverend Theophane Kalinowski, OFM, the Sisters met for ten days of reflection and discussion on the essentials of the religious life in a vastly changing world. The leading participants in this Period of Re-inspiration included Mother M. Beatrice Rybacki, the superior general; Sister M. Venantia Rec, the assistant superior general; Sister M. Gonzaga Raniszewski, the secretary general; Sister M. Doloretta Radzienda, the mistress of novices; Sister M. Rosalima Sierocki, the directress of the juniorate; Sister M. Rosemary Ferus, the directress of the postulants; and Sister M. Alphonsine Kobylinski,[1] who was slated to become the directress of postulants in January of 1966. The chairperson for the sessions in which position papers[2] on the renovation, adaptation, and implementation of religious life and spirit were read and discussed was Sister M. Hugoline Czaplinski, principal of Madonna High School.[3]

At this very significant gathering, Mother M. Beatrice informed the Sisters that as early as 1952, communications from the Holy See had strongly urged religious communities to simplify their headdress. By the late 1960s, for the communities who had heeded this directive, the result was a new and simple look in which the coife and guimpe were dispensed with leaving the hair revealed which was a radical departure from the traditional image of a Sister. In many religious communities, the members also chose to shorten and alter their habits in other ways in an effort to appear more contemporary.

As a result of the first Re-inspiration Period, a decision was made by Mother M. Beatrice and her general council to allow the Franciscan Sisters of Chicago to experiment with a new headdress and styles of habits under controlled circumstances. This experimentation and modification was to take place at Madonna High School. Eventually, the wearing of an experimental headdress and a shortened or altered habit became optional for all the Sisters in the congregation. For the Sisters who chose to wear the modifiedhabit, the Franciscan cord and chaplet were now dispensed with.[4]

Another group of Sisters met for the congregation's second Period of Re-inspiration held from July 10 to 17, 1966. Under the direction of the Reverend Colman Machrzak, OFM, forty-four Sisters participated in an intense program on the spiritual directives concerning the renewal of religious life based on the documents of the Second Vatican Council, chiefly *Perfectae Caritatis*.[5]

The Second Vatican Council convened by Pope John XXIII in 1959 had initiated reforms within the Church and urged the renewal of religious life. Sisters all over the world were spurred by Vatican II to reexamine their lives in terms of the Gospel, the charisms of their founder or foundress, and their mission in the Church and in the world. On October 2, 1966, Mother M. Beatrice informed the Franciscan Sisters of Chicago that in an attempt to put into motion the adaptation and renewal recommended to the religious congregations by the Second Vatican Council and the directives of Pope Paul VI, who had succeeded Pope John XXIII, all religious orders of men and women were mandated to hold an Extraordinary Chapter of Affairs within the next two years. The Constitutions, directories, custom books, books of prayer, and religious ceremonies of the congregation were to be suitably evaluated and adapted in the light of the Vatican decrees. While the First Extraordinary Chapter of Affairs was to be concerned with the progress of the entire congregation and would deal with the issue of necessary and meaningful change, Mother M. Beatrice cautioned the Sisters that every effort would be made to ensure that besides the external updating planned by the congregation, the focus of the chapter was spiritual renewal, both on the personal and community level.

Mother M. Beatrice and the general council scheduled the First Extraordinary Chapter of Affairs to convene from June 14 to July 12, 1968. On February 22, 1967, the Sisters met for the first of several regional meetings held in preparation for the chapter.[6] By April 3, in a spirit of gratitude and enthusiasm, Mother M. Beatrice addressed a letter to the Sisters:

Dear Sisters:

"The stone has started rolling" toward the preparations for our First Extraordinary Chapter of Affairs. In each of the five areas where preliminary meetings have been held in regard to the chapter preparations, the Sisters showed so much enthusiasm, willingness to help, and cooperation that it was a pleasure talking to them.

Sister M. Hugoline and I have been impressed by the enthusiasm of the participants. It has made our task so much easier. I wish to thank all of you—superiors and subjects—for your heartfelt cooperation. It seems that each and every one of you wants to do all you possibly can to help make our chapter successful.

Please do not extinguish the candle of fervor which you have lighted at these meetings. Keep the candle burning and may it enlighten your minds and enkindle zeal in your hearts to work for the good of the community.

Since every member of the community is involved, we are looking forward with great hope to hearing suggestions for our spiritual renewal. Read books and articles on the subject, take part in dialogues in your homes with one aim in mind—to make our First Extraordinary Chapter of Affairs successful.

May the Holy Spirit guide you always.

Devotedly yours,

Mother M. Beatrice[7]

To help implement the work of the First Extraordinary Chapter of Affairs and to bring about the research, analysis, and communication necessary for long-range planning in the whole congregation, Mother M. Beatrice and the general council created twelve commissions whose general purpose was to prepare the groundwork for a fruitful chapter and to stimulate the congregation to examine itself through careful self-study. The commissions were composed of Sisters who had voluntarily joined the particular group. Members of the commissions met with varying regularity, assembled and distributed bibliographies, consulted experts, sent out questionnaires to priests, Sisters, and the laity, addressed large and small groups on the missions, sponsored meetings and workshops, and, finally, summed up their work in five- to ten-page documented position papers which presented the rationale for the reorientation of the congregation. The commissions and their elected chairpersons consisted of the following: 1) Administrative Structure, Sister M. Concordia Lawrence; 2) Constitutions, Sister Kathleen Melia; 3) Customs and Garb, Sister Eleanor Marie Jadrych; 4) Education, Sister Joseph Marie Zenda; 5) Health Service, Insurance, and Retirement, Sister M. Natalie Uscinowicz; 6) Vows, Sister Marie Francis Moson; 7) Prayer Life, Sister Eileen Kazmierowicz; 8) Public Opinion, Sister Janice Piesko; 9) Sister Formation, Sister M. Francine Labus; 10) Liturgy, Sister M. Euphemia Switalski; 11) Apostolate, Sister M. Georgeann Kinel; 12) General Chapter, Sister M. Christine Brzozowski.[8]

In the summer of 1967, the members of the congregation elected a central committee called the General Chapter Commission to coordinate the chapter. The committee consisted of Sister M. Sponsa Bajorek, the chairperson; Sister M. Antonella Abramowicz; Sister M. Agnes Zywiec; Sister M. Rosemary Ferus; Sister M. Claritta Warchalowski; Sister M. Tarcisia Bucki; and Sister M. Gabriel Lazarski. The main purpose of the General Chapter Commission was to initiate the work of the twelve commissions and to evaluate the work periodically during the coming year so that the final position papers which were to be presented at the First Extraordinary Chapter of Affairs in 1968 would contain an authentic picture of the congregation's thinking, including its needs, hopes, and suggestions for relevancy.

One of the features of the First Extraordinary Chapter of Affairs was the invitation issued by the General Chapter Commission to the community-at-large to submit proposals for change and adaptation in order to assist the delegates in setting short- and long-range goals for the congregation. More than 551 proposals came in from individual Sisters, groups, missions, and regional committees. Those Sisters submitting proposals were asked to give reasons and documentation for their ideas and to suggest possible methods for implementation. As a consequence, careful study often preceded the writing of the proposals and the recommended implementations sometimes set up guidelines which expedited the chapter work.

Preparations for the important task of the First Extraordinary Chapter of Affairs were prayerful and intense. Expert consultants were frequently called in to talk to or work with the Sisters, bringing variety, excellence, and a desire to share in the Sisters' work. Among those invited to give lectures or workshops, for example, were such noted theologians as the Reverend Anselm Romb, OFM, Conv., who in "Blueprints for Renewal" explained the renewal process; the Reverend Nicholas Persich, CM, who also made himself available to the General Chapter Commission; the Reverend Edward Stokes, SJ, a well-known canonist who spoke on "The Structure and Procedure of the First Extraordinary Chapter of Affairs"; the Reverend Paul Boyle, CP, who conducted a workshop; the Reverend Kevin O'Rourke, who delivered a paper on "Obedience and Authority"; the Reverend Joseph Sedlak, who spoke on "The Dynamics of Change"; Sister M. Gerald, CSC, who spoke of personal budgeting and the spirit and vow of poverty in "Modern Management in Religious Congregations"; and Sister M. Dorita, OSF, who spoke on the "Procedures for a General Chapter."[9]

For the first time in the history of the congregation, a new method of electing chapter delegates was initiated.[10] This method relieved the Sisters from voting by geography and allowed them to choose leaders from the community-at-large. According to the old method, large houses or groups of small houses elected two delegates from their own number. With the permission of the Holy See, the congregation departed from this procedure and the result was the following plan:

1. Perpetually professed and junior Sisters could vote for delegates; only perpetually professed members, however, could be elected as delegates to the chapter.
2. The ex-officio members were the superior general, the four council members, the bursar general, and former mothers general.
3. The total number of members in the chapter was to be forty; these were to be nominated and elected by secret ballot. Seven of the members were ex-officio members and thirty-three were to be elected delegates.
4. Since the junior Sisters played a vital and indispensable role in the future of the community, they would be allowed to elect four Sisters

as representatives. Only junior Sisters could vote for their representatives.

5. Two ballots were to be sent to each member of the community: a nominating ballot and an elective ballot. In the nominating ballot the following procedure was to be used:

> From the age group of 61 and over: 8 sisters
> From the age group of 50–60: 12 sisters
> From the age group of 39–49: 12 sisters
> From the age group of 38–under: 8 sisters

6. From the returns of the nominating ballot, an elective ballot would be determined and include:

> From the age group of 61 and over: the 8 Sisters receiving the highest number
> From the age group of 50–60: the 18 Sisters receiving the highest number
> From the age group of 39–49: the 24 Sisters receiving the highest number
> From the age group of 39–under: the 16 Sisters receiving the highest number

7. The 66 names would be checked to determine which apostolate the Sisters represented. The following minimum representation would be reached in the particular apostolate:

> Apostolate of elementary and secondary education and formation: 15 names
> Apostolate of the care for the aged: 5 names
> Apostolate of nursing: 5 names
> Apostolate of care for children in day care centers, domestic, and general works: 4 names[11]

While many Sisters did not agree that electing by age groups or by certain numbers in each group was the best method, the majority of Sisters believed that the new plan was a vast improvement over the previous geographic method. When the elections took place six months before the First Extraordinary Chapter of Affairs convened, thirty-seven Sisters in addition to seven ex-officio members comprised the chapter delegation. Generally speaking, electing from the community-at-large seemed to provide a unified, well-prepared, vocal, and decisive group.[12]

When the election results were made known, Mother M. Beatrice asked the Sisters to support the nominated delegates with trust, affection, and prayer since the delegates were facing responsibilities such as forming policies, goals, principles, positions, and legislation for the common good in response to the needs of the Church, the congregation, and society. Every Sister, therefore, had the obligation to study, discuss, and inform the delegates of her views on pending issues. In turn, the delegates had the obligation to represent the best interests of the Sisters.

The Congregation of the Franciscan Sisters of Chicago had held a General Chapter of Elections every six years since its foundation. The Chapter of Elections was a meeting of Sister-delegates for the purpose of electing a superior general and her council and for dealing with matters pertaining to the entire congregation. A Chapter of Affairs, on the other hand, was to be a session of the General Chapter at which new legislation was introduced, new policies and practices decided upon, and articles of the Constitutions amended or reaffirmed. What is more, the First Extraordinary Chapter of Affairs was planned to be an "open chapter." Pre-Vatican chapters had always been closed to all but the delegates, and except for published enactments that legislated procedures for the congregation, non-delegates knew little of chapter activities.[13] Now, the First Extra-ordinary Chapter of Affairs to be held in the congregation was to be marked by its total openness and the sharing of reflections and opinions by its members.

An achievement of superb scientific and engineering skill occurred on July 15, 1968, when three American astronauts flying Apollo II landed on the moon, and two of them actually walked on it. The astronauts, Neil Armstrong and Edwin Aldrin planted the American flag on the lunar desert and completed a two-hour and twenty-minute moonwalk. The third astronaut, Michael Collins, monitored the descent of their command capsule *Columbia* to the earth on July 24.

For American Catholics, the year was one of stark tragedy. Robert F. Kennedy, the United States Senator from New York from 1965 to 1968, and brother to the assassinated thirty-fifth president of the United States, John F. Kennedy, was himself assassinated in June of 1968 in Los Angeles while campaigning for the Democratic presidential nomination.

During that memorable year of 1968, the Franciscan Sisters of Chicago prepared to meet for a historic "first"—an Extraordinary Chapter of Affairs—a momentous event in the history of all religious congregations.

The congregation's First Extraordinary Chapter of Affairs sounded the call to internal and external adaptation and a change in the spiritual, personal, communal, and apostolic life of the Sisters. The chapter was held in three sessions. The first session opened on June 24 and adjourned on July 12, 1968. It was slated to reconvene from December 27 to 30, 1968, but was cancelled due to a severe winter storm. Instead, the second session was held from January 29 to February 2, 1969. The third and last session was held from August 13 to 19, 1969.[14]

When the First Extraordinary Chapter of Affairs ended in August of 1969, it had opened the way for a long period of adequate and prudent experimentation with the decrees which had been passed by the chapter delegation. By 1970, Mother M. Beatrice Rybacki had completed her second six-year term as superior general. That year, the congregation made plans to convoke the Eleventh General Chapter of Elections during which time a new superior general and a general council would be elected. When the chapter opened on June 25, 1970, Sister M. Hugoline Czaplinski, who had served as second councilor during Mother M. Beatrice's second term of office, was elected the new superior general. In 1972, a Second Special Chapter of Affairs was convoked. Both the Chapters of 1970 and 1972 served as a coordinated community effort to evaluate all the new forms of experimentation initiated by the Decrees of Vatican II and the First Extraordinary Chapter of Affairs. In 1974, still another chapter, the Twelfth General Chapter of Elections met from June 24 to 29. This chapter dealt with the final compilation of the various decrees and proposals that had developed from the task of renewal and adaptation begun in 1968 at the First Extraordinary Chapter of Affairs and the subsequent Chapters of 1970 and 1972. The Twelfth General Chapter culminated in the unanimous re-election for another four-year term for Sister M. Hugoline, who, led by the creative action of the Holy Spirit, continued to guide the Franciscan Sisters of Chicago through the welcome, but oftentimes painful, phenomenon of renewal.

If all the events, decrees, and ramifications of the First Extraordinary Chapter of Affairs of 1968, the Eleventh General Chapter of Elections of 1970, the Second Special Chapter of Affairs of 1972, and the Twelfth General Chapter of Elections of 1974 were recounted in detail within these pages for historical purposes, they would, in fact, require a separate volume. The delegates to these four chapters realized, of course, that while some decrees passed at a particular chapter were fruitful and beneficial, other decrees needed more study and clarification. Thus it happened that decrees passed at one chapter were reassessed, restated, or revoked at a later chapter. On the other hand, many of the decrees were simply clarifications or reaffirmations of decrees passed at an earlier chapter. In order, therefore, to give a broader picture of the changes and adaptations in the congregation in the period from 1968 to 1978, the main decrees or prescriptions of the four chapters will be combined at this point and the final enactment or disposition of the particular decree will be given. In this fashion, it is hoped that the risk of repetition or confusion will be avoided and a clearer understanding will be provided of the congregation's manner of living, praying, governing, and working after the implementations of the Second Vatican Council and the decrees of the four separate chapters mentioned above were put into effect.

The opening of the First Extraordinary Chapter of Affairs in the congregation took place on June 24, 1968, at nine o'clock in the morning. It was preceded by a Mass to the Holy Spirit celebrated by the Most Reverend Alfred L. Abramowicz, auxiliary bishop of Chicago. The first formal assembly of the chapter in the Motherhouse in Lemont under the chairperson, Sister M. Hugoline Czaplinski, convened at one-thirty o'clock in the afternoon in the Sisters' community room. Mother M. Beatrice Rybacki greeted the forty-four delegates and stressed their privileged positions as elected representatives of the congregation and reminded them of their attendant responsibilities.

The very first session of the chapter began with the matter of a simplified name for the congregation. Early in 1967, the Apostolate Commission had sent a questionnaire to the community-at-large relating to the feasibility of a name change. The returns indicated that more than one-half of the Sisters favored dropping the name of Blessed Kunegunda[15] from the congregation's title; they also suggested possible new selections. At the chapter, a position paper on the subject was well received and supported by the delegates. Consequently, at a Community Study Day held in March of 1969, the membership voted from several possible new titles. It was apparent that the Sisters chose to be clearly identified with their Seraphic Father, St. Francis of Assisi, and like him, to be identified with their place of foundation. They chose to be called the Franciscan Sisters of Chicago. By February of 1970, the community title change was complete.

The chief element of renewal emphasized in the Second Vatican Council decree *Perfectae Caritatis* was renovation of the interior spirit, certainly a goal holding first place in the life of the congregation and of each member. Apart from dropping obsolete customs and adapting certain practical modifications in the externals of daily conventual life, the basic thrust of the renewal was an examination of the Sisters' spiritual life.

The traditional prayer life of the Sisters had always been highly structured with prescriptions relating to time, place, and length. There had always been a large amount of vocal prayer. Now, with the exception of the Liturgy of the Eucharist and the American Interim Breviary, the *Prayer of Christians*,[16] which was accepted as the official community prayer, the responsibility for cultivating a deep and vital prayer life was mainly the duty of the individual Sister. The rosary, the Franciscan chaplet, meditation, the Stations of the Cross, spiritual reading, the daily examen, litanies, novenas, the Franciscan Cross Prayers, Holy Hours, and visits to the Blessed Sacrament were now considered personal prayers. In the spirit of devotional prayer, individual mission homes were to make their own spiritual preparation for the following traditional feasts: the Sacred Heart of Jesus, the Immaculate Conception, St. Joseph, Blessed Kunegunda, St. Francis of Assisi, and the death anniversary of Mother M. Theresa Dudzik. In 1974, the feast of Christ the King was added. Some new methods of revitalizing the Sisters' spiritual life were also recommended: Scripture services, shared prayer groups, dialogue weekends, monthly home dialogues, and Bible vigils.

In keeping with the principle of respect for individual persons and their right to pray as the Spirit calls them, the new Spiritual Life Commission implemented programs such as the Annual Retreat, the Week-end Retreat, and Periods of Re-inspiration to meet the needs of the Sisters. The older or "traditional" method of a strictly structured retreat was discontinued.[17] The retreat program was now arranged to allow for group dialogue, shared prayer, and even periods of recreation. The Spiritual Life Commission was encouraged to obtain many and varied retreat masters[18] to ensure the Sisters a well-integrated spiritual life. The Sisters were encouraged to participate in a retreat or series of conferences outside the congregation when the opportunity presented itself.

In accordance with the decrees of 1970, Week-end Retreats were implemented. As many as five weekend retreats a year were offered centering on topics such as Scripture, personality, social awareness, and prayer. It was agreed that the community-at-large be made aware of post-conciliar concepts and terminology before they could accept implementation of chapter decrees with understanding. To foster this awareness, regular and mandatory Study Days were planned to substitute for what was previously the monthly retreat. The Study Days were considered a valuable means of deepening the knowledge of Scripture and developing new theological and liturgical insights. They also presented opportunities to the Sisters to become informed of the spiritual, apostolic, and financial concerns of the congregation.

Another valuable means of ongoing formation in the religious life was presented by the three-week Period of Re-inspiration held at the Motherhouse in the summers of 1971 and 1973. This was a time for reflection, more intense prayer, deeper liturgical experiences, and an occasion for sharing insights with other participants. More than one hundred Sisters registered for the two periods which were distinguished by their excellent staff and subject matter.[19]

Since Baptism for a Christian is a real birth into the Mystical Body of Christ, any Sister who wished could now use her baptismal and family name instead of the religious name she had received as a novice. The period from August 1, 1968, to January 1, 1969, was designated for this decision.[20]

A new and more contemporary formula for the profession of vows was approved.[21] Of the four formulas suggested at the chapter, the delegates voted for the following one to be adopted:

I, Sister N. N., in order to deepen my baptismal dedication, vow celibacy,[22] poverty, and obedience to be carried out in love and service. Before God, I dedicate my life and seek to take my place in the Church to build community in my congregation as well as among the People of God after the spirit of St. Francis. All this I promise (forever, for a year) in accordance with the norms of our congregation.[22]

In an effort to intensify the Sisters' spiritual life, the delegates wholeheartedly supported the proposal for the establishment of a Community House of Prayer.

By far one of the most important matters at the First Extraordinary Chapter of Affairs was the need to revise and update the Constitutions and the Directory in the light of the post-Vatican II era. The chapter proposed new Constitutions which would include two sections: the Spiritual Document meant to capture the essence of the congregation and reveal the charisms of St. Francis and Mother M. Theresa Dudzik, and the Precepts which were meant to express the positive means by which the ideals set down in the Spiritual Document could be lived.[23]

The Constitutions which resulted from the First Extraordinary Chapter of Affairs were the result of three years of renewal effort. The entire congregation contributed to their contents by being involved in the renewal through questionnaires, proposals, position papers, and dialogues. When completed, the Constitutions were experimental, that is, they could be retained, revised, or completely revoked at subsequent chapters. Consequently, they were referred to as Interim (temporary or provisional) Constitutions. The new Interim Constitutions called *For This Have We Come* published in 1970, were written by Sister Kathleen Melia, Sister Marie Francis Moson, Sister Jane Madajczyk, Sister M. Francis Clare Radke, and Sister Margaret Grempka. A Directory which correlated with the theme of the Constitutions was also compiled and called *To Respond in Community*. While the Interim Constitutions offered an acceptable way of life, they were very loosely structured and thus provided few rules, precepts, or obligations. The chapters of 1970, 1972, and 1974 produced their own sets of guidelines and legislation by which the Sisters lived experimentally as the Second Vatican Council had suggested. In 1975, however, during the administration of Sister M. Hugoline Czaplinski, a second book of Constitutions and a Directory were produced under the direction of Sister M. Antonissima Jamruk, the assistant general. Finally in 1982, during the term of Sister Martha Joan Sempolski, the Constitutions of the Franciscan Sisters of Chicago were approved by the Sacred Congregation for Religious and Secular Institutes. The Decree of Approbation urged the Franciscan Sisters of Chicago to an ever-deeper commitment to Christ and his Church.[24]

While the compilation of the Spiritual Document was in progress, the delegates at the First Extraordinary Chapter of Affairs discussed the charism of Mother M. Theresa Dudzik. A close reading of her "Chronicle" led the delegates to the meaning of her charism: to be subservient to the Church and ever aware of the Church's needs. Because the members of the congregation also wanted to read Mother M. Theresa's "Chronicle," it was photocopied and distributed to each Sister at the conclusion of the chapter. One of the direct consequences of the chapter was a decree that urged the continuation of the cause for the beatification of Mother M. Theresa Dudzik.

An immediate result of the First Extraordinary Chapter of Affairs was the change in structure of the government of the congregation. As far as possible, the principles of collegiality and subsidiarity as advocated by the Second Vatican Council were implemented in the government of the community. According to these principles, authority is not exercised autocratically, but is shared by all who are in a position to offer their advice or experience to maintain enlightened leadership. In an effort to promulgate the principles of collegiality and subsidiarity, certain prescriptions were proposed at the First Extraordinary Chapter of Affairs and passed at the Eleventh General Chapter of 1970. Collectively, they included:

1. That the superior general and the members of the general council be referred to as the collegial board.[25]
2. That the collegial board consist of the following: the superior

general, the assistant to the superior general, the secretary general, the treasurer general, and one councilor.[26]

3. That the councilor be referred to as the apostolate coordinator. In addition to other specified duties, she would be the member of the collegial board to assist the superior general in administering some of the apostolic works in the congregation.[27]

4. That the term of office for the superior general and the members of the collegial board be four years with a possible re-election for another four years. In 1978, this was amended to a five-year term with a possible re-election for another five-year term. This remains in effect today.

5. That a General Chapter of Elections be held every four years. A Chapter of Affairs would be convoked every two years before the General Chapter of Elections and when the need arose.[28]

6. That the superior general be addressed as "Sister." Her official title would remain "Superior General."

7. That the title of "Vicar General" be changed to "Assistant Superior General."

8. That the title "Treasurer" be adopted for the member of the collegial board in charge of finances rather than the title "Bursar" as was used formerly.

9. That to facilitate smooth functioning and continuity of work in the collegial board, the General Chapter of Elections take place during Easter week. The new administration would not assume office until the convocation of the General Chapter in June.

10. That to make known the areas of concern and progress in the congregation, an Advisory Board be formed. It would consist of three full-time directors in the areas of Education, Hospital-Nursing Homes, and Formation-Vocation. The board would serve for two years with a possible reappointment for three more years. A Health-Retirement Director's position would be held by a two-member team. The Religious Life Director's position was to be substituted by the Spiritual Life Commission.

One of the topics discussed at the General Chapter of Elections of 1974 was the request for participation of the community-at-large in the election of the superior general and the collegial board. It was resolved, therefore, that nominations for those offices be open to all professed members of the congregation. At the present time, the superior general and the members of the general council are nominated by the membership and elected by the delegates at the General Chapter of Elections.

In order to apply the principles of subsidiarity and collegiality promulgated by

Vatican II, in 1970 the congregation initiated an experimental program for the election of a local superior. Now the choice of a local superior could be made by members of the religious home. The congregation also initiated an experiment in collegial living that year which provided for team leadership. In this context, group authority was stressed rather than superior-subject relations, especially in small houses. Consequently, some small houses were granted permission to experiment with collegial government in which there was no religious superior, but all decisions were based on consensus. The group was headed by a "coordinator" or "sister-in-charge" as she was called. When the strengths and the weaknesses of the collegial government were evaluated by the members of the house experimenting with it, it was found that a number of problems presented themselves especially in the area of the lack of the personal authority of the coordinator. In 1974, therefore, the chapter delegates passed a decree to have every local house either elect a religious superior or have one appointed. The decree remains in effect today.[29]

In the area of formation, the program was revised and updated. The First Extraordinary Chapter of Affairs recommended a program of Sister formation based on the principles of renewal and adaptation of the religious life according to the Documents of Vatican II and the *Instruction on the Renewal of Religious Formation* issued in 1969 by the Sacred Congregation for Religious. Thus the Formation Program in the congregation which had always been rigidly structured now allowed for some changes in the various phases of formation.

At the June session of the First Extraordinary Chapter of Affairs, some recommendations were made for the Formation Program. For the first time in the history of the congregation, the delegates had voted to have the time of novitiate be of only one year's duration. At the August session of the chapter, the decree was rescinded and a novitiate of two years' duration was reinstated. A time element for temporary vows was suggested which fixed the length of temporary profession at six years, initially vowed for a two-year period, followed by a three-year period, and finally by a one-year period after which perpetual vows would be taken. This decree was also rescinded. It was replaced by a decree which stated that the period of temporary profession was to last no less than three years and no more than nine years. A Sister could request perpetual profession when she was firmly convinced of her commitment. The renewal of temporary vows was to be on an individual basis. This time period for the profession of vows in the congregation is in effect today.

At the First Extraordinary Chapter of Affairs, the possibility of replacing temporary vows with a commitment such as a "promise" to the congregation was discussed but rejected by the delegates.

In implementing the decrees passed by the First Extraordinary Chapter of Affairs and subsequent chapters, the delegates determined that the program in the postulancy was to be highly individualized and would include a prayer life, community living, ministerial experience, and instruction. In regard to the novitiate period which marked the formal beginning of religious life, a decree was passed to have the first year of the novitiate be a time of intense spiritual development, while in the second year, the novice could begin a part of her formal training for a particular ministry in the congregation.

By the Second Special Chapter of Affairs of 1972, the basic units of the postulancy, novitiate, temporary, and perpetual profession remained as part of formation, but two new features were introduced. The first new feature was the Affiliate Program which was initiated in order to offer young women interested in religious life an opportunity to continue human development and deepen spiritual growth through a program of experience and study leading to a personal decision regarding religious life. While the length of the Affiliate Program varied, it was a preparation for entrance into the postulancy of the congregation.

The second new feature of the Formation Program was the introduction of a Formation Team that would plan and implement the formation and vocation program of the congregation. The composition of the Formation Team at this period was structured to include the formation director, a full-time member of the team appointed to be the overall coordinator; the affiliate director and the vocation director who would serve as part-time members; and the assistant superior general, an ex-officio member.

Another change in the Formation Program was the Rite of Ceremony which was now based on the norms prescribed by the General Congregation for Divine Worship and continues today. The ceremony of initiation is simple and private in the presence of the members of the congregation and the novice's immediate family. During the ceremony, the novice receives a simple white veil and a medal on a chain. At first profession, temporary vows are made during the Liturgy of the Eucharist but without special ceremony. The community and family are present. The black veil and a crucifix to be worn around the neck are presented to the Sister after she makes her vows. The renewal of vows each year for three to nine years after first profession occurs during the Liturgy of the Eucharist but again, without solemnity. At her final profession, the Sister, called to the sanctuary, professes her vows in the presence of the celebrant, the superior general, members of the congregation, and the assembled family and guests. After professing her vows, the Sister signs the document of profession upon the altar itself. Then a ring is given to the Sister to symbolize her perpetual profession to God.

One of the major adaptations was made in the strictly regulated lives of the Sisters. For the first time, the Sisters of each home were permitted to plan their own daily horarium thereby flexibly changing the schedule to provide for individual needs. The purpose was to assure greater personal responsibility for their lives and to make the Sisters more available for the service of others.

In the past the Sisters had often been too work-oriented, and their lifestyle prescribed a very formalized type of recreation. As a consequence of the chapters, numerous changes were made in the area of recreational and social activities. Recreation was to be provided according to the needs of the individual home. The Sisters could choose from a variety of activities which were enjoyable, relaxing, profitable, and cultural. They were urged to take advantage of existing opportunities such as attending plays and concerts, reading novels, newspapers, and magazines; listening to tapes, watching television, visiting museums, eating out, or shopping. Other prescriptions included:

1. The Sisters could now participate in family celebrations such as weddings, anniversaries, graduations, Baptisms, First Holy Communions, and Confirmations.
2. An annual home visit or yearly vacation of three weeks was permitted; the Sisters who had an immediate family abroad were permitted to visit them every ten years at the expense of the congregation.[30]
3. The Sisters were now permitted to celebrate their birthdays.

As a consequence of the rescinding of so many restrictions, the Sisters could now be more actively involved in parish and community affairs as well.

At the First Extraordinary Chapter of Affairs, a resolution was passed to provide a monthly allowance of $3–$5 to each Sister for her incidental needs. In 1970, a decree was passed to provide an opportunity for the individual Sister to be immediately responsible for her own personal expenses and to be as radical as she wished in living out her personal expression of poverty. As a result, the congregation began an experiment with a personal budget. A $25.00 allotment was given to each Sister monthly to cover all expenses except medical charges, education, room and board, personal membership in professional organizations, transportation and registration for professional and religious meetings, and transportation for the annual home visit or vacation. The Motherhouse would continue to absorb the costs of retreats, workshops, study days, and other community functions. The budget, still in effect, has since been increased to $50.00 a month.

One of the position papers which was of noteworthy importance to the Sisters was that offered by the chairperson of the Customs and Garb Commission. It initiated a discussion during which positive and negative attitudes concerning the sensitive issue of modifying the religious habit were presented. Without a doubt, the habit was an issue at each of the chapters. Since the Second Vatican Council had stated in its decree *Perfectae Caritatis* that "the religious habit, an outward mark of consecration to God, should be simple and modest, poor and at the same time becoming," the delegates voted to adopt a dress code. The following code which emerged remains in effect today:

1. In wearing the habit, the Sisters give corporate witness of their consecration and external expression of Franciscan poverty. Therefore, they should be economical in purchasing simple and becoming apparel.
2. The Sisters may choose to wear the traditional habit or a modified habit, a jumper, a suit, a dress, or a skirt and weskit of solid brown only.
3. The blouse, simple in style, should be white, solid brown, or solid

beige with long or three-quarter-length sleeves.

4. A black veil with a peaked white trim (adopted by the congregation) should be worn.

5. The traditional crucifix is worn or a smaller one may be substituted.

6. The silver ring with the congregation's emblem is the uniform symbol of the perpetually professed members.

7. The Sisters should appear in full dress, that is, veil, suit or dress for all formal liturgical celebrations, such as the Eucharistic celebration, funerals, jubilees, profession ceremonies, and other special occasions.[31]

Another field in which change occurred on a large scale was in the matter of relating to the laity. Prior to the Second Vatican Council, for example, there were strict regulations in regard to dining with seculars so that the Sisters were not even allowed to dine with their own families when they came to visit. The Sisters rarely, if ever, socialized with the laity and even the cultivation of lay friendships was discouraged. There were strict regulations in regard to the "cloistered" areas in the convent where no lay person was allowed to enter. These basic restrictions were changed as a result of the First Extraordinary Chapter of Affairs, and, today, the lay person is made to feel genuinely "at home" in the convent. More essentially, the cultivation of lay friendships is supported and even encouraged. Probably one of the most obvious reasons for the change in attitude was due to the fact that because of the shortage of Sister-personnel, lay people were being employed by the Sisters in various capacities in their convents, infirmaries, schools, and institutions. It was inevitable then, that before long, the Sisters would employ more and more qualified lay men and women to administrative posts in the congregation's owned and operated institutions, a proposal which had also been supported at the First Extraordinary Chapter of Affairs and subsequent chapters.

Another issue the delegates dealt with was a change in community living. Many proposals advocated the experimentation with small groups of Sisters living in separate houses or apartments, a lifestyle unheard of before the Second Vatican Council.

Because of the shortage of Sister personnel, it was obviously impossible to carry out commitments made in times of stability and growth in membership. After much discussion, deliberation, and prayer, the chapter delegates recognized the necessity of eventually withdrawing the Sisters from some schools, hospitals, and institutions. Many Sisters were reaching retirement age, and many were suffering health deficiencies. There was a scarcity of new applicants and the congregation was unable to replace those Sisters who chose to leave. A profound need to study the congregation's apostolic activities existed. The delegates, therefore, voted to establish an Apostolate Commission which would determine the needs and trends in particular localities and propose recommendations. As a result of the Apostolic Commission's reevaluation of the congregation's institutional and corporate effectiveness, a decision was made in the early 1970s to withdraw from several schools, all the small hospitals, and some homes for the aged. The particular schools and institutions closed as a result of the deliberations of the four Chapters of 1968, 1970, 1972, and 1974 are identified within their historical context in this book.

In the schools and institutions in which the Sisters maintained their apostolates, there was, however, a determined effort to abandon some traditional tasks or make particular changes in areas such as directing choirs, maintaining the sanctuary and sacristy, serving the parish as organist, giving private piano lessons, training altar boys, counting church collections, and supervising playgrounds and cafeterias.

While the chapter members were evaluating the scope and intensity of the congregation's apostolic endeavors, they were, however, also aware of the fact that the areas of the Sisters' activities were no longer limited to the teaching and nursing profession or to working in the institutions owned and operated by the congregation. In the age of renewal, the Sisters could now express their preferences prior to an apostolic assignment. They could also choose to work outside the congregation in newly emerging apostolates or ministries as they were now called. The congregation was even open to the possibility of apostolic involvement in foreign countries as a real missionary venture.

In connection with the Sisters' ministries, the First Extraordinary Chapter of Affairs decreed that all Sisters have equal educational opportunities in the areas associated with their ministries. Every attempt was made to integrate the Sisters who as yet had no degrees into the total educative pattern as full-time students. The Sisters were resolved to carry out their ministerial commitments to serve in all areas with qualified and certified Sister-personnel.

To better understand and accept the physical, emotional, spiritual, and ministerial needs of the aging Sisters, a Retirement Program was organized. It was meant to ensure the individual Sister's continued growth, contribution, and personal happiness. In addition, the Retirement Program safeguarded the welfare, spirit, and productivity of the entire congregation. Some ministries that the Sisters were recommended to examine in preretirement or retirement were as diverse as the following: tutoring in all academic or specialized areas; acting as teacher aides or general clerical aides; proctoring study halls; assisting in school bookstores; assisting immigrants with language problems; writing letters for the patients in hospitals and the aged in nursing homes; and acting as receptionists in homes for the aged.

Perhaps one of the most beautiful decrees to emanate from the General Chapter of 1974 was the one which stated that the Motherhouse be recognized as the ministry of prayer and suffering, the special mission of the aged, retired, and ill Sisters.

While the emphasis of renewal was certainly not on mere externalism, there were certain exterior elements, prevalent in all religious orders from the time of their foundations, which had become outmoded and irrelevant. The delegates at the First Extraordinary Chapter of Affairs voted to discontinue a number of such customs in the area of religious discipline: asking the superior for a blessing when leaving the house; kneeling at table for meals on the vigil of a specific feastday; requesting a penance from the superior after breaking some small article; usage of bells to summon the Sisters to prayer and other conventual activities; silence at meals; "Grand Silence" after night prayers; censoring or restricting mail or the use of the telephone; restrictions on Sunday travel; time of rising and retiring; minute details restricting travel and the need for a companion; and elimination of "rank" in the chapel, refectory, or community gatherings, and confined only to the most formal assemblies such as a General Chapter of Affairs or of Elections.

It cannot be denied that the Franciscan Sisters of Chicago, like so many other congregations, experienced a crisis, both internal and external during this period of renewal. In 1969 alone, twelve Sisters left the congregation. In the ensuing years, the number rose to approximately 120 Sisters with few postulants making application. Although the departing Sisters gave many reasons for leaving, chief among them was what some imagined to be "reluctance" on the part of the congregation to effect change. They felt that they were in need of a more dynamic community or one that was more flexible. Some Sisters felt that they could accomplish more outside the community; others had become disillusioned with religious life and now took the opportunity to leave. There were those Sisters who wished to pursue a ministry or a lifestyle that was clearly not within the framework of the Franciscan Sisters of Chicago. Later, it was not surprising to learn that some Sisters who had departed the community came to the realization that the "changes" in religious life which they had envisioned and welcomed so enthusiastically in the beginning were not as satisfying after all, as they had thought they would be. In all truth, renewal and adaptation was a painful process causing confusion and sometimes misunderstanding among what could be termed conservative, moderate, and liberal Sisters. Many of the Sisters, particularly the older ones, did not understand the reasons behind some of the changes in the Church or in the congregation. While the community membership continued to express hope and trust for the future of the congregation, it could not be denied that the process of change, the loss of membership, and the idea of fading tradition caused turmoil and pain.

During the First Extraordinary Chapter of Affairs, the delegates studied and legislated in the areas of the spiritual life, personal growth, community life, government, finance, formation, apostolate, and communication. They particularly examined public and communal worship, forms of shared authority, and diversification of ministries and lifestyles as an extension of communal witness. At the end of these deliberations, the Sisters emerged with a fundamental focus for the congregation. After sincerely and seriously considering renewal and adaptation of the religious life in the light of a worldwide cultural transformation and in the spirit of the Church, the Sisters were determined to continue in a holy and intelligent renewal and in prudent experimentation. As a consequence, the conclusion of the First Extraordinary Chapter of Affairs saw the formation of the Implementation Committee whose purpose it was to undertake visits to the houses of the congregation in order to interpret the norms and guidelines of the chapter to the Sisters. Sister M. Sponsa Bajorek, elected the chairperson of the Implementation

Committee, selected the following Sisters to aid her: Sister M. Antonella Abramowicz, Sister M. Claritta Warchalowski, and Sister Madalyn Chwierut for the Illinois-Indiana region. Sister Andre Marie Clement and Sister Eileen Kazmierowicz were selected as representatives for the missions in the Ohio-Pennsylvania area. Sister M. Georgeann Kinel, Sister M. Marifilia Strzycki, and Sister M. Natalie Uscinowicz were chosen as representatives for the mission regions of the West.[32]

Shortly after the close of the first session of the First Extraordinary Chapter of Affairs in July of 1968, the congregation was saddened to hear of the illness of one of their most popular delegates and respected women, Sister M. Doloretta Radzienda, the novice mistress. No length of office for the mistress of novices had ever been established in the congregation and as a consequence, Sister M. Doloretta, appointed to that position in 1946, had served for seven consecutive terms for a total of twenty-two years. By November of 1968, however, Sister M. Doloretta, a woman of exemplary virtue and religious commitment, became ill. Acting on her doctor's orders, she resigned her position in the latter part of the month. On December 11, 1968, Sister M. Francine Labus was appointed to succeed Sister M. Doloretta as directress of novices and of the Sisters in temporary vows. Because she was only thirty-two years of age at the time of her appointment, it was necessary to obtain a special dispensation for Sister M. Francine to accept the position.[33]

Sister M. Francine entered the aspirancy of the Franciscan Sisters of Chicago from St. Hedwig's Church in Gary on August 22, 1952. Her postulancy began on February 2, 1953. She entered the novitiate on August 12, 1953, and made her first profession of vows on August 12, 1955. On August 12, 1960, she made her perpetual commitment to God and to the congregation.

Prior to her appointment to the office of directress of novices, Sister M. Francine taught in various elementary schools of the congregation in Chicago and in La Grange Park, Illinois; and in Indiana Harbor, Indiana. She received her bachelor's and master's degrees in education from Loyola University of Chicago.[34]

An amiable and deeply spiritual woman, Sister M. Francine had directed her energies to the service of God and neighbor since her entrance into the aspirancy. Sedate of manner and appearance, she possessed a refreshing image of a dedicated and devout Sister. Her splendid example of religious observance coupled with her genuine fondness for community life were assets in her new role as directress of formation.[35]

Another delegate to the First Extraordinary Chapter of Affairs who attended only the first session in June and was unable to participate in subsequent sessions was Sister M. Aloysetta Ciezadlo who for sixteen years had served very efficiently as the bursar in the general administration of the congregation.

After the conclusion of the first session of the chapter, the congregation learned that Sister M. Aloysetta was terminally ill with cancer. When the results of her condition

.l been made known to her at St. John Hospital, the congregation's medical center in Huron, South Dakota, this gentle, unassuming, and loving Sister informed Mother M. Beatrice: "By now, Sister M. Marifilia [Strzycki] has told you the results of my operation. If it is God's Will that I should die, I am ready."[36] Sister M. Aloysetta returned to Lemont expecting to die before Christmas. Sister M. Ralph Stawasz, who had arrived at the Motherhouse in August of 1968 after having served as the administrator and superior of Alvernia Rest Home (now Mount Alverna Home) in Parma, Ohio, was assigned to aid Sister M. Aloysetta in the execution of her duties as bursar. When Sister M. Aloysetta was, of necessity, forced to enter the infirmary, she humbly submitted to the Will of God: "I am only sorry that I can no longer work for the community."[37] Sister M. Aloysetta died on April 12, 1969, at the age of sixty-two. She had been a religious for forty-two years. Nearing the end of her life, she withstood her sufferings and embraced death with the same faith and courage that she had exemplified during her lifetime. Sister M. Gonzaga, who had worked very closely with the prayerful and conscientious Sister M. Aloysetta for sixteen years, and had known her for many more, paid her the supreme compliment by calling Sister M. Aloysetta "a good nun."[38]

In the midst of change and renewal, the Franciscan Sisters of Chicago reached a milestone in their history in 1969. The congregation was now seventy-five years old. The events of that Jubilee Year were in marked contrast to the celebrations which had characterized the congregation's modest 25th, 40th, and 50th Anniversaries.

The Seventy-fifth Jubilee Year began with a celebration of High Mass at Our Lady of Victory Convent Motherhouse in Lemont on December 8, 1969. Officiating at the mass was John Cardinal Cody who was assisted by the Most Reverend Alfred L. Abramowicz and the Most Reverend William E. McManus, both auxiliary bishops of Chicago, and the Reverend Eugene McClory, the secretary for religious matters in the Archdiocese of Chicago.

One of the highlights of the Seventy-fifth Jubilee Year celebration was a presentation at Madonna High School of an original musical, *Somebody, Somewhere,* based on the events of the congregation's beginnings as recorded in "The Chronicle of the Franciscan Sisters under the Patronage of St. Kunegunda in Chicago, Illinois" by Mother M. Theresa Dudzik.[39] The musical score, libretto, and dramatic narrative were the composition of Mr. Donn Manning and Mr. Don George[40] who had been commissioned by the congregation to write an original play suitable for the occasion. Messrs. Manning and George were no strangers to the Franciscan Sisters of Chicago since for years, the men had been associated with the elegant and celebrated musicals staged at Madonna High School. When *Somebody, Somewhere,* under the direction of Sister M. Dorothy Szostek, was presented to the public in December 1969, the musical met with instant success and its talented cast played to a crowded auditorium for many performances.[41]

Another dramatic highlight of the Seventy-fifth Jubilee Year celebration was the civic banquet held on Sunday, November 22, 1970, in the International and Grand Ballrooms of the Conrad Hilton Hotel in Downtown Chicago. Sister M. Alvernia Groszek, chairperson of the memorable evening's events, was assisted by Sister M. Alacoque Czartoryski, Sister Eleanor Marie Jadrych, and Sister M. Kingnetta Szczypula. The 1,200 guests celebrated the proud and historic event were witnesses to a series of outstanding presentations. The Reverend Walter Szczypula, brother of Sister M. Kingnetta, served as toastmaster. It was his privilege to present the world-renowned Father Flanagan's All-American Boys Town Choir under the direction of the Very Reverend Monsignor Francis Schmitt. The Franciscan Sisters of Chicago Choir, under the direction of Sister M. Euphemia Switalski and Sister M. Lucretia Kot, sang choral selections from the original musical *Somebody, Somewhere.* The junior professed Sisters, accompanying themselves with guitars, sang several musical numbers composed by Sister Kathleen Melia. A commemorative Jubilee Year booklet was also prepared for the occasion by Sister Kathleen Melia and Sister M. Sponsa Bajorek.

Among the distinguished guests who extended their greetings and congratulations to the Franciscan Sisters of Chicago were John Cardinal Cody, the Most Reverend Alfred L. Abramowicz, the Most Reverend Andrew Grutka, bishop of Gary; the Most Reverend Aloysius Wycislo, bishop of Green Bay; and the Most Reverend William McManus, auxiliary bishop of Chicago. Present also were the Right Reverend Monsignor Nicholas Wegner, director of Boys Town; the Reverend Edmund Raczka, provincial superior of the Congregation of the Resurrection; the Reverend Dacian Bluma, OFM, provincial superior of the Franciscan Fathers of the Assumption Province, Pulaski, Wisconsin; the Very Reverend Monsignor Ferdinand Melevage, superintendent of schools, Diocese of Gary; the Reverend H. Robert Clark, superintendent of schools, Archdiocese of Chicago; and the Honorable Roman Pucinski, congressman from Chicago. The observance of the Diamond Anniversary of the congregation called forth congratulary messages from a large group of well-wishers including Pope Paul VI who imparted his paternal apostolic blessing to Sister M. Hugoline Czaplinski, the superior general, and the Franciscan Sisters of Chicago.

The official closing of the Jubilee Year took place on December 6, 1970, at the Motherhouse in Lemont. The Mass of Thanksgiving was concelebrated by the Reverend Blase Chemazar, OFM, guardian of St. Mary's Seminary, Lemont; the Reverend Cletus Lynch, pastor of St. Louise de Marillac Church, La Grange Park, Illinois; the Reverend Casimir Szatkowski, pastor of St. John Berchmans Church, Chicago; the Reverend Leonard Wegiel, OFM, brother of Sister Therese Marie Wegiel; and the Reverend Sergius Wroblewski, OFM, who delivered the homily. The entire congregation was represented in the Offertory Procession as Sister M. Hugoline and the members of the collegial board offered gifts indicative of the congregation and its spirit. The Franciscan Sisters Choir, under the direction of Sister Emilie Marie Lesniak, enhanced the Sacred Liturgy.

At three o'clock in the afternoon, the Seventy-fifth Jubilee Year celebration came to an end with an open house at the Motherhouse for the families, friends, relatives, and benefactors of the congregation.

THE WINDS OF CHANGE: THE FIRST EXTRAORDINARY CHAPTER OF AFFAIRS

[1]Born in Cleveland, Sister M. Alphonsine entered the congregation on June 4, 1932, from Sacred Heart of Jesus Church in that city. Her novitiate began on August 15, 1934, and she made her first profession of vows on August 15, 1936. She professed her perpetual vows on August 12, 1942.

Sister M. Alphonsine served as a teacher for twenty-one years in the congregation's schools in Illinois and Indiana. She obtained her bachelor's degree at De Paul University and a certificate in theology from St. Xavier College in Chicago. From 1958 to 1964, she served as principal and superior at St. Leo the Great School in Cleveland. In September of 1965, she resided at St. Pancratius School in Chicago while she earned her master's degree in guidance and counseling from Loyola University of Chicago. In January of 1966, she moved to the Motherhouse in Lemont when she was named directress of postulants. At this time, the postulants attended St. Francis College in Joliet, Illinois, and studied theology with the Reverend Sergius Wroblewski, OFM. Some postulants were also sent to mission homes to gain experience outside the novitiate. Sister M. Alphonsine remained the mistress of postulants until August of 1967, when she was assigned to SS. Philip and James School in Cleveland as superior and principal. Assigned to St. Anthony Medical Center to the Department of Pastoral Care, she also served as superior from 1979 to 1984.

Sister M. Alphonsine was that happy combination of a good religious and a very likable person. A woman of great generosity, she was always helpful and dedicated to any duty to which she was assigned. She possessed a spirit of merriment and exuded a trust which made her extremely approachable. *Congregation Membership Records;* and *Interviews* with Sisters, September 1983 (AFSCL).

[2]Position papers are researched and original opinions on a particular subject or issue.

[3]Secretaries General, *Community Chronicle, 1957–1970* (AFSCL).

[4]Ibid.

[5]*Minutes of General Council Proceedings, 1956–1970* (AFSCL).

[6]Secretaries General, *Community Chronicle, 1957–1970.*

[7]*Book of Correspondence:* Letter from Mother M. Beatrice Rybacki to the Sisters, 3 April 1967 (AFSCL).

[8]*Franciscan Echo,* Vol. 10, No. 1, September 1967.

[9]Secretaries General, *Community Chronicle, 1957–1970* (AFSCL).

[10]On February 28, 1968, the congregation was notified by the Chancery Office of the Archdiocese of Chicago that the Holy See had granted permission to use the new proceedings for the election of the delegates. Secretaries General, *Community Chronicle, 1957–1970* (AFSCL).

[11]Secretaries General, *Community Chronicle, 1957–1970* (AFSCL).

[12]See Appendix K.

[13]A special "Chapter News Digest" was issued to inform members of the results of the chapter sessions. The delegates also decided that any changes voted upon should be implemented by the community-at-large immediately after receiving the "Chapter News Digest."

[14]*Minutes of First Extraordinary Chapter of Affairs, 1969* (AFSCL).

[15]See Chapter 6 for the reasons the Sisters chose Blessed Kunegunda as their patroness at their foundation.

[16]See Chapter 63.

[17]In the early days of the congregation, retreats were held at the Motherhouse for all the Sisters. Among the priests who were actively involved in conducting the retreats were members of the Congregation of the Resurrection, especially the Reverend Vincent Rapacz, CR; the Reverend John Zdechlik, CR; the Reverend John Drzewiecki, CR; the Reverend Joseph Zwierzycki, CR; the Reverend Joseph Tarasiuk, CR; and the Reverend Francis Dembiński, CR.

In later years, because of the growing number of Sisters and for the sake of economy, the Sisters gathered at particular convents. For example, the Sisters stationed in Cleveland and Youngstown, Ohio; and Conemaugh and Johnstown in Pennsylvania, gathered at Sacred Heart of Jesus Convent in Cleveland for their annual retreat.

From the 1930s through the early 1950s, the Sisters made the move to engage retreat masters of various congregations. As a consequence, the retreats were conducted by Cistercians, Passionists, Marianists, Salesians, Franciscans, Resurrectionists, Vincentians, and Redemptorists. In the latter part of the 1950s, and throughout the 1960s the Franciscan Fathers of the Assumption of the Blessed Virgin Mary Province of Pulaski, Wisconsin, conducted most of the congregation's retreats.

[18]The retreat masters engaged were some of the outstanding speakers of the times, for example the Reverend Sebastian Moore, OSB; the Reverend Rene Hayes, O. Carm.; the Reverend John Powell, SJ; the Reverend Joseph Stobba, OSA; the Reverend Mark Pesch, OFM Cap.; the Reverend Tad Guzie, SJ; the Reverend John Hardon, SJ; the Reverend Kenneth Roberts; and the Reverend Regis Barwig.

[19]A sample of the 1973 Period of Re-inspiration speakers proves the point: the Reverend Sebastian Moore, OSB, "A Call to Vocation in Scripture"; the Reverend Joseph Stobba, OSA, "Prayer as an Experience of Encounter as Related to Apostolic Involvement"; Dr. Richard Issel, "Self-understanding, Self-revelation and Dialogue"; the Reverend Mark Pesch, OFM Cap., "Community Living"; Reverend Cajetan Bogdanski, OFM, "Franciscanism"; and Sister Maristel, OSF, "Religious Relevancy in the Modern World."

[20]The name changes are indicated in Appendix G.

[21]The former formula for profession was: "I, Sister N. N., vow and promise to Almighty God, to ever-blessed Virgin Mary, to our Blessed Father Francis, to all the Saints, and to you, Mother Superior General N. N. (or her delegate N. N.) for a year, (or for life) to observe the Rule of the Third Order of St. Francis approved by His Holiness Pope Pius XI, to live in obedience, poverty, and in chastity according to the Constitutions of our congregation."

[22]The term *chastity* was changed to *celibacy*. Later, the term *chastity* was restored.

[23]Franciscan Sisters of Chicago, *For This Have We Come*, Interim Constitutions, Lemont, Illinois, 1970.

[24]See Appendix A.

[25]By 1978, the collegial board had reverted to being called the general council.

[26]Traditionally, the general administration had consisted of the following: the superior general, the vicar general and first councilor, a general bursar, and three other councilors one of whom served additionally as the secretary general.

[27]By 1978, the apostolate coordinator's position was dispensed with. Once again, four councilors made up the general council along with the superior general and the assistant superior general.

[28]This prescription did not hold since the only other General Chapter of Affairs in the congregation was the one held in 1972.

[29]Franciscan Sisters of Chicago, *Supplement Chapter Decrees*, Lemont, Illinois, 1972.

[30]One of the resolutions to emerge from the chapter was that the congregation would sponsor and pay for a group tour or an individual vacation for every Sister after she had completed twenty-five years of faithful service in the congregation. The congregation also sponsored the first Canadian Pilgrimage Tour for the Golden Jubilarians (retroactively) from June 26 to July 3, 1972. The sites included Niagara Falls, Toronto, Montreal, Quebec, and the Shrines of Ste. Anne de Beupre, Our Lady of the Cape, and the Shrine of the Martyrs at Auriesville, New York.

[31]Franciscan Sisters of Chicago, *Chapter Enactments of 1974*, Lemont, Illinois, 1974.

[32]*Franciscan Echo*, Vol. 11, No. 2, December 1968.

[33]The Constitutions stated that the directress of novices should be thirty-five years old.

[34]In 1972, she accepted the position of principal at St. Pancratius School and later, that of Five Holy Martyrs School. During this period she also served as a member of the formation team. When the St. Francis House of Prayer was opened in 1980, she was appointed its first superior. In 1983, at the Fourteenth General Chapter of Elections Sister M. Francine was elected the secretary general. *Congregation Membership Records* (AFSCL).

[35]*Interviews* with Sisters, 1985 (AFSCL).

[36]Secretaries General, *Community Chronicle, 1957–1970* (AFSCL).

[37]*Franciscan Echo*, April 1969.

[38]Ibid.

[39]A sample of the tender and fitting musical score is the title song, "Somebody, Somewhere":

> Somebody, somewhere has just got to care
> What happens in life's lonely day.
> Somebody somewhere has just got to share
> A moment of life's weary way.
> Somebody out there is wisely aware
> And caring and sharing with me.
> And someone one day had the wisdom to say
> Where there's some will there's always some way.
> Somebody somewhere has just got to care
> What happens to all of our dreams.
> Somebody out there is hearing my prayer
> No matter how distant it seems.
> Somebody somewhere, somebody out there,
> Somebody has just got to care.

[40]Manning and George were professionals in the performing arts. They were associated with the highly successful Car and Boat Shows presented yearly at McCormick Place in Chicago.

[41]A little-known anecdote related to *Somebody, Somewhere* is appropriate here. Miss Marilu Henner, a talented senior at the congregation's Madonna High School portrayed Mother M. Theresa Dudzik in the musical drama relating to her life. Miss Henner graduated in 1969, moved to Hollywood, achieved fame in the TV series, "Taxi," and went on to motion picture success.

CHAPTER 61

The Eleventh and Twelfth General Chapters: Sister M. Hugoline Czaplinski

The opening session of the Eleventh General Chapter of Elections on June 24, 1970, began with the celebration of a Votive Mass to the Holy Spirit by the Reverend Eugene McClory, vicar general for the religious of the Archdiocese of Chicago. At ten-forty o'clock in the morning in the presence of Father McClory, Sister M. Natalie Uscinowicz, official chairperson of the election, formally began the session. Immediately following the preliminary directions of procedure, the forty-five delegates[1] voted for a new superior general and her general council. Sister M. Hugoline Czaplinski, the principal of Madonna High School, was elected the eighth superior general of the congregation. In a very brief acceptance speech, Sister M. Hugoline spoke to the delegates:

> I shall strive to be the bridge that joins a proud and courageous past with a vital and changing future, that joins our laboring community with an anxious and lonely society, that joins the alienated man with the peace of Christ, that joins fresh and untried ideas with treasured customs, that joins the hearts of all our Sisters one with the other.[2]

The new superior general was born Jane Czaplinski in Dayton, Ohio, on November 28, 1911, the fifth of seven children born to Theophil and Elizabeth (née Suchodolski) Czaplinski. When a flood ruined the grocery store which her father owned and operated in Dayton, the family moved to Superior, Wisconsin. There her father sustained an injury for which he received no compensation thereby necessitating the family's return to Dayton. Later, the Czaplinski family moved to Hammond, Indiana, and made their home in the vicinity of St. Mary of Częstochowa Parish.

It seemed inevitable that Jane Czaplinski would one day become a Franciscan Sister. In the elementary grades she had been taught by the Congregation of the Sisters of St. Joseph of the Third Order of St. Francis, the Congregation of the Franciscan Sisters of Perpetual Help, and lastly, the Congregation of the Franciscan Sisters of Chicago which she entered following her graduation from the eighth grade. Her secondary education was completed at the congregation's Our Lady of Victory High School in Chicago.

Jane Czaplinski's postulancy began on October 4, 1926, and she was received into the novitiate on July 16, 1927. At her reception into the novitiate she received the name Sister M. Hugoline, after the illustrious first cardinal protector of the Franciscan Order. On July 17, 1929, she made her first profession; on July 24, 1933, she united herself perpetually to the congregation.[3]

After her first profession, Sister M. Hugoline was sent to St. Pancratius School in Chicago where she had already taught as a second-year novice. She remained there until 1934 as a teacher. In 1934, she was reassigned to St. Pancratius Parish as an organist and music teacher only and remained until 1940. Her next assignment was to Sacred Heart of Jesus School in La Porte, Indiana, where she served as teacher and organist from 1940 to 1952. She spent the next year at Sacred Heart of Jesus School in Gary (Tolleston), Indiana, before she was assigned to teach at Johnstown Central Catholic High School in Johnstown, Pennsylvania. In 1956, she was transferred to Madonna High School in Chicago where she served as the school's third principal. She also served as religious superior to the Sisters on the staff of the high school from 1963 to 1969. At the congregation's Tenth General Chapter of Elections held in 1964, she was elected second councilor for a six-year term. After fourteen years of inspired leadership as principal of Madonna High School,[4] she was elected superior general at the Eleventh General Chapter of 1970 for a term of four years.[5]

Sister M. Hugoline received her bachelor's and master's degrees from De Paul University in Chicago and did postgraduate work at Duquesne University in Pittsburgh; Washington University in St. Louis; and Georgetown University in Washington, DC. Because she herself took postgraduate courses and attended workshops, as superior general she always encouraged the Sisters to attend state and national meetings and to belong to professional organizations. Recognizing the individuality of the Sisters, she urged them to update the areas of their apostolates and encouraged their spiritual and academic development. In the emerging ministries or the traditional apostolates, she provided opportunities for Sisters to choose their area of service.

As a member of the general council from 1964 to 1970, Sister M. Hugoline was involved with the renewal program, adapting religious life according to post-Vatican II prescriptions. An active member of the Sisters' Advisory Council of Religious Women of the Archdiocese of Chicago, she also served on the Education Committee in the 1970s. She was chairperson of the Committee on Resolutions and Recommendations of Region VIII of the Leadership Conference of Women Religious.

Of average height and robust build, Sister M. Hugoline exuded an extremely sociable demeanor which placed her at ease with herself and with others. The noted American humorist Will Rogers is credited with saying: "I never met a man I didn't like." Much the same sentiments can be expressed regarding Sister M. Hugoline. She was always well liked, and she always returned the compliment. Because she was a stimulating conversationalist, possessed a good nature, and was pleasantly approachable, she was one of the congregation's best-known and most admired Sisters. Basically a very straight-forward person, she was quick to promote fun and laughter. Holding true to Franciscan ideals, her practice of poverty was especially noteworthy. A musician herself, she loved and appreciated the musical works of the masters.[6]

In life and service, she exemplified the eminent Franciscan, St. Bonaventure:

No reading without function
No speculation without devotion
No investigation without admiration
No observation without exultation
No industry without piety
No knowledge without love
No understanding without humility
No study without divine grace
No reflection in the soul without divinely-inspired wisdom.[7]

Elected to serve with Sister M. Hugoline on the general council, or the collegial board as it was now called, were Sister M. Antonissima Jamruk, director of nursing at St. John Regional Medical Center in Huron, South Dakota, now assistant superior general; Sister M. Alberta Bialas,[8] faculty member of Madonna High School since 1952 and community supervisor of schools, now the apostolate coordinator; Sister M. Alvernia Groszek,[9] science department chairperson at Madonna High School, now secretary general; and Sister M. Ralph Stawasz, past administrator of Mount Alverna Home in Parma, Ohio, elected to the office of treasurer.

Newly elected to the collegial board as the assistant general was one of the congregation's most gracious, unassuming, and devout women. Sister M. Antonissima, the former Josephine Jamruk, was born on October 14, 1919, in East St. Louis, Illinois. She entered the congregation from St. Adalbert's Church on August 13, 1937, and was received into the postulancy on February 2, 1938. On August 15, 1938, she was received into the novitiate and made her first profession of vows on August 15, 1940. She bound herself perpetually to the congregation on August 12, 1945.[10]

Sister M. Antonissima began her service in the congregation as a teacher in 1939. In 1948, however, she entered St. Joseph Hospital School of Nursing in Joliet, Illinois. At the completion of her studies in 1952, she was sent to St. John Hospital and School of Nursing in Huron, South Dakota, where she remained for thirteen years. Having already obtained her bachelor's degree from De Paul University in Chicago, she obtained her master's degree in nursing education from Marquette University in Milwaukee. Upon her return to St. John Hospital in 1967, she was named director of nursing services.[11] Of a peaceable nature herself, Sister M. Antonissima brought to all her efforts a spirit of loving dedication to duty governed by a boundless confidence in the Providence of God. Zealous for God's honor, she loved prayer and was self-disciplined and penitential.[12]

Also newly elected was the treasurer, Sister M. Ralph, the former Wanda Stawasz, who was born on August 11, 1918, in Chicago. She entered from St. Hedwig's Parish on October 4, 1933, became a novice on August 15, 1934, and professed her first vows on

August 15, 1936. Her perpetual vows were taken on August 12, 1942.

After professing her vows, Sister M. Ralph spent eighteen years as a teacher in the schools of the congregation. She received her bachelor's degree from De Paul University in Chicago. In April 1954, she became ill and was sent to St. John Hospital in Huron, South Dakota, where she remained until September when she was sent to Alvernia Rest Home (now Mount Alverna Home) in Parma, Ohio. With her characteristic vision, perception, and affectionate esteem for people, she served as the superior and administrator at the home until 1968. Returning to the Motherhouse that year, she assisted Sister M. Aloysetta Ciezadlo in her office as procurator general. When Sister M. Aloysetta died in 1969, Sister M. Ralph assumed the position of treasurer.[13]

A practical and efficient treasurer and possessed of a keen business sense which enabled her to handle the funds of the congregation to the best advantage, Sister M. Ralph was also a woman of great sensitivity. Her ability to share love, her devotion to prayer, and her faith like a mustard seed have made her one of the most zealous and respected Sisters in the congregation.[14]

Following the election of Sister M. Hugoline as superior general and the subsequent election of the collegial board, the afternoon proceedings of the Eleventh General Chapter opened with a report by Mother M. Beatrice Rybacki concerning her administration of the congregation during her second term of office from 1964 to 1970. In her final statements to the delegates, she expressed her hope for the future of the congregation and its renewed response to the ministerial needs of the Church. Expressing her gratitude to the entire congregation for its prayerful support of her administration, Mother M. Beatrice felt that it had been chiefly through the prayers of the Sisters that she had been sustained in her formidable second term of office during which the First Extraordinary Chapter of Affairs had taken place.

After twenty-two sessions, the Eleventh General Chapter of Elections of 1970 closed with the celebration of the Liturgy of the Eucharist. The ultimate purpose of the chapter had been achieved. It had successfully elected its community leaders, and its reviews, considerations, clarifications, and decrees provided and sustained a vision of the future for the congregation. Before the Sister-delegates left the Motherhouse to return to their homes, Sister M. Hugoline, the newly elected superior general, praised them for the zeal and competency they had exhibited during the chapter deliberations. She urged them to continue to work together to make the implementation of the chapter decrees[15] a success in the spirit of the Second Vatican Council and to remember that the spiritual and apostolic vitality of the congregation was of primary importance.[16]

In order to evaluate more fully the forms and decrees which emanated from the First Extraordinary Chapter of Affairs of 1968 and the Eleventh General Chapter of Elections of 1970, a Second Special Chapter of Affairs was convoked from August 14 to August 19, 1972. The delegates[17] were called to order by Sister M. Antonissima Jamruk, the assistant general and chapter coordinator, on Monday, August 14. The delegates had assembled on Sunday for a day of silence and prayerful reflection. In the evening of that day, Sister M. Hugoline, the superior general, addressed the delegates, emphasizing their influential role in the Second Special Chapter of Affairs and the impact of their chapter deliberations on the entire community. Her message was clear: "Strength in the chapter will beget strength in the whole community; weakness in the chapter will affect the whole social body to its last cell." To the young membership, she offered the challenge of leading an exemplary religious life sustained by prayer and union with God. To those over fifty, she proposed that they continue to have faith and to plan earnestly for the future. The day of reflection closed with a conference by the Reverend Sylvester Makarewicz, OFM, who addressed the issue: "Spiritual Renewal—A Chapter Priority."[18]

The Second Special Chapter of Affairs reexamined the Constitutions, the directives, and other bylaws so that they would always be relevant, updated, and effective. The chapter members examined the areas of spiritual life, formation, government, the apostolate, and finance.[19] At its conclusion, the chapter produced a resolution that the Sisters look and work hopefully toward the future as true ecclesial women, alive in the Spirit and witnesses of the Gospel message.[20]

In one area, however, the Second Special Chapter of Affairs had a character all its own. The procedure for electing the members of this chapter had been unprecedented. With the exception of the ex-officio members, there was an across-the-board election for the delegates. Each Sister in the community was allowed to indicate her willingness to serve as an active delegate and her name was placed on the nomination ballot. The ballot was divided into three equal parts according to the order of religious profession. Sixty-four names emerged forming the election ballot, and from this ballot, thirty-four Sisters were chosen. When the official delegate list was issued, many Sisters felt that the resultant chapter body was not representative of the congregation. Consequently, after the Second Special Chapter of Affairs ended, the Ad Hoc Committee formed at the chapter met in October of 1972 to review various methods of nominating chapter delegates for approval of the community-at-large in order to prepare the slate for the nomination of delegates to the Twelfth General Chapter of Elections scheduled for 1974.[21] An improved and more successful method for electing members of the chapter was used in the Twelfth General Chapter. In 1982, a handbook for the nomination and election of chapter delegates was formalized to carry out the procedures for the nomination and election of delegates to future chapters.

A strategic change occurred in the area of formation at the Second Special Chapter of Affairs. Sister Emilie Marie Lesniak, who had been appointed to the position of novice director in 1972, presented to the delegates the proposed program of formation which was to be initiated in the congregation that year—the Affiliate Program and the Formation Team concept.

The Affiliate Program was proposed as a period of prayerful discernment whereby the congregation would provide opportunities for women interested in religious life to get to know themselves and the Sisters better and to develop a sense of the spirit of the congregation and make a personal decision regarding religious life. The affiliate would meet regularly with the affiliate director and with other affiliates. The length of the Affiliate Program was to be determined by need. In 1973, the program was put into effect in the congregation.

The second new feature was the introduction of a Formation Team which would plan and implement the formation and vocation program of the congregation. The goals of the Formation Team were well defined: 1) to share the responsibility of the personal and spiritual development of each Sister in initial formation; 2) to share in the planning and implementation of a variety of programs for the various phases of formation; 3) to keep the congregation abreast of the goals, trends in formation, and current thinking applicable to religious life and community living by means of a newsletter;[22] and 4) to keep knowledgeable of formation programs in other congregations and seek ways to collaborate with other communities in formation.[23] It would be the responsibility of the Formation Team to provide a program that was flexible, psychologically sound, socially adequate, and academically suitable.[24]

The composition of the new Formation Team was structured to include the following: Sister Emilie Marie Lesniak, the formation director, a full-time member of the team appointed to be the over-all coordinator in order to ensure continuity in all stages of formation; Sister M. Francis Clare Radke, the affiliate director, a part-time member; Sister Chestine Marie Bugay, vocation director, a part-time member; and Sister M. Antonissima Jamruk, the assistant superior general, an ex-officio member of the team.

Sister Emilie Marie Lesniak,[25] appointed to the very important position as formation director in the post-conciliar age, was a native of Chicago. She entered from Five Holy Martyrs Parish on August 27, 1961, and was received into the novitiate on July 11, 1962. Her first profession of vows was made on August 12, 1964, and she pronounced her perpetual vows on August 12, 1969.

A graduate of St. Xavier College in Chicago, Sister Emilie Marie also held a bachelor of arts degree from the Music College of St. Francis in Joliet, Illinois. Her first assignment as a postulant was at Madonna High School where she taught theology. After the completion of her novitiate and juniorate, during which time she served as the organist at the Motherhouse, she was assigned to St. Stanislaus Bishop and Martyr School, and later, to Five Holy Martyrs School as teacher and organist. This gifted musician also obtained a master's degree in music education from De Paul University in Chicago and a master's degree in piano from the E.V. Eggert Academy of Music.[26] In 1971, she was selected to pursue special education in preparation for the position of formation director. After assuming the office in 1972, she served two consecutive four-year terms.[27]

Sister Emilie Marie possessed a gracious and delicate manner which endeared her to her novices. Affable, kind, and rooted in the interior life, she lived and gave direction to the novices and to the Sisters in temporary vows as one having experienced the faithfulness of Jesus. She was always a dedicated and supportive member of the congregation.[28]

The Second Special Chapter of Affairs had been held in 1972 in order to review and assess the implementations of the First Extraordinary Chapter of Affairs of 1968 and the Eleventh General Chapter of Elections of 1970. Now, in 1974, it was necessary to convoke another chapter, the Twelfth General Chapter of Elections, since the four-year term of Sister M. Hugoline, the superior general, and the members of her collegial board had come to an end.

On April 15, 1974, John Cardinal Cody presided at the election session of the Twelfth General Chapter of the Franciscan Sisters of Chicago. At this time, Sister Hugoline Czaplinski was unanimously re-elected for another four-year term as the superior general. Cardinal Cody[29] officiated at the Votive Mass to the Holy Spirit at nine-thirty o'clock in the morning prior to the election with the assistance of the Reverend John Mulvihill, secretary for religious matters of the Archdiocese of Chicago, and the Reverend Athanasius Lovrencic, OFM, superior of St. Mary's Retreat House in Lemont. Many Sisters from the mission houses were also present, eager to hear the results of the elections. They rejoiced in the choice of Sister M. Hugoline because of her innate ability to lead and because they envisioned the continuation of change and renewal within the community according to the directives and implementations of chapter decrees.

On April 18, 1974, Cardinal Cody sent a congratulatory message to Sister M. Hugoline, echoing the sentiments of the congregation. It read:

> Dear Sister Hugoline:
> Although I offered my heartfelt congratulations as a matter of record, I want to say how happy I am that your Sisters have chosen you again as the superior general of the Franciscan Sisters of Chicago . . .
>
> > Very gratefully yours in Christ,
> > John Cardinal Cody
> > Archbishop of Chicago[30]

Re-elected to the collegial board of the congregation by the delegates[31] as assistant to the superior general was Sister M. Antonissima Jamruk who had worked so earnestly and tenaciously with the Formation and the Spiritual Life Commission for four years. Also re-elected were Sister M. Alvernia Groszek as secretary general and Sister M. Ralph Stawasz as treasurer general. Newly elected to the collegial board was the principal of Five Holy Martyrs School, Sister M. Gabriel Lazarski, who replaced Sister M. Alberta Bialas, the former apostolate coordinator who had served for a four-year term.

Sister M. Gabriel, the only new member of the collegial board, was the former Irene Lazarski. She entered the congregation in 1947, was received into the novitiate on August 12, 1947, and pronounced her final vows on August 12, 1954.[32]

After her first profession of vows, Sister M. Gabriel was assigned to the teaching ministry. She obtained her bachelor's degree from St. Joseph's College in Rensselaer,

Indiana, and her master's degree from Loyola University of Chicago. As a teacher, she served in several schools of the congregation in Illinois and Indiana. At Five Holy Martyrs School, she acted as principal from 1969 to 1973. In addition to her position as apostolate coordinator while a member of the collegiate board, she was also appointed the superior of the Motherhouse from 1977 to 1979.[33]

An exemplary religious from her entrance into the congregation, Sister M. Gabriel possessed deep spiritual insight coupled with a loving and gentle demeanor which were well known and admired. She might well be an example of the contemplative life lived in splendid conjunction with the active. Sister M. Gabriel's administrative capabilities combined with her ardor for apostolic success made her an excellent choice for her role as apostolate coordinator.[34]

The Second Vatican Council and its aftermath created many roles and responsibilities for religious women in the mission of the Church, and the Franciscan Sisters of Chicago responded to them. The deliberations of the First Extraordinary Chapter of Affairs and subsequent chapter enactments of the General Chapters of 1970, 1972, and 1974 allowed the Sisters to provide a faith response to what some felt was God's personal appeal to them. As a result, with the permission of Sister M. Hugoline, the superior general, and the collegial board, the Sisters expanded their vision to recognize and engage in new interests and new ministries.

Religious education in the Catholic school has always been a most significant apostolic work. Before the Second Vatican Council, the responsibility to develop and coordinate parish religious education programs for children and teens who, for one reason or another, did not attend Catholic schools, was the duty of the pastor, the assistant pastor, or the Sisters at the parish. This was also the case with the Franciscan Sisters of Chicago. To assist in the religious instruction of children and teens in public schools,[35] the Sisters devoted their time and talent to the teaching of Confraternity of Christian Doctrine (CCD) classes on Saturdays, Sundays, and after school hours in the parishes to which they were attached. Many of the Sisters participated in a special "released time" program which meant that the students left their public schools during school hours to attend religious instruction classes held away from the public school premises. In most cases, the classes were held in their local parochial schools. Very often the Sisters taught catechism and prepared children for the sacraments in nearby parishes lacking parochial schools.

During the regular school year, there were missions to which the Sisters went weekly to give religious instruction or to prepare the children for the sacraments in small towns where there were no parochial schools. For example, the Sisters from St. Florian's Parish in Hegewisch went to Mother of God Parish in Burnham; the Sisters from St. Casimir Church in Cleveland met the needs of the public school children at St. Andrew Bobola Church in Sheffield, Ohio; the Sisters at Sacred Heart Parish in Gary (Tolleston) went to Immaculate Heart of Mary Church in Independence Hill, Indiana; the Sisters at St.

Stanislaus School in Youngstown traveled to St. Joseph's Church in Warren, Ohio. At the congregation's hospitals in Atkinson, Nebraska, and Gregory, Martin, and Huron in South Dakota as well as at Boys Town, Nebraska, the Sisters taught CCD classes. Oftentimes, even second-year novices conducted CCD classes at various parishes. Some Sisters were involved in religious instruction which required greater compassion and service. One of these services was SPRED (Special Religious Education Division) which directed religious education for the mentally handicapped. Several Sisters missioned at St. Louise de Marillac Parish in La Grange Park were master catechists in the SPRED program.[36]

The Franciscan Sisters of Chicago conducted numerous workshops and gave demonstrations in various methods of religious instruction. They participated in Institutes of Religion, gave teacher-training programs, and served on committees for religion education workshops for catechists in various dioceses.

The Second Vatican Council and its subsequent development gave rise to a whole new concept in religious education. It had long been felt that for the development of a solid Christian community, the Confraternity of Christian Doctrine program was in need of a general restructuring. During the post-Vatican era, therefore, pastors began to delegate their responsibility to develop and coordinate parish religious education programs for public school children and teens to competent and dedicated lay persons, clergy, and Sisters. An increased awareness on the part of the Church to provide a comprehensive, integrated, and total approach to religious education made it beneficial for parishes that were able, to hire and train a parish coordinator of religious instruction. The professional parish religious educator, engaged in this ministry in the Church on a full-time basis, was known as a director or coordinator of religious education. Such a person, it was expected, would possess a master's degree in religious education, its equivalent in study or experience, or would be a graduate student in the field of religious education. This person would be a professional, salaried, and full-time member of the parish pastoral staff. Thus, it would be the duty of the religious education coordinator to develop, organize, administer, and evaluate the religious education program in the CCD School of Religion. This included the recruiting and training of catechists and aides for the CCD School of Religion classes; working with parents in developing programs for the sacramental preparation of children; working with the catechists in developing liturgies and paraliturgies for groups within the program while consulting with the parish staff in the choice and direction of the curriculum to be used; preparing adults who were to celebrate in the communal Anointing of the Sick and also marriage preparation; and planning sessions in the continuing education of adults in the areas of theology and Bible study. Religious education coordinators were expected to develop their own faith and update their catechetical background by attending meetings, seminars, workshops, and taking university courses in order to be of greater service to the parish community.

During the First Extraordinary Chapter of Affairs held in 1968, the delegates had given serious consideration to training some Sisters as directors of religious education. As a consequence, several Franciscan Sisters of Chicago resolved to commit themselves to full-time religious education.

The services of the Franciscan Sisters of Chicago as religious education coordinators were first requested by the Reverend John Strebig, pastor of the new parish of St. Matthias. Located in the southern part of Crown Point, Indiana, the parish was founded in 1966 due to a large shift of population to that section of the state. At that time, there were approximately 291 families living in the area. Because the parish did not as yet have a place for liturgical worship on Sundays, the Franciscan Sisters of Chicago at the newly built St. Anthony Home in Crown Point granted permission to Father Strebig to use the chapel in the home.[37]

In June of 1969, construction began on Marshall Street for a multipurpose type of structure for St. Matthias Parish. The facility had been designed to accommodate the religious instruction program for children, various youth activities, and numerous social events of the parish. At the completion of the new facility, the work of the Franciscan Sisters of Chicago officially began in the parish with the assignment of Sister M. Claritta Warchalowski and Sister Doloria Kosiek in September of 1970.[38] Both Sisters were assigned to coordinate the religious education program for the children, the teenagers and the adults. When first assigned to St. Matthias Parish, the Sisters resided at Holy Name Convent in Cedar Lake, Indiana, with the School Sisters of St. Francis. After a few months, they moved to St. Mary's Convent in Crown Point where the pastor was the Reverend Joseph Hammes, an old and dear friend of the congregation. In 1971, however, Sister M. Claritta and Sister Doloria transferred their living quarters to Gary (Tolleston), Indiana, where the Franciscan Sisters of Chicago who taught at Blessed Sacrament School in Gary made their home. When Sister M. Claritta withdrew from the assignment near the end of 1971, Sister Doloria took up residence with the Sisters at St. Anthony's Medical Center convent in Crown Point.

In January of 1975, Sister Doloria terminated her services at St. Matthias Parish to become the religious education coordinator at St. Pascal Baylon Church in the Austin-Irving community in Chicago. Founded by Archbishop Quigley in 1914, the St. Pascal Baylon complex, with its combination of church and school in a beautiful Spanish mission-style motif, listed approximately 2,700 families.[39]

In 1976, Sister Theresa Mary Obremski assumed her duties as director of religious education in the residential district of Cragin at St. Genevieve's Church on the Northwest Side of the city. The parish, an offshoot of St. Sylvester's Church, was organized in 1889. St. Genevieve's Church, unique in its architectural beauty, serves approximately 4,500 families within its boundaries.[40] As religious education coordinator, Sister Theresa was provided with a parish house, formerly a private residence, from which she coordinates the successful and vibrant religious education program in that parish.

In 1980, Sister Doloria Kosiek left St. Pascal Baylon Parish and joined the parish community of Our Lady of Ransom established in 1960 in Niles, Illinois, from portions of the northwest suburbs of Niles, Park Ridge, and Des Plaines. When the church, school, and convent were dedicated on August 18, 1963, the membership consisted of 1,200 families.

By 1980, there were 2,225 families with approximately two hundred students in the CCD classes conducted by Sister Doloria.[41]

Several Sisters indicated their preference for direct parish ministry in the early 1970s, and several parishes were actively seeking Sisters to minister in this fashion. One of the parishes which was originally a mission of St. Mary's Church in Des Plaines, Illinois, was St. James Church in Arlington Heights. St. James had grown from a parish of twenty-six families to 2,400 families by 1970. The ever-increasing parish population meant, however, an increase in the number of schoolchildren. Parishioners at St. James Church were eager to have their children's spiritual needs met. With the burgeoning parish population, all the children could not be accommodated in the parish school. In the early 1970s, therefore, the parish developed a unique concept—the school of religion. A full-time administrator and four assistants were hired along with volunteer catechists to create and carry out a program of religious education.[42] In 1971, Sister Janice Piesko, a Franciscan Sister of Chicago, was hired as an administrator in two areas of stimulating and challenging work: the Family Christian Education Program and the Youth Ministry Program designed for the Christian formation of high school students and young adults. Sister Janice remained at St. James Parish until 1975.

One of the main recommendations approved by the Eleventh General Chapter allowed the Sisters to experiment with a new and radical change within the structure of community life called "small group living." This new lifestyle allowed groups of Sisters to live together voluntarily with common goals and definite commitments on a controlled experimental basis. The general chapter decreed that a concrete plan be worked out by the petitioning group and presented to the superior general and the collegial board for discussion and decision. Four Sisters, drawn together by common and specific goals and a mutual understanding of these goals, asked for and received permission to participate in the small group living experiment. They asked to be allowed, as a corporate expression of Franciscanism, to give religious witness by living and working in a crisis area. In a letter to the congregation, Sister M. Hugoline, the superior general, reminded the Sisters that according to the decrees issued after the general chapter, the experiment in small group living was not merely to be "tolerated" by the congregation but was to be "accepted and encouraged."[43]

The four Sisters began their experiment in small group living on August 10, 1971. They moved into a rented apartment on Logan Boulevard in the Logan Square district, a community located a few miles northwest of Downtown Chicago. They became members of St. John Berchmans Parish. The group was comprised of the following: a team member of the Religious Education Department at St. James parish in Arlington Heights, Illinois; a teacher of religion at Madonna High School; a junior high school teacher at St. Stanislaus Bishop and Martyr School in the Cragin area; and a teacher who was part of an inter-community faculty at St. Bonaventure School on West Diversey Parkway.[44] Together the four Sisters formed St. Francis Mission or Tau House.[45] The Reverend Sergius Wroblewski, OFM, for many years a friend of the Franciscan Sisters of Chicago, served as spiritual director and mentor to the Sisters at Tau House. In electing to live together as a small unit, the members of Tau House had listed certain aims that they hoped to achieve through this new form of Gospel witness in the Church. They outlined their aims in a letter to the congregation:

> Our specific goals and objectives lie in our desire to build community centered in prayer, in the midst of the lay community. As sisters, we hope to be an encouragement, an inspiration, and a support to one another in our efforts toward leading a good religious life, as well as to be an encouragement to one another in our professional endeavors. We believe that small group living will more readily facilitate means by which we may expand our goals of community living, prayer, and poverty.
>
> Essentially, we hope to cultivate and strengthen our witness to the Gospel message as religious women. We have accepted informal, communal prayer, and scriptural meditation as part of our lifestyle in addition to the celebration of the Eucharist and the recitation of the Office. Simplicity and moderation in food and furnishings and economic dependency through the budget will be our norm by which we may expand that type of femininity characterized by creative womanhood to impart warmth, graciousness and genuine concern to those in our surroundings.[46]

After a year, the experiment was to be evaluated by the superior general and the collegial board. If it proved successful, the four Sisters would be permitted to continue living at Tau House until the Second Special Chapter of Affairs scheduled for 1972 at which time the chapter delegates would review the worth and effectiveness of the experiment and recommend its continuance or suppression.

Permission was granted by the Second Special Chapter of Affairs of 1972 for the Sisters to continue living at Tau House. On April 9, 1973, near the close of the two-year experimental period, Sister M. Hugoline informed the four Sisters that their religious house was to be recognized as a unit comparable to the congregation's other mission homes.[47]

Earlier in 1972, another group of Sisters, encouraged by the apparent success of Tau House, asked for and obtained permission to live out their religious witness in small group living. The new group was composed of three teachers at Madonna High School and one day student at the University of Illinois Medical Center.[48] These Sisters also moved into an apartment on Logan Boulevard in the same Logan Square area as the Tau House group, and were, likewise, parishioners of St. John Berchmans Church. The second group elected to call their home the St. Paul Mission. The Reverend Sergius Wroblewski, OFM, provided guidance and spiritual direction for this group as well.[49] The Sisters had worked out a concrete plan for daily living and presented it to Sister M. Hugoline and the collegial board for discussion and decision. The board approved the St. Paul Mission experiment and asked the members of the congregation to accept the new lifestyle as a definite type of communal living in harmony with the goals of the Franciscan Sisters of Chicago.

In June of 1974, the Twelfth General Chapter of Elections convened. In her "Report to the General Chapter," Sister M. Hugoline reiterated the fact that the experiment in small group living was a valid one. She did, however, refer to Canon Law, Number 497 which stated:

> There is no objection to small communities provided that the "lifestyle" be that of a religious community with a person in authority no matter what the title. The experience of many institutes indicates that small communities should not be composed of peer groups only, nor should they be chosen according to personal preference.[50]

Sister M. Hugoline was forced to admit that after careful and concerned evaluation, the small group living experiment had been a "mistake."[51] Furthermore, she told the chapter delegates and later the entire congregation that the Sisters of Tau House and St. Paul Mission, almost all of whom were teachers at Madonna High School at this point in time, would be asked to leave the Logan Square area and take up residence at the new and large Madonna High School Residency which had been erected in 1974. The members of both Tau House and the St. Paul Mission chose to leave the congregation at that time.[52]

With the closing both of Tau House and the St. Paul Mission, experimentation in small group living for the Franciscan Sisters of Chicago ended since no other Sisters indicated a preference for this manner of living out their religious commitment.

Although in 1971 the congregation had been in existence for almost seventy-five years, it had never seriously considered sending its members to serve as foreign missionaries. Throughout the years, however, several requests had come in from places such as Shasi, China;[53] Rio de Janeiro and Santarem, Brazil; Phuket, Thailand; and Bombay, India.[54]

At the First Extraordinary Chapter of Affairs of 1968, the chapter delegates deliberated the issue of overseas assignments in the fertile mission fields. One of the chapter recommendations strongly urged that the congregation open a foreign mission either in India or Africa.

Sister Therese Marie Wegiel, who had made her perpetual profession of vows in 1968, and who had completed her training as a nurse anesthetist, sought permission from the superior general and the collegial board to volunteer three years of service in India. Without any mission bases of its own, the Franciscan Sisters of Chicago supported Sister Therese Marie's request. On February 11, 1971, she left for Jamshedpur, India, located approximately 150 miles from Calcutta, to serve as an anesthetist at a hospital conducted by the Congregation of the Sisters of Mercy. At the hospital which sought to provide assistance to the sick regardless of race, caste, creed, sex, or ability to pay, Sister Therese

Marie taught Indian nationals in the field of anesthesia. During her years of service in India, Sister Therese Marie received only a small subsidy from the government-approved hospital, and the Franciscan Sisters of Chicago assumed all her financial obligations as its contribution to the needs of the Church in India.[55]

After the Second Vatican Council, almost every private, public, or church-related college and university developed a program in campus ministry. The program was a replacement for the forms of pastoral care and religious education that Catholic bishops had initiated over seventy years ago in public colleges and universities and had been known as the Newman Club.[56] The campus ministry program developed as a pastoral apostolate of service to the members of the entire college and university community, both Catholic and secular. Its general aim was to make the Church present and active in the entire academic community. When an opportunity presented itself to respond to this emerging role of service for women as an extension of the Church's role in education in the 1970s, Sister Eileen Kazmierowicz obtained permission from Sister M. Hugoline and the collegial board to become part of the ecumenical campus ministry team at the University of Akron in Ohio.

Beginning in September of 1973, individually and as a team member, Sister Eileen served the University of Akron community in a pastoral, educational, and social capacity. Her basic function of "being present" to the entire university community was carried out through a number of programs which included the planning of liturgical celebrations, spiritual counseling, lectures, workshops, discussion groups, retreats, weekend encounter groups, and social action programs. Guided by the belief that the university community was in need of the Gospel to be made real by human interaction, Sister Eileen and the ecumenical campus ministry team offered opportunities to worship, to learn, and to share.[57]

While a member of the team, Sister Eileen participated in another unique experience by living in a diocesan house of prayer in Barberton, Ohio. Sister Eileen's "community" consisted of a member of the Congregation of the Sisters of the Divine Redeemer of Elizabeth, Pennsylvania, and two members of the Congregation of the Sisters of the Third Order of St. Dominic of Akron, Ohio, all who were engaged in various roles of ministerial service.[58]

The Church today, perhaps as never before in its history, is being challenged to demonstrate visibly its concern for the spiritual and social welfare of all the People of God. In its response to poverty, to the socially disadvantaged, and to discrimination in our time, the Church calls for involvement in all works of mercy. In Chicago at the Cook County Department of Corrections, commonly referred to as the Cook County Jail, at 25th Street and California Avenue, an educational program for non-adjudicated inmates had been started for those men who, having been charged with a crime, were behind bars and waiting for their cases to come before the judge. These were "trial prisoners," who had not yet been found guilty but were incarcerated in surroundings and under conditions that were in themselves punitive.[59] An education program for those awaiting trial had been initiated by the Reverend Joseph McDonnell, chaplain of Cook County Prison, for eight years. In this endeavor, he was aided by Lieutenant Danny Robinson of the prison staff. Classes were conducted by approximately thirty Sisters and lay women volunteers who met with inmates enrolled in the program every Tuesday evening for two hours from September through May.

Several Sisters of the Congregation of St. Felix of Cantalice (Felicians) at Good Counsel High School in Chicago had taught at the prison for a number of years. In 1974, however, important community commitments made it impossible for some of them to continue. Consequently, they asked the Franciscan Sisters of Chicago at Madonna High School to volunteer in their places. Five Sisters responded to their request: Sister Anne Marie Knawa, Sister M. Christine Brzozowski, Sister M. Jude Kruszewski, Sister Marie Frances Moson, and Sister Terri Slezak. On September 17, 1974, the Sisters visited the prison tiers for the first time and urged the men to "come back to school." In 1975, Sister M. Monica Sendlosky was added to the list of volunteers.[60]

The two-hour teaching session was conducted on a very personal basis; each teacher had only a few student inmates. This enabled the men to communicate freely and to receive the individual attention their situation demanded. The curriculum consisted of mathematics, typing, art, and the basic skills of reading, vocabulary study, grammar, spelling, and writing. Many of the men who participated had no educational background and had to begin at pre-elementary levels. Others were more advanced and were taught accordingly. Even at that, only a fraction of the prison's total population was reached. While there were many programs in the United States for sentenced criminals, the one for unsentenced men at the Cook County Jail was the only one in the country at the time.[61]

The Sisters continued to visit their student prisoners long after the prisoners had been sentenced to the state penitentiary at Joliet or Pontiac, Illinois. These visits impressed upon the offenders the appealing love and compassion which dwells in the hearts of all those who love God. If the message of the Gospel was extended to the imprisoned, then, the Sisters learned, the jailed in turn oftentimes responded with a message of hope and gratitude—sentiments the prisoners have expressed in letters to the Sisters:

> I would like to thank you for all the things you have done for me, and I will never forget this kindness and you . . . You know, Sister, Tuesday nights when you came to the prison was like getting good news from home . . . I owe you so much. Thank you for bringing me peace of mind.[62]

A letter from another inmate seemed to make "all the Tuesdays worthwhile":

I am writing these few lines to wish you a Merry Christmas and a Happy New Years. [*sic*] Also to hope it brings you all that you asked for in your prayers. [*sic*] God is always at your side because of the love you have to share with us who in the eyes of society are considered to be castaways. But its [*sic*] completely the reverse in the eyes of God and yours.

You bring us happiness just by being here on Tuesdays, and peace of mind, body, and soul when you mention us in your prayers. Thank you for being so kind to us. For its [*sic*] not many who understand our situation and try as hard as you to make [*sic*] more bearable. Thank you for remembering us when you kneel down before our God to give thanks for all of your blessings. Most of all thank you for being you. God bless you and keep you for you are part of what little light we have in here.[63]

Through the efforts of Father McDonnell, the Illinois Law Enforcement Commission funded the program for three years enabling the volunteer teachers to receive some compensation and to purchase needed materials for instruction. When the commission ended its three-year commitment to the program, Father McDonnell appealed to John Cardinal Cody, the archbishop of Chicago, who expressed great interest and concern in the work being done at the prison. Consequently, for the next few years, the Archdiocese of Chicago funded this unique and innovative educational program and gave it every encouragement and support.[64] Unfortunately, the program was suspended in early 1980 when the new addition to the prison was completed and the prisoners were transferred there making it difficult to consolidate the program because of reasons of security.

In 1972, Sister Chestine Marie Bugay took up residence at St. Louise de Marillac Convent in La Grange Park, Illinois, in order to become a part of the intercommunity staff at Immaculate Heart of Mary High School in Westchester, Illinois, conducted by the Sisters, Servants of the Immaculate Heart of Mary. Sister Chestine's main role as a teacher of religion was to "be present" to the Immaculate Heart of Mary High School community as a Franciscan. She remained on the staff until January of 1974.[65]

The faith response of the Franciscan Sisters of Chicago to the community of humankind through spiritually uplifting music resulted in another "first" venture for the congregation. Aided by a mutual love of song, musical talent, and a generous dose of good will, several Sisters came together in 1970 to form a community musical group called "Daybreak."[66] Having sung and played successfully at Catholic liturgies, Protestant services, and for various activities of lay organizations, the Sisters recorded an album of twelve original songs whose music and lyrics were composed by the spirited and creative leader of the group, Sister Kathleen Melia. The recording venture, done entirely in the

Sisters' free time and requiring almost a year to complete, was under the capable direction of Sister Emilie Marie Lesniak. The thirteenth member of the versatile group, Sister M. Sponsa Bajorek, designed the original jacket for the album which was entitled, "On the Way." After its release in 1971, the album sold over 2,000 copies.[67]

In 1982, during the celebration of the eighth centenary of the birth of St. Francis of Assisi, nine Sisters[68] recorded twelve modern, original religious songs in a new album which they called, "A New Kind of Freedom." This time, Mr. Patrick Ferreri acted as musical director and arranger for the group. The cover design, an illustration of Chicago's beautiful skyline, was once again executed by Sister M. Sponsa Bajorek. In April 1982, more than 1,000 record albums, and 500 cassettes and music books were released for sale and met with immediate success.[69]

Among the signs of reverence and faith emerging in the early 1970s, the extraordinary minister of the Eucharist assumed a unique function for the benefit of the People of God.[70] The genuine need for the assistance of Sisters and lay persons to facilitate the distribution of Holy Communion under certain circumstances and with proper permission encouraged many of the Sisters of the congregation to become extraordinary ministers of the Eucharist. With the permission of the Holy See and designated by the proper ecclesiastical authorities of the diocese in which they served, the Sisters' new task within the Christian community was to perform a pastoral act in the distribution of Holy Communion at mass, and in some dioceses, the distribution of the Eucharist to the sick, aged, and incapacitated in their homes or in hospitals. Each Sister attended a formation session provided by the Diocesan Liturgical Commission, and in a ceremony of deputation was designated publicly as an "ordinary Christian called to a role of extraordinary service," and "an embodiment of charity and a sign of hope to the Christian community."[71]

THE ELEVENTH AND TWELFTH GENERAL CHAPTERS:
SISTER M. HUGOLINE CZAPLINSKI

[1]See Appendix K.

[2]Address to the delegates of the Eleventh Chapter of Elections by Sister M. Hugoline Czaplinski, superior general, 24 June 1970 (AFSCL).

[3]*Congregation Membership Records* (AFSCL).

[4]See Chapter 51.

[5]*Congregation Membership Records* (AFSCL).

[6]*Interviews* with Sisters, September 1983 (AFSCL).

[7]*Madonna High School Dedication Book,* Chicago, Illinois, 1959.

[8]Sister M. Alberta is discussed at length in Chapter 51.

[9]Sister M. Alvernia is discussed at length in Chapter 51.

[10]*Congregation Membership Records* (AFSCL).

[11]Ibid.

[12]*Interviews* with Sisters, September 1983 (AFSCL).

[13]*Congregation Membership Records* (AFSCL).

[14]*Interviews* with Sisters, September 1983 (AFSCL).

[15]See Chapter 60.

[16]Address to the delegates to the Eleventh General Chapter of Elections by Sister M. Hugoline, superior general, June 1970 (AFSCL).

[17]See Appendix K. Address to the delegates to the Second Special Chapter of Affairs by Sister M. Hugoline, superior general, 14 August 1972 (AFSCL).

[19]*Minutes of General Chapter Proceedings, 1970–1974* (AFSCL).

[20]*Chapter Decrees Supplement,* 1972 (AFSCL).

[21]Procedures for election of delegates, Second Special Chapter of Affairs, 1972 (AFSCL).

[22]The Formation Team issued a newsletter called "Formation Notes" four times a year.

[23]One of the trends of the Formation Program in the 1970s which has successfully continued in the congregation is the Intercommunity Formation Program. When initiated, the novices of the Franciscan Sisters of Chicago joined with the novices of the Congregation of the Franciscan Sisters of Christ the King for courses in theology, Scripture, and religious life which were accredited by the College of St. Francis in Joliet, Illinois. Later the program was extended to include the Congregation of the Sisters of St. Casimir, the Congregation of the Sisters of St. Felix of Cantalice (Felicians) and the Congregation of the Mantellate Sisters, Servants of Mary. The Intercommunity Formation Program also included intercommunity days of prayer and days of recollection for the postulants, novices, and junior Sisters.

[24]Franciscan Sisters of Chicago Formation Committee, "Formation in the 1970s," Research report presented to the Second Special Chapter of Affairs, August 1972 (AFSCL).

[25]Sister Emilie Marie was the niece of the late Miss Berenice Lesniak who served the Congregation of the Franciscan Sisters of Chicago faithfully for many years. Miss Lesniak, who was a bank executive, savings and loan secretary, realtor, builder, appraiser and insurance broker, offered her invaluable services to the congregation and proved to be a good friend as well. Her sound advice and prudent counsel could always be counted on.

[26]*Congregation Membership Records* (AFSCL).

[27]In 1980, she was appointed principal of Five Holy Martyrs School.

[28]*Interviews* with Sisters, September 1983 (AFSCL).

[29]John Cardinal Cody, the sixth archbishop and the fourth cardinal of the Archdiocese of Chicago, was born on December 24, 1907, in St. Louis, Missouri. He attended Holy Rosary Parochial School and St. Louis Preparatory Seminary. An outstanding student at the North American College in Rome, he was ordained there on December 8, 1931. From 1938 to 1940, he served as secretary to Archbishop John Glennon of St. Louis, and rose to chancellor of the archdiocese holding that position until 1947. In 1955, he became the bishop of the diocese of St. Joseph, Missouri. A year later, he was transferred to the newly formed diocese of Kansas City-St. Joseph as the ordinary. During the Second Vatican Council, Pope John XXIII appointed Archbishop Cody one of the designers of the council and named him to the Liturgical Commission of the United States Bishops as well as the Commission for Seminaries and Studies. On November 8, 1964, Archbishop Cody was named to succeed Archbishop Joseph Rummel as ordinary of New Orleans. Here Archbishop Cody gained a reputation as a staunch upholder of civil rights and won recognition for his role in integrating the Catholic schools of that city.

Rome appointed him the successor to Albert Cardinal Meyer of Chicago. Two years later, he was named a cardinal by Pope Paul VI, thereby heading the nation's largest archdiocese. It was Cardinal Cody's responsibility to implement the liturgical, pastoral, and ecumenical directives which the Second Vatican Council promulgated. He exercised spiritual leadership by encouraging interdenominational cooperation in the whole religious community. Of the local developments which were an outgrowth of the council were the establishment of the clergy personnel board, the archdiocesan presbyterial senate, and the boards of conciliation and arbitration. He inaugurated a health program for priests and religious. He is credited with providing insurance and pension plans for archdiocesan lay employees, and with establishing a retirement and pension plan for priests. His attention to ministerial concern was evident in the establishment of the archdiocesan permanent deacon program. In 1967, he divided the huge archdiocese into seven districts and later into twelve vicariates in order to move its administration closer to the people. Cardinal Cody is credited with organizing the archdiocesan archives at St. Mary of the Lake Seminary in Mundelein, Illinois. He established a complete coverage plan for the archdiocesan newspaper, *The Chicago Catholic* (formerly *The New World*).

In 1978, Cardinal Cody participated in the conclaves which elected Pope John Paul I and John Paul II. In October of 1979, he hosted the visit of the Holy Father and all the United States bishops to Chicago during the Pope's pastoral visit to the nation. The cardinal's last major public appearance was on Christmas Eve 1981, his seventy-fourth birthday, when he celebrated Midnight Mass at Holy Name Cathedral. After another brief hospital stay, he went into seclusion at his home where he died on April 25, 1982, of cardiac arrest.

[30]*Book of Correspondence:* Letter from John Cardinal Cody, archbishop of Chicago to Sister M. Hugoline Czaplinski, superior general of the Franciscan Sisters of Chicago, 18 April 1974 (AFSCL).

[31]See Appendix K.

[32]*Congregation Membership Records* (AFSCL).

[33]*Book of Annual Assignments* (AFSCL).

[34]*Interviews* with Sisters, September 1983 (AFSCL).

[35]For a summary of the summer religious vacation schools conducted in places where there were no Catholic schools or where children were unable to attend parochial schools, see Chapter 35.

[36]*Book of Annual Assignments* (AFSCL).

[37]*Dedication of St. Matthias Church* (Crown Point, Indiana, 1970), no pagination.

[38]Ibid.

[39]*The Church of St. Pascal: A History of Fifty Years* (South Hackensack, New Jersey: Custombook, Inc., 1967), no pagination.

[40]Reverend Joseph Thompson, ed., *Diamond Jubilee of the Archdiocese of Chicago, 1920* (Des Plaines, Illinois: St. Mary's Training School Press, 1920), p. 541.

[41]Reverend Monsignor Harry C. Koenig, ed., *A History of the Archdiocese of Chicago: Published in Observance of the Centenary of the Archdiocese, 1980*, 2 vols. (Chicago: The Archdiocese of Chicago, 1980) 2:1372–1374.

[42]*St. James Church: Diamond Jubilee Book, 1902–1977* (Arlington Heights, Illinois, 1977), p. 31.

[43]*Bulletins of the Superiors General:* Letter from Sister M. Hugoline Czaplinski, superior general, to the congregation, 21 April 1971; and *Chapter Decrees, 1970*, p. 48.

[44]The Sisters were Sister Janice Piesko, Sister Kathryn Marie Zulaski, Sister Dawn Louise Capilupo, and Sister M. Francetta Glowinski.

[45]The *Tau* is a T-shaped cross, which for St. Francis, had mystic significance. He placed it in his writings and used it as his usual signature. It is, then, characteristically Franciscan.

[46]*Book of Correspondence:* Letter from the members of Tau House to the congregation, 24 April 1971 (AFSCL).

[47]*Book of Correspondence:* Letter from Sister M. Hugoline, superior general, to the members of Tau House, 9 April 1973 (AFSCL).

[48]The Sisters were Sister Margaret Grempka, Sister Jane Madejczyk, Sister Diane Przyborowski, and Sister M. Beatrice Hernandez.

[49]*Book of Correspondence:* Letter from members of St. Paul Mission to the congregation, 1972 (AFSCL).

[50]*Chapter News in Brief*, July 1974 (AFSCL).

[51]"Report to the General Chapter," Sister M. Hugoline, superior general, June 1974 (AFSCL).

[52]*Book of Departures* (AFSCL).

[53]The request from China came in 1937. Shasi is located 800 hundred miles west of Shanghai.

[54]*Book of Missions Refused* (AFSCL).

[55]*Bulletins of the Superiors General:* "From the Desk of Sister M. Hugoline Czaplinski," 1971 (AFSCL).

[56]"The Newman Apostolate," *The New World*, 20 February 1976.

[57]Campus Ministry Team, University of Akron, Ohio, "What is Campus Ministry?" Ohio, 1975. (Mimeographed).

[58]*Book of Correspondence:* Letter from Sister Eileen Kazmierowicz to author, 31 October 1973 (AFSCL).

[59]George M. Anderson, SJ, "Jails, Lockups, and Houses of Detention," *America*, January 1976, pp. 6–10.

[60]*Madonna High School House Journal* (AFSCL).

[61]"Keeping Heads Together Behind a Locked Door," *The New World*, 29 March 1974, sec. 2, p. 9.

[62]*Book of Correspondence:* Letter from prisoner to author, 3 June 1975 (AFSCL).

[63]*Book of Correspondence:* Letter from prisoner to author, 9 December 1975 (AFSCL).

[64]The information was supplied by the Reverend Joseph Bennett, the chaplain at Cook County Department of Corrections, in December of 1976. He had succeeded Father McDonnell that year. Father Bennett continued in the spirit of his predecessor in his dedication and responsibility in advancing this innovative and badly needed educational program, the most important feature being the promotion and restoration of human dignity to prisoners who, according to the Constitution of the United States, "are presumed innocent until the contrary has been proven." *Book of Correspondence:* Letter from the Reverend Joseph Bennett to author, 13 December 1976 (AFSCL).

[65]*Congregation Membership Records* (AFSCL).

[66]Included in the "Daybreak" group were Sister M. Beatrice Hernandez, Sister Dawn Louise Capilupo, Sister Diane Marie Collins, Sister M. Francetta Glowacki, Sister M. Francis Clare Radke, Sister Jane Madejczyk, Sister Joan Klimek, Sister Margaret Grempka, Sister Margaret Mary Peckenpaugh, and Sister M. Rosalima Sierocki.

[67]*Interview* with Sister Kathleen Melia, 15 September 1974 (AFSCL).

[68]The new musical group consisted of Sister M. Bernadette Bajuscik, Sister Diane Marie Collins, Sister Emilie Marie Lesniak, Sister Jean Therese Jarosz, Sister Joan Klimek, Sister Kathleen Melia, Sister Linda Marie Hughes, Sister Lora Ann Slawinski, and Sister Maureen Battista Tuohy.

[69]*Interview* with Sister Diane Marie Collins, 24 August 1982 (AFSCL).

[70]"Liturgy 70: A Ministry of Service: A Theological Insight into the Role of Extraordinary Ministers," Vol. 2, No. 4–5, Archdiocese of Chicago.

[71]"Sermon Outline III, Historical Perspective," Liturgy Training Program, Archdiocese of Chicago (1971).

CHAPTER 62

St. Anthony Medical Center

The Franciscan Sisters of Chicago reached a historic milestone in 1973 when in response to a call to meet the health care needs of the residents of Crown Point[1] and South Lake County in Indiana, they initiated construction of St. Anthony Hospital. The hospital is one structure in the medical complex, now called the St. Anthony Medical Center, which also contains the St. Anthony Home, the Holy Family Child Care Center, and a convent for the Sisters on the staffs of all three institutions.

In 1968, the Franciscan Sisters of Chicago, in keeping with the mandate issued by the Second Vatican Council, held their First Extraordinary Chapter of Affairs. During this historic meeting, a comprehensive study was made of all the congregation's corporate apostolates. Every school, hospital, and institution owned and operated by the Sisters was studied and evaluated in the spirit of the needs of the Church and of the times. At that strategic chapter, a decision was made to withdraw from the small hospitals operated by the Sisters in Atkinson, Nebraska; and Gregory and Martin, South Dakota. The only hospital left to the congregation was the St. John Regional Medical Center in Huron, South Dakota. The Sister-delegates to the chapter confirmed the congregation's belief that the influence of the Catholic Church in the health field continued to be highly desirable. The Sisters affirmed that their presence in the Catholic-sponsored health care facilities bore witness to Christ and fostered the charisms of St. Francis of Assisi and Mother M. Theresa Dudzik. As a consequence of this declared expression of continuing ministry to the sick and the dying, the Franciscan Sisters of Chicago resolved to construct a hospital on the grounds of St. Anthony Home in Crown Point with the assistance of the Lake County, Indiana, community.

As has already been noted in Chapter 59, the Franciscan Sisters of Chicago opened St. Anthony Home in Crown Point in 1939 to serve the needs of nineteen elderly men and women in a small house on the southeast corner of South Court Street and Franciscan Road. In 1966, a $3 million structure opened near that site as the new St. Anthony Home. The Sisters continued to minister to the aged in a spirit of love and dedication.

Early in 1970, an analysis of Lake County population profiles concluded that a diagnostic and acute care hospital was needed in Crown Point, Indiana.[2] A personal and mail survey conducted that year indicated that the Franciscan Sisters of Chicago had already established a record of extraordinary service in patient care at St. Anthony Home, and now petitions, both master and individual, urged the Sisters to build a general hospital near the site of St. Anthony Home.[3] Resolutions urging a "home hospital" were passed by city and town councils of South Lake County, by service clubs, other organizations, and by professional and business groups. After extensive studies, the Sisters agreed to invest $5.5 million from available funds and long-term borrowing for construction. A local fund drive was initiated on July 2, 1970, and the people of Crown Point and South Lake County pledged more than $1.2 million. A year earlier, in May of 1969, Mother M. Beatrice Rybacki, the superior general; Sister M. Venantia Rec, the assistant general; Sister M. Hugoline Czaplinski, the second councilor; and Lawrence T. Filosa,[4] the president of St. John Regional Medical Center in Huron, South Dakota, and executive director of health care facilities for the Franciscan Sisters of Chicago, had visited the Most Reverend Andrew Grutka, bishop of Gary, who gave the project his blessing.[5]

In January of 1971, the Leo A. Daly Company of St. Louis was contracted to design the hospital.[6] Hired to build the hospital structure itself was the Calumet Construction Company. The initial building was to be a large, one-story section suggesting expansion possibilities. All the scientific and technological advances were to be incorporated into the new St. Anthony Hospital, allowing for excellent comprehensive and personalized patient care. As progressive health care and public demand would warrant, complementary programs in addition to the proposed acute care hospital and existing long-term facility could be added.

On Sunday, May 21, 1972, at one-thirty o'clock in the afternoon, ground-breaking ceremonies were held during which the celebrant, the Most Reverend Andrew Grutka, bishop of Gary, blessed the construction site. After a musical interlude by the Crown Point High School Band, Bishop Grutka addressed the enthusiastic crowd. He called the plan of construction a "bold venture" and praised the dedication and courage of the Franciscan Sisters of Chicago for undertaking such a monumental task. He also congratulated the local citizens for their earnest efforts in helping to get the hospital built. Richard C. Collins, the mayor of Crown Point, termed the proposed construction of the hospital the "highlight" of his tenure of office.[7]

When the construction of St. Anthony Hospital began, it was necessary to build a convent to house the Sisters on the staffs of both the "Home" and the "Hospital." Early in 1973, therefore, a beautiful one-story Spanish-style convent was constructed west of the "Home" facing Franciscan Road. The following Sisters comprising the staffs of both institutions moved into the convent on July 6, 1973: Sister M. Agatha Walerski, Sister M. Andrea Puchalski, Sister M. Doloretta Radzienda, Sister M. De Sales Wyszynski, Sister M. Edwina Wilk, Sister M. Electa Rytel, Sister M. Emily Kowal, Sister M. Euphemia Switalski, Sister Frances Szczur, Sister Josephine Marie Haske, Sister M. Laetitia

St. Anthony Medical Center Convent
Crown Point, Indiana

Kolczak, Sister M. Lucille Klockowski, Sister M. Marifilia Strzycki, Sister Martha Joan Sempolski, Sister Michael Marie Golaszewski, Sister M. Mildred Bieda, Sister M. Natalie Uscinowicz, Sister M. Sigfrieda Scensny, Sister M. Tarcisia Bucki, and Sister M. Theresilla Ignasiak. By 1974, several other Sisters had joined the staff. They were Sister M. Alphonsine Kobylinski, Sister M. Carmel Rokicki, and Sister M. Olivia Pacek.[8]

The long-awaited dedication of the hospital took place on Sunday, February 24, 1974, at two o'clock in the afternoon. The invocation was delivered by Bishop Grutka, and the Honorable Otis Bowen, the governor of Indiana, gave the keynote address. The official ceremony was preceded by a dedication brunch at the Merrillville Holiday Inn Convention Center at ten-thirty o'clock in the morning of the same day. More than five hundred state, city, and religious dignitaries together with the Sisters, campaign workers, and supporters of St. Anthony Hospital braved the sub-zero temperatures to attend.[9]

The new St. Anthony Hospital, at South Main and Franciscan Drive, opened its doors on March 1, 1974, with a licensed capacity of 184 beds and twenty-two bassinets. The total cost of the hospital, including construction, equipment, furnishings, land acquisition, architects, other fees, and the first year anticipated operating expenditures was estimated at $11.5 million. The three-story structure contained 160 beds with fifteen to twenty private rooms. The remaining rooms were semiprivate. The building was designed to accommodate the major services department on the first floor. The patients' rooms were on the second and third floors. The hospital's design provided that the main chassis of the building at the center would permit upward expansion in phases to 450 beds making a sixth floor. An extension of ancillary services would broaden the first floor to accommodate the expected needs.

The hospital made provision for emergency room service, complete clinical laboratory service, automative machine testing, a surgical suite with five operating rooms and recovery rooms, outpatient services, radiology or X-ray, labor, delivery, and post-delivery services, a nursery for newborns, a surgery floor, a medical floor, a pediatrics department, coronary and intensive care, and respiratory therapy services. It also had a nuclear-medical department with diagnostic and therapeutic services.

With an interior in shocking yellows, blues, greens, and orange, the hospital was an innovative concept in health care. The draperies in the patients' rooms used lemon yellow and a green leaf motif. Off-white walls and matching flame-retardant cubicle curtains to provide privacy further added to the fresh, cheerful atmosphere. Much of the first floor and portions of the second and third floors had gold-green carpeting.

St. Anthony Medical Center, from its foundation, kept pace with the growing needs of all the people. In 1977, population increases in the area of Crown Point and South Lake County called for the initiation of construction in the expansion program. A fourth floor with ninety-six beds was added which now made St. Anthony's a 280-bed hospital. Medical facilities in other areas included a cardiovascular recovery area, a pediatrics intensive care area, a neonatal intensive care area, and outpatient specialties and offices.

The Grand Dedication Ceremony of the addition to the hospital was held on May 18, 1980, at two o'clock in the afternoon. The invocation was delivered by the Reverend Myron Lowisz, OFM, director of pastoral care at St. Anthony Medical Center. The Honorable Richard C. Collins, mayor of Crown Point, gave the keynote address. Sister Martha Joan Sempolski, the superior general of the Franciscan Sisters of Chicago, gave the welcome address. Amid a large gathering of community leaders and friends of St. Anthony Medical Center, the Reverend John P. Starr, pastor of the First Christian Church of Crown Point, gave the benediction.

Another major expansion project commenced in 1980 and was completed in 1983. The expansion project included the addition of three patient care floors and the addition of five one-story interconnected buildings or "pods" as an extension of the main inpatient care building. The pods contained the following: Pod one—Medical Library, Outpatient Waiting Area, Radiation Therapy, and Renal Dialysis; Pod two—Osteoporosis Diagnostic Office and Waiting Room, Non-Invasive Testing, CAT Scanner, Cardiac Rehabilitation, EKG (Electrocardiogram), and Pulmonary Rehabilitation; Pod three—Surgi Center; Pod four—MRI (Magnetic Resonance Imaging), Emergency, Security Office; Pod five—Admitting, Audiology, Multi-Purpose Room, EEG (Electroencephalogram), EMG (Electromyogram), and Public Relations.[10]

On May 31, 1983, Sister Martha Joan Sempolski, superior general and chairperson of the Board of Directors, officially announced the termination of Lawrence T. Filosa, as president of St. Anthony Medical Center; the dissolution of the Board of Directors of St. Anthony Medical Center; and the appointment of an interim administrator, Kenneth A. Eshak, to manage the day-to-day functions of the hospital. Mr. Eshak was an employee of the Alexian Brothers Health Management Corporation of Elk Grove Village, Illinois,[11] a health care management and consulting firm retained by the Franciscan Sisters of Chicago to provide interim management services.

St. Anthony Medical Center
Crown Point, Indiana (1974–   )

The members of the corporation continued to oversee the governance of the hospital by their involvement in the facility and by exercising their right to appoint new directors to the board of St. Anthony Medical Center. On August 19, 1983, Sister Joseph Marie Zenda, the new superior general and chairperson of the board, announced the appointment of Peter C. Rogan as president and chief executive officer of St. Anthony Medical Center.[12]

The year 1983 had indeed been a time of transition for the hospital. Internally, the new administration confronted many problems when it took office in September. This situation was made even more complicated by rapid and complex change in the American health care environment, but the challenges were met most successfully, and St. Anthony Medical Center emerged stronger and more committed than ever to providing the best possible health care services to the people of Northwest Indiana.[13]

The first measure of any health care facility is the quality of its medical staff. St. Anthony Medical Center owes its reputation as a regional health care leader to more than 260 physicians, representing fifteen specialties, on the staff. Five of these specialties were added in 1983 or early in 1985: clinical allergy and immunology, pediatric urology, pediatric orthopedic surgery, clinical psychology, and colon and rectal surgery.

Approximately three or four times each month, as part of its continuing medical education, the Medical Center provides ongoing professional instruction to the Medical Staff covering a broad variety of subjects. Educational programs, such as cardiopulmonary resuscitation, recertification, and intravenous therapy certification, are offered on a continuous basis to employees.

At its foundation, St. Anthony Medical Center employed a primary nursing concept called the "Friesen Concept" which eliminated the traditional nurses' station. This new concept with its innovative technological facilities interconnected by a sophisticated communications systems allowed for optimal utilization of material and manpower. Above all, it eliminated a myriad of time and energy-consuming duties which formerly would have been the responsibility of nurses, freeing the nurses to be with the patient.

St. Anthony's comprehensive capabilities in the diagnosis and treatment of cancer makes the Medical Center a leading community cancer center. Its linear accelerator and the corresponding treatment simulator represent the latest advance in cancer therapy. The addition of this sophisticated tool in 1983 enables the hospital to offer a full continuum of cancer care services including the following: both inpatient and outpatient cancer treatment programs; the development by the medical staff of special oncology and cancer treatment guidelines to assist in diagnosis, staging of the disease, and review of cancer care; a computerized tumor registry for the purpose of cancer study and survival follow-up; a rehabilitation program featuring recreational and other diverse activities for cancer patients and their families; a variety of special support programs for cancer patients and their families; and a mammography center.[14]

In 1985, the Medical Center opened the Oncology Family Room dedicated to providing cancer patients with a family-centered atmosphere in the hospital environment. The room is equipped with home entertainment devices, exercise machines, and a small

Aerial View, St. Anthony Medical Center Complex
Crown Point, Indiana

kitchen. The room is tacit recognition of the importance of family cohesiveness during a time of both physical and psychological distress.[15]

To enhance compassionate, comprehensive care for the terminally ill, St. Anthony's has implemented an Outpatient Hospice Program. The Medical Center is currently studying the feasibility of an Inpatient Hospice Program. To implement these programs, St. Anthony's has been working with various community groups to explore how its resources can best be utilized to provide counseling, spiritual guidance, and family-centered care for the terminally ill.

St. Anthony Hospital has always been in the vanguard of cardiovascular medicine—in diagnosis, in surgery, and in rehabilitation. In 1987, four open-heart surgery teams performed more than seven hundred major surgical procedures, including coronary bypasses, valve replacements, arterial bypasses, and aneurysm repairs. The twenty-three cardiologists performed more than 2,800 angiograms and angioplasties. Many other patients were treated medically with modern drugs such as beta-blockers and devices such as pacemakers.

From the diagnosis of cardiac disease with procedures such as thalium stress testing, nonevasive ultrasound, echocardiography and bi-plane imaging, to treatment such as the left ventricle assist pump and laser angioplasty, St. Anthony's possesses the modern technology to perform the necessary functions. The hospital has a ten-bed Cardiovascular Intensive Care Unit, staffed by nurses specially trained and highly dedicated to total patient care. To complete the recovery process, three phases of cardiac rehabilitation are provided along with nutritional counseling and exercise prescriptions to help patients regain a healthy lifestyle.

By the spring of 1985, the hospital had already built and opened the area's most advanced Cardiac Catheterization Laboratory. With this technology available, it is possible to perform treatments that actually prevent heart attacks, to mitigate the damage of infarctions in progress, and to perform a host of other procedures more efficiently. In technology and people, St. Anthony's is truly "The Heart Hospital."[16]

Special Services include the Intensive/Coronary Care Unit which is capable of providing for the care of medical/surgical patients in need of highly technical medical and nursing aid. The intensive care unit handles major surgical patients, massive trauma patients, dialysis patients, and other types of patients needing the close scrutiny of specially trained nurses and highly sophisticated equipment. The coronary care unit provides highly technical nursing and medical care for those patients with cardiac problems, metabolic disorders, and other anomalies not requiring surgical intervention. This combined unit monitors all patients for their cardiac status visually, with nursing personnel monitoring all equipment continuously.

St. Anthony Medical Center offers a family-centered maternity program which combines personal care, advanced medical facilities, and educational support to assure prospective parents of a rewarding, memorable childbirth. Among the services offered is a birthing room, sibling and grandparent visitation, rooming-in, mother/baby nursing, a comfortable homelike atmosphere throughout the unit, the famous and much-imitated Candlelight Dinner, and friendly nurses. The Teddy Bear Club for expectant parents is a new addition.

The Pediatric Unit at St. Anthony Medical Center provides care for all types of general, medical, and surgical cases for patients neonate to sixteen years of age. The neonatal unit cares for infants from birth to thirty days old who need close professional surveillance and sophisticated equipment to monitor vital functions. St. Anthony Medical Center's special pediatric programs meet the needs of the total child. These needs include pediatric presurgical tours, a pediatric oncology clinic, a pediatric play therapy program, and a pediatric intensive care unit.

Because children are an important focus of St. Anthony's caring mission, it was regionally one of the first to introduce the concept of "play therapy." Designed to divert a child's anger or frustration about being hospitalized, this program allows the child to act out feelings through the familiar routine of play. The program has recently been strengthened by adding a child life specialist to the staff. This specialist works closely with hospitalized children, observing and directing their behavior and creativity. The latest addition to the pediatric unit is a parents' lounge.[17]

The basic premise upon which St. Anthony Medical Center operates is that each and every patient is an individual and should be cared for by professionals with emphasis on meeting the patients' individual needs. The Dietary Service Department complements other professional departments by ensuring that patients are considered on the basis of their normal dietary habits as well as their medical dietary needs. The Dietary Department is responsible for regular and special diets with preparation and service designed to please the sight and appetite. Nutritionally fun pediatric menus have been developed for the young patients. The well-balanced fun foods provide a variety of food acceptable to youngsters. For new parents, a special gourmet meal is prepared. Another feature, "Meals on Wheels," is one of the cooperative efforts actively supported by the hospital. It is an innovative service that brings nourishing meals to the elderly, ill, or incapacitated in South Lake County.

The Department of Social Services at the Medical Center has qualified social workers available. These professionals provide personal and family counseling services for the patient and/or the patient's family, provide information about referral to appropriate community services and community resources, assist with discharge planning needs, and when requested, assist in arranging transfer to a nursing home.

Making action possible for the disabled individual is the goal of the hospital's Rehabilitation Services. Physically impaired individuals receive intensive, comprehensive treatment, and virtually any orthopedic or neurological physical impairment can be treated including paralysis, amputation, fracture, dislocations, birth defects, nerve damage, arthritis, stroke, brain damage, spinal cord injury or disease, and speech and hearing impairments. Because each client is unique, each is treated by his own "team." Headed by a physician, each team includes rehabilitation nurses, physical, occupational, and vocational therapists, speech pathologists, psychologists, pastoral care and social service staff members, and other specialists as needed. Respiratory therapy is a service provided to treat and prevent pulmonary complications.

St. Anthony Medical Center has an Occupational Therapy Department whose services are available to assist those patients who need to relearn the activities of daily living, as well as acquire lost manual dexterity skills. The Occupational Therapy Department is located in the Mother Theresa Pavilion which is attached to St. Anthony Home. Applying comprehensive treatment and positive motivation, the Medical Center helps disabled individuals attain their unique potential for a self-reliant, productive life.

The Emergency Unit at St. Anthony Medical Center provides care for those needing immediate medical attention and aids accident or disaster victims. A doctor and nurses are on duty twenty-four hours a day. Ambulances equipped with advanced life support equipment have a twenty-four-hour communication system with the emergency room at St. Anthony Medical Center to help administer care at the scene of an accident or illness and during transport.

In 1984 the new Night-Care Service for the treatment of minor illness or injury reduced the long visits and paperwork often associated with hospital emergency rooms. Minor medical problems that cannot wait until morning can now be treated promptly.

The Medical Center was officially designated a Poison Control Center in the State of Indiana in 1975. The Emergency Department is equipped with the "poisindex" which enables readouts (total identification and treatment needed) on more than eighty thousand identified poisons in less than thirty seconds.

St. Anthony Hospital also has a Surgi Center which provides same day surgery. Outpatient services for surgical procedures and recovery room facilities are available on a daily basis. Patients may receive the benefit of having surgical procedures carried out as well as post-surgical care without an overnight hospital stay. Treatment rooms are available for outpatient care for those receiving chemotherapy, blood transfusions, and other life-maintenance treatments.

A Trauma Center was opened in November 1983 and was one of the most advanced facilities of its kind in Indiana. All emergency services are located in the Trauma Center which includes two trauma rooms, each capable of handling two surgeries simultaneously; ten examination rooms; a separate X-ray area; improved access for emergency vehicles; and access to IHERN (Indiana Hospital and Emergency Room Network), an emergency information exchange system. Over 14,000 people annually use its twenty-four-hour emergency room service.

The helicopter's growing position as an important element in the rapid transfer of patients has brought about a keen awareness of the potential of this versatile aircraft. Recognizing its important role in life-threatening situations when every second counts, St. Anthony Medical Center has become the first health facility in Northwest Indiana to install its own heliport.

St. Anthony Medical Center participates in the Lake County Area Red Cross

Blood Program and has an agreement with the Mid-American Regional Red Cross Blood Program to provide patients with quality blood at low cost.

In the 1980s, St. Anthony Medical Center introduced a comprehensive range of medical specialties. In 1984, the Pho/Con 192, a sophisticated diagnostic camera used in a variety of procedures ranging from bone scanning to tumor screening was made available. The Medical Center was also the first to have a blood recyling program, in which blood normally lost during surgery is collected, cleaned, and reintroduced into the patient's system. The Medical Center installed a computerized blood chemistry analyzer whose speed and accuracy cut costs and dramatically improved quality. It also provides profiles of other bodily fluids.

The hospital has in operation a brand new type of equipment called a micro-dot imager. The hospital is the first in Northern Indiana with this equipment. The imager enables a closer look at an area of study—brain, heart, liver, lung, bone, spleen, pancreas—so that a clear and easier diagnosis can be made.

Magnetic resonance imaging, introduced in 1986, is the most modern method available for pictures (produced by the natural forces of magnetism and radio waves) of internal parts of the body.

Another example of advanced technology utilized at the Medical Center is ultrasound which is used in various applications to help physicians diagnose problems. These include echocardiograms, carotid doppler studies, and obstetrical sonograms.

In 1985, St. Anthony Medical Center initiated Tender Loving Care, Inc., (later changed to Staff Builders), a home health care service that provides a complete range of nursing and therapeutic services. The service, a joint venture between St. Anthony Hospital and Staff Builders, helps cut health care costs by allowing patients to return to the comfort and security of their homes more quickly.[18]

Throughout the years, St. Anthony's has continued to expand outpatient services. Cost effective and convenient, outpatient services are a growing aspect of health care made possible by advancing technology and improved techniques. Among the many services offered at the hospital are Physical Therapy, where conditions such as frozen shoulders, cervical strains, and low back pain are treated, and where rehabilitation after knee surgery, total hip replacement, and stroke is available; Clinical Laboratory, where diagnostic and therapeutic tests are performed on blood, tissues, and other body fluids; Radiology, where chest, skeletal, skull, and kidney X-rays are performed and fluoroscopy of the colon and upper gastrointestinal tract is available, as well as ultrasound, mammography, and CAT scan; Audiology, for individuals who need a hearing evaluation or who need an electronystagmogram (ENG) test for chronic dizziness; Renal Dialysis, for individuals with kidney failure who require mechanical removal of waste from their blood; Nutritional Counseling, for individuals who are on a specific medically prescribed diet or for those interested in a realistic and effective weight loss or weight control program; Examination Area and Physicians' Office Center, where patients can meet with their physicians for examinations and minor procedures; Electrocardiogram (EKG), a diagnostic test to determine how the heart is functioning; Electroencephalogram (EEG), a diagnostic test to determine the proper functioning of certain brain activity; Electomyogram (EMG), a diagnostic test for certain activities of the nervous system; Pulmonary Rehabilitation and Respiratory Therapy, for individuals suffering from chronic bronchitis, emphysema, asthma, or other obstructive lung diseases; Cardiac Rehabilitation, for individuals who have had heart surgery or who need a disciplined, medically based program to improve heart function; Radiation Therapy, for patients who require treatments by a linear accelerator; IV Therapy, for individuals who need certain nutritional supplements or a type of antiobiotic medication; Blood Transfusions, for individuals who are anemic for various reasons or have blood disorders; and Biofeedback, for individuals who suffer chronic pain, migraine headaches, hypertension, or stress and have unsuccessfully sought solutions; this noninvasive method teaches voluntary control of internal physiological processes.[19]

St. Anthony Medical Center already performs more eye surgeries than any other hospital in Northwest Indiana. With the addition of the YAG laser, the medical center has become the pre-eminent eye center in that service area.

A newly expanded gastroenterology laboratory now can produce esophageal motility studies. St. Anthony's is the only hospital in Northwest Indiana with this capability. Esophageal motility studies are useful in the diagnosis of chest pain, particularly in distinguishing between heart disease and motor disorders of the esophagus.

The only enterostolam therapist in Northwest Indiana has joined the staff to assist in caring for colostomy and ileostomy patients, as well as those with decubitus ulcers. The therapist provides patient education and staff development in this specialized field. Plans are on the drawing board for an ostomy clinic to open.

St. Anthony Medical Center recognizes its responsibility to promote good health services and thus offers the following: Physician Referral, where newcomers or any individual needing a family doctor or specialist can obtain the names, addresses, or phone numbers of physicians on St. Anthony's staff; Poison Control Center, where virtually every drug and toxic substance is listed in the hospital's Poisindex file which is updated regularly; and Officer UGG, a program that includes visual material to educate and warn children about the dangers of toxic substances. Schools, churches, and other groups can schedule an Officer UGG program. St. Anthony Medical Center also offers wellness and fitness classes, including aerobics, swimnastics, and "Aquababes"; Medi-Caring Hotline, where Medicare paperwork is explained and help offered by the Business Office; Nutrition Hotline, the source for the latest information concerning special diets, fad diets, and bad diets which can be discussed with a registered dietitian; Home Health Care, a service wherein registered nurses, therapists, companions, housekeepers, or virtually any home health care need can be met through St. Anthony Medical Center and Staff Builders; screenings for high blood pressure; skin, breast, and colon cancer; as well as diabetes, glaucoma, hypertension, and hearing impairment. A crippled children's clinic and other health maintenance programs are offered. Blood drives are held every third Friday of each month; educational programs include cardiac pulmonary resuscitation (CPR) and a freedom from smoking clinic. Support groups based at St. Anthony's include: SPARK (Support for Parents with Asthmatic Kids), BREATHING FREE (for chronic lung disease victims), COMPASSIONATE FRIENDS (for parents who have lost a child), CARING AND SHARING (for cancer patients and their families). The Speakers Bureau provides speakers for clubs, civic groups, and schools on a variety of health care topics, from the latest advances in cardiac care to ways of reducing hypertension.

St. Anthony Medical Center has a Health Science Library serving the informational, educational, and research needs of the medical staff and all personnel of the Medical Center. When the hospital opened, a small medical library was established primarily for the physicians. The book and journal collections grew progressively and the library subsequently expanded its services to meet the needs not only of the physicians but also of the administrators, nurses, employees of the Medical Center, and students enrolled in the training programs offered by the Center.

In July 1984, the library moved to a new wing of the hospital. The new facilities include two offices for the staff, a workroom, and a storage area. The attractive decor and furniture create a very pleasant atmosphere for its users. Presently the collection consists of more than 1,500 volumes of journals, and subscription holdings to about 200 major titles in clinical medicine, nursing, and administrative areas. The book collection of over 1,800 titles consists of well-balanced, authoritative books for physicians in each specialty and updated titles for nurses, allied health professionals, and health care administration. The library is a member of the National Medical Library Network which further adds to a real wealth of the library's resources. Sister M. Maurita Wszolek served as the overseer, researcher, and librarian from 1976 until her retirement in 1987.[20] She was succeeded by Monica Backe who is assisted by Sister M. Charitas Gajdzinski.[21]

A part of the total patient care at St. Anthony Medical Center includes the Department of Pastoral Care which meets the spiritual and emotional needs of the patient, family, and hospital personnel. The Reverend Myron Lowisz[22] is the director of the pastoral ministry team which also includes the Reverend Anthony Janik, OFM, and the Reverend Carmen Scuderi.[23] The coordinator of the department is Sister M. Alphonsine Kobylinski. Sister Jean Adamczyk, Sister M. Georgeann Kinel, and Sister M. Joella Bielinski are all assistant chaplains.[24]

The Department of Pastoral Care came into existence on March 1, 1974, the day the hospital opened. As an integral part of St. Anthony Medical Center, the Department of Pastoral Care provides excellent opportunities for spiritual assistance. The Liturgy of the Eucharist is celebrated every day in the small, lovely hospital chapel as well as in the large chapel of St. Anthony Home. The Eucharistic Liturgy and the rosary as well as other services from the hospital chapel can be viewed on closed circuit television in patient rooms. Daily distribution of the Holy Eucharist is made to patients in their rooms by a priest or a Sister. Benediction of the Blessed Sacrament is held every Friday at five o'clock in the evening in the nursing home chapel, and morning and night prayers are said over the public address system daily. The Sacraments of Reconciliation and the Anointing of the Sick are administered upon request and in times of need. Seasonal events such as distribution of ashes, the blessing of throats, and special prayer services at Christmas, Thanksgiving, and Easter are celebrated. Each new admission is visited by a member of the Pastoral Care Team as soon as possible after admission. Presurgical visits are made to those who are admitted to surgery, as well as to the Dialysis Unit, the Outpatient Surgical Waiting Area, all Critical Care areas, and the Emergency Department. Memorial prayer services of the Fulness of Life are conducted every three months for families of patients of St. Anthony Medical Center who are deceased. Because the Department of Pastoral Care provides spiritual aid to all the patients, clergy of all denominations are available upon request and are encouraged to visit their patients in the hospital. Interfaith services are also held as announced.

On August 1, 1986, Mr. Stephen Leurck was appointed the fourth president and chief executive officer of St. Anthony Medical Center. He brought to the Medical Center an excellent record of accomplishment in health care and an in-depth background in hospital administration. Appointed to serve as administrative assistant to the president was Sister M. Bernadette Bajuscik.[25]

Supporting the work of the physicians and nursing staff are employees in Pharmacy, X-ray, Laboratory, Administrative Services, Business Office, Dietary, Medical Records, Respiratory Therapy, Maintenance, Housekeeping, Physical Therapy, Plant Management, Public Relations, Materiels, In-Service, Social Services, Personnel, Security, Infection Control, and Laundry—all who join to deliver quality health care in an atmosphere of Christian love and compassion. As of August 1987, the Medical Center employs 1,116 persons, of whom 780 are full-time and 336 are part-time employees thus making the Medical Center the largest employer in Crown Point. A monthly newspaper, *Health Beat,* is published monthly for the staff and employees of St. Anthony Medical Center.

A very essential part of St. Anthony Medical Center is its active service program. Called the Auxilians, these "pink ladies" and "red coats" provide many services within the Medical Center and help make hospitalization as pleasant as possible for its patients. The Auxilians contribute more than thirty different indispensable services to others in a true Christian spirit of concern. With a membership of more than 250 women and men, the St. Anthony's Auxiliary volunteer over 55,000 service hours annually to attend to the needs of the patients, visitors, and residents of the Medical Center, St. Anthony Home, and the Holy Family Child Care Center. In addition, the fund-raising events of the Auxilians have enabled them to contribute more than $265,000 to the Medical Center during the past fourteen years.[26]

St. Anthony Medical Center, a part of the Franciscan Sisters of Chicago Health Services, Inc., is licensed by the Indiana State Board of Health. The Medical Center is a member of the American Hospital Association, the Catholic Hospital Health Association, the Indiana Hospital Association, and the Indiana Catholic Health Care Association. It is accredited by the Joint Commission on Accreditation of Healthcare Organizations.

St. Anthony Medical Center participates in a quality assurance program developed along standards prepared by the Joint Commission on Accreditation of Healthcare Organizations. This program assures that each one of the patients receives quality care based upon standards which are prepared by its own medical and hospital staff in cooperation with other hospitals across the nation. The Joint Commission on Accreditation of Healthcare Organizations is the assurance that the hospital is well run, well organized, and well staffed.

The continued growth and development of St. Anthony's has resulted in plans to erect the Medical Office Building of St. Anthony Medical Center on its Crown Point campus. The ground-breaking was scheduled for May 24, 1988.

The Mission Statement of the Franciscan Sisters of Chicago concerning St. Anthony Medical Center contains the reason for the existence of the facility. In the spirit of St. Francis of Assisi and Mother M. Theresa Dudzik, the Sisters and the staff of the Medical Center are committed to caring for the sick and suffering of all race, color, creed, sex, handicap, or financial status. This mission is carried out by providing Christian love, compassion, and respect for human dignity, and in offering services of professional excellence that attempt to heal the mind, body, and the spirit of its patients. The Mission Statement affirms the hospital's philosophy:

> Our mission at St. Anthony Medical Center is to continue the healing mission of Jesus Christ: to heal the sick, to calm the spirit, and to promote wellness in order to enrich the quality of life of all those we serve. Sharing in the spirit and tradition of Mother Mary Theresa Dudzik and the ministry of the Franciscan Sisters of Chicago, we strive to create a community of caring and compassion. Because we are morally bound to respect the dignity of all human life, we employ qualified staff, practice responsible management, maintain fiscal responsibility and utilize modern technology in order to achieve this end.[27]

With the passage of time, the social, political, economic, and technological climate in which health care is provided is hardly static, and new developments are sure to affect St. Anthony Medical Center. Two things, however, will never change: the commitment of the Franciscan Sisters of Chicago to excellence in health care and their dedication to enhancing the spiritual as well as the physical well-being of the Crown Point and South Lake County community. Each new or improved service at St. Anthony Hospital, the Holy Family Child Care Center, and St. Anthony Home expresses the commitment of the Franciscan Sisters of Chicago to the people of Northwest Indiana.[28] From the beginning of the hospital, the Franciscan Sisters of Chicago and the staff of St. Anthony Medical Center have been devoted to the concept of total health care in an atmosphere of love, sensitivity, and compassion through commitment, through understanding, through progress, and through leadership.[29] These qualities can be only enhanced as St. Anthony Medical Center enters the challenging era of the '90s and beyond.

ST. ANTHONY MEDICAL CENTER

[1]Crown Point is the county seat of Lake County, Indiana, and is located in central Lake County, approximately thirty-five miles southeast of Chicago and 150 miles northwest of Indianapolis. The city of Crown Point has an estimated population of 16,984.

[2]The need for comprehensive health services in the suburbs of Schaumburg and Downers Grove in Illinois was also studied before the decision to build in Crown Point was made. Both suburbs had indicated great interest in a medical complex.

[3]St. Anthony Hospital, "A Statement for the Case, 1970"; and "St. Anthony Hospital Brochure on Proposed Hospital, 1972" (AFSCL).

[4]At the First Extraordinary Chapter of Affairs, one of the immediate results of the chapter deliberations was the introduction of lay administrators into the congregation's schools and institutions.

[5]Report to the Second Special Chapter of Affairs by Sister M. Hugoline Czaplinski, superior general, 1974 (AFSCL).

[6]The firm is an international specialist in hospital construction.

[7]*Hammond Times*, 22 May 1972.

[8]*Book of Annual Assignments* (AFSCL).

[9]"From the Desk of Sister M. Hugoline," 26 February 1974 (AFSCL).

[10]*Book of Correspondence:* Letter from Sister M. Bernadette Bajuscik to author, 5 April 1988 (AFSCL).

[11]The management consulting firm was set up in 1978 in response to a growing demand for consultation services. The Alexian Brothers have been in the health care field since the Middle Ages. They celebrated their 650th anniversary in 1984.

[12]*Book of Correspondence:* Letter from Sister Joseph Marie Zenda, superior general, to author, 22 May 1988 (AFSCL).

[13]*St. Anthony Medical Center Annual Report, 1984* (AFSCL).

[14]*St. Anthony Medical Center Annual Report, 1983* (AFSCL).

[15]*St. Anthony Medical Center Annual Report, 1985* (AFSCL).

[16]*St. Anthony Medical Center Annual Report, 1985 and 1987* (AFSCL).

[17]St. Anthony Medical Center, "Pediatric Health Mecca for South Lake County," *Hammond Times*, 3 May 1985.

[18]*St. Anthony Medical Center Annual Report, 1985* (AFSCL).

[19]*St. Anthony Medical Center Annual Report, 1987* (AFSCL).

[20]See Chapter 49.

[21]See Chapter 51.

[22]See Chapter 49.

[23]They are all members of the Franciscan Fathers of the Assumption of the Blessed Virgin Mary Province of Pulaski, Wisconsin.

[24]Other department members are Sister M. Louise Nowicki, Sister M. Laetitia Kolczak, and Sister M. Amabilis Bellock who serve at St. Anthony Home.

[25]Sister M. Bernadette entered the Congregation of the Franciscan Sisters of Chicago on March 1, 1974 and professed her perpetual vows on June 10, 1976. She served as an elementary school teacher at Holy Trinity School, Gary, Indiana for nine years and at St. Louise de Marillac School in La Grange Park, Illinois, for seven years. In 1981, she was appointed director/assistant

administrator at Guardian Angel Day Care Center in Chicago and from 1983–1984, she served as administ. ator/director.

Sister M. Bernadette received a bachelor of science degree in elementary education from Calumet College, East Chicago, Indiana, in 1966, and a master of science degree from Indiana University Northwest, in Gary in 1974. In January of 1987, she received a master's degree in health administration from the Department of Hospital and Health Administration of St. Louis University, St. Louis. She is an associate member of the American College of Health Care Executives. *Congregation Membership Records* (AFSCL).

[26]St. Anthony Medical Center, *Patients' Handbook,* 1987.

[27]St. Anthony Medical Center, Office of Mission Effectiveness, 1985.

[28]*St. Anthony Medical Center Annual Report, 1987,* "Preface," by Sister Joseph Marie Zenda, superior general.

[29]*St. Anthony Medical Center Annual Report, 1984* (AFSCL).

CHAPTER 63

The Thirteenth General Chapter:
Sister Martha Joan Sempolski

The entire world mourned the loss of Pope Paul VI who died of a heart attack on August 6, 1978. The College of Cardinals, meeting in one of the largest and the shortest conclaves in history, chose as his successor, Albino Luciani, the Patriarch of Venice, who assumed the papacy on August 26 as Pope John Paul. After a span of only thirty-three days, the unbelievable occurred. By September 28, 1978, Pope John Paul, "the smiling pope," also was dead, a victim of a heart attack. On the second day of voting at the year's second conclave, history was made in the Roman Catholic Church with the election of the first non-Italian pope in 455 years, the first pope from a Communist nation, and the first Polish pope. He was Karol Wojtyla, since 1964 the cardinal-archbishop of Cracow in southern Poland. As the 263rd successor of St. Peter, he chose the name Pope John Paul II, keeping alive the names of his worthy predecessors. Amid unsuppressed jubilation over all the world, especially among the Poles, he assumed the papal office on October 22, 1978.[1]

While the entire Church greeted the new pontiff, the Franciscan Sisters of Chicago had additional cause for celebration. At the election session of the Thirteenth General Chapter held on Easter Monday, March 28, 1978, Sister Martha Joan Sempolski had been voted to the highest office in the congregation. She assumed her office as superior general at the convocation of the Thirteenth General Chapter of Elections on June 24, 1978. The Sisters chosen as members of the general council were Sister M. Antonissima Jamruk, re-elected to an unprecedented third term as assistant superior general; Sister M. Hugoline Czaplinski, who had just completed two terms as the superior general, elected first councilor; Sister M. Gabriel Lazarski, elected second councilor;[2] Sister M. Alvernia Groszek, re-elected secretary general for a third term and Sister M. Ralph Stawasz, also re-elected to a third term as treasurer general.

Sister Martha Joan Sempolski, the woman chosen to guide the congregation as its ninth superior general, was born in Kent, Ohio, on April 27, 1917. The daughter of Vincent and Stella (née Pilatowski) Sempolski, she spent her childhood and youth in Cleveland. She entered the congregation on January 31, 1931, from St. Casimir's Parish in Cleveland's once-famed *Poznań* district. Invested with the habit on August 15, 1932, she was given the name Sister M. Anatolia. Two years later, August 16, 1934, she made her first profession, and on August 16, 1938, she pronounced her perpetual vows.[3]

As a teacher, Sister Martha Joan was stationed at Five Holy Martyrs School in Chicago and St. John Cantius School in Indiana Harbor, Indiana, during which time she obtained her undergraduate degree at De Paul University. Sister Martha Joan was then sent to Mundelein College in Chicago to study dietetics. In 1947, upon completion of her apprenticeship as a dietitian at Good Samaritan Hospital in Cincinnati, Ohio, she was assigned to the congregation's newly built St. John Hospital and School of Nursing in Huron, South Dakota. She remained there for almost twenty-five years as director of the dietary department and instructor in the school of nursing. From 1969 to 1973, she also served as the religious superior. During this period, she reverted to her baptismal name. In 1973, she was assigned to St. Anthony Home in Crown Point, Indiana, where she served as administrative assistant.[4] Having been chosen as a delegate to the general chapter in 1978, she was elected by that body to the position of superior general for the newly established term of five years.

Lacking neither courage nor confidence in God, Sister Martha Joan assumed her duties as superior general with the qualities which, through the years of her religious life, had come to be associated with her: sincere humility, charming simplicity, deeply rooted piety, genuine concern and respect for each Sister, and Franciscan amiability. Distinguished by her tall stature and warm blue eyes, Sister Martha Joan possessed a benevolent expression which, at the same time, was indicative of firmness, conviction, and equanimity in facing the difficulties inseparable from her office.[5] A woman of prayer, she spared no effort to foster in the congregation the deep spirituality and dedication which she envisioned as necessary to maintain the integrity of religious life in the 1980s. She communicated this attitude in her personal contacts and visits with the Sisters and through the community newsletter which she wrote faithfully each month.[6] Warmly human, she took every occasion to exhort the Sisters to "preserve and strengthen the spirit of Mother M. Theresa Dudzik by fidelity to the vows, permanent commitment, selfless service, and loving concern for one another in Jesus through prayer and prayerful living."[7]

In their numerous deliberations at the Thirteenth General Chapter of Elections the Sister-delegates enacted decrees which dealt with spiritual, administrative, and community matters. While some of the decrees were new in origin, many were reaffirmations or restatements of decrees passed at the last chapter held in 1974.

Chief among the new decrees was the need to organize a committee to write the new Constitutions and Directory. Sister M. Antonissima Jamruk, the assistant general, and coordinator of the Thirteenth General Chapter was appointed to head the committee.[8]

One of the most significant and long-awaited decisions to emerge from the chapter was the adoption by the congregation of the restored and revised daily Liturgy of the Hours, the *Roman Franciscan Christian Book of Prayer.*[9] The delegates also stated that in all the homes of the congregation from the twelfth to the twentieth of each month, a petition for the intentions of the Mother M. Theresa Novena be presented during the recitation of the Liturgy of the Hours. In an effort to intensify the Sisters' continued spiritual growth, it was decided that a day of recollection be held each month. The time and type of program was to be determined by the individual mission home. The program could in some way creatively use spiritual discernment, dialogue, tapes, films, readings, slides, shared prayer, liturgical and paraliturgical services, and periods of silence.

The chapter delegates voted that the crest embossed on the cover of the booklet entitled *The Words of Mother M. Theresa Dudzik as Contained in the Chronicle of Mother M. Theresa* be accepted as the official emblem of the congregation. This emblem, executed artistically by Sister M. Sponsa Bajorek, is fully explained in Appendix C of this book.

Other changes occured in the formula for profession, now amended to read:

> I, Sister N. N., vow to you, Almighty God, poverty, chastity, and obedience (for one year; for all my life) according to the Rule of the Third Order Regular of St. Francis and the Constitutions of the congregation of the Franciscan Sisters of Chicago. I make my profession into the hands of Mother (N. N.), Superior General, and I entrust my vows to the Blessed Virgin Mary. I dedicate my life and seek to take my place in the Church, to build community in my congregation as well as among the People of God after the the spirit of St. Francis.

The formula for the devotional renewal of vows was also changed to read:

> On the solemn commemoration of the profession of St. Francis, April 16, and on the feast of the Immaculate Conception, December 8, and at the close of each yearly retreat, we shall make in common, a devotional renewal of vows:
>
> I, Sister N. N., renew my vows of poverty, chastity, and obedience to you, Almighty God, according to the Rule of the Third Order Regular of St. Francis and the Constitutions of the congregation of the Franciscan Sisters of Chicago. I entrust my vows to the Blessed Virgin Mary. I rededicate my life and seek to take my place in the Church, to build community in my congregation as well as among the People of God after the spirit of St. Francis.

There were several decrees which dealt with the administrative aspects of the congregation. In most cases they were amendments of the decrees of the Eleventh Chapter of Elections held in 1974 which remain in effect today:

> 1. That the election session of the general chapter take place on Easter Monday.The new administration would assume the duties of their office at the convocation of the general chapter in June.

2. That the term of the office of the superior general be five years. This office would be restricted to two consecutive terms.
3. That there be four general councilors to the superior general listed in the order of precedence:
   a. The first councilor would serve as assistant to the superior general.
   b. The second and third councilors would fulfill responsibilities delegated to them by the superior general.
   c. The fourth councilor would serve as the secretary general.
4. That the general councilors hold office until the next chapter. Re-election to the council for one additional consecutive term would be possible.
5. That the general treasurer be appointed by the superior general and her council and hold this position until the next chapter. Appointments for additional terms would follow.
6. That in discussions pertaining to the temporal administration, the treasurer general be called to the council meetings to furnish necessary documents and to give advice. She would not have active voice in matters voted upon by the general council.
7. That a handbook of procedures for implementing the method of nominating the superior general and councilors be prepared.
8. That in the area of formation, the following terms of office apply:
   a. Formation director: a four-year term with possible reappointment.
   b. Part-time members: a three-year term with possible reappointment.
   c. Ex-officio member of the administration: the assistant superior general.
   d. All the terms of office be restricted to two consecutive terms.[10]

Two other modifications, relating to the practice of poverty, emerged from the Thirteenth General Chapter and dealt with matters common only to the congregation. The first prescription designated which items the monthly budget would cover which included: clothing, personal items, stamps and stationery, personal books and periodicals, personal travel and recreation, long distance calls, and hobbies. The second prescription stipulated that each Sister would have an annual vacation not to exceed three weeks. A round trip fare to a resort, family home or another convent, plus $50.00 for incidentals would be paid by the congregation.

When the delegates to the Thirteenth General Chapter of Elections met in 1978, it had been almost twenty years since the Second Vatican Council had taken place. It had been ten years since the First Extraordinary Chapter of Affairs had been held, that strategic chapter which had ushered in an era of change and renewal in the congregation. It could not be denied that religious life had undergone a profound transition. Only time will be able to assess the developments and radical changes that revolutionized religious life in the post-Vatican period. One thing is certain. While participating in the renewal and adaptation recommended by the Second Vatican Council, the Franciscan Sisters of Chicago resolved at the Thirteenth General Chapter of 1978 to retain the habit as a sign of religious consecration, to emphasize communal worship, to share life in community, and to serve in their basic corporate apostolates. Their ongoing renewal and adaptation would always remain within the parameters of the Church and the charism of Mother M. Theresa Dudzik, their foundress.

The Constitutions of the congregation after the Second Vatican Council stated that while continuing to serve in traditional apostolates, the Sisters should be sensitive and open to the promptings of the Holy Spirit. Several Sisters in the congregation felt the urgency to respond to new ministries as these revealed themselves in the "signs of the times."

Among the members of society today who are most in need of service are the elderly, the disabled, the poor, the forgotten, and the lonely who are housebound. The main thrust of the new ministry of the Visitors Program to the elderly, sick, and poor is to provide companionship, love, support, and spiritual enrichment to such persons through personal contact. Indeed, the disabled, middle-aged, and senior citizens faced with losses of spouse, children, position, economic status, independence, and friendly neighbors because of a changing neighborhood may feel worthless, lonely, and depressed. Some parish churches, therefore, increasingly aware of the corporal and spiritual works of mercy which need to be met on the parish level, initiated the Community Parish Outreach Program. In 1978, Sister Martha Joan and her general council granted permission to Sister M. Mildred Bieda to begin such a program at St. Rose of Lima Parish on West 48th and Justine Streets on Chicago's Southwest Side.[11] She resided with the Sisters at the congregation's nearby Guardian Angel Day Care Center and Home for Ladies.

Sister M. Mildred's ministry encompassed a myriad of meaningful activities. She acted as extraordinary minister of the Holy Eucharist and head of the Parish Committee for the Anointing of the Sick. She dispensed home health care information and planned the admission of the ill to hospitals or nursing homes. Providing meals for the homebound from the parish food pantry—the congregation's Guardian Angel Day Care Center—or the "Meals on Wheels" project sponsored by the Chicago Nutrition Program for the Elderly was also part of her daily service. She arranged for the parish's Legion of Mary Organization to assist in transporting the homebound to clinics, to assist in shopping and in general visitation, and to accompany people to clinics when there was no family or friend to do so. Contacting lawyers for legal services, helping complete insurance forms, and informing home owners about such things as tax rebates were also part of her duties. Other services rendered by Sister M. Mildred were strictly personal in nature. Purchasing food and preparing meals at their homes, she established friendships with homebound persons, acting as interpreter for Polish-speaking parishioners and encouraging the homebound to join parish and local senior citizens' clubs. Sister M. Mildred's friendly and supportive visits were supplemented by telephone reassurances when home visits were not possible. Her apostolic service to the People of God was also concerned with the Maternity Hot Line, the Holy Cross Mission and its Al-Anon Program, the Illinois Public Aid Office in regard to food stamps, the Loop Family Services, and the Mayor's Office for Health and Home Care. In August of 1980, Jane Byrne, then the mayor of Chicago, sent a special congratulatory letter to Sister M. Mildred commending her outstanding contribution to the "Immunization in the Park" Program which provided vaccine for thousands of school children during the summer.[12]

The parishioners and the senior citizens' club members of St. Rose of Lima Parish were formally commissioned as Ministers of Praise by the pastor and his associates in 1984. Each person so commissioned received a cross of live wood from the Holy Land to be worn on the breast, and by the commissioning, to offer all prayers, joys, and sufferings for the salvation of souls. Each commissioned person also received a certificate and a book of prayers. Thus, the prayer ministry emerged as one of the most important activities of that parish.

The congregation was highly honored when on September 10, 1979, John Cardinal Cody, archbishop of Chicago, named the congregation's assistant superior general, Sister M. Antonissima Jamruk, the vicar delegate for women religious of the Archdiocese of Chicago. The gracious and grateful Cardinal Cody confirmed her appointment a few days later:

> I am very grateful to you for having consented to assist me in this very important part of archdiocesan administration and I am sure that our relationship in this apostolate will prove of great benefit to the parishes, the priests, and the religious who work so untiringly here in the Archdiocese of Chicago.[13]

In her new position, Sister M. Antonissima worked with the Reverend John E. Mulvihill, the cardinal's secretary for religious matters. The primary purpose of their joint roles was to be an ecclesial and pastoral presence to the religious in the archdiocese. Other facets of their office were to be supportive of the religious life in the archdiocese, to deal with crises and serious problems of religious, and to provide direction for religious in the local church.

With the coming of Joseph Cardinal Bernardin to the Archdiocese of Chicago in 1982, the Office for Religious Matters was reorganized. Sister M. Antonissima was asked to remain for the year 1984–1985 to act as consulting director for the Office for Religious Matters to allow maximum use of her expertise and insight so essential for the smooth functioning of the office. She remained until July 1, 1985. Earlier, in February, she had received a letter from Cardinal Bernardin in which he extended his deepest gratitude to her:

> Thank you for the wonderful contribution you have made to the Archdiocese of Chicago and especially to our religious during the past six years. You have brought a generous and committed spirit to this ministry. Just as you have given of yourself during this time, so also the Archdiocese has been enriched by your service.[14]

Another Franciscan Sister of Chicago who read the "sign of the times" resided at the Guardian Angel Day Care Center and was involved in direct service to the poor of the "Back of the Yards" neighborhood. Sister M. Claudiana Jachimowicz began her ministry to the poor at "The Port" in March of 1985. An inner city project, "The Port," which serviced the poor with a listening post, shelter, clothing, and a soup kitchen, took its name from *Portiuncula* meaning "Little Portion," the birthplace of the Franciscan Order in Italy.

The site of a former drug store at the corner of 51st Street and Ashland Avenue, "The Port" was a project of the Assumption Province of the Order of Friars Minor of Pulaski, Wisconsin, and was maintained by the Gospel Brothers of River Torto on South Justine Street. Directed by the Reverend Gus Milon, OFM, "The Port" was an outreach of the Franciscan Friars and a response to the Franciscan call to live the Gospel among the poor and to be of service to them—"to discover and touch Jesus in the distressing disguise of his poor."[15]

Sister M. Claudiana was directly involved with the poor by praying with them, listening to them, and counseling them spiritually. She coordinated activities such as crafts and games and was in charge of clothing distribution. When asked how she came to work at "The Port," Sister M. Claudiana was quick to reply: "Through the reading of Scripture, I felt called by the Lord. I believe the Lord had annointed me to work directly with the poor and to bring them the Good News."[16]

THE THIRTEENTH GENERAL CHAPTER:
SISTER MARTHA JOAN SEMPOLSKI

[1]The first Polish Pope was born Karol Wojtyla on May 18, 1920, in a town in southern Poland called Wadowice. He attended Cracow's Jagiellonian University where he was active in the theater group and wrote poetry. With the Nazi invasion of Poland at the start of World War II, Karol Wojtyla worked in a quarry and later as a chemical factory worker while secretly studying for the priesthood. He was ordained in 1946 and sent to Rome's Angelicum College where he earned a doctorate in philosophy. In the early years of his priesthood, he served on the faculties of the Catholic University of Lublin, the Jagiellonian University, and the University of Cracow. In 1958, he was made auxiliary bishop of Cracow and in 1964, he was named archbishop, the first residential head of the See since the death of Adam Cardinal Sapieha in 1951. He criticized the Communist government in Poland repeatedly and at the Second Vatican Council exhorted the leaders of the Church to champion the cause of religious liberty throughout the world. Pope Paul VI raised Archbishop Wojtyla to the College of Cardinals in 1967. Subsequently, Cardinal Wojtyla served actively in the Congregation for the Sacraments and Divine Worship, the Congregation for the Clergy, and the Congregation for Catholic Education. He was also a theological consultant to Pope Paul VI. The new Cardinal continued to win grudging but unavoidable concessions from the Communist government in his native Poland.

It was a man with this kind of spirit whom the College of Cardinals chose to become Pope in the election following the sudden death of Pope John Paul I. In his first year as pope, John Paul II wrote an encyclical, *Redemptor Homini* [The Redeemer of Man], criticizing totalitarian governments, the arms race, and the consumer society. This remarkable pope has created a new kind of papacy. He swims, skis, canoes, hikes, dances, holds campfire meetings, and joins in songfests. His faith and spirit appear indefatigable. In a most dastardly incident, an attempt was made on the life of Pope John Paul II on May 13, 1981, in St. Peter's Square by an alleged Turkish terrorist, Mehemet Ali Agca. By late June, the pope appeared to be thoroughly recovered. *Catholic Almanac, 1980;* and Felician A. Foy, OFM, ed., *Our Sunday Visitor,* October, 1975.

[2]In the previous administration, Sister M. Gabriel had served as the coordinator of community apostolates.

[3]*Spis Sióstr* (AFSCL).

[4]*Book of Annual Assignments* (AFSCL).

[5]*Interviews* with Sisters, 1980 (AFSCL).

[6]Sister Martha Joan, the superior general, continued to use the personal newsletter, "From the Desk of . . . " to communicate with the Sisters on a monthly basis. The traditional *Franciscan Echo* was published at Christmas and Easter only. To inform the Sisters of general community happenings, a publication aptly entitled, *Franciscan Brief,* edited by the secretary general, Sister M. Alvernia Groszek, was initiated and appeared monthly.

[7]*Community Newsletter,* No. 1, July 1978 (AFSCL).

[8]See Appendix A.

[9]The *Roman Franciscan Christian Book of Prayer* replaced the American Interim Breviary, the *Prayer of Christians.*

[10]*Minutes of General Chapter Proceedings, 1978* (AFSCL).

[11]St. Rose of Lima Parish was founded in 1881 on the South Side of Chicago to serve the Irish families who lived west of the Union Stock Yards in the Town of Lake area. By 1896, the parish numbered 700 families. As the number of families in the parish declined through the years, St. Rose of Lima School was closed in June of 1971 when the Sisters of Mercy withdrew. Reverend Monsignor Harry C. Koenig, ed., *A History of the Archdiocese of Chicago: Published in Observance of the Centenary of the Archdiocese, 1980,* 2 vols. (Chicago: The Archdiocese of Chicago, 1980) 1:153–157.

[12]*Franciscan Brief,* Vol. 3, Lemont, Illinois August 1980 (AFSCL).

[13]*Book of Correspondence:* Letter from John Cardinal Cody to Sister M. Antonissima Jamruk, 17

September 1970 (AFSCL).

[14]*Book of Correspondence:* Letter from Joseph Cardinal Bernardin to Sister M. Antonissima Jamruk, 2 November 1985 (AFSCL).

[15]Reverend Augustin Milon, OFM, ed., "The Port-Pourri," (Chicago: The Franciscan Friars, Assumption of the Blessed Virgin Mary Province, Gospel Brothers, February 1985), p. 1.

[16]*Book of Correspondence:* Letter from Sister M. Claudiana Jachimowicz to author, 22 September 1985 (AFSCL).

CHAPTER 64

Challenge and Response

The world watched with wonder in the fall of 1979 as Pope John Paul II, the "traveling Pope," took major excursions outside the walls of Vatican City during the first twelve months of his pontificate. His travels took him to Mexico, Poland, Ireland, and to the great delight of millions of Americans, to the United States. The Pontiff met with people in the great cities of Boston, Philadelphia, Des Moines, and Washington, DC. In addition, he went to New York to proclaim the message of Christ's peace to the United Nations before the General Assembly.[1]

On October 4, 1979, the TWA airship, appropriately named Shepherd I, brought to Chicago the Supreme Pontiff—the first pope ever to visit the Windy City. Here he was engaged in an almost nonstop program of activities. The Holy Father was greeted warmly by Chicago's Spanish-speaking residents of the Pilsen area at the Providence of God Church. He traveled to Quigley Preparatory Seminary on Chicago's Southwest Side where he met with more than 350 bishops from every state in the union. During his stay in Chicago, Pope John Paul II attended a ceremony of prayer and welcome at Holy Name Cathedral. The greatest spectacle of his trip, Chicagoans agreed, was the Eucharistic Liturgy he offered on the greenery of Grant Park near Lake Michigan before an enthusiastic crowd estimated at 1.5 million people.

For thousands of Poles, however, the highlight of the papal visit to Chicago was the Polish-language Liturgy of the Eucharist which the Holy Father offered for more than 200,000 pilgrims at Five Holy Martyrs Church at Richmond and 43rd Streets on Chicago's Southwest Side. The Holy Father had previously visited the parish twice as Karol Wojtyla, archbishop of Cracow—in 1969 and again in 1976—as the guest of the Most Reverend Alfred L. Abramowicz, auxiliary bishop of Chicago, the pastor of Five Holy Martyrs Church. These visits especially delighted the Franciscan Sisters of Chicago, who, since 1912, have staffed the elementary school.[2]

The visit of Pope John Paul II to the United States in 1979 proved to be a most fitting climax to the era of the 1970s. With the advent of the 1980s, the Franciscan Sisters of Chicago again welcomed the change and movement in the Church which thrust their congregation into renewed life and called forth a celebration of Franciscan mission.

In the years following the Second Vatican Council, the Franciscan Sisters of Chicago had a dream which they believed would enhance their spirituality. Ever since the First Extraordinary Chapter of Affairs held in 1968, there had been proposals submitted by the Sisters at subsequent general chapters regarding the establishment of a Community House of Prayer. A house of prayer, a lifestyle within the framework of the Constitutions and the Directory of the Franciscan Sisters of Chicago, would have as its purpose "to serve as a center of spirituality and renewal for the congregation thus witnessing to the primacy of prayer in every Christian life."[3] Many of the Sisters felt themselves called to a life of more intense prayer, while others, having experienced the pressures and tensions of twentieth century religious witness, indicated a need to revitalize their interior life by temporary residence in such a house. Having considered the evident needs of the Sisters and realizing that a house of prayer would be a source of countless blessings upon the entire congregation, a general chapter committee in 1978 recommended that concrete plans be formulated for the establishment of a house of prayer. The general chapter passed a decree to the effect that Sisters who were interested in becoming core members of a house of prayer make known their desire to the superior general. It was hoped that this core group would eventually form a liturgical and loving union which would witness to contemplative values.

The dream of establishing a Franciscan house of prayer became a reality in August of 1980, when the Sisters took up residence there. The St. Francis House of Prayer, as it had been named by the vote of the congregation, officially opened in a separate house on the grounds of Our Lady of Victory Convent, the General Motherhouse of the Franciscan Sisters of Chicago in Lemont, Illinois. The private house had served previously as a home for the chief custodian of the Motherhouse and his family and was now remodeled to serve its new purpose. All the furnishings for the house of prayer had been secured from the Motherhouse as well as from the recently closed St. John Regional Medical Center in Huron, South Dakota.

On August 12, 1980, the Very Reverend John W. Curran, the urban vicar of Region XI, as the delegate of John Cardinal Cody, blessed the house of prayer. On August 20, the official opening day of the St. Francis House of Prayer, the Liturgy of the Eucharist was celebrated in the Sacred Heart Chapel at the Motherhouse in thanksgiving for the establishment of the house of prayer and in petition for the blessing of Divine Providence upon its three core members: Sister M. Francine Labus, the superior; Sister Ann Rose Mroz, and Sister M. Tarcisia Bucki. At three o'clock in the afternoon of the same day, a scriptural prayer service was held in the new chapel in thanksgiving for this ministry which now more thoroughly integrated the contemplative and apostolic dimensions of the Sisters' lives. Four days later, on August 24, the Reverend Richard Hart, OFM, director of preachers for the Capuchin Province of St. Joseph in Milwaukee, Wisconsin, celebrated the Sacred Liturgy for the first time in the little chapel of the house of prayer.

The ministry of the three core members was twofold. Firstly, the Sisters believed

St. Francis House of Prayer
Lemont, Illinois (1980–   )

that this center of prayer, contemplation, and theological renewal genuinely supported the active ministries of the congregation. Secondly, the house of prayer provided an atmosphere of peace, prayer, and hospitality for all those Sisters who came to spend some time there. Here the individual Sister could deepen and revivify her spiritual life through extended prayer experiences, directed or private retreats, days of recollections or ongoing spiritual direction and return renewed to the active life. It was hoped that in the future, religious of other congregations, priests, brothers, and laity would be welcomed with Franciscan hospitality for periods of prayer and spiritual renewal.

The general goals and objectives of the house of prayer indicated the manner in which this twofold ministry was carried out by its core members. The Sisters aimed at developing a deeper, personal relationship with God through prayer, silence, solitude, and penance. They prayed for the needs of the Church, of the congregation, and of the world. Their lifestyle was simple. Because the ministry of prayer was primary in their lives, involvement in other areas was understandably limited. Nevertheless, some areas of service in which they engaged included teaching religious education classes, serving as lectors at the Liturgy of the Eucharist, acting as extraordinary ministers of the Eucharist, and conducting prayer groups at the Motherhouse. The members of the house of prayer also visited and prayed with the Sisters in the Motherhouse infirmary, prepared liturgies and paraliturgies, days of recollection, and offered spiritual counseling to those who requested it. The Sisters earned stipends by directing retreats outside the house of prayer, by sewing, and by accepting speaking engagements relative to the spiritual life.[4]

In 1982, Sister Rose Ann returned to the active ministry. Her place in the St. Francis House of Prayer was taken by Sister M. Bertille Geffert. A year later, Sister M.

Francine was elected fourth councilor and secretary general, and Sister M. Tarcisia was assigned to the infirmary of the Motherhouse as the chief pharmacist. From 1983 to 1985, Sister Martha Joan Sempolski, the former superior general, and Sister M. Cundette Minchuk, who withdrew from the field of teaching for a year, took up residence in the house of prayer. Today, the St. Francis House of Prayer continues to echo gently the simple invitation of Jesus to souls: "Come apart with me to an out-of-the-way place and rest awhile." The affirmative answers to the invitation on the part of Sisters, priests, and the laity continue to make this ministry a very fruitful and rewarding one.

By 1980, the second four-year term of Sister Emilie Marie Lesniak, the director of formation, had come to an end. Sister Martha Joan and her councilors, therefore, announced the appointment of Sister M. Francis Clare Radke as her successor.

Born in Chicago and a parishioner of St. Pancratius Church on Chicago's Southwest Side, Sister M. Francis Clare entered the congregation on August 27, 1961. Her novitiate began on August 11, 1962; she professed her first vows on August 12, 1964, and made her perpetual vows on August 12, 1969. Her juniorate was spent at the Motherhouse in Lemont, Illinois. A graduate of Loyola University of Chicago with a bachelor's and a master's degree, Sister M. Francis Clare joined the staff of Five Holy Martyrs School in 1965 where she remained for fifteen years. During that time she also served as the religious superior for three years.[5]

Zealous about the external works of the congregation and the spiritual dimensions of its members, Sister M. Francis Clare proved an exemplary person for the position of formation director. She possessed a natural gentility and gracious tact. Her keen awareness of the essentials of religious life helped her to achieve a balance and unity in her own life which was readily apparent to all and served as an inspiration to others, especially those in formation. She served with genuine sensitivity and efficiency until her election as assistant general in 1983.[6]

In answer to the needs of God's people, the congregation opened the doors of the Motherhouse in 1981 to a most significant enrichment program called "Marriage Encounter" offered to married couples.

The Office for Marriage and Family Life had been established in the Archdiocese of Chicago in 1974 as one of the main ministries within the framework and support of the Office of the Laity. The purpose of the Office for Marriage and Family Life was to coordinate the ministries, agencies, and movements that serve the couples and families of the Church of Chicago. The Marriage Encounter Program, aimed at the couples' enrichment and growth, was such a movement.[7]

In February of 1981, Sister M. Agnes Zywiec, the superior of the Motherhouse, was asked by the Marriage Encounter Group for use of the facilities of the Motherhouse to hold Marriage Encounter weekends. With the approval of Sister Martha Joan and the general council, the Marriage Encounter group and later, the Engaged Couples group, regularly held their meetings at the Our Lady of Victory Convent Motherhouse beginning with March 8, 1981. In that year alone, seven Marriage Encounter and thirteen Engaged Couples Encounter weekends were hosted. Sister Martha Joan encouraged the Sisters both at the Motherhouse and outside it to volunteer their services during these special weekends. Among the Sisters who eagerly donated their efforts were Sister Marianne Kaplan, Sister M. Petronia Budzinski, Sister M. Roberta Duda, Sister Victoria Valerie Smagacz, Sister M. Crescentine Oszuscik, and Sister M. Innocent Smagacz.[8] Many of the Sisters stationed at the Motherhouse throughout the year also extended their services to help make the Encounter Programs a success.

The participants of the Weekend Encounters attested to the success of the programs and the kindness of the Sisters:

Dear Sisters,

Your warmth and kindness have enriched our experience more than you could possibly realize. Being here has created a total feeling of peace and love that we feel we couldn't have captured in any other atmosphere. Your smiling faces have filled us with joy.

Thank you.

Gail and Jim Quinn[9]

Another group wrote:

Dearest Sisters:

We would like to thank you and all the beautiful Sisters who really made us feel at home. Your love and caring for us really put us at ease. Not only did you open your home to us, but you opened your hearts, and words are inadequate to express our appreciation and love for you. You will always be in our prayers, and we won't forget you, because you touched our hearts. Thank you for your prayers. We will tell the couples that you will be praying for them. We love you.

Tom and Lauretta Murphy
Mike and Aggie Weber
Bob and Sue Tapp
Fr. Tom Cleary and all the
couples and priests[10]

When the Franciscan Sisters of Chicago had settled in Lemont, Illinois, in 1926, they had been ministered to spiritually by the Franciscan Fathers of the Custody of the Holy Cross of Lemont. In 1981, the general council determined to name a resident pastoral director for the congregation. As a consequence, the Reverend Louis Fronczak, OFM, assumed this responsibility in January of that year. His appointment was confirmed by John Cardinal Cody and the Reverend Theodore Zaremba, OFM, minister provincial of the Province of the Assumption of the Blessed Virgin Mary of Pulaski, Wisconsin.

As pastoral director, Father Fronczak had many duties, chief among them being the daily celebration of the Liturgy of the Eucharist and the weekly Sacrament of Reconciliation. He acted as consultant for the St. Francis House of Prayer and directed retreats, study days, and days of recollection for the Sisters in the congregation. Father Fronczak also acted as instructor to the Sisters in formation. When he was transferred in 1984, the Reverend Reginald Maslinski, OFM, succeeded him as chaplain.

In a spirit of praise and thanksgiving to God for the Gift of St. Francis of Assisi to the Church and to the world, more than two hundred Franciscan Sisters of Chicago gathered at the Motherhouse on the weekend of April 16, 17, and 18 of 1982, for a grand celebration of his birthday. Earlier, in 1980, a year of prayer and renewal for all members of the Franciscan Order had been announced to prepare for the commemoration of the 800th anniversary of the birth of the Poverello of Assisi. Now, two years later, the Sisters came to the Motherhouse from Chicago and La Grange Park, Illinois; Crown Point and Gary, Indiana; Cleveland and Parma, Ohio; and Johnstown, Pennsylvania; at the invitation of Sister Martha Joan, who in February had written to the Sisters:

> Let us assemble to listen to the wisdom of our elder Sisters and to the dreams of our young . . . let us join to rekindle the fire of Christ within us . . . to deepen our Franciscan unity, surface our visions, and encourage new beginnings. Let us tell each other about our ministries, our endeavors, and our dreams for the future . . . believing in the innate goodness, truth, and beauty of each Sister . . . with the firm conviction that the Spirit is the unifying principle who will lead us forth.[11]

The Franciscan Weekend celebration opened on Friday evening, April 16, with a welcome address by Sister Martha Joan who reminded the Sisters of the theme of the assembly based on the words of St. Francis: "I have done my part; may Christ teach you yours." She was followed by the assistant general, Sister M. Antonissima Jamruk, who spoke on the topic of "Renewal in the Congregation." An update on the cause for the Beatification of the congregation's foundress, the Servant of God, Mother M. Theresa Dudzik, was presented by Sister M. Alvernia Groszek, the secretary general.

On Saturday, April 17, the meeting featured papers delivered by individual Sisters concerning the histories, present status, and future plans of the congregation's ministries. The papers were considered in the light of the Sisters' response to their old and new ministries based on the spirit of St. Francis and Mother M. Theresa Dudzik.

The Eucharistic Liturgies and paraliturgical services with the Reverend Louis

Fronczak, OFM, as celebrant were the highlights of the Franciscan weekend. Saturday's Eucharistic Liturgy, "The Witness of Our Message," included the offering of symbols of each mission and ministry during the presentation of the gifts at the altar. On the same day, a healing service for the "Suffering Church" was held for all the sick and infirm Sisters of the congregation and for those Sisters desiring to be anointed. The Eucharistic Liturgy on Sunday, April 18, "Show Forth the Fruits of Conversion," concluded with the Sisters' devotional renewal of vows. An impressive memorial service for the congregation's 241 deceased members was celebrated on Sunday afternoon in the Sacred Heart Chapel and concluded at the congregation's cemetery on the Motherhouse grounds.

The three-day celebration included such special projects as a shadow skit on the life of St. Francis and an extensive exhibit of the congregation's history as captured in cherished photographs. Several Sisters created special Franciscan banners which stood in the sanctuary of the chapel. An antependium relating to the life of St. Francis graced the main altar. Each day's celebration ended with refreshments and recreation in the social hall of Our Lady of Victory Convent.

A departure service in the Sacred Heart Chapel on Sunday ended with the distribution of relics of the Servant of God, Mother M. Theresa Dudzik. The Sisters left the Motherhouse in the late afternoon inspired by Sister Martha Joan's parting words: "Remember, Sisters, that your gifts and your uniqueness are for the service of the Church."

In conjunction with the celebration of the Eighth Centenary of St. Francis' Birth, each Sister received a Community Memorial Book entitled, *I Have Done My Part: May Christ Teach You Yours,* compiled and edited by Sister M. Jude Kruszewski. Each Sister also received a *Community Heritage Book* compiled and edited by Sister Lora Ann Slawinski. In addition, nine Sisters who comprised a musical group presented their new album, "A New Kind of Freedom," containing original songs and music. Sister M. Gabriel, a member of the general council, was the chairperson for this memorable weekend, the first such event in the history of the congregation.

CHALLENGE AND RESPONSE

[1]*The Pope in Chicago, A Commemorative Album* (Chicago: Follett Publishing Co., 1979), no pagination.

[2]*Pilgrim Among Us,* Catholic League for Religious Assistance to Poland (Chicago: 1979), no pagination.

[3]*My God and My All: Constitutions and Directory of the Franciscan Sisters of Chicago* (Lemont, Illinois, 1982) Art. 29, p. 54.

[4]"St. Francis House of Prayer: General Goals and Objectives": Lemont, Illinois, 1981 (Mimeographed).

[5]*Congregation Membership Records* (AFSCL).

[6]*Interviews* with Sisters, 1986 (AFSCL).

[7]Rev. Msgr. Harry C. Koenig, STD, ed. *Caritas Christi Urget Nos: A History of the Offices, Agencies, and Institutions of the Archdiocese of Chicago,* 2 vols. (Chicago: New World Publishing Company, 1981).

[8]"From the Desk of Sister Martha Joan Sempolski," (August 1981) p. 5.

[9]Ibid.

[10]Ibid.

[11]*Book of Correspondence:* Letter from Sister Martha Joan Sempolski to the Sisters, February 1982 (AFSCL).

CHAPTER 65

Further Ministerial Witness

The Franciscan Sisters of Chicago began their ministry to the residents of Crown Point, Indiana, in 1939, when they first opened St. Anthony's Home with nineteen aged residents. In 1966, a new structure was built to accommodate the many elderly men and women who sought admission. In a bold and creative apostolic move in 1974, the congregation constructed St. Anthony Hospital (now St. Anthony Medical Center) adjacent to the new St. Anthony Home. By the spring of 1982, the Sisters presented an additional ministry to the people of the Crown Point community. After prudent deliberation, the Sisters opened the Holy Family Child Care Center, a developmental care center designed to provide educational and child-related services to the children of the physicians, employees, and volunteers of St. Anthony Medical Center and St. Anthony Home. As enrollment allowed, other children of the Crown Point and South Lake community would be welcomed as well.

The formal groundbreaking ceremony for the Holy Family Child Care Center was held on June 27, 1980, at two o'clock in the afternoon. The actual construction of the child care facility involved two distinct buildings on the grounds bordered by Main Street, Franciscan Road, 125th Street, and Court Street. The main building was the old two-story structure which had been purchased by the Sisters in 1939 for use as a home for the aged and called St. Anthony's Home.[1] For over twenty-seven years, the needs of the elderly were met in that home until it became necessary to construct a larger and more serviceable facility. In 1966 a new St. Anthony Home rose on an adjacent piece of property. After that year, the old facility served as living quarters for the Sisters who staffed the new St. Anthony Home, and, later, as a temporary convent for the Sisters who came to Crown Point to staff the new St. Anthony Medical Center. In 1974, the old St. Anthony's Home resumed its place as a health care center where a staff dealt with the medical needs of children and where professional counselors were available to aid unwed mothers. The old St. Anthony's Home provided these services until 1979. When the decision was made to convert the home into the Holy Family Child Care Center, the venerable white house was thoroughly renovated. The extensive addition to the Holy Family Child Care Center was designed to complement and enhance the original style of the old white house,[2] while at the same time incorporating the most modern features available for a child care facility. The firm of Leo A. Daly of St. Louis, Missouri, designed the new complex which was built by the Calumet Construction Company of Indiana.

The Holy Family Child Care Center was dedicated on April 24, 1982. The Liturgy of the Eucharist was celebrated in the chapel of St. Anthony Home by the Most Reverend Andrew G. Grutka, bishop of Gary, with the Reverend Myron Lowisz, OFM, and the Reverend Anthony Janik, OFM, members of the Department of Pastoral Care as co-celebrants. A cocktail reception and brunch was held in the Mother Theresa Pavilion of St. Anthony Home during which Bishop Grutka delivered the invocation and blessed the facility. The keynote address was delivered by the president of the medical staff at St. Anthony Medical Center, Felipe S. Chua, MD, who congratulated the Sisters "on the establishment of the Holy Family Child Care Center in this 'decade of the family' thus making additional facilities available for extended services to the family."[3] The Honorable Richard C. Collins, mayor of Crown Point, and Sister Martha Joan Sempolski, superior general of the Franciscan Sisters of Chicago, delivered brief addresses. The final Benediction was rendered by the Reverend John Starr, minister of the First Christian Church of Crown Point. Tours were conducted throughout the new facility, and at their conclusion, a cake-cutting ceremony took place in the lobby of the Holy Family Child Care Center.

On May 3, 1982, the beautiful and modern facility was opened and occupied by 150 children under the direction of Miss Iole M. Vellutini. In September of 1983, Sister M. Christine Brzozowski was named the new director. Using the most modern concepts, the Holy Family Child Care Center provides for the South Lake community of Crown Point a facility uniquely designed to meet the needs of the changing times and an administration and staff devoted to providing superior child care services.

The Holy Family Child Care Center was designed and equipped to meet the needs of children from infancy through five years of age. Children participate in a program that is supervised by qualified instructors who meet the stringent educational standards required by the State of Indiana. With a genuine commitment on the part of the administration and staff, the program provides an extremely suitable structured educational and recreational environment. In conjunction with St. Anthony Medical Center, each child is given speech, hearing, and vision tests.[4]

Because one of the major goals of the Holy Family Child Care Center is the spiritual care and well-being of the child, the Franciscan Sisters of Chicago are actively involved in fulfilling this dimension and goal. The Sisters who minister at the center arrange religious services for the children on appropriate occasions. They also teach Bible stories, religious songs, and prayers. Among those who have contributed immeasurably to the children's growth in this area are Sister M. Purissima Babinski, Sister M. Julianne Markowicz, and Sister M. Edwinette Wisz.

All the rooms at the Holy Family Child Care Center are very attractive, extremely

Holy Family Child Care Center
Crown Point, Indiana (1980–   )

colorful, and most modernly equipped. The first floor of the center contains rooms for infants, toddlers, and two and three-year-olds. The second floor makes provision for the children who are four and five years old while the third floor contains offices and a conference room. On any given day, the number of children at the child care center can rise to 128.

The Holy Family Child Care Center has successfully achieved its goal of being a true "home away from home" providing the child with loving care, sound moral teaching, and an enriching educational experience. The beautiful statue of the Holy Family which graces the lawn directly in front of the center is a symbol of the purpose and devotion inside the lovely facility itself.

In the last year of her term of office as superior general, Sister Martha Joan received an invitation from the Reverend Ronald Bajorski, regional superintendent of Catholic schools in Ohio, to staff St. Anthony of Padua School in Parma. For the first time in the history of the congregation, Sister Martha Joan and her councilors invited the community-at-large to aid in the decision making.[5] With solid affirmation, the Sisters favored accepting the staffing of the school which, quite incidentally, was located directly across the street from Mount Alverna Home where the Franciscan Sisters of Chicago have ministered since 1952—a fact which, no doubt, contributed to the affirmative action.

St. Anthony of Padua Church in Parma, Ohio, was one of five parishes in metropolitan Cleveland and its suburbs staffed by the Franciscan Fathers of the Sacred Heart Province of St. Louis, Missouri. Erected canonically by the Most Reverend Edward F. Hoban, archbishop-bishop of Cleveland, on June 4, 1959, it had as its founding pastor the Reverend Jeremy Fischer. The property assigned to the new parish at that time was occupied by two private residences and the Holy Family Cancer Home conducted by the Congregation of the Third Order of St. Dominic of St. Rose of Lima (the Servants of Relief for Incurable Cancer). When the hospital which the Dominican Sisters were in the process of building for the cancer patients was completed and the patients were transferred to the new hospital across State Road, Father Fischer moved into the home which the Dominican Sisters had vacated in July of 1959.[6]

In order to provide a temporary church and a meeting place for the members of the new St. Anthony of Padua Parish, the Right Reverend Monsignor Frederic Mohan, director of diocesan charities, offered the facilities of Parmadale to the pastor.[7] Eventually, the men of the parish remodeled the old cancer home and the building was named "St. Anthony Hall." To enable more parishioners to participate in daily mass, the men built a chapel in St. Anthony Hall and called it the "Chapel on the Hill." The Holy Sacrifice of the Mass was offered there for the first time on December 21, 1959.[8] In the meantime, the children attended St. Francis de Sales School, and Confraternity of Christian Doctrine classes were conducted by the Congregation of the Sisters of Charity of St. Augustine at Parmadale.

St. Anthony of Padua School
Parma, Ohio (1983–   )

The building of the parish school-gym was so advanced by January of 1961, that it soon became the temporary church. The school, a one-story structure of contemporary design containing twenty-six classrooms, was also completed that year. On September 6, classes for 806 pupils began in sixteen classrooms with six Sisters of the Congregation of St. Joseph of Rocky River Drive and ten lay teachers on the staff.[9]

In the spring of 1961, the former cancer home was remodeled into a convent for the Sisters of St. Joseph. By 1963, more classrooms were opened in the school-gym making a total of twenty with 992 students enrolled and nine Sisters and eleven lay teachers. By 1966, there were 1,145 children in the school. The number of Sisters on the staff increased to ten, and larger convent facilities were needed. On April 6, ground-breaking ceremonies for the new convent were held and construction began in earnest. In August of 1966, the Reverend William Barnickel, who had been an assistant in the parish since its foundation, was appointed the new pastor. Under his direction, the convent was completed during the summer of 1967. The first floor of the Sisters' residence, built to house twenty-two Sisters, was of yellow brick; the second floor was finished in wood. The Sisters moved into their new home on August 12, 1967.[10] In June of 1968, Father Barnickel resigned his pastorate and was succeeded by the Reverend Donulus Wunderlich.

In the years that followed, the number of Sisters of St. Joseph assigned to St. Anthony's School was gradually reduced to three. Early in June of 1972, a decision was made to have the priests move into the Sisters' convent; the Sisters, on the other hand, were to move into the residence that had served as the rectory since the foundation of the parish. In 1973, a lay principal was appointed because of the dwindling number of Sister personnel. Finally, with only one Sister left on the staff in 1976, the Sisters of St. Joseph withdrew from the parish permanently.[11] Unwilling to leave the school without any Sisters on the staff, Father Wunderlich invited the Sisters of the Congregation of the Resurrection from Chicago to take charge. In September in 1976, the Sisters of the Resurrection began their ministry at the school with a total of 579 students.[12] In addition to the three Resurrectionist Sisters, there were two Sisters of the Congregation of St. Joseph and one Sister of the Congregation of St. Joseph of the Third Order of St. Francis on the staff. At the end of the 1981–1982 school year, there were 588 pupils with three Sisters of the Resurrection and eighteen lay teachers. Soon, however, because of the shortage of Sister-personnel, the Resurrectionist Sisters were forced to decrease the number of their ministries, and in 1983, they withdrew from St. Anthony's School. It was then that the diocesan superintendent, Father Bajorski, appealed to the Franciscan Sisters of Chicago to staff the school.

On July 5, 1983, three Franciscan Sisters of Chicago took up residence at St. Anthony of Padua Convent. They were Sister M. Josetta Kuczmarski, superior and teacher of grade five; Sister Elizabeth Marie Jadrych, teacher of grade three; and Sister M. Symphorosa Goryszewski, assigned to household duties. The Reverend Dolard Paulus, OFM, the pastor, and the parishioners of St. Anthony of Padua Church welcomed the Franciscan Sisters of Chicago warmly and enthusiastically. The Sacred Liturgy was

St. Anthony of Padua Convent
Parma, Ohio

celebrated in the convent chapel by the Reverend John McManamon, OFM, to ask God's blessing upon the Sisters and their new venture. In August of 1983, Sister M. Josetta and Sister Elizabeth Marie were reassigned to St. Anthony's School with Sister M. Pulcheria Mikolajczyk who lived with them but continued her ministry at Mount Alverna Home. When the Sisters had arrived in 1983 to staff St. Anthony's School, they moved into the old convent located on the grounds where the new church was scheduled to be built. When the construction of the new church was undertaken, another house at 6834 State Road was acquired for the Sisters. They moved into their convent on May 26, 1984, and their former convent residence was razed shortly thereafter.[13] With the beginning of the new school year in 1984, Sister M. Agnella Sieja was a welcome addition to the staff.

Today, there are approximately three Sisters and nineteen lay teachers at St. Anthony of Padua School with a total of 545 pupils in this stable and vibrant parish in Parma, Ohio.

FURTHER MINISTERIAL WITNESS

[1] For a more detailed history of this building, see Chapter 40.

[2] Because of the architectural significance of the old white house and its place in the cultural history of Crown Point, it was nominated for placement on the National Register of Historical Places. Sharon M. Clawson, *Holy Family Child Care Center: Dedication Book* (Crown Point, Indiana, 1982), no pagination.

[3] Ibid.

[4] *Book of Correspondence:* Letter from Sister M. Christine Brzozowski to author, 9 September 1985. (AFSCL).

[5] *Book of Correspondence:* Letter from Sister Martha Joan Sempolski to Sisters, 22 December 1982 (AFSCL).

[6] Diocese of Cleveland, Chancery Office, "Parishes in Ohio," p. 19.

[7] Parmadale, an orphanage of approximately 180 acres consisting of cottages for the care of orphaned and dependent children, is located in Parma. Parmadale has been operated by the Congregation of the Sisters of Charity of St. Augustine since 1947.

[8] "Parishes in Ohio," p. 20.

[9] Sisters of the Congregation of St. Joseph of Rocky River Drive, "Minutes of Council Meeting," 12 February 1961, Archives, St. Joseph Convent, Cleveland, Ohio.

[10] "Parishes in Ohio," p. 21.

[11] Ibid., p. 22.

[12] *Book of Correspondence:* Letter from Sister M. Monica, provincial secretary, Sisters of the Resurrection, Chicago, Illinois, to author, 22 September 1983 (AFSCL).

[13] *Book of Correspondence:* Letter from Sister M. Francine Labus to author, August 1985.

CHAPTER 66

The Fourteenth General Chapter:
Sister Joseph Marie Zenda

On Easter Monday, April 4, 1983, the Most Reverend Alfred L. Abramowicz, auxiliary bishop of Chicago, acting in place of the ordinary of the archdiocese, Joseph Cardinal Bernardin, celebrated the Mass of the Holy Spirit at ten-thirty o'clock in the Sacred Heart Chapel at the Motherhouse of the Franciscan Sisters of Chicago in Lemont, Illinois, where thirty delegates were assembled for the election session of the congregation's Fourteenth General Chapter of Elections.[1] Bishop Abramowicz was assisted by the Reverend John Mulvihill, vicar for religious of the Archdiocese of Chicago, and the Reverend Louis Fronczak, pastoral director of the congregation. At the conclusion of the Liturgy of the Eucharist, Bishop Abramowicz and Father Mulvihill met in the community room with the chapter delegates, and the Fourteenth General Chapter of Elections was called to order. The delegates proceeded to the matter of selecting the superior general who would lead the congregation for the next five years. Elected the superior general was Sister Joseph Marie Zenda, the principal of Madonna High School. Sister M. Francis Clare Radke, the director of formation, was elected assistant general and first councilor. Sister M. Alvernia Groszek, who had held the office of secretary general for thirteen years, was elected second councilor. Sister M. Hugoline Czaplinski, who had served as the first councilor in the former administration, was now elected the third councilor. Sister M. Francine Labus, the superior of the St. Francis House of Prayer, was elected fourth councilor and secretary general. Sister M. Ralph continued as treasurer general, an appointed office.[2]

The election of Sister Joseph Marie came as no surprise to most of the members of the congregation. Having distinguished herself as Madonna High School's zealous and clear-sighted principal for thirteen years and as a prudent and faith-filled superior for six, her name and her excellent qualifications were known to almost every Sister. Endowed with a pleasant personality and abiding spirituality, she proved circumspect, just, and industrious in all her dealings and endeavors.[3]

Sister Joseph Marie, the former Loretta Zenda, was born in Cleveland, Ohio. The daughter of Harry and Sophie (née Stefanski) Zenda, she entered the congregation from Sacred Heart of Jesus Church on the Southwest Side of that city. Her postulancy began on

Sister Joseph Marie Zenda
Tenth Superior General
1983–1988
1988–

February 2, 1956, and her novitiate on August 12, 1956. On August 12, 1958, in the company of two other young women, she made her first profession. At her profession of perpetual vows on August 12, 1963, she was the only member of her group remaining.[4]

Sister Joseph Marie received her bachelor's degree from St. John College of Cleveland and her master's degree from John Carroll University also in Cleveland. A teacher in the congregation's elementary schools for eleven years, she was appointed to Madonna High School in 1968 as assistant principal and teacher of religion. At the First Extraordinary Chapter of Affairs in 1968, she served as secretary as well as chairperson of the Education Commission of the chapter. In 1969, she was named Community Apostolate Coordinator and as such sought and compiled data which was used for a five-year projection of community personnel and apostolic activity. Her in-depth study and evaluation of twenty-two elementary schools was used to determine staff utilization patterns, create a new reading program, and establish programs and techniques for individualization. In 1970, she became the principal of Madonna High School and worked with untiring energy in a steady and dependable manner which inspired confidence in her leadership.[5] She served on the Board of Directors of the Illinois Association of Catholic School Principals and also held offices in the Archdiocesan High School Principals' Association. Her initiative and dedication were generally admired, and thus, she was easily cast into a leadership role early in her religious life.

Less than a week after her election, Sister Joseph Marie sent a letter to the members of the congregation. The tone and content were characteristic of her abiding faith, placable nature, and genuine love of community. In it she stated:

> Each of you is vitally important to me. As members of the Congregation of the Franciscan Sisters of Chicago, we are mutually responsible for the growth of the congregation, for the preservation of our religious identity, and for the proclamation of the Gospel message. To attain these goals, we must be of one mind, and one heart willing to share in both the glory of the cross as well as the glory of the Resurrection.[6]

The Fourteenth General Chapter was scheduled for June 23 to June 28, 1983. On June 22, all the delegates had assembled at the Motherhouse. While they were at supper in the evening on that day, they were shocked to learn of the death of one of the members of their delegation. Sister M. Alberta Bialas had just been released from Silver Cross Hospital in Joliet, Illinois, where she had been a patient for a week. She had been sitting in the lobby of Our Lady of Victory Convent Motherhouse waiting to be taken to her room when she was stricken. For the first time in the history of the congregation, a delegate had expired before the convocation of a chapter. When the Fourteenth General Chapter formally convened the next day, her assigned desk, empty except for her photograph and a rose, gave mute testimony to the dedicated, departed Sister M. Alberta— "mighty in stature, generous of heart, and gentle of spirit."[7]

On the morning of June 23, 1983, the chapter was called to order by Sister M. Antonissima Jamruk, the former assistant general. During the session, Sister Martha Joan Sempolski, the former superior general, presented her report on the state of the congregation during her administration from 1978 to 1983. During this five-year period, thirty-nine Sisters had died and fourteen Sisters had left the congregation. The total membership stood at 225 Sisters. At the conclusion of her presentation, Sister Martha Joan thanked the entire congregation for their prayers and support during her tenure of office. She urged the Sisters to "enter a new era of the congregation by wholehearted cooperation with the new administration."[8]

Sister Joseph Marie was formally installed as the tenth superior general of the Franciscan Sisters of Chicago on June 24, the feast of St. John the Baptist, in a very joyous ceremony held in the Sacred Heart Chapel of the Motherhouse. Many Sisters from the Illinois and the Indiana mission homes were present at the installation.

At the final session of the Fourteenth General Chapter, Sister Joseph Marie delivered an inspiring address to the delegates:

As we conclude this Fourteenth General Chapter, we ought to do so with gratitude in our hearts. We have seen God's hand, we have witnessed Christ's redemptive power, and we have felt the presence of the Spirit. There has been no other chapter delegation that has had this whole process more graphically displayed than we have in the passing of Sister M. Alberta Bialas.

I give you my word that the general council and I will try our very best to use our abilities and God-given skills to enact, to promulgate, and to execute that which this chapter has resolved. We are committed to it.

You have done some mighty things, but you have also exacted some mighty things from us. When we begin to execute them, communication, trust, support, service, respect, and sacrifice will be needed.

As you go forth from Our Lady of Victory Convent, our Mother-house, you have the responsibility to support that which you have enacted at this general chapter.

Now, go forth to live, to proclaim, and to promulgate the theme of this chapter: "Reverence the Lord and each other through love, service, and community; witness God's presence in the Church by living the paschal mystery in the spirit of St. Francis and Mother M. Theresa Dudzik. In patience, humility, and joy we will draw all to God, our Father."[9]

At the adjournment of the chapter, the delegates assembled in the Sacred Heart Chapel to recommit themselves to the essentials of religious life by declaring the following affirmations which were the result of their chapter deliberations and resolutions:

That we strive to make the Gospel message ever alive by proclaiming God's truth and love in the compassionate spirit of Saint Francis and Mother M. Theresa.

That through communication, trust, respect, sacrifice and service, we strive to live in a spirit of ongoing conversion.

That the service we render in our apostolates be a love-response to our being sent to continue the mission of Jesus in the world.

That as daughters of Mother M. Theresa, who always showed a special love and concern for the poor, we continue to minister to the spiritual and material needs of the People of God, supported by community and individual awareness and prayer.

That we, who are called to peace and unity reject all hostilities within ourselves and our community. We will work to break down barriers, ease tensions, and build bridges of hope and trust.

That in our interpersonal relationships, we constantly strive to create family by affirming, supporting, accepting, and loving one another.

That through our witness of patience, humility, and joy we become living signs of God's presence in the world. Such a witness proclaims the value of consecrated living and encourages others to come and follow us.[10]

One of the first decisions of the new administration was to appoint a postulant-novice director to replace Sister M. Francis Clare Radke who had been elected the assistant superior general. The woman selected by Sister Joseph Marie and her general council was Sister Joan Klimek. Mindful that initial formation in the congregation is the basis for continuing growth in the religious life, Sister Joseph Marie and the councilors proceeded to the task of selecting Sisters to complete the formation team. By July 19, in addition to Sister Joan Klimek, the following appointments were announced to the congregation: Sister M. Francis Clare Radke, director of the formation program; Sister M. Cundette Minchuk, vocation director; Sister Diane Marie Collins, affiliate director; Sister M. Christine Brzozowski, director of Sisters in temporary vows;[11] and Sister M. Francine Labus, advisor.

The new postulant-novice director, Sister Joan Klimek, was a peaceable, affable, and deeply religious woman. Upon her appointment, Sister Joan accepted the responsibility and in faith committed herself to the congregation as part of its vital formation team.

A native of Chicago, Sister Joan entered the congregation from St. Gall's Church on Chicago's Southwest Side on February 12, 1959. She was invested with the habit of St. Francis on August 11, 1959, and made her first profession of vows on August 12, 1961. Her perpetual consecration was made on August 12, 1966.

Sister Joan began her active ministry by training as a practical nurse at Mother Cabrini Hospital in 1962. She expressed a desire to enter the teaching apostolate, and after receiving her bachelor's degree from Loyola University of Chicago, she was assigned to St. Hedwig's School in Gary for seven years. She spent eight years as a junior high school teacher at St. Louise de Marillac School in La Grange Park, Illinois. After obtaining her master's degree from Loyola University of Chicago, Sister Joan was appointed to Madonna High School in 1968 where she served as guidance counselor until her appointment as postulant-novice director in 1983.[12]

In order to provide more formal training for Sister Joan, she was sent to the University of St. Louis in September of 1984 to participate in their well-known Institute on Religious Formation. During her absence of approximately one year, the postulants and novices were placed in the care of Sister M. Antonella Abramowicz.

Sister Joan resumed her duties as postulant and novice director in June of 1985. Unfortunately, within the space of a year, she became seriously ill, and in January of 1987, was granted a sabbatical leave. On February 14, Sister M. Gabriel Lazarski, who had been the representative for Mission Effectiveness at St. Anthony Medical Center in Crown Point, Indiana, was appointed to conclude Sister Joan's term of office. On August 18, 1987, with great sorrow and a profound sense of loss, the congregation learned that Sister Joan had succumbed to cancer.

Animated by faith and a sense of purpose, Sister Joseph Marie and her general council initiated a new program aimed to provide guidance and inspiration to the members of the congregation. In October of 1984, they arranged for a memorable celebration of the gift of Franciscanism when each Sister was given the opportunity to rediscover the spiritual treasures of St. Francis of Assisi through her attendance at a weekend workshop called "Roots and Wings." Conducted by Sister M. Francine Labus, Sister Frances Szczur, and Sister Carol Marie Schommer, the workshop consisted of a series of talks and activities on the Approved Rule of the Third Order Regular of St. Francis. The sessions included topics such as "The History of the Rule," "The History of the Penitential Movement and the Third Order," and "Conversion Spirituality" among others.[13]

Believing that music greatly enhances worship and is a mode of prayer, Sister Joseph Marie revived the Franciscan Sisters Choir. Sister M. Lucretia Kot agreed to direct the choir while Sister Marie Frances Niecikowski and Sister Emilie Marie Lesniak eagerly consented to accompany them as organists. The Franciscan Sisters Choir now sings at all formal community gatherings and celebrations.

Under the new administration, the first issue of the congregation's newsletter dropped the title *Franciscan Brief* and reverted to the *Franciscan Echo*. Both the *Franciscan Echo* and the monthly personal newsletter from Sister Joseph Marie continued to unite the membership in terms of genuine Sisterly concern and supportive action.

Fully aware of the number of senior Sisters who were in need of nursing care and therapy, a lay staff of nurses now assisted in the infirmary. The new administration also arranged for the updating of the infirmary's physical facilities. At the suggestion of Sister Joseph Marie, activity service projects were initiated for the Sisters in the infirmary and for other retired Sisters. Among other helpful activities, the senior Sisters bundled flyers and stitched various-sized bandages for the American Cancer Society. In the area of pastoral care, the spiritual needs of the Sisters in the infirmary were met by the ministrations of the Motherhouse chaplain, the Reverend Reginald Maslinski, OFM.

On December 8, 1984, nearly 85 percent of the congregation gathered at the Motherhouse to celebrate the 90th Anniversary of the founding of the Franciscan Sisters of Chicago. Joseph Cardinal Bernardin[14] offered the Liturgy of the Eucharist in the Sacred Heart Chapel of the Motherhouse. In his homily, Cardinal Bernardin spoke of Mother M. Theresa Dudzik's noble call and undertaking:

> Mother M. Theresa's great dedication and love in caring for the poor, the aged, the disabled, and the abandoned are so well known to all of us. Her extraordinary qualities continue to inspire the work of your community. As the chief shepherd of this local Church and in my own name,

> I want to thank you for all that you have done and all that you are doing for the Church in the United States, especially in the Archdiocese of Chicago.
>
> The Gospel which we have proclaimed this morning, bears witness to Mother M. Theresa's response to God's call, her trust and commitment to doing the will of the Father. Knowing her example of discipleship and service, we recognize that God was not only the source of her life but also the destiny of her journey of faith.[15]

Later, in the dining room, Sister Joseph Marie spoke to the Sisters and reminded them of their own commitment:

> You have taken the original inspiration of our foundress, you have consistently translated it into action and have made it an enduring reality—one that is the sustaining soul and spirit of our community. What I wish to impress you with today is that the origin of our congregation is to be found in the mind of God, communicated to our foundress, and ratified by the Church. God had a purpose for the existence of our congregation and what he needed was a human instrument to say "Fiat." Mother M. Theresa Dudzik said that "Fiat."[16]

In the afternoon, the Sisters gathered in the Social Hall to enjoy a drama entitled "Theresa, Flower of Faith," based on the life of Mother M. Theresa Dudzik and the beginnings of the congregation.

One of the main celebrations of the congregation's 90th Anniversary was a spiritual pilgrimage to St. Stanislaus Kostka Church, the site of the foundation of the congregation. On Sunday, April 14, the Sisters joined with clergy, relatives, friends, and those to whom and with whom they ministered, in a special journey of prayer to the church to praise and thank God for the blessings upon the congregation during the past ninety years. Since the Resurrectionist priests, in the persons of the Reverend Vincent Barzynski, CR, and the Reverend Andrew Spetz, CR, were instrumental in guiding Josephine Dudzik in founding the congregation and providing spiritual guidance to the pioneer Sisters, the Reverend Edwin Zygmunt, CR, superior of the Chicago Province of the Congregation of the Resurrection, was invited to be the principal celebrant and homilist. Concelebrating with Father Zygmunt were the Reverend William Gulas, OFM, superior of the Assumption of the Blessed Virgin Mary Province of the Order of Friars Minor from Pulaski, Wisconsin; the Reverend John Lewandowski, MS, the provincial of the Missionaries of Our Lady of La Salette; the Reverend Joseph Glab, CR, pastor of St. Stanislaus Kostka Church; and the Reverend Marion Matlak, vice-postulator of the cause for the beatification of Mother M. Theresa Dudzik.

Participants in the entrance procession included representatives of organizations in the area where the Sisters ministered and approximately fifty priests. Of the more than

1,000 people in attendance were members of many congregations of Sisters and brothers as well as some relatives of Mother M. Theresa.

During the Liturgy of the Eucharist, the Franciscan Sisters of Chicago sang, joined by the Five Holy Martyrs Church Jubilee Choir. Sister Emilie Marie Lesniak played the organ and Paul Tawech conducted the combined choirs. After the beautiful and inspiring liturgy, a simple reception in the cafeteria of St. Stanislaus Kostka School followed.

The culminating activity of the 90th Anniversary celebration was an outdoor Liturgy of the Eucharist and a community picnic on Sunday, June 23, 1985, on the spacious grounds of the Motherhouse in Lemont. Among the participants were the families, relatives, friends and benefactors of the congregation.

In connection with the 90th Anniversary celebration of the establishment of the congregation, the Mother M. Theresa Heritage Room containing her memorabilia and that of the early community was established on the first floor of the Motherhouse.

In January of 1986, Sister Paula Frances Howard was granted permission by the administration to begin a new form of ministerial service at St. Martin de Porres House of Hope, a Christian communal shelter located in Chicago's blighted Woodlawn area, for homeless women and their children. The shelter provides time and aid to allow the residents to stabilize their lives in a safe, secure, and loving place during crisis periods and to give them the peace and space they need to assess their life choices. The services offered by the shelter are high school (GED) programs in parenting, household management, budgeting, social services, art classes, child care, and housing. Sister Paula Frances serves as a staff social worker.

At the request of the Reverend James M. Lennon, the pastor of SS. Peter and Paul Church in Naperville, Illinois, four Franciscan Sisters of Chicago volunteered their services to that parish in conducting a census in the summer of 1986. Sister M. Mildred Bieda, Sister Victoria Valerie Smagacz, Sister M. Monica Sendlosky, and Sister M. Rosemary Ferus worked collaboratively with four Sisters of the Congregation of the Franciscan Sisters of the Sacred Heart from Mokena, Illinois, in canvassing the parish of more than 3,000 families. Through their efforts, Father Lennon hoped to identify sacramental and catechetical needs among his parishioners, as well as to identify families desiring reconciliation with the Church.

The Franciscan Sisters of Chicago opened a Home Office in the Motherhouse on July 1, 1986. The Home Office, which Sister Joseph Marie and her councilors envisioned at the beginning of their administration, was the concept of systematic management and service to the congregation's corporately owned institutions. The Fourteenth General

Chapter of Elections wisely recognized the increased involvement of dedicated men and women in the management of the congregation's institutions. As a consequence, they passed a Chapter Act directing the administration to set up such a central office. The Chapter Act reads:

> That since the laity are increasingly offered administrative positions in the Church and in Church-owned institutions, we, the Franciscan Sisters of Chicago, develop a management system for the operation of all our corporately owned institutions which would help instill and perpetuate our religious identity and spirit of Franciscanism, while the institution is administered by either religious or lay persons.[17]

In the process of working for three years to achieve the goal of providing a Home Office, the general administration learned the tremendous canonical responsibility a congregation has to preserve its mission, its identity, and its stewardship in all the facilities operated by the Franciscan Sisters of Chicago. The establishment of the Home Office was a step toward helping the administration improve its stewardship responsibilities.

The members of the Home Office staff consisted of Sister Joseph Marie Zenda, executive director; Sister M. Francis Clare Radke, director of mission effectiveness;[18] Sister M. Ralph Stawasz, treasurer; and Sister M. Helene Galuszka, director of fiscal services. The Home Office personnel's aim was to unite the efforts of the congregation's corporate members to continue the Gospel ministry of Jesus Christ in the spirit of St. Francis and Mother M. Theresa Dudzik and the traditions of the Franciscan Sisters of Chicago. All available resources and energies of each corporation were directed toward seeking out, initiating, promoting, sustaining, and supporting those services which enable persons to realize their full potential as God's creation. Through the congregation's exercise of responsible stewardship, the Franciscan Sisters of Chicago believe they will be better able to serve the poor and oppressed needing their help.[19]

In another administrative decision made in 1986, Sister Joseph Marie and her councilors appointed a Planning Committee whose general purpose was to serve the congregation by formulating goals for short- and long-range planning in an organized, consistent, and creative manner. Their statement of purpose specifically indicated that they were to identify significant trends that were impacting on the Church, the congregation, and society; to relate these trends to the mission and identity of the congregation; and to recommend some action that the Franciscan Sisters of Chicago might take to enhance their mission and to respond to these trends. Appointed to this special Planning Committee were Sister M. Gabriel Lazarski, chairperson; Sister M. Hugoline Czaplinski, Sister M. Marinella Gubala, Sister M. Helene Galuszka, and Sister Lora Ann Slawinski. While the total community would be involved in the planning process in some instances, the Planning Committee's role was to be strictly advisory to the administration and to the congregation. The over-all responsibility for congregational planning rests with the superior general and her councilors.

The prophet Jeremiah says: "I [Yahweh] know the plans I have for you, plans for peace not disaster, reserving a future full of hope for you." In this spirit, Sister Joseph Marie and her councilors have, since the beginning of their administration, expresssed their commitment to a "future full of hope" for the Franciscan Sisters of Chicago. As a consequence, they have announced plans for the construction of a 150-bed nursing home to be erected at the present site of Mother Theresa Home in Lemont, Illinois, which will provide sheltered, intermediate, and skilled-care beds. Because of the antiquated building structure plus the limited number of resident rooms, lounges, office space, and other common areas, the Franciscan Sisters of Chicago sought permission to build a new Mother Theresa Home. The construction of the new replacement facility will represent the first phase in long-range plans for a comprehensive retirement community called "Franciscan Village," to be built around the nursing home on the property in Lemont.[20]

In June of 1988, the Fifteenth General Chapter of Elections will take place. In her address to the delegates[21] at a pre-chapter meeting in April of 1987, Sister Joseph Marie emphasized the need for "faith" and for "work." She stressed:

> We must live, breathe, and speak *with faith* and *in faith*, for to do anything else is to have renounced the actions of a loving God to His people . . . it is our faith that will sustain us, both in the pursuit of holiness and in our apostolic endeavors.[22]

If it is an example of faith the Franciscan Sisters of Chicago seek today, they need look no further than that of their beloved foundress. To Mother Mary Theresa Dudzik—Woman, Social Service Pioneer, Religious Sister, and Venerated Foundress— can aptly be applied the words of Jesus as found in the Gospel of St. John: "You have not chosen Me; but I have chosen you and have appointed you, that you should go and bear fruit, and that your fruit should remain." Her "Chronicle" reveals the source of her unwavering faith in the midst of the trials and discouragements which she faced during the pioneer days of the congregation: "The thought that I had freely agreed upon this undertaking for the love of Jesus Christ sustained me."[23] The Franciscan Sisters of Chicago, under the patronage of the Immaculate Conception, look to the future imbued with the same vision, hope, and courage which first inspired their cherished foundress. The "Chronicle" of Mother M. Theresa Dudzik ends with the following words:

> And now I am closing this chronicle of the community. It contains many deficiencies and inadequacies because I cannot recall the happenings. I did not have the opportunity to write down all the minor occurrences from the beginning of the community. The more important ones I have written down insofar as I can remember them. Now I beg you to forgive me for all the inaccuracies and my terrible handwriting. I believe that the Sisters are aware of my lack of higher education in recording such matters. Again I humbly beg the Sisters for pardon. Praised be Jesus Christ.[24]

There are many greetings and partings which are graced with expressions indicative of the Catholic faith. In rural parts of some countries, the old religious salutations and responses are still widely used. Mother M. Theresa expressed one of the most beautiful and enduring in closing her "Chronicle" with the words: "Praised be Jesus Christ." This history of the Franciscan Sisters of Chicago closes with the words generally given in response to that salutation: "For Ages and Ages. Amen."

THE FOURTEENTH GENERAL CHAPTER: SISTER JOSEPH MARIE ZENDA

[1]See Appendix K.

[2]These Sisters have all been mentioned at length in previous chapters.

[3]*Congregation Membership Records;* and *Interviews* with Sisters, 1985 (AFSCL).

[4]*Congregation Membership Records* (AFSCL).

[5]See Chapter 51.

[6]*Book of Correspondence:* Letter from Sister Joseph Marie Zenda, superior general, to the Franciscan Sisters of Chicago, 12 April 1983 (AFSCL).

[7]"The Chapter Briefly," June 1983 (AFSCL).

[8]*Minutes of General Chapter Proceedings, 1983* (AFSCL).

[9]Address delivered by Sister Joseph Marie Zenda, superior general, to delegates to the Fourteenth General Chapter, June 1983 (AFSCL).

[10]Affirmations of the Fourteenth General Chapter, June 1983 (AFSCL).

[11]See Appendix J.

[12]*Congregation Membership Records* (AFSCL).

[13]*Franciscan Echo,* Vol. 23, No. 4, December 1984.

[14]Joseph Cardinal Bernardin is Chicago's fifth cardinal, seventh archbishop, and twelfth bishop in her 142-year history. The son of immigrants from Northern Italy, Joseph Louis Bernardin was born on April 2, 1928, in Columbia, South Carolina. He was ordained a priest for the Diocese of Charleston on April 26, 1952. On the same day in 1966, he was named the auxiliary bishop of New Orleans. Bishop Bernardin was named first secretary general of the National Conference of the Catholic Bishops United States Conference from 1968 to 1972. Just a few months after the Vatican Council's final session, Bernardin was appointed the archbishop of Cincinnati.

In 1974, his peers elected him to a three-year term as president of the National Conference of Catholic Bishops. During these years, he was the official spokesman for American Catholicism while continuing to serve as spiritual leader of his own archdiocese. His talents continued to gain him international as well as national recognition. Elected as an American delegate to the World Synod of Bishops, Bernardin was named at the end of the session to the fifteen-man permanent council that advises the Pope on synodal business between the triennial sessions. Ten weeks after the death of John Cardinal Cody, Archbishop Bernardin was appointed to head the Archdiocese of Chicago. The Reverend John Keating (now Bishop Keating of Virginia) then the administrator of the Archdiocese of Chicago said this of him: "The Pope is sending us a gift of God. Archbishop Bernardin is an outstanding choice, an excellent leader. We are absolutely thrilled and delighted at his appointment."

On August 25, 1982, Bernardin was installed as the seventh archbishop of Chicago at Holy Name Cathedral. One of the most widely known, respected and admired Catholic bishops in the nation, Bernardin was made a cardinal in 1983. "The Installation of Archbishop Bernardin," *Chicago Catholic,* September 5, 1982, 96 pp.; and *Chicago Catholic,* Special Edition, July 16, 1982, Vol. 90, No. 27, pp. 1–28.

[15]Homily delivered by Joseph Cardinal Bernardin to Franciscan Sisters of Chicago, 8 December 1984.

[16]Address by Sister Joseph Marie Zenda, superior general, to the Congregation, 8 December 1984.

[17]Chapter Act, Fourteenth General Chapter, June 1983.

[18]Sister M. Francis Clare was appointed to this position in 1984. After study and projection, she actively began her responsibility of planning and coordinating all mission awareness activities. Several Sisters were appointed to aid her as mission effectiveness persons in each of the

congregation's health care facilities. The primary objective of the mission effectiveness personnel was to develop a basic orientation program for presentation in each health care facility based upon the history, philosophy, and mission of the Franciscan Sisters of Chicago and of the respective institution.

[19]*Book of Correspondence:* Letter from Sister Joseph Marie Zenda, superior general to the congregation, June 1986.

[20]Newsletter from Sister Joseph Marie Zenda, superior general, to the congregation, March 1987; and *Lemont Metropolitan,* 31 December 1987.

[21]See Appendix K.

[22]*Grand Chapter Bulletin,* 30 May 1987, No. 1.

[23]Matka Maria Teresa Dudzik, "Kronika Sióstr Franciszkanek pod opieką Św. Kunegundy w Chicago, Illinois" [The Chronicle of the Franciscan Sisters under the patronage of St. Kunegunda in Chicago, Illinois] Chicago, 1910 (Unpublished manuscript, AFSCL), p. 6.

[24]Ibid., p. 103.

Ordinaries and Bishops

Most Rev. Paul Peter Rhode
Auxiliary Bishop of Chicago 1908–1915
Bishop of Green Bay, Wisconsin
1915–1945

Most Rev. Edward F. Hoban
Archbishop–Bishop of Cleveland
1945–1966

George Cardinal Mundelein
First Cardinal, Third Archbishop
and Eighth Bishop of Chicago
1915–1939

Samuel Cardinal Stritch
Second Cardinal, Fourth Archbishop
and Ninth Bishop of Chicago
1939–1958

John Cardinal Cody
Fourth Cardinal, Sixth Archbishop and
Eleventh Bishop of Chicago
1965–1982

Albert Cardinal Meyer
Third Cardinal, Fifth Archbishop
and Tenth Bishop of Chicago
1958–1965

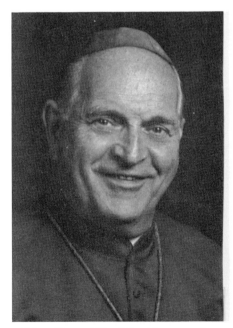

Most Rev. Alfred L. Abramowicz
Auxiliary Bishop of Chicago
1968–

Religious Habit: Past and Present

A postulant in the garb
adopted in 1899

A novitiate class in the 1930s

Reception Ceremony at Our Lady of Victory
Convent, Lemont, Illinois, c. 1942

Postulants in the garb
adopted c. 1924

A group of Sisters in the garb worn c. 1945

A Professed Sister in the
religious garb c. 1950

The "new look" worn by
the Sisters for the first
time in 1959

A modified habit
after the First
Extraordinary Chapter
of Affairs of 1968

APPENDIX A

THE CONSTITUTIONS OF THE CONGREGATION OF
THE FRANCISCAN SISTERS OF CHICAGO

The Constitutions of a congregation are the regulations which, briefly and clearly formulated, govern a religious institute in all the phases of its daily life. They are the principles on which, besides the Rule and the Book of Customs, a particular congregation is built. When the small band of Franciscan tertiaries met on December 23, 1894, to begin their life in common as religious, they elected to follow the Tertiary Rule of St. Francis of Assisi. A year later, Father Vincent Barzynski, CR, presented the Sisters with a horarium (the order of the day) and a number of brief observances or recommendations for living the religious life in common based again on the Tertiary Rule of St. Francis. These observances were the congregation's first Constitutions. The Sisters realized, of course, that the formation of a definitive set of Constitutions would have to evolve as the little community developed and grew in number.[1]

By 1898, Father Barzynski was shifting more of the responsibility for the spiritual leadership of the Sisters to Father Andrew Spetz, CR. Father Spetz was aware that the Sisters were in need of a more definable and adaptable set of Constitutions based on the Rule of the Third Order Regular of St. Francis. To this end, Father Spetz contacted the Congregation of the Sisters of the Third Order of St. Francis in Milwaukee, Wisconsin,[2] to provide him with a copy of their Constitutions. The Sisters very willingly sent a copy of their Constitutions of 1874 to Father Spetz, who, in turn, used them as a guide in writing the Constitutions for the small community of Franciscans in Avondale since the Sisters' objectives in serving God and the Church as Franciscans were similar.[3] After completing the Constitutions, Father Spetz gave a copy to Sister M. Theresa Dudzik and Sister M. Anna Wysinski for approval.[4] The Sisters returned the Constitutions to Father Spetz several times asking him for greater clarification concerning some article or prescription. By 1909, the Constitutions based on the Rule of the Third Order Regular of St. Francis for the Congregation of the Franciscan Sisters of Blessed Kunegunda were approved by the Most Reverend James Quigley, archbishop of Chicago, and each Sister was given a copy.[5]

The aforementioned Constitutions were practiced by the Sisters through the years as part of their religious consecration. The pioneer Sisters were aware of the fact that the Constitutions acquire a special force and create a special bond between the congregation and the Church when the Constitutions receive the approval of the Holy See thereby designating the congregation as valid. To secure this privilege, however, it was necessary to acquire the *Decree of Praise—Decretem Laudis*—which would be a sign of the Church's acknowledgment and authorization of the congregation, that is, granting it the right to exist. It is due to the vision and merit of Mother M. Vincent Czyzewski and her general council that at the convocation of the Third General Chapter in 1922, one of the chief topics on the agenda was the need to secure papal approbation of the Constitutions.

When the delegates to the Third General Chapter met in 1922, they agreed to the appointment of a committee of Sisters to study the Constitutions. Appointed to this committee were Sister M. Benigna Jakajtis, Sister M. Emily Kondziolka, Sister M. Hedwig Kubera, Sister M. John Barczak, Sister M. Kunegunda Pinkowski, Sister Mary Welter, Sister M. Sylvestra Pelczar, and Sister M. Zita Kosmala. In 1918, the Code of Canon Law—*Codex Juris Canonini*—the body of laws by which the Church is governed had become effective. The chief function of the Committee on the Constitutions, therefore, was to revise the Constitutions of the congregation in accordance with the Code of Canon Law as it applied to religious. The committee was to study the Constitutions and to outline any additions or corrections. Upon the committee's completion of the study, the Constitutions were to be translated into English, submitted to Archbishop Mundelein for approval and, then sent to the Sacred Congregation for Religious Affairs in Rome for approbation and, hopefully, the desired *Decree of Praise*.

On August 7, 1922, Mother M. Vincent Czyzewski and Sister M. Philipine Lama, the assistant general, paid a visit to the Right Reverend Monsignor Francis Rempe, the vicar general for women religious of the Archdiocese of Chicago, to give an account of the chapter proceedings. At this meeting, the Sisters asked Monsignor Rempe to present their revised Constitutions to Archbishop Mundelein for his approval and to obtain from him a Letter of Approbation or Recommendation which was required from the Ordinary of the Archdiocese. At a subsequent visit to Monsignor Rempe in January of 1923, Mother M. Vincent and Sister M. Philipine discussed the matter of securing Letters of Approbation which were also required from the bishops in whose dioceses the congregation was located. At this visit, the Sisters received a draft of the petition sent by Monsignor Rempe to Archbishop Mundelein for his final approval before the actual petition would be drawn up. It read:

> The Franciscan Sisters of St. Kunegunda have their headquarters here in Chicago where their congregation was founded thirty years ago. Spurred by charity, the Sisters initially dedicated themselves to the care of the seriously ill and aged; then, in response to the counsel and urging of many pastors, they wholeheartedly assumed the education of youth, so that at present they teach with distinction in nineteen schools in various dioceses.
>
> We hereby praise their Rule, discipline, and dedication. Moreover, we willingly grant the approbation which they petition.
>
> Given in Chicago . . .
>
> Fr. Rempe[6]

Monsignor Rempe further informed Mother M. Vincent and Sister M. Philipine that it would be necessary for him to conduct a canonical visitation of the congregation before he could give the Sisters the Letter of Approbation from Archbishop Mundelein.

The canonical visitation, Monsignor Rempe cautioned, was a very complex and careful examination of the congregation's spiritual life and the specific ends for which it was founded.

On July 30, 1923, Monsignor Rempe made his proposed canonical vision during which he asked Mother M. Vincent and her general council for an account of the congregation's development in regard to members, locations, and kinds of apostolates in which the congregation was involved. He inquired about the number of Sisters in the congregation, the dioceses in which they served, and the number of persons in their care. Monsignor Rempe also inquired about the congregation's financial state. At the conclusion of the examination, he promised to send a Letter of Approbation to the congregation from Archbishop Mundelein. He also advised Mother M. Vincent that Letters of Approbation be obtained at this time from the bishops in whose dioceses the congregation was located. Correspondence in the archives indicates that requests for these testimonial letters were sent to bishops of the dioceses of Fort Wayne, Indiana; Cleveland, Ohio; Altoona and Pittsburgh, Pennsylvania; and Belleville, Illinois. The following letter was dispatched:

> Very Reverend Bishop:
>
> We humbly and respectfully request Your Lordship to write a Letter of Recommendation on behalf of our Community for the purpose of obtaining the *Decree of Praise—Decretum Laudis*—from the Holy See.
>
> Thus far our Order is diocesan since we have not yet received the approval of the Holy Father but only that of the Archbishop of Chicago.
>
> We now desire to obtain such an approval, and having already secured the Letter of Recommendation from His Grace, the Most Reverend Archbishop George W. Mundelein, it is necessary that we obtain similar ones from all the Right Reverend Bishops in whose dioceses the Sisters are engaged in work. All these letters will be sent to the Sacred Congregation of the Religious Affairs in Rome.
>
> Therefore, I humbly beg again and hope that our request will be granted. I beg to remain,
>
> Sincerely yours in Domino,
> Mother M. Vincent[7]

In September of 1924, Mother M. Vincent obtained the services of the Reverend Cyril Mitera, OFM,[8] a priest well known to the congregation, to help Sister M. Benigna Jakajtis revise the Constitutions according to the new Code of Canon Law with the anticipation of eventual papal approval of the Constitutions. Father Mitera recommended that Mother M. Vincent secure the services of the scholarly Reverend Jasper Thoennessen,[9] who had long distinguished himself as an advisor to various Sisterhoods working on their Constitutions. Mother M. Vincent, grateful for the opportunity to have Father Thoennessen's expert guidance on the project, sent Sister M. Benigna Jakajtis and Sister M. Sylvestra Pelczar to confer with him in Odanah, Wisconsin, where he was stationed. The Sisters met with Father Thoennessen on October 12, 1924, and minutely examined the Constitutions of the congregation paragraph by paragraph.[10]

One of the notable changes made in the Constitutions pertained to the novitiate. Father Thoennessen strongly advocated a two-year novitiate whose purpose in the first year would be the building of a strong spiritual foundation; in the second year, the novice could prepare for her eventual assignment in one of the congregation's various apostolates. In the first year of the novitiate, therefore, concentration was to be placed on the spiritual formation of the novice with the study of the religious vows, the Rule, the Constitutions, the Book of Customs, and the cultivation of virtue and related matters. Besides that of the mistress of novices, spiritual guidance would also be provided by the weekly confessor. In keeping with the congregation's emphasis on Franciscan spirituality, the confessors and spiritual directors for both the novices and the professed Sisters at Our Lady of Victory Convent in Lemont would be the priests of the Assumption Province of the Order of Friars Minor from Pulaski, Wisconsin. Eventually serving as confessors and conference masters were the Reverend Dionysius (Dennis) Babilewicz, OFM,[11] the Reverend Lawrence Konieczka, OFM,[12] and the Reverend Luke Pedtke, OFM.[13]

On October 26, 1924, Sister M. Benigna and Sister M. Sylvestra reported to Mother M. Vincent and the general council that more corrections and revisions were needed in the Constitutions. According to the directions of Father Thoennessen, the following revisions were also suggested:

1. The congregation should be known as the Franciscan Sisters of Blessed Kunegunda rather than the Franciscan Sisters of Saint Kunegunda since she had not as yet been listed among the saints of the Church.

2. Because the Sacred Congregation in Rome demanded of each congregation of the Third Order of St. Francis a *Decree of Aggregation* to the First Order, Father Thoennessen recommended to Father Mitera that he secure, through the provincial, this *Act of Aggregation* from the Father General of the Franciscan Order in Rome.

3. The Rule of St. Francis of the Third Order Regular approved by Pope Nicholas IV and revised by Pope Leo X should be placed before the Constitutions according to the demands of Rome.[14]

Another session of the general council was held on November 27, 1924, at which time these changes were suggested:

1. The scrutiny[15] before entering the novitiate and the professing of first vows should be taken under consideration. The scrutiny is not stated in Canon Law and, therefore, is unnecessary. These scrutinies belong to the customs of the congregation rather than to the articles of the Constitutions.

2. Father Thoennessen advocated the bestowal of rings at the making of

perpetual vows. He urged the practice to be accepted for the following reasons:

   a. Rings are a symbol of the perpetual union with God by means of the three vows.

   b. The Father General of the Order of Friars Minor who aggregates the Third Order to the First Order, anticipates and places the obligation upon the Sisters to accept the *Franciscan Ceremonial.*

   c. Since the bestowal of rings is a part of the *Franciscan Ceremonial,* all Franciscans should wear rings.[16]

During the next three sessions of the general council, the Constitutions were read from beginning to end and explained according to the directions of Father Thoennessen.

On April 18, 1925, the congregation received the long-desired *Decree of Aggregation* which Mother M. Vincent had labored to secure and which now joined the congregation to the First Order of Franciscans:

DECREE OF AGGREGATION
The Minister General of the
Entire Order of Friars Minor
Frater Bernardine Klumper
to the
Venerable Sisters of the Third Order
of Our Holy Father Saint Francis of
the Congregation of Blessed Kunegunda
whose Motherhouse is in the city of
Chicago, United States of America

HEALTH AND SERAPHIC BENEDICTION

Desiring to increase in you that praiseworthy attachment of your hearts to the Seraphic Order from which you have received your holy habit and your rule of life, as is evident from the documents which you have submitted to us at the same time being anxious to satisfy, as far as lies within our power, the wishes you have lately expressed to us; and having, moreover, the assured confidence that your fidelity and charity will grow from day to day by the granting of these new favors and graces, so that the strength which emanates from the Seraphic Spirit will, through you continue to produce ever increasing fruits—we aggregate all the Sisters of your Community and all those to be received in the future, by authority of these present letters, to our Order, from which you have taken your name and habit; and we declare you are so aggregated with this effect, that you may participate according to the Decree of the Sacred Congregation of Indulgences and Holy Relics, dated August 28th, 1903, in all the Indulgences which have been granted directly by the Roman Pontiffs only to the First and Second Orders, and that your churches may enjoy the same indulgences as the churches of the aforesaid Orders enjoy.

Farewell, and may you be mindful in your prayers before God of us and our Seraphic Order.

Given at Rome, St. Antonio, March 20th, 1925.

Fr. Bernadine Klumper, OFM

Minister General

When the congregation began to implement the revised Constitutions, and because of the *Decree of Aggregation* which linked the congregation with the First Order of Friars Minor, there was a stronger emphasis on the cultivation of Franciscan spirituality and devotions. As a consequence of the desire to be rooted in Franciscanism, the Sisters turned repeatedly for spiritual guidance especially to the Franciscan Fathers of the Assumption of the Blessed Virgin Mary Province of Pulaski, Wisconsin.[17] Since 1925, the Franciscan Fathers of Pulaski have served as retreat masters, confessors, advisors, and very good friends to the congregation.

On October 7, 1925, Mother M. Vincent and Sister M. Benigna Jakajtis paid a visit to Cardinal Mundelein with a special plea. The Sisters needed his signature on a letter being sent to Rome which contained a request to allow the congregation to celebrate July 27 as the feast of their patroness, Blessed Kunegunda. Cardinal Mundelein received the Sisters warmly, signed the letter, and commended the Sisters for their action.[18]

On October 23, Mother M. Vincent and Sister M. Benigna visited Monsignor Rempe for the express purpose of giving him a copy of the revised Constitutions prepared by Father Thoennessen and Sister M. Benigna. The Sisters pointed out some of the additional changes in the Constitutions to Monsignor Rempe:

1. The secondary aim of the Congregation namely, the care of the sick and of children in orphanages should be stricken, since that care was not being given at that point in time. Monsignor Rempe suggested, however, that the Sisters not delete that secondary aim from the Constitutions altogether.

2. Perpetual vows should be made after three years of temporary vows instead of after six years as had been the practice since 1918. Monsignor Rempe advised the Sisters to begin this practice in 1926.[19]

3. A half-hour of meditation should be added in the afternoon. Monsignor Rempe did not recommend this suggestion.

4. The Stations of the Cross should be said in common at least once a week.

5. The Franciscan Crown should be recited in homes where the Sisters could not pray the *Little Office of the Blessed Virgin Mary.*

6. On Saturdays, meat should be eaten only once a day; on Wednesdays,

there should be total abstinence from meat.[20]

7. An article should be inserted pertaining to "Admonitions and Punishments."

8. An article should be inserted concerning "Expulsions."

9. The number of deceased persons to be remembered in prayer should be increased to include the Pope, the Cardinal Protector,[21] the Ordinary of the Diocese, the Superior General, the Sisters Superior, and the parents of the Sisters.

10. The method of nominating delegates to the general chapter should be changed as well as the manner in which the general chapter was conducted. There should be an increase in the number of delegates.

11. Regulations and guidelines should be inserted for the Sisters engaged in teaching, taking care of the aged and the hospitalized as well as the residents of the home for working girls.

Monsignor Rempe was pleased with the revised Constitutions and gave his whole-hearted approbation to the above-mentioned articles.

The requested Letters of Approbation from the bishops of each diocese in which the Sisters exercised the corporal and spiritual works of mercy were obtained. Along with these Letters of Approbation and that of Archbishop Mundelein, other essential information was also gathered by Mother M. Vincent for the Sacred Congregation of Religious. This included the origin of the congregation; the name of the foundress and her principal human and spiritual qualities; the statistics concerning Sister personnel; the disciplinary condition; the material and economic conditions; and other details about the postulancy, the novitiate, and the congregation's educational requirements. All this material plus the Constitutions, the Book of Customs, and the designated daily prayers of the congregation were presented to Vincent Cardinal La Puma, prefect of the Sacred Congregation of Religious on August 16, 1926. Cardinal La Puma then presented the material to the Holy See for a thorough examination. Only after such an exhaustive examination could the Congregation of the Franciscan Sisters of Blessed Kunegunda be recognized in the family of congregations and be declared of pontifical right.[22]

The Sisters rejoiced when after waiting four years for the approbation of the Constitutions, the news arrived that Pope Pius XI had granted the temporary approval of the Constitutions for a period of seven years by way of experimentation. The bishops had submitted favorable reports to the Holy See commending the spirit and ministry of the Franciscan Sisters of Blessed Kunegunda working in their dioceses. The rigorous examination of the congregation had proved successful as well. As a result, Mother M. Aloysia Holysz, who had succeeded Mother M. Vincent Czyzewski as superior general, the general council, and all the Sisters were filled with joy when the congregation received the *Decree of Praise* on December 9, 1930. It was the first step to final approbation of the congregation by the Holy See. With this *Decree of Praise,* the congregation was now declared of pontifical right. After receiving the news, Mother M. Aloysia sent an announcement to all the houses urging the Sisters to recite or sing the "Te Deum" and offer a novena of thanksgiving to St. Francis for this grace. Because the text of the approved Constitutions was written in English, the Reverend Ferdinand Pawłowski, OFM,[23] from Pulaski, Wisconsin, was asked to translate the Constitutions into Polish.[24] The *Decree of Praise* read:

DECREE

In the year of the Lord, 1894, in the city of Chicago, with the approbation of legitimate Church authority, a pious Congregation of Sisters was formed under the title of Blessed Kunegunda of the III Order of the Seraphic St. Francis,—the work principally of two devout ladies: Josephine Dudzik and Rose Wysinski by name. Soon after, a Motherhouse was legally established in the same city.

The Sisters spoken of, besides a general aim, that is, of personal sanctification, set for themselves a particular goal, namely: the education of children of both sexes in parochial schools and orphanages, as well as young ladies in high schools, and also: care of the sick in hospitals and bringing aid to the elderly and to working ladies.

All members of the Congregation lead a life-in-common under the authority of the Superioress General, who is chosen every six years; then after legitimately completing the novitiate, they profess simple vows: namely, poverty, chastity and obedience,—first, for a time; then, in perpetuity.

When under the propitious influence of God's grace the modest number of Sisters grew and twenty-two homes were established in many dioceses with the favorable agreement of the Bishops, who in fact express their joy because of the abundant fruits of salvation accruing from it, the Superioress General together with her Council recently had sent His Holiness Pope Pius XI a most humble request, asking that he deign to approve the aforementioned Congregation and its Constitutions with his Apostolic Authority.

Consequently, His Holiness, by Divine Providence Pope Pius XI, at an audience granted on December 9, 1930, to the Most Reverend Secretary of the Sacred Congregation in charge of Affairs Pertaining to Religious, after taking into account the laudatory letters of the Most Reverend Bishops, in whose dioceses the homes of the Congregation exist, and acceding to the wishes of Their Eminences, the Very Reverend Cardinals of the Holy Roman Church at the head of this Holy Congregation, who at a Plenary Session of November 29 of this year, held in the Vatican Palace, had completely discussed the whole matter, the Holy Father, in the most flattering terms, deigned to praise and command the aforementioned Institute as a religious Congregation of simple vows under the authority of the Superioress General; in addition, he favorably approved and confirmed for a seven-year trial the Constitutions expressed in Latin in the form they are contained in the copy whose original is preserved in the archives of this same Congregation; and likewise, on the strength of this decree, he praises and commends the Institute itself and, as was mentioned above, he approves and confirms the Constitutions thereof, safeguarding the jurisdiction of the local Ordinaries in accordance with the prescriptions of the Holy Canons.

Given in Rome, from the Holy Congregation in charge of Affairs of Religious, December 9, 1930.

Alex Henry M. Card. Lepicier, OSM, Prefect
Vincent La Puma, Secretary[25]

Seven years had passed since the Holy See had approved the Constitutions of the congregation and had granted it the *Decree of Praise*. It was necessary, therefore, in 1937, to submit the Constitutions to Rome for final approval. The period of experimentation had shown that the Constitutions were practical and capable of being observed by the Sisters. Mother M. Antonina Osinski and her general council arranged for the Reverend Conradin Wallbraun, OFM,[26] a member of the Chicago-St. Louis Province of the Sacred Heart, to examine the Constitutions according to the Code of Canon Law before submitting them for examination.[27] Once again, testimonial letters were requested from the bishops of the dioceses where the Sisters were engaged in the apostolate.[28] The following letter is an example of the response of the bishops:

January 8, 1938

Mother M. Antonina
Superior General
Franciscan Sisters of St. Kunegunda
2649 North Hamlin Avenue
Chicago, Ill.

Dear Mother Antonina:

It gives me great pleasure to recommend the Franciscan Sisters of St. Kunegunda.

Their service as teachers in two of the parochial schools of the Diocese of Altoona, in St. Casimir's Parish, Johnstown, and in Assumption Parish, Conemaugh, are deeply appreciated.

Because of their devoted lives and their faithful attention to duty, they earned the favorable commendation of our Predecessors and we confidently trust that, with the blessing of God, they will continue to further the interests of Holy Mother Church.

Wishing you and the Sisters under your care every success and blessing, I am,

> Very sincerely in Christ,
> Richard T. Guilfoyle
> Bishop of Altoona[29]

In March 1940, Father Wallbraun informed Mother M. Antonina that the congregation had received its second or final approbation on December 9, 1939. While there were several minor changes in the Constitutions, one article was of paramount importance. It specified that the Sisters should make vows for one year and renew them annually for five years. After six years of temporary vows, the Sisters should be admitted to perpetual vows.[30] The text of the *Decree of Final Approval* of the Constitutions read:

DECREE OF FINAL APPROVAL OF THE
CONSTITUTIONS OF THE INSTITUTE
OF THE SISTERS OF BLESSED KUNEGUNDA
OF THE THIRD ORDER OF THE SERAPHIC SAINT FRANCIS

The Institute of the Sisters of Blessed Kunegunda of the Third Order of the Seraphic Saint Francis, whose principal house exists in the Archdiocese of Chicago, has obtained from the Holy See, the approval of the Constitutions on December 9th, 1930, for seven years by way of experiment.

However, in order that this Institute might flourish daily with more abundant fruits for the good of the Church, the superior general with the Council most humbly requested the final approval of the Constitutions by the Holy See.

Our Most Holy Father, by Divine Providence, Pope Pius XII, in audience on the fourth day of July, 1939, granted to His Eminence, the Cardinal Prefect of the Sacred Congregation of Religious, in consideration of the commendatory letters of the Right Reverend Bishops in whose dioceses the houses of the Institute are found, and after hearing the vote of the Commission of Consultors, has deigned most kindly, definitely to approve and confirm the Constitutions with some changes and additions, a copy of which is preserved in the Archives of the Sacred Congregation. Accordingly, by the tenor of the present Decree, the same Constitutions are approved and confirmed, notwithstanding whatsoever to the contrary.

Given at Rome from the Secretariate of the Sacred Congregation of Religious on December 9th, 1939.

> Vinc. Card. La Puma, Prefect
> Fr. S. N. Pasetto, Secr.

The *Decree,* ratifying the Constitutions as well as a copy with corrections of the Constitutions dated December 9, 1939, was given to Reverend Ferdinand Pawłowski, OFM, to translate from Latin to Polish.

Through the ensuing years, the Constitutions remained stable. In the 1960s, however, the Second Vatican Council challenged religious congregations to renewal; the Franciscan Sisters of Blessed Kunegunda (soon to be renamed the Franciscan Sisters of Chicago) immediately began years of research, study, and heartfelt probing of their true mission in the Church. The First Extraordinary Chapter of Affairs was held in 1968 and produced the first new Constitutions entitled *For This Have We Come.* These Interim Constitutions (temporary or provisional) dated 1970 proved to be very loosely structured. While they offered an acceptable way of life, they provided few rules, precepts, or obligations. The General Chapter of Elections held in 1970 plus the Second Special Chapter of Affairs held in 1972 and the General Chapter of Elections of 1974 produced their own sets of guidelines and legislation by which the members of the congregation lived experimentally as the Second Vatican Council had suggested and the Church had encouraged.

In 1975, a second book of proposed Constitutions and Directory (formerly called the Book of Customs) showed a marked improvement providing more stability and guidance to the members of the congregation. The Constitutions and Directory were written chiefly by a committee under the direction of the chapter coordinator, Sister M. Antonissima Jamruk, the assistant general. But still another general chapter followed and more changes were made in the Constitutions by the delegates at the Thirteenth General Chapter of 1978.

In 1979, a committee of four Sisters,[31] under the direction of Sister M. Antonissima, was formed by the superior general to incorporate the recommendations made by the Reverend Basil Heiser, OFM, of the Sacred Congregation for Religious and Secular Institutes, into the new Constitutions. The members of this committee also rearranged many of the articles for consistency and clarity. Articles dealing with aspects of religious life which were important and permanent were included in the new Constitutions. Nothing of the basic text was changed unless certain articles were inconsistent with the wishes of the Sacred Congregation; no change was made without the approbation of the superior general and her council. The committee's intentions were to provide a document which would eventually warrant the approval of Rome.

The following is the *Decree* obtained by the Franciscan Sisters of Chicago and given at Rome on October 4, 1982:

Sacred Congregation for Religious and for Secular Institutes

DECREE

This Sacred Congregation for Religious and for Secular Institutes, by virtue of its authority to erect, guide, and promote institutes of the consecrated life, after careful examination of the Constitutions of the

Franciscan Sisters of Chicago, acceding to the petition of the Superior General and her Council, hereby approves these Constitutions within the limits of common law and as amended according to the observations made by this Sacred Congregation. May the generous living of these Constitutions encourage all the Franciscan Sisters of Chicago to an ever-deeper commitment of their consecrated life, to Christ and to his Church in the spirit of Mother Mary Theresa Dudzik and under the protection of their holy father, St. Francis.

Given at Rome, October 4, 1982
Feast of St. Francis of Assisi

E. Card. Pironio, Pref.
+Augustine Mayer, OSB[32], Sec.

The next step in the entire process was to send copies of the Rule, Constitutions, and Directory to the Sacred Congregation for Religious and Secular Institutes for approval. The final approval of the Constitutions and Directory came on the 800th anniversary of the birth of St. Francis, in the 88th year of the congregation's existence, that is, October 4, 1982.

On February 16, 1983, Ash Wednesday, a lovely ceremony of the distribution of the Constitutions and Directory was held in the Sacred Heart Chapel at the Motherhouse in Lemont. During this special prayer service, Sister Martha Joan Sempolski, the superior general, shared some reflections with the Sisters on the implementation of the Constitutions after which the new Constitutions and Directory were handed to each member of the congregation by Sister Martha Joan who was aided by Sister M. Antonissima, the assistant general. What remained now was for each Franciscan Sister of Chicago to accept and live the Rule and the Constitutions and Directory in the spirit of the foundress of the congregation, Mother M. Theresa Dudzik. For this self-imposed but loving task, the Sisters had the inspiration of the prophet Isaiah to whom God had promised: "Fear not, for I am with you, be not dismayed, for I am your God; I will strengthen you, I will help you, I will uphold you with my victorious right hand."[33]

APPENDIX A

THE CONSTITUTIONS OF THE CONGREGATION OF
THE FRANCISCAN SISTERS OF CHICAGO

[1]Siostra M. Gonzaga Raniszewski, OSFK, *Rys historyczny Zgromadzenia Sióstr Franciszkanek Błogosławionej Kunegundy. Część pierwsza*, 1860–1910 [A historical survey of the Franciscan Sisters of Blessed Kunegunda. Part one, 1860–1910] (Chicago: By the Author, 1947), p. 27.

[2]The Sisters of the Third Order of St. Francis of Assisi, also known as the Sisters of Penance and Charity, trace their origin to the year 1849, when six women, Tertiaries of the Third Order of St. Francis of Augsburg, Germany, came to Milwaukee, Wisconsin, and established one of the first Motherhouses to be founded in that state.

[3]*Book of Correspondence:* Letter from Sister Diana Tergerson, OSF, to author, 27 August 1975 (AFSCL).

[4]The original Constitutions are preserved in the archives in Lemont.

[5]Raniszewski, p. 61.

[6]Archives, Archdiocese of Chicago, Mundelein, Illinois: Sample copy of petition from the Right Reverend Monsignor Francis Rempe to Archbishop Mundelein, 1923.

[7]*Book of Correspondence:* Letter from Mother M. Vincent Czyzewski to bishops of dioceses served by the Franciscan Sisters of Chicago, 23 August 1923 (AFSCL).

[8]The Reverend Cyril Mitera, OFM, was born in Tarnów, Poland in 1875. He entered the Sacred Heart Province of the Order of Friars Minor in St. Louis and received his habit in 1893. Father Mitera made his simple profession of vows in 1894 and pronounced his solemn vows in 1897. Ordained in 1899 by the Most Reverend John Kain, archbishop of St. Louis, he served in various parishes in Omaha before his transfer to St. Stanislaus Church in Cleveland in 1915. In 1927, he became a member of the Assumption Province of the Order of Friars Minor in Pulaski, Wisconsin, but rejoined the Sacred Heart Province in 1943. He died in 1961 in Joliet, Illinois.

While Father Mitera was stationed at St. Stanislaus Church in Cleveland in 1915, he became acquainted with the Franciscan Sisters of Chicago who staffed St. Casimir's School in that city. He directed many Sisters into the congregation among whom were Sister M. Fidelia Armatys, Sister M. Gonzaga Raniszewski, Sister M. Sylvia Lewandowski, and Sister M. Pius Wojcicki. Biographical sketch received from secretary of Chicago-St. Louis Province of the Sacred Heart.

[9]The Reverend Jasper Thoennessen, OFM, was born in Aachen (Koeln), Germany in 1873. He entered the Sacred Heart Province of the Order of Friars Minor in St. Louis and was invested with the habit in 1892. He made his simple profession of vows in 1893 and his solemn profession in 1896. Father Thoennessen was ordained a priest on July 2, 1898, by the Most Reverend John J. Kain, archbishop of St. Louis. Throughout his religious life, he served as pastor, lector of theology, guardian, and definitor. He died on January 24, 1932, at St. Augustine Friary in Chicago.

For fifteen years he devoted himself to the work of assisting various congregations in writing their Constitutions and obtaining the approval of the Sacred Congregation of Religious for them. He was the author of a brochure entitled "Religious Communities of Women," containing a clear and concise presentation of the legislation of the Church concerning religious orders and congregations of women. Biographical sketch received from secretary of Chicago-St. Louis Province of the Sacred Heart.

[10]*Minutes of General Council Proceedings, 1910–1934;* and Secretaries General, *Community Chronicle*, pp. 82–84. (AFSCL).

[11]The Reverend Dionysius (Dennis) Babilewicz was born in 1888 in Poland and came to the United States at the age of fourteen. At the invitation of the Reverend James Schneider, OFM, he arrived in Pulaski, Wisconsin, to begin his formal education for the priesthood. The Most Reverend

Paul Rhode, bishop of Green Bay, ordained him to the priesthood in 1919.

In 1928, he was sent to Des Plaines, Illinois to assume the chaplaincy in the provincial house of the Congregation of the Sisters of the Holy Family of Nazareth. The next year he was commissioned to plan the construction of St. Francis Monastery and College in Burlington, Wisconsin. From 1934 to 1937, he held the office of First Definitor of the Assumption of the Blessed Virgin Mary Commissariate and Guardian of Assumption BVM Friary in Pulaski. In a series of assignments he served as chaplain at homes for the aged, guardian of St. Anthony Friary in Pittsburgh, master of brothers and assistant master of novices in Pulaski, and vice-guardian of Stella Maris Retreat House in Cedar Lake, Indiana. From 1963 to 1967, he took up residence at Christ the King Seminary in West Chicago, Illinois. He died on February 28, 1968, in Sheboygan, Wisconsin. Archives: Assumption BVM Province, Pulaski, Wisconsin.

[12]The Reverend Lawrence Konieczka, OFM, was born in Poland in 1886. He entered the novitiate in Pulaski, Wisconsin, in 1906 and professed his solemn vows in 1910. He completed his education in the United States at St. Joseph Minor Seminary, Teutopolis, Illinois, and St. Bonaventure Minor Seminary in Sturtevant, Wisconsin. His theological studies were made in Quebec, Canada, where he was ordained on July 20, 1913.

Father Konieczka was appointed master of novices at the age of twenty-eight thereby requiring a canonical dispensation for the office. He served as pastor and guardian until his death in 1932 at forty-seven. Archives: Assumption BVM Province, Pulaski, Wisconsin.

[13]Father Pedtke was born in Ashley, Illinois, in 1900. His high school, college, and theological training were pursued at St. Bonaventure Minor Seminary in Sturtevant, Wisconsin. In 1926 he was ordained in Green Bay, Wisconsin, by Bishop Paul Rhode. His provincial appointments included duties as chaplain, pastor, superior, and master of clerics in theology at Green Bay, Wisconsin, and Cedar Lake, Indiana. He rendered pastoral-parochial assistance at various friaries, and, in 1974, became a chaplain in New Britain, Connecticut. Archives: Assumption BVM Province, Pulaski, Wisconsin.

[14]*Minutes of General Council Proceedings*, 26 October 1924 (AFSCL).

[15]The scrutiny was a method of election or an examination of the candidate by Sister-examiners and a Sister-delegate. If three-fourths of the votes were against a Sister's reception to the novitiate, first vows, or perpetual vows, the Sister was dismissed at once. If the majority of votes was in favor of the Sister, she was admitted to the novitiate, first vows, or perpetual profession. *Konstytucja Sióstr III Zakonu Św. Ojca Franciszka pod Wezwaniem Św. Kunegundy w Chicago, Illinois* (Chicago: *Dziennik Chicagoski*, 1909) pp. 10–11.

[16]The *Franciscan Ceremonial* was the book containing the ritual for ceremonies such as the investiture of novices, first profession of vows, perpetual profession of vows, and the silver anniversary of profession.

[17]The Franciscan Fathers of the Assumption of the Blessed Virgin Mary Province of Pulaski, Wisconsin, were founded by Brother Augustine Zeytz. Born in Poland, Brother Augustine left for America when the Russians suppressed religious orders in his country. Upon his arrival in the United States on December 10, 1872, he took temporary refuge with the Franciscan Fathers in Cincinnati, Ohio. Here Brother Zeytz conceived the idea of restoring or upholding the faith among immigrant Lithuanians and Poles in the Shenandoah Valley of Pennsylvania. He became enthused with the idea of founding a Franciscan monastery in the United States, but the vicious anti-clericalism and equally vicious nationalism so discouraged him that he returned to Europe.

In 1886 he returned to America, once again imbued with the spirit of ministering to the spiritual needs of the Poles and the Lithuanians. He received a free land grant in a tiny Polish community called Pulaski in Wisconsin. On April 19, 1887, the Holy See approved his new foundation of Franciscans and thus began the history of the Assumption Province. In April of 1888 two other Franciscan priests joined him in this new venture, and by winter, the Reverend James Schneider had arrived from France. Soon the group rose to thirteen friars. When their superior died, Father Schneider was appointed. The external difficulties the friars experienced were superseded by the internal conflicts among the new community. Father Schneider immersed himself in missionary activities throughout the East and Midwest, thus leaving the small community and the parish without a priest. Severe misunderstandings arose between Father Schneider and Brother Zeytz. This resulted in Brother Augustine and eleven other Brothers leaving the Pulaski community and joining the Franciscan Fathers of the Sacred Heart Province of St. Louis, Missouri. Because of this unfortunate occurrence, the minister general of the Order of Friars Minor placed the Pulaski community under the jurisdiction of the St. Louis Province of the Order of Friars Minor from 1894 to 1910.

By 1897 Rome was prepared to abandon the Pulaski project, but the Reverend Stanislaus Jeka, the superior since 1895, strongly defended the foundation. With the arrival of new friars prepared for leadership and authority, the men were convinced that Divine Providence intended their community to exist. The Pulaski community regained its autonomy by official decree from the order's generalate in Rome on December 17, 1910.

The community grew with vigor. The Reverend Francis Manel established St. Bonaventure College in Pulaski in 1901. In 1907, he founded the Franciscan printery and edited a monthly magazine for Polish-speaking Americans, the *Franciscan Message*. Through the years, the friars authored thousands of pamphlets and articles. Soon the bishops entrusted the organization of several parishes to the new community. In 1922, St. Bonaventure College in Pulaski was transferred to Sturtevant, Wisconsin; St. Francis College was built in Burlington, Wisconsin. In April of 1939, the Assumption Commissariat was elevated to the status of a province. The Very Reverend Isidore Cwiklinski was appointed the first provincial superior. In 1940, Lake Geneva, Wisconsin, was made the site of the new novitiate. A vocational school for the training of Franciscan Brothers was founded in Pulaski in 1952. In that year also, the province began its missionary work on the island of Samar in the Philippine Islands. In West Chicago, Illinois, a new theologate was built in 1955. A retreat house for men was opened in Cedar Lake, Indiana, in 1956. The work of the province today is as varied as the work of the Church itself in religious, missionary, and educational activity. *Franciscan Message*, September 1962; Majchrzak, Reverend Colman, OFM, *And God Gives Increase*, no pagination; and Strykowski, Reverend Gordion, OFM, Press Release, Franciscan Information Office, Pulaski, Wisconsin, 1963.

Brother Stanislaus Furman, the brother of Sister M. Evelyn and Sister M. Seraphinia of the Franciscan Sisters of Chicago, has been a member of the Assumption of the Blessed Virgin Mary Province since May 17, 1927.

[18]Secretaries General, *Community Chronicle*, p. 87 (AFSCL).

[19]In the Constitutions approved by Rome in 1930, a change occurred; temporary vows were to be made for three years and renewed for another three. If the Sister were of age after six years in temporary vows, she was permitted to make perpetual vows.

[20]In 1926, this was changed to: "On all Wednesdays the Sisters may eat meat once a day and on Saturdays, there is no abstinence from meat." Secretaries General, *Community Chronicle*, 3 July 1926 (AFSCL).

[21]The congregation never had a Cardinal Protector. The article was inserted at the insistence of Father Thoennessen. In any serious case, the superior general turned to the archbishop of Chicago for guidance or advice.

[22]Secretaries General, *Community Chronicle*, 23 October 1926 (AFSCL).

[23]The Reverend Ferdinand Pawłowski, OFM, was born in Radom, Illinois, in 1896. He was invested with the Franciscan habit in 1913, and Bishop Paul P. Rhode ordained him a priest on August 28, 1920.

From 1923, Father Pawłowski served as an educator. His other assignments included serving as master of clerics, prefect of studies, local superior, and provincial board member. He was editor of the *Miesięcznik Franciszkanski* and *Posłaniec*, director of the printery, columnist for the *Miesięcznik* and the pastor of St. Mary of the Angels Church in Green Bay, Wisconsin. As late as 1968, he was a member of the faculty of Christ the King Theological Seminary in West Chicago, Illinois. He died in 1974 in Green Bay. Archives: Assumption BVM Province, Pulaski, Wisconsin.

[24]Siostra M. Gonzaga Raniszewski, OSFK, "Rys historyczny Zgromadzenia Sióstr Franciszkanek Bł. Kunegundy. Część druga, 1910–1940" [A historical survey of the Franciscan Sisters of Blessed Kunegunda. Part two, 1910–1940] Typewritten, unpublished manuscript (AFSCL), p. 178.

[25]This *Decree* was translated from the Polish to English by the Reverend Edward Janas, CR, at the request of the author.

[26]Born in Germany in 1878, Father Conradin was invested with the Franciscan habit on July 31, 1897, in Teutopolis, Illinois. He was ordained a priest on July 25, 1903, in Rome, where he remained for two years. From 1906 to 1910, he was lector of theology in Santa Barbara, California, and from 1910 to 1913, he served as the master of clerics. Sent to St. Louis in 1913, Father Conradin remained there for two years in the same capacity. From 1921 to 1922, he served in Chicago at the Old St. Peter's Church. He became lector of theology again in 1922 and taught in Teutopolis and St. Louis. Father Conradin died on October 29, 1956, in St. Louis. Biographical sketch received from the Reverend James Perluzzi, OFM, secretary of the Sacred Heart Province of the Order of Friars Minor, 21 November 1974 (AFSCL).

[27]*Minutes of General Council Proceedings,* 1934–1956; and *Community Chronicle,* p. 178 (AFSCL).

[28]By this time, the congregation also had houses in the dioceses of Gary, Indiana, and Bismarck, North Dakota.

[29]*Book of Correspondence:* Letter from the Most Reverend Richard T. Guilfoyle to Mother M. Antonina Osinski, 8 January 1938 (AFSCL).

[30]*Minutes of General Council Proceedings,* 4 May 1939 (AFSCL).

[31]These Sisters were Sister Emilie Marie Lesniak, Sister Kathleen Melia, Sister M. Marifilia Strzycki, and Sister M. Theophane Rakowski.

[32]*My God and My All: Constitutions of the Franciscan Sisters of Chicago* (Lemont, Illinois, 1982), p. 1.

[33]Isaiah 41:10.

APPENDIX B

THE BEATIFICATION AND CANONIZATION PROCESS OF THE SERVANT OF GOD, MOTHER MARY THERESA DUDZIK, FOUNDRESS OF THE CONGREGATION OF THE FRANCISCAN SISTERS OF CHICAGO

Canonization is a solemn declaration by the Pope that a person is in heaven and entitled to the full honors of the Catholic Church. Basically, canonization entails two steps. The person's cause, that is, the process of beatification and canonization, must be introduced. During the cause, the Congregation of Rites declares whether or not the person whose cause is under consideration showed virtue to a heroic degree and is, therefore, entitled to be referred to as "Venerable." This preliminary process is long and arduous with a detailed examination of the person's life, writings, reputation, and accomplishments. If the person was not a martyr, miracles must be proved to have resulted from prayers to that person. If the Congregation of Rites rules in favor of the person, the Pope names the person "Blessed" and this is called beatification. A "Blessed" is honored locally or in a religious community. The process continues by a re-examination of the "Blessed's" life, and two new miracles must be proved. If this part of the process is successful, the declaration of canonization is made to the whole Church, and the person is then called "Saint."[1]

The Catholic Church has always considered it a duty to search and proclaim the "wonderful works of God,"[2] those whom we call saints, and to show them as examples to others for their edification and imitation. If it is the Will of Divine Providence that Mother M. Theresa Dudzik should be declared a "wonderful work of God," it is of interest and of necessity to review the steps taken in the attempt to bring Mother M. Theresa Dudzik to the honors of the altar.

When Mother M. Vincent Czyzewski was elected the superior general in 1922, she entrusted Sister M. Benigna Jakajtis with the task of updating the Constitutions of the congregation. Sister M. Benigna was guided in this assignment by the Reverend Jasper Thoennessen, OFM.[3] Acting as consultor to the congregation, Father Thoennessen urged the Sisters to keep the memory of the foundress and her co-foundresses alive by speaking of them, printing their photographs, and saving memorabilia. To this end, Mother M. Vincent and the general council voted to have large portraits of Mother M. Theresa Dudzik and Mother M. Anna Wysinski painted and displayed in the community room at the Motherhouse. Copies of the portraits 15-1/2 inches by 19 inches, were also distributed to all the mission homes.[4] The administration also arranged to distribute to each Sister a medallion of Mother M. Theresa and Mother M. Anna. The Sisters were encouraged to speak about Mother M. Theresa and Mother M. Anna and the foundation of the congregation at evening recreation.

When Mother M. Aloysia Holysz was elected to the office of superior general in 1928, leaflets were printed with short biographies of Mother M. Theresa and Mother M. Anna and given to the Sisters to distribute to their families, friends, relatives, and

937

acquaintances. The specific purpose of the leaflets was to have the faithful notify the congregation concerning any favors granted through the intercession of either Mother M. Theresa Dudzik or Mother M. Anna Wysinski.

At the Fifth General Chapter held in 1934, one of the delegates, Sister M. Helen Swiszcz, proposed that biographies of Mother M. Theresa and Mother M. Anna be written and published. The delegates agreed and passed a decree to that effect.

During the Fifth General Chapter, Mother M. Antonina Osinski became the superior general. Shortly thereafter, she chose Sister M. Gonzaga Raniszewski as her private secretary. It was now sixteen years after the death of Mother M. Theresa. At the beginning of her term, Mother M. Antonina, anxious to have the saintly Mother M. Theresa Dudzik proclaimed the foundress of the congregation and raised to the altar, entrusted Sister M. Gonzaga with the task of gathering facts for a history of the congregation.[5] In 1935, Mother M. Antonina and the general council made several attempts to present the case for the beatification process to the Church authorities, but because of World War II, little or no progress was made. During this period, Sister M. Gonzaga continued to gather documented information from many living witnesses who had known Mother M. Theresa personally. She consulted other available sources, especially the "Chronicle" of Mother M. Theresa as well as the "Community Chronicle," a journal kept by Sister M. Philipine Lama, the secretary general during the first term of Mother M. Aloysia Holysz, that is, from 1916 to 1922. On the 45th anniversary of the congregation in 1939, Mother M. Antonina read excerpted chapters from Sister M. Gonzaga's as yet unpublished history to the Sisters at the Motherhouse during the recreation hour. Many Sisters learned for the first time about the congregation's foundation and about the sufferings, trials, and hardships of Mother M. Theresa Dudzik. Because Sister M. Angeline Topolinski emerged from the pages of the history as one of the pioneer Sisters, Mother M. Antonina referred to her as a co-foundress. To that effect, a photograph of Mother M. Theresa, Mother M. Anna, and Mother M. Angeline, encased in a 2-1/2 inch by 3 inch standing gold metal frame, was given to each Sister. Each mission home was sent a necrology list which was prominently displayed in the community room of every home. At the top of the necrology list were the photographs of Mother M. Theresa, Mother M. Anna, and Mother M. Angeline.[6]

During the general chapter held in 1940, which resulted in the election of Mother M. Mechtilde Zynda as the superior general, Sister M. Gonzaga's unpublished historical material was read to the Sister-delegates during the lunch hour and after chapter sessions. Many Sisters who were not delegates but who had lived with Mother M. Theresa, Mother M. Anna, and Mother M. Angeline were invited to these readings and were asked to comment, make corrections, or add information which could be included in the history before its publication. Among those present at the readings were Mother M. Aloysia Holysz, Mother M. Vincent Czyzewski, and Mother M. Antonina Osinski, all former superiors general. It was at this significant chapter that Sister M. Theresa Dudzik was given the title "Mother" and since then has always been referred to as Mother M. Theresa Dudzik.

In 1944, the congregation celebrated its Golden Jubilee. Two publications in honor of this event proved to be very valuable for their historical data. The first, the *Golden Jubilee of the Franciscan Sisters of Bl. Kunegunda, 1894–1944,* written by Sister M. Paul Kirschbaum, included a short sketch of the work of Mother M. Theresa and Mother M. Anna. The second, *Zarys Półwiecza Dziejów Zgromadzenia Sióstr Franciszkanek Błog. Kunegundy, Chgo. Ill., 1894–1944* [Sketch of the fifty–year history of the Congregation of the Franciscan Sisters of Bl. Kunegunda, Chicago, Illinois, 1894–1944] was written by Sister M. Gonzaga Raniszewski and contained a brief biography of Mother M. Theresa and Mother M. Anna.

Mother M. Jerome Dadej was elected the superior general in 1946. At a meeting of the general council in February of 1949, Mother M. Jerome suggested that the process of the canonization of Mother M. Theresa be revived.[7] She informed her councilors that she had given one of the congregation's most prestigious retreat masters, the Reverend Francis Cegiełka,[8] a Pallotine priest, a copy of Mother M. Theresa's "Chronicle" to read while he was conducting a retreat at the Motherhouse. Upon learning that Mother M. Jerome had been one of Mother M. Theresa's novices, Father Cegiełka had urged Mother M. Jerome to begin the process for the canonization of this "extraordinarily holy person." The priest-theologian had determined from his reading of the "Chronicle" that Mother M. Theresa was not merely "another Sister in the congregation." He believed that her exercise of the virtues of faith, hope, and charity in the face of extreme hardships and suffering was truly heroic. Father Cegiełka informed Mother M. Jerome that she had an obligation to undertake the cause of the canonization of Mother M. Theresa Dudzik.[9]

Mother M. Jerome began her pursuit to open the cause of Mother M. Theresa Dudzik by consulting with Sister M. Theodosia Szrom, CR, a member of the Congregation of the Sisters of the Resurrection, who had been instrumental in inaugurating the cause of their foundress, Mother M. Celine Borzecki. Sister M. Theodosia, in turn, advised Mother M. Jerome to consult with the Right Reverend Aristeo Simoni[10] who had been instrumental in the process of the canonization of Chicago's "Citizen Saint," St. Frances Xavier Cabrini, the foundress of the Congregation of the Missionary Sisters of the Sacred Heart.[11] At a meeting with Mother M. Jerome on March 25, 1950, Monsignor Simoni expressed interest in the cause of Mother M. Theresa Dudzik and heartily encouraged it. Because of Monsignor Simoni's involvement in the processes of beatification of other persons, he felt he could not take on another cause and, therefore, suggested that Mother M. Jerome confer with the Right Reverend Monsignor Edward Smaza.[12] Monsignor Smaza, on the other hand, was extremely busy with his duties in the Matrimonial Court of the Metropolitan Tribunal of Chicago and could not handle another assignment at the time. Instead, he scheduled an audience for Mother M. Jerome with Samuel Cardinal Stritch, the archbishop of Chicago, since it was necessary to secure his permission before progressing any further. On March 31, 1950, Mother M. Jerome and Sister M. Gonzaga were received by Cardinal Stritch at which time Mother M. Jerome presented him with a copy of the "Chronicle" of Mother M. Theresa. Before Cardinal Stritch could again confer with Mother M. Jerome, he was called to Rome to serve as Pro-prefect of the Sacred Congregation for the Propagation of the Faith.[13] His secretary, in rearranging his papers, found the "Chronicle" and returned it to Mother M. Jerome without any comment.

In June of 1958, Mother M. Beatrice Rybacki was elected the congregation's seventh superior general. Earlier in February of that year, the Reverend Henry M. Malak[14] had visited the Motherhouse for the first time to give a retreat to the members of the Our Lady of Częstochowa Society. At that time, he had been engaged to present a series of retreats to the Sisters at the Motherhouse. Father Malak eagerly consented to the request for his services as a retreat master and expressed a great interest in the congregation. He specifically asked for the history of the congregation so that he might incorporate it into his lectures. Upon reading the "Chronicle" of Mother M. Theresa, Father Malak recognized her as a woman of eminent and heroic virtue.[15] He became a most enthusiastic supporter of Mother M. Theresa and suggested that the Sisters who had known and lived with her give oral testimony concerning any personal contact they had had with her. This action resulted in one hundred sixteen depositions from Sisters, relatives of Mother M. Theresa, and other eyewitnesses.

On June 30, 1960, a small pamphlet with the picture of Mother M. Theresa and a prayer for her beatification was published in the English and the Polish languages. It bore the *Imprimatur*[16] of Albert Cardinal Meyer.

The 100th anniversary of the birth of Mother M. Theresa was celebrated on August 30, 1960. A Solemn High Mass was celebrated at the Motherhouse by the Reverend John Grabowski, CR, who was assisted by the Reverend Casimir Polinski, CR, the Reverend Anthony Laskowski, CR, and the Reverend Stanley Ziemba, CR, as master of ceremonies. The Reverend Henry M. Malak delivered a sermon in which he acquainted the assembled group with the life of Mother M. Theresa. The chapel was filled with clergy, relatives of Mother M. Theresa, many lay friends of the congregation, and about one hundred fifty Sisters. In commemoration of the centenary of the birth of Mother M. Theresa, the administration of the congregation decided that a mass for the beatification of Mother M. Theresa was to be offered at the Motherhouse on the twentieth day of each month, a custom which still prevails.[17]

In 1961, a brief biography, *Apostołka Miłosierdzia z Chicago* [The Apostle of Mercy of Chicago] was published by Father Malak and was translated into English by Sister M. Hugoline Czaplinski. An *Imprimatur* was obtained from the Most Reverend Martin McNamara, bishop of Joliet. A three-fold leaflet, with a brief resume of the life of Mother M. Theresa, a prayer for her beatification, and her photograph on the top fold was printed and distributed to the faithful. By now, several Sisters had presented sketches of the life of Mother M. Theresa at meetings of the Polish American Historical Association. These were later printed in *Polish American Studies*.[18] In addition, several newspapers carried articles concerning Mother M. Theresa, *The New World* (now *The Chicago Catholic*) among them.

Albert Cardinal Meyer became the new archbishop of Chicago in 1962. Mother

M. Beatrice sent a letter informing the Cardinal of all the details concerning the congregation's efforts to promote the cause of Mother M. Theresa. Cardinal Meyer, who proved to be extremely supportive, advised Mother M. Beatrice to consult with the Right Reverend Monsignor Alfred Abramowicz of the Archdiocesan Chancery Office. The meeting with Monsignor Abramowicz was most successful; he exhibited genuine interest in the cause and its promotion.[19]

In January of 1962, a quarterly, *The Apostle of Mercy of Chicago Bulletin,* was issued.[20] It was edited and published by Father Malak in both the Polish and the English languages. Because of the countless letters of inquiry received concerning the cause of Mother M. Theresa, the League of Mother M. Theresa was formed and coordinated by Sister M. Venantia Rec. With the assistance of Sister M. Jeannette Golojuch, the *Bulletin* was mailed to all subscribers informing them of the life of Mother M. Theresa Dudzik and the vigorous efforts to promote her beatification. All incoming mail pertinent to graces and favors received as well as petitions for prayer were handled by the league. Its members shared in the prayers, sacrifices, and good works of the Franciscan Sisters of Chicago and in the Holy Masses offered for the intention of the members of the league. At this time, a hymn to Mother M. Theresa was composed by Father Malak and translated into English by Sister M. Theophane Rakowski. This hymn is now sung during the monthly novena in her honor.

By 1963, the cause of Mother M. Theresa had matured to such a degree that Mother M. Beatrice, Sister M. Venantia, and Father Malak visited Cardinal Meyer with the request that Father Malak be appointed the postulator in the Archdiocese of Chicago for the beatification of Mother M. Theresa. A postulator is one who prosecutes, either in his own name or in that of others, the cause of the beatification of a Servant of God or the canonization of a "Blessed" before the Congregation of Rites and other competent tribunals. On September 11, 1963, the cause of Mother M. Theresa Dudzik was formally opened. On September 14, 1963, a document was officially signed, approving the appointment of Father Malak as postulator who, as a consequence of the appointment, took up residence in the former novitiate house in Lemont.[21] In the following year, the Mother M. Theresa Museum was established in the novitiate house by Father Malak and Sister M. Venantia. Memorabilia of Mother M. Theresa together with artifacts of the congregation collected when the first Motherhouse in Chicago was dismantled were displayed.

The years passed in quiet activity, and in 1968, Father Malak added pertinent documentary materials and an illustrated section with footnotes to the "Chronicle" of Mother M. Theresa. The 172-page spiral book, typed and translated into English by Sister M. Hugoline Czaplinski, was mimeographed and distributed to all the Sisters in the congregation.

On September 20, 1968, the 50th anniversary of the death of Mother M. Theresa, the Eucharistic Liturgy was celebrated at the Motherhouse in Lemont by the Most Reverend Alfred L. Abramowicz with numerous clergy, Sisters, relatives, and friends in attendance. The next year, on the occasion of the congregation's 75th Anniversary of foundation, an original musical in two acts entitled *Somebody, Somewhere,* based on the life of Mother M. Theresa, was staged at the congregation's Madonna High School.[22]

By 1972, the beatification cause had advanced to the stage where it was now necessary to present it to the authorities in Rome in order to secure a postulator for the cause in Rome. Sister M. Hugoline Czaplinski, who had succeeded Mother M. Beatrice Rybacki as superior general in 1970, turned to the Most Reverend Ladislaus Rubin, secretary of the International Synod of Bishops and president of the Postulators' Center for Studies. A kind and sympathetic letter arrived from Bishop Rubin informing Sister M. Hugoline that the Reverend Michael Machejek, OCD, had been appointed postulator in Rome for the cause of the beatification of Mother M. Theresa. After the postulator in Rome was approved, the cause of Mother M. Theresa Dudzik was entered into the Books of the Sacred Congregation for the Cause of Saints. In the Archdiocese of Chicago, the Reverend Chester Konsowski, pastor of St. Florian's Church, was named vice-postulator.[23]

When Father Machejek was appointed the postulator in Rome in 1972, he began to study the researched materials and documents pertaining to the cause. He submitted two proposals to Sister M. Hugoline, the superior general, namely, to consider seriously furthering the beatification cause and to arrange for the exhumation of the remains of Mother M. Theresa. Thus, on Friday, October 13, 1972, the mortal remains of Mother M. Theresa were exhumed from their resting place in St. Adalbert's Cemetery in Niles, Illinois. At the graveside were present members of a special tribunal delegated by John Cardinal Cody: the Most Reverend Alfred Abramowicz, auxiliary bishop of Chicago; the Reverend Michael Machejek, OCD, official postulator of the cause in Rome; the Reverend Chester Konsowski, vice-postulator; the Reverend Henry Malak, archdiocesan postulator; Dr. Gissur Brjnjolfsson, pathologist from Loyola University of Chicago's Stritch School of Medicine, accompanied by Dr. Zenon Kowaliczko; Sister M. Hugoline Czaplinski, superior general of the Franciscan Sisters of Chicago, along with the other members of the collegial board; Sister M. Venantia Rec, coordinator of Mother M. Theresa's cause; Adam Bona, director of St. Adalbert's Cemetery, and his assistant, Anthony Urbanski; and more than seventy-five other official witnesses of the exhumation. Included were relatives of Mother M. Theresa as well as numerous clergy, Sisters, and friends of the congregation.[24]

At nine o'clock in the morning, the special tribunal assembled in the mausoleum of the Resurrectionist Fathers and opened the solemn rites of the exhumation with a prayer. Authorized personnel proceeded to the graveside of Mother M. Theresa directed by Sister M. Praxeda Ostrega who had been a novice of Mother M. Theresa and who had attended her simple funeral on September 18, 1918. The Reverend John Rolek, the official notary for the cause of Mother M. Theresa, recorded all pertinent information and observations made at the graveside and the actual exhumation proceedings. The tribunal proceeded in formal procession into the mausoleum with the remains of Mother M. Theresa and also the remains of the original casket and other personal articles found within the grave. In the mausoleum, positive identification of the bones took place. These were enclosed in a metal casket bearing the seal of John Cardinal Cody. The metal casket was placed in an outer wooden casket and was also sealed. Other articles were placed in plastic boxes and likewise sealed.[25] Late Friday evening, the hearse bearing the remains of Mother M. Theresa was escorted by the police and authorized personnel to the General Motherhouse in Lemont, Illinois. The remains of Mother M. Theresa were waked until Sunday, October 15, 1972, when at four o'clock in the afternoon a liturgical service was conducted by the Most Reverend Alfred L. Abramowicz. In the congregation were members of the tribunal, the postulator, the vice-postulator, and many Sisters, relatives, and friends of the congregation. The casket bearing the remains was reinterred in the rear of the Sacred Heart chapel in a niche and sealed within a granite sarcophagus. The Reverend Theophane Kalinowski, OFM, delivered the homily.[26]

In May of the next year, the soil covering the gravesite of Mother M. Theresa's original grave in St. Adalbert's Cemetery was transferred to a plot in the Congregation's cemetery in Lemont where a gravesite monument slab, three feet by six feet, covers the area and reads: "Intended gravesite of Mother M. Theresa Dudzik." The memorial stone was officially installed and blessed at a special liturgical ceremony on May 6, 1973. From that day on, the daily prayer for the beatification of the servant of God, Mother M. Theresa was initiated in all the houses of the congregation.[27]

In January of 1973, a desperate mother, whose son lay in a coma as the result of the Illinois Central Railroad crash in October of 1972, had come to pray and beg the intercession of Mother M. Theresa Dudzik at the sarcophagus in the Sacred Heart Chapel at the Motherhouse. Roseann Lisiecki claimed that her son, Jerry, was cured shortly after her visit to the sarcophagus. Three large medical volumes on Jerry Lisiecki's condition were sent to Rome for translation and investigation. The authorities in Rome have yet to make a decision on any facts presented. The publicity of Jerry Lisiecki's case resulted in the visitation to Mother M. Theresa's remains by hundreds of persons who came to the Sacred Heart Chapel in Lemont to pray through her intercession. From that time on, due to the popular demand of the public, novena pamphlets have been published. Also, every month from the twelfth to the twentieth, a novena of masses is celebrated at the Motherhouse for all petitions received requesting favors through the intercession of Mother M. Theresa.[28] Daily and weekly visitations to the sarcophagus continue in the form of Sunday pilgrimages and retreat days for various parishes and clubs from Chicago and nearby areas.

On December 8, 1976, the Reverend Michael Machejek, in the name of the Franciscan Sisters of Chicago, presented documented volumes concerning Mother M. Theresa's cause to the Chancery Office of the Archdiocese of Chicago with a petition to open the beatification process of Mother M. Theresa. After prayerful and serious deliberation, Cardinal Cody supported this petition and presented all the necessary documents to the Sacred Congregation for the Cause of Saints on June 6, 1977, asking for the decree *Nihil Obstat*[29] to open formally the beatification process in the Archdiocese of

Chicago. The Sacred Congregation for the Cause of Saints in Rome accepted these documents on the feast of St. Francis, October 4, 1977, and began to study and discuss the materials relevant to the life and heroic virtue of the Servant of God, Mother M. Theresa Dudzik.

Sister Martha Joan Sempolski was elected superior general of the congregation in 1978. That year, a prayer composed by Mother M. Theresa called "A Prayer for Our Daily Needs" and found on the flyleaf of her prayer book was translated into English by Sister Anne Marie Knawa, printed, and distributed to the Sisters. In addition, a spiral-bound stand-up booklet entitled *The Words of Mother M. Theresa* containing fifty-five pages and collated by Sister Anne Marie Knawa and Sister M. Jude Kruszewski was printed and distributed to each Sister.

Sister Martha Joan attended the meeting of the International Union of Superiors General in Rome in November of 1978. She met with Father Machejek at the offices of the Sacred Congregation for the Cause of Saints. They also met with Monsignor Cajetan Stano, a Conventual Franciscan, the promoter of causes. In the company of the Most Reverend Alfred Abramowicz, auxiliary bishop of Chicago, they also met with Conrad Cardinal Bafile, the cardinal prefect of the Sacred Congregation for the Cause of Saints. Father Machejek prepared the necessary documents for Cardinal Cody to sign giving permission for opening the cause of Mother M. Theresa Dudzik in the Archdiocese of Chicago.[30]

At the beginning of May 1979, Father Machejek informed Sister Martha Joan that he would come to Chicago in September to open the diocesan process.[31] On May 11, the Sacred Congregation agreed to grant permission for a Cognitive Process to be opened in the Archdiocese of Chicago. The prefect of the Sacred Congregation for the Cause of Saints, Cardinal Bafile, obtained the ratification of the decree *Nihil Obstat* with the signature of Pope John Paul II. On June 1, 1979, additional information for opening the beatification process was submitted to Cardinal Cody through the postulator from Rome.

The Cognitive Process for the Beatification of the Servant of God, Mother M. Theresa Dudzik, foundress of the Franciscan Sisters of Chicago, was opened officially in the Archdiocese of Chicago by the ordinary, John Cardinal Cody, on September 8, 1979. He celebrated a Pontifical Mass in the Sacred Heart Chapel at the Motherhouse with the Most Reverend Alfred Abramowicz, auxiliary bishop of Chicago; the Most Reverend Joseph Imesch, bishop of Joliet; and many attending clergy. The homilist, the Reverend Marion Matlak, who had been appointed vice-postulator after the death of the Reverend Chester Konsowski,[32] emphasized Mother M. Theresa's compassionate love for the poor, aged, crippled, and abandoned. The Tribunal Court was appointed and consisted of the following: the Most Reverend Alfred Abramowicz, presiding judge; the Right Reverend Monsignor Theodore Kaczorowski, co-judge; the Right Reverend Monsignor Edward Smaza, co-judge; the Right Reverend Monsignor Stanislaus Piwowar, promoter of the faith; the Reverend John Rolek, notary; the Reverend Joseph Nowak, notary; the Reverend Edward Janas, notary; Sister M. Alvernia Groszek, tribunal secretary; and Mr. Edward

Walera, courier. Along with the members of the Tribunal Court, the postulator, the Reverend Michael Machejek, and the vice-postulator, the Reverend Marion Matlak, took oaths at the opening public session of the Cognitive Process during the Eucharistic Liturgy.[33]

Investigation of the documents and the interrogation of witnesses was begun formally by the Tribunal Court at the Motherhouse on October 15, 1979. Subsequently, the Tribunal Court met every Monday at the Motherhouse of the Franciscan Sisters of Chicago for a period of two years. The sessions began at nine-thirty o'clock in the morning and continued until six o'clock in the evening. In the ninety-one sessions held, thirty-four Sisters, ten lay persons, one priest, two nieces of Mother M. Theresa, one grandniece and one grandnephew, and witnesses who testified to alleged miracles were interrogated. The testimonies were then sent to the Sacred Congregation for the Cause of Saints in Rome.[34]

A thirty-six page booklet entitled *Sprawa Chicagoska Beatifikacji i Kanonizacji Służebnicy Bożej Marii Teresy Dudzik Fundatorki Sióstr Franciszkanek Bł. Kunegundy, Chicago, Illinois* [The Matter of the Chicago Beatification and Canonization of the Servant of God, Mother M. Theresa Dudzik, the Foundress of the Franciscan Sisters of Blessed Kunegunda, Chicago, Illinois] was published by the postulator, Father Michael Machejek, in Rome in 1979. This was presented as documentary material to the Sacred Congregation for the Cause of Saints in Rome.

The Chicago Catholic, along with the *Chicago Sun-Times* and the *Chicago Tribune,* carried notices relating to the process of the beatification of Mother M. Theresa Dudzik. A "last call" for evidence pertaining to the cause for sainthood of Mother M. Theresa was one of the requirements of the process. It read:

FINAL CALL FOR DOCUMENTS IN THE
BEATIFICATION PROCESS OF
MOTHER MARY THERESA DUDZIK

The Cognitive Process in the Cause of the Beatification of the Servant of God, Mother Mary Theresa Dudzik, is drawing to a close. Mother Mary Theresa Dudzik was the foundress of the Congregation of the Franciscan Sisters of Blessed Kunegunda, (1894) now known as the Franciscan Sisters of Chicago since 1970, with the headquarters in Lemont, Ill.

In a few weeks the Tribunal in this Process will send to Rome all the Acts of this Cause. The Sacred Congregation for the Cause of Saints will then begin the study of the evidence and testimony of the witnesses concerning the heroic virtues of the Servant of God.

Before the transmission of these Acts to Rome, the Tribunal once again calls upon all possessing documents, writings, letters, or mementos of the Servant of God, to present them to the Tribunal for inspection.

All such information should be sent, at the latest, by May 15, 1981, addressed as follows:

The Reverend Marion Matlak,
Vice-postulator of Mother Theresa's Cause
c/o St. Cornelius Church
5205 Lieb
Chicago, Illinois 60630[35]

On Monday, July 27, 1981, three large boxes of original written testimony submitted by witnesses from 1970 to 1981 and two large boxes of transcripts were presented to Cardinal Cody. The Tribunal Court appointed by Cardinal Cody had met in September of 1979 in the Chancery Office for the ninety-first and last session to gather the final testimony and evidence concerning the life and heroic virtues of Mother M. Theresa. The transcripts were sent to the Apostolic Delegate in Washington, DC, who arranged to have them transported by way of diplomatic pouch to the Sacred Congregation for the Cause of Saints. The volume of materials was received by the postulator, Father Machejek, in August. In October of 1982, he, in turn, sent the Franciscan Sisters of Chicago a copy of a forty-page booklet entitled *Positio Super Scriptis* collated by the Sacred Congregation for the Cause of Saints. It presented a statement of the Sacred Congregation on the life and "Chronicle" of Mother M. Theresa Dudzik.[36]

The Franciscan Sisters of Chicago continue to work and pray for the cause of their holy foundress. In *Foundresses, Founders, and Their Religious Families*, the Reverend John Lozano, CMF, quotes from the Reverend Jerome Nadal, SJ, in *Commentarii de Instituto Societatis Jesu*:

> When God wishes to help His Church, He first raises up a person and gives him a special grace and a motion under which he must serve in a special way. This is what He did with St. Francis: He gave him a particular grace both for his personal advancement and for that of his companions . . . . In the same way He raised up Ignatius and gave him a gift, and through him, He gave it to us.[37]

Is it too presumptuous to believe that God raised up Mother M. Theresa Dudzik and gave her a special grace and a motion to serve Him in a special way? Is it too presumptuous to believe that God raised up Mother M. Theresa Dudzik and gave her a gift, and through her, He gave it to her daughters, the Franciscan Sisters of Chicago?

THE BEATIFICATION AND CANONIZATION PROCESS OF THE SERVANT OF GOD, MOTHER MARY THERESA DUDZIK, FOUNDRESS OF THE CONGREGATION OF THE FRANCISCAN SISTERS OF CHICAGO

[1]Jacques Douillet, *What Is a Saint?* (New York: Hawthorn Books, 1958), p. 89.

[2]Acts 2:13.

[3]See Appendix A.

[4]Years later, Sister M. Bridget Czuj painted beautiful oil paintings of Mother M. Theresa and Mother M. Anna which hung in the main lobby of St. Joseph Home for the Aged. Presently they are in the Mother M. Theresa Museum in Lemont.

[5]*Minutes of General Council Proceedings, 1934–1956* (AFSCL).

[6]Secretaries General, *Community Chronicle, 1939* (AFSCL).

[7]*Minutes of General Council Proceedings, 1934–1956* (AFSCL)

[8]The Reverend Francis Cegiełka, a member of the Society of the Catholic Apostolate founded by St. Vincent Pallotti, was born and educated in Poland. He was ordained in Rome and obtained his doctorate in theology at the Pontifical Gregorian University. His early years of priestly ministry were spent in France. In 1937, he was appointed by August Cardinal Hlond to take care of 500,000 Poles and about 100 Polish priests working among the Poles in France. During the German occupation of France in 1940, he was arrested and incarcerated in nine prisons as well as in the concentration camps of Sachsenhausen and Dachau. Liberated by the American Seventh Army in 1945, he returned to France where he received the "Legion d'Honneur."

From his arrival in the United States in 1948, he worked as a retreat master for religious women and priests. He served as a faculty member at Felician College, Lodi, New Jersey, and Holy Family College in Philadelphia, Pennsylvania. In 1970, he traveled to Pakistan, India, Thailand, and Japan studying the religions of Asia. He published a number of books in Polish and English dealing with the religious life. Biographical sketch received from the Reverend M. Leszczynski, SAC, Society of the Catholic Apostolate, Pallottine Fathers, North Tonawanda, New York (AFSCL).

In 1952, Father Cegiełka gave conferences to the novices at Our Lady of Victory Convent about two or three times a year.

[9]*Book of Correspondence:* Letter from the Reverend Francis Cegiełka to Mother M. Jerome Dadej, 1949 (AFSCL).

[10]Born in Rome, the Very Reverend Aristeo Simoni made his profession in the Congregation of the Resurrection in 1897, and was ordained in Rome in 1901. While in the congregation, he was assigned to St. Jerome's College, Kitchener, Canada; St. Mary's College, St. Mary, Kentucky; and St. Stanislaus Kostka Church and St. Stanislaus College, Chicago. He was a chaplain in the United States Army for many years and was decorated with the Distinguished Service Cross.

In 1922, he left the Resurrectionist community and transferred to the Rockford Diocese. In 1952, he was incardinated into the Archdiocese of Chicago and became vice-postulator in the beatification cause of Mother Cabrini, America's citizen saint. Chairperson of the Mother Cabrini League in Chicago, he was also a literary contributor to the *Mother Cabrini Messenger*. He retired with residence at Columbus Hospital in Chicago where he died in 1958. Edward T. Janas, CR, *Dictionary of American Resurrectionists, 1865–1965* (Rome: Gregorian University Press, 1967) pp. 111–112.

[11]*Minutes of General Council Proceedings, 1934–1957* (AFSCL).

[12]Secretaries General, *Community Chronicle,* p. 282 (AFSCL).

[13]Ibid.

[14]The Reverend Henry Malak was born on November 1, 1912, in Poland. After completing junior college, he passed a state examination and continued his education in Gniezno and Poznań. He was ordained in 1938. The outbreak of the Second World War cut short his priestly work. He spent six years in Nazi concentration camps including the last four in Dachau before being liberated. He then served as a pastor in Germany from 1945 to 1950 when he came to the United States. He worked for the Franciscan Publishers in Pulaski, Wisconsin, where he edited articles and pamphlets. He also gave retreats to various Sisterhoods including the Franciscan Sisters of Chicago. Father Malak, a perpetual tertiary of the Third Order of St. Francis, died in the infirmary of the Franciscan Sisters of Chicago on July 19, 1987.

[15]Secretaries General, *Community Chronicle, 1957–1960* (AFSCL).

[16]This is a permission from a competent ecclesiastical authority to publish a book that may be safely read without damage to faith or morals. The *Imprimatur* may be obtained where the work is written, printed, or published.

[17]Secretaries General, *Community Chronicle, 1957–1960* (AFSCL).

[18]In December of 1951, Sister M. Alvernia Groszek presented a paper "The Franciscan Sisters of Bl. Kunegunda" at the Polish American Historical Association convention in Chicago. The paper was published in *Polish American Studies,* Vol. VIII, No. 3–4, July–December1951, pp. 92–96. In 1961, Sister Clarent Marie Urbanowicz presented a sketch of Mother M. Theresa's life at the 17th Annual Meeting of the Polish American Historical Association in Buffalo, New York. The paper was also published in *Polish American Studies*. In 1977, Sister Anne MarieKnawa presented a paper entitled "Jane Addams and Josephine Dudzik: Social Service Pioneers," at the Polish American Historical Association convention in Dallas, Texas. The paper was published in *Polish American Studies,* Vol. XXXV, No. 1–2, Spring–Autumn, 1978.

[19]Secretaries General, *Community Chronicle, 1957–1970* (AFSCL).

[20]Ibid.

[21]*Franciscan Echo,* (Lemont, Illinois: 1963).

[22]See Chapter 61.

[23]*Minutes of General Council Proceedings, 1934–1974* (AFSCL).

[24]Ibid.

[25]Sister M. Alvernia Groszek, "Written Report Concerning the Cause of Mother M. Theresa Dudzik," 1983 (AFSCL).

[26]Ibid.

[27]Reverend Henry M. Malak, ed., *The Apostle of Mercy from Chicago* (Lemont: December 1973), pp. 9–10.

[28]Secretaries General, *Community Chronicle, 1934–1974* (AFSCL).

[29]This phrase is used by the censor of books to indicate that he has examined the book and found nothing against faith and morals that would prevent its publication.

[30]*Minutes of General Council Proceedings, 1957–1980* (AFSCL).

[31]*Bulletins of the Superior General,* "From the Desk of Sister M. Hugoline," November 1978.

[32]Father Konsowski died in 1974.

[33]Groszek, "Written Report" (AFSCL).

[34]*Franciscan Brief,* vol. 3 (Lemont Illinois: November–December 1980).

[35]*Chicago Catholic,* 10 April 1981.

[36]*Franciscan Brief,* vol. 5 (Lemont Illinois: September–October 1982).

[37]Jerome Nadal, SJ, "Exhortions 1555 in Hispania" nn. 4–5, in *Commentarii,* cited by John M. Lozano, CMF, *Foundresses, Founders, and Their Religious Families* (Chicago: Claret Center for Resources in Spirituality, 1983), p. 22.

THE EMBLEM OF THE CONGREGATION OF
THE FRANCISCAN SISTERS OF CHICAGO

949

The Franciscan Sisters of Chicago have chosen as the basis of their emblem[1] the ancient *Chi Rho,* the Greek symbol for Christ whose Holy Gospel they have promised to observe. The letter *M,* with its ulterior curved lines, rises from the stem of the *Chi Rho* and symbolizes Mary, the Mother of God, whom Saint Francis of Assisi chose as patroness and advocate of his Order for all times.[2] The Madonna lily represents Mary under her title, the Immaculate Conception, to whom Mother Mary Theresa Dudzik had a profound and fervent devotion, and to whose patronage she entrusted the congregation from its foundation.[3]

Transversed at the base of the *Chi Rho* are the pierced hands of Jesus and Saint Francis whose ardent love for the Crucified Christ resulted in the impression of the sacred stigmata on his body. The crossbar and the stem of the *Chi Rho* form the *Tau,* a T-shaped cross, sometimes called the Old Testament cross, a sign of God's love and salvation for his Chosen People.[4] The *Tau* engendered in Saint Francis a great reverence for its mystic significance; consequently, he placed it in his writings and used it as his usual signature.[5] These graphic symbols combine to identify the Sisters as members of the Third Order Regular of Saint Francis of Assisi.

The specific character of Franciscanism is the commitment of its members to live the Gospel message of charity toward God, humanity, and all of God's creation; to embrace penance and poverty; to render joyful and dedicated service to the people of God; and to be messengers of peace and Christian community according to the example of their Seraphic Father, Saint Francis. The essence of Franciscan spirituality is contained in the constant aspiration of Saint Francis, "My God and my All," which the congregation has accepted as its motto. This motto best expresses the ideal which the Franciscan Sisters of Chicago strive to imitate.[6]

NOTES AND REFERENCES

[1]The emblem of the Franciscan Sisters of Chicago was designed by Sister M. Sponsa Bajorek, OSF.

[2]*Vita Secunda* or *Second Life of St. Francis* by Thomas of Celano cited by Marion H. Habig, ed., *St. Francis of Assisi, Writings and Early Biographies: English Omnibus of the Sources for the Life of St. Francis* (Chicago: Franciscan Herald Press, 1972), p. 521.

[3]Matka Maria Teresa Dudzik, "Kronika Sióstr Franciszkanek, pod opieką Św. Kunegundy w Chicago, Illinois" [The Chronicle of the Franciscan Sisters under the patronage of St. Kunegunda in Chicago, Illinois] Unpublished manuscript, Chicago, 1910 (AFSCL).

[4]F. R. Webber, *Church Symbolism,* 2nd ed. rev. (Cleveland: J. H. Hansen, 1938), p. 104.

[5]*Major Life of St. Francis* by St. Bonaventure cited by Marion H. Habig, ed., *St. Francis of Assisi, Writings and Early Biographies: English Omnibus of the Sources for the Life of St. Francis* (Chicago: Franciscan Herald Press, 1972), p. 660.

[6]The interpretation of the emblem of the Franciscan Sisters of Chicago was formulated by Sister Anne Marie Knawa, OSF.

APPENDIX D

MAJOR SUPERIORS OF THE CONGREGATION OF THE
FRANCISCAN SISTERS OF CHICAGO

MOTHERS SUPERIOR	TERM OF OFFICE
Sister M. Theresa Dudzik	December 23, 1894–October 4, 1898
Sister M. Anna Wysinski	October 4, 1898–October 4, 1905
Sister M. Vincent Czyzewski	October 4, 1905–January 1, 1909
Sister M. Theresa Dudzik	January 1, 1909–August 12, 1910

MOTHERS GENERAL	TERM OF OFFICE
Mother M. Anna Wysinski	August 12, 1910–July 20, 1916
Mother M. Aloysia Holysz	July 20, 1916–July 20, 1922
Mother M. Vincent Czyzewski	July 20, 1922–June 29, 1928
Mother M. Aloysia Holysz	June 29, 1928–July 2, 1934
Mother M. Antonina Osinski	July 2, 1934–June 29, 1940
Mother M. Theresa Dudzik*	
Mother M. Mechtilde Zynda†	June 29, 1940–March 16, 1946
Mother M. Jerome Dadej**	March 16, 1946 July 2, 1946–July 2, 1952 July 2, 1952–June 20, 1958
Mother M. Beatrice Rybacki	June 30, 1958–July 2, 1964 July 2, 1964–June 24, 1970
Sister M. Hugoline Czaplinski***#	June 24, 1970–June 24, 1974 June 24, 1974–June 24, 1978
Sister Martha Joan Sempolski=	June 24, 1978–June 24, 1983
Sister Joseph Marie Zenda††	June 24, 1983–

* The sixth general chapter held in 1940 unanimously agreed to accord the title "Mother" to Sister M. Theresa Dudzik.

† Mother M. Mechtilde died on March 16, 1946.

** Sister M. Jerome Dadej, assistant general, completed Mother M. Mechtilde's term.

*** The title of "Mother" was changed to "Sister" by the Eleventh General Chapter held in 1970 in an effort to effect collegiality.

Sister M. Hugoline was re-elected for another four-year term at the election session of the Twelfth General Chapter on April 15, 1974.

= Sister Martha Joan was elected for a five-year term at the election session of the Thirteenth General Chapter on March 28, 1978. She took office on June 24, 1978.

†† Sister Joseph Marie was elected for a five-year term at the election session of the Fourteenth General Chapter on April 4, 1983. She took office on June 24, 1983.

APPENDIX E

SUPERIORS GENERAL AND MEMBERS
OF THE GENERAL COUNCIL OF THE CONGREGATION OF
THE FRANCISCAN SISTERS OF CHICAGO

FIRST GENERAL CHAPTER OF ELECTIONS: 1910–1916

Superior general	Mother M. Anna Wysinski
Assistant general and first councilor	Sister M. Vincent Czyzewski
Second councilor	Sister M. Hedwig Kubera
Third councilor	Sister M. Andrea Zawadzki
Secretary general	Sister M. Aloysia Holysz
Procurator	Sister M. Salomea Grabowski

SECOND GENERAL CHAPTER OF ELECTIONS: 1916–1922

Superior general	Mother M. Aloysia Holysz
Assistant general and first councilor	Sister M. Clara Ogurek
Second councilor	Sister M. Hedwig Kubera
Third councilor	Sister M. Andrea Zawadzki
Secretary general	Sister M. Philipine Lama
Procurator	Sister M. Salomea Grabowski

THIRD GENERAL CHAPTER OF ELECTIONS: 1922–1928

Superior general	Mother M. Vincent Czyzewski
Assistant general and first councilor	Sister M. Philipine Lama
Second councilor	Sister M. Sylvestra Pelczar
Third councilor and secretary general	Sister M. Benigna Jakajtis
Procurator	Sister M. Leona Pochelski

FOURTH GENERAL CHAPTER OF ELECTIONS: 1928–1934

Superior general	Mother M. Aloysia Holysz
Assistant general and first councilor	Sister M. Benigna Jakajtis
Second councilor	Sister M. Seraphine Zamrowski
Third councilor	Sister M. Innocenta Antosz
Fourth councilor and secretary general	Sister M. Leona Pochelski

FIFTH GENERAL CHAPTER OF ELECTIONS: 1934–1940

Superior general	Mother M. Antonina Osinski
Vicar general and first councilor	Sister M. Innocenta Antosz
Second councilor	Sister M. Salomea Grabowski
Third councilor	Sister M. Stephanie Pinkowski
Fourth councilor and secretary general	Sister M. Jerome Dadej
Procurator	Sister M. Raphael Bogalecki

SIXTH GENERAL CHAPTER OF ELECTIONS: 1940–1946

Superior general	Mother M. Mechtilde Zynda
Vicar general and first councilor	Sister M. Jerome Dadej
Second councilor	Sister M. Philipine Lama
Third councilor and secretary general	Sister M. Paul Kirschbaum
Fourth councilor	Sister M. John Barczak
Procurator	Sister M. Raphael Bogalecki

SEVENTH GENERAL CHAPTER OF ELECTIONS: 1946–1952

Superior general	Mother M. Jerome Dadej
Vicar general and first councilor	Sister M. Felixa Jorz
Second councilor	Sister M. John Barczak
Third councilor	Mother M. Antonina Osinski
Fourth councilor and secretary general	Sister M. Gonzaga Raniszewski
Procurator	Sister M. Raphael Bogalecki

EIGHTH GENERAL CHAPTER OF ELECTIONS: 1952–1958

Superior general	Mother M. Jerome Dadej
Vicar general and first councilor	Mother M. Antonina Osinski
Second councilor	Sister M. Edward Nowak
Third councilor and secretary general	Sister M. Gonzaga Raniszewski
Fourth councilor	Sister M. Alberta Bialas
Procurator	Sister M. Aloysetta Ciezadlo

NINTH GENERAL CHAPTER OF ELECTIONS: 1958–1964

Superior general	Mother M. Beatrice Rybacki
Vicar general and first councilor	Sister M. Venantia Rec
Second councilor	Sister M. Crescencia Chmiel
Third councilor and secretary general	Sister M. Gonzaga Raniszewski
Fourth councilor	Sister M. Edward Nowak
General bursar	Sister M. Aloysetta Ciezadlo

TENTH GENERAL CHAPTER OF ELECTIONS: 1964–1970

Superior general	Mother M. Beatrice Rybacki
Vicar general and first councilor	Sister M. Venantia Rec
Second councilor	Sister M. Hugoline Czaplinski
Third councilor and secretary general	Sister M. Gonzaga Raniszewski
Fourth councilor	Sister M. Rosalima Sierocki
General bursar	Sister M. Aloysetta Ciezadlo

FIRST EXTRAORDINARY CHAPTER OF AFFAIRS: 1968

ELEVENTH GENERAL CHAPTER OF ELECTIONS: 1970–1974

Superior general	Sister M. Hugoline Czaplinski
Assistant superior general	Sister M. Antonissima Jamruk
Apostolate coordinator	Sister M. Alberta Bialas
Secretary general	Sister M. Alvernia Groszek
Treasurer	Sister M. Ralph Stawasz

SECOND SPECIAL CHAPTER OF AFFAIRS: 1972

TWELFTH GENERAL CHAPTER OF ELECTIONS: 1974–1978

Superior general	Sister M. Hugoline Czaplinski
Assistant superior general	Sister M. Antonissima Jamruk
Apostolate coordinator	Sister M. Gabriel Lazarski
Secretary general	Sister M. Alvernia Groszek
Treasurer	Sister M. Ralph Stawasz

THIRTEENTH GENERAL CHAPTER OF ELECTIONS: 1978–1983

Superior general	Sister Martha Joan Sempolski
Assistant superior general	Sister M. Antonissima Jamruk
First councilor	Sister M. Hugoline Czaplinski
Second councilor	Sister M. Gabriel Lazarski
Secretary generel	Sister M. Alvernia Groszek
Treasurer	Sister M. Ralph Stawasz

FOURTEENTH GENERAL CHAPTER OF ELECTIONS: 1983-1988

Superior general	Sister Joseph Marie Zenda
Assistant superior general and first councilor	Sister M. Francis Clare Radke
Second councilor	Sister M. Alvernia Groszek
Third councilor	Sister M. Hugoline Czaplinski
Fourth councilor and secretary general	Sister M. Francine Labus
Treasurer	Sister M. Ralph Stawasz

APPENDIX F

HOUSES AND INSTITUTIONS STAFFED BY THE
CONGREGATION OF THE FRANCISCAN SISTERS OF CHICAGO

YEAR ACCEPTED	YEAR RELINQUISHED	NAME	LOCATION	MINISTRY
1898		St. Joseph Home for the Aged and Crippled / St. Joseph Home of Chicago	Chicago, Illinois	Home for the aged
1899	1911	St. Vincent Orphan Asylum	Chicago, Illinois	Home for orphans
1901	1903	SS. Peter and Paul	Spring Valley, Illinois	Elementary school
1902		St. Stanislaus Bishop and Martyr	Chicago, Illinois	Elementary school
1903	1976 *	St. Casimir	Cleveland, Ohio	Elementary school
1904	1915	St. Elizabeth's Day Nursery	Chicago, Illinois	Day care center
1904	1907	St. Michael	Berlin, Wisconsin	Elementary school
1905	1906	St. Casimir	St. Louis, Missouri	Elementary school
1905	1911	St. Josaphat	Oshkosh, Wisconsin	Elementary school
1906	1913	St. Adalbert Bishop and Martyr	Whiting, Indiana	Elementary school
1906	1912	St. Stanislaus Kostka	St. Louis, Missouri	Elementary school
1907	1979	St. John Cantius / Indiana Harbor Catholic Elementary School	Indiana Harbor, Indiana	Elementary school

*In 1976, the school closed and the Sisters' ministry was that of sacristans and parish visitors. Ten years later they withdrew completely.

954

Year	Name	Location	Type
1907	St. Adalbert	East St. Louis, Illinois	Elementary school
1908	St. Florian	Chicago, Illinois	Elementary school
1909	St. Hedwig Day Nursery	Chicago, Illinois	Day care center
1909	St. Hedwig	Gary, Indiana	Elementary school
1909	St. Stanislaus Kostka	Youngstown, Ohio	Elementary school
1910	SS. Peter and Paul	Spring Valley, Illinois	Elementary school
1911	St. Stanislaus Bishop and Martyr	Posen, Illinois	Elementary school
1911	Holy Trinity	Falls City, Texas	Elementary school
1911	St. Stanislaus Kostka	Falls City, Texas	Elementary school
1911	St. Roch	La Salle, Illinois	Elementary school
1912	Five Holy Martyrs	Chicago, Illinois	Elementary school
1912	St. Casimir / West End Consolidation School	Johnstown, Pennsylvania	Elementary school
1912	Assumption of the Blessed Virgin Mary / Conemaugh Catholic Consolidation School	Conemaugh, Pennsylvania	Elementary school
1914	St. Mary of Częstochowa	Hammond, Indiana	Elementary school
1915	Sacred Heart of Jesus	Gary (Tolleston), Indiana	Elementary school
1916	Sacred Heart of Jesus	La Porte, Indiana	Elementary school
1917	St. Michael	Glen Campbell, Pennsylvania	Elementary school
1917	St. Adalbert	Farrell, Pennsylvania	Elementary school
1917	SS. Peter and Paul	Arcadia, Pennsylvania	Elementary school
1917	St. Mary of Częstochowa	Madison, Illinois	Elementary school

Year	Institution	Location	Type
1917	St. Casimir	Streator, Illinois	Elementary school
1917	St. Joseph	East Chicago, Indiana	Elementary school
1917	Guardian Angel Day Nursery and Home for Working Girls / Guardian Angel Day Care Center and Home for Ladies †	Chicago, Illinois	Day care center and home for ladies
1918	Assumption of the Blessed Virgin Mary	New Chicago, Indiana	Elementary school
1919	Sacred Heart of Jesus	Cleveland, Ohio	Elementary school
1920	St. Elizabeth's Day Nursery	Chicago, Illinois	Day care center
1924	St. Pancratius	Chicago, Illinois	Elementary school
1926	Our Lady of Victory Convent	Lemont, Illinois	Novitiate house
1934	Our Lady of Spring Bank Cistercian Abbey	Okauchee, Wisconsin	Domestic department
1936	Mount Alvernia Convent	East Cleveland, Ohio	House of studies / home for aged women
1936	St. Florian	Chicago, Illinois	Parochial commercial high school
1936	Our Lady of Victory Convent	Lemont, Illinois	Home for retired Sisters
1938	The Catholic Sisters College The Catholic University of America	Washington, DC	Domestic department
1939	South Heart Public School	South Heart, North Dakota	Elementary and high school
1939	St. Anthony Home	Crown Point, Indiana	Home for the aged

† In 1983, the ministry to the Home for Ladies ceased to exist and the institution was called Guardian Angel Day Care Center.

1940	Boys Town	Boys Town, Nebraska	Domestic, religion, bookkeeping, and sewing departments
1940	Our Lady of Victory Convent	Lemont, Illinois	Novitiate house
1943	St. Peter Claver	Mobile, Alabama	Elementary school
1943	St. Joseph Home for the Aged	Cleveland, Ohio	Home for the aged
1944	St. John the Baptist / St. Joseph the Provider	Campbell, Ohio	Elementary school
1946	Madonna Hall	Cleveland, Ohio	Home for aged women
1947	St. John Hospital and School of Nursing / St. John Regional Medical Center	Huron, South Dakota	Hospital and school of nursing
1948	Mother of Grace (Gregory Community Hospital)	Gregory, South Dakota	Hospital
1948	St. Philip of Jesus Community Center	Chicago, Illinois	Social center
1949	Madonna High School	Chicago, Illinois	Secondary school
1950	SS. Philip and James	Cleveland, Ohio	Elementary school
1952	Mount Alverna Home	Parma, Ohio	Home for the aged
1952	St. Anthony Hospital	Martin, South Dakota	Hospital
1952	Our Lady of the Sandhills (Atkinson Memorial Hospital)	Atkinson, Nebraska	Hospital
1953	Johnstown Central Catholic High School	Johnstown, Pennsylvania	Secondary school
1955	St. Leo the Great	Cleveland, Ohio	Elementary school
1956	St. Louise de Marillac	La Grange Park, Illinois	Elementary school
1960	Blessed Sacrament	Gary, Indiana	Elementary school

1963		Our Lady of Victory Convent	Lemont, Illinois	Motherhouse and Novitiate
1964		Mother Theresa Home	Lemont, Illinois	Home for the aged
1970	1975	St. Matthias	Crown Point, Indiana	Religious education
1971	1975	St. James	Arlington Heights, Illinois	Youth ministry
1974		St. Anthony Medical Center	Crown Point, Indiana	Hospital
1976		St. Genevieve	Chicago, Illinois	Religious education
1976	1980	St. Pascal Baylon	Chicago, Illinois	Religious education
1978		St. Rose of Lima	Chicago, Illinois	Parish ministry
1980		Our Lady of Ransom	Niles, Illinois	Religious education
1980		St. Francis House House of Prayer	Lemont, Illinois	House of prayer
1980		Holy Family Child Care Center	Crown Point, Indiana	Child care center
1983		St. Anthony of Padua	Parma, Ohio	Elementary school
1984		The "PORT"	Chicago, Illinois	Shelter for hungry and homeless
1986		St. Martin de Porres House of Hope	Chicago, Illinois	Shelter for homeless women and children

APPENDIX G

PRESENT MEMBERSHIP OF THE CONGREGATION
OF THE FRANCISCAN SISTERS OF CHICAGO

(As of September 1, 1987)

Sister Anne Marie Knawa
Sister Ann Rose Mroz (Nazaria)
Sister Bernice Marie Junio (Stanisia)
Sister Carol Marie Schommer (Jane Frances)
Sister Clarent Marie Urbanowicz (Clarenta)
Sister Diane Marie Collins
Sister Doloria Kosiek
Sister Dorothy Joan Lagocki (Anthony)
Sister Eleanor Marie Jadrych (Ignatius)
Sister Elizabeth Marie Jadrych (Stephanilla)
Sister Emilie Marie Lesniak
Sister Frances Szczur (Heliodore)
Sister Helen Marie Zasadzinski (Emerentia)
Sister Jean Adamczyk (Seraphica)
Sister Jeanne Marie Toriskie
Sister Jean Therese Jarosz (Michael Therese)
Sister Josephine Marie Haske (Humiliata)
Sister Joseph Marie Zenda
Sister Julianne Markowicz (Euphrasia)
Sister Kathleen Melia (Agnes Ann)
Sister Leona Watroba (Hedwinella)
Sister Lillian Watroba (Sidonia)
Sister Linda Therese Holmes
Sister Lois Marie Rossi
Sister Lora Ann Slawinski
Sister Lora Marie Frantz
Sister Louise Ann Glowacki (Amalia)
Sister Marianne Kaplan (Fortunata)
Sister Marie Dominic Wyza
Sister Marie Frances Niecikowski (Innocent)
Sister Martha Joan Sempolski (Anatolia)
Sister Mary Adelaide Szyper
Sister Mary Adelma Walkowski
Sister Mary Agatha Walerski
Sister Mary Agnella Sieja
Sister Mary Agnes Zywiec
Sister Mary Alacoque Czartoryski
Sister Mary Albertine Schab
Sister Mary Alcantara Ochwat
Sister Mary Alice Klepek
Sister Mary Aloysilla Kedzior
Sister Mary Alphonsine Kobylinski
Sister Mary Altissima Netzel
Sister Mary Alvernia Groszek

Sister Mary Amabilis Bellock
Sister Mary Ambrosia Tworek
Sister Mary Andrea Puchalski
Sister Mary Angelica Seidl
Sister Mary Angeline Kedzior
Sister Mary Annuncia Milanowski
Sister Mary Antonella Abramowicz
Sister Mary Antoniana Stanczak
Sister Mary Antonissima Jamruk
Sister Mary Antonita Waloch
Sister Mary Aquinas Rosky
Sister Mary Arcadia Chmiel
Sister Mary Archangela Tyranski
Sister Mary Aurelia Zyla
Sister Mary Basil Ochocinski
Sister Mary Beata Klecha
Sister Mary Beatrice Rybacki
Sister Mary Bernadette Bajuscik
Sister Mary Bertha Kaminski
Sister Mary Bertille Geffert
Sister Mary Boniface Pranke
Sister Mary Bronisia Kapusnik
Sister Mary Carmel Rokicki
Sister Mary Cecilia Trocki (Leonard)
Sister Mary Celeste Walkowski
Sister Mary Charitas Gajdzinski
Sister Mary Christine Brzozowski
Sister Mary Clare Brunkala
Sister Mary Clarissa Kolupka
Sister Mary Clarissima Zielaskiewicz
Sister Mary Claudia Bomba
Sister Mary Claudiana Jachimowicz
Sister Mary Clemensa Klepek
Sister Mary Colette Kwieczka
Sister Mary Colombiere Piotrowski
Sister Mary Concordia Lawrence
Sister Mary Consilia Przybyl
Sister Mary Consolata Markowicz
Sister Mary Crescencia Chmiel
Sister Mary Crescentine Oszuscik
Sister Mary Cundette Minchuk
Sister Mary De Chantal Mazuryk
Sister Mary Delphine Brzozowski
Sister Mary Deofilia Piaskowy

Names in parentheses were given to each Sister on entering the congregation; these names were relinquished in 1968 when Sisters were permitted to reassume their baptismal names.

Sister Mary De Sales Wyszynski
Sister Mary Dolores Radziwiecki
Sister Mary Doloretta Radzienda
Sister Mary Dolorine Piwowarski
Sister Mary Donald Urban
Sister Mary Dorothea Micek
Sister Mary Dorothy Szostek
Sister Mary Dosithea Ruz
Sister Mary Dulcissima Kaczmarek
Sister Mary Edward Nowak
Sister Mary Edwina Wilk
Sister Mary Edwinette Wisz
Sister Mary Elaine Bartkowski
Sister Mary Electa Rytel
Sister Mary Emily Kowal
Sister Mary Ephrem Soprych
Sister Mary Epiphany Gorski
Sister Mary Equitia Nawracaj
Sister Mary Ernestine Radecki
Sister Mary Esther Obuchowski
Sister Mary Eucheria Obara
Sister Mary Eusebius Kolupka
Sister Mary Eymard Sanok
Sister Mary Felicia Wierciak
Sister Mary Francesca Janowicz
Sister Mary Francine Labus
Sister Mary Francis Clare Radke
Sister Mary Gabriel Lazarski
Sister Mary Gaythee Young
Sister Mary Gemma Stanek
Sister Mary Generose Siepak
Sister Mary Georgeann Kinel
Sister Mary Gracianne Fibich
Sister Mary Hedwinette Burliga
Sister Mary Helene Galuszka
Sister Mary Hermenegilde Moszczynski
Sister Mary Honoria Urbaniak
Sister Mary Hubert Jasinski
Sister Mary Hugoline Czaplinski
Sister Mary Illuminata Szczepanski
Sister Mary Innocent Smagacz
Sister Mary Irmina Kon
Sister Mary Jeanette Golojuch
Sister Mary Joella Bielinski
Sister Mary Joseph Grochowski
Sister Mary Josephine Penza
Sister Mary Josette Kuczmarski
Sister Mary Jude Kruszewski
Sister Mary Julitta Szczepanik
Sister Mary Kinga Repinski
Sister Mary Kingnetta Szczypula
Sister Mary Laetitia Kolczak
Sister Mary Leonida Bywalec
Sister Mary Leonilla Stogowski
Sister Mary Liliosa Hoinski
Sister Mary Lillian Szura
Sister Mary Louise Nowicki
Sister Mary Loyola Dymanowski

Sister Mary Lucille Klockowski
Sister Mary Lucretia Kot
Sister Mary Ludmilla Fedak
Sister Mary Marifilia Strzycki
Sister Mary Marinella Gubala
Sister Mary Maristella Skrzynski
Sister Mary Marylla Stanislawczyk
Sister Mary Maurita Wszolek
Sister Mary Maximina Pachut
Sister Mary Michael Siebab
Sister Mary Mildred Bieda
Sister Mary Monica Sendlosky
Sister Mary Natalie Uscinowicz
Sister Mary Olga Kulik
Sister Mary Olivia Pacek
Sister Mary Pachomia Rychlicki
Sister Mary Petronia Budzinski (Piotronia)
Sister Mary Placidia Rzonca
Sister Mary Praesentia Grzybowski
Sister Mary Pulcheria Mikolajczyk
Sister Mary Purissima Babinski
Sister Mary Ralph Stawasz
Sister Mary Regina Krolak
Sister Mary Renata Krukowski
Sister Mary Richard Duszynski
Sister Mary Roberta Duda
Sister Mary Rosalima Sierocki
Sister Mary Rosaria Frodyma
Sister Mary Rose Ann Zmich
Sister Mary Rosemary Ferus
Sister Mary Rose Wilbur Flower
Sister Mary Salomina Rzonca
Sister Mary Seraphinia Furman
Sister Mary Simon Glowacki
Sister Mary Sponsa Bajorek
Sister Mary Symphorosa Goryszewski
Sister Mary Tarcisia Bucki
Sister Mary Teresita Kuczmarski
Sister Mary Thaddea Duran
Sister Mary Therese Grajek
Sister Mary Theresilla Ignasiak
Sister Mary Theresine Wojciechowicz
Sister Mary Tyburcia Sliwa
Sister Mary Venantia Rec
Sister Mary Veronica Blaszkiewicz
Sister Mary Vincent Swies
Sister Mary Virgina Murawski
Sister Mary Virginette Rokicki
Sister Paula Frances Howard
Sister Rose Therese Bzibziak
Sister Sharon Marie Haugh
Sister Sophie Marie Kierszke (Henry)
Sister Susan Catherine Bayliss (Matthew)
Sister Susan Diane Brunovsky
Sister Theresa Mary Obremski (Stanislaus Marie)
Sister Therese Agnes Kniola (Plautille)
Sister Victoria Valerie Smagacz (Silveria)

APPENDIX H

DECEASED MEMBERS OF THE CONGREGATION
OF THE FRANCISCAN SISTERS OF CHICAGO
(As of September 1, 1987)

Sister M. Delphine Myszewski	July 30, 1908
Sister M. Ignatia Dukowski	July 6, 1911
Sister M. Bernadine Narozny	January 24, 1912
Sister M. Bonaventure Blazek	November 10, 1912
Sister M. Philomena Marszalkowski	August 6, 1914
Sister M. Pelagia Bywalec	November 15, 1914
Mother M. Anna Wysinski	January 27, 1917
Sister M. Theodore Laski	August 17, 1918
Sister M. Josepha Suchomski	August 30, 1918
Mother M. Theresa Dudzik	September 20, 1918
Sister M. Boleslaus Nagorski	December 3, 1918
Sister M. Gertrude Haniewicz	April 10, 1919
Sister M. Felixa Karwata	April 24, 1920
Sister M. Melanie Stoinski	July 3, 1920
Sister M. Clemensa Steczko	August 11, 1920
Sister M. Caroline Cabaj	November 18, 1920
Sister M. Methodia Pajdo	March 23, 1921
Sister M. Leonarda Dzierwa	May 5, 1923
Sister M. Simplicia Bloch	June 12, 1923
Sister M. Emily Kondziolka	October 27, 1923
Sister M. Bernarda Jagiello	March 21, 1928
Sister M. Kinga Gajda	December 28, 1928
Sister M. Lucy Murdza	January 24, 1929
Sister M. Andrea Zawadzki	August 15, 1929
Sister M. Pancratius Pankowski	June 25, 1930
Sister M. Chrysostom Keller	June 27, 1930
Mother M. Angelina Topolinski	December 4, 1930
Sister M. Agnes Roszak	April 7, 1931
Sister M. Gabriela Moskal	March 11, 1932
Sister M. Cyrilla Gawlowicz	March 18, 1932
Sister M. Angela Kolodziej	April 28, 1934
Sister M. Annunciata Klimasz	July 5, 1934
Sister M. Rufina Klucznik	August 10, 1934
Sister M. Ignatia Hodkiewicz	September 5, 1934
Sister M. Veronica Maka	October 31, 1934
Sister M. Agatha Kostka	April 24, 1935
Sister M. Michael Sobieszczyk	October 15, 1935
Sister M. Dorthea Tomon	January 23, 1936
Sister M. Christine Zborowski	February 1, 1936
Sister M. Bonaventure Paprocki	August 18, 1936
Sister M. Salesia Rzeszutko	February 1, 1937
Sister M. Dominic Makowski	February 10, 1937
Sister M. Claudia Florek	February 11, 1937
Sister M. Innocenta Antosz	March 6, 1938
Sister M. Rosalie Scepuniak	July 14, 1940
Sister M. Florentine Karasek	October 16, 1940

Sister M. Alexa Olszewski	January 29, 1941
Sister M. Kostka Baron	May 1, 1941
Sister M. Peter Ostrega	June 3, 1941
Sister M. Francis Drufke	October 21, 1941
Mother M. Vincent Czyzewski	April 22, 1942
Sister M. Marcelline Molek	July 7, 1942
Sister M. Augustine Malinowski	August 3, 1942
Sister M. Regina Iwan	November 11, 1942
Sister M. Cantius Gruca	April 28, 1944
Sister M. Colette Nowak	September 25, 1945
Mother M. Mechtilde Zynda	March 16, 1946
Sister M. Casimir Janowiak	June 28, 1947
Sister M. Margaret Nawracaj	August 29, 1947
Sister M. Nicholas Poterek	January 14, 1949
Sister M. Seraphine Zamrowski	September 7, 1949
Sister M. Paulette Barnak	October 1, 1949
Sister M. Stephanie Pinkowski	February 17, 1950
Sister M. Theophilla Stasiek	January 26, 1951
Sister M. Celestine Potwora	September 29, 1951
Sister M. Constance Pajdo	December 14, 1951
Sister M. Wenceslaus Gorski	March 10, 1952
Sister M. Monica Frankowski	May 16, 1953
Sister M. Cajetan Tabasz	June 10, 1953
Sister M. Thecla Gawlowicz	February 10, 1954
Sister M. Leona Pochelski	October 23, 1954
Sister M. Berchmans Fidler	November 11, 1954
Mother M. Aloysia Holysz	March 18, 1955
Sister M. Alphonsa Makowski	July 7, 1955
Sister Mary Welter	October 17, 1955
Sister M. John Barczak	December 11, 1955
Sister M. Sylvestra Pelczar	January 10, 1956
Sister M. Bernice Stefanski	March 16, 1956
Sister M. Philomena Wasik	March 31, 1956
Sister M. Victoria Modelski	June 15, 1956
Sister M. Pontiana Nowakowski	July 15, 1957
Sister M. Urban Klimek	November 15, 1957
Sister M. Philipine Lama	January 11, 1958
Sister M. Kunegunda Pinkowski	January 27, 1958
Sister M. Stanislaus Reich	April 27, 1958
Sister M. Appolonia Stozek	June 19, 1958
Sister M. Blase Wojcik	February 9, 1959
Sister M. Arsenia Krolikowski	February 10, 1959
Sister M. Blanche Bartkowski	February 12, 1959
Sister M. Gerardette Molda	June 7, 1959
Sister M. Clothilde Stefiej	June 11, 1959
Sister M. Rose Gorski	July 2, 1959
Sister M. Patricia Eiress	September 29, 1959
Sister M. Raphael Bogalecki	November 7, 1959
Sister M. Laurentine Trocki	December 31, 1959
Sister M. Bibianna Wiza	February 26, 1960
Sister M. Elizabeth Baut	June 18, 1960
Sister M. Anastasia Halcerz	August 18, 1960
Sister M. Leocadia Das	August 23, 1960
Sister M. Louis Scibior	September 9, 1960
Sister M. Benilda Walkowski	October 26, 1960
Sister M. Luciana Konrad	November 14, 1960
Sister M. Rudolpha Trytek	November 29, 1960
Sister M. Paul Kirschbaum	March 13, 1961

Sister M. Barbara Grochola	May 11, 1961
Sister M. Lauretta Partyka	June 18, 1961
Sister M. Angela Jasinski	August 4, 1961
Sister M. Joanna Trojak	January 4, 1962
Sister M. Herman Pieniazek	February 11, 1962
Sister M. Catherine Bobula	May 13, 1962
Sister M. Gertrude Zwierzycki	June 2, 1962
Sister M. Pascaline Dudek	June 22, 1962
Sister M. Chester Dziarnowski	January 19, 1963
Sister M. Martina Gazda	March 27, 1963
Mother M. Antonina Osinski	May 4, 1963
Sister M. Sabina Bujak	May 30, 1963
Sister M. Helen Swiszcz	May 31, 1963
Sister M. Immaculate Matuszewski	October 24, 1963
Sister M. Cyprian Lewandowski	January 24, 1964
Sister M. Sylvia Lewandowski	February 2, 1964
Sister M. Gerard Gorzkowski	February 2, 1964
Sister M. Humilianna Lemanczyk	March 15, 1965
Sister M. Ladislaus Wroblewski	March 20, 1965
Sister M. Ann Francis Grosh	May 10, 1965
Sister M. Imelda Derbin	September 5, 1966
Sister M. Camilla Radlowski	September 13, 1966
Sister M. Callista Gach	October 22, 1966
Sister M. Isabelle Sutor	November 18, 1966
Sister M. Eleanor Bomba	November 28, 1966
Sister M. Ursula Murdza	December 6, 1966
Sister M. Conrad Kempisty	January 4, 1967
Sister M. Hilary Dadej	May 3, 1967
Sister M. Hedwig Kubera	May 25, 1967
Sister M. Rita Schmitt	May 8, 1968
Sister M. Adolpha Waranowski	August 1, 1968
Sister M. Magdalen Schreiber	October 7, 1968
Sister M. Bernarda Urbanski	October 26, 1968
Sister M. Michaeline Tabor	November 11, 1968
Sister M. Humilia Proc	December 5, 1968
Sister M. Laurentia Owczarzak	December 20, 1968
Sister M. Thomas Halgas	December 25, 1968
Sister M. Amata Holub	January 16, 1969
Sister M. Salomea Grabowski	February 13, 1969
Sister M. Aloysetta Ciezadlo	April 12, 1969
Sister M. Samuel Maziarka	June 27, 1969
Sister M. Mercy Witczak	September 25, 1969
Sister M. Irene Stojak	September 26, 1969
Sister M. Virginia Minta	November 16, 1969
Sister M. Zygmunta Zebracki	March 5, 1970
Sister M. Benigna Jakajtis	March 16, 1970
Sister M. Felixa Jorz	March 30, 1970
Sister M. Brunona Szwagiel	April 9, 1970
Sister M. Josephata Tadych	April 27, 1970
Sister M. Celine Madaj	May 19, 1970
Sister M. Jolanta Nowak	August 17, 1970
Sister M. Dolorosa Bojanowski	September 23, 1970
Sister M. Marcianna Mysliwiec	September 27, 1970
Mother M. Jerome Dadej	November 1, 1970
Sister M. Bridget Czuj	January 28, 1971
Sister M. Gonzaga Raniszewski	March 5, 1971
Sister M. Romana Szkutak	April 13, 1971
Sister M. Susanna Pietrzycki	May 13, 1971
Sister M. Sophie Ciurkot	June 13, 1971
Sister M. Floriana Milanowski	June 14, 1971

Sister M. Valeria Szkutak	October 26, 1971
Sister M. Clara Ogurek	December 18, 1971
Sister M. Petronella Kuta	January 19, 1972
Sister M. Pius Wojcicki	February 20, 1972
Sister M. Cherubim Madaj	February 29, 1972
Sister M. Edmunda Siernicki	April 16, 1972
Sister M. Felicita Pajor	April 26, 1972
Sister M. Theodore Madaj	May 1, 1972
Sister M. Ottilia Madaj	July 4, 1972
Sister M. Hyacinth Barczewski	November 5, 1972
Sister M. Bernadine Ostrega	December 8, 1972
Sister M. Raymond Tabor	March 3, 1973
Sister M. Philip Galinski	March 13, 1973
Sister M. Euphrosine Tryjanowski	March 28, 1973
Sister M. Pauline Dydo	May 8, 1973
Sister M. Damian Graczyk	May 21, 1973
Sister M. Germaine Moson	May 24, 1973
Sister M. Eugenia Detlaf	May 25, 1973
Sister M. Anselma Pasternacki	June 13, 1973
Sister M. Nepomucene Kulesza	October 16, 1973
Sister M. Maxima Wozniczka	December 12, 1973
Sister M. Athanasia Murzyn	December 17, 1973
Sister M. Clementine Ficek	December 20, 1973
Sister M. Redempta Demski	December 21, 1973
Sister M. Albina Bieszczad	June 27, 1974
Sister M. Bogumila Swiech	July 25, 1974
Sister M. Pelagia Szczurek	August 11, 1974
Sister M. Ludwina Prokuszka	August 18, 1974
Sister M. Simplicita Mruczkowski	October 1, 1974
Sister M. Marcella Turlinski	December 27, 1974
Sister M. Zita Kosmala	December 31, 1974
Sister M. Blandina Orlowski	January 18, 1975
Sister M. Sigfrieda Scensny	January 29, 1975
Sister M. Leontina Gawlik	March 3, 1975
Sister Mary Kulik (Mamerta)	February 5, 1976
Sister M. Ernest Blazonczyk	February 10, 1976
Sister M. Martha Bywalec	March 2, 1976
Sister M. Innocentia Sierocki	April 15, 1976
Sister M. Loretta Ruminski	June 14, 1976
Sister M. Vincenza Lech	June 23, 1976
Sister M. Cecilia Janicki	July 6, 1976
Sister M. Praxeda Ostrega	September 12, 1976
Sister M. Francis Swider	April 6, 1977
Sister M. Maxencia Pozniakowski	July 23, 1977
Sister M. Lucy Drozdz	August 17, 1977
Sister M. Febronia Morzuch	January 18, 1978
Sister M. Euphemia Switalski	April 26, 1978
Sister M. Leontia Swiech	June 29, 1978
Sister M. Desideria Grendys	September 30, 1978
Sister M. Sebastianna Nowak	December 20, 1978
Sister M. Benedict Polcyn	February 18, 1979
Sister M. Carol Rychlicki	April 12, 1979
Sister M. Aurea Cyburt	May 13, 1979
Sister M. Grace Kujawa	June 20, 1979
Sister M. Xavier Wroblewski	August 29, 1979
Sister M. Carmelita Szczepanski	September 12, 1979
Sister M. Narcissa Skomski	October 31, 1979
Sister M. James Rucinski	December 18, 1979
Sister M. Scholastica Jakubski	December 29, 1979
Sister M. Mirone Koziol	January 28, 1980
Sister M. Emerentiana Sztuka	February 15, 1980

Sister M. Norberta Haas	July 3, 1980
Sister M. Aquiline Jakubski	August 19, 1980
Sister M. Antonia Polcyn	September 7, 1980
Sister M. Honorata Makowski	October 22, 1980
Sister M. Antoinette Tadych	November 20, 1980
Sister M. Fidelia Armatys	December 28, 1980
Sister M. Isidore Wilkos	January 5, 1981
Sister M. Eulalia Sierocki	January 27, 1981
Sister M. Dionysia Baron	May 21, 1981
Sister M. Anna Radzienda	June 27, 1981
Sister M. Olimpia Wroblewski	July 6, 1981
Sister M. Hilariona Murczek	July 13, 1981
Sister M. Clavera Papiernik	November 18, 1981
Sister M. Balbina Olszewski	December 23, 1981
Sister M. Fabian Owczarzak	April 6, 1982
Sister M. Theophane Rakowski	April 9, 1982
Sister M. Rosaline Lenart	September 10, 1982
Sister M. Canisia Niemiec	October 4, 1982
Sister Helen Marie Mackowiak (Antonima)	October 8, 1982
Sister M. Ferdinand Skiba	January 6, 1983
Sister M. Sebastia Podraza	January 20, 1983
Sister M. Assumpta Repinski	April 2, 1983
Sister M. Perpetua Sulski	April 24, 1983
Sister M. Alexandra Jablonski	May 5, 1983
Sister M. Alberta Bialas	June 22, 1983
Sister Eleanor Plocki (Aloysius Ann)	April 26, 1984
Sister M. Methodia Ryzner	June 5, 1984
Sister M. Borgia Lesiak	June 7, 1984
Sister M. Teresanna Bartuszewski	August 17, 1984
Sister M. Theresia Rybak	August 26, 1984
Sister M. Theresa Dadej	September 9, 1984
Sister M. Severine Mical	January 16, 1985
Sister M. Ligoria Motyka	January 18, 1985
Sister M. Hildegarde Demps	January 26, 1985
Sister M. Ildephonsa Bidus	January 28, 1985
Sister M. Seraphia Bejrowski	January 28, 1985
Sister M. Edna Perciach	June 2, 1985
Sister M. Evelyn Furman	October 3, 1985
Sister M. Eustace Borowski	December 17, 1985
Sister M. Theodosia Biss	January 27, 1986
Sister Maryanne Pawlikowski (Modesta)	June 30, 1986
Sister M. Daniel Gach	August 15, 1986
Sister M. Genevieve Swiatowiec	December 23, 1986
Sister M. Leonia Mszanski	July 25, 1987
Sister Joan Klimek	August 18, 1987

Names in parentheses were given to Sisters on entering the congregation; these names were relinquished in 1968 when Sisters were permitted to reassume their baptismal names.

APPENDIX I

KEY PERSONNEL OF THE CONGREGATION OF THE FRANCISCAN SISTERS OF CHICAGO

ELEMENTARY SCHOOLS
Assumption of the Blessed Virgin Mary / Conemaugh Catholic Consolidation School
Conemaugh, Pennsylvania (1912–1979)

1912	(Mission school of St. Casimir, Johnstown, Pennsylvania)		
1922–1924	Sister M. Salomea Grabowski	Superior	Principal
1924–1929	Sister M. Eusebius Kolupka	Superior	Principal
1929–1933	Sister M. Peter Ostrega	Superior	Principal
1933–1935 (Jan.)	Sister M. Angela Jasinski	Superior	Principal
1935–1937 (Jan.)	Sister M. Theresia Rybak	Superior	Principal
1937–1937 (Aug.–Nov.)	Sister M. Zygmunta Zebracki	Superior	Principal
1937–1940	Sister M. Theresia Rybak	Superior	Principal
1940–1943	Sister M. Humilia Proc	Superior	Principal
1943–1946	Sister M. Teresita Kuczmarski	Superior	Principal
1946–1952	Sister M. Michael Siebab	Superior	Principal
1952–1958	Sister M. Thaddea Duran	Superior	Principal
1958–1959	Sister M. Tyburcia Sliwa	Superior	Principal
1959–1962	Sister M. Ferdinand Skiba	Superior	Principal
1962–1968	Sister M. Aurelia Zyla	Superior	Principal
1968–1969	Sister M. Adelma Walkowski	Superior	Principal
1969–1971	Sister M. Michael Siebab	Superior	Principal
1971–1973	Sister M. Evelyn Furman		Principal
	Sister M. Michael Siebab	Superior	
1973–1977	Sister M. Evelyn Furman	Superior	Principal
1977–1978	Sister M. Michael Siebab	Superior	
	Sister M. Evelyn Furman		Principal
1978–1979	Sister M. Evelyn Furman	Superior	

Assumption of the Blessed Virgin Mary
New Chicago, Indiana (1918–1969)

1919–1920	Sister M. Dominic Makowski	Superior	Principal
1920–1921	Sister M. Salomea Grabowski	Superior	Principal
1921–1922	Sister M. Genevieve Swiatowiec	Superior	Principal
1922–1925	Sister M. Alphonsa Makowski	Superior	Principal
1925–1928	Sister M. Boniface Pranke	Superior	Principal
1928–1931	Sister M. Edmunda Siernicki	Superior	Principal
1931–1935	Sister M. Josephata Tadych	Superior	Principal
1935–1939	Sister M. Edmunda Siernicki	Superior	Principal
1939–1942	Sister M. Chester Dziarnowski	Superior	Principal
1942–1945	Sister M. Berchmans Fidler	Superior	Principal
1945–1951	Sister M. Emerentiana Sztuka	Superior	Principal
1951–1952	Sister M. Aloysetta Ciezadlo	Superior	Principal
1952–1954	Sister M. Eymard Sanok	Superior	Principal
1954–1960	Sister M. Irmina Kon	Superior	Principal
1960–1962	Sister M. Georgeann Kinel	Superior	Principal
1962–1968	Sister M. Petronia Budzinski	Superior	Principal
1968–1969	Sister Ann Rose Mroz	Superior	Principal

Blessed Sacrament
Gary, Indiana   (1960–1987)

1960–1968	Sister M. Theodore Madaj		Principal
1968–1969	Sister M. Maurita Wszolek		Principal
	Sister M. Gabriel Lazarski	Superior	
1969–1970	Sister M. Maurita Wszolek		Principal
	Sister M. Theodore Madaj	Superior	
1970–1971	Sister M. Virginette Rokicki		Principal
	Sister M. Deofilia Piaskowy	Superior	
1971–1972	Sister M. Virginette Rokicki		Principal
(Sept.–Jan.)	Sister M. Colette Kwieczka	Coordinator	
(Jan.–Feb.)	Sister M. Laurentine Michalowski	Coordinator	
(Feb.–Mar.)	Sister M. Deofilia Piaskowy	Coordinator	
(Mar.–Apr.)	Sister M. Virginette Rokicki	Coordinator	
(Apr.–May)	Sister M. Innocent Smagacz	Coordinator	
(May–June)	Sister M. Colette Kwieczka	Coordinator	
(June–July)	Sister M. Elaine Bartkowski	Coordinator	
(July–Aug.)	Sister M. Theodore Madaj	Coordinator	
1972–1973	Sister M. Gemma Stanek		Principal
(Sept.–Feb.)	Sister M. Colette Kwieczka	Coordinator	
(Feb.–Aug.)	Sister M. Laurentine Michalowski	Coordinator	
1973–1975	Sister M. Gemma Stanek		Principal
	Sister M. Laurentine Michalowski	Superior	
1975–1976	Sister M. Gemma Stanek		Principal
	Sister M. Deofilia Piaskowy	Superior	
1976–1977	Sister M. Gemma Stanek		Principal
	Sister M. Laurentine Michalowski	Superior	
1977–1979	Sister M. Gemma Stanek		Principal
	Sister M. Colette Kwieczka	Superior	
1979–1984	Sister M. Colette Kwieczka		Principal
	Sister M. Elaine Bartkowski	Superior	
1984–1987	Sister M. Colette Kwieczka		Principal
	Sister M. Edwinette Wisz	Superior	

Five Holy Martyrs
Chicago, Illinois   (1912–   )

1912–1916	Sister M. Clara Ogurek	Superior	Principal
1916–1919	Sister M. Jerome Dadej	Superior	Principal
1919–1925	Sister M. Benigna Jakajtis	Superior	Principal
1925–1931	Sister M. Eugenia Detlaf	Superior	Principal
1931–1934	Sister M. Scholastica Jakubski	Superior	Principal
1934–1940	Sister M. Eugenia Detlaf	Superior	Principal
1940–1946	Sister Bernice Marie Junio	Superior	Principal
1946–1948	Mother M. Antonina Osinski	Superior	Principal
1948–1954	Sister M. Edward Nowak	Superior	Principal
1954–1960	Sister M. Theodore Madaj	Superior	Principal
1960–1966	Sister M. Alice Klepek	Superior	Principal
1966–1967	Sister M. Teresita Kuczmarski	Superior	Principal
1967–1969	Sister M. Claudiana Jachimowicz	Superior	Principal
1969–1970	Sister M. Gabriel Lazarski	Superior	Principal
1970–1973	Sister M. Gabriel Lazarski		Principal
	Sister M. Rosalima Sierocki	Superior	
1973–1974	Sister M. Gabriel Lazarski		Principal
	Sister Therese Agnes Kniola	Superior	

1974–1975	Sister Dolores Jean Molik		Principal
	Sister Therese Agnes Kniola	Superior	
1975–1979	Sister M. Francine Labus		Principal
	Sister M. Francis Clare Radke	Superior	
1979–1980	Sister M. Francine Labus		Principal
	Sister M. Rosalima Sierocki	Superior	
1980–1981	Sister Emilie Marie Lesniak		Principal
	Sister M. Rosalima Sierocki	Superior	
1981–1984	Sister Emilie Marie Lesniak	Superior	Principal
1984–	Sister Emilie Marie Lesniak	Principal	
	Sister M. Innocent Smagacz	Superior	

Holy Trinity
Falls City, Texas   (1911–1914)

1911–1912	Sister M. Vincent Czyzewski	Superior	Principal
1912–1914	Sister M. Colette Nowak	Superior	Principal

Sacred Heart
Gary, Indiana   (1915–1968)

1918–1922	Sister M. Alphonsa Makowski	Superior	Principal
1922–1925	Sister M. Jerome Dadej	Superior	Principal
1925–1931	Sister M. Hilary Dadej	Superior	Principal
1931–1932	Sister M. Sylvestra Pelczar	Superior	Principal
1932–1933	Sister M. Angela Jasinski	Superior	Principal
1933–1934	Sister M. Eugenia Detlaf	Superior	Principal
1934–1936	Sister M. Benigna Jakajtis	Superior	Principal
1936–1942	Sister M. Theodore Madaj	Superior	Principal
1942–1944	Sister M. Zygmunta Zebracki	Superior	Principal
1944–1950	Sister M. Alberta Bialas	Superior	Principal
1950–1956	Sister Bernice Marie Junio	Superior	Principal
1956–1962	Sister M. Hilary Dadej	Superior	Principal
1962–1968	Sister M. Kinga Repinski	Superior	Principal

Sacred Heart of Jesus
Cleveland, Ohio   (1919–1979)

1919–1922	Sister M. Innocenta Antosz	Superior	Principal
1922–1928	Mother M. Aloysia Holysz	Superior	Principal
1928–1933	Sister M. Philipine Lama	Superior	Principal
1933–1934	Sister M. Ignatius Hodkiewicz	Superior	Principal
1934–1935	Sister M. Herman Pieniazek	Superior	Principal
1935–1940	Sister M. Dolorosa Bojanowski	Superior	Principal
1940–1946	Sister M. Philomena Wasik	Superior	Principal
1946–1949	Sister M. Dolorosa Bojanowski	Superior	Principal
1949–1952	Sister M. Euphemia Switalski	Superior	Principal
1952–1958	Sister M. Michael Siebab	Superior	Principal
1958–1964	Sister M. Liliosa Hoinski	Superior	Principal
1964–1966	Sister M. Alcantara Ochwat	Superior	Principal
1966–1968	Sister M. Equitia Nawracaj	Superior	Principal
1968–1972	Sister M. Pachomia Rychlicki	Superior	Principal
1972–1974	Sister M. Thaddea Duran	Superior	Principal
1974–1975	Sister M. Thaddea Duran		Principal
	Sister M. Eucheria Obara	Superior	
1975–1977	Sister M. Thaddea Duran	Superior	Principal
1977–1979	Sister M. Thaddea Duran		Principal
	Sister M. Equitia Nawracaj	Superior	

Sacred Heart of Jesus
La Porte, Indiana   (1916–1969)

1916–1919	Sister M. Seraphine Zamrowski	Superior	Principal
1919–1922	Sister M. Martha Bywalec	Superior	Principal
1922–1925	Sister M. Genevieve Swiatowiec	Superior	Principal
1925–1931	Sister M. Felicita Pajor	Superior	Principal
1931–1934	Sister M. Jerome Dadej	Superior	Principal
1934–1940	Sister M. Martha Bywalec	Superior	Principal
1940–1946	Sister M. Sylvestra Pelczar	Superior	Principal
1946–1949	Sister M. Philomena Wasik	Superior	Principal
1949–1955	Sister M. Carmel Rokicki	Superior	Principal
1955–1961	Sister M. Archangela Tyranski	Superior	Principal
1961–1964	Sister M. Virginette Rokicki	Superior	Principal
1964–1967	Sister M. Gemma Stanek	Superior	Principal
1967–1969	Sister M. Elaine Bartkowski	Superior	Principal

St. Adalbert
East St. Louis, Illinois   (1907–1969)

1907–1910	Sister M. Salomea Grabowski	Superior	Principal
1910–1911	Sister M. Clemensa Steczko	Superior	Principal
1911–1913	Sister M. Philipine Lama	Superior	Principal
1913–1916	Sister M. Leona Pochelski	Superior	Principal
1916–1918	Sister M. Chester Dziarnowski	Superior	Principal
1918–1924	Sister M. Zita Kosmala	Superior	Principal
1924–1927	Sister M. Salomea Grabowski	Superior	Principal
1927–1931	Sister M. Raphael Bogalecki	Superior	Principal
1931–1937	Sister M. Zita Kosmala	Superior	Principal
1937–1938	Sister M. Sylvestra Pelczar	Superior	Principal
1938–1940	Sister M. Carmel Rokicki	Superior	Principal
1940–1944	Sister M. Emerentiana Sztuka	Superior	Principal
1944–1948	Sister M. Edward Nowak	Superior	Principal
1948–1954	Sister M. Irmina Kon	Superior	Principal
1954–1960	Sister Mary Kulik	Superior	Principal
1960–1966	Sister M. Remigia Lewandowski	Superior	Principal
1966–1969	Sister M. Clemensa Klepek	Superior	Principal

St. Adalbert
Farrell, Pennsylvania   (1917–1918)

| 1917 (Sept.–Dec.) | Sister M. Francis Drufka | Superior | Principal |
| 1917–1918 (Dec.–June) | Sister M. Eugenia Detlaf | Superior | Principal |

St. Adalbert
Whiting, Indiana   (1906–1913)

| 1906–1911 | Sister M. Aloysia Holysz | Superior | Principal |
| 1911–1913 | Sister M. Hugoline Wojciechowski | Superior | Principal |

St. Anthony of Padua
Parma, Ohio   (1983–   )

| 1983– | Sister M. Josetta Kuczmarski | Superior | |

St. Casimir
Cleveland, Ohio   (1903–1986)

1903–1904	Sister M. Clara Ogurek	Superior	Principal
1904–1909	Sister M. Stanislaus Reich	Superior	Principal
1909–1912	Sister M. Leona Pochelski	Superior	Principal

1912–1915	Sister M. Aloysia Holysz	Superior	Principal
1915–1919	Sister M. Innocenta Antosz	Superior	Principal
1919–1921	Sister M. Casimir Janowiak	Superior	Principal
1921–1925	Sister M. Eugenia Detlaf	Superior	Principal
1925–1931	Sister M. Jerome Dadej	Superior	Principal
1931–1932	Sister M. Ignatius Hodkiewicz	Superior	Principal
1932–1937	Sister M. Sylvestra Pelczar	Superior	Principal
1937–1943	Sister M. Beatrice Rybacki	Superior	Principal
1943–1949	Sister M. Euphemia Switalski	Superior	Principal
1949–1952	Sister M. Dolorosa Bojanowski	Superior	Principal
1952–1958	Sister M. Beatrice Rybacki	Superior	Principal
1958–1964	Sister Julianne Markowicz	Superior	Principal
1964–1966	Sister M. Michael Siebab	Superior	Principal
1966–1971	Sister M. Edward Nowak	Superior	Principal
1971–1973	Sister M. Clemensa Klepek	Superior	Principal
1973–1974	Sister M. Clemensa Klepek		Principal
	Sister M. Daniel Gach	Superior	
1974–1976	Sister M. Clemensa Klepek	Superior	Principal
Parish ministry			
1976–1979	Sister M. Clemensa Klepek	Superior	
1979–1986	Sister M. Celeste Walkowski	Superior	

St. Casimir / West End Catholic Consolidation School
Johnstown, Pennsylvania   (1912–1982)

1912–1916	Sister M. Chester Dziarnowski	Superior	Principal
1916–1917 (Sept.–Jan.)	Sister M. Leona Pochelski	Superior	Principal
1917–1922 (Jan.)	Sister M. Stephanie Pinkowski	Superior	Principal
1922–1928	Sister M. Hyacinth Barczewski	Superior	Principal
1928–1934	Sister M. Michaeline Tabor	Superior	Principal
1934–1936	Sister M. Aloysia Holysz	Superior	Principal
1936–1942	Sister M. Ambrosia Tworek	Superior	Principal
1942–1946	Sister M. Benigna Jakajtis	Superior	Principal
1946–1951	Sister M. Teresita Kuczmarski	Superior	Principal
1951–1957	Sister M. Liliosa Hoinski	Superior	Principal
1957–1960	Sister M. Felixa Jorz	Superior	Principal
1960–1966	Sister Therese Agnes Kniola	Superior	Principal
1966–1970	Sister M. Irmina Kon	Superior	Principal
1970–1971	Sister M. Irmina Kon	Superior	
1971–1972	Sister M. Irmina Kon		Principal
	(Sept.–Oct.) (Jan.–Feb.) (May–June)		
	Sister M. Angeline Kedzior	Coordinator	
	(Oct.–Nov.) (Feb.–Mar.) (June–July)		
	Sister M. Marylla Stanislawczyk	Coordinator	
	(Nov.–Dec.) (Mar.–Apr.) (July–Aug.)		
	Sister M. Hermenegilde Moszczynski	Coordinator	
	(Dec.–Jan.) (Apr.–May) (Aug.–Sept.)		
	Sister M. Irmina Kon	Coordinator	
1972–1975	Sister M. Irmina Kon	Superior	Principal
1975–1979	Sister M. Hermenegilde Moszczynski	Superior	
1979–1982	Sister M. Irmina Kon	Superior	

St. Casimir
St. Louis, Missouri   (1905–1906)

1905–1906	Sister M. Aloysia Holysz	Superior	Principal

St. Casimir
Streator, Illinois   (1917–1924)

1917–1910 (Jan.)	Sister M. Antonina Osinski	Superior	Principal
1918–1921	Sister M. Chester Dziarnowski	Superior	Principal
1921–1921 (July–Oct.)	Sister M. Casimir Janowiak	Superior	Principal
1921–1922 (Oct.)	Sister M. John Barczak	Superior	Principal
1922–1924	Sister M. Edmunda Siernicki	Superior	Principal

St. Florian
Chicago, Illinois   (1908–   )

1908–1910	Sister M. Colette Nowak	Superior	Principal
1910–1912	Sister M. Chester Dziarnowski	Superior	Principal
1912–1914	Sister M. Innocenta Antosz	Superior	Principal
1914–1915	Sister M. Coletta Nowak	Superior	Principal
1915–1916	Sister M. Seraphine Zamrowski	Superior	Principal
1916–1917	Sister M. Francis Drufke	Superior	Principal
1917–1917 (Sept.–Nov.)	Sister M. Leona Pochelski	Superior	Principal
1918–1919	Sister M. Edmunda Siernicki	Superior	Principal
1919–1921	Sister M. Paul Kirschbaum	Superior	Principal
1921–1922	Sister M. Hyacinth Barczewski	Superior	Principal
1922–1927	Sister M. Paul Kirschbaum	Superior	Principal
1927–1934	Sister M. Antonina Osinski	Superior	Principal
1934–1939 (Sept.–Nov.)	Sister M. Emmanuel Dogorski	Superior	Principal
1939–1940	Sister M. Philipine Lama	Superior	Principal
1940–1946	Sister M. Ottilia Madaj	Superior	Principal
1946–1952	Sister M. Eustace Borowski	Superior	Principal
1952–1958	Sister M. Zita Kosmala	Superior	Principal
1958–1961	Sister M. Eustace Borowski	Superior	Principal
1961–1967	Sister M. Crescentine Oszuscik	Superior	Principal
1967–1969	Sister M. Cundette Minchuk	Superior	Principal
1969–1970	Sister M. Cundette Minchuk		Principal
	Sister Maryanne Pawlikowski	Superior	
1970–1972	Sister M. Cundette Minchuk		Principal
	Sister M. Louise Nowak	Superior	
1972–1973	Sister M. Cundette Minchuk		Principal
(Sept.–Mar.)	Sister Therese Agnes Kniola	Coordinator	
(Mar.–Sept.)	Sister M. Maximina Pachut	Coordinator	
1973–1974	Sister M. Cundette Minchuk		Principal
	Sister Ann Rose Mroz	Superior	
1974–1975	Sister M. Cundette Minchuk		Principal
	Sister M. Marylla Stanislawczyk	Superior	
1975–1976	Sister M. Agnella Sieja		Principal
	Sister M. Theresine Wojciechowicz	Superior	
1976–1979	Sister M. Agnella Sieja		Principal
	Sister Maryanne Pawlikowski	Superior	
1979–1984	Sister M. Agnella Sieja		Principal
	Sister M. Marylla Stanislawczyk	Superior	
1984–1985	Sister Jeanne Marie Toriskie		Principal
	Sister M. Crescentine Oszuscik	Superior	
1985–1987	Sister Jeanne Marie Toriskie		Principal
	Sister M. Maristella Skrzynski	Superior	
1987–	Sister Jeanne Marie Toriskie		Principal
	Sister M. Marylla Stanislawczyk	Superior	

St. Hedwig
Gary, Indiana   (1909–1978)

1909–1910	Sister M. Jerome Dadej	Superior	Principal
1910–1911	Sister Mary Welter	Superior	Principal
1911–1912	Sister M. Susanna Kielpinski	Superior	Principal
1912–1915	Sister M. Humilianna Lemanczyk	Superior	Principal
1915–1917	Sister M. Bernice Stefanski	Superior	Principal
1917–1918	Sister M. Benedict Polcyn	Superior	Principal
1918–1921	Sister M. Eugenia Detlaf	Superior	Principal
1921–1924	Sister M. Wenceslaus Gorski	Superior	Principal
1924–1931	Sister M. Zita Kosmala	Superior	Principal
1931–1932	Sister M. Paul Kirschbaum	Superior	Principal
1932–1937	Sister M. Felicita Pajor	Superior	Principal
1937–1943	Sister M. Zita Kosmala	Superior	Principal
1943–1946	Sister M. Eustace Borowski	Superior	Principal
1946–1952	Sister M. Zita Kosmala	Superior	Principal
1952–1955	Sister M. Euphemia Switalski	Superior	Principal
1955–1961	Sister M. Carmel Rokicki	Superior	Principal
1961–1964	Sister M. Hermenegilde Moszczynski	Superior	Principal
1964–1966	Sister M. Edward Nowak	Superior	Principal
1966–1970	Sister M. Rosaline Lenart	Superior	Principal
1970–1972	Sister M. Equitia Nawracaj	Superior	Principal
1972–1973	Sister M. Equitia Nawracaj		Principal
	Sister M. Claudiana Jachimowicz	Superior	
1973–1974	Sister M. Claudiana Jachimowicz	Superior	
1974–1978	Sister M. Louse Nowicki	Superior	

St. John Cantius / Indiana Harbor Catholic Elementary School
Indiana Harbor, Indiana   (1907–1979)

1907–1909	Sister M. Kunegunda Pinkowski	Superior	Principal
1909–1910	Sister M. Stephanie Pinkowski	Superior	Principal
1910–1916	Sister M. Zita Kosmala	Superior	Principal
1916–1918	Sister M. Berchmans Fidler	Superior	Principal
1918–1919 (Mar.)	Sister M. Francis Drufke	Superior	Principal
1919–1924 (Mar.)	Sister M. Felicita Pajor	Superior	Principal
1924–1926	Sister M. Josephata Tadych	Superior	Principal
1926–1928	Sister M. Chester Dziarnowski	Superior	Principal
1928–1931	Sister M. Bogumila Swiech	Superior	Principal
1931–1934	Sister M. Hilary Dadej	Superior	Principal
1934–1935	Sister M. Narcissa Skomski	Superior	Principal
1935–1936	Sister M. Bonaventure Paprocki	Superior	Principal
1936–1939	Sister M. Benigna Jakajtis	Superior	Principal
1939–1940	Mother M. Aloysia Holysz	Superior	Principal
1940–1946	Sister M. Philipine Lama	Superior	Principal
1946–1948 (Feb.)	Sister M. Immaculate Matuszewski	Superior	Principal
1948–1948 (Feb.–June)	Sister M. Bibianna Wiza	Superior	Principal
1948–1954	Sister M. Theodore Madaj	Superior	Principal
1954–1957	Sister M. Julitta Szczepanik	Superior	Principal
1957–1963	Sister M. Teresita Kuczmarski	Superior	Principal
1963–1969	Sister M. Arcadia Chmiel	Superior	Principal
1969–1971	Sister Marianne Kaplan	Superior	
1971–1972	Sister M. Eymard Sanok	Superior	
1972–1977	Sister Marianne Kaplan	Superior	
1977–1979	Sister Rose Therese Bzibziak	Superior	

St. John the Baptist / St. Joseph the Provider
Campbell, Ohio   (1944–1987)

1945–1946	Sister M. Euphrosine Tryjanowski	Superior	Principal
1946–1952	Sister M. Theresia Rybak	Superior	Principal
1952–1958	Sister M. Hubert Jasinski	Superior	Principal
1958–1964	Sister M. Julitta Szczepanik	Superior	Principal
1964–1969	Sister M. Marylla Stanislawczyk	Superior	Principal
1969–1973	Sister Therese Slezak	Coordinator	Principal
1973–1977	Sister M. Clarissima Zielaskiewicz	Superior	Principal
1977–1981	Sister M. Clarissima Zielaskiewicz		Principal
	Sister M. Annuncia Milanowski	Superior	
1981–1987	Sister M. Clarissima Zielaskiewicz	Superior	Principal

St. Josaphat
Oshkosh, Wisconsin   (1905–1911)

1905–1906	Sister M. Gerard Gorzkowski	Superior	Principal
1906–1909	Sister M. Seraphine Zamrowski	Superior	Principal
1909–1910	Sister M. Alphonsa Makowski	Superior	Principal
1910–1911	Sister M. Jerome Dadej	Superior	Principal

St. Joseph
East Chicago, Indiana   (1917–1968)

1918–1924	Sister M. Berchmans Fidler	Superior	Principal
1924–1929	Sister M. Peter Ostrega	Superior	Principal
1929–1934	Sister M. Martha Bywalec	Superior	Principal
1924–1935	Sister M. Fabian Owczarzak	Superior	Principal
1935–1936	Sister M. Herman Pieniazek	Superior	Principal
1936–1942	Sister M. Berchmans Fidler	Superior	Principal
1942–1946	Sister M. Dolorosa Bojanowski	Superior	Principal
1946–1952	Sister M. Josephata Tadych	Superior	Principal
1952–1958	Sister M. Rosalima Sierocki	Superior	Principal
1958–1964	Sister M. Olivia Pacek	Superior	Principal
1964–1968	Sister Marianne Kaplan	Superior	Principal

St. Leo the Great
Cleveland, Ohio   (1955–   )

1955–1958	Sister M. Virgina Murawski	Superior	Principal
1958–1964	Sister M. Alphonsine Kobylinski	Superior	Principal
1964–1969	Sister M. Hubert Jasinski	Superior	Principal
1969–1970	Sister M. Eileen Kazmierowicz		Principal
	Sister M. Theresia Rybak	Superior	
1970–1971	Sister M. Eileen Kazmierowicz	Superior	Principal
1971–1972	Sister M. Eileen Kazmierowicz		Principal
	Sister Dolores Bysiek (Sept.–Oct.) (Mar.–Apr.)	Coordinator	
	Sister Patricia Witkiewicz (Oct.–Nov.) (Apr.–May)	Coordinator	
	Sister M. Georgene Wilson (Nov.–Dec.) (May–June)	Coordinator	
	Sister M. Joella Bielinski (Dec.–Jan.) (June)	Coordinator	
	Sister M. Eileen Kazmierowicz (Jan.–Feb.)	Coordinator	
1972–1973	Sister M. Eileen Kazmierowicz		Principal
	Sister Sharon Rock (Sept.–Oct.) (Feb.–Mar.)	Coordinator	

	Sister Dolores Jean Molik (Oct.–Nov.) (Mar.–Apr.)	Coordinator	
	Sister M. Joella Bielinski (Nov.–Dec.) (Apr.–May)	Coordinator	
	Sister M. Aurelia Zyla (Dec.–Jan.) (May–June)	Coordinator	
	Sister M. Eileen Kazmierowicz (Jan.–Feb.) (June)	Coordinator	
1973–1974	Sister Dolores Jean Molik	Coordinator	
1974–1975	Sister M. Aurelia Zyla	Superior	
1975–1976	Sister M. Joella Bielinski	Superior	
1976–1978 (Jan.)	Sister M. Virgina Murawski	Superior	
1978–1980 (Jan.)	Sister Elizabeth Marie Jadrych	Superior	
1980–1987	Sister M. Dolorine Piwowarski	Superior	
1987–	Sister M. Celeste Walkowski	Superior	

St. Louise de Marillac
La Grange Park, Illinois (1956–1987)

1956–1962	Sister M. Edward Nowak	Superior	Principal
1962–1968	Sister M. Louise Nowicki	Superior	Principal
1968–1970	Sister M. Agnella Sieja		Principal
	Sister Elizabeth Marie Jadrych	Superior	
1970–1971	Sister M. Agnella Sieja		Principal
	Sister M. Joella Bielinski	Superior	
1971–1972	Sister M. Agnella Sieja		Principal
	Sister Theresa Mary Obremski (Sept.–Oct.)	Coordinator	
	Sister M. Petronia Budzinski (Oct.–Nov.)	Coordinator	
	Sister M. Eucheria Obara (Nov.–Dec.)	Coordinator	
	Sister M. Leonida Bywalec (Dec.–Jan.)	Coordinator	
	Sister Patricia Ann Pokropinski (Jan. 1–15)	Coordinator	
	Sister Sharon Rock (Jan. 15–31)	Coordinator	
	Sister Julianne Markowicz (Jan.–Feb.)	Coordinator	
	Sister M. Julitta Szczepanik (Feb.–Mar.)	Coordinator	
	Sister M. Georgeann Kinel (Mar.–Apr.)	Coordinator	
	Sister Chestine Bugay (Apr.–May)	Coordinator	
	Sister M. Julianna Podraza (June–July)	Coordinator	
	Sister M. Crescentine Oszuszcik (July–Aug.)	Coordinator	
1972–1973	Sister M. Agnella Sieja		Principal
	Sister M. Georgeann Kinel (Sept.–Feb.)	Coordinator	
	Sister M. Julitta Szczepanik (Feb.–Aug.)	Coordinator	
1973–1974	Sister M. Agnella Sieja		Principal
	Sister Patricia Ann Pokropinski	Coordinator	

1974–1975	Sister M. Agnella Sieja		Principal
	Sister M. Petronia Budzinski	Superior	
1975–1979	Sister M. Petronia Budzinski	Superior	
1979–1984	Sister Marianne Kaplan	Superior	
1984–1987	Sister M. Petronia Budzinski	Superior	

St. Mary of Częstochowa
Hammond, Indiana   (1914–1970)

1914–1916	Sister M. Gerard Gorzkowski	Superior	Principal
1916–1919	Sister M. Hyacinth Barczewski	Superior	Principal
1919–1925	Sister M. Josephata Tadych	Superior	Principal
1925–1927	Sister M. Alphonsa Makowski	Superior	Principal
1927–1928	Sister M. Domitilla Swiech	Superior	Principal
1928–1934	Sister M. Hyacinth Barczewski	Superior	Principal
1934–1934 (Aug.–Sept.)	Sister M. Kunegunda Pinkowski	Superior	Principal
1934–1937	Sister M. Dionysia Baron	Superior	Principal
1937–1937 (Sept.–Dec.)	Sister M. Theresia Rybak	Superior	Principal
1937–1939 (Dec.–March)	Sister M. Delphine Brzozowski	Superior	Principal
1939–1940 (March)	Sister M. Marcianna Mysliwiec	Superior	Principal
1940–1946	Sister M. Theresia Rybak	Superior	Principal
1946–1952	Sister M. Ottilia Madaj	Superior	Principal
1952–1955	Sister M. Louise Nowicki	Superior	Principal
1955–1961	Sister M. Hildegarde Demps	Superior	Principal
1961–1967	Sister M. Pachomia Rychlicki	Superior	Principal
1967–1969	Sister M. Dolorine Piwowarski	Superior	Principal
1969–1970	Sister M. Equitia Nawracaj	Superior	Principal

St. Mary of Częstochowa
Madison, Illinois   (1917–1920)

1917–1920	Sister M. Euphrosine Tryjanowski	Superior	Principal

St. Michael
Berlin, Wisconsin   (1904–1907)

1904–1905	Sister M. Rose Gorski	Superior	Principal
1905–1907	Sister M. Salomea Grabowski	Superior	Principal

St. Michael
Glen Campbell, Pennsylvania   (1917–1928)

1917–1919	Sister M. Boniface Pranke	Superior	Principal
1919–1922	Sister M. Edmunda Siernicki	Superior	Principal
1922–1925	Sister M. Bibianna Wiza	Superior	Principal
1925–1928	Sister M. Ambrosia Tworek	Superior	Principal

St. Pancratius
Chicago, Illinois   (1924–   )

1924–1926 (Feb.)	Sister M. Sylvestra Pelczar	Superior	Principal
1926–1926 (Feb.–June)	Sister M. Philipine Lama	Superior	Principal
1926–1928	Sister M. Helen Swiszcz	Superior	Principal
1928–1934	Sister M. Innocenta Antosz	Superior	Principal
1934–1940	Sister M. Euphrosine Tryjanowski	Superior	Principal
1940–1943	Sister M. Euphemia Switalski	Superior	Principal
1943–1946	Sister M. Josephata Tadych	Superior	Principal
1946–1949	Sister M. Euphrosine Tryjanowski	Superior	Principal
1949–1955	Sister M. Hildegarde Demps	Superior	Principal
1955–1961	Sister M. Louise Nowicki	Superior	Principal

1961–1967	Sister Maryanne Pawlikowski	Superior	Principal
1967–1972	Sister M. Rosetta Kiernicki	Superior	Principal
1972–1973	Sister M. Francine Labus		Principal
1972–1973 (Sept.–Feb.)	Sister M. Francine Labus	Coordinator	
1972–1973 (Feb.–Aug.)	Sister M. Julianna Podraza	Coordinator	
1973–1974	Sister M. Francine Labus	Superior	Principal
1974–1977	Sister M. Concordia Lawrence	Superior	Principal
1977–1979	Sister M. Concordia Lawrence		Principal
	Sister M. Maximina Pachut	Superior	
1979–1983	Sister M. Concordia Lawrence		Principal
	Sister M. Cundette Minczuk	Superior	
1984–1985	Sister M. Concordia Lawrence		Principal
	Sister M. Thaddea Duran	Superior	
1985–	Sister M. Antonella Abramowicz		Principal
	Sister M. Thaddea Duran	Superior	

SS. Peter and Paul
Arcadia, Pennsylvania (1917–1928)

1917–1919	Sister M. Dionysia Kujanek	Superior	Principal
1919–1925	Sister M. Raphael Bogalecki	Superior	Principal
1925–1928	Sister M. Bonaventure Paprocki	Superior	Principal

SS. Peter and Paul
Spring Valley, Illinois (1901–1903) (1910–1918)

1901–1903	Sister M. Kunegunda Pinkowski	Superior	Principal
1910–1911	Sister M. Colette Nowak	Superior	Principal
1911–1912	Sister M. Francis Drufke	Superior	Principal
1912–1913	Sister M. Leona Pochelski	Superior	Principal
1913–1915	Sister M. Seraphine Zamrowski	Superior	Principal
1915–1917	Sister M. Benedict Polcyn	Superior	Principal
1917–1918	Sister M. Bernice Stefanski	Superior	Principal

SS. Philip and James
Cleveland, Ohio (1950–1982)

1950–1952	Sister M. Alberta Bialas	Superior	Principal
1952–1958	Sister M. Venantia Rec	Superior	Principal
1958–1964	Sister M. Elizabeth Marie Jadrych	Superior	Principal
1964–1968	Sister M. Maristella Skrzynski	Superior	Principal
1968–1969	Sister M. Clarissima Zielaskiewicz	Superior	Principal
1969–1972	Sister M. Alphonsine Kobylinski	Superior	Principal
1972–1973	Sister M. Alphonsine Kobylinski	Superior	Principal
	Sister M. Teresita Kuczmarski	Coordinator	
1973–1974	Sister M. Alphonsine Kobylinski	Coordinator	Principal
1974–1975	Sister Elizabeth Marie Jadrych		Principal
	Sister M. Josetta Kuczmarski	Superior	
1975–1977 (Dec.)	Sister Elizabeth Marie Jadrych	Superior	Principal
1978–1981 (Jan.)	Sister M. Teresita Kuczmarski	Superior	
1981–1982	Sister M. Josetta Kuczmarski	Superior	

St. Peter Claver
Mobile, Alabama (1943–1949)

1943–1946	Sister M. Blanche Bartkowski	Superior	Principal
1946–1949	Sister M. Theresa Grajek	Superior	Principal

St. Roch
La Salle, Illinois   (1911–1913)

| 1911–1913 | Sister M. Simplicia Bloch | Superior | Principal |

St. Stanislaus Bishop and Martyr
Chicago, Illinois   (1902–   )

1902–1905 (Jan.)	Sister M. Aloysia Holysz	Superior	Principal
1905–1909	Sister M. Philipine Lama	Superior	Principal
1909–1910	Sister M. Gerard Gorzkowski	Superior	Principal
1910–1913 (Jan.)	Sister M. Dominic Makowski	Superior	Principal
1913–1919 (Jan.)	Sister M. Benigna Jakajtis	Superior	Principal
1919–1920	Sister M. Leona Pochelski	Superior	Principal
1920–1926	Sister M. Helen Swiszcz	Superior	Principal
1926–1931	Sister M. Euphrosine Tryjanowski	Superior	Principal
1931–1934	Sister M. Narcissa Skomski	Superior	Principal
1934–1940	Sister M. Hilary Dadej	Superior	Principal
1940–1946	Sister M. Immaculate Matuszewski	Superior	Principal
1946–1951	Sister M. Blanche Bartkowski	Superior	Principal
1951–1957	Sister M. Teresita Kuczmarski	Superior	Principal
1960–1964	Sister M. Rosalima Sierocki	Superior	Principal
1964–1967	Sister M. Dolores Radziwiecki	Superior	Principal
1967–1970	Sister M. Gemma Stanek	Superior	Principal
1970–1971	Sister Clarent Marie Urbanowicz		Principal
	Sister M. Alice Klepek	Superior	
1971–1973	Sister M. Edward Nowak		Principal
	Sister M. Alice Klepek	Superior	
1973–1974	Sister M. Edward Nowak		Principal
	Sister Lillian Watroba	Superior	
1974–1975	Sister M. Edward Nowak		Principal
	Sister M. Mirone Koziol	Superior	
1975–1979	Sister M. Alberta Bialas		Principal
	Sister M. Mirone Koziol	Superior	
1979–1982	Sister M. Alberta Bialas		Principal
	Sister M. Gabriel Lazarski	Superior	
1982–1984	Sister M. Gabriel Lazarski	Superior	
1984–1985	Sister M. Gabriel Lazarski		Principal
	Sister M. Antonissima Jamruk	Superior	
1985–	Sister Lora Ann Slawinski		Principal
	Sister Doloria Kosiek	Superior	

St. Stanislaus Bishop and Martyr
Posen, Illinois   (1911–1918)

1911–1912	Sister M. Innocenta Antosz	Superior	Principal
1912–1913	Sister M. Helen Swiszcz	Superior	Principal
1913–1915	Sister M. Bernice Stefanski	Superior	Principal
1915–1915 (Sept.–Dec.)	Sister M. Simplicia Bloch	Superior	Principal
1915–1916 (Dec.–June)	Sister M. Josephata Tadych	Superior	Principal
1916–1916 (Sept.–Dec.)	Sister M. Dominic Makowski	Superior	Principal
1916–1917 (Dec.–June)	Sister M. Salomea Grabowski	Superior	Principal
1917–1918 (Sept.–Apr.)	Sister M. Clemensa Steczko	Superior	Principal
1918–1918 (Aug.–June)	Sister M. Rose Gorski	Superior	Principal

St. Stanislaus Kostka, Falls City, Texas   (1911–1913)*

*See Holy Trinity School, Falls City, Texas

St. Stanislaus Kostka
St. Louis, Missouri   (1906–1912)

1906–1908	Sister M. Colette Nowak	Superior	Principal
1908–1909	Sister M. Zita Kosmala	Superior	Principal
1909–1911	Sister M. Innocenta Antosz	Superior	Principal
1911–1912	Sister M. Stephanie Pinkowski	Superior	Principal

St. Stanislaus Kostka
Youngstown, Ohio   (1909–1982)

1910–1912	Sister M. Casimir Janowiak	Superior	Principal
1910–1912 (Sept.–Jan.)	Sister M. Seraphine Zamrowski	Superior	Principal
1912–1912 (Jan.–June)	Sister Mary Welter	Superior	Principal
1912–1913	Sister M. Susanna Kielpinski	Superior	Principal
1913–1916	Sister M. Philipine Lama	Superior	Principal
1916–1916 (Sept.–Dec.)	Sister M. Antonina Osinski	Superior	Principal
1917–1918 (Jan.–June)	Sister M. Zita Kosmala	Superior	Principal
1918–1919	Sister M. Bernice Stefanski	Superior	Principal
1919–1920	Sister M. Seraphine Zamrowski	Superior	Principal
1920–1926	Sister M. Euphrosine Tryjanowski	Superior	Principal
1926–1927	Sister M. Stephanie Pinkowski	Superior	Principal
1927–1933	Sister M. Ottilia Madaj	Superior	Principal
1933–1936	Sister M. Chester Dziarnowski	Superior	Principal
1936–1940	Sister M. Immaculate Matuszewski	Superior	Principal
1940–1942	Sister M. Benigna Jakajtis	Superior	Principal
1942–1946	Sister M. Bogumila Swiech	Superior	Principal
1946–1952	Sister M. Beatrice Rybacki	Superior	Principal
1952–1958	Sister M. Daniel Gach	Superior	Principal
1958–1964	Sister M. Clemensa Klepek	Superior	Principal
1964–1970	Sister M. Leonida Bywalec	Superior	Principal
1970–1972	Sister M. Rosaline Lenart		Principal
	Sister Dolores Jean Molik	Superior	
1972–1973	Sister M. Rosaline Lenart		Principal
	Sister M. Purissima Babinski	Superior	
1973–1977	Sister M. Rosaline Lenart		Principal
	Sister M. Pachomia Rychlicki	Superior	
1977–1981	Sister M. Rosaline Lenart		Principal
	Sister M. Hubert Jasinski	Superior	
1981–1982	Sister M. Rosaline Lenart	Superior	Principal

South Heart Public School
South Heart, North Dakota   (1939–1941)

1939–1941	Sister M. Bogumila Swiech	Superior	

HIGH SCHOOLS

Johnstown Central Catholic High School, Johnstown, Pennsylvania   (1953–1960)†

Madonna High School
Chicago, Illinois   (1949–   )

1949–1951	(Motherhouse)		
	Sister M. Crescencia Chmiel		Principal
	Sister M. Kunegunda Pinkowski	Superior	
1951–1953 (Aug.)	Sister M. Crescencia Chmiel		Principal
	Sister M. Hilary Dadej	Superior	
1953–1954	Sister M. Alberta Bialas		Principal
	Sister M. Hilary Dadej	Superior	

† See St. Casimir / West End Catholic Consolidation School, Johnstown, Pennsylvania

1954–1956	Sister M. Alberta Bialas		Principal
	Sister M. Dolorosa Bojanowski	Superior	
1956–1957	Sister M. Hugoline Czaplinski		Principal
	Sister M. Dolorosa Bojanowski	Superior	
1957–1963	Sister M. Hugoline Czaplinski		Principal
	Sister M. Alberta Bialas	Superior	Principal
1963–1969	Sister M. Hugoline Czaplinski	Superior	Principal
1969–1970	Sister M. Hugoline Czaplinski		Principal
	Sister M. Sponsa Bajorek	Superior	
1970–1971	Sister Joseph Marie Zenda		Principal
	Sister M. Kingnetta Szczypula	Coordinator	
1971–1974	Sister Joseph Marie Zenda		Principal
1971–1973 (Dec.)	Sister M. Rosemary Ferus	Coordinator	
1974–1974 (Jan.–Sept.)			
Residency 1B	Sister Carol Marie Schommer	Coordinator	
Residency 2A	Sister Eleanor Marie Jadrych	Coordinator	
Residency 2B	Sister Helen Marie Mackowiak	Coordinator	
Residency 3A	Sister Joseph Marie Zenda	Coordinator	
Residency 3B	Sister M. Jude Kruszewski	Coordinator	
1974–1975	Sister Joseph Marie Zenda		Principal
Residency 1B	Sister Carol Marie Schommer	Superior	
Residency 2A	Sister Eleanor Marie Jadrych	Superior	
Residency 2B	Sister M. Kingnetta Szczypula	Superior	
Residency 3A	Sister Joseph Marie Zenda	Superior	
Residency 3B	Sister M. Jude Kruszewski	Superior	
1975–1977	Sister Joseph Marie Zenda		Principal
Residency 1B	Sister M. Sponsa Bajorek	Superior	
Residency 2A	Sister Eleanor Marie Jadrych	Superior	
Residency 2B	Sister M. Kingnetta Szczypula	Superior	
Residency 3A	Sister Joseph Marie Zenda	Superior	
Residency 3B	Sister M. Jude Kruszewski	Superior	
1977–1979	Sister Joseph Marie Zenda		Principal
Residency 1B	Sister M. Sponsa Bajorek	Superior	
Residency 2A	Sister M. Antonella Abramowicz	Superior	
Residency 2B	Sister M. Kingnetta Szczypula	Superior	
Residency 3A	Sister M. Charitas Gajdzinski	Superior	
Residency 3B	Sister Therese Slezak	Superior	
1979–1980	Sister Joseph Marie Zenda		Principal
Residency 1B	Sister M. Marinella Gubala	Superior	
Residency 2A	Sister M. Antonella Abramowicz	Superior	
Residency 2B	Sister M. Georgeann Kinel	Superior	
Residency 3A	Sister Joseph Marie Zenda	Superior	
Residency 3B	Sister Therese Slezak	Superior	
1980–1981	Sister Joseph Marie Zenda		Principal
Residency 1B	Sister M. Marinella Gubala	Superior	
Residency 2A	Sister M. Antonella Abramowicz	Superior	
Residency 2B	Sister M. Charitas Gajdzinski	Superior	
Residency 3A	Sister Joseph Marie Zenda	Superior	
Residency 3B	Sister Therese Slezak	Superior	
1981–1982	Sister Joseph Marie Zenda		Principal
Residency 1B	Sister M. Marinella Gubala	Superior	
Residency 2A	Sister Eleanor Marie Jadrych	Superior	
Residency 2B	Sister M. Charitas Gajdzinski	Superior	
Residency 3A	Sister Joseph Marie Zenda	Superior	
Residency 3B	Sister M. Jude Kruszewski	Superior	
1982–1983	Sister Joseph Marie Zenda		Principal
Residency 1B	Sister M. Marinella Gubala	Superior	

Residency 2A	Sister Carol Marie Schommer	Superior	
Residency 2B	Sister M. Charitas Gajdzinski	Superior	
Residency 3A	Sister Joseph Marie Zenda	Superior	
Residency 3B	Sister M. Jude Kruszewski	Superior	
1983–1984	Sister M. Alvernia Groszek		Principal
Residency 1B	Sister M. Marinella Gubala	Superior	
Residency 2A	Sister Carol Marie Schommer	Superior	
Residency 2B	Sister M. Charitas Gajdzinski	Superior	
Residency 3A	Sister M. Rosemary Ferus	Superior	
Residency 3B	Sister M. Jude Kruszewski	Superior	
1984–1985	Sister M. Alvernia Groszek		Principal
Residency 1B	Sister M. Sponsa Bajorek	Superior	
Residency 2A	Sister M. Alvernia Groszek	Superior	
Residency 2B	Sister M. Charitas Gajdzinski	Superior	
Residency 3A	Sister M. Rosemary Ferus	Superior	
Residency 3B	Sister M. Jude Kruszewski	Superior	
1985–1986	Sister M. Alvernia Groszek		Principal
Residency 2A	Sister M. Alvernia Groszek	Superior	
Residency 2B	Sister M. Kingnetta Szczypula	Superior	
Residency 3A	Sister M. Rosemary Ferus	Superior	
Residency 3B	Sister M. Jude Kruszewski	Superior	
1986–	Sister Carol Marie Schommer		Principal
Residency 2A	Sister Carol Marie Schommer	Superior	
Residency 2B	Sister M. Kingnetta Szczypula	Superior	
Residency 3A	Sister M. Rosemary Ferus	Superior	
Residency 3B	Sister M. Jude Kruszewski	Superior	

St. Florian High School, Chicago, Illinois   (1936–1943)‡

HOMES FOR THE AGED

Madonna Hall
Cleveland, Ohio   (1946–1970)

1946–1950	Sister M. Hilary Dadej	Superior	Administrator
1951–1954	Sister M. Bronisia Kapusnik	Superior	Administrator
1954–1960	Sister M. Agnes Zywiec	Superior	Administrator
1960–1966	Sister M. Illuminata Szczepanski	Superior	Administrator
1966–1970	Sister M. Colombiere Piotrowski	Superior	Administrator

Mother Theresa Home
Lemont, Illinois   (1964–   )

1964–1969 (July)	Sister M. Virginia Minta		Administrator
1969–1970 (July)	Sister M. Agnes Zywiec		Administrator
1970–1972 (Jan.)	Sister M. Agnes Zywiec	Superior	Administrator
1972–1973 (Feb.–Jan.)	Sister M. Liliosa Hoinski	Superior	Administrator
1974–1975 (Jan.–July 1)	Sister M. Mildred Bieda	Superior	Administrator
1975–1977 (July)	Sister M. Liliosa Hoinski	Superior	Administrator
1977–1978	Sister Patricia Ann Pokropinski	Acting Administrator	
	Sister M. Generose Siepak	Superior	
1978–1979 (Feb.)	Sister Patricia Ann Pokropinski	Superior	Administrator
1979–1983	Sister Margaret Mary Peckenpaugh	Superior	Administrator
1983–1984 (Nov.)	Sister M. Dorothea Micek		Administrator
1984–1987	Sister M. Dorothea Micek	Superior	Administrator

‡ See St. Florian School, Chicago, Illinois

Mount Alverna Home
Parma, Ohio   (1951–   )

1952–1955	Sister M. Benigna Jakajtis	Superior	Administrator
1955–1956	Sister M. Philomena Wasik	Superior	Administrator
1956–1962	Sister M. Immaculate Matuszewski	Superior	Administrator
1962–1968	Sister M. Ralph Stawasz	Superior	Administrator
1968–1970	Sister M. Aquinas Rosky	Superior	Administrator
1970–1974	Mother M. Beatrice Rybacki	Superior	Administrator
1974–1975	Sister M. Aquinas Rosky		Administrator
	Mother M. Beatrice Rybacki	Superior	Administrator
1975–1979	Mother M. Beatrice Rybacki	Superior	Administrator
1979–1984	Sister M. Aloysilla Kedzior	Superior	Administrator
1984–1986	Sister M. Aloysilla Kedzior		Administrator
	Sister M. Natalie Uscinowicz	Superior	
1986–	Sister M. Natalie Uscinowicz	Superior	

St. Anthony Home
Crown Point, Indiana   (1939–1974)

1939–1942	Sister M. Marcelline Molek	Superior	Administrator
1942–1948	Sister M. Theodore Madaj	Superior	Administrator
1948–1950	Sister M. Stephanie Pinkowski	Superior	Administrator
1950–1956	Sister M. Sylvestra Pelczar	Superior	Administrator
1956–1962 (Jan.)	Sister M. Ottilia Madaj	Superior	Administrator
1962–1968 (Aug.–Aug.)	Sister M. Cherubim Madaj	Superior	Administrator
1968–1972 (Aug.)	Sister M. Mildred Bieda	Superior	
1972–1973 (Jan.)	Sister M. Mildred Bieda	Superior	Administrator
New facility:			
1973–1974	Sister M. Mildred Bieda	Interim Superior	Administrator
1975–1979	Sister Frances Szczur	Superior	
1979–1984	Sister M. Alphonsine Kobylinski	Superior	
1984–	Sister Dorothy Joan Lagocki	Superior	

St. Joseph Home for the Aged and Crippled / St. Joseph Home of Chicago
Chicago, Illinois   (1897–   )

1894–1898	Sister M. Theresa Dudzik	Superior	
1898–1905	Sister M. Anna Wysinski	Superior	
1905–1909 (Oct.–Jan.)	Sister M. Vincent Czyzewski	Superior	
1909–1910 (Jan.–Aug.)	Sister M. Theresa Dudzik	Superior	
1910–1911	Sister M. Clara Ogurek	Superior	
1911–1912	Sister M. Andrea Zawadzki	Superior	
1912–1916	Sister M. Vincent Czyzewski	Superior	
1916–1919	Sister M. Kunegunda Pinkowski	Superior	
1919–1922	Sister M. Gerard Gorzkowski	Superior	
1922–1928	Sister M. Martha Bywalec	Superior	
1928–1931	Sister M. Chester Dziarnowski	Superior	
1931–1934	Sister M. Bogumila Swiech	Superior	
1933–1934	Sister M. Ladislaus Wroblewski		Administrator
1934–1935	Sister M. Paul Kirschbaum	Superior	
	Sister M. John Barczak		Administrator
1935–1940	Sister M. Stephanie Pinkowski	Superior	
	Sister M. John Barczak		Administrator
1940–1941 (Oct.)	Sister M. Francis Drufke	Superior	
	Sister M. Scholastica Jakubski		Administrator
1941–1948	Sister M. Stephanie Pinkowski	Superior	

1946 (Feb.)	Sister M. Scholastica Jakubski		Administrator
1946 (Aug.)	Sister M. Rosaria Frodyma		Administrator
1948–1948 (Feb–Nov.)	Sister M. Felixa Jorz	Superior	
	Sister M. Rosaria Frodyma		Administrator
1948–1952 (Nov.–Jan.)	Sister M. Kunegunda Pinkowski	Superior	
	Sister M. Rosaria Frodyma		Administrator
1952–1958 (Jan.–Aug.)	Sister M. Ambrosia Tworek	Superior	
1953–1958	Sister M. Olimpia Wroblewski		Administrator
1958–1960 (Oct.)	Sister M. Venantia Rec	Superior	
	Sister M. Olimpia Wroblewski		Administrator
1960–1963 (Oct.–June)	Sister M. Venantia Rec	Superior	
	Sister M. Agnes Zywiec		Administrator
1963–1969	Sister M. Agnes Zywiec	Superior	Administrator
1969–1970 (Sept.)	Sister M. Angelica Seidl	Superior	
	Sister Josephine Marie Haske		Administrator
1970–1970 (Sept.–Dec.)	Sister M. Angelica Seidl	Superior	Administrator
1971–1972 (Jan.–Aug.)	Sister M. Leonilla Stogowski	Superior	
	Sister M. Concordia Lawrence		Administrator
1972–1975 (Dec.)	Sister M. Leona Watroba	Superior	
	Sister M. Agnes Zywiec		Administrator
1975–1976 (Feb.)	Sister M. Agnes Zywiec	Superior	
1976–1977 (Feb.)	Sister M. Leona Watroba	Superior	
	Sister M. Agnes Zywiec		Administrator
1977–1979 (Mar.)	Sister M. Agnes Zywiec	Superior	Administrator
1977–1981 (Jan.)	Sister Patricia Ann Pokropinski	Superior	Administrator
1981–1982 (Jan.)	Sister M. Amabilis Bellock	Superior	
	Sister Kathleen Melia		Administrator
1982–1982 (May–Sept)	Sister M. Amabilis Bellock	Superior	
	Sister M. Agnes Zywiec		Administrator
1982–1984 (Sept.–Feb.)	Sister Paula Frances Howard	Superior	
1984–1984 (Feb.–Sept.)	Sister M. Ephrem Soprych		
1984–1985	Sister M. Agnes Zywiec	Superior	
1985–1987 (May)	Sister Martha Joan Sempolski	Superior	
1987– (Sept.)	Sister M. Antonissima Jamruk	Superior	

St. Joseph Home for the Aged
Cleveland, Ohio   (1943–1966)

1943–1944 (Dec.–Feb.)	Sister M. Hilary Dadej	Superior	Administrator
1944–1950 (Feb. 1)	Sister M. Virginia Minta	Superior	Administrator
1950–1956	Sister M. Euphrosine Tryjanowski	Superior	Administrator
1956–1959	Sister M. Virgina Minta	Superior	Administrator
1959–1962	Sister M. Olga Kulik	Superior	Administrator
1962–1966	Sister M. Colombiere Piotrowski	Superior	Administrator

RELIGIOUS EDUCATION

Our Lady of Ransom
Niles, Illinois   (1980–   )

1980–	Sister Doloria Kosiek	Director of Religious Education

St. Genevieve
Chicago, Illinois   (1976–   )

1976–	Sister Theresa Mary Obremski	Director of Religious Education

St. James
Arlington Heights, Illinois   (1971–1975)

| 1971–1975 | Sister Janice Piesko | Director of Religious Education |

St. Matthias
Crown Point, Indiana   (1970–1975)

| 1970–1975 | Sister Doloria Kosiek | Director of Religious Education |

St. Pascal Baylon
Chicago, Illinois   (1976–1980)

| 1976–1980 | Sister Doloria Kosiek | Director of Religious Education |

DOMESTIC WORK

The Catholic Sisters College
The Catholic University of America   (1938–1946)

| 1938–1940 | Sister M. Felixa Jorz | Superior |
| 1940–1946 | Mother M. Antonina Osinski | Superior |

Our Lady of Spring Bank
Cistercian Abbey
Okauchee, Wisconsin   (1934–1942)

1934–1935 (July–Oct.)	Sister M. Humilianna Lemanczyk	Superior
1935–1936 (Oct.–Feb.)	Sister M. Gonzaga Raniszewski	Superior
1936–1938 (Feb.–Dec.)	Sister M. Ottilia Madaj	Superior
1939–1942 (Jan.–June)	Sister M. Hyacinth Barczewski	Superior

CONVENTS

Motherhouse: Our Lady of Victory Convent
Lemont, Illinois   (1964–   )

1964–1970	Sister M. Pelagia Szczurek	Superior
1970–1974	Sister M. Innocentia Sierocki	Superior
1974–1975	Sister M. Alberta Bialas	Superior
1975–1976	Sister M. Innocentia Sierocki	Superior
1976–1977 (Apr.)	Sister M. Theophane Rakowski	Superior
1977–1979	Sister M. Gabriel Lazarski	Superior
1979–1982 (May)	Sister M. Agnes Zywiec	Superior
1982–1984 (May)	Sister M. Electa Rytel	Superior
1984–1987	Sister M. Bertille Geffert	Superior
1987–	Sister M. Petronia Budzinski	Superior

Mount Alvernia
East Cleveland, Ohio   (1936–1952)

1936–1937	Sister M. Chester Dziarnowski	Superior
1937–1940	Sister M. Felicita Pajor	Superior
1940–1946	Sister M. Hilary Dadej	Superior
1946–1952	Sister M. Benigna Jakajtis	Superior

Our Lady of Victory Convent for Retired and Infirm Sisters
Lemont, Illinois   (1936–1963)

1935–1938	Sister M. Salomea Grabowski	Superior
1938–1940	Sister M. Sylvestra Pelczar	Superior
1940–1943	Sister M. Marcianna Mysliwiec	Superior

1943–1946	Sister M. Eugenia Detlaf	Superior	
1946–1949	Sister M. Praxeda Ostrega	Superior	
1949–1952	Sister M. Martha Bywalec	Superior	
1952–1958	Sister M. Pelagia Szczurek	Superior	
1958–1963	Sister M. Eugenia Detlaf	Superior	

Our Lady of Victory Novitiate House
Lemont, Illinois   (1926–1935)

1927–1928 (Sept.)	Sister M. Mechtilde Zynda	Superior	
1928–1935 (Sept.)	Mother M. Vincent Czyzewski	Superior	

St. Francis House of Prayer
Lemont, Illinois   (1980–)

1980–1983	Sister M. Francine Labus	Superior	
1983–1984	Sister M. Bertille Geffert	Superior	
1984–1985	Sister Martha Joan Sempolski	Superior	

HOSPITALS

Mother of Grace Hospital (Gregory Community Hospital)
Gregory, South Dakota   (1948–1962)

1948–1952	Sister M. Innocentia Sierocki	Superior	Administrator
1942–1959	Sister M. Aquinas Rosky	Superior	Administrator
1959–1960	Sister M. Aquinas Rosky		Administrator
	Sister M. Colombiere Piotrowski	Superior	
1960–1961	Sister M. Colombiere Piotrowski	Superior	Administrator
1961–1962 (Oct.–May)	Sister M. Leonia Mszanski	Superior	Administrator

Our Lady of the Sandhills (Atkinson Memorial Hospital)
Atkinson, Nebraska   (1952–1972)

1952–1958 (Jan.–July)	Sister M. Antonita Waloch	Superior	Administrator
1958–1961	Sister M. Antonita Waloch		Administrator
	Mother M. Antonina Osinski	Superior	
1961–1962 (Oct.–Dec.)	Sister M. Bertille Geffert		Administrator
	Mother M. Antonina Osinski	Superior	
1962–1969 (Dec.–Apr.)	Sister Josephine Marie Haske	Superior	Administrator
1969–1972	Sister M. Amabilis Bellock	Superior	Administrator

St. Anthony Hospital
Martin, South Dakota   (1952–1971)

1952–1955	Sister M. Paul Kirschbaum	Superior	Administrator
1955–1961	Sister M. Bertilla Geffert	Superior	Administrator
1961–1964	Sister M. Basil Ochocinski	Superior	Administrator
1964–1966	Sister M. Antonita Waloch	Superior	Administrator
1966–1971	Sister M. Bertille Geffert	Superior	Administrator

St. Anthony Medical Center
Crown Point, Indiana   (1974–)

1974–1979	Sister Frances Szczur	Superior	
1979–1984	Sister M. Alphonsine Kobylinski	Superior	
1984–	Sister Dorothy Joan Lagocki	Superior	

St. John Hospital and School of Nursing / St. John Regional Medical Center
Huron, South Dakota (1947–1978)

1945–1946 (Sprague Hospital)

	Sister M. Leonia Mszanski	Superior	
1946–1948 (Aug.–Sept.)	Sister M. Innocentia Sierocki	Superior	

1947–1948 (St. John Hospital)

(Nov.–Sept.)	Sister M. Innocentia Sierocki	Superior	Administrator
1948–1952 (Sept.–June)	Mother M. Antonina Osinski	Superior	Administrator
1952–1958	Sister M. Innocentia Sierocki	Superior	Administrator
1958–1961 (Aug.)	Sister M. Innocentia Sierocki		Administrator
	Mother M. Jerome Dadej	Superior	
1962–1967 (Jan.–Nov.)	Sister M. Innocientia Sierocki	Superior	Administrator
1967–1968 (Sept.)	Sister M. Amabilis Bellock		Administrator
	Sister M. Marifilia Strzycki	Superior	
1968–1969 (June)	Sister M. Marifilia Strzycki	Superior	
1969–1969 (June–Aug.)	Sister Jean Adamczyk	Superior	
1969–1974 (Aug.–Jan.)	Sister Martha Joan Sempolski	Superior	
1974–1974 (Jan.–Sept.)	Sister M. Olga Kulik	Superior	
1974–1977	Sister M. Alacoque Czartoryski	Superior	
1975–1977	Sister M. Aloysilla Kedzior		Administrator
1977–1978	Sister M. Aloysilla Kedzior	Superior	Administrator

DAY CARE CENTERS

Guardian Angel Day Nursery and Home for Working Girls Guardian Angel
Day Care Center and Home for Ladies / Guardian Angel Day Care Center
Chicago, Illinois (1918–   )

1917–1922	Sister M. Ladislaus Wroblewski	Superior	Administrator
1922–1928	Sister M. Innocenta Antosz	Superior	Administrator
1928–1931	Sister M. Francis Drufke	Superior	Administrator
1931–1934	Sister M. Edmunda Siernicki	Superior	Administrator
1934–1938	Sister M. Perpetua Sulski	Superior	Administrator
1938–1940	Sister M. Innocentia Sierocki	Superior	Administrator
1940–1946	Sister M. Praxeda Ostrega	Superior	Administrator
1946–1949	Sister M. Martha Bywalec	Superior	Administrator
1949–1955	Sister M. Praxeda Ostrega	Superior	Administrator
1955–1961	Sister M. Dionysia Baron	Superior	Administrator
1961–1967	Sister M. Dosithea Ruz	Superior	Administrator
1967–1969	Sister M. Dionysia Baron	Superior	Administrator
1969–1973	Sister M. Carmel Rokicki	Superior	Administrator
1973–1974	Sister M. Carmel Rokicki		Administrator
	Sister M. Innocent Smagacz	Superior	
1974–1977	Sister M. Innocent Smagacz	Superior	Administrator
1977–1979	Sister M. Innocent Smagacz		Administrator
	Sister M. Vincent Swies	Superior	
1979–1983	Sister M. Hugoline Czaplinski	Superior	Administrator
1983–1984	Sister M. Bernadette Bajuscik	Superior	Administrator
1984–	Sister Marianne Kaplan	Superior	Administrator

Holy Family Child Care Center
Crown Point, Indiana (1982–   )

1984–	Sister M. Christine Brzozowski	Administrator

St. Elizabeth's Day Nursery
Chicago, Illinois   (1904–1915)(1920–1959)

1904–1911	Sister M. Angeline Topolinski	Superior	Administrator

1911–1915	Sister M. Ladislaus Wroblewski	Superior	Administrator
1920–1924	Sister M. Francis Drufke	Superior	Administrator
1924–1931	Sister M. Anselma Pasternacki	Superior	Administrator
1931–1934	Sister M. Raphael Bogalecki	Superior	Administrator
1934–1940	Sister M. Anselma Pasternacki	Superior	Administrator
1940–1946	Sister M. Ladislaus Wroblewski	Superior	Administrator
1946–1952	Sister M. Eugenia Detlaf	Superior	Administrator
1952–1955	Sister M. Philomena Wasik	Superior	Administrator
1955–1959	Sister M. Praxeda Ostrega	Superior	Administrator

St. Hedwig Day Nursery
Chicago, Illinois   (1909–1909)

| 1909–1909 (Feb.) | Sister M. Josepha Suchomski | Superior |

St. Vincent's Orphan Asylum, Chicago, Illinois   (1899–1911)§

SPECIAL SERVICES

Boys Town
Boys Town, Nebraska   (1940–1976)

1940–1946	Sister M. Innocentia Sierocki	Superior
1946–1949	Sister M. Bogumila Swiech	Superior
1949–1951 (Dec.)	Sister M. Ambrosia Tworek	Superior
1952–1958 (Jan.)	Sister M. Humilia Prock	Superior
1958–1960	Sister M. Hyacinth Barczewski	Superior
1960–1963	Sister M. Clarissa Kolupka	Superior
1963–1969	Sister M. Georgeann Kinel	Superior
1969–1971	Sister M. Theophane Rakowski	Superior
1971–1972	Sister M. Sebastia Podraza	Superior
1972–1973	Sister M. Angelica Seidl	Superior
1973–1976	Sister M. Equitia Nawracaj	Superior

St. Philip of Jesus Community Center, Chicago, Illinois   (1948–1951)#

St. Rose of Lima
Chicago, Illinois   (1978–   )

| 1978– | Sister M. Mildred Bieda | Parish minister |

The "PORT"
Chicago, Illinois   (1984–   )

| 1984– | Sister M. Claudiana Jachimowicz | Hungry and homeless ministry |

St. Martin de Porres House of Hope
Chicago, Illinois   (1986–   )

| 1986– | Sister Paula Frances Howard | Homeless women and children ministry |

§ See St. Joseph Home for the Aged and Crippled / St. Joseph Home of Chicago, Chicago, Illinois
# See Guardian Angel Day Nursery and Home for Working Girls / Guardian Angel Day Care Center, Chicago, Illinois

DIRECTRESSES OF FORMATION AND FIELD SUPERVISORS
OF INSTRUCTION IN THE CONGREGATION OF THE FRANCISCAN SISTERS OF CHICAGO

DIRECTRESSES OF NOVICES	TERM OF OFFICE	LOCATION	SUPERIOR GENERAL
Sister M. Theresa Dudzik	1899–1905	Motherhouse/St. Joseph Home Chicago, Illinois	Sister M. Anna Wysinski (Mother Superior)
	1905–1909	Motherhouse/St. Joseph Home Chicago, Illinois	Sister M. Vincent Czyzewski (Mother Superior)
Sister M. Kunegunda Pinkowski	1909–1910	Motherhouse/St. Joseph Home Chicago, Illinois	Sister M. Theresa Dudzik (Mother Superior)
	1910–1916	Motherhouse/St. Joseph Home Chicago, Illinois	Mother M. Anna Wysinski
Sister M. Gerard Gorzkowski	1916–1919	Motherhouse/St. Joseph Home Chicago, Illinois	Mother M. Aloysia Holysz
Assistant: Sister M. Zita Kosmala Sister M. Martha Bywalec	1916–1917 1917–1919		
Sister M. Jerome Dadej	1919–1922	Motherhouse/St. Joseph Home Chicago, Illinois	Mother M. Aloysia Holysz
Assistant: Sister M. John Barczak Sister M. Kunegunda Pinkowski	1919–1921 1922–1925		
Sister M. John Barczak	1922–1928	Motherhouse/St. Joseph Home Chicago, Illinois	Mother M. Vincent Czyzewski
Assistant: Sister M. Raphael Bogalecki Sister M. Mechtilde Zynda	1925–1927 1927–1928	Our Lady of Victory Convent Lemont, Illinois	Mother M. Vincent Czyzewski
Sister M. Gonzaga Raniszewski	1928–1931	Our Lady of Victory Convent Lemont, Illinois	Mother M. Aloysia Holysz
	1931–1934	Motherhouse/St. Joseph Home Chicago, Illinois	Mother M. Aloysia Holysz
Assistant: Sister M. Mechtilde Zynda	1931–1934		

Name	Dates	Location	Superior
Sister M. Mechtilde Zynda	1934–1940	Motherhouse/St. Joseph Home Chicago, Illinois	Mother M. Antonina Osinski
Assistant: Sister M. Rosaria Frodyma	1938–1939		
Sister M. Isabelle Sutor	1939–1940		
Sister M. Felixa Jorz	1940–1946	Our Lady of Victory Convent Lemont, Illinois	Mother M. Mechtilde Zynda
Assistant: Sister M. Isabelle Sutor	1940–1946		
Sister M. Doloretta Radzienda*	1946–1958	Our Lady of Victory Convent Lemont, Illinois	Mother M. Jerome Dadej
	1958–1968	Our Lady of Victory Convent Lemont, Illinois	Mother M. Beatrice Rybacki
Assistant: Sister M. Isabelle Sutor**	1946–1966		
Sister M. Francine Labus	1968–1970	Our Lady of Victory Convent Lemont, Illinois	Mother M. Beatrice Rybacki
	1970–1972	Our Lady of Victory Convent Lemont, Illinois	Sister M. Hugoline Czaplinski
Sister Emilie Marie Lesniak	1972–1976	Our Lady of Victory Convent Lemont, Illinois	Sister M. Hugoline Czaplinski
	1976–1978		Sister M. Hugoline Czaplinski
	1978–1980		Sister Martha Joan Sempolski
Sister M. Francis Clare Radke	1980–1883	Our Lady of Victory Convent Lemont, Illinois	Sister Martha Joan Sempolski
Sister Joan Klimek	1983–1984(Aug.)	Our Lady of Victory Convent Lemont, Illinois	Sister Joseph Marie Zenda
Sister M. Antonella Abramowicz***	1984(Aug.)–1985(June)	Our Lady of Victory Convent Lemont, Illinois	Sister Joseph Marie Zenda
Sister Joan Klimek†	1985(June)–1987(Jan.)	Our Lady of Victory Convent Lemont, Illinois	Sister Joseph Marie Zenda
Sister M. Gabriel Lazarski	1987–(Feb.)	Our Lady of Victory Convent Lemont, Illinois	Sister Joseph Marie Zenda

* Sister M. Doloretta Radzienda resigned on December 3, 1968, due to ill health.

** Sister M. Isabelle Sutor died on November 18, 1966.

*** Sister M. Antonella Abramowicz was appointed to take the place of Sister Joan Klimek who attended the Institute on Religious Formation at St. Louis University.

DIRECTRESSES OF POSTULANTS / ASPIRANTS	TERM OF OFFICE	LOCATION	SUPERIOR GENERAL
Sister M. Theresa Dudzik	1894–1898	Motherhouse/St. Joseph Home Chicago, Illinois	Sister M. Theresa Dudzik (Mother Superior)
Sister M. Hedwig Kubera	1898–1905	Motherhouse/St. Joseph Home Chicago, Illinois	Sister M. Anna Wysinskj (Mother Superior)
Sister M. Clara Ogurek	1905–1908	Motherhouse/St. Joseph Home Chicago, Illinois	Sister M. Vincent Czyzewski (Mother Superior)
	1908–1909(Jan.)	Motherhouse/St. Joseph Home Chicago, Illinois	Sister M. Vincent Czyzewski (Mother Superior)
Sister M. Gerard Gorzkowski	1909(Feb.)–1909(Aug.)	Motherhouse/St. Joseph Home Chicago, Illinois	Sister M. Theresa Dudzik (Mother Superior)
	1910–1914	Motherhouse/St. Joseph Home Chicago, Illinois	Mother M. Anna Wysinski
Sister M. Hedwig Kubera	1914–1916	Motherhouse/St. Joseph Home Chicago, Illinois	Mother M. Anna Wysinski
Sister M. Martha Bywalec	1917–1919	Motherhouse/St. Joseph Home Chicago, Illinois	Mother M. Aloysia Holysz
Sister M. John Barczak	1919–1922	Motherhouse/St. Joseph Home Chicago, Illinois	Mother M. Aloysia Holysz
Sister M. Kunegunda Pinkowski	1922–1925	Motherhouse/St. Joseph Home Chicago, Illinois	Mother M. Vincent Czyzewski
Sister M. Raphael Bogalecki	1925–1927	Motherhouse/St. Joseph Home Chicago, Illinois	Mother M. Vincent Czyzewski
Sister M. Hedwig Kubera	1928–1934	Motherhouse /St. Joseph Home Chicago, Illinois	Mother M. Aloysia Holysz
	1934–1940	Motherhouse/St. Joseph Home Chicago, Illinois	Mother M. Antonina Osinski
Sister M. Stephanie Pinkowski	1940–1941	Motherhouse/St. Joseph Home Chicago, Illinois	Mother M. Mechtilde Zynda
Sister M. Felixa Jorz	1940–1946	Our Lady of Victory Convent Lemont, Illinois	Mother M. Mechtilde Zynda
Sister M. Doloretta Radzienda	1946–1953	Our Lady of Victory Convent Lemont, Illinois	Mother M. Jerome Dadej

†Sister Joan Klimek was granted a sabbatical because of serious illness. She died on August 18, 1987.

Sister M. Therese Grajek	1949–1953 (Aspirants only)	Madonna High School Chicago, Illinois	Mother M. Jerome Dadej
Sister M. Maristella Skrzynski	1953–1958 (Aspirants and Postulants)	Madonna High School Chicago, Illinois	Mother M. Jerome Dadej
	1958–1962 (Aspirants and Postulants)	Madonna High School Chicago, Illinois	Mother M. Beatrice Rybacki
Sister M. Edward Nowak	1962–1963 (Aspirants and Postulants)	Madonna High School Chicago, Illinois	Mother M. Beatrice Rybacki
Sister M. Crescencia Chmiel	1963–1964 (Aspirants and Postulants)	Madonna High School Chicago, Illinois	Mother M. Beatrice Rybacki
Sister M. Rosemary Ferus	1964–1965 (Aspirants and Postulants)	Madonna High School Chicago, Illinois	Mother M. Beatrice Rybacki
	1965–1967 (Aspirants only)*	Madonna High School Chicago, Illinois	Mother M. Beatrice Rybacki
Sister M. Alphonsine Kobylinski	1966–1967 (Postulants only)**	Our Lady of Victory Convent Lemont, Illinois	Mother M. Beatrice Rybacki

*The Postulants were under the care of Sister M. Doloretta Radzienda, the Novice Mistress, at Our Lady of Victory Convent, Lemont, Illinois.
**The Aspirant Program at Madonna High School was phased out.

JUNIORATE DIRECTRESSES	TERM OF OFFICE	LOCATION	SUPERIOR GENERAL
Sister M. Crescencia Chmiel†	1961–1962	Motherhouse/St. Joseph Home Chicago, Illinois	Mother M. Beatrice Rybacki
Sister M. Doloretta Radzienda††	1961–1963	Our Lady of Victory Convent Lemont, Illinois	Mother M. Beatrice Rybacki
Sister M. Venantia Rec	1963–1964	Our Lady of Victory Convent Chicago, Illinois	Mother M. Beatrice Rybacki
Sister M. Rosalima Sierocki†††	1964–1967	Our Lady of Victory Convent Lemont, Illinois	Mother M. Beatrice Rybacki

† Sister M. Crescencia was in charge of the Junior Sisters who attended Mundelein College and St. Francis Xavier Cabrini School of Practical Nursing.

†† Sister M. Doloretta, the Novice Mistress, was also in charge of the Junior Sisters who attended St. Francis College in Joliet, Illinois.
††† The Juniorate was discontinued.

DIRECTRESSES OF SISTERS IN TEMPORARY VOWS	TERM OF OFFICE	LOCATION	SUPERIOR GENERAL
Sister M. Francine Labus	1968–1972	Our Lady of Victory Convent Lemont, Illinois	Mother M. Beatrice Rybacki
			Sister M. Hugoline Czaplinski
Sister Emilie Marie Lesniak	1972–1980	Our Lady of Victory Convent Lemont, Illinois	Sister M. Hugoline Czaplinski
			Sister Martha Joan Sempolski
Sister M. Francis Clare Radke	1980–1983	Our Lady of Victory Convent Lemont, Illinois	Sister Martha Joan Sempolski
Sister M. Christine Brzozowski*	1983–1983		Sister Joseph Marie Zenda
Sister M. Rosemary Ferus**	1983–		Sister Joseph Marie Zenda

* Sister M. Christine had been appointed in July. Due to the conflicting duties connected with her appointment as director of the Holy Family Child Care Center in Crown Point, Indiana, she relinquished the position.

** Sister M. Rosemary assumed the position in December.

FIELD SUPERVISORS OF INSTRUCTION	TERM OF OFFICE§	GRADES	SUPERIOR GENERAL
Sister M. Philipine Lama	1922–1928		Mother M. Vincent Czyzewski
Sister M. Benigna Jakajtis	1922–1928		
Sister M. Paul Kirschbaum	1922–1928		
Sister M. Josephata Tadych	1922–1928		
Sister M. Jerome Dadejš§§	1922–1928		
Sister M. Benigna Jakajtis	1926–1928	EDUCATION COMMISSION	Mother M. Vincent Czyzewski

APPENDIX J

Name	Date	Level (Location)	Supervisor
Sister M. Antonina Osinski	1928–1934	Primary/Intermediate/Upper (Illinois)	Mother M. Aloysia Holysz
	1930–1934	Primary/Intermediate/Upper (Indiana)	
Sister M. Euphemia Switalski	1932–	Prepared/Supervised Music Methods	
Sister M. Blanche Bartkowski	1934–1937	Intermediate/Upper	Mother M. Antonina Osinski
	1937–1940	Primary/Intermediate/Upper	
Sister M. Eymard Sanok	1934–1937#	Primary	Mother M. Antonina Osinski
Sister M. Bernice Marie Junio	1940–1946	Primary/Intermediate/Upper (Indiana)	Mother M. Mechtilde Zynda
Sister M. Alberta Bialas	1949–1950	Primary/Intermediate/Upper (Illinois)	Mother M. Jerome Dadej
Sister M. Edward Nowak	1950–1954	Primary/Intermediate/Upper (Illinois)	Mother M. Jerome Dadej
Sister Bernice Marie Junio	1950–1954	Primary/Intermediate/Upper (Indiana)	Mother M. Jerome Dadej
Sister M. Edward Nowak	1954–1958	Intermediate/Upper	Mother M. Jerome Dadej
Sister M. Theresine Wojciechowicz	1954–1958	Primary	Mother M. Jerome Dadej
Sister M. Alberta Bialas	1958–1961	Primary/Intermediate/Upper (Illinois)	Mother M. Beatrice Rybacki
Sister M. Crescencia Chmiel	1961–1964	Primary/Intermediate/Upper (Illinois)	Mother M. Beatrice Rybacki
Sister M. Kinga Repinski	1962–1968	Primary/Intermediate/Upper (Indiana)	Mother M. Beatrice Rybacki

Sister M. Rosemary Ferus	1968–1970	Educational Consultant	Mother M. Beatrice Rybacki
Sister M. Hugoline Czaplinski (Madonna High School)			
Sister M. Alberta Bialas (Illinois)	1968	Education Coordinators ##	Mother M. Beatrice Rybacki
Sister M. Maurita Wszolek (Indiana)			
Sister M. Antonissima Jamruk (South Dakota and Nebraska)			
Sister M. Leonida Bywalec (Ohio and Pennsylvania)			
Sister M. Alberta Bialas	1970–1974	APOSTOLATE COORDINATOR	Sister M. Hugoline Czaplinski
Sister M. Gabriel Lazarski	1974–1978	APOSTOLATE COORDINATOR	Sister M. Hugoline Czaplinski
Sister M. Hugoline Czaplinski	1978–1983	Director of Education	Sister Martha Joan Sempolski

§ In some instances, the exact dates have been difficult to determine.

§§ Sister M. Sylvestra Pelczar was appointed in place of Sister M. Jerome Dadej when the latter was sent to St. Casimir School in Cleveland as superior and principal.

In 1937, Sister M. Eymard Sanok was the recipient of a scholarship to the University of Warsaw in Poland.

The Education Coordinators were named by the First Extraordinary Chapter of Affairs held in June of 1968.

APPENDIX K

DELEGATES TO THE GENERAL CHAPTERS
AND SPECIAL CHAPTERS OF AFFAIRS OF THE CONGREGATION OF
THE FRANCISCAN SISTERS OF CHICAGO

FIRST GENERAL CHAPTER: 1910

1. Sister M. Aloysia Holysz
2. Sister M. Andrea Zawadzki
3. Sister M. Angeline Topolinski
4. Sister M. Anna Wysinski
5. Sister M. Clara Ogurek
6. Sister M. Elizabeth Baut
7. Sister M. Hedwig Kubera
8. Sister M. Josepha Suchomski
9. Sister M. Kunegunda Pinkowski
10. Sister M. Leona Pochelski
11. Sister M. Philipine Lama
12. Sister M. Salomea Grabowski
13. Sister M. Theresa Dudzik
14. Sister M. Vincent Czyzewski

SECOND GENERAL CHAPTER: 1916

1. Sister M. Aloysia Holysz
2. Sister M. Andrea Zawadzki
3. Mother M. Anna Wysinski
4. Sister M. Chester Dziarnowski
5. Sister M. Clara Ogurek
6. Sister M. Hedwig Kubera
7. Sister M. Innocenta Antosz
8. Sister M. Kunegunda Pinkowski
9. Sister M. Leona Pochelski
10. Sister M. Philipine Lama
11. Sister M. Salomea Grabowski
12. Sister M. Theresa Dudzik
13. Sister M. Vincent Czyzewski
14. Sister M. Zita Kosmala

THIRD GENERAL CHAPTER: 1922

1. Mother M. Aloysia Holysz
2. Sister M. Andrea Zawadzki
3. Sister M. Angeline Topolinski
4. Sister M. Anselma Pasternacki
5. Sister M. Benigna Jakajtis
6. Sister M. Clara Ogurek
7. Sister M. Domicela Swiech
8. Sister M. Emily Kondziolka
9. Sister M. Eugenia Detlaf
10. Sister M. Euphrosine Tryjanowski
11. Sister M. Gerard Gorzkowski
12. Sister M. Hedwig Kubera
13. Sister M. Helen Swiszcz
14. Sister M. Hilary Dadej
15. Sister M. Hyacinth Barczewski
16. Sister M. Innocenta Antosz
17. Sister M. John Barczak
18. Sister M. Kunegunda Pinkowski
19. Sister M. Ladislaus Wroblewski
20. Sister M. Leona Pochelski
21. Sister M. Marcelline Molek
22. Sister M. Philipine Lama
23. Sister M. Salomea Grabowski
24. Sister M. Seraphine Zamrowski
25. Sister M. Sylvestra Pelczar
26. Sister M. Vincent Czyzewski
27. Sister Mary Welter
28. Sister M. Wenceslaus Gorski
29. Sister M. Zita Kosmala

FOURTH GENERAL CHAPTER: 1928

1. Mother M. Aloysia Holysz
2. Mother M. Vincent Czyzewski
3. Sister M. Angelina Topolinski
4. Sister M. Antonina Osinski
5. Sister M. Benigna Jakajtis
6. Sister M. Berchmans Fidler
7. Sister M. Brunona Szwagiel
8. Sister M. Chester Dziarnowski
9. Sister M. Eugenia Detlaf
10. Sister M. Euphrosine Tryjanowski
11. Sister M. Felicita Pajor
12. Sister M. Francis Drufke
13. Sister M. Gerard Gorzkowski
14. Sister M. Helen Swiszcz
15. Sister M. Herman Pieniazek
16. Sister M. Hilary Dadej
17. Sister M. Hyacinth Barczewski
18. Sister M. Immaculate Matuszewski
19. Sister M. Innocenta Antosz
20. Sister M. Jerome Dadej
21. Sister M. Leona Pochelski
22. Sister M. Martha Bywalec
23. Sister M. Mechtilde Zynda
24. Sister M. Ottilia Madaj
25. Sister M. Paul Kirschbaum
26. Sister M. Philipine Lama
27. Sister M. Raphael Bogalecki
28. Sister M. Salesia Rzeszutko
29. Sister M. Salomea Grabowski
30. Sister M. Seraphine Zamrowski
31. Sister M. Stephanie Pinkowski
32. Sister M. Sylvestra Pelczar
33. Sister M. Ursula Murdza
34. Sister M. Zita Kosmala

FIFTH GENERAL CHAPTER: 1934

1. Mother M. Aloysia Holysz
2. Mother M. Vincent Czyzewski
3. Sister M. Antonina Osinski
4. Sister M. Benigna Jakajtis
5. Sister M. Berchmans Fidler
6. Sister M. Bogumila Swiech
7. Sister M. Chester Dziarnowski
8. Sister M. Dionysia Baron
9. Sister M. Dominic Makowski
10. Sister M. Edmunda Siernicki
11. Sister M. Euphrosine Tryjanowski
12. Sister M. Fabian Owczarzak
13. Sister M. Felicita Pajor
14. Sister M. Helen Swiszcz
15. Sister M. Herman Pieniazek
16. Sister M. Hilary Dadej
17. Sister M. Hyacinth Barczewski
18. Sister M. Ignatia Hodkiewicz
19. Sister M. Innocenta Antosz
20. Sister M. Jerome Dadej*
21. Sister M. Leona Pochelski
22. Sister M. Marcianna Mysliwiec
23. Sister M. Martha Bywalec
24. Sister M. Mechtilde Zynda
25. Sister M. Michaeline Tabor
26. Sister M. Monica Frankowski
27. Sister M. Narcissa Skomski
28. Sister M. Pascaline Dudek
29. Sister M. Paul Kirschbaum
30. Sister M. Philipine Lama
31. Sister M. Philomena Marszalkowski
32. Sister M. Raphael Bogalecki
33. Sister M. Salomea Grabowski
34. Sister M. Scholastica Jakubski
35. Sister M. Seraphine Zamrowski
36. Sister M. Stephanie Pinkowski
37. Sister M. Sylvestra Pelczar
38. Sister M. Zita Kosmala

* Summoned to the Fifth General Chapter as a result of having been elected secretary general and fourth councilor.

SIXTH GENERAL CHAPTER: 1940

1. Mother M. Aloysia Holysz
2. Mother M. Antonina Osinski
3. Mother M. Vincent Czyzewski
4. Sister M. Beatrice Rybacki
5. Sister M. Bibianna Wiza
6. Sister M. Bogumila Swiech
7. Sister M. Chester Dziarnowski
8. Sister M. Consolata Markowicz
9. Sister M. Desideria Grendys
10. Sister M. Dionysia Baron
11. Sister M. Dolorosa Bojanowski
12. Sister M. Eugenia Detlaf
13. Sister M. Euphemia Switalski
14. Sister M. Euphrosine Tryjanowski
15. Sister M. Fabian Owczarzak
16. Sister M. Felicita Pajor
17. Sister M. Felixa Jorz
18. Sister M. Francis Drufke
19. Sister M. Helen Swiszcz
20. Sister M. Hilary Dadej
21. Sister M. Immaculate Matuszewski
22. Sister M. Innocenta Antosz
23. Sister M. Jerome Dadej
24. Sister M. John Barczak*
25. Sister M. Josephata Tadych
26. Sister M. Marcelline Molek
27. Sister M. Mechtilde Zynda
28. Sister M. Ottilia Madaj
29. Sister M. Paul Kirschbaum
30. Sister M. Philipine Lama
31. Sister M. Raphael Bogalecki
32. Sister M. Salomea Grabowski
33. Sister M. Scholastica Jakubski
34. Sister M. Stephanie Pinkowski
35. Sister M. Sylvestra Pelczar
36. Sister M. Zita Kosmala
37. Sister Sophie Marie Kierszke

* Summoned to the Sixth General Chapter as a result of having been elected fourth councilor.

SEVENTH GENERAL CHAPTER: 1946

1. Mother M. Aloysia Holysz
2. Mother M. Antonina Osinski
3. Sister Bernice Marie Junio
4. Sister M. Alberta Bialas
5. Sister M. Assumpta Repinski
6. Sister M. Basil Ochocinski
7. Sister M. Berchmans Fidler
8. Sister M. Bibianna Wiza
9. Sister M. Blanche Bartkowski
10. Sister M. Bogumila Swiech
11. Sister M. Crescencia Chmiel
12. Sister M. Damian Graczyk
13. Sister M. Dionysia Baron
14. Sister M. Edward Nowak
15. Sister M. Eugenia Detlaf
16. Sister M. Euphemia Switalski
17. Sister M. Eustace Borowski
18. Sister M. Felicita Pajor
19. Sister M. Felixa Jorz*
20. Sister M. Gonzaga Raniszewski
21. Sister M. Hildegarde Demps
22. Sister M. Honoria Urbaniak
23. Sister M. Immaculate Matuszewski
24. Sister M. Innocentia Sierocki
25. Sister M. Jerome Dadej
26. Sister M. John Barczak
27. Sister M. Josephata Tadych
28. Sister M. Louise Nowicki
29. Sister M. Ottilia Madaj
30. Sister M. Paul Kirschbaum
31. Sister M. Pelagia Szczurek
32. Sister M. Philipine Lama
33. Sister M. Philomena Marszalkowski
34. Sister M. Praxeda Ostrega
35. Sister M. Raphael Bogalecki
36. Sister M. Salomea Grabowski
37. Sister M. Stephanie Pinkowski
38. Sister M. Venantia Rec
39. Sister M. Virginette Rokicki
40. Sister M. Virgina Minta
41. Sister M. Zita Kosmala

* Summoned to the Seventh General Chapter as a result of having been elected assistant superior general and first councilor.

EIGHTH GENERAL CHAPTER: 1952

1. Mother M. Aloysia Holysz*
2. Mother M. Antonina Osinski
3. Mother M. Jerome Dadej
4. Sister M. Alberta Bialas**
5. Sister M. Alice Klepek
6. Sister M. Aloysetta Ciezadlo***
7. Sister M. Ambrosia Tworek
8. Sister M. Angelica Seidl
9. Sister M. Antonita Waloch
10. Sister M. Benigna Jakajtis
11. Sister M. Clemensa Klepek
12. Sister M. Consolata Markowicz
13. Sister M. Cyprian Lewandowski
14. Sister M. Doloretta Radzienda
15. Sister M. Dolorosa Bojanowski
16. Sister M. Edward Nowak
17. Sister M. Euphemia Switalski
18. Sister M. Euphrosine Tryjanowski
19. Sister M. Eustace Borowski
20. Sister M. Felixa Jorz
21. Sister M. Fidelia Armatys
22. Sister M. Gonzaga Raniszewski
23. Sister M. Hilary Dadej
24. Sister M. Hildegarde Demps
25. Sister M. Humilia Proc
26. Sister M. Hyacinth Barczewski
27. Sister M. Innocentia Sierocki
28. Sister M. John Barczak
29. Sister M. Louise Nowicki
30. Sister M. Ludmilla Fedak
31. Sister M. Martha Bywalec
32. Sister M. Mercy Witczak
33. Sister M. Narcissa Skomski
34. Sister M. Praxeda Ostrega
35. Sister M. Raphael Bogalecki
36. Sister M. Sylvia Lewandowski
37. Sister M. Teresita Kuczmarski
38. Sister M. Tyburcia Sliwa
39. Sister M. Venantia Rec
40. Sister M. Virgina Minta
41. Sister M. Zita Kosmala

* Hospitalized; did not participate.
** Summoned to the Eighth General Chapter as a result of having been elected fourth councilor.
*** Summoned to the Eighth General Chapter as a result of having been elected procurator general.

NINTH GENERAL CHAPTER: 1958

1. Mother M. Antonina Osinski
2. Mother M. Jerome Dadej
3. Sister Bernice Marie Junio
4. Sister M. Alberta Bialas
5. Sister M. Alice Klepek
6. Sister M. Aloysetta Ciezadlo
7. Sister M. Ambrosia Tworek
8. Sister M. Antonita Waloch
9. Sister M. Basil Ochocinski
10. Sister M. Beatrice Rybacki
11. Sister M. Benigna Jakajtis
12. Sister M. Clemensa Klepek
13. Sister M. Crescencia Chmiel
14. Sister M. Dionysia Baron
15. Sister M. Dolores Radziwiecki
16. Sister M. Doloretta Radzienda

17. Sister M. Edward Nowak
18. Sister M. Eugenia Detlaf
19. Sister M. Euphrasia Markowicz
20. Sister M. Eustace Borowski
21. Sister M. Felixa Jorz
22. Sister M. Gonzaga Raniszewski
23. Sister M. Hilary Dadej
24. Sister M. Immaculate Matuszewski
25. Sister M. Innocentia Sierocki
26. Sister M. Irmina Kon
27. Sister M. Leonia Mszanski
28. Sister M. Louise Nowicki
29. Sister M. Michael Siebab
30. Sister M. Mirone Koziol
31. Sister M. Narcissa Skomski
32. Sister M. Pelagia Szczurek
33. Sister M. Sigfrieda Scensny
34. Sister M. Theodore Madaj
35. Sister M. Theresia Rybak
36. Sister M. Tyburcia Sliwa
37. Sister M. Venantia Rec
38. Sister M. Zita Kosmala
39. Sister M. Zygmunta Zebracki

TENTH GENERAL CHAPTER: 1964

1. Mother M. Beatrice Rybacki
2. Mother M. Jerome Dadej
3. Sister Ann Rose Mroz
4. Sister M. Agnes Zywiec
5. Sister M. Alice Klepek
6. Sister M. Aloysetta Ciezadlo
7. Sister M. Alphonsine Kobylinski
8. Sister Maryanne Pawlikowski
9. Sister M. Antonella Abramowicz
10. Sister M. Aquinas Rosky
11. Sister M. Basil Ochocinski
12. Sister M. Borgia Lesiak
13. Sister M. Bronisia Kapusnik
14. Sister M. Clemensa Klepek
15. Sister M. Crescencia Chmiel
16. Sister M. Crescentine Oszuscik
17. Sister M. Dionysia Baron
18. Sister M. Doloretta Radzienda
19. Sister M. Edna Perciach
20. Sister M. Edward Nowak
21. Sister M. Eugenia Detlaf
22. Sister M. Eulalia Sierocki
23. Sister M. Euphrasia Markowicz
24. Sister M. Evelyn Furman
25. Sister M. Georgeann Kinel
26. Sister M. Gonzaga Raniszewski
27. Sister M. Hugoline Czaplinski
28. Sister M. Innocentia Sierocki
29. Sister M. Laurentia Owczarzak
30. Sister M. Leonida Bywalec
31. Sister M. Liliosa Hoinski
32. Sister M. Lillian Watroba
33. Sister M. Louise Nowicki
34. Sister M. Maurita Wszolek
35. Sister M. Ottilia Madaj
36. Sister M. Pachomia Rychlicki
37. Sister M. Pelagia Szczurek
38. Sister M. Ralph Stawasz
39. Sister M. Rosalima Sierocki
40. Sister M. Rosaline Lenart
41. Sister M. Venantia Rec
42. Sister M. Xavier Wroblewski
43. Sister Therese Agnes Kniola

FIRST EXTRAORDINARY CHAPTER OF AFFAIRS: 1968

1. Mother M. Beatrice Rybacki
2. Mother M. Jerome Dadej*
3. Sister Andre Marie Clement
4. Sister Anne Marie Knawa
5. Sister Doloria Kosiek
6. Sister Eleanor Marie Jadrych
7. Sister Jane Madejczyk
8. Sister Joseph Marie Zenda
9. Sister Kathleen Melia
10. Sister Margaret Grempka
11. Sister M. Agnella Sieja
12. Sister M. Agnes Zywiec
13. Sister M. Alacoque Czartoryski
14. Sister M. Alberta Bialas
15. Sister M. Aloysetta Ciezadlo**
16. Sister M. Alphonsine Kobylinski
17. Sister M. Alvernia Groszek***
18. Sister M. Angelica Seidl
19. Sister M. Antonella Abramowicz
20. Sister M. Antonissima Jamruk
21. Sister M. Christine Brzozowski
22. Sister M. Clarissa Kolupka
23. Sister M. Claritta Warchalowski
24. Sister M. Concordia Lawrence
25. Sister M. Doloretta Radzienda†
26. Sister M. Felixa Jorz
27. Sister M. Francesca Janowicz††
28. Sister M. Francine Labus
29. Sister M. Francis Clare Radke
30. Sister M. Georgeann Kinel
31. Sister M. Gonzaga Raniszewski
32. Sister M. Hugoline Czaplinski
33. Sister M. Innocentia Sierocki
34. Sister M. Kingnetta Szczypula
35. Sister M. Madalyn Chwierut
36. Sister M. Marifilia Strzycki
37. Sister M. Natalie Uscinowicz
38. Sister M. Pelagia Szczurek
39. Sister M. Ralph Stawasz†††
40. Sister M. Rosalima Sierocki
41. Sister M. Rosemary Ferus
42. Sister M. Sponsa Bajorek
43. Sister M. Tarcisia Bucki#
44. Sister M. Venantia Rec

   * Resigned due to illness; replaced by Sister M. Euphemia Switalski.
  ** Did not participate in II or III sessions; replaced by Sister M. Amabilis Bellock.
*** Did not participate in II session; replaced
   † Did not participate in II or III sessions; replaced by Sister M. Crescencia Chmiel.
  †† Did not participate in II or III sessions; replaced by Sister Marie Francis Moson.
††† Did not participate in I session; replaced by Sister Marie Francis Moson; returned for II and III sessions.
  # Did not participate in II or III sessions; replaced by Sister M. Tyburcia Sliwa.

ELEVENTH GENERAL CHAPTER: 1970

1. Mother M. Jerome Dadej
2. Sister Clarent Marie Urbanowicz
3. Sister Dawn Louise Capilupo
4. Sister Diane Przyborowski
5. Sister Emilie Marie Lesniak
6. Sister Joseph Marie Zenda
7. Sister Kathleen Melia
8. Sister Margaret Grempka
9. Sister Margaret Mary Peckenpaugh
10. Sister M. Agnella Sieja
11. Sister M. Agnes Zywiec
12. Sister M. Alberta Bialas
13. Sister M. Alvernia Groszek
14. Sister M. Amabilis Bellock
15. Sister M. Angelica Seidl
16. Sister M. Antonella Abramowicz
17. Sister M. Antonissima Jamruk
18. Sister M. Beatrice Rybacki
19. Sister M. Christine Brzozowski
20. Sister M. Claritta Warchalowski
21. Sister M. Colombiere Piotrowski
22. Sister M. Concordia Lawrence
23. Sister M. Cundette Minczuk
24. Sister M. Doloretta Radzienda
25. Sister M. Euphemia Switalski
26. Sister M. Francetta Glowinski
27. Sister M. Francine Labus
28. Sister M. Francis Clare Radke
29. Sister M. Gonzaga Raniszewski
30. Sister M. Hugoline Czaplinski
31. Sister M. Innocentia Sierocki
32. Sister M. Kingnetta Szczypula
33. Sister M. Marifilia Strzycki
34. Sister M. Mildred Bieda
35. Sister M. Natalie Uscinowicz
36. Sister M. Pelagia Szczurek
37. Sister M. Petronia Budzinski
38. Sister M. Ralph Stawasz
39. Sister M. Roberta Duda
40. Sister M. Rosalima Sierocki
41. Sister M. Rosaline Lenart
42. Sister M. Rosemary Ferus
43. Sister M. Sponsa Bajorek
44. Sister M. Tarcisia Bucki
45. Sister M. Venantia Rec

SECOND SPECIAL CHAPTER OF AFFAIRS: 1972

1. Sister Clarent Marie Urbanowicz
2. Sister Doloria Kosiek
3. Sister Dolores Jean Molik
4. Sister Emilie Marie Lesniak
5. Sister Frances Marie Niecikowski
6. Sister Joan Klimek
7. Sister Kathleen Melia
8. Sister Margaret Mary Peckenpaugh
9. Sister M. Agnes Zywiec
10. Sister M. Alacoque Czartoryski
11. Sister M. Alberta Bialas
12. Sister M. Aloysilla Kedzior
13. Sister M. Alvernia Groszek
14. Sister M. Antonissima Jamruk
15. Sister M. Beatrice Rybacki

16. Sister M. Clarissa Kolupka
17. Sister M. Clemensa Klepek
18. Sister M. Colombiere Piotrowski
19. Sister M. Concordia Lawrence
20. Sister M. Cundette Minczuk
21. Sister M. Doloretta Radzienda
22. Sister M. Dorothea Micek
23. Sister M. Electa Rytel
24. Sister M. Ephrem Soprych
25 .Sister M. Euphemia Switalski
26. Sister M. Francine Labus
27. Sister M. Francis Clare Radke
28. Sister M. Gabriel Lazarski
29. Sister M. Georgeann Kinel
30. Sister M. Hildegarde Demps
31. Sister M. Hugoline Czaplinski
32. Sister M. Innocentia Sierocki
33. Sister M. Liliosa Hoinski
34. Sister M. Natalie Uscinowicz
35. Sister M. Ralph Stawasz
36. Sister M. Rosalima Sierocki
37. Sister M. Sponsa Bajorek
38. Sister M. Tarcisia Bucki
39. Sister M. Theophane Rakowski
40. Sister M. Theresia Rybak

TWELFTH GENERAL CHAPTER: 1974

1. Sister Clarent Marie Urbanowicz
2. Sister M. Agnella Sieja
3. Sister M. Agnes Zywiec
4. Sister M. Alacoque Czartoryski
5. Sister M. Alberta Bialas
6. Sister M. Aloysilla Kedzior
7. Sister M. Alphonsine Kobylinski*
8. Sister M. Alvernia Groszek
9. Sister M. Antonella Abramowicz
10. Sister M. Antonissima Jamruk
11. Sister M. Beatrice Rybacki
12. Sister M. Concordia Lawrence
13. Sister M. Crescencia Chmiel
14. Sister M. Electa Rytel
15. Sister M. Euphemia Switalski
16. Sister M. Francis Clare Radke
17. Sister M. Gabriel Lazarski
18. Sister M. Georgeann Kinel
19. Sister M. Hugoline Czaplinski
20. Sister M. Kingnetta Szczypula
21. Sister M. Leonida Bywalec
22. Sister M. Liliosa Hoinski
23. Sister M. Marifilia Strzycki
24. Sister M. Mildred Bieda
25. Sister M. Ralph Stawasz
26. Sister M. Sponsa Bajorek
27. Sister M. Tarcisia Bucki
28. Sister M. Theophane Rakowski
29. Sister M. Theresia Rybak
30. Sister M. Venantia Rec

* Resigned due to illness; replaced by Sister
M. Bertille Geffert.

THIRTEENTH GENERAL CHAPTER: 1978

1. Sister Clarent Marie Urbanowicz
2. Sister Emilie Marie Lesniak
3. Sister Frances Szczur
4. Sister Martha Joan Sempolski

5. Sister M. Agnella Sieja
6. Sister M. Agnes Zywiec
7. Sister M. Alacoque Czartoryski
8. Sister M. Alberta Bialas
9. Sister M. Alvernia Groszek
10. Sister M. Antonella Abramowicz
11. Sister M. Antonissima Jamruk
12. Sister M. Beatrice Rybacki*
13. Sister M. Clemensa Klepek
14. Sister M. Concordia Lawrence
15. Sister M. Cundette Minczuk
16. Sister M. Electa Rytel
17. Sister M. Francine Labus
18. Sister M. Francis Clare Radke
19. Sister M. Gabriel Lazarski
20. Sister M. Hugoline Czaplinski
21. Sister M. Liliosa Hoinski
22. Sister M. Louise Nowicki
23. Sister M. Natalie Uscinowicz
24. Sister M. Petronia Budzinski
25. Sister M. Ralph Stawasz
26. Sister M. Rosalima Sierocki
27. Sister M. Sponsa Bajorek
28. Sister M. Tarcisia Bucki
29. Sister M. Theophane Rakowski
30. Sister M. Venantia Rec

* Resigned due to poor health; replaced by
Sister M. Leonida Bywalec.

FOURTEENTH GENERAL CHAPTER: 1983

1. Sister Anne Marie Knawa
2. Sister Clarent Marie Urbanowicz
3. Sister Joseph Marie Zenda
4. Sister Margaret Mary Peckenpaugh
5. Sister Marianne Kaplan
6. Sister Martha Joan Sempolski
7. Sister M. Agnella Sieja
8. Sister M. Alacoque Czartoryski
9. Sister M. Alberta Bialas*
10. Sister M. Alphonsine Kobylinski
11. Sister M. Alvernia Groszek
12. Sister M. Amabilis Bellock
13. Sister M. Antonella Abramowicz
14. Sister M. Antonissima Jamruk
15. Sister M. Charitas Gajdzinski**
16. Sister M. Dorothea Micek
17. Sister M. Electa Rytel
18. Sister M. Frances Clare Radke
19. Sister M. Francine Labus
20. Sister M. Gabriel Lazarski
21. Sister M. Hugoline Czaplinski
22. Sister M. Jude Kruszewski
23. Sister M. Kingnetta Szczypula
24. Sister M. Louise Nowicki
25. Sister M. Natalie Uscinowicz
26. Sister M. Ralph Stawasz
27. Sister M. Sponsa Bajorek
28. Sister M. Tarcisia Bucki
29. Sister M. Venantia Rec
30. Sister Paula Frances Howard

* Died on June 22, 1983, the day before the
Fourteenth General Chapter was
convoked; replaced by Sister Victoria
Valerie Smagacz.
** Hospitalized; replaced by Sister M.
Clarissa Kolupka.

APPENDIX L

A PRAYER FOR OUR DAILY NEEDS WRITTEN BY MOTHER MARY THERESA DUDZIK, FOUNDRESS OF THE CONGREGATION OF THE FRANCISCAN SISTERS OF CHICAGO

Let us pray:

O God, you have enriched your Church with a religious family, the Franciscan Sisters of Chicago. Give us the grace to reject the goods of this world and to direct our desires to heavenly things. We ask your mercy; forgive us our sins. Through the intercession of the Blessed Virgin Mary and all your saints, especially St. Francis of Assisi, keep us your faithful servants, our families, relatives, friends, benefactors in constant holiness. Cleanse us from our sins and adorn us with virtue. Grant us peace and salvation. Deliver us from our enemies, seen and unseen. Help us to overcome our bodily desires. Provide us with healthful air and fertile land. Support our friends with love; look kindly upon our enemies. Keep our country, Chicago our city, and all the faithful who live here from flood, famine, fire, war, and especially from loss of faith in you.

Sister M. Theresa

(The prayer, handwritten on the fly-leaves of Sister M. Theresa's *Little Office of the Blessed Virgin Mary,* was translated from the Polish by Sister Anne Marie Knawa, OSF, and published for the first time in 1978.)

APPENDIX M

PRAYER FOR THE BEATIFICATION OF THE SERVANT OF GOD, MOTHER MARY THERESA DUDZIK, FOUNDRESS OF THE CONGREGATION OF THE FRANCISCAN SISTERS OF CHICAGO

Let us pray:

O God of infinite love and mercy, Who hast inflamed the humble heart of Mother Mary Theresa with the virtues of love and mercy, which flow abundantly from the Sacred Heart of Thy Son and from the Immaculate Heart of His Blessed Mother, grant, we beseech Thee, that Mother Mary Theresa may become our constant intercessor before Thy Divine Throne. Grant, O Lord, that the virtues of charity and mercy, which Mother Mary Theresa exercised on this earth toward the needy, abandoned and suffering, may also be obtained for us from Thee. Through Christ Thy Son, Our Lord.

O Mother Immaculate, whose honor was promoted by Mother Mary Theresa, we implore Thee, that through her intercession before Thy Divine Son, we may be granted the favor we humbly request. . . .

Our Father, Hail Mary, Glory be.

Immaculate Heart of Mary, pray for us.

Nihil obstat: Alfred L. Abramowicz, J. C. L.
                Censor Deputatus
Imprimatur: + Albert Cardinal Meyer, D.D.
                Archbishop of Chicago

BIBLIOGRAPHY

ARCHIVAL MATERIALS

(The reference abbreviation, AFSCL, represents Archival Materials of the Franciscan Sisters of Chicago, Lemont.)

Administrative Records.

Amo Christum. Kocham Chrystusa, oblubienica przed Obliczem Boga, Książka do nabozeństw Sióstr Franciszkanek pod wezwaniem Bł. Kunegundy. [I love Christ, the spouse before the Face of God, a book of devotions of the Franciscan Sisters under the patronage of Blessed Kunegunda.] Chicago, Illinois, 1932.

Book of Admittances.

Book of Admittances, St. Joseph Home for the Aged and Crippled, Chicago, Illinois.

Book of Annual Assignments.

Book of Closed Schools and Institutions.

Book of Contracts.

Book of Correspondence.

Book of Deceased Sisters.

Book of Departures.

Book of Depositions.

Book of Testimonials.

Bulletins of the Superiors General.

Bywalec, Sister M. Martha, OSFK. "The Chronicle of St. Joseph Home for the Aged." (Unpublished manuscript.)

Chapter Decrees and Chapter Decrees Supplements.

Chapter News in Brief.

Civil Documents.

Community Chronicle of the Franciscan Sisters of Chicago.

Community Newsletters.

Congregation Membership Records.

Constitutions Committee. *Interim Constitutions for the Franciscan Sisters of Chicago.* Lemont, Illinois, 1970.

Constitutions of the Congregation of the Franciscan Sisters of Chicago.

Directory of the Franciscan Sisters of Chicago. (Formerly known as the *Book of Customs, Dyrektorium* or *Regulamin.*)

Documents of Beatification Process.

Document of Erection from the Most Reverend Patrick A. Feehan, Archbishop of Chicago, 18 October 1899.

Dudzik, Matka Maria Teresa,"Kronika Sióstr Franciszkanek pod opieką Św. Kunegundy w Chicago, Illinois" [The Chronicle of the Franciscan Sisters under the patronage of St. Kunegunda in Chicago, Illinois], Chicago, Illinois, 1910. (Unpublished manuscript.)

Echo Avondalskie [Avondale Echo].

Formation and Vocation Standing Committee. "Formation and Vocation: A Progress Report Presented to the Twelfth General Chapter." Lemont, Illinois, June 1974.

Formation Committee. "Formation in the 1970s: A Research Report Presented to the 1972 Special Chapter of Affairs." Lemont, Illinois, August 1972.

"Founding of St. Anthony's Home for the Aged." Crown Point, Indiana.

Franciscan Brief.

Franciscan Echo.

"History of Mother Theresa Home," 12 November 1973.

Holysz, Sister M Aloysia, OSFK. "Franciscan Sisters of St. Kunegunda Chronicle, 1894–1922." Chicago, Illinois, 1922. (Unpublished manuscript.)

House Journals.

Institution Journals.

Kirschbaum, Sister M. Paul, OSFK, ed. *The Congregation of Franciscan Sisters of Bl. Kunegunda: A Sketch of Its Foundation and Progress, 1894–1944.* Niles, Illinois: St. Hedwig Printery, 1944.

Marian Year File, 1954.

Minutes of Extraordinary Chapters of Affairs Proceedings.

Minutes of General Chapter Proceedings.

Minutes of General Council Proceedings.

Newsprints and Photos.

Old Peoples Board and Dowries. St. Joseph Home for the Aged and Crippled, Chicago, Illinois.

Personal Diaries.

Personal Interviews.

Personal Notes and Memoirs.

Rachunki Domu Św. Józefa dla Polskich Starców i Kalek w Avondale, Illinois.

Rachunki z Oranżerii, l lipca 1915–1918 września 1917 [Greenhouse records, 1 July 1915–1918 September 1917]. Chicago, Illinois, 1917.

Raniszewski, Sister M. Gonzaga, OSFK. *Blessed Kinga or Kunegunda.* Chicago: Franciscan Sisters of Bl. Kunegunda, 1950.

――――. "Rys historyczny Zgromadzenia Sióstr Franciszkanek Bł. Kunegundy. Cześć druga, 1910–1940" [A historical survey of the Franciscan Sisters of Blessed Kunegunda. Part two, 1910–1940], Chicago, Illinois, 1940. (Unpublished manuscript.)

Record of Birth and Baptism. Register of Parish Church in Kamień Krajeński.

Record of Summer Schools and Catechetical Centers.

Reports to the General Chapters by Superiors General.

Reports to the Holy See.

Rules and Constitutions.

St. Anthony Hospital. "A Statement for the Case, 1970."

――――. Brochure on Proposed Hospital, 1972.

St. Anthony Medical Center. *Patients' Handbook. 1987.*

――――. *Annual Reports.*

St. Francis House of Prayer: General Goals and Objectives, 1981. Lemont, Illinois, 1981.

St. John Regional Medical Center, Board of Directors and President of St. John Regional Medical Center. "Report to the Franciscan Sisters of Chicago. Subject: St. John School of Nursing." Huron, South Dakota, 1976.

St. Vincent's Orphan Asylum. "Financial Reports, 1898–1911." Chicago, Illinois.

School Journals.

Siatka, Stanislaus, CR, ed. *Sierota* [The Orphan]. Chicago: *Dziennik Chicagoski,* 1899.

Spetz, Rev. Andrew, CR. "Annual Report to the Board of State Commissioners of Public Charities at Springfield, Illinois." Chicago, Illinois, 30 January 1908.

――――. "A Report to the Chicago Association of Commerce." Subscriptions Investigating Committee, 27 April 1911.

Spis Sióstr. (Inviddual files with biographical data of each member from 1894 to 1940.)

Stawasz, Sister M. Ralph. "Summary of Activities of Corporation," Alvernia Rest Home, Parma, Ohio, 5 October 1960.

BOOKS

Abbelen, P. M. *Venerable Mother M. Caroline Friess. A Sketch of Her Life and Character.* Translated by the School Sisters of Notre Dame. 2nd ed. St. Louis: B. Herder Book Co., 1917.

Abbot, Walter M., ed. *The Documents of Vatican II.* New York: American Press, 1966.

Abbott, Edith. *The Tenements of Chicago, 1908–1935.* Chicago: University of Chicago Press, 1936.

Addams, Jane. *Twenty Years at Hull-House.* New York: Macmillan Co., 1910.

Ahles, Sister M. Assumpta, OSF. *In the Shadow of His Wings.* Saint Paul: North Central Publishing Co., 1977.

Angle, Paul M., ed. *Prairie Street: Impressions of Illinois, 1673–1967, by Travelers and Others.* Chicago: The University of Chicago Press, 1968.

Appleton, Ted. *Your Guide to Poland.* New York: Funk & Wagnalls, 1971.

Armstrong, April. *What's Happening to the Catholic Church?* Garden City: Doubleday & Co., 1966.

Attwater, Donald, ed. *A Catholic Dictionary.* New York: Macmillan Co., 1961.

Balch, Emily Greene. *Our Slavic Fellow Citizens.* New York: Charities Publication Committee, 1910.

Barnett, Clifford, et al. *Poland: Its People; Its Society; Its Culture.* New York: Grove Press, 1958.

Beuckman, Rev. Frederick. *History of the Diocese of Belleville, 1700–1914. Section One: St. Clair County.* Belleville, Illinois: Buechler Publishing Co., 1914.

Bishop, Glenn A., and Gilbert, Paul T. *Chicago's Accomplishments and Leaders.* Chicago: Bishop Publishing Co., 1932.

Bishops' Committee of the Confraternity of Christian Doctrine. *The New American Bible.* Translated by Members of the Catholic Biblical Association of America. New York: P. J. Kenedy & Sons, 1970.

Blanshard, Brand. *The Church and the Polish Immigrant.* (No imprint.) 1920. Available at Harvard University.

Bluma, Dacian, OFM, and Chowaniec, Theophilus, OFM, comps. *A History of the Assumption of the Blessed Virgin Mary Province.* Pulaski, Wisconsin: Franciscan Publishers, 1966.

Blunden, Godfrey, and the Editors of *Life. Eastern Europe.* New York: *Time,* 1965.

Bolek, Francis, ed. *Who's Who in Polish America: A Biographical Directory of Polish American Leaders and Distinguished Poles Resident in the Americas.* 3rd ed. New York: Harbinger House, 1943; Arno Publishers, 1970.

Borgia, Sister M. Francis. *He Sent Two.* Milwaukee: Bruce Publishing Co., 1965.

Borromeo, Sister Charles, CSC. *The New Nuns.* New York: New America Library, 1967.

Breton, Valentin, OFM. "Franciscan Spirituality." In *Some Schools of Catholic Spirituality.* Edited by Jean Gautier. New York: Desclee Co., 1959.

Bridgwater, William, and Kurtz, Seymour, eds. *The Columbia Encyclopedia.* 3rd ed. New York: Columbia University Press, 1963.

Brown, Francis J., Ph.D., and Roucek, Joseph A., Ph.D., eds. *Our Racial and National Minorities: Their History, Contributions, and Present Problems.* New York: Prentice-Hall, 1937.

Brusher, Joseph, SJ. *Popes Through the Ages.* Princeton, New Jersey: D. Van Nostrand Co., 1959.

Carpenter, Allan. *Illinois, Land of Lincoln.* Chicago: Childrens Press, 1968.

Chicago Plan Commission. *Forty-Four Cities in the City of Chicago.* Chicago: City of Chicago, 1942.

Chrypinski, Anna, ed. *Polish Customs.* Detroit: Friends of Polish Art, 1972.

Code, Rev. Joseph B. *Great American Foundresses.* New York: Macmillan Co., 1929.

Cogley, John. *Catholic America.* New York: Dial Press, 1973.

Coogan, M. Jane, BVM. *The Price of Our Heritage.* 2 vols. Dubuque, Iowa: Mount Carmel Press, 1975.

Coughlin Roger J., and Riplinger, Cathryn A. *The Story of Charitable Care in the Archdiocese of Chicago, 1844–1959.* Chicago: Catholic Charities, 1959.

Coulson, John, ed. *The Saints.* New York: Guild Press, 1957.

Crosby, Alfred W. *Epidemic and Peace, 1918.* Westport: Greenwood Press, 1976.

Crowe, Frederick E., SJ. *A Time of Change.* Milwaukee: Bruce Publishing Co., 1968.

Cuban, Larry, and Hansen, Rita. *People and the City Neighborhoods.* Glenview, Illinois: Scott, Foresman, & Co., 1974.

Currey, J. Seymour. *Chicago: Its History and Its Builders.* Vol. 3. Chicago: S. J. Clarke Publishing Co., 1912.

De Chantal, Sister M., CSFN. *Out of Nazareth, A Centenary of the Sisters of the Holy Family of Nazareth in the Service of the Church.* New York, New York: Exposition Press, 1974.

Dedmon, Emmett. *Fabulous Chicago.* New York: Random House, 1953.

Delaney, John J., and Tobin, James E., *Dictionary of Catholic Biography.* Garden City, New York: Doubleday & Co., 1961.

Di Donato, Pietro. *Immigrant Saint: The Life of Mother Cabrini.* New York: McGraw-Hill Book Co., 1960.

Dolan, Jay P. *The American Catholic Experience: A History from Colonial Times to the Present.* Garden City, New York: Doubleday & Co., 1985.

Domanski, F., et al. *The Contribution of the Poles to the Growth of Catholicism in the United States.* Rome: 1959.

Donnelly, Sister Gertrude Joseph. *The Sister Apostle*. Notre Dame, Indiana: Fides Publishers, 1964.

Douillet, Jacques. *What Is a Saint?* New York: Hawthorn Books, 1958.

Dvornik, Francis. *The Slavs in European History and Civilization*. New Brunswick, New Jersey: Rutgers University Press, 1962.

Dworaczyk, Rev. Edward J., comp. *The First Polish Colonies of America in Texas*. San Antonio: Naylor Co., 1930.

——. *The First Polish Colonies in Texas*. San Antonio: Naylor Co., 1936.

——. *The Millennium History of Panna Maria, Texas, the Oldest Polish Settlement in America, 1854–1966*. San Antonio: Naylor Co., 1966.

Dyboski, Roman. *Outlines of Polish History*. 2nd ed. London: George Allen and Unwin, 1941.

——. *Poland in World Civilization*. Edited by Ludwik Krzyżanowski. New York: J. M. Barrett Corp, 1950.

Ellis, John Tracy. *American Catholicism*. Chicago: University of Chicago Press, 1956.

Englebert, Omer. *St. Francis of Assisi: A Biography*. Translated by Eve Marie Cooper. Chicago: Franciscan Herald Press, 1965.

English-Speaking Conference of the Order of Friars Minor. *I Have Done My Part; May Christ Teach You Yours*. Pulaski, Wisconsin: Franciscan Publishers, 1981.

Esser, Cajetan, OFM. *The Order of St. Francis*. Translated by Ignatius Brady, OFM. Chicago: Franciscan Herald Press, 1959.

Faherty, William Barnaby, SJ. *Dream by the River: Two Centuries of St. Louis Catholicism, 1766–1967*. St. Louis: Piraeus Publishers, 1973.

Farr, Finis. *Chicago: A Personal History of America's Most American City*. New Rochelle, New York: Arlington House, 1973.

Federal Writers' Project of the Work Projects Administration for the State of Illinois. *Illinois: A Descriptive and Historical Guide*. Chicago: A. C. McClurg & Co., 1939.

Federation of Franciscan Sisters of U.S.A. *Go To My Brethren: A Spiritual Document for Apostolic Communities of Franciscan Women*. Pittsburgh: Federation of Franciscan Sisters of U.S.A., 1969.

Finck, Sister Mary Helena. *The Congregation of the Sisters of Charity of the Incarnate Word of San Antonio, Texas*. Washington, DC: The Catholic University of America, 1925.

Fink, Salvator, OFM, and Hanley, Boniface, OFM. *The Franciscans: Love At Work*. New Jersey: St. Anthony Guild Press, 1963.

Fox, Paul. *The Poles in America*. New York: Arno Press and the *New York Times,* 1970.

Frederic, Sister M. Catherine, OSF. *The Handbook of Catholic Practices*. New York and London: Hawthorn Books, 1964.

Gambari, Rev. Elio, SMM. *Renewal in Religious Life*. Boston: Daughters of St. Paul, 1947.

Garraghan, Gilbert, SJ. *The Catholic Church in Chicago, 1673–1871*. Chicago: Loyola University Press, 1921.

Gautier, Jean. *Some Schools of Catholic Spirituality*. New York: Desclee Co., 1959.

Giejsztor, Aleksander; Kieniewicz, Stefan; Rostwoworski, Emanuel; Tazbir, Janusz; and Wereszycki, Henry. *History of Poland*. Warsaw: PWN: Polish Scientific Publishers, 1968.

Gilbert, Paul, and Bryson, Charles Lee. *Chicago and Its Makers*. Chicago: Felix Mendelsohn, 1929.

Golawski, M. *Poland Through the Ages*. London: Orbis Limited, 1971.

Górska, Małgorzata, ed. *Poland: The Country and Its People*. Warsaw: Interpress Publishers, 1969.

Graham, Jory. *Chicago: An Extraordinary Guide*. Chicago: Rand McNally & Co., 1967.

Greeley, Andrew. *Neighborhood*. New York: Seabury Press, 1977.

Greene, Victor R. *For God and Country: The Rise of Polish and Lithuanian Ethnic Consciousness in America, 1860–1910*. Madison, Wisconsin: State Historical Society of Madison, Wisconsin, 1975.

Habig, Marion A., ed. *St. Francis of Assisi, Writings and Early Biographies: English Omnibus of the Sources for the Life of St. Francis*. Chicago: Franciscan Herald Press, 1972.

Haiman, Miecislaus. *Polish Past in America, 1608–1865*. Chicago: Polish Museum of America, 1975.

——. "The Poles in Chicago." In *Poles of Chicago: A History of One Century of Contribution to the City of Chicago, Illinois, 1837–1937*. Edited by Polish Pageant, Inc. Chicago: By the Author, 1937.

Halecki, Oscar. *A History of Poland*. 2nd rev. ed. London: J. M. Dent & Sons, 1955.

Hanley, Boniface, OFM, and Fink, Salvator, OFM. *The Franciscans: Love at Work.* Paterson: St. Anthony's Guild, 1962.

Heise, Kenan, and Edgerton, Michael. *Chicago Center for Enterprise. Vol. I: The 19th Century.* Woodland Hills: Windsor Publications, 1978.

——. *Chicago Center for Enterprise.* Vol. II: *The 20th Century.* Woodland Hills: Windsor Publications, 1978.

Heming, Harry H., comp. *History of the Catholic Church in Wisconsin, 1895–1898.* Milwaukee: Catholic Historical Publishing Co., 1898.

Hill, Commissioner Lewis W. *Historic City: the Settlement of Chicago.* Chicago: Department of Development and Planning, 1976.

Hinnebausch, Paul, OP. *The Signs of the Times and the Religious Life.* New York: Sheed & Ward, 1967.

Hoag, Edwin. *American Cities: Their Historical and Social Development.* Philadelphia: J. B. Lippincott Co., 1969.

Holli, Melvin G., and Jones, Peter d'A., eds. *The Ethnic Frontier.* Grand Rapids, Michigan: William B. Eerdmans Publishing Co., 1977.

Holt, Glen E., and Pacyga, Dominic A. *Chicago: A Historical Guide to the Neighborhoods—The Loop and South Side.* Chicago: Chicago Historical Society, 1979.

Howard, Robert. *Illinois: A History of the Prairie State.* Grand Rapids, Michigan: William B. Eerdmans Publishing Co., 1972.

Hynes, Michael J. *History of the Diocese of Cleveland.* Cleveland: World Publishing Co., 1953.

Illinois Guide and Gazetteer. Chicago: Rand McNally & Co., 1969.

Iwicki, John J., CR. *The First One Hundred Years: A Study of the Congregation of the Resurrection in the United States, 1866–1966.* Rome: Gregorian University Press, 1966.

Janas, Edward T., CR. *Dictionary of American Resurrectionists, 1865–1965.* Rome: Gregorian University Press, 1967.

John, Eric, ed. *The Popes: A Concise Biographical History.* Vol. 2. New York: Hawthorne Books, 1964.

Kalinowski, Sister Mary Theophane, CSSF. *Felician Sisters in the West.* Ponca City, Oklahoma: Bruce Publishing Co., 1967.

Kaniewicz, Stefan. *The Emancipation of the Polish Peasantry.* Chicago: University of Chicago Press, 1969.

Kantowicz, Edward R. *Polish-American Politics in Chicago, 1888–1940.* Chicago: University of Chicago Press, 1975.

——. "Polish Chicago: Survival Through Solidarity." In *The Ethnic Frontier,* pp. 180–209. Edited by Melvin G. Holli and Peter d'A. James. Grand Rapids, Michigan: William B. Eerdmans Publishing Co., 1977.

Kaplan, Herbert A. *The First Partition of Poland.* New York: Columbia University Press, 1962.

Kennedy, Eugene. *The Joy of Being Human.* Chicago: Thomas More Press, 1974.

Kennedy, John. *A Nation of Immigrants.* New York: Harper & Row, 1964.

Kilduff, Dorrell, and Pygman, C. H. *Illinois: History, Government, Geography.* Chicago: Follett Publishing Co., 1962.

King, Martha Bennett. *The Key to Chicago.* New York: J. B. Lippincott Co., 1961.

Koenig, Rev. Msgr. Harry C., ed. *A History of the Archdiocese of Chicago: Published in Observance of the Centenary of the Archdiocese, 1980.* 2 vols. Chicago: Archdiocese of Chicago, 1980.

——. *Caritas Christi Urget Nos: A History of the Offices, Agencies, and Institutions of the Archdiocese of Chicago.* 2 vols. Chicago: New World Publishing Co., 1981.

Kogan, Herman, and Cromie, Robert. *The Great Fire: Chicago, 1871.* New York: G. P. Putnam's Sons, 1971.

Kogan, Herman, and Wendt, Lloyd. *Chicago: A Pictorial History.* New York: Bonanza Books, 1958.

Kruszka, Wacław. *Historya Polska w Ameryce* [The history of the Poles in America]. New ed. Milwaukee: Kuryer Publishing Co., 1937.

——. *Siedm Siedmiolece Czyli Pół Wieku Życia i Pamiętnik i Przyczynek do Historii Polskiej w Ameryce* [Seven times seven or the half-century of my life: A memoir and aid to the history of the Poles in America]. 2 vols. Milwaukee: Kuryer Press, 1924.

——. *Historya Polska w Ameryce* [The history of the Poles in America]. 13 vols. Milwaukee: Kuryer Press, 1905–1908.

Kuniczak, W. S. *My Name is Million.* New York: Doubleday & Co., 1978.

Kuznicki, Ellen Marie, CSSF. "The Polish American Parochial Schools." In *Poles in America,* pp. 435–60. Edited by Frank Mocha. Stevens Point, Wisconsin: Worzalla Publishing Co., 1978.

Kuzniewski, Anthony J., SJ. "The Catholic Church in the Life of the Polish-Americans." In *Poles in America,* pp. 399–422. Edited by Frank Mocha. Stevens Point, Wisconsin: Worzalla Publishing Co., 1978.

Ledit, Joseph, SJ. *Archbishop John Baptist Cieplak.* Montreal: Palm Publishers, 1963.

Lekeux, P. Martial, OFM. *20th Century Litany to the Poverello.* Chicago: Franciscan Herald Press, 1958.

Leslie, Robert. *Reform and Insurrection in Russian Poland, 1856–1865.* London: Athlone Press, 1963.

Lilien, Marya, and Pyrek-Ejsmont, Malgorzata. *Polish Churches along the Kennedy Expressway.* Chicago: Chicago Historical Society, 1980.

Linn, James Weber. *Jane Addams: A Biography.* New York: D. Appleton-Century Co., 1943.

Long, Leonard, CR. *The Resurrectionists.* Chicago: By the Author, 1971.

Longstreet, Stephen. *Chicago, 1860–1919.* New York: David McKay Co., 1973.

Lopata, Helena Znaniecka. *Polish Americans: Status Competition in an Ethnic Community.* Englewood Cliffs: Prentice-Hall, 1976.

Lord, Robert Howard. *The Second Partition of Poland.* Cambridge: Howard University Press, 1915.

Lozano, John M., *Foundresses, Founders, and Their Religious Families.* Translated by Joseph Daries, CMF. Chicago: Claret Center for Resources in Spirituality, 1983.

Maisel, Albert Q. *They All Chose America.* New York: Thomas Nelson & Sons, 1957.

Masseron, Alexandre, and Habig, Marion A., OFM. *The Franciscans.* Chicago: Franciscan Herald Press, 1959.

Mausolff, A. J. M., and Mausolff, M. K. *Saint Companions for Each Day.* St. Paul: St. Paul Publications, 1954.

Mayer, Harold M., and Wade, Richard E. *Chicago: Growth of a Metropolis.* Chicago: University of Chicago Press, 1969.

Maynard, Theodore. *The Story of American Catholicism.* New York: Macmillan Co., 1954.

McCarthy, Thomas P., CSV, comp. *Guide to the Catholic Sisterhoods in the United States.* Foreword by the Most Reverend Amleto Giovanni Cicognani. Washington, DC. Catholic University of America Press, 1958.

McCullough, David G. "The Johnstown Flood." In *Reader's Digest Condensed Books.* Vol. 4. Pleasantville, New York, 1968.

Meadows, Denis. *A Short History of the Catholic Church.* New York: Guild Press, 1959.

Meagher, Rev. George, TCSC. *With Attentive Ear and Courageous Heart.* Milwaukee: Bruce Publishing Co., 1957.

Meigs, Cornelia. *Jane Addams, Pioneer for Social Justice.* Boston: Little, Brown and Co., 1970.

Meyers, Sister Bertrande, DC. *Sisters for the 21st Century.* New York: Sheed & Ward, 1965.

Miller-Fulop, Rene. *The Saints That Moved the World.* New York: Thomas Y. Crowell Co., 1945.

Mocha, Frank, ed. *Poles in America.* Stevens Point, Wisconsin: Worzalla Publishing Co., 1978.

Mondadori, Arnoldo. *The Life and Times of St. Francis.* Philadelphia and New York: Curtis Publishing Co., 1967.

Moorman, John R. H. *Richest of Poor Men.* Huntington, Indiana: Our Sunday Visitor, 1977.

Muckenheim, Sister Charles Borromeo, CSC. *The Implications of Renewal.* Notre Dame, Indiana: Fides Publishing, 1966.

Neuwien, Reginald A., ed. *Catholic Schools in Action: The Notre Dame Study of Catholic Elementary and Secondary Schools in the United States.* Notre Dame, Indiana: University of Notre Dame, 1966.

Notre Dame, A School Sister of. *Mother Caroline and the School Sisters of Notre Dame in North America.* 2 vols. St. Louis: Woodward and Tiernan Co., 1928.

Oursler, Fulton, and Oursler, Will. *Father Flanagan of Boys Town.* Garden City, New York: Doubleday & Co., 1949.

Pacyga, Dominic A., and Skerrett, Ellen. *Chicago: City of Neighborhoods.* Chicago: Loyola University Press, 1986.

Parot, Joseph J. *Polish Catholics in Chicago, 1850–1920.* De Kalb: Northern Illinois University Press, 1981.

Pierce, Bessie Louise. *A History of Chicago.* Vol. 3: *The Rise of a Modern City, 1871–1893.* New York: Alfred A. Knopf, 1957.

Pierce, Richard. *The Polish in America.* Chicago: Claretian Publications, 1972.

Polzin, Theresita. *The Polish American: Whence and Whither.* Pulaski, Wisconsin: Franciscan Publishers, 1973.

Przygoda, Jacek. *Texas Pioneers from Poland: A Study in the Ethnic History.* (No imprint.) 1971.

Raniszewski, Siostra M. Gonzaga, OSFK. *Rys historyczny Zgromadzenia Sióstr Franciszkanek Błogosławionej Kunegundy. Część pierwsza, 1860–1910* [A historical survey of the Franciscan Sisters of Blessed Kunegunda. Part one, 1860–1910] Chicago: By the Author, 1947.

Reddaway, W. F., et al. *From the Origins to Sobieski (to 1696).* Vol. 1: *The Cambridge History of Poland.* Cambridge: Cambridge University Press, 1950.

———. *From Augustus II to Piłsudski (1697–1935).* Vol. 2: *The Cambridge History of Poland.* Cambridge: Cambridge University Press, 1941.

Reed, Earl H. "Belmont-Cragin, Montclare, Hermosa, Community Areas Nos. 18, 19, and 20." *Forty-Four Cities in the City of Chicago.* Chicago: Chicago Plan Commission, 1942.

Renkiewicz, Frank. *The Poles in America, 1608–1972: A Chronology and Fact Book.* Dobbs Ferry, New York: Oceana, 1973.

Ricciardi, Antonio. *His Will Alone.* Translated by Regis N. Barwig. Rome: Edizioni Agiografiche, 1970.

Rodriguez, Alphonse, SJ. *Progress in Perfection and Virtues.* 3 vols. Translated by Casimir Riedl, SJ. Krakow: X. Michale Mycielski, 1894.

Roemer, Theodore, OFM Cap. *The Catholic Church in the United States.* St. Louis: B. Herder Book Co., 1940.

Romb, Anselm W., OFM Conv. *The Franciscan Charism in the Church.* Paterson, New Jersey: St. Anthony Guild Press, 1969.

Roucek, Joseph S. *Poles in the United States of America.* Gdynia, Poland: Baltic Institute, 1937.

Ryan, Sister Mary Philip, OP. *Amid the Alien Corn.* St. Charles: Ones Wood Press, 1967.

St. John, Christopher. *A Little Book of Polish Saints.* London: Burns and Oates, 1918.

Schmitt, Bernadotte E., ed. *Poland.* Berkeley and Los Angeles: University of California Press, 1964.

Schimberg, Albert Paul. *The Larks of Umbria.* Milwaukee: Bruce Publishing Co., 1942.

Stephenson, George. *A History of American Immigration, 1820–1924.* Boston: Ginn & Co., 1926.

Sullivan, Kay. *The Catholic Tourist Guide.* New York: Meredith Press, 1967.

Super, Paul. *The Polish Tradition: An Interpretation of a Nation.* London: Maxlove Publishing Co., 1939.

Swastek, Rev. Joseph. *Priest and Pioneer: Rev. Leopold Moczygemba.* Detroit: Conventual Press, 1951.

———. *The Polish American Story.* Buffalo: Felician Sisters, 1955.

Świętosławski, Wojciech. "Education." In *Poland,* pp. 257–273. Edited by Bernadotte E. Schmitt. Berkeley and Los Angeles: University of California Press, 1964.

Szawlewski, Mieczysław. *Wychodztwo Polskie w Stanach Zjednoczonych Ameryki.* Lwów: Narodowego Imenia Ossolinskich, 1924.

These United States. New York: Readers Digest Association, 1968.

Thompson, Rev. Joseph, ed. *Diamond Jubilee of the Archdiocese of Chicago, 1920.* Des Plaines, Illinois: St. Mary Training School Press, 1920.

Thurston, Herbert, SJ, and Atwater, Donald, eds. *Butler's Lives of the Saints.* 4 vols. London: Burns and Oates, 1956.

Tims, Margaret. *Jane Addams of Hull House, 1860–1935.* London: George Allen and Unwin, 1961.

Tomczak, Anthony C., ed. *Poles in America: Their Contribution to a Century of Progress.* Chicago: Polish Day Association, 1933.

Tours, Cesaire De, OFM Cap. *Franciscan Perfection.* Translated by Paul Barrett, OFM Cap. Westminster, Maryland: Newman Press, 1956.

Van Doornik, Father N. G. *Francis of Assisi. A Prophet for Our Time.* Translated by Barbara Potter Fasting. Holland, 1977.

Vann, Father Joseph, OFM, ed. *Lives of the Saints: With Excerpts from Their Writings.* Introduction by Father Thomas Plassman, OFM. New York: John J. Crawley & Co., 1954.

Vatican Council II. "Declaration on Christian Education." In *The Documents of Vatican II,* pp. 634,

646–47. Edited by Walter M. Abbott. New York: Herder & Herder, 1966.

——. "Decree on the Apostolate of the Laity." In *The Documents of Vatican II*, pp. 490–91. Edited by Walter M. Abbott. New York: Herder & Herder, 1966.

——. "Decree on the Appropriate Renewal of Religious Life." In *The Documents of Vatican II*, pp. 464–472, 478. Edited by Walter M. Abbott. New York: Herder & Herder, 1966.

——. "Decree on the Instruments of Social Communications. "In *The Documents of Vatican II*, p. 322. Edited by Walter M. Abbott. New York: Herder & Herder, 1966.

——. "Dogmatic Constitution on the Church." In *The Documents of Vatican II*, p. 59. Edited by Walter M. Abbott. New York: Herder & Herder, 1966.

Vincent, Msgr. Francis. "The Spirituality of St. Francis of Sales." In *Some Schools of Catholic Spirituality*. Edited by Jean Gautier. New York: Desclee Co., 1959.

Wachtel, Karol. *Polonja w Ameryce* [The Poles in America]. Philadelphia: Polish Star Co., 1944.

Walton, Clyde C., ed. *An Illinois Reader*. De Kalb: Northern Illinois University Press, 1970.

Wandycz, Peter. *The Lands of Partitioned Poland, 1795–1918*. Seattle: University of Washington Press, 1974.

Webber, F. R. *Church Symbolism*. 2nd rev ed. Cleveland: J. H. Hanson, 1938.

Wegenknecht, Edward. *Chicago*. Oklahoma: University of Oklahoma Press, 1964.

Weiser, Francis C. *Handbook of Christian Feasts and Customs*. New York: Harcourt, Brace & Co., 1952.

Wittke, Carl. *We Who Built America: The Saga of the Immigrant*. Cleveland: Press of Western Reserve University, 1964.

Włoszczewski, Stefan. *History of Polish American Culture*. Trenton, New Jersey: White Eagle Publishing Co., 1946.

Wycislo, Aloysius J. "The Polish Catholic Immigrant." In *Roman Catholicism and the American Way of Life*. Edited by Thomas T. McAvoy. Notre Dame, Indiana: University of Notre Dame Press, 1960.

Wytrwal, Joseph A. *America's Polish Heritage: A Social History of the Poles in America*. Detroit: Endurance Press, 1961.

——. *Poles in American History and Tradition*. Detroit: Endurance Press, 1969.

——. *The Poles in America*. Minneapolis: Lerner Publications Co., 1969.

Zawistowski, Theodore L. "The Polish National Catholic Church: An Acceptable Alternative." In *Poles in America*, pp. 423–34. Edited by Frank Mocha. Stevens Point: Worzalla Publishing Co., 1978.

Zglenicki, Leon, ed. *Poles of Chicago, 1837–1937*. Chicago: Polish Pageant, 1937.

Zieleniewicz, Andrzej. *Poland*. Translated, revised, and edited by R. Strybel, L. Chrobot, R. Geryk, J. Swastek, and W. Ziemba, in cooperation with Edward Piszek. Orchard Lake: Center for Polish Studies and Culture, 1971.

Zurawski, Joseph W. *Polish American History and Culture: A Classified Bibliography*. Chicago: Polish Museum of America, 1975.

SOUVENIR BOOKS

Adamczyk, Sister Jean, and Kedzior, Sister M. Aloysilla, eds. *St. John School of Nursing: Graduates 1948–1976*. Special edition. Huron, South Dakota, St. John School of Nursing, 1976.

Album Jubileuszowy Każimierzowo, 1890–1940 [A Jubilee Album of St. Casimir Parish, 1890–1940]. Chicago, Illinois, 1940.

Album Pamiątkowy Złotego Jubileuszu Parafii Świętego Stanisława Kostki, 1867–1917 [A Commemorative Album of the Golden Jubilee of St. Stanislaus Kostka Parish, 1867–1917]. Chicago, Illinois, 1917.

Album Srebrnego Jubileuszu Parafii Św. Jana Kantego, 1904–1929 [An Album of the Silver Jubilee of St. John Cantius Parish, 1904–1929]. Indiana Harbor, Indiana, 1929.

Alerding, H. J., Rt. Rev. *The Diocese of Fort Wayne 1857–September 1907: A Book of Historical Reference, 1669–1907*. Fort Wayne, Indiana: Archer Publishing Co., 1907.

Alvernia Rest Home: Souvenir Book of Dedication. Parma, Ohio, 14 June 1953.

Annals of St. Boniface Parish, 1862–1926. Chicago, Illinois, 1926.

Archdiocese of San Antonio: Diamond Jubilee, 1874–1949. San Antonio, Texas, 1949.

Archdiocese of San Antonio, 1874–1974. San Antonio, Texas, 1974.

Assumption of the BVM Church, A Pictorial Directory: Golden Jubilee Year, 1922–1972. Conemaugh, Pennsylvania 1972.

Assumption of the BVM Church: Souvenir Book of Dedication. Conemaugh, Pennsylvania, 1958.

Ave Maria: Pamiętnik Złotego Jubileuszu Parafii Św. Kazimierza, 1902–1952 [Golden Jubilee of St. Casimir's Parish, 1902–1952]. Johnstown, Pennsylvania, 1952.

Boys Town: Memories and Dreams. Boystown, Nebraska, 1976.

Buschman, Barbara, ed. *Lemont, Illinois: Its History in Commemoration of the Centennial of Its Incorporation, 1873–1973.* Des Plaines, Illinois: King/Mann Yearbook Center, 1973.

Cathedral of Our Lady of Perpetual Help: Dedication Book. Rapid City, South Dakota, 1963.

Centennial History of the Founding of the Nativity of the Blessed Virgin Mary Parish in Częstochowa, Texas, 1873–1973. Częstochowa, Texas, 1973.

Centennial Year, 1873–1973, Holy Trinity Church: A Historical Review. Chicago, Illinois, 1973.

Chicago's Tribute to His Excellency Most Rev. Bernard J. Sheil, DD, on the 25th Anniversary of His Consecration. Chicago, Illinois, 1935.

Church of St. Pascal: A History of Fifty Years. South Hackensack, New Jersey: Custombook, 1967.

Clawson, Sharon M., ed. *Holy Family Child Care Center: Dedication Book.* Crown Point, Indiana, 1982.

———. *The Nursing Home.* Crown Point, Indiana: St. Anthony Medical Center, 1977.

Commemoration of Blessed Sacrament Church and School: Blessing and Dedication. Gary, Indiana, 1971.

Commemorative Booklet: St. Michael and SS. Peter and Paul, 145 Years of Faith. Glen Campbell and Arcadia, Pennsylvania, 1975.

Commemorative Book: The Diamond Jubilee of St. Stanislaus Parish. Posen, Illinois, 1970.

Cyryla, Siostra Maria, CSSF. *Wśród Dusz Dla Dusz, 1910–1953: Dzieje i Dorobek.* Chicago: Nakładem Sióstr Felicjanek, 1953.

Dadej, Mother M. Jerome, OSFK, and Gorzkowski, Sister M. Gerarda, OSFK, eds. *Pamiętnik z Okazjii Złotego Jubileuszu Zgromadzenia, 1944.* Niles, Illinois: St. Hedwig Printery, 1944.

Dedication Book of the New Sacred Heart of Jesus Church. La Porte, Indiana, 1971.

Dedication Book: St. Louise de Marillac Church and School. La Grange Park, Illinois, 1958.

Dedication of St. Matthias Church. Crown Point, Indiana, 1970.

Dedication of the New St. Mary Church. Madison, Illinois, 1954.

Diamond Jubilee, 1867–1942: St. Stanislaus Kostka Church. Chicago, Illinois, 1942.

Doman, Sister M. Tullia. "Polish Americans and Their Contributions to the Catholic Church in the United States." *Sacrum Poloniae Millenium* 6 (1959): 371–602.

Farrell Golden Jubilee Book. Farrell, Pennsylvania, 1951.

Fiftieth Anniversary of St. Peter Claver Church, 1911–1961. Mobile, Alabama, 1961.

Fiftieth Anniversary of St. Stanislaus Bishop and Martyr Church. Chicago, Illinois, 1943.

Five Holy Martyrs Church: Golden Jubilee Souvenir Book, 1909–1959. Chicago, Illinois, 1959.

Franciscan Sisters of Perpetual Help: Golden Jubilee Book, 1901–1951. St. Louis, Missouri, 1951.

Golden Jubilee Souvenir Book, 1902–1952: St. Stanislaus B. & M. Parish. Chicago, Illinois, 1952.

Golden Jubilee Souvenir Booklet, 1916–1967: Sacred Heart Church. La Porte, Indiana, 1967.

Golden Anniversary of St. Peter Claver Church, 1911–1961. Mobile, Alabama, 1961.

Golden Anniversary of St. Stanislaus Kostka Church, 1902–1952. Youngstown, Ohio, 1952.

Golden Jubilee Book of St. Stanislaus Parish. Posen, Illinois, 1970.

Golden Jubilee of St. Mary's Church, 1912–1962. Madison, Illinois, 1962.

Golden Jubilee of St. Stanislaus College-Weber High School, 1890–1940. Chicago, Illinois, 1940.

Golden Jubilee, 1899–1949: St. Mary of the Angels Church. Chicago, Illinois, 1949.

Golden Jubilee, 1909–1959: SS. Peter and Paul's Catholic Church. Spring Valley, Illinois, 1959.

Golden Jubilee Year of St. Hedwig's Parish, 1908–1958. Gary, Indiana, 1958.

Guardian Angel Day Nursery and Home for Girls: Golden Jubilee Souvenir Book, 1915–1965. Chicago, Illinois, 31 October 1965.

Haiman, Mieczysław. *Zjednoczenie Polskie Rzymsko-Katolickie w Ameryce, 1873–1948* [The History of the Polish Roman Catholic Union of America]. Chicago, Illinois, 1948.

"History of Cestohowa Parish." *The Centennial History of the Founding of the Nativity of the Blessed Virgin Mary Parish in Częstochowa, Texas, 1873–1973*. Częstochowa, Texas, 1973.

Immaculate Conception BVM Diamond Jubilee, 1882–1957. Chicago, Illinois, 1957.

Indiana Harbor Catholic Elementary School Yearbook, 1976. Indiana Harbor, Indiana, 1976.

Iwicki, Rev. John, CR. "The Novitiate Story." *St. Joseph's Novitiate Dedication Booklet* (September 1960).

Jakajtis, Sister M. Benigna, OSFK, and Swiech, Sister M. Bogumila, OSFK. "Brief Sketch of the Work of the Community in Cleveland." In the *Souvenir Book of Dedication of Alvernia Rest Home*. Parma, Ohio, 1953.

Jubileusz 25cio-lecia Parafii Św. Floriana, 1905–1930: Księga Pamiątkowa [A Dedication Book: Silver Jubilee of St. Florian's Parish, 1905–1930]. Hegewisch, Illinois, 1930.

Komar, Paul A., ed. *Farrell Golden Jubilee, 1901–1951*. Farrell, Pennsylvania, 1951.

Kruszewski, Sister M. Jude, ed. *I Have Done My Part: May Christ Teach You Yours*. Marceline, Missouri: Walsworth Publishing Co., 1982.

Kruszka, Ks. Wacław. *Pamiętnik Złotego Jubileuszu Parafii Św. Każimierza w Cleveland, Ohio, 1892–1942* [Golden Jubilee of St. Casimir's Parish, Cleveland, Ohio]. Cleveland, Ohio, 1942.

Książka Pamiątkowa z Okazji Upomiętnienia Srebrnego Jubileuszu Polskiej Parafii Najsłodszego Serca Jezus [A Silver Jubilee Book: Sacred Heart of Jesus Parish]. La Porte, Indiana, 1938.

Księga Srebrna Wydana Staraniem Komitetu Jubileuszowego z okazji i ku czci 25-lecia Pracy w Winnicy Panskiej w Parafii Św. Józefa w Chicago Wiel. Ks. St. Cholewinskiego: Dnia 7-go lipca, 1935 r. [A Silver Jubilee Book in Honor of the Reverend Stanislaus Cholewinski, Pastor of St. Joseph Parish]. Chicago, Illinois, 1935.

Księga Wspomnien Parafii Najsłodszego Serca Jezus, 1891–1941 [Book of Memories: Sacred Heart of Jesus Parish, 1891–1941]. Cleveland, Ohio, 1941.

Madonna High School Dedication Book. Chicago, Illinois, 1959.

Memento of the 50th Anniversary of the Church of St. Joseph. East Chicago, Indiana, 1967.

Memorare: St. Mary's College, 1821–1971. St. Mary, Kentucky, 1971.

Mruz, Sister M. Carolyn and a Book of Celebration Staff. *Franciscan Sisters of Our Lady of Perpetual Help, 1901–1976*. Ferguson, Missouri, 1976.

Nasz Pamiętnik Parafialny Wydanie Jubileuszowego w Okazji Uroczystości Dwudziestopięcialecie Założenia Parafii SS. Pięciu Braci Polaków i Męczenników [Our Parish Record on the Occasion of the Silver Jubilee of Five Holy Martyrs—Poles and Martyrs Parish]. Chicago, Illinois, 1934.

New St. Casimir, the Prince Church: Commemorative Book of Dedication. St. Louis, Missouri, 1977.

Nyka, Leon C., ed. *Poles in America: Their Contribution to a Century of Progress*. Chicago: *Polish Daily Zgoda*, 1933.

Our Golden Jubilee, 1897–1947: St. Josaphat's Catholic Church. Oshkosh, Wisconsin, 1947.

Our Lady of Victory Convent: Dedication Book. Lemont, Illinois, 1963.

Our Lady of Victory Convent: Souvenir of Dedication. Lemont, Illinois, 1937.

Pamiątka Złotego Jubileuszu Parafii Św. Jana Kantego [A Souvenir of the Golden Jubilee of St. John Cantius Parish]. Chicago, Illinois, 1943.

Pamiątka Złotego Jubileuszu Parafii Św. Stanislawa Kostki, 1880–1930 [Souvenir of the Golden Jubilee of St. Stanislaus Kostka Parish, 1880–1930]. St. Louis, Missouri, 1930.

Pamiętnik Jubileuszowy ki czci Ks. Ludwika Grudzinskiego, Proboszcza Parafii Św. Jana Bożego, 1903–1928 [A Jubilee Souvenir in Honor of the Reverend Louis Grudzinski, Pastor of St. John of God Church, 1903–1928]. Chicago, Illinois, 1928.

Pamiętnik Obchodu 25-letniego Jubileuszu Ochronki Św. Elżbiety Pod Opieką Sióstr Franciszkanek, 1920–1945. [A Souvenir of the 25th Jubilee of St. Elizabeth's Nursery under the Direction of the Franciscan Sisters, 1920–1945]. Chicago, Illinois, 1945.

Pamiętnik Srebnego Jubileusza Parafii Św. Jadwigi, 1908–1933 [A Souvenir of the Silver Jubilee of St. Hedwig's Parish, 1908–1933]. Gary, Indiana, 1933.

Pamiętnik z Okazji Poświęcenia Nowego Kościoła Św. Jadwigi [A Souvenir on the Occasion of the Dedication of the New St. Hedwig Church]. Gary, Indiana, 1942.

Pamiętnik z Okazji Srebrnego Jubileuszu Parafii Wniebowzięcia Najświetszej Marii Panny [A Souvenir Book: Silver Jubilee of Assumption of the Blessed Virgin Mary Parish]. New Chicago, Indiana, 1942.

Parafii Św. Trójcy: Książka Jubileuszowa, 1893–1943 [Holy Trinity Parish Golden Jubilee Book, 1893–1943]. Chicago, Illinois, 1943.

Poland's Millennium of Christianity: Indiana Observance Souvenir Book. Hammond, Indiana: Klines Printers, 1966.

Poles in America: Their Contribution to a Century of Progress: A Commemorative Souvenir Book Compiled and Published on the Occasion of the Polish Week of Hospitality, July 17 to 23: A Century of Progress International Exposition. Chicago, Illinois, 1933.

Pope in Chicago: A Commemorative Album. Chicago: Follett Publishing Co., 1979.

Poverello: St. John's School of Nursing. Huron, South Dakota, 1963.

Pylon '74: Father Flanagan's Boys' Home. Vol. 23. Boys Town, Nebraska, 1974.

Pylon '76: Father Flanagan's Boys' Home. Vol. 24. Boys Town, Nebraska, 1976.

Raniszewski, Siostra M. Gonzaga, OSFK. *Zarys Polwiecza Zgromadzenia Sióstr Franciszkanek Bł. Kunegundy* [Sketch of the fifty-year history of the Congregation of the Franciscan Sisters of Bl. Kunegunda]. Chicago: By the Author, 1944.

Ryba, Sister Ellen Marie, CSSF, ed., in collaboration with Felician Sisters of American Provinces. *Response, 1874–1974.* Canada and Brazil: Felician Sisters, 1974.

Sacred Heart of Jesus Church: Golden Jubilee Book, 1910–1960. Chicago, Illinois, 1960.

St. Adalbert: A Tribute to 100 Years of Service, 1874–1974. Chicago, Illinois, 1974.

St. Albertus, Detroit's Oldest Parish: Centennial Book, 1872–1973. Detroit, Michigan, 1974.

St. Casimir Parish: Diamond Jubilee, 1890–1965. Chicago, Illinois, 1965.

St. Casimir's Catholic Church: Album Directory. St. Louis, Missouri, 1975.

Saint Casimir's Catholic Church: Golden Jubilee, 1916–1966. Streator, Illinois, 1966.

St. Cecilia's Church: Diamond Jubilee, Louisville, Kentucky, 1948.

St. Hedwig Church: Diamond Jubilee, 1888–1963. Chicago, Illinois, 1963.

St. Hyacinth Church: Golden Jubilee, 1894–1944. Chicago, Illinois, 1944.

St. Hyacinth Parish, 1894–1969. Chicago, Illinois, 1969.

St. James Church: Diamond Jubilee Book, 1902–1977. Arlington Heights, Illinois, 1977.

St. John Cantius Church: Diamond Jubilee Book, 1905–1980. Indiana Harbor, Indiana, 1980.

St. John Cantius Church, 1893–1968. Chicago, Illinois, 1968.

St. John Cantius Church: Golden Jubilee Book, 1905–1955. Indiana Harbor, Indiana, 1955.

St. John of God Church: Golden Jubilee Book, 1907–1957. Chicago, Illinois, 1957.

St. John Reports: 30th Anniversary Issue. Huron, South Dakota: St. John Regional Medical Center, 1977.

St. Joseph the Provider: Dedication Book. Campbell, Ohio, 1963.

St. Mary of Częstochowa: 50th Anniversary. Hammond, Indiana, 1963.

St. Mary's College. *Memorare, 1821–1871.* St. Mary, Kentucky, 1871.

St. Pancratius Church Dedication Book. Chicago, Illinois, 1960.

St. Roch's Diamond Jubilee. La Salle, Illinois, 1975.

Saints Cyril and Methodius Church: Diamond Jubilee, 1884–1959. Lemont, Illinois, 1959.

SS. Philip and James: 25th Anniversary, 1950–1975. Cleveland, Ohio, 1975.

St. Stanislaus B. and M. Church: Anniversary, 1893–1968. Chicago, Illinois, 1968.

St. Stanislaus Kostka Centennial Book, 1867–1967. Chicago, Illinois, 1967.

75th Anniversary: St. Stanislaus Kostka Church, 1902–1977. Youngstown, Ohio, 1977.

Solemn Dedication of Our Lady of Loretto Church and School Commemorative Booklet. St. Louis, Missouri, 1962.

Souvenir Booklet: Dedication of Alvernia Rest Home: Convalescent and Home for the Aged. Parma, Ohio, 1953.

Souvenir Booklet: Dedication of St. Leo the Great Church and School. Cleveland, Ohio, 1951.

Souvenir Book of Dedication of the Assumption of the Blessed Virgin Mary Church, 1922–1972. Conemaugh, Pennsylvania, 1958.

Srebrny Jubileusz Parafii Św. Wojciecha, 1905–1930 [Silver Jubilee: St. Adalbert Parish, 1905–1930]. East St. Louis, Illinois, 1930.

Thompson, Rev. Joseph, ed. *Diamond Jubilee of the Archdiocese of Chicago, 1920.* Des Plaines, St. Mary's Training School Press, 1920.

Weber's New Frontier: Souvenir Book of Dedication. Chicago, Illinois, 1962.

Zarys Historii Parafii Św. Wojciecha B. i M., 1902–1927, oraz szkice Towarzystwo istniejących przy tej parafii [Record of the history of St. Adalbert B. and M. Parish, 1902–1927, together with a sketch of the parish organizations.] Whiting, Indiana, 1927.

Złoty Jubileusz Parafii Św. Jacka, 1875–1929 [Golden Jubilee: St. Hyacinth Parish, 1875–1925]. La Salle, Illinois, 1925.

Złoty Jubileusz Parafii Św. Kazimierza, 1889–1939 [Golden Jubilee: St. Casimir Church, 1889–1939]. St. Louis, Missouri, 1939.

NEWSPAPERS

"Arcybiskup Jan Cieplak." *The New World,* 27 February 1976.

Besser, James David. "A Street Called Home: Why Milwaukee Avenue is Really Chicago's Main Street." *Chicago Sun-Times Midwest Magazine,* 3 November 1974.

Boys Town Times, 12 October 1973.

Catholic Week, 9 May 1947; 21 October 1960.

"Chicago and the U.S.A.: A Special Issue on a Great City's Contribution to the Nation." *Chicago Tribune Magazine,* 23 May 1976.

Chicago Daily News, 2 September 1954; 19 September 1969.

Chicago Sun-Times, 24 October 1976; 19 December 1976; 1978.

Chicago Tribune, 7 May 1982.

Cross, Robert. "The Heartland in World History. " *Chicago Tribune Magazine,* May 1976.

Drury. John. "Chicago Homes." *Chicago Daily News,* 12 April 1940.

Dziennik Chicagoski (1890–1963), Editorial Library, Chicago, Illinois.

Fetcko, Dolores. "St. Anthony–Vital Part of Area History." *Northwest Indiana Post-Tribune,* 26 July 1981.

Friedan, Betty. "The Men I Most Admire." *Chicago Sun-Times Parade Magazine,* 12 August 1984.

"Golden Jubilee of the Diocese of Grand Island." *Nebraska Register Supplement,* 14 September 1962.

"Golden Priestly Jubilee: The Most Reverend Gerald T. Bergen, Archbishop of Omaha." *True Voice: Official Newspaper of the Archdiocese of Omaha* 63 (1965).

Greeley, Andrew M. "The Unwanted People Who Proved Indispensable." *Chicago Tribune Magazine,* 23 May 1976.

Gregory Times-Advocate (Gregory, South Dakota), 23 June 1937; 7 June 1962.

Hammond Times, 2 October 1967.

"Honoring His Excellency, The Most Reverend Thomas J. Toolen, Archbishop of Mobile-Birmingham, on the Occasion of the Golden Jubilee of His Ordination." *Catholic Week: Official Publication of the Catholic Church in Alabama and Northwest Florida,* 21 October, 1960.

Hurst, Jack. "Polish-American and Proud." *Chicago Tribune Magazine,* 15 February 1976.

Janas, Rev. Edward T., CR. *Dziennik Chicagoski,* 28 October 1967.

Johnstown Tribune-Democrat, 7 December 1977.

"Keeping Heads Together Behind a Locked Door." *The New World,* 29 March 1974.

Kraus, Herbert M. "They're Still Fighting Over 'Saint Jane'." *Chicago Daily News,* 22 September 1977.

Kuzniewski, Anthony J., SJ. "Polish Catholics in America."*The New World,* 30 January 1976.

Lemont Herald, 27 February 1974.

Madaj, Rev. Menceslaus J. "Chicago: The Polish Capital of the United States." *New World,* 9 April 1971.

———. "The Third Cardinal of the Archdiocese of Chicago." *The New World,* 21 February 1975.

———. *The New World,* 30 August 1964; 16 August 1974.

"The Miraculous Our Lady of Częstochowa." *Naród Polski,* August 1966.

The New World, 3 March 1944; 23 July 1971.

Omaha World Herald, 1973.

Our Sunday Visitor (Gary, Indiana), 15 January 1961; 1 May 1966; September 1974; October 1975.

"St. Josephat—Landmark for Poles." *Milwaukee Sentinel,* 2 May 1964.

"St. Michael's Souvenir Dedication Number." *Berlin* (Wisconsin) *Evening Journal,* 26 October 1927.

San Antonio Daily Herald, 18 November 1869.

Schoneck, Harold M. "Drive Against Swine Flu Recalls the Pandemic of 1918." *Chicago Daily News,* 11 October 1976.

Segal, Eugene. "Why Neighborhoods Stay Good: Polish Traditions Help Cleveland's Poznan Defy Rot." *Cleveland Plain Dealer,* 20 September 1959.

Solemn Observance of the Fortieth Episcopal Anniversary and the Fifty-seventh Sacerdotal Anniversary of the Most Reverend Thomas J. Toolen, Archbishop of the Diocese of Mobile Birmingham. *Catholic Week,* 25 October 1967.

"The Newman Apostolate." *The New World,* 20 February 1976.

"The Ties That Bind Are Lasting." *Chicago Sun Times Midwest Magazine,* 28 July 1968.

Western Catholic Supplement, Souvenir Number, 25 April 1924.

MAGAZINES AND JOURNALS

Anderson, George M., SJ. "Jails, Lockups, and Houses of Detention." *America,* January 1976.

Andrea, Sister M., SSND. "The Societies of St. Stanislaus Kostka Parish." *Polish American Studies* 9 (January–June 1952); 27–37.

Apostolate for Vocations, Archdiocese of Newark, N.J. "Meet The Daughters of the Heart of Mary." *Careers with Christ Magazine* 5 (1973).

Baker, T. Lindsay. "The Early Years of Rev. Wincenty Barzynski." *Polish American Studies* 32 (1975): 29–52.

"The Reverend Leopold Moczygemba, Patriarch of Polonia." *Polish American Studies* 41 (Spring 1984): 66–109.

"Bł. Kunegunda, 1224–1292." *Posłaniec.* Pulaski, Wisconsin: Franciscan Fathers, Assumption of BVM Province, 1937, pp. 206–209.

Brennan, Margaret, IHM. "Standing in Experience: A Reflection on the Status of Women in the Church." *Catholic Mind,* May 1976, pp. 19–32.

Brozek, Andrzej. "Polish Migration to Texas." *Polish American Studies* 30 (1973): 20–27.

Busyn, Helen. "Peter Kiołbassa—Maker of Polish America." *Polish American Studies* 8 (1951): 65–84.

Cada, Brother Lawrence J., SM, and Fitz, Brother Raymond L., SM. "The Recovery of Religious Life." *Review for Religious* 34 (1975): 690–718.

Catholic Education Press. *The Catholic Educational Review* 89 (September 1951): 433.

Conventual Franciscan Friars. *The Immaculate* 17 (1966).

"Częstochowa: National Shrine of Poland." *The Grail,* March 1945, pp. 83–86.

Greeley, Andrew M. "Catholicism in America: 200 Years and Counting." *The Critic,* Summer 1976, pp. 14–47; 54–70.

Greene, Victor E., "Pre-World War I Polish Emigration to the United States: Motives and Statistics." *The Polish Review* 6 (Summer 1961): 68.

Groszek, Sister M. Alvernia, OSFK. "The Franciscan Sisters of Blessed Kunegunda." *Polish American Studies* 8 (1951): 92–96.

Haiman, Miecislaus. "J. E. Ks. Biskup Paweł P. Rhode, Jego Życie i Czyny." *Przegląd Katolicki* 9 (March–April 1934): 22.

Inviolata, Sister M. "Noble Street in Chicago." *Polish American Studies* 11 (1954): 1–8.

Janas, Rev. Edward T., CR. "Father Peter Semenenko, CR, and His Message." *Polish American Studies* 13 (1956): 1–18.

Josephite Harvest 78 (July–August 1966): 11.

Jubilee Magazine. December 1962, p. 26.

Knawa, Sister Anne Marie, OSF. "Jane Addams and Josephine Dudzik: Social Service Pioneers." *Polish American Studies* 35 (1978): 13–22.

Kulik, Al T. "A Review of *Rys Historyczny Zgromadzenia Sióstr Franciszkanek Błogosławionej Kunegundy. Część pierwsza, 1860–1910*" [A Review of *The Franciscan Sisters of Blessed Kunegunda. Part one, 1860–1910*]. *Polish American Studies* 9 (January–June 1952).

Kurtz, Robert, CR. *Resurrection Studies.* July 1980.

"Lesser Brothers." *Quarterly Chronicle of the Franciscan St. Louis-Chicago Province of the Sacred Heart* 14 (January 1980): 1–64.

Lucille, Sister M., CR. "The Causes of Polish Immigration to the United States." *Polish American Studies* 8 (1951): 85–91.

Madaj, Rev. Menceslaus J. "The Polish Immigrant and the Catholic Church in America." *Polish American Studies* 6 (1949): 1–8.

———. "The Polish Immigrant, the American Catholic Hierarchy, and Father Wenceslaus Kruszka." *Polish American Studies* 26 (1969): 16–29.

Monzell, Thomas I. "The Catholic Church and the Americanization of the Polish Immigrant." *Polish American Studies* 26 (1969): 1–18.

Nobilis, Sister M., SSND. "The First Polish School in the United States." *Polish American Studies* 4 (January–June 1947): 1–5.

———. "The School Sisters of Notre Dame in Polish American Education. " *Polish American Studies* 12 (1955): 77–83.

"O Kanonizacje Błog. Kingi, Królowej Polski i Klaryski." *Kronika Seraficka*. Hartland, Wisconsin, pp. 289–294.

Orzell, Lawrence. "A Minority Within a Minority: The Polish National Catholic Church, 1896–1907." *Polish American Studies* 36 (1979): 1–32.

Oswald, Ruth. "Our Lady of Częstochowa." *Action Now* 4 (1951): 1–3.

Our Colored Missions 27 (February 1941); 32 (March 1946); 33 (March 1947).

Palmer, Rev. Jerome, OSB, ed. "Częstochowa: National Shrine of Poland." *The Grail,* March 1945, pp. 83–86.

Paxton, Arnold. "Polish People in America." *Franciscan Message* 28 (November 1974).

Population Studies: A Journal of Demography. Vol. 6, No. 3. London: Cambridge University Press, 1953.

Przegląd Katolicki [The Polish Ecclesiastical Review]. 7 vols. Chicago: The Polish Publishing Co., 1913–1920.

Purcell, Richard J. "Polish Immigration a Century Ago." *America,* 9 June 1934, pp. 27–32.

Raniszewski, Sister M. Gonzaga, OSFK. "Siostry Franciszkanki pod Wezwaniem Bł. Kunegundy." *Przegląd Katolicki* [The Polish Ecclesiastical Review], 1933, pp. 6–11.

Roberts, William P., SJ. "The Religious Habit and Contemporary Witness." *Sisters Today* 37 (April 1967).

Stevens, Clifford. "The Founder of Boys Town." *Catholic Digest,* May 1972, pp. 37–42.

Stoler, Peter. "Plagues of the Past." *Time,* 16 August 1976, pp. 66–67.

Swastek, Rev. Joseph. "A Critical Examination of Father Kruszka's *Historya Polska w Ameryce.*" *Polish American Studies* 14 (1957): 103–110.

———. "Priest and Pioneer: Reverend Leopold Moczygemba." *The Seraphic Chronicle.* Detroit: The Conventual Press, 1951.

———. "The Contribution of the Catholic Church in the U.S.A." *Polish American Studies* 14 (1947): 15–26.

Syski, Rt. Rev. Msgr. Alexander, STM. "The Nestor of Polish Historians in America: Reverend Wacław Kruszka." *Polish American Studies* I (1944): 62–70.

Terbovich, Fr. John B., OFM Cap. "Poland's Culture and Its People." *The Immaculate* 17 (1966): 49–53.

Time 116 (December 1980): 26.

Tomczak, Anthony C. "The Poles in Chicago." *Poland* 12 (1931).

Urbanowicz, Sister Clarent Marie, OSF. "Mother Mary Theresa Dudzik." *Polish American Studies* 19 (1962): 42–45.

Zubrżycki, J. "Emigration from Poland in the 19th and 20th Centuries." *Population Studies,* 7 vols. (11 March 1976).

ENCYCLOPEDIAS

Catholic Encyclopedia. 1938. Vol. II; Vol. VIII.

"Makers of America—Natives and Aliens." *Encyclopedia Britannica.* 11th ed. 1891–1903. Vol. V.

National Catholic Almanac. 1959. Vol. III; 1971. Vol. VI; 1980. Vol. II.

New Catholic Encyclopedia. 1966. Vol. VI.

New Catholic Encyclopedia. 1967. Vol. VII.

Official Catholic Directory. 1896; 1901; 1975.

Polish American Encyclopedia. 1954. Vol. I.

Suzanne Cita-Malard. "Religious Orders of Women." *Twentieth Century Encyclopedia of Catholicism.* 1964. Vol. LXXXVI.

Wille, Lois. "Chicago." *The World Book Encyclopedia.* 1987. Vol. III.

DISSERTATIONS AND THESES

Baker, Lindsay T. "The Early History of Panna Maria, Texas." Ph.D. dissertation, Texas Tech University, 1975.

Ciesluk, Joseph E. "National Parishes in the U.S." D.C.L. dissertation, The Catholic University of America, 1944.

Ditlinger, Sister M. Julia, OSF. "A Study of Franciscanism in 80 Secondary Schools During 1947–1948." M.A. thesis, De Paul University, 1951.

Drobka, Frank J. "Education in Poland, Past and Present." Ph.D. dissertation, The Catholic University of America, 1927.

Ficht, Sister M. Inviolata. "Noble Street in Chicago: Socio-cultural Study of Polish Residents Within Ten Blocks." M.A. thesis, De Paul University, 1952.

Givens, Willard E. "Galician Immigration." M.A. thesis, Columbia University, 1915.

Grajewski, Henry C. "The Founding of the Polish School System—The First Universal Public-School Program in Europe." M.A. thesis, Marquette University, 1973.

Kalinowski, Sister M. Theophane, CSSF. "The First Decade of the Sisters of St. Felix in America, 1874–1884." M.A. thesis, Loyola University, Chicago, 1956.

Karolczak, Mary Valentia. "Some Aspects of Polish Immigration to the United States with Special Reference to the Period 1870–1905." M.A. thesis, Marquette University, 1942.

Lenczyk, Peter P. "Origins and Early Development of the Congregation of the Resurrection." M.A. thesis, St. Louis University, 1936.

Lopata, Helen Znaniecka. "The Function of Voluntary Association in an Ethnic Community: Polonia." Ph.D. dissertation, University of Chicago, 1954.

Magierski, Louis. "Polish-American Activities in Chicago, 1919–1939." M.A. thesis, University of Illinois, 1946.

Małolepszy, Sister Mary Dulcissima. "A Historical Study of the St. Hedwig's Home, An Institution for the Care of Dependent Children, Archdiocese of Chicago." M.A. thesis, Loyola University, Chicago, 1945.

Mueller, Marie, SSND. "Parish Jubilee Booklets: A Problem in Historiography." M.A. thesis, St. Louis University, 1952.

Mysliwiec, Rev. John, CR. "The History of the Catholic Poles of St. Louis." M.A. thesis, St. Louis University, 1936.

Pacyga, Dominic A. "Villages of Packinghouses and Steel Mills: The Polish Worker on Chicago's South Side." Ph.D. dissertation, University of Illinois at Chicago Circle, 1981.

Parot, Joseph J. "The American Faith and the Persistance of Chicago Polonia 1870–1920." Ph.D. dissertation, Northern Illinois University, 1971.

Pogorzelska, Mary Assumpta. "A Historical Study of Religion and Education as Underlying Influences in the Localization of the Poles of Cleveland up to 1915." M.A. thesis, St. John's College of Cleveland, 1951.

Runge, Fenton J. "National Parishes in the City of St. Louis." M.A. thesis, St. Louis University, 1955.

Stec, Casimir. "The National Orientation of the Poles in the United States 1608–1935." M.A. thesis, Marquette University, 1946.

Wargin, Lucille. "The Polish Immigrant in the American Community." M.A. thesis, De Paul University, 1948.

Wilczak, Paul. "The Polish National Catholic Church." M.A. thesis, The Catholic University of America, 1966.

Wisniewski, Joseph A., CR. "St. Stanislaus Kostka Parish in Chicago: Its Spiritual, Educational, and Cultural Legacy to the 6,000,000 Americans of Polish Extraction, 1869–1908." M.A. thesis, De Paul University, 1964.

MISCELLANEOUS

Annals of the Sisters of Charity of the Incarnate Word, Motherhouse Archives, San Antonio, Texas.

Antosz, James, CR. "A Short History of the Congregation of the Resurrection." Chicago, 1972. (Mimeographed.)

Archives of the Archdiocese of Chicago. St. Mary of the Lake Seminary. Mundelein, Illinois.

Barrett, Edward J. County Clerk, State of Illinois. Certificate of death #24434, photocopied from the original. (AFSCL).

"Brief History of St. Peter Claver Church, Mobile, Alabama," 6 June 1953. (Typewritten.)

"Brief History of the Formative Years of the Polish Community in Chicago and the State of Illinois." Press release of the Polish National Alliance, 29 April 1975.

Campus Ministry Team, University of Akron, Ohio. "What is Campus Ministry?" Ohio, 1975. (Mimeographed.)

Chicago, Illinois. Department of Health. "A Report on an Epidemic of Influenza." Pamphlet file: Cc H42 1918a.

Congregation of the Sisters of Charity of the Incarnate Word. "Addresses to the Parents of Our Postulants," no. 55. Texas: 28 October 1883.

Department of Health of the City of Chicago. "Report on an Epidemic of Influenza in Chicago Occurring During the Fall of 1918." In *Report and Handbook of the Department of the City of Chicago for the Years 1911–1918, Inclusive.* Chicago: House of Severinghaus, 1919.

Diocese of Cleveland. The Chancery Office. "Parishes in Ohio." (Typewritten.)

XXVIII Międzynarodowy Kongres Eucharystyczny w Chicago, Illinois, 20–24 June 1926. *Program Polskiej Sekcji Kongresu.* Niles, Illinois: St. Hedwig's Orphanage Printery, 1926.

Emil, Sister M., IHM. President of Marygrove College. *Sister Formation Bulletin, Supplement.* Detroit, Summer 1956.

Franciscan Educational Conference, Sisters' Division. *Franciscan Education, Report of the First National Meeting of Franciscan Teaching Sisterhoods.* Chicago: Franciscan Educational Conference, 1953.

Groszek, Sister M. Alvernia. "Report Concerning the Cause of Mother Theresa Dudzik." Lemont, Illinois, 1983.

Hidden Power. Chicago: Franciscan Herald Press, 1960.

Kitagawa, Evelyn M., and Taeuber, Karl E., eds. *Local Community Fact Book, Chicago Metropolitan Area. 1960.* Chicago: Community Inventory, University of Chicago, 1963.

Kusper, Stanley T. Jr., County Clerk. *Bureau of Vital Statistics, Undertakers' Report.* Chicago: Department of Health, 1976.

Letter from Mother M. Raphael Lubowidzka, first provincial superior of the Congregation of the Sisters of the Holy Family of Nazareth, Holy Family Academy, Chicago, Illinois, to Mother Mary of Jesus the Good Shepherd (Frances Siedliska) foundress of the Sisters of the Holy Family of Nazareth, in Rome, 14 September 1887 (Original copy in the archives at the Motherhouse of the Congregation of the Holy Family of Nazareth in Rome, Italy).

"Liturgy 70: A Ministry of Service: A Theological Insight into the Role of Extraordinary Ministers," Volume 2, No. 4–5.

Milon, Rev. Augustin, OFM, ed. "The Port-Pourri." Chicago: The Franciscan Friars (Assumption BVM Province) Gospel Brothers, February 1985.

Mobile Birmingham Diocesan Record Sheets.

Molik, Sister Dolores Jean. "The Black Non-Catholic Child in the Catholic School." Gary, Indiana, 1978 (Typewritten).

Mundelein, The Most Reverend George. "Sermon" at the dedication of the Five Holy Martyrs Church and School. Chicago, 1920 (Archdiocesan Archives at St. Mary of the Lake Seminary, Mundelein, Illinois).

"Our Polish Pioneers, 1855–1936." San Antonio: St. Michael's School, 1937. (Typewritten.)

Peckenpaugh, Sister Margaret Mary. "Mother Theresa Home." Talk delivered 17 April 1982.

"Pilgrim Among Us." Catholic League for Religious Assistance to Poland. Chicago: 1979.

Polish Texan. San Antonio: University of Texas, 1972.

Price, Surgeon A. B. *Hospital Survey of Huron, South Dakota,* December 10, 1943. Kansas City, Missouri: U.S. Public Health Service District Number 7, pp. 1–11.

Province of the Assumption of the Blessed Virgin Mary. *Catalogus.* Pulaski, Wisconsin: Order of Friars Minor, 1960.

Robertson, John Dill, MD, commissioner of health, *A Report on an Epidemic of Influenza in the City of Chicago in the Fall of 1918,* Reprinted from the *Octennial Report 1911–1917,* Educational Series, No. 15, Department of Health (Chicago: 1918). Contains a report of the 1890 epidemic by Swayne Wickersham, commissioner of health, 1890 under "Previous Influenza Epidemics in Chicago."

St. Elizabeth's Hospital Archives. Chicago, Illinois.

"St. Mary's Church Bulletin." Hammond, Indiana, 12 April 1970.

St. Joseph Home. "Candle," Vol. 13, No.1 (Cleveland, 1966).

St. Stanislaus Kostka Church. *Book of Records.* Chicago, Illinois.

———. *Burial Register. Vol. 2: 1877–1882.* Chicago, Illinois.

———. *Burial Register. Vol. 3: 1882–1890.* Chicago, Illinois.

———. *Burial Register. Vol. 14: 1904–1907.* Chicago, Illinois.

———. *Registram Matrimonioram. Vol. 1: 1869–1882.* Chicago, Illinois.

———. *Zapowiedzie. Vol. 13: 1890.* Chicago, Illinois.

School Sisters of Notre Dame. "Obituaries 1931." Motherhouse Archives, Mequon, Wisconsin.

———. "Candidature Records, 1871–1880 and 1881–1890." Motherhouse Archives, Mequon, Wisconsin.

Seraphic Institute of Theology for Sisters. "Bulletin of Information." College of St. Francis, Joliet, Illinois, 1959.

"Sermon Outline III, Historical Perspective." Liturgy Training Program. Archdiocese of Chicago, 1971.

Sisters of Charity of the Incarnate Word. "The Motherhouse Diary, 1883–1889." Motherhouse Archives, San Antonio, Texas.

Sisters of the Congregation of St. Joseph of Rocky River Drive. "Minutes of Council Meeting, 13 February 1961." Archives, St. Joseph Convent, Cleveland, Ohio.

Soukup, Gayle, RRA. Medical Records Department. St. Elizabeth's Hospital, Chicago, Illinois. Microfilm of Surgery Registers and Patient Register, 10 February 1976.

Spetz, Rev. Andrew, CR. *Epistolae, 1893–1912.* Archives of the Congregation of the Resurrection, Rome, Italy.

"Statement of the Case for the Proposed St. Anthony Hospital." Crown Point, Indiana: St. Anthony Hospital, 1969.

Texas Department of Health, County of Bexar. Bureau of Vital Statistics. Standard Certificate of Death, p. 41, No. 49.

U.S. Congress, Senate. *Reports of the Immigration Commission.* "Dictionary of Races or Peoples." S. Doc. 622, 61st Congress, 3rd session, 1911.

———. Reports of the Immigration Commission. S. Doc. 747, 61st Congress, 3rd session, 1911.

———. *Statistical Review of Immigration, 1820–1910.* S. Doc. 756, 61st Cong., 3rd session, 1911.

U.S. Department of Labor. *The Report of the Commissioner General of Immigration,* Vol. 12. Washington, DC: 1901.

Abramowicz, Bishop Alfred L., 293, 358, 430–431, 445, 701, 793, 807, 824, 836, 837, 887, 902
Addams, Jane, 48–49, 71 n.6, 441
Advanced Catechism, 102 n.10
Advisory Council, 224
Affiliate Program, 830, 845–846
Aged, infirm, needy, mission to the, 64, 65, 66, 68, 84, 85, 520, 617, 743, 882. *See also names of individual institutions*
Aggiornamento, 780, 781
Agnes Dzik, Sister M. (Pauline), 87, 93 n.33, 138, 139, 144
Agnes Zywiec, Sister M., 445–446, 555, 561, 798, 801 n.11, 820, 890
Alberta Bialas, Sister M., 319, 431, 438, 687, 688–689, 693, 694, 700, 719 n.109, 720, 723, 770, 843
Alerding, Bishop Herman J., 201–202, 333, 344, 389
All Saints Cathedral Polish Old Catholic Church (Independent), (Chicago, Illinois), 83, 84, 89 nn.1, 2
Alms, collecting of, 87
Aloysetta Ciezadlo, Sister M., 523, 535 n.2, 597 nn.17, 19, 720, 721, 774, 804, 835–836
Aloysia Holysz, Mother M.: 326–327; advisory council, 224; Archbishop Glennon, 188–189; Assumption staffing, 390; Blessed Sacrament rescue, 166; catechetical missions, 448; charter signing, 254; Commission appointments, 436; community prayer book, 436; councilor, 248; delegate, 247; Eighth General Chapter, 720; Guardian Angel staffing, 352; Holy Trinity refusal, 284; illness and death, 454; land purchase, 415; lay retreats, 454; letters, 227, 299–301; Mother-house goal, 421, 422; musical education, 438; novitiate decision, 329; recall of Sisters, 337, 343; St. Stanislaus Bishop and Martyr School (Chicago, Illinois), 154; school staffing, 333, 335, 394; Second General Chapter, 327–328; second term, 438; Sister-nurse refusal, 581; superior general, 325, 435

Aloysilla Kedzior, Sister M., 463, 633, 644–645, 646, 654, 655, 747, 751
Alphonsine Kobylinski, Sister M., 761 n.2, 763, 864, 873
Alvernia Groszek, Sister M., 295, 686, 692, 703, 837, 878, 885 n.6, 892, 902
Alvernia Rest Home for the Convalescent and Aged (Parma, Ohio). *See* Mount Alverna Home and Annex
Amabilis Bellock, Sister M., 463, 473, 474, 633, 641, 645, 646, 647, 650, 734, 812
American Catholic hierarchy, 198, 211 n.15
Amo Christum, 436, 776
Andrea Zawadzki, Sister M., 237, 248, 251, 256, 325, 327, 366, 402
Andrusiewicz, Theodosia, 234
Andrzejkiewicz (Andrews), Rev. Felix, 526, 527, 528, 529, 531, 532–533, 534
Angeline Topolinski, Sister M. (Mother): 451–453; advisor and bursar, 196; advisory council, 224; Charter signature omission, 254; Constitutions, 436; day care support, 179; finances, 402; first vows, 139; move to Avondale, 107; perpetual vows, 236; renewal of vows, 143–144; responsibilities, 138; St. Elizabeth's Day Nursery (Chicago, Illinois), 178; seamstress work, 85; secretary, 327; steadfastness in Congregation, 84. *See also* Topolinski, Constance
Anna Wysinski, Mother M.: acceptance of orphan care, 132–133; admonition received, 260; anniversary as superior, 196; appointment as superior, 110; approval of Constitutions, 110; burial, 91 n.16; burial of Sister M. Theresa, 368; Charter signing, 254; concerns about community, 98; death and funeral 249, 364–366; decisions on day care, 180–181; early steadfastness, 84; failing health, 324; family concerns, 86, 100–101; First General Chapter, 247, 248, 251, 254; first vows, 139; fund raising, 98; general council, 256, 259; Holy Trinity, (Falls City, Texas), 270, 283, 275–276; home for aged, 94; illness and Quigley visit, 171; inaccuracies regarding, 371 n.6; last

mission accepted, 317; legacy, 250, 369, 281, 297; life before Sisterhood, 248–249; offer of Sisters, 290; novitiate, 121; perpetual vows, 236; personal qualities, 249; plans to reside with community, 99; reburial, 372; renewal of vows, 143–144; requests for teaching Sisters, 186, 296; residence expansion, 162–163; responsiveness to parish needs, 289; St. Casimir's (Cleveland, Ohio), 164, 165; St. Casimir's (St. Louis, Missouri), 188; St. Elizabeth's Day Nursery (Chicago, Illinois), 178; St. Joseph's Home (Chicago, Illinois), 86; St. Roch's (La Salle, Illinois), 268; St. Stanislaus (Posen, Illinois), 266; SS. Peter and Paul School (Spring Valley, Illinois), 149–150; search for quarters, 94–95; Second General Chapter, 324, 325; superior general, 247; withdrawal from St. Louis, Missouri, 192. *See also* Wysinski, Rosalie

Anne Marie Knawa, Sister, 698, 719 n.110, 726 n.20, 763, 768, 855

Anniversaries: community, 101, 112, 236, 397–398, 521, 541–542; congregation, 632, 790, 806, 836–837, 907–909; members, 608, 776, 793; St. Francis of Assisi, 892–893

Anti-garb act of North Dakota, 534

Antonina Osinski, Mother M.: aged Sisters care, 488; assistant superior general, 639; beatification cause, 465; *Book of Customs,* 613; Boys Town, Nebraska, 549, 550–551; Catholic Sisters College superior, 480, 481; Church Vestment Workshop, 256; college degrees, 407; committee service, 436; convent teacher, 407; councilor, 604, 720; Crown Point, Indiana property, 515, 516, 519; document signature, 491; domestic service support, 463, 472, 476–477, 482–483; donation for vestment workshop, 234; *Echo Avondalskie,* 466; financial proposal from St. Florian's (Chicago, Illinois), 218; financial struggle with Father Mielcarek, 231; Gregory Hospital (Gregory, South Dakota) staffing, 584; Guardian Angel Day Nursery (Chicago,

Illinois) negotiation, 355; health care ministry support, 629; hospital inspection, 668; hospital purchase questions, 582, 583; hospital refusals, 582–583; hospital staffing question, 728–729; icon instructions, 496; influenza nursing, 354, 369–370; land purchase, 679, 680; later service, death, 523; Mayor Kelly visit, 522; 458–461; Motherhouse plans, 488; Mount Alvernia Convent (East Cleveland, Ohio), 505–509; novena permission, 496; novitiate transfer, 489; nurse's training, illness, reassignment, 198; nursing study promoted, 462–463; province proposal, 505; Sacred Heart High School (Cleveland, Ohio), 396; scholarships forfeited, 467; school visit, 723; South Heart Public School (South Heart, North Dakota), 526, 527, 528, 529–530, 533; superior general, 458; teacher, superior, 341; teacher training encouraged, 463–464; teaching agreement, 227

Antonissima Jamruk, Sister M., 447, 639, 652, 827, 843, 844–845, 846, 847, 878, 883–884, 892, 904

Archconfraternity of the Immaculate Heart of Mary, 124–125

Archdiocesan Reading Program (Chicago, Illinois), 770–771

Aspirancy program, 679, 680–681, 684, 685, 698, 785, 805, 816

Assumption of the Blessed Virgin Mary School / Conemaugh Catholic Consolidation School (Conemaugh, Pennsylvania), 303–307

Assumption of the Blessed Virgin Mary School (New Chicago, Indiana), 389–392

Atkinson Memorial Hospital (Atkinson, Nebraska). *See* Our Lady of the Sandhills Hospital; West Holt Memorial Hospital

Avondale, 67, 72 n.17

Babilewicz, Rev. Dionysius, OFM, 420, 421

Back of the Yards, 116 n.6, 350, 358–359

Back of the Yards Neighborhood Council, 358, 362 n.45

Badarzynski, Rev. Rembert, OFM, 643, 653

Bakalarczyk, Rev. Richard, 480

Bakanowski, Rev. Adolph, CR, 23, 24–27

Bak, Rev. Bernard, CR, 804, 807

Baltimore Catechism, 314

Baniewicz, Rev. Joseph, CR, 408, 494, 521, 537, 595, 682, 685

Baron, Wanda, 698

Barrett, Msgr. John W., 586

Barth, Rev. Pius J., OFM, 757

Barton Hospital (Watertown, South Dakota), 582

Bartylak, Rev. Walter, CR, 423, 465

Barzynski, Rev. Joseph, CR, 89 n.1

Barzynski, Rev. Vincent M., CR: 27–31; absence, 85; accident, 120; appointment changes, 110; building advice, 87; building loan, 98–99; building plans rebuke, 94; counsel to Josephine Dudzik, 69–70; counsel to tertiaries, 67; horarium creation, 77; illness, death, funeral, 121–123; Independent Church crisis, 83; influence recalled, 908; mission for Josephine Dudzik, tertiaries, 67; orphanage involvement, 131–132; orphanage named for, 133; parish founding, 90 n.16, 154, 285 n.2; pastoral concerns and Josephine Dudzik, 56; pastoral success, 54; pastorate, 89 n.1; proposals for tertiaries, 67; regard for Sister M. Theresa, 382; reprimand of Sister Theresa, 78, 113, 114; rumors about, 98, 110; St. Joseph Home (Chicago, Illinois), 109; site suggestion, 85; spiritual life of Sister M. Theresa, 381; support for Josephine Dudzik, 66

Beatrice Rybacki, Mother M.: 774–775; administration report, 805, 844; aspirancy program, 785; Blessed Sacrament (Gary, Indiana), 782; building plans, 520; cemetery development, 795; chapel dedication, 809; Church Vestment Workshop, 235; *Echo Franciszkanski,* 777; First Extraordinary Chapter of Affairs, 819–820, 822; Guardian Angel Day Care Center Jubilee, 358; home for aged, 797; hospital refusal, 585; hospital withdrawal, 672, 673–674; Madonna High School (Chicago, Illinois) addition, 697–698; medical center plans, 863; Motherhouse rehabilitation, 789; Our Lady of Victory Motherhouse (Lemont, Illinois), 789, 792, 796; recall of Sisters, 320; re-election, 804; *Regina Mundi,* 759; Re-inspiration, 818; relic transport, 494; response to change, 209; St. Leo (Cleveland, Ohio), 764; scholarship, 466; special education plan, 559; superior general term, 824

Belinski, Klemens J., 87, 91 n.26

Belmont Community Hospital (Chicago, Illinois), 582–583

Benedictine Sisters, Congregation of, (Yankton, South Dakota), 667, 668, 669, 728, 741, 742–743

Benigna Jakajtis, Sister M., 198, 259, 290, 305, 402, 404, 406, 407, 408, 435, 436, 438, 509–510, 511, 582, 691, 743, 744, 746

Bennett County Community Hospital (Martin, South Dakota). *See* St. Anthony's Hospital (Martin, South Dakota)

Bennett, Rev. Joseph, 860 n.64

Bergan, Bishop Gerald T., 729, 732

Bernardin, Joseph Cardinal, 883–884, 907

Bernice Marie Junio, Sister, 218, 320, 395, 407

Black Death Pox, 131

Blanche Bartkowski, Sister M., 395, 431, 450, 464, 466, 570, 573, 592, 640–641

Blessed Sacrament: and Sister Theresa Dudzik, 111–112, 125; daily reception, 375

Blessed Sacrament School (Gary, Indiana), 782–785

Blondis, Ernest, MD, 585

Boleslaus II, King of Poland, 159–160 n.34

Bona, Bishop Stanislaus, 420, 421, 435, 453, 483, 541–542

Bona, Msgr. Thomas, 406, 432, 442, 490, 493

Bonnan, Joseph, 446

Bonzano, Giovanni Cardinal, 432

Boys Town (Boys Town, Nebraska), 548–563, 564 n.5, 849

Brady, Bishop William O., 584, 631, 635, 648, 651, 652, 667

Brady Hall (Washington, DC). *See* Catholic Sisters College, The

Buczyna, Rev. Joseph, 335, 345–346

Budnik, Anne, 5

Budnik, August, 5, 11 n.13

Budnik, Marianne, 5
Butoric, William M., 521
Campus ministry, 854
Canonical houses, 324
Canonical novitiate, 150
Canon Law, Code of, 162, 247, 414, 422, 425 n.1, 488, 853
Carol Marie Schommer, Sister, 703–704, 802 n.15
Casey, Msgr. George, 527
Cassidy, Rev. Frank P., 481
Catechetical mission, 448–451, 526, 591
Catechism of the Vows, 314
Cathedral of the Holy Angels School (Gary, Indiana), 320
Catholic Charities (Chicago, Illinois), 332, 443, 797, 800
Catholic High School Building Fund, 683, 685, 694
Catholic Sisters College, The (Washington, DC), 477–484
Catholic Social Mission House (Youngstown, Ohio), 589, 590
Catholic University of America, The (Washington, DC), 477, 483
CCD. *See* Confraternity of Christian Doctrine classes
Cebula, Rev. Sebastian, 190
Cegiełka, Rev. Francis, SAC, 613
Chamberlain, South Dakota, 668
Chapin Street (Chicago, Illinois), 42 n.97, 57, 73 n.22
Chaplains: St. Joseph Home, 216–217, 221 n.6
Chapter of faults, 438, 805
Charism: Mother M. Theresa Dudzik, 383, 827
Charter of Incorporation, State of Illinois, 254–255, 263 n.34
Chelewski, Susanna, 66, 67
Chester Dziarnowski, Sister M., 188, 217, 297, 324, 327, 436, 443, 450, 499, 505, 507
Chicago: comparison with Babylon, 112, 118 n.33; economic growth, 21; exploration and founding, 43–44; funeral prohibition, 56–57; immigrant neighborhoods, 45–46; labor unrest and strikes, 47; Polish immigrant settlements, 17; population growth, 22; public health problems, 46–47; social service in 1893, 48

Chicago Fire Department, 789
Chicago First Grade Organization, 295
Chicago free clinics, 355
Chicago Park District, 592–594
Chicago World's Fair (1893). *See* World's Columbian Exposition
Child care mission: day nursery, 228; expanding community works, 178–182; maternity service, 180; proposal for facility, 259. *See also names of individual institutions*
Chodniewicz, Rev. Florian, 217
Choir controversy, 259
Choir direction and training, 206, 220, 294, 319, 389, 397
Chojnice, 3
Cholewinski, Msgr. Stanislaus, 350, 356, 357, 365, 611
Christine Brzozowski, Sister M., 641, 696, 715 n.75, 820, 855, 896
Christmas Eve supper, Polish tradition, 76, 80 n.4
"Chronicle": absence of joy, 79; benefaction to Sisters, 163; Blessed Sacrament, 377–378; community meal preparation, 80 n.3; concern for others, 382; departures from congregation, 85; distribution of, 827; doubts about vows, 138; Father Barzynski, 382; Father Rodowicz recalled, 216; first profession of vows, 139–140; *Godzinki* in Latin, 164; gratitude to Klemens Beliński, 91 n.26; hardships and suffering, 98; help for unfortunate, 64; Immaculate Conception devotion, 378; loss of employment, income, 86–87; parishoners, 88; permanent residence goal, 67; prayers with residents, 455 n.7; promise to care for community, 69–70; relocating, 101; removal as superior, 111; Rule, 113, 114; rumors, 98; St. Joseph, 380; source of faith, 911; submission to God's Will, 380–381; support for community, 381; tasks, 78. *See also* "Kronika Sióstr Franciskanek pod opieką Św. Kunegundy w Chicago, Illinois"
Church Vestment Workshop: 414, 480; fund raising, 234–236; Sister workers, 240–241 n.49
Cich, Rev. Wenceslaus, OFM, 444, 492

Cicognani, Archbishop Amleto, 480

Cieplak, Archbishop John B., 431

Clara Ogurek, Sister M., 100–101, 104 n.40,
118 n.23, 133, 151–152, 153, 165, 178,
201, 236, 247, 251, 253, 256, 290, 324,
325, 327, 402, 608, 686, 794

Clarent Marie Urbanowicz, Sister, 232, 295,
687, 689, 761 n.2, 763, 808

Cody, John Cardinal, 445, 701, 795, 836, 837,
847, 856, 883, 892

Collins, Hon. Richard C., 863, 865, 896

Commission on Spiritual Affairs, 253

Commissions: apostolate, 832–833;
Constitutions, 401, 436, 879; discipline,
education, 402, 406–408, 436; finance,
402, 436; novices, postulants, 327, 329;
planning, 910; school affairs, 327;
spiritual affairs, 253, 327

Conference of Major Religious Superiors of
Women, 773

Confraternity of Christian Doctrine classes,
294, 319, 397, 708 n.2, 724, 848, 849

Congregation of the Resurrection: and St.
Stanislaus Kostka Parish (Chicago,
Illinois), 23; chaplains for St. Joseph
Home (Chicago, Illinois), 217; Chicago
parishes, 29; confessors and retreat
masters, 314–315; day-care mission,
178, founding, 23–24; influence
recalled, 908; missions in the United
States, 24; missions to Texas, 27–28

Constitutions: 110, 223, 235, 252–253;
apostolates, 882; changes, 405–406,
826–827; First Extraordinary Chapter of
Affairs, 819; General Chapter
consideration, 823; local superior, 328;
new, 879; papal ratification, 438;
review and update, 845; teaching
purpose, 722; Third Order Rule, 436

Constitutions of the Third of May, 14

Contracts, 273–275, 279, 533

Cook County Department of Corrections
(Chicago, Illinois), 854–856

Cook County Zoning Board of Appeals, 797

Cooke, Msgr. Vincent, 621, 625

Coordinator of Religious Education, 849–851

Crawley-Boevey, Rev. Mateo, SSCC, 539

Crescencia Chmiel, Sister M., 339, 407, 408,
438, 466, 681–682, 686, 688, 694, 700,
762, 763, 774, 785, 808

Cronin, Rev. Francis, 629, 667

Cross Prayers, 437

Custom Book of the Franciscan Sisters of
Chicago. *See Directory* of the
Franciscan Sisters of Chicago

Cwiklinski, Rev. Isidore, OFM, 542

CYO Vacation Centers and School, 592–594,
596 n.12

Dąbkowski, Rev. Stephen, CR, 138

"Daybreak," 856–857

Decree of Aggregation, 405

Dembiński, Rev. Francis, CR, 126, 314, 365,
367, 838 n.17

Depression of 1893, 48

Dimmerling, Bishop Harold J., 741, 742

Directory of the Franciscan Sisters of
Chicago, 253–254, 613, 826, 879

Doloretta Radzienda, Sister M., 218, 407,
530, 531, 609–611, 785, 792, 818, 835,
863

Domestic service apostolate, 463, 472–473.
See also names of individual missions

Dorhmann, George, Sr., MD, 198, 370

Dorney, Rev. Maurice J., 524 n.5

Dramatic Circle, 40 nn.84–85

Dramatic direction and training, 157, 294, 397

Drengacz, Rev. Thomas A., 449–450

Drewniak, Rev. Adolph, CR, 315

Drewnicki, Rev. Andrew, 149

Drzewiecki, Rev. John, CR, 367, 368, 838
n.17

Dubuis, Bishop Claude-Marie, 28

Dudzik, Agnes (née Polaszczyk), 3, 5, 172

Dudzik, Frances (Sister M. Leovina), 5–6, 53

Dudzik, John, 3, 5, 56

Dudzik, Joseph, 5, 52, 57, 63 n.45, 107

Dudzik, Josephine: age upon arrival in
America, 58 n.5; baptism, 3; compared
with Jane Addams, 71 n.6; compared
with St. Theresa of Avila, 63 n.38;
confirmation, 6; daily life in Płocicz,
10; education, 6–7; employment, 52;
founding members, 66; friendship with
Rosalie Wysinski, 249; good works,
dedication to, 5, 7–8, 9–10; land of
birth, 13; motivation for religious life,
53–54; parish participation, 54–56;
paternal grandparents, 5; personal
qualities, 7, 8; physical appearance, 8;
promise to care for community, 69–70;
religious education, 7; religious fervor,
10; religious order plans, 65; religious

superior, 76; religious upbringing, 6; St. Stanislaus Kostka Parish (Chicago, Illinois), 17, 32; schooling, 6–7; shelter to the needy, 64–65; spirituality, 8; Third Order admission, 55–56; Third Order profession, 56; with her mother, 57. *See also* Theresa Dudzik, Mother M.; Theresa Dudzik, Sister M.

Dudzik, Katharine, 3, 6, 53. *See also* St. Barbara of the Blessed Sacrament Dudzik, Sister

Dudzik, Marianne (Budnik), 5

Dudzik, Rosalie (Frank), 5

Dunne, Rev. Dennis, 365

Dyniewicz, Ladislaus, 35 n.23

Dziennik Chicagoski, 28, 29, 365

Dziennik Związkowy, 366, 368

East Cleveland Zoning Ordinance, 506, 510–511

Echo Avondalskie (Avondale Echo), 514, 530–531

Education of Sisters, 329, 407, 539, 593, 678–679, 681, 684, 722, 784–785

Edward Nowak, Sister M., 467, 697, 720–721, 768, 769, 774, 787 n.18

Eighth General Chapter of Elections, 499, 519, 720, 721–722, 773

11 Chapin Street, 57, 73 n.22

Eleventh General Chapter of Elections, 694, 824, 827–829, 841, 844, 851

Elizabeth Baut, Sister M., 101, 103 n.12, 104 n.42, 236, 247

Emigration to America, 19 n.19, 52

Emilie Marie Lesniak, Sister, 697, 812, 845, 846, 857, 861 n.68, 890, 907, 909

Employments: early efforts, 77–78; laundry, housekeeping, sewing, 85, 97; loss of income, 109

Engaged Couples Encounter, 891

Ephpheta School for the Deaf, 679, 682

Euphemia Switalski, Sister M., 697, 723, 820, 837, 863

Extraordinary ministers of the Eucharist, 857

Eymard Sanok, Sister M., 343, 346, 466–467, 771

Fabianski, Rev. Jerome, CR, 161 n.55, 452, 490, 495, 595, 635, 679

Family Christian Education Program, St. James Church (Arlington Heights, Illinois), 851

Farm (Lemont, Illinois), 498–500, 722

Father Flanagan of Boys Town. *See* Flanagan, Msgr. Edward J.

Father Flanagan's All-American Boys Town Choir, 837

Federal aid, 670, 671, 739, 740, 808

Feehan, Archbishop Patrick A., 68, 89 n.1, 123, 133–134, 149–150, 154, 162, 266

Felicita Pajor, Sister M., 436, 491, 499, 508

Felixa Jorz, Sister M., 479, 480, 540–541, 584, 604, 609, 635, 668, 680, 684, 686

Felixa Steltman, Sister (Marianne), 66, 76, 84

Fifteenth General Chapter of Elections, 911

Fifth General Chapter of Elections, 458, 462

Filipek, Rev. Fidelis, OFM, 638, 640, 647, 648

Filipski, Rev. Ladislaus, CR, 205

Filosa, Lawrence T., 642, 732, 733, 734, 742, 863, 865

Finances and financing, 651, 674, 731, 744, 863. *See also under names of individual institutions*

Fiołek, Rev. Stanislaus, CR, 495, 595, 687

First Extraordinary Chapter of Affairs: 209, 819–835; apostolate evaluations and changes, 335, 392, 559–560, 732, 741, 832–833; beatification cause, 827; *Book of Customs,* 819; business of, 618; change and renewal, 881; charism of Mother M. Theresa, 827; collegial government, 829; commissions, 820; Community House of Prayer, 826; community life, 832; Constitutions and Directory, 826–827; consultants for, 821; conventual practices, 825; dates of sessions, 823; deliberations and decisions, 642; directors of religious education, 849; educational opportunities, 833; events, decrees, ramifications, 824; focus on spiritual renewal, 819; Implementation Committee, 834–835; open conduct of, 823; opening, 825–826; overseas missions, 853; plans, preparations, purpose, 785, 819–823; postulancy, novitiate, vows, 826, 829–830; prayer life, 825; religious disciplines, 833–834; retreats and retreat masters, 825–826; Sister Formation, 829–830; spiritual life, 825–826; study days, 826; traditional tasks, 833

First General Chapter of Elections, 223, 235, 237, 247–248, 251, 252–254

First National Meeting of Franciscan Teaching Sisters, 757–758

Five Holy Martyrs Church Jubilee Choir, 909

Five Holy Martyrs School (Chicago, Illinois), 289–295, 308, 428, 887

Flanagan, Msgr. Edward J., 481, 548–550, 551–552, 555–557, 564 nn.17, 18, 612

Floods (Johnstown, Pennsylvania), 297–301

Foley, Bishop Thomas, 22, 23, 24–25

Formation Program and Team, 785, 830, 845, 846, 881

For This Have We Come, 827

Forty Hours Devotion, 164

Fourteenth General Chapter of Elections, 902, 904–906, 909–910

Fourth General Chapter of Elections, 435–439

Frances Marzanek, Sister (Katherine), 66, 76, 83, 84, 90 n.4

Frances Troeder, Sister (Theodosia), 100, 104 n.39

Francine Labus, Sister M.: 451, 906; commission chair, 820; councilor, 902; house of prayer, 888; novice mistress, 835; secretary general, 890

Francis Clare Radke, Sister: Constitutions, 827; councilor, 890, 902; formation director, 846, 906

Franciscan Brief, 885 n.6

Franciscan Ceremonial, 383, 437

Franciscan Crown, 378. *See also* Rosary of the Seven Joys of the Blessed Virgin Mary

Franciscan Echo, 66, 707, 885 n.6, 907

Franciscan Fathers of the Assumption of the Blessed Virgin Mary Province (Pulaski, Wisconsin), 420, 436, 437, 638

Franciscan Fathers of the Custody of the Holy Cross (Lemont, Illinois), 416, 426 n.11, 891

Franciscan National Marian Commission, 760

Franciscan Rule, 113, 376

Franciscan Sisters of Chicago Choir, 357, 812, 837, 907, 909

Franciscan Sisters of Chicago, Congregation of: administration, 827–829, 839 n.26, 880–881; aged, retired, ill sisters, 833; apostolate coordinator, 828, 839 n.27; apostolate expansion, 808, 848–851; Archbishop Feehan importance, 73 n.26; assistant superior general, 828; benefactor, 166, 360 n.4; changes and adaptations, 756–757; collegial board, 827; day of grace, 806; day of recollection, 806, 889; dedication of, 632; departures and dismissals, 834; early candidates, 137–138; Eucharistic Congress, 432; Father Barzynski's death, 123; feast days, 806, 825; financial hardships, 231, 232, 669, 737; first historian, 607; founding, 8, 70, 71–72 n.10; founding members, 76; garb and social standing, 260; growth, 137, 149, 162; hardships, 95–96, 109, 141, 152, 165, 266–267, 299–301, 302–303, 310 n.38; Health Services, Inc., 874; Holy Hour, 776; hunger among, 133; influenza affliction, 369–370; intercommunity living, 764–765; laity and friendships, 832; legal recognition of, 254; Marian features, ideals, symbols, 378; meditation, 776; membership, 324, 421, 454, 603, 773, 788, 805, 904; Millenium of Christianity, 808; monthly allowance, 831, 881; move to Avondale, 106–107; musical groups and recordings, 856–857; name of congregation, 825; naming of Sisters, 826; original mission, 67; praise for, 199, 307, 309 n.14, 611, 645, 675, 742, 810; prayer recitation, 722; provincial house proposal, 744; rebels among, 260; recreation, social activities, 830–831; refugee vocations plan, 612; requests for Sisters, 625; retirement program, 833; Rule, 110, 382; small-group living, 851–853; spirit of dedication, 138; standards of, 141; study rules, 776; superior general, 828, 881, 910; visiting privileges, 608, 806; vocations, 881

Franciscan Sisters of Our Lady of Perpetual Help, Congregation of (St. Louis, Missouri), 343

Franciscan Village (Lemont, Illinois), 911

Francis de Sales, Saint, 374–375

Francis of Assisi, Saint, 376, 377, 378, 384, 386 n.13, 388 n.26

Frank, Adam, 5, 52, 97–98

Frank, Rosalie, 8, 52, 98

Free health care, 180

"From the Desk of . . . ," 885 n.6

Fronczak, Rev. Louis, OFM, 892, 902

Fulgens Corona, 759

Furman, Rev. Adalbert, 168 n.4, 234, 365

Gabriel Lazarski, Sister M., 320, 346, 747, 782, 820, 847–848, 878, 893, 906, 910

Gapczynski, Ignatius Rev., 318–319, 334, 335, 389, 515

Gawlina, Bishop Joseph, 466
Gawronski, Dr. Wacław, 465
Genevieve Swiatowiec, Sister M., 390, 473, 474, 515, 516
George, Don, 836
Georgi, Louis, MD, 581
Gerard Gorzkowski, Sister M., 155, 174, 224, 251, 252, 315, 328, 402, 407, 428, 429, 436, 466, 467, 682, 686
Germanization of Poland, 13–14
Gettysburg Memorial Hospital, (Gettysburg, South Dakota) 582
Gieburowski, Rev. Joseph, CR, 126–127
Gill, Catherine. *See* Josepha Gill, Sister M.
Gilmour, Bishop Richard, 393
Gleason house (East Cleveland, Ohio), 505
Glennon, Archbishop John, 187, 188, 188–189
Gnielinski, Rev. Francis, 186–188
Gniot, John, 103 n.21, 106–107
Godzinki (Little Hours), 77, 164
"Golden Age" of Poland, 13
Gonzaga Raniszewski, Sister M.: 606–607; *Book of Customs,* 613; Boys Town, Nebraska, 553; building loan, 789; building plans, 510; Catholic Sisters College (Washington, DC), 483; charter signatures, 255; congregation history, 465; contract, 671; *Echo Avondalskie,* 466; *Echo Franciszkanski,* 777; fund raising effort, 683; hospital inspection, 729; land purchase, 680; Marian Congress, 760; mistress of novices, 420, 436; Mother M. Antonina, 461; praise for *Rys,* 612; *Regina Mundi,* 759; Re-inspiration, 818; St. Anthony's Home (Crown Point, Indiana), 514, 517, 520; secretary general, 462, 604, 720, 774, 804; Sister M. Theresa's suffering, 366; superior, 474
Góralski, Brother Adalbert, CR, 113
Gordon, Rev. Francis, CR, 29, 31, 123, 369, 441–442
Górek, Rev. Anthony, 315, 389, 390
Grabowski, Rev. John, CR, 790, 793
Graff, Antoinette, 109
Great Chicago Fire, 25, 44–45, 131
Great Depression, 226–227, 230–231
Greenhouse, 329
Gregory Community Hospital (Gregory, South Dakota). *See* Mother of Grace Hospital (Gregory, South Dakota)

Greinader, Rev. Linford F., 762
Grevenbroek, Rev. Joseph von, So. Cist., 476
Grudzinski, Rev. Louis, 181, 350, 351–352, 356, 410, 414–415
Grutka, Bishop Andrew, 346, 520, 521, 809, 810, 811, 812, 837, 863, 864, 896
Guardian Angel Day Care Center and Home for Ladies. *See* Guardian Angel Day Nursery and Home for Working Girls
Guardian Angel Day Nursery and Home for Working Girls: 350–359; assembly hall, 360 n.7; chapel, 357; dispensary, 353; during World War II, 354; Father Grudzinski, 181; financial support sources, 355; free services, 354; Golden Jubilee, 357–358; growth and services, 351; infant services, 352–353; influenza epidemic, 354; medical services, 352–354; ownership, 355–356; property of Sisters, 356; purpose and plan, 350; women's services, 352
Gużiel, Rev. Casimir, CR, 595
gymnasium, 39 n.63
Habit, religious: 437, 462, 541, 607–608, 640, 722, 776, 818, 831–832, 882; aspirant garb, 684
Haiman, Miecislaus, 19 n.28, 21
Hamlin Park Center, 592
Hammes, Rev. Joseph, 515, 517
Hardin Square, 592, 593
Health care ministry, 581–582, 584–585, 620, 629, 631, 642, 646, 727, 743, 875. *See also names of individual institutions*
Hedwig Kubera, Sister M., 133, 196–197, 234, 236, 247, 248, 251, 254, 256, 325, 327, 401, 422
Hegener, Rev. Mark, OFM, 357, 619, 621
Heruday, Rev. Thaddeus, 588, 589, 590
Hickey, Bishop James A., 747, 748
High Mass, 102 n.8
Hillinger, Bishop Raymond P., 694, 768
Hlond, August Cardinal, 432, 444
Hoban, Bishop Edward J., 429, 509, 510, 511, 542–543, 544, 617, 618, 743, 744, 745, 754 n.63, 763, 898
Hoch, Bishop Lambert A., 643, 645, 652
Holy Family Child Care Center, (Crown Point, Indiana), 895–897
Holy Family Orphanage (Chicago, Illinois), 28, 131–132
Holy Trinity Church (Chicago, Illinois), 25, 37 n.55

Holy Trinity School (Falls City, Texas), 269–278, 280–284
Home Planning Committee, 87, 94, 95–96, 97
Horarium, 76, 77, 95, 112, 253, 806
Hubsch, Rev. Arthur, 278, 281–282, 283
Hugoline Czaplinski, Sister M.: 167, 841–843; assignment changes, 759; Boys Town, Nebraska, 560; councilor, 804, 878, 902; First Extraordinary Chapter of Affairs, 824–826; hospital withdrawals, 732, 741–742; Johnstown Central Catholic High School (Johnstown, Pennsylvania), 762; Madonna High School (Chicago, Illinois) principal, 693, 697, 698–699, 700, 762; medical center plan, 863; music education, 439; Planning Committee, 910; Re-inspiration Period, 818; St. Anthony Home (Crown Point, Indiana), 811; Second Special Chapter, 845; small group living, 851, 852, 853; superior general, 698, 824, 847
Hull House, 48, 50 n.14, 71 n.6
Humboldt Park, 592
Hupp, Rev. Robert P., 560
Huron Regional Medical Center (Huron, South Dakota), 645
Hyacinth Barczewski, Sister M., 83, 84, 103 n.12, 178, 402, 436, 474, 475, 476, 517, 561
Hyacinth Bezler, Sister (Marianne), 71 n.8, 78
Illinois High School Association, 699
Immaculate Conception, Feast of, 112, 378, 494
Immaculate Conception of the Blessed Virgin Mary, Centennial Observance, 760
Immaculate Heart of Mary Church (Independence Hill, Indiana), 848
Independent physicians (Huron, South Dakota), 636–637
Indiana Harbor Catholic Elementary School, (Indiana Harbor, Indiana). *See* St. John Cantius School (Indiana Harbor, Indiana)
Infant Welfare Station, 180
Influenza epidemic (Chicago, Illinois), 56–57, 131, 370
Ingraham Street, 94–95, 102 n.6
Innocenta Antosz, Sister M., 193 n.12, 266, 324, 327, 394, 395, 402, 435–436, 458, 488, 489, 491, 505, 522

Innocentia Sierocki, Sister M., 348 n.34, 463, 554, 555, 563, 634, 639, 640, 641–642, 669, 671, 674, 686, 816 n.6
Intercommunity Formation Program, 858 n.23
International Eucharistic Congress, 431–432
Interim Constitutions, 827
Ivanko, Msgr. Michael, 544
Jadwiga, Queen of Poland, 13
Janik, Reverend Anthony, OFM, 812, 873, 896
Jansenism, 386 n.10
Jasna Góra, 502–503 n.22
Jański, Bogdan, 24
Jeanne Marie Toriskie, Sister, 220, 239 n.38, 718 n.101, 802 n.15
Jennings Hall for the Aged (Cleveland, Ohio), 509, 743
Jerome Dadej, Mother M.: 604–606; Alvernia Rest Home (Parma, Ohio), 743, 744, 745; Archbishop Noll letter, 317; Boys Town, Nebraska visit, 550; chapter report, 773; committee membership, 436; community center, 618–619, 621; cornerstone document, 491; council membership, 458, 522, 537; CYO staffing, 593; debt cancellation, 227; farm retention, 499; final years, 771; fund raising, 182; ground breaking, 647–648; health care apostolate, 727; home proposal, 509; hospital staffing, 557, 564 n.17, 584, 585, 668, 728, 729–730, 731, 734–735, 737–738; land transactions, 511, 519, 679, 680, 682; letters, 207; Madonna Hall (Cleveland, Ohio), 617; Madonna High School (Chicago, Illinois) financing, 683, 684, 685, 687, 691, 692, 694; Madonna High founding, 564 n.9, 686, 696, 754 n.63; Marian Year, 760; Mother of Grace Hospital (Gregory, South Dakota), 670, 671; novitiate move, 495; ownership negotiation, 356; property inspection, 505; *Regina Mundi* support, 759; *Rys* publication, 612; Sacred Heart High School (Cleveland, Ohio), 396; St. Hedwig's (Gary, Indiana), 225; St. John Hospital (Huron, South Dakota), 634, 635; school staffing, 346, 723, 762–763, 766, 767, 782; Special Reading Program, 770; staff recalling, 558–559, 574–575, 576, 624; superior,

640; superior general, 555–556, 603, 720; trustees meeting, 636; vocation efforts, 611–612, 678–679, 698

Joachim Milewski, Sister (Victoria), 66, 76, 77–78

Joan Klimek, Sister, 239 n.24, 717 n.100, 787 n.17, 861 n.68, 906

John Barczak, Sister M., 401, 405, 408, 462, 537, 604

John Paul, Pope, 878

John Paul II, Pope, 294, 878, 887, 885 n.1

Johnstown Central Catholic High School (Johnstown, Pennsylvania), 762–763

John XXIII, Pope, 780–781, 786 n.2

Jordan, Msgr. Edward B., 477–478, 479, 480

Josepha Gill, Sister M., 79, 84, 85, 109

Josepha Suchomski, Sister M., 224, 247, 370

Joseph Marie Zenda, Sister: 902–904; commission chair, 820; congregation guidance, 907, 911; Home Office, 909–910; letter to congregation, 904; Madonna High School (Chicago, Illinois) principal, 698, 699, 700, 702; planning committee, 910; St. Leo School (Parma, Ohio), 765; St. Louise de Marillac residence (La Grange Park, Illinois), 770; sisters choir revival, 907; speech, 908; staff recall, 591–592, 784; superior general, 702, 902

Joseph, Saint, 3, 96, 116 n.1, 163, 380, 825

Juniorate, 784–785

Juszkiewicz, Rev. Joseph, 23

Kahellek, Rev. Peter, 318, 389

Kajsiewicz, Rev. Jerome, CR, 23, 24, 25

Kalinowski, Rev. Theophane, OFM, 640, 790, 791, 818

Kamien Krajeński, 3, 7

Karabasz, Msgr. Francis, 350, 356, 357, 360 n.5

Karcz, Rev. John, 270, 271–272, 275, 287 n.46

Karcz, Rev. Valerian, 391

Kashubes, 173

Kasprzycki, Rev. John, CR, 31, 134, 442, 452

Kelly, Hon. Edward J., 292, 519, 522

Kennedy Expressway, 32, 89 n.1. See also Northwest Expressway

Kiley, Rev. Moses, 410

Kiołbassa, Peter, 22, 23, 86, 97

Kloska, Rev. Andrew, CR, 693, 696

Knapik, Rev. Joseph, CSSR, 364, 365, 366

Kobrzynski, Rev. Simon, CR, 77, 86, 87

Kocham Chrystusa . . . , 436

Koerner, Edward W., 815

Kolęda, 297

Komirowo, 5

Kopciak, Josephine, 55, 57

Kowalczyk, Rev. Stephen, CR, 126, 314, 367, 452

Kozłowski, Rev. Anthony, 83, 89 nn.1, 2

Krol, John Cardinal, 744

"Kronika Sióstr Franciszkanek pod opieką Św. Kunegundy w Chicago, Illinois" (Dudzik), 8. See also "Chronicle"

Kruszka, Rev. John, 289, 290, 364, 365, 366

Kruszka, Rev. Wacław, 173–174, 211–212 n.17

Kruszynski, Rev. John, CR, 133, 315

Kubiaczyk, Rev. Francis, CR, 157

Kucera, Archbishop Daniel, OSB, 766

Kulinski, Rev. Francis, 218–220

Kulturkampf, 25

Kunegunda, Blessed, 68–69, 74 n.28, 206, 494

Kunegunda Pinkowski, Sister M., 151–152, 202, 224, 236, 247, 251–252, 254, 324, 327, 401, 405, 801 n.11

Kwasigroch, Andrew, 113

Kwasigroch, Rose, 113

Ladislaus Wroblewski, Sister M., 8, 180, 198, 327, 328, 351, 353, 402, 415, 444, 582

Ładon, Rev. Felix, CR, 137

Land grant of Congress, 21

Latko, Rev. Ernest, OFM, 758

League of Mother M. Theresa, 778

Lemont, Illinois, 415–416, 425–426 n.8, 585–586

Lengerich, Msgr. Vincent, 810

Leona Pochelski, Sister M., 247, 253, 324, 325, 327, 402, 404–405, 435, 436

Leovina Dudzik, Sister M., 59 n.9. See also Dudzik, Frances

Lesniak, Berenice, 692, 858

Leurck, Stephen, 874

Ligman, Rev. Thaddeus, CR, 314

Little Office of the Blessed Virgin Mary, 259, 328, 377, 378, 806

Lora Ann Slawinski, Sister, 702, 705, 718 n.101, 719 n.109, 861 n.68

Lovrencic, Rev. Athanasius, OFM, 847

Lowisz, Rev. Myron, OFM, 643, 653, 811, 812, 865, 873, 896

Low Mass, 126

Lowney, Rev. James, CSV, 687

Lusk, Robert D., 583, 629, 633, 646, 652

Lux, Rev. Sylvester, 763, 764

Lynch, Rev. Cletus J., 766, 767, 768, 769, 793, 837

Mabon, Rev. Thomas K., 307

McCarty, Bishop William T., CSSR, 584, 585, 669, 670, 673, 674–675, 734–736, 737

McCort, Bishop John J., 304, 305

McDowell Avenue (Chicago, Illlinois), 360 n.10

McFadden, Bishop James, 509

McManus, Bishop William E., 696–697, 770, 836, 837

Maday, Rev. Edward A. 293

Madejczyk, Rev. Louis, 782

Madic, Rev. Aloysius, OFM, 610, 615 n.30

Madonna Hall (Cleveland, Ohio), 617–618

Madonna High School (Chicago, Illinois): 91 n.16, 169 n.11; accreditation, 687, 693, 697, 706; Advanced Placement Courses, 699; Alumnae Association, 700; building addition, 697–698; College Acceleration Program, 699; construction, 693, 694–696; curriculum, 682, 684–685, 686, 688, 693, 699, 700, 703, 704; enrollment, 681, 684, 686, 687, 689, 693, 694, 696, 697, 698, 700, 706; facilities, 681, 684, 686, 689, 694–695, 697–698, 699, 700, 702; faculty, 682, 684–685, 686, 687, 689, 691, 694, 696, 697, 698, 700, 703; Fathers' Club and Auxiliary, 693; financing, 679–680, 681, 682–684, 685, 687–688, 689–693; founding, 564 n.9; fund raising, 683, 691, 692–693, 700; Glee Club, 696; growth, 762; idea and purpose of, 678–679; Marian observance, 760; Mothers' Club and Auxiliary, 686, 692; Office of School Development, 700; "Old Building" razing, 700; principals and administration, 681, 686, 687, 688, 693, 698–699, 700, 702–703, 704; religious vocational purpose, 680–681; school song, 719 n.112; Silver Anniversary, 701–702; *Somebody, Somewhere*, 836; student activities and organizations, 704–706; student publications, 705, 719 nn.109, 110; student services, 687, 698, 699, 700, 705; vocations from, 685

Magdalen Schreiber, Sister M., 83–84

"Magnificat," 126, 806

Malak, Rev. Henry M., 778, 798

Manning, Donn, 836

Manual Training Act, 264 n.54

Marianne Kaplan, Sister, 346, 359, 392, 476, 553

Maristella Skrzynski, Sister M., 431, 592, 594, 689, 723–724

Marquard, Rev. Philip, OFM, 618

Marriage Encounter, 890–891

Martha Bywalec, Sister M., 356, 405, 408, 423, 436, 499, 561, 619

Martha Joan Sempolski, Sister: 878–879; administration report, 904; Alvernia Rest Home, (Parma, Ohio), 592, 747; Constitutions approval, 827; dietitian, 635; formation appointment, 890; Holy Family Child Care Center (Crown Point, Indiana), 896; house of prayer, 890; Marriage Encounter Groups, 891; newsletter, 885 n.6; nutrition instructor, 651; outreach program, 882; pastoral care, 447; St. Anthony Medical Center (Crown Point, Indiana), 864, 865; St. Francis anniversary, 892; St. Martin's celebration, 645; school staffing, 897; superior, 878; withdrawal of staff, 397, 725

Mary of Jesus, the Good Shepherd, (Frances Siedliska), Mother, 60 n.11

Maslinski, Rev. Reginald, OFM, 799, 892, 907

Matlak, Rev. Marion, 908

May, Bishop, John L., 576

Mechtilde Zynda, Mother M.: 537–539; art studies, 408; assistant superior general, 420; convent superior, 418; *Echo Avondalskie,* 466; finance commission, 436; hospital commitment, 633–634; illness and death, 482, 574, 594–595; letter to Bishop Noll, 391–392; mission staffing, 531–534, 542–543, 553, 554, 555, 569, 583, 592, 631; novice, postulant mistress, 436, 462, 493; recall of Sisters, 475, 481–482; repainting of chapel, 542; requests for Sisters, 450, 629; superior general, 475, 480

Meegan, Joseph, 358, 363 n.46

Mendicancy, 92–93 n.32

Meyer, Albert Cardinal, 430, 696, 769, 778, 789, 793–794, 796, 804

Mielcarek, Msgr. John, 450, 458, 473, 488, 527

Mieszko I, King of Poland, 13

Millenium of Poland's Christianity, 32, 807–808

Milon, Rev. Gus F., OFM, 884

Milwaukee Avenue, 116 n.3

Misiura, Adalbert, 595

Moczygemba, Rev. Leopold, 22, 39, 40 n.69, 193 n.4

Modjeska (Modrzejewska), Helena, 41 n.84

Monighan, Msgr. Frank, 667, 668, 736

Motherhouse (Chicago, Illinois): councils, 327, 405; Częstohowa Society, 496; expansion need, 788–789; first days, 107; library, 460; overcrowding, 414, 505; rebuilding, 608; years of service, 792. *See also* Our Lady of Victory Convent, General Motherhouse (Lemont, Illinois)

Mother M. Theresa Novena, 880

Mother of God Church (Burnham, Illinois), 220, 222 n.23, 848

Mother of Grace Hospital (Gregory, South Dakota), 584, 667, 668, 669–674, 675

Mother Theresa Home (Lemont, Illinois): accreditation, 797–800; facilities and services, 799; license change, 799; plans, 793; replacement structure, 911; staff, 798

Mother Theresa Museum (Lemont, Illinois), 495

Mount Alverna Home and Annex (Parma, Ohio), 743–751

Mount Alvernia Convent (East Cleveland, Ohio), 505–511, 743

Mundelein, George Cardinal, 218–219, 290, 328, 365, 369, 428, 441, 444, 582, 583, 679

Mungovan, Rev. Edward, 517

Municipal Tuberculosis Dispensary, 180

Murphy, Msgr. Albert G., 544

Musical direction and training, 157, 294, 395, 438–439

Muzillo, Mark, 751

Napieralski, Stella, MD, 353, 356, 362 n.40

Natalie Uscinowicz, Sister M., 633, 645, 646, 650–651, 653–654, 820, 835, 841, 864

National Archives, Washington, DC, 58 n.3

National Polio Foundation, 639

Nawrocki, Msgr. Stanislaus, 367

"New Kind of Freedom, A," 857, 893

Newman Club, 854

Night Adoration of the Blessed Sacrament, 539, 721

Nimeth, Rev. Albert J., OFM, 357, 619

Ninth General Chapter of Elections: 773–774, 776–778

"Noah's Ark," 217, 218, 219, 632

Noble Street (Chicago, Illinois), 21

North Central Association of Colleges and Secondary Schools, 687

North Dakota public schools, 528

Northwest Expressway, 32. *See also* Kennedy Expressway

Novitiate, 118 n.29: changes, 778; elements of, 829–830; first, 120–121, 126; novice assignment, 418; novitiate house and housing, 172, 417–418, 423, 489, 493, 792; preparation for vows, 421; reception of candidates, 125–126, 140, 143, 144, 168 n.1, 171, 199, 205, 210 n.7, 255, 327, 418, 493, 494, 542, 760, 794; record admission, 327; study program, 329; suggestion, 488; teacher needs and change, 409; two-year, 405; visits and letters, 805

Nowicki, Rev. Vincent, 430, 490, 493

Nursing education. *See* St. John Hospital and School of Nursing (Huron, South Dakota)

Nursing mission. *See* Health care ministry *and names of individual institutions*

O'Brien, Rev. James, 723

Obyrtacz, Rev. John, CR, 154, 442, 452

O'Meara, Msgr. William, 582

O'Neill, Rev. John J., 583, 629, 632, 634, 635, 639, 646, 647, 648

Orphanage, 131. *See also names of individual institutions*

Our Lady of Częstochowa: icon, 502–503 n.22; icon copy, 496–497, 791–792; Society, 496

Our Lady of Grace Society, 182

Our Lady of Lourdes Grotto (Lemont, Illinois), 494–495, 521

Our Lady of Ransom Parish (Niles, Illinois), 850–851

Our Lady of Spring Bank Abbey (Okauchee, Wisconsin), 472–476

Our Lady of the Angels School (Chicago, Illinois), 182

Our Lady of the Sandhills Hospital (Atkinson, Nebraska), 727–734. *See also* Atkinson Memorial Hospital (Atkinson, Nebraska); West Holt Memorial Hospital

Our Lady of Victory Convent Cemetery (Lemont, Illinois), 795–796

Our Lady of Victory Convent for the Aged and

Infirm Sisters (Lemont, Illinois), 488–496, 501–502 n.14, 585–586, 789, 792

Our Lady of Victory Convent, General Motherhouse (Lemont Illinois): chapel, 791–792; communications media library, 796; dedication, 793, 794; Exposition of the Blessed Sacrament, 796; functions served, 796–797; Home Office, 909–910; house of prayer, 888; icon transfer, 497; infirmary, 907; novitiate site, 495; plans for, 488, 789–790; reconstruction, 796; site selection, 789; structure and facilities, 790–791, 794, 796; transfer to Lemont, 235. *See also* Motherhouse (Chicago, Illinois)

Our Lady of Victory Convent (Walker Mansion, Lemont, Illinois): 414–423, 488–496, 501–502 n.14, 585–586, 789, 792

Our Lady of Victory High School (Chicago, Illinois), 407–408

Our Lady of Victory Society, 421

Our Lady of Victory: statue, 125; title, 128–129 n.29

Palubicki, Ignatius, 85

Panna Maria (Texas), 28, 39 n.69

Pan-Slavism, 37 n.42

Partitions of Poland, 13, 14

Paul Kirschbaum, Sister M.: 540; Boys Town, Nebraska, 553; committees, 406, 436; education, 407, 439, 463; Holy Trinity School (Falls City, Texas), 276; hospital review, 633, 634; postulancy, 236; profession, 199; Redfield Hospital (Redfield, South Dakota) visit, 629; secretery general, 518, 537; superior, 462, 736, 740; teaching, 407–408

Paul VI, 781, 788, 837, 878

Pawłowski, Rev. Ferdinand, OFM, 612

Pecasse, Rev. Romuald, So Cist., 474, 475, 476

Pelczar, Bishop Sebastian, 81 n.8

Percy, Nelson, MD, 594

Perfectae Caritatis, 781, 825, 831

Period of Re-inspiration, 818–819, 825, 839 n.19

Philipine Lama, Sister M.: 324, 325, 326, 327, 328, 406, 407, 522, 537; Assumption, 305; Blessed Sacrament rescue, 154–155; First General Chapter, 247

Piechowski, Rev. John, CR, 89 n.1, 103 n.19, 126, 145 n.8, 366, 367, 368

Pieczynski, Rev. Francis, CR, 314

Pilgrimages (Lemont Illinois), 421, 422

Piotrowski, Nikodem L., 99, 442

Pius X, Saint., 386 n.10

Pius XII, 756, 759–760, 784

Plagens, Bishop Joseph C., 450

Plank Road, 21

Plaza, Stanislaus Rev., 188, 189, 193–194 n.22

Płocicz, 3, 5, 6, 7

Pociask, Alyce, 496

Poland, history of: 11 nn.4, 7, 13–17, 18 n.3, 19 n.13; Christianity introduced, 816 n.14; German invasion, 467

Poles: anticlericalism among exiles, 24; cultural and religious tenacity, 16; emigration, 16–17, 19 n.28, 21–22, 25; exile in France, 24; patriotism and passion for freedom, 13

Poliomyelitis epidemic, St. John Hospital (Huron, South Dakota), 639

Polish American Studies, 613

Polish Daily News (Chicago, Illinois), 368

Polish immigrant settlements: Catholic parishes in Chicago, Illinois, 21, 45, 169 n.11, 217, 289; Church-centered life, 54; Cleveland, Ohio, 392–393; community names, 34 n.15; complaints of Catholics, 198; East St. Louis, Illinois, 206; Falls City, Texas, 269–271; Gary, Indiana, 224; Indiana Harbor, Indiana, 201; Johnstown, Pennsylvania, 296; La Porte, Indiana, 333; Madison, Illinois, 342; Oshkosh, Wisconsin, 173; Polish-language schools, 140; Posen, Illinois, 266; private schools, 39 n.69; religious unrest, 89 n.1; St. Louis, Misouri, 186; social problems, 131; Texas, 39 n.69; Whiting, Indiana; 200; Youngstown, Ohio, 229, 350, 428, 588

Polish language, suppression of, 16

Polish Manual Training School For Boys and St. Hedwig's Industrial School for Girls (Niles, Illinois), 257

Polish National Alliance, 38 n.55

Polish National Catholic Church, 89–90 n.2, 90 n.5

Polish Old Catholic Church, 89 n.2, 90 n.16

Polish Past in America, 1608–1865 (Haiman): statistics on Polish settlements in the U.S., 19 n.28

Polish Publishing Company, 29
Polish Roman Catholic Union of America, 29,
    38 n.55
Polonia, 22
Popieluszko, Rev. Jerzy, 18 n.3
Portiuncula, 168 n.9, 387 n.13, 884
Portiuncula Indulgence, 164
"Port, The," (Chicago, Illinois), 884
Postulancy: 118 n.28; changes, 778;
    education, 838 n.1; first, 112, 126; garb,
    329; housing, 423, 493, 792, 805;
    length, 405; teacher preparation, 150
Postulate to Rome, 773
Poznań, 3, 11 n.2, 266
Prayer of Christians, 825
Prison teaching apostolate, 854–856
Progressive Series School of Music, 438–439
Przegląd Kościelny (The Polish Ecclesiastical
    Review), 489
Purcell, Msgr. Harold, 568
Pursley, Bishop Leo A., 320
Queen of Angels Society, 358
Quigley, Archbishop James E., 164, 171, 180,
    252, 256, 258
Raczka, Rev. Edmund, CR, 445, 837
Radecki, Msgr. Andrew, 166–167, 507, 508,
    583, 744, 807
Radniecki, Rev. Stanislaus, 428, 430
Radziejewski, Rev. John, 87
Ralph Stawasz, Sister M., 597 n.19, 746, 747,
    836, 843–844, 847, 878, 902, 910
Rapacz, Rev. Vincent, CR, 126, 314, 838 n.17
Raphael Bagulecki, Sister M., 49, 436, 458,
    451–462, 522, 537
Regina Mundi, 759
"Released time" program, 848
Religious education apostolate, 764, 769,
    848–851. *See also* Confraternity of
    Christian Doctrine classes
Religious habit, 72 n.12: Franciscan Sisters of
    Chicago, 67, 88, 109, 121, 127 n.6
Religious Vacation School. *See* Catechetical
    mission
Rempe, Msgr. Francis, 330, 365, 367, 406,
    409, 414, 415, 435, 582
Resurrectionists. *See* Congregation of the
    Resurrection
Resurrection Mausoleum, 808
Retreats: 112, 777, 806, 838 n.17, 889; lay,
    454
Rhode, Bishop Paul Peter, 199, 236, 256–257,
    258, 260, 289, 333

Rings, wearing of, 437–438, 806
Rite of Ceremony, 830–831
Rogalski, Rev. Stanislaus, CR, 235–236
Rogeria, Sister M., SSND, 30
Roman Franciscan Christian Book of Prayer,
    879
Roman Institute of Sacred Studies, 759
Roos, Rev. Thomas A., So Cist., 472, 474
Roots and Wings, 907
Rosalima Sierocki, Sister M., 295, 348 n.34,
    439, 777, 785, 804–805, 818
Rosary of the Seven Joys of the Blessed
    Virgin Mary, 121. *See also* Franciscan
    Crown
Rosemary Ferus, Sister M., 698, 726 n.20,
    818, 820, 909
Rozmarek, Wanda, 697
Rubin, Bishop Ladislaus, 808
Rusch, Msgr. Francis S., 257, 264 n.54
Ryan, Bishop James H., STD, 552–553
Ryan, Bishop Vincent J., 536 n.26
Rybacki, Rev. Stanislaus, 395
"Rys historyczny Zgromadzenia Sióstr
    Franciszkanek Błogosławionej
    Kunegundy. Część druga, 1910–1940,"
    465, 521, 607
*Rys historyczny Zgromadzenia Sióstr
    Franciszkanek Błogosławionej
    Kunegundy. Część pierwsza,
    1860–1910,* 8–10, 68
Sabbatine Privilege, 614 n.18
Sacred Congregation of Religious Affairs, 611
Sacred Heart Chapel (Lemont, Illinois),
    791–792, 794, 802–803 n.17
Sacred Heart of Jesus School (Cleveland,
    Ohio), 392–397
Sacred Heart of Jesus School (Gary, Indiana),
    317–320
Sacred Heart of Jesus School (La Porte,
    Indiana), 333–335
St. Adalbert's Cemetery, 123, 795
St. Adalbert's Church (Chicago, Illinois), 92
    n.26
St. Adalbert's School (East St. Louis,
    Illinois), 206–209
St. Adalbert's School (Farrell, Pennsylvania),
    335–337, 347 n.11
St. Adalbert's School (Whiting, Indiana),
    200–201
St. Anne's Infirmary, 163, 172
St. Ann's School (Spring Valley, Illinois),
    153

St. Anthony Home (Crown Point, Indiana): 808–815; accreditation, 815; auxiliary, 815; building addition, 814; dedication, 810; design and construction, 809–810; diet supervision, 813; facilities, 811; history of, 895; medical care, 812–813; nursing care, 813; opening, 808; pastoral care service, 812; recreational activities, 814; rehabilitative services, 813; Respite Care Program, 814; skilled-care unit, 814; social services, 813. *See also* St. Anthony Medical Center; St. Anthony's Home for the Aged (Crown Point, Indiana)

St. Anthony Hospital, (Crown Point, Indiana). *See* St. Anthony Medical Center

St. Anthony Medical Center, 583, 862–875; accreditation, 874–875; auxiliary service, 874; blood recycling, 870–871; cancer treatment, 867; cardiovascular service, 868; convent, 863; decor, 865; design and construction, 863; dietary service, 869; directors, 865; educational programs, 866; emergency room service, 864, 870; establishment, 642; expansion program, 865; facilities, 864–865; financing, 863; health services, 872; helicopter, 870; history of, 895; home health care, 871; library, 873; maternity program, 868–869; medical staff, 866; nursing service, 866–867; occupational therapy, 870; Oncology Family Room, 867–868; Outpatient Hospice Program, 868; outpatient services, 871–872; outpatient surgery, 870; pastoral care, 873–874; pediatric service, 869; poison control, 870, 872; rehabilitative services, 869; social services, 869; supporting staff, 874; terminally ill care, 868. *See also* St. Anthony Home for the Aged (Crown Point, Indiana); St. Anthony Home (Crown Point, Indiana)

St. Anthony of Padua School (Parma, Ohio), 897, 899–900

St. Anthony's Home for the Aged (Crown Point, Indiana), 514–521, 808. *See also* St. Anthony Home (Crown Point, Indiana); St. Anthony Medical Center

St. Anthony's Hospital (Martin, South Dakota), 584, 734–742

St. Barbara of the Blessed Sacrament Dudzik, Sister, 53. *See also* Dudzik, Katharine

St. Barbara School (Brookfield, Illinois), 767–768

St. Casimir's School (Johnstown, Pennsylvania), 296–307, 762

St. Casimir School (Streator, Illinois), 340–342

St. Casimir's School (Cleveland, Ohio), 164–167

St. Casimir's School (St. Louis, Missouri), 186–190

St. Elizabeth Hospital Training School (Lafayette, Indiana), 197–198

St. Elizabeth's Day Nursery (Chicago, Illinois), 178–182, 362 n.36

St. Florian's Commercial High School, 218

St. Florian's School (Chicago, Illinois), 217–220

St. Francis Home (Chicago, Illinois), 443–444

St. Francis Home (Lemont, Illinois), 420, 422

St. Francis House of Prayer (Lemont, Illinois), 888–890

St. Francis Mission (Chicago, Illinois), 852, 853

St. Francis Villa (Lemont, Illinois): convent grounds, 491, 493

St. Genevieve Church (Chicago, Illinois), 850

St. Hedwig's Church and Parish (Chicago, Illinois), 83, 89 n.1, 238 n.7

St. Hedwig's Industrial School for Girls, 257. *See also* St. Hedwig's Orphanage, (Niles, Illinois)

St. Hedwig's Orphanage (Chicago, Illinois), 224

St. Hedwig's Orphanage (Niles, Illinois), 258, 264 n.54. *See also* St. Hedwig's Industrial School for Girls

St. Hedwig's School (Gary, Indiana), 225–228

St. Hyacinth's Church (Chicago, Illinois), 90–91 n.16

St. James Church (Arlington Heights, Illinois), 851

St. Joachim Home, 152, 162

St. John Cantius Church (Chicago, Illinois), 92 n.29

St. John Cantius School (Indiana Harbor, Indiana), 201–205

St. John Hospital (Huron, South Dakota): 629–646, 651; accreditation, 638; board, 636, 637; bylaws, 637; fund raising, 633; medic staff bylaws, 636–637; service figures, 641. *See also*

St. John Regional Medical Center

St. John Hospital and School of Nursing (Huron, South Dakota), 576, 583–584, 640, 646–655, 670

St. John Hospital School of Nursing Alumni Association, 649

St. John Regional Medical Center, 642–645, 654, 655; directors, 643, 644; law suit, 644–645; medical staff bylaws, 643; pastoral care, 643; Silver Jubilee, 643. *See also* St. John Hospital (Huron, South Dakota)

St. John the Baptist School, (Campbell, Ohio), 232, 590–591. *See also* St. Joseph the Provider School (Campbell, Ohio).

St. Josephat's School (Oshkosh, Wisconsin), 173–175

St. Joseph Benevolent Society (Gary, Indiana), 514–515, 518

St. Joseph Church (Chicago, Illinois), 360 n.4

St. Joseph Home for the Aged (Chicago, Illinois): blessing, 444; chaplain, 444; Diamond Jubilee, 445; chapter concern, 327; dignitaries' visit, 432; financial support, 443; mayoral visit, 522; medical care providers, 443; Motherhouse site, 789; name change, 445; new facilities, 441–445; renaming, 443; services, 444. *See also* St. Joseph Home for the Aged and Crippled; St. Joseph Home of Chicago

St. Joseph Home for the Aged (Cleveland, Ohio), 542–545

St. Joseph Home for the Aged and Crippled (Chicago, Illinois): Blessed Sacrament at, 125; blessing, 109; building progress, 99–100; chapel, 125-126, 255–256; divestiture proposal, 410; document of erection, 133–134; expansion and funding, 409–410; first adult male resident, 105 n.44; food shortage, 108; fund raising, 232–233; greenhouse venture, 232–233; laundry addition, 172; name proposal, 96; naming of and move to, 106; need to expand, 171; number of residents, 176 n.6; overcrowding, 132–133; panic after funeral, 123; problems upon opening, 107–108; Quigley support, 171; Sisters' workload, 133. *See also* St. Joseph Home for the Aged; St. Joseph Home of Chicago

St. Joseph Home of Chicago (Chicago, Illinois), 445–448. *See also* St. Joseph Home for the Aged (Chicago, Illinois); St. Joseph Home for the Aged and Crippled (Chicago, Illinois)

St. Joseph School (East Chicago, Indiana), 344–346

St. Joseph the Provider School (Campbell, Ohio), 591–592. *See also* St. John the Baptist School

St. Joseph's Church (Warren, Ohio), 232

St. Joseph's Home Florists, 232–233

St. Leo the Great School (Parma, Ohio), 167, 763–765

St. Louise de Marillac School (La Grange Park, Illinois), 721, 765–770

St. Margaret's Maternity Home (Chicago, Illinois), 180, 181

St. Martin de Porres House of Hope (Chicago, Illinois), 909

St. Mary of Częstochowa School (Hammond, Indiana), 315–317

St. Mary of Częstochowa School (Madison, Illinois), 342–344

St. Mary's College (St. Mary, Kentucky), 321 n.1, 368–369

St. Mary's Church (Orwell, Ohio), 232

St. Matthias Parish (Crown Point, Indiana), 850

St. Michael the Archangel School (Glen Campbell, Pennsylvania), 337–340

St. Michael's Parish (San Antonio, Texas), 28

St. Michael's School (Berlin, Wisconsin), 172, 173

St. Pancratius School (Chicago, Illinois), 292, 428–431, 771

St. Pascal Baylon Church (Chicago, Illinois), 850

St. Paul Mission (Chicago, Illinois), 852, 853

St. Peter Claver School (Mobile, Alabama), 568, 577

St. Philip of Jesus Community Center (Chicago, Illinois), 618–625

St. Roch's School (LaSalle, Illinois), 268–269

St. Rose of Lima Parish (Chicago, Illinois) 882, 883

St. Stanislaus Bishop and Martyr Church (Cleveland, Ohio), 392–393

St. Stanislaus Bishop and Martyr School (Chicago, Illinois), 153–157

St. Stanislaus Bishop and Martyr School Band (Chicago, Illinois), 493

St. Stanislaus Bishop and Martyr School (Posen, Illinois), 266–268

St. Stanislaus Kostka Church (Chicago, Illinois): dedication, 25; design, 22; expansion, 25; masses, 40 n.83; new structure, 30–31; rebuilding, 40 n.82; role in Polish-American religious life, 32; Sisters' pilgrimage, 908–909

St. Stanislaus Kostka College (Chicago, Illinois). *See* Weber High School

St. Stanislaus Kostka Parish (Chicago, Illinois), 88; Archconfraternity of the Immaculate Heart of Mary, 54–55; dissidence within, 24; Dramatic Circle, 40 n.84; establishment, 17; Golden Jubilee, 368; infant mortality, 180; obtaining a pastor, 22; organizations, 54; pastorate of Rev. Barzyski, 27; Sunday masses, 102 n.9; Third Order founding, 55

St. Stanislaus Kostka Parish (Youngstown, Ohio), 229–232

St. Stanislaus Kostka School (Chicago, Illinois), 31–32, 40 n.81, 368

St. Stanislaus Kostka School (Falls City, Texas), 278, 279

St. Stanislaus Kostka School (St. Louis, Missouri), 186, 190–192

St. Theresa Home, 162

St. Vincent's Orphan Asylum (Chicago, Illinois): chapel, 134–135; document of erection, 133–134; financial hardships, 257; funding and founding, 133–137; Motherhouse site, 789; need to expand, 171, 256; Quigley support, 171; razing, 444

SS. Peter and Paul School (Arcadia, Pennsylvania), 338–340

SS. Peter and Paul School (Spring Valley, Illinois), 149–153

SS. Phillip and James School (Cleveland, Ohio), 167, 722–725

Salesia Rzeszutko, Sister M., 229, 297, 300, 301, 311 n.53

Salomea Grabowski, Sister M., 152, 172, 206, 247, 248, 251, 305, 325, 327, 390, 402, 435, 436, 458, 473, 491, 505, 522, 686

Samborski, Rev. Joseph, CR, 452, 497

Saurenhaus, Ernest, MD, 205, 366

Schmitt, Msgr. Francis, 561–562, 837

Schneider, W.J., MD, 353

Schoenewald House, 178, 182

School Sisters of Notre Dame, Congregation of, 29–30, 32, 58–59 n.7

Schools. *See names of individual schools and* Catechetical mission; Confraternity of Christian Doctrine classes; "Released time" program; Teaching apostolate

Schrembs, Archbishop Joseph, 395, 507, 509

Scuderi, Rev. Carmen, 873

Second General Chapter of Elections, 324–330

Second National Meeting of Franciscan Sisters, 758

Second Plenary Council of Baltimore, 147

Second Special Chapter of Affairs, 844–847, 852

Second Vatican Council: aim, 780–781; collegiality, governing structures; 827, 828–829; consequences of, 882; impact on religious communities, 819; living guidelines, 827; new concepts in religious education, 849; new roles for religious women, 848; religious habits, 831; spiritual renewal, 825

Sedlaczek, Rev. Eugene, CR, 109

Semenenko, Rev. Peter, CR, 19, 24

Seraphic Institute of Theology for Sisters, 757–758

Seraphic Society for Vocations, 611

Seraphine Zamrowski, Sister M, 151–152, 165, 229, 333, 395, 402, 404, 435, 436, 462

Seventh General Chapter of Elections, 499, 603–604, 607–608, 612

Seventy-fifth Jubilee Year, 836–838

Shaw, Bishop John William, 270, 277–278, 280, 281, 282, 283

Sheil, Bishop Bernard J., 363 n.46, 592–593, 594

Sheil School of Social Studies, 592

Shircel, Rev. Cyril, OFM, 610, 758

Shirley, J.C., 583, 629–630, 632, 633, 635, 636, 646

Siara, Rev. Francis, CR, 314

Siatka, Rev. Stanislaus, CR, 137

Sierota, 137, 139, 232

Sister Formation Conference and Program, 784–785

Sister shortage, 520, 542, 574–576, 592, 593, 626, 735, 738, 766, 770, 784, 899

Sisters of Charity of the Incarnate Word, Congregation of, 59–60 nn.10, 11

Sisters of St. Elizabeth, Congregation of (Kamien Krajeński), 7

Sisters of St. Felix of Cantalice, Congregation of, 268, 393

Sisters of the Holy Family of Nazareth, Congregation of, 60 n.11, 534

Sisters of the Third Order of St. Francis under the patronage of Blessed Kunegunda: 68; official recognition, 162; registration of incorporation, 254. *See also* Franciscan Sisters of Chicago, Congregation of

Sixth General Chapter of Elections, 537, 541

Skrzypinski, Rev., Julius, 201–202

Slovenians (La Salle, Illinios), 268

Smallpox epidemic, 152

Smarzewski-Schermann, Anthony, 21

Society of Night Adoration, 539

Society of St. Joseph (Chicago, Illinois), 25

Society of St. Stanislaus Kostka (Chicago, Illinois), 22, 25

Society of the Daughters of the Heart of Mary, 679, 682, 685

Somebody, Somewhere (Manning and George), 836, 837

South Heart Public School (South Heart, North Dakota), 526–534

Spetz, Rev. Andrew, CR, 123–124: admonition of Sisters, 260; appointments of Sisters, 196, 223–224; association with Sisters, 110; bishops' representative, 247; care for the sick, 581; clinic role, 179–180; Constitutions, 110; death, 368; departure for Kentucky, 368; Father Karcz negotiations, 273; First General Chapter postponement, 236; first teaching mission of Sisters, 151; funeral, 369; health-care mission, 197–198; illness, Jubilee, 235; influence recalled, 908; legacy, 369; letter to Bishop Shaw, 280–281; potential for Sisters, 149; regard of Sister M. Theresa, 382; residence at St. Joseph Home (Chicago, Illinois), 236; return from Europe, 236; St. Elizabeth's Day Nursery (Chicago, Illinois), 178; saintliness of Mother Anna, 249; Southern mission, 372 n.21; spiritual director, 164; transfer from Chicago, 180; visit to Sisters, 368–369

Spetz, Rev. George, CR, 369

Spetz, Rev. Theobald, CR, 369

Spiritual Life (Pelczar), 77, 81 n.8

Sprague, B.H., 630

Sprague Hospital and School of Nursing (Huron, South Dakota), 630–632, 633, 635, 646. *See also* St. John Hospital and School of Nursing (Huron, South Dakota)

SPRED (Special Religious Education Division), 769, 849

Stanisia, Sister M., SSND, 408, 412 n.32

Stanislaus Bishop and Martyr, Saint, 159–160 n.34

Stanislaus Kostka, Saint, 34 n.17

Stanisławowo (Chicago, Illinois), 15, 25, 27, 35 n.23, 45–47

Stanowski, Rev. Urban, OFM, 190–191, 192

State of Illinois Department of Health, 798

Stations of the Cross, 138

Stations of the Seven Sorrows of the Blessed Virgin Mary, 490–491

Stephanie Pinkowski, Sister M., 160 n.40, 202, 436, 458, 461, 473, 491, 522

Strebig, Rev. John, 850

Stritch, Samuel Cardinal: 542, 569, 576, 595, 611, 621, 679, 683–684, 765; and Madonna High School (Chicago, Illinois), 682, 684–685, 687, 689, 690, 694

Strzycki, Msgr. James J., 290, 292, 293, 423, 491, 494, 537

Stuczko, Rev. Casimir, CSC, 38 n.55, 401, 410 325, 397

Stunek, Rev. Howard, OFM, 640, 653, 749

Summer Reading Programs, 771

Świątkowski, Rev. Luke, CR, 216, 238 n.17

Świerczek, Rev. Stanislaus, CR, 157, 364, 365

Sylvestra, Pelczar, Sister M., 402–403, 408, 436

Symon, Archbishop Albin, 198–199

Szczypula, Rev. Walter, 692, 696, 837

Szrambek, Clara, 66, 70

Szulak, Rev. F.X., SJ, 22, 23

Szypkowski, Rev. Theophilus, CR, 315, 322 n.10, 367

Tarasiuk, Rev. Joseph, CR, 315, 322 n.10, 329, 364, 366, 367, 368, 418, 431, 444, 452, 595, 838 n.17

Tarcisia Bucki, Sister M., 211 n.13, 643, 684, 686, 687, 692, 734, 758, 777, 820, 864, 888, 890

Tau House. *See* St. Francis Mission (Chicago, Illinois)

Tau, 860 n.45

Teacher training and workshops, 150, 295, 329, 406–408, 431, 438, 722

Teaching apostolate: Boys Town, 555; decision affecting, 897; expansion plan, 678–679; first, 151; number of schools, 722; poor, 335; public school children, 619–620; remedial reading centers, 593; requests for Sisters, 588; school staffing, 409. *See also* Catechetical mission; Confraternity of Christian Doctrine classes; CYO Vacation Centers and School; Religious education apostolate; *and names of individual schools*

Tenth General Chapter of Elections, 453, 804, 805–806

Theological Institute (St. Xavier College, Chicago, Illinois), 757

Theresa Dudzik, Mother M.: beatification cause, 778, 795, 892; charism, 827; feast day honoring, 806; foundress recognition, 612; grave of, 795; portrait, 430; relics, 893; remains of, 792; sainthood candidate, 368; tributes to, 907–908, 911–912; works of mercy, 745. *See also* Dudzik, Josephine; Theresa Dudzik, Sister M.

Theresa Dudzik, Sister M.: abandonment to Divine Providence, 375, 380–381; ability to inspire, 223–224; alms collecting, 87; appearance, 249; appointments objection, 328; approval of Constitutions, 110; assistant superior, 327; basic devotions, 376; benefactors, attitudes toward, 382; biographical sources, 374; Blessed Sacrament desired, 111–112; change of candidates, 138; chapter representative, 324; charism, 384; charter signing, 254; Commission on Spiritual Affairs, 248, 253; committee member, 327; concern for Sisters, 459; concern over building, 99–100; concerns about vows, 138; criticism of, 142; deathbed concern, 366–367; death, funeral, 367–368; devotion to Blessed Sacrament, Blessed Virgin Mary, St. Joseph, 377–378, 380; devotion to Church, 383; diligence, 384; duties, 171, 194, 248; example of, 385; failure to be elected superior general, 248; Father Barzynski's death,

121–122; final illness, 366–368; financial hardships of community, 232; First General Chapter, 247; generosity of spirit, 384; greenhouse director, 233; growth of order, 137; home for aged and crippled, 85, 94; humility, 384; illness and surgery, 205; joy in life, 383; kindness, 383; legacy, 369; loans to relatives, 86; *metanoia* and penance, 381; mother superior, 153, 223; name-day, 142–143; novice, mistress, postulant, 140–141; need for spiritual director, 115; opposition to, 140–141; orphanage plans, 132; orphan care, 132–133; patience, 383; postulancy, reflection on, 112; postulant mistress, 114; poverty, 382; leaving community, thoughts on, 114–115; rededication to God, 115; regard for Rev. Spetz, 123–124; religious life reflections, 84; removal as superior, 110; reprimand from Father Barzynski, 78; resemblance with St. Francis, 384; residence expansion, 163; restoring household peace, 78; rumors against, 97–98, 110–111; Saint Joseph, faith in, 96; St. Joseph Home (Chicago, Illinois), 86, 107–108; saints' influence, 376–377; search for quarters, 94–95; self-doubts, 99, 114; sensitivity to others, 382; service mission, 384; spiritual advice, 383; spirit of sacrifice, 113; superior general candidate, 325; teaching apostolate, 149–150; title "Mother" accorded, 541; toils, 85, 100, 109; vows, 139, 143–144, 236; withdrawal of teachers, 174–175. *See also* Dudzik, Josephine; Theresa Dudzik, Mother M.

Theresa of Avila, Saint, 62–63 n.38

Therese Grajek, Sister M., 570, 573, 576, 685, 686, 689, 719 n.110, 749, 758

Third General Chapter of Elections, 401, 410

Third Order of St. Francis, 55, 72 n.10

Thirteenth General Chapter of Elections, 879–882

Thym, John, 258

Toolen, Archbishop Thomas J., 568, 574–576, 578 n.2

Topolinski, Constance, 76. *See also* Angeline Topolinski, Sister M. (Mother)

Trójcowo, 25

Tschetter-Hohm Clinic, 630, 636–637

Tuberculosis: mortality, 354; patient care, 488; Sister deaths, 216, 256, 276, 292, 297, 354

Twelfth General Chapter of Elections, 824, 847

XXVIII International Eucharistic Congress, 431–432

21st Ecumenical Council, 780

Tworek, Felix, 498–499

Typhoid epidemics, 131

Union Stock Yards, 116 n.6

Urban Apostolate of Sisters, 239 n.24

Uzdrowski, Rev. Francis, CR, 452

Vatican I, 780

Vatican II. *See* Second Vatican Council

Venantia Rec., Sister M., 348 n.34, 523, 724, 774, 775–776, 792, 795, 796, 804, 818, 863

"Veni, Creator," 125

Vicar general for women religious, 329–330

Vincent Czyzewski, Mother M.: 402–403; administration, 405; advisory council, 224; Archbishop Cieplak visit, 431; art studies, 408; assistant general, first councilor, 248; charter signing, 254; Constitutions, 401, 436; convent superior, 420; convent visit, 418; death, 432; decline of office, 328, 435; education concern, 406, 407; financial solutions, 409; First General Chapter, 247; Franciscan conferences, 420; Holy Trinity School (Fall City, Texas), 275, 276; House Affairs Commission, 327; mother superior, 196, 223, 256; Motherhouse election, 405; musical education, 438; new Motherhouse, 414, 415; new St. Joseph Home (Chicago, Illinois), 424, novice mistress, 327, 421; nurse request, 581–582; recall of sisters, 189, 305; refusal of staff, 343; school staffing, 190, 200–201, 206, 217; superior general, 325, 402; Walker Home (Lemont, Illinois) renovation, 416

Virnig, Rev. Charles, 584

Visitation Nuns, 572

Visitors Program, 882

Vocations: sources of, 92 n.29, 153, 160 n.41, 259, 678–679, 680–681, 698

Vows: 329, 406, 437, 826, 829, 880; first professions, 139, 168 n.1, 178, 212–213 n.22, 255, 420–421, 494, 794; perpetual professions, 255, 437

Wachtel, Karol, 41 n.84, 150

Wałęsa, Lech, 18 n.3

Walker Family, 425 n.4

Walker, George, 415

Warszawa, 392

Way of the Cross, 147 n.36, 405

Weber, Archbishop Joseph, CR, 314, 321 n.3, 325

Weber High School (Chicago, Illinois), 28, 132, 145 n.8

Wegner, Msgr. Nicholas H., 558–560, 562, 807

West End Catholic Consolidation School (Johnstown, Pennsylvania). *See* St. Casimir's School (Johnstown, Pennsylvania)

West Holt Memorial Hospital, 734. *See also* Atkinson Memorial Hospital; Our Lady of the Sandhills Hospital

West Pope John Paul II Drive, 294

"White City" (Chicago, Illinois), 47–48

"White House," (Lemont, Illinois) 420, 489, 493

Wieczorek, Rev. Simon, CR, 22–23

Wiedemann, Emil, 113

"Windy City," 48

Władysław II Jagiełło, King of Poland, 13

Wołłowski, Rev. John, CR, 5, 23

Women's Rosary Sociey, 98, 125

World Federation of Poles Abroad, 466

World's Columbian Exposition, 47–48

Wroblewski, Rev. Sergius, OFM, 610, 697, 837, 852

Wycislo, Bishop Aloysius, 445, 612, 794, 837

Wysinski Family, 248

Wysinski, Matilda, 94

Wysinski, Rosalie: friendship with Theresa Dudzik, 249; parish society participation, 54; postponement of joining community, 67; support for Josephine Dudzik plan, 65; Third Order admission, 55–56. *See also* Anna Wysinski, Mother M.

Wyszynski, Stefan Cardinal, 807, 808

Year of Christ, The, 77

Youche, Vincent, 517, 519

Youngkin, Rev. Edwin F., SSJ, 569–570, 573, 576

Young Ladies' Rosary Society, 54, 98, 113, 256, 257

Zahajkiewicz, Szczęsny, 40 n.81, 41 n.84, 150

Zapała, Rev. Ladislaus, CR, 205

Zdechlik, Rev. John, CR, 315, 365, 838 n.17

Zock, Msgr. Raymond, 492, 603, 625, 693, 774

Zukotynski, Tadeusz, 40 n.82

Zuroweste, Bishop Albert T., 207–208, 209

Zwiardowski, Rev. Felix, CR, 27, 60 n.11, 286 n.33

Zwierzycki, Rev. Joseph, CR, 314, 367, 838 n.17